RUSSIAN CAMPAIGN

Miles

0   100   200   300   400   500

Main Railways   Oil Pipelines — — — — —

WITHDRAWN

Archangel 320 m
Perm 450 m
Baku 50 m

Kalinin
Gorki   R.Volga   Kazan
R.Oka
MOSCOW
Mozhaisk
Tula
Sukhinichi
U. S. S. R.
Orel
Kursk   Voronezh
Svoboda
Belgorod   Pavlovsk
Kharkov   R. Don
Poltava
Krasnograd   Millerovo   Kalach   Stalingrad
Izyum   Voroshilovgrad   Labachov
Gorlovka   R.Donets   R.Volga
Dniepr   Stalino   Tsimlyanska
rivoi-   Zaporozhye   R. Mius   Kotelnikovo
Rog
Nikopol   Taganrog   Astrakhan
Mariupol   Rostov
SEA OF
AZOV   CASPIAN
Kerch   SEA
RIMEA   Tikhoretsk
Krasnodar   Armavir
Sevastapol   Novorossiisk   R.Kuban
Taman Pen.   Maikop   R.Terek
Tuapse   Makhach-Kala
Grozny
K   S E A   Sukhumi   Ordzhonikidze
Tiflis
Batum

BRITISH INTELLIGENCE IN THE SECOND WORLD WAR

ITS INFLUENCE ON STRATEGY AND OPERATIONS

VOLUME TWO

The authors of this, as of other official histories
of the Second World War, have been given free access
to official documents. They alone are responsible
for the statements made and the views expressed.

BRITISH INTELLIGENCE IN THE SECOND WORLD WAR

Its Influence on Strategy and Operations

VOLUME TWO

by

F. H. HINSLEY

President of St John's College and
Professor of the History of International Relations
in the University of Cambridge

with

E. E. THOMAS
C. F. G. RANSOM
R. C. KNIGHT

CAMBRIDGE UNIVERSITY PRESS
NEW YORK

Published in the USA by the
Syndicate of Cambridge University Press
32 East 57th Street, New York, NY 10022, USA

Printed in England for Her Majesty's Stationery Office
by The Pitman Press Ltd, Bath
Dd 699439 K88 2/81

ISBN 0 521 242908

CONTENTS

v

PART VII:
THE FIRST HALF OF 1943

A bibliography covering the whole of this history will be included in the third, and final, volume.

PREFACE

W E THINK it will be helpful if we repeat here the conditions under which we have worked as we stated them in the preface to Volume I.

In carrying out our brief, which was to produce an account of the influence of British intelligence on strategy and operations during the Second World War, we have encountered two problems of presentation. The first was how to furnish the strategic and operational context without retelling the history of the war in all its detail; we trust we have arrived at a satisfactory solution to it. The second arose because different meanings are given to the term intelligence. The value and the justification of intelligence depend on the use that is made of its findings; and this has been our central concern. But its findings depend on the prior acquisition, interpretation and evaluation of information; and judgment about its influence on those who used it requires an understanding of these complex activities. We have tried to provide this understanding without being too much diverted by the problems and techniques associated with the provision of intelligence. Some readers will feel that we have strayed too far down the arid paths of organisation and methods. Others, to whom such subjects are fascinating in themselves, will wish that we had said more about them.

It is from no wish to disarm such criticisms that we venture to point to the novel and exceptional character of our work. No considered account of the relationship between intelligence and strategic and operational decisions has hitherto been possible, for no such account could be drawn up except by authors having unrestricted access to intelligence records as well as to other archives. In relation to the British records for the Second World War and the inter-war years, we have been granted this freedom as a special measure. No restriction has been placed on us while carrying out our research. On the contrary, in obtaining access to archives and in consulting members of the war-time intelligence community we have received full co-operation and prompt assistance from the Historical Section of the Cabinet Office and the appropriate government departments. Some members of the war-time community may feel that we might have made our consultation more extensive; we have confined it to points on which we needed to supplement or clarify the evidence of the surviving archives. As for the archives, we set out to see all; and if any have escaped our scrutiny we are satisfied that over-sight on our part is the sole explanation.

In preparing the results of our research for publication we have
been governed by a ruling that calls for a brief explanation. On 12
January 1978, in a written reply to a parliamentary question, the
Secretary of State for Foreign Affairs advised war-time intelligence
staff on the limited extent to which they were absolved from their
undertakings of reticence in the light of recent changes of policy
with regard to the release of war-time records. He drew a distinction between the records of the Service intelligence directorates,
which will be placed with other departmental archives in the Public
Record Office, and 'other information, including details of the
methods by which this material was obtained'. He explained that
this other information 'remains subject to the undertakings and to
the Official Secrets Acts and may not be disclosed'. And he
concluded with a reference to this History: 'if it is published, the
principles governing the extent of permitted disclosure embodied in
the guidance above will apply in relation to the Official History'.
This statement has not prevented us from incorporating in the
published History the results of our work on records which are not
to be opened. The records in question are the domestic records of
some of the intelligence-collecting bodies. We have been required
to restrict our use of them only to the extent that secrecy about
intelligence techniques and with respect to individuals remains
essential.

The need to apply this restriction to the published history has
at no point impeded our analysis of the state of intelligence and
of its impact, and it has in no way affected our conclusions.
It has, however, dictated the system that we have adopted when
giving references to our sources. Government departments, inter-
governmental bodies and operational commands – the recipients,
assessors and users of intelligence – have presented no difficulty; to
their intelligence files, as to their other records, we have always
supplied precise references. This applies not only to documents
already opened in the Public Record Office, and those to be opened
after a stated period of extended closure, but also to individual files
and papers which, though they may not be available for public
research for a considerable time to come, nevertheless fall into
categories of war-time records whose eventual opening in the
Record Office may be expected. But it would have served no useful
purpose to give precise references to the domestic files of the
intelligence-collecting bodies, which are unlikely ever to be opened
in the Public Record Office. We have been permitted – indeed
encouraged – to make use of these files in our text and we have done
so on a generous scale, but in their case our text must be accepted
as being the only evidence of their contents that can be made
public. This course may demand from our readers more trust than
historians have the right to expect, but we believe they will agree

that it is preferable to the alternative, which was to have incorporated no evidence for which we could not quote sources.

The above limitations have arisen from the need for security. We turn now to others which have been imposed on us by the scale on which we have worked. The first of these is that not merely when security has required it but throughout the book – in the many cases where security is no longer at stake and where readers may regret our reticence – we have cast our account in impersonal terms and refrained from naming individuals. We have done so because for our purposes it has generally sufficed to refer to the organisations to which individuals belonged; the exceptions are a few activities which were so specialised or were carried out by such small staffs, and thus became so closely associated with individuals, that it has been convenient sometimes to use names. In addition, however, we must admit to a feeling for the appropriateness of Flaubert's recipe for the perfect realistic novel: *pas de monstres, et pas de héros*. The performance of the war-time intelligence community, its shortcomings no less than its successes, rested not only on the activities of a large number of organisations but also, within each organisation, on the work of many individuals. To have identified all would have been impossible in a book of this canvas; to have given prominence to only a few would have been unjust to the many more who were equally deserving of mention.

As for the organisations, it has been impossible to deal at equal length with all. In some cases we have had to be content with a bare sketch because they kept or retained few records. With others we have dealt briefly because most of their work falls outside our subject. This applies to those responsible for counter-intelligence, security and the use of intelligence for deception purposes; like the intelligence activities of the enemy, we have investigated them in these volumes only to the extent that they contributed to what the British authorities knew about the enemy's conduct of the war. Lack of space has restricted what we have been able to say about intelligence in the field – about the work that was carried out, often in hazardous conditions, by Service intelligence officers with fighting units and by the people who were responsible in the field for signal intelligence, for reporting to the SIS and SOE, for examining enemy equipment and for undertaking photographic interpretation, POW examination and many similar tasks. As for the contribution of the many men and women who carried out essential routine work at establishments in the United Kingdom and overseas – who undertook the continuous manning of intercept stations or of cryptanalytic machinery, the maintenance of PR aircraft and their cameras, the preparation of target information for the RAF or of topographical information for all three Services, the monitoring of foreign newspapers, broadcasts and intercepted mail, and the endless indexing, typing, teleprinting, cyphering and transmitting of the intelligence output – only occasional references to it have been possible in an account which sets out to reconstruct the influence of intelligence on the major decisions, the chief operations and the general course of the war.

Even at this last level there are unavoidable omissions. The most important of these is that we have not attempted to cover the war in the Far East; when this was so much the concern of the United States, it is not possible to provide an adequate account on the basis of the British archives alone. A second derives from the fact that while the archives are generally adequate for reconstructing the influence of intelligence in Whitehall, there is practically no record of how and to what extent intelligence influenced the individual decisions of the operational commands. It has usually been possible to reconstruct what intelligence they had at their disposal at any time. What they made of it under operational conditions, and in circumstances in which it was inevitably incomplete, is on all but a few occasions a matter for surmise. And this is one matter which, after stating the facts to the best of our ability, we have left to the judgment of our readers and to the attention of those who will themselves wish to follow up our research by work in the voluminous records which are being made available to the public.

That room remains for further research is something that goes without saying. Even on issues and episodes for which we have set out to supply the fullest possible accounts, the public records will yield interpretations that differ from those we have offered. At the opposite extreme there are particular undertakings and individual operations to which we have not even referred. In our attempt to write a co-ordinated yet compact history we have necessarily proceeded not only with a broad brush but also with a selective hand, and we shall be content if we have provided an adequate framework and a reliable perspective for other historians as well as for the general reader.

□

We wish to express our indebtedness to Mr M Davenport CBE for the valuable assistance we have received from his war-time knowledge of the German effort against British cyphers. We must again make special reference to the contribution of Miss Eve Streatfeild. In addition to sharing in the research, she has for several years carried out with great skill and patience the bulk of the administrative work that the project has involved.

We cannot let this volume go to press without expressing our regret at the death, at a late stage in its preparation, of Dr R C Knight OBE, MSc, PhD.

ABBREVIATIONS

AAPIU   Army Air Photographic Interpretation Unit
ACAS (I)   Assistant Chief of Air Staff (Intelligence)
ADI (K)   Assistant Director Intelligence (Prisoners of War)
ADI (Ph)   Assistant Director Intelligence (Photographic)
ADI (Sc)   Assistant Director Intelligence (Science)
ADIC   Assistant Director Operational Intelligence Centre (Admiralty)
ADNI (PW)   Assistant Director Naval Intelligence (Prisoners of War)
AFHQ   Allied Force Headquarters
AFV   Armoured Fighting Vehicle
AI   Air Intelligence (Branch of the Air Ministry)
ASI   Air Scientific Intelligence
ASV   Anti-Surface Vessel Radar

BJSM   British Joint Services Mission (Washington)
BMM   British Military Mission (Moscow)
BNLO   British Naval Liaison Officer
BSC   British Security Co-ordination (New York)

'C'   also CSS: Head of the Secret Service
CAIO   Chief Air Intelligence Officer, Algiers
CAS   Chief of the Air Staff
CBME   Combined Bureau Middle East
CCS   Combined Chiefs of Staff (Anglo-US)
CIC   Combined Intelligence Committee (Anglo-US)
CIGS   Chief of the Imperial General Staff
CIU   Central Interpretation Unit
CNO   Chief of Naval Operations (US)
CNS   Chief of Naval Staff (First Sea Lord)
COHQ   Combined Operations Headquarters
COS   Chiefs of Staff (British)
CSDIC   Combined Services Detailed Interrogation Centre
CSS   Chief of the Secret Service, also 'C'

DAK   Deutsches Afrika Korps
DD (C)   Deputy Director (Civil) (at GC and CS)
DD (Ph)   Deputy Director (Photography) (Air Ministry)
DD (S)   Deputy Director (Services) (at GC and CS)
DDI   Deputy Director of Intelligence (Air Staff)
DDIC   Deputy Director Operational Intelligence Centre (Admiralty)
DDMI   Deputy Director Military Intelligence
DDMI (I)   Deputy Director Military Intelligence (Intelligence)
DDMI (O)   Deputy Director Military Intelligence (Operations)

xiii

xiv

DDMI (PW)	Deputy Director Military Intelligence (Prisoners of War)
DDMI (Y)	Deputy Director Military Intelligence (Y Service)
DDNI	Deputy Director of Naval Intelligence
DF	Direction Finding
DMI	Director of Military Intelligence
DNI	Director of Naval Intelligence
DSD	Director Signal Division (Admiralty)
ETOUSA	European Theatre of Operations United States Army
GAF	German Air Force
GC and CS	Government Code and Cypher School
GS Int	General Staff Intelligence
HDU	Home Defence Units
IAF	Italian Air Force
IS (O)	Intelligence Section (Operations)
ISSB	Inter-Service Security Board
ISTD	Inter-Services Topographical Department
JIC	Joint Intelligence Sub-Committee (of the COS)
JIS	Joint Intelligence Staff
JPS	Joint Planning Staff (of the COS)
LRC	London Reception Centre
LRDG	Long Range Desert Group
MEIC	Middle East Intelligence Centre
MEW	Ministry of Economic Warfare
MI	Military Intelligence (Branch of the War Office)
MIRS	Military Intelligence Research Section
NAIU	North African Interpretation Unit
NCXF	Naval Commander Expeditionary Force (*Torch*)
NID	Naval Intelligence Division
OCI	Office of the Co-ordination of Information (US)
OIC	Operational Intelligence Centre (Admiralty)
OKH	Oberkommando des Heeres (High Command of the German Army)
OKL	Oberkommando der Luftwaffe (High Command of the German Air Force)
OKM	Oberkommando der Kriegsmarine (High Command of the German Navy)
OKW	Oberkommando des Wehrmacht (High Command of the German Armed Forces)
ONI	Office of Naval Intelligence (US)
OSS	Office of Strategic Services (US)

PAIC	Persia and Iraq Command
PDU	Photographic Development Unit
PIU	Photographic Interpretation Unit
PR	Photographic Reconnaissance
PRU	Photographic Reconnaissance Unit
PWE	Political Warfare Executive
PWIS (Home)	Prisoners of War Intelligence Service
Pzkw	Panzerkampfwagen
RAE	Royal Aircraft Establishment
RFP	Radio Finger Printing
RSS	Radio Security Service
R/T	Radio Telephony
SALU	Sub-section of Air Section GC and CS, specialising in the fusion of high and low-grade GAF Sigint (not strictly an abbreviation)
SCU	Special Communications Unit
SD	Sicherheitsdienst
Sigint	Signal Intelligence – the general term for the processes of interception and decryption and the intelligence they produced
SIME	Security Intelligence Middle East
SIS	Special or Secret Intelligence Service
SLU	Special Liaison Unit
SOE	Special Operations Executive
TA	Traffic Analysis – the study of wireless communication networks and procedure signals, call-signs, low-grade codes and plain language, together with DF (see above)
TINA	Study of morse characteristics of individual wireless operators (not an abbreviation)
TRE	Telecommunications Research Establishment
VCAS	Vice-Chief of the Air Staff
VCIGS	Vice-Chief of the Imperial General Staff
VCNS	Vice-Chief of the Naval Staff
WIDU	Wireless Intelligence and Development Unit
W/T	Wireless Telegraphy
Y	The interception, analysis and decryption of wireless traffic in low and medium-grade codes and cyphers. The term 'low-grade' refers to the degree of security provided by a code or cypher and does not imply that the traffic in it was either unimportant or easy to break and interpret

LIST OF MAPS

PART IV

Developments in the Organisation of
Intelligence and in overall Strategic
Intelligence Assessments from mid-1941
to mid-1943

CHAPTER 15

Developments in the Organisation of Intelligence

IN THE two years following the German attack on Russia the work of the intelligence bodies in the United Kingdom was steadily adjusted to the change in the character of the war. Apart from expanding to keep pace with the enormous increase in intelligence that came with the extension of Germany's operations and the growth of their own experience and resources, they had now to take particular account of the entry as Allies of the Soviet Union and the United States and of the need to apply their knowledge of the enemy to the planning of British and Allied offensives.

Like much of the responsibility for developing intelligence arrangements with the Allied powers,* much of the work of supervising the expansion of the intelligence bodies and regulating their relations with the planning authorities fell to the Joint Intelligence Committee (JIC). It was therefore fortunate that the most important war-time step in the reorganisation of the JIC had already taken place in the spring of 1941. Once the Axis Planning Section had evolved into an inner Committee of the JIC, composed largely of its junior members and known as the Joint Intelligence Staff (JIS),† the JIC itself was able to concentrate on its responsibility for guiding intelligence policy and supervising the administration of the growing number of inter-Service intelligence bodies in the knowledge that in the JIS it had, for the first time, a body to carry out the JIC's other task of co-ordinating, assessing and disseminating strategic intelligence in considered inter-Service appreciations.

The establishment of the JIS was all the more timely because it took place just when the flow of intelligence was undergoing an enormous expansion, with dramatically beneficial effects on the quality of JIS appreciations. But it did not on that account eliminate all friction between the JIC and the Whitehall departments. Indeed, the increase in high-grade Sigint made so great an impression with its scope and its authenticity that it produced arrangements which at first threatened to undermine such progress as Whitehall had made towards accepting the principle of central

---

* See below, Chapter 16.
† See Volume I, p 298.

inter-Service assessment for strategic intelligence. By the middle of 1941 the daily supply of Enigma items which the Prime Minister had requested from 'C' on 27 September 1940* had developed into a routine by which, every day when he was in London, the Prime Minister received a selection of the more important Service Sigint and, less frequently, decrypts of Axis diplomatic telegrams and of Abwehr and German police signals, most of it in the form of the decrypts as they had been translated at GC and CS but otherwise unprocessed. He also continued to receive as part of this routine memoranda on the progress, procedure and security of the cryptanalytic programme, and later some of the more interesting SIS reports were added.† When the Prime Minister was abroad other arrangements were made. When he went to Cairo in August 1942 he was kept in touch through the service from GC and CS to the Special Liaison Unit (SLU) there;[1]‡ and when he went on to Moscow it appears that he relied on the intelligence that was being sent to the British Military Mission. While he was at the Casablanca conference in January 1943, on the other hand, he received a morning telegram 'from Boniface'§ in addition to the evening 'Sunset' telegram.‖ On the basis of this material he frequently made proposals and enquiries to the Chiefs of Staff or to theatre commanders.¶ It was partly on this account, to arm them against his proddings and questions, that each of the Service departments began to issue Sigint summaries to a small circle of their officers. In the Admiralty, for example, a new sub-section of NID 17 (later NID 12) was set up for this purpose in July 1941; by November it was delivering summaries to the First Sea Lord three or four times a day,[4] and in December, after complaining that 'C''s bulletins were being drawn up without a naval commentary, the DNI took further steps in an attempt to ensure that the First Sea Lord was

---

* See Volume I, pp 295–296.
† These papers are henceforth referred to as the Dir/C Archive.
‡ For the development of the SLU link to the Middle East see Volume I, Appendix 13.
§ See Volume I, p 138 and below Appendix 1 (ii), p 646.
‖ For the 'Sunset' telegrams see below, p 47.
¶ His consuming interest in the material is illustrated by his correspondence with 'C' during the Casablanca conference. Before leaving London he requested that 'C' should 'repeat all really important messages to me textually'.[2] On 18 January he sent the following signal from Casablanca: 'Why have you not kept me properly supplied with news? Volume should be increased at least five-fold and important messages sent textually.'[3] No SCU/SLU link was provided for the Casablanca conference and it was as a result of the Prime Minister's discontent with the amount of information sent to him that such a link was provided for subsequent conferences.

1.   Dir/C Archive 497 of 24 August 1942.
2.   ibid, 2031 of 11 January 1943.
3.   ibid, Stratagem 71, from HMS *Bulolo* to Admiralty, 1226/18 January 1943.
4.   C Morgan, *NID History 1939–1942*, p 147.

adequately briefed for his dealings with the Prime Minister. It is not difficult to imagine the problems which these developments created for the JIS by prompting different reactions to the same intelligence from different quarters.

Other problems arose in the opposite direction, from the understandable concern for the security of Sigint. The greatest of them arose from the fact that, whereas the Service members of the JIS were privy to intelligence reaching their departments from all sources, including the diplomatic as well as the Service Sigint, the Foreign Office for reasons of security did not at this stage receive any military Sigint; indeed, apart from the Permanent Under-Secretary and its representative on the JIC, it did not know of the existence of the Enigma. In addition, the members of the JIS had to deal with non-indoctrinated staff in their own departments. These restrictions seriously complicated the discussion of JIS drafts and delayed the production of JIS appreciations.[5] Another cause of delay, to which the JIC itself drew attention in the spring of 1942, was the insistence of the senior JIS team on seeing every paper, however minor, before it was circulated[6] and yet another was the tendency of the Directors of Intelligence on the JIC to water down or even to disown the JIS's conclusions.[7] As early as July 1941, however, the DMI was satisfied that 'the JIS are . . . to an increasing extent and at all stages, working in direct contact with the various Joint Planning Staffs so as to ensure that the best possible information regarding the probability or feasibility of enemy action in any theatre and at any future time, is made available to the Planners. This results in a balanced machinery in which the JIS is in fact the inter-Service enemy planning section . . .'.[8] And in November 1941 the Joint Planners were describing their relations with the JIS as 'entirely satisfactory.'[9]

The JIC was no less content with the JIC's relations with the Planners, though it would have liked the JIS to be housed in closer proximity to the planning staff.[10] From the spring of 1942 it renewed its pressure for this requirement and in August, when planning for the Allied landings in French north Africa (Operation *Torch*) and other large-scale Allied operations was at last getting into its stride and the JIS was being consulted about the drafting of most planning papers with an intelligence content, the Planners

---

5. ADM 223/107, Value and Use of Special Intelligence in JIC Work, paras 4, 5 and 7.
6. JIC (42) 8th (o) Meeting, 10 March; JIC (42) 11th and 39th Meetings 16 March and 28 July.
7. ADM 223/107, JIC 345/44 of 4 March 1944.
8. JIC (41) 297, Annex (DMI to CIGS, 19 July 1941).
9. CAB 84/37, JP (41) 988 of 20 November.
10. JIC (41) 28th Meeting, 14 October.

conceded that it was desirable.[11] Between then and the beginning
of 1943, when the JIS and the Joint Planners were at last housed
under the same roof, regular meetings were instituted between the
Directors of Plans and the Deputy Directors of Intelligence, the
first of which took place at the beginning of October 1942, and
early in November, these meetings having failed to eliminate every
disagreement about strategic assessments, it was laid down that the
JIC could request a meeting with the Planners whenever it thought
fit.[12]

The desirability of the reform which inaugurated the JIS, indeed
the necessity for it, was confirmed not only by the closer relations
with the Planners which it opened up, but also by the continual
increase in the JIC's administrative labours. Its work as the
organiser of a confidential information bureau for British missions
and Cs-in-C overseas mounted every month from the summer of
1941. In July 1941 it had to consider the security aspect of the
decision to despatch intelligence summaries to the British Mission
in Moscow.[13]* During August it had first to brief the British
representatives to the strategic conference with the USA in Newfoundland and then to help in compiling for them a daily operational and intelligence summary.[14] In September, prodded by complaints from Gibraltar,[15] it introduced more systematic arrangements for keeping the overseas commands abreast of its intelligence
summaries,[16] and from the beginning of December it had to
supplement the new arrangements by organising the despatch of a
daily telegram on the general war situation to the Cs-in-C in the
Far East.[17] Once inaugurated, these various series of bulletins and
summaries were drafted by the JIS, as were the appreciations and
the daily Intelligence Summary† which the JIC circulated in

---

* See below, pp 59–60.
† This, temporarily suspended in November 1940 and revived sometime in 1941, was
finally suspended in June 1942.[18]

11. JIC (42) 10th, 35th, 39th and 41st Meetings, 10 March, 28 July, 18 and 27
     August.
12. CAB 84/4, JP (42) 162nd, 168th Meetings, 2 and 19 October; CAB 84/5,
     172nd and 179th Meetings, 23 October and 6 November; JIC (42) 54th (o)
     Meeting, 27 October.
13. CAB 79/12, COS (41) 230th Meeting, 1 July; JIC (41) 20th Meeting,
     1 July.
14. CAB 80/30, COS (41) 505, Annexes II and IV; CAB 120/21, PM file
     402/1/1.
15. CAB 79/14, COS (41) 304th and 307th Meetings, 30 August and
     2 September; JIC (41) 25th Meeting, 2 September; JIC (41) 354 of
     4 September.
16. JIC (41) 25th Meeting, 2 September.
17. CAB 79/16, COS (41) 403rd and 405th Meetings, 1 and 2 December.
18. JIC (42) 28th Meeting, 30 June.

Whitehall. But only the JIC itself could negotiate the administrative and security problems associated with their introduction.

Similar problems arose for the JIC out of its supervision of inter-Service bodies and arrangements, both old and new. Throughout the second half of 1941 it was preoccupied with the development of the Inter-Service Topographical Department (ISTD), which was still encountering many difficulties.* In October it was wrestling with CSDIC's need for additional accommodation and was making new arrangements to meet the increasing demands on CSDIC's services.† In December it was mediating in a quarrel between the Foreign Office and the Air Ministry about how to reduce the inconvenience to intelligence work caused by delays in the transport of diplomatic bags and personnel.[19] And by the end of the year, after much detailed discussion, it had set up two new inter-Service organisations – the Inter-Service Cypher and W/T Security Committee, which was made responsible under the JIC, and in place of a hitherto *ad hoc* Inter-Service Cypher Security Committee, for the security of British wireless communications, not least in the light of British progress against enemy communications;[20]‡ and the Intelligence Section (Operations) (IS (O)), the organisation that was set up in an attempt to collate the intelligence required for operational planning.§

During 1942 the administrative and co-ordinating work of the JIC continued to expand into new fields. In April it began to supervise the work of the Hartley Technical Sub-Committee on Axis Oil, the successor to the Hankey and the Lloyd committees, and thus became the channel through which technical reports on the enemy's oil position reached the Chiefs of Staff and, when necessary, the Defence Committee.[21]‖ In August it temporarily assumed responsibility for co-ordinating intelligence that was being collected from different sources on German, Italian and French morale by the Foreign Office, MEW and PWE.¶ Between then

---

* See below, p 9 et seq.   † See below, p 32 et seq.
‡ See Appendix 1 (Part (1)).   § See Below, p 12 et seq.
‖ See below, Chapter 18.
¶ PWE, the Political Warfare Executive, was established in August 1941. It grew out of SO I, the propaganda arm of SOE which was itself a development of Department EH (Electra House), the organisation which had been responsible for propaganda and political warfare in 1939 and 1940. Although it had an intelligence department, it was a user rather than a supplier of intelligence except on one subject: its analysis of enemy propaganda, based on its regular digesting of foreign Press and radio, had a bearing on the study of enemy morale and was 'the one field of intelligence in which PWE made an original contribution to the study of enemy military strategy'.[22]

19. JIC (41) 36th and 37th Meeting, 3 and 9 December; JIC (41) 480 of 17 December.
20. JIC (41) 26th and 29th Meetings, 26 September and 21 October; JIC (41) 416 of 21 October.
21. CAB 66/23, WP (42) 163 (JIC (42) 147 of 20 April)
22. CAB/HIST/P/1/1, Garnett, *The Political Warfare Executive*, p 11.

and the autumn it produced four consolidated but inconclusive reports on this subject.[23] Nor did its existing supervisory commitments become less onerous. By April its agenda had become so much preoccupied with the procedural problems of the various inter-Service bodies which it supervised – CSDIC, ISTD, IS(O), the Central Interpretation Unit and the Photographic Reconnaissance Unit* – that it took the obvious step of instituting regular meetings of the Deputy Directors of Intelligence to deal with such matters and refer only questions of principle to the senior committee.[24] From October 1942, however, the Deputy Directors increasingly attended the meetings of the senior committee in place of the Directors, whose time and energies were more and more absorbed in administering their own intelligence branches.

☐

The further expansion of the Service intelligence branches took place within the organisational framework they had adopted by the middle of 1941, the only important modifications being those that were called for by the increase in the amount of intelligence, by the need for relations with Allies and, above all, by the growth in the demand for intelligence from those responsible for planning British and Allied operations – a growth which began in the middle of 1941 and which was to continue for the remainder of the war.†

At the highest level of planning, where what was required was strategic intelligence assessments by a single central body, the demand was met with little further reorganisation by the system which was by then ensuring, after considerable delay and several abortive experiments, the efficient analysis and dissemination of what was known about the enemy's intentions and capacities: the evolution of the JIS within the JIC and the establishment of ever closer relations between the JIC, the JIS, the Joint Planners and the Service intelligence branches. It was otherwise when it came to the provision of highly detailed background information to the variety of different and frequently competing planning groups – notably Combined Operations HQ, GHQ Home Forces and separate force commanders – that were responsible for special types of undertaking or particular areas or individual operations.

---

* See below, p 36 et seq.
† For a summary of developments within the Service branches see Appendix 2.

23. JIC (42) 365 of 18 September, 381 of 2 October, 395 of 9 October and 404 of 14 October.
24. JIC (42) 11th and 12th Meetings, 31 March and 3 April; JIC (42) 105 of 27 March.

For this no adequate arrangements yet existed and many administrative and security problems were encountered in the course of developing them.

It had already been decided that topographical intelligence, on terrain, beaches, ports and transport communications, should be collated and disseminated on an inter-Service basis by a single organisation – the Inter-Service Topographical Department.* But in the autumn of 1941 several steps were taken which indicate that ISTD was having difficulty in meeting the growing demands upon it. In September the JIC authorised it to receive SIS reports containing topographical information, whereas hitherto it had had to depend on digests of these reports made in the Service intelligence branches.[25] At the end of the year the JIC empowered it to approach the Allied governments-in-exile with a view to making greater use of refugee aliens as a source of topographical intelligence.[26] It had by then also acquired the right to make requests for assistance direct to the CIU; but in October the JIC decided that all such requests should pass through ADI (Ph) at the Air Ministry, who had the task of handling all other requests, the Air Intelligence Branch having expressed anxiety about the insecurity that might result if the ISTD continued to make direct approaches to the CIU.[27]

Not surprisingly, perhaps, the accumulation of information and of staff at ISTD from the beginning of 1942 combined with the proliferation of demands from the various planning agencies to produce new problems and fresh sources of friction. In June 1942 the Air Ministry and MEW complained that in response to questionnaires from the Joint Planners, which were intended only to indicate the types of information that were likely to be required, ISTD was producing over-elaborate reports and was including in them ephemeral intelligence that was out-of-date before it was circulated – that it was, in other words, exceeding its responsibility to provide topographical intelligence. This led the JIC to lay down stricter guidelines for the contents of ISTD reports and to attempt to demarcate the respective responsibilities of ISTD and CIU in relation to photographic intelligence on aviation matters such as airfields. As a further means of restricting ISTD to topographical intelligence, the JIC at the same time ruled that responsibility for assembling and circulating 'non-permanent' intelligence, on such matters as order of battle and mobile defences, must lie with the

---

* See Volume I, pp 161, 292.

25. JIC (41) 27th Meeting, 23 September.
26. JIC (41) 34th and 37th Meetings, 26 November and 9 December; JIC (41) 438 of 12 November and 445 of 23 November.
27. JIC (41) 29th Meeting, 21 October; JIC (41) 407 of 12 October and 418 of 24 October.

Intelligence Section (Operations),[28] an organisation which had been set up at the end of 1941 on the initiative of the Joint Planning Staff and Combined Operations HQ. At the end of September the JIC again curbed the zeal of ISTD by refusing its request to receive copies of POW interrogations on the ground that the circulation of unevaluated and uncollated intelligence beyond the Service intelligence branches was undesirable.[29]

Although friction continued between ISTD and, on the other hand, AI and CIU, it was gradually eliminated during the autumn of 1942 at the working level without further appeal to the JIC.[30] With somewhat greater difficulty, the JIC managed by that time to clarify the function of the Intelligence Section (Operations) – IS (O) – and to smooth its relations with ISTD and the Service intelligence branches. In arguing for the establishment of the IS (O) the Joint Planners had drawn a distinction between the excellent supply of 'strategical information' they were now obtaining from the JIS and, on the other hand, the delays and the difficulties experienced by their operational planning sections in getting from the Service intelligence branches and the ISTD the more detailed intelligence required for the planning of British operations. To overcome this problem – and also to reduce the danger that uncontrolled planning requests for intelligence about a particular area might endanger the security of British operational projects – they advocated a system by which a single department of the JIC, analogous to the JIS, should assemble, collate and disseminate all operational intelligence required by themselves, by Combined Operations HQ, GHQ Home Forces and the force commanders for planning purposes.[31] Led by the DNI, but against the wishes of the DMI, the JIC tried to avoid the new responsibility.[32] It only partly succeeded. The IS (O), its staff drawn from the three Services and MEW, was placed under the 'general guidance' of the JIS.[33] It was responsible for indicating to ISTD what topographical information was required for an operation, for co-ordinating and submitting demands for photographs through ADI (Ph) and then for the collation and reconciliation of all the intelligence obtained from ISTD, from the Service intelligence departments and from such bodies as MEW and SOE. It was required to work in close touch with the Service intelligence departments, whose own direct contact with the planning staffs and

28.   JIC (42) 26th, 28th and 29th Meetings, 12 and 30 June and 3 July.
29.   JIC (42) 49th Meeting, 29 September.
30.   JIC (42) 44th Meeting, 8 September; JIC (42) 420 of 23 October.
31.   CAB 84/37, JP (41) 988 of 20 November.
32.   JIC (41) 37th Meeting, 9 December; CAB 84/3, JP (41) 172nd Meeting, 18 December.
33.   JIC (41) 40th Meeting, 30 December.

force commanders continued 'in all cases where personal explanation of matters within the respective provinces of the intelligence sections is desirable'. The minor operations carried out by Combined Operations did not fall within the IS (O)'s brief.[34]

The additional burden soon proved too heavy and too administrative in character for the JIS. By March 1942 the JIC itself had assumed direct administrative charge of the IS (O).[35] During April it discussed ways of preserving security and reducing demands on the staffs of the intelligence branches of the Service departments by, on the one hand, encouraging the various planning groups to submit their intelligence requirements only to the IS (O) and, on the other hand, by persuading the Joint Planners to allow the IS (O) to be represented at their discussions while the preparation of British operations was still in the early stages.[36] A directive incorporating these improvements, and now emphasising IS (O)'s role as more of a clearing house than an agency to collate intelligence, was drawn up in May,[37] but it could not be issued until the JIC had settled with 'C' the difficult question of the extent to which IS (O) should have access to the product of the various sources of intelligence. The JIC believed that if it was to work efficiently the IS (O) must have full knowledge of all the sources, including the most secret ones. Reporting back to the JIC on 26 June, 'C' accepted this requirement on certain conditions.[38] The conditions were presumably concerned to regulate the extent to which IS (O) made use of the most sensitive sources in the papers it drew up for the planners; the JIC showed that this was tightly controlled when, in August, it agreed that IS (O) papers might include extracts from JIC papers only with the approval of the secretary of the JIC.[39]*

The JIC's new directive to the IS (O) was eventually issued at the end of July 1942.[41] Before it was sent out it had become clear that the attempt to regulate and rationalise the demands for intelligence from the growing number of planning staffs by channelling them through an expanded IS (O) would run into other difficulties. On 17 July the JIC reaffirmed that requests to the

---

* The JIC had earlier agreed with great reluctance that GHQ Home Forces should receive such of its papers as dealt with Germany, Occupied France and Belgium, though it had refused the GHQ's request to be represented at JIC and JIS meetings.[40]

34. JIC (41) 499 of 30 December.
35. JIC (42) 8th (o) Meeting, 10 March.
36. JIC (42) 135 of 14 April; JIC (42) 16th, 17th and 18th Meetings, 21, 24 and 28 April; CAB 84/4, JP (42) 63rd Meeting, 3 April, Annex II.
37. JIC (42) 172 of 6 May.
38. JIC (42) 27th Meeting, 26 June.
39. JIC (42) 42nd Meeting, 28 August.
40. JIC (42) 9th and 23rd Meetings, 17 March and 2 June.
41. JIC (42) 269 of 24 July.

ISTD for topographical intelligence must pass through the IS (O) and be monitored by it in conjunction, if necessary, with the secretary of the JIC.[42] In August the JIC had to deal with an accusation from the DNI that the reports drawn up by the IS (O) were overlapping those of his brain-child, the ISTD, and straying into its territory. But once the JIC had insisted that such duplication was justifiable, in view of the overwhelming importance of providing planners and force commanders with single short papers on their requirements, at least initially, the two bodies worked out amicable working arrangements.

If it took some time to smooth relations between the ISTD and the IS (O), two bodies under the jurisdiction of the JIC, it was also difficult at first to persuade planning staffs, over which the JIC had no control, to conform to the new arrangements. Despite its early interest in establishing IS (O), Combined Operations HQ had formed its own inter-Service team of intelligence officers in December 1941; this preferred to maintain direct if informal relations with the Service intelligence branches and ISTD,[43] and even with the CIU and SOE,[44] rather than channel its requirements through the IS (O), and the JIC had to be content with asking COHQ to avoid duplication of demands on the Service departments by keeping IS (O) generally informed of the intelligence it was collecting.[45] GHQ Home Forces received a similar request. Its Intelligence Section expanded after the autumn of 1941, when C-in-C Home Forces' responsibilities were extended to include the planning and execution of a large-scale cross-Channel operation.[46] In July 1942, by which time it had acquired its own sub-sections studying relevant Sigint and collecting such photographic interpretations as it required and had its own representatives in MI and AI, it was further agreed that, in an attempt to avoid duplication, there should be a geographical division of labour between GHQ Home Forces and IS (O). Except for the provision of order of battle intelligence, which remained with MI, GHQ Home Forces was made responsible for collating all intelligence for

42. JIC (42) 33rd Meeting, 17 July.
43. CAB 106/3, History of the Combined Operations Organisation, 1940–45, pp 12, 20; ADM 223/90, Basset and Wells, *ISTD*, para 29; Morgan, op cit, pp 34–35, 247–248.
44. Morgan, op cit, p 247; Air Historical Branch, *Air Ministry Intelligence*, p 53; CAB 79/15, COS (41) 387th Meeting, 14 November; JIC (41) 945 and 947, both of 10 November.
45. JIC (41) 470 of 24 December; JIC (42) 31st (o) Meeting, 10 July; 33rd Meeting, 17 July; ADM 223/107, Note to NID 17S, 2 September 1943, para 2.
46. CAB 79/14, COS (41) 314th Meeting, 8 September; CAB 80/59, COS (41) 192 (o) of 6 September, 589 of 27 September; CAB 80/31, COS (41) 630 of 16 November (revised as CAB 80/32, COS (41) 733 of 10 December).

the area 30 miles from the coast between Den Helder and the Loire, and this area was excluded from IS (O)'s jurisdiction.[47]

By that time further complications had arisen from the decision of the Chiefs of Staff in March 1942 to set up the Combined Commanders Group, consisting of C-in-C Home Forces, AOC-in-C Fighter Command, the Chief of Combined Operations and, later, a naval C-in-C, to plan a cross-Channel invasion in 1942 (*Sledge-hammer*), and, from April 1942, a cross-Channel invasion in 1943 (*Roundup*). They were met in the first instance by the decision of the JIC in July that, since the collection and preparation of intelligence for the Combined Commanders Group was being carried out main-ly by the Intelligence Section of GHQ Home Forces, the IS (O) should be excluded from the preparations for *Roundup*.[48] Later in the same month, however, the Anglo-American decision to carry out operation *Torch* in 1942 opened the way to a longer-term solution by precipitating the establishment of Allied Force HQ (AFHQ), with its own Combined Intelligence Section, at Norfolk House.* The Combined Intelligence Section of AFHQ was theoretically responsible for collecting the intelligence required not only for the planning of *Torch*, for which General Eisenhower was appointed C-in-C Allied Expeditionary Force in August 1942, but also for the planning of the cross-Channel invasion, though the latter continued to be carried out by the British Combined Commanders Group until the formation of COSSAC – the fore-runner of SHAEF – in April 1943.

It was not long before the various planning groups began to see the merits of a system for centralising and rationalising, within reason, the ever mounting flow of their requests for intelligence, and the JIC's exclusion of the IS (O) from the *Roundup* planning proved to be unworkable. In the autumn the IS (O) and the ISTD, hard-pressed on other time-consuming projects, were in-structed by the JIC and the Joint Planning Staff to devote 25 per cent of their time to *Roundup* in order that all requirements for this operation should be met early in the new year.[49] Both organisations received compliments from AFHQ for their contributions to the success of the north African landings and the JIC added its own congratulations during a discussion of the staff increases both would need to enable them to meet the still heavier demands AFHQ would make in the future.[50]

---

* See below, p 50.

47. Morgan, op cit, p 55; ADM 223/107, NID 0668 of 25 July 1942; Mockler-Ferryman, *Military Intelligence Organisation*, pp 124–125.
48. JIC (42) 31st (o) Meeting, 10 July.
49. CAB 84/5, JP (42) 179th Meeting, 6 November.
50. JIC (42) 431 (o) of 30 October, 440 (o) of 10 November and 444 of 13 November; JIC (42) 55th Meeting, 3 November; ADM 223/90, paras 91, 99.

In the case of another issue involving co-ordination between the planning of operations and the provision of intelligence – relations between SOE and the SIS and the exercise of direction over their activities – the combined efforts of the JIC and the Joint Planners met with less success. The question was brought to the fore in the spring of 1942 when the JIC drew attention to the lack of intelligence about the European area and the Chiefs of Staff instructed it to 'focus a spotlight on our intelligence system' on the continent.[51] The JIC's first response was to point out that SOE's operations might alert enemy authorities and hamper the collection of intelligence unless there was close co-operation at all stages of planning between SOE, Combined Operations and the SIS.[52] It was perhaps all the more anxious on this score because in March, after a protracted battle and with 'C''s very reluctant consent, SOE, whose communications requirements had expanded beyond anything that the SIS could provide, had acquired its own codes and wireless organisation and no longer depended on those of the SIS. The Chiefs of Staff instructed the Directors of Plans and the Directors of Intelligence to examine the best ways of co-ordinating the activities of SOE with those of the SIS[53] and, pending the outcome of this enquiry, issued two directives to SOE. The first of the directives specified that, with reference to the continent of Europe, SOE must maintain constant collaboration with the Joint Planners and the commanders, conform to their general strategic plans, and take care to avoid precipitating premature patriotic risings.[54] The second dealt with French north Africa; in that theatre it instructed SOE to maintain at all times the closest touch with the SIS in the delicate task of persuading the French to react favourably to Allied operations.[55]

The report commissioned from the Joint Planners and the JIC on relations between the SIS and SOE followed on 15 May. It stressed that the clash of interest between the two bodies was so fundamental that it could not be resolved by enjoining them to work together or laying down general indications of priorities to which they should conform. What was called for was nothing less than their amalgamation into a single service under the general direction of the Chiefs of Staff. It should not be placed under one of the Service ministers or the Foreign Secretary, but be given an executive head on a level with the Chiefs of Staff who would attend all Chiefs of Staff meetings which discussed subjects affecting him.

51.   CAB 80/62, COS (42) 103 (o) of 18 April.
52.   JIC (42) 156 (o) of 29 April.
53.   CAB 79/20, COS (42) 135th and 136th Meetings, 30 April and 1 May.
54.   CAB 80/62, COS (42) 133 (o) of 12 May.
55.   ibid, COS (42) 134 (o) of 12 May; CAB 79/21, COS (42) 147th Meeting, 11 May.

Special arrangements would have to be made to safeguard the interests of the Foreign Office.[56]

Nothing came of this recommendation. The SIS and SOE, no doubt stimulated by the agitation and certainly encouraged by the Prime Minister's staff, made attempts to improve liaison between themselves by discussing the idea of joint attendances at meetings with the Vice-Chiefs of Staff and – though this, too, came to nothing – by considering the formation of a co-ordinating committee.[57] From June 1942 the SIS, at 'C''s suggestion and in order to reduce friction with SOE, maintained a liaison officer with the Joint Planners, who had from time to time expressed regret at the lack of direct contact.[58] But the joint report of the Planners and the JIC was not even discussed by the Chiefs of Staff, and it was left to the Prime Minister's staff, in the person of Major Morton, to continue to use its good offices to improve relations between SOE and the SIS.[59] From the records the reasons for the inaction of the Chiefs of Staff are not entirely clear. It owed something to the fact that they had already been irritated by suggestions from SOE that, as the 'Fourth Arm' in modern warfare, it should be granted full membership of the Chiefs of Staff organisation, especially of the Joint Planners and the JIC. Beyond that it may safely be surmised that an investigation which had had its origin chiefly in an anxiety to curb the operational activities of SOE, but which had ended in advocating the association of the SIS with the Chiefs of Staff, from whom it had been kept separate as a matter of principle, was felt on all sides to have raised more problems than it could possibly solve.

As relations between the SOE and the SIS were thus left unsettled, friction between the two organisations naturally increased when, following the expansion of the war to those areas, the SOE began to be active in Vichy France and French north Africa. Locally, mutual mistrust and friction had been alleviated in the spring of 1942 when the 'private navies' of the SIS, SOE and MI 9, which were each carrying out clandestine operations along the coast of southern France and north-west Africa, were amalgamated into a single Coast Watching Flotilla. But after the *Torch* landings 'C', worried lest his own attempts to rebuild networks in Vichy France would be endangered by the decision that the SOE should organise sabotage there, asked the Prime Minister to impress on the SOE the need to keep in close touch with the SIS.[60] As the

---

56. CAB 80/45, JP (42) 502 of 15 May.
57. CAB 121/305, SIC file B/Special Operations/1, folios 29, 30.
58. CAB 84/4. JP (42) 111th Meeting, 5 June; CAB 121/232, SIC file B/Departments/3, folios 27 a, c, d (correspondence between 'C' and Ismay, 4 and 5 June 1942).
59. CAB 121/305, folios 27b–f.
60. Dir/C Archive 1375 of 13 November 1942.

Joint Planners and the JIC had foreseen, the plea was to no avail. Throughout 1943, and into 1944, the SIS was complaining that agents who had been recruited in France for intelligence purposes were being used in SOE operations. The SIS complaints were all the more sharp, we may assume, because the SOE itself provided an increasing amount of intelligence from the spring of 1943, notably about enemy strengths in Tunisia and the state of the resistance movements in France.[61] The SIS was also smarting in the spring of 1943 from a setback in the eastern Mediterranean. The authorities in London had recently authorised additional flights for the SOE in that area at the expense of the SIS, and had done so in part as a result of an approach by SOE (Middle East) to the Prime Minister during his visit to Cairo in January. But the SOE also had grounds for complaint. Despite the 1941 agreement between the two bodies which had arranged that the SIS would limit its activities in Denmark to its existing agents, and otherwise permit the SOE to act for it there,* the SIS built up a number of new contacts in Denmark during 1942, and it further offended the SOE in August 1943, when the HQ of the Danish MI's network was forced to retreat to Sweden, by demanding direct communications with the HQ in Sweden. Thanks to its excellent relations with the Swedish intelligence service, the Danish organisation was able to maintain constant touch from Sweden with its network in Denmark, which remained intact for the rest of the war.

Relations in north Africa improved in the spring of 1943 when a Special Duties (SD) Squadron was formed for the combined use of the SIS, SOE and MI 9, an arrangement which was extended later in the year with the formation of a combined flight to operate into southern France. But two more attempts to end the bickering between the London HQs, and between their representatives in the European theatre, proved abortive. The first was a proposal made at the instigation of the Security Service (MI 5) in March 1943; it was killed by the Prime Minister. The more so because it felt that such a reform would become essential after the war, MI 5 argued that steps should be taken at once to merge the SIS, the SOE and itself into a single Intelligence Service. The Prime Minister replied that 'every Department which has waxed during the war is now considering how it can quarter its officials on the public indefinitely when peace returns. The less we encourage these illusions the better . . .. I have a feeling that it would be a mistake at the present time to stir up all these pools, and I do not think that the kind of Committee you propose would be fruitful'. He suggested that 'cases

---

* See Volume I, p 278.

61. JIC (43) 12th (o) Meeting, 9 March; JIC (43) 114 and 119 of 13 and
  . 17 March; JIC (43) 325 (o) of 1 August.

of friction could be smoothed out and common action promoted' if the heads of the SIS, the SOE and MI 5 met monthly with his representative, Major Morton. Such meetings were instituted, but only two were held, in April and July.[62] In July, called upon to investigate SIS indications that some of SOE's groups in France had been penetrated, the JIC again pressed for measures that would ensure closer collaboration between the two organisations. Its representations were considered by the Chiefs of Staff and the Defence Committee in August, to little avail as we shall see.[63]*

□

In the quarrels between the SIS and the SOE the bodies which received intelligence from them – the Foreign Office, the JIC and the Service intelligence branches – generally sympathised with the SIS. From the middle of 1941, moreover, by which time the SIS networks and their Allied counterparts were beginning to recover from the disruption they had suffered when Germany had extended her conquests in Europe in the spring and summer of 1940,[†] the Service branches became temporarily less critical of the SIS's performance. In the second half of that year the DMI commended the SIS for its contribution to the success of the Bruneval raid –[‡] 'a very remarkable piece of first-class intelligence such as is rarely obtainable' – and the NID was congratulatory about the naval intelligence it was obtaining from Brest and Lorient, while from the beginning of 1942 the Air Ministry was receiving SIS reports which 'added very considerably' to its knowledge of the German night-fighter organisation in the Low Countries.[§] By then, however, the discontent of the Service branches with the SIS was resurfacing, as it was always liable to do.

One reason for this was that the SIS was still making no progress against some important targets, notably the Army's order of battle in Germany and naval and shipping movements in north German ports, on which Sigint could throw very little light.[64] Another was that its coverage in some areas was undergoing another decline in the wake of a marked tightening up of Germany's counter-espionage measures. It now emerged that the Polish network in Europe had been penetrated in November 1941; it did not begin to

---

* See Volume III.   † See Volume I, especially pp 171, 226.
‡ See below, p 249.   § See below, p 250.

62. Correspondence retained in the Private Office of the Secretary of the Cabinet.
63. CAB 79/63, COS (43) 173rd (o) Meeting 27 July, 178th (o) Meeting, 2 August, 180th (o) Meeting, 4 August; CAB 69/5, DO (43) 7th Meeting, 2 August; JIC (43) 325 (o) of 1 August.
64. WO 208/3573, MI 14 Appreciation for the CIGS, 26 January 1942.

recover until the following summer. Though less seriously affected, the other networks in France were also curbed. Colonel Bertrand,* who had managed to continue operating from unoccupied France and had formed especially useful contacts at the German Embassy in Vichy and the German naval HQ in Paris, was forced to cut back his activities, and the coverage provided by the SIS's own Vichy network was also greatly reduced. The Czech intelligence service underwent a more drastic decline. By June 1942 practically no information was being received from it despite the fact that the SIS had increased its W/T facilities; nor were things improved by the appointment at that time of an SIS liaison officer to the Czechs. To add to SIS's misfortunes, the Czech intelligence service now lost A-54, who had rendered such valuable service from Germany since before the outbreak of war.† A marked man from October 1941, he was finally arrested in March 1942.[65]

In these circumstances the Service Directors of Intelligence were again pressing for reform of the SIS from the beginning of 1942, and in February they secured a reorganisation at SIS HQ by which the three Services each released a senior officer to be a deputy director there who would ensure that the requirements of his intelligence branch were better understood. 'C' formed the three Service deputy directors, together with a fourth appointed from his own staff, into a board responsible for directing the activities of the SIS throughout the world, with each deputy in charge of a different theatre. In June the DNI, who had led the campaign for reform, protested against this way of implementing it: it made it impossible for the deputy directors to carry out the supervision of the work of the SIS on behalf of their own branches. But he received no support from the other Directors of Intelligence and no further change was made until the autumn of 1943, when SIS HQ itself concluded that the deputy director system was unsatisfactory. Another reorganisation at that time removed responsibility for SIS operations from the Service representatives by replacing the deputy directors with regional controllers.

If little further was heard after the middle of 1942 of the complaint that the SIS was failing to understand the needs of its customers, the reason lay partly in the fact that there was less and less substance in it. On the one hand, the Service branches came to recognise that, if the SIS was still not meeting some of their important needs, the reason lay rather with difficulties in the field over which it had little control or with the intractability of the more important targets. On the other, to compensate for the setbacks it received in some areas during 1942, it gained ground in others. In

---

* See Volume I, Appendix 1.   † See Volume I, p 58.

65. Amort and Jedlica, *The Canaris File* (1970), pp 141, 145.

Norway it now established ship-watchers in all the main ports except Bergen and at several other places overlooking the shipping routes – though the station at Trondheim was still handicapped by W/T difficulties, and no agent was able to penetrate Altenfjord until 1943.* From the middle of the year the agents it had installed in Denmark were supplying details about the GAF's night-fighter and radar defences. Though the number of agents in the Netherlands remained small, it improved its contacts with the Dutch who, in a reorganisation in 1942, established a new Intelligence Bureau. In Spain the ban imposed by the British Ambassador on the operation of clandestine W/T sets† was lifted in the spring of 1942, enabling it to set up coastal stations and supply some naval and shipping intelligence.[66] Penetration of the south of France and of north-west Africa from Gibraltar greatly improved with the creation of the Coast Watching Flotilla,‡ and some progress was also made in establishing a network in Tunisia and Libya that was controlled from Malta. In the Middle East, where the networks, starved of resources, especially of air transport, had produced nothing of value up to the middle of 1942, things so much improved that by the end of the year the SIS was at last accepted as 'a serious intelligence agency' and granted close contacts with the C-in-C and the Minister of State.

In consequence of some of these developments the SIS was providing good coverage of the western Mediterranean in the weeks before the Allied landings in French north-west Africa in November 1942; and after the landings, when SIS Algiers and SIS Middle East were able to co-operate on the SCU/SLU link between First and Eighth Armies, it was to supply some intelligence of operational value.§ In Europe, on the other hand, operation *Torch* led to a further setback for the SIS by precipitating the German occupation of Vichy France, where its own and the Polish and Free French networks suffered heavy casualties and widespread arrests and Bertrand, forced to retreat to the Italian-occupied zone in the south, lost most of his remaining contacts. In addition it was later to emerge that one of the largest Free French networks was penetrated to the extent that from early in 1943 two of its senior members were Abwehr agents.[67] But the SIS recovered from this blow more quickly than from earlier setbacks. By March 1943 four of its networks of Vichy contacts were again reporting and, although Bertrand's reduced organisation encountered growing

---

* See below, p 203.   † See Volume I, pp 275–276.
‡ See above, p 15.   § See below, Chapters 24 and 27.

66.   CAB 79/14, COS (41) 307th Meeting, 1 September.
67.   G Bertrand, *L'Enigma ou la plus grande énigme de la guerre 1939–1945* (1973), p 147.

difficulties, the Polish and Free French networks had also resumed communication with London. And from the middle of 1943 there was to be continued expansion and improvement in the SIS's coverage, of France as of other areas, despite the recurrence from time to time of setbacks at the hands of the enemy's intelligence and security organisations.

□

In struggling to mitigate the effects of its own reverses, as in carrying out with MI 5 the work of inflicting reverses on its enemy counterparts, the SIS derived increasing assistance after the end of 1941 from the cyphers used by the German espionage and counter-espionage authorities, particularly the Abwehr and the Security Police. Decrypts of the Security Police traffic gave information about clandestine German operations against Allied agents.* GC and CS, having broken some of the hand cyphers of the Abwehr at different dates during 1940,† was by December 1941 at last obtaining enough intercepts to enable it to break the Enigma key used by the Abwehr for W/T communications between Berlin and its main stations in occupied and neutral countries; and from February 1942 it read the traffic in a separate key that was used between Berlin and the Abwehr's espionage stations in the Straits of Gibraltar.‡ From June 1941 CBME supplemented the work of GC and CS by decrypting the locally intercepted signals in the hand cyphers used by the Abwehr in Turkey and later by the Abwehr and the Sicherheitsdienst in the Balkans, the Aegean and north Africa. As a result of these developments the number of Abwehr and SD signals decrypted, most of them currently, doubled during 1942. By the spring of 1943, when decrypts numbered some 3,000 a week, the British authorities had been reading a large proportion of the Abwehr's total wireless traffic for over a year, and they continued to do so even after the Abwehr improved its cyphers and its wireless security in the latter part of 1943. These measures made it virtually impossible to exploit the hand cyphers at GC and CS for several months. Meanwhile, however, the initial break into the new cypher systems was made at CBME, and in January 1944 the head of the CBME Abwehr section returned to GC and CS to assist in extending to other areas the success achieved in the Middle East.

The Abwehr decrypts were valuable above all for counter-intelligence purposes, for which reason the SIS's Radio Security

---

* See Appendix 5.   † See Volume I, p 120 fn.
‡ See Appendices 4 and 15.

Service (RSS) retained responsibility for intercepting them and became the chief adviser on the use to which they were put. But from its scrutiny of such things as the questions the Abwehr was putting to its agents and the adjustments it was making to its organisation the RSS could sometimes extract intelligence of operational and political interest; and it developed a section to look after the interests of other customers than MI 5 and the SIS and appointed watchkeepers to the GC and CS section which undertook the decryption and translation of the decrypts. From the summer of 1942 intelligence from the Secret Service Sigint began to be passed with the Service Sigint direct from GC and CS to the Middle East on the SCU/SLU link. Partly because the most important part of its output was derived from the breaking of machine cyphers, it had already been decided that GC and CS's Secret Service Section should remain at Bletchley Park when, in a major reorganisation in the spring of 1942, the commercial and diplomatic sections were hived off from the remainder of GC and CS.

The reorganisation of GC and CS was preceded, in the winter of 1941–42, by another attempt to wrest control of it from 'C'. Like that of the previous winter,* the demand for change was made by the War Office; and more determined than on the earlier occasion, when he had requested that the Y Committee should investigate and report to the JIC, the DMI now proposed that the JIC should replace the Y Board in control of Sigint policy.

When the DMI opened his new campaign in September 1941 the very fact that the Sigint service was expanding so fast emphasised the extent to which it still suffered from shortages of manpower and equipment. If it had acquired the facilities it needed for intercepting, decrypting and translating all the enemy's wireless traffic, which was far from being the case, it would have suffered even more than it did from the inadequacy of communications for Sigint purposes. In the autumn of 1941, for example, enemy high-grade signals which were intercepted in the Middle East but which had to be forwarded to GC and CS for exploitation† were being received there with a delay of between two and five days if transmitted by wireless in cypher, and were often subjected to as much as a month's further delay before Bletchley's Cypher Office could decypher them; while less urgent intercepts, sent from the

---

* See Volume I, p 270 et seq.

† A GC and CS officer, known as the Fort Control Officer, operated at CBME from May 1941. His function was to arrange for the interception by Middle East resources of networks exploitable by Bletchley Park for the benefit of Middle East Command. It was not until after the GSO I responsible for Sigint at GHQ, ME visited Bletchley in June 1941 that it was appreciated in Cairo that such interception was not, as had previously been thought, a diversion of Middle East resources to meet War Office intelligence priorities.

Middle East by air, took three weeks to arrive.* At the same time, while all three Services complained of these delays, the War Office resented them most bitterly because it was still benefiting less than the other two Services from GC and CS's cryptanalytic successes. The Air Ministry was profiting from the solution of more and more GAF Enigma keys; the Admiralty had the satisfaction that the naval Enigma had been read regularly since May 1941 and that since the summer of that year GC and CS had also broken into the cypher used by the Italian Navy to carry the bulk of the enemy's communications about his Mediterranean shipping;† but GC and CS was still achieving only occasional solutions of Enigma keys used by the German Army on the Russian front and in Libya, so that, apart from what it obtained from GC and CS's reading of German police traffic and a railway Enigma key, the War Office was receiving little high-grade Sigint that was of direct importance to it.‡ To make matters worse, the quarrels between GC and CS and MI 8, which had precipitated the enquiry of the winter of 1940–1941, had not died down.

These quarrels centred on the fact that while MI 8 was responsible for intercepting German Army and GAF traffic and subjecting it to Traffic Analysis, and GC and CS controlled cryptanalysis, cryptanalysis and Traffic Analysis were inseparable, or at least not easily separated.§ MI 8, which had amalgamated its scattered Traffic Analysis parties into a single unit in the spring of 1941, was by the summer, following the extension of German operations to Libya, the Balkans and Russia, acquiring a thorough understanding of the behaviour of the Enigma W/T networks of the German Army and the GAF. In July it solved the complicated German Army call-sign system. This achievement greatly simplified GC and CS's task of deciding what cryptanalytic priority to give to the various Enigma keys. At the same time, it greatly strengthened MI 8's insistence that it must undertake its Traffic

---

* By this time GC and CS's UK communications were 'good, if not very good'. Its overseas communications were 'woefully inadequate'. For example, Cypher Office, which had taken over responsibility for the Middle East from Air Section in April 1941, was so completely swamped by the end of that year by the amount of intercepts being transmitted from the Middle East that a million groups of undecyphered backlog had to be destroyed in January 1942; as an indication of the scale of expansion in the total communications sent out from GC and CS, which was much increased by the US entry into the war, the weekly total of groups encyphered grew from $\frac{1}{4}$ million at the end of 1941 to 1 million at the end of 1942 and to 2 million by the middle of 1943.

† The Italians had adopted this system under pressure from the Germans who claimed that the existing Italian cyphers were vulnerable. It was a medium-grade cypher which had first been intercepted in December 1940, when the Italian Navy's use of its version of the Enigma machine was declining, and which turned out to be based on a modification of the commercially available Swedish C38 machine. It is referred to hereafter as the C38m for reasons of brevity.

‡ For further details of GC and CS's progress against enemy cyphers see below p 27 et seq and Appendix 4.

§ See Volume I, pp 269–270.

Analysis at GC and CS, in close proximity to the decryption of the Enigma traffic; but while GC and CS had now welcomed the transfer to Bletchley of MI 8's Traffic Analysis section, 100 strong, the transfer was still being delayed by accommodation problems, which were not solved until May 1942. Meanwhile, MI 8 was equally insistent that it could not carry out its responsibility for directing interception policy, so as to meet the operational needs of the General Staff, while GC and CS exercised the chief influence on what was intercepted; particularly in view of the continuing grave shortage of intercept sets and resources, it must itself control the interception programme.

It was in these circumstances that in September 1941 the DMI complained to the Y Board that, though it was 'vital', the Sigint programme was suffering from shortage of equipment and a lack of effective operational control and that, briefed by MI 8, he suggested that the direction of Sigint policy should be taken out of the hands of the Y Board and given to the JIC. The Y Board, he argued, was exercising only very general control, as could be judged from the fact that it met less than once a month; actual control, such as it was, was being exercised by GC and CS, and thus by people 'who rightly have no touch with the Operational and Planning Directorates of the Ministries, and no knowledge of our future operations'.

In the discussions at the Y Board which followed this démarche GC and CS justified its executive direction of the interception programme without disputing the need for instructions from Whitehall: the operational control of interception was an hour-to-hour business which had to be left to its own experts, but they should work to a general policy that was laid down and kept under review by higher authority. GC and CS might well have added that, as well as calling for decisions about the priority to be given to work for the Navy, the Air Force and the Army, general policy was unavoidably influenced by the cryptanalytic situation as well as by strategic need – by what GC and CS could do, as much as by what Whitehall might wish. At any rate the other Directors of Intelligence, tolerably satisfied with the existing arrangements, again failed to back up the War Office's demand for reorganisation, and the DMI resorted to bringing pressure to bear on the Y Board via the Chiefs of Staff.

At their weekly meeting with the JIC on 23 December 1941 the Chiefs of Staff, at the instigation of the CIGS, asked the Y Board to make an urgent examination of the organisation of the Sigint service and to make proposals for meeting its needs for extra equipment, accommodation and staff.[68] On 9 January 1942 they

---

68. CAB 79/16, COS (41) 432nd Meeting, 23 December.

approved the Y Board's recommendations.[69] Most of these dealt
with the needs of the service. As well as a crash programme to
increase staff and equipment for the intercept stations and at GC
and CS, they included the creation of a special W/T network
reserved for the transmission of the raw material and the product of
Sigint; the allocation of space in transport aircraft for the same
purpose; the granting of absolute priority to demands for the
requisitioning of premises in the neighbourhood of GC and CS and
of intercept stations; the request that cryptanalysis should be
treated as a reserved occupation. But two of the recommendations
reaffirmed the principle that the Sigint service should be controlled
from the United Kingdom: high-grade cryptanalysis and research
must continue to be concentrated in Bletchley and Washington;
and in their breaking and exploitation of low and medium-grade
systems, overseas bureaux must be guided and directed from home.
Against this principle, as a result of the continuing grave shortage
of W/T communications for Sigint purposes and of the recent
capture of Army Enigma keys in the Western Desert,* Whitehall
had received renewed proposals from the Middle East for the
decryption of high-grade Sigint in the theatre† and a demand from
India for independence from GC and CS, and GHQ Home Forces
had suggested even that work on the Enigma in the United
Kingdom should be decentralised. But the Y Board was unanimous
in maintaining that all such requests must be rejected.

On the questions that had precipitated its inquiry – Who should
control the Sigint programme in the United Kingdom and exercise
the United Kingdom's direction over the Sigint effort overseas?
Through what machinery? – the Y Board similarly reaffirmed that
it exercised these powers itself under the authority of the Chiefs of
Staff. Nor was its jurisdiction ever challenged again.‡ At the same
time, it recognised that over and above its other recommendations
it would have to take steps to improve the direct relations,
complicated, fractious but at the same time flexible and increasing-

---

* See below, pp 310, 374.

† See Volume I, p 219 et seq for earlier proposals of this kind. But the subject was to be
raised again from time to time, see, for example, below p 423.

‡ Between October 1942 and the spring of 1943 the War Office again advocated a
reorganisation of the Sigint system, one by which GC and CS should be responsible for
interception, Traffic Analysis and cryptanalysis in all theatres of war, exercising its function
through a subordinate Y centre in each theatre, while the processing and assessment of
decrypts was carried out by separate Sigint units for each of the three Services in each
theatre, at home and abroad. The War Office put these proposals before the Y Board. The Y
Board was all but unanimous in deciding that they were impracticable; by the spring of 1943,
indeed, when communications for Sigint purposes were rapidly improving, it was beginning
to contemplate the closing down of all overseas cryptanalytic bureaux in favour of
centralisation at GC and CS, and their replacement by a GC and CS adviser at each
command.

69.   CAB 79/56, COS (42) 1st (o) Meeting, 9 January.

ly informal, between GC and CS and the intelligence branches in Whitehall.

□

The most important of these steps was a programme to rectify the managerial weaknesses of GC and CS. These weaknesses had attracted criticism from the intelligence branches of the Service departments in the winter of 1940–1941.* Since that time they had become more pronounced as an organisation which had started life as a small cryptanalytic bureau dealing predominantly with Axis diplomatic cyphers had evolved not only into the main Sigint production centre concerned primarily with enemy military cyphers but also into the headquarters of a Sigint network that was virtually world-wide. Having increased four-fold to about 900 between the outbreak of war and the beginning of 1941, the number of people it employed had grown to nearly 1,500 by early 1942, and it was clear by then that its expansion must be continued at a still more rapid rate.[†]

Even in dealing with straightforward difficulties – housing, feeding, transport and welfare for the expanding staff, and physical security for Bletchley Park and its expanding annexes and out-stations – the administration, carried out by 'C''s officers with advice from a Joint Committee of Control comprising representatives from the SIS and GC and CS, was proving ineffective. For more complicated matters like forward planning for GC and CS's future needs in staff and equipment and the energetic presentation of these requirements to the Y Board, the administrative system was still more inadequate, not to say wholly unsuitable – and so much so that in October 1941 the cryptanalysts who headed the attack on the Enigma keys took the desperate, but not unprofitable, step of appealing for help directly to the Prime Minister.[‡] But matters were brought to a head in the autumn of 1941 by the friction which arose within GC and CS from the employment of civilians and Service officers alongside each other and from disputes between officers seconded to GC and CS from the different Services.

This friction, negligible so long as GC and CS had been composed mainly of civilian and Service cryptanalysts, had steadily become more explosive after the Air Ministry and the War Office, following the first breaks into the Enigma, had seconded intelligence officers to that section of GC and CS which translated and

---

* See Volume I, p 273 et seq.

† It employed 3,293 staff (1,727 civilian, 1,566 Services) in December 1942; 5,052 (2,635 civilian, 2,417 Services) in June 1943. In March 1943 the Chiefs of Staff authorised the expansion of its staff by a further 1,760, most of which it had received by June 1944.

‡ See Appendix 3.

elucidated the Air Force and Army Enigma decrypts and disseminated the resulting intelligence. In order to avoid conflict – and also in order to preserve the principle that the production of Sigint was the preserve of the SIS, whose authority must be interpolated between the Sigint product and its consumers – it had been laid down that on secondment to GC and CS these officers were attached to the SIS; and it had been understood by the civilian administration at GC and CS that their functions would be to ensure that the Enigma output was sent to the Service intelligence branches and the Middle East commands in the form most suitable to their needs and, secondly, to assist the watches which translated and elucidated the Enigma decrypts by advising on the needs and priorities of their Services. The seconded officers, maintaining not unnaturally that their first duty was to AI or MI, quickly developed a different view of their functions, and by October 1941 their discontent, mounting in step with the ever-increasing stream of Enigma decrypts, had culminated in the demand that they should have total operational control of the staff engaged in translating and elucidating the decrypts, and selecting from them those which should be passed to Whitehall and operational theatres, the head of that staff being restricted to its administration. In November 'C' granted this demand, which was supported by the AI and MI sections at the SIS. But the new system proved to be no easier to operate than that which it replaced – not least because the senior AI and MI officers at GC and CS began to quarrel with each other as well as with the administrator.

In January 1942, when the spate of argument and recrimination was damaging efficiency and threatening a breakdown of discipline, 'C' in his capacity as Director of GC and CS appointed an independent investigator, a former DDMI, to report not only on the dispute about the handling of the product of Air Force and Army Enigma and on the administrative control of GC and CS, but also on the functioning of GC and CS's Naval and Air Sections. In February 'C' implemented the recommendations that came out of the inquiry. The administration of GC and CS by the Joint Committee of Control was abolished in a process by which the civil (that is the diplomatic and commercial cryptanalysis) sections were withdrawn from Bletchley and placed under a Deputy Director (C) while the Service sections, those which had grown up around the core of the pre-war GC and CS and which had now added to their cryptanalytic work intelligence functions of great significance, were placed under a Deputy Director (S). Subject only to control by 'C', who remained Director of GC and CS, and by the Y Board on which he was GC and CS's representative, the DD (S) was given undisputed responsibility for all work done at Bletchley for the Service ministries, including intelligence, and was provided with new administrative staff to replace the SIS administrators who accompanied the DD (C) to his new quarters. It was also laid down that DD (S)'s heads of sections, although many of them were civilians, should have operational control of their Service personnel, and on that basis what had been the two most controversial issues were now settled. With the arrival of the whole of MI 8's Traffic Analysis staff at Bletchley in May 1942 the quarrel about who should control Army/GAF interception and Traffic Analysis subsided. The dispute about the day-to-day control over the processing of Army and Air Force Enigma decrypts was terminated by the appointment of a new head of the section who was made directly responsible only to the DD (S) and who, though an RAF officer, was not only to act for AI and MI but also to look after NID's interests on an inter-Service basis.*

In the relations between GC and CS and the intelligence branches in Whitehall the reorganisation of February 1942 inaugurated a period of continual improvement. The improvement owed much to the fact that GC and CS had at last acquired an administrative structure that was adequate for the proper direction of its increasingly complex and varied activities. But it was also brought about because GC and CS's work had already entered upon a new phase when the reorganisation was effected. It so happened that the reorganisation coincided not only with the final abandonment of the attempt to read the Italian Navy's high-grade book cyphers, which was rendered hopeless when the Italians made fundamental changes in February 1942, but also with another setback, one that was far more serious if less permanent. At the beginning of February 1942 the introduction by the U-boat Command of a separate Enigma key, one that used four wheels, deprived GC and CS of the ability to decrypt signals to and from U-boats.[†] Against these disappointments, however, may be set the fact that from the middle of 1941 GC and CS had embarked upon what was to become an all-but unbroken chain of success against the enemy's high and medium-grade Service and police cyphers.[‡]

---

* For some time the GAF/Army Enigma section had selected Enigma shipping intelligence for transmission to the Middle East and a Mediterranean watch in the Naval Section had selected the C38m decrypts. In the reorganisation of February 1942 the naval Mediterranean watch was attached to the GAF/Army Enigma watch and, to ensure that all Sigint about the maritime situation in the Mediterranean was properly processed and selected before despatch from GC and CS, the NID reinforced the watch with naval officers.

† See below, p 179.

‡ For details of these successes down to the middle of 1943 see Appendix 4. Greater difficulty was encountered, on the other hand, in the work against Axis diplomatic cyphers. The Japanese systems continued to be read regularly, but Italy introduced more difficult cyphers in the summer of 1942, which were not mastered until the end of that year, and Vichy introduced new cyphers in November 1942 in Europe and the Middle East; these remained insoluble, so that Vichy's traffic with the Far East, where the old cyphers were only modified, was all that was read for the remainder of the war. As for the German diplomatic

By the summer of 1942 it was reading 4 SS Enigma keys in addition to medium and low-grade hand cyphers used by the German police* and it had so extended its mastery over the GAF Enigma that it was regularly reading 22 different keys. By the same date, as we have seen, it had done much to off-set its failure against the Italian naval book cyphers, and the disuse by the Italian Navy of its version of the Enigma cypher, by breaking, from the summer of 1941, the C 38 m.[†] And not less important, it had at last broken into the Enigma keys of the German Army. The first Army key to be broken regularly was one that was in use on the Russian front: GC and CS read it from soon after the invasion of Russia, on 27 June 1941. From November 1941 it was reading regularly the two main Army keys in use in the Middle East. By the summer of 1942 it had broken two more Army keys.

In the year beginning the summer of 1942 GC and CS continued to enlarge on these successes. By that summer it was solving each day the daily settings of some 26 Army and GAF keys, these being usually the most important and most heavily used of the 50 or so different keys then in force throughout the Army and the GAF, and with only a brief reduction in January 1943, caused by the introduction of a new call-sign system for some of the networks of the German Army, this figure steadily increased during the next twelve months as staff and equipment limitations at GC and CS were reduced. From the summer of 1942, moreover, it broke regularly the Süd Enigma key (named Porpoise by GC and CS), then being used by German naval commands in the Mediterranean, the Balkans and the Black Sea.[‡] In December 1942 it at last solved the separate four-wheel Enigma key that had been used by the U-boat Command since the previous February.[§] And already by the same date it had all but completed the enormous feat of creating the new sections and developing the new techniques in

---

cyphers, some were broken by GC and CS from October 1942. But despite close collaboration between the US and GC and CS none of the traffic was read currently until early in 1943; and what was read was not of the highest importance, the most secret German correspondence being transmitted in one-time pad. The first decrypt from this traffic to reach the Prime Minister was sent on 5 October 1942; it was of no importance. The next went to him on 29 March 1943, but it was a decrypt of a telegram dated 29 June 1942 which told all German missions that their most important task was to discover the place of the Allied invasion.[70] The Enigma key used by the German Naval Attaché in Tokyo (known to GC and CS as Seahorse) was not broken until the autumn of 1943.

  * For the nature of the intelligence obtained from these cyphers see Appendix 5.
  † See above, p 22 fn†.

  ‡ This key had been introduced in the Mediterranean and the Balkans in 1941 but its traffic had been put aside at GC and CS on the assumption that it would not be breakable until its quantity increased; but when it was examined in the summer of 1942, when it was also being used in the Black Sea, it turned out that it was encyphered on a relatively uncomplicated pre-war machine and could be decrypted with no special difficulty.

  § See below, pp 233, 548, 551–552.

70.   Dir/C Archive 2771 of 29 March 1943.

interception and cryptanalysis that enabled it from the end of 1942 to read the high-level operational communications for which the German Army had recently introduced new links using encyphered non-morse transmissions.

In terms of the amount of intelligence it yielded, GC and CS's success in solving the cypher system (Geheimschreiber; named Fish by GC and CS) used for these non-morse transmissions was never to be as valuable as its mastery of the Enigma keys. During 1943 the number of decrypts it yielded – about 330 per month at the beginning of the year, dropping to less than 250 per month at the end – was a trickle compared with the output of Enigma decrypts, which rose from some 39,000 per month (25,000 Army and GAF; 14,000 Navy) in the early part of 1942 to over 84,000 per month (48,000 Army and GAF; 36,000 Navy) between the autumn of 1943 and the end of the war.* In terms of the intelligence value of their contents, on the other hand, the decrypts of Geheimschreiber were commonly more important than the Enigma; moreover, a Fish decrypt commonly incorporated a large number of individual signals. Whereas the bulk of the Enigma traffic was at and below Army level, the Fish links were confined to communications at Army level and above, that is between Armies and Army Groups and OKH; this being so, they carried orders, appreciations and situation reports, and even routine returns of strength and supplies, of which the decrypts were of exceptional significance.

This was one reason why comparatively little Fish traffic was intercepted, the Fish networks being less numerous and carrying far less traffic than the Enigma. But it was not the only reason for the huge discrepancy between the amount of Fish and the amount of Enigma that GC and CS produced. Still more relevant is the fact that at every stage of exploitation – at the point of interception; in the work of solving the basic settings of its cypher machine; at the stage of decrypting the transmissions even after the basic settings had been solved – the attack on Fish had to surmount intellectual, technological and organisational problems of a still higher order than those presented by the Enigma machine, and even than those which GC and CS overcame in breaking the four-wheel Enigma by the end of 1942. That it had solved them to the extent that a proportion of the Fish intercepts could be decrypted nearly current-ly on a regular basis from the beginning of 1943, at a time when the Germans were making only limited use of the new system and were still intending to improve it in the light of experience, is an impressive tribute to GC and CS's work. It need not be doubted, moreover, that at the time the vigilance with which it had monitored the Fish system from the outset, the ingenuity with

---

* Compare also GC and CS's output of Axis diplomatic decrypts; they totalled 14,050 in 1943, the best year of the war.

which it had exploited the failure of the Germans themselves to uphold the rigorously high standards of operating which the system called for, and the resourcefulness with which it had invented and organised novel advances in machine-construction and Traffic Analysis, and co-ordinated them in an immensely intricate programme, did more than add a highly-prized new element to the range of its increasing Sigint output. Its achievement against Fish consolidated the enhanced prestige which the sheer bulk of this output, increasing with its very new success, had brought to GC and CS since the autumn of 1941.*

From as early as the end of 1941 GC and CS's growing prestige and output had brought about the transfer to Bletchley of more and more Service personnel, many of them war-time recruits from the occupations which were supplying Bletchley's civilians, and had produced between Bletchley and the intelligence branches in Whitehall growing mutual recognition of each other's knowledge and experience. It was thanks to these developments that the rigid barriers of jealousy and incomprehension which had initially separated cryptanalysis from intelligence – the techniques of producing Sigint from those required for interpreting, understanding and disseminating it – had already begun to dissolve when the administration of GC and CS was reformed in February 1942. And from that date, under the combined impact of the reorganisation of GC and CS and its continuing successes, they finally collapsed. The intelligence branches accepted that GC and CS did not infringe their rights if, as well as deciding on interception and cryptanalytic priorities, it interpreted the Sigint material it produced and disseminated the intelligence direct to overseas commands; and they recognised that, the better to perform these functions, no less than to carry out its cryptanalysis, GC and CS must be given intelligence from other sources and, under safeguards, even knowledge of future Allied operational intentions and the needs they were likely to generate. They recognised, indeed, that GC and CS was on some matters better placed to interpret Sigint than they were themselves – that its research methods and voluminous indexes, initially developed to help it to attack cyphers and to elucidate and reconstruct the texts of decrypts, gave it unrivalled expertise on subjects like enemy cover-names, proformas, technical terms and signals routines which not infrequently provided the best or the sole clues to the operational significance of the enemy's messages. Nor was their growing appreciation of the value of this expertise confined to the work of the numerically small sections of GC and CS which processed the high-grade decrypts. By the beginning of 1942 they were increasingly aware that at

---

* For further details of Fish see Volume III.

Bletchley, where alone the outputs of the enemy's high, medium and low-grade communications were studied in close proximity, the research of those sections which concentrated on the enemy's tactical codes and W/T and R/T procedures – notably the Air Section – had much to contribute to the improvement of current or operational intelligence.* From the same date GC and CS responded by steadily improving the procedures by which it regulated its interception and cryptanalytic priorities, as between the needs of the three Services and of different theatres of war, in close consultation with the Service intelligence branches; and it became less academic in presenting what it had to offer, less narrow in its conception of its functions and, as it ceased to be treated as a Foreign Office body dabbling in Service affairs, less defensive in presenting its requirements. Talk about the needs or the responsibilities of the three Services and GC and CS gave place on both sides to willing partnership in the task of operating and developing a single Sigint service; and it was in this spirit that for the remainder of the war Whitehall and Bletchley shared the work of wrestling with continuing but declining shortages, of adjusting to recurring but diminishing setbacks and thus of providing both a constantly increasingly supply of Sigint to the operational authorities and increasingly effective guidance and control for Sigint authorities and stations overseas.

□

As with the organisation of Sigint, so with that of two other sources that were of growing importance as supplying intelligence on a continuous basis – prisoners of war and photographic reconnaissance – the period from the middle of 1941 to the middle of 1943 was one in which, while difficulties persisted, inter-Service and other conflicts were steadily reduced by the expansion of resources and the accumulation of experience.

The organisation for handling POW naturally expanded most in the Middle East. Equally naturally, though it developed under the general supervision of CSDIC (ME), its expansion there took place chiefly on separate Service lines. Thus, from the spring of 1942 a small interrogation staff was attached to C-in-C Mediterranean to be responsible for all naval POW intelligence in the Mediterranean and the Indian Ocean, while a primarily Army mobile unit was set up in the Western Desert; and thereafter the CSDIC detachments that were set up elsewhere were mainly air or

---

* Work on the German Army's field cyphers was not properly organised in the United Kingdom, as opposed to the Middle East and north Africa, before the spring of 1943–see below, Appendix 18 and Volume III. For the work done in the United Kingdom on the GAF's tactical communications see below, Chapter 20.

mainly naval or mainly army, as operational requirements demanded. CSDIC (ME) and its detachments concentrated on obtaining operational and tactical intelligence; more valuable POWs,
such as General von Thoma after the battle of Alamein, were sent
back after initial interrogation to the United Kingdom, where the
more long-term and the more technical results of interrogation
were collated with other intelligence before being disseminated to
the commands.[71] The same procedure was followed by the
interrogation teams which, separate from CSDIC (ME), were
formed to accompany the Allied landings in French north Africa in
November 1942. Initially these teams, one British and one American, operated independently, but in February 1943 they were
amalgamated with US and British technical officers into the Allied
Captured Intelligence Centre (ACIC) at Algiers. In the following
month French representatives were attached to the ACIC and in
May, following discussions with CSDIC (ME), the interrogation
sections of the Centre were formed into CSDIC (Algiers).[72]

In the United Kingdom, despite the fact that before the end of
1942 most POW were air or naval, CSDIC and other organisations closely associated with it continued to be administered by the
War Office.* In October 1941 the War Office established a new
section (MI 9(a)) to administer CSDIC and the POW Interrogation Service (PWIS), which undertook the preliminary interrogation of POW on their arrival in the country and which supplied
interrogators to accompany such British raids as those against St
Nazaire and Dieppe. In January 1941 a centre was established
under the ministerial control of the Home Office at the Royal
Victoria Patriotic Schools at Wandsworth, and later known as the
London Reception Centre (LRC), for the reception and interrogation of alien escapees and refugees. In December 1941 a new
section (MI 19) was created to be responsible on behalf of the
Services for the military work of these three organisations, leaving
MI 9 the work of questioning escaped British POW and, increasingly, of developing in conjunction with the SIS an organisa-
tion to assist them to escape, and an additional DDMI – DDMI
(PW) – was appointed to take charge of both sections.[73]

---

* See Volume I, p 283.

71. Mockler-Ferryman, op cit, p 185; *Air Ministry Intelligence*, p 100; Morgan,
     op cit, pp 16, 72; ADM 223/84, Draft History of POW Intelligence, p 56.
72. Mockler-Ferryman, op cit, pp 169–170, 185; *Air Ministry Intelligence*, pp
     126–127.
73. Mockler-Ferryman, op cit, pp 17, 48, 52–56; ADM 223/84, pp 5–6; *Air
     Ministry Intelligence*, pp 100, 118, 143; JIC (41) 398 (o) of 7 October, 425 (o)
     of 31 October; CAB 79/15, COS (41) 352nd, 358th, 377th and 382nd
     Meetings, 13 and 17 October, 5 and 10 November; CAB 80/60, COS (41)
     247 (o) of 6 November. For the work of MI 9 see M R D Foot and J M
     Langley, *MI 9: Escape and Evasion* (1979).

Together with administrative control by the War Office on behalf of the other Services and other departments, the principle of inter-Service collaboration in the operation of a single organisation was in general maintained at the CSDIC and the associated bodies. At the LRC, where refugees arriving mainly from France, Denmark and Norway provided a steady flow of information about conditions in occupied Europe, all three Services maintained interrogators as did MI 5 and the SIS and, later, PWE and MEW.[74] Although the CSDIC had already evolved as three Service sections, each reporting separately to its own Service intelligence branch, all three sections moved together during the first half of 1942 to new quarters at Latimer in Buckinghamshire, where they worked in comparative harmony despite some divergencies about methods.[75]

Some light is thrown on these divergencies by the air and naval accounts of CSDIC. The Air Ministry account shows that the Air Section at CSDIC maintained a comprehensive index of GAF personalities and order of battle, based on all available sources, and emphasises that experience showed that better results were obtained if interrogators had a breadth of knowledge over and above their specialist interests.[76] The Admiralty account, on the other hand, explains that the NID deliberately refrained from supplying its interrogators with much information from other sources in the belief that their interrogations would be distorted and their reports adulterated by too wide a knowledge; and it contrasts its own procedure with that of the Air Section at CSDIC, whose reports it criticises for mixing up POW remarks with other information and glossing the factual reports of interrogations with the conjectures and interpretations of the interrogators.[77]

Whatever may be thought about these different approaches, the accounts agree that with occasional notable exceptions it was not until 1942 that POW interrogations came to be classed among the reliable sources of intelligence. According to the Air Ministry, the intelligence branches and the operational authorities did not accept them as authoritative during the first two years of the war.[78] The NID account illustrates the low regard for POW intelligence in the intelligence and operational branches of the Admiralty, instancing their refusal to believe POW claims that U-boats could dive to a depth of 600 feet, that the U-boat command had developed supply U-boats* and that *Narvik*-class destroyers had 15 cm guns, but

---

* See below p 229.

74.   Mockler-Ferryman, op cit, p 56.
75.   ibid, p 54.
76.   *Air Ministry Intelligence*, Chapter 7.
77.   ADM 223/84, pp 31–32, 51.
78.   *Air Ministry Intelligence*, Chapter 7, para 86.

confesses that it was due in some measure to the fact that naval POW intelligence did not get into its stride until the middle of 1942. On the other hand, it claims that improvements in interrogation methods and the recruitment of stool-pigeons in sufficient numbers produced from that date both an increasing supply of specialised and technical information and a healthy respect for the intelligence obtained from POW.[79]* The growth in the amount of intelligence and in the attention paid to it was to be reflected in the up-grading of the naval and air elements of CSDIC in the summer of 1943, when additional Assistant Directors of Intelligence – ADNI (PW) and ADI (K) – were appointed in NID and AI to watch over the interests of the Services.[80]

The Service departments were far less slow to recognise the value of photographic reconnaissance. In the summer of 1941 the importance attached to this source had already produced, against a background of inter-Service recrimination about its neglect, the decision to give priority to its expansion and agreement on two organisational measures for maximising the employment of its scarce resources in high-performance aircraft and trained interpreters. One of these steps was the establishment of the CIU as the inter-Service centre for the interpretation of photography under the control of the Assistant Chief of Staff (Intelligence) at the Air Ministry (ACAS (I)) and for all training in interpretation. The other was the amalgamation into a single formation in Coastal Command, under the operational control of ACAS (I), of the main operational PR units in the United Kingdom.† Of these two measures the former required little subsequent revision. From September 1941, when a new inter-Service School of Photographic Intelligence was set up, doubling the previous capacity to 40 trainees,[81] the CIU expanded up to and then beyond its initial establishment – 104 RAF and WAAF officers – and set about developing additional specialised sections to meet the increasingly varied demands that were made upon it by the intelligence bodies. It had 14 interpretation sections by February 1942 which included, as well as those for the Navy and Army, sections on airfield construction and development, factories, bomb-damage assessment, W/T installations and, its newest, a section for the interpretation of night photographs. To these it added in August 1942 a section which was responsible for special reports on the north

---

* In June 1942 the Army Enigma disclosed that in the fighting in north Africa the Germans had captured a great number of British documents revealing a large-scale 'betrayal' of important military secrets through POW interrogation.

† See Volume I, pp 279–280.

79.   ADM 223/84, pp 9–10, 36–37.
80.   ibid, p 34; *Air Ministry Intelligence*, p 101.
81.   AIR 41/7, *Photographic Reconnaissance*, Vol II, p 25.

African coast in preparation for operation *Torch*, and which then remained in existence to do similar work for subsequent Allied operations, and, at the end of the year, a section to meet the requirements of Special Duty (clandestine) Operations in Europe.[82] By that time some sections had been reorganised and enlarged to meet the increased need for bomb-damage assessment that accompanied the intensification of US Eighth Army Air Force's offensive from the United Kingdom against industrial targets.* Eighth USAAF had its own PR squadrons and photographic interpreters but did not set up a separate interpretation unit; its interpreters were attached to the CIU, as were interpreters from the US Army and Navy.† By June 1943 the RAF establishment at the CIU had grown to 314 officers.[83]

Within the United Kingdom, as a result of the accumulation of experience and of records at the CIU, the centralisation of interpretation worked to the general satisfaction of all three Service departments, and not least to that of the Admiralty,[84] and difficulty was encountered in only two directions.

In the first place, in the autumn of 1941 it emerged that the capacity of the School of Photographic Intelligence was insufficient for training the large numbers of officers which the Army would in due course need to attach to its field units for photographic interpretation for tactical purposes. As it was also judged that such interpretation could not easily be supervised by the CIU, the Army and the RAF reached an agreement by which, while the CIU continued to be the centre for all strategic interpretation, tactical interpretation would be undertaken at Command HQs when interpreters became available, and by which the War Office would set up a separate school of photographic intelligence under MI 4 for training in tactical interpretation. In May 1942, when this agreement was implemented, the Army contingent was divided into two sections, of which one was withdrawn by GHQ Home Forces to meet tactical requirements and the other remained at CIU.[85] From then on the Army interpretation staff at the CIU was responsible for artillery and anti-aircraft intelligence as well as for inter-Service studies, while the interpretation staff at Home Forces HQ concentrated on intelligence against the enemy's 'minor defences'.[86]

The second source of pressure, Bomber Command's objection to

---

82.   ibid, p 42; *Air Ministry Intelligence*, p 53.
83.   AIR 41/7, pp 42, 77–78.
84.   Morgan, op cit, p 60.
85.   AIR 41/7, p 40.
86.   Mockler-Ferryman, op cit, p 59.

the transfer to the CIU of responsibility for the photographic assessment of bomb damage, was dealt with less amicably. When No 1 and No 3 PRU were amalgamated under the Air Ministry in the summer of 1941 GOC-in-C Home Forces was allowed to retain control of the reconnaissance flight, later No 140 (Army Co-operation) Squadron, which had been formed to meet his requirements in the event of invasion.[87] But No 3 PRU, which had specialised in sorties flown to photograph bomb damage, was moved from the control of Bomber Command to form a single unit with No 1 PRU, and at the same time Bomber Command's responsibility for bomb-damage assessment was transferred to the CIU. Thereafter, Bomber Command not only complained that its need for bomb-damage sorties was suffering as a result of the higher priority that was being given to the PR requirements of the Admiralty, but also insisted that only a separate bomb-damage Flight under its own control, doing its own photographic interpretation, could meet its need. Early in 1942 the Air Ministry peremptorily refused its request for an independent Flight,[88] but Bomber Command continued to complain. In October 1942 the question of forming a special bomb-damage assessment unit was again considered and again rejected in favour of centralised control over all PR resources.[89]

Except for the difficulties with Bomber Command, the centralisation of photographic reconnaissance worked well. To begin with, indeed, when PRU was under Coastal Command, there was some difficulty in settling priorities in requests for cover. The Admiralty and Bomber Command made their requests direct to Coastal Command HQ, but other requests passed through ADI (Ph). In January 1942 a complaint from the DMI led the JIC to institute a weekly review of the requests made for PR and of the extent to which they had been met.[90] But the difficulty was overcome from February 1942, when a part of ADI (Ph)'s section was located at Coastal Command HQ to carry out the examination of all requests and decide on their priority. In November 1942 ADI (Ph)'s staff returned to the Air Ministry, and all requirements for PR were received and co-ordinated there until early in 1944. Only one further adjustment was made before that date: in July 1942 ADI (Ph)'s section at the Air Ministry was placed under the Director of Intelligence (Operations) in order to ensure that priorities for PR cover were settled in the light of the operational intelligence derived from Sigint.[91]

---

87.   AIR 41/7, pp 6, 48.   88.   ibid, p 4.
89.   ibid, pp 8–9.   90.   JIC (42) 2nd Meeting, 4 January.
91.   AIR 41/7, pp 4–5.

The problem of regulating competing demands for photographic reconnaissance was in any case becoming easier from the autumn of 1941 as a result of an increase in the number of suitable aircraft and the introduction of longer-range aircraft. During the first half of 1941 a committee of the JIC, set up to assess the size of the requirement for PR and the number of aircraft needed, had been much delayed by inter-Service disputes and differences between experts. In August it recommended that the Chiefs of Staff should give the highest priority to the provision of specialised aircraft to enable the PRU to undertake as early as possible a programme of 24 sorties a day. The Chiefs of Staff gave their approval on 6 August.[92] In October 1941 the United Kingdom establishment in PR aircraft was set at 43 Type D Spitfires plus 7 Type G (armed) Spitfires in five Flights, 8 Mosquitoes in two Flights, and a Flight of 2 Glen Martin Marylands.

The two Marylands had been chosen to minimise any Spanish suspicions that Britain was not abiding by her undertaking of November 1939 to use Gibraltar only for Fleet Air Arm or training purposes. Since June 1941, for the same reason, they had operated only for short periods from Gibraltar but their photographs had been interpreted there by a small CIU detachment.[93] They continued to operate in this way until June 1942, when the JIC decided under pressure from the Admiralty and the War Office that they should be based permanently at Gibraltar.[94] The first two Mosquitoes, of which the Air Ministry had ordered 50 at the end of 1939, became available in September 1941. As a two-seater aircraft, it brought about improvement in navigation and target location, and with its greater range (2,350 miles compared with the 1,700–1,800 miles of the Spitfire Type D) it rapidly proved itself in PR work.

By December 1941 No 1 PRU was up to establishment in Spitfires and had received 6 of its 8 Mosquitoes.[95] Together with successive improvements in cameras and in the methods of installing and operating them – improvements which ensured ever better photographs* – the increase in the number and range of the

---

* In January 1942 the F 52 camera, with 14″, 20″ and 36″ focal lengths, was introduced, producing a scale of 1/10,000 at 30,000 feet, and in May 1942 this camera was fitted with a magazine capable of taking up to 500 exposures. At the end of the year a great advance was made when new methods of camera installation were introduced into Mosquitoes and Spitfires which doubled the large-scale cover of each sortie and therefore reduced the number of sorties or runs necessary to cover one target when assessing bomb damage.[96]

92. JIC (41) 63 of 10 February; JIC (41) 7th Meeting, 25 February; JIC (41) 114, last revise dated 21 April; JIC (41) 18th and 23rd Meetings, 19 June and 2 August; JIC (41) 312 of 30 July; CAB 79/13, COS (41) 278th Meeting, 6 August.   93. AIR 41/7, pp 47, 98.
94. JIC (42) 203 of 1 June; JIC (42) 24th Meeting, 5 June.
95. AIR 41/7, p 48.   96. ibid, pp 22–24.

aircraft more than doubled the PR coverage obtained from the United Kingdom in 1941, as compared with 1940, and after the spring of 1942 little further expansion was called for. During 1940 there had been 1,198 sorties, of which 835 were successful. In 1941 the PRU flew 2,676 sorties (1,855 successful), in 1942 2,777 sorties (2,203 successful) and in 1943 2,989 sorties (2,252 successful). This expansion, one of the most notable developments in war-time intelligence, was most rapid between April 1941, when the number of sorties averaged 4·1 a day, and April 1942, when it averaged 9·6. By the spring of 1942 there was no shortage of aircraft for PR requirements from the United Kingdom, and the only serious limitation was the weather. And from the beginning of 1942 the Mosquito extended the range of operations 'from Tromso to Prague and Pilsen'; the longest flights of the year, to Bodo and Königsberg, were flown in March, by which date routine coverage of Norway and the east Baltic ports was being undertaken.[97]

In the United Kingdom it remained only to develop night reconnaissance, a refinement which might be of value by reducing delay in detecting enemy moves. During 1941 experiments in night reconnaissance had been precluded by shortage of suitable aircraft and the lack of night equipment, and during 1941 trials were made with aircraft which proved unsatisfactory. In August 1942, how-ever, the Air Staff allocated two Wellingtons to No 1 PRU for the work, and the first operational sortie took place in December.[98]*

To meet the more urgent requirement of the build-up of PR resources in the Middle East and the Mediterranean after the establishment of No 2 PRU in September 1940†, progress was slow during 1941 and it was not until February 1942 that the PRU had long-range Spitfires at its disposal. Meanwhile other units had been formed in 1941 to carry out PR, both strategic and tactical, and there were two interpretation units – the Army/Air Photographic Interpretation Unit (AAPIU) in the forward area in the Western Desert and the CIU ME with HQ in Cairo. By the summer of 1942 duplication of effort was such that a new unit – No 285 Wing RAF – was set up to co-ordinate all visual and photographic reconnaissance in the desert, and AAPIU and the detachment from the CIU ME with Eighth Army were also brought into close collaboration by being placed under the control of the new Wing.[99] A new unit – No 4 PRU – was formed to serve the British forces which took part in the Allied invasion of French north Africa.

---

* See Volume III.
† See Volume I, pp 207–208.

97.   ibid, pp 109–111, 133.
98.   ibid, pp 25–26.
99.   ibid, pp 59–61, 98.

Initially it operated independently of its US counterpart, USAAF 3rd Reconnaissance Group, and neither they nor their accompanying interpretation units made any effective contribution to the Tunisian campaign before February–March 1943, when the US and British PR units in Tunisia were amalgamated into a single organisation under the North African PR Wing, which carried out PR operations and interpretation on an integrated basis.*

---

* For a fuller description of the development of PR in north Africa and the Mediterranean see below, Part VI and Appendix 21, p 757 fn.

CHAPTER 16

Intelligence Arrangements with
the United States and
the Soviet Union

THE GERMAN attack on Russia produced no effective arrangements for the exchange of intelligence between the British and Soviet governments.* With the American intelligence authorities, in contrast, Whitehall had made provisional arrangements as early as the spring of 1941, and within a few months of the entry of the United States into the war in December 1941 these had been replaced by agreements which in due course established intimate collaboration between the two countries.

The provisional arrangements of the spring of 1941 had included, for the exchange of evaluated intelligence, the arrival of a US Mission in Whitehall and the formation within the British Joint Staff Mission in Washington (BJSM) of a JIC (Washington) – JIC (W).† The London JIC had laid it down that the JIC (W) was to send Whitehall a daily telegram on intelligence developments in Washington, to keep a 'library' for the BJSM and the US intelligence authorities of the intelligence appreciations sent to it from Whitehall, and to do what it could to assist the US authorities to establish a JIC of their own.[1] It was Whitehall's view that the exchange of intelligence must as soon as possible take place directly between the Service intelligence branches and the US Mission in London (as yet known as the Special Observers Group) and between the JIC and a US JIC when one was formed. The JIC was thus at pains to discourage the JIC (W) from assuming that it would itself become the main channel, least of all for the exchange of the volume of up-to-date information that would be required for planning purposes.[2] But this view of the matter encountered two difficulties. First, it did not satisfy the JIC (W), which felt that it would be in an impossible position if it did not know what

---

* See below, p 58 et seq.
† See Volume I, pp 313–314.

1. CAB 122/1584, Minute 23 September 1941, summarised in MM (41) 191 of 21 October, MM (41) 214, Annex I of 12 November 1941 and Annex II of 13 October 1941, GI 'Notes on the Organisation and Responsibilities of the British JIC Washington', 8 December 1941, para 2.
2. JIC (41) 38th Meeting, 16 December.

Whitehall was passing to the US authorities.[3] In the second place, it could not be implemented until the US authorities had established a JIC and settled the organisation of their Mission in London.

The JIC (W) complained in the autumn of 1941 that it was not receiving enough intelligence from London.[4] Nor was it satisfied when, upon the entry of the United States into the war, the JIC agreed to telegraph summaries of JIC appreciations but refused its request for a daily summary of Whitehall's intelligence.[5] In January 1942 the BJSM, at the request of the JIC (W), took the question to the 'Arcadia' (Washington) conference of the two governments. At the conference the British Chiefs of Staff consented to the despatch of more information to the JIC (W) – it was allowed to receive a summary of the intelligence discussed at the Chiefs of Staff's weekly meeting with the JIC – and the Combined Chiefs of Staff (CCS)* accepted the principle of exchanging 'complete military intelligence' in both capitals.[6] In February, after further discussion, the Combined Planning Staff recommended, and the CCS approved, the establishment of a US JIC, the free exchange of intelligence between the US JIC and the JIC (W) and, further, the formation by these two bodies of the Combined Intelligence Committee (CIC) to prepare appreciations for the Combined Chiefs of Staff. The free exchange of intelligence was to apply to all theatres and was to extend beyond Washington to field echelons at all levels. The British contribution to joint appreciations was to be supplied by the JIC in London through the JIC (W).[7]

When these proposals received prior approval in London on 10 February 1942 the JIC expressed the hope that the US authorities would complete the arrangements by establishing an American JIC in Whitehall,[8] and this further step was taken by the beginning

---

* At the 'Arcadia' conference it was decreed that the word 'combined' was to be applied to Allied collaboration: 'joint' to inter-Service collaboration within one nation.

3. CAB 122/1584, JIC (W) Meeting, 19 December 1941.
4. ibid, Minute 23 September 1941, in MM (41) 191, GI notes, para 2.
5. JIC (41) 39th Meeting, 23 December; CAB 122/1584, Minutes of JIC (W) Meetings 8 and 9 December 1941.
6. CAB 122/1584, JIC (W) Meeting 19 December and JIC (W) minute to JSM 29 December 1941; CAB 80/34, COS (42) 78 (p 44), Annex VI of 31 December 1941, COS (42) 79 (pp 77–78) Annex XXXI and (p 85) Annex XXXIV both of 13 January.
7. CAB 80/33, COS (42) 75 (p 17), Annex V of 14 January, reproduced in Gwyer and Butler, *Grand Strategy*, Vol III Part II (1964), Appendix II; CAB 122/1584, CPS 1 of 22 January 1942, (reproduced in CAB 80/34, COS (42) 112 of 16 February); CAB 88/5, CCS 23/1 of 11 February 1942; CAB 88/1, CCS 4th Meeting, 10 February 1942.
8. JIC (42) 41 (o) of 6 February and 42 (o) of 9 February; CAB 79/18, COS (42) 43rd Meeting, 9 February.

of March. Hitherto, while relations between the US Special Observers Group in London and the US attachés had remained unsettled, the JIC had applied some restrictions to the exchange of intelligence with the Group: exchange took place only between the Group and the Service intelligence branches, not by American attendance at inter-Service meetings, and, except for the Far Eastern theatre, information was withheld about the nature of the most secret intelligence and the methods by which it was acquired.[9] Now, the US JIC in London was invited to attend the meetings of the intelligence staff officers which prepared routine summaries for the JIC, and by the end of March the JIC had agreed that the JIS should pass to the American body drafts of the appreciations it drew up for transmission to Washington and that the two bodies should discuss the drafts together if time permitted.[10*]

Because the normal channel for the transmission of its appreciations to Washington was to be the JIC (W), not the US JIC in London, and also out of the need to adjust to the creation of the US JIC in Washington, the JIC strengthened the JIC (W) during March 1942. The JIC (W) was divided into a junior, or drafting committee, and a senior committee, the latter being expected to join with its US opposite number in formal meetings of the CIC only in the event of irreconcilable differences at the junior level. It was given a permanent secretary, who was made jointly responsible with the secretary of the US JIC for ensuring that the US and British elements of the CCS received simultaneously identical CIC appreciations. Nor was it any longer questioned that the JIC (W) must receive the fullest possible supply of intelligence from London. The JIC agreed that, except for those of purely domestic interest, all its papers should be telegraphed to the JIC (W) in summary, the full texts following by the quickest possible means, and that the JIC (W) should be told in a weekly telegram what papers were being prepared in Whitehall. It authorised the Service intelligence branches to send to their individual representatives on the JIC (W) whatever information they might need. And it gave the JIC (W) complete freedom to disclose its intelligence to its American opposite numbers, and to discuss it with them, except when specifically instructed to the contrary.[11]

---

* For the arrangements made by the JIC for American representation on its Hartley Sub-Committee on Axis Oil see below, p 46.

9. JIC (41) 39th Meeting, 23 December; CAB 79/16, COS (41) 440th Meeting, 30 December.
10. JIC (42) 7th Meeting, 3 March; JIC (42) 97 of 20 March; JIC (42) 11th Meeting, 30 March; JIC (42) 110 of 30 March, Part I.
11. JIC (42) 9th Meeting, 17 March; JIC (42) 110 of 30 March, Part 2 and Annex; CAB 122/1584, MM (S) (42) 15th Meeting, 17 March, and Feudal telegram No 3 of 11 April 1942; CAB 121/230, SIC file B/Departments/2, folio 26a, Telegram to JIC (W), 9 June 1942.

From March 1942 to May 1943 it proved necessary to make few changes of any importance to these arrangements. The JIC (W)'s Service members chafed at the fact that both its chairman and its deputy chairman were civilians from MEW, particularly after May 1942 when, on the first occasion when it proved necessary to hold a meeting of the CIC – to discuss a difference of opinion about German intentions – the chairman attended alone. Although the JIC decreed that he must be accompanied by his Service colleagues at future CIC meetings,[12] allegations of undue MEW and Foreign Office bias in the work of the JIC (W) continued to be made[13] until in February 1943 the London JIC abolished the division of the JIC (W) into a senior and a junior committee. By that time the division had become unnecessary: the JIC (W)'s so-called junior membership had had to be made more senior to match the standing of the Americans with whom they worked. Thereafter, allegations of undue civilian influence died away and in May, to match the representation of the State Department on the US JIC, the Foreign Office's representation on the JIC (W) was strengthened.[14]

Day-to-day co-operation with the Americans had meanwhile worked smoothly. A second meeting of the CIC – to discuss the possibility of a German threat to Spain – did not take place till 11 February 1943.[15] But the US JIC and the JIC (W) had since the previous August met increasingly frequently as the Combined Intelligence Sub-Committee (CISC), and by the autumn of 1942 the work of the CISC had been put on a regular basis, with short meetings daily for the presentation of 'the enemy intelligence situation' and a meeting once a week for general discussion and a review of the world situation.[16] At the beginning of 1943 the London JIC remained distinctly unimpressed by the quality of the summaries and appreciations made by the CISC for the CCS and by the US JIC for the American Joint Chiefs of Staff, while the London JIS, which had already had the task of supplying Washington with briefs and data for these papers, was wilting under the increasing burden of having to send Washington its comments on them. But Whitehall was also gratified by the increasing readiness of the US JIC to seek British help via the CISC when preparing its own papers,[17] and only two anxieties disturbed its otherwise complete satisfaction with the progress of

12. JIC (42) 22nd Meeting, 26 May.
13. CAB 122/1584, GI Notes, 8 December 1942.
14. JIC (43) 6th (o) Meeting, 2 February, 43rd (o) Meeting 24 August.
15. CAB 88/57, CIC 2nd Meeting, 11 February 1943.
16. CAB 88/61, CISC 11th Meeting, 23 July 1942; JIC (42) 36th (o) Meeting, 4 August.
17. CAB 122/1584, GI Notes, 8 December 1942.

the Anglo-American partnership in the exchange of evaluated intelligence. The first concerned the need within the BJSM to make relations between the JIC (W) and the Joint Planners as close as those which at last existed between the Planners and the JIC in Whitehall.[18]* The second concerned the confusion that might arise if British intelligence reached the US planning authorities through too many different agencies.

□

This second anxiety was an extension, though a considerable one, of the concern which the JIC displayed about arrangements in Whitehall throughout 1942, as the growing number of British planning authorities threatened to bring delay and duplication into the communications between those authorities and the intelligence bodies.† From February 1942, when the CCS decided that the free exchange of intelligence should apply everywhere, and at all levels,‡ closer links were established not only between the JIS and the US JIC in London and between British representatives and the US intelligence bodies in Washington, but also between the US London JIC and the British Service intelligence branches and between the Service branches and US commands in the United Kingdom. And when intelligence thus began to pass by several different routes – between Whitehall and Washington by both British and US channels; from Whitehall to US authorities in Britain; and between US authorities in Washington and Britain – there was much scope for duplication and misunderstanding, quite apart from such difficulties as the rivalry between the US Navy and War Departments and the non-existence of a separate US Air Force. On the other hand, the JIC's own responsibility was largely confined to developing and regularising the exchange of strategic intelligence appreciations. Other arrangements, particularly those for the exchange of operational intelligence, it necessarily left in the hands of the separate departments, and they necessarily made different arrangements with their different opposite numbers.

Liaison between British and American authorities concerned with economic intelligence depended upon a variety of channels. In the spring of 1941 the Commercial Secretary of the US Embassy in London established liaison with MEW,[19] and at the same time MEW developed close contacts with the US Military Attaché.[20] British government experts involved in official conversations with

---

* See above, pp 5–6.   † See above, p 8.
‡ See above, p 42.

18.   JIC (43) 6th (o) Meeting, 2 February.
19.   Medlicott, *The Economic Blockade*, Vol I (1952), p 501.
20.   ibid, p 500.

the Americans on aspects of economic warfare could draw upon factual and analytical information originating in the Intelligence Department of MEW.

Systematic British-American intelligence exchange and collaboration developed earlier in the study of enemy oil than in more general economic matters. The Lloyd Committee in London, although occasionally able to draw upon information or estimates from independent American bodies,[21] was not matched by a similar American organisation. Early in 1942, however, an Enemy Oil Committee including representatives of the US Services and other interested agencies was established in Washington as a Sub-Committee of the Joint Chiefs of Staff, the British being in liaison with it by means of an official of MEW attached to the British Embassy.[22] When in March 1942 the British Lloyd Committee was replaced by the Hartley Technical Sub-Committee on Axis Oil of the JIC, liaison with the Americans was fully established and in September 1942 the JIC agreed that the Americans should be represented on the Hartley Committee.[23] The Petroleum Attachés of the US Embassy in London successively became members of the Committee.[24]*

Anglo-American intelligence collaboration on important aspects of industrial production, raw materials and labour resources in Germany and German Europe was slower to develop and less effective than liaison in the oil sector. The London-Washington JIC arrangements brought comparatively slight American weight to bear upon MEW and JIC appreciations of the German economy even when American opinions differed from British. The USA had no central economic intelligence staff comparable with that in MEW and encountered difficulties in establishing one. The State Department, which exercised authority in the sphere of economic warfare, formed its own Board of Economic Operations in October 1941, and complex relationships between that Board and the inter-departmental Economic Defence Board, formed in July 1941 and later re-named the Board of Economic Warfare, hampered the development of a single economic intelligence organisation,[25] while Colonel Donovan's COI† was unable to establish its own economic section until August 1942.[26] Throughout 1942 and 1943 British appreciations of the German economy were heavily drawn upon by the Americans.[27]

---

* See below, pp 136–137.   † See further below, p 52 et seq.

21. See for example CAB 77/29, AO (46) 1, p 92.   22. ibid, p 90.
23. JIC (42) 49th Meeting, 29 September.
24. CAB 77/29, AO (46) 1, p 116.
25. Medlicott, op cit, Vol I, p 62.
26. CAB 122/1584, Washington to MEW 29 August 1942; JIC (42) 36th (o)
     Meeting 4 August.   27 Medlicott, op cit, Vol I, p 62.

The Admiralty had set up in 1941 an intelligence section (NID 18) in the British Admiralty Delegation in Washington, and worked out with the Navy Department a system whereby, while all Admiralty requests for intelligence from the Navy Department were channelled through NID 18, all Navy Department requests for intelligence from the Admiralty were channelled through the US Naval HQ in London.[28] This system, by-passing the Naval Attachés and leaving them to concentrate on their accustomed task of providing information about the US and British navies, continued to operate, and to be effective in avoiding duplication, even after December 1941, when the requirement of requests for information ceased to be important with the development of closer collaboration. From that date representatives of the US Naval HQ made daily visits to the NID and the OIC, and the NID provided the head of the US Naval HQ with a daily intelligence bulletin from which, on instructions from the Chief of the Naval Staff, nothing was withheld. From the same date NID 18 had a desk in the Navy Department and made daily visits to collect operational intelligence.[29] From the summer of 1942, because Admiral Cunningham, the new head of the British Admiralty Delegation, felt that deficiencies in the supply to him of information from high-grade Sigint were putting him at a disadvantage in discussions with the Navy Department, NID started a special series of telegrams (the 'Sunset' series), which were despatched daily to Washington via 'C'.*

Close as it became during 1942, the naval collaboration naturally left room for improvement. But some attempts to improve it were counter-productive. Thus the appointment of British liaison officers to the US Naval HQ in London produced, unfortunately but unintentionally, a temporary cessation of the daily visits from the HQ to the Admiralty.[30] Other attempts at improvement came to nothing. From the middle of 1942 the DNI urged that misunderstandings would not be eliminated until US officers were seconded to work as members of the NID and British officers were taken into the Office of Naval Intelligence (ONI). This proposal made no progress, the shortage of suitable officers being given as the main

---

* To begin with NID's 'Sunset' telegrams also included military and air Sigint. In the autumn of 1942, after AI and MI had protested at this incursion into their fields and the BJSM had in turn protested at the resulting drop in the usefulness of 'Sunsets' from which air and military intelligence was excluded, a joint Service 'Sunset' system was inaugurated. It, too, was operated daily through 'C'.

28.   ADM 223/108, Barrett report on Anglo-American Co-operation, pp 3–7, ADM 223/107, NID 03545/46 of 4 June 1946, History of NID 18, paras 1, 3 and 5.
29.   ADM 223/108, Barrett, op cit, pp 1–2; ADM 223/107, History of NID 18, para 29.
30.   ADM 223/108, Barrett, op cit, p 8.

reason.[31] But other considerations – residual national susceptibilities; the fact that relations between the operational and the intelligence branches of the Navy Department were different from those prevailing in the Admiralty – suggest that, if it had been implemented, the proposal would not at that stage have been as fruitful as was hoped. On the other hand, such obstacles to effective collaboration were overcome without immense difficulty when operational needs required that they should be set aside. The US Admiral operating with the Home Fleet received intelligence, including Ultra messages, from the OIC. Though not without delay – it arose partly from differences of organisation between the Navy Department and the Admiralty, and partly from the wish of the Navy Department, even at the height of the U-boat sinkings on the eastern seaboard, to learn from its own mistakes rather than from the Admiralty's experience – the Navy Department in the spring of 1942 invited the OIC to send someone to advise it on the establishment of a U-boat tracking room. This advice was at once accepted and a direct signal link set up to the OIC's Tracking Room. From then on communication between the two rooms, which were later joined by one in Ottawa,* was so good that they operated virtually as a single organisation without any need to exchange or integrate their staffs.[32]

Unlike the NID, AI quickly supplemented exchange of intelligence via the RAF Delegation in Washington and the US air authorities in London by the direct exchange of intelligence staff. A US representative was taken on to the staff of ACAS (I) from the beginning of 1942. His appointment persuaded the Washington authorities and the US operational HQs to trust AI's intelligence appreciations. It was followed in March 1942 by an American request for the loan of trained air intelligence officers, a request that was met by posting an RAF officer to form and run a training school in the United States.[33] Nor did this development and the formation in the US War Department in the spring of 1942 of a separate intelligence organisation for the Army Air Corps bring to an end the attachment of US officers to AI and, for anti-aircraft work, to MI.[34] US representatives from Washington and from the operational and intelligence sections of US air commands served as working members of AI, undertaking duties over and above that of

---

* See below, p 551.

31. ADM 223/107, NID 005790/42, DNI Report of 1 November 1942.
32. Beesly, *Very Special Intelligence* (1977), pp 106–110; McLachlan, *Room 39* (1968), pp 237–239; ADM 223/107, NID 002956/42, Winn Report of Mission, 3 June 1942.
33. Air Historical Branch, *Air Ministry Intelligence*, p 22; JIC (42) 110 of 30 March.
34. Mockler-Ferryman, *Military Intelligence Organisation*, p 26.

ensuring that US interests were safeguarded. The GAF sub-division of AI's Aircraft Production Section had a US officer as its deputy head; US officers served full-time in the Airfield Intelligence Section before going on to join the US intelligence staffs at Allied HQs. The Technical Intelligence and Target Intelligence Sections were virtually Anglo-American organisations.[35] The same was true of the Order of Battle and Operational Intelligence Section, and this established with the US air commands in the United Kingdom the same direct communications and the exchange of intelligence appreciations that existed between AI and the RAF commands. Moreover, the US Eighth Army Air Force made no attempt to develop its own Y service; from the first USAAF air raid on Europe, in August 1942, to the end of the war, its commands received Y intelligence direct from Cheadle, Kingsdown and GC and CS.[36]

Exchange of intelligence staff on a permanent basis between the US War Department and MI began in the autumn of 1942. By that time, the exchange of information via the British Army Staff in Washington and US representatives in Whitehall having proved incapable of settling differences about such complex problems as enemy order of battle, the two establishments had resorted to exchanges of missions and visits to hammer out the methods and the considerations they would jointly apply in calculating the order of battle of the German Army, and had tacitly agreed that MI would be primarily responsible for German order of battle and the War Department primarily responsible for the order of battle of the Japanese. But in the autumn of 1942 this understanding, which was not made formal until September 1944, was supplemented by the appointment of US officers to MI and of British officers to the US War Department to work in all fields, Japanese and Italian as well as German, and in particular by the creation under MI 14 of an Anglo-US Section that was responsible for pooling all evidence bearing on enemy order of battle.[37]

The War Department-War Office Section in MI 14 was renamed the Military Intelligence Research Section (MIRS) in the summer of 1943. From that date, with branches in both London and Washington, with power to attach specialists temporarily to theatre, force and field army HQs for the rapid collection of order of battle intelligence from captured documents, and with the responsibility for supplying such intelligence direct to theatre and force commanders in Europe and Africa, it was to effect the total

---

35. *Air Ministry Intelligence*, pp 22–24, 214, 242, 266–267.
36. ibid, pp 89–91, 169, 178.
37. JIC (42) 36th (o) Meeting, 4 August, JIC (42) 314 (o) of 14 August, JIC (42) 49th and 51st Meetings, 29 September and 6 October; Davidson Papers (King's College, London), H, Part I, pp 13–16; Mockler-Ferryman, op cit, pp 66–68.

integration of British and US Army intelligence at the research level.* Meanwhile total integration, with the emphasis on a division of labour in which the American operational authorities relied on the British intelligence bodies, had perforce been adopted for the provision of intelligence for army planning from the time when, for operation *Torch*, Allied Force Headquarters under General Eisenhower was established in August 1942.

General Eisenhower acquired an inter-Service intelligence staff that was mainly composed of British officers, including one who had worked at GC and CS. This staff, headed by a British army officer with an American deputy, received intelligence, including Enigma decrypts, from the British authorities on the same footing as the Service ministries and the British overseas commands. Apart from providing the American members of AFHQ's intelligence staff, the United States had sent representatives to the United Kingdom to set up Y stations and to form the Sigint units that would be attached to the US forces for operation *Torch*. In the course of this work they profited from British experience and maintained close collaboration with the British authorities, General Eisenhower's chief Sigint officer attending meetings of the Y Committee when he needed help and when matters of interest to him were on the agenda.

In the early days at AFHQ the development of the intelligence arrangements was inevitably attended by some degree of strain and confusion. The creation of a completely integrated Allied HQ was itself a novel undertaking. Outside a narrow circle at the top level, very little was known about the purpose of the new command. When experienced British officers were working with untrained American colleagues in an organisation where the Supreme Commander, his Chief of Staff and the heads of all sections but the Intelligence Section were American, and when the organisation depended almost entirely on British-supplied intelligence, it is not difficult to see that there was scope for resentment on both sides. Nor was it easy to align the integration that was proceeding at AFHQ with the more cumbersome exchange arrangements that were developing between London and Washington. Thus in August 1942 the BJSM was complaining that General Eisenhower was receiving a great deal of intelligence that was not available in Washington and that he was sending reports to Washington that were not shown to the British authorities there.[38] At AFHQ, however, these and similar problems turned out to be no more than teething-trouble, as we shall see when we turn to the contribution of intelligence to the planning of operation *Torch*.†

□

* See Volume III.   † See below, Chapter 24.

38. CAB 121/284, SIC file B/Information/3, LETOD telegram 248 of 17 August 1942.

When these various arrangements were bringing about the unrestricted exchange of evaluated intelligence, the British and American authorities could not avoid a further problem. Washington demanded, and London desired, that the United States should participate in the process of producing intelligence, but if Washington were to insist on complete self-sufficiency in this respect, and London on retaining it, the outcome would be rivalry and waste of effort. In these circumstances, how could they ensure that their collaboration in this process was, as far as possible, both effective and economical?

For some of the intelligence sources co-operation was established without difficulty. From December 1941 the United States and Great Britain were, together with Canada, co-ordinating their censorship activities as fully as possible. By the summer of 1943 a US POW section was working alongside MI 9, a USAAF officer had joined ADI (K) and US interrogators had been attached to CSDIC (UK).[39] US officers participated fully in the examination of captured equipment in the UK.[40] The ISTD met all US requests for topographical intelligence, directly within the UK, via NID 18 in Washington until the ISTD established its own section there in the summer of 1944.[41] In relation to photographic reconnaissance, also, a settlement was easily achieved. In August 1941, as part of the provisional arrangements reached during the spring, the Air Ministry undertook to train US officers in the technique of interpretation; by October eleven officers had passed through the training course and returned as instructors to the United States. In the spring of 1942, in preparation for the arrival in the United Kingdom of the first units of the US Eighth Army Air Force, it was agreed that, while the USAAF should have its own operational reconnaissance units, the interpretation of reconnaissance photographs in the United Kingdom should be carried out jointly at one place. The CIU thus became inter-Allied as well as inter-Service, US officers being assigned to it from the Army and the Navy as well as from US Eighth Air Force. In June 1943 their number was 71, 30 from US Eighth Air Force, 30 from the Army and 11 from the Navy. In addition, a US officer was initially attached to ADI (Ph), and from the start of USAAF operations in Europe in August 1942, ADI (Ph)'s staff, assisted by an Anglo-American Committee

39. ADM 223/84, History of POW Interrogation, pp 53–55; Mockler-Ferryman, op cit, p 53; *Air Ministry Intelligence*, p 101.
40. CAB 88/61, CISC 18th, 19th, 21st and 22nd Meetings, 2, 9, 23 and 30 October 1942; JIC (42) 55th (o) Meeting, 3 November.
41. ADM 223/108, Barrett, op cit, p 8; ADM 223/107, DNI Minute 03234/42 of 22 June, NID 005790/42 of 1 November 1942, Report of DNI visit to Washington, History of NID 18, paras 21–22; ADM 223/90, Bassett and Wells, History of ISTD; JIC (42) 440 (o) of 10 November.

for Co-ordination of Current Air Operations, handled all American and British requests for reconnaissance flights and settled priorities. Until October 1942, when the first US reconnaissance unit arrived in the United Kingdom, the US forces relied on the PRU; thereafter US requirements were met by the US units as far as possible, but the RAF helped when needed and in return could call on the units of the US 7th Photo Group (four squadrons by March 1943) in emergencies.[42]

Relations between the SIS and its nearest US counterpart, though always close, and eventually harmonious, were not always so smooth. The combined intelligence and special operations organisation which was set up by the President in June 1941 as the Office of the Co-ordination of Information (COI) under Colonel Donovan was the first attempt to centralise the espionage activities of the USA. It opened its European headquarters in London in November 1941. The SIS, which had been training Colonel Donovan's first recruits in London since the previous February* and which from November provided him with training facilities in Canada, assumed that at least in Europe the COI would agree to allow the activities that it organised from London in the European theatre to be carried out under direction from its own larger and more experienced staff; and it had good reason to be apprehensive about the incursion of yet another organisation into the delicate and narrow field of agent recruitment. Equally naturally, perhaps, the COI, while accepting that there must be close collaboration, felt that its operations ought to be conducted independently of the authorities of another state and, when that seemed called for, without their knowledge.

The friction engendered by such divergent positions was not something that could be eliminated by general understandings. In the summer of 1942, following a reorganisation of the COI which re-named it the Office of Strategic Services (OSS) and placed it under the US Chiefs of Staff instead of the President, Colonel Donovan met the British Chiefs of Staff, attended by the JIC, in London. They had learned that the COI, to the consternation of the SIS, had established direct contacts in London with the intelligence services of the governments-in-exile,[43] and they warned him of the dangers that would arise if too many organisations acted independently. He assured them that the OSS would maintain the closest collaboration with the SIS and SOE.[44] But the satisfaction

---

* See Volume I, p 313.

42.   AIR 41/7, *Photographic Reconnaissance*, Vol II, pp 77–78.
43.   US War Department History Project, Strategic Services Unit, *War Report of the OSS*, Vol 2 (New York 1976), p 4.
44.   CAB 79/22, COS (42) 180th Meeting, 16 June.

of both sides with this discussion at the highest level was not shared lower down. There were those in the OSS who suspected that it was 'probably at SIS insistence' that in July 1942 the US operational command in Europe (ETOUSA) demanded to be informed whenever the OSS sent out an agent and that in August, as the JIC was advised, the US Chiefs of Staff ordered the OSS to carry out no operations without the consent of the theatre commander.[45] They felt that the explanation for these restrictions lay 'not only in the American command's siding with the British against a US unit, but also in ETOUSA's playing into the hands of SIS in the latter's efforts to curtail the development of an independent American SI [Secret Intelligence] Service'.[46] And after the invasion of French north Africa they welcomed the opportunity to work from Algeria in a US-controlled theatre where their operations could not be hampered by 'British services, in particular SIS'.[47] On the other hand, it was with great reluctance that the SIS accepted that the freedom of the OSS to operate independently should be subject only to operational authorities. In November 1942, when the OSS was at last ready to operate agents in Europe, the SIS, with General Eisenhower's support, was unwilling to permit such agents to report to London, as opposed to direct to the USA. In January 1943 the OSS defeated an SIS proposal that the two organisations should use joint codes and a single communications system. In the OSS's view, the proposal would have enabled the SIS to keep its own activities secret while obtaining full knowledge of those of the OSS; for the SIS, sceptical of the OSS's security standards, the rejection of the proposal justified the retention of its existing policy of normally forbidding the exchange of intelligence between SIS and OSS agents in the field. In the spring 1943 the two bodies again clashed about the control of secret missions which OSS Algiers was sending into France.

Despite latent mutual suspicion, however, and the recurrence of open disagreements, the SIS and the OSS had struck up a reasonably harmonious relationship on many fronts by the beginning of 1943. Sir William Stephenson, head of the British Security Co-ordination (BSC) in New York and the SIS's liaison officer with the OSS in the USA, continued to support the OSS with advice and training facilities, as he had done since it was established, receiving from it in return assistance in carrying out BSC's responsibility for British blockade intelligence and counterespionage in the western hemisphere. Intelligence was exchanged freely on a reciprocal basis between London and Washington, the

---

45.   US War Department, op cit, p 6; JIC (42) 36th (o) Meeting, 4 August.
46.   ibid, p 7.
47.   ibid, p 166.

normal system being that OSS reports from Europe were sent from Washington to London if of special value to the SIS and that SIS material of special value was passed to the London office of the OSS. From the spring of 1942, however, the SIS agreed that the intelligence reports of its Cairo office on the Middle East and south-eastern Europe might be passed to the OSS's newly-opened Cairo office for transmission to Washington, in return for which the OSS helped the SIS in Cairo by supplying equipment and motor transport,[48] and from the time of his arrival in the autumn of 1942 the OSS representative in Switzerland collaborated closely with the SIS office there. In London, at the same time, relations became increasingly close. By 1943 OSS staff had been taken into the SIS's counter-intelligence section, where it had complete access to the files,[49] and although for understandable reasons the SIS still placed some restrictions on the Sigint it passed to the OSS in London, these restrictions did not apply to its exchanges with OSS HQ in Washington.[50]

In relation to that part of the OSS's activities which corresponded to SOE's there were similar difficulties. The OSS and SOE reached a general understanding which was approved by the American and the British Chiefs of Staff in September 1942. It provided for close collaboration between the two headquarters but except in those parts of Europe marked out for Allied invasion, where the SOE and the OSS would jointly direct an integrated field force, divided the world into British and American areas of responsibility.[51] The agreement fell short of what Whitehall had pressed for – a single Allied organisation directing the pooled resources of the two bodies;[52] and in some 'grey' areas like the Middle East and the Balkans, where the two bodies over-lapped but did not closely co-ordinate their activities, it operated poorly at the working level. In Norway, however, the OSS accepted without difficulty the existing Anglo-Norwegian system of control, while in western Europe and north Africa the SOE and the OSS, beginning with their preparations for operation *Torch*, learned to work as one, the SOE benefiting from US stores and aircraft, the OSS relying on British organisation and prior experience, and both accepting the decisions of a joint controlling committee that was set up in February 1943 to arbitrate in their sometimes lively disagreements.[53]

As the relations of the SIS and SOE with the OSS settled down,

---

48.   US War Department, op cit, p 47.
49.   ibid, p 149.
50.   JIC (42) 28th Meeting, 30 June.
51.   US War Department, op cit, p 4.
52.   CAB 84/46, JP (42) 632 of 23 June: CAB 84/47, JP (42) 707 of 30 July.
53.   US War Department, op cit, pp 135, 225–226.

the work of the BSC in New York on their behalf underwent a change. It had originally been active as their liaison office in the western hemisphere in collecting intelligence and conducting counter-espionage operations for them, but as these functions passed to the OSS and the FBI it became chiefly the channel through which an increasing amount of intelligence was exchanged between those organisations and Whitehall. In the same way, as arrangements were developed for exchanging Sigint with the United States the BSC, from being the channel by which Sigint items were occasionally brought to the attention of US authorities, developed the important additional function of providing in north America the security arrangements and the communications facilities that were required for the passing of intercepts between London and Washington.

Intelligence derived from Sigint had begun to be exchanged in the spring of 1941, when the US Navy and War Departments had established small delegations to the US Mission in London to represent them in discussions with the intelligence branches of the Whitehall Service departments, and those branches had appointed officers to the BJSM.* At the same time 'C' had appointed a Chief Liaison Officer to the BJSM to advise him on problems that might arise in connection with the exchange of intelligence derived from cryptanalysis. Until the American entry into the war the amount of such intelligence exchanged remained small, not least because the highest US authorities, although now aware that the British were reading some German Enigma, agreed that they should not receive its results. At the end of June 1941, however, this arrangement began to break down. The Prime Minister began to press 'C' to pass to Washington the contents of Enigma decrypts containing instructions as to the attitude U-boats should adopt towards US naval units in the Atlantic. 'C' initially advised against any relaxation on the ground that no adequate security cover could be provided if the contents of precise Enigma signals were to be distributed in the US.[54] But relaxation was gradually permitted as the US Navy became more involved in patrolling the Atlantic and escorting shipping; and the outcome was uncertainty in Whitehall as to the extent to which US representatives there might be indoctrinated into the Enigma secret and complaints from Washington that Whitehall was withholding intelligence.

By the autumn of 1941 it was clear to the Whitehall authorities that if the US entered the war it would be necessary to arrange 'a full and firm alliance' in the Sigint field. But when the attack on

---

* See Volume I, pp 313–314.

54. Dir/C Archive, 6863 of 24 June 1941.

Pearl Harbour in December 1941 had removed the deeper obstacles to such an alliance, it was equally clear that the negotiation would be difficult. Quite apart from British susceptibilities – the anxiety about security in the USA and, perhaps, a concern to minimise any decline of influence that might come with the injection of superior US resources – differences of organisation between London and Washington were bound to cause complications. In the absence of a single body for the control of American Sigint, comparable to the Y Board, negotiations had to be conducted separately with the Navy and War Departments, and each of these was so organised that both GC and CS and the British Service departments had to be parties to agreements about the interception, production and dissemination of Sigint.

It was in these circumstances that two UK deputations visited the United States in the spring of 1942. The first, a mission from the Y Committee comprising representatives of the three Services and the Foreign Office, had no difficulty in achieving its objective: a series of agreements about the co-ordination of British and US intercept and DF programmes, the exchange of intercepted material, co-operation in the development of RFP and TINA equipment and techniques and (though this understanding never developed into a formal organisation) the eventual establishment of an Allied Y Committee. The second mission went from GC and CS. Its purpose was to bring the US authorities abreast of Bletchley's progress with all enemy cyphers and to persuade them to accept the British view that while so much work remained to be done against the Japanese cyphers, they should not duplicate GC and CS's work on the European, particularly the Enigma, but should be content to receive copies of such decrypts as they required. In this it did not entirely succeed. It found that the War Department was anxious to be in a position to exploit the Enigma if it wished, though disclaiming any intention of doing so at once, and that the Navy Department, not unnaturally in view of its own operational concern with the U-boat war and the fact that GC and CS had not succeeded in breaking the U-boat Enigma key that had come into force at the beginning of February,* was determined to begin cryptanalytic work on the Enigma as soon as possible. A compromise was reached. One US Army cryptanalyst and two from the US Navy would work at Bletchley; they arrived in June 1942. In addition, GC and CS would provide the Navy Department with a 'Bombe' to save it the trouble of designing its own machine.

The compromise entirely satisfied the War Department for the time being. With the Navy Department, on the other hand, GC

* See below, p 179.

and CS's relations were strained in June by American complaints at GC and CS's delay in sending the Bombe, and in September the Navy Department announced that it had developed a more advanced machine of its own, would have built 360 copies of it by the end of the year, and intended to attack the U-boat Enigma settings forthwith. But in October a second deputation from GC and CS to Washington negotiated another compromise. GC and CS 'acceded to US desires to attack the [German] naval and submarine problems' and agreed to supply the Navy Department with the intercepts and with technical assistance. In return the Navy Department, in addition to agreeing to supply GC and CS with Japanese naval decrypts and other intelligence for onward transmission to British Sigint groups in the Far East, undertook to construct only 100 Bombes,* accepted that GC and CS should be responsible for co-ordinating the work done by the American machines on the Enigma with that done by the British, and agreed to the complete and immediate exchange of the cryptanalytic results.

This arrangement between the Navy Department and GC and CS worked smoothly for the remainder of the war; from early in 1943 – by which time the four-wheel U-boat Enigma had at last been broken – the British and the American work on naval Enigma settings was carried out according to a single programme, and GC and CS increasingly profited from its freedom to use the ever-growing number of American Bombes against non-naval settings. However, the Navy Department entered into the arrangement without informing the War Department, and the British unfortunately bore the brunt of the War Department's recriminations. These began with the accusation that GC and CS was withholding Sigint data and culminated in February 1943 in the demand that the British authorities should send Enigma intercepts to Washington, the War Department having launched out on building its own Bombe. Nor was it until May 1943, after GC and CS had sent another mission to Washington and the CIGS had intervened on its behalf with General Marshall,[55] and when a War Department mission to GC and CS had familiarised itself with the system in force there for processing high-grade Sigint and disseminating it to ministries and commands, that a settlement was reached.

The settlement, which owed much to satisfaction with the GC and CS system of those US Army officers who, in Britain and at AFHQ, had seen it in operation, was one in which the US War Department, more completely than the US naval authorities,

---

* The American Bombe had an output capacity of only half that of the British machine.

55.   CAB 80/70, COS (43) 287 (o) of 7 June, p 4 (COS (T) 11th and 13th Meetings, 12 and 13 May).

accepted the British arguments. It laid it down that GC and CS alone should exploit all German and Italian military cyphers and that the War Department should concentrate on the Japanese Army cyphers, each side providing the other with all decrypts and undertaking the complete exchange of views and information at all levels. It further arranged that the War Department should strengthen the cryptanalytic and intelligence delegations it maintained at GC and CS, where they participated fully for the remainder of the war in the cryptanalytic programme, in intelligence research and as members of the watches which supplied the Sigint product direct to all commands in the European theatre, British, combined and American alike.

□

The movement towards collaboration between the British and the American intelligence communities stood in sharp contrast to the fact that the British and Soviet authorities made little progress towards the exchange of intelligence.

The British attitude in this matter was partly conditioned by the extreme secretiveness and defensiveness of the Russians. The Russians dropped their reserve from time to time at meetings between the two governments on the highest level. Otherwise, except when they were looking for immediate help, in such operations as the running of the Arctic supply convoys, they suspended all contacts and withheld all information about themselves at times of crisis. In less critical months they permitted the British Military Mission to make visits to the fronts and entertained requests for information about the operations and dispositions of their armed forces, but these requests they either left unanswered or answered only after a long delay. As a result, as we shall see, the best source of British information about the Russian fronts was not the Soviet government, or the Russian Military Mission in London, but GC and CS's decrypts of the Enigma traffic of the German forces on the eastern front.* By the end of 1942, moreover, a particularly ironical situation was developing. GC and CS was by then undertaking on behalf of the authorities responsible for strategic deception the continuous study of German estimates of Allied order of battle, and decrypted appreciations of the Soviet order of battle made by the GAF intelligence organisation were proving to be the best source of information about the state of the Soviet forces.

At the end of 1941 the British government protested at the highest diplomatic level against the obstructiveness of the Soviet

---

* See below, Chapter 17.

authorities in supplying information about themselves: and it repeated the protest at the end of 1942 and in January 1943.[56] On none of these occasions, however, did it complain that the Russians were being no more forthcoming in response to its efforts to improve the exchange of intelligence about the enemy. For one thing, it was for its own purposes well enough supplied from its own resources with intelligence about Germany's eastern front. For another, it had set limits on security grounds to what it was prepared to offer until Russia had reciprocated; the prospect of receiving intelligence from the Soviet authorities never became bright enough to justify lowering the restrictions.

As in the months preceding the German attack on Russia, Whitehall's anxiety to do what it could to strengthen Soviet resistance to the German offensive led it to take the initiative when Russia entered the war. Whitehall at no time contemplated that the British success with Enigma should be revealed to the Russians but after much hesitation, and all but deterred by the early disclosure in Enigma decrypts that the Germans were reading a number of Soviet codes and cyphers,* the Chiefs of Staff and 'C' accepted early in July 1941 the risk of allowing them to receive the more important Enigma intelligence on a regular basis in camouflaged form. In doing so they gave way to pressure from the Prime Minister. On 24 June, in reply to his request that some unspecified item should be sent to the Russians, 'C' advised against divulging Enigma intelligence to them in view of the insecurity of their cyphers, but the Prime Minister instructed him to proceed 'provided no risks are run'.[58] And once the regular service had started, the Prime Minister often enquired whether a particular decrypt had been sent or demanded to know why it had been withheld.[59†]

The method adopted for passing the intelligence was that each of the Service intelligence branches drew up its own telegrams and cleared them internally at a high level (DDNI and DDIC in NID; DMI in MI; ACAS (I) in AI) before submitting them to 'C' for

---

* By the middle of July Enigma decrypts had revealed that the Germans were reading signals from Russia's 17th Air Division, understood the signalling system used by Russian aircraft in the Leningrad area and were decrypting some Russian naval traffic; and the BMM was asked to alert the Russians.[57]

† The earliest of several interventions by him occurred on 17 July 1941; a typical one came on 6 December 1942 when he enquired: 'Has any of this been passed to Joe?'.[60]

56. CAB 66/20, WP (42) 8 of 5 January, p 17; CAB 121/465, SIC file D/Russia/5, JIC (43) 25 of 2 February; Morgan, *NID History 1939–1942*, p 105 et seq; ADM 223/107, Skeleton History of NID 16, pp 7–8 and NID 0066, minutes of meeting 28 April 1943.
57. London/Moscow Signals file, unnumbered telegrams of 7 and 13 July 1941.
58. Dir/C Archive, 6863 of 24 June 1941.
59. ibid, 7098 of 17 July 1941.
60. ibid, 1645 of 6 December 1942.

further scrutiny and despatch to the British Military Mission in Moscow (BMM).[61] Obvious formulas – 'a well-placed source in Berlin', 'a most reliable source' – provided the cover, but care was taken to withhold details like unit identifications that could only have been obtained from decrypts,* and the BMM was instructed to take the further precaution of asking the Russians not to disclose by W/T that they were receiving intelligence from British sources.[63]† There is no truth in the much-publicised claim that the British authorities made use of the 'Lucy' ring, a Soviet espionage organisation which operated from Switzerland, to forward intelligence to Moscow.

A good deal of operational intelligence was sent through the BMM up to the summer of 1942.‡ By the spring of that year, however, the BMM and the British Embassy had become frustrated by the cumbersome liaison protocol which the Russians had insisted on applying to most of their contacts;[65] and though constantly bombarded by Soviet requests for further information about German strengths, dispositions and intentions, they had failed to elicit

---

* For example, a decrypt of 11 July 1942 from Luftflotte 4 to Fliegerkorps VIII on operations in the area of Army Group B read: '1) Increasing enemy pressure on the front of the Second Army is to be expected. The pinning-down of strong enemy forces on the Army's front is desirable taking into account the operations of the Eastern Army as a whole. 2) The task of the Army Group von Weichs is with the Second Hungarian Army to hold the Donets front between the mouth of the Potudan and the mouth of the Voronezh, and, together with the Second Army, to hold the bridgehead Voronezh, and the present position on the general line Olchowatka-Oserk-Bork-Kotysch railway station (east of Droskowo)'. This was sent to the BMM in Moscow by MI on 13 July – after a warning telegram that it came from a 'most reliable and occasional source' – as: 'For information of Russian General Staff. Our picture from various sources gives clear indication that Germans, including Hungarians, intend to hold Russians on front Livni-Voronezh-Svoboda, while armoured forces push southeastwards between rivers Don and Donets'. On the original decrypt MI had commented that it could not locate Oserk and Kotysch, but that the general line did not indicate any considerable change on the Voronezh front; that although 'Donets' was clearly written it was presumably an error for 'Don'; that there were other indications that the armoured spearhead was to push south-east between the Don and the Voronezh-Rostov railway; and that this was the first mention of an army group on the Russian front as Army Group B.[62]

† The Prime Minister was as anxious about the camouflage as he was to help the Russians. In September 1941, when the head of the BMM reported that the Russian intermediaries revealed the source of British information only to Stalin and Marshal Shaposhnikov, the Chief of the General Staff, he demanded an explanation. 'C' replied that he was confident that the BMM had not exceeded its instructions; it gave the source to the Russians only when they showed incredulity, and they were then told that it was an officer in the German War Office.[64]

‡ The texts of the telegrams cleared by ACAS (I) are in the London/Moscow Signals file. This does not contain the telegrams issued by NID and MI, but these can sometimes be found in other files, including the Dir/C Archive, see below Chapter 17.

61.   ibid, 6908 of 28 June 1941; JIC (41) 20th Meeting, 1 July.
62.   Dir/C Archive, MI telegrams to BMM 167 and 168/MI 14 of 13 July 1942, CX/MSS/1179/T23.
63.   ibid, 6908 of 28 June and 7098 of 17 July 1941.
64.   ibid, 7666 of 28 September 1941.
65.   Morgan, op cit, p 111.

either a regular intelligence bulletin from the Russians or, even, answers to specific enquiries from the United Kingdom about, for example, unidentified GAF units and GAF aircraft that were known to have fallen into Russian hands.[66] At the same time, the Service intelligence branches had encountered a wall of resistance to their efforts to exchange intelligence via the Soviet Military Mission in London. They had begun them with instructions to hold discussions on a barter basis about sources, methods and results. By the beginning of 1942 AI had found the Russians unwilling to exchange even technical intelligence about captured enemy equipment; thereafter, while continuing to supply the Mission unilaterally with regular reports on the order of battle, the operations and the intentions of the GAF on the Russian front, AI confined itself to answering specific Russian questions.[67] The special section of MI that was set up in August 1941 to liaise with the Soviet Mission, under the direct control of the DMI,[68] has left no record of its activities. Its experience was presumably similar to that of AI except that it is known that some military technical intelligence was obtained from the Russian front.[69] The NID persevered for somewhat longer than AI. In April 1942 the DNI was reasonably satisfied with the exchange of intelligence about the German Navy;[70] in January the Russians had provided useful information from the Black Sea about the German magnetic mine, and they provided more in June.[71] In May the DNI instituted weekly NID meetings with the Russian Mission.[72] But in London, as in Moscow, the attempt to increase contacts seems only to have increased the reticence of the Russians.

In these circumstances, and also because it continued to get evidence from the Enigma that Germany was reading Soviet communications, the Y Board decided that the supply of high-grade Sigint via the BMM must cease, or at least be greatly reduced. From the end of June 1942 the telegrams despatched by 'C' on behalf of AI dwindled to a trickle. On evidence of the total flow of Army and Air Force Enigma decrypts, the MI series suffered a similar fate: it is clear that from the middle of 1942 items bearing on the Russian front were commonly not forwarded to Moscow. However, despite the fact that on 15 November the BMM was informed that the service was being discontinued

---

66. London/Moscow Signals file, unnumbered telegrams of 7 and 13 July 1941 and telegram MI6/4/23 of 13 September 1941.
67. *Air Ministry Intelligence*, pp 25–26, 267.
68. Mockler-Ferryman, op cit, pp 18, 27, 28.
69. For example, WO 208/3580, MEF/6000/MI 10 of 12 August 1943, part 5.
70. Morgan, op cit, p 109.
71. ADM 223/107, Black Sea Diary, pp 4–5.
72. ibid, Skeleton History of NID 16, pp 7–8.

altogether for the time being,[73] it did not cease. It appears that the NID continued to send information from the Enigma to the BMM and the British naval liaison officers in Russia when it was 'really important' that the Russians should have it, and it is clear that, particularly during the Soviet counter-offensive at Stalingrad which opened on 19 November 1942, operational intelligence about German Army and Air Force intentions was still passed to Moscow, some of it marked 'reports sent by the JIC' and some of it at the Prime Minister's insistence, as a special measure. On 22 November 'C' expressed his concern that the Prime Minister was requiring him to forward intelligence derived solely from the Enigma when the Germans were tightening their signals security: 'it is for this reason that I am always embarrassed at sending the Russians information only obtainable from this source, owing to the legibility of many Russian cyphers'.[74]*

In the first half of 1943, after the German collapse at Stalingrad, Whitehall returned to, and intensified, its more cautious attitude. Russia was still given warning of Germany's main intentions – at the beginning of April she was warned of the plan to move against Novorossiisk, and at the end of April of the preparations for the Kursk offensive –[†] but much less Enigma was now forwarded to Moscow. Relations with the Soviet Mission in London became more guarded, the NID adopting a policy of tough bargaining[75] and the War Office transferring responsibility for liaison with the Mission from MI to the Director, Liaison Missions, who acted for the Deputy Chief of the Imperial General Staff.[76] And while one consideration in British minds was the decline in the German threat on the eastern front, and another the knowledge that Germany was still reading at least Russian medium-grade cyphers without great difficulty, Soviet suspiciousness and unreadiness to reciprocate were no less influential. In the autumn of 1942 the British Naval Liaison Officer with the Black Sea Fleet had been charged with discourtesy to the Soviet regime; in November the Soviet authorities reprimanded his successor for collecting intelligence about communications in the Caucasus.[77] In February 1943 they summarily closed down the small intercept station which, with limited facilities for transmitting its intercepts back to the United Kingdom, they had permitted the Admiralty to establish near

---

* See below, pp 109–110.
† See below, p 624 and Appendix 22.

73. London/Moscow Signals file, Y Committee Chairman to BMM, SJ 60 of 15 November 1942.
74. Dir/C Archive, 1473 of 22 November 1942.
75. ADM 223/107, NID 0066 of 28 April 1943.
76. Mockler-Ferryman, op cit, pp 19, 28–30.
77. Morgan, op cit, pp 109–110.

Murmansk in July 1941 in support of the defence of the Arctic convoys. By that time, moreover, it was obvious that, as well as failing to respond to the receipt of intelligence, they were unwilling or unable to collaborate in producing it.

In the spring of 1942, at the invitation of the Soviet authorities, the NID had discussed with them ways and means of improving Sigint collaboration in Murmansk for the benefit of the Arctic convoys. In exchange for copies of their intercepts of German naval transmissions, an expansion of the British intercept station and better facilities for transmitting the intercepts to the United Kingdom, it had offered them information about German naval W/T procedure and British methods of Traffic Analysis and had obtained permission to build on these beginnings by handing over some minor German naval and air codes and captured documents if the partnership prospered. It had failed to do so. The agreed extension of the British intercept and transmitting stations had provoked the recurring bouts of suspicion on the part of the Soviet authorities in the area which in February 1943 produced the closure of the stations.* Meanwhile the efforts of MI and AI had fared even less well than the NID's. In the summer of 1941, at the suggestion of the British Military Mission, AI had sent a Y officer to Russia to explain the RAF Y organisation to the Soviet authorities and, in the hope of a quid pro quo, to give them the GAF tactical codes and details about the GAF's beacons and navigational aids and its tactical and ground-station call-signs. He had been given similar material in return – GAF tactical codes and call-signs and some intercepts.[78] His visit was followed by one on behalf of MI 8. Its representative had handed over captured documents on German Army W/T procedure and apparatus, and the methods developed for solving German police cyphers. He had obtained captured documents, but no cryptanalytic material, and waited for a Soviet follow-up approach. Although none had come, he had in August 1942 been appointed to the British Military Mission as 'the accredited representative of the Y Services in Russia'; there was still some hope that the Russians might reciprocate by posting a Russian Y officer to the United Kingdom and showing some interest in Sigint collaboration in limited fields – the exchange of German intercepts, low-grade German codes and cyphers and possibly Japan's codes and cyphers. In December, in the hope that that would produce some reaction, he had been authorised to hand

---

* Collaboration in PR for the Arctic convoys proceeded somewhat more smoothly, see below p 222.

78. CAB 79/13, COS (41) 280th Meeting, 7 August; CAB 121/465, BMM and WO telegrams of 30 July and 9 August 1941.

over information about how to read the Abwehr hand cyphers.[79]*
But by February 1943 no progress had been made and the
accredited Y representative was recalled for further consultation.

A few days after the closure of the Admiralty's intercept station
in February 1943 the Russian naval authorities, conceding that
Russia needed to acquire more experience, proposed to the British
Military Mission that two officers should visit the United Kingdom
for three months to study British interception and wireless intelligence. The Y Board's immediate reaction was to reject the
suggestion. Over and above its annoyance with the Russian action,
it had by then considered a depressing report from its representative at the BMM on his efforts to work with the Russian Army's Y
authorities: they had agreed in August 1942 to provide Japanese
intercepts and German intercepts and captured documents in
return for information about the Japanese military attaché code
and GAF tactical codes and cyphers; as we have seen, they had
subsequently been given information about the Abwehr hand
cypher keys and they had been allowed to know that the British
were able to read some of the medium-grade cyphers of the German
Army; but the Y Board's representative had failed to obtain access
to them after the middle of October, and in December he had been
told that they wanted to terminate the agreement. Moreover, GC
and CS warned the Board that Russia might demand more
cryptanalytic assistance if the visit went forward; in which case a
refusal might make co-operation with her even more difficult, while
further concessions would carry the risk that, because of the
insecurity of Russian cyphers, Germany would learn that her own
cyphers were being read. But GC and CS also stressed the
importance of receiving Russian intercepts of German signals that
were inaudible in the United Kingdom, particularly of naval traffic
from the Arctic and of police and army field traffic in Russia, and
was inclined to agree with the Board's Moscow representative that,
provided it was accompanied by firm conditions, acceptance of the
proposal of the Russian naval authorities might be a means of
forcing a better response from the Russian Army. Meanwhile the Y
Board had consulted the British Ambassador in Moscow and he
had advised against a hasty decision 'in view of our present efforts
to establish a new relationship with the Russians in matters of this

---

* At the end of the previous month 'C' had proposed to send this information to the
Russians. He thought it possible that the Russians were reading these cyphers themselves in
any case, but the SIS was unable to judge whether the decrypts carried genuine intelligence
or intelligence planted by the Russians, who alone could decide on their value.[80]

79. London/Moscow Signals file, Y Board Chairman to BMM, SJ 86 of 23
    December 1942.
80. Dir/C Archive, 1487 of 23 November 1942.

kind and of Stalin's declared intention to see to it that his people co-operate with ourselves'.

In April, accordingly, the Y Board decided to permit two naval officers to visit some UK Y establishments (but not Bletchley) for a month, on condition that a British officer returned with them to Russia and was given equal access to similar Russian naval establishments, and on condition that the Soviet Army authorities reversed their policy of non-co-operation. In addition, the Russians were again given evidence of the insecurity of their cyphers and informed that they would be given no further enemy codes and cyphers until the Y Board was satisfied that they had improved their own; and they were asked to do what they could to increase their interception of German naval traffic in the north. At the same time, however, the Board also decided that its permanent representative at the BMM should not return to Moscow but should continue to advise on Anglo-Soviet Sigint relations from GC and CS; from July 1943 a newly-appointed SIS representative at the BMM became responsible for liaison with the Y authorities in Moscow.

In June 1943 it emerged that the Russians had captured the Auka code, used by the GAF for air to ground signalling, and a naval Enigma machine; the Soviet naval authorities asked for advice on how to exploit the Auka and enquired whether the British knew how to use the naval Enigma machine. In July the British and Soviet naval authorities in the Murmansk area held a satisfactory meeting to discuss the exploitation of Auka and the interception of German naval traffic; and the British followed this up by presenting the Russians with a captured Enigma machine and a book of instructions for its use – though not with advice about how to solve the keys.* In the meantime, however, the BMM had reported a total lack of progress with the Soviet Army authorities – cordial enough but 'swollen-headed with success', they were evading serious negotiations – and on 21 July the British Ambassador took the matter up with Molotov. His intervention produced meetings with a general who knew nothing of the previous discussions and who, while suggesting that he might send two officers to England, was principally interested in discovering the sources of

---

* It was learned during July 1943 that the Russians were getting results from the Auka code, and it was presumed that they exploited the GAF tactical codes and the police and Abwehr hand cyphers that had been handed to them. But the secretiveness of the Soviet authorities, and the impossibility of knowing what interpretation to put on their occasional confessions of inexperience, and on the limited interest they appeared to show in the operational intelligence that was passed to them, kept Whitehall uncertain of the extent of their Sigint achievements. In particular, while there was some slight evidence that their principal sources of intelligence about the German Army in the autumn of 1941 were DF, POW and captured documents, it could not thereafter be established whether and, if so, from what dates they succeeded in reading Enigma keys.

the British evidence about Soviet cypher insecurity and establishing which codes and cyphers it applied to. He was given more information on this subject, the British evidence being attributed to such enemy cypher systems as had been handed to the Russians and to a disaffected Austrian POW, but was also advised that until the Soviet authorities showed a genuine interest in co-operation they would not receive any further Sigint assistance or be free to send the two naval officers to the United Kingdom. This final British démarche had no effect. In sporadic meetings during the remainder of 1943 the Russians confined themselves to requesting more material without offering anything in return, and in 1944, as British interest in obtaining intercepts from Russia declined, negotiations on Sigint shrank to a desultory exchange of telegrams before lapsing altogether.

In these final stages the British willingness to keep the liaison alive owed more to a wish to forward the SIS's efforts to make contact with the Russians than to the belief that the Russians would change their attitude where Sigint was concerned. These efforts began from July 1943 when the SIS appointed a representative to the BMM with instructions to discuss with the Russians German Secret Service activities behind their lines and to stress to them the need to improve their cypher security. But he, too, had no success, the few occasions when it seemed that a promising opening had been made all foundering on the replacement of the Russian official.

To some extent the SOE made greater progress. In September 1941 it reached a formal agreement with the NKVD providing for full collaboration in subversion and propaganda in all countries outside the USSR and the British Commonwealth. Thereafter, there was an SOE Mission in Moscow and an NKVD Mission in London which maintained fairly frequent contact with the appropriate authorities. Early in 1942, however, by which time it was clear that collaboration was to be anything but full, the Foreign Office insisted on limiting the agreement so that it did not apply to neutral countries or permit the entry of Russian agents into western enemy-occupied countries without the consent of the governments-in-exile. From then on the SOE liaison in Moscow often complained that its existence was futile, but it retained some contact with unofficial Russians and was occasionally permitted to visit areas where other British officers were not welcomed.

CHAPTER 17

Strategic Assessments from June 1941 to the Fall of Stalingrad January 1943

THE INHIBITIONS which so severely limited the exchange of intelligence with Russia, and restricted even the receipt of information in Whitehall about Russia's own forces, had two consequences for British strategic assessments. The first was that, in conjunction with the poverty of British intelligence about Russia up to June 1941, the lack of reliable information about the general situation on the eastern front in the month following the German attack intensified the disposition to assume that she was in no state to withstand so large an offensive and kept alive the fear that Germany would soon be free to advance on the Middle East through the Caucasus or resume her preparations for an invasion of Britain. In the second place, it was because Whitehall had good intelligence about the Russian front from the German Enigma that it was able thereafter to revise its initial assessments and to establish a reasonably accurate coverage of the progress of the eastern campaigns at a time when those campaigns were exerting an ever-increasing influence on Allied strategy and the entire course of the war.

On 14 June 1941, in its first comprehensive review of Russia's capacity to resist, the JIC judged that the first phase on the eastern front, in which Germany would occupy the Ukraine and Moscow, would last something under four and something over six weeks, and strongly implied that it would be followed by a total Soviet collapse.[1] In further papers dated 3 and 23 July it put no figures on its estimates, but continued to discount the prospect of prolonged Soviet resistance.[2] On 28 and 31 July, however, it excluded the possibility of total collapse to the extent that it expected only that Germany would be sufficiently successful to enable her to disengage some forces for other theatres,[3] and in another paper on 1 August it was so much more encouraging about the continuation of Russia's resistance that the Prime Minister and the Chiefs of Staff

---

1. CAB 121/412, SIC file D/Germany/1, JIC (41) 234 (Revise) of 14 June.
2. JIC (41) 265 and 294 (o) of 3 and 23 July.
3. JIC (41) 288 of 28 July; CAB 121/464, SIC file D/Russia/4, JIC (41) 290 of 31 July.

decided to relax the highest state of readiness that was then in force against the threat of a German invasion of Britain (operation *Sealion*).[4]* A week later the JIC concluded that Russia's resistance had ruled out any German troop movements down to the end of 1941 other than for consolidation of the eastern front; there would be no full-scale operations elsewhere.[5]

The JIC's revision of its initial assessments owed little to information from the Soviet authorities, which was confined to what they released in their communiqués about the progress of the fighting and to occasional assurances from Stalin that Russia would hold out. In the middle of September, when it attempted in collaboration with MEW to study the effect on Russia's war potential of her hypothetical withdrawal to four successive defence lines, it could offer no firm conclusions because its knowledge of her resources, her existing stocks and the actual and potential size of her armed forces was 'inexact'.[6] On these matters it was never to become so well informed that it could offer reliable estimates. As late as the autumn of 1942 the Anglo-American Combined Intelligence Committee reported that neither London nor Washington had succeeded in obtaining from Russia any intelligence of value about Germany's operations and intentions,[7] and at the Casablanca conference in January 1943 the United States and British Chiefs of Staff were still complaining of the difficulty of getting information from Russia to facilitate sending aid to her.[8] From soon after the German attack on Russia, however, Whitehall was receiving a regular supply of accurate intelligence about the course of operations from the Enigma.

The intelligence provided by this source was by no means complete. It was limited by the extent to which the German forces could rely on land-lines and by the difficulty of intercepting their W/T transmissions in the United Kingdom; for these reasons it was patchy for the Leningrad sector and negligible for the extreme north. It was obtained with some delay: GC and CS was sometimes held up by interception difficulties, which produced corrupt texts, and it not unnaturally gave a lower priority to the traffic from the Russian front than to that which was of immediate operational value to Whitehall and the British commands. This is all the more understandable because it soon emerged that the Germans were

---

* See Vol I, p 483, and below, p 78 et seq.

4. JIC (41) 307 (o) of 1 August.
5. CAB 121/412, JIC (41) 311 of 8 August.
6. CAB 121/464, JIC (41) 357 of 13 September.
7. CAB 88/61, CISC 19th Meeting, 9 October 1941.
8. CAB 121/145, SIC file A/Strategy/2, CSCS 56th Meeting, 14 January 1943, pp 3–4.

not employing new weapons or novel tactics or strategic methods; in particular the GAF, operating once again in close support of the Army against an inferior enemy, was relying on the organisation, the tactics, the equipment and the type of operation with which Whitehall was already sufficiently familiar. But when all this has been said, it still remains the case that by providing the only reliable guide to events on the eastern front, and by yielding a good deal of intelligence about the central and southern sectors, the Enigma made an invaluable contribution to Whitehall's strategic assessments.

To begin with, the intelligence was derived mainly from the GAF's general key (Red) and although other GAF and a number of Army keys were to contribute, this always remained the steadiest source of Enigma decrypts on the eastern front. Of the further GAF keys only one other was intercepted in 1941. This was the key of the GAF field Sigint service on the eastern front (named Mustard at GC and CS).* This was broken on 12 days between June and September, but not again till April 1942. It was then broken with fair frequency and provided a comprehensive picture of the order of battle of the Soviet Army and Air Force. Of the Army Enigma keys the most important appeared at the beginning of the campaign. It was used for communications on a highly complex network between armies and army groups on the eastern front and the Army High Command (OKH). Called Vulture by GC and CS, it was broken a few times between June and September, but from October till mid-December with some regularity. From the end of 1941, however, largely owing to the introduction of land-lines, it was lost for over a year. It provided regular and detailed operational reports as well as occasional high-level appreciations, statements of intent and some supply information which came on no other key, and from no other source, until GC and CS regularly broke the German non-morse teleprinter traffic in 1943.† Only two other Army keys were broken before 1943. One was an army/air co-operation key (Kestrel to GC and CS) which was read fairly frequently in the autumn of 1941 and then lapsed in March 1942. It yielded mostly air reconnaissance reports. The other (Kite to GC and CS) was concerned with army supply matters; it was read occasionally in the early part of 1942.

The decrypts of the Red key, supplemented by Vulture and Kestrel, soon yielded a tolerably complete tally of the GAF units engaged in the fighting and a fair amount of information on their strengths and the scale of their operations. It was also possible to identify army formations down to corps and, with somewhat more

---

* Other variants of the Mustard key, used by the GAF field Sigint service in the Mediterranean and in the west appeared in 1943 and later.

† See above, p 29 and, for further details, Volume III.

delay, down to division. Together with the GAF's frequent references to positions reached by the Army, they thus provided a good guide to the scale, the objectives and the progress of the German offensive. As we shall see, valuable information on these subjects was also obtained from time to time from other Sigint sources, notably the Japanese diplomatic decrypts of which the Japanese reports from Berlin were especially valuable on German intentions. And the decrypts established from the middle of July that, after making enormous gains, the offensive was beginning to falter.

On 17 July the Chiefs of Staff résumé reported that it was emerging 'from several sources' that Germany had been surprised by the scale of Russian resistance, was disturbed by her own casualties and was preparing for a slowing down of her advance;[9] in particular, there were signs that the GAF was ceasing to be able to give adequate protection both to the Panzer formations and to concentrations and strategic positions to the rear of the tremendously long front.[10] Although they were not specified, and cannot now be traced, the 'several sources' probably included A-54 and diplomatic and SIS reports like that which reached Whitehall at the end of July from a Swedish source with good contacts in OKH who said that the German estimate for the defeat of the USSR was then three months at the least.[11] But it is clear that MI 14's best indications that Germany was being forced to modify her plans were being derived from the Enigma decrypts, and that this is why Whitehall had decided early in July 1941 to send a regular selection of the important Enigma items to the Russian authorities via the British Military Mission. On 14 July MI signalled to Moscow its estimate of the dispositions of the German armies and army groups in Russia, together with what it knew of the order of battle of Panzer and motorised divisions. On 16 July it sent its appreciation of German intentions in the Smolensk and Dnieper areas and the news that the GAF was to prevent Russian withdrawals by attacks on the railways.[12]*

In Germany the process of revising the *Barbarossa* plans for the attack on Russia culminated in the directive for the next phase of the offensive which Hitler issued on 21 August. This laid it down that the most important objectives before the onset of winter were

---

* This last item of intelligence was sent at the request of the Prime Minister. For the inauguration of the supply of Enigma to Moscow see above pp 59–60.

9.   CAB 80/29, COS (41) 441 (98th Résumé), para 22.
10. ibid, para 69.
11. WO 208/3573, MI 14 Appreciation for the CIGS, 28 July 1941; Amort and Jedlica, *The Canaris File*, (1970), pp 113–114.
12. Dir/C Archive 6976 of 14 July 1941, covering WO telegrams to BMM Moscow, Nos 91 and No 26/MI 14 of 14 July; No 28/MI 14 of 16 July 1941; CX/MSS/59/T10.

the seizure of the Crimea and the industrial region of the Donets, the cutting of Russia's oil route from the Caucasus and the investment of Leningrad; only after these targets had been achieved would the offensive be resumed on the central front. A week later Hitler approved a review of future intentions which assumed for the first time that the objectives could not all be reached before the winter. In coming to these conclusions he overruled protests from the General Staff and the commanders in the field, who urged that Moscow should be the main objective, and was swayed by a number of considerations. By early in August the German intelligence staffs had identified 50 Russian armoured divisions, an unexpectedly large number; and while they did not realise until October that the initial *Barbarossa* plans had been wholly mistaken in assuming that Russia would be broken if deprived of the industrial areas of Moscow, Tula, Kursk and Kharkov, they had already discovered that her industrial potential was greater than they had allowed. The progress of the fighting on the various sectors of the front was no less influential. The first definite check to the German advance had come early in August, when the attempt by Army Groups North and Centre to clear the Velikie Luki pocket on the Smolensk front miscarried in the face of savage Soviet attacks; but this setback had coincided with spectacular successes on the part of Army Group South. Early in August Army Group South's encircling movement west of the Dnieper had destroyed all organised resistance in the western Ukraine; by the last week of the month it had overrun the Ukraine up to the Dnieper and captured Dniepropetrovsk, the Black Sea base of Nikolayev and the metallurgical centres of Krivoi Rog and Nikopol.[13]

Of the Hitler directive of 21 August, as of the objections to it that were voiced in the highest circles in Germany, no word reached Whitehall. Nor was there much improvement in the supply of information from Moscow about Russia's military and industrial position. In talks with Harry Hopkins, the special adviser of President Roosevelt, at the end of July, and in one of his rare interviews with the head of the British Military Mission early in August, Stalin had been reassuring: he believed that Leningrad, Moscow and Kiev would hold out until the winter set in, claimed that he had 240 divisions, plus 20 in reserve, and felt that Russia had adequate capacity for a war of three to four years provided he could overcome a serious shortage of aluminium.[14] But there was no way of checking these claims, and as late as the end of

13. Gwyer and Butler, *Grand Strategy*, Vol III (1964) Part I, pp 99–105, 193; Cabinet Office Historical Section EDS/Appreciation/5 Supp 1, pp 2–3; Woodward, *British Foreign Policy in the Second World War*, Vol II (1971), p 3 fn.

14. Gwyer and Butler, op cit, Vol III, Part I, pp 106–109.

September the Beaverbrook supply mission to Moscow was unable to elicit any details.[15] In the middle of August, however, the British Military Mission learned that the Russians had 'much evidence' that German operations were being hampered by shortage of oil;[16] and by the beginning of September several reports from the SIS and from diplomatic sources had suggested that Germany was anxious about the degree of Russian resistance and was preparing for a winter campaign.[17] And some confirmation of this evidence and of these reports was being obtained from the GAF Enigma.

Between the middle of August and the middle of September AI was able to discern from the study of the Enigma decrypts that the GAF was suffering supply and maintenance difficulties. It was finding it impossible to provide close support on the required scale, was being forced to transfer close support units from one sector to another, and was reporting that the serviceability of its units was no more than 50 per cent.[18] From the same source MI was able to follow the German setback at Velikie Luki, to sense that this would induce the Germans to give highest priority to the advance of Army Group South in the Ukraine and, after the fall of Dniepropetrovsk on 26 August, to forecast that the next major German thrust would be carried out by the combined Panzer forces of Army Group Centre and Army Group South against Kiev.[19]

During September the GAF Enigma provided a considerable amount of intelligence about the fighting on the southern sector. It gave full details of the battle of Kiev, from which Whitehall could see – though without being able to judge to what extent – that the Russians had succeeded in extricating some of their forces.[20] It showed that by the end of the month Soviet resistance had stopped the German advance from Uman towards Kharkov[21] and had frustrated the German attempt to drive into the Crimea through the Perekop isthmus.[22] On the northern front, where the German advance was threatening the Leningrad–Moscow railway at the end of August, intelligence was much less plentiful. Beyond the fact

---

15. CAB 66/19, WP (41) 238 of 8 October.
16. CAB 120/25, PM Registered file 402/1/1D, Abbey telegram No 57 to Riviera Conference, Newfoundland, 17 August 1941.
17. CAB 80/29, COS (41) 478 (101st Résumé), para 25; WO 208/3573 of 11 August and 1 September.
18. CAB 80/30, COS (41) 513 (103rd Résumé), para 60; COS (41) 563 (106th Résumé), paras 63, 66; COS (41) 575 (107th Résumé), para 75.
19. eg CX/MSS/121, 152, 183, 212, 239; CAB 80/29, COS (41) 478 (101st Résumé), paras 21, 65; CAB 80/30, COS (41) 563 (106th Résumé), para 25.
20. eg CX/MSS/245, 253, 259, 262, 283; CAB 80/31, COS (41) 600 (109th Résumé), para 18; CAB 65/19, WM (41) 97 of 25 September.
21. eg CX/MSS/278, 293.
22. eg CX/MSS/239, 272, 293.

that by 4 September the railway had been cut and the German
advance was continuing, little was learned until 25 September,
when there were signs that the Germans were preparing a siege of
Leningrad.[23] By that time, however, the Enigma and MI 8's
Traffic Analysis on the frequencies which carried it* had disclosed
that most of the GAF formations on the northern front, together
with Panzer divisions from Army Groups North and South, were
being transferred to Army Group Centre.[24] As early as 9 September
GC and CS had decrypted Kesselring's order for the fulfilment of
the Führer's 'great plan' to destroy the three Russian armies of the
centre.[25] On this and similar evidence, GC and CS having
predicted as much on 22 September,[26] the possibility that the
Germans were about to resume the thrust on Moscow was mentioned in the Chiefs of Staff résumé on 25 September.[27] Between 20
and 24 September a series of warnings was sent from Whitehall to
Russia.†

The German drive on Moscow was re-started on 2 October. By
20 October it had reached Mozhaisk, 65 miles from the capital, and
Soviet government departments had been evacuated temporarily to
Kuibyshev, Stalin and most of his ministers remaining in Moscow.
But the advance then lost impetus and a final effort to reach
Moscow, ordered by Hitler on 13 November against the advice of
von Bock, C-in-C Army Group Centre, ended in failure.[30] The
Enigma ensured that Whitehall was fully and promptly informed of
the scale and the fortunes of the offensive. No sooner had the
Kestrel decrypts divulged that the attack had begun than there was
a big increase in GC and CS's success against the Vulture key. The
Vulture decrypts quickly established that, in terms of the number
of armoured and motorised divisions committed, the drive on
Moscow constituted the greatest offensive effort that Germany had

* Cheadle's analysis of the German air to ground communications appears to have
produced no intelligence about the GAF on the eastern front. This was no doubt partly on
account of lack of resources and partly because of inability to intercept the traffic.

† On 2 October the Prime Minister minuted 'C': 'Are you warning the Russians of the
developing concentration [on the central front]? Show me the last five messages you have
sent out to our missions on the subject'. In reply 'C' reported that nine warnings had been
sent during the four days 20–24 September.[28] The text of one of these warnings remains in
the files; it stated that enemy air and ground concentrations in the Smolensk area indicated
impending major operations there.[29]

23. CAB 80/30, COS (41) 533 (104th Résumé), paras 18–20; COS (41) 553
    (105th Résumé), para 20; COS (41) 585 (108th Résumé), para 20.
24. eg CX/MSS/251, 258, 263, 264, 274, 281.
25. CX/MSS/224, para 3; Dir/C Archive 7518 of 9 September 1941.
26. AI/MSS/3.
27. CAB 80/30, COS (41) 585 (108th Résumé), para 27.
28. Dir/C Archive 7706 of 20 October 1941.
29. Telegram to BMM No 71/MI 14 of 20 September 1941.
30. Gwyer and Butler, op cit, Vol III, Part I, pp 194–197.

yet mounted, involving as it did 14 of her 21 armoured divisions*
and 8 motorised divisions from the 16 she was believed to have
available. But by disclosing the day-by-day movements and problems of enemy formations they also established that the advance
was slowing down as it encountered increasingly bad weather,
mounting fuel shortages, Soviet counter-attacks and evidence that
the Soviet Air Force was gaining superiority.[31] From this evidence
it was known from mid-November that the German forces were
having increasing difficulties in dealing with the Russian winter.[32]
By 5 December other decrypts had reported that the extreme cold
had made guns, vehicles and tanks unusable.[33] Another contained
a report by von Bock on 16 November, the first day of the final
push, to the effect that on the whole of Army Group Centre's 900
kilometre front he had only one reserve division.[34] And in the last
days of the push the GAF liaison officer with Second Army, which
was then fighting in the Kursk sector, complained that no German
fighters had been seen for two weeks.[35] The Mustard decrypts had
meanwhile disclosed that the Russians had brought forces from the
Far East into action.[36]

From 3 December the Enigma indicated that the Germans were
preparing to withdraw on the Moscow sector, and on 6 December
the decrypts included the general order for a 'wheel-back'.[37] By
then the German armies on the other sectors of the front, which at
the beginning of November had either gained the objectives laid
down in Hitler's directive of 21 August or had seemed to be within
easy grasp of them, had all suffered delays and reverses; and this
was in some cases known from the Enigma. From the Leningrad
area, where the German advance east of the city had taken Tikhvin
on 10 November and temporarily cut the last rail link, there was, as
before, no Enigma of value; the news that the German advance was
weakly supplied and that the Russians had captured Tikhvin was
presumably obtained from communiqués and the British Military
Mission.[38] But following Eleventh Army's forcing of the Perekop
isthmus the Enigma provided good coverage of the fighting in the
Crimea, where it showed that the German advance had been

---

* Enigma revealed that, of this total, two armoured divisions were in Africa and the
remaining five elsewhere on the Russian front.

31. eg CX/MSS/333, 339, 346, 351, 380, 404, 437, 438, 440.
32. CX/MSS/439/T4, 441/T5; Dir/C Archive 8077 and 8080 of 17 and 18
    November 1941.
33. CX/MSS/509.
34. CX/MSS/440.
35. CX/MSS/501.
36. CX/MSS/441.
37. CX/MSS/508.
38. CAB 80/32, COS (41) 739 (119th Résumé), para 20.

stopped before Sevastopol and in the Kerch peninsula.[39] And from Army Group South there was sufficient Enigma to show that its forces, over-extended by their success in reaching the line Kursk–Kharkov–Stalino–Taganrog, and in capturing Rostov on 21 November, had been retreating since then before Timoshenko's counter-offensive and had by early December given up all the ground they had gained in the past month.[40]

It was in these circumstances that on 8 December a Führer directive, the gist of which was repeated in an official German communiqué, stopped all large-scale offensives on the eastern front and put Germany's forces on the defensive for the winter.[41]

□

On 11 December Germany and Italy declared war on the United States, the Japanese attack on Pearl Harbour having taken place on 7 December 1941 (on 8 December by Japanese time).

Germany's response to Pearl Harbour came as no surprise. In August 1941 the Japanese Ambassador in Berlin had reported to Tokyo a conversation in which Hitler had assured him that 'in the event of a collision between Japan and the United States Germany would at once open hostilities with the United States'. On seeing GC and CS's decrypt of this telegram the Prime Minister asked for confirmation that the President had also seen it: 'C' replied that Washington had had the decrypt.

As for the Japanese attack, an analysis of the intelligence that was available about Japan's intentions after the middle of 1941 is beyond the scope of this volume. The intelligence that was available to the US authorities was the subject of a Congressional enquiry in 1946 and a study of it was published in 1962, which reached the following conclusions. 'The Peal Harbor air attack was the only part of the Japanese war plan that took Washington unawares'. 'It is clear enough that Japan was preparing for an all-out war with England and America, but it is nowhere clear whether she intended to make the first move by attacking either power directly, or whether she was preparing to meet a sudden blow from England or America . . . in response to further Japanese moves to the south'. However, although the Magic signals* were 'not unambiguous' on these two issues, 'they indicated quite clearly a level of tension where an accident on either side could open a full-scale war' – in which respect the intelligence picture after the

___

* Magic was the US cover-word for intelligence derived from high-grade Japanese Sigint.

39. eg CX/MSS/316, 323, 327, 356, 387, 438; CX/MSS/228/T15.
40. eg CX/MSS/347, 427, 442, 452, 487, 497.
41. CAB 80/32, COS (41) 739 (119th Résumé), para 21; *Führer Directives 1939–1941*, pp 231–232.

beginning of November differed significantly from that which had existed in July and October, the two periods earlier in 1941 in which US-Japanese relations had become tense.[42] In the British archives there is no intelligence of any importance that was not available to the Americans, who, indeed, had much that was not available in Whitehall, and the British appreciations do not call for any departure from the above conclusions.

Throughout the period between the German attack on Russia and the beginning of November 1941 the JIC consistently emphasized two theses. The first was that Japan, preferring to continue her expansion southwards, would not intervene against Russia. The second was that in her southward expansion she would make every effort to avoid provoking the United States. It expressed the first view for the first time on 25 June.[43] On 4 July it repeated it when commenting on an appreciation received from the US Special Naval Observers in London to the effect that, while it was clear that Japan was now embarking on a policy that would probably involve war, it looked as if her action in the south would for the present stop at Indo-China and that she would make a major military effort against Russia before the end of July; the JIC still held that Japan would not act against Russia but would take advantage of any opportunity to expand southwards beyond Indo-China.[44] On 2 August it judged that Japan's further expansion in the south, avoiding the Netherlands East Indies as being too provocative to the United States, would make for Thailand via the Kra isthmus so as to put her in a position to attack Malaya should she decide to resort to force against Great Britain.[45] On 11 August, having received more reports of Japanese concentrations against Russia, it conceded that an attack on Russia was feasible simultaneously with the occupation of Thailand, but thought this was unlikely.[46] A month later it noted that a change from defensive preparations to preparations for an offensive had taken place in Japan's dispositions against Russia, and concluded that she would not risk war against the United States and Great Britain by attacking Malaya until Russia had been so weakened that she was compelled to reduce her forces in the Far East below their present level; but it added that 'sooner or later' economic stringency would compel Japan to choose between a forcible expedition in the south and an accommodation with the United States.[47]

The next JIC assessment of Japan's intentions was issued on 18

42.   R Wohlstetter, *Pearl Harbor; Warning and Decision* (1962), pp 210–211, 227.
43.   JIC (41) 261 of 25 June.
44.   CAB 121/748, SIC file G/Japan/1, 4 July 1941.
45.   JIC (41) 309 of 2 August.
46.   CAB 121/748, JIC (41) 320 of 11 August.
47.   ibid, JIC (41) 362 of 13 September.

November. Begun on 11 November 'in the light of the most recent intelligence', which included the Sigint disclosure that Japan had fixed 25 November as the deadline for a successful outcome to her negotiations in Washington,[48] it stressed that Japan was at last being driven by the effects of the US–British economic sanctions to make this fundamental decision. But it also concluded that, if the negotiations broke down and Japan decided to risk war, the first move would be against Thailand: this was suggested by her recent military movements and by the fact that it would be a sound preliminary to safeguard operations against Malaya or the Netherlands East Indies, but above all by the consideration that by acting in that way she would incur the least risk of war with the United States.[49] And in a paper issued on 28 November the JIC implicitly excluded the prospect of a direct Japanese attack on US possessions: it calculated that if Japan broke off the negotiations she would move against Thailand very early in 1942 in order to be ready for an attack on Malaya in the favourable spring weather.[50] Except for a paper on 5 December which canvassed the advantages and disadvantages of Russia's participation in a war with Japan,[51] there was no further JIC appreciation of the situation in the Far East before the Japanese attack.

□

In the European theatre the first important intelligence development following Germany's assumption of the defensive in Russia and the extension of the war to the Far East was the disclosure by the GAF Enigma that units of Fliegerkorps II – four bomber Gruppen, three dive-bomber Gruppen, three fighter Gruppen and two reconnaissance Staffeln – were to be withdrawn from the Russian front to Sicily.[52] The Enigma decrypts had foreshadowed the eventual transfer from Russia of Luftflotte 2, of which Fliegerkorps II was a component,* as early as 27 October.[53] In the middle of November they had confirmed that the transfer was about to take place, and by the beginning of December they had established that Sicily was the destination and that north Africa was to be part of the Luftflotte's new command.[54] But uncertainty as to whether the situation on the Russian front would permit the move

---

* For the operational chain of command of the GAF see Volume I, Appendix 10.

48. JIC (41) 32nd Meeting, 11 November; Wohlstetter, op cit, p 210.
49. CAB 121/748, JIC (41) 439 of 18 November.
50. JIC (41) 449 of 28 November.
51. JIC (41) 460 (o) of 5 December.
52. CAB 121/464, JIC (41) 469 (o) of 11 December.
53. WO 208/3573 of 27 October 1941.
54. eg CX/MSS/359/T24, 487/T17, 492/T5.

persisted until the end of December, when a series of returns listed the units of Fliegerkorps II that were en route to the Mediterranean.[55]* By then MI 14 was 'certain' that there had been no large-scale withdrawal of German troops from Russia.[56]

The knowledge that the Germans were making no large army withdrawals from Russia and the discovery that Luftflotte 2 was moving to Sicily, and not returning to France as had been assumed in October,[57] had obvious consequences for Whitehall's assessment of the threat from *Sealion*. The danger that Germany would renew her attempt to invade the United Kingdom in the spring of 1942 had been effectively discounted by September 1941 in the light of her progress on the eastern front. By the end of the year it was eliminated by these positive and negative disclosures about her redeployment.

In the first few weeks following the German attack on Russia, while uncertainty prevailed as to Russia's ability to survive it, the threat from *Sealion* had remained in the forefront of attention in Whitehall. On 25 June the Chiefs of Staff had insisted that British defences must be at the highest state of readiness by 1 September.[58] Nor had they changed their minds by 18 July when they instructed the JIC to re-examine the threat; this decision followed a discussion about the possible reinforcement of the Middle East in which the Prime Minister had suggested that the invasion of Russia had made it less likely that *Sealion* would be attempted in the autumn, but in which the Chiefs of Staff had emphasised the risk of reducing the limited number of tanks available for Home Forces.[59]

On 23 July the JIC had pronounced that *Sealion* was unlikely to be attempted in 1941. But it had not supported this judgment with the argument that Russia was now sure to avoid collapse. Its thesis was that, whatever happened to Russia, *Sealion* was becoming an increasingly hazardous undertaking, as German resources came under increasing strain and British resources expanded, and that as it was unlikely that Germany could withdraw forces from Russia before the end of August, and would need at least six weeks to re-deploy them in the west, the weather would be unpropitious before she was ready for an invasion in 1941. Moreover, it had not ruled *Sealion* out for a later date: Germany was still building

---

* It emerged from later decrypts that not all the units listed had in fact left Russia; see below, p 344–345.

55. eg CX/MSS/573/T8, 669/T8, 674/T52, 851, 886/T2.
56. WO 208/3573 of 8 December 1941; CAB 80/32, COS (41) 723 (118th Résumé), para 42.
57. WO 208/3573 of 27 October 1941.
58. CAB 79/12, COS (41) 234th Meeting, 25 June.
59. CAB 79/12, COS (41) 250th Meeting, 17 July; CAB 79/13, COS (41) 251st Meeting, 17 July; CAB 69/2, DO (41) 51st Meeting, 17 July.

landing-craft; she might develop new methods and weapons even if there were as yet no signs of this; and not unnaturally at a time when the situation on the eastern front was critical and Whitehall still lacked any firm intelligence about it, the JIC had added that it was impossible to predict when Moscow would fall.[60] In its next review of the effects of the campaign in Russia on the prospects for *Sealion* the JIC on 1 August had done little more than restate these same conclusions more emphatically. Without categorically excluding an invasion attempt in 1941, it had reckoned that as it was 'inconceivable' that Germany would break off the campaign before achieving a major success – the capitulation of the Russian Army or the capture of sufficient territory to prevent a Soviet counter-offensive – the earliest date from which she could begin to disengage her forces was the last week of August, and that as all her transport and supply arrangements were directed against Russia, and substantially all her first-line forces were engaged there, the winter would be approaching before she could mount an invasion attempt.[61]

It was in the light of this assessment, if not solely as a result of it, that the Prime Minister and the Chiefs of Staff on 2 August relaxed the highest state of readiness against *Sealion* and notified the authorities concerned that they could expect to receive one month's notice if the threat of invasion returned.[62] Thereafter, the JIC would continue to refer to it in its general assessments of the enemy's intentions; as late as 30 September it was still asserting that an invasion of England in the spring of 1942 would be Germany's 'most certain road to victory'.[63] But it devoted no further separate report to *Sealion* until it completed in November 1941 a revision of the paper on invasion that it had compiled the previous January.[64]* By then, despite a resurgence of references in Axis diplomatic decrypts during the autumn to the danger of invasion,† the revision had become a somewhat routine exercise; it had been in train since the previous July. And that *Sealion* was by then looked upon as a somewhat remote threat may be judged from the response to the JIC's paper. The paper was considered by the

---

* See Vol I, p 262 et seq.

† On 22 October the Prime Minister upbraided his staff and 'C' for withholding from him the decrypt of 7 October of a report in which the Japanese Ambassador in Berlin had given details of German invasion preparations seen during a tour of the Boulogne area. Perhaps for this reason, several other diplomatic references to the invasion project are to be found in the Dir/C Archive from this date.[65]

60. JIC (41) 294 (o) of 23 July.
61. JIC (41) 307 (o) of 1 August.
62. CAB 79/13, COS (41) 272nd Meeting, 2 August.
63. JIC (41) 380 of 30 September.
64. JIC (41) 427 of 4 November.
65. Dir/C Archive, 7871 of 23 October 1941.

Vice-Chiefs of Staff; at the end of December, after a considerable delay, they set up an inter-Service Committee on the Invasion of Britain, composed of members of the Joint Planning Staff and the JIC, and instructed it to produce an operational plan for a German invasion in the spring of 1942 'on the following assumptions –

"That the Germans will remain on the defensive on all other fronts and subject only to this limitation they will employ the maximum possible forces for the attack on England." '[66]

□

By December 1941 it was obvious not only that Germany's opportunities for taking offensive action outside Russia before the spring had been considerably reduced, but also that her progress in Russia had ceased to constitute an immediate danger to the Middle East. In the previous August the continuation of Russian resistance had deferred the threat from *Sealion*. As a result of the rapidity of the German advance in the south, on the other hand, the danger of a German attack on the Middle East from the Caucasus had replaced *Sealion* as the greatest of Whitehall's anxieties. But by the beginning of December 1941 this threat, too, had been reduced by the Soviet counter-offensive.

At the end of July the JIC had speculated that, with Russia defeated, the German Army and the GAF might redeploy between mid-September and mid-November for a variety of further operations but had made no attempt to arrange them in an order of priority. As well as *Sealion*, these operations had included a drive against Turkey or Syria, an offensive against Malta, an offensive through Spain against Gibraltar and French north Africa, and an eastward advance in north Africa from Libya.[67]* On 8 August, in a more considered study of German intentions down to the end of 1941, it had argued that the collapse of Russia would be followed down to the end of 1941 by a period of economic reorganisation, regrouping and consolidation on Germany's part; in that period Germany would intensify her pressure on Turkey, Vichy and Spain but would undertake operations only in the Western Desert and against Britain and her trade routes.† But it had also argued that as

---

    * This comprehensive programme, as it happens, was identical with that envisaged by the Germans for the period following the defeat of Russia, as may be seen from a draft Führer Directive of 11 June and OKW's amended version of 30 June.[68]

    † For disagreements between Whitehall's and Cairo's assessments of the northern threat see below pp 278–279.

66.   CAB 79/15, COS (41) 380th Meeting, 7 November, COS (41) 382nd
       Meeting, 10 November; CAB 80/60, COS (41) 283 (o) of 31 December.
67.   JIC (41) 290 of 31 July.
68.   *Führer Directives*, pp 186–190.

soon as she was ready for larger operations she would probably give first priority to a drive through the Caucasus because of her shortage of oil.[69]*

The view of the JIC had been reflected in the appreciation that was handed by the Chiefs of Staff to the US authorities at the 'Riviera' conference at Placentia, Newfoundland, later in August 1941. Discounting the possibility that Russian resistance could have any decisive influence on the course of the war, and assuming that shipping restrictions would more or less permanently dictate the shape and restrict the scope of Allied strategy, this appreciation had argued that it would be impracticable to seek to defeat Germany in Europe until her war machine had been worn down by attrition, perhaps by the autumn of 1942, and had urged that priority should meanwhile be given to containing her in the Middle East.[71]† And on 25 August, as one step in this direction, British and Russian troops had embarked on the occupation of Iran following joint démarches to Tehran on 19 July and 16 August in which Great Britain and Russia had demanded the expulsion of specified German nationals 'known to be engaged in political activities'.[72]

The occupation of Iran had been undertaken as a precautionary measure; firm intelligence of an imminent Axis threat to the country or of Iranian collusion with the Axis was lacking. It is true that on 2 June, no doubt prompted by developments in Iraq,‡ the JIC had estimated that the number of German nationals in Iran had reached 5,000 and had argued that they constituted 'a very highly developed German Fifth Column', with 'well-advanced' plans for exerting pressure on the Iranian government.[73] During July, however, MI and the Foreign Office had both judged that this figure, which had been influenced by Russian claims, was

---

* The JIC has also thought it possible that in this period, after achieving outstanding military successes against Russia, Germany might make a peace offer to Great Britain. In an earlier paper, in an attempt to assess the form the offer would take and what would be world reactions to it, it had reviewed reports on this subject from diplomatic sources, from the SIS and from the Press and radio.[70]

† In annexes attached to this appreciation Whitehall had presented, for the first time, background intelligence for possible Allied operations against French Morocco, Dakar and Norway, the last being included at the insistence of the Prime Minister, who had not accepted the COS view that an operation against Norway was impracticable.

‡ See Volume I, pp, 409–414.

69. CAB 121/412, JIC (41) 311 of 8 August.
70. ibid, JIC (41) 288 of 28 July.
71. CAB 80/30, COS (41) 505 of 20 August; Gwyer and Butler, op cit, Vol III, Part 1, pp 125–129.
72. For the details see Woodward, op cit, Vol II, pp 23–26; Gwyer and Butler, op cit, Vol II, Part 1, pp 185–188.
73. JIC (41) 228 of 2 June.

exaggerated,[74] and neither had been much impressed by the threat of Axis political influence. On 1 August the Foreign Secretary had told the Defence Committee that 'though they might be well organised, [the Germans] did not appear to have much political influence as they had been unable to make the Shah take any steps to support Rashid Ali when he made his coup d'état in Iraq'.[75] In the War Office's weekly intelligence summary for 30 July and again on 4 August, in a report to the British Military Mission in Moscow, MI had dismissed recent rumours to the effect that the Axis was preparing a rebellion or a coup: unless, as was unlikely, they were supported by the Iranian Army, the Germans as yet were in no position to undertake anything beyond sabotage, and the rumours were probably being put about by the Russians as a means of justifying an Anglo-Russian occupation.[76]* Between then and the Anglo-Russian occupation no reliable intelligence had been received which ran counter to this scepticism or cast doubt on the protestations of the Iranian government that its policy was to preserve the strictest neutrality. On the contrary, the Italian diplomatic decrypts had disclosed in the second week of August that the German attempts to organise subversion in the Caucasus from Iran had run into difficulties and that the Iranian government was hoping that the first of the Anglo-Russian démarches would induce the Axis 'to give up any suspicious activities which there might have been'. It was also clear that the Iranian government had imposed close supervision over the 'more formidable Germans'.[77]

Decrypt evidence of Axis under-ground activity in Iran had not been entirely lacking. At the end of July an Abwehr decrypt had established that German agents were collecting information on the Iranian oil-fields,[78] and from the Italian diplomatic decrypts it had been learned that an Italian Intelligence Centre for the collection of political and military intelligence was being formed in Tehran. On 2 August an Italian diplomatic decrypt had shown that the

---

* MI gave no evidence for this suggestion and it was clear from Allied diplomatic reports and Axis diplomatic decrypts that some at least of the rumours, which were repeated in the Press and on the radio, had emanated from Free French sources; these were claiming that German residents in Iran, taking advantage of Germany's advance into Russia, were planning to seize Iranian oil wells.

74. CAB 121/654, SIC file F/Persia/1, correspondence of 11, 18 and 21 July 1941; WO 208/2259, War Office Weekly Intelligence Summaries, Nos 99 and 102 of 9 and 30 July 1941.
75. CAB 121/654, DO (41) 53rd Meeting, 1 August.
76. WO 208/2259, No 102 of 30 July 1941; CAB 105/6, Hist (B) 6, No 138 of 4 August 1941.
77. WO 208/2260, WO Weekly Intelligence Summary No 104 of 13 August 1941.
78. WO 208/3573 of 28 July 1941.

Italians were suspecting that Germany had been talking to the Iranians about the territorial expansion of Iran in the event of a Soviet collapse. On 22 August another Italian diplomatic decrypt had reported that Germany was continuing to transport arms and ammunition to Iran via Turkey. Meanwhile, in yet another decrypt of 8 August, the Italians had quoted Rashid Ali as believing that the Iranian government was 'substantially favourable' to the Axis and would throw off the mask as soon as German troops appeared in the Caucasus. But before the receipt of any of this intelligence Whitehall had already begun to plan for the Anglo-Russian intervention, urged on by General Wavell, now C-in-C India, who stressed the need to avoid a repetition of the coup in Iraq,[79] and by General Auchinleck, C-in-C Middle East, who stressed the necessity of extinguishing German influence before Germany was in a position to influence Iran.[80] On 26 July, moreover, the Joint Planners had noted that while the immediate aim of the intervention was the expulsion of the German colony, 'our real military requirements' were to ensure the defence of the oil-fields and refineries against air attack and sabotage and to prevent the Iranian government from adopting a policy hostile to British interests.[81]

In further assessments during the autumn of 1941 the JIC had become more optimistic about Russia's ability to hold on until the winter, but also more convinced of Germany's concern to reach the Caucasus. On 30 September it had held that while she might attack elsewhere if forced to stabilise the front in Russia, her primary objective would be the Caucasus.[82] At the end of October it had felt that her need to capture the Caucasian oil was so desperate that she might take numerous risks to do so during the winter.[83] On 8 November it had concluded that her forces were unlikely to reach the Caucasian range before Christmas and that her present supreme effort to take Moscow and possibly Leningrad would probably fail, but that in the spring of 1942 her objective would be an offensive against Russia in full strength. She would thereafter undertake a full-scale attack against British positions in the Middle East through Iran and probably also through Turkey;[84]* and she

---

* The possibility of a German attack on Turkey had been reported in September 1941 by A-54 in the last identifiable report to be received from him.[85] In October the subject had reappeared in the Axis diplomatic decrypts. On 3 October, for example, the Prime

79. Churchill, *The Second World War*, Vol III (1950), p 424.
80. CAB 105/6, No 82 of 20 July 1941.
81. CAB 121/564, JP (41) 594 of 26 July.
82. JIC (41) 380 of 30 September; CAB 79/14, COS (41) 342nd Meeting, 3 October.
83. JIC (41) 347 of 22 October, 420 (o) of 26 October; CAB 121/472, SIC file D/Russia/8, JIC (41) 419 of 27 October.
84. CAB 121/412, JIC (41) 433 of 8 November.
85. Amort and Jedlica, op cit, p 127.

would avoid additional commitments in Spain and north Africa, or an attempt to mount *Sealion*, until she had secured her oil.

During the remainder of November, while the Germans were advancing rapidly on the southern sector, and before the British authorities had come to realise the scope of Timoshenko's counter-offensive there, which began on 20 November, Whitehall continued to predict that while the other fronts would probably be stabilised for the winter, operations into the Caucasus would go on.[88] On 2 December the JIC noted that these depended on the capture of Sevastopol, without which the Germans could not cross the Kerch straits into the Caucasus, and that they would be strategically unsound unless the Germans could recapture Rostov, which had just been retaken in the Russian counter-offensive, but it calculated that the Germans would be at the Maikop oilfields by late January and in Grozny by mid-February if they gained Rostov by 15 December. The JIC also noted, however, that if the other fronts were stabilised, the Russians would be able to transfer forces to the south and that as the Russians seemed fully determined to deny the Caucasus to the Germans, and were already operating with 1,000 aircraft in the south, the Germans were unlikely to achieve the timetable it had worked out.[89]

By 11 December the JIC felt certain – more so than ever – that the original *Barbarossa* plan 'must' have envisaged the German conquest of the Caucasus, to be followed by operations through Iran, Iraq or Turkey. But it now thought it too early to predict what Germany would do in the spring of 1942, so obvious was it that her original plan had failed.[90]

Later in December, during the debate which took place between the Prime Minister and the Chiefs of Staff before they went to the 'Arcadia' conference with the US authorities in Washington at the end of the year, opinion in Whitehall about the imminence of the threat from the Caucasus remained divided. But it was no longer doubted that Russia had demonstrated her capacity to avoid defeat and that her continued resistance would be a central assumption in the planning of the western Allies. Two papers from the Prime Minister initiated the debate. In the first he favoured an Allied attempt to occupy French north Africa in 1942, by agreement if

---

Minister's daily selection of decrypts included a report from the Italian Minister in Istanbul to the effect that Turkey would maintain her neutrality against any aggressor; he had marked it: 'This is important'.[86] On 14 October 'C' advised the Prime Minister that his man in Ankara had consulted one of his well-placed contacts who had confided that the Turkish General Staff expected Turkey to be invaded in the spring.[87]

86. Dir/C Archive, 7697 of 2 October, 7707 of 3 October 1941.
87. ibid, 7795 of 14 October 1941.
88. WO 208/3573 of 17 and 24 November 1941.
89. CAB 121/464, JIC (41) 452 of 2 December.
90. ibid, JIC (41) 469 (o) of 11 December.

possible but by force if necessary,* and he supported his case with the argument that while Germany might retaliate by occupying Vichy France and forcing her way into Spain, her failure in Russia had made it far less likely that she would be strong enough to counter-attack through Syria, Iraq and Iran.[91] In the second he contemplated an Allied entry into Europe in 1943 against German Army and Air Force resistance 'at the present level', but against an increased U-boat effort, on the assumption that Allied operations in north Africa in 1942 had prospered and that the Russians had remained strongly established on the eastern front.[92] In their first response to these papers the Chiefs of Staff and the Joint Planners advocated giving all possible aid to Russia – her continued resistance was, they now argued, of primary importance to any Allied strategy for the defeat of Germany – but otherwise confined themselves to listing the most likely dangers from Germany. Apart from an intensification of the U-boat effort involving her possible seizure of Casablanca, Dakar and Madagascar† as U-boat bases, they judged these to be the invasion of Britain (unlikely, but not to be ruled out), the occupation of Spain and French north Africa (in reaction to the British advance in the Western Desert) and an advance to the Middle East from the north. Unlike the Prime Minister, they felt that the last of these threats was the most serious; the fighting on the eastern front might give some respite, but there was 'ample evidence' of German plans for very heavy pressure in this direction from the Caucasus even before the spring.[93]

Despite this difference of opinion, the Chiefs of Staff and the Prime Minister, at one in regarding a large-scale land offensive in the west against Germany as impracticable until 1943, had little difficulty in concerting an agreed statement of proposals for 1942 for presentation to the 'Arcadia' conference. It recommended that while giving all possible aid to Russia and undertaking the arming of Turkey, the Allies should gain possession of north-west Africa (*Gymnast*), build up their strength in the Middle East and stage

---

* The occupation of French north Africa in response to an invitation from the French authorities (operation *Gymnast*) had been under consideration in Whitehall since October 1941, when the Defence Committee had rejected a proposal for attacking Sicily (operation *Whipcord*). By the time of the 'Arcadia' conference it had in British discussions developed into a project for landing uninvited but with the hope of French collaboration.

† On 20 March 1942 the decrypt of a report from the Japanese Ambassador in Berlin was to reveal that the Germans were pressing Japan to land in Madagascar. The President asked that the Prime Minister's attention should be drawn to this.

91. Churchill, op cit, Vol III, pp 574–578; Gwyer and Butler, op cit, Vol III, Part 1, pp 325–329.
92. CAB 69/4, DO (42) 6 of 22 January, Part III; Gwyer and Butler, op cit, Vol III, Part 1, pp 334–336.
93. CAB 80/61, COS (42) 15 (o) of 14 January; Gwyer and Butler, op cit, Vol III, Part 1, pp 339–344.

limited land operations in north-west Europe or across the Mediterranean.[94]

□

Before the 'Arcadia' conference met the Russians had opened their first counter-attacks on the Moscow front, and the Prime Minister had already, on 10 December 1941, spoken to the War Cabinet of a serious German defeat.[95] By 23 December he thought it 'almost a miracle' that Russia's counter-attack in the centre showed no signs of slackening and that she was extending her attacks to the northern and southern fronts.[96] And by 18 December Whitehall realised that the Russians had removed the threat to Moscow, at any rate for the winter.[97]

Some information on the new situation and on Russia's improving prospects was obtained first-hand from Stalin when the Foreign Secretary and the VCIGS visited Moscow in the second half of December. Stalin thought it would be two months before Germany could reorganise her Army and bring forward new formations. He was determined to exploit this breathing space by continuing the counter-offensive; and its prospects were good because he had a slight superiority in the air and, to off-set Germany's great superiority in tanks, her Army lacked winter equipment and its morale was low. Germany would resume the offensive in the spring, but he agreed with the VCIGS that she had no strategic reserve and felt that she would have to carry it out with reconstituted divisions that had already fought in Russia; and he thought it not unlikely that their fighting efficiency had been permanently impaired. Meanwhile Russia's war industries were fast recovering. The VCIGS was impressed by Stalin's assessment of the longer-term prospects and although he did not expect striking Russian successes unless the German morale cracked, he thought it 'would indeed be surprising' if the morale of the German Army came through the winter unimpaired.[98]

With regard to the immediate fighting Stalin's optimism was borne out by the Enigma. Before the end of December there was ample evidence from this source that the Russian action in saving Moscow was not merely a defensive operation, but a major

94. Gwyer and Butler, op cit, Vol III, Part 1, pp 344–348.
95. CAB 65/24, WM (41) 126 of 10 December.
96. CAB 121/150, SIC file A/Strategy/6, Meeting with Dominion representatives during Arcadia Conference; CAB 80/32, COS (41) 754 (121st Résumé), paras 16, 20.
97. CAB 80/32, COS (41) 749 (120th Résumé), para 23.
98. CAB 121/459, SIC file D/Russia/1, VCIGS Report of Military Conversations during Mr Eden's visit to Moscow December 1941, pp 1–3, 6–7 and Annexes 1, 2, 2A and 2B.

offensive in which all Russian successes were being followed up by deployment in strength, and that the German forces of Army Group Centre were as unprepared for the counter-offensive as they were for the intense cold of the Russian winter. It was clear that Panzergruppe 4, the army most closely threatening Moscow at the start of the Soviet counter-attacks, had collapsed with severe losses, that Panzergruppe 3 to the north-west of Moscow had been reduced from a striking force to an ineffective remnant on the defensive, and that its perilous position had forced the withdrawal of Ninth Army further north. To the south-west of Moscow the right wing of Fourth Army had been smashed and in the south Second Army and Panzergruppe 2, exposed in the Tula salient, had carried out a confused retreat in face of the Russian attack towards Kursk.[99]

From the middle of December the breaking of the Vulture settings, the main source of this intelligence about Army Group Centre, became spasmodic, and from the end of 1941 the key defied the best efforts of GC and CS. This was mainly the direct consequence of the reduction of traffic following the large-scale construction of land-lines by the German Army, and more than another year was to pass before GC and CS again – and then by no means regularly – decrypted high-grade Army Enigma traffic from the Russian front. During the huge Soviet counter-offensive along the whole front which was launched in the first week of January 1942 the supply of Sigint was accordingly largely confined once again to what could be derived from the GAF Enigma keys, though Kestrel continued to be read occasionally until March 1942. The general GAF key continued to be broken daily, and Mustard, valuable for the light it threw on Soviet strengths and activities, was still broken from time to time. In addition GC and CS now broke further GAF keys. It was at this point that the GAF introduced separate Enigma keys for each of its Fliegerkorps and of those used on the eastern front GC and CS broke two: that of Fliegerkorps VIII on Army Group Centre's front (which it named Beetle) and that of Fliegerkorps IV with Army Group South (named Hornet). By March 1942 it had also broken the key of Luftgau Ost (named Foxglove). The product from GAF keys was supplemented by other sources. There were decrypts of the traffic between Rome and the Italian Air Force on the eastern front and from the German General in Rome to the Army HQ in Africa,

---

99. eg for Pzgr 3 CX/MSS/501/T7, 508/T11 and 19, 509/T32, 525/T4, 551, 552/T4, 554/T2, 580/T1; for Ninth Army 520/T40, 525/T14, 551, 554/T2; for Pzgr 4 508/T13, 525/T2, 532/T18, 538/T4, 551/T8, 555/T1, 567/T9; for Fourth Army 545/T12, 547/T9; for Pzgr 2 507/T12, 508/T5, 509/T15 and 28, 522, 524/T11, 529/T10, 553/T10, 541/T6, 551/T17, 552/T8, 564/T10.

which proved to be increasingly useful during 1942; there were also decrypts of the Enigma keys used by the Abwehr and the SS in Russia and of a police hand cypher, broken from the autumn of 1941, though these yielded less operational information.*

The Enigma was particularly valuable because other information about the eastern front – from the SIS, the British Military Mission, the official communiqués – was either untrustworthy or too general and too belated to be of great operational interest. From the Sigint, in contrast, MI 14 obtained enough reliable data with so little delay that it was able to follow the progress of the Russian counter-offensive in some detail. It could see that in the centre, where the Germans had been driven back some 100 to 150 miles, Army Group Centre was in a precarious position by the end of January 1942.[100] By the same time, on the other hand, it knew that the supporting Russian offensive in the Ukraine was faltering after securing the Izyum bridgehead over the northern Donets – a salient from which Soviet forces threatened Kharkov and had hoped to force the Germans to abandon operations in the Crimea[101] – and that the Russian counter-attacks in the Crimea had as yet achieved no decisive results.[102] And from the end of February, when the initial Soviet successes against Army Group North were also being reversed,† it became clear that the Russians would be unable to hold on to the favourable position they had won on the central front. Early in March the Germans were strongly entrenched there and a final Soviet push had to be called off early in April.[104]

---

* See Appendices 4 and 5.

† The GAF Enigma disclosed during April that in the northern sector a large-scale operation was taking place to supply by air German ground forces cut off in the Demyansk area south-east of Lake Ilmen. The COS decided that the Russians must be told of this. It was the success of this supply operation that led to the similar attempt, this time disastrously, to supply the encircled 6th Army at Stalingrad in the winter of 1942–1943.[103]

100. eg CX/MSS/625/T5, 633/T9, 642/T16, 656/T21, 659/T15, 660/T12, 19 and 24, 669/T5, 15 and 17, 670/T21 and 112, 671/T25, 678/T5. See also eg CAB 80/33, COS (42) 25 (12th Résumé), COS (42) 43 (125th Résumé), COS (42) 63 (126th Résumé); CAB 80/34, COS (42) 90 (127th Résumé); WO 208/3573 of 26 January 1942; Seaton, *The Russo-German War 1941–1945* (1971), pp 233–237.
101. eg CX/MSS/648/T16, 654/T1, 656/T21, 659/T18, 663/T4, 674/T6 and 43, 679/T4, 681/T26, 682/T8; CAB 80/33, COS (42) 11 (123rd Résumé), COS (42) 25 (124th Résumé), COS (42) 43 (125th Résumé), COS (42) 63 (126th Résumé); CAB 80/34, COS (42) 104 (128th Résumé), COS (42) 122 (129th Résumé). See also Seaton, op cit, pp 248–250; Erickson, *The Road to Stalingrad* (1975), pp 326–329.
102. eg CX/MSS/565/T21 and 29, 603/T2, 5 and 11, 606/T2, 610/T14; CAB 80/33, COS (42) 3 (122nd Résumé), COS (42) 25 (124th Résumé).
103. eg CX/MSS/871, 884/T4, 886/T8, 890/T13, 893/T8, 895/T2, 901/T17; CAB 79/20, COS (42) 119th Meeting, 15 April; Seaton, op cit, pp 246–247.
104. Seaton, op cit, pp 238–239; Erickson, op cit, pp 311, 322–328, 331–333.

The change in the situation on the eastern front was reflected in Axis diplomatic decrypts. On 17 January 1942 the Japanese embassy in Moscow had appreciated that Germany might have to evacuate the whole of Russia. But by March 1942 the diplomatic decrypts began to carry rumours to the effect than Japan might intervene against Russia; on 4 March the Prime Minister asked that one such decrypt should be passed to the President.[105] On 12 April 1942 the Japanese decrypts indicated that Japan was anxious to discover whether the Germans were negotiating a compromise peace with the Russians and the Prime Minister wondered whether Stalin should be informed. The Foreign Office dissuaded him for obvious reasons.

The faltering of the Russian offensive exerted a profound influence on British planning. Up to the end of January 1942, while the intelligence was telling of Russian successes, Whitehall's knowledge of the Soviet advance had not only contributed to the decision to defer operation *Gymnast*; however temporarily, it had even inspired the hope that a landing in Europe in 1942 could be substituted for *Gymnast*. *Gymnast* had suffered a severe setback as a result of Rommel's counter-attack from Agheila within days of the conclusion of the 'Arcadia' conference. But it was with arguments derived from the situation in Russia that at the end of January the Joint Planners had recommended its deferment. They reasoned that the French in north Africa would not invite an Allied occupation until Eighth Army broke into Tripolitania and unless it began to look as if Germany might collapse in the face of Russia's offensive, but that in that eventuality the Allies should attack in Europe itself instead of in Africa. By quoting the opinion of the JIC to the effect that, in view of the Soviet successes, it was now unlikely that Germany would move against Spain except to forestall or counter Allied action in north Africa, they urged that the need to carry out *Gymnast* had in any case become less urgent.[106] And on 11 February the Joint Planners, more optimistic about the Russian advance than ever, had even suggested that Soviet successes might have brought about by the autumn so great a decline in German morale and German strength in the west as to permit the western Allies to revive the cross-Channel operation *Sledgehammer* and make a 'hasty return' to the continent in 1942.[107] On 13 February the Chiefs of Staff directed the C-in-C Home Forces to begin to prepare both for this eventuality and for an Allied cross-Channel invasion in 1943 (operation *Roundup*).[108] A month

---

105. Dir/C Archive, 8875 of 4 March 1942.
106. CAB 121/489, SIC file E/North Africa/2, JP (42) 83 of 28 January, COS (42) 5th (o) Meeting, 31 January.
107. CAB 84/41, JP (42) 124 of 11 February.
108. CAB 80/61, COS (42) 40 (o) of 13 February.

later, however, when *Gymnast* was finally deferred until the autumn,[109] the discussion of operation *Sledgehammer* became still more urgent under the very different impetus of alarm and disappointment produced by the knowledge of Soviet setbacks.

On 14 February the CIGS was already cautioning that the next two weeks would show whether the Russians were capable of further advances in the face of stiffening German resistance.[110] On 7 March the Joint Planners no longer doubted the outcome;[111] on the evidence of what they knew of the military situation but, as they admitted, without any intelligence which specifically suggested that she was disintegrating, they warned the Chiefs of Staff that Russia stood in very urgent need of help.[112] The Chiefs of Staff met with the Directors of Intelligence to consider this plea on 10 March; they concluded that no cross-Channel operation that was practicable was likely to do much to divert German forces from the eastern front.[113] The only action that proved possible at this juncture followed on 24 March, when the RAF, in an effort to divert German fighter forces from Russia, resumed the sweeps over north-west France which had been abandoned at the end of 1941.[114]*

The conclusion of 10 March conformed to the agreement of the Combined Chiefs of Staff, recorded in December 1941 at the 'Arcadia' conference, to rule out a continental invasion until Germany showed signs of weakening.[115] Nor was it changed after a further month of active discussion. On 21 March, prompted by further papers from the Joint Planners, the Chiefs of Staff appointed a Combined Commanders Group to plan *Sledgehammer*.[116] By 7 April the Group had collated all available intelligence relating to a cross-Channel invasion and circulated it in the first detailed paper on that subject.[117] But the available intelligence – about Germany's military strengths and dispositions and her capacity to reinforce them – had already led it to the view that *Sledgehammer* was impracticable, and on 14 April it finally concluded that no Allied action to help Russia was possible in

---

* See below, pp 269–270.

109.   CAB 79/19, COS (42) 81st Meeting, 12 March.
110.   CAB 79/18, COS (42) 50th Meeting, 14 February.
111.   CAB 84/43, JP (42) 243 of 7 March.
112.   Gwyer and Butler, op cit, Vol III, Part II, pp 567–569.
113.   CAB 79/87, COS (42) 78th Meeting SSF, 10 March.
114.   AIR 41/49, *Air Defence of Great Britain*, Vol V, p 103.
115.   CAB 80/34, COS (42) 79, Annex VII: Gwyer and Butler, op cit, Vol III, Part I, pp 357–358.
116.   CAB 84/43, JP (42) 274 (S), 17 March, JP (42) 298 of 19 March; CAB 79/56, COS (42) 12th (o) Meeting, 21 March.
117.   CAB 80/62, COS (42) 92 (o) of 7 April.

Europe in 1942 apart from limited raids.[118] Before long, as a natural corollary to this conclusion, Whitehall would be pressing Washington to agree to the reactivation of operation *Gymnast.**

□

During March 1942, despite the alarm of the Joint Planners, the intelligence authorities in Whitehall had continued to derive satisfaction from the knowledge that the Soviet forces were maintaining heavy pressure at a time when Germany badly needed to rest and refit for her spring offensive.[119] At the beginning of April, however, they were warning that the thaw might bring Germany the relief she needed,[120] and by 23 April they had turned their attention to the problem of forecasting the timing and the objectives of the next German offensive.[121]

Since the last weeks of 1941, when it had been convinced that Germany's major effort in 1942 would be launched against Russia and that her main thrust would be towards the Caucasian and Middle Eastern oil,† the JIC had found no grounds for changing its opinion. It is true that on 17 January 1942 it had conjectured that, in the light of the recent GAF concentration in the Mediterranean, the thrust to the Middle East would be made through Syria and Turkey, rather than through Rostov, so as to associate it with the current Axis effort to control the central and eastern Mediterranean.[122] But by 25 January it had reverted to the view that it would maintain throughout the winter: the attack would be made into the Caucasus via the Ukraine.

The JIC had supported this view with evidence from several intelligence sources, including Sigint. The evidence showed that Russia was still managing to maintain air superiority – so much so that only part of the substantial GAF withdrawals from Russia to the Mediterranean that had been ordered towards the end of 1941 were being carried out, while other GAF units withdrawn for rest and refitting were being sent back to Russia after a minimum time away – and this suggested that Germany would have to limit herself to a single front, and to one where she could concentrate sufficient air power to achieve local superiority. This front was sure

---

* See below, p 100 et seq.   † See above, p 83 et seq.

118. CAB 80/62, COS (42) 99 (0) of 14 April; Gwyer and Butler, op cit, Vol III, Part II, pp 569–572.
119. CAB 80/35, COS (42) 171 (132nd Résumé), para 18, COS (42) 178 (133rd Résumé), para 22.
120. CAB 80/36, COS (42) 213 (136th Résumé), para 18, COS (42) 227 (137th Résumé), para 19.
121. ibid, COS (42) 232 (138th Résumé), paras 20–23.
122. CAB 121/412, JIC (42) 19 of 17 January.

to be against the Soviets because, apart from the fact that the GAF build-up in the Mediterranean was smaller than had been intended, there was still no evidence of large-scale German Army withdrawals from Russia.* And it was likely to be the southern sector of the eastern front because the Germans were sending increasing reinforcements there.[127]

In January the evidence for this last conclusion had been slight; and some of it, notably diplomatic decrypts to the effect that Germany was applying pressure on Hungary and Romania for maximum military support, had been less than conclusive proof that Germany would concentrate against the southern Soviet sector.[128] On 14 March the JIC reported that the evidence had become substantial. The railways in the Ukraine were being developed in a programme to be completed by 15 March; airfields were being constructed south of Kharkov; troop movements to the south were taking place in excess of defence needs. No such preparations were being made in the areas of Army Group Centre and Army Group North and, since there were indications that the Germans were still withdrawing troops from the Balkans, an attack on the Caucasus through Turkey could be ruled out. On these grounds and also because other signs were more and more suggesting that Germany had the strength for only one major offensive in 1942 the JIC was now convinced that she would deliver her coming attack against the southern Russian front, with the double objective of defeating the Soviet Army and seizing the Caucasian oil. It added that there was 'evidence' that the start of the attack had been postponed to 15 May.[129]† The JIC's conclusion formed the basis of

---

* Since December 1941 there had been conflicting reports about Army withdrawals from Russia in connection with a spate of rumours about an imminent German invasion of Spain and a German attack on Turkey.[123] But by 26 January 1942 MI had received from the SIS 'a most valuable report' which clarified the situation in France by showing that some 7 weak divisions had left France for Russia and been replaced by about the same number of severely reduced divisions from the eastern front.[124] And by the end of January it was estimating, to some extent with Sigint evidence, that the number of German divisions in the Balkans had dropped from 14 in December to 6.[125] At the least, therefore, withdrawals from Russia had so far been compensated by movements to Russia.[126]

† Although it is not now possible to track down the source of all the intelligence used in this appreciation, there are some indications that the picture was less clear than the JIC allowed. MI 14 had drawn attention to reports – unattributed, but presumably received from the SIS or its Polish or French counterparts – to the effect that the gauge on the Ukrainian railways was being changed.[130] On the other hand, the information about

123. WO 208/3573 of 15 and 29 December 1941.
124. ibid, 26 January 1942.
125. ibid, 1 February 1942.
126. CAB 80/33, COS (42) 43 (125th Résumé).
127. CAB 121/412, JIC (42) 34 of 25 January.
128. WO 208/3573 of 19 and 26 January, 9 February 1942.
129. CAB 121/412, JIC (42) 75 of 14 March.
130. WO 208/3573 of 23 February and 2 March 1942.

the British draft for an Anglo-US Combined Intelligence Committee paper.

Between the middle of March and the beginning of May, while the final draft of the combined paper was debated, the JIC's conclusion received further support, both negative and positive, from the intelligence sources. It became a constant theme of the intelligence summaries that there was no evidence of German preparations for an advance through Turkey. It was now, also, that chiefly on strategic and logistical grounds, but also on the basis of negative and positive intelligence, the *Sealion* threat was finally dismissed. In April the Joint Planners issued guidelines to the departments to help them to avoid discrepancies in the drafting of planning papers; they included a JIC assessment of February 1942 to the effect that the Germans would not attempt *Sealion* before defeating Russia and that not even the preliminary air attack on Great Britain could begin before three months after Russia's defeat.[134]* Of the positive intelligence, two GAF Enigma decrypts

---

German airfield construction in the south, some of which came from the Enigma, did not find its way into the COS résumés or MI 14's summaries, perhaps from the feeling that the Enigma coverage of the Russian front was incomplete, and MI 14's summaries were less positive than the JIC in drawing conclusions from German troop movements. They noted on 9 March that there was some evidence of German preparations for operations against Leningrad and in the extreme north;[131] they detected no further troop movements out of the Balkans after December 1941;[132] and with regard to troop movements generally, they now stressed that the information was 'most scanty' and that there was 'no reliable evidence' about the extent to which the withdrawal of troops from Russia was being counter-balanced by reliefs from the west.[133]

* After the circulation of the Joint Planners' guidelines in April 1942 the JIC still occasionally reviewed the threat of invasion in response to enquiries. On 19 April it supplied a paper to the inter-Service Committee on the Invasion of Britain (see above, p 80) on the state of Germany's resources in which it did not think the threat a serious one.[135] In June 1942, in reply to a request from the Home Fleet for an assessment of the prospects for invasion or raids up to November 1942, it dismissed the latter as uncharacteristic of the enemy and repeated that the former was ruled out while Russia remained undefeated, and for three months afterwards.[136] By then it had decided, on 2 June 1942, not to abolish the Combined Intelligence Committee which it had established in May 1940 to co-ordinate all intelligence with a bearing on the threat of invasion (see Volume I, pp 168–169), but to reduce its meetings to one a week.[137] In the autumn of 1942 this Combined Intelligence Committee helped the JIC to prepare answers to further enquiries from the inter-Service Home Defence Committee[138] and the Chiefs of Staff – the latter an enquiry as to the likelihood of *Sealion* in the event of the failure of the Allied landings in north-west Africa and a Russian collapse, to which the JIC replied that even on these assumptions Germany would be unable to build up 4,000 aircraft, 'the irreducible minimum' for an invasion, by August 1943, and that in the absence of German air superiority *Sealion* would be far less likely than the enemy's exploitation of Britain's weakened position in the Middle East.[139]

---

131. ibid, 9 March 1942. 132. ibid, 1 Feb 1942.
133. ibid, 16 and 23 February, 9 March 1942.
134. JIC (42) 62 of 23 February; CAB 84/44, JP (42) 371 (S) of 14 April.
135. JIC (42) 145 (o) of 19 April. 136. JIC (42) 232 of 17 June.
137. JIC (42) 23rd Meeting, 2 June.
138. JIC (42) 367 (o) of 20 September.
139. JIC (42) 392 (o) of 6 October; CAB 121/145, COS (42) 139th (o) Meeting, 6 October.

must have reinforced this assessment in March. One disclosed that on Göring's authority anti-aircraft protection in Germany was being weakened in order to give protection to railways on the eastern front; on his copy of it, for the attention of the CAS, the Prime Minister remarked: 'This is important. It shows that the attack on Russia is paramount, and no feint or truce. It shows how needful it is now for us to keep bombing them as the weather improves'.[140] The other decrypt contained a GAF appreciation that 'under Soviet pressure the English with US reinforcements are going to land in north-west Europe'; it was read out at a COS meeting on 28 March.[141]

Despite this sign of Germany's anxiety for north-west Europe, however, the bulk of the positive intelligence left no doubt that she was giving priority to the coming offensive in Russia and that she intended to concentrate it in the south against the Caucasus. One important pointer in this direction was contained in the decrypts of the signals from the Japanese Ambassador in Berlin. Between 8 February and 10 March he had several times reported that the important or the initial objective of the German offensive was to be an attack in the south, and that a Caucasus campaign would be followed by an advance on the Near East. On 21 March a further report from him reproduced a statement from Ribbentrop to the effect that when Germany had 'struck a mortal blow' at Russia during 1942 an invasion of the Near East both from Africa and the Caucasus would follow. President Roosevelt thought this so significant that he drew the Prime Minister's attention to it. SIS information included advice from Bertrand that the main German effort was to be against the Caucasus and that success in the Caucasus would be followed by a descent on the Persian Gulf through Iraq and Iran, and reports from Switzerland to the effect that although she would not confine the offensive to the southern front, Germany attached great importance to seizing the Caucasian oil by the autumn. The Polish SIS supplied more details about the preparation of airfields in southern Russia and reported a large increase of rail traffic to the area.[142] At the end of May an SIS agent operating in the Baltic area reported that Stalingrad was to be the first objective in the drive to the Caucasus. The British Military Attaché in Madrid had by then reported that the Spanish military had reached the same conclusion after talks with the German General Staff.[143] These other sources were borne out by GAF Enigma. By the end of April it had disclosed that Flak Korps I, which had co-operated with the spearhead formations in the

---

140.   Dir/C Archive, 8934 of 12 March 1942, covering CX/MSS/786/T17.
141.   ibid, 9053 of 26 March 1942; CX/MSS/828/T8.
142.   WO 208/3573 of 20 April 1942.
143.   WO 208/3573 of 13 April 1942.

major German offensives of 1940 and 1941, most recently in that of
Army Group Centre during 1941, was to operate with Army Group
South; that the volume of air transport in southern Russia had
doubled since February; and that the GAF's plans for reinforcing
the southern sector by approximately 300 aircraft would raise the
total aircraft there to 950 by early May.[144] This figure may be
compared with AI's April estimate of the total GAF strength on
the eastern front; this had risen to 2,000 from 1,600 at the
beginning of 1942.[145] On 4 May MI noted that Sigint evidence of
the presence of Fliegerkorps VIII in the Crimea, where since the
beginning of the year it had been known that HQ Fliegerkorps V
had returned, reconstituted as Special Staff Crimea,[146] provided
further confirmation that the main weight of the German attack
would fall in the south even if it also indicated that the main attack
would be preceded by an attempt to force the Kerch straits and
reduce Sevastopol.[147]

Despite the strength of this evidence the combined intelligence
paper that was finally issued by the British and the American JICs
on 6 May concluded that Germany's primary objective during 1942
would take the form of an initial attack in the south that would be
accompanied by containing operations in the centre and the
north.[148] To the extent that this assessment modified the views of
the London JIC, the change was perhaps partly due to other items
of intelligence. By 20 April Whitehall had learned that von Kuchler
had succeeded von Leeb in command of Army Group North;[149] this
clearly suggested the possibility that Germany was planning an
attack on Leningrad, although MI 14 was still uncertain on this
score on 1 June.[150] By 4 May the Enigma had disclosed that troop
movements in excess of defence needs were taking place in Norway;
and by mid-May, after examining the evidence and consulting the
British attachés in Stockholm, the JIC had concluded that the
Germans were probably intending an attack on Murmansk.[151] But
what chiefly influenced the JIC was the disagreement of the
American JIC with its argument that the condition of the German
Army and the strain on the German economy were such that

144. ibid, 20 and 27 April 1942; eg CX/MSS/892/T4, 902/T6, 906/T21, 937/T1
      and 938/T15.
145. CAB 80/36, COS (42) 213 (136th Résumé).
146. CX/MSS/633/T14, 657/T11.
147. WO 208/3573 of 4 May 1942; eg CX/MSS/937/T1, 938/T15.
148. CAB 88/58, CIC 8 of 6 May 1942.
149. WO 208/3573 of 20 April 1942.
150. ibid, 1 June 1942.
151. ibid, 4 and 11 May 1942; CAB 121/412, JIC (42) 172 (o) of 8 May, JIC
      (42) 186 (o) of 15 May; CAB 66/25, WP (42) 246 of 6 June (JIC (42) 200 of
      1 June); CAB 79/21, COS (42) 169th Meeting, 4 June; CAB 79/56, COS
      (42) 51st (o) Meeting, 8 June; CX/MSS/843/T6.

Germany would be capable of a main offensive on only one sector of the Russian front.

In February the US JIC had argued that, as Germany had already withdrawn from Russia for rest and refit the bulk of the GAF and numerous divisions, including armoured divisions, she would be able to take the offensive as soon as the weather permitted.[152] On 14 March the British JIC had rebutted this argument: the strength of the GAF in Russia had increased from 1,250 to 1,900 since October 1941 and MI's order of battle intelligence did not suggest that any armoured divisions had been withdrawn.[153] During April Washington had again insisted that not more than 40–70 German divisions had been involved in the winter fighting; the remainder had been rested and 25 armoured divisions, 35 motorised divisions and some 200 from an overall total of 240 infantry divisions would be available for the spring offensive. It had insisted, further, that the London JIC was exaggerating Germany's need for the Caucasian oil and was being over-optimistic about the extent to which Germany's preparations were weakening her war production. Whitehall had maintained that there were already 179 German divisions in Russia and that the maximum ground force she could assemble was 196 divisions, of which 10 armoured and 20 infantry divisions, the maximum that she could have managed to rest and refit during the winter, would make up the spearhead. It had also remained adamant about the importance for Germany of the oil.[154] On 6 and 25 April it had updated its March appreciation without modifying it in any important respect.[155] Moreover, it adhered to these positions in the combined paper of 6 May, which stated the different assessments of the two JICs and noted, also, that, whereas the Americans assessed the total GAF first-line strength available for the eastern front as 3,000 aircraft, the British assessed it at between 2,000 and 2,400. But in this joint paper the London JIC modified its assessment of the strain on the German economy to the extent of agreeing that after the coming Russian campaign the Germans could hope to restore production before they had to meet an Allied offensive, even as it modified its assessment of the German objective to the extent of allowing for operations on sectors of the front other than the Caucasus.

In the event the British estimates of the scale of the total German effort were the more accurate. When the German Army went over

---

152. JIC (42) 64 (o) of 23 February.
153. CAB 121/412, JIC (42) 75 of 14 March.
154. JIC (42) 132 and 137 of 12 and 14 April.
155. JIC (42) 152 of 25 April; CAB 66/23, WP (42) 158 of 11 April (JIC (42) 121 of 6 April); CAB 79/20, COS (42) 110th Meeting, with the Prime Minister, 8 April.

to the offensive there were 172 German divisions on the eastern front, including Finland, out of an overall total of 221; and Army Group South had 68 of them, including 9 armoured and 7 motorised, plus 28 satellite divisions.[156]* The GAF strength was some 2,640 on the front as a whole, with 1,500 on the southern sector.[158] But the Americans proved to be nearer the mark in suspecting that the German offensive might not be confined to the south. The revised German plan of October 1941 had set the seizure of the Caucasian oil as the first objective of the spring offensive, this to be followed by an advance through the passes from Iraq to Iran and, in the autumn of 1942, the conquest of Iran. On 5 April 1942, when the Soviet winter offensive had frustrated this timetable, Hitler had issued a new directive. This had stated that the general objectives of the coming campaign were the destruction of 'the entire defence potential remaining to the Soviets' and the cutting of their most important sources of supply; and it had left the objective in the south unchanged: 'to destroy the enemy before the Don in order to gain the oil region of the Caucasus area and to cross the Caucasian mountains'. But it had insisted against the advice of OKH that, as well as attacking in the south and holding in the central sector, the Army was to capture Leningrad and join up with the Finnish Army as soon as sufficient forces could be made available.[159]†

---

* By July the total for motorised divisions had dropped to 5.[157]

† Whereas the American and British intelligence authorities at least agreed that the initial attack and the main effort in the German offensive would be made in the south, it has been claimed that the collective opinion of the Soviet military authorities in March and April was that the offensive would come in the centre, against Moscow; that this was so despite the fact that Soviet intelligence, including the 'Lucy' ring, took the same view as Anglo-American intelligence; and that not even the Russian capture of the German outline plan on 19 June persuaded Stalin to change his mind.[160] These claims may be contrasted with the evidence in the British archives. In March the Chiefs of Staff understood that the Soviet High Command expected the spring offensive to come in the south:[161] and in March and April Enigma and Abwehr decrypts indicated that the German intelligence authorities judged that Russia expected the German objectives in the spring offensive to be against the Caucasus and the Caspian and was herself sending reinforcements to those areas.[162] Between mid-May and mid-June Whitehall sent two series of appreciations to Russia. The first, from MI, culminated on 23 May in the warning that Germany intended to concentrate between 13 and 16 Panzer divisions in a southern army group before launching her main offensive, which would not be possible before June.[163] The second, from AI, concluded with a general assessment of Germany's intentions: based on Kursk, she would operate in the direction of Voronezh and towards the Don as soon as the operation against Sevastopol was

156. Seaton, op cit, p 270 and fn 12.
157. ibid, p 271 and fn 14.
158. AIR 41/49, p 178.
159. Seaton, op cit, pp 256, 258–259, 266; Gwyer and Butler, op cit, Vol III, Part II, pp 442–445, 447, 594.
160. Seaton, op cit, p 262; Erickson, op cit, pp 337, 338, 340, 342, 354–355.
161. CAB 79/19, COS (42) 76th meeting, 9 March.
162. CX/MSS/827/T16, 879/T12.
163. Telegram to BMM 150/MI 14 of 23 May 1942.

Whitehall was uncertain whether Russia could survive the German offensive. In a paper of 1 June the JIC emphasised that it still knew 'considerably less' about Russia's dispositions, resources and war potential than it did about Germany's. In this, its first attempt to foresee the course of the campaign and to calculate the implications for the course of the war as a whole, it guessed, however, on the basis of Russia's performance hitherto, that the outcome would be touch-and-go. Favourably placed for attack and possessed of the better fighting machine, Germany would have the initial advantage. But the Russians ought to be able to bring the advance to a halt, perhaps on the line Tula–Voronezh–Donets–Rostov. With such large forces engaged over so large an area of manoeuvre, the decisive phase would not come before August. But between August and October events might move rapidly to a climax, with both sides suffering very heavily, and for each side the margin between success and failure might become very narrow. For each side, too, failure might be catastrophic. If Germany realised that she had to face yet another winter in Russia her 'collapse . . . as in 1918 may ensue with startling rapidity'. If Russia collapsed Germany would make good use of the winter, in circumstances that could not yet be foreseen, to build up either against Allied invasion or for offensive operations against the Middle East. With regard to Russia, however, the JIC allowed that the loss of Leningrad and of the Moscow industrial area would not affect her ability to maintain her land and air forces for a considerable time and that the loss of the Caucasian oil, some 75 per cent of her total production, would probably not limit her capacity to carry on the war for about a year.[167]

Although they thought them 'slightly over-optimistic' about the immediate prospects for the Russians, who might not be able to hold the line suggested by the JIC, the Chiefs of Staff accepted these general conclusions, with which those of the US JIC were in

---

completed.[164] In the second week of June the retiring Head of the British Military Mission reported that at the time of his recent departure from Moscow it had still been the Soviet view that the German offensive would be on the southern sector; indeed he felt that the Russian dispositions to meet the southern attack might well induce Germany to decide to switch the attack to the centre.[165] By 8 June, on the other hand, MI 14 had received two reports to the effect that the Russians thought the main offensive was likely to come in the central sector. Nothing is known about the origin or reliability of these two last reports. But whatever the truth may be about the Soviet assessment, MI's treatment of the reports suggests that Whitehall was far from sure that it knew the Soviet mind: since there was no evidence that the Germans were making any preparations north of Kursk, it could not accept the reports unless by 'the central sector' the Russians meant the Kursk region.[166]

164. AI 1 (c) 75 and 78 of 2 and 11 June 1942.
165. CAB 79/21, COS (42) 178th meeting, 13 June.
166. WO 208/3573 of 8 June 1942.
167. CAB 66/25, WP (42) 246 of 6 June (JIC (42) 200 of 1 June).

broad agreement,[168] in the first week of June.[169] At that time, as during the past month, the German offensive had been expected to begin about 8 June,[170] and MI had correctly appreciated that the German clearance of the Crimea, which began on 8 May, and the German attack on the Russian salient at Izyum, which began on 17 May, were but necessary preliminaries to the main campaign.[171] By the end of May, however, despite lacking details about the course of the fighting, Whitehall knew from the Enigma and from the Soviet General Staff that in these preliminary operations the German Army had been forced to use spearhead formations which it had wanted to reserve for the main attack and that the GAF's dispositions for the main attack had been dislocated.[172] By 22 June it knew that the German timetable had also been upset by the unexpectedly strong Russian resistance at Sevastopol, which was delaying the transfer of Fliegerkorps VIII to the Kursk area.[173] On 29 June, however, when the Enigma showed that 75 per cent of the Fliegerkorps was concentrated at Kursk and there were signs that Hitler had been at Poltava for the past few days,[174] the Chiefs of Staff notified the Cabinet that Germany had opened her long-expected offensive in the south.[175] It had begun on 28 June.

On 14 July Whitehall sent a formal warning to Russia that the German intention was to hold the Soviet forces on the Voronezh front and make the main summer offensive south-eastwards between the Don and the Donets; two Panzer armies would swing south-eastwards east of the Donets while Seventeenth Army would attack eastwards from the Stalino area.[176]

□

Until the middle of August the progress of the German advance was almost as rapid as the fastest of the 1941 offensives. By the end of July it was thrusting in three directions – eastwards against the middle Don towards Stalingrad; south-eastwards over the Don

---

168. JIC (42) 239 (o) of 26 June; JIC (42) 254 (o) of 11 July.
169. CAB 79/21, COS (42) 169th meeting, 4 June; CAB 79/56, COS (42) 51st (o) meeting, 8 June.
170. CAB 66/24, WP (42) 219 of 10 June; WO 208/3573 of 13, 20 and 27 April, 4 and 18 May.
171. WO 208/3573 of 11 May 1942; CAB 80/56, COS (42) 261 (141st Résumé), COS (42) 472 (142nd Résumé).
172. CX/MSS/1001/T18; WO 208/3573 of 25 May and 15 June 1942; CAB 80/36, COS (42) 283 (143rd Résumé).
173. WO 208/3573 of 22 June 1942; CAB 80/37, COS (42) 320 (147th Résumé).
174. CX/MSS/1113/T6, 1118/T13, 1127/T20; WO 208/3573 of 29 June 1942.
175. CAB 65/26, WM (42) 83 of 29 June.
176. Dir/C Archive, 56 of 14 July 1942; CX/MSS/1179/T46.

against the railway from Stalingrad to Tikhoretsk; south-westwards over the Don near Rostov towards the line Armavir–Maikop–Tuapse – and no doubt remained about its objectives. By 21 July, as the British Military Mission reported, the Soviet General Staff thought that the objective was 'undoubtedly' the Caucasus, perhaps accompanied by a simultaneous drive on Stalingrad to secure the German left flank.[177] By 3 August Whitehall learned from Sigint that Germany's intention was to take Stalingrad and advance into Caucasia.[178] On 6 August the southern thrust broke the Russian front at Armavir, reached the Caucasian foothills and seized Maikop. By the end of August the German troops in the south were within 60 miles of Grozny and despite stiffer Russian resistance the other thrusts had all but encircled Stalingrad.

Even before events had confirmed that the main German effort was being made in the south, with the Caucasus as one of its objectives, the momentum of the German advance had precipitated a conclusion to the postponed Anglo-American debate about the form and time of the second front – about the rival claims for *Roundup* in 1943 or *Gymnast* before the end of 1942.

The US authorities had virtually agreed to the abandonment of *Sledgehammer* on 14 April, at the conclusion of a visit to London by Marshall and Hopkins, but they had then secured for the first time British agreement that *Roundup* should go forward, being preceded by raids and possibly the seizure of a bridgehead in Europe if opportunity offered. In May, however, the Combined Commanders Group had warned Whitehall that *Roundup* would be impossible in 1943 if Russia were to be defeated by Germany's coming offensive, and the Prime Minister, influenced also by Russian pressure for an earlier second front, had suggested to the President that *Gymnast* should be revived. On 20–21 June, in discussions with the Prime Minister and the Chiefs of Staff in Washington, the US authorities had held the British to the agreement to carry out *Roundup*, but the President had been persuaded by the British argument that an earlier alternative operation, which could only be *Gymnast*, must be prepared against the eventuality of an emergency on the Russian front.[179]

On 7 July after the opening of the German offensive, the Cabinet decided that the Prime Minister should press the President to adopt *Gymnast*; it felt that some action in 1942 had become imperative but that *Sledgehammer* was not feasible. The Prime

---

177. CAB 121/464, BMM telegram MIL 6319 of 15 July 1942.
178. CX/MSS/1230/T9, 1237/T2, 1241/T23, 1263/T11; WO 208/3573 of 3 August 1942.
179. Gwyer and Butler, op cit, Vol III, Part II, pp 567–581, 618, 620, 622–629.

Minister's approach to Washington caused some consternation there and precipitated a second visit to London by Marshall and Hopkins. On 17 July, the day before the Americans arrived, the Joint Planners summed up their views on Allied strategy 'in view of the possibility of Russian defeat': if Russia were to be defeated before the spring, *Roundup* would be totally impracticable; even if Russia survived the German onslaught Germany might still be able to reinforce western Europe in 1943 on such a scale as to make it uncertain whether *Roundup* could go forward in 1943. They accordingly recommended that the Allies should proceed with *Gymnast* and establish a hold on French north Africa before Germany could recover from the present campaign in Russia.[180] They had reached this conclusion after discussions with the JIC. But the JIC had remained confident that Russia would not collapse. On 15 July, and again on the following day, it had refused to alter the assessment of Russia's chances that it had made on 1 June.[181]*

On 22 July, while the American visitors were still in London, the Cabinet decided to accept the Joint Planners' recommendation, and the President and the Combined Chiefs of Staff fell in with the decision on 23–24 July. The US military authorities did so on the understanding that *Gymnast* (now re-named *Torch*) should involve no avoidable reduction in the preparations for *Roundup*. But because they realised that it would probably rule out *Roundup*, they also stipulated that the final decision to undertake *Torch* as soon as possible before December 1942 should be deferred until it could be judged whether Russia's position would be so weak by 15 September that it made *Roundup* impracticable for 1943. Despite this reservation, however, the President and the Prime Minister both understood that the decision now reached was that *Torch* would be launched as soon as possible.[182] And in the event the preparations for *Torch* went ahead on this assumption against a background of considerable uncertainty about prospects on the eastern front.†

The JIC continued to discount on 30 July the 'worst case' hypothesis of a total Russian collapse, but it admitted that light German forces could reach Iran by November.[183] On 2 August, in an appreciation that was forwarded to Cairo, it enlarged on Russia's capacity to resist: the loss of Stalingrad and of the northern Caucasus would greatly strain her economic resources, but there was no reason why her military collapse should follow before the winter; in particular, her Air Force had numerical superiority and

---

* See above, p 98.   † See below, Chapter 24.

180. CAB 84/47, JP (42) 679 of 17 July.
181. JIC (42) 264 of 15 July; CAB 121/412, JIC (42) 265 of 16 July.
182. Gwyer and Butler, op cit, Vol III, Part II, pp 631–636.
183. CAB 121/638, SIC file F/Mideast/6, JIC (42) 285 of 30 July.

remained an effective force.[184] In this appreciation, however, the JIC conceded that it was handicapped by the lack of an 'authentic Russian picture' and that there was no intelligence as to what Germany intended after reaching Stalingrad and the Caucasus,* and on 3 August it advised that, to ensure that *Torch* took place while Germany was still heavily engaged in Russia, the earliest possible date should be set for it.[185] After the fall of Maikop in the first week of August there was some evidence that the German advance was slowing down, but evidence, also, of 'some disorganisation' among the Russian forces.[186] On 19 August, in a review of future German strategy drawn up in connection with the *Torch* planning, the JIC repeated the conclusion that Russia would not collapse in 1942 and was insistent that Germany would be unable to make any substantial withdrawals from the Russian front until well into October without jeopardising her objective in Russia, which must at least be to leave the Russian forces north of the Don incapable of offensive action in 1943. But it again admitted that it lacked all knowledge of Russian plans or of the state of her forces and that intelligence about German intentions was scanty and conflicting.[187]

On the same day – 19 August 1942 – Canadian and British forces carried out the raid on Dieppe.† Since 14 April, when the discussion of *Sledgehammer* by the Combined Commanders Group had pointed to the impracticability of any cross-Channel action in 1942 other than raids‡ and the British authorities had agreed with General Marshall that *Roundup* should be preceded during 1942 by raids and possibly the seizure of a bridgehead if opportunity offered,§ active preparation by GHQ Home Forces and Combined Operations HQ for a raid had proceeded alongside continuing investigation into the practicability of *Roundup*. By 11 June, when the Cabinet concluded that *Sledgehammer* was out of the question and that a raid on the French coast, or possibly the Prime Minister's project for operations in north Norway, was all that could be attempted in time to have any influence in reducing the impact of Germany's impending eastern offensive, the needs of the planners had inaugurated that process by which the work of the

---

* During July the SIS's contacts in Switzerland were maintaining that Berlin accepted that Germany could not advance beyond Maikop in 1942 and was making preparations for a second winter campaign in Russia; but there is no reference to these reports in the JIC assessments, and no support for them from other sources.

  † See Appendix 13.   ‡ See above, pp 90–91.
  § See above, p 100.

184.   CAB 121/464, JIC (42) 298 (o) of 2 August, COS (ME) 282 of 3 August.
185.   CAB 121/490, SIC file E/North Africa/3A, JIC (42) 299 (o) of 3 August.
186.   CAB 80/37, COS (42) 373 (154th Résumé), para 27.
187.   CAB 121/497, SIC file E/North Africa/3G, JIC (42) 316 (o) of 19 August.

JIC, in addition to assessing Germany's long-term intentions, was devoted to organising, to an ever-increasing extent down to the end of the war, the intelligence required for the planning of Allied operations. But these needs had also emphasised that detailed intelligence was in short supply for north-west Europe, particularly in relation to the enemy's Army strengths and ground defences. It was at this time, and in response to complaints from the Planners,[188] that the Chiefs of Staff ordered the intelligence bodies to 'focus a spotlight' on Europe.*

□

By August 1942 Whitehall's anxiety about the German danger to the Middle East, which had declined with the opening of the Soviet counter-offensive in December 1941, was again acute. During July the JIC had argued that Germany could not move into Iraq and Iran before defeating the Russians and had ruled out a major threat in that direction before the spring of 1943.[189] On 19 August it calculated that, as well as being incapable of any offensive in the west or the Mediterranean in response to *Torch* before October 1942, including even the occupation of Vichy France, Germany would not move into Turkey and could not act against Iran before the spring of 1943.[190] But in relation to the Middle East threat the VCIGS in London thought that this calculation was too optimistic,[191] and the CIGS, then in Moscow with the Prime Minister, shared the VCIGS's doubts. The Prime Minister, on the other hand, was inclined to accept Stalin's assurance that the Caucasus front would hold till the winter. On their return from Moscow he drew the attention of the CIGS to the decrypt of a Japanese diplomatic signal which said that Germany was greatly exaggerating the casualties she had inflicted on Russia during the recent fighting and that even if the Caucasus fell the Russians would be able to continue: the Japanese authorities believed the Russians had sufficient strength to stop a German advance to Baku before the winter. But the CIGS remained convinced that planning must continue on the assumption that light German forces would attack northern Iran before the end of the year.[192] It was at his

---

* See above, p 14.

188. CAB 106/107, Combined Commanders File for 2nd Meeting, 22 May 1942; GHQ Home Forces note of 21 May.
189. CAB 121/412, JIC (42) 265 of 16 July; CAB 121/638, JIC (42) 285 of 30 July.
190. CAB 121/497, JIC (42) 316 (o) of 19 August.
191. CAB 79/57, COS (42) 98th (o) Meeting, 24 August.
192. Gwyer and Butler, op cit, Vol III, Part II, pp 661–662; CAB 66/28, WP (42) 373 of 23 August, Annexes III and VI; CAB 80/64, COS (42) 245 (o) of 25 August, Annex X.

instigation that on 2 September the JIC produced another appreciation of the threat to the Middle East.[193] It allowed that, if Russia's resistance flagged, a German advance could reach north Iran by the end of December, when winter conditions would close down operations until the spring. But it clung to the view that Russia would succeed in delaying the German advance; it had been heartened by the information brought back from Moscow,[194] which indicated that Russia had more forces available for the Caucasus than it had thought and that she intended to make a fighting withdrawal into southern Caucasus and into Iran, if necessary. With this assessment the Prime Minister generally agreed,[195] but the CIGS still thought it was 'perhaps on the optimistic side'.[196]

At the time of these exchanges in Whitehall General von List, in command of Army Group A,* was already resisting pressure from Hitler for an advance in strength down the Black Sea coast to Batum, a move which would have split the Army Group in two on both sides of the mountains and for which List felt that the supply arrangements were inadequate. List was dismissed in the first week of September. OKW having supported him, his dismissal was followed by a breach between Jodl and Hitler, who himself took over command of Army Group A till November. Halder, Chief of OKH, was also dismissed at the end of September, from which time, as it was to be learned after the war, close observers in Germany dated Hitler's withdrawal into grim solitude and attributed it to his realisation that his last throw had failed.[198] Except for rumours in October that Halder had been dismissed and that von Bock was opposed to a winter campaign against the Caucasus, Whitehall had no inkling of the extent of the crisis in the German High Command until November, when the SIS began to report on it. On 7 September, however, Sigint had established that the main German effort was to be devoted to the attack on Stalingrad by Army Group B,[199] and during the next two weeks it became clearer with every day that passed that the outcome of the struggle

---

* After the opening of the German offensive, Army Group South had been split into Army Group A (List) and Army Group B (Bock), the former to be responsible for the eventual Caucasus campaign. MI 14 learned of the reorganisation from the Enigma, and correctly appreciated the purpose of it, on 20 July.[197]

193. CAB 121/638, JIC (42) 332 of 2 September.
194. CAB 121/460, SIC file D/Russia/1, Vol 2, War Cabinet print of unofficial meeting of the Prime Minister and Stalin, 15 August 1942.
195. CAB 120/744, PM Registered file 413/1, 12 September 1942.
196. CAB 79/23, COS (42) 255th Meeting, 4 September.
197. WO 208/3573 of 20 July 1942.
198. Howard, *Grand Strategy*, Vol IV, (1972), p 32; Seaton, op cit, pp 285–286, 301–304.
199. eg CX/MSS/1354/T20, 1368/T4 and 19, 1372; WO 208/3573 of 7 September 1942.

on the whole of the Soviet southern front hinged on the result of the Stalingrad battle.

By the beginning of September the Germans had reduced the defensive perimeter at Stalingrad to a perilously small area, but the defenders were being reinforced. On 7 September Army Group B resumed its attack in a supreme effort to complete the capture of the city before the Russians completed its reinforcement. On the same day MI 14 noted that the final stage of the battle was beginning,[200] and on 14 September, after a week of intense fighting, it judged that Stalingrad was about to fall and speculated on what Germany would do in the few remaining weeks before the winter with the troops that would now become available for other operations.[201] But the Russian resistance continued, and in the second half of September, Whitehall having learned from Japanese diplomatic decrypts that Japan had definitely rejected a German appeal that she should turn on Russia, its appreciations brightened up. By 17 September the Chiefs of Staff résumé had calculated that after rest and refit the German troops would be left with only some six to eight weeks in which further operations would be possible, and it had noted that the possibility of an offensive on the central sector receded with every day that the Russian resistance was prolonged.[202] A week later it was using far more confident language: Germany now faced the prospect of a second winter in Russia on a greatly extended line against a Russian Army that would still be capable of engaging large enemy forces.[203] On 18 September, in a contribution to the re-examination of Allied strategy that was being made in preparation for the Casablanca conference, the JIC repeated its view that Germany's military action was unlikely to put Russia out of the war in 1942;[204] on 14 September it had already reiterated its assumption that Russia would still be holding Moscow and the southern Caucasus in January 1943 even if she had lost Stalingrad and Leningrad.[205] On 28 September, when Sigint had confirmed earlier indications that Germany was moving Eleventh Army to the Leningrad front from the Crimea[206]* and there was a 'considerable mass' of other

* This move, ordered by Hitler at the end of July because he was so impressed by Eleventh Army's performance in the capture of Sevastopol, denuded his armies in the south during the later stages of the battle of Stalingrad.[207]

200. WO 208/3573 of 7 September 1942.
201. ibid, 14 September 1942; eg CX/MSS/1379/T3, 1396/T18, 1399/T5, 1403/T12.
202. CAB 80/38, COS (42) 404 (159th Résumé).
203. ibid, COS (42) 410 (160th Résumé).
204. JIC (42) 358 of 18 September.
205. CAB 121/412, JIC (42) 355 (0) of 14 September.
206. WO 208/3573 of 21 September 1942.
207. Seaton, op cit, pp 263–264; Erickson, op cit, p 362.

intelligence suggesting that she was preparing an attack on Leningrad, MI 14 thought that this attack might be ruled out for 1942 unless Stalingrad fell before the end of September,[208] and by 1 October it was prepared to say that 'it is doubtful whether it can take place this year'.[209]

In the Caucasus, too, the Russians continued their stubborn resistance. Whitehall's information about the situation in the Caucasus came partly from the GAF Enigma and the occasional reports from the Moscow Mission, the two sources which also kept it in touch with the Stalingrad fighting, but it also received reports from the British Naval Liaison Officer, Black Sea[210] and, beginning in September 1942, from the decrypts of signals in the Porpoise Enigma key.* Although it was far from perfect, the coverage provided by these sources was enough to show that the German advance was being slowed down. On 17 September the Chiefs of Staff résumé declared that 'unless . . . the Germans can accelerate their progress over the mountains or succeed in by-passing them, they may well find themselves baulked this year of southern Caucasia'.[211] On 2 October the JIC felt that the most recent intelligence fully confirmed its earlier opinion that there was no real danger to Iraq and Iran before the spring of 1943. The Russians had checked the German advances towards Grozny and Sukhumi; the Germans were making only slow progress towards the Georgian pass and Tuapse; and since it was reported that the Russians now had 50 divisions in the Caucasus, the JIC felt confident that German forces would not penetrate beyond the Caucasian range during the coming winter.[212]

The Chiefs of Staff, accepting this assessment, deferred defence preparations by Persia and Iraq Command (PAIC), which would have cut across the supply programme to Russia by the southern route, early in October.[213]† Nor was the JIC's optimism misplaced. For some weeks the intelligence sources produced conflicting evidence as the situation in the Caucasus moved to its climax. On 5 October the GAF Enigma reported that bombs were being diverted there from Stalingrad; but a German police decrypt suggested that Germany had decided not to press on.[214] On 19

---

* See above, p 28 and Appendix 4.
† See further below, p 430.

208. WO 208/3573 of 28 September 1942.
209. CAB 80/38, COS (42) 419 (161st Résumé).
210. ADM 223/107, Black Sea Diary, pp 7, 8.
211. CAB 80/38, COS (42) 404 (158th Résumé).
212. CAB 121/638, JIC (42) 383 of 2 October.
213. CAB 79/24, COS (42) 279th Meeting, 5 October; Howard, op cit, Vol IV, p 57.
214. WO 208/3573 of 5 October 1942.

October, against a 'probably reliable' report, probably from the SIS, that further German operations had been cancelled, MI 14 was weighing Sigint indications that this decision applied only to the southern Caucasus.[215] By 2 November delayed GAF Enigma decrypts had disclosed preparations to transfer aircraft to Terek as soon as Stalingrad had fallen and, although these plans might have been overtaken by events, another 'well informed' source had reported that operations in the Caucasus were to continue.[216] This other source was probably the BNLO Black Sea; at the beginning of November he twice warned Whitehall that the Soviet authorities expected a strong German effort to reach Grozny, where the position was 'anything but rosy for the Russians'.[217] In the Porpoise decrypts, on the other hand, which earlier in October had shown that Sevastopol was being opened as a supply base for the Army and that preparations were being made for operations in the Sea of Azov and the Caspian, there were from the end of October signs that these preparations were being cancelled, complaints of the complete lack of GAF support for naval operations, and reports about the increasingly grim plight of the German troops.[218] As it happened, in the third week of October the advance of the German Seventeenth Army on Tuapse was fought to a standstill and on 2 November First Panzer Army, in its approach to Sukhumi and Grozny, was stopped at the most easterly point ever reached by German troops. On 5 November the Chiefs of Staff résumé at last committed itself to the view that any further German advance was unlikely,[219] and on 9 November MI 14 was confirmed in this view by an Enigma decrypt which disclosed that Hitler had issued instructions for the bombing of Baku.[220]

By 16 November the possibility of a further German advance in the south was ruled out by the weather – the passes were now snowbound – and by the situation at Stalingrad. Already on 22 October, commenting on the tremendous surge of fighting at Stalingrad that had lasted since the last few days of September, the COS résumé had concluded that, whatever the outcome, the Germans had been held long enough to rule out any major enemy offensive further north in 1942.[221] In fact, Germany's final desperate offensive effort was by then petering out, and by 9 November it was so clear that it had failed that Whitehall took GAF Enigma

215. ibid, 19 October 1942.
216. ibid, 2 November 1942.
217. ADM 223/107, Black Sea Diary, pp 8–9.
218. eg DEFE 3/581, ZTPGM 1591, 1837, 1870, 1887, 1909; DEFE 3/582, ZTPGM 2308, 2513, 2581, 2590; DEFE 3/583, ZTPGM 3421; DEFE 3/584, ZTPGM 4196.
219. CAB 80/38, COS (42) 447 (166th Résumé).
220. WO 208/3573 of 9 November 1942; CX/MSS/1635/T26.
221. CAB 80/38, COS (42) 435 (164th Résumé).

revelations of the move of German Army and GAF reinforcements to the central sector to be evidence of preparations to meet a Russian attack.[222] On 12 November, by which time the Enigma had produced a wealth of detail about the strain that the Stalingrad fighting had put on the German supply situation,[223] the COS résumé announced that, except for local German operations in the area of Tuapse and Ordzhonikidze, stalemate reigned on the entire eastern front.[224]

□

The Soviet counter-offensive at Stalingrad, a huge double envelopment to cut off the German salient, was launched on 19 November 1942. By 21 November it broke through on the front of Third Romanian Army. On 27 November it had surrounded the German Sixth Army and the German force in the Caucasus was threatened by its extension to Rostov. By 17 December the Russians had frustrated the attempt of von Manstein, commander of the newly formed Army Group Don, to relieve Sixth Army. A week later they had put the Italian Eighth Army to flight in their advance towards Rostov, and were threatening to cut off Army Group Don and Army Group A. On 28 December Hitler was forced to agree that both Army Groups should withdraw to a general line some 150 miles west of Stalingrad. It was too late to save Sixth Army. On 14 October he had ordered that there were to be no withdrawals from the positions then reached; and in the few days before Christmas he had refused to rescind this order when Manstein was discussing with Sixth Army the possibility, then rapidly fading, of a break-out.

Stalin informed the Prime Minister of the start of the counter-offensive on 20 November.[225] Thereafter, Whitehall was able to follow its early progress through official communiqués, information from the British Military Mission in Moscow, which temporarily found the Soviet authorities more forthcoming than usual, and – a valuable supplement to, and check upon, these other sources – plentiful Enigma decrypts, which were being circulated with a delay of two to three days. The GAF Enigma decrypts of 22 November included Hitler's instructions for restoring the situation, which confirmed the seriousness of the German position, and a warning from the Chief Quartermaster of Luftflotte 4 to the effect that Sixth Army could not be supplied by air; he had only 80 transport aircraft.[226] On 25 November they included a report to the

---

222. WO 208/3573 of 9 November 1942.
223. ibid, 16 November 1942; eg CX/MSS/1669/T27, 1637/T25.
224. CAB 80/38, COS (42) 453 (167th Résumé).
225. Howard, op cit, Vol IV, p 48.
226. CX/MSS/1728/T13.

effect that 'the armoured forces at Stalingrad are surrounded and cannot be supplied with fuel on any large scale'; this was one of the many decrypts from Stalingrad shown to the Prime Minister.[227] By 26 November they had revealed that 60 additional transport aircraft had been sent to Luftflotte 4.[228] A Porpoise decrypt of 27 November from the naval liaison officer with Army Group A confirmed that Sixth Army had been surrounded and announced Manstein's appointment to command 'Stab Don'.[229] By 30 November the GAF decrypts had disclosed that the GAF had only weak forces on the Don front[230] and they provided other indications that, except in relatively narrow sectors, it could afford no more than the absolute minimum of support for the ground forces.[231]

From the end of November the GAF Enigma provided full coverage of the enormous effort made by the GAF to maintain air supply of the beleaguered Sixth Army. It revealed that FW 200s from Bordeaux and Trondheim were being brought in to assist;[232] that transport aircraft reinforcements and bomber pilots to fly them were being withdrawn from the training schools; and, still more significant, that other transport aircraft were being taken back from the Mediterranean. As late as 10 December AI had calculated that some 200 transport aircraft had been transferred from the Russian front to meet the German Army's requirement in Tunisia; but by 26 December it knew that 150 Ju 52s had been returned to Russia in the past six days.[233] It was clear, moreover, that but for the fact that the GAF had recently incurred heavy losses in transport aircraft en route to Tunisia and on African airfields* and was compelled to retain a large fleet of them there, it would have recalled still more to Russia: some of the December decrypts showed that, great as it was, the diversion of aircraft to the Stalingrad battle was proving inadequate. Detailed intelligence about the movement of transport aircraft, first from Russia and then back to Luftflotte 4's area, and of the airfields they were using for the supply of Stalingrad, formed an important part of the information which Whitehall forwarded to Moscow after the beginning of the Soviet offensive; this information also included the

---

* See below, p 494 et seq.

227. Dir/C Archive, 1525 of 25 November 1942.
228. CX/MSS/1730/T8.
229. CX/MSS/1741/T3, 1743/T14, 1747/T10; WO 208/3573 of 7 December 1942.
230. eg CX/MSS/1749/T4.
231. CAB 80/38, COS (42) 474 (170th Résumé), para 54.
232. CX/MSS/1897/T2; AIR 41/10, *The Rise and Fall of the German Air Force*, pp 217–218, 225.
233. Air Sunset No 37 of 26 December 1942; CAB 80/38, COS (42) 477 (171st Résumé), para 56.

gist of the more valuable decrypts about the situation in Stalingrad, estimates of German aircraft production and 'reports sent by the JIC'.[234]

On 22 December the British Mission was informed by the Soviet General Staff that the offensive continued to make good progress: the Germans had withdrawn in disorder once their defences in the central Don area had been pierced and, in the absence of a strategic reserve on the eastern front as a whole, they were reinforcing the southern sector by withdrawing front line units from other sectors and throwing them in piecemeal; the General Staff expected that the Russian rate of advance would be governed by the physical endurance of its troops, rather than by the enemy's resistance.[235] The decrypts available in Whitehall during December contained little information about the ground fighting, but they gave some support to the Soviet appreciation by establishing that the Germans were still retreating before strong Russian forces; and they showed that these forces had crossed the Don north of Kotelnikovo and reached the Don bend south-east of Tsymlyanskaya by the end of December.[236]

During January 1943 the Russians completed the annihilation of the Sixth Army, which formally surrendered on 2 February. They recaptured Velikie Luki in an offensive on the central front. They raised the siege of Leningrad in the north. In relation to these operations Sigint added little to the general knowledge that Whitehall was deriving from the communiqués. It was otherwise in the south, where Russia's advance on Rostov and her counter-offensive on the upper Don were sweeping away what remained of Army Group B and threatening the communications of Army Group Don and Army Group A. Between the end of December 1942, when Hitler reluctantly accepted a partial and gradual withdrawal of Army Group A to the Kuban – though still insisting that it should hold Maikop and form bridgeheads over the Kerch straits and the lower Don as bases from which a later campaign might be launched towards the Caspian – and the end of January 1943, when he was forced to order a final withdrawal from the Caucasus across the Taman bridgehead into the Crimea, the Porpoise Enigma decrypts provided an invaluable commentary on the German retreat.

On 30 December 1942 they disclosed the decision to shorten Army Group A's line.[237] By the end of January 1943 they showed that, as a result of the shortage of fuel and of air support, the

234. Dir/C Archive, 1489 of 23 November 1942.
235. WO 208/3573 of 28 December 1942; CAB 121/464, MIL 7912 of 23 December 1942.
236. CX/MSS/1858/T34, 1885/T30, 1897/T2.
237. DEFE 3/586, ZTPGM 6493.

Germans had decided to fall back on two bridgeheads, one in the Taman-Novorossiisk area and the other around Rostov, and had ordered the transport by air to the Crimea of all army personnel not needed for the defence of the Taman.[238]

On 23 January, in the light of this evidence and of the information it was receiving from the Military Mission in Moscow, the JIC calculated that the Germans might be able to evacuate the troops from the northern Caucasus, but not their equipment, and that few of the troops would escape if the Russians were able to press home their advance from Rostov and Mariupol.[239] Such an advance, together with an attempt to free the Kharkov area by two simultaneous thrusts towards Kursk and Kharkov, was in fact the next Soviet objective.

□

An unexpectedly favourable turn had thus come about in the position on the Russian front, off-setting the disappointment arising from the unexpected difficulties encountered in the Tunisian campaign,* when the western Allies reviewed their future strategy at the Casablanca conference ('Symbol') in the second half of January 1943. At the conference they reaffirmed that victory over Germany should continue to be given priority over the needs of the war in the Far East. To the even greater satisfaction of the British authorities, the Americans also agreed that as a means of maintaining the pressure on Germany and of relieving the Russians, further operations in the Mediterranean, designed to bring about the collapse of Italy, were preferable to an attempt to invade north-west Europe in 1943.[240]

The decision of July 1942 to mount operation *Torch* before the end of the year had been followed by some signs of an American retreat from the agreement of the 'Arcadia' conference in December 1941 to give priority to the defeat of Germany. Whitehall, however, had continued to have no doubts about the wisdom of that policy. On 18 September and again in October the JIC, weighing the relative merits of a Germany-first or a Japan-first strategy, had argued on the one hand that Germany's economy was becoming steadily less able to meet her needs† and, on the other, that if

---

* See below, Chapters 24 and 27.   † See below, Chapter 18.

238. Naval Headlines, Nos 530 and 540 of 16 and 26 December 1942, 551, 552 558, 572, 574 of 6, 7, 13, 27 and 29 January 1943; DEFE 3/585, ZTPGM 5596, 5819; DEFE 3/586, ZTPGM 6065; DEFE 3/587, ZTPGM 7284; DEFE 3/588, ZTPGM 8424, 8485 and 8493.
239. CAB 121/472, SIC file D/Russia/8, MIL 8123 of 21 January, JIC (43) 30 of 23 January.
240. Howard, op cit, Vol IV, Chapters XI and XII.

Germany were to defeat Russia and the western Allies were not operating against her, she would quickly rebuild her strength and possibly go over to the offensive through Spain or Turkey or the Caucasus.[241] On 18 October the Joint Planners had supported the retention of a Germany-first strategy both in order to forestall such German threats and on the ground that Germany's industry, her manpower and her armed forces were now 'strained to the utmost'.[242] And just as the Planners had merely enlarged on the arguments of the JIC, so their own assessment provoked no debate.

As for the form that the Germany-first strategy should take, Whitehall had become increasingly convinced after the decision to launch operation *Torch* that, alongside the bombing offensive against Germany, further extensive operations should be undertaken in the Mediterranean, in preference, if necessary, to re-entry into north-west Europe in 1943. That the main effort after *Torch* should be directed against Italy had been advocated by the Chiefs of Staff on operational grounds on 20 October 1942.[243] By 15 November, when the Prime Minister had concurred in this argument,[244] the JIC had made only two brief pronouncements on the subject. On 11 November, after the launching of *Torch*, it had cautioned that Italy was unlikely to collapse before the Allies had invaded Sardinia, and possibly Sicily too; on 14 November it had suggested that a successful operation against Sardinia, coming on top of *Torch* and the British advance towards Tripoli, might produce something close to panic in Italy.[245] Later in November, after the opening of the Russian offensive at Stalingrad, it had argued that whereas Germany would not otherwise move additional forces to the Mediterranean, if Allied operations against Italy forced Germany to occupy Italy and reinforce the Balkans she would need 20 to 30 additional divisions, the bulk of which would have to come from Russia with 'devastating results' on the Russian front.[246] The JIC had made this calculation in the course of supporting the Foreign Office against the Prime Minister's suggestion that Italy might be suborned out of the war. The Foreign Office had dismissed the possibility that any group of Italians would treat with the Allies before an increased weight of attack on Italy had provoked internal upheaval, but it had urged that

241. JIC (42) 358 of 18 September; CAB 121/145, COS (42) 345 (0) of 30 October, para 3.
242. CAB 121/145, JP (42) 880 of 18 October.
243. CAB 121/127, SIC file A/Policy/ME/2, COS (42) 354 (0) of 20 October, paras 6–12.
244. ibid, COS (42) 182nd (0) Meeting, 15 November.
245. JIC (42) 422 (0) of 11 November; JIC (42) 447 (0) of 14 November.
246. CAB 84/5, JP (42) 192nd Meeting, 27 November; JIC (42) 466 (0) of 28 November.

political and prestige considerations would force Germany to send troops to the Balkans as well as to Italy if Italy showed signs of collapsing.[247] While agreeing with the Foreign Office's view, the JIC had qualified it by arguing that in the last resort Germany would abandon Italy in order to concentrate on the Balkans; for the Balkans she would need 12 additional divisions, and in order to find them she would even be prepared to shorten her line in Russia.

It is possible that these arguments had had some influence on the statement drawn up by the Joint Planners on 5 December as a brief for use by the Chiefs of Staff at the Casablanca conference. While expressing the hope that the Allied seizure of Sicily, or preferably Sardinia, would bring about the collapse of Italy, this had recommended that after her collapse the war should be carried into the Balkans, rather than to the Italian mainland.[248]* But intelligence had not affected the outcome when, at the beginning of December, the Prime Minister had directed that the case for a Mediterranean strategy should be re-examined.

It is true that two items of intelligence had prompted the Prime Minister to call for the re-examination. Under interrogation after his capture at el Alamein, General von Thoma had described Germany's 180 divisions in Russia as being 'in many cases little more than brigades'; and evidence from Sigint and the SIS had disclosed that Germany's occupation of Vichy France in response to the Allied landings in French north Africa had absorbed 11 of the 39 divisions she had kept in northern France and the Low Countries.[249] What had chiefly weighed with him, however, was the knowledge that, in view of the promises he had made to Stalin in August 1942, the abandonment of *Roundup* might have serious political implications; and it was no doubt for this reason that he had hoped that the re-examination would show that it would be possible both to extend the present Mediterranean operations and to re-enter Europe in 1943. But he had not questioned its findings when, on 12 December, the Joint Planners had reported that to aim at the attrition of Germany by following *Torch* with further Mediterranean operations and continuing the bomber offensive was preferable to reverting to preparation for the earliest possible invasion of north-west Europe.[250]

The Planners' arguments were twofold. The first was based on

---

* For a more detailed account of the debates which accompanied the planning of the Allied operations against Sardinia and Sicily and in the Balkans see Volume III.

247. CAB 66/31, WP (42) 545 of 24 November, WP (42) 546 of 25 November.
248. CAB 121/127, JP (42) 990 of 5 December; Howard, op cit, Vol IV, pp 228–233.
249. CAB 121/145, COS (42) 429 (o) of 3 December.
250. CAB 121/145, JP (42) 1005 of 12 December (revised 10 January 1943), Annex VI of which is JIC (42) 490 of 11 December.

detailed order of battle calculations provided by the JIC. To plan for *Roundup* in 1943 would involve the Allies in six months of inactivity, which would give Germany the opportunity to recuperate and enable her to avoid withdrawing divisions from Russia or any other front until August 1943; whereas the other course would produce a decline in Italian morale, and perhaps even Italy's collapse, and might force Germany, while still having to maintain 39 divisions in France and the Low Countries, to replace the 9 Italian divisions in Russia and send some 12 divisions to the Balkans in the spring of 1943 and might also, should she have to garrison Italy as well, increase her commitments in the Mediterranean to 20–30 divisions. The second argument was the now familiar one that Germany's manpower shortages, transport difficulties and increasingly critical oil situation all pointed to the need for the Allies to keep up a relentless pressure on her. It had been repeated by the JIC on 3 December in a review of Germany's future strategy which had mentioned the evidence recently received of friction between the Army High Command and Hitler,* had emphasised the weakness of the GAF as being 'probably the most serious limiting factor' in the German military machine† and, after noting that the German authorities were becoming concerned at the state of civilian morale, had even considered the possibility of a German collapse. Though it dismissed this last possibility for the immediate future, the JIC did not exclude it as a contingency for 1943 and still felt, as it had in its paper of 1 June,‡ that when collapse did come 'it might come with startling rapidity'.[251]

From the second of these arguments Whitehall made use at the Casablanca conference only of the evidence that Germany's oil supplies might be in a critical state in another five months; it urged that this was 'the strongest argument' against allowing her any respite in the near future.[252] But it was on the first argument that the Chiefs of Staff chiefly relied when presenting their case for a Mediterranean strategy. As drawn up by the JIC, this had taken the form of a 'very rough balance sheet',[253] submitted with every reserve because its figures rested on so many imponderables, of the different degrees of strain that would be imposed on the German Army and the GAF during 1943 by a variety of different situations; but it had suggested that the greatest strain would result – that Germany would incur the worst deficits below the minimum number of divisions and aircraft she would need on all her fronts –

---

* See above, p 104.
† See Chapter 20 for Enigma disclosures of GAF weaknesses by the end of 1942.
‡ See above, p 98.

251. CAB 121/412, JIC (42) 462 of 3 December.
252. CAB 121/145, COS (42) 452 (o) of 31 December.
253. JIC (42) 477 of 7 December.

if, while she remained on the defensive in the west and in the Mediterranean but held the present line in Russia and continued fighting in the Caucasus, Italy had been knocked out of the war. As well as tabling these calculations at the conference, the Chiefs of Staff drew attention to the size of these worst-case deficits – 54 divisions and some 2,000 aircraft – in the report in which they listed the arguments which favoured the conclusion that a Mediterranean strategy would do most to relieve the pressure on Russia.[254]

A full analysis of how the British delegation at the Casablanca conference, by deploying these arguments, succeeded in the main in winning American agreement to its long-prepared objective, has been given in the official history of Allied Grand Strategy.[255] The intelligence archives contain little that needs to be added to it, and since that little refers to the second stage of the conference, which discussed how to put the agreed strategy into effect, it is best added when we deal with the post-conference planning of operations in the individual theatres of war.* At this point it is enough to record that on 19 January 1943 the Combined Chiefs of Staff brought the first stage of the conference to a close by approving the following recommendations for the conduct of the war in Europe in 1943:[256]

'1. *Security*
The defeat of the U-boat must remain a first charge on the resources of the United Nations.

2. *Assistance to Russia*
The Soviet forces must be sustained by the greatest volume of supplies that can be transported to Russia without prohibitive cost in shipping.

3. *Operations in the European Theatre*
Operations in the European Theatre will be conducted with the object of defeating Germany in 1943 with the maximum forces that can be brought to bear upon her by the United Nations.

4. *The main lines of offensive action will be:*
In the Mediterranean
(a) The occupation of Sicily with the object of:
    (i) Making the Mediterranean line of communications more secure.
    (ii) Diverting German pressure from the Russian front.
    (iii) Intensifying the pressure on Italy.
(b) To create a situation in which Turkey can be enlisted as an active ally.

---

* In Volume III.

254. CAB 121/145, COS (42) 452 (o) of 31 December, Annex.
255. Howard, op cit, Vol IV, Chapters XIII and XIV.
256. ibid, Appendix III (D).

In the United Kingdom

(c) The heaviest possible bomber offensive against the German war effort.

(d) Such limited offensive operations as may be practicable with the amphibious forces available.

(e) The assembly of the strongest possible force (subject to (a) and (b) above and paragraph 6 below)* in constant readiness to re-enter the continent as soon as German resistance is weakened to the required extent.'

□

When these decisions were reached the Allies remained uncertain about the enemy's policy with regard to chemical warfare – so much so that in the month following the Casablanca conference the British authorities were more disturbed than at any previous point in the war by the prospect that Germany might be preparing to resort to the use of gas. In the same month, February 1943, in an operation approved the previous summer as a result of uneasiness about Germany's nuclear research programme, the Allies attacked the plant that was producing heavy water for Germany in Norway. During the past two years the state of intelligence in each of these directions had been such that Whitehall's strategic assessments had been unable either to exclude the possibility of developments which would have incalculable consequences for the course of the war or to provide firm estimates of the enemy's progress and intentions.

From the beginning of 1942, after declining for almost a year,† rumours that Germany intended to resort to gas warfare again became insistent; they were associated with the fear that she might use gas in her coming spring offensive on the Russian front and came at a time when the Germans themselves were beginning to be anxious that Russia might resort to gas warfare.[257] In February the possibility that Germany might use gas was the subject of an exchange of telegrams between the War Office and the C-in-C Middle East[258] and in March the Soviet authorities expressed their anxiety to Whitehall; they were always to be more forthcoming on this subject than on others. The Prime Minister, with the approval

---

* Paragraph 6 dealt with operations in the Pacific and Far East.
† For a summary of the evidence available about the threat of chemical warfare up to the beginning of 1942 see Appendix 6.

257. WO 208/3576, Porton file CDR 5, p 740, Intelligence Summary No 84 of 29 October 1945.
258. CAB 121/100, SIC file A/Policy/Chemical Warfare/1, telegrams 0/59560 of 10 February, 73141 of 26 February 1942.

of the Defence Committee, replied by assuring Stalin that Great Britain would treat the German use of gas against Russia exactly as if it had been directed against herself, and would immediately retaliate.[259] On 1 April the Prime Minister informed the US President of Stalin's approach and his own statement in reply,[260] and on the recommendation of the Chiefs of Staff the views of the Chemical Warfare Committee on the gases most likely to be used and on counter-measures were passed to the US authorities and to the British Military Mission in Moscow for the information of the Russians.[261] On the same date, in response to further Soviet requests for the British opinion on the likelihood of the threat, MI advised the Mission that over and above 'the usual crop of rumours' there were indications that it 'was a definite possibility if all else fails'.[262] It is clear from an exhaustive inter-Service report of 31 March that the indications did not include positive intelligence on German intentions. The report dealt mainly with British preparedness to engage in chemical warfare in the light of what was known of Germany's preparedness, but with regard to her likely policy it confined itself to expressing the opinion that Whitehall had held since the outbreak of war: in view of the measures she had taken to protect her civilians, the fear of retaliation was not likely to deter her from using gas if it was likely to be to her military advantage; it was probable that she would not hesitate to use it if it suited her.[263]

Throughout the spring of 1942 rumours persisted about the enemy's intention to resort to gas in Russia and, although they were unconfirmed by any reliable source,* Whitehall continued to be seriously concerned not only about the threat but also about the possibility that the undertaking given to the Russians might tempt them to claim that Germany had used gas when they had no evidence that she had done so, in order to bring about British retaliation. It was in the hope of deterring both combatants that in a broadcast on 10 May the Prime Minister publicly announced the

---

* The first reference to German interest in gas on the Russian front to be provided by the Enigma was received early in May 1942, but it was ambiguous about Germany's own intentions and the interest shown did not appear to have an urgent character. The decrypt ordered an investigation into reports that newly-formed Russian divisions were practically without gas training; and some GAF units were instructed to report on the state of such training of their own personnel.[264]

259. CAB 69/4, DO (42) 8th Meeting, 18 March; CAB 121/100, COS (42) 70 (o) of 21 March; Churchill, *The Second World War*, Vol IV (1951) p 279.
260. Churchill, op cit, Vol IV, p 294.
261. CAB 121/100, COS (42) 78 (o) of 28 March; CAB 79/19, COS (42) 100th Meeting, 30 March.
262. Telegram to BMM MI 10/6 of 1 April 1942.
263. CAB 121/100, COS (42) 81 (o) of 31 March.
264. WO 208/3573 of 11 May 1942.

British commitment to retaliate.[265] The anxiety then assumed wider proportions.* On 6 June the President publicly declared that the US would retaliate if Japan used gas against China and other United Nations countries. During July Whitehall considered a long report from the Chinese Ambassador describing the use of gas by Japan in China, and also the interest Japan had shown in bacteriological warfare there.[269] With reference to the Russian front, however, rumours of Germany's intention to use gas died out after the opening of her long-expected offensive at the end of June; and Whitehall did not again give special attention to the danger until the autumn.

On 28 September, discussing a memorandum from the Ministry of Supply on the progress of British measures in readiness for chemical warfare, the Chiefs of Staff made the point that, since Germany had still not resorted to gas on the Russian front and was unlikely to do so if she was in danger of defeat, the threat had begun to subside;[270] the underlying reason for this view was probably Germany's growing disadvantage in chemical warfare as a result of increasing Allied air superiority. The JIC, instructed to examine this judgment 'from the enemy's point of view', reported in its favour on 5 October. Given the course the war was taking, it felt that the likelihood that Germany would use gas was becoming more remote; except in retaliation, it was reasonable to assume that she would do so only in support of an operation, like the invasion of Great Britain, from which she expected a victorious end to the war, and she could contemplate no such operation until she had eliminated Russia.[271] In their discussion of this report the Chiefs of Staff noted that the JIC had not allowed for a 'mad dog act' by Hitler; bearing that possibility in mind, they decided that British preparations for gas warfare should continue.[272] In December, in a further review, the JIC conceded that it could not entirely rule out the possibility that Hitler might order the use of gas if faced with

---

* During May the Enigma decrypts disclosed enemy precautions in the Western Desert: an anti-gas instructional unit went to Benghazi[266] and 2,000 respirators were sent there from Tripoli.[267] Occasional items concerned with gas warfare continued to appear in the decrypts until the end of the north African campaign but were never of an alarmist nature; in July 1942 they revealed an intention to equip camels with gas masks.[268]

265. CAB 121/100, JP (42) 382 of 10 April, DO (42) 45 of 29 April, COS (42) 183rd Meeting, 19 June.
266. CX/MSS/980/T4.
267. CX/MSS/1009/T23.
268. CX/MSS/1157/T4.
269. CAB 121/100, Pacific War Council (42) 11 of 14 July, PWC (42) 12th Meeting, 20 July.
270. ibid, COS (42) 273 (o) of 25 September, COS (42) 274th Meeting, 28 September.
271. ibid, JIC (42) 388 of 5 October.
272. ibid, COS (42) 282nd Meeting, 7 October.

military disaster, but again concluded that the danger was other-wise remote.[273] Later in December 1942, when the fighting at Stalingrad was moving to its climax, MI drew attention to the recurrence of rumours to the effect that Germany intended to resort to gas warfare in Russia, but treated the reports sceptically.[274]

In February 1943, however, following the fall of Stalingrad and the conclusion of the Casablanca conference, there was another alarm in Whitehall. It was started by an Enigma decrypt which gave an estimate of the number of replacement gas masks that would be required by all units of the German Army, other than those in Germany, Poland and Czechoslovakia, as at 1 April 1943. The Prime Minister regarded the decrypt as 'most important' and called for comments. The CIGS was disposed to agree. He replied in the following terms:

'In the past new types of anti-gas stores and equipment in the German Army have always been introduced gradually, as they became available from production. An exchange of respirator containers throughout the German field army by a specific date cannot therefore be without significance.

Technical sections have so far been of the opinion that existing German respirators would give adequate protection against any new gas likely to be developed in this war, though they have never gone so far as to say that the discovery of a new gas by the Germans is impossible.

A possible explanation appears to be that the Germans may now have stocks of a new gas against which their present containers are not proof. Even if this is so, however, they do not propose to make use of it before April'.[275]*

---

* In fact the Germans had begun to produce Tabun, a new nerve gas more lethal than any available to either side in the Second World War, in April 1942.[276] A second and even more toxic nerve gas, Sarin, was on the point of being produced at the end of the war and a third, Soman, even more lethal, was also under development. These gases 'were the only significant advance in chemical warfare weapons since the development of mustard gas in World War I'.[277] Allied intelligence failed 'to secure any definite lead on the German work on their Tabun type gases' in or before the Second World War. Although Allied intelligence frequently received reports of new German chemical warfare agents with 'astounding properties', these reports were rated low in reliability and little credence was given to them.[278] Many of the reports can be seen with hindsight to have referred to Tabun.[279] The Allies did not receive confirmed intelligence of German work on nerve gases until the first stocks of Tabun weapons had been captured in 1945.[280]

273. JIC (42) 472 (o) of 5 December.
274. WO 208/3573 of 14 December 1942.
275. Dir/C Archive, 2277 of 14 February 1943, covering CX/MSS/2109/T38, 2305 of 16 February 1943 with CIGS reply.
276. Stockholm International Peace Research Institute (SIPRI), *The Problems of Chemical and Biological Warfare*, Vol 1 (1971), pp 72, 87.
277. ibid, p 73.
278. ibid, p 315, quoting Chemical Corps Journal I (3), 40–43, 48; 1947.
279. WO 208/3576, pp 878–881, Intelligence Summary No 90 of 25 January 1946.
280. SIPRI, op cit, p 315.

And just when this exchange was taking place Whitehall began to receive agitated signals from Russia.

On 16 February the BNLO Black Sea reported that 'due to information from captured documents[and] interrogation of prisoners of war Russians convinced Germans will resort to use of gas in near future'.[281] On 25 February the BMM reported that the Soviet authorities were 'convinced Germans will not scruple to use gas and have following concrete evidence of intended use near future' – the evidence consisting of (a) the knowledge that 30 to 40 trains of gas containers had recently been transferred to the Russian front, (b) the discovery that German Army gas masks had been recently fitted with new filters, (c) the fact that German troops were carrying gas masks at all times, (d) references by German prisoners in coversation among themselves to the intention to use gas soon or in the spring, (e) the capture of equipment and (f) a report to the effect that the chemical plant at Ludwigshafen was working to full capacity.[282] On 27 February, in response to this telegram, the Prime Minister minuted the COS that they must be ready to retaliate promptly and with severity and be prepared for enemy counter-measures.[283] On 1 March the COS ordered the Chemical Warfare Committee to review the state of British preparedness, asked the JIC to report again, as a matter of urgency, on the evidence for the threat and instructed the Joint Planners to consider the operational implications of any conclusions reached by the Chemical Warfare Committee and the JIC.[284]

On 1 March MI 14 circulated somewhat dismissive comments on the Enigma decrypt and the telegram from the BMM.[285]* In its further assessment, issued on 3 March, the JIC considered the same evidence together with such other indications as had recently come to hand: a report from a source 'hitherto found to be reliable' that Hitler would accept defeat only after employing all means of warfare including chemical and bacteriological warfare; reports that respirators were being provided for German civilians; evidence† that the Germans were anxious to assess the Allied state of

---

* Of the items of 'concrete evidence' submitted from Moscow it said that (a) was quite likely but was unconfirmed by British evidence, that (b) was a routine precaution unless the decrypt implied that a change of gas masks was to be carried out in April prematurely, that (c) was standard procedure, that (d) was not a new development, even though rumours were more prevalent than usual, and that (e) was normal.

† The JIC did not specify this evidence. It was perhaps referring to the fact that at the end of 1942 and in the early months of 1943 the Enigma decrypts disclosed that the Germans had issued alerts about the danger that the Allies would resort to gas in Tunisia. They began when the Germans, in their turn, decrypted an Allied signal which referred ambiguously to

281.　CAB 121/100, BNLO Black Sea to Admiralty 0845/16 February 1943.
282.　ibid, BMM to War Office, MIL 8451 of 25 February.
283.　ibid, COS (43) 66 of 27 February, PM Minute 27/3.
284.　ibid, COS (43) 53rd Meeting, 1 March.
285.　WO 208/3573 of 1 March 1943.

readiness for chemical warfare. It pointed out that none of the evidence directly suggested that the Germans intended to initiate gas warfare and concluded that, 'though less remote than hitherto', the danger remained slight so long as the decision rested with the German military authorities; action by Hitler could not be discounted, however.[289] On 20 March the Chemical Warfare Committee agreed with this view, adding that Italy might be deterred even more than Germany by the fear of retaliation and that Japan would probably be deterred by her weakness in the air.[290] On 31 March the Joint Planners stressed that whereas the introduction of gas warfare would still be to the disadvantage of the Allies in every theatre outside Europe, in contrast to the position in 1942 the Allies were now better placed to use gas against Germany than was Germany to use it against them.[291] By that time the subject was being discussed by the Anglo-American Combined Intelligence Committee; at meetings on 18 March and 1 April this committee re-drafted and approved a paper on Germany's capacities and intentions which concluded that Germany and Japan were unlikely to initiate gas warfare in the near future and that Italy was unlikely to act except in concert with Germany.[292]

On 19 April, in a memorandum to the Prime Minister summarising the arrangements that had by then been made to co-ordinate the response of British and US forces in all theatres to the use of gas, the COS gave him the latest estimate of the state of the threat from Germany in the words used by the JIC on 3 March. 'Although recent reports from Russia and other sources confirm that the Germans are fully prepared for gas warfare, and imply their intention to use it, full analysis of the evidence suggests that the chances of their starting chemical warfare, though less remote than hitherto, are still small. The possibility cannot be excluded, however, that Hitler, faced with imminent military disaster, might order it to be introduced.'[293] On the day of the COS memorandum

---

the delivery of gas containers and prompted them to warn Fifth Panzer Army that 'the enemy possibly intends to use poison gas'. This warning was decrypted in the Enigma on 22 December 1942.[286] It was followed by decrypts of general warnings from the Italian Supreme Command[287] and several local alerts. On 26 March 1943, for example, Army Group Rommel ordered counter-preparations against gas attack.[288]

286. CX/MSS/1852/T30 of 21 December 1942, CX/MSS/1853/T10 of 22 December 1942.
287. CX/MSS/2148/T36, 2326/T25.
288. VM 7599 of 26 March 1943; CX/MSS/2326/T25.
289. CAB 121/100, JIC (43) 87 (0) of 3 March.
290. ibid, COS (43) 139 (0) of 20 March (CCW (43) 11 (Final)).
291. ibid, JP (43) 96 of 31 March.
292. CAB 88/57, CIC 4th Meeting, 18 March and 6th Meeting, 1 April 1943; CAB 88/58, CIC 15/1 of 2 April.
293. CAB 121/100, COS (43) 198 (0) of 19 April.

the Prime Minister took the question up with Stalin: as 'we have a rumour from Spain of the intention of the Germans to use gas on the Russian front and I understand you also have some indications of the same kind', did Stalin want Great Britain to renew her declaration of the previous year on retaliation?[294] On 21 April the British government repeated the declaration.[295]

On the same day MI 14 informed AFHQ Algiers of Whitehall's latest assessment of the threat from Germany and requested that particular attention should be directed to it during the interrogation of prisoners. AFHQ reported back early in May: there were no rumours among its POW about gas; they were receiving no training or special equipment that suggested an intention to use it; and the general belief at AFHQ was that the enemy would not use it even in defeat.[296] Within a month the German collapse in Tunisia had confirmed the accuracy of this estimate. By then, moreover, it was beginning to emerge that, while evidence of unusual anti-gas precautions on the part of the enemy might still imply that he was preparing for the offensive use of gas, this evidence had as yet almost always coincided with renewals of German suspicions that the Allies might initiate gas warfare; and it was no doubt on this account, as well in the light of operational experience up to the summer of 1943, that the Allies were not again to be as seriously occupied by this problem as they had been in the weeks following the Casablanca conference.

The spring of 1943 was also the date from which the Allied authorities began to feel increasingly reassured in relation to Germany's nuclear research programme, another problem on which they had experienced increasing anxiety, especially since the spring of 1941, on account of the fact that their knowledge of their own preparations was not matched by firm intelligence about the enemy's.

The results of splitting an atom of uranium had been discovered in April 1939, when Professor Joliot-Curie's French team had shown that in this fission spare neutrons were released, so that a chain reaction was possible. Scientists had quickly foreseen that uranium fission might be an immense source of heat and power and that there was also a possibility that it might provide an extraordinarily powerful explosion. However, two days before the outbreak of war Niels Bohr of Denmark and John Wheeler of Princeton had published a theoretical explanation of the fission process showing that it occurs only in the uranium 235 isotope and not in the 238 isotope. Since a lump of uranium contains only one 235 atom to one

294. ibid, PM telegram T 540/3.
295. *The Times*, 22 April 1943.
296. CAB 121/100, WO to AFHQ, 72185 of 21 April; AFHQ to WO, 9832 and T87 of 6 and 8 May 1943.

hundred and forty 238 atoms, and separation is extremely difficult, the prospect of atomic bombs receded. A chain reaction would succeed only if the neutrons released by fission were slowed down before they hit the 235 atoms. This process would make nuclear power possible but the reaction would not be fast enough for a bomb.

The publication of this basic information on fission had led before or just after the outbreak of war to the opening of secret government files in the United States, France, Britain, Germany, Russia and Japan. A further basic discovery was made in conditions of war-time secrecy: that in the course of slow chain reactions in unseparated uranium a new element would be formed which would behave like U 235 and be usable for bombs. The new element was plutonium.

In April 1940 two refugee scientists in Britain, Otto Frisch and Rudolf Peierls, wrote a crucial memorandum showing how and why a U 235 bomb was possible. This led the British government to set up under the Ministry of Aircraft Production the MAUD Committee which reported most lucidly and cogently in July 1941 that an atomic bomb was feasible, certainly with U 235 and possibly with plutonium. The Prime Minister, advised by Lord Cherwell, had no doubt that Britain should proceed with the bomb. The Chiefs of Staff and, subsequently, the Scientific Advisory Committee agreed.

At that time no firm evidence had been obtained about the German programme since the outbreak of war. But it was known that shortly before the Germans invaded Norway the French had foiled a German attempt to obtain heavy water, a material that facilitated slow chain reaction, from Norsk Hydro at Vemork, near Rjukan in southern Norway,* and the French had also reported that the Germans were making great efforts to find out what they were doing.[298] Subsequently it became known that as a result of the occupation of Belgium the Germans had acquired access to the largest stock of uranium oxide in Europe – that held at the refinery of the Union Minière at Oolen[299] – and the SIS reported that they were taking steps to increase the production of heavy water at Vemork. It was known that supplies of uranium much in excess of normal industrial requirements were essential for any large-scale programme whether as a source of power or as a military weapon

---

* These supplies of heavy water were brought to London by French scientists after the fall of France[297] and later used at Cambridge.

297. M Gowing, *Britain and Atomic Energy 1939–1945* (1946), p 50.
298. ibid, pp 43, 50. See also D Irving, *The Virus House* (1967) which describes investigations he made in Germany after the war on the German work and its relation to the Anglo-American project.
299. Gowing, op cit, p 101.

and that, though heavy water was not the only moderator for slowing down neutrons, only an interest in nuclear development could explain its production in large quantities; but it was still not known whether work on a bomb was included in the German programme. The MAUD Committee, in its report of July 1941, summed up the position in the following terms:

'We know that Germany has taken a great deal of trouble to secure supplies of . . . heavy water. In the earlier stages we thought this substance would be of great importance for our work. It appears in fact that its usefulness in the release of atomic energy is limited to processes which are not likely to be of immediate war value but the Germans may not have realised this, and it may be mentioned that the lines on which we are now working are such as would be likely to suggest themselves to any capable physicist'.[300]

The fear that Germany might already be working on a bomb, which had been an important consideration for Lord Cherwell, the Chiefs of Staff and the Scientific Advisory Council when they decided to recommend that Britain should proceed with a bomb, now made it urgent to find out whether the German programme was ahead of, or likely to go ahead of, the British. Hitherto, though any report or rumours received about Germany's programme had of course been noted,[301] there had been 'little serious effort . . . to get information as to what work was actually being done in Germany'.[302] But from the beginning of 1942 special efforts were made to improve the supply of intelligence and systematise its study.

By the end of 1941 responsibility for the atomic energy problem had been transferred from the Ministry of Aircraft Production to a 'Directorate of Tube Alloys' (the cover name for the project), with its own Technical Committee, in the Department of Scientific and Industrial Research under the direct responsibility of Sir John Anderson. By the same date, after an exchange of letters between the Prime Minister and the President, collaboration had been established between the Directorate and a corresponding organisation in the United States, where the receipt of the MAUD report had focussed attention on the need for a co-ordinated nuclear programme. In May 1942, with the approval of 'C', a member of the SIS was assigned to the Directorate of Tube Alloys to organise the collection and help with the interpretation of intelligence, with such support as he might need from ADI (Sc) in the Air Ministry.

This last task was not easy. Sigint was silent on the subject. PR could not be turned to account until other sources pointed to the

---

300.   Ibid, Appendix 2, p 395.
301.   ibid, p 87.
302.   CAB 126/184, Anderson Papers, Report No 55 of 5 October 1944, p 1.

whereabouts of constructional activities which suggested the development of large-scale plants of an unusual type; in the event this source was valuable during the planning of attacks on Vemork in 1943* but otherwise made no contribution until the second half of 1944, when it established that Germany had made no great effort to increase the production of uranium in Czechoslovakia and that no large-scale plant had been constructed at one suspected site in Germany.[303] Even had it been practicable to maintain agents in Germany, it would have been difficult for them to obtain reliable evidence on so complex a technical problem, and dangerous on grounds of internal security to brief them adequately. Considerations of internal security obstructed not only the collection of intelligence but also the process of scrutinising such evidence as was collected. In these circumstances all that could be done was to alert the intelligence-collecting agencies to the importance of obtaining information on general topics, such as the whereabouts and activities of specified German scientists, the building of unusual constructions and the production of unusual materials, so that the Technical Committee of Tube Alloys could mate any intelligence that might come in with British research findings and the scrutiny of such research papers as continued to be published abroad.[304]

By the beginning of 1942 the SIS had established a young scientist in the University of Stockholm to report on his own work, on the whereabouts of German scientists and on the contacts of Swedish scientists with Germany, and he was still reporting in 1943. But his reports have not been retained in the files. The same applies to reports from a well-placed writer for a German scientific journal who was in touch with the SIS from spring 1942 and to those from a Norwegian scientist who provided information about German scientists from the same period. But the minutes of the meetings of the Tube Alloys Technical Committee indicate that no important intelligence had been obtained by May 1942, and from the occasional summaries that remain in their files it is safe to conclude that the SIS and SOE had by that date succeeded only in confirming in general terms that the Germans remained active.†

It was thus on scientific grounds – 'since recent experiments in Cambridge have confirmed that element 94 (plutonium) can be as

---

* See below, p 127 et seq.

† On 22 May 1942 the SOE reported from Stockholm that it had heard that the heavy water from Vemork was being used in Germany in attempts to develop a bomb; it added the comment that these attempts might not succeed, but said that the information had come from more than one source.

303. CAB 126/244, Anderson Papers, Report No 67, Part 1 of 28 November 1944, pp 3, 7.
304. CAB 126/184, p 1; CAB 126/244, pp 2, 9–10.

good as U 235 for military purposes, and since it would best be prepared in systems using heavy water' – that on 23 April 1942 the Tube Alloys Technical Committee, still lacking any firm intelligence about the German programme, recommended that an attempt should be made to stop the production of heavy water in Norway[305] and were informed, by 7 May, that this was being studied by SOE.[306]

In June 1942 what appears to have been the first positive warning was received that Germany was working on a bomb. This came in a letter from Professor Waller in Sweden to a friend in London to the effect that, under the direction of Professor Heisenberg, experimental work was in progress in several laboratories on the fission of uranium and that 'results must not be excluded'. In July Professor Conant in the USA reported to the Directorate of Tube Alloys that Doctor Szilard had heard from a friend in Switzerland that the Germans had a 'power machine' working and might use the radio-active fission products as a military weapon, while in August a German professor who had left Germany for Norway sent a message that Heisenberg was working on a U 235 bomb and a 'power machine'. Heisenberg was said to be doubtful about the former but certain of the latter and satisfied with progress.

It was clear that Heisenberg's work involved the use of some heavy hydrogen (deuterium) compound and he was stated to have had half a ton of heavy water and to be due to receive a further ton. This information was considered by the Tube Alloys Technical Committee at meetings in July and August at which it was noted that it was not supported by such intelligence as had been obtained from British sources.[307]*

It may be added, however, that the report from Professor Conant was followed by a British investigation into the practical problems of detecting the dissemination of radio-active material and decontaminating areas affected by it. The conclusions were reported to the Technical Committee in September and October[309] and approved by Sir John Anderson and his Consultative Council.

The Directorate of Tube Alloys, while remaining uncertain about the scope of the German programme, had been kept well informed about the production of heavy water in Norway and the

---

* It seems likely that Professor Waller's letter was inspired by Professor Bohr in Denmark and, as it happens, the July report had accurately reflected Heisenberg's views. After the war he claimed that 'we saw an open road ahead of us, leading to the atomic bomb', from September 1941. But in the summer of 1942, though confident that a reactor could be built, he doubted that it would be possible to develop a bomb with the resources allowed to him.[308]

305. UK Atomic Energy Agency Archive, TATC (42) 4th Meeting, 23 April.
306. ibid, 5th Meeting, 7 May 1942.
307. ibid, 6th Meeting of 9 July, 8th Meeting of 14 August 1942.
308. Irving, op cit, pp 93, 105–106.
309. TATC (42) 9th and 10th Meetings, 9 September and 13 October.

importance Germany attached to increasing it. Professor Leif Tronstad, a former head of the Department of Industrial Chemistry at the Trondheim Technical Institute who had been involved in setting up the heavy water plant at Vemork, had been evacuated to Britain in the autumn of 1941. He had provided precise details about the expansion of heavy water production.[310] In March 1942 SIS established contact with a well placed employee of the heavy water plant at Vemork and with his help obtained photographs and drawings of the Vemork plant and details of the German plans for increasing its output. From April 1942 the SOE in Stockholm had been trying to find out by what routes the heavy water was reaching Germany and what its destinations were; by October 1942 it had established that the supplies were being sent by rail to Oslo but had failed to discover their onward routes and destinations.

On 18 October 1942, after two postponements during the previous month, an SOE advance party parachuted into Norway to establish a base camp some 30 miles from Rjukan. On 19 November, finally briefed by a former employee of the heavy water plant using plans and documents previously obtained, a Combined Operations party of 34 men was towed to Norway in two gliders. The gliders crashed on landing and the survivors were captured and shot.[311]

After the failure of the first operation the SOE's advance party continued to supply weather reports from the area and, assisted by the SIS and informants in the factory, operational intelligence about the defences of the factory, including such things as the times its guards were changed and its alarm procedures. In London, where it had been agreed that a second attempt to sabotage the factory should be made, this time to be carried out by SOE and using volunteers from the Norwegian Army, this local intelligence was supplemented by information provided by the Norwegian High Command and plans of Vemork based on aerial photography. The second attack on Vemork followed on 28 February 1943; it was confined to the high concentration plant, where it inflicted serious damage without sustaining any casualties. On 4 August 1943, however, the SOE reported that Vemork had re-started all apparatus on 15 April and had again been producing concentrated heavy water in small quantities by June. In the light of this and other evidence of the German determination to restore the position it was decided that the United States Army Air Force should attack Vemork.[312] The USAAF attack, which virtually put an end to the production of heavy water, followed in November 1943.

310.   UKAEA Archive, DSIR file TA 8, Ms note November 1941.
311.   For an account of the attacks on Vemork see the series of articles in *Aftenposten Oslo*, April 1969.
312.   CAB 126/244, p 8.

It was to emerge at the end of the war that when it sustained these severe blows the German nuclear research programme had for some time been faltering, partly on account of the division of the work between researchers backed by the War Office and a group of academic scientists, and partly from waning support at the highest level. At the time the authorities in Whitehall could not be sure that this was so. The reports which continued to reach London from physicists in Scandinavia and also, from 1943, in Switzerland left no doubt that nuclear research was still being carried out in Germany;[313] but as late as November 1944 an analysis of these reports confessed that 'it is extremely difficult to form a definite opinion as to the urgency and purpose of this work'.[314] At the same time, it seems clear from another analysis of the available intelligence that the British authorities were coming to believe by the summer of 1943 that the Germans, having concluded that they could not produce a weapon in time for use in the present war, had since the beginning of that year reduced the priority attached to the nuclear research programme. This report, too, was compiled after the event – it is dated 5 October 1944.[315] But the evidence it summarised included the fact that from the beginning of 1943 the German scientific journals had been allowed to publish, with an abnormally long delay between the date of compilation and the date of publication, papers which had a bearing on 'the design of a nuclear power unit of a 94[plutonium]-producing pile.' It also noted evidence that the German nuclear effort had been stepped up again from the end of 1943, but judged that the explanation might be the fact that the Germans had learned of the scale and progress of the Allied nuclear programme, rather than their belief that the German programme could be retrieved before the end of the war.

To this extent the threat from Germany's nuclear programme, like that which was produced by the knowledge that she was prepared for chemical warfare, was ceasing to be a source of grave anxiety to the Allied governments by the summer of 1943, and in this respect it stood in sharp contrast to the threat presented by her development of rocket weapons. As we shall see, reports on this subject had begun to reach Whitehall at the end of 1942, and by May 1943 the intelligence which had accumulated was causing serious alarm.*

---

* See Volume III.

313. ibid, p 3 et seq.
314. ibid, p 5.
315. CAB 126/184.

CHAPTER 18

Intelligence on the German Economy from June 1941 to the Summer of 1943

BETWEEN mid-1941 and mid-1943 Whitehall's assessments and forecasts of Germany's economic situation were not notably more reliable than those made in the first two years of the war. They improved to the extent that from early in 1943 MEW's Enemy Branch became more aware of the shortcomings of earlier estimates and approached its task with increasing caution. But that task had meanwhile been made still more difficult by the expansion of the scale of the war – an expansion that was not accompanied by any improvement in the quantity or quality of the information obtained by the intelligence sources.

The most important sources of intelligence continued to be censorship material, photographic reconnaissance, captured documents, reports from the British diplomatic missions, reports from agents, the output of the foreign Press and Sigint. In April 1942, surveying these sources, the JIC noted that Sigint and PR were 'most valuable',[1] but it added that PR could rarely be devoted exclusively to economic intelligence tasks, so large were other demands upon it, and in this area Sigint certainly remained more valuable as a check on other sources than as a primary source in itself. The JIC also singled out the British missions in Sweden and Switzerland as the most important diplomatic sources, but it noted that the contributions received from the American government were 'steadily increasing in value', and it held out the hope that the difficulty of getting captured documents and material from Russia might soon be overcome.[2] Referring to the work of agents, it credited to the SIS 'valuable economic intelligence', although reports on the output of factories were 'not often forthcoming' and could not be increased unless the more important work of the SIS in gathering operational intelligence was reduced, and noted that the Czechs and the Poles were also making an important contribution.[3] By the end of 1941 the collection of economic intelligence was becoming a major commitment for the SIS in Switzerland, the Poles had established a network throughout

---

1. JIC (42) 145 (o) of 19 April.　　2. ibid.　　3. ibid.

France which was providing industrial intelligence from both French zones, and intelligence from the Polish underground about the conditions in Poland was reaching the SIS via the Polish government in London. It may be added that from 1941 until the German occupation of Vichy France after the Allied landings in north-west Africa, the reports which Colonel Bertrand sent to the SIS included information on the French economy. The JIC also described the Press, including technical publications and the texts of official decrees, as 'most important';[4] and it is clear that the Intelligence Branch of MEW depended more heavily on published material than on the secret sources.*

While intelligence from secret sources was only marginally increasing, the problems to which it was applied were becoming more complex. The success of the German campaigns in western Europe in 1940 had confirmed Hitler's belief in Blitzkrieg economics and the management of the German economy had therefore remained unchanged. But the failure of the German attacks in Russia in June 1941 and the spring of 1942, and the entry of the United States into the war, enforced changes in German economic policy and in the structure and management of the German economy. Whitehall discerned that changes were taking place, but the changes were not completed by the summer of 1943 and their consequences for the German economy were difficult to calculate. Moreover, the outcome of the fighting in Russia hung in the balance until the second German offensive ended in disaster at Stalingrad. Until then, since a total German victory would so enrich Germany's resources as to render her economy virtually impregnable whereas her defeat must exhaust her resources, it would have been impossible to make long-term forecasts of German economic strength even if British intelligence had possessed an intimate knowledge of the German economy. Although it was clear by the beginning of 1943 that a German victory in Russia was unlikely, and that the cost of the attack on Russia was mounting rapidly, estimating the current and future means and resources of Germany and German Europe presented exceptional difficulties.

□

* The weekly intelligence summary issued by Enemy Branch contained a section entitled Current Intelligence Notes until September 1942 and thereafter Miscellaneous Reports until the end of the year. A new section entitled Classified Intelligence Reports was introduced in January 1943. Current Intelligence Notes and Miscellaneous Reports for 1942 comprise some 2,200 items on economic matters throughout German Europe; of the total number of reports some three-fifths were based upon the Press, broadcasts and official statements, and the remainder upon reports of varying reliability (the originals of which have been destroyed). The main subjects covered were labour, industry and supply, transport and communications, food, agriculture and finance; armament production rarely. As an

4. ibid.

By the end of 1941 MEW was over-estimating the rate of decline of German stocks of raw materials but it did not consider the situation yet to be critical, even after allowing for the heavy demands of the fighting in Russia.[5] Supplies of copper, lead, tin, aluminium and magnesium were thought to be adequate for 1942. The Germans now controlled the manganese resources of Nikopol in the USSR; increasing tonnages of chrome were coming from Yugoslavia and Greece. If the Germans could put the nickel mines at Petsamo in Finland into full operation deficiencies could be overcome; if Spain and Portugal could rise to the occasion a deficiency of 4,000 tons of tungsten could be overcome; French Morocco was a potential source from which to replenish the low stocks of cobalt, used as a catalyst in the Fischer-Tropsch synthetic oil plants. A large deficiency in rubber was evident, but that might be remedied by the production of synthetic rubber – of which very little was known.

By the end of 1942 MEW detected signs of deterioration in the German raw material situation.[*] It estimated that heavy air raids on the Ruhr and Saar areas had led to a decline of $1\frac{1}{4}$ million tons in annual steel capacity[†] and that iron ore imports from Sweden had declined; those from Spain were expected to decline from the spring of 1943.[‡] MEW further estimated that, unexpectedly, the margin between supply and demand for aluminium had sharply narrowed, that a copper shortage leading to an intensive scrap-collection campaign had developed and that, owing to the success of Russian 'denial' operations, the supply of manganese from Nikopol had increased less rapidly than expected. Germany had no immediate problems with tungsten, produced by Spain in increasing quantities, and the cobalt situation was approximately in balance; but she depended for molybdenum upon the Knaben mines in Norway, the chromium position was deteriorating and stocks were expected to fall in 1943, and a major accident had stopped output at the Petsamo nickel smelter in Finland.[7] Meanwhile, by the end of 1942 the blockade-running from the Far East, which had greatly assisted Germany's supplies of rubber and vegetable oil, was being seriously interrupted.[§]

---

indication to sources the series of Classified Intelligence Reports introduced in 1943 is of greater historical value.

  * For MEW's intelligence on the German shortage of shipping for the transport of raw materials see below, pp 198–199, 538.

  † In fact in the fourth quarter of 1941 steel production in Greater Germany was 7,085,000 tons, in the first quarter of 1942 6,424,000 tons, in the second quarter 6,850,000, in the third 7,419,000 and in the fourth 8,051,000.[6]

  ‡ See below, p 538.
  § See below, pp 190, 540 et seq.

  5. FO 837/14, MEW Summary of Enemy Economic Developments No 119 of 29 December 1941.
  6. U S Strategic Bombing Survey, Synoptic Volume (1945), Table 72, p 252.
  7. FO 837/15, MEW Weekly Intelligence Report No 45 of 24 December 1942.

Although at the end of 1942 MEW under-estimated, in the same manner as a year before, the German stocks of raw materials, Enemy Branch did not conclude that the balance was already critical for the German economy.*

In the spring of 1942, it is true, a more optimistic view had prevailed, the JIC forecasting in March that the renewed campaign in Russia would leave Germany with stocks of war materials exhausted and industrial potential impaired.[10] But the American view had been that the British emphasis on materials was leading to an under-estimate of Germany's powers of recovery.[11] This had been communicated to the British JIC in April 1942 and by May

* The following tables are provided only to indicate the general trends.

MEW Estimates of materials in German Europe (1941 and 1942) (000 metric tons)[8]

	1941			1942			1943
	Stocks at 1.1.41	Current Supplies	Consumption	Stocks at 1.1.42	Current Supplies	Consumption	Stocks at 1.1.43
Chrome ore (all grades)	123	118	191	50	140	205	Nil
Molybdenum (metal)	2.0	2.0	3.0	1.0	3.0	3.5	0.5
Wolfram	8.4	2.9	8.5	2.8	3.7	6.0	0.5
Manganese (50% Mn Ore)	620	220	650	190	370	650	Nil
Copper	225	175	300	100	250	275	75
Nickel (metal)	12.2	4.2	11.0	5.4	3.5	9.0	Nil
Tin (metal)	20.2	5.6	12.0	13.7	5.1	12.0	6.8
Asbestos Textile	3.7	0.6	4.3	Nil	Nil	Nil	Nil
Other	10.0	13.0	18.0	5.0	12.0	18.0	Nil
Bauxite	1,350	1,100	1,400	1,050	1,250	1,450	850
Alumina	Very small	550	550	Very small	575	575	Very small
Aluminium Metal and Scrap	Stocks less than 50,000 tons						

Official German Statistics showing Stocks 1941 and 1942 (000 metric tons)[9]

	1941			1942			1943
	Stocks at 1.1.41	Current Supplies	Consumption	Stocks at 1.1.42	Current Supplies	Consumption	Stocks at 1.1.43
Chrome ore	36.8	11.2	43.3	18.8	42.1	38.4	22.6
Molybdenum	1.9	0.5	2.2	1.8	0.5	1.8	0.6
Wolfram	3.1	1.0	3.4	2.7	1.9	3.0	1.6
Manganese ore	164.8	73.5	152.1	91.3	154.4	124.1	54.0
Copper	209.0	329.0	372.0	167.0	344.0	238.0	265.0
Nickel	11.3	8.8	9.2	10.9	5.5	8.0	10.4
Tin	10.0	11.7	10.9	10.9	14.0	8.3	16.7
Bauxite	n.a.	272.4	250.2	220.1	332.4	275.4	213.8
Aluminium	54.0[a]	385.6[b]	289.8	76.4[a]	382.1[b]	291.3	90.8[a]

(a) Calculated from production and imports, less consumption in previous year given in the table.
(b) Primary and secondary production plus imports.

8.   FO 837/15, MEW Weekly Intelligence Report No 45 of 24 December 1942; FO 837/17, WIR No 72A of 3 July 1943 and No 108 of 31 December 1943.
9.   US Strategic Bombing Survey, Synoptic Volume, Table 83, pp 263–264.
10. CAB 121/412, SIC file D/Germany/1, Vol I, JIC (42) 75 of 14 March.
11. JIC (42) 132 of 12 April.

the JIC had modified its position and now held that deterioration would be 'gradual'.* In the first six months of 1943 MEW made no major alterations to its estimates of the raw material situation at the end of 1942.

More calculable than changes in German stocks of raw materials, a decline in production and consumption of foodstuffs in Germany in the first half of 1942, for the first time since the beginning of the war, was evident to MEW. In April substantial cuts were made in the bread, meat and fats rations; potatoes were in short supply. MEW estimated that in June the ordinary consumer was obtaining rather less than 2,000 calories and the heavy worker rather less than 3,000 calories a day. Ascribing the difficulties in part to the indifferent harvest of 1941, MEW also emphasised that the levels of imports expected by Germany had not been realised. German imports of grain from south-eastern Europe stood at only 20 per cent of the pre-war figure and this region, where harvest prospects for 1942 were poor, could be written off as a source for 1942–1943. No return was expected from the Ukraine in the coming harvest year. Meat supplies were precarious. In MEW's view Germany was now virtually dependent upon her own production in conditions of shortages of labour, machinery and fertilisers.[12]

The food situation improved very greatly in the second half of the year. In October the bread ration was fully, and the meat ration partially, restored. In western and northern Europe the 1942 grain harvest was much larger than expected and the German potato crop, an important source of calories, was very good. At the end of 1942 MEW conceded that there had been a marked increase in the level of food consumption in Germany, representing a rise in the calorie intake from 2,500 to (for heavy workers) 3,000 per head,[13] although there was little change in the other countries of German Europe. No estimate could be made of any dividend the Germans might be securing from occupied Soviet Ukraine.

In short, it was recognised during 1942 that Germany herself had largely recovered from an incipient crisis and although in some sectors of agricultural production supplies were precariously balanced, there was no general shortage of food.

□

In the period under review British intelligence estimates detected no shortage of fuels, other than oil, severe enough to imperil current

---

* See below, p 158 and above, pp 95–96.

12.   FO 837/15, MEW Weekly Intelligence Report No 20 of 30 June 1942.
13.   ibid, No 45 of 24 December 1942.

production to the detriment of the German armed forces. Oil apart, shortages requiring special measures such as rationing were detected, but no absolute dearth.

With one basic fuel, coal, Germany was plentifully supplied. In 1942 MEW thought that a shortage of skilled underground workers and railway wagons might reduce output in Germany, and expected a 'very bad situation' to arise in Western Europe.[14] But it later conceded that Germany had experienced no difficulties and at the end of 1942 it identified Germany as the only important country in Europe not rationing electricity.[15] While the supply of energy from coal and electricity was judged to be adequate for requirements and secure in provenance, oil, directly related to the fluctuating requirements of the armed forces, was known to be subject to precarious balancing and, in particular, to be dependent upon the military outcome in Russia. The intelligence bodies therefore continued to give close attention to oil.

British estimates of the oil position at the beginning of operation *Barbarossa* in June 1941 gave the Axis a stock of 4,850,000 tons, of which 2,850,000 tons were in transit and distribution, leaving a margin of 2,000,000 tons freely available.[16] It was estimated in July 1941 that if fighting were to continue on the current scale consumption in enemy and enemy-occupied territories would exceed new supplies by 250,000 tons a month, and that after eight months it would no longer be possible for Germany to maintain the existing scale of fighting unless some of the 'immobilised' 2,850,000 tons could be drawn upon. In August the estimate of withdrawal from stocks was tentatively raised to 375,000 tons a month and MEW commented: 'it does appear highly probable that a prolongation of the Russian campaign for even a few months will, through its effect on oil, begin to affect Germany's war potential or her strategic mobility, or both'.[17]

In fact during the campaign of 1941 the operations of the German forces in Russia were not decisively affected by lack of oil, nor did the German General Staff plead oil supply difficulties as an excuse for military failures.[18] But it was apparent to Whitehall, as it was to the German authorities, that this would not be the case in 1942 if operations were to continue on the scale of 1941. The newly created Hartley Technical Sub-Committee on Axis Oil,* examining the situation in December 1941, considered that the Germans

---

* See Volume I, pp 102–3 and above, p 7.

14.   ibid, No 20 of 3 June 1942.
15.   ibid, No 45 of 24 December 1942.
16.   FO 837/14, MEW Summary of Enemy Economic Developments No 95 of 14 July 1941.
17.   ibid, No 99 of 11 August 1941.
18.   CAB 77/29, AO (46) 1 of 9 March, p 32.

would save 300,000 tons of oil a month if the whole eastern front
were to become static during the winter or 200,000 tons if the
southern front alone remained active.[19] But the eastern front did
not remain static. On 6 December 1941, the day after the German
advance upon Moscow came to a halt, the Russians launched their
counter-offensive and the Germans were engaged in a hard-fought
retreat until the end of March 1942. In the opinion of MEW the
Germans, denied the substantial savings in oil which a lull in the
fighting might have assured them, were worse off in the spring of
1942 than they had been in December 1941 without any 'cushion'
of free stocks.[20] This opinion followed the conclusion jointly
reached by the Hartley and Lloyd Committees in December 1941
that, since consumption between July and October 1941 had
exceeded production by 1,500,000 tons, total stocks at 1 January
1942 would be near the distributional minimum of 2,800,000 tons
and the oil position at a 'crucial' stage.[21]*

  This appreciation of the oil situation was among the factors
which led the JIC to predict with confidence in March 1942 that
the main thrust of Hitler's renewed attack upon Russia in the
summer would occur in the south and be directed at the Russian
oilfields.[23]† Intelligence could also forecast with confidence that in
order to keep their forces adequately supplied during the summer
campaign of 1942 the Germans must make strenuous efforts to
increase synthetic production and reduce civilian consumption. In
May 1942 it was estimated that total production for the year would
be 15 million tons, as against 13.75 million tons in 1941; 35 per cent
of this would come from synthetic plants and a further 10 per cent
from substitute fuel processes, the flexibility of the industry permit
ting resources to be switched from one product to another in
response to current requirements. Even allowing for the expansion
of synthetic production which, as PR showed, was being hindered
by delays in the construction of new plants, such as that at Brüx in
Czechoslovakia, it was felt that intense activity on one half of the
Russian front at any given time would cause supplies to fall short of
current military and civilian needs by 150–200,000 tons a month
and that such a shortfall would necessitate cutting civilian consumption to about 25 per cent below the amount needed for 'a full
industrial war effort'. It was expected that the effect would fall

---

  * Although German figures for the distributional minimum were lower than the British,
official German statistics show that stocks were in fact at this point in January 1942.[22]
  † See above, p 92.

19.   CAB 66/20, WP (41) 300 of 15 December.
20.   FO 837/15, MEW Weekly Intelligence Report No 20 of 30 June 1942.
21.   CAB 66/20, WP (41) 300 of 15 December.
22.   CAB 77/29, AO (46) 1, Chart facing p 40.
23.   CAB 121/412, JIC (42) 75 of 14 March.

mainly upon Germany, all other countries with the exception of Romania being already reduced to subsisting on a bare minimum.[24]

A severe cut was in fact made in German civil consumption during 1942. In 1941 the civil economy of Axis Europe consumed 8 million tons of oil products, of which Germany's share was 3.97 million tons; in 1942 the comparable quantities fell to 5.2 million tons and 2.47 million tons. But contrary to British expectations, production in the main German industries continued to rise.*

At the end of 1942 the Hartley Committee recorded that reports were being received of drastic steps to reduce civil consumption in Germany and, after August 1942, of interruption of Service training, especially in the GAF. These reports were in fact correct, but the Hartley Committee, impressed by the expansion of synthetic oil production, which was expected to yield an additional 1 million tons per annum by mid-1943 and another 500,000 tons per annum by the end of 1943, was not prepared to forecast that a fuel shortage would immobilise the German armed forces. Written in December 1942, before the outcome of the battle of Stalingrad could be known, its paper estimated that the Germans should be able to renew operations against the Caucasus in the latter half of 1943.[25]

At the beginning of 1943 British and American assessments of trends in the German oil situation were broadly in agreement, but there was a discrepancy between their estimates of stocks. When this was brought to the attention of the Combined Chiefs of Staff on 19 January 1943 at the Casablanca conference the Combined Chiefs asked their Combined Intelligence Committee to secure an agreed Anglo-American assessment.[26] In February 1943 Sir Harold Hartley, Chairman of the Hartley Committee, wrote to the Chairman of the United States Enemy Oil Committee suggesting that, rather than attempt to reconcile their differing estimates of German stocks, the two committees should agree to a general statement that on 1 January 1943 stocks were so low that withdrawals to make up any material deficit were no longer possible.[27] To this proposal the United States Chairman gave his agreement in April, suggesting also that it might be practicable for the two committees to agree on a common figure for 1 January 1943 'even if it were to be somewhat arbitrary'.[28] Between 28 June and 12 July 1943 the committees met

---

* See below, p 141.

24.   FO 837/15 MEW WIR No 20 of 30 June 1942; CAB 66/28, WP (42) 396 of 5 September (JIC (42) 309 of 5 September).
25.   CAB 60/32, WP (42) 596 of 18 December.
26.   CAB 121/152, SIC file A/Strategy/8, CCS 62nd meeting, 19 January 1943.
27.   CAB 121/418, SIC file D/Germany/3, JIC (43) 340 of 18 August, Annex A (JIC (43) 253 of 25 June).
28.   ibid.

in London for conversations ranging over the whole German oil situation. They agreed that their earlier studies had shown the same trends since 1939. There had been an initial period in which consumption had exceeded production but in which stocks had been restored, roughly by June 1941, to the 1939 level by loot. The expenditure of the Russian campaign and the failure to reach the Caucasian oilfields had compelled Germany in the autumn of 1941 to enforce rigid economy and the use of substitute fuels, but, even so, the stock position had deteriorated during 1942, reports coming in since the autumn showing that the oil shortage was beginning to affect the armed forces. Thereafter, the two committees also agreed, Germany had been able by the end of 1942 to improve her stock position by enforcing rigid economy in civilian consumption and benefiting from increased synthetic production. During their discussions, however, the estimates of the two committees of Germany's actual stocks diverged. Because their starting points were differing estimates of the position in 1939, the American figure was 5 million tons, the British 3 million. To resolve this discrepancy the committees decided to adopt a 'provisional datum point' of 4 million tons for 1 January 1943.[29]

The conflict between stock estimates, now reconciled by the simple device of taking a point midway between them, had little affected the independent assessments of the overall German oil position made by the committees in June before their meetings took place.[30] These proved to be almost identical[31] and for the rest of the war British and American estimates of the German oil situation were in close agreement. The British assessment of the overall position, made in June 1943, was that during the six months prior to April 1943 Germany had succeeded in increasing her oil stocks by over 500,000 tons, thus restoring them to the minimum necessary for efficient distribution. Total production had amounted to 8,477,000 tons and total consumption to 7,552,000, giving a theoretical increase in stocks of 925,000; from this, however, losses of 416,000 tons due to the bombing of synthetic plants, sinkings of tankers and abandonment of fuel reserves in Russia and north Africa had to be deducted, leaving an estimated net increase in stocks of 509,000 tons. The situation was 'tight' enough to cause the Germans serious anxiety, the shortage of diesel fuel being a pointer to general difficulties, but because the future held so many imponderables the British committee was not prepared to give a firm forecast of trends. On the one hand Germany's loss of the military initiative would lead to increased requirements for stocks

---

29. CAB 77/21, AO (43) 33 of 29 July (JIC (43) 312).
30. JIC (43) 266 of 25 June; CAB 121/418, JIC (43) 340 of 18 August, Annex A.
31. CAB 77/21, AO (43) 33 of 29 July (JIC (43) 312).

and to the curtailment of civil consumption directly affecting the war effort. On the other hand there was now a possibility that Italy would soon be out of the war, thereby releasing an additional 1 million tons per annum of Romanian oil for German use: and when the new synthetic plants under construction came into production at the beginning of 1944 Germany's 'essential needs' should be met.[32]

□

The labour situation in Germany was considered by MEW to be one of increasing stringency as early as December 1941,[33] the civilian labour force having declined by 2 million workers between mid-1939 and the end of 1940. Enemy Branch estimated that during 1941, despite the expansion of the armed forces by 2 million to a total of 10 million, Germany had been able to recruit an additional 1¾–2 million workers from the natural growth of population, the increased employment of women and the acquisition of foreign workers. But it also estimated that, if the numbers of the working population were 'weighted according to the estimated capacity of each group', the German labour force was, in effect, one million less at the end of 1941 than at the end of 1940, and that over the war period to the end of 1941 effective civilian labour had probably declined by at least 12 per cent as compared with the last full pre-war year.[34]

These calculations led MEW to forecast in December 1941 that, because the 'safe' margin of withdrawals of manpower from industry and agriculture for the armed forces had now been exceeded, Germany must release men from the forces for civilian work during the winter in order to maintain industrial output, and that, if factory leave were not given to men serving with the forces, Germany would begin the campaign of 1942 with a much lower scale of equipment than that of 1941.[35] The forecast proved to be wrong. MEW accepted in June 1942 that there had been no factory leave for the armed forces in the winter 1941–1942, Germany having been able to enter 1942 with the same numbers of workers as at the beginning of 1941 by virtue of the increased employment of women and the use of foreigners and POW. But it believed that the labour force was less efficient than before, the 1942 spring comb-out having affected all economic sectors including the war industries, and that to deal with the resultant manpower shortages the Germans had instituted a great labour drive, curtailing consumption-goods industries and concentrating production in more

---

32.   CAB 121/418, JIC (43) 340 of 18 August, Annex A.
33.   FO 837/14, MEW Summary of Enemy Economic Developments No 119 of 19 December 1941.
34.   ibid.   35.   ibid.

efficient units. It also believed that the curtailment of consumption-goods industries had freed no more than a half-million workers and that increased output had been achieved, in the main, not by greater efficiency but by longer hours (a ten-hour day being the general rule). Sauckel's appointment as labour dictator for the Nazi party* was thought to have secured direct party influence on the mobilisation of labour throughout the whole of German-occupied Europe, where the stage of full labour mobilisation was rapidly approaching.[36]

A memorandum circulated by MEW to the War Cabinet in October 1942 argued that labour supplies had become a bottleneck in Germany about a year earlier than in Great Britain and that in view of the prolonged fighting in Russia and growing British and American war production, the Germans had realised the necessity for great economies in manpower and a thorough-going re-organisation of the whole German war economy.[37]†

At the end of 1942 MEW considered that the German labour position was relatively satisfactory in agriculture but less so in industry. 'The movement for the concentration of industry which was carried out last spring has produced very little labour either for transfer from less essential industries to the war industries or for re-allocation within the war industries themselves'. '. . . this year there is the familiar picture of a civilian labour force remaining fairly stable in terms of numbers, but declining steadily in quality'. Various forms of wage changes were aimed at extracting greater output, but 'Germany has reached a stage in the war at which an increase in money earnings alone is not enough to call forth increased output . . . '.[38] This assessment held during the first half of 1943.

□

Enemy Branch's estimate of the capabilities of the engineering industries in general provides a background for its conclusions on the industries manufacturing war material. By the end of 1942 MEW[39] had acquired evidence that German capacity for producing certain types of machine tool, although insufficient for requirements in the aircraft and motor vehicle industries, was still providing an excess of productive capacity for the manufacture of heavy tools such as boring mills, heavy lathes and presses; products of this kind were being offered for export although certain types of tool were being obtained, on an increasing scale, from France and

---

* See below, p 151.   † See below, pp 149–153.

36. FO 837/15, MEW WIR No 20 of 30 June 1942.
37. CAB 66/29, WP (42) 437 of 9 October.
38. FO 837/15, MEW WIR No 45 of 24 December 1942.
39. ibid.

Belgium. Other sectors of the engineering industry seemed to be performing at least adequately. Exceptional measures to raise the output of steam locomotives by standardisation which had come into force earlier in the year were producing impressive results. Maximum use was being made of French and Belgian facilities for the production of motor vehicles and the output of the Renault works had risen above the level it had reached before the works had been bombed in March 1942. Ample capacity existed for the production of diesel engines and tractors. Factory capacity in electrical engineering was sufficient for all needs, although there was probably a shortage of skilled labour.

As seen from London the German engineering industries therefore showed few signs of weakness as the second winter of war in Russia closed in.

From 1940 onwards resources in Germany were being transferred from the civil building and associated industries to the armaments industries,* but in the armaments industries themselves as late as the autumn of 1941 considerable productive capacity existed which was not fully used for essential or priority tasks.† While in 1941 and 1942 MEW correctly discounted the possibility that German industrial production as a whole might greatly increase,‡

---

* *Percentage Share of Industrial Groups in National Industrial Production*[40]

	1939	1940	1941	1942	1943	1944
Basic Industries	21	22	25	25	24	21
Armaments	9	16	16	22	31	40
Construction	23	15	13	9	6	6
Other Investment Goods	18	18	18	19	16	11
Consumer Goods	29	29	28	25	23	22

---

† The United States Strategic Bombing Survey describes the situation of the German economy at the end of 1941 as being an 'equilibrium of excess capacity in which high costs were protected, production of superfluous goods . . . and scarce materials allocated to non-essential programmes'. An increase of armament output could have been easily obtained in 1942 by altering these conditions. It concluded that: 'German production during the early years of the war expanded but little. From 1939 to 1942 the gross national product of pre-war Germany . . . rose by only five billion, less than 4 per cent'. 'Preparations for the second campaign against Russia and its continued supply increased the outlay for principal finished munitions . . . eight billion more than in 1941'.[41]

‡ 'In fact industrial output increased between 1939 and 1942 by about 20 per cent whereas total output increased by only 6 per cent. In manufacturing industry productivity increased about 15 per cent over the same period'.[42] An index compiled after the war puts the rate of expansion lower:[43]

Industrial Production

1939	1940	1941	1942	1943	1944
100	96	99	100	112	110

40. D Petzina, *Autarkiepolitik im Dritten Reich 1939–45* (Stuttgart 1960).
41. US Strategic Bombing Survey, Synoptic Volume, pp 23, 24.
42. A S Milward, *War, Economy and Society 1939–1945* (1977), p 77.
43. R Wagenführ, *Die deutsche Industrie im Kriege 1939–45* (1963).

Enemy Branch failed to detect either the availability of considerable under-used industrial capacity or the transference of resources to the armaments industries. While realising the rather moderate increase in general production, it did not envisage the massive transfer of resources from building and investment to armaments.* In this situation, assuming that the German economy was fully stretched, MEW adhered to the view that Germany's production of armaments was already in decline and found it difficult to abandon its view until early in 1943. It was not until July of that year that, after stating that 'the view that has hitherto been held is that the output of the German engineering and armaments industries as a whole reached its peak in the early part of 1941, and that since that date it has tended to fall off somewhat', MEW added the following significant qualification: 'It has never been contended that the output of particular products may not have expanded . . . Although the production of finished munitions may have been maintained or even increased, there has undoubtedly been a marked fall in the output of less essential products . . .'.[44]

This was the first explicit reference by Enemy Branch to serious uneasiness about the reliability of earlier assessments. In June 1942 MEW had commented on the 'astonishing feat' permitting Germany to begin her second year's attack on Russia with forces little weaker in equipment (with the important exception of aircraft) than she had commanded in 1941.[45†] In October 1942 the JIC had recognised that while armaments production was 'not altogether satisfactory', there was still no evidence that the needs of her armed forces (again with the possible exception of aircraft) could not be met.[46] In December 1942, shaken now by evidence of the expansion of GAF fighter production, Enemy Branch admitted that Germany was still turning out armaments 'on an exceedingly formidable scale'; 'it would seem that the German engineering industries have so far lost little of their resourcefulness in meeting the constant demands of the fighting forces for new types of weapons, ammunition and equipment'.[47] In February 1943 the JIC, though still

---

* In June 1941 Enemy Branch was divided into six sections: (1) Enemy and Occupied Territories, of which sub-sections were General, Food, Metal, Chemicals, Arms and Far East; (2) Commodities; (3) Oil and Transport; (4) Shipping; (5) Enemy Transactions; (6) Services Co-operation. There was no section especially concerned with the study of German construction.

† See further below, p 152.

44. FO 837/17, MEW WIR No 72A of 3 July 1943, p 9.
45. FO 837/15, MEW WIR No 30 of 30 June 1942.
46. JIC (42) 368 of 6 October.
47. FO 837/15, MEW WIR No 45 of 24 December 1942.

asserting that Germany's output of armaments had fallen and would continue to fall, admitted that there was no evidence that reduced production had begun to affect the scale of equipment for the German Army.[48] A month later it thought that Germany's recent heavy losses of material on the Russian front and the decline in her industrial output 'may make it impossible for Germany adequately to equip in 1943 her own armed forces and still less those of her satellites',[49] but in May it reported that there was no sign of any significant deterioration in the quality of captured enemy material, and concluded that 'it is impossible to forecast with accuracy when, and on what fronts, shortages will seriously hamper German operations'.[50]

Except in relation to U-boat construction, Whitehall was slow to reach this conclusion because it continued to encounter serious difficulties in obtaining evidence upon which to base detailed estimates of the German output of weapons; and those difficulties were compounded by the fact that in 1940 and 1941 its detailed estimates had been exaggerated.

Air Intelligence recognised early in 1942 that the unexpected depletion and weakness of the GAF after six months of war in Russia threw considerable doubt upon the British estimates of German aircraft production which had been hitherto accepted. A new sub-section (AI 2(a)) was accordingly entrusted with the task of re-examining the estimates. It quickly concluded that output had been over-estimated in 1940 and 1941.[51]

Although receiving from time to time SIS reports containing official statistics of the production of German aircraft in France and details of the production of certain components in Poland, the new sub-section depended chiefly upon plotting graphs of the works numbers and dates of manufacture carried by enemy aircraft, a process by which an average monthly rate of output could be obtained. Crashed aircraft inspected by RAF officers in the field were the principal source of this type of information, but estimating was a slow process and liable to error. AI 2(a) also used whatever intelligence it could obtain from the interception of W/T call-signs from enemy aircraft in operation. GAF fighter aircraft fitted with W/T were mainly twin-engined types, single-engined fighters carrying R/T. While R/T could not be intercepted systematically except at comparatively short range, W/T call-signs of twin-engined aircraft, especially during tests or delivery flights, provided

48.   JIC (43) 40 of 11 February.
49.   CAB 121/419, SIC file D/Germany/4, JIC (43) 99 of 9 March.
50.   CAB 66/36, WP (43) 189 of 3 May (JIC (43) 142 (o) of 2 April).
51.   Air Historical Branch, *Air Ministry Intelligence*, p 169.

a better, if irregular, source of information.[52] By combining this intelligence with SIS reports and information from crashed aircraft, AI 2(a) could estimate a pattern of trends in aircraft production, but only several weeks in arrears.

The method adopted by the sub-section, reinforced by order of battle intelligence on the front-line strength of the GAF in Russia, led to the retrospective scaling down of British estimates of German production for 1940–1941 and of forecasts of output in 1942. A paper issued on 15 October 1942[53] put the average monthly production of operational types in January–June 1940 at 925, in July–December 1940 at 1,015 and in January–June 1941 at 1,035. The previous figures for each of these periods had been 1,250, 1,200–1,500 and 1,255–1,500 respectively.* The retrospective estimates thus reduced over-estimates current in 1940–1941.

The trend of estimates made in 1942 and 1943 on the basis of the method used by AI 2(a) can be followed in the details of fighter and bomber production issued in monthly reports:†

	Estimated Monthly Production[55]		Actual Monthly Production[56]	
	Fighters	Bombers	Fighters	Bombers
April 1942	470	765	427	552
September 1942	525	555	492	520
October 1942	535	600	502	590
November 1942	560	575	488	509
January 1943	600	560	512	674
February 1943	600	510	858	757
March 1943	780	435	962	757
April 1943	820	435	936	735
May 1943	765	420	1,013	718
June 1943	880	440	1,134	710
July 1943	980	455	1,236	743
August 1943	1,020	435	1,135	710
September 1943	880	455	1,072	678

* See Volume I, pp 227–229, 308–309.

† The Air Ministry estimates of fighter production for 1942 to February 1943 do not tally with estimates adopted by the Combined Chiefs of Staff at their conference in Washington in May 1943, when output was charted at c 730 per month in August 1942, c 760 in September 1942, c 775 October 1942–January 1943 and 810 in February 1943.[54]

52. ibid, pp 230, 233–235.
53. AIR 19/543, AI 2 (a) Report 2/42 of 15 October 1942.
54. CAB 80/70, COS (43) 286 (o) of 7 June (CCS 87th Meeting 14 May 1943 and CCS 217).
55. JIC (42) 113 of 10 April; AIR 19/543, AI 2(a) Reports, 8 September 1942 et seq.
56. US Strategic Bombing Survey, Synoptic Volume, Table 102, p 277.

The effect of revising estimates of production is shown by the following figures from JIC reports:

Estimated Monthly Rates of Production
of all operational types

April 1942	1,640[57]
June 1942	1,200–1,400[58]
October 1942	1,250[59]

It is clear that it was the new system of estimating production which accounted for the loss of 400 a month in the JIC figures between April and October. Neither JIC nor MEW reports suggest that the reduced rates of monthly production accepted by the JIC reflected a belief that *actual* output was declining. MEW, reviewing the German aircraft industry at the end of 1942, took the view that the average rate of production in the second half of the year exceeded the average rate in the first half of the year by a small margin.[60]

On the other hand, while AI 2(a)'s estimates were virtually accurate between September and November 1942, by January 1943 the new method was under-estimating the actual production of bombers, and by February 1943 the magnitude of the actual increase in fighter production was eluding the British intelligence authorities. The method of calculating output adopted in 1942 proved to be fallible by mid-1943; it was to break down in the spring of 1944.*

Up to the spring of 1943 the under-estimate of aircraft production was not large enough to mislead JIC assessments of GAF strength or seriously to conflict with order of battle intelligence. As early as January 1943, however, the fact that the fighter force was expanding was obvious from order of battle intelligence. In February the JIC concluded that re-equipment of the GAF in 1942 had been mainly confined to fighter units and that 'some' increase in the single-engined fighter force was to be expected.[61] And in April the JIC regarded the expansion of the fighter force as a move to strengthen the defensive arm of the GAF, a development which if not checked might gravely impede the Allied air offensive; it thought that the German achievement in increasing the fighter establishment from 1,360 in operational units in August 1940 to

---

* See Volume III.

57. JIC (42) 113 of 10 April.
58. JIC (42) 224 of 20 June.
59. JIC (42) 468 of 6 October.
60. FO 837/15, MEW WIR No 45 of 24 December 1942.
61. JIC (43) 40 of 11 February.

2,050 in April 1943, accompanied by the re-equipment of practically the whole single-engined fighter force with Me 109s and FW 190 aircraft, was remarkable.[62]

This achievement reflected a wholesale reorganisation of the German aircraft industry. When Germany invaded Russia in June 1941 Göring issued instructions that the front line strength of the GAF should be quadrupled. General Udet, Director of Air Armament, could see no way of implementing the order, complaining that the requirements of the GAF had for too long been subordinated to those of the Army and that the industry was short of raw materials and manpower. Field Marshal Milch (the State Secretary for Air), endowed with overriding powers to solve problems of shortages of engines, manpower and aluminium, realised that quadrupling the strength of the GAF was impossible and that the production programme was in a state of chaos. He demanded a rationalisation of the entire industry. On 17 November 1941 Udet committed suicide and Milch was immediately made Director of Air Armament. In partnership with Speer he radically reorganised the industry. Despite great difficulties with manpower, the output of aircraft was increased in the autumn of 1942 to a level 50 per cent above that of June 1941.[63]

There is no evidence in available documents that the British intelligence authorities were aware before the end of 1942 of the impact of Milch and Speer upon the aircraft industry. It was not until the middle of 1943 that MEW concluded that the increase in the output of fighters was due to the reorganisation of the aircraft industry in 1942.[64] One reason for the delay was that even after order of battle intelligence had begun to throw doubts on the new methods of computing aircraft production, from the spring of 1943, the work of estimating production continued to be bedevilled by another problem. Estimates of aircraft production and intelligence about the performance of the aircraft industry and its rapidly increasing capacity were not co-ordinated. Co-operation between AI 2(a) and MEW, 'for various reasons . . . never very practicable',[65] failed to bring together effectively such intelligence as AI 2(a) and MEW possessed. And the division of responsibilities between MEW and the Air Ministry – the former for estimates of the capacity of the aircraft industry and the latter for estimates of output – also partly explains the continuing gap between estimated and actual German fighter output, a gap which began to increase rapidly in the summer of 1943.

British current assessments of German production of land arma-

62. CAB 121/413, SIC file D/Germany/1, Vol II, JIC (43) 185 of 23 April.
63. D Irving, *The Rise and Fall of the Luftwaffe* (1974), pp 125, 145 et seq.
64. FO 837/17, MEW WIR No 72 A of 3 July 1943.
65. *Air Ministry Intelligence*, p 239.

ments in 1941, 1942 and the first half of 1943 were uncertain and subject to adjustment. MEW Enemy Branch in June 1942 took the view that armament production had declined in the previous twelve months but that the output of tanks had not been affected by the decline. Enemy Branch could find 'no indication of appreciable variation in AFV production or design since September 1941.'[66]*
In December 1942 Enemy Branch reported that 'whatever the difficulties, German armament is still on an exceedingly formidable scale' and 'both the quality and performance of the arms turned out continue to be of a high standard' but, as for tanks, 'such indirect evidence as is available . . . suggests that tank output during 1942 was not, at least in respect of numbers, as high as in 1941'. Enemy Branch added: 'it is possible that by now industry is being called on to prepare for new and heavier types'.[67]†

In its review of intelligence covering the first six months of 1943[70] MEW summed up: 'In a speech by Speer, Reichsminister for Armaments and Munitions . . . delivered at the NSDAP Rally on 5 June, very large percentage increases were claimed in the production of certain types of shells and artillery, and at the same time it was claimed that there had also been increases in the output of tanks, aircraft and locomotives. It is significant that the increases claimed were based on a comparison of the output in May 1943 with the average output in 1941 . . .'. MEW concluded that 'many of the claims made regarding large percentage increases in particular (and mostly new) types of weapons, ammunition and armoured fighting vehicles can be accepted'.

Alerted in the spring of 1943 to new products from the German tank manufacturers MEW Enemy Branch also recognised the necessity of revising British estimates of the quantity of German tank output. In April 1943 a JIC report put the annual rate of

---

* See Appendix 14.

† *Actual German Production of Tanks*
Number and Weight of tanks (Quarterly mean averages of monthly production)

	1941				1942				1943			
	Jan–Mar	Apl–June	July–Sept	Oct–Dec	Jan–Mar	Apl–June	July–Sept	Oct–Dec	Jan–Mar	Apl–June	July–Sept	Oct–Dec
No. of Tanks[68]	196	256	300	329	342	361	326	353	330	500	544	655
Weight in metric tons[69]	3,900	5,030	5,800	6,270	6,770	8,030	7,630	8,930	8,030	16,730	19,460	23,650

66. FO 837/15, MEW WIR No 20 of 30 June 1942.
67. ibid, No 45 of 24 December 1942.
68. US Strategic Bombing Survey, Synoptic Volume, Table 104, p 278.
69. ibid, Table 105, p 279.
70. FO 837/17, MEW WIR No 72A of 3 July 1943.

German output of tanks during 1942 at 1,000 a month:[71] the actual monthly average of output in 1942 was 345.[72]* The April estimate was severely reduced in a JIC report issued in August which put current German output at 700 a month.[73] Although German output was beginning to rise steeply, actual output at 500 a month[74] was well below this estimate, but the reduction made in August from the estimate made in April 1943 marked the initiation of new calculations undertaken in co-operation between MEW Enemy Branch and the American embassy in London. Completed in 1944 Anglo-American revised estimates for the years 1941, 1942 and 1943 were approximately correct.†

Intelligence estimates of U-boat production in 1941–1943 rarely deviated from the actual position. The difficulties facing NID were more manageable than those confronting the departments studying the output of aircraft and land armaments, and by June 1941 NID's knowledge of the yards had become detailed, the principal sources of information being PR, U-boat prisoners and Home Waters Enigma on U-boats passing forward to their trials.‡ In June 1941 NID set out the numbers of boats on the slips and fitting out and the tonnages launched at each of the nine principal German yards (Bremen, Bremerhaven, Emden, Flensburg, Hamburg, Kiel, Lübeck, Vegesack and Wilhelmshaven).[75] Instead of issuing an estimate of the number of boats completed since 1939, the practice followed in earlier NID reports, the report of June 1941 assessed the number of boats in service on 3 June 1941 at 120.§ This was slightly below the actual figure of 137, which can be calculated from the German official account.[76] The NID paper forecast that the number of U-boats in service by the end of 1941

---

* If in its report the JIC was referring not to tanks only but to *all* armoured fighting vehicles (AFVs) the British estimate was still exaggerated. Actual monthly average output of all AFV in 1942 was 516.

†	Anglo-American 1944 Estimates of Monthly average output	Actual Monthly average of output
1941	240	270
1942	330	345
1943	480	500

For the methods and results of the Anglo-American intelligence study of German tank production see Volume III.

‡ See Volume I, pp 336–339 and below, p 163.

§ 'In service' means the number of boats commissioned since 1939 (including those currently under trial or training) less losses since 1939.

71. CAB 121/413, JIC (43) 171 of 28 April
72. US Strategic Bombing Survey, Table 104, p 278.
73. JIC (43) 282 of 1 August.
74. US Strategic Bombing Survey, Synoptic Volume, Table 104, p 278.
75. ADM 223/107, NID 002322/41 of 16 June 1941.
76. ADM 186/802, *The U-boat War in the Atlantic*, Vol 1, Appendix II.

would be 210. This forecast fell short of what was to be achieved; the number of boats in service at the beginning of 1942, as derived from the official account, was 249. The NID under-estimate was based upon forecasting an incorrect average monthly output of 14.3; actual monthly output rose to 19.4 and planned output to 20.[77]

The under-estimate was corrected by MEW and NID between June and October 1941. By October the estimated monthly rate of output was raised to 20 a month,[78] a figure very close to the true one. The effect of this revision, reinforced by constantly increasing PR coverage of the German yards, is shown in NID estimates of July 1942 which put the number of U-boats then in operational service at between 140 and 150.[79] The actual figure was 140.[80]* The total number of U-boats in service in July 1942 was 331, a figure reached by adding to the 140 operational boats a further 191 under training and trials, as given in official German statistics. NID's estimate of the number of boats 'completed' by July 1942 was 335.[†] Correspondence between the estimated and the actual figure was thus remarkably close.

In March 1943 NID estimated that 420 U-boats were in commission and between 240 and 250 in operational service.[81] Both estimates were correct. When in September 1943 NID reviewed the situation[82] it estimated that in August 400 U-boats were in commission, of which 180–200 were in operational service. In fact the number of boats in commission was 403 and those in operational service 164.

□

As well as making assessments of the performance of particular sectors of the German economy MEW had to grapple with three broader problems in its effort to arrive at an overall appreciation of the enemy's economic situation. What was the nature of the administrative reforms of 1942–1943 and what were their effects upon the efficiency of war industries? What were the effects of Allied bombing upon German war output? What was the value to

---

* 'In operational service' in both NID estimates and the German official statistics excludes the number of boats undergoing training and trials.

† 'Completed' is clearly identical with 'in service' used in the official German statistics.

77.   ibid.
78.   JIC (41) 412 of 23 October.
79.   ADM 223/107, NID 03619/42 of 11 July 1942.
80.   ADM 186/802, Appendix II. See also S W Roskill, *The War at Sea*, Vol 1, (1954), Appendix Q.
81.   ADM 223/107, NID 01730/43 of 15 March 1943.
82.   ibid, NID 06496/43 of 3 September 1943.

the German economy of the contribution of its allies and the occupied territories?

The failure of the Blitzkrieg campaigns in Russia in 1941 and 1942 forced upon Hitler the reorganisation of central control over German war production. An article published in *Die Deutsche Wirtschaft* on 30 January 1942 led MEW to realise that 'Germany's war effort is not running as smoothly as the comprehensive system of controls would seem to suggest'.[83] Thereafter Enemy Branch observed with care the programme of economic administrative reform and Speer's rise to power as Minister of Armaments and Munitions.

When the German advance upon Moscow was halted in the winter of 1941 the Minister of Armaments and Munitions, Fritz Todt, influenced Hitler in the preparation of a series of Führer directives on industrial rationalisation designed to concentrate production in plants with the best working methods and to use greater mass production. The directive 'Armament in 1942' of 10 January 1942, demanding very large increases in production, strengthened the argument not only for rationalisation of production but also for greater centralised control over war production. At the end of January 1942 Todt proposed himself to Hitler as head of a centralised system. General Thomas of the Wehrwirtschafts-und Rüstungsamt (Wi Rü)* had argued for the creation of a centrally directed war economy even in pre-war years but he was disappointed by Todt's proposal because he had hoped that the Army would retain and extend its authority over war production. On 6 February 1942 Todt took the chair at the first meeting ever to be held of the chairmen of all the committees concerned with war production. Two days later he was killed in an air crash.[84]

Albert Speer succeeded Todt as Reich Minister for Armaments and Munitions on 18 February 1942. MEW thought that Speer, like Todt, was 'an organisation expert rather than a politician'. It thought that he had been given by Göring responsibility under the Four Year Plan for questions on armaments concerned chiefly with administration and that responsibility for armaments production remained with Wi Rü.[85] In fact Speer had been appointed by Hitler, and he immediately demonstrated his influence with the Führer by securing for himself the power to appoint the heads of all committees, including those created by Todt, and by persuading Hitler to modify the call-up for the armed forces in the spring of 1942 in order to provide labour for the construction of new factory space. By March he had extended the committee system, which

---

* See Volume I, Appendix 3.

83. FO 837/15, MEW WIR No 3 of 8 March 1942.
84. A S Milward, *The German Economy at War* (1965), pp 68, 70.
85. FO 837/15, MEW WIR No 6 of 28 March 1942.

under Todt had applied only to land armaments, so as to include shipbuilding and U-boat construction and, despite Göring's opposition, to anti-aircraft guns and bombs. On 4 April Hitler agreed to the formation of a Central Planning Board to control the allocation of raw materials to each sector of the economy. The Board had three members – Milch, Dr Körner of the Four Year Plan office and Speer himself, who was also to be the ultimate judge of appeals lodged against the Board's decisions. In the first week of May Wi Rü, symbol and instrument of the Army's economic powers, was split and a part transferred to Speer's ministry.[86]

In May MEW recognised that the issue of decrees, many of them signed by Hitler, demonstrated that 'the crisis for some time inherent in the German administration has come to a head'.[87] It missed the formation of the Central Planning Board, which was not mentioned in its intelligence papers in 1942. But in June MEW concluded that, representing something new in the German system, the ministry under Speer had acquired 'much more unity of command and control to give a peak impulse to armament production'.[88] It also knew in June that the functions of Wi Rü which 'dealt with the planning of arms production' had been transferred in part to Speer and that General Thomas would in future report to Speer on matters for which the Ministry of Armaments and Munitions was not responsible.[89] By the end of the year it knew that the arms inspectors formerly belonging to Wi Rü had become members of Speer's ministry and concluded that the ministry now held a key position in the German economic system.[90]

By the summer of 1942 MEW had discerned four new types of industrial organisation in Germany. Main commissions (Hauptausschüsse), established by Speer in March to work out technical procedures and control orders for the production of the more important mass-produced war materials 'such as tanks and aircraft;* industrial rings (Industrieringe), directly under the control of Speer to co-ordinate the main commissions; producer associations (Herstellerringe), voluntary and temporary unions of private firms acting as a unit under the leadership of parent firms; Reich associations (Reichs Vereingungen) of public bodies, formed

---

* Speer's ministry did not take over aircraft production at this point. The first step towards this, its assumption of control of fighter production, was taken in February 1944 and completed in March. Control over all branches of aircraft was delayed until April 1944.[91]

86. Milward, *The German Economy at War*, p 82.
87. FO 837/15, MEW WIR No 13 of 16 May 1942.
88. ibid, No 20 of 30 June 1942.
89. ibid, No 16 of 6 June 1942.
90. ibid, No 41 of 28 November 1942.
91. JIC (46) 33 of 20 October. See also A Speer, *Inside the Third Reich* (1971) pp 450, 471–473.

by the Ministry of Economics, membership of which was compulsory for firms in the industries affected. Associations for iron and steel, bast fibres, chemical fibres, textiles and coal were brought into being to ensure that production was concentrated in efficient firms.[92] Summing up the 'huge reorganisation' in June 1942[93] MEW considered the armament sector to be the focus; in this sector complete and unified control, both central and regional, 'ensured a more efficient basis than before'. Measures in the civil sector had not conformed to the uniform pattern; 'on balance it would appear that the system has become even more complicated'.

As we have seen, MEW had noted by April 1942 the appointment of Fritz Sauckel as General Plenipotentiary for Labour, regarding it as 'an attempt to concentrate control in the field of labour management',[94] but it had not learned of the relationship between him and Speer. At the same time it had observed that the reorganisation had not yet affected the allocation of raw materials to industry. This was, indeed, one of the most complex of the problems still facing the German government in 1942. Until the end of the year this task rested with Reich offices (Reichsstellen)* each of which was responsible for the supply, both domestically produced and imported, of one material. Armaments factories had therefore to deal with as many Reichsstellen as the number of materials they required. MEW knew by the beginning of 1943 that this system was about to be changed. In November 1942 Funk, the Minister of Economics, under whose jurisdiction the Reichsstellen fell, published a summary of all the regulations relating to them. This proved to be a signal for change. MEW correctly analysed the new measures now introduced, the main effect of which was to regroup the controls of materials to meet the total requirements of manufacturers, in several cases subordinating them to Reich associations responsible for production and in others handing over their functions completely to the producer association, as in the case of the iron industry. The outcome was the creation of 'fields of control' in which manufacture and the allocation of raw materials were linked.[95] This reform paved the way for the establishment of a single controlling authority for industrial production, the position to which Hitler appointed Speer on 2 September 1943. MEW interpreted this move, correctly, as a defeat for Funk, now left with responsibility for general economic policy, the supply of consumer goods, foreign trade questions and monetary policy, but deprived of authority in manufacturing industry. By the end of 1943 it was

---

* See Volume One, Appendix 3.

92. FO 837/15, MEW WIR No 21 of 17 July 1942.
93. ibid, No 20 of 30 June 1942.
94. ibid, No 8 of 3 April 1942.
95. FO 837/17, MEW WIR No 49 of 21 January 1943.

recognised in MEW that the concentration of power in Speer's hands had been a 'logical move' on Hitler's part.[96]

It was much more difficult to assess the effects of the German re-organisation upon production than it was to understand the new administrative structure. In May 1942 MEW reported that despite the intensity of the drive for increased production which had been going on for three months, there was little evidence of substantial results.[97] In June it thought that the new methods had caused a further restriction in the supply of consumption-goods and services, but that the scope for 'rationalisation' of industrial output was limited because a high degree of modernisation had already been achieved in the post-inflation period of the 1930s. 'If the German regime is successful in effecting the switchover without undue friction, there is reason to expect that Germany's future output will be bigger, not necesssarily than present production, but bigger than it would have been if no reorganisation had taken place'. As for the 'astonishing feat' by which Germany was beginning her second year's attack on Russia with forces little weaker in numbers or equipment (with the important exception of aircraft) than she had commanded a year before, it judged that this had been achieved by 'further extremes in efficiency and economy in the use of materials and labour' of which the effects were shown in falling output, deteriorating transport and a rapid worsening of the food situation.[98] In December 1942 MEW, noting that the German Press had taken a cautious view of the results of rationalisation, concluded that output as a whole had apparently not increased and that the supply of consumer goods had decreased. In its view such gains as were being secured from rationalisation were being off-set by deterioration in the labour situation.[99]

By the summer of 1943, however, MEW discerned that Germany was obtaining the first dividends from Speer's reorganisation and mobilisation measures; full production was at last being attained in factories put under construction in 1941 or even 1940. Allowing that many of Speer's public claims for the output of land armaments could be accepted, it concluded that the German position would have been much more serious than it was had the programme of rationalisation and standardisation not been carried out. During the first six months of 1943 MEW estimated that Germany had suffered military disasters and serious air raid damage to basic industries; the wastage of armaments and loss of consumer goods had denied success to the war production

---

96.   FO 837/18, MEW WIR No 108 of 29 February 1944.
97.   FO 837/15, MEW WIR No 13 of 16 May 1942.
98.   ibid, No 30 of 30 June 1942.
99.   ibid, No 45 of 24 December 1942.

emergency programme (Kriegsauflage), introduced in the autumn of 1942 to provide goods for the victims of air raids; in fact civilian standards would be cut further.[100] But it is notable that this review of the German situation in the summer of 1943 identified no decline in the output or the quality of war material.

☐

In their judgments on war output of the German economy as a whole in the period under review, the intelligence authorities did not regard Allied bombing as a major factor operating directly upon the level of German industrial production.

In December 1941, granting that the effect of bombing could not be estimated with any degree of precision, MEW considered that direct injury inflicted on plant had not been on a severe scale; public utilities, railways and the efficiency of workers had been adversely affected in areas frequently visited by the RAF, but German production, with the exception of submarine construction, had not been delayed 'to any serious extent'.[101]

Reviewing the effects of the heavy raids on western and north-western Germany in the spring of 1942 MEW estimated that the 'fair measure of direct damage' done to industrial plant and equipment was likely to have had less effect than the dislocation of transport and essential services and the interruption of work, casualties, absenteeism and general disorganisation resulting from the raids, but it conceded that 'at this stage of the war, when all economic activities have been planned within fine limits to the detriment of the flexibility of the industrial machine as a whole, the effects, and the accumulation of effects, on war output of such interferences are likely to spread wider and sink deeper than they would have done twelve months ago'. The most important econo-mic aspect of the raids was considered to have been their effects on the living conditions of the civilian population; to meet distress on this scale the German government had been forced, at the dictation of British air power, to divert resources from the production of war material to civil defence.[102]

At the end of 1942 MEW still held the same view; in the course of the year 'direct damage to plant and equipment, though substantial, has been a less potent factor in the reduction of industrial output than the general influences of transport disloca-tion, absenteeism, loss of working hours and increased fatigue due to nights spent in shelters and the difficulties of workers' travel'.

---

100.   FO 837/17, No 72A of 3 July 1943.
101.   FO 837/14, MEW Summary of Enemy Economic Development No 119 of 29 December 1941.
102.   FO 837/15, MEW WIR No 20 of 30 June 1942.

The coal mining industry was thought to have been particularly susceptible to dislocation from indirect causes, to the extent that the loss of output during the year might have been 5–10 million tons out of a total production of 150 million tons. About 10 per cent of the total numbers of dwellings in the raided areas had been rendered uninhabitable. The destruction caused by air raids had 'created demands upon manpower which in the long run cannot be met except at the expense of the productivity, or at least the expansion, of other branches of the war effort'. In the autumn of 1942, as we have seen, it had been announced in Germany that a Kriegsauflage programme had been set up to provide consumer goods for the victims of air raids: in December MEW already had some evidence that orders on that account were being placed in the occupied territories.[103] One of the principal results of the British air offensive in 1942 was, therefore, in MEW's assessment of the situation, the diversion to the production of consumer goods of some resources which would otherwise have been used in the expansion of war production. As to whether the offensive was having wider consequences, MEW remained sceptical. In November 1942, in one of a series of articles prepared for the *Army Quarterly*, Enemy Branch concluded in respect of industrial bombing: 'The plain fact is that no one yet knows how large a part the use of large-scale bombing against industrial objectives – a new weapon and a new form of warfare – can play in reducing Germany's power and will to fight'.[104]

In July 1943 the CAS asked the JIC to prepare quarterly analyses of the Anglo-American bombing offensive.[105] The first of this new series, which was to be continued up to the start of operation *Overlord* in June 1944, was issued by the JIC on 22 July. As American views had been taken into account, this and the later reports in the series represent the best opinion of the intelligence community in London on the general effects of the Anglo-American air offensive upon the German economy. In the first report[106] the JIC acknowledged the complexity of the task it faced and its conclusions reflected the caution of its approach. It pointed out that a nation's economic and industrial structure and the endurance of its population and its capacity to work formed an organic whole: injury caused by bombing could not be assessed 'by counting houses and factories'. In truth there could be no yardstick with which to measure the extent to which the German industrial system was already softened by bombing. With this proviso the JIC saw the principal effects of the bombing up to and including

103.   ibid, No 45 of 24 December 1942.
104.   *Army Quarterly*, Vol XLV No 1 of November 1942.
105.   JIC (43) 272 of 1 July.
106.   JIC (43) 294 of 22 July.

the second quarter of 1943 as the devastation of great industrial centres on such a scale that they were now regarded as front-line zones, with a corresponding effect on morale; severe effects on housing, transport, administration and the supply of consumer goods, so that the Kriegsauflage programme was much reduced; and considerable physical destruction of production capacity. This last, however, represented only a small proportion of the total impact. Few, if any, industries had lost a critical number of their factories and small reserves of manufacturing capacity and possible spheres of retrenchment still remained on a scale sufficient to cushion the supply of armaments; and since the greater part of the damage had been done to industries producing for other industries, there would be a time-lag before the effects became fully apparent. The JIC estimated that because of air attacks the steel industry in the Ruhr-Rhineland region was operating by the end of June at only 50 per cent of capacity, a loss of output equivalent to a 15 per cent reduction of total Axis output.* The attack on the Knaben molybdenum mines in Norway was expected to stop output for three months, reduce output to 50 per cent for a further three months and cause an alteration in the composition of some alloy steels. The JIC thought that the equivalent of 12–13 U-boats had been lost through bomb damage to the building yards, but did not consider losses in armaments production to have been critical; very little damage to factories engaged in aircraft production had occurred.

☐

In its efforts to make reliable assessments of Germany's general economic situation Whitehall was handicapped not only by the difficulties of computing the effects of the German economic administrative reform and of Allied bombing but also by that of calculating the contribution to Germany's war effort of the economies of her European allies and of the occupied territories. The economies of the occupied countries, external to and not integrated with the German economy, under the so-called New Order, presented acute problems to MEW's Enemy Branch. 'The occupied countries are an immense German commitment. Is the commitment on balance a benefit or a burden? The answer to this question decisively affects the course of the war: it . . . is one of the principal elements of uncertainty and instability in assessing

---

* The estimate of 15 per cent was exaggerated. Steel production in Greater Germany stood at 8,051,000 metric tons in the fourth quarter of 1942, 8,062,000 in the first quarter of 1943 and 7,532,000 in the second quarter. For Germany plus enemy-occupied territory total production in respect to the corresponding quarters was 9,018,000, 8,956,000 and 8,554,000, an overall decline of 5.1 per cent.[107]

107. US Strategic Bombing Survey, Synoptic Volume, Tables 71 and 72, pp 250–252.

German Europe's war potential.'[108] In effect Enemy Branch set for itself two questions: firstly, what was the magnitude of German Europe's contribution to the German economy, and secondly, how far could the contribution be further mobilised and increased in value?

In March 1942 MEW estimated that the occupied countries were providing in the form of raw materials, agricultural supplies and industrial production 15–20 per cent of Germany's requirements.[109] In April 1942 the JIC, including Italy as well as the occupied countries in its figures, set their total contribution to the German war economy at 25 per cent, and noted that in these countries the Allied blockade and the diversion of resources to war production had reduced civilian consumption to a very low level.[110]

MEW was also calculating the value, in Reichsmarks, of war expenditure on German account and of German Europe's contribution to it. The results of these calculations, tabulated in November 1942, showed that 68.6 per cent of the Axis war effort was carried by Germany itself, 14.9 per cent by the Axis allies, 16.1 per cent by the occupied countries and 0.4 per cent by the European neutrals.[111]* Aggregated contributions of the Axis allies and occu-

*

	War Expenditure				
	Nature of Contribution RM 000,000,000			Total Contribution	
Countries	Direct	War Indemnity Occupation Costs	Unpaid Exports[1]	RM 000,000,000	% of Axis War Effort
Germany	73.3	—	0.1	73.4	68.6
Italy	10.5	—	0.4	10.9	10.2
Other Axis Allies	3.6	0.2	1.2	5.0	4.7
All Axis Allies	14.1	0.2	1.6	15.9	14.9
France	—	7.0	1.0	8.0	7.5
Belgium	—	1.2	1.6	2.8	2.6
Holland	—	1.6	1.3	2.9	2.7
Other Occupied Countries	—	2.7	0.8	3.5	3.3
All Occupied Countries	—	12.5	4.7	17.2	16.1
European Neutrals	—	—	0.4	0.4	0.4
TOTAL	87.4	12.7	6.8	106.9	100.0

(1) Note: 'Unpaid Exports' should have read 'Unrequited Exports'. Countries exporting to Germany were 'paid' not in the form of German exports but by additions to their Reichsmark credit balances. According to MEW in June 1941 these amounted to 3,530 million RM (excluding Italy) and a year later to 9,175 million RM; in November 1942 MEW calculated that they were rising by 6,805 million RM per annum.[112]

108.   FO 837/15, MEW WIR No 3 of 8 March 1942.   109.   ibid.
110.   JIC (42) 113 of 10 April.
111.   FO 837/15, MEW WIR No 38 of 7 November.
112.   ibid.

pied territories, expressed in Reichsmarks, amounted to 30.1 per cent of the Axis war effort, almost one-half of that of Germany herself in 1942.

These estimates were not far from the mark. A post-war estimate of the output taken from 'territories annexed, occupied or intimidated', expressed in Reichsmarks and forming that part of the German total available product expended on government supplies and equipment, is similar to, although not identical with, MEW's assessment.[113]*

At this stage of the war, therefore, the economic value of German Europe to the Reich was no longer being under-estimated. On the other hand, MEW held the view that while fighting continued in Russia the contribution of the occupied territories to Germany could not be increased. In March 1942 MEW concluded that Europe presented 'a picture of fading rather than increasing activity'[116] in all the countries of German Europe, with few exceptions. This conclusion was somewhat premature. In fact Europe's contribution rose during 1942. It reached a peak at the end of the year, but began to decline in 1943.[117]†

□

By the beginning of 1943 MEW was having to accept that, when examined sector by sector, the German economy was still performing impressively; and what it knew about the economic impact of Germany's administrative reforms, the effects of Allied bombing and the situation in occupied Europe contained no indication that the crisis which it had long expected to arise for Germany by that date, if not even earlier, was at all imminent. Its economic assessments accordingly became increasingly cautious and, while recognising that Germany's economy could only deteriorate as the course of the war continued to turn against her, they ceased to forecast when the deterioration might be expected to set in.

In June 1942 MEW had believed that 'like an army in the later stages of a battle, Germany's economic resources are wholly

---

* A special paper by the Overall Economic Effects branch of the US Strategic Bombing Survey estimates that in November 1942 foreign contributions amounted to approximately one half of German government expenditure, excluding the pay of the armed forces and interest on the national debt.[114] The Survey's estimate of foreign contributions to the German economy has been criticised in post-war historical work.[115] It is not within the scope of this book to re-examine the Survey.

† See Volume III.

113. US Strategic Bombing Survey, Synoptic Volume, p 21.
114. ibid, p 22.
115. For example, Milward, *War, Economy and Society 1939–1954*, p 141.
116. FO 837/15, MEW WIR No 3 of 8 March 1942.
117. US Strategic Bombing Survey, Synoptic Volume, Table p 22.

mobilised and wholly engaged. They cannot be much further
developed or differently employed until the strain upon them has
been relieved by victory or ended by defeat'.[118] At the end of 1942,
however, it was allowing that the German economy had 'come
through the strains of the last six months better than might have
been expected'. 'Germany's war economy is being continually
adjusted with considerable skill to . . . shortage of materials and
shortage of men'. 'Economically she will not be able to support in
1943 a military effort as great as that of 1942, still less that of 1941;
but this weakening can be turned into failure and defeat only if the
United Nations can face her with challenges beyond her power to
meet'.[119] And in February 1943 it repeated this new-found insistence that Germany's economic decline should not be expected to be
rapid or automatic. In view of the military situation, her war
potential would continue to decline; but only Allied attack would
accelerate it.[120]

The greater caution of MEW's Enemy Branch was reflected in
the assessments of the JIC. In March 1942 the JIC had maintained that the German economy was already at the limit of its
capacity – and so much so that in her efforts to ensure that the
coming offensive in Russia was decisive, she was taking the risk of
weakening her industry and reducing her future war production.
By May, influenced by American scepticism, it had modified this
judgment to the extent of agreeing that after the coming Russian
campaign the Germans could hope to restore production before
they had to face a western offensive.* In September, in its
contribution to the world-wide review which the Joint Planners
were preparing for the Casablanca conference, it had returned to
the view that Germany must fail to maintain her economic war
potential in 1943 unless she could reduce the scale of her military
effort. With essential production affected by reduced supplies of
some raw materials, with armaments reserves depleted and manpower over-mobilised, with supplies of food, clothing and housing
progressively worsening, with transport receiving priority over
armaments and with the occupied territories yielding diminishing
returns, she must steadily lose the ability to maintain both a high
scale of military effort and a tolerable civil standard of living.[121] By
December the JIC was urging, however, that the strain on the
German economy was one of the factors which pointed to the need

---

* See above, pp 95–96, 132–133.

118.   FO 837/15, MEW WIR No 20 of 30 June 1942.
119.   ibid, No 45 of 24 December 1942.
120.   CAB 66/31, WP (43) of 5 February. See also W W Medlicott, *The Economic
       Blockade*, Vol II (1959), p 383 et seq.
121.   JIC (42) 358 of 18 September.

for the Allies to keep up a relentless pressure on her.* And by June 1943 there had been a further shift in its views.

In December 1942 the JIC had still not excluded the possibility of a German collapse in 1943 if the pressure on her was maintained; when it did come, collapse might occur 'with startling rapidity'.† In the first half of 1943 no JIC paper repeated the sweeping generalisations of the September 1942 assessment; and in June 1943, required by the Chiefs of Staff to examine the possibility of a German collapse, it reported that although there had been drastic alterations in plans and failures with individual programmes, there was no evidence of a general breakdown of economic planning.[122] A month later, using similar language in its half-yearly intelligence review, MEW completed the retreat from the expectations that had been harboured in Whitehall during the first three years of the war: the blows sustained by Germany in the first half of 1943 had been heavier than in any previous period, but there had been no corresponding deterioration in her power to fight.[123]

---

* See above, pp 111–112.
† See above, p 114.

122. CAB 121/419, JIC (43) 239 (o) of 5 June.
123. FO 837/17, MEW WIR 72A of 3 July 1943.

PART V

The War at Sea and the Air War in North-west Europe from mid-1941 to December 1942

CHAPTER 19

The War at Sea and
the Battle of the Atlantic
from June 1941 to the end of 1942

IN THE war at sea the situation was profoundly altered when GC and CS began to read continuously and with little or no delay the wireless traffic in the Home Waters (Heimisch) settings of the German naval Enigma that were common, as yet, to the entire German surface navy in the Atlantic area and to the U-boats. GC and CS's first substantial break into these settings had come in the second half of March 1941, when it had read the traffic for February. By 10 May it had read most of the traffic for April. The traffic for the month of May was read with a delay of between three and seven days. During May the capture of U-110 yielded the short-signal code books, which enabled GC and CS to read from May onwards the Kurzsignale, the short signals in which the U-boats transmitted their sighting reports and weather information. Captures enabled GC and CS to read all the traffic for June and July, including 'officer-only' signals, currently. By the beginning of August it had finally established its mastery over the Home Waters settings, a mastery which enabled it to read the whole of the traffic for the rest of the war except for occasional days in the second half of 1941 with little delay. The maximum delay was 72 hours and the normal delay was much less, often only a few hours.*

This change on the Sigint front coincided with a reduction in the activities of the main units of the German surface fleet. None succeeded in leaving Germany – and only one attempted to do so – between the loss of the *Bismarck* in May 1941 and the beginning of 1942, when the German Naval Command decided to concentrate its main units in north Norway. But the fact that GC and CS was now reading the naval Enigma did not enable the Admiralty to rule out a repetition of that period earlier in 1941 in which, in three short cruises,† one German battleship, two battle-

---

* See Volume I, pp 337–338. A feature of the naval Enigma machine was that while its outer settings changed daily, its inner settings changed only every other day. It was more difficult to break the inner than the outer setting, and the breaking of the outer setting normally followed within an hour or two of the beginning of the second day's traffic.

† See Volume I, p 331.

cruisers and a cruiser had sunk over 150,000 tons of shipping. From time to time, moreover the Enigma evidence created unavoidable alarm by being incomplete and tantalisingly allusive about the enemy's intentions.

At the end of August 1941 it revealed that the *Scheer* had been allotted a 'special task to the northward' and when Traffic Analysis, confirmed by the Enigma, showed her moving to Oslo from the Baltic in the first days of September, the Admiralty had to make extensive preparations against a move into the Atlantic until, on 10 and 11 September, the Enigma made it clear that she was returning to Swinemünde.[1] Nor was this the last alarm about the *Scheer*. On 2 November 1941, on the basis of Enigma evidence which could only be construed as indicating preparations for a raiding cruise, the OIC warned that she would be 'proceeding to sea outside the Baltic in the near future'; and between then and January 1942, at a time when the *Scheer* was known to be moving in and out of Swindemünde, it issued frequent, and as it turned out, inaccurate warnings that she was about to sail.[2] But if the regular reading of the Enigma did not eliminate anxiety, and even created it from time to time, it did provide invaluable reassurance from the middle of 1941, at a time when the resources of the Home Fleet were severely stretched, by establishing the presence and the whereabouts in the Baltic of the German main units, which PR could only occasionally do. No less important, it generated increasing confidence that, should any of these units attempt further sorties, the Admiralty would have nearly current, and perhaps even prior, intelligence about their movements.

That this confidence was justified was illustrated as early as June 1941. An Enigma message of 10 June, inaugurating a new series of signals for the pocket battleship *Lützow*, enabled the OIC to issue in the early hours of 11 June the warning that this ship might be intending to break out into the Atlantic: a new series of signals had been opened up in this way for the *Bismarck* and the *Prinz Eugen* immediately before their departure from the Baltic. Coastal Command reinforced its patrols, but by the evening of 12 June the ship had not been sighted. On 11 June, however, the Enigma messages transmitted to her were switched from the Baltic to the North Sea operational frequency, a strong indication that she was at least proceeding to Norway, and during 12 June their contents provided

---

1. ADM 223/79, Ultra signals 1712/31 August, 2006/2 September, 0058/6 September 1941; ADM 223/109, Ultra signals 0047/7 September, 1604/10 September, 1849/11 September 1941. Compare S W Roskill, *The War at Sea*, Vol 1 (1954), p 493.
2. ADM 223/103, Ultra signal 0010/2 November 1941 and, as an example of the latter warnings, ibid, 2316/19 November; ADM 223/92, OIC SI Nos 53, 56 of 7 and 12 January 1942.

precise information about her progress. The Admiralty was able to announce at 1250 on 12 June that she was passing the latitude of the Skaw at 1230, north-bound and probably at 20 knots. At 2119 on 12 June it could report that she had passed the line Naze to Lobjerg at 2030.[3] It was on the basis of this information that Coastal Command despatched at about 2300 the striking force, 14 torpedo bombers, which at 0218 on 13 June, two hours after she had been briefly sighted off the Naze by a Coastal Command patrol, scored a hit on the *Lützow*. Although only one torpedo found its mark, and although further attacks on the ship up to 0500 failed to do further damage, the first attack left her severely crippled.[4] The Enigma confirmed by 0525 that she had been hit. During the rest of 13 June it showed her creeping back under heavy escort through the Kattegat.[5]

The speed and accuracy of the Admiralty's intelligence during this episode, improving even on its performance during the sailing of the *Bismarck*, and forming a striking contrast with the Admiralty's lack of information about almost all the earlier sorties of the German surface units, was a striking illustration of the change that had been brought about by the break into the Home Waters settings of the naval Enigma, a change that was soon to have still greater effect on the Battle of the Atlantic.* But to some less important Allied advances in the war at sea at this time the Enigma either made no contribution or was only a marginal asset. It was thanks to the insecurity of the Abwehr hand cyphers that in August 1941, after earlier failures during 1940, the Germans were frustrated in their attempt to establish a meteorological station in Greenland; they did not renew the attempt until August 1942.† Between May and November 1941 they lost three of their commerce-raiding auxiliary cruisers, but the Enigma contributed to only one of these British successes.

Before leaving Germany, and on their return, these disguised raiders used the Home Waters settings; but the seven that were at sea at the beginning of May 1941 had all sailed during 1940, before the Enigma had become available. Between August and the end of November 1941 four of them returned to Germany. But the Enigma, the only source that could give advance information about such movements, did so only about the last of them. On the basis of accurate warnings from the Admiralty that a raider was returning to Biscay and would from there pass up the Channel on 27

---

* See below, p 167 et seq.   † See Appendix 7.

3. ADM 223/78, Ultra signals 0420, 1632, 1724, 2341 and 2345/11 June, 1250 and 2119/12 June 1941.
4. Roskill, op cit, Vol 1, p 484.
5. ADM 223/78, Ultra signals 0525, 0644 and 1211/13 June 1941.

November,[6] unsuccessful attempts were made by British surface ships and aircraft to intercept her. In December the Enigma revealed that one of the returned raiders was about to move down the Channel on a second cruise.[7] Air strikes were sent out but failed to find her in bad weather. These two movements at the end of 1941 showed that, even when the Enigma was being read, it remained extremely difficult to prevent the Germans from passing fast ships through the Channel if they chose their weather carefully and provided powerful escort.[8]

Once they had put to sea the raiders, operating mainly in the south Atlantic, the Indian Ocean and Australasian waters, transferred from the Home Waters settings of the Enigma to the Ausserheimisch (Outside Home Waters) settings; and GC and CS was never able to read the latter settings. That three of the seven raiders at sea at the beginning of May were sunk during the remaining months of 1941 was thus only partly due to the breaking of the Enigma. It owed something to the progress the OIC and other naval authorities were making in the difficult task of tracking the raiders on the basis of their sinkings, of rare sightings and occasional distress signals – a task which the raiders made difficult by avoiding the regular shipping routes, by doing their utmost to prevent their victims, independently routed merchant ships, from sending distress signals, and by maintaining almost complete wireless silence. It owed something, also, to the improvement that was taking place in British precautions. The earliest of the three sinkings came in May as a result of the receipt of a distress call, and this was the first time that a raider was caught with help from one of her victims.[9] It was directly as a result of the Enigma, however, that the third raider was sunk on 22 November. She was ordered to refuel U-boats that were to operate off the Cape of Good Hope; although GC and CS could not read her instructions, it could read the instructions sent to the U-boats, which remained on the Home Waters settings even when they were working so far south, and it was in this way that *HMS Devonshire* caught the raider *Atlantis* at the refuelling rendezvous.[10]

□

6. ADM 223/109, Ultra signals 0926 and 1630/27 November, 0905/28 November, 1835/30 November 1941; AIR 41/47, *The RAF in Maritime War*, Vol III, pp 136, 179.
7. ADM 223/109, Ultra signals 1710/9 December, 1600/26 December 1941; AIR 41/47, p 141.
8. Roskill, op cit, Vol I, p 505.
9. ibid, p 385.
10. ibid, p 545; ADM 223/103, Ultra signal 2004/21 November 1941.

The sinking of three of Germany's auxiliary raiders during the second half of 1941 was followed, as we shall see, by a decline in the activities of these ships from the beginning of 1942.* Even when these activities had been at their height, however, the raiders had been by no means the gravest threat to British shipping. Between the outbreak of war and March 1943, when their operations were coming to an end, they sank 129 ships, totalling 800,310 tons. These figures by no means reflect the full impact of the raiders, whose chief functions were to disperse Great Britain's naval resources and to dislocate the flow of her merchant shipping. Even so, they do not bear comparison with the ravages of the GAF and the U-boats. During the three months of March, April and May 1941 alone, the losses in the United Kingdom and Atlantic areas directly attributable to air attack had mounted to 88 ships of 247,118 tons,† and a further 27 ships had been sunk by mines laid by the GAF,‡ while the U-boats had accounted for 140 ships of 812,733 tons, an average of over 270,000 tons a month.

Except for reconnaissance by the Focke Wulf Kondors of I/KG 40, whose activities continued to be followed by the RAF, the GAF's anti-shipping effort had begun to decline after the beginning of April 1941. But the threat at sea remained the most immediate and pressing danger to Great Britain because by June the successes obtained by the U-boats since the opening of their new offensive in the spring showed every sign of continuing and of achieving a decisive result. It is true that great improvements, both in organisation and equipment, were now being made to the British defences.[11] As against that, the number of U-boats was increasing. In April Germany had still had only 26 operational U-boats, and many of them had operated practically continuously since the outbreak of the war. But the Admiralty knew from the Enigma that new U-boats were steadily coming into service, and it estimated that these would raise the number of operational U-boats to 60 in July and to as many as 100 by the end of 1941. Nor was this estimate much at fault; the actual position at the end of the year was that 249 U-boats were in commission, of which 91 were operational. As well as growing in numbers, moreover, the U-boats had improved their performance against convoys by adopting new tactics.

In the discussion of British anti-submarine policy the main dispute until May 1941 had centred on the question whether it would be more effective to counter the U-boats by hunting for them

---

* See below, pp. 190–191.

† These figures exclude losses sustained during the operations in Greece and Crete.

‡ Losses from mining had been heavier in 1940 and had reached their peak in November and December 1940, with 21 ships sunk in each month.

11.   Roskill, op cit, Vol I, Chapter XXI.

or by escorting convoys as strongly as possible. In May 1941 an Admiralty committee had reached the conclusion that 'we cannot afford to weaken our convoy escorts to provide the ships required for searching forces until far greater strength is available than is at present in prospect'.[12] By then, however, the fundamental problem was coming to lie elsewhere. Since the spring, as a result of the adoption by the U-boat Command of wolf-pack tactics in the north Atlantic, it had begun to emerge that, beyond the range of air cover, the available escorts could not protect convoys from mass attack by U-boats operating on the surface at night, and from massive losses, once convoys had been sighted. Although Dönitz, the C-in-C U-boats, had advocated them in a book in 1939, the adoption of these tactics had taken the Admiralty by surprise. The problems they posed would gradually be reduced as the supply of ship-borne radar and HF/DF improved.[13] Meanwhile, however, as the number of operational U-boats increased, the problem would mount unless means were found of so routeing shipping that the chances of sightings by U-boats were drastically reduced.

The Admiralty, advised by OIC's Submarine Tracking Room, had attempted the evasive routeing of convoys, as of independent shipping, since the outbreak of war, even though it had rarely been able to do more than guess at the whereabouts of the U-boats.* Since the beginning of 1941 its work in this direction had begun to improve. The extension of Coastal Command's patrols had forced the U-boats to concentrate in the central Atlantic and given the Admiralty more sea-room for the diversion of shipping. The adoption by the U-boats of wolf-pack tactics had made it necessary for those which sighted convoys to transmit homing signals for the benefit of the other U-boats on patrol, and these signals could be DFd. The better to exploit these opportunities, the Tracking Room had developed closer relations with the convoy authorities, which were reorganised as Western Approaches Command in February, and with Coastal Command. At the beginning of June, however, when the Joint Planners took stock of the situation, it seemed not improbable that this improvement, and any further advances by the British defences, would be more than off-set by increases in the weight of the German attack.

The Joint Planners noted that the combined output of all Commonwealth yards did not exceed one million tons of new shipping a year, but that on the most conservative estimate the merchant fleet would have suffered a further loss of 4 to 5 million tons by the end of 1941. An appeal for a building programme had

---

* See Volume I, p 333 et seq.

12.   ibid, pp 134–135, 481.
13.   ibid, pp 355–358; AIR 41/47, pp 40–61.

already gone out to the United States. Even if it were answered, however, Great Britain could not benefit from this source for at least eighteen months. Meanwhile, in order to feed her population and maintain her war production, she must import at least 36 million tons of dry cargo during 1941 and not less than 720 tanker-cargoes of oil, but at the rate at which cargo was being landed, she would receive only 28.5 million tons of dry cargo and 660 tanker-cargoes. By the end of the year there would be a deficit of 7 million tons of supply imports and 2 million tons of food; oil stocks, already nearing the danger point, would have shrunk by another 318,000 tons; and imports of manufactured goods would also be in arrears. During the rest of 1941 all these shortages except the last could be met by withdrawals from stock, but they necessitated the greatest possible economy in the use of available shipping and 'no new large-scale military commitments involving an ocean passage can be justified'. Thereafter the outlook was bleak unless the U-boats could be brought under control. 'We conclude from the foregoing statement of the position that it is only by a reduction of the rate of loss that a real margin of safety can be achieved.'[14]

The Joint Planners were not being unduly gloomy. Even as things turned out, it was only by the narrowest of margins that, despite the suspension of raids by the German surface fleet and the decline in the contribution of the GAF to the Battle of the Atlantic, the U-boat campaign failed to be decisive during 1941, and it is safe to assume that by the end of the year, before other developments had begun to increase the supply of shipping, the campaign would indeed have reached crippling proportions if its returns had gone on expanding at anything like the rate obtained during the first half of the year. But from the end of June, far from continuing to rise with the increase in the number of U-boats at sea, the amount of shipping sunk by U-boats was reduced to well below a half of the level the U-boats had achieved since March. In the four months to the end of June they had sunk shipping at the rate of 282,000 tons a month. In the months from July to the end of the year their monthly toll averaged 120,000 tons.*

For the reduction in actual shipping losses the main cause was a change in the Admiralty's policy. From 18 June it raised the minimum speed limit for independently routed ships from 13 to 15 knots, and there followed a dramatic decline in losses of 'independents', from 120 ships in the three months April to June to 25 ships between the beginning of July and the end of September. In contrast, the number of ships sunk in convoy or straggling from

---

* See Appendix 8 and Roskill, op cit, Vol I, Appendix R, Table I.

14. Gwyer and Butler, *Grand Strategy*, Vol III, Part I (1964), pp 9–12.

convoy increased from the beginning of July. But this reflected the fact that more ships were being taken into convoy and the fact that the U-boats, the number on patrol increasing significantly at last from the end of August, continued to improve their performance against such convoys as they were able to attack, and what is more significant is that despite these developments so many convoys made an undisturbed passage, the U-boats being more and more occupied in fruitless search operations. The difference between what the U-boats now achieved over-all and what they might have achieved – and, indeed, expected to achieve – was due to the great improvement in the evasive routeing of the convoys that took place when GC and CS began to read the naval Enigma.

That the Enigma breakthrough made a decisive contribution in this way, over and above such assistance as it gave in the routeing of independent ships, may be judged by the scope of the intelligence it provided. From May onwards, with the British intercept stations receiving every signal transmitted by or to the U-boats, and with the U-boat Command employing the Home Waters settings of the Enigma, every signal was being decyphered. Nor was that all. Although the U-boats rarely transmitted except to send their short signals, the U-boat Command had decided that in the north Atlantic it must exercise a centralised co-ordination over their dispositions and attacks, at least until the steady increase in the number of U-boats at sea had significantly reduced the difficulty of contacting convoys. This involved it in transmitting comprehensive situation reports and patrol instructions on the basis of which the OIC and GC and CS were able to make a detailed study of the capacities, the tactics and the methods of attack of the U-boats and the OIC was able to produce, day after day, a virtually complete chart of their dispositions. This intelligence did not exert its full impact until the end of June. From then to the end of 1941 operational circumstances were to reduce its value in particular areas and technical difficulties were to impede its flow from time to time. But the occasional interruptions serve only to confirm the extent to which the reading of the Enigma had transformed the situation. There was to be a close correlation between the periods when they were being encountered and those in which the performance of the U-boats temporarily recovered.

During May and June the shipping losses would have been even more appalling than they were if the Enigma had not already been available to some extent; but its value was cut back by cryptanalytic delays. In May the delay in breaking the daily Enigma settings was still as much as seven days at some times. Thus on 19 May, when convoy HX 126 ran into the U-boat pack and lost eight ships before the escort joined, the OIC had not received the U-boat Command's instructions which had redisposed the pack on 14

May, and did not do so until 21 May.[15]* From the beginning of June the Enigma traffic was at last read currently for two months – decrypted, that is, within an hour of its transmission – but now another problem was encountered. In the middle of June the U-boat Command, taking the first of a series of steps which showed that it was becoming disturbed that the U-boats were experiencing so much difficulty in intercepting convoys, and was suspecting internal insecurity, introduced a more complicated system of coding the positions at sea which figured within the encyphered Enigma signals. The OIC and GC and CS had largely solved the new system by the beginning of July, but during June it delayed and occasionally prevented identification of the U-boats' dispositions.[†]

Despite this technical handicap, the current decryption of the Enigma traffic from the beginning of June enormously improved the effectiveness of the OIC's evasive routeing. So much was this so that U-boats in the north Atlantic made no sightings between the beginning of the month and 23 June. What was equally important, the Admiralty's knowledge from the Enigma that the homeward-bound convoy HX 133 had been sighted on 23 June,[17] and that the U-boats were converging on it, enabled it to strip the escorts from two outward-bound convoys in order to reinforce HX 133 before the attack. In the subsequent convoy battle the escort outnumbered the U-boats and was able to keep the losses down to five ships, and also to sink two U-boats.[18]

In these circumstances it was for operational reasons that the total of sinkings by U-boats remained high till the end of June 1941: in an area outside the north Atlantic the U-boats were still being successful. Since the spring Type IXB[‡] (1,050-ton) U-boats had been operating off the west coast of Africa, close to Freetown and the Cape Verde Islands. In April the amount of shipping sunk south of 35°N had risen to two-thirds of that sunk north of 57°N, though the number of U-boats there had never exceeded six. In May the five U-boats in the area had sunk 32 ships, mostly independents, as compared with the 25 sunk in the north Atlantic. In June they were joined for the first time by one of the latest

---

* It was this encounter that led to the immediate introduction by the British authorities, with the aid of the Canadian Navy, of the system of complete trans-Atlantic escort. Hitherto the escorts of westbound convoys had left them in mid-ocean to proceed alone while the escorts picked up an eastbound convoy for the passage to the United Kingdom.[16]

† See Appendix 9.   ‡ For technical intelligence on U-boats see Appendix 10.

15. DEFE 3/1, ZTP 601 of 14 May 1941.
16. Roskill, op cit, Vol 1, p 463.
17. ADM 186/802, German Naval History Series, *The U-boat War in the Atlantic*, Vol 1, p 75.
18. Roskill, op cit, Vol 1, p 466; ADM 186/804, Naval Staff History, BR 1337.

U-boats (Type IXC, 1,120-ton) that were now becoming available, which was sent to operate in the Freetown–Lagos area,[19] and their successes remained high until the end of the month. But at this distance from home they could not operate for long – 47 days at sea – without being refuelled, and by the end of June, with the loss or capture of almost every German tanker in the sweep that followed the destruction of the *Bismarck*,* they had to be withdrawn. They were given the opportunity to refuel in Spanish colonial ports and the Portuguese Cape Verde islands, and six of them had done so by the end of September 1941, but the fact that the OIC could establish this from the Enigma and other sources enabled the British government to take diplomatic action to stop it.[20]

It was not until mid-September that a second wave of U-boats reached the west African area. But then, after July and August had seen virtually no ships sunk there, the U-boat Command failed to recover the initiative because the better organisation of shipping at last enabled the OIC to route it in the light of the Enigma information about the U-boat dispositions. In September, with five U-boats off Freetown and two further south, only three Allied ships were sunk, though U-boats outward-bound for Freetown sank seven other merchant ships from convoy SL 87.[21] In November and December British ships, directed by the Enigma, sank the raider† and a supply ship with which the Germans had hoped to re-fuel these U-boats. At this the U-boat Command abandoned operations in the area.

From the beginning of July the decline in sinkings off west Africa and the introduction of the higher minimum speed for independents brought about for the first time a dramatic drop in the monthly total of U-boat successes, for in the north Atlantic the failure of the U-boats to sight convoys continued. In July the U-boats on the trans-Atlantic routes again patrolled for three weeks without seeing a convoy; and the only convoy (OG 69) attacked during the month was on the north–south route between Africa and the United Kingdom through the eastern Atlantic. In August the Enigma ceased to be read absolutely currently. But much of the traffic was still decrypted within a few hours, and none was delayed for more than three days, and the operational pattern was very similar to that of July. To begin with, most of the U-boats were retained on the north–south route, where they succeeded in

---

* See Volume I, p 339 et seq.
† See above, p 166.

19.   ADM 186/802, pp 94–95.
20.   ibid, pp 95–96; ADM 223/92, OIC SI Nos 5 and 6 of 15 July 1941; Roskill, op cit, Vol 1, p 479; DEFE 3/3, ZTP 2090, 2537; DEFE 3/20, ZTPG 538.
21.   ADM 186/802, p 96.

finding another convoy (HG 70), but when they were redisposed on the strategically more vital trans-Atlantic route, from 10 August, they again patrolled fruitlessly for ten days until, in desperation, the U-boat Command moved them eastward in an attempt to make contacts closer to the United Kingdom, between Ireland and Iceland. In this they did not succeed. Since the Admiralty had been forewarned – the Enigma was being read at the time with a delay of 50 hours – and since the area was well within range of Coastal Command's patrols, they were subjected to intensive air and surface attacks. In eighteen attacks one U-boat was sunk and a second forced to surrender.[22] Such was the effect of the successes against the U-boats during these two months that the War Cabinet was inclined to believe that a corner has been turned in the Battle of the Atlantic and that Coastal Command's few long-range bombers might be diverted to targets in Germany. That proposal was successfully opposed by the Admiralty and Coastal Command.[23]

In September the fortunes of the U-boats improved. In addition to convoy SL 87, they attacked two other convoys on the north–south route and two trans-Atlantic convoys, sinking 34 ships from them. The improvement was partly due to the increasing number of U-boats at sea, which enabled the U-boat Command to form them into several groups for the first time, but it owed much to the difficulties occasioned for the OIC Tracking Room by the fact that the U-boat Command introduced on 11 September a new and more complex method of disguising the positions contained in the Enigma traffic. For weeks after this change the identification of the positions given in the instructions to the U-boats was a protracted process involving some guesswork.* However, the recovery by the U-boats was by no means proportionate to the increase in the number of U-boats at sea: although the number was nearly double what it had been in the first six months of 1941, the shipping sunk was below the monthly average for that period. The recovery was, moreover, short-lived. In October the U-boats attacked only one trans-Atlantic convoy (SC 48) and one convoy on the north-south route, and although these were subjected to heavy attack, Allied shipping losses were cut back by 25 per cent from the September level. And in November this comparative decline in the rate of the U-boat successes was followed by a landslide. The U-boats sank in that month only 62,000 tons of shipping, less than in any month since May 1940.

For this débacle, which marked the defeat of the U-boat

* See Appendix 9.

22. Roskill, op cit, Vol 1, p 467.
23. ibid, p 467; AIR 41/47, p 29.

Command in the major offensive against the convoys which it had launched in the spring, the growing expertise of the OIC in evasive routeing, based on the reading of the Enigma, was a fundamental cause. It is true that since the convoy battles of July the Enigma had revealed that in exploiting their sightings of convoys the U-boats were being increasingly hampered by the convoy escorts as well as by the arrival of less experienced U-boat commanders.[24]* During September and October, on the other hand, the heavy losses sustained by such convoys as were attacked demonstrated that beyond the areas within the range of land-based air cover, which the U-boats now avoided, the continual improvement in the Allied defences was still not keeping pace with the continual increase in the number of U-boats that could be massed into an attack if a convoy was contacted. But during October GC and CS had further reduced the delay in reading the Enigma to an average of 26 hours, as compared with 50 in August and 41 in September – to be precise, it was breaking the settings of the first of each pair of days with an average delay of 48 hours and the settings of each second day within a few hours – and GC and CS and the OIC had jointly gone far towards solving the latest method, introduced in September, by which the Germans disguised within the Enigma signals the positions on the German naval grid. It was as a result of these advances that during the last three weeks of October none of the U-boat patrol lines in mid-Atlantic succeeded in finding a convoy. Fifteen Atlantic convoys were successfully diverted, three were

---

* The escorts were now being reinforced by the US Navy. Intelligence documents released by the US government show that, as well as progressively extending its patrol zones to the eastward from April 1941, and assuming responsibility for escorting fast convoys in the western Atlantic from September 1941, the US Navy participated in the conduct of convoy operations in the western Atlantic from September 1941 – receiving from the Admiralty recommended routes before the departure of east-bound convoys, both fast and slow; diverting convoys, both east-bound and west-bound, as advised in signals from the Admiralty, even if they had no US escorts; and switching escorts from safe to threatened convoys in collaboration with the Admiralty. USS *Kearney* was sunk on the night of 16–17 October in the attack on convoy SC 48 after she and four other US destroyers, diverted from a west-bound convoy to reinforce the escort of convoy SC 48, had taken over tactical control of the battle.[25]

Apart from the direct assistance they provided to convoy defence, the US escorts hampered the freedom of action of the U-boats. From early in June 1941, as the Enigma disclosed, the U-boats received frequent instructions designed to avoid clashes with the USA; this was particularly true of the orders issued on the eve of operation *Barbarossa*. However, the attack on USS *Kearney* was covered by an order issued early in June, and never rescinded, by which 'darkened warships acting as convoy escorts are only to be attacked if the situation makes it necessary.'[26]

24. ADM 186/802, p 96; Roskill, op cit, Vol 1, p 470.
25. J Rohwer, '"Special Intelligence" und die Geleitzugsteuerung im Herbst 1941' in *Marine Rundschau*, November 1978 and 'Der Einfluss der allierten Funkaufklärung auf den Verlauf des Zweiten Weltkrieges' in *Vierteljahrshefte für Zeitgeschichte*, Heft 3 1979, pp 353–354.
26. DEFE 3/1, ZTP 725; ZTPGU 1652, 1668, 1777 and 6896.

sighted by U-boats that were on passage to and from the patrol lines, and of these three only SC 48 was sighted near enough to a patrol line to enable the U-boats to develop their attack.[27]

Until the end of October, despite the evidence that individual U-boats on passage were sighting convoys more frequently while the patrol groups were failing to do so, the U-boat Command had clung to the policy of disposing the U-boats in close-knit patrol lines, of which the object was to maximise the weight of attack if a convoy was contacted, but evasive routeing based on the Enigma information had forced it to spread the patrol lines over an ever-increasing frontage, so that the U-boats were too far apart to achieve a concentrated attack. In November it abandoned its single patrol line in the north Atlantic in favour of four shorter lines of U-boats, which were to keep continually on the move in the search for targets.[28] But on 22 November, before these groups had had time to form, it ordered all U-boats to concentrate in the Gibraltar area and virtually abandoned the offensive against the trans-Atlantic convoys. On 8 December all the U-boats operating in the Atlantic were in the Gibraltar area.[29]

If the main reason for the lack of sightings by U-boats during November was that the flow of Enigma intelligence into the OIC about their dispositions was so complete, another reason was that, despite the continual increase in operational U-boats, the number on patrol in the Atlantic, and the number on passage to and from their patrol areas, was declining on account of the withdrawal of U-boats from the Battle of the Atlantic to the Mediterranean and to Norwegian waters. Six were sent to the Mediterranean at the end of September, two more at the beginning of November. When the British offensive in Libya began on 18 November eleven further U-boats were earmarked for this theatre, and by 15 December a total of twenty had passed through the Straits of Gibraltar.* In October a Northern Waters group of U-boats was formed in Norway on Hitler's personal orders. Three more U-boats had to be spared to relieve this group at the end of November. At the end of December the U-boat Command resisted the request for three more. But on 24 January 1942 Hitler again intervened to order that eight U-boats must be kept stationed in the Iceland–Scotland area for the defence of the Norwegian coast, and during March 1942 the number of operational U-boats assigned to the Northern Waters group had risen to twenty-four.[30]

---

* See below, pp 327–328.

27. Rohwer, loc cit.
28. ADM 186/802, p 96.
29. ibid, pp 90–91.
30. Naval Historical Branch, BR 305 (2), *The U-boat War in the Atlantic*, Vol II, pp 8–10.

The Enigma did not give explicit information about these withdrawals, and it was some time before the OIC worked out the scale on which they were taking place. The impact on Atlantic operations of the withdrawals was, however, disclosed in the Enigma without delay. In September twenty U-boats had been on patrol in the Atlantic, leaving aside the U-boats on passage. On 1 November there were ten in the north Atlantic and six off Gibraltar. On 8 December there were only twelve U-boats on patrol in the Atlantic, all of which were concentrated off Gibraltar,[31] and on 20 December, when there were five in the north Atlantic but when four of them were known to be on passage to the Mediterranean, the OIC's U-boat situation report commented that 'the primary object seems, at least temporarily, to be no longer the destruction of merchant shipping'.[32] By 1 January 1942 only six U-boats remained on Atlantic patrol, and all were in the vicinity of the Azores.[33] These, the remnants of the group that had been moved to the area west of Gibraltar by the beginning of December, would have been more numerous had it not been the case that, over and above the withdrawal of U-boats to other theatres, December had proved to be an expensive month for the group. Between 17 and 21 December, in an attack on convoy HG 76, homeward bound from Gibraltar, it had lost no less than four U-boats and, although it had done considerable damage to the escort, including the sinking of HMS *Audacity*, the escort carrier, which had been attached primarily to deal with the FW 200s from Bordeaux, it had sunk only two merchant ships. This was the first convoy battle in which the escort had included an escort carrier.[34]

□

Despite the decline in the number of U-boats on patrol, the shipping sunk by U-boat in the Atlantic increased in December 1941; twenty merchant ships were lost there, including those sunk in the attack on convoy HG 76.[35] Nor need it be doubted that this recovery on the part of the U-boats reflected two important changes on the intelligence front. The first was a marked improvement in the performance of the German naval B-Dienst against British naval codes and cyphers. From September 1941, after

---

31.   ADM 223/109, Ultra signals 1658/6 December and 2347/9 December 1941.

32.   ADM 223/92, OIC SI No 40 of 20 December 1941.

33.   BR 305 (2), p 3.

34.   Roskill, op cit, Vol 1, pp 478–479.

35.   Naval Historial Branch, BR 1736 (51) (IB), *Defeat of the Enemy Attack on Shipping 1939–1945*.

experiencing considerable difficulty with it since August 1940, it again read much more of the traffic in the main Royal Navy Cypher (Naval Cypher No 2) with much less delay. By December 1941 it was also beginning to read the traffic in a special cypher (Naval Cypher No 3) which the Admiralty had made available for Anglo–US–Canadian communications in the Atlantic in the previous summer.* But the B-Dienst's success against Naval Cypher No 3 was limited before the beginning of 1942 and the recovery in its fortunes was more than off-set by the intelligence produced by GC and CS from the naval Enigma until, at the end of November 1941, the U-boat Command effected a second change in the situation by introducing a still more complex method of coding the positions given in the Enigma messages. In December 1941 and January 1942 it was not uncommon for the OIC and GC and CS to fail, despite all their efforts, to decode the positions given in the Enigma instructions sent to the U-boats.† And from the beginning of February 1942 they sustained a still more serious setback on the cryptanalytic front.

Since the middle of 1941 the British authorities had been faced with the problem of making use of the available intelligence without alerting Germany to the fact that the naval Enigma had been compromised. In dealing with the problem they had taken all possible precautions and, where the U-boats were concerned, they had also been helped by a fortunate combination of circumstances. Once the Enigma intelligence began to flow, the Admiralty had assumed over convoy movements in the Atlantic a more direct control than it normally exercised and had developed a technique for making maximum use of its information without compromising its source – routeing shipping either without the need to resort to further instructions once convoys had received their sailing instructions or, if subsequent changes became essential, issuing instructions of which the origin in the Enigma intelligence was concealed by reference to the sighting of a U-boat or to a DF fix on a U-boat's transmissions or to operational requirements. For the purposes of internal security these precautions were effective enough, but they did not help to lull German suspicions. Although this became known only at the end of the war, the U-boat Command was anxious and puzzled by the declining success of the U-boats in finding convoys as early as May 1941. It was on this front, however, that good fortune smiled on the Admiralty: for a variety of reasons, the Germans deferred taking decisive action on their suspicions until 1942.

In the first place, the fact that the performance of the German naval intelligence service against the Royal Navy's communica-

---

* See Appendix 1 (Part (1)).   † See Appendix 9.

tions had slumped between August 1940 and September 1941* – the period in which, as a result of GC and CS's success against the naval Enigma, that of British intelligence against the U-boats had so greatly improved – had had two important consequences. It had helped to prevent the U-boat Command from detecting the connection which existed, despite the Admiralty's precautions, between British evasive routeing and the reading of the Enigma; and it had presented the Command with one explanation for the failure of the U-boats. For this failure, moreover, there was no lack of other explanations. Except against convoys on the United Kingdom–Gibraltar route, where the U-boat Command was also well informed by agents in Spain of the movements of convoys using Gibraltar,† the fact that British air patrols had driven the U-boats into the central Atlantic had deprived them of reconnaissance assistance from the Focke Wulf aircraft of I/KG 40. The adoption by the U-boats of close-formation dispositions, in order to maximise their attack when a convoy was contacted, had reduced their own reconnaissance range, and until the steady increase in the number of operational U-boats began to make a significant difference to the numbers on patrol, which it did not do before 1942, the numbers on patrol were still very restricted in comparison with the vast expanse of ocean they had to cover. Even so, the U-boat Command remained so unsatisfied that it more than once questioned the security of the Enigma – only to be reassured by the naval staff that the cypher was invulnerable.

In these circumstances the U-boat Command, suspecting internal insecurity, introduced from June 1941, as a means of disguising U-boat positions from prying eyes, the series of coding devices to which we have already referred. Except for the last of them, introduced at the end of November, these handicapped British intelligence only temporarily. From 1 October 1941 the Command segregated its own communications from those of other users of the Home Waters Enigma by adopting modified Home Waters Enigma settings for the U-boats. But this measure, too, created only minor difficulties for GC and CS.‡ There followed on 19 November a review of the situation by the U-boat Command in which the Command confessed itself mystified: it accepted that the Enigma was secure and it was also satisfied that internal security was as complete as it could be made, but it remained convinced that

---

* See above, pp 176–177.
† See Appendix 15.
‡ It prevented GC and CS from reading U-boat traffic until 7 October and occasioned more than average delay in breaking the settings for 12 and 13 October.[36] A similar modification, less drastic but made with the same purpose, had been introduced as early as 1 April 1941; it had given GC and CS no trouble.

36. Dir/C Archive, 7731 and 7744 of 7 October 1941.

British intelligence was in possession of regular information about its dispositions and that British sightings, DF fixes and Traffic Analysis were not sufficient to account for it.*

Of these investigations in Germany the British authorities of course received no inkling until the end of the war. But they were soon to learn the outcome of the enemy's continuing anxiety. On 1 February 1942 the U-boat Command added a fourth wheel to the Enigma machine for the communications of its Atlantic and Mediterranean U-boats, and this step, though devised as a further measure against internal insecurity, was at last effective against GC and CS. Except for occasional days, GC and CS was unable to solve the U-boat settings until December 1942.† During this long interval the effects of this great loss of intelligence were to be all the more serious because, as chance would have it, February 1942 was the month in which the B-Dienst completed its reconstruction of Naval Cypher No 3, the cypher which carried the bulk of Allied communications about the north Atlantic convoys; from then until June 1943, with only one short interruption in December 1942 and January 1943, the enemy would read a large proportion of its signals with little delay.‡ It was for these reasons, as well as because the U-boats exploited a new operational area off the north American coast from early in the year, that the first half of 1942 was to see a startling recovery in their performance and that, despite continuous improvements in Allied defences and resources, there was to be no decline in the level of their successes until the beginning of 1943.

□

The German surface fleet continued to use the Home Waters settings of the Enigma, as did the U-boats in the Baltic and in Norwegian waters, and those settings continued to be read currently, or nearly currently, without interruption. But this fact did not enable the OIC to avert, later in February 1942, a further, though slighter, British misfortune – the failure to prevent the *Scharnhorst*, the *Gneisenau* and the *Prinz Eugen* from passing from Brest up the Channel.

From the time of their arrival in Brest these ships had been kept under close surveillance by PR§ and by the SIS,‖ whose agents in

---

* Dönitz's suspicions had been strengthened by, among other things, the arrival of British submarines at a rendezvous for three U-boats in the Cape Verde islands at the end of September 1941.

† See below, pp 233, 548, 551–552.   ‡ See Appendix 1 (Part (i)).

§ The very large PR effort against Brest from 28 March 1941 to 12 February 1942 totalled 729 sorties, flown with the loss of 9 Spitfires.[37]

‖ See Volume I, p 332.

37. AIR 41/7, *Photographic Reconnaissance*, Vol II, p 95.

Brest assisted further by supplying the Admiralty with documents
and photographs, including a plan of Brest's harbour defences. The
ships had also been subjected to continuing RAF attacks. The
Gneisenau was hit on 6 April 1941, the *Prinz Eugen* on 1 July, the
Scharnhorst at La Pallice on 24 July when an agent's report of her
movement from Brest had led to an RAF attack. The damage was
so serious that the Germans estimated that the *Gneisenau* and the
Prinz Eugen would not be operational before the end of the year.
The Admiralty knew by the end of April that the *Gneisenau* had
been seriously damaged, and by October had received reports from
SIS and PR that all three ships had been hit,[38] but it could not on
the basis of SIS and PR evidence be sure of their operational state.
At the end of 1941, however, it received the first indication that
they might be preparing to move. Between 16 December, when PR
disclosed that the *Prinz Eugen* was undocked, and 23 December,
when PR disclosed that the *Gneisenau* was also alongside a jetty,[39]
the Enigma revealed that the gun crews of all three ships were
carrying out firing practice in the *Admiral Scheer* and the *Hipper* in
the Baltic.[40] On 24 December the Admiralty informed the three air
commands that a breakout from Brest was likely at any time.[41]

Between 19 and 23 January 1942 the Enigma showed that the
Scharnhorst gun crews were still with the *Scheer*,[42] but by 1 February
evidence pointing to a break-out had accumulated. PR, which
during January had shown the ships sometimes in and sometimes
out of dock, had established that all three were undocked on 31
January.[43] From the Enigma, from PR and from SIS reports it was
apparent by then that they were leaving port at night for steaming
trials and returning each morning.[44] PR, the Enigma and the SIS
also revealed the reinforcement of the Channel by 2 destroyers, 5
torpedo boats and 8 minesweepers,[45] and enemy minesweeping and
GAF reconnaissance were noted in the vicinity of Brest.[46] On 1
February the OIC concluded that the departure of the ships was
'near at hand',[47] and on 2 February the Admiralty distributed an
appreciation of the possible destination of the ships.

---

38.   CAB 80/27, COS (41) 248 (85th Résumé), COS (41) 279 (87th Résumé);
       Roskill, op cit, Vol 1, pp 393–394, 483, 486–487, 491; AIR 41/47, p 191.
39.   ADM 223/92, OIC SI No 56 of 12 January 1942.
40.   Unless otherwise stated, the subsequent paragraphs in this section of the
       text are based on ADM 223/88, Colpoys, *Admiralty Use of Special Intelligence
       in Naval Operations*, pp 84–93.
41.   AIR 41/47, p 208.
42.   ADM 223/92, OIC SI No 82 of 5 February 1942.
43.   AIR 41/47, p 212.
44.   ibid, p 221 fn; ADM 223/92, OIC SI No 74 of 1 February 1942.
45.   AIR 41/47, pp 211–212; ADM 223/92, OIC SI No 74 of 1 February 1942.
46.   Cmd 6775 (HMSO 1946) Report of the Bucknill Enquiry, Appendix I,
       Admiralty Appreciation of 2 February 1942.
47.   ADM 223/92, OIC SI No 74 of 1 February 1942.

While admitting that there was 'little evidence to show which way the Brest ships will go if and when they leave Brest', the appreciation concluded that 'the Channel passage appears to be their most probable direction . . .'[48] Neither up to this time nor later was any hint received from any intelligence source that Hitler, his fears of an invasion of Norway increased by the British raids on Vaagsö and the Lofotens in December 1941, had insisted that the ships must be brought back to Germany through the Straits of Dover in daylight, a daring undertaking which relied heavily on surprise but made the best use of fighter cover.[49] Apart, therefore, from the evidence that the enemy was assembling additional naval forces in the Channel,[50] the Admiralty's conclusion was based only on operational considerations: the Channel represented less risk to the enemy than the ocean passage, particularly in view of the absence of British heavy ships in the area and the weakness of the British torpedo-armed forces there. On similar grounds the OIC had already leaned to the same view on 19 January,[51] and the C-in-C Home Fleet had expressed it almost a year earlier, when the squadron was first located in Brest.[52]

On 3 February the First Sea Lord, at a meeting of the Chiefs of Staff, referred to a concentration of enemy fighters on the Channel coast as perhaps indicating the intention to move the ships through the Straits.[53] By that date, moreover, the Enigma and PR showed that the enemy's naval reinforcements between Brest and the Hook had risen to 7 destroyers, 10 torpedo boats, over 30 minesweepers, 25 E-boats and many other minor warships.[54] And on the same day British preparations were put in train on the assumption that the enemy would move up-Channel. The Admiralty passed its appreciation of the previous day to the Cs-in-C of Coastal, Bomber and Fighter Commands, who at once alerted their groups.[55] The Air Ministry brought into force operation *Fuller* – the plan, drawn up nine months earlier for dealing with a possible Channel breakthrough, which placed all the air forces concerned at indefinite short notice.[56] A system of special air patrols was instituted; designed chiefly to detect the ships if they sailed round Ushant, this also allowed for the unlikely case that they might break out in other

---

48. Cmd 6775, Appendix I.
49. Roskill, op cit, Vol II (1957), pp 150, 152–153; D Richards, *The RAF 1939–45*, Vol I (1953), p 360; Cmd 6775, paras 105–108.
50. ADM 223/92, OIC SI No 92 of 13 February 1942.
51. ibid, OIC SI No 64 of 19 January 1942.
52. Roskill, op cit, Vol I, p 392.
53. CAB 79/18, COS (42) 37th Meeting, 3 February.
54. ADM 223/92, OIC SI No 77 of 3 February 1942.
55. AIR 41/47, p 213.
56. Richards, op cit, Vol I, p 364.

directions.[57] The Admiralty also diverted six destroyers from convoy duties, holding them at short notice in the Thames Estuary, and made other redispositions. It had already despatched two submarines, all that could be spared, to patrol off Brest.

Though the destination of the ships now seemed virtually certain, the problem remained of finding out the time of their departure, and it was vital to solve this since the effectiveness of the planned counter-measures depended on the earliest possible notice. On 5 February the Enigma revealed that Admiral Commanding Battleships had hoisted his flag in the *Scharnhorst* and the OIC, which also knew that the battle cruisers had recently carried out further exercises, took this as indicating 'an impending departure'.[58] On 8 February, however, a lift in the weather permitted PR to establish that all three big ships were still in Brest, the *Scharnhorst* being in dock,[59] and had been joined by two further destroyers, making four in all,[60] and at this news – prompted perhaps by the strain to which the RAF was now being subjected – AOC-in-C Coastal Command issued an appreciation to Bomber and Fighter Commands. This repeated the Admiralty's earlier conclusion about the destination of the ships and added that departure was likely to take place 'any time after Tuesday 10th February'.[61] On the same day, he issued detailed operational orders to Coastal Command's groups and individual stations[62] and took the risk of ordering the Beaufort torpedo bomber squadron stationed at Leuchars and charged with watching the *Tirpitz*, which had recently arrived at Trondheim,* to fly south.[63] No 11 Group, Fighter Command, which was responsible for co-ordinating all fighter forces engaged in operation *Fuller*, also issued additional orders on receiving AOC-in-C Coastal Command's appreciation.[64] On 10 February, however, without informing the Admiralty, AOC-in-C Bomber Command stood down more than a half of his *Fuller* force, leaving only 100 bombers at four hours' instead of two hours' notice.[65]

By that time the Enigma had been providing for the past week scraps of evidence to the effect that German minesweepers were clearing a new passage through the Bight. As well as removing

---

* See below, p 200.

57.   Roskill, op cit, Vol II, p 151.
58.   ADM 223/92, OIC SI No 82 of 5 February 1942.
59.   AIR 41/47, p 214.
60.   ibid, p 215.
61.   Cmd 6775, Appendix 6.
62.   ibid, Appendix 5.
63.   ibid, para 12.
64.   AIR 41/47, p 213.
65.   ibid, p 225.

virtually all doubt about the enemy's intention to go up-Channel, these clues, elucidated with the help of captured charts of enemy swept channels, had enabled the OIC gradually to establish the lie of the new passage.[66] Shortly after 1800 on 11 February further decrypts were received on the strength of which the OIC that night completed the plotting of the route.[67] At 1229 on 12 February the Admiralty promulgated the information that 'the most probable route for the battle cruisers will be from 53°36' N 05°15' E through 53°43' N 05°57' E to 54°00' N 06°04' E and thence along 54°00' N'.[68]

This information was issued after the *Scharnhorst*, the *Gneisenau* and the *Prinz Eugen* had been detected in the Channel. Except that PR on 11 February had shown that all the ships were again out of dock,[69] no last-minute intelligence of their departure had been received before they sailed at 2245 that day, nor was it till 1125 on 12 February, when they had already passed Boulogne, that 'news of the identification of the squadron was transmitted from Fighter Command to the Admiralty and all other authorities concerned'.[70]

The lack of current and near-current Enigma decrypts was not the least important reason why so much time elapsed before it was discovered that the ships had sailed. As luck would have it, the delays in breaking into the daily naval Enigma settings at this time were such that the traffic for 10, 11 and 12 February was not decrypted until 15 February, while – beyond the information about minesweeping in the Bight, which may have entered into the appreciation issued by Coastal Command on 8 February to the effect that the ships were likely to leave any time after 10 February – the Enigma traffic decrypted up to 10 February had contained no indications about the enemy's timing.[71] But in this situation it was all the more unfortunate that during the night of 11–12 February the plans that had been made for getting early warning by other means were dogged by a series of operational mishaps and failures.

On 6 February the Admiralty had given HMS *Sealion*, the only modern submarine available, 'discretion to penetrate inside Brest roads, to try to catch the German ships in the enclosed waters where they had been seen to carry out their trials and exercises'.[72] To assist her in this most dangerous patrol she was provided with

66.   Morgan, *NID History 1939–1942*, p 220.
67.   ibid, p 200.
68.   ibid, p 220, quoting Admiralty message 1229/12 February.
69.   Cmd 6775, para 102.
70.   ibid, para 23.
71.   ADM 223/92, OIC SI No 93 of 15 February.
72.   Cmd 6775, para 15; Roskill, op cit, Vol II, p 141; McLachlan, *Room 39* (1968), p 358; Beesly, *Very Special Intelligence* (1977), p 121.

information about the minefields and swept channels off Brest and with the details of the German exercise areas which the OIC had obtained from the Enigma.[73] On the afternoon tide on 11 February she had penetrated into the approaches to Brest, had seen nothing, and had withdrawn at 2035 to charge her batteries in preparation for renewing her attempt the next day.[74] Meanwhile, the German ships had been preparing to sail at 1930,[75] but their departure was delayed till 2245 by an RAF raid which was carried out when PR, the first that had been possible since 9 February, had disclosed that they were still in harbour, with torpedo booms still in position, at 1615.[76] But for their delay in sailing, they might well have been seen by the *Sealion*.

As it happened, they were missed not only by the *Sealion* but also by the three special night air patrols that were being flown by Coastal Command. The aircraft flying the earliest and most easterly of these patrols, that which covered the coast round Brest and was designed to detect the ships in whatever direction they sailed, reached the patrol area soon after 1900 on 11 February. At 1925 it signalled that its ASV was defective and returned to base. By 2238 its crew was back in the patrol area in a stand-by aircraft, and for some minutes early on 12 February the stand-by aircraft was in ASV range of the German ships. But the ASV registered no blips.[77]* The second patrol ran from Ushant towards Jersey. Its aircraft reached the line on schedule at 2015 on 11 February. But at 2055 it, too, reported that its ASV was not working; and, as the aircraft was not replaced, there was no patrol when the ships passed the line at 0050 on 12 February.[79]† The third patrol fared equally badly. Designed to cover the area from Le Havre to Boulogne up to daylight, it was terminated at 0613 on 12 February, about an hour before schedule, because of a fog forecast; the ships were then still to the westward of it.[81] There remained only the routine first-light patrol that was flown daily by Fighter Command

---

* The Board of Enquiry into the escape of the ships (the Bucknill Enquiry) concluded that they had passed by during the gap in the patrol. This has been shown to be incorrect, but no explanation has been found for the failure of the stand-by aircraft to detect the ships. Its ASV was in working order; but, as the Board of Enquiry recognised, ASV was known to be only 50 per cent reliable.[78]

† The break-down of this patrol was not reported to the naval authorities at Dover or to Fighter Command.[80]

73.   McLachlan, op cit, p 358.
74.   AIR 41/47 p 225; Cmd 6775, para 15; Beesly, op cit, p 122.
75.   Roskill, op cit, Vol II, p 154.
76.   AIR 41/47, pp 216, 221.
77.   ibid, p 222; Roskill, op cit Vol II, p 154; Richards, op cit, p 366 and fn.
78.   Cmd 6775, para 91.
79.   AIR 41/47, pp 222, 223; Cmd 6775, para 100.
80.   Roskill, op cit, Vol II, p 154.
81.   AIR 41/47, p 223; Richards, op cit, Vol I, p 366.

between Ostend and the mouth of the Somme, and the German ships were some distance west of the Somme when this patrol ended just before 1000 on 12 February.[82] To complete the tale, PR of Brest after daylight on 12 February was prevented by low cloud and a smoke screen from discovering whether or not the ships had sailed.[83]

There had been no alert since Coastal Command's appreciation of 8 February when, later in the morning, the first signs of enemy activity in the Channel were detected by British coastal radar stations. Between 0825 and 0959 they registered four plots of enemy aircraft circling in small areas just north of Le Havre.* The plots were of a type that was by no means uncommon, and it was not until about 1000 that No 11 Group, Fighter Command, realising that the areas being circled were moving north-east at a speed of 20 to 25 knots, decided to send two Spitfires to investigate. They took off at 1020.[84] By that time Fighter Command HQ had learned that enemy attempts to jam the coastal radar screen had begun at 0920 and that the radar station at Beachy Head was beginning to record indications of surface vessels, and at 1052 the stations in Kent reported 'two fairly large ships' off Le Touquet.[85] But when these developments were reported to No 11 Group and the naval authorities at Dover, just before 1100, the pilots of the two Spitfires were already being interrogated; having observed their routine instructions not to report by W/T, they had landed back at 1050, and the senior pilot was reporting that he had seen an escorted convoy of 20 to 30 ships and a group of E-boats. This information was rushed to No 11 Group and to Dover – where it arrived at 1105 – before the junior pilot added that he had also seen a vessel with a tripod mast and superstructure.[86] And before his interrogation could be completed, two other Spitfires, on a sweep that had no connection with operation *Fuller*, had returned to base at 1109 to announce that they had sighted the German squadron at 1042, 16 miles west of Le Touquet. It was their report, thus delayed by their observation of routine instructions not to break W/T silence, that Fighter Command transmitted to all concerned at 1125.[87]

All the attempts that were made to attack the ships during the

---

* It appears that similar activity was noted by an Army Y unit in training at Chertsey. Intercepting GAF traffic for practice, the unit claims to have detected small orbiting groups of aircraft going up-Channel and to have reported this to GHQ Home Forces to whom it was of no interest. The records of the RAF Y organisation make no reference to such intercepts.

82.   Cmd 6775, para 24; AIR 41/47, p 226.
83.   AIR 41/47, p 223.
84.   ibid, p 226; Cmd 6775, paras 25, 26.
85.   Cmd 6775, paras 27, 32; AIR 41/47, p 227; Richards, op cit, Vol 1, p 367.
86.   Cmd 6775, paras 28–30; ADM 186/803, BR 1736 (7) 48, p 7; AIR 41/47, p 227; Richards, op cit, Vol 1, p 367.
87.   Cmd 6775, paras 23, 30; ADM 186/803, p 7; AIR 41/47, pp 227–228.

rest of 12 February came to nothing. Although there were other reasons for their failure – the weather was foul and the available British forces were limited – it was mainly due to the lateness of the alert. The subsequent Board of Enquiry attributed this to two things in the first instance. It drew attention first to the neglect of the authorities to rectify some of the breakdowns in the night air patrols, and particularly to their omission to strengthen and extend Fighter Command's routine first-light patrol in the Channel after the night patrols had proved defective.[88] Secondly, it criticised the slowness of the authorities in taking action on the earliest indications that were received of the enemy's move – the circling plots registered by coastal radar, and the enemy's attempts to jam the coastal radar stations.[89] And by way of accounting for these shortcomings it emphasised that it had been 'the general opinion among those who were dealing with the problem . . . that the enemy's most probable course would be to try to pass through the Straits of Dover by night'.[90] In the Admiralty appreciation of 2 February this had indeed been assumed, though not specifically stated, and the same assumption had been made by AOC-in-C Coastal Command in his appreciation of 8 February,[91] though Coastal Command's detailed operational orders of 8 February had allowed for the possibility that the ships might attempt to pass the Straits by day.[92] As late as 10 February, moreover, as the Board of Enquiry discovered, some officers in the Admiralty were still leaning to this assumption,[93] and it was shared by Vice-Admiral Dover,[94] and it perhaps also influenced the timing of HMS *Sealion*'s movements on 11 February. But if this misjudgment 'influenced the arrangements made for the [air] patrols, both as to their design and application',[95] it does not sufficiently explain the slowness to act on the earliest indications that the enemy was on the move.

On the delay in investigating the first plots of circling aircraft, the Board of Enquiry commented that 'unfortunately No 11 (Fighter) Group . . . were not sufficiently alive to the fact that the German ships might be coming out at about this time'.[96] For similar reasons, while the operators at the coastal radar stations were quickly aware that an unusual situation was developing, there was delay in reporting and acting on their plots of ships.[97] It may be added that the two Spitfire pilots who ultimately identified the battle cruisers did not know that their move was thought to be

---

88.   Cmd 6775, paras 93, 98, 99, 134.
89.   ibid, paras 103, 104.   90.   ibid, paras 110, 132.
91.   AIR 41/47, p 215.
92.   Cmd 6775, Appendix IV.   93.   ibid, para 132.
94.   ADM 186/803, p 2; Roskill, op cit, Vol II, p 159.
95.   Cmd 6775, para 133.
96.   ibid, para 102.   97.   Beesly, op cit, p 122.

imminent,[98] and that, in circumstances that can scarcely have justified this, both they and the pilots who took off at 1020 to investigate the radar plots observed the routine instructions not to use W/T. In the light of these facts it may be concluded that, whatever circulation was given to the Admiralty and Coastal Command appreciations of 2 and 8 February – and how wide this was is not known – their contents did not filter down to 'many men in important positions – commanders of stations and squadrons – [who] knew only, as they had known for months, that the German vessels might try to put to sea, but not that there was special reason to believe that they would emerge between 10 and 15 February . . .'[99]

When all this has been said, however, it must be allowed that the German authorities had planned the operation meticulously, choosing ideal weather and sea conditions and making excellent use of the element of surprise; and it may be added that, even so, intelligence, and good liaison in making use of it on the British side, turned the successful transit of the Straits by German capital ships into a Pyrrhic victory. On the strength of the intelligence made available by the Admiralty about the minesweeping in the Bight, Bomber Command had laid 69 magnetic mines along the new swept way on 6 February and 25 more on 7 February.[100] On 11 February, when the route of the new channel was established more precisely, it had laid four more mines,[101] and further mines were laid on 12 February, when it was learned that the enemy was in the Straits.[102] On the evening of 12 February in the vicinity of these mines the two German battle cruisers were each mined once, the *Scharnhorst* being severely damaged, the *Gneisenau* less so, and both were thus prevented from joining the *Tirpitz* in Norway. The *Scharnhorst* had earlier hit another mine, in a position too far to the westward for that to be attributable to the recent minelaying, but the previous damage to her had been less serious.[103]

That both ships had been mined was soon established by the Enigma,[104] but the news was not published for some time: the temptation to release it, and mitigate the indignation that swept the United Kingdom, was resisted. It was not till much later that the Admiralty learned that on the night of 26–27 February, when she was in the floating dock at Kiel, the *Gneisenau* was further damaged

98.   Richards, op cit, Vol 1, p 367.
99.   ibid, p 375.
100. Morgan, op cit, p 220; AIR 41/47, p 213 fn.
101. AIR 41/47, p 213 fn.
102. Morgan, op cit, p 220; Beesly, op cit, p 119.
103. ADM 223/88, p 92.
104. Naval Headlines No 234 of 20 February 1942; Dir C/Archive 8815 of 22 February 1942.

by two heavy bombs in a Bomber Command raid. This attack, on top of the damage she had sustained in Brest and during the passage to Germany, left her needing a year under repair, and in January 1943, the month in which the *Scharnhorst* at last succeeded in making the passage from the Baltic to Norway, the *Gneisenau*'s refit was abandoned.

□

The German Naval Command assessed the move of the Brest ships through the Channel as 'a tactical victory, but a strategic defeat'. It recognised that by concentrating its ships, and that partly for defensive purposes, it was abandoning the threat from Brest to the Atlantic convoys that it had maintained for so long. During most of 1942, however, it continued to achieve tactical successes in Biscay and the Channel, getting blockade runners in and out of Biscay and sending auxiliary raiders to sea via the Channel, the only possible route since the middle of 1941.

Between April 1941 and May 1942, in the first instalment of an Axis programme of sailing German and Italian blockade runners between Japan and the Biscay ports, with scarce raw materials for Germany and machinery and machine tools for Japan, six ships got away from Biscay and twelve out of sixteen ships succeeded in reaching Biscay from the Far East. No advance warning had been received before the sailings began. Nor did intelligence about the blockade runners quickly improve after PR and the naval Enigma had established in June 1941 that one of them had reached Biscay[105] – in fact it was the second – and the SIS had reported in September 1941 that yet another had arrived.

The news of these arrivals prompted the establishment in October 1941 of a joint Admiralty/MEW committee to consider what could be done. Operationally it was agreed that Coastal Command's Biscay patrols against the U-boats and the Brest squadron should be diverted whenever a blockade runner was expected to be moving in or out of the area. On the intelligence side an effort was made to get advance warning of sailings from missions and naval reporting authorities in the Far East.[106] As it happened, however, the main source of information about the Axis plans turned out to be the Japanese diplomatic cypher traffic, and even when this gave the date of departure of a ship from Japan, which it did only on rare occasions,[107] that information was not a sufficiently precise basis for mounting special Biscay patrols. The naval

---

105.   ADM 223/94, OIC SI No 223 of 6 June 1942.
106.   AIR 41/47, p 534; Roskill, op cit, Vol II, p 183.
107.   ADM 223/99, OIC S No 222 of 21 January 1942.

Enigma evidence suffered from the same limitation with respect to inward-bound ships. Although it suggested from time to time that a movement through Biscay was being prepared, it only once revealed the position of a blockade runner on the high seas.[108] It was with assistance from the Enigma that the Coastal Command patrols sighted a blockade runner for the first time on 11 January 1942 and that the ship – the *Elsa Essberger* – was successfully attacked and driven to off-load her cargo in Ferrol,[109]* but the only other sighting of an inward-bound ship up to June 1942 was a chance sighting on 15 May.[111] The Enigma traffic more commonly gave warning that a ship was about to leave the Bay – for the blockade runners usually got U-boat or torpedo-boat escort on arriving at or departing from a Biscay port – and the OIC had some knowledge of the routes that the ships would take across Biscay. Almost always, however, the Enigma warnings came too late for action, as did PR and SIS warnings of impending departures.[112]

By June 1942 only three blockade runners had been sunk – two by routine naval patrols and, as the Enigma disclosed, one accidentally by a U-boat.[113] On the other hand, the intelligence sources were leaving no doubt that the ships were arriving in and getting away from Biscay regularly. As the OIC reported in June, 12 arrivals had been detected in the past twelve months, mainly by the naval Enigma or PR,[114] and six departures had been noted.[115] In the same month MEW expressed considerable anxiety about the success of the Axis programme. It calculated that in the first six months of the year nine blockade runners had reached the French ports carrying 60,000 to 65,000 tons of rubber and valuable supplies of tin, wolfram, hemp, hides, silk and vegetable oils, and that if the total were to reach 100,000 tons for the whole of 1942 Germany's essential needs in some of these commodities would have been met.[116] But despite the introduction of stricter measures

---

* This ship eventually reached Bordeaux despite the fact that a good deal of information about her was obtained from Sigint – and despite diplomatic pressure on Spain to stop her and her cargo.[110]

108. ibid, OIC S No 223 of 22 January 1942.
109. ibid, OIC S No 219 of 16 January 1942.
110. ibid; AIR 41/47, p 438.
111. AIR 41/47, p 439.
112. ADM 223/99, OIC S Nos 250 of 23 March, 259 of 11 April, 278 of 11 May, 285 of 18 May 1942; ADM 223/94, OIC SI No 223 of 6 June 1942.
113. AIR 41/47, p 436; ADM 223/99, OIC S No 229 of 2 February 1942.
114. ADM 223/94, OIC SI No 223 of 6 June 1942.
115. Roskill, op cit, Vol II, p 183.
116. FO 837/15, MEW Weekly Intelligence Reports Nos 18 and 20 of 20 and 30 June 1942.

by the Admiralty* the expanded blockade running programme launched by the enemy for the winter of 1942–1943 was not seriously interrupted until the middle of November. As we shall see, moreover, the Allies owed their first successes against it to a combination of good luck and increased operational activity; not until the end of 1942 did intelligence about the blockade runners undergo any marked improvement.†

Until the autumn of 1942 the same was true of intelligence about the passage of auxiliary raiders through the Channel. For a short period at the end of 1941, with the loss or the return to Germany of all the ships that had sailed in 1940, the Germans had no auxiliary cruiser at sea. In January 1942 a second series of cruises began with the departure from Biscay of the *Thor* (Raider E), the ship which had moved down the Channel during the previous month.‡ She was followed by the *Michel* (Raider H) in March and the *Stier* (Raider J) in May. Their movement down the Channel was disclosed by the Enigma, but attempts to intercept them failed.[118] In all three cases the Home Waters Enigma enabled the Admiralty only to give warning that they had left Biscay for their cruise.[119]

In October 1942, in contrast, with fuller Enigma intelligence to help them, strengthened British striking forces foiled the next German attempt to get such ships down the Channel. The Admiralty was able to warn the naval commands on 29 September 1942 that the *Komet* (Raider B) was about to leave Germany on a second cruise. As early as July the Enigma had revealed that she had completed her trials in the Baltic. In August she was photographed in Wilhelmshaven, and on 17 August PR established that she had left that port, but on 18 September the Enigma showed that she had been delayed by faults in her echo-sounding gear. On 2 October the Admiralty's warning was confirmed by an Enigma message announcing that she was to be employed on a further

---

* They included the preparation for RAF pilots by the CIU of photographs of likely blockade runners and of all neutral vessels that might be encountered in Biscay, and the request that the governments of Spain, Portugal and Eire should give notice of the movements north of 42°15′ N of all their ships over 2,500 tons.[117]

† See below, p 540 et seq.

‡ See above, p 166.

117.   AIR 41/47, pp 447–448.

118.   For the evidence on the *Michel* see ADM 223/109, Ultra signal 0555/11 March 1942. For that on the *Stier* see ADM 223/99, OIC SI Nos 196 and 199 of 18 and 20 May 1942. For the attempts to intercept these ships see Roskill, op cit, Vol II, pp 163–164 and AIR 41/47, p 251 and Appendix XVIII, p 7.

119.   ADM 223/109, Ultra signal 1030/17 January 1942 warned that the *Thor* was outward bound; ibid, Ultra signal 1237/23 March 1942 warned that the *Michel* had left on 20 March; ADM 223/111, Ultra signal 1642/22 May 1942 for the *Stier*.

cruise, and on 4 October another message reported her passage through the Kiel Canal.[120]

This was the last reference to her in the Enigma under her own name. But when auxiliary cruisers were moving through the Channel, and using the Home Waters Enigma settings, the German Naval Command had for some time past adopted the precaution of allotting them cover names. In November 1941, on completing her first cruise, the *Komet* (Raider B) had gone up the Channel disguised as *Sperrbrecher 52*. On 5 October 1942 *Sperrbrecher 12*, a minesweeper which was known from GC and CS's voluminous Enigma indexes to have been sunk some time before, was informed in the Enigma that mark-boats were being laid out for her off Flushing from the evening of 7 October. On the surmise that this information was addressed to the raider, the Admiralty issued it on 7 October, by which time it also knew that three torpedo-boats at Brest had moved to Le Havre.

Between 7 and 13 October, when the raider reached Le Havre, the Enigma was being read with a delay of 36 hours, and on the German side there were unexpected delays in the ship's nightly passages from port to port. For these reasons the earliest attempts to intercept her, one by destroyers on 10 October and one by aircraft on 12 October, were unsuccessful.[121] But on the night of 13–14 October, on passage from Le Havre to Cherbourg, the *Komet* was sunk by a force of motor torpedo boats and destroyers. They had been despatched on the assumption that she would be leaving Le Havre that night – the Enigma signal announcing her departure was not decyphered till the following night, but this assumption had been supported by Traffic Analysis. The destroyers worked with the additional advantage that, on the basis of many months of Enigma traffic, the Admiralty knew precisely the route the raider would follow.[122]

☐

The difficulty that the Germans were beginning to encounter when moving their auxiliary raiders through the Channel was not the only indication that the initiative in European coastal waters was beginning to pass from the Germans to the British during 1942. Since the spring of 1942 the British had carried out raids on German-occupied France and throughout the year, while German successes against British coastal shipping were steadily reduced, the British offensive against German coastal shipping no less steadily increased.

---

120. ADM 223/88, pp 193, 194.   121. ibid, pp 194–195.
122. ibid, pp 196–197; Roskill, op cit, Vol II, pp 256–257.

Raids were carried out against Bruneval in February,* against St Nazaire in March and against Dieppe in August.† The raid against St Nazaire, with the object of denying the use of its dock to the *Tirpitz*, was suggested by the NID in the autumn of 1941 and planned on the intelligence side in close collaboration between the intelligence staff of Combined Operations HQ, which was responsible for the operational planning, and several other bodies.[123] NID 1, with assistance from the ISTD, compiled the shore information, some of which came from detailed plans of St Nazaire provided by the SIS. Information about the dock itself was obtained overtly from pre-war technical journals. Other information about shore defences, including coastal artillery, was provided by MI, with whom another section of NID now worked so closely on these topics as to constitute an inter-Service organisation.‡ The OIC determined the approach route and the timing of the raid in the light of the Enigma intelligence about the enemy's swept channels and recognition signals and AI's knowledge of the GAF's routine patrols. The CIU supplied a special detailed interpretation of photographs of the area and also the model that was used in the training of the raiding force.[124]

In contrast to the mass of static information that the intelligence authorities put into the planning of the raid, no current intelligence became available during the operation, and it was not until the raid was almost over that the naval Enigma began to reveal some of the enemy's reactions to it.[125] In time the Enigma gave useful details about the defence measures introduced at other ports in consequence of the raid – though these did not include the fact that Hitler ordered Dönitz to withdraw to Paris the U-boat control room that had been set up at Lorient towards the end of 1940.[126] From other sources than the Enigma Whitehall received evidence of the damage done and confirmation that the operation had been successful. PR established the extent of the damage on the evening of 29 March,[127] further details came in from the SIS during the following month,[128] and in December 1942 the London Reception Centre, the inter-departmental refugee centre at Wandsworth, obtained a full and reliable account of the damage done by the raid, and of the panic it had caused, from a French mechanic.[129]

The raid on St Nazaire was followed during the remainder of

---

* See below, p 249.   † See Appendix 13.
‡ See Volume I, p 286 and below, Appendix 2.

123.   Morgan, op cit, p 54: Roskill, op cit, Vol II, p 168.
124.   Morgan, op cit, pp 53–54, 56, 247.
125.   ADM 223/93, OIC SI No 138 of 29 March 1942.
126.   Roskill, op cit, Vol II, p 173.
127.   AIR 41/47, pp 143, 274.
128.   Morgan, op cit, p 59.
129.   ibid, p 58.

1942 by a slow but steady reversal of fortunes in the war against coastal shipping. The German offensive against British coastal shipping, in the form of bombing raids by the GAF and of minelaying by the GAF and by E-boats, had been intensified during the spring of 1941* as part of the programme for stepping up the blockade of the United Kingdom, and the Germans had introduced more sophisticated mines, including a magnetic/acoustic mine.† By the end of 1941, however, British coastal shipping losses had begun to decline.[130] By the end of 1942, after a further cut-back in the German effort from September of that year, it was 'plain that a turning point in coastal warfare had been reached' and that, in particular, the menace of enemy minelaying had been 'overcome to a large extent'.[131] The period March–June 1941, on the other hand, had seen the beginning of the British offensive on Germany's coastal shipping,[132] and both in scale and in the results, particularly from minelaying by the RAF, this offensive grew steadily throughout 1942.

The decline in Germany's successes against coastal shipping was closely associated with the reduction of the forces she could spare. From June 1941 the GAF's previous unremitting assault on coastal shipping had given way to sporadic bombing raids and minelaying sorties, mainly at night, because so many of its units had been transferred to the Russian front. E-boat operations had been reduced from the same date, the flotillas being transferred to the Baltic. They returned in October 1941 to north German ports but subsequently had to be dispersed to Norway and Sicily as well as being used against the United Kingdom. The further slump in the GAF's successes during 1942 was similarly due to the fact that it was being stretched elsewhere; it ceased to mine off the west coast of the United Kingdom from February and from July the E-boats were laying more mines in United Kingdom waters than the GAF.[133] Hardly less important in bringing down the British losses was another operational factor – the fact that the British air and naval arrangements for shipping protection were steadily improved. But British intelligence was also improving and the part it played in assisting the British offensive was by no means negligible.

Against the GAF's raids Cheadle's exploitation of low-grade Sigint‡ continued to be the chief source. By the middle of 1941 this had already reached the point at which Cheadle could give

---

* See above, p 167.
† The first specimen of the magnetic/acoustic mine was recovered on 5 September 1941. See also below, p 288.
‡ Throughout this book the term 'low-grade' refers to the degree of security provided by a code or cypher and does not imply that the traffic in it was either unimportant or easy to break and interpret.

130.   BR 1736 (51) (IB); Roskill, op cit, Vol I, pp 330–332, 500.
131.   Roskill, op cit, Vol II, p 255.
132.   ibid, Vol I, pp 336, 502: AIR 41/47, p 97.   133.   BR 1736 (51) (IB).

several hours' warning of most GAF attacks,* and from that time, with the GAF making low-level and sporadic attacks which were difficult to detect by radar, the Sigint predictions became more valuable.[134] Nor did they lose their value when British low-scanning radar was eventually introduced, for they still helped to identify the radar plots as they had done for Fighter Command during the Battle of Britain.[135] Cheadle's techniques had by now been extended, moreover, to include that of using the GAF's MF navigational beacons to give notice that activity was to be expected from certain airfields or by certain units. Numerous raids were predicted by this method during 1942, in many cases an hour ahead of the radar alert. Fighter patrols flown with the convoys as a result of these warnings often deterred the GAF from making its attacks. The warnings were also useful in deflecting GAF mine-laying sorties against the east coast estuaries and in helping Bomber Command to carry out intruder operations against the GAF's minelayers.[136]

Another source of information, the interception and interpretation of German plain language and low-grade R/T signals on VHF, was useful both against the GAF and against the E-boats. This Y Service activity had been undertaken since 1940 by RAF and naval coast stations. From the spring of 1941 more coast stations were brought into service, R/T intercept staff called 'Headache' parties were installed in the destroyers of the Nore Command and communications were improved between the stations and the naval commands – and between the stations and GC and CS, which helped them in the work of interpretation. Until the middle of 1944 more and more ships were fitted with 'Headache' and the ship-borne Y-branch operations contributed to the saving of many ships for, although the use of radar was spreading, centimetric sets were not generally fitted in anti-E-boat ships before 1942 and Plan Position Indicators, whose panoramic displays eliminated the delay associated with compiling a plot, did not become available till 1944.

Unlike 'Headache', the Enigma could rarely give tactical warning of E-boat raids and could not supply up-to-the-minute intelligence during E-boat engagements. From October 1941, however, when the Germans re-established a force of 20 E-boats for operations in British coastal waters, the regular reading of the Enigma produced a large amount of information about the movements of this force between different bases, the routes the E-boats used on their sorties

---

* See below, p 241.

134. *Air Ministry Intelligence*, pp 80–81.
135. Roskill, op cit, Vol II, p 148: B Collier, *The Defence of the United Kingdom* (1957), p 316.
136. *Air Ministry Intelligence*, pp 81, 85: AIR 41/47, pp 561–562.

and the areas they had mined. This information did not always prevent the E-boats from achieving surprise with alterations in their areas of operation. In July 1942, in particular, despite warning from the Enigma that they were moving down to Cherbourg, the E-boats launched surprise attacks in Lyme Bay.[137] The Enigma contributed heavily, however, to the growing efficiency of Coastal Command and the naval defences, a process which forced the E-boats from the middle of 1942 to operate only at night.[138] Technical intelligence from the Enigma about enemy mines and minelaying was invaluable to the British minesweeping effort: it was channelled through the Admiralty's unindoctrinated Deputy Director of Torpedoes and Mining for whom special arrangements for passing the information were made.[139]

From the autumn of 1942 the naval Enigma was being used, as was 'Headache' and work done at Cheadle, less for defensive purposes than in support of the mounting British offensive against the enemy's coastal shipping. It had been of some value in the early stages of this offensive by enabling the Admiralty to do something to correct the greatly exaggerated successes claimed by the RAF for its raids on enemy shipping. In July 1941 an Anti-Shipping Operations Assessment Committee had been established, and this committee was advised by an inter-departmental Enemy Shipping Losses Assessment Committee (ESLAC) consisting of indoctrinated people who, under the chairmanship of ADIC at the OIC,* relied heavily on the naval Enigma in the scrutiny of the British claims. No great accuracy was at first attainable in this direction. In the period from March to the end of June 1941 Bomber Command had claimed to have sunk 104 ships and to have damaged 72. ESLAC reduced these claims to 31 ships sunk and 55 damaged; the actual figures were 7 sunk and 7 damaged.[140] Nor was the Enigma often of direct importance in guiding the RAF's bombing attacks on coastal shipping to their targets; for this purpose, though 'Headache' assisted, the most useful sources of information were air reconnaissance, coastal radar and the rapidly improving ability of the CIU to make operationally important deductions from its interpretation of the PR photographs.[141] But the regular reading of the Enigma was invaluable in providing the

---

* For the appointment of this assistant director to co-ordinate the action taken by NID on material provided by GC and CS see Volume I, p 274.

137. ADM 223/94, OIC SI No 227 of 9 June 1942; ADM 223/111, Ultra signals 1216/29 June, 1540/9 August, 1702/15 August; ADM 223/112, 1100/17 August 1942.
138. AIR 41/47, p 259
139. Roskill, op cit, Vol I, pp 498, 510; Vol II, p 254.
140. Roskill, op cit, Vol I, p 503; AIR 41/47, p 98(n).
141. AIR 41/47, p 120 and Appendix XVIII.

OIC with the framework into which it could fit the information obtained from these other sources – and also from captured documents and, particularly from Norway where reconnaissance was less complete, from SIS and SOE reports – and thus build up the virtually complete knowledge of the enemy's coastal shipping routines in the entire area from the North Cape to the Spanish frontier which in turn determined the RAF's reconnaissance programme.

The research on this subject, which was summarised in regular bulletins to the operational commands from the beginning of August 1941,[142] was co-ordinated in the OIC. It required an enormous effort, larger than that applied to any other problem not excluding the tracking of U-boats. It required, also, the collaboration of many other authorities. The country sections of NID, the heads of which were now aware of the existence of the Enigma traffic, supplied much of the information on ports, shore defences and enemy naval organisation. GC and CS specialised in working out those features for which the bulk of the information came from putting together the often esoteric evidence of the Enigma signals with that obtained from captured documents – the enemy's swept channels, minefields, navigational markings and patrol routines. There was continuous contact, also, between the OIC and the naval liaison officers at the air commands and the SO (1)'s and air liaison officers at the naval commands, and their close knowledge of enemy movements in their areas, derived from sightings, radar plots and British operations did much to fill out the picture.

From August 1941 the evidence began to show that the increasing British offensive was forcing the enemy to stop daylight sailings. By the autumn, although he could still pass ships through the Channel if he took great care, only a few strategically important ships were venturing south of Rotterdam. By November, on the other hand, improvements by the enemy to his defences between Rotterdam and the Elbe were forcing the RAF to reduce its offensive in that area, while in Norway and Biscay strikes against shipping, though increasing, remained on a restricted scale. At the end of the year, therefore, although the initiative in the war against coastal shipping had passed from Germany to Great Britain, the British air offensive was still obtaining only moderate results from its direct attacks. But the fact that the number of sorties had greatly exceeded the number of successful attacks strongly suggests that this was not for lack of intelligence about targets. Between April and December 1941 the RAF sank 42 merchant ships and damaged about 25.[143]

---

142.   ADM 223/92, OIC SI No 7 of 1 August 1941.
143.   Roskill, op cit, Vol I, p 507, Table 15.

During 1942, again mainly for operational reasons, the results obtained by direct attacks did not greatly improve. More of the RAF's maritime effort was now diverted against the U-boats; the enemy's shipping defences were still improving; torpedo aircraft were still in short supply. From June 1942 there was even a decline in the number of successful direct attacks because the German counter-measures forced Coastal Command to bomb from medium and high levels. In the whole of 1942, for these reasons, the RAF sank only 42 ships in 1,565 direct attacks.[144] But it was otherwise with the minelaying raids by Bomber Command, which formed another part of the RAF's maritime offensive. This activity grew in scale and effectiveness from the beginning of 1942: the Enigma fully disclosed the extent of its success and no source other than the Enigma could have done so.

From the end of 1940 Bomber Command had reduced the minelaying operations, mainly in the western Baltic, that it had carried out from time to time since the outbreak of war. Apart from preferring to use its long-range bombers against targets in Germany, it had not known that, as Germany was ill-supplied with minesweepers, minelaying had been a particularly effective form of attack on her shipping.[145] From the spring of 1941, however, as a result of the breaking of the naval Enigma, the Admiralty became so well informed about the enemy's shipping casualties from mining that it could begin to demonstrate how much more effective the minelaying was than direct attacks. By April 1942 the Enigma had revealed that all forms of minelaying had destroyed 191 enemy ships, of which 140 had been sunk by mines laid by the RAF. It was chiefly on this account that, after the end of 1941, at a time when the evidence was casting doubts on the effectiveness of its raids on Germany,* Bomber Command became more and more prepared to devote a part of its effort to minelaying.[146]

Because the effectiveness of the minelaying offensive depended on detailed knowledge of when and where the enemy's shipping was most vulnerable, the Admiralty's knowledge of shipping routines, exercise areas, swept ways, navigational arrangements and coastal defences, derived as we have shown from the Enigma – and in the Baltic more than elsewhere from captured documents and from the work of the Naval Attaché, Stockholm – was vitally important. From the summer of 1941 the amount of information on these subjects that the OIC sent to Bomber and Coastal Commands by special letter and telephone grew steadily, and much of it

---

* See below, p 261.

144. ibid, Vol II, p 260, Table 18, p 165, Table 12; AIR 41/47, p 281.
145. Roskill, op cit, Vol I, pp 334–337.
146. ibid, Vol I, p 510; ADM 223/107, Role of Special Intelligence in Bomber Command's Minelaying Campaign in the Baltic, p 2.

was the result of research on the voluminous naval Enigma traffic from minor war vessels and authorities mostly remote from the war's operational areas. Because it took time and patience, however, to build up this kind of intelligence, it was not until the middle of 1942 that a complete grasp of the situation was established.[147] As late as the spring of 1942, for example, the Admiralty did not realise that, partly because of the losses inflicted by the British and partly because of poor organisation and expanding demands, Germany's shortage of coastal shipping was reaching crisis proportions and requiring emergency measures.[148] There were also operational shortcomings to be dealt with before the minelaying campaign could be expanded. But by the beginning of 1942 the Admiralty was increasing the production of mines, Bomber Command was steadily replacing the single-mine-carrying Hampden with aircraft that could carry between two and six mines, and from the middle of the year the campaign got into its stride.

Its success is illustrated by the following figures:[149]

Period	Mines sown by Bomber and Coastal Commands	Enemy ships sunk by mine	Enemy ships damaged by mine
April–Dec 1941	1,150	35	39
Jan–July 1942	4,366	71	47
Aug–Dec 1942	5,345	93	64

A further indication of its effectiveness is the fact that during August–December 1942, while all other forms of attack on shipping caused the loss of only 20 ships in return for the loss of 197 aircraft, the minelaying during that period cost 93 aircraft.[150]

Thanks largely to the Enigma, the authorities in Whitehall had at the time a reasonably accurate knowledge of the enemy's casualties and of the extent to which they stemmed from the minelaying offensive. Not less important, they recognised increasingly clearly after the middle of 1942 that, as was indeed the case, the offensive was largely responsible for the fact that a shortage of shipping was handicapping the German war effort. Though MEW did not realise that the shortage had already reached crisis proportions, demanding emergency measures,[151] it detected signs of it in the first half of 1942, when it noted a falling off in the German–Swedish trade and the fact that Germany had been requisitioning Norwegian fishing vessels for cargo work.[152] By

147.   ADM 223/107, pp 2, 5, 20–21.
148.   Roskill, op cit, Vol II, p 359; AIR 41/47, pp 395–398.
149.   Naval Historical Branch, BR 1736 (56)(1), *British Mining Operations 1939–1945.*   150.   Roskill, op cit, Vol II, p 264, Table 20.
151.   ibid, p 259; AIR 41/47, pp 393–398.
152.   FO 837/15, Nos 9, 17 and 20 of 18 April, 13 June and 30 June 1942.

October it knew that the Germans had appointed a special Reichskommissar for shipping and that a serious 'operational shortage' existed.[153] At the end of the year it estimated that the Reichskommissar had done little to alleviate the shortage, which it attributed not only to a decline in shipping but also to shortage of officers and crews, the immobilisation of diesel ships by fuel shortage, and the diversion of shipping to meet Sweden's coal requirements.[154] In March 1943 it emphasised that by the end of 1942 the shipping situation in northern waters had 'deteriorated to the point where a shortage of serviceable shipping has become a limiting factor in the German supply programme'. In this report, moreover, while allowing that other causes were at work – an increasing demand by the enemy's armed forces for naval auxiliary vessels and a low rate of replacement and repair were now mentioned, as well as shortages of crews and of diesel fuel – it gave pride of place to the heavy losses brought about by the Allied anti-shipping offensive, especially to ships of between 3,000 and 8,000 tons, and stressed that there would be a progressive deterioration in Germany's shipping position if the offensive was maintained at the existing level.[155]

□

If the end of 1942 saw a distinct change to the disadvantage of Germany in the war in coastal waters, as the beginning of the year had seen with the withdrawal of the battle cruisers from Brest a reduction of the threat to Atlantic shipping, the intervening months had been marked not only by the serious deterioration in intelligence against the Atlantic U-boats to which we have already drawn attention,* but also by the rise of a new problem – the need to pass convoys to and from Russia's Arctic ports against increasing enemy opposition.

These convoys had begun in August 1941. Until the end of the year they had been run without interference from the enemy, using Archangel as their terminus. Thereafter, despite the freezing of the White Sea, they were able to continue by switching to Murmansk in the Kola inlet, the Germans having failed in their attempt to cut this off by land,† and they had lost only one merchant ship and one

---

* See above, pp 178–179.

† The work of the British and Russian submarines had made a considerable contribution to this failure by dislocating Germany's coastal shipping in north Norway and, although it had rarely been possible to predict the movement of this shipping, the British submarines had been greatly assisted by the fact that the OIC had excellent background intelligence from the naval Enigma about Germany's patrols, harbour installations, routes, escorts and other convoy arrangements.[156]

153.   FO 837/16, Nos 30 and 33 of 12 September and 3 October 1942.
154.   ibid, No 43 of 12 December 1942.
155.   FO 837/17, No 55 of 4 March 1943.
156.   ADM 223/92, OIC SI No 3 of 12 July 1941 and No 21 of 18 October 1941: Roskill, op cit, Vol I, pp 485, 495.

destroyer to U-boat attack up to the beginning of March 1942. By December 1941, on the other hand, the Germans had established a new command, Admiral Commanding Northern Waters, to be responsible for U-boat and surface ship operations in this area, and had decided to move U-boats and destroyers to the far north, as well as to reinforce the GAF there. And between then and the spring, as they came to realise the scale on which supplies were reaching Russia, and as their determination to interrupt the convoys supplemented the original reason for the decision to divert forces to Norway, which was the fact that Hitler's anxiety about a possible Allied descent on the Norwegian coast had been intensified by British commando raids in the Vestfjord and at Vaagsö* in December 1941, they built up a balanced force of surface units, U-boats and aircraft in the Norwegian theatre with the double purpose of attacking the shipping on the Arctic route and of defending Norway.

The GAF reinforcements – bombers and torpedo-bombers, backed by long-range reconnaissance aircraft – began to arrive in January 1942, when new air commands were set up at Stavanger and Kirkenes. In February a third new GAF command, *Flieger-führer Lofoten*, was given the dual role of defending Norway and working against the convoys. In the same month the number of U-boats allocated to the far north for anti-convoy operations was increased from three to nine, and six others were distributed between Narvik, Trondheim and Bergen for reconnaissance and defence against landings. In May all U-boats that had been diverted to the Norwegian theatre were transferred to the Arctic Command. On 23 February the *Scheer* and the *Prinz Eugen* joined the *Tirpitz*, which had reached Trondheim on 16 January. The *Hipper* joined them there on 21 March, and on 26 May the *Lützow* reached Narvik, to which area the *Scheer* had moved earlier in the month.[157]

Of these redispositions the British authorities were kept closely informed throughout. From the GAF Enigma and the low-grade GAF Sigint provided by Cheadle they had a detailed knowledge of all the changes that were taking place in the GAF order of battle; and of the more important of these changes – the various stages by which the GAF brought about the very considerable increase in its strength; its preparations for operations against naval units; its development of a torpedo-bomber force; the arrival of FW 200s at Trondheim for long-range reconnaissance in northern waters – they had notified the Home Fleet long before the Germans made their first air sighting of an Arctic convoy, PQ 12, on 5 March and

---

* Documents captured in the Vaagsö raid, as well as producing cryptanalytic material, provided full details of German coastal defences from Norway to France.

157. Roskill, op cit, Vol I, pp 492–3, 495; Vol II, pp 116, 118–119, 125, 130, 135.

their first air attack on one, PQ 13, on 27 March.[158] With the aid of
the naval Enigma they quickly detected the first important reinforcement of the U-boats in the Arctic in February, and were able
to keep track of the further increase in Arctic U-boats to 12 in
March and to estimate that the total number in Norwegian waters
was about 21 by August,[159] when the actual figure was 23.[160] From
the same source they received in advance warning of the transfers
of the main units of the German Fleet from the Baltic to Norway. It
was as a result of these warnings, aided occasionally by low-grade
Sigint indications, that, at a time of great shortage of long-range
reconnaissance aircraft and other demands on them, the Admiralty
laid on the special reconnaissance which sighted some of the ships.
These transfers alone presented possibilities for interference with
the German build-up. The failure to stop them showed how
difficult it was to turn the available intelligence to operational use.

As early as 12 February the Admiralty knew from the Enigma
that further large warships were to join the *Tirpitz* at Trondheim,[161]
and on the morning of 20 February it obtained indications from
Traffic Analysis that a naval movement from Germany had begun.
On the strength of this evidence a reconnaissance aircraft sighted
two large warships off Jutland at 1100 on that day. It was unable to
keep contact in bad weather, but from the evening of 21 February
detailed Enigma intelligence came in about the future movements
of the ships.[162] It was as a result of this information that the ships
were sighted twice on 22 February and, four submarines having
already been sent to patrol off Trondheim, one of them, HMS
Trident, torpedoed the *Prinz Eugen* on the morning of 23 February as
she and the *Scheer* approached that base. By the afternoon of 24
February the Admiralty knew from the Enigma that the *Prinz Eugen*
had been hit.[163] With this exception, however, it proved impossible
to intercept the main units while they were on passage to Norway.
One difficulty was that except for a brief period during January
1942, when it was read currently, the Enigma was still being read
with some delay.* Another was that, beginning with the transfer of
the *Tirpitz*, the ships in most cases avoided the more usual exit

---

* See above, p 163. By January 1942 delay had been reduced to an average of 32 hours
and from then on there were times when the material was current, or nearly so, but there
were other periods when it came to hand too late for operational purposes.

158.   ADM 223/109, Ultra signals 1904 and 2253/27 December 1941, 1051/5
       February, 2119 and 2234/10 February 1942; ADM 223/92, OIC SI Nos 79
       and 96 of 4 and 16 February 1942.
159.   ADM 223/92, OIC SI No 86 of 9 February 1942; ADM 223/94, OIC SI
       No 275 of 27 July and No 297 of 10 August 1942.
160.   AIR 41/47, Appendix II.   161.   CX/MSS/708/T7.
162.   ADM 223/109, Ultra signals 2211/21 February and 0059/22 February
       1942.
163.   ibid, 2312/18 February, 1010/20 February, 1654/24 February 1942; Roskill,
       op cit, Vol II, pp 118–119.

route through the Belts and the Kattegat and moved to Norway via the Kiel Canal and the North Sea. This was partly for security reasons: the German Naval Command, which had persuaded the Swedish authorities to keep a close watch on the movements of the British Naval Attaché in Stockholm after learning that the Admiralty had received a report of the *Bismarck*'s departure from the Baltic, had taken this additional precaution after the attack on the *Lützow* in June 1941 had given it further evidence of the speed and accuracy of the Admiralty's intelligence.[164] It had thus turned out that the Admiralty was able to warn that the *Tirpitz* had left Germany only on 17 January, the day after her arrival in Trondheim,[165]* though it had known from the Enigma since December that she was to be ready for operations by 10 January, and, the Enigma having shown that she had embarked neither an Admiral nor an intelligence detachment as the *Bismarck* had done, it had informed the Home Fleet from 7 January that it was unlikely that she would immediately try to break out into the Atlantic.[169] In the same way, all efforts to attack the *Hipper* came to nothing. Special reconnaissance was laid on when low-grade Sigint pointed to the possibility of an imminent naval move. But it was not until the early hours of 20 March that the Enigma confirmed that she was at sea and gave details of her route. She was sighted off Norway on the afternoon of the 20th.[170] In May the *Lützow* also escaped attack while moving to Norway, as did the *Prinz Eugen* during her return to the Baltic.

In the case of the *Lützow* the Admiralty was warned by the Naval Attaché, Stockholm on 13 May that she would probably be leaving the Baltic on 15 or 16 May bound for north Norway. On 14 May

---

* The *Tirpitz*'s working-up had been watched closely by the authorities in Whitehall since the destruction of the *Bismarck*. On estimates of her state depended the disposition of Britain's major units. Thus it was on the calculation that she would not be ready to break out from the Baltic before the *Duke of York* was ready in December 1941 that it was decided in October of that year to send the *Prince of Wales* to Singapore.[166] Sources of information included POW, the SIS and the Naval Attaché Stockholm, but the most important were PR and the Enigma. The Enigma revealed that the *Tirpitz* would be at sea in the east Baltic from the end of September 1941.[167] And in early November the Prime Minister was shown an analysis by GC and CS of an exercise in which, on her own, she had been confronted by greatly superior forces. It was concluded that this, and the fact that she was known from the Enigma to have been fitted with upper-deck torpedo tubes, reflected the experience of the loss of the *Bismarck*.[168]

164.   Roskill, op cit, Vol 1, pp 474–475.
165.   ADM 223/109, Ultra signals 0850, 1005 and 1519/17 January 1942.
166.   Churchill, *The Second World War*, Vol III (1950), pp 768–774.
167.   ADM 223/109, Ultra signal 1017/24 September 1941.
168.   Dir/C Archive 7954 of 3 November 1941, covering ZG/114 of 2 November.
169.   ADM 223/109, Ultra signals 1925/7 January and 1853/21 January; ADM 223/92, OIC SI Nos 38 of 17 December 1941 and 53 of 7 January 1942.
170.   ADM 223/109, Ultra signals 0047, 0134 and 0413/20 March 1942; AIR 41/47, p 303.

the Enigma confirmed that a warship was in the Great Belt, northward bound, and the Admiralty laid on air patrols which sighted the ship at 1100 on 16 May. But she reversed course on being sighted, and contact with her was not regained despite the fact that her change of course and her subsequent movements during her passage to Narvik were disclosed by the Enigma without much delay.[171] In the case of the *Prinz Eugen* the Enigma gave no advance warning, but PR reported on 16 May that her berth was empty and four of the W/T ship-watching stations which the SIS had now established in Norway reported her movements between Trondheim and Christiansand in time for the Admiralty to have her sighted by air reconnaissance and subjected to air attack.* The attack was unsuccessful.[172]

Once the German reinforcements, naval and air, had reached their bases in Norway they presented a formidable threat to the Arctic convoys, and in its efforts to use intelligence against this threat the Admiralty again encountered grave difficulties in a strategic situation in which the advantages were all on the German side, so much so that the Arctic convoys would have been suspended but for the fact that powerful political considerations demanded their continuation. These difficulties were particularly severe when it came to protecting the convoys against the GAF and the danger of sorties by the German battleships.

Against the U-boats in the Arctic the Admiralty could not practise evasive routeing to anything like the extent that it could in the Atlantic: the room for manoeuvre was heavily restricted and little deviation from the convoy routes was possible. As against that, the forces supporting the convoys were invariably commanded by Flag Officers and to them, as Ultra recipients, the Admiralty relayed a constant supply of Enigma in addition to other intelligence. Other factors played their part in limiting the success of the U-boats – the persistence and the efficiency with which the escorts took the offensive against them; the fact that the U-boat Command did not use its most experienced commanders on the Arctic route; the fact, which emerged unmistakably from the Enigma, that Admiral Commanding Northern Waters operated the U-boats much less efficiently than the U-boat Command operated the

---

* The SIS was unable to establish an agent in the vicinity of the fleet anchorage in Trondheim itself before the summer of 1942 and it did not succeed in installing one in Altenfjord until the autumn of 1943.

171. ADM 223/111. Ultra signals 2016/14 May, 1724 and 2105/16 May, 0134/17 May, 1039/18 May, 0130/19 May, 0745/25 May; AIR 41/47, p 309.
172. ADM 223/111, Ultra signal 1055/19 May; ADM 223/99, OIC S No 198 of 19 May; AIR 41/47, p 311.

Atlantic U-boats.[173] But the intelligence thus sent out, primarily the Enigma, provided the support forces with a comprehensive and precise account of the number of U-boats on patrol, their movements and dispositions and their operational reports throughout the passage of the convoys, and it may be assumed that this was not the least reason why the U-boats did comparatively little damage except when they were exploiting the disorganisation imposed on the convoys by GAF attacks or the fear of raids by the main units.*

The GAF, which in fact accomplished most of the damage, presented a problem to which intelligence could contribute much less. For all their intimate knowledge of the enemy's order of battle in the Arctic area, the authorities in the United Kingdom were seldom able to warn the convoys in advance that an attack was coming. The evidence for the details of impending attacks, as of the patrols and sighting reports of the enemy's reconnaissance aircraft, was provided mainly by the GAF's low-grade W/T traffic. Not all of this could be intercepted in the United Kingdom; inferences from the considerable amount that was intercepted there could not often be relayed in time. To overcome these difficulties the NID and AI developed a system by which parties of so-called 'computers' from Cheadle accompanied the Home Fleet's cruiser admirals who commanded the close support for the convoys. These parties received via the Admiralty details about the GAF's frequencies, call-signs and daily-changing low-grade codes. With this assistance, and given their understanding of the GAF's signals procedure, they were able to provide the convoy escorts with a fairly good picture of the enemy's reconnaissance activity, and they could sometimes predict an attack twenty minutes ahead of radar. But this system was not introduced until May 1942 – the parties sailed for the first time with PQ 16 – and by then the scale of the GAF's effort had so much increased that tactical intelligence, however good, was of little avail. Against PQ 16 the GAF deployed 129 attack aircraft and 72 assorted reconnaissance aircraft, and it made 230 bomber sorties and 42 torpedo bomber attacks.[174] Against PQ 18 in September 1942 it made an even bigger effort – the biggest, indeed, against any Arctic convoy, for in November the bulk of its Arctic squadrons were to be moved to the Mediterranean – and PQ 18 lost 13 out of 40 ships, most of them to GAF attack.

For nine weeks before the sailing of PQ 18 the Arctic convoys were suspended. In part the result of the diversion of Home Fleet

* Between 21 August 1941 and 30 December 1942 306 merchant ships sailed to Russia of which 53 were lost, 36 to aircraft and 17 to U-boats. In the return convoys the total was 227 ships, of which 17 were lost, 2 to aircraft, 8 to U-boats, 2 to surface attack and 4 merchant ships and an escort in a British minefield off Iceland.

173.   ADM 223/93, OIC SI No 141 of 30 March 1942.
174.   ADM 223/94, OIC SI Nos 236 of 15 June, 237 of 18 June 1942.

forces to the Mediterranean, the suspension was also accepted because of the difficulty of defending the convoys against air attack and because the problem of dealing with the menace from the German surface fleet had proved unmanageable during the sailing of PQ 17. This problem had first arisen at the end of February with the arrival at Trondheim of the *Scheer*, the *Prinz Eugen* and enough destroyers to provide a screen for the *Tirpitz*. Moreover the Enigma had disclosed at that time that the German Admiral Commanding Battleships, who had not accompanied the *Tirpitz* when she sailed in January, had now embarked.[175] Accordingly, distant cover by battleship and aircraft carrier was provided for the convoys for the first time when PQ 12 and QP 8 sailed on 1 March, the two convoys were sailed simultaneously to maximise the protection and Coastal Command flew special patrols off Trondheim.

At that point there was no certainty either that the enemy would move his surface ships or that, if he did, he would move them against the convoys. Partly because the C-in-C Home Fleet was unable to rule out the possibility of an enemy breakthrough to the Atlantic, partly because he was anxious to husband the Home Fleet's resources against the time when the Trondheim squadron might be reinforced by the *Scharnhorst* and the *Gneisenau*,[176] and partly for a reason not mentioned in his report of proceedings – his wish to remain in telephone contact with such intelligence as the OIC would acquire – he would have preferred to keep the *King George V* and the *Victorious* at Scapa while the remainder of the battle fleet supported the convoys. But on 3 March he was over-ruled by the Admiralty, which accepted responsibility for any breakout into the Atlantic, and at 1030 on 6 March he joined the rest of the fleet in the area east of Jan Mayen, south of PQ 12's route. At about 1100 on 6 March the *Tirpitz* sailed from Trondheim with three destroyers for the same area, an FW 200 having sighted PQ 12 at mid-day on 5 March.

Up to 6 March, as well as learning from the convoy that it had been sighted by the GAF,[177] the C-in-C had received several items of intelligence from the OIC. Three Ultra signals had told him that 17 U-boats were either in the Norwegian area or on passage to it, but that no details were available about their patrol areas.[178] He had been given an estimate of the numbers and types of GAF aircraft at Norwegian bases which contained the reassurance that there was no threat from torpedo aircraft.[179] He had learned that

---

175.   ADM 223/93, OIC SI No 110 of 3 March 1942.
176.   Naval Historical Branch, BR 1736 (44), *Arctic Convoys 1941–1945*, p 6.
177.   ADM 199/347, HMS *Kenya* telegram 1326/5 March 1942.
178.   ADM 223/109, Ultra signals 1748/2 March, 1152/4 March and 2015/5 March 1942.
179.   ibid, Ultra signal 1951/2 March 1942.

PR of Trondheim had found all three German ships in their usual position at 1230 on 4 March and that the Naval Attaché Stockholm had confirmed PR evidence that the *Prinz Eugen* was heavily damaged.[180] On 5 March, however, PR of Trondheim had failed on account of bad weather; and on 6 March, when it failed again, the extra seaward patrol that had been arranged was not flown 'apparently for lack of aircraft'.[181] Nor was it till midnight on 6–7 March that the C-in-C learned that HM submarine *Seawolf* had sighted a battleship or a cruiser leaving Trondheim by the northern exit at 1801 that day[182] – though he had earlier received from the OIC a warning that W/T traffic at Trondheim was heavy and (apparently on the basis of DF evidence) that a surface unit might be west of that port.[183]

The C-in-C judged that the *Seawolf* had sighted the *Tirpitz* and that the *Tirpitz*'s objective was convoy PQ 12. Before leaving Scapa he had agreed with the OIC that, if she sailed, she would give priority to PQ 12; furthermore, he personally believed that her motive was 'defensive and based on the possibility of convoy PQ 12 containing a military force bound for north Norway'.[184] He accordingly set course for a position from which the *Victorious* could fly and search south of the convoy at 1000 on 7 March. Unfortunately – for the planned search would have straddled the *Tirpitz* and her destroyers at a time when the Home Fleet was within a hundred miles of her and steering on a converging course[185] – icing made flying impossible; and at 1130 on 7 March the C-in-C turned south-west. He made this decision in the hope of finding weather more suitable for flying and from the wish to move his forces into waters where they would be less vulnerable to chance torpedo hits.[186] When he made it he believed that the convoy would be comparatively safe in the low visibility,[187] and he had received no intelligence about the enemy since the previous midnight.

The C-in-C kept on his new course until the intelligence picture changed. It was not changed when the Enigma, which was being decrypted with a delay of between 16 and 24 hours, told him in the afternoon that the *Tirpitz* had been informed on the evening of 6 March that GAF reconnaissance for the convoy on the morning of 7 March would concentrate south of Bear Island but would also

---

180.   ADM 199/347, Admiralty signals 1618/4 March and 1223/5 March 1942.
181.   BR 1736 (44), p 8.
182.   ADM 199/347, Admiralty signal 2350/6 March 1942. (*Seawolf's* 1940/6 March was not received by the C-in-C).
183.   ibid, Admiralty signal 2027/6 March 1942, C-inC Home Fleet's Report of Proceedings, 13 March 1942, para 6.
184.   ADM 199/347, C-in-C's Report, para 7.
185.   ibid, para 12; BR 1736 (44), p 13; Roskill, op cit, Vol II, p 121.
186.   ADM 199/347, C-in-C's Report, para 7; BR 1736 (44), pp 12–13.
187.   ADM 199/347, C-in-C's Report, para 7; BR 1736 (44), p 12.

include an area off the Norwegian coast as far south as Trondheim;[188] this last detail did, however, strengthen the C-in-C's belief that the *Tirpitz* was on an anti-invasion sortie.[189] But at 1632 the flagship intercepted a distress message from a ship belonging to convoy QP 8, the position of which was ambiguous as received in the flagship, and this was followed at 1640 by the interception of a lengthy German transmission on which the flagship's DF bearing pointed to a position in the estimated area of PQ 12. At this the C-in-C, thinking it 'probable that if this bearing was of the *Tirpitz*, who I am convinced was highly nervous of being in such waters, she would consider her presence compromised and would return immediately to her base', ordered six destroyers to act on this assumption and attempt to intercept her while he proceeded north-eastwards with the battle fleet in case the *Tirpitz* continued to look for PQ 12.[190]

The transmission of 1640 had in fact been made by a U-boat; and had the C-in-C's staff been familiar with the enemy's W/T procedure they would have know that, if the *Tirpitz* were to transmit at all, she would do so only in short signals – a precaution of which she had been reminded in Enigma instructions of 6 March which, however, did not reach the Admiralty till 1707 on 7 March. But further Enigma intelligence, reaching the C-in-C before the Home Fleet's destroyers were detached, led him to cancel their sweep and confirmed, and perhaps even prompted, his decision to take the fleet to the north-east, the course he finally shaped at 1923.[191] In an Ultra signal from the Admiralty, timed 1518, he was told that the *Tirpitz* had indeed left Trondheim on 6 March 'to operate against the convoy' accompanied by three destroyers, and that at 2000 on 6 March the enemy had been unaware that the Home Fleet was at sea.[192] At the same time, in a general signal timed 1519, the Admiralty warned the convoy that enemy forces might be in its vicinity and instructed it to steer an evasive course.[193] A second Ultra signal, timed 1652, reproduced orders sent to eight U-boats on 6 March, disclosed that five of them were not to attack west of the meridian of North Cape (thus indicating that the area in which the *Tirpitz* might operate extended to the east of Bear Island) and revealed that the German destroyers were to be prepared to oil at sea (thus indicating that the *Tirpitz* might remain at sea for some time).[194] A third Ultra signal, timed 1934,

---

188. ADM 223/109, Ultra signal 1350/7 March 1942.
189. ADM 199/347, C-in-C's Report, para 7.
190. ibid, para 9.
191. BR 1736 (44), p 14.
192. ADM 223/109, Ultra signal 1518/7 March 1942.
193. BR 1736 (44), p 9 (n); L Kennedy, *Menace* (1979), p 40.
194.   ADM 223/109, Ultra signal 1652/7 March 1942.

also indicated that on 6 March the *Tirpitz* might operate east of the meridian of North Cape.[195]

Before receiving this last signal – and not long after he had turned north-east – the C-in-C again changed his plans when, at 1940 on 7 March, the flagship intercepted another enemy transmission. The C-in-C's report of proceedings shows that his staff now piled upon the belief that the first transmission might have been made by the *Tirpitz* the assumption that the second transmission had come from the same unit: 'at 1940, however, another DF bearing from the same unit showed that she was moving south at high speed'.[196] This was an unwarranted assumption; it was rarely possible to tell whether or not signals had come from the same transmitter. The OIC was aware that this was the case and, having the benefit of GC and CS's familiarity with German naval W/T procedure, it had not associated the first transmission with the *Tirpitz*. At the same time, not thinking that the flagship would place more weight on the German transmissions than it did itself, it did not signal any comment on them to the C-in-C. The result was that the C-in-C returned to his initial appreciation that the *Tirpitz* would be anxious to return to base. He accordingly detached his destroyers to intercept her on her way back to Norway, while he himself 'awaited' Admiralty confirmation of the identity of the ship whose signals had been DFd, 'and then, at midnight, having heard nothing', turned the battle fleet south so as to be within air striking range if the *Tirpitz* was intercepted by the destroyers.[197]

But for the flagship's mistaken assumption about the second German transmission – like the first, it was a signal from a U-boat – it is improbable that the C-in-C would have taken these decisions. And but for a further intelligence mishap it is conceivable that he might have retrieved the situation during 8 March. At 0400 that day, having heard nothing from his destroyers, he concluded that the *Tirpitz* had eluded them, and being unprepared to operate close to U-boats without a screen, he turned away towards Iceland to collect destroyers.[198] At that time the *Tirpitz* was 250 miles NE of the Fleet and 90 miles SE of PQ 12, from which position she searched for the convoy south and west of Bear Island throughout the day,[199] but the C-in-C had received only one item of Enigma intelligence since the early evening of 7 March: in a signal timed 0057 on 8 March the Admiralty had informed him that on the evening of 7 March the Enigma had revealed that the Germans had had no further sighting reports and still did not suspect that the Home Fleet was at sea.[200] At 0656 and at 1225,

195.   ibid, Ultra signal 1934/7 March 1942.
196.   ADM 199/347; C-in-C's Report, para 10.   197.   ibid, para 10.
198.   ibid, para 11.   199.   BR 1736 (44), pp 15–16.
200.   ADM 223/109, Ultra signal 0057/8 March 1942.

however, the OIC sent the C-in-C the contents of two further Enigma decrypts. The first gave the areas which the GAF would reconnoitre during 8 March: Bear Island–North Cape; the sea area between Norway; the Home Fleet's bases. The second reported that British W/T was still normal.[201] In themselves these signals threw no positive light on the *Tirpitz*; but the OIC omitted to notify the C-in-C that they were based on decrypts of signals issued by Gruppe Nord to the German Admiral Commanding Battleships – decrypts which thus gave unmistakable indications that at the time of their despatch, in the early hours of 8 March, the *Tirpitz* had not abandoned the search for the convoy.

It is not unreasonable to conclude that the C-in-C would have turned back at once if the OIC had not omitted this evidence; he was to do so as soon as he received firmer intelligence. On the other hand, it is difficult to decide how to account for the OIC's omission. Unaware that the C-in-C had concluded that the *Tirpitz* had broken off – for the Fleet had been keeping wireless silence and had failed in its efforts to contact the Admiralty by Special W/T (SWT)* – and thinking that he was still in hot pursuit, it may have taken it for granted that he would understand that the decrypts had been addressed to the *Tirpitz*. Alternatively, it may itself have missed the significance of that fact, for it had had no previous experience in handling Enigma intelligence in the course of a complicated operation.

Whatever the explanation, the confusion was cleared up in the afternoon of 8 March. At that point the Enigma, which, as luck would have it, had defied early decryption since the Home Fleet had put to sea, began to be broken so nearly currently that, for the first time in the war during an important operation involving surface ships, the OIC received the decrypts within two or three hours of their German time of origin. In a signal timed 1500 it informed the C-in-C that at 1116 Admiral Commanding Battleships had been instructed to return to Trondheim if the *Tirpitz* had not found the convoy by nightfall on 9 March, and that at 1233 he had been advised that British W/T was still considered to be normal.[202] At 1820, on receipt of this signal, the C-in-C, then 300 miles to the south-east, hauled round to make for the Bear Island area; and at 1830, after fruitlessly trying to contact the Admiralty by SWT during the past two days, he broke wireless silence to announce his position and his intentions and, so that he could

---

* SWT procedure used special frequencies, dispensed with call-signs and disguised the transmission in such a way as to make it difficult to identify them as British naval messages. It was used only by the Home Fleet.

201.   ibid, Ultra signals 0656 and 1225/8 March 1942.
202.   ibid, 1500/8 March 1942

avoid further signalling, to ask the Admiralty to operate the cruisers and destroyers of the Home Fleet.

While the C-in-C continued on his new course the OIC warned him that the enemy's U-boats had been ordered to attack surface forces south-east of Jan Mayen.[203] It also notified him in a signal timed 2331 on 8 March that the *Tirpitz* would rendezvous with her destroyers at 0700 on 9 March halfway between Bear Island and North Cape and would search westward from there along the converse of the convoy's estimated route.[204] At 0137 on 9 March, however, the Admiralty signalled him the bare instruction: 'Steer 120° maximum speed'. It had received at 0102 the decrypt of a message timed 2232 on 8 March in which Gruppe Nord had repeated back to the *Tirpitz*, by way of acknowledgment, the contents of a short signal from her timed 2025. The contents themselves were sent to the C-in-C in an Ultra signal timed 0148: she had cancelled her intended operation for 9 March and would now rendezvous with destroyers off the Lofoten Islands at 0700 9 March.[205] The Home Fleet altered course for the Lofoten Islands at 0242. In a signal timed 0248 it was informed that the *Tirpitz* would pass 65°38′ N, 10°52′ E at 1300 en route for Trondheim, this being the contents of a decrypt timed 2336 on 8 March which the OIC had received at 0212.[206]

The Fleet was then 200 miles to the westward but it was able to make up enough ground for aircraft from the *Victorious* to sight the *Tirpitz* at 0800 and attack her at 0917. The attack was unsuccessful, and on the morning of 10 March the Enigma divulged that on the previous evening the *Tirpitz* had put in at Narvik and would return to Trondheim when conditions were favourable. Attempts were made to intercept her with destroyers and submarines on her way to Trondheim; but the weather was so thick that her departure from Narvik was delayed until the early hours of 13 March by which time, to make things more difficult, GC and CS had ceased to decypher the Enigma currently. It did not disclose that she had left Narvik until many hours after the event. Nor was it till 18 March that a Coastal Command reconnaissance aircraft located her at Trondheim.[207]

Against the next convoys – PQ 13 and QP 9, which sailed on 20 and 21 March – the Germans deployed ten U-boats, the GAF and

203.   ibid, Ultra signal 1658/8 March 1942.
204.   ibid, Ultra signal 2331/8 March 1942.
205.   ibid, Ultra signal 0148/9 March. The file copy of the signal bears a
        pencilled note to the effect that the time of origin on the original draft was
        0118/9 March 1942.   206.   DEFE 3/88, ZTPG 37257.
207.   ADM 223/109, Ultra signals 0640, 0825, 0920 and 1250/10 March,
        1122/11 March, 0005/14 March 1942; ADM 223/93, OIC SI No 117 of 12
        March 1942; BR 1736 (44), p 19; Roskill, opcit, Vol II, p 123.

three destroyers. The Admiralty was able from the Enigma to provide the support forces with details of the U-boat patrol areas, to warn them to expect the GAF and destroyer attacks and to advise them that the GAF had sighted PQ 13 on the morning of 27 March. About the destroyers the Enigma supplied considerable advance information,[208] their movement to Kirkenes on 26 March, notice of their intention to attack, and indications of where their attack was to be expected all being relayed to the support force of PQ 13 well before the encounter on 29 March in which the support force, led by the cruiser *Trinidad*, sank one enemy destroyer and damaged the other two, in exchange for damage to herself and the loss of one merchant ship.[209] PQ 13 was the first of the convoys to suffer appreciable losses – two ships sunk by aircraft, two by U-boats and one by destroyers – but the ships sunk were either stragglers or had been scattered by a gale, and were thus unable to benefit from the intelligence sent to the support forces.[210] Not less important, the Enigma provided the Admiralty with negative evidence that none of the larger enemy ships had moved north with the destroyers,[211] and subsequent negative evidence – the absence in the Enigma decrypts of signals to the main units or of reference to main units in the signals to the U-boats and the destroyers – was accepted as a reliable guide throughout the operation.

In this last respect, as in the fact that it provided the support forces with a stream of information about the current strength and dispositions of the U-boats and the GAF, about the GAF's sightings of the convoys, and about the movements and intentions of the destroyers in the north, the pattern of the intelligence sent out during the passage of PQ 13 was repeated for the next few convoys. On two occasions during the passage of PQ 14 and QP 10 in the middle of April the Admiralty assured the Home Fleet that there was no evidence that the enemy's main units were at sea.[212] At the end of April the Home Fleet was alerted in the early stages of the passage of PQ 15 and QP 11, in response to Enigma evidence that the GAF had brought some units to one hour's notice for anti-shipping attacks. Although it soon emerged that the enemy's state of readiness was in part associated with an anti-invasion scare in the Lofoten area,[213]* the convoys were duly subjected to air

---

* Since October 1941 either the naval or air Enigma had disclosed several such German alerts; one on 21 April 1942 brought the *Tirpitz* and the *Hipper* to short notice.[214]

208. ADM 223/110, Ultra signals 2325/26 March, 0020, 1645, 1826 and 2148/27 March 1942.

209. Roskill, op cit, Vol II, pp 126–127.   210. BR 1736 (44), p 32.

211. ADM 223/110, Ultra signal 0020/27 March 1942.

212. ibid, Ultra signals 0506/13 April, 2357/14 April 1942.

213. ibid, Ultra signal 1635/30 April 1942.

214. ADM 223/109, Ultra signals 1540/19 October 1941, 0250/ February 1942; ADM 223/111. Ultra signal 1553/21 April 1942.

attack without further warning. In addition, on 1 May, QP 11 was attacked by three German destroyers which sank one merchant vessel and the cruiser *Edinburgh*, previously damaged by a U-boat. The Admiralty was able to warn the Flag Officer Commanding 18 Cruiser Squadron (CS 18) in the *Edinburgh* at 1420 on 1 May that the destroyers had sailed from Kirkenes at 0100 that day with orders to operate against the cruiser; this warning, reaching CS 18 soon after the destroyers began their attack on the convoy, probably underlay the instructions he issued to his own escorting destroyers on the assumption that the enemy would shift his attention to the *Edinburgh*. The *Edinburgh* was sunk on 2 May, but – as the Admiralty at once learned from the Enigma – she and her destroyers sank one of the German destroyers and damaged the other two.[215]

With every subsequent convoy operation the convoys themselves were increased in size, the days lengthened, and the strain of watching for any sign of movement by the large German ships steadily mounted. After the arrival of PQ 15 the movement of the *Scheer* from Trondheim to Narvik, which was revealed in the Enigma on 10 and 11 May and checked by PR the next day, added considerably to the strain and delayed the sailing of PQ 16 from 16 to 21 May.[216] The movement more than offset the fact, which had also been established by the Enigma, that the threat from German destroyers had been greatly reduced in the engagement with the *Edinburgh*. In addition, the Enigma disclosed that Admiral Northern Waters had moved his HQ to Narvik[217] and that the Kirkenes U-boats had been transferred to Narvik, a move which led the OIC to believe that the Germans aimed to bring a bigger weight of attack against the Russia-bound convoys at an earlier stage in their passage.[218] By the end of April, moreover, the Enigma had established that the *Tirpitz* had escaped damage during Bomber Command's latest attempt to put her out of action: the Enigma decrypt reporting on the raid that was carried out against her on 27 April described the attack as 'most courageous' but said that there was no damage to the ship, smoke having provided the best possible protection.[219] It was perhaps with these developments in mind that on 18 May the First Sea Lord reiterated that the passage

---

215.   ADM 223/110, Ultra signals 1402/1 May, 2105/2 May 1942; BR 1736 (44), p 40; Roskill, op cit, Vol II, pp 129–130.

216.   ADM 223/111, Ultra signals 2248/10 May, 0126/11 May 1942; AIR 41/47, pp 310–311.

217.   ADM 223/99, OIC S No 283 of 16 May 1942.

218.   ADM 223/93, OIC SI No 195 of 18 May 1942.

219.   ADM 223/110, Ultra signal 0011/29 April 1942; DEFE 3/96, ZTPG 45822.

of the Arctic convoys was 'a most unsound operation, with the dice loaded against us in every direction',[220] and that on 23 May, when the Admiralty replied to an enquiry from the C-in-C Home Fleet as to the extent to which he could expect to receive intelligence from the Enigma during the next few days, it warned him that 'it is not usually possible to forecast when source will recommence' and that 'movements of German units are not certain to be detected by this source'.

On the same day the Admiralty was able to tell the Home Fleet that the *Scheer* and her four destroyers had been put at short notice on 21 May.[221] On the evening of 25 May the Enigma reported that the *Lützow* would reach Narvik on the following day.[222] But in the event, although PQ 16 was subjected between 25 and 28 May to intensive attack by U-boats and the GAF, the GAF again doing most of the damage, the *Scheer* and the *Lützow* made no move against it. On 28 May, moreover, when the battered convoy was approaching Bear Island, the Enigma revealed that the *Tirpitz* would be exercising at Trondheim between 28 and 30 May.[223] The inactivity of the main units probably resulted from Hitler's insistence that the Navy should not risk a serious reverse, an insistence which had led him to instruct Admiral Raeder that the heavy ships must not be used against a convoy unless the whereabouts of the British aircraft carriers had previously been established. It was the need to adjust to these instructions, which made it unlikely that the ships could otherwise sail in time to attack the convoys, that took Raeder to Trondheim at the end of May to work out with Admiral Commanding Battleships a plan for sending the ships to temporary bases in the extreme north as soon as the next Russia-bound convoy was known to have sailed, and for using all of them against it only after it had passed 20° E.[224]

Of Hitler's prohibition and the German Navy's reaction to it the Admiralty learned nothing from the Enigma beyond the fact that Raeder visited Trondheim on 31 May.[225] On 18 June, however, it received from the Naval Attaché Stockholm an account of how the Germans planned to attack the next Arctic convoy with U-boats, air forces and two groups of surface ships.[226]* It was thus with

---

* This was the first information obtained from a source subsequently graded A 2 by the Admiralty (Enigma was graded A 1) via the Naval Attaché Stockholm. He had succeeded at this point in obtaining via the Deputy Chief of the Swedish Combined Intelligence Staff decrypts of German operational orders passing from Berlin to the German naval commands in Norway by land-line,[227] presumably in the Fish cypher (see above, p 29).

220.   Roskill, op cit, Vol II, p 130.
221.   ADM 223/111, Ultra signal 1759/23 May 1942.
222.   ibid, Ultra signal 2030/25 May 1942.
223.   ibid, Ultra signal 1135/28 May 1942.
224.   Roskill, op cit, Vol II, pp 135–137.
225.   ADM 223/99, OIC S No 297 of 3 June 1942.
226.   Morgan, op cit, pp 80, 81.   227.   ibid, pp 73–82.

every expectation that the German surface ships would intervene, and with considerable foreboding, that the Admiralty made its preparations for the sailing of the next convoy, PQ 17. It gave orders that the cruiser covering force should not proceed east of Bear Island unless it was clear that the convoy was threatened by an enemy force which did not include the battleship; and in a last-minute telephone discussion with the C-in-C the First Sea Lord told him that the Admiralty might order the convoy to scatter if it appeared to be in imminent danger of attack from the enemy's surface fleet.[228] By this time 13 Allied submarines had been deployed to cover the exits from the north Norwegian bases and the approaches to the convoy route to counter the enemy's surface forces and, in an attempt to improve the chances of detecting the enemy's warship movements, arrangements had been made for RAF Catalinas to land at Russian bases after patrolling off north Norway and to work from them for a time before returning to the United Kingdom.[229]

□

When PQ 17 sailed on 27 June 1942 the Enigma intelligence about the strengths and dispositions of the U-boats and the GAF's forces was, as usual, excellent, and it included details of the arrangements made by the GAF for finding and shadowing the convoy and numerous German reports of the position of the ice-edge.[230] In view of the British intention to route the convoy as far to the northward as possible, the latter were a valuable guide to enemy expectations even though British reconnaissance was to show that the ice-edge was much further north than they had indicated. As for the German surface ships, the Home Fleet had recently been informed that there was no evidence from the Enigma that the *Tirpitz* had left Trondheim.[231] It was now told that, while 'from negative information' it was 'probable' that the *Scheer* and the *Lützow* were still at Narvik, nevertheless the fact that the GAF was preparing some special operation was 'probably concerned with movements of main units'.[232] Late on 30 June the Admiralty sent the C-in-C and the cruiser admirals a further negative report: 'it appears from negative information that there was no movement of a main unit on the Norwegian coast on 27, 28 and 29 June'.[233] On the afternoon of

228.   Roskill, op cit, Vol II, pp 135–136.
229.   ibid, p 133; BR 1736 (44), p 54.
230.   ADM 223/111, Ultra signals 1557/27 June, 1605/28 June, 1215/29 June 1942.
231.   ibid, Ultra signal 1044/17 June 1942.
232.   ibid, Ultra signal 1657/28 June 1942.
233.   ibid, Ultra signal 2316/30 June 1942.

1 July they were informed that it was known that the Germans expected the convoy to be passing Jan Mayen at about that time, but that 'on negative evidence it would appear that there had been no movement of main units and no sighting of PQ convoy up to 1200 on 1st July'.[234] The C-in-C was fully aware of the basis of these negative reports. On 28 June he had asked to be kept informed 'of times at which current Special Intelligence becomes available'.[235]* Thereafter the Admiralty sent him regular messages telling him when the OIC expected the Enigma to be broken, when the Enigma had been broken and, from time to time, when the OIC had completed the study of the latest period of decrypts.†

At 1432 on 1 July the GAF's sighting report of PQ 17 was intercepted in the United Kingdom, and at 1900 the Admiralty relayed the news to all ships. On 2 July it added to this two items of Enigma intelligence for the Ultra recipients. At 1313 it warned them that the GAF had ordered a torpedo-bomber attack for 2100.[236]‡ At 2349 it informed them that there were 'no direct indications of movements of enemy main units', but drew their attention to the possible significance of the fact that the GAF had placed its coastal fighters on the alert and had flown reconnaissance patrols during 2 July in an effort to locate the C-in-C's heavy covering forces.[237] During 3 July, however, the intelligence issued to them by the Admiralty established that two German fleet movements had taken place earlier that day, and left little doubt that one was the transfer of the *Scheer* to a base north of Narvik and the other the movement of the *Tirpitz* and the *Hipper* from Trondheim northwards up the coast. That the *Scheer's* northern base was probably Altenfjord was known to the Admiralty from the fact that the Enigma had revealed in June that nets were to be laid out there and by a report from the Naval Attaché Stockholm, also in June, that two major warships were expected there.[238] Although the Enigma indicated that the *Lützow* was not in company with the *Scheer*, it did not disclose until 8 July that she had remained in the Narvik area, where she had run aground and become non-operational. During 4 July the Admiralty accordingly had to

* For an earlier exchange on this subject see above, p 213. 'Special Intelligence' was a term used by the Admiralty, and to a lesser extent other authorities, when referring to Ultra, ie to the results of high-grade cryptanalysis.
† See Appendix 11 for the Ultra signals sent out by the Admiralty during the passage of PQ 17.
‡ In fact the GAF brought the time of this attack forward to 1800 and it took place before the Home Fleet could receive the revised warning.

234. ibid, Ultra signals 1326, 1550 and 1719/1 July 1942.
235. ibid, C-in-C Home Fleet to Admiralty 1912/28 June 1942.
236. ibid, Ultra signal 1313/2 July 1942.
237. ibid, Ultra signal 2349/2 July 1942.
238. ADM 223/99, OIC S No 300 of 7 June 1942.

assume that she, too, would be available.[239] As for the *Tirpitz* and the *Hipper*, it had not been possible for air reconnaissance to throw any light on their whereabouts.[240]

The information about the movements of 3 July derived from the fact that GC and CS was reading the Enigma traffic for the period 1200 on 1 July to 1200 on 3 July from about 0500 on 3 July.* In the Arctic theatre at this time the Enigma settings were changed daily at noon and, as we have already explained,† the settings of the second pair of days were usually broken within a few hours once the settings of the first day of the pair had been broken. The Enigma traffic for the first of the next pair of days – that for the period from 1200 on 3 July to 1200 on 4 July – was broken at 1837 on 4 July, after a long delay during 3 and 4 July, and the decrypts began to reach the OIC about 1900. This unreadability gap, stretching from 1200 on 3 July to 1900 on 4 July, was made all the more agonising by the fact that an accident had interrupted the air reconnaissance patrols off North Cape between 1100 and 1700 on 4 July.[241] While it lasted, apart from reporting that the GAF had sighted PQ 17 at 0726 and again at 1630 on 4 July,[242] the OIC sent only two items of intelligence to the C-in-C Home Fleet. One at 0250 on 4 July suggested that a sequence of German naval transmissions, transmitted at hourly intervals since 1407 on 3 July, might remain indecypherable when the Enigma was next broken and 'may indicate the commencement of a special operation by main units',‡ and the other, at 1145, confirmed the move of the *Scheer* to Altenfjord. At 1203, however, the Admiralty gave the Flag Officer

---

* At the beginning of July 1942 the shortages of Bombes at GC and CS necessitated difficult decisions about priority as between PQ 17 and the fighting in the Western Desert which had become critical after Rommel's Gazala offensive. After consultation with Whitehall, highest priority was given to the Home Waters traffic in view of the threat to PQ 17.

† See above, p 163 fn*.

‡ This surmise was based on the decrypt of a signal from the *Scheer* timed 1158 on 3 July in which she reported to Naval Communications Office Narvik that she had been unable to decypher two recent signals on the Kootwyk frequency, and on the fact that the signals had also proved to be indecypherable at GC and CS.[243] The signals differed from signals using the Offizier settings; in these the originator and the recipient and a statement that an Offizier message followed were encyphered in the ordinary Enigma setting. They may have been indecypherable either because of an error on the part of the W/T operator or because they were encyphered in a new four-wheel Enigma key that was coming into use for communication between Flag Officers during fleet operations. Named Barracuda at GC and CS and Neptun by the Germany Navy, there is some evidence that this key, which was rarely used and never broken, was made available to the Fleet in time for the intended operation against PQ 17. But apart from the two received on the morning of 3 July no indecypherable signals were received at GC and CS during that operation.

239.   ADM 223/111, Ultra signals 1754/3 July, 1311/8 July 1942.
240.   AIR 41/47, pp 328–329.
241.   Roskill, op cit, Vol II, p 139; AIR 41/47, p 329.
242.   ADM 223/111, Ultra signals 1720 and 1806/4 July 1942.
243.   DEFE 3/110, ZTPG 59645, teleprinted to the OIC at 0001/4 July 1942.

Commanding First Cruiser Squadron (CS 1) discretion to continue east of the limit of 25° E 'should the situation demand it'. The C-in-C, having received no intelligence to account for this change of plan, at once qualified the Admiralty's instruction by ordering CS 1 to leave the Barents Sea when the convoy was east of 25° E, or earlier at his discretion, unless the Admiralty assured him that the *Tirpitz* 'cannot be met'. At 1800 CS 1 announced his intention of withdrawing at 2200. But at 1930, having heard that the Enigma for the period to noon on 4 July had been broken, the Admiralty signalled him to this effect: 'Further information may be available shortly. Remain with convoy pending further instructions'.[244]

When GC and CS reported that it had broken the Enigma for the 24 hours up to noon on 4 July the First Sea Lord was visiting the OIC with the Assistant Chief of Naval Operations and the Director of Operations Division (Home). The first of the OIC's signals conveying to the Home Fleet the intelligence derived from the latest decrypts was despatched after some discussion between them, the DDIC – the head of the OIC – and Commander Denning, the officer responsible under DDIC for appreciations about the German surface fleet.* As despatched at 1918 it announced that the *Tirpitz* had arrived at Altenfjord at 0900 that morning and that her destroyers and torpedo-boats had been ordered to refuel at once; it added that the *Scheer* was also at Altenfjord and that at 1622 on 3 July two U-boats had been ordered to shadow the convoy.[247]† Denning recollected that he had wanted to add the comment that all the indications suggested that the *Tirpitz* was still in Altenfjord, that after some argument the comment was deleted before the signal was sent and that Admiral

---

* There is no contemporary record of these exchanges. The only participant who left a written account of them was the late Vice-Admiral Sir Norman Denning; by courtesy of his executors, the reconstruction which follows makes use of his personal testimony.[245] One unofficial account has been published,[246] but it appears to be only a garbled version of Vice-Admiral Denning's recollections.

It states that when the First Sea Lord asked whether he could be assured that the *Tirpitz* was still in Altenfjord, Denning replied: 'No. I shall have firm indications only when the *Tirpitz* has left'. It claims that the First Sea Lord put a further question, 'Can you at least tell me whether the *Tirpitz* is ready to go to sea?' and was told that 'she would not leave within the next few hours'. Apart from the internal inconsistency of the first of these reported replies and the implausibility of the second of the reported questions, such answers could not have been given at the time of the meeting, as we shall see, and this version of them probably represents that part of Vice-Admiral Denning's argument in which he said he was confident that in the next few hours decrypts of the Enigma for the period since noon on 4 July would confirm his view that the *Tirpitz* had not yet sailed.

† See Appendix 11 for the text of this and subsequent Admiralty Ultra signals.

244. Roskill, op cit, Vol II, p 138.
245. A copy of Vice-Admiral Denning's account is preserved in the archives of Churchill College, Cambridge under reference ROSK 5/72.
246. McLachlan, op cit, p 286.
247. DEFE 3/110, ZTPG 59870.

Pound then asked him why he thought the *Tirpitz* had not yet sailed. He recollected that he gave the following reasons. He was convinced that in view of her experience while operating against PQ 12 the Germans would not allow her to sail until they had satisfied themselves that she would not be in danger from the Home Fleet, particularly its aircraft carriers. Another newly arrived Enigma decrypt had disclosed that at 0015 on 4 July a German aircraft had sighted CS 1's force and reported that it included a battleship,[248] and together with the fact that there was no evidence that the GAF had sighted the Home Fleet since 1 July, this led him to believe that the enemy could not disregard the possibility that CS 1's force might be a major force. Up to noon the Enigma had provided no decrypt ordering the U-boats to keep clear of the convoy, and he thought that transmissions by the U-boats since noon, though as yet unreadable, showed that they were still in contact with it. Finally, he argued, other German naval W/T traffic since noon had exhibited none of the characteristics normally associated with the presence of surface ships at sea, and no sighting reports had been received from British and Russian submarines on patrol off the North Cape.* According to Denning, the First Sea Lord reflected on all this and then asked, as he left, 'Can you assure me that the *Tirpitz* is still in Altenfjord?' and Denning replied that, although he could not give an absolute assurance, he was confident that she was, and expected that his opinion would be confirmed when, in the fairly near future, GC and CS broke the Enigma for the 24 hours beginning at noon.

In the event GC and CS broke the Enigma for this period almost immediately; the decrypts began to reach the OIC at 2000. But it had provided no new positive intelligence bearing on the First Sea Lord's questions by the time the DDIC left to attend a staff meeting which the First Sea Lord had called for 2030. One new decrypt, which Denning remembered showing to the DDIC as he was leaving, did indeed virtually prove that the *Tirpitz* had not sailed by noon. Timed 1130 on 4 July but not received in the OIC until 2031,[250] it was summarised in an Ultra signal timed 2110; it had informed the U-boats that no German surface ships were then in their operational area and that the British heavy ships were to be the main target for the U-boats when they encountered them. But. this intelligence did not change the situation; the assumption had already been made that the *Tirpitz*'s destroyers and torpedo-boats

---

* As we have seen the SIS had no agent inside Altenfjord before August 1942 and it was not until November 1943 that one of its agents was able to penetrate the closely-guarded area of of the fleet anchorage.[249] At the time of PQ 17 there was an agent between the mouth of the fjord and North Cape but he was able to report only intermittently and could not be counted on.

248.   ibid, ZTPG 59868.   249.   McLachlan, op cit, pp 40–41.
250.   DEFE 3/110, ZTPG 59910.

would not have completed refuelling until about noon. As for the decrypts transmitted since noon, one had established that a U-boat had sighted CS 1's force at 1327, reporting it as 'heavy enemy forces'[251]; another at 1458 had ordered this U-boat to shadow 'the battleship formation' and had repeated that the other U-boats were to attack the heavy ships; but the third had disclosed that the GAF had correctly reported at 1455 that CS 1's force consisted of four heavy cruisers with destroyers.[252] Ultra signals summarising these decrypts were sent to the C-in-C Home Fleet and CS 1 at 2108 and 2110, in the DDIC's absence. Otherwise, the Naval Section at GC and CS, which shared Denning's judgment, could support it only with the strong negative evidence that in the latest decrypts there was as yet no reference to the German ships, no Offizier signals and no indecypherable messages. It had notified the OIC at 1837, 1839 and 1931 on 4 July that C-in-C Fleet had sent Offizier signals to Gruppe Nord in Berlin timed 1758, 1802 and 2247 on 3 July;[253] and later on the evening of 4 July it was to report that on the afternoon of 3 July three Offizier signals had been transmitted from Admiral Commanding Northern Waters to C-in-C Fleet and one Offizier signal from a U-boat to Admiral Commanding Northern Waters.[254] But it had identified no Offizier signals and encountered no indecypherable transmissions in the traffic intercepted since *Tirpitz*'s arrival at Altenfjord.

On the strength of this intelligence the DDIC either could not prevail against the decisions reached at the staff meeting or did not feel that he could counsel against them. He returned to the OIC about 2130 to report that the meeting had decided that it must be assumed that the *Tirpitz* had sailed; that for this reason, and on account of the threat from U-boats, CS 1 should be ordered to withdraw; and that since the German surface ships could reach it at 0200 on 5 July if they had sailed as soon as the destroyers and torpedo-boats had refuelled, the convoy should be scattered. Nor did he have any success when he was persuaded to go back to the First Sea Lord to say that the OIC still wished to advise the Home Fleet that it believed not only that the *Tirpitz* had not sailed by noon, but also that she had not yet done so, and would not until the Germans had established the location and strength of the forces supporting the convoy. In the absence of positive evidence that the enemy had not sailed since noon, the First Sea Lord would not approve such a signal or countermand the recent decisions. The Admiralty's orders were despatched at 2136 on 4 July.*

---

* There is no contemporary record of the proceedings at the staff meeting, and for the DDIC's report on it and for his return to the First Sea Lord we again rely on Vice-Admiral Denning's testimony.

251. ibid, ZTPG 59895. 252. ibid, ZTPG 59896.
253. ibid, ZTPG 59863, 59864, 59876.
254. ibid, ZTPG 59925, 59930, 59935, 59938.

It was indeed the case that positive evidence that the *Tirpitz* had not sailed was lacking when the orders went out. Although the Enigma had just become current, and although GC and CS was giving priority to decrypting the most recent transmissions, the decrypts had not yet fulfilled Denning's expectation that they would confirm his appreciation. More than that, the negative evidence was subject to serious and growing reservations. The latest decrypt bearing on the problem was that of the signal transmitted at 1458; and given the necessary presumption that the ships in Altenfjord had been ready to sail by about noon, the absence of reference to them in decrypts since 1458 was having to contend with the anxiety that every next decrypt might disclose that they were at sea. It was because delays and uncertainties of this kind had been experienced with the Enigma on earlier occasions that the OIC had warned the C-in-C Home Fleet on 23 May that 'movements of German units are not certain to be detected by this source'.* As for the arguments on which Denning had based his appreciation, it was not the OIC's practice to accept that, particularly in the Arctic where 100 per cent interception of signals could not be guaranteed, the presence at sea of surface ships could be disproved by the behaviour of undecyphered wireless traffic, or by the lack of sighting reports by Allied forces, unless there was supporting evidence; and the other evidence on which Denning had relied was losing its force with the passage of time. It was by no means clear since the receipt of the decrypt timed 1455 that the Germans were confusing CS 1's force with the Home Fleet, the more so as British heavy ships had never been sent as far to the east as the position in which CS 1 had been first sighted; DF fixes on the U-boat transmissions were too few and too inaccurate to prove that the U-boats had not yet been ordered out of the convoy's vicinity. While it would be wrong to suggest that the First Sea Lord and his staff recognised the force of all these reservations, it is easy to see why Denning's appreciation fell short of their demand for conclusive evidence; and it is easy to see why they demanded conclusive evidence. They had to consider what would happen if the convoy was not scattered, if the supporting force were not withdrawn, and if the *Tirpitz*, the *Hipper*, the *Scheer* (and, for all they knew, the *Lützow*) and their seven destroyers had indeed already sailed.

At the same time, the operational authorities had to recognise that the convoy would in any case suffer heavily if it was scattered – it in fact lost 14 out of its 37 ships to air attack and 10 to U-boats, of which 8 or 9 were known to have kept almost continuous contact with it since 1 July[255] – and this makes it tempting to argue that,

---

* See above, p 213.

255. ADM 223/94, OIC SI No 257 of 6 July 1942.

instead of setting aside the OIC's appreciation, they might at least have deferred their decision pending the receipt of further decrypts, in the same way as they had earlier instructed CS 1 to remain with the convoy pending further information. But apart from the consideration that delay had come to seem hazardous once the Enigma had disclosed that the *Tirpitz* had reached Altenfjord and that her destroyers were to refuel at once, deferment would not have enabled them to get the convoy safely to its destination. In appreciating that the enemy's ships had not sailed by the evening of 4 July Denning was right, and right for the right reasons; but they sailed the next day after a calculated delay.

The scattering of the convoy was followed by a continuing lack of reference in the decrypts to the German surface ships. This strengthened the belief that they had not yet sailed, and it explains why at 0238 on 5 July, at about the time previously calculated to be the earliest at which the *Tirpitz* could reach the convoy, the DDIC at last authorised a signal advising the Home Fleet that 'it is not known if German heavy forces have sailed from Altenfjord, but they are unlikely to have done so before 1200/4th'. The signal also said, as Denning had earlier argued, that the enemy might be uncertain whether a battleship was in company with CS 1 and did not appear to know the whereabouts of the Home Fleet; and these were indeed the reasons why the German ships had not yet sailed. In view of the limitations that Hitler had imposed on the use of the German ships,* Raeder had ordered the *Tirpitz* and the *Hipper* to Vestfjord and the *Scheer* and the *Lützow* to Altenfjord as soon as he knew that the convoy had sailed, and hoped to get permission to send them to sea as soon as the Home Fleet had been located. During the night of 3–4 July, the GAF having failed to sight the Home Fleet on 3 July, he had moved the *Tirpitz* and the *Hipper* to Altenfjord to join the *Scheer*, and he kept the whole force ready to sail until Hitler's permission came. It came in the forenoon of 5 July. The *Tirpitz*, the *Hipper* and the *Scheer* began to leave Altenfjord with 7 destroyers and 2 torpedo-boats between 1100 and 1130, with the intention of attacking convoy PQ 17 on the morning of 6 July.[256] And at 1145, fifteen minutes before the Enigma settings changed again at noon and brought about another temporary intelligence blackout, the *Tirpitz* reported that she would be ready at Rolvsöysund, one of the exit routes from Altenfjord, at 1430. The decrypt of her signal was relayed to the Home Fleet at 1517. The German squadron was sighted by a Russian submarine at 1700 and by an aircraft at 1816, and at 2029, steering an easterly course off the North Cape, 300 miles from where the convoy had scattered, it was sighted by a British submarine.[257]

---

* See above, p 213.

256.   Roskill, op cit, Vol II, pp 138, 142.
257.   ibid, p 142 and map 13; AIR 41/47, p 329.

The enemy's sortie finally confirmed the accuracy of Denning's judgment during the previous evening that the ships had not sailed at the time the decision was taken to withdraw CS 1 and scatter the convoy. It does not justify the conclusion that the operational authorities in the Admiralty could have saved the convoy if they had accepted the judgment. This conclusion requires us to believe that the enemy would have gone on confusing CS 1 with the Home Fleet, and would thus not have sailed his ships at all if CS 1 had not been withdrawn. But aside from the fact that the GAF had correctly identified CS 1's force as consisting of 4 cruisers as early as the afternoon of 4 July, the enemy waited until the GAF had also sighted the Home Fleet, as it did at 0700 on 5 July, some 500 miles from the scattered convoy. And we have to recognise that in the Arctic conditions of nearly total daylight it is unlikely that the German authorities would have failed to establish that the Home Fleet was in no position to interfere with their delayed attack. If the First Sea Lord had been convinced by Denning's appreciation on the evening of 4 July he could have made use of the breathing space to order the convoy to reverse course with its covering force and fall back towards the Home Fleet until the situation was clearer. But if the appreciation had persuaded him to allow the convoy to proceed, he would have had no choice but to order it to scatter on 5 July when the Enigma reported that the *Tirpitz* was about to leave Altenfjord.

At 2219 on 5 July the German ships were recalled; it subsequently emerged that they were ordered to do so when the enemy realised the extent of the damage that was being inflicted on the ships of the scattered convoy by U-boats and the GAF.[258] Since the Enigma for the period from noon on 5 July to noon on 6 July was not broken until the morning of 6 July, the Admiralty's signal to the Fleet announcing that the Germans had called off their operation was not sent until 1317 on 6 July. The ships were sighted at Altenfjord at 1045 on 7 July,* and although attempts were made to intercept them with submarines, they reached Narvik without incident at 0200 on 8 July – as the Enigma, readable once again, disclosed

---

* This was the first occasion on which a PRU Mosquito flew to Vaenga, in Arctic Russia, refuelled and returned to the United Kingdom.[259] After this the Soviet authorities were persuaded to allow a detachment of the PRU to operate Spitfires from Vaenga. Arriving in September 1942, the Spitfires carried out a number of successful sorties before the end of October, when the weather deteriorated. The detachment was then withdrawn, but it handed over its Spitfires, cameras and equipment to the Russian Air Force. During its stay it discussed PR techniques with the Russians and was allowed to examine Russian photographs of the area. Though limited in scope, these exchanges interested AI and MI in the possibility of future collaboration against enemy-held positions in Norway, and further PR detachments were to be sent to the area in September 1943 and March 1944.[260]

258.   ADM 223/111, Ultra signal 1317/6 July 1942.
259.   AIR 41/47, p 330.   260.   AIR 41/7, p 102.

within a few hours.[261] Later on 8 July the Enigma indicated that one or more warships might be leaving Narvik for the south.[262] It was not until 13 July, however, that it confirmed that the *Lützow* had moved to Trondheim during the night of 9–10 July. But the same day it threw some light on the damage that had prevented her from taking part in the operation against PQ 17 and established that 3 destroyers had also grounded in the Narvik area on 3 July.[263]

□

In the interval before the sailing of the next convoy to Russia on 2 September the Germans withdrew the *Lützow* to Germany and sent the 6-inch cruiser *Köln* from the Baltic to Trondheim. As with most of the enemy's movements along the Norwegian coast earlier in 1942, it proved impossible to interfere with these transfers, but intelligence – chiefly the naval Enigma and NA Stockholm's A 2 source – gave advance warning of them and confirmed with little or no delay that they had taken place. In the case of the *Lützow* the Enigma indicated that she would probably go right through to the Baltic by giving details of fighter preparations both south and north of Trondheim, and her departure from Narvik was reported by an agent and confirmed by Coastal Command. But the attempts to sight her on passage came to nothing.[264] Of the extraordinary operation *Wunderland*, carried out in the Kara Sea by the *Scheer* between 16 and 29 August in search of a large Russian convoy reported to be approaching through the Arctic ice from the east, the Admiralty was kept fully informed by the Enigma but could not intervene.[265] Against another enemy operation, however, it was able to turn intelligence to practical use. On 10 August it learned from the Enigma that the minelayer *Ulm* was approaching Narvik from the south. On 25 August the Enigma gave details of the area off the north-west coast of Novaya Zemlya in which the *Ulm* was to lay her mines and of the route she was to take. On the strength of this information the Admiralty ordered the US cruiser *Tuscaloosa* to detach along a given course the three British destroyers which were

---

261.   ADM 223/111. Ultra signal 0508/8 July 1942.
262.   ibid, Ultra signal 1805/8 July 1942.
263.   ibid, Ultra signal 1850/13 July 1942.
264.   For the *Köln* see ADM 223/111, Ultra signal 1542/14 July 1942 and ADM 223/100, OIC S No 330 of 15 July 1942. For the *Lützow* ADM 223/111, Ultra signals [TOO illegible] of 23 July, 2222/6 August, 2135/8 August and 1452/10 August 1942; Roskill, op cit, Vol II, p 277. See also AIR 41/48, *The RAF in Maritime War*, Vol IV, p 346 and A R Wells, *Studies in British Naval Intelligence 1880–1945*, p 235 (1972, unpublished thesis, University of London).
265.   ADM 223/112, Ultra signals 1423/17 August, 1010/30 August 1942; Morgan, op cit, p 81.

accompanying her; as a result the *Ulm* was sunk that night.[266] This was one of the rare occasions on which orders based on Ultra intelligence were sent to ships not privy to the Ultra secret.

The sinking of the *Ulm* greatly reduced the threat of large-scale mining to the Arctic route. At the beginning of October the Enigma showed that the Germans had been reduced to using the *Hipper* for minelaying off Novaya Zemlya – though it failed to give advance warning of her sortie, and NA Stockholm's A 2 report that she had left on a short cruise on 24 September did not reach the Admiralty until 27 September.[267] Until the end of September, however, these two sources left no doubt that the Germans had every intention of repeating against the next convoy the combined attack by surface ships, U-boats and aircraft that they had planned against PQ 17. On 1 August they warned their U-boats, of which 20 had already been disposed on the assumption that the next Russia-bound convoy would sail soon, to expect co-operation from surface ships.[268] On 5 August, on receiving from one of the U-boats a false sighting of a convoy, they sailed the *Köln* from Trondheim to join the *Tirpitz*, the *Hipper* and the *Scheer* in the Narvik area and ordered the transfer of an additional Gruppe of Ju 88 torpedo-bombers (up to 30 aircraft) to north Norway. The GAF Enigma gave advance notice of the move of the aircraft and reported their arrival;[269] but for all that it was as usual giving the fullest details about the dispositions of the U-boats, and advance general notice of the enemy's plans, the performance of the naval Enigma in relation to the movement of the *Köln* was a reminder, if any was needed, that it remained difficult to get advance tactical information about the movements of the German surface ships. It gave a hint during 6 August that some warship movement was taking place, but the Admiralty did not learn that the *Köln* had moved until an hour after her arrival at Narvik.[270]

By the time PQ 18 actually sailed on 2 September, nearly a month after this false alarm on the part of the Germans, the British authorities had set up for the first time a balanced force of strike and reconnaissance aircraft in north Russia. Two squadrons of RAF Hampden torpedo aircraft, a squadron of Catalina flying boats and, as we have seen, four PR Spitfires were despatched at the beginning of September, the first priority of the reconnaissance aircraft being to watch the German surface ships. To accompany

266.   ibid, Ultra signals 1212/19 August, 1355/25 August and 1734/2 September 1942; Roskill, op cit, Vol II, p 279.
267.   ibid, Ultra signals 1319/27 September, 0213/2 October and 1220 of 4 October 1942.
268.   ADM 223/111, Ultra signal 1826/1 August 1942.
269.   ibid, Ultra signals 1615/5 August, 1053/8 August 1942.
270.   ibid, Ultra Signals 1725 and 2222/6 August 1942.

the convoy through the critical area a large number of destroyers replaced the earlier system of a cruiser covering force in the hope that with their torpedoes they would either deter the *Tirpitz* or damage her if she attacked. Against the expected heavy attacks by the GAF an escort carrier was included in the convoy. The chances that the convoy would escape detection and attack were known to be slim, and it came as no surprise when low-grade Sigint showed that FW 200s had sighted the close escort in Iceland on 6 September and the convoy itself on 8 September. By then the Admiralty had issued, as usual, a comprehensive statement of the whereabouts of the 20 U-boats that could be expected to attack and an estimate of the GAF forces that would be used. This estimate – 65 torpedo-bombers and 120 bombers[271] – understated the number of torpedo-bombers – 92[272] – which the GAF had assembled; but it left no doubt that PQ 18 must expect a higher scale of air torpedo attack than any convoy had yet experienced.

On 9 September, after further air sightings of the convoy, the Germans re-disposed their U-boats and the OIC relayed the new patrol areas to Ultra recipients on the following day.[273] On 10 September they moved the *Scheer*, the *Hipper* and the *Köln* from Narvik to Altenfjord. The ships were sighted by British submarines but were out of range. The submarines had been stationed in the light of a considerable amount of intelligence, mainly from the Enigma, about the routes followed by the German ships during their sorties against PQ 17; this had been promulgated by Flag Officer Submarines in August.[274] But the Enigma provided no news of the German move until the early hours of 11 September, when the Admiralty reported that Admiral Commanding Cruisers in the *Hipper* was due at Altenfjord at 0900 that day.[275] Nor was it until the afternoon of 11 September that the OIC was able to conclude from some signs in the Enigma and photographic reconnaissance of Altenfjord that the *Tirpitz* had probably remained at Narvik.[276]

On 13 September, as well as giving the latest instructions sent to the U-boats, the Enigma became momentarily more revealing about the surface units in Altenfjord. At 1650 the ships were brought to one hour's notice, a fact which the Admiralty brought to the attention of the Flag Officer with the convoy's covering force at

---

271. ADM 223/112, Ultra signals 1228/30 August, 1037 and 1145/2 September 1942.
272. Roskill, op cit, Vol II, p 282.
273. ADM 223/112, Ultra signal 1839/10 September 1942.
274. ibid, signal from FOS 1219/20 August, retransmitted as Ultra signal 1605/21 August 1942.
275. ibid, Ultra signal 0740/11 September 1942.
276. ibid, Ultra signal 1603/11 September 1942.

2325.[277] Thereafter, the ships in Altenfjord were kept under observation by the PRU on 14, 15 and 16 September, the Enigma enabled the Admiralty to confirm on 15 September that the *Tirpitz* was still at Narvik on 14 September,[278] and the Admiralty learned from NA Stockholm's A 2 source on 16 September that the Germans intended to employ only the *Hipper*, the *Scheer* and the *Köln* against PQ 18, and that the *Tirpitz* was suffering from some defect and would not sail unless the situation required her.[279] But by 16 September the German naval authorities had decided not to use any of the ships. Although the Admiralty did not learn this at the time, they had on 13 September wanted to sail the Altenfjord squadron against the west-bound convoy, QP 14, but on 14 September, having once again been warned by Hitler that they must take no undue risks on account of the importance of the squadron for the defence of Norway, they had cancelled the operation.[280]

Within a fortnight NA Stockholm's A 2 source reported that the *Tirpitz* had bearing trouble and would undergo a refit,[281] and she was photographed by a PR Mosquito from Leuchars at Narvik on 28 September.[282] There followed in October further temporary relief. After indicating on 21 and 22 October that the *Scheer* was moving from Altenfjord to Narvik and that she or another main unit might move further south,[283] the naval Enigma disclosed on the evening of 23 October that 'a formation' was to pass a point between Narvik and Trondheim at 1100 on 24 October.[284] By midnight on 23/24 October it added that two ships, presumed by the OIC to be main units, would enter Trondheim fjord on 24 October.[285] There is no evidence that any steps were taken to intercept, probably because once again, as so often before, these clues were an insufficient basis for an attempt at interception by the Home Fleet or submarines or Coastal Command, all of which needed timely notice and good luck if they were to overcome in operations on the Norwegian coast the obstacles created by bad weather and great distances.* Nor was it until 24 hours later that

---

* But it is possible that the operational authorities held back because another and less orthodox operation was already being planned against the *Tirpitz*. On 26 October Leif Larsen sailed from the SOE's Shetland base in an attempt to sink the *Tirpitz* with the newly developed one-man torpedoes (Chariots). His mission, originally planned for Narvik but

277.   ibid, Ultra signal 2325/13 September 1942.
278.   ibid, Ultra signal 1125/15 September 1942; compare Roskill, op cit, Vol II, pp 283–284.   279.   ADM 223/111, Ultra signal 0400/16 Sept 1942.
280.   Roskill, op cit, Vol II, p 282.
281.   ADM 223/111, Ultra signal 1319/27 September 1942.
282.   AIR 41/7, p 102.
283.   ADM 223/112, Ultra signals 0807/21 October and 2100/22 October 1942.
284.   ibid, Ultra signal 2215/23 October 1942.
285.   ibid, Ultra signal 0040/24 October 1942.

the OIC learned from another source, presumably the Naval Attaché Stockholm, and certainly to its surprise – for the earlier Stockholm reports had said that the labour and equipment for *Tirpitz*'s refit were being sent to Narvik – that the two ships were the *Tirpitz* and the *Scheer*.[287] This was confirmed by the Enigma during 25 October.[288]

The *Tirpitz* stayed at Trondheim, but early in November the *Scheer* went back to Germany for a refit. No attempt was made to intercept her, most probably because intelligence about her move, such as it was, arrived too late. As early as 6 November the OIC suspected from Enigma indications that she might move south, and on 7 November it learned that she was at sea. But her movement was evidently not reported by the SIS's ship-watching stations – they were often prevented from signalling by difficult W/T conditions – and it was not until the evening of 7 November that the Enigma disclosed that she had been off Stavanger at 1430 that day; and not until 11 November did it report that she had reached the Baltic.[289]

By then the GAF in north Norway was also being reduced. The GAF, unlike the surface fleet, had made heavy attacks on PQ 18, its torpedo-bombers being especially effective though with heavy losses to themselves. These attacks would have been more damaging but for the fact that, for the first time, steps had been taken to have the GAF's R/T traffic intercepted by a 'Headache' operator in the ship of the cruiser admiral in command of the close escort; the intercepts gave advance warning of some of the attacks, thus enabling the escort carrier to fly off her aircraft in good time. The attacks marked the peak of the GAF's effort against the Arctic route. Before the sailing of the last convoy in the PQ/QP series – that of QP 15 from Archangel on 17 November – the GAF Enigma had disclosed at the beginning of November that torpedo-bombers and long-range bombers were being moved from north Norway to the Mediterranean to counter the Allied landings in north Africa.[290]*

□

switched at the last minute to Trondheim, came close to succeeding. He bluffed his way to a position from which the attack could be mounted but lost his Chariots in an unlucky squall.[286]

   * See below, p 480.

286.   Roskill, op cit, Vol II, p 258; Woodward, *Tirpitz* (New English Library edn 1974), p 86.
287.   ADM 223/112, Ultra signal 0054/25 October 1942.
288.   ibid, Ultra signal 1150/25 October 1942.
289.   ibid, Ultra signal 1019/6 November; ADM 223/113. Ultra signals 0300 and 1935/7 November 1942; Naval Headlines 490 of 7 November, 495 of 11 November 1942.
290.   ADM 223/112, Ultra signal 1326/5 November 1942.

In November 1942, when the British authorities were thus obtaining some relief on the Arctic route, no relief was in sight in the Battle of the Atlantic. Since the introduction of a separate Enigma key for U-boats on 1 February 1942 the Atlantic communications of the U-boat Command had all but completely defied cryptanalysis at GC and CS; the setting of the new key had been broken for only three days – 23 and 24 February and 14 March – and it had taken 6 three-wheel Bombes 17 days to solve each of these settings. For some months after 1 February, as we shall see, the operational consequences of the loss of the U-boat Enigma had been mitigated by the fact that it had all but coincided with the decision of the U-boat Command, following the entry of the United States into the war, to concentrate its main effort against shipping on the American and Canadian coasts. But from August 1942, when the U-boats had returned to the convoy routes, the continuing lack of intelligence about their movements and dispositions, combined with their ever-increasing numbers, had been reflected in the fact that their sinkings of Allied ships, both in the open Atlantic and in terms of their total success, had risen beyond all previous levels.

On 1 January the first six U-boats (Type IXB and IXC, of 1,050 and 1,120 tons) were heading for the new operational area off north America. They sank their first ship there on 12 January. On 24 January – such were the pickings, according to the reports of the first U-boats to arrive, and so poor the defences – Dönitz ordered 12 U-boats on patrol west of the United Kingdom to return to port for servicing and immediate redeployment against the area. In the event only four of them got to the east coast of the USA, for early in February Dönitz was ordered to deploy 20 operational U-boats to Norway. Otherwise, except that he despatched two Type IX U-boats to the Freetown area in February, he gave absolute priority to the offensive in the Americas, where the area of operations had been extended by the despatch of 5 U-boats (Type IXB and IXC) to the Caribbean in the second half of January.[291] No further U-boats were transferred to the Mediterranean until September 1942; not till July 1942 did U-boats return to the Gibraltar area, and not till the autumn did they seriously resume the search for convoys in the north Atlantic.

The level of the U-boats' successes recovered rapidly in the wake of their transfer to the new operational area. Of the total of 327,000 tons of Allied shipping sunk in January 1942 two-thirds was sunk by U-boats in American and Canadian waters in the last third of the month. In every month but one from January to June, inclusive, the amount of shipping sunk by the U-boats mounted sharply, and by far the largest number of the sinkings occurred

291.   BR 305 (2); Roskill, op cit, Vol II, pp 94–95.

either off the American and Canadian eastern sea-board or, as they slowly extended their operational area, in the Gulf of Mexico and the Caribbean.* Nor is it difficult to say why. The operational U-boat force was at last increasing steadily: the average number of Atlantic U-boats at sea each day increased from 22 in January to 61 in May.[292] With this force – its effective time on patrol extended by refuelling from tanker U-boats, of which the first became available in April 1942,[†] and by the activities of an enemy refuelling network in central America, based on British Honduras, which the British and American security authorities could not break up until June – it soon became possible for the U-boat Command to keep between 10 and 15 U-boats permanently on patrol between Boston and Trinidad, despite the long period they had to spend on passage to the area. Until June, on the other hand, the American and Canadian authorities were able to make only slow progress towards organising anti-U-boat defences, especially in instituting coastal convoys and providing air cover. Two U-boats were sunk by aircraft off Newfoundland in March, but there was no further success until a U-boat was sunk off Bermuda on 30 June and the first sinking of a U-boat by air attack off the US coast did not occur till 7 July.[294]

When operational conditions were obviously among the main reasons why the U-boats were able to achieve in the first half of 1942, in return for negligible losses, their greatest sustained period of success in the whole course of the war, it is difficult to assess the extent to which the recovery of their fortunes was also due to the loss of intelligence about them that followed from their adoption of the four-wheel Enigma on 1 February. Not even the best intelligence about their activities off the American coast would have facilitated either an effective counter-attack on them or the effective evasive routeing of shipping so long as the U-boats were at liberty, in the absence of air cover, to operate close inshore and, in the absence of a convoy system, to do so against unprotected shipping. From June 1942, on the other hand, by which time the Allies had made no progress against the U-boat Enigma, it was because of the extension of US and Canadian air patrols and the introduction of

---

* See Roskill, op cit, Vol I Appendix R and Vol II, Appendix O.

† The first intelligence about plans for the development of supply U-boats for refuelling at sea was produced by the SIS in March 1941 and was later supported by a Japanese diplomatic decrypt. It was discounted in the Admiralty until air photographs of a broad-beamed U-boat, taken in Kiel in April 1942, gave some credence to it. But the existence of supply U-boats was not generally accepted until one was sunk and its crew captured in August 1942.[293] See Appendix 10.

292.   AIR 41/47, Appendix II.

293.   Morgan, op cit, p 253; ADM 223/94, OIC SI No 216 of 1 June and No 321 of 24 August 1942; Beesly, op cit, p 115.

294.   BR 1736 (51) (1A).

convoys, that the U-boats began to report that they were encountering growing difficulties; and only then did the U-boat
Command reduce its offensive in the western Atlantic, except in the
Caribbean and off Brazil, and turn its attention back to the convoy
routes to and from the United Kingdom. In these circumstances, it
may well be the case that the most serious operational consequence
of the loss of the U-boat Enigma during most of 1942 was that the
Admiralty and the US Navy Department had to wait until the
beginning of 1943 for firm evidence that the enemy was reading the
cypher which carried the inter-Allied signals about Atlantic shipping movements. The loss of the Enigma, which coincided with the
beginning of the period in which the U-boats derived maximum
benefit from the B-Dienst's exploitation of Naval Cypher No 3, goes
some way to explain why steps to improve the security of that
cypher, and eventually to replace it, were delayed until the early
summer of 1943.* As for Allied intelligence, moreover, it may even
have been fortunate that the introduction of the fourth wheel for the
Atlantic Enigma also coincided with the German decision to
concentrate the U-boat offensive against the American coasts. Had
the U-boats continued to give priority to attacks on Atlantic
convoys after the Enigma had been changed, it is likely that there
would have been such an improvement in their performance
against convoys that the U-boat Command might have concluded
that its earlier difficulties had been due to the fact that the
three-wheel Enigma was insecure.

However that may be, it was not long before the extent of the
change that had come over the intelligence situation was borne in
upon the OIC. On 9 February 1942, in its first weekly U-boat
situation report after the new Enigma settings came into force, the
Tracking Room in the OIC announced that 'since the end of
January no Special Information has been available about any
U-boats other than those controlled by Admiral Norway'. 'Inevitably', it added, 'the picture of the Atlantic dispositions is by now
out of focus and little can be said with any confidence in estimating
the present and future movement of the U-boats'.[295] With every
week that passed after this report the picture did, indeed, inevitably
become more indistinct, as is shown in the OIC's successive weekly
U-boat situation reports.

It is true that the tracking of the U-boats was not again reduced
to that state of pure guesswork, relieved only by what was learned
from British sighting reports, the attacks made by the U-boats and
the DF-ing of their few transmissions, which had prevailed before
the spring of 1941. The German Navy used the Home Waters

---

* See above, p 177, below, p 553, and Appendix 1 (Part (i)).

295.   ADM 223/92, OIC SI No 86 of 9 February 1942.

Enigma settings in the western Baltic until January 1944, when it introduced a separate Enigma key for the entire Baltic. Between November 1941 and May 1942 it also used the Home Waters settings in the eastern Baltic, an area in which separate (and unreadable) settings were otherwise in force up to January 1944. Primarily from the Home Waters Enigma – though German naval low-grade codes also helped – the OIC still obtained regular information about the commissioning and working up of new U-boats in the Baltic, which enabled it to keep a reliable check on the numbers coming into service and to identify the type of each newly numbered U-boat, and was usually warned when a U-boat left the Baltic or Norway or the Bay of Biscay for an operational cruise and when it had returned to base. In addition, the Home Waters Enigma continued to provide detailed intelligence on the routes followed by the U-boats when entering or leaving the Biscay ports.[296] Further, after reading the Home Waters Enigma for a whole year before the U-boats in the Atlantic abandoned the use of it – February 1941 to January 1942 – the OIC and GC and CS had built up an enormous fund of knowledge about every aspect of the U-boat Command – its routine procedures, its tactical methods, including the methods it used for pack attacks, its strategic ideas, the endurance of each of its types of U-boat.[297] During 1942, finally, other sources – POW and captured documents, PR, diplomatic reports and the SIS – continued to supply new information not only of this kind but also on the performance, armament and other characteristics of each type of U-boat.* With this information the OIC maintained accurate estimates of the number of U-boats at sea at any one time, had a good idea of how many were homeward and outward bound and how many were on patrol, kept a good check on the claims of Allied forces to have destroyed U-boats, and was sometimes able to deduce, from its type or from information about the experience of its commander, the operational area to which a U-boat was proceeding. But it was still the case that the Enigma now vouchsafed no information about the U-boats between the time they left harbour and the time they returned from patrol.

In this situation, despite every effort to forecast the daily movement of each U-boat after it had left harbour, the daily plot of U-boat dispositions soon ceased to be reliable. And this was now more clearly recognised than had been the case before the spring of 1941 because research undertaken on the basis of the Enigma decrypted up to the beginning of February 1942 had established

---

* See Appendix 10.

296. ADM 223/93, OIC SI No 128 of 21 March 1942.
297. ADM 223/94, OIC SI No 265 of 13 July 1942.

that little reliance could be placed on other aids to the tracking of U-boats. Checked against the decrypted signals, RFP and TINA had shown a high rate of failure, and one that had increased in parallel with the increase in the number of U-boats at sea. It had to be accepted that RFP and TINA could only distinguish supply and minelaying U-boats, which were being identified by PR in the Biscay bases, from the much larger fleet of standard U-boats. Another analysis had checked the positions of U-boats given in the decrypts against the DF bearings on the transmissions of the signals and had shown that DF fixes, although more reliable than RFP or TINA, were somewhat erratic, and that it was possible to improve them by applying regular corrections to the bearings taken at individual DF stations. But in the absence of a regular supply of decrypted positions these regular corrections could no longer be made.

It was thus with understandable anxiety that the Admiralty watched, as it was able to do, the steady increase in the daily average number of U-boats at sea in the Atlantic, from 22 in January and 61 in May to 86 at the beginning of August, and that it awaited the time when, with the improvement of the defences on the American seaboard, the U-boats would be redisposed for another offensive against the convoy routes. This time came in August. The Admiralty had expected it since July, when the U-boat successes in American waters began to decline[298] and when the operational evidence showed that U-boats, though as yet operating singly, were back in some numbers in the area between Gibraltar and the Azores. Between 5 and 10 August a pack of U-boats – in fact 18 of them – fought the first in the new round of convoy battles in the north Atlantic against convoy SC 94, sinking 11 out of its 33 ships, 53,000 tons of merchant shipping. During the two months August and September 1942 the U-boats located 21 of the 63 convoys that were sailed, made sustained attacks on 7 of them and sank 43 of their ships. In those months they were still sinking less shipping in the Atlantic than on the American seaboard, where they continued to find soft spots in the Caribbean and make surprise attacks in the St Lawrence. During October, however, when the number of U-boats at sea in the Atlantic was known to have reached just over 100,[299] their total monthly sinkings in the open Atlantic exceeded for the first time the figure of half a million tons as compared with 85,000 tons sunk off the American coast.

In November there was a small decline in the number of ships sunk in the trans-Atlantic convoys because many U-boats were

298. Roskill, op cit, Vol II, p 199.
299. ADM 223/95, OIC SI No 394 of 12 October 1942.

diverted to operate, without success, against the Allied landings in north-west Africa. But the total amount of Allied shipping lost to U-boat attack reached, at 721,700 tons, the highest figure for any month in the entire war. At the same time, the number of U-boats sunk in the north Atlantic area, including the Americas, again fell back. During the first six months of 1942 only eleven U-boats had been sunk in the area, eight of them by convoy escorts; in July 6 had been sunk, in August 5, in September 3, in October 8. But in November only 2 were sunk.[300] And at the end of December another convoy battle, the attack on convoy ON 154, showed how much the U-boats had regained the upper hand outside the range of air cover. In this attack 11 U-boats sank 13 ships and lost only one of their number.

There is no difficulty in these circumstances in imagining the relief with which the Admiralty received in mid-December the news that GC and CS had begun to make its way into the four-wheel Enigma settings and was at last confident that it would continue to make progress against this most formidable of all the Enigma keys. Indeed, its satisfaction can be sensed in the caution-ary signal which the First Sea Lord sent to the US Chief of Naval Operations on the evening of 13 December 1942, and which read as follows:

'As the result of months of the most strenuous endeavour a few days' U-boat traffic will be readable in the immediate future and this may lead to better results in the near future.

You will, I am sure, appreciate the care necessary in making use of this information to prevent suspicion being aroused as to its source. We have found this especially difficult when action by routeing authorities outside the Admiralty is required.

It would be a tragedy if we had to start all over again on what would undoubtedly be a still more difficult problem.'

---

300. BR 1736 (51A and 51B).

CHAPTER 20

The Air War in the West from May 1941 to the end of 1942

IN MAY 1941 the transfer of most of the German bombers to the Russian front brought to a close the first and the most sustained of the GAF's offensives against the United Kingdom. Two main developments thereafter changed the character of the air war in western Europe. The RAF, later reinforced by the US Eighth Army Air Force, intensified the bombing of Germany and also undertook daylight fighter sweeps and light bomber raids with the object of bringing the GAF to battle and inflicting casualties. The GAF, on the other hand, partly because of the consequent development of its defensive fighter forces at the expense of its bomber and reconnaissance forces, and partly because of the gradual dilution of its over-all resources by the demands of the Russian and the Mediterranean theatres, proved all but unable to resume the bombing of the United Kingdom. Only briefly, between April and October 1942, did it make the attempt in the period down to the beginning of 1943 and then its effort was on a much smaller scale than during the winter of 1940–1941.

While this reversal of roles and of scales of effort was taking place the British intelligence authorities, having already built up a considerable fund of knowledge on these matters from a wide range of sources – high and low-grade Sigint, PR, POW, captured material and the SIS – continued to increase their familiarity with the over-all state of the GAF and with its strength, deployment and order of battle on every front. Nor need it be doubted that this fact conferred an important, if impalpable, benefit on the Allied air authorities by reducing their uncertainty about the strategic situation in which they made their major operational decisions. But if general or strategic intelligence about the state of the GAF continued to improve, it was otherwise with the availability of intelligence that could influence the outcome of operations. Far from increasing, the contribution made by Sigint to the more effective conduct of air operations now underwent a marked, if a temporary, decline. Though radar plots became of increasing value, the distinction between Sigint as a source of general information and Sigint as a source of day-to-day operational intelligence that was of practical use, a distinction that was always sharpest in the context of the air war, was never so prominent as it was in this phase of the struggle with the GAF in western Europe.

To the extent that this decline was due to difficulties in procuring intelligence it owed much to the fact that, for all but its tactical communications, the GAF in Germany itself and the western theatre as a whole made little use of W/T, and therefore transmitted little Enigma. As a result of GC and CS's ability to read so many of them, the GAF Enigma keys in force elsewhere continued to provide an accurate tally of the movements into and out of this theatre of the GAF's formations, and did so with such regularity that the Air Ministry could be confident of learning in advance of their redeployments. From time to time the GAF in the theatre itself resorted to transmitting signals encyphered in the Enigma for special purposes; it was in this way that GC and CS was able to throw light on the organisation of the GAF's night-fighter system, though not on its deployment, by breaking the key used by Fliegerkorps XII from early in 1942.* But these were exceptions. The general rule in relation to the operational intentions, the order of battle, the scale of effort and the types of aircraft of the GAF was that 'whenever a piece of Ultra information was received . . . during 1941 and 1942 on matters concerning the Western Front it was looked upon as an event of great note'.[1]

This situation, so different from that obtaining in theatres where the enemy was operating beyond the range of land-lines, was to change later on; but not until the approach of D-day in Normandy did it change sufficiently to justify the establishment of SCU/SLU links to carry high-grade Sigint from GC and CS direct to the principal home commands. Until then intelligence on the operations of the GAF within western Europe was derived chiefly from low-grade Sigint, PR and POW interrogation and was sent direct to the home commands of the RAF by those who procured it – by Cheadle and Kingsdown, by the CIU and by CSDIC. It was backed up by regular digests and appreciations on order of battle and other longer-term matters, based on all these sources, and on SIS reports, and on such Enigma as was available, which the commands received from the Air Ministry, and it was supplemented also by continuous discussions and direct contacts with the Ministry. For applying the intelligence to the planning and conduct of their operations, however, the commands themselves were responsible on the principle that they alone could mate it with experience derived from operational contact with the enemy.

Down to the end of 1942 the commands discharged this responsibility with little success – or at least with little benefit to themselves. To some observers, notably the Air Section at GC and CS, it

---

* See below, pp 252–253.

1.   The Use of Sigint in AI 3(b), p 1.

seemed that the reason for this was the fact that the arrangements in force for utilising the available operational intelligence were too inflexible; they believed that the commands needed more help in interpreting the evidence, particularly that from low-grade Sigint, and that this requirement called for contact between the commands and those who, like themselves, were closer to the sources. But the Air Ministry's view was that, over and above what the commands did for themselves on the basis of reports reaching them direct from Cheadle and Kingsdown, they should receive appreciated intelligence only from the Air Intelligence Branch; and, perhaps not surprisingly, it maintained the belief that only the Air Intelligence Branch could judge what would be useful to the commands until it was clear how in the new circumstances the low-grade Sigint could best be used for operational purposes.

We shall see that in few, if any, directions was this point reached before the end of 1942, and that by that time, on the other hand, experiments in improving the supply of operational intelligence to the commands were in train.

□

After the middle of May 1941 night raids by the GAF against the United Kingdom were infrequent and on a small scale, and they were supplemented by irregular day-time attacks on shipping and coastal towns by fighters and fighter-bombers only up to July 1941. Thereafter, except that minelaying operations off the British coasts continued, the air defence of Great Britain presented few problems until the end of April 1942, when the small GAF bomber force available in the west, reinforced by anti-shipping, minelaying and training units, and often flying multiple sorties, resumed heavy night bombing with the Baedeker raids.

Beginning on a modest scale, these attacks on cities like Exeter, Norwich, York, Bath and Canterbury rose in intensity during May 1942. During that month, however, the raids became less accurate and effective. Nor did the GAF's performance improve when, in June, it switched its targets on most nights to ports and industrial towns. By early September 1942 – except for an attack on Canterbury on 31 October – its night offensive was over. Its day-time attacks with fighter-bombers, which had also been resumed in the spring of 1942, were relatively more effective. Delivered by 2, 4 or 8 aircraft at low level to avoid radar, and using FW 190s in place of Me 109s from July, they were difficult to counter. But the force engaged seldom mustered more than 20 serviceable aircraft, and after a raid on 31 October – again on Canterbury – it suspended operations on being called away to take part in the occupation of Vichy France.[2]

---

2.   AIR 41/49, *The Air Defence of Great Britain*, Vol V, p 171.

The failure of the GAF's 1942 offensive was due in large measure to the GAF's limitations. The forces it could make available were small. The bombers – though not the fighter-bombers – were not all of modern design. A shortage of experienced pilots and crews, brought about by the enemy's enormous losses on the Russian front but accentuated by the casualties imposed by Fighter Command's growing night-fighter force, reduced the effectiveness of the raids. But the failure was by no means unqualified. Opening the offensive with some 200 bombers and a few fighter-bombers, the GAF held down no fewer than 1,400 British fighters throughout 1942, at a time when they were urgently needed in other theatres, not to speak of 6,000 guns and the large forces of Service and civil defence manpower that were otherwise occupied in the air defence of the United Kingdom.

Whatever may be said of the decision to retain such a powerful fighter force in the United Kingdom – it is a decision that was subsequently severely criticised[3] – it owed nothing to faulty strategic intelligence. Soon after the beginning of the offensive the Air Intelligence Branch accurately forecast the probable scale of the enemy's effort – as many as 150 aircraft might take part in a raid, but it was unlikely that the figure would normally exceed 80 – and from its knowledge of the state of the GAF and of its commitments in other theatres it realised that there was little chance that the enemy would be able to resume the bombing of the United Kingdom on a larger scale.[4]

For the accuracy of these assessments, and for the fact that it remained confident that they did not need revision, Air Intelligence was indebted to Sigint. From early in 1942 the Enigma had disclosed that the GAF was beginning to suffer from an over-all manpower shortage, the first of the enemy's armed forces to do so.[5] In March 1942 it indicated that the GAF's fighter arm was most seriously affected. At the end of the year, discussing the fact that the GAF's Emergency Defence Units, newly created to take some of the strain off the Army, were not standing up well to winter conditions on the eastern front, it revealed that the over-all shortage had become so grave that, despite its own difficulties, the GAF had had to sacrifice a large amount of its manpower to these ground fighting divisions;[6] this significant development had begun in October.[7] At the same time, the Air Ministry could be sure that, should the GAF decide to increase its effort against the United Kingdom despite its other commitments, the change of policy would be disclosed by the Enigma and by the GAF's low-grade

3.   ibid, Preface, p iv.   4.   ibid, pp 37–38.
5.   For example, CX/MSS/646/T2.
6.   CX/MSS/1899/T15 of 4 January.   7.   AIR 41/49, pp 33–34.

communications. Early in April, before the beginning of the 1942 offensive, it had learned from these two sources that the GAF was increasing its bomber strength in north-west Europe; the new arrivals had included II/KG 100, ordered home from the eastern front,[8]* and IV/KG 40, identified in Holland,[9] together with Reserve Training Units. There were good grounds for believing that the Enigma, supplemented by the order of battle intelligence that Cheadle was deriving from low-grade Sigint,[†] would give notice of any further reinforcements.[10]

Even so, intelligence gave 'no indication of the much increased scale of enemy attacks which began towards the end of April', and no warning that they would be directed against undefended Baedeker targets.[11] Although the suspicion existed that the GAF might resume the bomber offensive in retaliation for the RAF's raids on Lübeck and Rostock,[‡] the arrival of bomber reinforcements in the west was interpreted as being a precaution against repetitions of the British raid on St Nazaire, which had taken place on 27–28 March.[12]§ Nor did the British defences derive much benefit from operational intelligence during the course of the 1942 offensive. Against the fighter-bomber raids no effective system of alert was developed until the end of 1943; what provided it from that date was not an improvement in operational intelligence but the introduction of 'low-looking' radar to counter the fighter-bombers' low-flying tactics.[13] As for the night offensive, the long-range bombers adopted tactics designed to elude or confuse the now extended warning radar chain, and the Sigint sources were usually able to predict GAF activity only in general terms. The Enigma key used in connection with *X-Gerät* occasionally gave advance warning of a particular target but notice of individual raids and of their targets was not often received. The earliest of the raids, those against Exeter on the nights of 23 and 24 April, were all the more unexpected because, as a POW revealed early in May, the GAF, at pains to secure surprise, moved its bombers into position at low altitude and in W/T silence.[14] There was no warning of a raid, still less of its target, before the attacks on Bath

---

* It will be noted that this and other source references in this Chapter are to reports by the OIC in the Admiralty. Very few of the Air Ministry's intelligence appreciations for 1941 and 1942 have survived. The gap is partly filled by the GAF notes of the OIC, which were repeating material provided by the Air Intelligence Branch.

† See below, p 242.   ‡ See below, p, 267.
§ See above, p 192.

8.   ADM 223/93, OIC SI 131 and 150 of 22 March and 5 April 1942.
9.   ibid, OIC SI 155 of 12 April 1942.
10. AIR 41/49, pp 134, 166; JIC (42) 62 of 23 February; The Work of AI 3(b), p 6 para 8.   11.   AIR 41/49, p 43.
12. ADM 223/93, OIC SI 150 of 5 April, 161 of 15 April, 182 of 2 May 1942.
13. AIR 41/49, p 15.   14.   ibid, p 53.

on the nights of 25 and 26 April, on Norwich and York at the end of April and on Exeter on 3 May,[15] though low-grade Sigint was able during the raids to estimate their strength and detect the use of double sorties.[16] Thereafter the raids continued to take place without notice – thus Canterbury was attacked three times without warning at the beginning of June.[17] The Air Ministry was surprised, moreover, by their increased frequency. By 9 May, at a time when the GAF's bombing of Malta was in progress, the Enigma had disclosed that two Gruppen of long-range bombers had been transferred to France from Sicily. But Air Intelligence judged that they would 'probably be non-operational owing to the almost certain necessity for re-equipping;[18] nor was it until 23 May that it reported that these units had been participating in the offensive.[19]

It will be evident from this summary that intelligence had now lost the chief means of determining the enemy's operational intentions which had stood it in good stead during the Blitz of 1940–1941. From some months after the introduction of the beam systems Enigma intercepts had commonly revealed the target for the night, and timely notice of coming raids and good indications of their intended targets had also been provided by the interception and laying off of the beams from the *Knickebein* and *X-Gerät* transmitters, which had been switched on long before each raid.* But the GAF, as well as ceasing to transmit Enigma instructions for the beams from June 1941, had progressively reduced the interval between the switching on of the beam transmitters and the launching of the attacks. By May 1941 it had been operating a procedure by which the transmissions did not begin until its aircraft had crossed the English coast. Thereafter the GAF had developed a more sensitive *Knickebein* receiver, as we shall see, but it did not use it for operational purposes during the bombing campaign of 1942. At the same time, it occasionally switched the system on in order to mislead the defences, for example by setting the beams to intersect in the south while a raid was taking place in the north.[20]

As a result of other GAF security precautions it proved impossible during 1942 for Cheadle to make up for the loss of this source of detailed advance warning from its study of the MF beacons and the broadcast transmitters which the GAF used for marking turning points on raids and for homing on the return flight. From April

---

* See Volume I, pp 324–6 and its Appendix 11 (ii) and (iii).

15.   AIR 41/10, *The Rise and Fall of the German Air Force*, p 195; B Collier, *The Defence of the United Kingdom* (1957), p 307.
16.   Air Historical Branch, *Air Ministry Intelligence*, pp 70–71.
17.   AIR 41/49, p 55.   18.   ADM 223/93, OIC SI 189 of 9 May 1942.
19.   ADM 223/94, OIC SI 205 of 23 May 1942.
20.   AIR 41/46, No 80 Wing RAF Historical Report, p 32.

1941, in an effort to counter British 'meaconing' of the beacons and also presumably to prevent the expanding RAF effort from making use of the beacons for its own navigation, the GAF had introduced more complex changes of call-signs and frequencies.* These changes had caused little difficulty for Cheadle; though now made at varying times instead of at midnight, they had continued to take place only once a day. In September 1941, moreover, the GAF had introduced other changes of beacon procedure which made it temporarily possible for Cheadle to derive advance notice of the GAF's then infrequent raids. The broadcast transmitters were from that date operated in synchronous groups except when the GAF needed to use them during its own operations. And from the same date the MF beacons were switched on only when the GAF was operating; hitherto they had transmitted throughout the 24 hours on a more or less constant schedule.[21] But from 10 October 1941 the enemy had begun to change the beacon call-signs and frequencies much more frequently; they changed 6 times a day until August 1942, 15 times a day thereafter. This placed an onerous burden on Cheadle. After the autumn of 1941 it was rarely able to give advance warning of an enemy raid and it often encountered delays before it could report the call-signs, frequencies and locations of the beacons for 'meaconing' purposes.

Despite its inability to provide early warning, the study of the GAF's low-grade communications continued to be improved as a source of intelligence on the dispositions and order of battle of the enemy's long-range aircraft. By the middle of 1942 Cheadle had refined its methods to the point at which this study was 'a matter of routine', and until April 1943, when the GAF abandoned self-evident aircraft call-signs, it provided 'the greater part of the material' on which the Air Intelligence Branch based its order of battle calculations. In the same way, despite the added difficulties with the beacon call-signs and frequencies, the 'meaconing' organisation continued to function efficiently and to be a serious embarrassment to the GAF, as was shown when the GAF introduced a restricted frequency band for the beacons in September 1942 and additional beacon frequencies in 1943.[22] Nor was 'meaconing' the only counter-measure which helped to reduce the effectiveness of the GAF's night-bombing offensive. During the lull since May 1941 the British counter-measure authorities had anticipated the improvements the enemy might make to the equipment and procedure of his navigational beam systems, and the preparations they had made were largely successful in preventing the GAF from using these aids after April 1942.[23]

---

* See Volume I, Appendix 11 (i).

21. ibid, p 36.   22. ibid, pp 36, 37.   23. ibid, p 30.

As early as May 1941 POW and captured documents had revealed that, as was expected, the GAF was planning to introduce a more sensitive *Knickebein* receiver, one that could be used on any one of 34 spot frequencies between 30 and 33.3 M/cs instead of on these frequencies only, and to increase the number of *Knickebein* sites from 9 to 12.[24] This intelligence enabled No 80 Wing RAF to rule out, at least for the time being, the possibility that it might have to counter more radical modifications – a change of audio modulation frequency or the adoption of frequency modulation – as well as to put in hand the extension of its jamming equipment. The required extension called for aerial modifications and additional listening posts, but especially for an increase, from 32 to 66, of jamming transmitters; it was not completed until November 1941, by which time the recovery of a model of the new receiver from a Dornier 217, which, confused by 'meaconing', had landed at Lydd, had confirmed that the audio filter remained unchanged and that no modification to the jamming transmitters would be needed.[25] Although the transmissions on the new *Knickebein* frequencies were first intercepted in September 1941,[26] the GAF used them only for exercise purposes and deception during its bombing campaign against the United Kingdom in 1942. Not until after the beginning of 1943 – and then to little effect* – was it often used operationally over the United Kingdom.[27]

The *X-Gerät*, the second of the GAF's beam systems, ceased to be used operationally in June 1941; the last of the daily Enigma messages relating to it was decrypted on 16 June and later in the summer the Enigma confirmed that KG 100, the formation which had been using the system, had been transferred to the Russian front.[28] But the *X-Gerät* transmitters continued to radiate for long periods at a time, and while this was obviously for the purpose of deception, there were indications that the *X-Gerät*, too, was being improved. In their continuing search for new transmitters the PRU and the CIU noticed from July 1941 that while aerial arrays were being removed from some areas, in others they were being grouped close together – a modification which would enable aircraft to maintain course with less deviation when changing from the beam of one frequency to that of another.[29] In October 1941 a POW reported that a 'dog whistle' frequency was likely to be used – a statement which was interpreted correctly to mean that a supersonic frequency was involved. This was initially thought to be connected with *Knickebein*, but the capture of the new *Knickebein*

---

* See below, p 511.

24.   ibid, pp 12, 30.   25.   ibid, p 31.
26.   ibid, p 31.   27.   ibid, p 32.
28.   CX/MSS/41/T4.   29.   AIR 41/46, p 32.

receiver from the Dornier showed that this was not so and it was then assumed that it was associated with the *X-Gerät*. During the spring of 1942 the Enigma disclosed that a new variant of the *X-Gerät*, known as *Taub* (deaf), was being developed and thereafter further information on the subject was obtained from a POW. Appropriate modulations to the jamming transmitters were then introduced operationally.[30] It was then noticed that the Cherbourg *X-Gerät* transmitter had radiated during a raid by a single aircraft on the Bristol aircraft factory on 3 April, and after another by three aircraft on Brockworth airfield on the following day the Enigma disclosed that II/KG 100 had been involved and confirmed that the Germans were now introducing the modified *X-Gerät* system.[31] It was not before 23–24 May, however, after the Baedeker raids had virtually come to an end, that the *X-Gerät* was detected operating with supersonic modulation and that its jamming was taken in hand, and it appears that the delay was due to a limitation in the design of the intercept receivers.[32]

Once the jamming started *X-Gerät* was of little value to the GAF, the average percentage of bombs on targets being reduced to 13 per cent. After being used seven times in May, it operated four times in June, once in July and once in September 1942, and its signals ceased altogether from the middle of November. While the complexity of the system, and the fact that only one unit was equipped to use it, were probably the main reasons why it was abandoned, the discovery that the British had counter-measures capable of dealing with the additional modulation no doubt contributed to the enemy's decision.[33]

Y-Gerät, like *Knickebein*, was not reintroduced for operations against the United Kingdom till 1943. But the GAF continued to radiate the beams after May 1941 without making use of them during its infrequent attacks, and the preparation of counter-measures against the time when the system might be brought back into service presented no problem. The capture of a complete *Y-Gerät* early in May 1941* showed that the most effective counter-measure was a transmitter that sent out dash signals at a slightly different keying rate from that of the German signals. Thirty such transmitters covering the six known *Y-Gerät* stations had been deployed by September 1941.[34]

□

---

* See Volume I, p 328 and its Appendix 11 (iv).

30.   ibid; R V Jones, *Most Secret War* (1978), p 251.
31.   AIR 41/46, pp 32–33.   32.   Jones, op cit, pp 252–253.
33.   AIR 41/46, p 33.   34.   ibid, p 34 and Appendix K.

The reduction of the GAF's bombing of the United Kingdom from May 1941 was accompanied by an increase in the RAF's offensive against Germany. The offensive was to be enormously costly on account of the efficiency of the enemy's defences – a subject on which intelligence was for long unable to give Bomber Command much practical assistance. Much was known of the radars from early in 1941, and from the autumn of 1941 this enabled tactical counter-measures to be taken against the German defences well before their extent or location were known.* But it was not until the middle of 1942 that the intelligence authorities began to build up an understanding of the German radar and night-fighter aircraft systems, and not until early in 1943 did they influence the introduction of Allied technical counter-measures and begin to contribute heavily to the adoption of more effective bombing policies.

At the outbreak of war the British authorities had assumed that the RAF's attacks on Germany would encounter heavy anti-aircraft opposition. But, despite the fact that they were experimenting with various advanced systems of air defence, their assessment of the strength of those defences was based on information about pre-war guns and aircraft and was over-optimistic. In particular, although they themselves had developed to the point of deployment a radar system for the location of enemy aircraft, they discounted the possibility that Germany might also be developing an early-warning radar system. But operational experience quickly forced the RAF to revise its pre-war expectations. By the beginning of 1942 it realised that 'in general, German radio equipment has been built to a standard well above our own. It is probably safe to say that up to a few months ago, German output of RDF† equipment has been numerically inferior to our own. Since the beginning of the year however, there has been a very considerable increase in development of DT† equipment of all kinds. If Germany is driven to the defensive we may expect her RDF output to soar past ours, at the expense of the more aggressive applications of radio'.[35]

In its first raids on Germany – daylight attacks against warships in harbour – the RAF had discovered that her fighters had a speed far superior to its bombers and could shoot at a greater range than expected, that her anti-aircraft fire was accurate and that she possessed an efficient organisation for co-ordinating her fighters and her AA guns; and even at that early stage the suspicion

---

* See below, p 256.
† RDF (Radio Direction Finding) was the early name for Radar (*R*adio *D*etection and *R*anging). The German equivalent was DT (Detektor).

35.   AIR 20/1629, ASI Report No 13 of 10 January 1942.

dawned that if this organisation was so efficient it was because it made use of early-warning radar. Nearly a year had elapsed, however, before Enigma decrypts and POW reports, received between June and December 1940, finally established that the Germans had a radar known as the *Freya*.

Germany had started a radar research and development programme in 1934; by the outbreak of war she was deploying an early-warning system, had installed a naval set in some ships and had brought an AA fire-control set to a late stage of development.* The British intelligence and scientific authorities appear to have obtained no hint as to the existence of this programme until they received the Oslo report in November 1939.† The Oslo report had described two systems. It had stated that the first used 20 kw 'short wave' transmitters with short pulses, but had not specified the frequencies; had added that a chain of these transmitters already existed along the German coast and that they were to be installed throughout Germany by April 1940; and had claimed that during the RAF raid on Wilhelmshaven in September 1939 the aircraft had been detected by radar at a range of 120 miles. The report had mentioned a second radar set described as 'in preparation'; it used dishes and the wavelength was 50 cm.

Up to the middle of 1940 only one further item of information had been received. After the *Graf Spee* had blown herself up after the battle of the River Plate on 18 December 1939, the report of the technical team which examined the wreck had described an aerial and concluded that she had possessed a gun-ranging radar set having a wavelength of 57 (or 114) cm. A search of previous intelligence on the *Graf Spee* had then produced a photograph taken in 1938 which showed the aerial in position but covered in canvas; no record exists of any earlier attempt to interpret the photograph.[37]

In May 1940 Dr R V Jones had reviewed reports of a scientific or technical nature received since the previous September and, relying

---

* 1. *Freya* Early in 1936 the Gema company started developments on a frequency of 150 Mc/s, which led to the *Freya*, which by the end of the year had achieved an aircraft detection range of about 50 miles. Production for the German Navy and Air Force started in 1938.

2. *Seetakt* The radar gun-ranging set, also produced by Gema, operated on 375 Mc/s. It was tested at sea in the autumn of 1937 with a range of 9 miles on other ships and a sufficient accuracy for its purpose. An early model was mounted on the *Graf Spee*. It was used for fire control of the Channel coastal batteries.

3. *Würzburg* In 1936 Telefunken developed a set on 560 Mc/s, primarily as a Flak fire-control unit, designed to be used with the 88 mm Flak gun, having an acceptable accuracy for this purpose up to a range of about 25 miles.[36]

† See Volume I, pp 99–100 and its Appendix 5.

36. A Price, *Instruments of Darkness* (1977), pp 59–60.
37. AIR 20/1629, para 2.4; Admiralty Report of Technical Mission, April 1940.

heavily on the Oslo report and the *Graf Spee* evidence and 'other vague indications', had concluded that it was certain that the Germans had some form of radar, and that it must be assumed that they had some knowledge of the British system.[38] This conclusion had been confirmed by Sigint and POW during the following summer. On 30 June 1940 a GAF Enigma message had referred to the fact that German aircraft had been able to intercept armed reconnaissance owing to excellent *Freya* reporting. On 10 July the Enigma had disclosed that there was a *Freya* north of Lannion, and on 14 July it had revealed that there was one on the Cap de la Hague.[39] POW interrogations were also now beginning to contribute. One had referred to German naval experiments with an apparatus for range and direction finding by means of reflected radio beams; another to experiments by the Flak command with a system known as EEMG.* These and similar scraps of information had by August 1940 made it clear that the *Freya* was some form of RDF.[41]

Once this conclusion had been reached, it had become possible to understand the complexity of the German nomenclature and to interpret other items of intelligence, such as a report to the effect that 'the Germans had RDF controlled fighters in Norway in July 1940'.[42] In August, moreover, the intelligence sources had provided some details about the enemy's radar procedures. POW had disclosed that air crews had to notify the *Freya* station so that their radar tracks might be identified, and on 8 August two Enigma decrypts had enabled further deductions to be made. The first had again referred to reporting methods and, with the POW reports, had made it certain that radio, rather than visual or some other means of detection, was employed. The second had been concerned with tactics to be employed in flights to England: as far as possible they should assemble over France, not out at sea, to prevent the British stations (*DT Gerät*) from giving warning to the RAF fighters. From this indication of the order of range that the Germans ascribed to the British stations, the British authorities had been able to estimate that the range of the German equipment was less than 70 miles.[43]

Once *Freya* had been identified as a radar, and the evidence had indicated that its function was probably early warning, it had not

---

* In a review in 1942, an Air Scientific Intelligence report described how a large number of different names for radar sets made early correlation and interpretation difficult – *Freya*, EEMG (Elektrische Entfernungs Messgerät), Heavy DT, Matratzen, Made, Sichtgerät etc.[40]

38. AIR 20/1622, ASI Report No 5 of 23 May 1940.
39. AIR 20/1625, ASI Report No 8 of 14 August 1940.
40. AIR 20/1629, para 2.5.   41.   AIR 20/1625, AIR 20/1629, para 2.3.
42. AIR 20/1629, para 2.5.   43.   ibid, para 11.

proved difficult to build up a general knowledge of the deployment, the organisation and the operational methods of the enemy's coastal early-warning system. In July 1940 it had been discovered that German stations were reporting aircraft plots by W/T in minor codes. From August the GAF Enigma had also provided an increasing number of references to the location and administration of these stations. Thereafter these two sources had provided a good deal of general information about what was now seen to be the *Freya* chain at a time when the Germans were extending it beyond the eight stations that had existed in the Frisian islands in October 1939 and were themselves learning how to operate it.[44] About the characteristics of the *Freya* apparatus, however, little more had been learned until February 1941 when the GAF Enigma, which had made few references to equipment and none to frequencies, disclosed that one *Freya* and two *Würzburg* were being sent to Romania and two *Würzburg* to Bulgaria, and added that 'the apparatus is absolutely essential since only in this way can aircraft-reporting cover of the coast be guaranteed'.[45] This intelligence confirmed that two radars existed – probably the two described in the Oslo report – and when related to the lengths of the Romanian and Bulgarian coastlines it provided a crude estimate of their ranges.

Later in February, 'within a few hours on 24 February 1941, the main coastal chain was doubly unmasked'[46] by photographic reconnaissance and the first interception of *Freya* signals.* From the preceding July a *Freya* was known to be in the neighbourhood of Auderville, at the Cap de la Hague station, and attempts had been made, without success, to photograph the equipment. The main difficulties had been the scale of reconnaissance photography, and the suspicion that the equipment was small. In November 1940 improvements in reconnaissance had produced photographs of greater scale which showed two circles to the west of Auderville of about 20 ft in diameter which could not be interpreted. Slight

---

* The first radar transmissions had been intercepted on 28 September 1940 by the Telecommunications Research Establishment (TRE) searching in the Dover area. Pulses were heard on about 80 cm (375 Mc/s), but it turned out that they were not what was being looked for. A set was being used to direct the fire of the German long-range batteries between Calais and Boulogne which were shelling Channel convoys.[47] Eventually half a dozen such stations were located in the area, all operating in the 78–85 cm band. A relatively low pulse repetition frequency (prf) of 1,000 was used, which suggested that the DT range was greatly in excess of the gun range. The counter-measure problem was examined by the Royal Navy who succeeded in jamming the transmissions.[48] It was later found that these sets were similar to that whose aerial had been found on the *Graf Spee*.[49]

44. ibid, paras 3.1, 5.2.5, 5.2.9, 5.2.10, 5.3, 11.
45. ibid, para 2.9.   46. ibid, para 2.9.
47. ibid, para 2.8; *Air Ministry Intelligence*, p 295.
48. AIR 20/1629, para 3.6.1.
                                                             49. Price, op cit, p 75.

changes were noted between successive frames, and as a consequence it was decided to fly a low-level sortie against what was now
a priority target. The first attempt failed on 16 February, but six
days later the necessary photographs were obtained.[50] Also on 24
February, before the photographs could be exploited, DT transmissions were intercepted and their characteristics and origin determined. They were on 120 Mc/s (2.5 m) with a prf of 1,000, giving a
maximum range of about 150 km. The rotatable array seen in each
of the circles in the photographs was of a type and of the right
dimensions for the transmissions, and DF evidence supported the
identification of this set as the *Freya*.[51]

During the remainder of 1941 more information accumulated
about *Freya* and the preparation of counter-measures was taken in
hand. SIS and POW reports threw light on its method of
operation. From interception and PR evidence it was possible to
keep step with the changes that were being made to the
equipment – to establish, for example, that some sets had a different pulse rate of 500, and thus twice the earlier maximum range of
150 kms; to assess its accuracy at about 1 km; and to take
signal-strength measurements which suggested a power of
100 kw.[52] But the *Würzburg* continued to be a more elusive target.
In March transmissions were heard on a frequency of 560 Mc/s
(53 cm) and with a prf of 5,000, suggesting a maximum range of
30 km. During the summer many intercepts were made, mainly by
No 109 Squadron RAF, some with slightly different characteristics.
The pulse rate became 3,700, thus increasing the maximum range;
the newer signals had a change in polarisation. The pulse length
was thought to be less than a microsecond, which led to the
speculation, correct as it turned out, that, as this precision was
unnecessary for early warning and aircraft reporting, the *Würzburg*
had been designed primarily for gun-ranging or AA prediction. But
no progress was made in identifying the apparatus from which
these pulses came, or in associating it with the *Würzburg*, until, late
in November 1941, the examination of small-scale photographs
showed an unexplained mark near to the cliffs at St Bruneval, near
Cap d'Antifer, from which area 53 cm signals had been intercepted. On 3 December a low-level sortie was flown, and although
no photographs were taken, the pilot reported that the object was
'an electric bowl fire about ten feet across'. Photographs were
obtained on 5 December; they showed that the apparatus had a
3 m dish.[53]

---

50. AIR 41/6, *Photographic Reconnaissance*, Vol I, Part IV, 2.
51. *Air Ministry Intelligence*, p 295; AIR 20/1629, paras 2.11, 2.12, 3.1; Jones, op
     cit, Chapter 23.   52. AIR 20/1629, para 3.1.
53. ibid, paras 2.15, 3.2; AIR 41/7, *Photographic Reconnaissance*, Vol II, Part II,
     1c.

Although it seemed reasonably certain that this apparatus was responsible for the 53 cm transmissions, proof was still lacking. The need for proof and for the acquisition of more detailed technical information led to the decision to make a raid on St Bruneval with the object of capturing the set. The plan for the raid was worked out on the basis of good photographic reconnaissance. The answers to further questions – whether the beach was mined; what gun defences existed; what troops were deployed in the area – were obtained by the SIS from its contacts in France.[54] The raid took place on 27–28 February 1942. It succeeded in capturing the receiver, amplifier, the pulse generator, the transmitter, the aerial element, and, together with one of the operators, full details of the operating method. Examination of the equipment showed that it had no anti-jamming devices and that there were other weaknesses in its design. In addition, the study of the factory markings on the captured equipment gave some idea of the rate of production, and thus of the extent of deployment, of what was now definitely identified as the *Würzburg*. Not less important, it was at last possible to compare German and British radar techniques. While the German designs incorporated no item that was unknown in the United Kingdom, the apparatus was technically in advance of British centimetric equipment, which did not achieve a range of 40 km on 50 cm until 1941.[55]

Even before photographs of the *Würzburg* were obtained in November 1941 the first clue was received to the existence of a third enemy radar. In September 1941 the RAF delegation in Washington had been given indistinct photographs of an apparatus mounted on a tower in the Berlin Tiergarten. Further information – some of it from a Chinese scientist who had seen this apparatus and described its general construction, and some from vertical photographs of Berlin taken by the PRU – made it possible to deduce that the apparatus was at least 20 feet in diameter; and the probability that it was a third type of radar was confirmed by the fact that the Bruneval photographs had shown that the diameter of the *Würzburg* was only about 10 feet.[56]

Further examples of the new radar, called the *Giant Würzburg*, were next found on operational sites. After the Enigma had referred to equipment having a range of 60 kms, a Belgian agent of the SIS reported in March 1942 that there was a *Freya* station at Nieuwerken near St Trond. Since this was in a known German night-fighter

54. Price, op cit, pp 81–86; G Millar, *The Bruneval Raid* (1974) pp 88–95; Jones, op cit, Chapter 27.
55. AIR 20/1631, ASI Report No 15 of 13 July 1942; Price, op cit, pp 81–86; Jones, Broadcast of 25 July 1974.
56. *Air Ministry Intelligence*, p 298; AIR 20/1633, ASI Report No 17 of 12 February 1943, p 3.

area, and might be expected to have Ground Controlled Interception (GCI) equipment, a PR sortie was flown. The photographs showed two radar sets similar to that in the Tiergarten and the circumstances suggested that they were an essential element in the night-fighter control system. In April a similar site was photographed on Walcheren Island, at Domburg. This last photograph, a low oblique, was important in two ways. It provided sufficient detail of the externals of the new radar to enable some estimates to be made. It also gave the layout of a GCI site, disclosing that it had a *Freya*, two *Giant Würzburg* and two *Würzburg*. The *Giant Würzburg* transmissions had still not been heard, but sufficient evidence had been accumulated to suggest that its frequency and prf were 560 Mc/s and 2,000. A directional aerial was then pointed at Domburg, and in May 1942 it received the pulses on 560 Mc/s at a prf of 1,875.[57]

At this juncture, in the spring of 1942, having reconstructed the characteristics of three ground radars and established their maximum ranges – 150 km for *Freya*; 60 km for the *Giant Würzburg*; 40 km for the *Würzburg* – the British authorities could see that the *Freya* was used for early warning and the *Würzburgs* for Flak control and night-fighter operations. From the same date, with this framework of knowledge helping them to assess new intelligence, they also benefited from a marked improvement in the supply of radar intelligence from the GAF Enigma, the SIS, the reconnaissance and photographic interpretation work of the PRU and the CIU,* and the interception of the radar transmissions by TRE and No 80 Wing. They accordingly experienced far less difficulty than before in keeping abreast of the continuing development, quantitatively and qualitatively, of the enemy's ground radar programme. By the spring of 1943 they knew that the number of *Freyas* in service had grown to about 300, of *Würzburgs* to about 1,000, of *Giant Würzburgs* to nearly 300; and it was clear that the *Giant Würzburg* was gradually replacing the *Würzburg* for height-finding at the early-warning stations. And before the end of 1942 they learned that the *Freyas* in the early-warning chain were gradually being replaced by larger sets.[58]

The first information about this new apparatus was received in July 1942 from the SIS, which reported that a square steel construction, 10 metres high by 35 long, with a fixed north–south direction, had been seen near a suspected *Freya* site near The Hague. In August the CIU reported that camouflaged erections at the site, which had been thought to contain a *Freya*, had been

---

* See below, pp 253–254.

57.   AIR 20/1629.
58.   AIR 20/1679, ASI Interim Report on 'Chimney', 17 March 1943, para 1.

replaced by a long raised girder, and in September it detected a
similar construction, about 96 feet long and supported on four
uprights, near Plougasnou in Brittany. Two further constructions
of the same kind were then photographed at known radar stations,
behind Cap Gris Nez and north of Domburg. By the end of
November 1942 the new sets were associated with references made
in German fighter R/T in the previous July to an apparatus called
Mammoth (*Mammut*) and with transmissions on 125 Mc/s in the
Freya band, but of abnormal strength, which had also been
intercepted since July. Although the particular reason for the
introduction of *Mammut* still remained uncertain – it might have
been easier searching, greater range, better low cover, greater plot
precision, smaller susceptibility to jamming or some combination
of these desiderata – it was obvious by then that the *Mammut*
presented a considerable advance on the *Freya*. It incorporated
electrical rather than mechanical means for swinging the radar
beam, which was a new departure in German design. Moreover, if,
as seemed probable, it used a phasing device to scan from a fixed
structure, its introduction meant that the Germans had mastered a
technique which the British had regarded as presenting too many
difficulties.[59]

From the fact that *Mammut* was an improvement on *Freya* for
early-warning tracking, it could be deduced that to obtain maximum benefit from it the enemy would be introducing better
equipment for height-finding at his early-warning stations, for
which purpose the *Giant Würzburg* had already gradually replaced
the *Würzburg*. This suspicion was confirmed in March 1943. Since
the previous summer GAF Enigma decrypts had made occasional
references to the installation of another new radar apparatus, the
Wassermann, in the Mediterranean and at sites on the North Sea
coast. They made it clear that the *Wassermann* was bigger than the
Freya and that it required special construction and extensive
foundations, but otherwise provided no details; nor was any
suspicious construction detected at the sites by the PRU. Early in
November 1942 the CIU reported the appearance at another site,
north of Boulogne, of a chimney-like object some 120 feet high.
Erected over underground buildings, and having extensive scaf-
folding or curtaining hanging down its sides, its purpose could not
at first be discerned. In February 1943, however, when the PRU
photographed a similar installation on Heligoland and *Mammut*
had already been identified, it was tentatively concluded that this
further development must be the *Wassermann* and that it had the
additional function of long-range height-finding. In March this
conclusion was strengthened by SIS reports of tall structures being

---

59. AIR 20/1677, ASI Interim Report on '*Hoardings*', 21 November 1942.

built at a site in Norway and at sites on the Dutch coast. At one of the Dutch sites, Bergen-aan-Zee, a tower had been photographed in December, but it had hitherto been thought to be dissimilar to the chimneys photographed near Boulogne and on Heligoland. One of the SIS reports added the information that the tower rotated. Another of the reports referred to the installation at this site as a *Wassermann*. *Wassermann* transmissions had still not been intercepted. On the other hand, the evidence indicated that the introduction of the set into service was a recent development and that it was as yet operational only on Heligoland, at Bergen-aan-Zee and possibly at Boulogne.[60]

□

By the end of 1942 the characteristics of the German ground radars were well understood; indeed, equipment for jamming them had been in existence and under continual development since May 1942, and only the feeling that the benefits of jamming would be more than off-set by the effects of enemy interference with British radar had delayed its introduction. It had been more difficult to acquire intelligence about the deployment and the equipment of the German night-fighter organisation, including the procedures by which the ground radars controlled the night-fighters opposing Bomber Command.

The German night-fighter organisation presented the British intelligence bodies with a formidable problem. Not least because the organisation itself was undergoing continual extension and improvement, they did not arrive at a thorough understanding of how it worked until the end of September 1942 despite the steady accumulation of information about it from the summer of 1940, when night-fighters first attacked Bomber Command.

For information about the enemy organisation the British authorities were in the first instance indebted to Sigint. Among the Sigint sources the Enigma yielded only occasional references until 1942. In June 1940 it reported that with the aid of something called *Freya*, JG 51 had destroyed nine British bombers;[61] and as early as August 1940 it disclosed the existence of NJG 1,[62] the first night-fighter Gruppe which had been created by the GAF in June, following the appointment of General Kammhuber to command the defences against night bombing. He constructed and rapidly expanded a defence belt based on night-fighter sectors or 'boxes'. By the end of 1941, when it showed that NJG 1 had been renamed Fliegerkorps XII and allotted its own Enigma key (named Cockroach at GC and CS), the Enigma had thrown next to no light on the equipment, tactics, deployment and expansion of the enemy's

---

60.   AIR 20/1629.   61.   RDF 1 and 2.   62.   CX/JQ 205A.

organisation. Nor did this situation immediately improve when GC and CS broke the Cockroach key in February 1942. Because of the difficulty of this key and because of competition for priority between it and other Enigma keys not much of the traffic was read until September 1942; and because the essential facts about the night-fighter system and its method of control had still not been determined, little could be made until then of the decrypts of Fliegerkorps XII's signals.[63]

The other Sigint source was provided by the encoded signals to and from the ground-controlled fighters for which, as for its regular day-fighter communications, the GAF used R/T on HF. Intercepted by the BBC and the HDUs* from September 1940, this new type of traffic was first studied by ADI (Sc), who was charged by ACAS (I) early in 1941 with the responsibility of 'compiling the intelligence picture of the German night defences'. Before long, however, the Air Intelligence Branch decided that the task of analysing the intercepts should be carried out by the Air Section at GC and CS.[64] The Air Section found it to be 'one of the toughest intelligence problems ever tackled', and one of the most tedious. The night-fighters observed highly rigid and secure signalling procedures. The intercepts of their traffic, though plentiful, were corrupt and often unintelligible. DF on HF R/T was poor. To make matters worse, the Air Section's early attempts to understand the traffic were unsuccessful because the interpretations were coloured by a knowledge of the British night-fighter system; this had from the outset placed emphasis on Air Interception (AI) and it seems clear that until well into 1941, before the GAF had introduced AI, the investigators tried to fit the R/T intercepts to the assumption that AI was already in use. For these reasons – and in the absence of any valuable assistance from the Enigma – the Air Section had learned little about the order of battle, the deployment, the operational procedures and the equipment of the night-fighter system by the beginning of 1942.

From March 1942, slowly but steadily, ADI (Sc) began to work out the elements of the night-fighter system, and to understand its method of control, with evidence provided by the SIS, the CIU and the PRU. From the end of 1941 SIS agents had been given special training in how to report on radar matters; by the following spring more than half of the reports from them that were sent to the CIU to assist its photographic interpretation were concerned with radar. Many of them were reports of radar sites, some of which, like that from the St Trond area in March 1942,† were followed up with

---

* See Volume I, p 180.   † See above, p 249.

63.   AIR 20/1629; CX/MSS/398/T1, 436/T8.
64.   AIR 20/1663, ASI Report No I of 29 December 1942.

valuable results by the PRU. One dated 20 April enclosed a stolen map, which gave the deployment of a searchlight regiment throughout the southern half of Belgium, and full details of the radar and searchlight dispositions within a single sector of the air defence belt. By May the evidence had made it possible to deduce how a typical sector was organised and equipped. At that point it became clear that some reorganisation was taking place in the main defensive zones. The SIS began to report that the searchlights were being removed; by 20 May the PRU had confirmed that all had gone. For some time thereafter, moreover, it remained difficult to identify the sectors; by the beginning of September only seven GCI stations had been located. But from that date the knowledge that had been built up with the PRU and SIS evidence made it possible to compare the German reported raid tracks and the actual flight paths of the RAF bombers. The comparison enabled the position of one of the radars to be located and then related to Fliegerkorps XII's decrypts. This allowed a full interpretation of the decrypts and made it possible to locate more and more of the sectors in the main belt and to keep track of their steady proliferation.[65] By the end of 1942 ADI (Sc) had located over 50 GCI stations and identified their sectors, and it was clear that the German expansion programme had concentrated on two areas. One lay along the coasts of Holland and the Bight; the other was an inland belt – known by the British as the *Kammhuber* line – which stretched from Schleswig Holstein to eastern France and the Swiss frontier.

To determine how the ground radars were used to control the fighters proved to be even more difficult. By the end of 1940 POW interrogations had established that the *Freya* could not identify unless the aircraft gave notice of their times and routes,* and thus that the fighters were not equipped with Identification Friend or Foe (IFF) equipment. From February 1941, however, evidence began to accumulate from a variety of sources – references by POW; the study of the night-fighter R/T traffic; the examination of a crashed aircraft, which proved to be wired for the device though it did not carry it – that the enemy was introducing IFF equipment and that the device went under the name of FuGe 25. And in October 1941, when an Enigma decrypt disclosed that a Staffel of Ju 87s in Libya had been fitted with the device and a POW described its method of operation, it became virtually certain that the German IFF equipment was operational but that its use was being restricted to aircraft operating over friendly territory.[66] Even then, however, there remained some uncertainty as to whether the

---

* See above, p 246.

65. *Air Ministry Intelligence*, p 303; AIR 20/1629; AIR 20/1663; Jones, op cit, pp 271–272; CX/MSS/2748, para 20 and 2942, para 11.
66. AIR 20/1629, para 4.

identification of the equipment as FuGe 25 was correct – for other names that might be associated with it were appearing in the intelligence sources[67] – and it was possible only to speculate about its characteristics and the way it was used for GCI and IFF until, from the spring of 1942, the equipment captured at St Bruneval* provided first-hand knowledge of the level of radar technology that the enemy was applying to the night-fighter control system[68] and the Enigma decrypts of Fliegerkorps XII established that there were two versions of the airborne device: FuGe 25 which worked with the *Giant Würzburg*, and FuGe 25A which worked with the *Freya* stations.[69]

It still remained to intercept the Air Interception transmissions. As in the case of the ground radars, none of the sources disclosed the essential details about frequencies and pulse rates. Moreover, the transmissions of the airborne sets could not normally be intercepted without the use of airborne search receivers. By September 1942 airborne signals had been intercepted by a special ground station in Norfolk but it could not be confirmed that these transmissions were from airborne equipment until a listening aircraft of No 1474 Flight RAF had flown in a night-fighter area and observed whether the transmissions grew in intensity up to the time it was attacked. This hazardous exploit was carried out successfully on 3 December 1942.[70] It confirmed that the transmissions were taking place on a wavelength of 61 cm and with a prf of 2,700.

With this technical advance ADI (Sc)'s section finally obtained a complete understanding of the German defence system as it was at the beginning of 1943.[71] By combining technical and order of battle intelligence it was at last able to describe how the night-fighter organisation had evolved and how it now functioned. It realised that the radius of operation of the radar-controlled night-fighters, initially 25 miles, had been extended by the introduction of the *Giant Würzburg* early in 1941 to about 40 miles, this being the extent of the 'box' within which each GCI station controlled the defensive activities of its night-fighters. From photographic reconnaissance of the GCI stations it could see that up to May 1942 there had been minor differences between the typical layout and equipment of the stations in the inland belt and those of the stations in the coastal belt, but that these differences, of which the most important was that the coastal belt had made no use of search-

---

* See above, p 249.

67. ibid.   68.   Jones, op cit, p 245.
69. AIR 20/1633, p 8.
70. AIR 20/1629; AIR 20/1633; Jones lecture, reprinted in *Journal of the Royal United Services Institute*, August 1947, p 360; Price, op cit, pp 106–107.
71. *Air Ministry Intelligence*, p 304.

lights, had disappeared when the inland belt adopted the same tactics as the coastal defences. Since then the organisation and the procedure in the two belts had been identical.

The organisation was divided into sectors, each consisting of three GCI stations and three boxes, one station to a box. The sector controller ordered up the fighters, one to each box, when an alert was sounded for his area. Each fighter then came under the direction of a GCI control officer who had a *Freya* and two *Giant Würzburgs* at his disposal. He used the *Freya* for early warning, tracked the fighter with one of his *Giant Würzburgs* and turned the other *Giant Würzburg* on to the enemy bomber once it was sighted. Thereafter, by comparing the radar plots of the bomber and of his own fighter he determined the vector position of the bomber relative to the fighter and passed this information to the fighter. If the fighter was equipped with AI he vectored it to within $1\frac{1}{4}$ miles of the bomber; otherwise he vectored it to within visual contact. Throughout an engagement the station was fully occupied with one target; it could not direct its attention to other bombers within its box. After an engagement the station vectored its fighter back to a beacon to await the next target. Additional evidence, derived from the operational experience of the British bomber crews as well as from intelligence, suggested that the German fighters established contact with bombers in about 20 per cent of the attempts, that about 60 per cent of the contacts led to successful attacks, and that the attack was usually made from behind and below, sometimes from as close as 20 to 50 yards.

From the autumn of 1941 partial knowledge of this system had enabled tactical measures to be taken against the *Kammhuber* line; the chief of the counter-measures was to fly the bombers in a compact force through a single box in as short a time as possible, since the controller could handle only one target at a time. But it was not possible to take technical counter-measures before ADI (Sc)'s comprehensive report giving the above description was issued on 29 December 1942.[72]* This paid tribute to the help received from a large number of sources – the SIS, PR, 1474 Flight, the Enigma (referred to obliquely), TRE, POW interrogation, even the pigeon service which carried messages locating stations from areas where there were no other communications. With regard to the work of the Air Section at GC and CS in interpreting the night-fighter R/T intercepts, it acknowledged a number of particular contributions it had made. By December 1941 the Air Section had confirmed that something called *Kleine Schraube* was a

---

* An abbreviated copy suitable for circulation down to command staffs and crews was issued on 12 February 1943.[73]

72. AIR 20/1663.   73. ibid.

radio beacon around which the German night-fighter orbited while waiting to be vectored on to its target,[74] and in May 1942, by fusing the R/T with W/T intercepts, it had established the frequency and the characteristics of the *Kleine Schraube* – which made it possible for Cheadle to DF the beacons and locate many of the fixed points of the night-fighter areas. In June 1942 it had thrown light on the problem of the FuGe 25A by showing that the night-fighters carried an apparatus which they called *Stern* and which was used to identify them by the ground controller.[75] In July 1942 the appearance in practice signals late in 1941 and in operational traffic from early in 1942 of a new R/T code signal *Emil Emil* led to the suggestion that the signal indicated that the night-fighter had now been brought close enough to the bombers to pick up its target by its own detector; this was the *Lichtenstein* apparatus which had been mentioned by a POW in April 1941 and was first referred to in the Enigma decrypts in July 1942.[76] But in addition to making these contributions to knowledge about the deployment and the control procedure of the enemy system, subjects which were of first concern to ADI (Sc) but on which the Air Section was only one of his several sources, the study of the R/T traffic had provided evidence about the tactics of the night-fighters; since the beginning of 1942, indeed, this had been the staple subject of the Air Section's daily retrospective analyses of the traffic. By the autumn of 1942 these reports were regularly recording the number of enemy aircraft that had operated the previous night, the number of interceptions they had attempted, the number of successes they had scored; and from such data the Air Section was working out the mean height at which interceptions were made and establishing such general findings as the fact that twice as many Allied bombers were intercepted on their way home as on their way to their targets. Of more importance, the traffic provided some understanding of the functions of a night-fighter controller operating the aircraft within the box for which he was responsible.

□

Despite the fact that a big effort went into the study of bombing targets,* intelligence could do little before the end of 1942 to increase the effectiveness of the British bombing raids. Until then, moreover, it exerted no influence on the evolution of bombing policy except for a brief period from January to March 1941 in which the primary target of Bomber Command was the destruction of Germany's synthetic oil installations.

The evolution of bombing policy was dictated by strategic

---

* See Appendix 2, p 654.

74. AIR 20/1663.   75. ibid, p 205.   76. ibid.

considerations and the operational and technical limitations imposed on Bomber Command by its training and equipment.
Among the strategic considerations the most important were the
strength of pre-war doctrines about the potentiality of strategic
bombing and the fact that those doctrines were buttressed after
1940 by, on the one hand, the call for retaliation for the GAF's
raids on the United Kingdom and, on the other hand, the
argument that, apart from the naval blockade and such subversion
as SOE might accomplish, the bomber had become Great Britain's
only offensive weapon. The chief limitations on the effectiveness of
Bomber Command were the fact that the enemy's defences made
day bombing of pin-point targets too hazardous and the fact that it
then encountered technical difficulties in finding and hitting precision targets at night. It was on account of these difficulties, as much
as under the influence of the general arguments for strategic
bombing, that Bomber Command, which had abandoned day
bombing as early as April 1940, embarked on the transition from
precision to area bombing in October 1940, from which date it had
concentrated its night bombing against single towns or industrial
areas instead of against specific industrial installations. In June
1941 the Air Staff, taking another large step towards area bombing,
decided that while Bomber Command should concentrate on
moonlight nights against railway centres and other transport
targets, it should otherwise – that is, for about three-quarters of the
time – continue its offensive with raids on such large and easily
located targets as Cologne, Düsseldorf, Duisburg, Hamburg,
Bremen, Hanover, Frankfurt, Mannheim, Stuttgart and Berlin,
with the double aim of achieving economic dislocation and reducing civilian morale.

In reaching this decision the Air Staff was influenced by its
growing recognition of the limitations facing Bomber Command,
and particularly by the fact that those limitations had been
underlined during a short-lived offensive against Germany's oil
installations between January and March 1941. The oil raids had
been undertaken in the light of intelligence put forward by the
Lloyd Committee since the summer of 1940, and after urgent
representations by the Hankey Committee for quick action, the Air
Staff having been persuaded by the Fifth Report of the Lloyd
Committee that Bomber Command could play a large part in
applying what the committee's chairman called the 'quick death
clinch on the whole enemy oil position' of which that report had
spoken.[77]* Within a few weeks, however, it had become clear that
they were proving to be no more effective than Bomber Command's

---

* See Volume I, pp 233, 241–244.

77.   CAB 66/14, WP (41) 2 of 2 January (POG (L) (40) 18 of 16 December).

earlier offensives. The campaign against oil had been abandoned in March 1941, when Bomber Command was temporarily diverted against defensive targets during a period of emergency in the Battle of the Atlantic, and, despite continued pressure from the Hankey Committee during the rest of 1941, the Joint Planners and the Air Staff now accepted that Bomber Command lacked the accuracy in navigation and bomb aiming that was necessary for effective attacks on such targets at night.*

The oil offensive had finally established that, in these circumstances, it was to no avail that MEW could provide Bomber Command with good information about targets – in this case, detailed evidence about the location of Germany's oil installations and reasonably accurate estimates of the state of her oil supplies. It had also confirmed that a second form of intelligence – Cheadle's ability to supply the RAF with the call-signs, frequencies and locations of the German MF beacons – could do little to reduce Bomber Command's navigational problems. If they were equipped with appropriate receivers, British aircraft could use these beacons to check their navigation on the way to their targets. Fighter Command had made use of Cheadle's ability to forecast the frequencies from December 1940, in its 'intruder' raids against GAF airfields. Thereafter arrangements had been made to get Cheadle's information to Bomber Command; and from October 1941, when Cheadle began to experience delays as a result of more rapid changes in the German frequencies,† these arrangements, which remained in force until 1943, included the transmission of beacon information to RAF crews after take-off if they had not received it beforehand.[78] But while this procedure was valuable for general navigational purposes, neither it nor traditional navigational methods were adequate for the accurate location and bombing of targets at night. This called for equipment and training that remained, as yet, beyond the reach of Bomber Command.

In addition to target information and information about the German beacons the photographing and assessment of bomb-damage had a bearing on the bombing effort, unlike information about the enemy's defence systems. This form of intelligence underwent a steady improvement from November 1940. But it was this improvement that established beyond doubt by the spring of 1941 that Bomber Command was unable to make effective night attacks against precision targets. MEW and the Air Ministry had recognised that photographic reconnaissance could be the only reliable method of assessing bomb damage, but with PR of the areas attacked at first limited and only gradually improving and

---

* See Appendix 12.   † See above, p 241.

78.   AIR 41/46, p 8.

with the small scale of the photographs making assessment difficult, there was until the end of 1940 a tendency to prefer air crew claims and the occasional report from Germany to the evidence of PR which was detecting little damage. Thereafter, with Spitfires available for photographing bomb damage and improved cameras making it possible to produce large-scale photographs, the true situation gradually emerged. After the first mass raid by all available aircraft on a selected industrial area – that against Mannheim on 16 December 1940 – all the air crew reports claimed that most bombs had fallen in the target area and that the centre of the town had been left in flames. But on 21 December, as its second attempt, a PRU Spitfire succeeded in photographing Mannheim in daylight, with distinctly sobering results. The photographs showed that, although considerable, the damage had been widely dispersed and that much of it was outside the target area. At the end of December a PR report on recent attacks on two oil plants at Gelsenkirchen showed that neither plant had suffered major damage. It was not until April 1941, however, after detailed study of large-scale daylight reconnaissance photographs of further raids, that the Directorate of Bomber Operations recognised that the estimate of 300 yards for bombing accuracy at night in good conditions was unattainable. This figure had been taken, without justification, from a pre-war estimate for daylight bombing; the correct figure was 1,000 yards, though 600 yards might be achieved in the best conditions.[79]

With the resumption of the bombing offensive in June 1941 a further advance in bomb-damage assessment showed that Bomber Command had neither sufficient accuracy in target location nor adequate bomb-aiming equipment even to produce the results that had been expected from area bombing. That this was so was finally established in August 1941, when Lord Cherwell instituted the first thorough survey of Bomber Command's operational summaries and of the night photographs taken by bombers during their operational sorties as a means of confirming their location and pinpointing bomb bursts.* This survey, undertaken by Lord Cherwell's secretary, Mr D M B Butt,[80] showed that since the

---

* These photographs should be distinguished from night photographic reconnaissance. This was still in the experimental stage and it was not until the end of 1942 that the first operational night PR sortie took place.

79.   Webster and Frankland, *The Strategic Air Offensive against Germany* (1961), Vol 1, pp 163–164, 220–222, 227, 245–247; AIR 41/40, *The RAF in the Bombing Offensive against Germany*, Vol II, pp 153–154.
80.   AIR 41/41, *The RAF in the Bombing Offensive against Germany*, Vol III, pp 41–43; Webster and Frankland, op cit, Vol I, pp 178, 247 and Vol IV, Appendix 13 (the Butt Report); C Babington Smith, *Evidence in Camera* (1958), pp 95–101; Jones, op cit, p 210.

beginning of June, of the aircraft which had claimed to have attacked within five miles of their targets, only about 1 in 3 had done so. This proportion, moreover, was the general average: 2 in 3 had done so when attacking French ports, but only 1 in 4 in raids on Germany, and only about 7 in 100 when the target was in the Ruhr, where industrial haze was common and the German defences were at their most formidable.

The Butt investigation led to the creation at Bomber Command of a small unit to carry on this kind of research; this was the origin of the Operational Research Section (ORS) in Bomber Command. The survey also brought about for the first time a full realisation of the need for urgency in introducing the new navigational equipment and new techniques that were already under development. The use of these in selected aircraft with expert crews to produce a Pathfinder force after the fashion of the GAF was now urgently examined.[81] But none of the new equipment came into service before March 1942, and some of it was delayed until 1943, while the Pathfinder force was not created until August 1942. Meanwhile, as well as achieving meagre results, the latest offensive was already faltering because the size of the available bomber force was quite inadequate for the task that had been imposed on it. From as early as 30 June 1941 the need to conserve the force was creating severe problems, and the casualty rate was being anxiously discussed by the Cabinet.[82] By the end of the year the offensive was breaking down 'owing to the limitations of the force, especially in face of cloud and haze which persisted over the targets and of the weather at home bases, which imposed too great demands on inadequately trained crews and sent the wastage figures soaring'.[83]

When this phase of the offensive came to an end in February 1942 it had done little damage to Germany's military potential despite absorbing about 60 per cent of Bomber Command's total efforts for seven months. It may therefore be wondered why the authorities persisted with the offensive when intelligence could now make accurate assessments of the effect of the bombing even if it could still make little positive contribution to its effectiveness. The RAF's own narrative on the offensive has maintained that one of the main reasons why this phase of the bombing was not called off earlier was that, despite the progress made in the assessment of bomb damage, 'the picture was never painted as gloomily at the time as it appears in retrospect'. The narrative continues –

---

81. Webster and Frankland, op cit, Vol I, pp 178, 247–250.
82. AIR 41/41, pp 39–42; CAB 65/18, WM (41) 64 of 30 June; CAB 65/19, WM (41) 68 and 84 of 10 July and 19 August.
83. AIR 41/41, pp 64–65.

'Crews' reports of what they believed they had accomplished were treated as reliable. Proved cases of error, usually revealed by daylight PR, came as a great shock, and at first threw doubt on the efficiency of the PI [Photographic Intelligence] rather than on the visual reports. Furthermore, the crews' belief usually received a good measure of confirmation from the bulk of "intelligence reports" percolating through at a lapse of a week or two. These told of heavy damage and lengthy disruption of transport and other facilities; or bolstered up current belief in the effect of that imponderable weapon, the attack on morale, giving rise to the impression that whenever our Wellingtons, Hampdens and Whitleys flew by night the population of western Germany took to its shelters, cowered under an incessant rain of high explosive and plotted rebellion against the hated Nazi regime.

There could be no greater contrast imaginable than that between the enthusiastic "travellers' tales" from Germany via Sweden or Switzerland on the one hand, and on the other the bleak pictures of scarcely damaged towns brought back by PRU Spitfires and the tell-tale night photographs [revealing bombing] of fields and open country. Rarely can there have been a campaign in which intelligence was so conflicting.'[84]

But the narrative adds that –

'realists in the Service accepted the irrefutable "evidence in camera" and, under the cloak of complacent publicity which kept the British people happy, went to work on schemes to improve matters and build up a force that could do what the optimists imagined was already being done.'[85]

In its accounts of individual raids, moreover, it frequently comments that at the time their uneconomical nature was 'fairly accurately guessed'.[86] It stresses, finally, that there was another reason for the duration of the campaign – the need to gain experience for the future. When we add that previous experience had established that attacks on precision targets would be still more uneconomical until bombing accuracy had been achieved, and that this was being confirmed by the lack of success in the attacks which continued on German warships in port, it seems safe to assume that it was for these other reasons, political and operational, that the authorities persisted, not because they ignored the results of accurate bomb-damage assessment, and still less because the intelligence bodies were failing to provide this information.

It was on these strategic and operational grounds that the Air Staff recommended, even when the previous offensive was being abandoned, that bombing should be resumed at an early date and that, with the aim of breaking Germany's civilian morale, and particularly the morale of her industrial workers, still greater emphasis should be placed on area bombing. On 14 February 1942, the Air Staff having argued that given that Bomber Command was

---

84.   ibid, pp 64–65.   85.   ibid, p 65.   86.   ibid, pp 67–69, for examples.

expanding, was about to introduce a new bomber and would now
be benefiting from 'Gee', the first of its radio navigation aids,*
bombing would produce better results than in the past, the Chiefs
of Staff accepted the recommendation.[87] But they did so with some
misgivings. Sceptical of the results achieved so far, the other two
Services were also beginning to insist that the demands of the RAF
were clashing seriously with their own defence requirements and to
feel, perhaps, that Bomber Command was ceasing to be the only
arm capable of taking the offensive. On 14 February, without
objecting to the RAF's plans, the First Sea Lord requested the
transfer of squadrons from Bomber Command to Coastal
Command.[88] On 6 March, the Admiralty again pressed for an
increase of land-based aircraft for work at sea, especially for
long-range reconnaissance for convoy support and attacks on
U-boats, and claimed that the Admiralty should control all aircraft
engaged on naval operations.[89] Four days later the CIGS expressed grave dissatisfaction at the Air Ministry's failure to provide
aircraft for army air support and also demanded that the Army
should control its own aircraft.[90]

Under this pressure the Chiefs of Staff agreed to review existing
air strategy and on 23 March 1942, to assist their review, they
called for the first time for a report from the JIC on the results
achieved so far by the bombing of Germany and the effects of
continuing the policy, in so far as they could be assessed.[91] But the
JIC's report made it clear that intelligence could not answer these
questions. No doubt because area bombing with new equipment
and new tactics had only recently begun, it made no use of the
evidence, such as it was, about the damage done by previous RAF
bombing; in any case, that evidence was limited to photographic
reconnaissance which could detect only visible damage, and in the
absence of reliable reports from Germany there was no way of
calculating the wider effects of visible damage on the economy or
the morale of the enemy. For these reasons the JIC suggested that
a study of the effectiveness of German bombing of the United
Kingdom might provide some pointers on the likely effects of
continued bombing, but stressed that these would depend on a host
of operational uncertainties.[92] Meanwhile, it concluded that given

---

* For details of 'Gee' see Webster and Frankland, op cit, Vol IV, Annex I; and for the
contribution of intelligence to the safeguarding of 'Gee' see ibid, Vol I, p 248, Price, op cit,
p 100 et seq, Jones, op cit, Chapter 25.

87.   Webster and Frankland, op cit, Vol I, pp 320–322 and Vol IV, Appendix 8
      (xxii); CAB 69/4, DO (42) 14 of 9 February.
88.   CAB 69/4, DO (42) 15 of 14 February.   89. ibid, DO (42) 23 of 6 March.
90.   CAB 80/35, COS (42) 164 of 10 March.
91.   CAB 79/19, COS (42) 80th Meeting of 11 March, 92nd Meeting of 23
      March.   92. JIC (42) 117 (o) of 6 April.

good operational conditions over six months air bombing was capable of bringing about an increasing reduction in Germany's war effort, but that the reduction could not be quantified. This conclusion was dismissed as useless by the Chiefs of Staff on 10 April.[93] By this time Lord Cherwell had intervened with his own analysis of the effects on houses of the GAF bombing of the United Kingdom. Its assumptions were questioned by Sir Henry Tizard, scientific adviser to the Air Ministry, who doubted whether such figures provided a reasonable guide to the destruction likely to be caused by the RAF up to the middle of 1943.[94]

In these circumstances the government again called in Mr Justice Singleton, asking him to estimate 'in the light of our experience of the German bombing of this country, and of such information as is available of the results of our bombing of Germany, what results are we likely to achieve from continuing our air attacks on Germany at the greatest possible strength during the next six, twelve and eighteen months respectively?'[95] His report, submitted on 20 May 1942, found, as had the JIC, that the available intelligence was not illuminating. It concluded that there was little prospect that in its attack on German morale Bomber Command would have any great results within six months; for the longer term, the state of German morale would depend not merely on the bombing but also on whether Germany suffered reverses, or failed to achieve successes, in Russia. And it was for its indirect effects in forcing the GAF to retain resources in Germany, which would be 'of incalculable value to Russia', rather than for its direct effects on German morale, which were 'much more difficult' to assess, that the report favoured a continuation of the bomber offensive.[96]

In addition to offering these general conclusions Mr Justice Singleton had to pronounce on protests which MEW was now making against the manner in which Bomber Command had been carrying out the new directive since February. MEW had not disagreed with the directive; it did not regard the bombing offensive as likely to have an important effect on the level of Germany's industrial production, and it accepted that its most important effects, even on industry, were likely to be those which it had on the living conditions of the civilian population.* But in the belief that the policy of area bombing should be combined with concentration against specific industries it had advised that targets selected according to a variety of economic criteria should be listed

---

* See above, pp 153–154.

93.   CAB 79/20, COS (42) 114th Meeting of 10 April.
94.   Webster and Frankland, op cit, Vol I, pp 331–337.
95.   CAB 79/20, COS (42) 114th Meeting of 10 April.
96.   Webster and Frankland, op cit, Vol IV, Appendix 17.

in the directive, particularly those that were known to be important for electric power, synthetic rubber, special components for the air and armaments industries, oil and substitute fuels, aluminium and soda ash, and diesel engines and accumulators for U-boats. And before very long it was complaining that Bomber Command was paying no attention to even this generously comprehensive list of priorities.

MEW's dissatisfaction came to a head after Bomber Command's attack on the MAN submarine diesel factory at Augsburg on 17 April. This was an experimental raid: the new Lancaster bombers were used for the first time in daylight and in routeing them to the target use was made of intelligence about the air defences over a wide area of Europe. But Bomber Command had chosen the target without consulting MEW and MEW protested strongly to the Prime Minister that the target, which in February it had put at the bottom of its recommended list, should not have been chosen in preference to others of greater economic importance.[97]

MEW's protest was referred to Mr Justice Singleton. In his report he accepted MEW's argument that 'to assess the probable effect on Germany's war effort of different degrees of damage to different parts of her economy is difficult, but it is essential in the framing of an effective bombing policy'.[98] At the same time, however, he recognised the force of Bomber Command's view that the prime criteria in selecting targets must be vulnerability and feasibility and, having conceded that 'the final choice of the target for the night must always rest with the C-in-C Bomber Command', he suggested that the bombing would produce better results if it gave priority to industrial areas rather than to houses and that liaison might possibly be improved between Bomber Command and the Bomb Target Committee which met once a fortnight under the chairmanship of the Air Ministry's Director of Bomber Operations.

To the general objective laid down in the directive of February 1942 the Air Ministry itself provided more effective opposition than did MEW because it could support its arguments with firmer intelligence. As early as January 1942 the Air Intelligence Branch had urged that the offensive should be directed against the German aircraft industry. On 28 February it went further and recommended a switch back to day bombing in a campaign of attrition against the GAF. It rested its argument on the fact that the Enigma evidence on the German order of battle was beginning to

---

97.   ibid, Vol I, pp 463–464.
98.   ibid, p 465. The quotation was from a letter from MEW to the Secretary of State for Air.

suggest that, as a result of the heavy strain of the Russian fighting, the GAF, and particularly its fighter arm, was weaker than at any time since the outbreak of the war.[99] These pleas were rejected on operational grounds – the RAF lacked the technology to mount precision attacks on the aircraft industry and its bombers were not equipped to engage in daylight combat with the GAF. On 8 April, however, the Chiefs of Staff were sufficiently impressed by the Air Ministry's evidence to instruct Fighter and Bomber Commands to consider plans for inflicting wastage on the GAF,[100] and early in May the Air Staff made a still greater concession. On 1 May the Director of Intelligence (Operations) at the Air Ministry pressed once again for a new directive to Bomber Command that would give priority to aircraft industry targets. He did not succeed in getting a new directive but on 5 May the Air Staff amended the February directive, giving high priority to the three aircraft industry targets that figured at the bottom of its list of targets and adding that when precision attack was possible consideration should be given to selecting as targets the factories that were believed to be responsible for nearly all of the GAF's fighter production.[101]

If the views of the Air Staff were changing, it was not only because it was beginning to be impressed by Air Intelligence's evidence about the critical situation in the GAF. It was under pressure from the Anglo-American Combined Planners, who also stressed that the reduction of the GAF's fighter force would be the best way of giving assistance to Russia.[102] By May, moreover, its resolve was weakening because it was having to face the fact that, so far as could be judged, the latest phase of the bomber offensive was having no appreciable effect on German industry. And it was also emerging that even indirectly, through the attack on civilian morale, its results were disappointing.

Considerable improvement had been expected in the accuracy and effectiveness of bombing from March 1942 following the introduction of 'Gee' which, it was hoped, would also provide a means of blind bombing. But in the event the photographic intelligence soon established that 'Gee', while fulfilling expectations as a navigational aid in getting aircraft over their target, and particularly in enabling aircraft to keep a tight schedule, was of little value to blind bombing, for which indeed it had not been designed.

In the first raid in which it was used, an attack on Essen on 8

99.   AIR 20/26, 25 January, 28 February and 4 March 1942.
100. CAB 79/56, COS (42) 21st (o) Meeting, 8 April: CAB 80/62, COS (42) 106 (o) of 19 April.
101. AIR 2/4476, Air Historical Branch file II/70/272(B)m Enclosure 28a.
102. AIR 41/42, *The RAF in the Bombing Offensive against Germany*, Vol IV, p 151.

March 1942, 80 per cent of the aircraft claimed to have attacked, but of the night photographs brought back from the raid the majority could not be interpreted, few were within five miles of the aiming point and none showed the centre of Essen. It was clear that the main weight of the attack had bombed on fires started away from the target. During March and April, in eight raids on Essen, 1,081 out of 1,555 aircraft claimed to have attacked, but only 22 out of 212 photographs taken during the raids proved the attacks to be within five miles of the town.[103] A specific blind-bombing attack on Cologne on 22 April confirmed that more than this was not to be expected. In all raids during the two months night photographs showed that 40 per cent of the aircraft had bombed within five miles compared with 26 per cent in the previous three months. In conditions when visual aiming had been impossible the evidence from the photographs was scanty, but it suggested that 50 per cent of bombs fell within five miles of the target and only 20 per cent within two miles. On the whole, the results up to the end of April were superior to those obtained by visual attack in poor weather but inferior to visual bombing in average or good weather.[104]

As well as using 'Gee', the RAF was at this time developing new tactics by introducing flares and a high proportion of incendiary bombs into air attacks. In March it used these tactics successfully in raids against the Renault works at Billancourt on the 3rd and against Lübeck on the 28th, in both of which low-level bombing proved possible. The raid against the Renault works – the first against a French target – was assisted by the SIS which had good intelligence about the target and about the likely reactions of the French, and could also give first-hand reports of the damage. Its agents reported a serious set-back in production which could not be resumed for three months.[105] At Lübeck incendiary bombs caused great destruction to the city's dense and largely timbered mediaeval buildings, as was confirmed by PR. The attack on Lübeck was followed by a series of raids on Rostock in April. It was in retaliation for these raids that Hitler ordered the Baedeker raids on the United Kingdom.* In April and May precision attacks with the new tactics were continued from time to time with varying success, but with poor results when low-level bombing was impossible. Night photographs and day-time PR frequently showed negligible damage against the main targets in May.[106]

It was in these circumstances that Bomber Command obtained

---

* See above, pp 237, 239–240.

103. Webster and Frankland, op cit, Vol I, p 390.
104. AIR 41/42, pp 56–57.
105. CAB 66/19, WP (41) 260 of 6 November: CAB 65/25, WM (42) 3 of 6 January and WM (42) 14 of 2 February.
106. AIR 41/42, p 158 et seq.

approval for its wish to revert to the policy of confining itself to mass bombing, and to do so by committing its entire force in thousand-bomber raids against a single town. The first thousand-bomber raid took place on 30 May 1942 against Cologne. It caused immense damage to the city, destroying 3,300 houses and rendering 45,132 people homeless. The extent of this damage was accurately enough assessed at the time as 3,000 houses and 50,000 homeless – though the number of deaths, actually 474, was greatly exaggerated in MEW's estimate of 1,000 to 6,000 – and it was far more serious than the total damage Bomber Command had done to Cologne with 1,364 sorties in smaller raids during the previous nine months. To that extent the experiment was a success. At the beginning of July, however, MEW recognised that the city was functioning normally again within two weeks of the raid.[107] Two further raids on the same scale, moreover, were distinctly less successful. 956 bombers attacked Essen on 1 June and 767 claimed to have bombed in or near the town. But none of the night photographs showed the target, and only 8 out of 73 photographs were within five miles of it. PR over the next few days confirmed that little damage had been done to the town and none to the Krupp works.[108] On 25 June 904 aircraft bombed Bremen with results that were almost as disappointing. PR showed damage to parts of the town and to the Focke Wulf factory, but established that the docks – the chief objective – had escaped injury.[109] These poor results brought the thousand-bomber raids to an end.

The discontinuation of the thousand-bomber raids was followed by further set-backs. Although its life was prolonged by the introduction of a second chain of stations and by the use of a different frequency from October, 'Gee' was being jammed by the Germans from the beginning of August 1942. From 18 August Bomber Command introduced the Pathfinder force, a further innovation which had been advocated since September 1941,* but until the end of 1942, when Bomber Command brought its next navigational aids into use,† the force had little impact in improving Bomber Command's ability to mark and accurately bomb its targets.

□

The reduction in the GAF's bombing of the United Kingdom from May 1941 was accompanied by an increase not only in Bomber

---

* See above, p 261.   † See below, pp 513, 515.

107.   ibid, pp 171–173; Webster and Frankland, op cit, Vol I, p 486.
108.   AIR 41/42, pp 174–176; Webster and Frankland, op cit, Vol I, pp 410–411.
109.   AIR 41/42, p 181.

Command's night offensive but also in the frequency of daylight sweeps over north-west Europe by Fighter Command, supplemented by aircraft of Coastal Command and the day bombers of Bomber Command and from mid-1942 the bomber formations of US Eighth Air Force, with the aim of destroying GAF fighters. The daylight offensive had begun at the beginning of 1941. From June of that year it was intensified in an effort to help the Russians by reducing or reversing the flow of GAF formations to the eastern front and disrupting communications in western Europe. Although Bomber Command soon withdrew from it, Fighter Command kept up the offensive with one-third of its total strength until the end of 1941. The offensive failed in its aims; the GAF did not have to reinforce the two Geschwader of fighters that it had maintained in the west.[110] At the same time, Fighter Command incurred heavy casualties. Having lost 51 pilots in these sweeps by June 1941, it lost a further 411 in the second half of the year, more than the number it had sacrificed during the Battle of Britain between July and October 1940. Not the least reason why the offensive was nevertheless continued is to be found in the fact that Fighter Command produced 'enormously exaggerated estimates of German losses'.[111] Between June 1941 and the end of the year it claimed to have destroyed 731 aircraft whereas the GAF lost only 154, of which 51 were not destroyed by British action.[112]

The exaggeration persisted because, as in 1940, the intelligence sources were unable to provide any check on the reliability of the claims made by British pilots. While the other sources – Enigma, POW, PR and the SIS – had nothing to offer, the study of the tactical communications of the GAF's day-fighter formations had not yet been developed. Cheadle could usually, if with some delay, determine the losses of enemy aircraft using W/T, but the GAF fighters used R/T. Nor did matters improve during the first half of 1942, when, after being suspended during January and February from the need to conserve Fighter Command's resources, the daylight offensive was resumed. It was again prolonged despite heavy casualties, largely as a result of the continuing inability of the intelligence authorities to produce a reliable method of estimating enemy losses.

From the end of January 1942 indications that the GAF was reducing its day-fighter force and its Flak organisation in north-west Europe[113] to meet the demands of other fronts coincided with the faltering of the Soviet counter-offensive and an anxiety in

---

110. AIR 41/49, p 87.
111. Collier, op cit, p 294: *Air Ministry Intelligence*, p 85.
112. Collier, op cit, p 294 fn.   113. AIR 41/49, p 102; CX/MSS/786/T16.

Whitehall to provide all possible relief to the Soviet forces.*
Furthermore, by the end of January the Enigma had disclosed that
30 of the latest type of single-engined fighter were being transferred
to Russia[114] and on 6 March 40 single-engined fighters were known
to be moving from the Pas de Calais to provide protection for
the strike force assembling in north Norway against the Arctic
convoys.[115] The CAS now pressed for a resumption of Fighter
Command's offensive and for a reconsideration by Bomber Command of the possibility of daylight raids on Germany.[116] The
daylight offensive re-commenced on 24 March and, as had been
hoped, the GAF responded energetically: at the end of March the
Enigma disclosed that fighter reinforcements were arriving in
France[117] and on 19 April it revealed that 120 out of 180 single-
engined fighters in the Pas de Calais were the new FW 190.[118] As a
result of the prompt action of the GAF, however, and of the
superiority of the FW 190, Fighter Command's casualties were
again severe. By mid-June it had lost 259 aircraft in return for the
destruction of 58 German fighters.[119] As before, on the other hand,
Fighter Command continued to over-estimate the enemy's losses;
when his actual losses were 58 aircraft, it claimed to have destroyed
197 by that date[120] – and the Air Ministry remained unable to
correct the exaggeration. On 6 July, when it had learned from the
Enigma that the GAF was finding it difficult to supply aircraft to
north Africa, had imposed flying restrictions in Russia and had
decided to quintuple fighter aircraft production at Wiener-
Neustadt, Air Intelligence judged that Fighter Command's operation had 'contributed substantially to the present satisfactory
situation' and urged that 'further intensive operations would be
likely to cause the Germans most serious embarrassment'.[121] It was
as a result of this appreciation that, despite growing anxiety about
Fighter Command's casualties, the offensive was kept up on a
reduced scale until it reached its climax in the Dieppe raid on 19
August.†

In so far as one of its main objects was to impose wastage on the
GAF and thus provide relief to Russia, the Dieppe raid was a
resounding failure, though the extent of its failure was partly
concealed by the fact that the RAF again over-estimated the
GAF's losses. It claimed to have destroyed 92 German aircraft,

---

* See above, p 89 et seq.   † See Appendix 13.

114.   CX/MSS/647/T5.
115.   ADM 223/93, OIC SI 115 of 8 March 1942; AIR 41/49, p 103.
116.   AIR 41/49, pp 103, 105.
117.   ADM 223/93, OIC SI 137 of 30 March 1942.
118.   ibid, OIC SI 167 of 19 April 1942.
119.   AIR 41/49, pp 110, 114.
120.   ibid, p 115.   121.   ibid, p 114.

with 39 probably destroyed and 140 damaged, in return for the loss of 106 Allied planes.[122] The German records give the German actual losses as 25 bombers and 23 fighters, plus damage to 16 bombers and 8 fighters.[123] As a result of the raid, however, the GAF increased its fighter force in north-west Europe. At the same time, the raid coincided with the opening of the day-time offensive against Europe by the bomber formations of US Eighth Air Force, which made its first cross-Channel raid on 17 August. In the light of these two developments the continuing inability of Allied intelligence to find reliable methods of establishing enemy losses after the middle of 1942 acquired still greater significance as a handicap to the conduct of Allied operations and the efficient use of Allied resources. The US force was dedicated to precision daylight bombing with its Norden bombsight; its confidence in its mission was sustained initially by its own small losses, but when these were replaced by heavy casualties, as they soon were, it was almost wholly its belief in its large claims against enemy aircraft that persuaded it to continue the offensive until the autumn of 1943. Its claims were more exaggerated than those made by the RAF – so much more so that the Air Ministry early distrusted them. In October 1942 for example, when US Eighth Air Force claimed to have destroyed 102 GAF fighters in an attack on Lille, the Air Intelligence Branch estimated that the figure could not have been more than 60.[124] As it happens, however, the enemy lost only one fighter during this raid.[125]

Air Intelligence's estimate was taken in consultation with the Air Section at GC and CS, which, allowing for the limitations of R/T as evidence, agreed that the American claim was much exaggerated. It may thus be safely concluded that the absence of even remotely reliable estimates of the GAF's losses was due not to a failure of communication between the Air Ministry and GC and CS, but to the lack of evidence. When the other sources were silent on the subject, it is clear that Air Section's study of the GAF's day-fighter R/T was failing to fill the gap.

Undertaken by the Air Section, this study took the form of daily analyses of the R/T traffic for the previous 24 hours from May 1941. From September of that year it was producing solutions of the GAF's R/T codes, and by the end of 1941, by which time the range of R/T interception had been extended to include all the main fighter areas between Norway and the Spanish border, the Air Section was able without delay, in advance of identifications obtained from POW and crashed aircraft, to identify individual

---

122. ibid, p 124. 123. ibid, p 124.
124. Craven and Cate, *The Army Air Forces in World War II*, Vol II (1949), p 221.
125. ibid, p 222.

fighter formations and to establish the total numbers of GAF day-fighters. At that time the Air Section established a specialised Fighter Intelligence sub-section. Before long, as well as becoming the main source of the Air Ministry's intelligence about the order of battle of the day-fighters, the sub-section was producing information of the kind which the Kingsdown chain of HDUs could not derive from the traffic – information about the number of fighters that had been airborne the previous day, about their positions and about the instructions they had received as to heights, courses and landings – and its daily summaries had become indispensable to the work of the HDU stations. That this was so was due to the fact that it was only at GC and CS that the R/T intercepts could be mated with the Enigma and with low-grade GAF W/T traffic. Three types of such traffic were immediately relevant. That of the German Observer Corps (Flugmeldedienst) provided a fairly accurate picture of the observer post layout in France and the Low Countries. That of the point-to-point service of the GAF fighter organisation (Jägerführer 2 and 3) in the Pas de Calais area yielded intelligence about fighter readiness, weather conditions at airfields and, from time to time, the enemy's operational orders. In addition the GAF's long-range radar stations reported the range and bearing of hostile aircraft in the *Freya* reporting code; this code was initially solved by ADI (Sc)'s section which also used its transmissions for plotting the stations of the enemy's radar chain.

From the spring of 1942, as the R/T traffic was more and more understood, the Air Section pressed for the circulation of its summaries of the traffic of the previous day to the RAF commands, which received the R/T intercepts direct from the HDUs but were unable to make much of them. AI (4) – the section controlling the RAF Y service and GC and CS's Air Section – vetoed this suggestion for some time on the ground that it was no part of GC and CS's duties to produce operational intelligence for the commands. From 1 June, however, it gave way to the pressure and approved the circulation of the reports; known as BMPs, they were sent to the RAF commands from 1 June 1942 and US Eighth Air Force from September. But just as the Air Section was unable to correct Allied estimates of enemy losses, so its reports on the tactics, procedures and dispositions of the enemy's day-fighters were not assisting the Allied commands to reduce their own heavy casualties before the end of 1942. For a whole year after the commencement of the BMPs, indeed, the Section was still acquiring experience; it was not until the middle of 1943, when it was providing the RAF with 75 per cent of its intelligence on the GAF's single-engine fighters, that against the day-fighters, as against the night-fighters, it became master of its trade.

It seems unlikely that this delay would have been greatly

reduced if the Air Ministry had not frowned on direct contacts between the Air Section and the commands. For one thing, the analysis of the R/T traffic encountered new difficulties in the autumn of 1942 when VHF began to replace HF for R/T purposes in the GAF fighter formations, and although the VHF traffic was audible until operations retreated into Germany from the end of 1943, this change was accompanied by the introduction of new fighter-control systems. Then again, the Air Section, working on the basis of the R/T logs it received from the Kingsdown stations, necessarily concentrated on providing retrospective analyses of the traffic of the previous 24 hours, and while its analyses theoretically provided the intelligence staffs at the commands with information that was useful to them when planning operations and devising tactics, they were practically of little value. It has been argued that things would have been different had the commands been in direct contact with GC and CS. The experience of US Eighth Air Force does not support this view. US Eighth Air Force, which did not of course come under the Air Ministry, made direct contact with the Air Section from the autumn of 1942, and there is no doubt that the Air Section's analyses benefited from this. But it is equally clear that US Eighth Air Force's operations derived little advantage before the middle of 1943.*

What the intelligence staffs at the commands needed most from the R/T was interpretation of operational intelligence while operations were in progress. But formidable organisational problems had to be overcome before such a service could be provided, and they had not been overcome by the beginning of 1943. A first attempt to provide the operational authorities with current interpretations of the low-grade Sigint, including the R/T intercepts, made during the Dieppe raid at the suggestion of the Sigint bodies, broke down for lack of adequate arrangements.† Its failure made it clear that if such a service was to be effective all low-grade Sigint must be collected and interpreted for the commands at one point and that, such was the complexity of the R/T traffic and the process of fusing it with other sources, that point could only be GC and CS's Air Section, at least until Kingsdown had been able to absorb the Air Section's experience and refine its techniques. But months of discussion followed before, again from mid-1943, the resulting system – the 'Kingsdown Hook-up' – became efficient.‡

---

* See below, p 519 et seq.   † See Appendix 13.   ‡ See Volume III.

PART VI

The Mediterranean and North Africa
from July 1941 to January 1943

CHAPTER 21

The Mediterranean and North Africa
from July 1941 to February 1942

IN THE summer of 1941 the chief problem in the Middle East
for the British was when and in what form they should resume
the offensive against the Axis forces in north Africa. As they
debated the problem they assumed that Russia might collapse as
early as August or September. They also assumed that Germany
took the same view and was already planning large-scale offensives
elsewhere. Nor were they wrong in their judgment that although
they could not rule out the possibility of a renewed attempt to
invade the United Kingdom – the Germans did not formally
abandon *Sealion* until February 1942[1] – the main thrust of Germany's next moves would be towards the Middle East and the
Mediterranean. But they were far from sure where and when she
would strike on that front and their uncertainty was unrelieved by
the receipt of any reliable intelligence about the enemy's intentions.

Unaware that early in June 1941, because of the losses she had
sustained in Crete and in any case unable to spare the necessary
forces from her coming attack on Russia, Germany had rejected an
airborne assault on Malta for the present,[2] they had to allow for
that possibility. Nor could they yet exclude the possibility of an
attack on Gibraltar. On 20 June the Joint Planners judged that
both threats were real.[3] At the end of July the C-in-C Middle East
and the C-in-C Mediterranean felt that there was 'always the
danger' of an attempt to capture Malta.[4] Thereafter, in view of the
absence of alarming reports from any source, these anxieties
declined, and from October 1941 intelligence confirmed the withdrawal of German divisions from the Franco-Spanish frontier.[5] In
the summer, however, the threat in the western Mediterranean
seemed to be surpassed only by the still greater danger to the
Middle East. About the Middle East there was further uncertainty.

---

1. Gwyer and Butler, *Grand Strategy*, Vol III, Part II (1964), p 540.
2. ISO Playfair, *The Mediterranean and Middle East*, Vol II (1956),
   pp 257–258.
3. CAB 84/32, JP (41) 467 of 20 June.
4. CAB 105/6, Hist (B) 6, Nos 78 and 129.
5. CAB 80/31, COS (41) 654 (113th Résumé); CAB 80/32, COS (41) 693
   (116th Résumé); WO 208/3573, MI 14 Appreciations for the CIGS, 20
   and 27 October, 17 and 24 November 1941.

Despite the fact that they agreed that Russia's collapse would be followed by a German offensive in that direction from the north, Whitehall and Cairo held different views as to how soon this offensive could be launched.

In Whitehall the JIC issued two papers on the subject at the request of the Joint Planners on 3 and 4 July. In these papers, the first of many such hypothetical studies it was to make for the JIC, the JIS estimated that the Germans were more likely to attack from Turkey than through the Caucasus. If she could disengage troops from Russia by mid-August, and if she could secure Turkey's acquiescence, Germany would be able to advance in strength from the Anatolian frontier into Iraq via Syria from November 1941, but not earlier. This advance might be combined with an attack on Cyprus. During the spring of 1942 it would be supplemented by a thrust from the Caucasus by troops which Germany would have brought into northern Iran and which would advance on Abadan after clearing northern Iraq.[6] These views were accepted, or shared, by the Defence Committee, which felt on 17 July that the threat from the north would take 'months' to develop,[7] and the Prime Minister used them in his attempt to persuade the C-in-C Middle East to take the offensive in Africa in September, before Rommel could take Tobruk – the 'indispensable preliminary to serious invasion of Egypt'.[8]

The JIS estimates bore a close similarity to the calculations the OKH was making for the timing and the direction of its advance into the Middle East.* They were not backed up, however, by any recent reliable intelligence about Germany's intentions. Thus the judgment that Germany would advance through Anatolia, rather than attack through the Caucasus, rested mainly on the interest she had shown in Syria earlier in the year and the fact that she had signed a Treaty of Friendship with Turkey on 18 June.[9] Not unnaturally, perhaps, in these circumstances, General Auchinleck, the new C-in-C Middle East, proved less ready than Whitehall to accept the JIC conclusions. On 4 July he had proposed delaying an offensive against Rommel on two grounds. His forces needed strengthening and time for training. No less important, he felt he should give priority to consolidating his positions in Syria, Cyprus and Iraq against the dangers of an early German attack from the north. In further exchanges with London during July he argued

---

* See above, pp 80–81.

6. JIC (41) 265 and 268 of 3 and 4 July; CAB 84/32, JP (41) 532 of 9 July.
7. CAB 69/2, DO (41) 51st Meeting, 17 July.
8. CAB 105/6, No 81; Churchill, *The Second World War*, Vol III (1950), pp 355, 359.
9. Gwyer and Butler, op cit, Vol III, Part I (1964), p 173.

that, since winter conditions might permit Germany to switch forces even while Russia continued to resist, the threat to Syria from Anatolia might develop as early as the first half of September. It was largely because 'the north may become the decisive front' that he wanted to delay until the end of 1941 before making a move in north Africa.[10]

At the end of July and the beginning of August, during a brief visit by the C-in-C to London, the two sides agreed on a compromise.[11] Both accepted the compromise reluctantly. The C-in-C subscribed to the view of the Chiefs of Staff that 'the immediate danger' from the north 'was diminished by the continued resistance of Russia', and that a full-scale attack through Turkey was extremely improbable before 1 November.[12] But he still offered only to make his advance on 1 November, and this was in part at least because he remained unconvinced by Whitehall's assessment.[13] The London authorities accepted his offer, but as well as feeling that he was exaggerating the imminence of the threat through Turkey, they regretted the delay for other reasons. They were aware of the current weakness of Rommel's position; they were also afraid of the possibility that, particularly in the event of an early Russian collapse, his forces could be reinforced and resupplied more quickly than the British forces in Egypt.

□

In contrast to the lack of information about Germany's strategic plans for the Middle East, some reliable intelligence was available about the enemy's supply difficulties in north Africa from the GAF Enigma. Although the Army Sigint authorities in the Middle East were at last beginning to make progress against the German Army's field codes and cyphers from the summer of 1941, these sources as yet yielded little intelligence.* Against the Enigma keys used by the German Army in north Africa GC and CS had still had no success.† But GC and CS continued to break virtually every day, and to do so almost currently, both the general GAF Enigma settings (the Red) and the modified settings that had been allotted to Fliegerkorps X and Fliegerführer Afrika (the Light Blue) and that remained in use by them until 1 January 1942 when all Fliegerkorps were issued with separate keys; and while this traffic was mainly concerned with GAF activities and supply operations,

---

* See below, pp 293–294.   † See below, pp 294–295 and Appendix 4.

10.   ibid, pp 171, 177, 182; CAB 105/6, Nos 57, 78, 81, 91.
11.   Churchill, op cit, Vol III, pp 354, 359, 361, 364.
12.   CAB 79/13, COS (41) 270th Meeting, 31 July, 274th Meeting, 2 August.
13.   Gwyer and Butler, op cit, Vol III, Part I, p 182.

it also carried some information about the ground situation in north Africa.

The GAF Enigma had provided in May 1941 the Paulus report on the exhaustion of Rommel's troops.* Since then it had shown that, as a result partly of the German operations against Crete and partly of Rommel's effort in June in beating off operation *Battleaxe* and taking Halfaya, the supply position of the enemy ground and air forces in north Africa was becoming increasingly precarious. From the opening of the Crete campaign it had revealed that the sailing of Axis supply convoys to north Africa had been reduced from every three to four days to every ten days. Thereafter it had carried frequent complaints that British attacks were also severely hampering the coastal shipping that took the supplies forward from the convoy terminals, frequent reports of a grave shortage of motor transport, spares and drivers for the long overland haul to the Egyptian frontier, and abundant evidence that German emergency measures were failing to overcome the difficulties. On 21 July it revealed that the Germans feared that British attacks on shipping in the eastern Mediterranean, mainly by submarines, would jeopardise future operations, and had ordered Fliegerkorps X to concentrate on anti-submarine work.[14] On 24 July it reported that submarines off Benghazi were 'creating a very serious supply position for the DAK', and on 1 August that the fuel situation of the German Afrika Korps (DAK) would be extremely grave if the British attacks continued.[15] On 22 and 29 July it reported that the GAF's supply position was critical and on 1 August that the GAF's fuel stocks in the forward area were sufficient for only two days' operations.[16]

By 28 July MI in London concluded that these supply difficulties alone would delay any general Axis offensive in north Africa.[17] By then, moreover, the Enigma had provided evidence that even an attack on Tobruk was not yet likely. Up to 10 July MI had allowed that this might come in the near future.[18] But by 14 July, having learned from the Enigma that the Germans were still buying siege artillery in Tunisia, it had concluded that Rommel's preparations for an assault on Tobruk were probably not completed.[19] This conclusion was supported by a report received from a well-placed SIS source, and passed to the CIGS on 21 July, to the effect that

---

 * See Volume I, pp 396–397.

14. OL 768 of 21 July 1941; CX/MSS/76/T3; ADM 223/102, Ultra signal 1803/22 July 1941.

15. OLs 805 of 25 July, 861 of 1 August 1941; CX/MSS/93/T11, 113/T2.

16. OLs 769 of 22 July, 835 of 29 July 1941; CX/MSS/76/T8, 77/T8, 103/T7.

17. WO 208/3573 of 28 July 1941.

18. CAB 80/29, COS (41) 421 (47th Résumé).

19. WO 208/3573 of 14 July 1941.

the Axis would undertake no large-scale operations in Libya before the end of October.[20] In an appreciation of 8 August the JIC accepted this conclusion.[21]

If their knowledge of the enemy's difficulties increased the preference of the London authorities for early British action, the setting aside of their immediate fears about Tobruk did something to reduce their apprehension at the C-in-C's insistence on delay. But they still feared that the Axis would overcome its difficulties and manage to get reinforcements to Africa while the C-in-C reorganised and trained for a set-piece battle, and for this anxiety, too, there were good grounds in the available intelligence. As early as 11 June the GAF Enigma had revealed that the Axis had decided to reduce the demand on motor transport and coastal shipping by sailing single ships direct to Benghazi, though only four ships were yet available for the service.[22] By the beginning of July it had emerged from the C 38m traffic* that four Italian 20,000-ton liners were being used to transport Italian troops to Tripoli.[23] The COS résumé for the week ending 3 July estimated that one division had already made the crossing.[24] By 22 July it was clear from the GAF Enigma that Italian troops were relieving forward elements of the DAK.[25] More disturbing, reports were then coming in, presumably from the SIS, of the southward movement of German troops through Italy en route to Libya.[26] These reports, received before the C-in-C's arrival in London at the end of July, were corroborated soon after his departure. The GAF Enigma identified a new German infantry regiment (the 361st) in Libya in the middle of August and soon afterwards established that it belonged to a new division (Division zbV Afrika, later renamed 90th Light).[27] On 4 August MI emphasised that although the Axis supply situation remained bad in the forward area, many ships – troopers included – had succeeded in getting through to north Africa during July despite increased sinkings by British forces.[28]

□

The intelligence about north Africa failed to deflect the C-in-C in the direction of the Prime Minister's preference for a quicker and

---

* See above, p 22 and below, pp 283–284.

20. ibid, 21 July 1941.   21. JIC (41) 311 of 8 August.
22. OL 570 of 11 June 1941; CX/JQ/1048/T 19; Playfair, op cit, Vol II, p. 257.
23. CAB 105/6, No 4.
24. CAB 80/29, COS (41) 407 (46th Résumé).
25. OL 777 of 22 July 1941; CX/MSS/78/T8.
26. CAB 80/29, COS (41) 458 (49th Résumé); WO 208/3573 of 21 July 1941.
27. CX/MSS/176, para 13.   28. WO 208/3573 of 4 August 1941.

less well prepared advance than the offensive he had agreed to launch in November. But during the second half of 1941 the continuation and improvement of this intelligence conspired with other developments to make that period one of sustained British successes against the Axis supply routes to north Africa, successes which were to have considerable importance for the future course of the fighting on land.

Of the other developments that now occurred, one was the transfer at the beginning of June 1941 of Fliegerkorps X from Sicily to Greece to replace Fliegerkorps VIII, which had gone to the Russian front. In the first half of 1941 Fliegerkorps X's operations from Sicily had greatly restricted British anti-shipping attacks from Malta. Its transfer to Greece, of which the GAF Enigma provided full details,[29] left the Italians to protect Axis shipping on the Tripoli route, though Fliegerkorps X continued as far as it could to help on the route to Benghazi. The other important development was an increase in the British anti-shipping forces in the Mediterranean. The number of submarines operating from Malta, Alexandria and Gibraltar, which had been nearly doubled in the second quarter of 1941, was increased again during the next three months. In July Malta's air striking force, hitherto limited to Swordfish of the Fleet Air Arm, was considerably strengthened, the reinforcements including a number of Blenheims whose crews had experience of anti-shipping operations over the North Sea. So was Malta's force of fighter aircraft. This improvement in the defences further extended the effectiveness of the naval and air striking forces that worked from the island, as did the lifting of some of the restrictions which had previously limited attacks by submarines on merchant shipping.[30]

These favourable developments in the operational situation, which put the British authorities in a better position to use the available anti-shipping intelligence, coincided with a significant increase in the amount and operational value of the intelligence. This increase was partly the result of additions to the number of reconnaissance aircraft working from Malta. In addition to the Hurricanes and Marylands of No 69 GR Squadron RAF, which could cover Tripoli, Sicily and the south Italian ports visually, regular photographic sorties were flown from the middle of 1941, and although Malta did not yet have a fully trained photographic interpretation unit, the local study of the photographs was also providing the naval and air staffs with some information about the enemy's convoy routes and routines. Until September 1941, how-

---

29.   OLs 527 and 549 of 1 and 8 June 1941; CX/MSS/1014/T21, 1035/T14.
30.   Roskill, *The War at Sea*, Vol 1 (1954), pp 438, 525; Playfair, op cit, Vol II, pp 57, 270, 278, 280.

ever, when Malta received a Spitfire from the United Kingdom, the photographic reconnaissance was restricted in its range, while much of Malta's limited reconnaissance effort had to be devoted to watching the Italian main fleet.[31] In these circumstances the Mediterranean authorities were fortunate in that an advance on the Sigint front helped them to use their restricted reconnaissance resources to maximum effect.[32]

In the first half of 1941 Sigint, supplementing reconnaissance, had already provided much useful information about Axis supplies and reinforcements. It had been obtained, as we have seen,* mainly from the GAF Enigma traffic with occasional contributions from the high-grade book cyphers of the Italian Army and Air Force. In the value of the GAF Enigma for anti-shipping intelligence there was some decline with the removal of Fliegerkorps X from the central Mediterranean. But both of these sources continued to be available, and the decline in the amount of Enigma was more than off-set by the product of the C 38m.† By the end of June GC and CS had broken the C 38m settings for May and June and was reading a few messages currently. The first intelligence from the source that it transmitted to the Middle East was sent out on 23 June: it gave details of the sailing of a convoy of four liners to Africa with Italian troops.[33] On 10 July GC and CS broke the July settings. Thereafter, with routine and progressively shorter interruptions at the end of each month,‡ when the Italians introduced new settings, and with more serious interruptions on one or two occasions during 1942,§ it was to go on reading the traffic with little or no delay until the Italian armistice.

The C 38m was a most valuable acquisition. Almost all the traffic could be intercepted in the United Kingdom. In the year after it was broken the Italians made steadily increasing use of it: the number of signals rose from 600 in August 1941 to nearly 4,000 in July 1942, the peak month. As it was used by Italian naval shore authorities and fleet units, it often provided information about the intentions of the enemy's main fleet. It was also used by non-Service organisations such as the Italo-French Armistice Commission for general purposes. Most important of all, however, it

---

* See Volume I, pp 400–401 and above, p 279.

† See above, p 22.

‡ By the end of 1941 the monthly interruption had been reduced to less than three days; by the end of 1942 it was less than 24 hours.

§ See below, pp 283, 348.

31. Playfair, op cit, Vol II, pp 56, 278, 280; AIR 41/7, *Photographic Reconnaissance*, Vol II, pp 47, 98.

32. ADM 223/88, Colpoys, *Admiralty Use of Special Intelligence in Naval Operations*, p 326.

33. OL 659 of 23 June 1941; ZTPI 22 and 23.

regularly carried information about forthcoming Axis shipping operations between Italy and north Africa, all of which came under the control of the Italian Admiralty. It was chiefly as a result of its reading of the C 38m, indeed, that GC and CS was able from July 1941 to give the operational authorities advance notice of virtually every convoy and important independent ship that sailed with troops or supplies across the Mediterranean, and usually to identify the ships and the escorting forces involved. About shipping movements in other areas – for example the Gulf of Genoa and the oil route through the Aegean – the C 38m provided similar information, but did so less regularly.

In the production of its intelligence about the north African routes other problems were encountered in addition to the need to overcome and reduce the monthly cryptanalytic interruptions. The routes given in the messages were disguised, and GC and CS, which did the research on them, was increasingly impeded by the fact that the code systems became extremely complicated, with cover names for ports, co-ordinates, positions and bearings, and also by the fact that dates of sailing and arrival times began to be coded. Until December 1941, however, the Italians used only a simple system of coded positions and GC and CS had little difficulty in providing the Middle East with the routes to be followed by enemy shipping and with its times of departure and arrival. Another problem grew in complexity as the British attack on the supply routes mounted. The enemy frequently changed the timing, composition, escort and route of convoys after they had originally been announced. At times when his plans were disturbed by British operations the situation was especially confused by his recall of convoys and his postponement or cancellation of sailings.

On account of this problem, no less than from the need to provide security cover for the source of their information, the Mediterranean commands as far as possible undertook air reconnaissance of the targets before acting on the intelligence sent to them. They were also under strict instructions to avoid sending signals that might betray the fact that they had learned the contents of enemy messages, and were reprimanded whenever London discovered that they had transgressed.* In the period before the British re-established a surface ship striking force at Malta, towards the end of October 1941, it remains difficult for these reasons to establish exactly what proportion of the attacks on and sinkings of Axis supply ships were directly attributable to the C 38m decrypts. But the Cs-in-C Middle East reported to the Chiefs of Staff on 17 September 1941 that 'the success of air and submarine attack has been very largely due to Special

---

* See Appendix 1 (Part (1)).

Intelligence'[34] and their testimony is borne out not only by the Admiralty, which stated at the end of the war that 'the bulk of the intelligence on which these operations were based was from this source',[35] but also by the contemporary records.

These establish that the high-grade Sigint and the C 38m decrypts commonly guided the reconnaissance which preceded the vast majority of the British anti-shipping strikes and that the timing of such other operations as the bombing and mining of the Axis ports often hinged on what Sigint had to say about the arrival or imminent arrival of supply ships and convoys. Towards the end of June the enemy was forced to recall the four liners which formed the first convoy to be reported by the C 38m because all available aircraft at Malta were concentrated against it.[36] The liners sailed again on 27 June and reached Libya safely. But the success of the submarine HMS *Upholder* in sinking two of these liners – the *Neptunia* and the *Oceania* – on 18 September stemmed directly from the fact that their route and time of sailing had been signalled to the Middle East on 15 September.[37] On 25 September the GAF Enigma showed that a ship containing the Axis's entire north African stock of one type of bomb had been blown up in an RAF raid on Benghazi, and the raid took place after Sigint had revealed that the ship was due to arrive on 23 September.[38] Apart from its contribution to individual operations, moreover, of which these few examples from this period must suffice, the Sigint was invaluable for the light it threw on general changes in the enemy's supply arrangements. It gave advance notice that from the beginning of August 1941, partly to give the Malta forces a wider berth and partly to reduce the long haul in north Africa from Tripoli to the forward area, the enemy would increase the number of sailings to Benghazi and thus sail more ships from the Aegean.[39] At the end of September the decrypts showed that Fliegerkorps X had been ordered to discontinue its raids on Egypt and concentrate on shipping protection and that it was transferring one Gruppe of long-range bombers and one of Me 110s to Sicily.[40] In the middle of October it revealed that the Italians had suspended all sailings to Tripoli as a result of their increasing losses on that route, where four ships had been sunk in the past fortnight.[41]

---

34. CAB 105/7, Hist (B) 7, No 161.   35. ADM 223/88, p. 321.
36. ADM 186/801, BR 1736 (49) (2), p 126.
37. OLs 1145 and 1149 of 15 September 1941; ZTPI 641; Roskill, op cit, Vol 1, p 526.
38. OLs 1235 of 20 September, 1290 and 1291 of 25 September 1941; ZTPI 772; CX/MSS/276/T9, 10 and 11.   39. eg ZTPI 313, 315, 316.
40. ADM 186/801, p 170; OLs 1247 and 1263 of 21 and 23 September 1941; CX/MSS/262/T24, 268/T12, 18 and 19.
41. OL 1587 of 18 October 1941; ZTPI 1417.

Up to the time of this suspension the monthly average of Axis tonnage sunk had been running since June at about double what it had been in the first half of the year,[42] and there was no lack of evidence that the losses were creating supply difficulties in north Africa. On 27 September the JIC calculated that Rommel's supplies were sufficient only for a limited campaign of not more than a fortnight.[43] It based this conclusion not only on the GAF Enigma, which showed that GAF stocks continued to be low, but also on a new source – signals in the German Army Enigma which were first decrypted at GC and CS on 17 September.* These showed that on 22 September the DAK had been ordered to reduce consumption of water, food and fuel.[44] On 10 October they showed that Rommel was also short of 88 mm anti-tank ammunition.[45] By the middle of October – this emerged from the C 38m – the Italians were being driven to take emergency measures to maintain essential supplies, transporting troops by air and in destroyers and sending submarines to Bardia and Derna with fuel and other stores.[46] Nor is there any doubt that these shortages had important operational consequences. Although at the time there was no intelligence about Rommel's plan or its postponements, it was on their account that he was forced to put off, first from September to October and then from October to late in November, an attack on Tobruk.†

Despite its contribution to this result, however, the anti-shipping intelligence showed that mainly as a result of his greater use of Benghazi, where British submarines had had little success since the beginning of August, no fewer than 24 ships had arrived between then and the beginning of September. This improvement in the Axis supply position aroused anxiety in both Whitehall and Alexandria. Towards the end of August, almost simultaneously, the Prime Minister and the C-in-C Mediterranean revived the idea of using naval surface forces based on Malta to boost the effectiveness of the attack on enemy convoys.[47]‡ Surface attack had been

---

* See below, pp 294–295.　　　　† See below, p 300 et seq.

‡ On 22 and 23 August respectively the Prime Minister and the C-in-C separately mooted this idea. On 24 August, almost certainly before he had seen the C-in-C's signals of the day before, the Prime Minister was provoked by a decrypt about further sailings to minute the First Sea Lord: 'What action will C-in-C Mediterranean take on this information? Surely he cannot put up with this kind of thing. . . . Is he going simply to leave these ships to the

---

42.　Playfair, op cit, Vol II, p 280.　　　43.　JIC (41) 388 (o) of 27 Sept 1941.
44.　OL 1250 of 22 September 1941; CX/MSS/256/T7, 265/T6.
45.　OL 1475 of 10 October 1941; CX/MSS/324/T4.
46.　ADM 233/102, Ultra signal 1836/13 October 1941; OL 1525 of 13 October 1941; ZTPI 1261, 1262, 1263.
47.　Churchill, op cit, Vol III, p 434; CAB 105/7, No 161: ADM 186/801, p 189.

effective in April 1941* and since then the C 38m decrypts had become available to provide reliable and comprehensive advance intelligence. Discussion of the operational factors continued during September, by the end of which intelligence began to produce indications that Rommel might at last be getting ready to attack Tobruk. On 21 October, as soon as fuel supplies were adequate, Force K – consisting of the cruisers HMS *Aurora* and *Penelope* and two destroyers – arrived in Malta.[49] Its exploits during the next two months were to be an outstandingly successful exercise in the operational use of intelligence. The attack on Axis supplies had already greatly increased in efficiency by October and had forced Rommel to postpone his attack on Tobruk. The still greater depredations brought about by Force K were not only to impose further delay on him, and thus to be instrumental in enabling the British to launch their offensive before he could strike; by keeping his supplies in a parlous state during the first month of the British advance, they were also to play a large part in forcing him to retreat.

□

The anti-shipping campaign interlocked with the overland operations of the RAF in the Middle East. By keeping the enemy air forces short of supplies and by increasingly diverting them to the protection of shipping, it reduced the RAF's main defensive problem – the protection of the great assemblage of shipping in the Canal and on the supply route to Tobruk and of the workshops and aircraft parks in the Cairo area. In return the RAF was better able to concentrate on its offensive tasks, some of which – bombing attacks and minelaying operations at the enemy's disembarkation ports,[†] interference with the supply routes between his ports and his depots, and raids on the communications between his rear areas and the front – were an extension of the anti-shipping campaign. The others, no less important during the planning of the British offensive, were the supply of information about the enemy's preparations and dispositions and the need to thwart his own

---

chance of a submarine without making any effort by his surface forces to intercept them? Please ask specifically what if anything he is going to do. We are still at war.'[48] The First Sea Lord's reply drew attention to the difficulties of intercepting shipping bound for Benghazi.

  * See Volume I, p 400.

  † See p 285 above. The bombing of Benghazi, which derived much help from Sigint notification of arrivals, was conspicuously successful, so much so that Hitler ordered special measures for the defence of the port.[50]

48. Dir/C Archive, Minute of 24 August 1941.
49. ADM 186/801, pp 189–190.
50. OL 1365 of 30 September 1941; CX/MSS/291/T7 and 15.

efforts to acquire such information about the British, and these, too, were made less difficult by the enemy's shortages.

In its defensive role the RAF was also directly assisted by intelligence, especially by the GAF Enigma. This warned it of GAF reinforcements – of the fact, for example, that six FW 200s of KG 40 and 'six He 111s had arrived at bases in the eastern Mediterranean in August for operations against the Canal and the Red Sea[51] – and kept it informed that Fliegerkorps X was consistently below strength. More important, it provided detailed tactical information on the GAF's day to day operations, and commonly did so in time for the information to reach the Middle East before the operations took place. GC and CS frequently predicted Fliegerkorps X's attacks against the Tobruk convoys, and practically all GAF mining operations off Tobruk, off Alexandria and in the Canal were either forecast or known about on completion, with full details of the number, type and claimed position of the mines dropped.[52] On 23 July 1941 it reported information which made it clear that the enemy was about to use a combined magnetic-acoustic mine in the Mediterranean. C-in-C Mediterranean was told that magnetic and acoustic sweepers must be used together. Fortunately the LL/SA sweep had in any case just been introduced into Egypt. From September 1941 the RAF Y Field Unit at Alexandria was supplementing the GAF Enigma by monitoring the GAF's tactical W/T activity, though it was not until 1942 that the RAF Y organisation in the Mediterranean got into its stride.*

The intelligence used in the RAF's offensive activities came from a greater variety of sources, of which photographic reconnaissance was not the least valuable. But the development of PR in the Mediterranean theatre was painfully slow following the formation of No 2 PRU in September 1940.† In July 1941 the establishment of the PRU was set at 20 Mosquitoes; two of these had been sent out by the end of 1941, but were destroyed by enemy action and not replaced until the end of 1942. Until the despatch of 12 Type D Spitfires in February 1942 the PRU had to depend for its operations in the Western Desert on Hurricanes, modified for PR but still unsuitable for the work. By the end of 1941 other units besides No 2 PRU were carrying out PR in the Western Desert, notably a newly formed Strategic Reconnaissance Unit operating under Air HQ, ME, Army Co-operation squadrons attached to each of

---

* See below, p 377 et seq.   † See Volume I, pp 207–208.

51. ADM 223/102, Ultra signal 1717/30 August 1941; OLs 1022 of 30 August, 1952 of 3 September 1941; CX/MSS/192/T4, 206/T11.

52. OLs 731, 784, 789, 836 of 4 to 29 July, OL 1097 of 11 September, OLs 1845 and 2002 of 8 and 17 November 1941 for some representative signals; CX/MSS/32/T14, 84/T4, 86/T11, 103/T10, 229/T2, 412/T21 and 24, 439/T16.

Eighth Army's two corps for tactical reconnaissance and No 60 SAAF Survey Flight which provided Eighth Army with photographs for mapping purposes.* Meanwhile difficulties between the RAF and the Army authorities about priorities for PR and photographic interpretation had been overcome since the formation in Cairo early in 1941 of an Army/Air Photographic Interpretation Unit (AAPIU). Initially staffed by only two fully trained interpreters from the CIU at Medmenham, their efforts were augmented by locally trained officers so that it was possible to provide interpreters at Air HQ No 204 Group RAF in the desert and with the advanced Interpretation Section at Army HQ. In November 1941 it was decided to form a ME CIU with detachments in the Western Desert, the Levant, Iraq and Malta and, to meet operational demands, interpeters from it were attached to lower formations for first phase interpretation. For administrative reasons and accommodation difficulties it was several months before the ME CIU was fully established, but as a result of these measures, and of close co-operation between Cairo and the advanced sections, five to six sorties a day were being flown for the Army during the planning of the British attack and PR was making a considerable contribution not only to the RAF's excellent information about the state of activity of the GAF units and their facilities but also to the stock of knowledge about the enemy's Army formations, his dispositions, defences, dumps and minefields, his roads, tracks and ports, and the movement of his supplies.[53]

As a source of intelligence captured documents and POW interrogations were of little importance compared with air reconnaissance in the weeks before the British offensive (operation *Crusader*). But the high-grade Sigint and the work of the Army's forward patrols supplemented the air reconnaissance in the collection of information about ground targets for the RAF; and for the RAF's operations against the enemy's air forces, and its watch on them, Sigint was the outstanding source. The GAF Enigma provided regular reports by the GAF on its tactical policy, its strengths and serviceability, the state of its airfields and its locations, transfers and reinforcements, as well as about its supply situation; and virtually every day it contained details of the day's targets and intended scale of effort and retrospective operational summaries. Such was the flow of this intelligence, and so slight the

---

* The multiplicity of units taking photographs caused confusion and duplication and this, together with the increase of air operations in May and June 1942, led to the formation of No 285 Wing RAF to co-ordinate both photographic and visual reconnaissance – see below, pp. 380, 402–403.

53.   Playfair, op cit, Vol III (1960), p 15; AIR 41/7, pp 59–60, 98; AIR 41/25, *The RAF in the Middle East Campaigns*, Vol II, pp 96, 131.

delay with which it was received, that it is no exaggeration to claim that the British authorities were as well informed as were its own commanders about the GAF's state and order of battle. They knew in advance, for example, that the Germans intended to equip one fighter unit with Me 109 Fs, which were superior to any RAF fighter then in the theatre, and the Enigma confirmed the presence of a few of these aircraft in October.[54] About the IAF, Sigint provided similar information, though there was less of it and it was obtained with more delay.[55] The surviving records do not state to what extent and in exactly what ways this knowledge influenced the RAF's day to day activities. But it is reasonable to assume that by influencing the PR programme, and by entering into the planning of the RAF's other operations and the briefing of its air crews, it played a large part in enabling the RAF to establish air supremacy in the weeks before the British advance.

It was also important in determining the air power the enemy would deploy in the coming battle, a matter on which it was obviously vital that the estimates should be correct and which on this occasion was especially important because the New Zealand Prime Minister had expressed concern at the need to be sure of air superiority. In the first half of October AI in Whitehall calculated that the establishment strength of the GAF in the Mediterranean was 420 aircraft and that, with serviceability at about 50 per cent, it had about 252 operational aircraft – 128 at Cyrenaican bases and the remainder able to supply a supporting effort from Crete and Greece. It estimated the establishment of the IAF in Cyrenaica at 295 aircraft, of which 180 were serviceable, but allowed that the serviceable figure might rise to 237 by D-day.[56] In Cairo up to mid-October it was calculated that the Axis would be able to muster 300 German and 350 Italian aircraft without reinforcement and that these figures might rise to 420 and 370 if the fighting in Russia died down in October and Germany transferred aircraft to north Africa.[57] These figures ignored the serviceability rate and took no account of the fuel and other restrictions that would limit the reinforcements that the GAF could use in north Africa – subjects on which Sigint was supplying full information – and the Prime Minister also insisted that they were 'misleading especially in their reference to the eastern front, which will certainly not be stabilised as early as October'.[58] By 20 October, however, after a

---

54.   CAB 80/31, COS (41) 616 (110th Résumé); OL 1140 of 14 September 1941; CX/MSS/241/T4.
55.   eg OLs 1136 of 14 September and 1172 of 17 September 1941 reporting the arrival of night fighters in Africa; CX/MSS/239/T16, 249/T15.
56.   AIR 41/25, p 21 and Appendix G.
57.   ibid, p 21.
58.   Gwyer and Butler, op cit, Vol III, Part I, p 229.

visit to Cairo by the Vice-Chief of the Air Staff, Whitehall and Cairo reached agreement on a new set of estimates. It was accepted that against an RAF strength of 528 serviceable aircraft, plus reserves of 50 per cent, an Axis establishment of 642 would yield 385 serviceable aircraft in Cyrenaica but no reserves apart from 156 German aircraft in Greece and Crete which might be used at long range for attacks on British lines of communication.[59]

In the event the Air Ministry's October estimates had given an accurate forecast of the enemy strengths at the beginning of the battle. The Italian establishment in Cyrenaica was 296 (estimate 295) and the GAF's was 423 (estimate 420), of which 244 were in Cyrenaica and the remainder in Greece and Crete. Of the total Axis establishment of 540 in Cyrenaica, 313 were serviceable (estimate 308). Of the total German establishment in Cyrenaica, Greece and Crete, 254 were serviceable (estimate 252).[60] On the other hand, the GAF Enigma had shown that Cairo's anxiety about the possibility that the GAF would send reinforcements to the Mediterranean was not entirely misplaced. On 25 October the Prime Minister stressed the necessity of making the maximum use of 'the next few weeks . . . while the enemy is disentangling his surplus air forces from the Russian front'.[61] He had been alerted by an Enigma report of the arrival in Rome of a GAF signals company which GC and CS, as a result of the progress it had made in disentangling the intricate numbering system used in the GAF signals organisation, was able to identify as belonging to Luftflotte 2, then on the central front in Russia.[62] But the British offensive had been launched before the Enigma announced the appointment of Kesselring, AOC of Luftflotte 2, to a Mediterranean command on 29 November.[63]* During December, when it gave full details of the transfer from Russia, it became clear that Fliegerkorps II and the HQ of Luftflotte 2 were moving to Sicily.[65] The movement, which Hitler had decided on in October, was one of the measures taken by Germany to counter Malta's blockade of Rommel's supplies.

□

---

* It subsequently emerged that he had been given the title of Oberbefehlshaber Süd (OBS), which GC and CS, at first uncertain as to its significance, translated as AOC-in-C South.[64]

59. AIR 41/25, pp 22–23 and Appendix G; Gwyer and Butler, op cit, Vol III, Part I, p 230.   60. AIR 41/25, pp 23, 88 and Appendix G.
61. Churchill, op cit, Vol III, p 487.   62. CX/MSS/466/T2.
63. MK 342 of 29 November 1941 (OLs were renamed MKs from 20 November 1941); CX/MSS/478/T2.
64. MK 834 of 14 December 1941; CX/MSS/476.   65. CX/MSS/558/T6.

As we have already seen, the Sigint about the Axis convoys provided a considerable amount of information about the supply situation of the Axis forces. Except that it distinguished tankers from dry cargo vessels, it disclosed advance information about the cargoes only on special occasions until GC and CS began to read the German Army Enigma currently. On this account it was not yet possible, as it was to be from the summer of 1942, to identify the ships that were carrying the supplies and reinforcements that Rommel most needed at any one time and to give priority to attacking them.* But already during the second half of 1941 the British authorities in Egypt were receiving a continuous account of the enemy's shipping arrivals and of his losses en route to the African ports. Without this – forced to rely on what they could obtain from sightings, from POW and from occasional agents' reports – they would have been reduced to guesswork. As it was, MI in Whitehall and sections at the Service HQs in Egypt concerned with the correlation of what was known from Sigint with other information about Axis deliveries were able to speculate with some confidence about the state of the enemy's supplies.† For the Army authorities, however, other information about the enemy's ground forces, particularly about his order of battle, was still more valuable.

Until the middle of September, order of battle intelligence was in short supply. Italian POW taken on the Tobruk front provided some details about Italian divisions in that area, and captured Italian correspondence established that a Mobile Corps had been formed round the Ariete Division.[66] But few documents were captured and few prisoners were taken during the lull in the fighting: the only other important item of this kind came when men of the 361st Regiment, former German members of the Foreign Legion, crossed to the British lines,[67] and the arrival of this unit was in any case being learned from the Enigma. The SIS contributed little: it had by now established an advanced station in the desert, but its few reports dealt only with activity in the enemy's rear areas.[68] As we have already seen, PR and other reconnaissance, air and ground, yielded much information about the enemy's dispositions, movements and defences,‡ but by itself this source was at its most useful when all the enemy's forces could be covered in one day, and this was rarely possible. Moreover – and this was a

---

* See below, p 423 et seq. † See further below, pp 423–424.
‡ See above, pp 288–289.

66. D Hunt, *A Don at War* (1966), p 67; WO 169/1010, Eighth Army Weekly Intelligence Review No 1 of 4 October 1941.
67. Hunt, op cit, p 65.
68. WO 208/3575, Williams, The Use of Ultra by the Army, p 2; WO 169/1107, XIII Corps Intelligence Summary, 3 November 1941.

particularly important limitation where tanks were concerned – it could not provide identifications of units seen, or even determine their nationality, unless it was supplemented by Sigint, of which little was yet available about the enemy's ground forces.

For the Army's Y organisation, which exploited the enemy's medium and low-grade communications,* the months before the British offensive were a period of discovery and preparations. The first positive steps were now made towards what was later to become one of the major intelligence achievements of the war. In France and Greece the Y organisation had exploited mainly tactical GAF traffic, and that under conditions of retreat. In July 1941 CBME, on the basis of intercepts of communications used during German mopping-up operations in Crete, broke the medium-grade field cypher used by the German Army in north Africa.† A start was also made in breaking certain simpler codes – that of the DAK's armoured car reconnaissance units, and the code used for relaying to units of the Army their 'thrust lines' or axes of advance – and all these, and others, were to yield an increasing amount of useful operational intelligence. They were judged suitable for exploitation forward, alongside comparable Italian codes and cyphers, and provision was made for this in the British plan through the attachment of units to HQ Eighth Army, to XIII Corps and, as a short-lived but apparently successful experiment, to 7th Armoured Division of XXX Corps.[69] During the lull the support organisation in Cairo also made progress with the task of reconstructing the networks, frequencies, call-signs and code names used by the German Army in Libya, and from this it was at last becoming possible to identify German units and formations. Since DF was as yet inadequate, however, locating the enemy transmitters was not possible; and the forward Y units, accustomed to handling Italian decrypts which were altogether simpler, not to say self-explanatory, had not yet built up the experience needed for interpreting the obscurities in the German signals. For these reasons, and also because of the paucity of enemy traffic, it was not until the time of the British attack that the Y organisation began to make progress against the German

---

* Army Y was the phrase commonly used for the conduct by the Army of Sigint in the field, viz, interception, DF, Traffic Analysis and the decryption and interpretation of low-grade field codes and cyphers.

† Very little traffic in this cypher had been intercepted by the British before the summer of 1941. It was based on the same system as the cyphers used by the German police and the GAF (see Appendix 5) and was also available to the GAF and the Army as a stand-by substitute for the Enigma. Towards the end of 1941 the police and the GAF replaced the simpler version by more sophisticated ones, but the German Army did not make this change until August 1942.

69.   WO 169/1175, 7th Armoured Division War Diary, 7 December 1941.

communications, although the Italian lower grade Army codes provided some information about personalities and, to a lesser extent, order of battle, and continued to do so until Italy left the war. Thus Army Y, like every other source, failed to give advance warning of the important reconnaissance in force made by 21st Panzer Division on 14 September.[70]*

From the middle of September, however, a new source of high-grade Sigint made it possible to work out the details and the significance of the changes that were reflected in the renaming of Rommel's command. Hitherto called the DAK, this was rechristened Panzergruppe Afrika on 31 July, when Rommel was put in control of the Italian XXI (infantry) Corps as well as of the DAK, the latter comprising the Italian Savona Infantry Division as well as 15th Panzer Division, 21st Panzer Division (formerly 5th Light Division) and the motorised Division zbV Afrika (later renamed 90th Light Division). When the GAF Enigma first mentioned Panzergruppe Afrika on 10 August[71] it was assumed by analogy with what MI was learning about the structure of Panzergruppen on the Russian front that the new title might portend the arrival in Africa of another German corps, perhaps of infantry. By the end of September, however, MI had established that the German forces in Africa consisted of two armoured divisions, now brought up to strength, and at least two regiments of a third which, though possibly motorised, was not armoured.[72] This correct conclusion, which guided the planning of the British offensive, was based on the fact that after the GAF Enigma had made reference to the 361st Regiment on 15 August and 21st Panzer Division on 5 September, the earliest regular decrypts of Army Enigma in north Africa had made it clear that while Division zbV Afrika, of which the regiment formed a part, was a new formation, 21st Panzer Division was a reinforced version of 5th Light Division.[73]

Of the various sub-divisions of Army Enigma keys, of greater complexity than those of the GAF, and also more securely used, one on the Russian front (Vulture) had first been broken in June 1941, but those in use in north Africa had resisted the efforts of GC and CS except for an occasional day. On 17 September, however GC and CS broke into one of them (which it named Chaffinch) on a substantial scale for the first time. From 17 September to 19

---

* See below, p 296. The raid was first spotted by the RAF.

70.   WO 169/1107 of 5 November 1941.
71.   CX/MSS/148, para 53.
72.   WO 208/3573 of 29 September and 13 October 1941; CAB 80/31, COS (41) 601 (109th Résumé).
73.   OL 1259 of 22 September 1941; CX/MSS/265/T1 and 7.

October 1941, and again from 2 November to 6 December, it read it with some regularity, though always with great effort and often a week or more late. Chaffinch turned out to consist of three related keys. Two of these were used between all the main supply bases in Africa, Rome and Salonika, and the third for special communications, such as daily appreciations, between Africa, Rome and Berlin. The settings for November were captured on 28 November, in the early days of *Crusader*, and helped GC and CS belatedly to complete its reading of the November traffic. The same haul of captured documents* also enabled GC and CS to break one week's traffic in a further African Army Enigma key (named Phoenix at GC and CS) which was used for operational communications between division and corps, and corps and army.†

During the planning of the British offensive the new source provided valuable information on German order of battle. It filled out the sparse ground force information being provided by the GAF Enigma at this time and the two sources together provided a reliable background against which the considerable, but irregular and incomplete, information from British reconnaissance patrols and low-grade local intelligence sources could be weighed and some of the wilder rumours dismissed.‡ The Army Enigma also provided many valuable identifications of German units and formations – such as those which helped clarify the composition of the Panzergruppe[75]§ – though it rarely located these units or identified Italian formations.[76]‖ More usefully it established or confirmed certain important enemy redispositions on the eve of the British offensive. By then it had disclosed the move of the Ariete Division to Bir Gubi and, with the help of POW and reconnaissance, had established the presence of the Trieste Division in the

---

* See below, p 310.

† See below, p 374.

‡ For example, on 6 November 1941 the Naval Attaché Ankara reported 'reliable information' that the Axis intended to have 40 divisions in Libya shortly, including 5 German divisions.[74]

§ The assessment was at fault only in minor matters. It was not known whether Division zbV Afrika was subordinated to the DAK. It was assumed that the Trento Division was part of the Italian XXX Corps, which was correctly identified as the Mobile Corps, when in fact the division was part of XXI Corps.

‖ The Enigma helped to identify XX and XXI Corps. Italian field Sigint gave details of the divisions subordinated to XXI Corps, and located its Corps HQ. But in addition to uncertainty about which Italian formations were included in Panzergruppe Afrika it was impossible to settle whether the Littorio Armoured Division was in Tripoli. This difficulty continued to complicate calculations of enemy armoured strength in the early months of 1942.

74.   CAB 105/8, Hist (B) 8, No 22.

75.   CAB 80/32, COS (41) 703 (117th Résumé); WO 169/1107 of 5 and 17 November 1941; CAB 44/91, AL 1200/22, p 44.

76.   WO 169/1010, No 1 of 4 October 1941; WO 169/1107 of 5 November 1941.

southern sector, at Bir Hacheim,[77] and thus that that part of the British plan which was intended to deceive the enemy into thinking that there would be a threat to his southern flank was meeting with some success. On 16 November, having already located 15th Panzer Division and Division zbV Afrika in the battle zone, it established that 21st Panzer Division was arriving at a point north-west of Capuzzo, between Tobruk and the Egyptian frontier, and that the DAK's two ground reconnaissance units were covering the gap between the Ariete Division and the sea.[78] This information assisted the interpretation of the last-minute comprehensive air reconnaissance which on 17 and 18 November showed no change throughout the battle area.[79]

The Enigma provided valuable last-minute information about the strength of Rommel's armour as well as about its dispositions. Until November 1941 there was no Sigint on this subject, but British calculations, based on what was believed to be the enemy's establishments, on POW and reconnaissance, and on assumptions of tank casualties and of time taken for repairs, were tolerably accurate. At the end of August, when the actual figures were 180 and about 50,[80] Cairo put the figures at 224 German tanks and 64 Italian but was uncertain whether replacements might have raised the German figure to 301.[81] London agreed with these estimates: it was almost certain that no reinforcements had been received.[82] On 6 October Cairo put the total of serviceable Axis tanks at 138, a figure which took account of the drastic reduction in the number of serviceable German tanks following 21st Panzer Division's reconnaissance in force of 14–15 September,[83] but recognised that this low figure would be temporary. During September planning proceeded on the assumption that in November the ratio of Axis to British tank strength (479 tanks) would be 4:6.[84] This forecast was corrected when the second break into the Chaffinch traffic from the beginning of November produced on 13 November the first decrypt of a type that was to be regularly available from the middle of 1942. It gave the following return of German tanks ready for action, total 244:

---

77. OL 1931 of 13 November 1941; CX/MSS/426/T9; WO 169/1123, XXX Corps Intelligence Summary No 1 of 10 November 1941; CAB 44/91, p 35; Playfair, op cit, Vol III, p 40 fn.

78. OLs 1175, 1259 and 1318 of 17, 24 and 27 September 1941; CX/MSS/249/T13, 265/T1 and 7, 282/T2.

79. WO 169/1107 of 17 and 18 November 1941; AIR 41/25, p 126.

80. Playfair, op cit, Vol II, p 262.

81. CAB 105/6, No 182.   82. AIR 41/25, Appendix F.

83. CAB 105/7, No 313; Playfair, op cit, Vol III, p 9.

84. Playfair, op cit, Vol III, p 6.

Formation	Pzkw II	Pzkw III	Pzkw IV
15th Panzer Division	38	75	20
21st Panzer Division	32	64	15[85]*

At the beginning of the British offensive MI estimated that the combined total of German and Italian serviceable tanks was 385.[86] This was remarkably accurate, for the actual number was 390 if the Italian light tanks were excluded.[87] MI also correctly assumed that, whereas the British had a sizeable reserve, the Axis had virtually none.

Neither in London nor in Cairo, on the other hand, did the intelligence appreciations of the enemy's order of battle dwell on a matter on which high-grade Sigint and PR naturally threw no light, but to which Wavell had drawn attention at the start of *Battleaxe* in May – the inferiority in some respects of British to German Armoured Fighting Vehicles (AFV) and their vulnerability to anti-tank guns. During the summer of 1941 technical intelligence had gradually improved.† Its sources, in addition to battle experience, were POW reports, captured documents and, above all, captured weapons and equipment which could be examined and tested. By the autumn all types of tank had been inspected, and a great deal learned of their armour and armament, and some idea had been obtained of their vulnerability to anti-tank guns. It was found that some tanks, particularly the Pzkw III, 'the work horse of the tank versus tank battle in the desert', and Pzkw IV had been fitted with extra armour plates, but it was not known in November 1941 how many had been so modified. Nor was it until March 1942 that tests established that the extra plates were face-hardened so that the two-pounder uncapped shot of most of Eighth Army's anti-tank and tank guns did not penetrate. A Pzkw IV had been captured in July 1941 in a fairly complete condition, and after a preliminary examination was shipped to the United Kingdom for a complete study. But neither examination apparently disclosed the face-hardening. Information on the anti-tank guns was also increasing. A 50 mm Pak 38, which was to do much damage during the coming campaign, had been captured. But details of the 88 mm dual-purpose Flak and anti-tank gun, which

---

* Pzkw was the abbreviation for Panzerkampfwagen and the Roman figures denoted the type of mark. Pzkw II was by now of little fighting value.

† See Appendix 10 for further details of technical intelligence on German tanks and anti-tank weapons.

85.   OL 1931 of 13 November 1941; CX/MSS/426/T9.
86.   CAB 80/32, COS (41) 703 (117th Résumé).
87.   Playfair, op cit, Vol II, p 262, Vol III, pp 29–30.

had caused so much trouble during *Battleaxe*, still remained unknown.[88] By November 1941 technical intelligence was thus failing to warn that the Pzkw III and IV were superior to most British tanks. On this score there was to be much recrimination when it was seen that Rommel's counter-attack in January 1942 had been a resounding success.[89] On 7 February 1942 the C-in-C Middle East insisted that to redress British inferiority in tank performance he must have 50 per cent superiority in numbers before he attempted another offensive.[90]* But in the period before the British offensive began, and in its successful phase, although many technical reports were issued by MI 10 ME and republished in London in the War Office intelligence summaries, the subject was rarely, if ever, referred to in the British appreciations.

If under-estimation of the quality of Rommel's equipment was one reason why British confidence was high when the *Crusader* offensive began, another was the failure to allow for the efficiency of his field intelligence. By August 1941 the Germans were regularly reading the War Office high-grade hand cypher which carried a good deal of Eighth Army's W/T traffic down to division level, and they continued to do so until January 1942. Until then, when their success was progressively reduced by British improvements to the recyphering system, whereas GC and CS's success against the German Army Enigma continued to expand, this cypher provided them with at least as much intelligence about Eighth Army's strengths and order of battle as Eighth Army was obtaining about those of Rommel's forces.[†] More important, while the British Y organisation in the Middle East was still in its infancy in the autumn of 1941, at least in its work on the communications of the German Army, Rommel's was already highly efficient and was greatly valued by himself and his commanders. It derived great benefit from British carelessness with regard to tactical codes and wireless procedure, particularly the use of uncontrolled R/T, of plain language and of an unsound call-sign procedure on the brigade-to-battalion links in the forward areas. The extent of its success was not suspected until the capture of part of Rommel's field Sigint unit and a large quantity of its records in July 1942.[‡]

---

* As late as June 1942 Whitehall was to have the mortification of reading a diplomatic decrypt in which Hitler was stated to have described British tanks as 'tin'.

† An example of the intelligence obtained by the enemy was revealed in the Army Enigma in October in a summary of information about recent increases in British ground force strength in Egypt. This gave so accurate an estimate of British tank strength that the War Office was 'very concerned'.

‡ See below, p 404.

88.   Playfair, op cit, Vol III, Appendix 8; WO 208/3580, MEF/9000 (I)/MI 10, MEF/6000/MI 10.   89.   Churchill, op cit, Vol IV (1951), pp 28–31.
90.   CAB 105/16, Hist (B) (Crusader) 2, No 194.

Until then German field Sigint was for Rommel a prolific source of information about Eighth Army's order of battle and, especially during battle, it frequently alerted him to Eighth Army's tactical intentions.*

□

On the subject of Rommel's operational intentions after the middle of 1941 the intelligence sources were less helpful than they were about his supplies and the order of battle and dispositions of his forces. This was partly because the operational value of the newest and most important of the sources on Rommel's intentions – the Army Enigma – was restricted by interruptions and delays in reading the traffic, and by the fact that only part of it could be intercepted in the United Kingdom. But these difficulties only accentuated the more fundamental handicap to which attention has already been drawn on several occasions. Except in special situations like that which was presented by the dependence of the Axis forces in north Africa on supplies by sea, even intelligence from high-grade Sigint rarely provided direct evidence of an intended future operation by the enemy or of his strategic plans. In the desert at this time the great majority of decrypts concerning the enemy ground forces were about the daily activities and adminis- tration of the units, formations and staffs of an army marking time before major operations.† Even they were but a small proportion of the enemy's total communications. Most internal communications went by courier and – where it existed – land-line, and those about future operations certainly did so. Such as went by W/T to and from the HQs in Rome and Berlin were mostly about drafts, supply and equipment. Such internal communications as rated despatch by W/T dealt with urgent requests for reinforcements, stores and equipment; local movement of units and supplies; exercises, patrols, complaints etc.; and by no means all decrypts of such messages were sent out from GC and CS to the Middle East on the SCU/SLU link.‡ With the Chaffinch break of September the study of the intercepts yielded – when supplemented by local intelligence sources whose evaluation they assisted – not only a knowledge of the enemy's order of battle but also a rounded picture of capabilities and behaviour. But in the lulls between battles the

---

* See Appendix 1 (Part (i)) for further details.

† A high proportion of the GAF's decrypts, on the other hand, concerned its daily operations and intentions. There was, of course, no lull for the air forces.

‡ For details of the special signals service from GC and CS to the Middle East see Volume I, Appendix 13, and below, pp 316–317, fn †.

only decrypts containing the clues about enemy intentions or plans were those which deviated from what the intelligence officer, on the evidence of this study, held to be the normal state of affairs. And although the amount of Sigint was at last making it possible for the intelligence officer to establish the routine and to pick out the abnormal there remained much room for uncertainty and disagreement when it came to forecasting the enemy's detailed intentions. Later in the war, when many additional Sigint sources became available, this difficulty was to be reduced; but it was never to be avoided entirely.

As it applied in north Africa in the second half of 1941, this problem meant that while the British authorities were able to deduce with some confidence from an early date that Rommel was in no position to launch an offensive against Egypt, they could by no means rule out the possibility that he would make an assault on Tobruk. For that he did have the capacity, and since the Tobruk garrison would otherwise threaten his supply line when he did try to reach Egypt, its elimination was an obvious preliminary. More to the point, they feared that, whereas his attack on Tobruk in April and May had failed because it had followed the most strongly defended access route, he had now discovered 'the right way in' and would succeed in his next attempt unless his attack was spoiled by an earlier British advance.[91] But in these circumstances, so crucial to the planning and timing of their own advance, they received no firm intelligence about Rommel's plan to make this assault in September and about the successive German postponements of the date to 23 November,* and could guess at it only by correlating what they knew about his preliminary moves and preparations with the information that was available about his supplies and reinforcements.

Until well into September there was little cause for anxiety. On 8 August the JIC agreed with the view already expressed by MI: there would be no Axis offensive before the end of October.† A fortnight later, although the operational authorities in Whitehall feared that Axis reinforcements might enable Rommel to move before the British, the C-in-C still calculated that Rommel's supply problems 'almost certainly' made it impossible for him to mount an offensive;[92] and the intelligence authorities in London agreed with the C-in-C. On 28 August they judged that supply and maintenance difficulties made it 'impossible' for the Axis to undertake

---

* See above, p 286. It was not until the end of the year that captured documents and late decrypts of Enigma messages disclosed these facts.

† See above, p 281.

91.   Hunt, op cit, pp 65, 71.
92.   Churchill, op cit, Vol III, p 434; CAB 105/6, Nos 191, 201.

intensified operations for any length of time, and on 25 August MI had ruled out 'immediate operations' on learning from the GAF Enigma that Fliegerführer Afrika was to be away from the theatre until mid-September.[93] By this last date, however, the Enigma was beginning to provide specific evidence of the preparations that the enemy was making for an operation against Tobruk.

By 12 September, when PR had already observed some reinforcement of the Tobruk perimeter,[94] the GAF Enigma revealed that Panzergruppe Afrika had asked urgently for maps and overlays of the Tobruk defences and that Fliegerkorps X was preparing for some special activity against Tobruk.[95] On 21 September it again referred to a 'special operation' by Fliegerkorps X against Tobruk.[96] Between then and 26 September the GAF and Army Enigmas reported further activity: HQ Division zbV Afrika had arrived in the forward area and some of its units were moving to the front from Tripoli; conferences were taking place between Rommel, AOC Fliegerkorps X and the German authorities in Rome; all parts of HQ Panzergruppe Afrika were being transferred to Gazala, 30 miles west of Tobruk; a conference was to be held at Gambut, Rommel's HQ 30 miles east of Tobruk.[97]

On this evidence, which was all the more disturbing because it was coming in at a time when the Australian forces were being withdrawn from Tobruk on the insistence of the Australian government, and on the strength of other more general pointers, the JIC concluded on 27 September that, although a major Axis offensive before mid-October remained unlikely, action against Tobruk could come earlier than 15 October, a date which had been mentioned by another source, presumably POW or SIS.[98] On 29 September MI agreed that an attack on Tobruk in the immediate future was more than likely, adding to the information used by the JIC the fact that references were being received to an operation *Beta* involving the Italian navy.[99]* But on 3 October a Chaffinch decrypt again put an end to immediate anxiety by reporting that the disruption of traffic between Italy and Africa was causing delays to the return of troops on leave which could not be made up for two or three weeks.[100] The signal conveying this intelligence to

---

* See below, p. 324, fn *.

93. CAB 80/30, COS (41) 533 (104th Résumé); WO 208/3573 of 25 August 1941.   94. WO 208/3573 of 1 September 1941.
95. OL 1108 of 12 September 1941; CX/MSS/232/T5.
96. OL 1241 of 21 September 1941; CX/MSS/262/T26.
97. OLs 1255, 1265 and 1306 of 22, 23 and 26 September 1941;
    CX/MSS/265/T17, 268/T16, 278/T1.
98. JIC (41) 388 (o) of 27 September.
99. WO 208/3573 of 29 September 1941.
100. OL 1379 of 3 October 1941; CX/MSS/296/T4.

Cairo concluded with a special instruction: 'The Minister of Defence directs that General Auchinleck should see'. On at least two further occasions before *Crusader* the Prime Minister directed that the C-in-C should be shown decrypts revealing the build-up of Rommel's anti-tank strength.[101]

During October the disruption of Axis traffic increased, with shipping to Tripoli suspended from 18 October, and the intelligence picture led the London authorities to the conclusion that, far from intending to launch an attack of his own, the enemy was now expecting a British offensive and was straining every nerve to be ready for it. This was particularly the view of AI and of the RAF officers at GC and CS who, in reply to a demand from Cairo for further evidence that its own secret preparations might have been compromised, summarised the evidence for it on 26 October. Apart from 'subtler shades of meaning impossible to express' in signals from GC and CS, the evidence consisted of increases in fighter strength in north Africa and of GAF PR activity, the ferrying of German troops in Italian destroyers and the enemy's anxiety about fuel, as well as of explicit Sigint references to the fact that the Germans were on the look-out for signs of a British attack.[102] There had been other such references since the beginning of the month. On 4 October the British Military Attaché in Ankara had reported information to the same effect that he had obtained from the Romanian Military Attaché: the Germans, though confident that they could hold it, were more concerned with the expected British attack than with launching an offensive of their own.[103] The appreciation of 26 October added on the basis of an IAF high-grade decrypt that 'Italian information was available to suggest that they expected an offensive and had so told the Germans'. On 27 October MI thought that a further Enigma item, to the effect that troops on leave from Libya were to be brought back urgently 'because of British dispositions', confirmed the view that the Axis expected some British action.[104] But if this interpretation posed the new threat that the enemy had detected the British preparations, which were now well advanced, the evidence did not exclude the possibility that he would try to forestall them by launching his own attack. On the contrary, from 17 October Sigint references to Rommel's preparations for the attack on Tobruk became so frequent as to suggest that it could not be far off. On 17, 19 and 21 October requests for flame-throwers (believed to be for assaulting concrete emplacements), for other assault equipment and for maps

101. Dir/C Archive, 7861 of 22 October and 7973 of 5 November 1941, covering CX/MSS/359/T15, 400/T16.
102. OL 1698 of 26 October 1941.
103. CAB 105/7, No 302.
104. WO 208/3573 of 27 October 1941.

of Tobruk were decrypted. On 20 October 17 Ju 52 loads of anti-tank guns were reported arriving at Gazala.[105]

At this juncture the British offensive was itself subjected to a series of postponements. The first, moving the date from 1 to 11 November, evoked the intense displeasure of the Prime Minister on 18 October; a second postponement till 15 November was followed by a request from a divisional commander for a further delay either of six days to 21 November or of a minimum of three days to 18 November.[106] But it was also followed on 2 November by the second of GC and CS's breaks into the Chaffinch traffic. Between 3 and 11 November the decrypts contained requests for maps and a large mosaic of Tobruk and for more assault equipment, with expressions of anxiety that this might not arrive 'in time'; a demand by Rommel for 100 more anti-tank guns 'by mid-November'; and a demand by Fliegerkorps X for a large quantity of aircraft fuel by 20 November. On 7 November they referred to an 'impending attack'. On 10 November they revealed that the Panzergruppe had suspended leave and that the Trento Motorised Division had been brought up to Tobruk, and mentioned 'landing boats'.* On 12 November they showed that 15th Panzer Division had asked for 800 assault badges as 'rewards of valour'. On 16 November it was learned that the Italian San Marco marine battalion had just arrived in Africa, a fact which, like the reference to landing boats, pointed to Rommel's intention to supplement his assault on Tobruk by a landing from the sea.[108] On 17 November, having already disclosed that Rommel had flown to Rome on 1 November, the Army Enigma reported that he would return to north Africa on the evening of 18 November.[109]†

After the event those who were at GC and CS at the time had no doubt that, although the British authorities were not yet familiar with Rommel's habit of visiting Europe in the last stage of the

---

* Rommel's plans included a sea-borne landing at Tobruk, and 500 rubber boats were found later.[107]

† Despite this information a raiding party led by Colonel Keyes landed by submarine on the night 17–18 November and Keyes lost his life in an attack on what was wrongly believed to be Rommel's house at Apollonia.[110] The news of 17 November that Rommel was returning on 18 November was sent to the Middle East in an emergency signal[111] but was obviously received too late to stop the operation. On 15 November the C 38m had disclosed that the Italians had learned from various reliable sources that the British intended to make a landing near Apollonia.[112]

105. OL 1637 of 21 October 1941; CX/MSS/359/T4.
106. Churchill, op cit, Vol III, p 481; Playfair, op cit, Vol III, pp 11–12.
107. CAB 44/92, AL 1200/27B, p 67.
108. OLs 1790, 1793, 1832, 1902 of 3 and 11 November 1941; CX/MSS/396/T3 and 5, 398/T10, 400/T5, 411/T12, 408/T12, 422/T14; WO 208/3573 of 2 October 1941.   109. OL 1770 of 3 November 1941; CX/MSS/396/T15.
110. Hunt, op cit, p 134.
111. OL 2008 of 17 November 1941; CX/MSS/440/T24.   112. ZTPI 2050.

preparations for his attacks, 'all these details gave Eighth Army a clear indication of the objective and nature of the German attack, and an indication of its timing sufficiently clear for the British offensive to start first'. 'The fact that Eighth Army was able to strike before Panzergruppe Afrika . . . was doubtless as much due . . . to appreciation of Rommel's timing' as it was to the harassing of Rommel's supplies. That Eighth Army was well aware that the Germans intended to move against Tobruk in the last ten days of November is borne out by the recollection of one who was then an intelligence officer in the Middle East and who also claims 'that, therefore, the offensive was timed for just before'.[113] This much is further supported by contemporary documents. On 16 and 17 November GHQ informed XIII and XXX Corps, which up to 10 November had appreciated that Rommel's dispositions were 'entirely defensive' and that, far from preparing to attack, he was ready to retreat,[114] that an enemy attack on Tobruk was imminent and that his order of battle showed that he was prepared to resist any British attempt to relieve the fortress.[115] GHQ stated that this intelligence was derived from POW interrogation but it is safe to assume that the appreciation was based on the Enigma or on POW evidence that had been evaluated in the light of the Enigma.

□

The British offensive of 18 November, operation *Crusader*, took the enemy by surprise. During October the authorities both in Berlin and Rome had issued warnings of a possible offensive.[116] By the end of that month there had been several Enigma items showing that the Germans were preparing to meet an attack in Libya, and Abwehr decrypts had reported that a large-scale attack on Libya was in preparation rather than action in Iran. Thereafter, however, the Italian C-in-C in Africa and Rommel were both discounting an imminent attack.[117] To this initial advantage, which chiefly derived from the success of the Army patrols and of the RAF in keeping the enemy's air and ground reconnaissance at a distance before the offensive began, another was added when, partly because Eighth Army kept W/T silence and partly because heavy rainstorms grounded the GAF during 18 and 19 November, Rommel's HQ failed at first to appreciate the scope of the British operation. On

---

113. Hunt, op cit, pp 71–72.
114. WO 169/1107 of 5 November 1941; WO 169/1123 of 10 November 1941.
115. WO 169/1010 of 16 and 17 November 1941; CAB 44/91, p 54.
116. Playfair, op cit, Vol III, p 20.
117. Playfair, op cit, Vol III, p 21.

his return to Africa on the evening of 18 November Rommel took the first news of it to mean that the British were making a reconnaissance in force, and ordered no change in his dispositions. On the evening of 19 November he ordered his Panzer divisions forward on the assumption that the British were trying to interfere with his own planned attack on Tobruk. It was not until the evening of 20 November that he realised that they had launched an all-out offensive.[118] Nor was this all. Although the bad weather hampered the RAF as much as the GAF, intelligence left the authorities in Cairo in no doubt that Rommel had been taken by surprise and was now failing to understand that major operations were afoot.[119]

In the absence of air reconnaissance, this appreciation was based during 18 and 19 November mainly on the fact that there had been no increase in the enemy's W/T activity. On the evening of 19 November it was confirmed by Cairo's receipt of the first high-grade Sigint decrypts about the enemy's reaction. These indeed included the news that the GAF had ordered dive-bomber and other units to leave Crete for north Africa 'because of a strong British thrust towards Tobruk' and the fact that the Italian naval authorities felt that movements by the Mediterranean Fleet were consistent with the beginning of 'a land offensive in Cyrenaica'.[120] But they also showed that at midday on 19 November the HQ of Panzergruppe Afrika had judged that the British were making no more than a reconnaissance in strength.[121]

By the time Rommel did recognise the scope of the British thrust, on 20 November, his delay had led the British forces to depart from their prearranged plan. The plan was for XXX Corps with the main British armour to move as though it was trying to relieve Tobruk, the assumption being that this threat would attract the enemy's armour, but then to wait near Gabr Saleh, 30 miles into Cyrenaica, until the enemy reacted, the object being to destroy that armour in a single short-lived battle. XIII Corps, mainly infantry, was to advance along the coast only when the enemy's armour was 'firmly engaged'. 70th Division was to sortie from Tobruk, but only when the enemy's armour had been defeated.[122] XXX Corps' waiting position was decided in the light of the locations of the enemy's armoured divisions, these being fully established by intelligence.* On reaching this position on the evening of 18

---

* See above, pp 295–296.

118. ibid, pp 39, 44.
119. CAB 105/15, Hist (B) (Crusader) 1, Nos 24, 27, 41.
120. OL 2052 of 19 November 1941; CX/MSS/446/T4; ADM 223/103, Ultra signal 1740/19 November 1941.
121. OL 2051 of 19 November 1941; CX/MSS/444/T2.
122. Playfair, op cit, Vol III, p 7.

November, however, the Corps in the absence of any move by the enemy divided its armour, 22nd Armoured Brigade making for Bir Gubi, where it attacked the Ariete Division the next morning, 7th Armoured Brigade occupying Sidi Rezegh, one of the heights commanding the approaches to Tobruk, and 4th Armoured Brigade staying in position, where it skirmished with 21st Panzer Division on 19 November and was attacked by 15th Panzer Division on 20 November. In addition, the sortie from Tobruk was now ordered for 21 November.[123] The result of these moves was disaster for the British in the battle that began when Rommel, finally responding on the evening of 20 November, ordered the whole of the DAK to attack at Sidi Rezegh on the following day.

During the forenoon of 20 November XXX Corps had received warning that 4th Armoured Brigade was to be attacked by 15th and 21st Panzer Divisions at midday that day;[124] this was the first contribution of Army Y. But there was no warning on the morning of 21 November when 15th and 21st Panzer Divisions attacked 7th Armoured Brigade as it was preparing to fight its way to a link-up with 70th Division's sortie from Tobruk. Air reconnaissance spotted some 200 enemy tanks moving north-eastward.[125] But either this information failed to reach 7th Armoured Brigade or it was assumed in the absence of further sightings and of any other intelligence that the enemy was withdrawing and being pursued by 4th and 22nd Armoured Brigades, which was how the situation was interpreted by the intelligence staffs of Eighth Army and XXX Corps.[126] The outcome was a day-long battle in which the British forces suffered the loss of 200 tanks, although the depleted 7th Armoured Brigade held on at Rezegh. In further heavy fighting the next day the DAK completed its defeat of XXX Corps' armour. In five days the Corps' 450 tanks had been reduced to about 50. The Germans, starting with 250 tanks, still had 173, although this was not known at the time.

The extent of the British losses was not appreciated by XXX Corps or Eighth Army until the morning of 23 November.[127] During 21 and 22 November, moreover, unit reports greatly over-estimated the enemy's losses. On 21 November XXX Corps thought these amounted to half of the German tanks; early on 22 November XIII Corps estimated that the Germans might be down to as few as 60 tanks.[128] Eighth Army accepted the view that the fighting had gone well – and so much so that it ordered XIII Corps to begin the move along the coast that had been planned to take

123.   ibid, p 42.   124. WO 169/1123 of 20 November 1941.
125.   AIR 41/25, pp 140 (n), 142.
126.   WO 169/1010 of 21 November 1941; Playfair, op cit, Vol III, p 46.
127.   Playfair, op cit, Vol III, p 48.
128.   WO 169/1123 of 21 November 1941; WO 169/1107 of 22 November 1941.

place only when the enemy's armour had been 'firmly engaged'.[129] The C-in-C also judged that 'the prospects of achieving our immediate object, namely destruction of German armoured forces, seem good'.[130] But no intelligence was cited in support of these optimistic appreciations apart from one Army Y intercept in which one enemy unit on 21 November had described the situation as 'one of extreme urgency'.[131] It is true that the C-in-C commended on the evening of 22 November the 'extraordinarily accurate and far-seeing' appreciations he had received from his intelligence staff.[132] In all probability, however, he was referring to the calculations made before the fighting began, which had correctly predicted the direction from which Rommel would intervene, rather than to subsequent appreciations. We cannot be sure because the records of GS Int, GHQ ME for this period have not survived.

By the morning of 23 November the facts were emerging. Eighth Army commander then calculated that he had only 44 fit tanks left, and since initial estimates of the enemy's losses had been revised to give the Germans 120 tanks, he felt that there were great risks in continuing. But that evening the C-in-C ordered that the offensive should press on; two days later he replaced the Army commander. He based his order partly on the calculation that the enemy's tank strength had been further reduced during fighting on 23 November from about 100 to 50, but mainly on the conviction that whereas reinforcements were available for Eighth Army, the enemy 'is fully stretched and desperate . . .'[133] As to the enemy's strength, there was still no reliable intelligence; in fact in the fighting of 23 November in which the DAK had destroyed 5th South African Brigade (one of the two brigades of 1st South African Division, the only infantry division with XXX Corps) the South African gunners had reduced the German tank strength from 173 to between 100 and 110.[134] On Rommel's lack of reinforcements and general supply difficulties, on the other hand, the British information was good. The C-in-C knew by 23 November that Rommel had fielded virtually his entire force of fighting tanks and could replace losses only by local recovery and repair. He had learned from Sigint on the evening of 22 November that the only Italian convoy to have left Italy since 8 November with ships capable of carrying tanks had been turned back by British forces on 21 November.[135]* During 23 November he had received a summary of

---

* See below, p 320.

129.   Playfair, op cit, Vol III, p 46.
130.   CAB 105/15, No 55; Churchill, op cit, Vol III, p 504.
131.   WO 169/1123 of 21 November; CAB 105/15, No 45.
132.   CAB 105/15, No 55.   133.   ibid, No 71.
134.   Playfair, op cit, Vol III, p 50.
135.   MK 58 of 22 November 1941; ZTPI 2364, 2367 and 2368.

Panzergruppe Afrika's report on the operations of 21 November. This revealed that the Panzergruppe had intended to go over to the defensive on 22 November because of the fuel position and the estimated strength of the thrust towards Tobruk by XIII Corps; although it had been overtaken by the DAK's attacks during 22 and 23 November, it thus confirmed that fuel shortage was another of Rommel's difficulties.[136] The other information available to the British commanders from Sigint was the news that late on 22 November the enemy was about to abandon Gambut, which showed that the advance of XIII Corps along the coast was increasing the strain on Rommel;[137] several messages indicating enemy anxiety about the danger of a thrust against Benghazi in his rear by the force that had gone towards Gialo, well to the south of the battlefield;[138] and the GAF's report that its operations were being 'severely hampered' by the loss of the *Procida* and the *Maritza*.[139]*

Early on 24 November intelligence provided – for the first time in the fighting, indeed in the whole war – timely warning of the operational intentions of the enemy's main ground forces. Realising that he retained a decisive superiority in tanks, Rommel decided to lead the two Panzer divisions and the Ariete Division from the scene of his victory over XXX Corps near Tobruk on a 60-mile easterly sweep back to the frontier area with the object of relieving his garrisons at Bardia and Sollum/Halfaya, of striking at Eighth Army's communications and of perhaps bringing about once again a general British withdrawal.[140] Early air reconnaissance on 24 November showed no signs of a fresh advance on his part,[141] but Eighth Army HQ had already received from the GAF Enigma a report from Fliegerführer Afrika of the previous day in which he announced that the Panzergruppe was confident of destroying the British forces at Rezegh and then intended operations on the Sollum front.[142] On this information it was correctly appreciated that Rommel's object would be to strike at communications and relieve Halfaya.[143]

The warning did not put the British forces in a position to prevent Rommel from overrunning HQ XXX Corps and causing

---

* See below, pp 320, 321–322.

136. MK 98 of 23 November 1941; CX/MSS/456/T14.
137. MK 90 of 22 November 1941; CX/MSS/456/T1.
138. MKs 37, 70 and 96 of 21, 22 and 23 November 1941; CX/MSS/450/T22, 454/T7, 456/T15.
139. MK 116 of 23 November 1941; CX/MSS/457/T10.
140. Playfair, op cit, Vol III, p 53.
141. ibid, p 54; AIR 41/25, p 151.
142. MK 138 of 0030/24 November 1941; CX/MSS/458/T38.
143. WO 169/1107 of 24 November 1941.

chaos in the British rear.[144] During his dramatic advance, moreover, little or no intelligence was forthcoming about his movements. Air reconnaissance got numerous sightings of the enemy's columns, but the picture was confused and the close links between the tactical reconnaissance squadrons and the Corps HQs were temporarily broken.[145] Army Y threw little light on the situation though 4th Indian Division, which played a large part in halting the raid, got some indirect help from XXX Corps' Y unit, whose product influenced Corps' situation reports.[146] None of the instructions and counter-instructions issued by the German formations, themselves in considerable confusion, found their way into the high-grade decrypts. But the Army Y organisation intercepted the signals in which Rommel recalled his forces to the approaches of Tobruk early on 27 November and in which he described the situation there as 'extremely critical'.[147] More important, the high-grade Sigint sent to the Middle East during the raid confirmed the GAF's deepening fuel crisis and its chronic shortage of fighters, and contained its warnings to the effect that British air superiority was overwhelming.[148] We may judge from the fact that the C-in-C referred to the 'untold value' of this information on 24 November,[149] and again emphasised its importance on 25 November,[150] that it played some part in his appreciation that the enemy had regained the initiative 'locally and temporarily only', and had 'little behind his effort', and thus in his refusal to change his recent decision to press on with his own advance.

On the coast the British advance, having taken Gambut on 23 November, was by 26 November ejecting the infantry forces Rommel had left to guard the heights dominating the approaches to Tobruk. Together with shortage of supplies, it was this development which forced Rommel to pull his armour back on 27 November. But the British had no success in their attempts to cut off its retreat, and on the morning of 28 November Rommel mounted an encircling movement against Rezegh, retaken by the New Zealanders the previous day. On 30 November he recaptured Rezegh; by 1 December he had forced the British to withdraw and had once again cut off Tobruk.

During this second round of the struggle for the heights above

---

144. Playfair, op cit, Vol III, p 53; WO 169/1010 of 25 November 1941.
145. Playfair, op cit, Vol III, p 56.
146. CAB 44/92, AL 1200/27A, p 124.
147. Playfair, op cit, Vol III, p 62; AIR 41/25, p 160; Hunt, op cit, p 70; CAB 105/15, No 96.
148. MKs 133 and 136 of 23 November, 138 of 24 November, 191 and 202 of 25 November 1941; CX/MSS/458/T26, 38 and 40, 462/T21, 464/T17.
149. CAB 105/15, No 71.
150. ibid, No 87.

Tobruk British tactical intelligence, though still exerting no decisive influence on the outcome, underwent a distinct improvement. Air reconnaissance, hampered by bad weather up to 27 November, now provided detailed and up-to-date reports on the enemy's formations.[151] Documents captured during the enemy's advance, including important signals material taken from 15th Panzer Division on 28 November and maps giving enemy identifications and dispositions, were put to good use.[152]* POW taken included von Ravenstein, commander of 21st Panzer Division, and his maps gave information about enemy minefields and the plans for the current attack on the British positions.[153] Army Y profited from the fact that during the attack the enemy resorted to plain language for all his operational orders. By the afternoon of 29 November the intercepts had established the latest positions of the enemy armour which was resuming its attack after heavy and inconclusive fighting during the previous day, and had shown that the attack was to be pressed again on 30 November despite the fact that its units, particularly 21st Panzer Division, were experiencing great difficulties.[154] High-grade Sigint also contributed. The enemy's operational orders for the encircling attack of 29 November were decrypted at GC and CS in the Army Enigma in time to reach the Middle East before the attack began.[155] On the morning of 1 December Eighth Army received the contents of an Enigma report of the previous evening from Rommel to Berlin in which he announced his intention to renew his attack the following morning.[156]

In addition to contributing to the tactical intelligence from which Eighth Army obtained 'a pretty good grasp of the battle',[157] high-grade Sigint was of some help to Cairo and Eighth Army commander at the time of the decision on 1 December to resume the offensive as soon as possible despite the latest setbacks. It is true that by the end of November, while the British forces were receiving reinforcements, 'signs of enemy supply shortage' were becoming visible.[158] But it must have been valuable to have the visible evidence confirmed by Sigint. The Middle East had received

---

* These documents also included the Enigma keys referred to on p 295 above and material that was of great use to the Army Y organisation.

151.   AIR 41/25, pp 170–171.
152.   WO 169/1010 of 28 November 1941; WO 169/1107 of 27 November 1941.
153.   WO 169/1010 of 29 and 30 November 1941; WO 169/1123 of 4 December 1941.
154.   CAB 44/92, AL 1200/27B, p 225; CAB 105/15, Nos 120, 121, 130; WO 169/1010 of 29 November 1941.
155.   MK 337 of 0645/29 November 1941; CX/MSS/476/T43.
156.   MK 418 of 0730/1 December 1941; CX/MSS/483/T20.
157.   Hunt, op cit, p 80.   158.   WO 169/1123 of 30 Nov 1941.

a series of decrypts about Rommel's supply situation on 21 November. These disclosed that Army supplies in north Africa as a whole had risen since the return of 13 November,* but that Benghazi held stocks for only two or three days and could not be replenished while the threat from 'the British desert raid' held up the supply columns, and that stores forward of Benghazi were so short that the supply of Derna by submarine and destroyer was 'of the utmost importance'.[159] The same source showed that the situation at Benghazi had not improved by the end of the month, when it also reported that there were not enough supply columns to meet the needs of the German forces.[160]

By the beginning of December Rommel had indeed decided that the fighting was becoming a battle of attrition and that the outlook for his forces was 'grave'.[161] On 4 December he decided to withdraw from the eastern face of Tobruk to a line running from El Adem to Bir Gubi. On 7 December, by which time he had been told that he could not expect his supply position to improve until the end of December, when GAF reinforcements to Sicily might once again enable convoys to get through to north Africa, he decided to withdraw to the Gazala position under cover of rearguard actions.[162] Largely because GC and CS had ceased to be able to read the Army Enigma on 6 December,† intelligence gave no advance notice of these decisions, and did not disclose the gloomy warning which Rommel had received about the supply situation. The first signs of the first withdrawal were obtained on the morning of 5 December from air and ground patrols and from Y intercepts, which showed that all Axis forces except those in the frontier garrisons were being pulled back and that the Panzer divisions were leaving the Rezegh area.[163] By the morning of 6 December, when these sources made it clear than an orderly movement was in progress towards Gazala,[164] the C-in-C and Eighth Army commander were already working on the assumption that the first withdrawal had been the beginning of a more general retreat.[165] They had received only two items of high-grade Sigint about the enemy's ground forces between 1 and 6 December, but the difference between them marked a turning point in the battle. The first was a

---

* See above, pp 296–297.   † See above, p 295.

159.   MK 98 of 23 November 1941; CX/MSS/456/T14.
160.   MK 309 of 28 November 1941; CX/MSS/475/T9.
161.   Playfair, op cit, Vol III, p 69.
162.   ibid, pp 74, 76–77.
163.   WO 169/1123 of 5 and 6 December 1941; WO 169/1010 of 5 December 1941; AIR 41/25, p 183.
164.   WO 169/1010 of 9 December 1941; AIR 41/25, p 185.
165.   CAB 105/15, Nos 161, 162; CAB 80/32, COS (41) 739 (119th Résumé); Playfair, op cit, Vol III, p 78.

confident report from Panzergruppe Afrika for 1 December.[166] The second was the Panzergruppe's report for 4 December, which they received on 5 December; this saw no evidence of a British withdrawal and expected that the British forces, refitted and reinforced, would renew the attack.[167]

Intelligence was similarly of no decisive importance after the beginning of the British advance to Gazala on 9 December. During the planning of *Crusader* it had been assumed that, once he had been forced to withdraw, Rommel would have to quit Cyrenaica. Now, although Eighth Army recast its plans on the assumption that he would stand and fight at Gazala,[168] the temptation remained strong to believe that he would withdraw his armour 'far to the westward'[169] and there was no conclusive evidence either way until the tough resistance encountered by the British forces in their first brush with the enemy at Gazala on 13 December convinced them that Rommel had located all his formations there.[170] The problem was that although the chief remaining sources – the GAF Enigma, Y and reconnaissance – were yielding fuller information than they had done during the previous three weeks, the information was confused by the enemy's own uncertainty as to how long he should hold Gazala and what position he should withdraw to next.

This uncertainty was reflected especially clearly in the GAF Enigma decrypts relayed to the Middle East. On 11 December they contained an indication that the enemy might continue his withdrawal beyond Tmimi, a base between Gazala and Derna.[171] On 12 December they reported that the Germans had discovered that there were no British forces west of Gazala and that the DAK was establishing itself there.[172] On 13 December they first confirmed that Gazala 'was being held', then reported that Rommel considered withdrawing to 'the Derna position' as early as 13–14 December and that the GAF was discussing the evacuation of its Derna base, and then disclosed that Kesselring had advised Rommel to hold a position forward of Derna since GAF support would otherwise be impossible.[173] On 14 December they announced that Rommel intended to hold Gazala 'until the Derna positions are partly manned'.[174] On 15 December, however, they

---

166. MK 439 of 3 December 1941; CX/MSS/489/T19.
167. MK 488 of 5 December 1941; CX/MSS/498/T11.
168. CAB 105/15, No 188.   169. ibid, Nos 188 and 203.
170. CAB 44/94, AL 1200/36, p 12.
171. MK 718 of 11 December 1941; CX/MSS/519/T42; WO 169/1010 of 12 December 1941.
172. MK 743 of 12 December 1941; CX/MSS/521/T8.
173. MKs 765, 767, 775, 783 and 788 of 13 December 1941; CX/MSS/524/T3 and 7, 525/T7, 526/T12 and 17.
174. MK 823 of 14 December 1941; CX/MSS/527/T4.

first carried the news that the Panzergruppe had ordered a withdrawal to Derna for the evening of the previous day, and had directed the DAK to Mechili,[175] and then contradicted it by reaffirming that the Panzergruppe was to continue to hold Gazala while the Derna position was extended.[176]

In these changing circumstances, the intelligence can have been of little help during the planning of the attack on the Gazala position. Whether it handicapped the planning, by creating the impression that the enemy was more disorganised than he was in fact, it is impossible to say. In the event, XIII Corps met with unexpectedly heavy resistance when it advanced against the north and centre of the line on 15 December with the intention of pinning the enemy down while 4th Armoured Brigade swept round the south and took him in the rear. Once the fighting had begun, moreover, the Y intelligence added to the confusion. During 14 December Y intercepts had suggested that Rommel was cancelling his plan to defend the line.[177] By the evening of 15 December, however, Y was reporting that he had been ordered to 'continue his attack and destroy the British completely';[178] and though Rommel never deviated from his plan to retreat, it had by the morning of 16 December created the impression that he was not fighting a rearguard action but aiming to halt the British advance.[179]

During 16 December the movement of 4th Armoured Brigade persuaded Rommel that he must pull out his main force during the night of 16–17 December, and the situation became clearer. On 16 December Y detected a westward movement of the enemy's HQ without being able to say that a withdrawal was imminent,[180] but two GAF Enigma decrypts established this beyond doubt. The first reported that a retreat to Derna on the night of 16–17 December was 'probably unavoidable'; the second confirmed that the retreat was to be made that night.[181] Late on 16 December Eighth Army passed the gist of these decrypts to XIII Corps, urging it to do all in its power to prevent the enemy's escape, and XIII Corps alerted 4th Armoured Brigade.[182] On the morning of 17 December, however, Eighth Army realised that 'the enemy's main body had evaded our armour and made good its escape'.[183]

Rommel now decided to retreat all the way to the Tripolitanian border at El Agheila. Air reconnaissance, Y and high-grade Sigint provided good intelligence during this stage of his withdrawal. On

---

175.   MK 861 of 15 December 1941; CX/MSS/530/T31.
176.   MK 870 of 15 December 1941; CX/MSS/531/T30.
177.   CAB 44/94, p 24.   178. ibid, p 28.
179.   ibid, p 28.   180. WO 169/1010 of 16 Dec 1941.
181.   MKs 916 and 930 of 16 December 1941; CX/MSS/535/T2 and 30.
182.   CAB 44/94, p 33; AIR 41/25, p 206.
183.   WO 169/1010 of 17 December 1941.

18 December Y and air reconnaissance made it clear that the enemy was retreating beyond Derna.[184] And a Sigint message of the previous day, in which the Italians requested that all available empty ships be sailed for Benghazi, suggested that he would make no attempt to hold on there – and might even be preparing to evacuate his infantry by sea.[185] This so excited the CAS that he sent a personal message to the AO C-in-C which said: 'It might be deduced that a Dunkirk is to be attempted. In this event, fighter cover may be difficult. This may well be our opportunity to turn it into another and better Crete'.[186] On 19 December Y showed that the German and Italian armour was retreating along the route Mechili-El Abiar, via Benghazi, rather than by more direct but more difficult routes inland.[187] The next day the Enigma confirmed this by revealing that the GAF had been given the task of protecting the landward flank of the retreat against British attempts at envelopment; by locating HQ DAK there it also confirmed that Rommel was making for Agedabia.[188] On 21 December air reconnaissance discovered a great deal of movement south of Benghazi and the Enigma disclosed that some German forces with the DAK commander had reached the Antellat area.[189] During 20 and 21 December, while reconnaissance showed the Italian XXI Corps retreating through Benghazi, the Enigma showed the Panzergruppe preparing to hold a line east of Benghazi for as long as possible, to enable stores to be got away, and thinking it might be able to hold Benghazi until 22 December in view of the slowness of the British pursuit.[190] In addition the Enigma gave full information about the airfields being used by the GAF for its operations and for the ferrying of fuel.[191] On 20 December an urgent message from Rommel complained that he was being handicapped by lack of fighter protection and requested that all available transport aircraft should be used to take in fuel.[192]

In their continuing attempts to interfere with the enemy's retreat the British forces were unable to turn this intelligence to account. How far this was due to the fact that they themselves were becoming overstretched as their lines of communication length-

---

184. ibid, of 19 December 1941.
185. MK 938 of 17 December 1941; ZTPI 3385.
186. MK 965 of 18 December 1941.
187. WO 169/1010 of 19 December 1941.
188. MKs 1076 and 1084 of 20 December 1941; CX/MSS/545/T26, 546/T14.
189. MK 1124 of 21 December 1941; CX/MSS/547/T34; WO 169/1010 of 22 and 23 December 1941.
190. MK 1140 of 21 December 1941; CX/MSS/549/T8; WO 169/1010 of 20 December 1941.
191. eg MKs 903 and 930 of 16 and 18 December 1941; CX/MSS/533/T27, 535/T30.
192. MK 1080 of 20 December 1941; CX/MSS/546/T8.

ened, or to operational difficulties plus the fact that, with every minute counting, they were unable to get information through to the advance formations, cannot now be established. There is some evidence, however, that the gist of the high-grade decrypts was getting as far as HQ XIII Corps.* At 0645 on 22 December Eighth Army commander sent a staff officer to XIII Corps commander with a letter which said: 'I felt that I had made it abundantly clear yesterday that there were good indications that [the enemy] would do all he could to cover the withdrawal southwards of his forces by holding [a line east of Benghazi]. From the most reliable of secret sources I know this to be so'. The letter urged XIII Corps to attack Magrun, just south of Benghazi, which was 'absolutely vital' to the enemy's operations: 'every effort is being made by him today, as yesterday, on an increasing scale to fly aviation spirit to Magrun'. No doubt because of the importance attached to the high-grade Sigint, it also urged XIII Corps to keep in touch with Eighth Army 'at all times'.[194]

More serious was the fact that the British forces suffered unexpected reverses. On 23 December 15th Panzer Division attacked without warning the force that was trying to cut the coastal road at Antelat, repulsing it and thus enabling the infantry divisions of the Italian XXI Corps to slip through to Agedabia. In two battles on 28 and 30 December the DAK attacked 22nd Armoured Brigade, the force that had been sent to storm Agedabia, inflicting on it heavy losses including 60 out of its 90 tanks. Of these attacks, as of that on 23 December, intelligence gave no tactical warning.[195] The Enigma had revealed only that the Panzergruppe had requested air reconnaissance of the approaches to Agedabia for 26, 27 and 28 December; Y identified the enemy formations once the fighting had begun but gave no advance notice; air reconnaissance failed to spot the enemy's approach.[196] More important, the British forces were completely surprised by the enemy's tank strength. On 19 December convoys had in fact reached Benghazi and Tripoli with tank reinforcements. By 20 December 21st Panzer Division had had no serviceable tanks, 15th Panzer Division had been reduced to between 20 and 23, the Italians to 15; in addition there were about a dozen German tanks in the workshop. A company of 21 tanks unloaded at Benghazi from the freighter *Ankara* had brought the DAK strength up to 68 in time for its counter-attack of

---

* The existence of high-grade Sigint was withheld from British corps, though whenever possible the officer selected for the senior intelligence post was one who had experience of this source in a previous appointment.[193]

193. WO 208/3575, p 6.
194. CAB 44/94, p 58.
195. WO 169/1010 of 30 December 1941; CAB 105/16, No 27.
196. WO 169/1010 of 29 and 31 December 1941.

23 December. By 28 December these reinforcements, together with repairs and 23 tanks unloaded at Tripoli from the *Mongenevro* had raised its number of serviceable tanks to 93.[197] But to 22nd Armoured Brigade it came as 'a matter of surprise, indeed a contradiction of the intelligence provided, that the enemy were able to attack with so many tanks', which it estimated at 60 plus 20 in reserve.[198]

The Army authorities had been kept fully informed by GC and CS since 8 December of the approach and arrival of these convoys.* On 18 December the C-in-C took them into account in his general appreciation of the enemy's position. 'Enemy's fuel, ammunition and general supply situation believed to be critical, and unless ships carrying fresh supplies reach Benghazi or Tripoli in the next few days Rommel may have to choose between risk of losing his forces in Cyrenaica, thereby leaving the way open to Tripoli; or of withdrawal from Cyrenaica. If fresh supplies arrive he will probably continue to fight in Cyrenaica'.[199] As luck would have it, however, GS Int GHQ, ME and Eighth Army appear to have overlooked a single reference in the Sigint that was being sent to them from GC and CS to the fact that one of the ships in these convoys was carrying 17 Pzkw III tanks. There is no reference to the information in Eighth Army's intelligence summaries or in GHQ, ME's signals to London. Nor did MI draw attention to this oversight.† This also applies to the only other Sigint evidence of tank reinforcements that was received at the time – the less important news which GC and CS sent out on 18 December that

---

* See below, p 322 et seq.

† The oversight may have been due in some measure to the difficulty which GC and CS encountered in interpreting the high-grade decrypts referring to these convoys. The system by which GC and CS forwarded the gist of its decrypts to the Middle East was by now improving fast, though it was to run into difficulties when the volume and complexity of the traffic increased from the beginning of 1942 (see below, pp 358–359). Texts of all signals sent to the Middle East were teleprinted, together with the full texts of the decrypts, to the appropriate Service intelligence branch in Whitehall, so that it could intervene if it thought a point had been neglected or misinterpreted; it did so in the course of a regular exchange of views with GC and CS, which usually drafted the agreed additional or corrective signals, and a comparison of the signals with the complete decrypts will show that little intelligence of any significance failed to reach the Middle East. On this occasion, however, the significance of the single reference to tanks was perhaps obscured by a chain of uncertainties. It occurred in association with an unspecified ship in a list of advance details about cargoes which GC and CS sent to Cairo and Eighth Army on 13 December.[200] There followed some difficulty in interpreting code-names associated with the convoys, but on 18 December, when the convoys were at last on passage, GC and CS advised the Middle East that it thought that the ship referred to in its signal of 13 December was among those which were by then known to be making for Tripoli.[201] At Eighth Army HQ this deduction may have been reinforced by

197. CAB 44/94, p 69.
198. ibid, p 79.
199. CAB 105/15, No 228.
200. MK 801 of 13 December 1941; CX/MSS/526/T43.
201. MK 1000 of 18 December 1941; CX/MSS/531 of 17 December 1941.

an unspecified number of tanks had arrived by air at Benina for 15th Panzer Division.[204]

By 24 December, before learning of the setback of the previous day, the C-in-C ME was discounting in his signals to London the possibility that the arrival of the Axis convoys would affect the situation. In his report of that day he estimated that the German forces concentrating at Agedabia had '30 to 40 tanks, many of which are thought to be light or obsolete types', that this remnant 'will almost certainly try to get away to the west', but that 'we may be able to bring it to battle despite our maintenance problems, which are tremendous'.[205] Thereafter GHQ made no reference to enemy tank strengths in its reports to London until 29 December when its account of the engagement of 28 December mentioned 50 or 60 tanks. But on 29 December it still felt that there were no signs that the enemy had been reinforced.[206]

Further forward, the estimates of the enemy's position made by Eighth Army and XIII Corps were equally 'out of touch with the realities of the situation'.[207] By 26 December Eighth Army had indeed concluded that 'Rommel intends staying where he is until turned out',[208] but it assured XIII Corps on that day that he was down to 30 tanks and that 22nd Armoured Brigade thus had a 'unique opportunity' to finish him off.[209] On 24 December XIII Corps had already assured 22nd Armoured Brigade that it was greatly superior in armour and that the enemy was in distress;[210] on 26 December it, too, gave the figure of 30 for total enemy serviceable tanks.[211] These estimates derived from the calculation that on 18 December, at the start of the pursuit, the DAK and the Italians had already each been reduced to 30 medium tanks.[212] At the time it was made, the original calculation was correct and Eighth Army cannot be faulted for ignoring an Italian POW report that the Germans had about 50 tanks on 18 December.[213] But the

---

reports to the effect that conditions at Benghazi made it impossible for the enemy to unload tanks there.[202] In the event, however, the tanks were in the ship that had reached Benghazi, the *Ankara*. In the signal of 18 December and in a further signal of 20 December GC and CS sent out details obtained from further decrypts about the cargoes of the ship that had reached Benghazi and of one of the Tripoli-bound ships,[203] but as these decrypts had made no further reference to tanks, these signals could have suggested to Cairo that neither ship was carrying tanks.

202. R Lewin, *Ultra goes to war* (1978), p 170.
203. MK 1111 of 20 December 1941; ZTPI 3600.
204. MK 933 of 18 December 1941; CX/MSS/539/T8.
205. CAB 105/15, No 266.
206. CAB 105/16, Nos 18, 20, 21.   207.   CAB 44/94, p 67.
208. ibid, p 68; WO 169/1010 of 26 December 1941.
209. CAB 44/94, p 68; WO 169/1010 of 26 December 1941.
210. CAB 44/94, p 67.
211. WO 169/1107 of 26 December 1941.
212. ibid, 18 December 1941.   213.   CAB 44/94, p 94.

subsequent estimates discounted a report which XIII Corps had circulated on the evening of 23 December. This had claimed that 50 enemy tanks had been in action at Antelat that day and that they had included nine Pzkw IVs, but XIII Corps concluded that the total had been made up by including light or obsolete tanks normally used on non-operational duties.[214] The estimates also took no account of an RAF sighting of 30 to 40 tanks some 100 miles west of Agedabia on 24 December. On 25 December XIII Corps had commented that this 'might be the first indication of possible tank reinforcements', but had decided that it 'should be treated with reserve pending confirmation'.[215] It seems reasonable to claim that it would have given more weight to this evidence if it had been alerted to the single Sigint reference to the shipment of tanks.

As it was, still further clues were overlooked when they came to light. On 27 December 22nd Armoured Brigade reported encountering Pzkw III tanks in the Agedabia area that were apparently newly arrived in the Middle East since they were freshly painted and bore no DAK signs; one was taken and showed only 400 km on its speedometer.[216] XIII Corps received on the same day a 'reliable report' that five German tanks had been landed at Benghazi on 21 December.[217] But on 28 December XIII Corps and Eighth Army were both expressing surprise at Rommel's evident determination to stand at Agedabia, and assuming that he must have under-estimated British tank strength.[218] And in its inquest of 30 December on the fighting of 28 December XIII Corps, while admitting that 'the question of possible reinforcements of medium tanks must be seriously considered', concluded that 'in spite of this evidence' – 22nd Armoured Brigade's claim to have been attacked by over 60 tanks had now added itself to the other clues – 'there is still no indication that any large numbers of German tanks have been landed in Africa, nor that Germany possesses any considerable reserves'.[219] When this was being written 22nd Armoured Brigade was taking the second round of severe punishment which finally convinced XIII Corps that Rommel had received tank reinforcements: in the action of 30 December 57 enemy tanks were counted, none of them a light tank, most of them Pzkw III or IV, and many of them looked new.[220]

Apart from the operations in which Eighth Army reduced Rommel's frontier garrisons at Bardia and Halfaya/Sollum in the first half of January 1942, there was no further fighting in north

214.   WO 169/1107 of 23 and 26 December 1941.
215.   CAB 44/94, p 69.
216.   Hunt, op cit, p 73.
217.   WO 169/1107 of 28 December 1941.
218.   CAB 44/94, p 78.
219.   WO 169/1107 of 30 December 1941.
220.   ibid, 31 December 1941.

Africa till Rommel launched his counter-offensive on 21 January. Despite his successes in the battles of 28 and 30 December, Rommel adhered to his plan to retreat to El Agheila, to take advantage of its natural defences and shorten his lines of communication with Tripoli. As a result of their reverses in those battles the British forces were too weak to interfere before he had completed his further withdrawal on 10 January. Despite those reverses, on the other hand, and their disappointment at seeing Rommel escape, the British authorities remained confident, as they planned for Eighth Army to renew its advance in the middle of February, that as a result of his losses, his lack of reinforcements and his supply difficulties, Rommel would be incapable of a serious attack on them before their own offensive was ready. But this calculation made no allowance, among other things, for the change that had taken place in the Mediterranean. By the end of 1941 the British ability to interfere with Axis supplies had been severely weakened by the elimination of Force K as a fighting force and by Axis measures to reduce British freedom of action in the central Mediterranean.

□

In the two months up to the middle of December 1941 the combination of high-grade shipping intelligence and the presence of Force K in Malta enabled the British forces to bring about a virtual stoppage of Axis supplies to north Africa. It is true that the Admiralty refused to countenance GC and CS's suggestion, now made for the first time, that the operational value of the Sigint would be distinctly improved if the C 38m were to be decrypted at Malta. In consequence of this cautious but understandable decision the Sigint passing on the SCU/SLU link from GC and CS to Vice Admiral Malta and from him in the form of operational orders to the Senior Officer Force K, who was not himself an Ultra recipient, was sometimes received too late for action. This happened during Force K's first sortie on 25 October, when it failed to intercept a group of Italian destroyers that was ferrying troops to north Africa. Commonly, however, and perhaps as frequently as was consistent with maintaining the security of the source, the information reached Malta in good time.

Force K's first and biggest success came in its attack on the first convoy to sail to Tripoli after the Italians had reopened the route. Full details of the route and composition of the convoy – it was a large one after the recent suspension of sailings to Tripoli – were sent out in time for Malta to have it sighted by Maryland reconnaissance aircraft of No 69 Squadron RAF on the afternoon of 8 November.[221] In the ensuing attack Force K sank all seven ships in the convoy despite a radio and radar failure in the Wellington that was detailed to direct it on to its target, and escaped unscathed despite the fact that the Italians had provided a cruiser covering force to supplement the destroyer escort.[222] Sigint, which had been silent about the covering force, confirmed next day that the entire convoy had been destroyed and that it had carried fuel for the GAF and badly needed equipment, including a large consignment of motor transport for the Army.[223] The next success, scarcely less decisive, followed on 21 November. By 15 November C 38m had established that, as part of a larger movement, a convoy of four large supply ships and seven destroyers, covered by cruisers and other destroyers, was to sail for Tripoli on 20 November, two days after the start of *Crusader*; by 18 November, not without difficulty, GC and CS had worked out its exact route.[224] On 21 November the convoy was sighted and attacked by aircraft and submarines; they did no damage to the merchant ships but torpedoed two of the Italian cruisers, and on 22 November the C 38m revealed that the convoy was being withdrawn to Taranto for fear of a follow-up attack by Force K.[225] Its retention in Taranto for more than a fortnight substantially added to Rommel's difficulties. Except that this time the intelligence came from the GAF Enigma, the procedure that had proved to effective on 8 November – the transmission of advance notice of the enemy's departure and route to the Mediterranean; a British air sighting; an attack by Force K followed by Sigint confirmation of the damage it had done – accompanied the sinking on 24 November of two ships, the *Maritza* and the *Procida*, that were carrying to Benghazi ammunition and what the Sigint had described as fuel cargo of decisive importance to the GAF.[226] The Prime Minister had been most anxious that action should be taken against these ships; he asked whether Admiral Cunningham had seen the decrypts describing their arrival as decisive.[227]

221.   OLs 1847, 1848 and 1849 of 8 November 1941; ZTPI 1800, 1803, 1820, 1829.
222.   Playfair, op cit, Vol III, p 103; ADM 186/801, p 190.
223.   OLs 1850 and 1858 of 9 November, 1881 of 10 November 1941; CX/MSS/415/T1, 419/T1.
224.   OLs 1963 of 15 November, 1984 of 16 November and 2023 of 18 November 1941; ZTPI 2073, 2074, 2078, 2111, 2118, 2194.
225.   MK 58 of 22 November 1941; ZTPI 2364, 2367, 2368.
226.   ADM 186/801, p 201; OLs 1793 of 5 November, 1811 of 7 November 1941; MKs 116 of 23 November, 191 of 25 November 1941; CX/MSS/396/T3 and 5, 398/T10, 457/T10, 462/T24.
227.   Dir/C Archive, 8142 of 23 November 1941; MKs 81 and 93 of 22 November 1941; CX/MSS/456/T8, 457/T10; Cabinet Office file 82/43/1, Part 2, PM to C-in-C Mediterranean 1431/23 November 1941.

These and other successes in November seriously disturbed the flow of Axis supplies to north Africa at a crucial time, just before and just after the beginning of the British offensive. Between June and the end of October about 16 per cent of the cargo sailed had failed to get through. In November, quite apart from an increase in the delays and dislocations caused by the British operations and by the frequent bombing and mining of the convoy terminals, the percentage rose to 62, so that, although the cargo loaded in Italy was up to the previous monthly average, the amount reaching north Africa was roughly halved.* Nor was there any lack of evidence that, besides having helped to delay Rommel's attack on Tobruk until after the British had begun their advance, the sinkings were now impeding his operations. On 25 November the GAF Enigma reported that the destruction of the *Maritza* and the *Procida* had placed German operations in 'real danger' and had necessitated the ferrying of fuel by all available aircraft and by

---

* I: *Number of merchant ships over 500 tons sunk at sea or at the ports of loading or unloading.*[228]

Month 1941	By Surface Warship	By Submarine	By Aircraft	From Other Causes	Number	Total Number	Total Tonnage (1,000)
June		3	2	1	6	—	17
July		3	4		7	—	28
Aug		2	7		9	—	35
Sept		4	6		10	—	65
Oct		2	5		7	—	33
Nov	9	1	3	1	14	—	59
Dec	2	5	1		8	—	39
				Total	61	—	276

The high tonnage sunk in September was largely due to the sinking of the large liners *Neptunia* and *Oceania* by HM Submarine *Upholder* who had received routeing details.

The November high total was due to the successes of Force K.

The reduction in the losses following these two successful months was due in part to a reduction of the number of cargoes sent.

II: *Cargoes disembarked in north Africa and percentage lost on passage.*[228]

Month 1941	Cargo embarked (1,000s)	General military cargo and fuel disembarked (1,000s)	Percentage lost on the way
June	131	125	4
July	76	63	18
Aug	96	84	12
Sept	94	67	28
Oct	92	74	20
Nov	79	30	62
Dec	48	39	18

Figures for fuel alone are available for the first five months. They show that, except for July when about 40 per cent of the fuel loaded was lost, percentage losses were less than for other supplies. In terms of quantities, whereas during the first three months 28,000 out of 31,000 tons, on the average, were successfully landed, in September and October an average of only 13,000 out of 16,000 tons arrived.

228.   Playfair, op cit, Vol II, p 281, Vol III, p 107.

Italian destroyers.[229] By the end of the month the Sigint showed that Italian destroyers were carrying deck cargoes of petrol to Derna and floating the drums ashore in order to cut their time in harbour and reduce the danger of RAF attack.[230] At the same time, however, the British successes forced the Axis powers to redouble their efforts to protect their supply convoys. At the end of November the C 38m gave details of the next convoy and information about its covering force. It turned out to be the first convoy for which the Italians were forced to provide battleship support.[231]

With this information, which was fortunately obtained just before the monthly change in the C 38m settings,* the RAF from Malta sank one ship and damaged a destroyer and a tanker carrying troops and petrol, and while Force B (HMS *Ajax* and HMS *Neptune* from Alexandria) acted in support, Force K first dashed towards Benghazi and sank a defensively-armed merchant ship and then re-crossed the Gulf of Sirte at high speed to finish off the destroyer and the tanker. On 5 and 8 December C 38m showed that the Italians were extending their use of warships for ferrying fuel by announcing that the 6-inch cruisers *Barbiano* and *Giussano* were to sail with fuel from Palermo to Tripoli. When the RAF obtained the confirmatory sighting of these ships on 12 December Force K was immobilised because its recent operations had run down Malta's fuel stocks. But HMS *Sikh* and three other destroyers which were off Algiers, hundreds of miles to the west, en route for Alexandria, increased speed to 30 knots and sank both cruisers off Cape Bon on 13 December.[233]

By that time the C 38m had established that the Italians were to repeat their attempt to sail convoys with heavy naval protection: on 12 December several ships, including some which had been turned back to Italy on 22 November, were to sail in three groups, each with battleship cover, and with further protection for the whole movement from the battleship *Littorio*. On the basis of this information C-in-C Mediterranean sailed three cruisers from Alexandria and ordered Force K, Force B and the *Sikh* group of destroyers to join them from Malta. Unable to take the *Queen Elizabeth* and the

---

* While the new settings were being worked out the First Sea Lord on 2 December personally directed the Mediterranean authorities to maintain air reconnaissance and Force K's activity during the next three or four days so as not to arouse enemy suspicions.[232]

229.   MKs 191 and 202 of 25 November 1941; CX/MSS/462/T24, 464/T17.
230.   MK 353 of 29 November 1941; CX/MSS/478/T14.
231.   ADM 223/103, Ultra signals 2010/28 November, 1628/30 November, 1908/30 November 1941; MKs 307, 346 and 376 of 28 November 1941; ZTPI 2617, 2623, 2669, 2696, 2710; ADM 186/801, pp 218–219.
232.   ADM 223/103, Ultra signal 0047/2 December 1941.
233.   MKs 485 of 5 December and 593 of 8 December 1941; ZTPI 2835, 2941; Roskill, op cit, Vol I, p 534; Playfair, op cit, Vol III, pp 109–110; ADM 186/801, p 217.

Valiant to sea for lack of a destroyer screen, he also carried out W/T deception in an attempt to persuade the Italians that he had sailed with the battleships. The ruse succeeded.* The Italian Fleet and convoys returned to base, but not before British submarines had torpedoed the battleship *Vittorio Veneto* and two merchant ships, and two other merchant ships had collided.[234]

On 16 December the C 38m and the GAF Enigma made it clear that the enemy was planning to re-sail these convoys, with the protection of the *Littorio* and other heavy ships, between that day and 19 December.[235] By then, if the Italians were being made bolder by desperation, the British forces were becoming over-stretched and in the action which followed – the first battle of Sirte – luck turned against them. When he received the intelligence, the C-in-C Mediterranean had already despatched the *Breconshire* to Malta with the fuel which, as we have seen, was now urgently needed. He decided that her escort of cruisers and destroyers under Admiral Vian, commanding 15 Cruiser Squadron (CS 15), while maintaining the primary aim of protecting the *Breconshire*, should try to attack the Italian convoy at night while Force K, coming out from Malta for the purpose, returned to the island with the tanker. But during 17 December it proved impossible to provide con-tinuous or accurate air reconnaissance of the Italian Fleet, and Sigint provided no further information beyond the course and speed (but unfortunately not the position) of the *Littorio*. Malta's air reconnaissance was, however, good enough to enable CS 15 to keep the *Breconshire* out of danger until dusk, when the squadron met the greatly superior Italian naval force and held it off for long enough for the tanker to reach Malta. CS 15 had made no contact with the enemy convoy but, after disengaging from the enemy battleships, he patrolled for a few hours either side of midnight across what GC and CS – with some difficulty – had estimated to be the route originally laid down for the convoy's Benghazi section.[236] By that time, however, following his fight with CS 15, the Italian C-in-C in the *Littorio* had changed these arrangements,[237] with the result that the Benghazi section – the *Ankara* with its highly important cargo of tanks – was not detached until late on 18 December.[238] All that CS 15 learned of the enemy's

---

* Such ruses drew extensively on the conclusions, known from the C 38m decrypts, extracted by the Italians from their study of British naval W/T.

234. MKs 617 of 8 December, 664 of 10 December, 698 of 11 December 1941; ZTPI 2978, 3049, 3110.
235. MK 895 of 16 December 1941; ZTPI 3335; ADM 223/103, Ultra signal 1030/16 December 1941.
236. MK 932 of 17 December 1941; ZTPI 3348.   237. ADM 186/801, p 222.
238. ADM 223/103, Ultra signal 1307/18 December 1941; MK 998 of 18 December 1941; ZTPI 3502, 3506.

change of plan was an Ultra message sent late on 17 December showing that the *Littorio* had been given discretion to alter the convoy's route.[239] It was probably this intelligence which caused him to break off his search soon after midnight and shape course for Alexandria.

When CS 15 was halfway home the C 38m revealed the positions of the enemy convoys[240] and the fact that the Italians had decided to send their main naval force back to Taranto at 1400 on 18 December.[241] At 1830 on 18 December, when this intelligence had been supplemented by aircraft sightings, Force K, scarcely back in Malta with the *Breconshire*, sailed again in an attempt to intercept the four important ships of the main Tripoli section, the RAF having delayed them by laying mines in their path. Just after midnight 18–19 December, before Force K could reach its quarry, it ran into an Italian minefield off Tripoli which sank the *Neptune* and *Kandahar* and damaged the *Aurora* and *Penelope*.* It was the arrival of these supplies in north Africa which permitted Rommel to mount his successful counter-offensive of 21 January 1942.[†]

□

The arrival at Benghazi and Tripoli of the Axis supply ships, and especially of their tank reinforcements, transformed the tactical situation in north Africa.[‡] What was more serious, at a time when their recovery of Cyrenaica would otherwise have enabled them to increase their maritime offensive, the British were now deprived of the ability to cut off supplies and reinforcements to Rommel which had played so large a part in forcing him to retreat. This turn-about, which was to be an important factor in the success of Rommel's counter-offensive in January 1942, resulted in part from

---

* C 38m had disclosed at the end of October that the Italians had carried out a large-scale minelaying operation (operation 'B') off Benghazi (see also above, p 301) and that a similar operation (operation 'T') had taken place during June, but had given no details of the lays.[242] The information about operation 'T' was sent only to the C-in-C Mediterranean and it is not known whether any hint of it had reached Force K, whose Senior Officer, as we have seen, was not an Ultra recipient and was normally briefed on such matters by Malta. In any case, the disaster occurred close to the 100-fathom line, a depth in which the British considered the laying of moored mines to be impossible.

† See below, p 330 et seq.   ‡ See above, p 316 et seq.

239. ADM 223/103, Ultra signal 2220/17 December 1941; MK 961 of 17 December 1941; ZTPI 3438.

240. ADM 223/103, Ultra signals 1246 and 1907/18 December 1941; MK 992 of 18 December 1941; ZTPI 3489.

241. ADM 223/103, Ultra signal 1430/18 December 1941; MK 1009 of 18 December 1941; ZTPI 3526.

242. ADM 223/102, Ultra signals 1825/13 September, 0050/9 October 1941; ADM 223/103, Ultra signal 1712/30 October 1941; OLs 1497 of 11 October and 1745 of 31 October 1941; ZTPI 1192.

the elimination of Force K and in part from the arrival of Fliegerkorps II in Sicily,* a move which in any case severely restricted Malta's value as an offensive base. But it was all the more complete because the Axis powers had taken other steps to maintain their own supplies and to stop British supplies from reaching Malta and Tobruk. By the end of 1941, as a result of these measures, British naval forces in the Mediterranean had suffered other serious losses and the task of sustaining Malta had been greatly increased.

The build-up and support of Malta's anti-shipping forces since July 1941 had been a difficult undertaking from the outset, necessitating special operations to pass convoys from Gibraltar since the island could be supplied only at still greater risk from the east while Rommel held Cyrenaica, but until the end of September the enemy had made no serious attempt to interfere.† Towards the end of September the C 38m did, however, show that the Italians intended to intervene against the next Gibraltar–Malta convoy with their Fleet as well as with their Air Force, and there were some signs that the GAF might support them. Before this convoy sailed on 24 September Force H knew from C 38m messages that the Italians had learned from an agent that a large convoy was mustering in Gibraltar, and that they were sending additional torpedo aircraft to Sardinia. On 27 September the intelligence showed that the Italians thought the British covering force in- cluded at most two battleships – that Admiral Somerville had thus succeeded in his attempt to deceive them by various means including sailing his heavily reinforced squadron on different courses but that the GAF had received indications that, as was the case, the Mediterranean Fleet from Alexandria had also sailed. Early in the afternoon Italian torpedo bombers hit and slowed down HMS *Nelson*, Admiral Somerville's flagship, and half an hour later the RAF sighted an Italian squadron, including two battle-

---

* See above, p 291.

† For this reason there had been no intelligence about the Italian Fleet's movements, though the Gibraltar-based Force H had been kept informed from the IAF high-grade cypher about the strength and movements of the Italian Air Force. This had prompted Admiral Somerville to make a second complaint to the COS in August[243] (for his first complaint see Volume I, p 211). By the end of August, however, the C 38m had already lifted the veil which, largely because of GC and CS's continued inability to break into the Italian high-grade naval book cyphers had shrouded the movements of the Italian main units. Thus between 22 and 26 August C 38m decrypts reporting the intentions of two Italian squadrons had enabled Force H to stand clear of superior enemy forces while it was covering a minelaying operation in the Gulf of Genoa.[244]

243. CAB 79/14, COS (41) 304th and 307th Meetings, 30 August and 2 September; JIC (41) 25th Meeting, 2 September; JIC (41) 354 of 4 September.

244. ADM 223/102, Ultra signals 1241 and 1805/23 August, 0310 and 1641/24 August 1941. See also Playfair, op cit, Vol II, p 273.

ships making for Force H. Within a couple of hours, when the two fleets had been within 50 miles of each other, it was seen by RAF reconnaissance to have turned away, presumably in response to instructions to the Italian C-in-C which had not been intercepted. But at midday on 28 September the Admiralty warned Force H that the Italian C-in-C in the *Littorio* with a second battleship in company was still at sea and, an hour earlier, had been ordered to make for the British covering force. Two hours later the Admiralty informed Force H that the Italian squadron had been ordered to return to Naples. The convoy was then arriving in Malta, having lost one ship to Italian torpedo aircraft.[245]

Despite its evident interest the GAF did not intervene against the September convoy. While the operation was taking place, however, GC and CS was receiving the first indications that the Germans were about to divert U-boats from the Atlantic to the Mediterranean. Between 27 and 29 September it decyphered messages in the Home Waters naval Enigma addressed to a group of U-boats in the Atlantic and containing cryptic references which led it to believe by 30 September that the group was bound for the Mediterranean and might begin to enter from 1 October.[246] Although no inkling had been received of the German decision at the end of August to transfer U-boats, minesweepers, R-boats (for minesweeping and coastal escort) and E-boats to the Mediterranean, or of Rommel's warning on 12 September that he would have to put off his attack on Tobruk unless these and other measures to safeguard his supplies were implemented,[247] all the clues that GC and CS assembled from its knowledge of German W/T procedure and grid references, and from its analysis of the whereabouts of the U-boats that were then at sea, strongly supported its deduction, as did the fact that the Germans had named the U-boats the *Goeben* group after the German cruiser that had been famous for its Mediterranean exploits in the First World War. The Tracking Room in the OIC was reluctant to accept the evidence; but on 3 October, when the *Goeben* group was warned that it might meet a French warship whose whereabouts – known from SIS reports – put the matter beyond doubt, the Admiralty notified the commands that an unknown number of U-boats might soon be operating east of Gibraltar and that two might have already passed the Straits.[248]

---

245.   ADM 223/102, Ultra signals 1856/7 September, 1300/22 September, 1240/23 September, 1933/27 September, 0106, 1214, 1215 and 1432/28 September 1941; Playfair, op cit, Vol II, p 275; ADM 186/801, pp 179, 180.

246.   eg DEFE 3/29, ZTPG 9799 of 27 September 1941.

247.   Playfair, op cit, Vol II, p 262; ADM 186/801, p 170.

248.   ADM 223/102, Ultra signals 1532, 1846 and 2306/3 October, 1347/4 October 1941. Compare Roskill, op cit, Vol 1, p 474.

Little more was learned about the *Goeben* group, which in fact consisted of six U-boats, beyond the fact that by 10 October some of them were on the Alexandria–Tobruk route,[249] where British forces made several attacks on them in the second half of October, and the fact that La Spezia would be one of their bases and that the Piraeus would be one of their ports of call.[250] U-boats in the Mediterranean used the modified form of the Home Waters naval Enigma introduced for all U-boats on 1 October 1941, and GC and CS was therefore able to read their traffic until the separate U-boat settings were introduced on 1 February 1942.* But because they were operating individually, and had received instructions beforehand, the traffic seldom disclosed anything precise about their positions and intentions. On 11 November, however, the Home Waters Enigma did reveal that the first six U-boats to enter the Mediterranean were to be followed by two more, and that these were to operate in the western Mediterranean; and on 12 November it gave full details of the areas in which they were to patrol.[251] The Admiralty promulgated these on the evening of 12 November as being in an area bounded on west and east respectively by Meridian 5°34′ W and by a line joining 36°51′ N, 1°50′ W and 33°57′ N, 0°22′ W, with one U-boat to the south and the other to the north of 36° N.[252] Later on 12 November it warned Flag Officer Force H, then on his way back to Gibraltar with HMS *Ark Royal* in company, that his position and course during the afternoon had been reported to the two U-boats;[253] it had already informed him during October that an Italian agent was watching the *Ark Royal's* movements and that the enemy had a reporting station in the area of the patrolling U-boats, on Alboran island.[254]† Despite the fact that Force H acted on these warnings, making a 'dog-leg' around Alboran island to confuse the watchers and zig-zagging to avoid the U-boats, one of the U-boats torpedoed the *Ark Royal* at 1541 on 13 November. She sank the following day.[255]

By that date – in fact, as soon as they learned of Force K's arrival at Malta towards the end of October – the Germans had decided that no less than 15 further U-boats, as well as E-boats and inshore

---

* See above, p 179. The U-boats east of Messina used the Offizier key associated with the Süd setting from 6 November until 12 December 1941. This was also readable.

† See Appendix 15.

249. ADM 223/102, Ultra signal 1700/10 October 1941; OL 1564 of 17 October; ZTPI 1356, 1370 and 1371.
250. ADM 223/103, Ultra signal 1337/22 October 1941. Dir/C Archive 8232 of 3 December 1941.
251. ADM 223/103, Ultra signal 2006/11 November 1941.
252. ibid, 1715/12 November 1941.   253. ibid, 2349/12 Nov 1941.
254. ADM 223/102, Ultra signals 1055 and 1750/14 October, 2121/16 October 1941.
255. ADM 186/801, pp 194–196.

craft, should follow the *Goeben* group into the Mediterranean, and that Fliegerkorps II should be transferred to Sicily. Unlike the plan to move Fliegerkorps II, the naval transfer was not immediately disclosed by Sigint. But by 26 November the Admiralty knew that the number of U-boats in the Mediterranean had grown to eleven, and on that day it warned that another fourteen to sixteen would pass the Straits between 27 November and 1 December.[256] This was incorrect and seems to have sprung from misinterpretation of orders to boats in fact directed to the Gibraltar approaches. The Admiralty's version, however, caused the Gibraltar authorities to intensify their patrols. These were now aided by the ASV Swordfish aircraft disembarked from the *Ark Royal*, which were able to detect U-boats on the surface at night. They sank one and turned back, badly damaged, four U-boats during December.[257] The Straits thus became increasingly hazardous and in mid-December the naval Enigma disclosed precise instructions to U-boats as to how, submerged if necessary, they were to make the transit.[258] Even so, as the Admiralty informed operational commands, by 15 December nineteen boats had succeeded in doing so since September.[259]*

As before, the naval Enigma continued to give little or no information about the movements and patrol positions of these U-boats. Perhaps for this reason, it was not until January 1942 that a member of the OIC was sent to Alexandria to set up a Mediterranean Tracking Room. During November and December 1941 no less than seven of the U-boats were sunk, but there is no evidence that Sigint contributed to these sinkings. Nor did it help to avert further successes by the U-boats. On 25 November, within days of the torpedoing of the *Ark Royal*, a U-boat sank the battleship HMS *Barham* when she was on her way back to Alexandria after operating in support of the recent Gibraltar–Malta convoy. On 14 December another U-boat sank the cruiser HMS *Galatea* off Alexandria.

The Mediterranean Fleet suffered another serious setback in the early hours of 19 December, when Italian human torpedoes (charioteers) penetrated Alexandria harbour and badly damaged the battleships *Queen Elizabeth* and *Valiant*. Of this attack intelligence did give some warning. Perhaps on account of GC and CS's inability to read the Italian naval book cyphers, earlier operations of a similar kind had gone on without any notice from Sigint. At the

---

* The actual number was 20.

256.   ADM 223/103, Ultra signal 1100/26 November 1941.
257.   ADM 186/801, p 209.
258.   ADM 223/103. Ultra signals 1930/13 December, 1309/14 December 1941.
259.   ibid, 1938/15 December 1941.

end of July motor torpedo boats had failed in an attack on Malta's Grand Harbour because they had been detected by the coastal radar;[260] but there had been no other warning. On 20 September, again, no warning had been received of the attack by human torpedoes from the submarine *Sciré* against shipping in Gibraltar; and it was not then known that this attack – it was the first to succeed, sinking an oil fuel hulk and badly damaging two merchant ships – was the fourth which the Italians had attempted against Gibraltar.[261] But that something was being planned against Alexandria in December was indicated by C 38m signals a few days before the attack.

By 17 December GC and CS had alerted the C-in-C Mediterranean to C 38m messages which showed the Supreme Command of the Italian Navy expressing interest in some project there which might, however, be no more than an air raid.[262] On 17 December the C-in-C was informed that a reconnaissance sortie on that day had shown the Italians that the two battleships were at their usual moorings and – an unusual touch – that the sea was calm. On 18 December GC and CS added the information that the Italians had stated that the reconnaissance was urgent.[263] It was on the strength of these warnings, which, vague as they were, sharpened the feeling of the C-in-C's staff that the Italians might take some desperate action against the Fleet in an effort to prevent its interference with their convoys to Africa at a time when Rommel was retreating, that the C-in-C issued a general alert at 1025 on 18 December: 'Attacks on Alexandria by air, boat or human torpedo may be expected when calm weather prevails. Look-outs and patrols should be warned accordingly'. But despite the alert the Italians succeeded in entering Alexandria, and despite preventive action in the two battleships, taken after an explosion in a near-by tanker, they severely damaged both ships.

The C 38m decrypts enabled the Admiralty to withhold publication of the damage, and of the loss of the *Barham*, until the end of January 1942. It showed that the enemy did not realise that the *Barham* had sunk[264] and that the damage to the *Queen Elizabeth* and the *Valiant*, which had settled at their moorings, at first went undetected by enemy reconnaissance.[265] But it also showed that by 30 January the Italians had learned of their success at Alexandria from a POW;[266] and if the enemy did not at once learn of all his

---

260. ADM 186/801, p 150.
261. ibid, pp 174–177.   262. ZTPI 3409.
263. ADM 223/103, Ultra signal 1637/17 December 1941; MK 956 of 17 December 1941; ZTPI 3371, 3424.   264. ADM 186/801, pp 203, 219.
265. ADM 223/103, Ultra signal 2248/19 December 1941; MK 1060 of 19 December 1941; ZTPI 3584, 3586, 3591.
266. ADM 223/103, Ultra signal 2006/30 January 1942.

latest successes, he did not delay before taking advantage of the changed situation at sea. From 29 December the C 38m traffic revealed that the Italians were preparing to sail a second convoy to Tripoli under battleship cover and gave full details in advance of its composition – nine merchant vessels of 10,000 tons – and its route. On 5 January 1942 C 38m reported the safe arrival of the convoy.[267] As a result of shortage of reconnaissance aircraft at Malta and of heavy GAF attacks on the island, it had not been sighted until it was nearing Tripoli, and an air strike had failed to find it.[268] Though the fact was not known, this convoy carried 54 tanks.[269]* A further convoy with battleship cover reached Tripoli virtually unscathed on 24 January. The C 38m gave details about its movements and the covering forces, and the information that it was carrying a large consignment of motor transport.[270] It did not mention that its cargoes included 71 tanks, but there were grounds for suspecting that it was also carrying tanks: on 14 January GC and CS had decrypted a C 38m message enquiring whether Tripoli could handle tanks of 25 tons.[271] The Chiefs of Staff urged the Cs-in-C ME to do their utmost to destroy this convoy.[272] But although Malta's aircraft sighted it on 23 January, air attacks succeeded in sinking only one ship. The C 38m revealed that most of its survivors – it was a troopship – managed to reach north Africa.

□

After Rommel's withdrawal to El Agheila at the beginning of 1942 Eighth Army accepted that it could not resume its own advance until the middle of February. At the same time, however, it reckoned – and GHQ ME agreed – that the enemy, though still perhaps able to make local attacks, was too weak and disorganised to attempt a counter-offensive, or at least to succeed with one, before then.[273] Rommel, aware of British weakness, disproved this assumption by counter-attacking on 21 January and by at once following up his first success when he found that he had taken the

---

* See below, p 336.

267. MK 1425 of 29 December 1941 and numerous further MKs to MK 1639 of 6 January 1942; ZTPI 4053, 4352, 4354, 4359.
268. CAB 105/8, Hist (B) 8, Nos 251, 274, 276.
269. Playfair, op cit, Vol III, p 159.
270. MKs 1935 of 18 January, 2020 and 2031 of 23 January, 2040 of 24 January 1942; ZTPI 4922, 5088, 5091, 5118, 5119; CX/MSS/646/T5.
271. MK 1847 of 14 January 1942; ZTPI 4739.
272. CAB 105/8, No 290.
273. Playfair, op cit, Vol III, p 137; Gwyer and Butler, op cit, Vol III, Part II, p 439; CAB 105/16, Nos 21, 25; CAB 44/94, p 104; CAB 44/96, AL 1200/71, p 2.

British forward units by surprise. He was greatly helped by the fact that it was at this time that the Germans began to read the cypher in which the US Military Attaché in Cairo was making regular reports about the state and intentions of Eighth Army.*

The fact that the British were surprised by his attack was partly due to his success in concealing his preparations in the few days before 21 January. Air reconnaissance, though greatly curtailed by gales, rain and sandstorms, had reported that the enemy was bringing supplies right up to the Agheila position by sea and, on 20 January, that there was an unusually heavy concentration of vehicles behind the enemy's front. But a 'successful PR' of Agheila by No 2 PRU on the morning of 20 January showed nothing untoward.[274] Nor did the observations by British forward troops, which were restricted by the temporary withdrawal for repairs of most of the armoured cars. On 21 January Eighth Army's intelligence summary mentioned without comment the sighting of a large number of vehicles on the previous day, and on 18 January it had noted that the enemy had made use of sandstorms to recover ground 'which denies us observation'. But on 16 January it had reported that his ground forces were on the defensive and digging in on all sectors, and on 17, 19 and 20 January it reported that activity remained normal. On 21 January weather restricted RAF reconnaissance and the first sign that the enemy was on the move came only when his columns were sighted by the British forward troops.[275]

When weather conditions and the withdrawal of patrol cars were restricting reconnaissance the British were unfortunate – and the extent of Rommel's tactical surprise was all the more complete – because other sources of intelligence produced no clear indication of the enemy's plans. GC and CS had ceased to be able to break the Chaffinch traffic since 6 December and by January it was finding that the Italian Army high-grade book cypher was becoming unreadable. The IAF's high-grade book cypher also became more difficult from the end of 1941, though something could be made of it until the end of 1942. Neither it nor IAF low-grade Sigint produced any clues in January 1942. Against that GC and CS intermittently read from that date the traffic of Fliegerkorps II and Fliegerkorps X in the new Enigma keys (Locust and Gadfly) in addition to the GAF general Enigma key. But the GAF Enigma produced only one decrypt which might have been interpreted as pointing to an impending attack. It was a message of 17 January from Flieger-

---

* See below, p 361 and Appendix 1 (Part (i)) p 640.

274. AIR 41/25, p 268.
275. WO 169/3803, Eighth Army Intelligence Summaries of 16–21 January, 27 January 1942.

führer Afrika to Kesselring complaining about the shortage of 50 kg bombs and requesting that he use every means to send 50 to the GAF's forward airfields 'in view of the operations of the next few days'. When relaying the message to the Middle East on 19 January GC and CS drew attention to this phrase but had to allow that it might relate only to the GAF's routine ground attack activities, which had already been increased.[276] Nor would it be reasonable after the event to suggest that more than this should have been read into the Fliegerführer's few words when there were no other clues. In the lull before 21 January Army Y produced a good deal of information, but it was mainly about the Italian ground forces and contained nothing to indicate an early attack. POW produced one piece of information on 18 January – a report that the whole of 8th Tank Regiment, the armoured regiment of 15th Panzer Division, was deployed in Wadi Faregh, the point from which 15th Panzer Division in fact attacked on 21 January.[277] On 20 January, on the other hand, the local Senussi informed the British forward troops that the enemy was preparing to withdraw further west.[278]

Of the enemy's intention to attack there was thus little, if any, evidence. But as well as achieving tactical surprise – and so much so that on 21 January the C-in-C Middle East was in Palestine and Eighth Army's commander was in Cairo making arrangements for the advance to Tripoli – Rommel found that the British forces were unprepared for an enemy offensive. One reason for this was the extent to which the British commands had been distracted by other preoccupations. Rumour – but not, as yet, reliable intelligence – was beginning to point to Axis plans for an assault on Malta,[279] and between 16 and 19 January the despatch of a convoy to Malta monopolised the attention of some of the operations and intelligence staffs. Intelligence staffs were also busy with security and censorship, matters which had been neglected during the British advance, and with briefing newly-arrived units and formations.[280] Above all, preparations for the continuation of the advance into Tripolitania made large calls on their time. It was essential, on the other hand, to speed up British supplies to the front, where maintenance conditions were parlous, and for this reason to reduce the garrisons the enemy had left behind astride the road at Bardia and Halfaya; but Bardia did not fall until 2 January, in part because the size of its garrison had been greatly under-estimated,[281]

---

276.   MK 1943 of 19 January 1942; CX/MSS/634/T25.
277.   WO 169/3803 of 19 January 1942.   278. CAB 44/96, p 2.
279.   Playfair, op cit, Vol III, p 156; WO 208/3573 of 19 January 1942.
280.   WO 169/3803 of 4, 13, 17 and 18 January 1942.
281.   WO 169/1123 of 20 December 1941; WO 169/1010 of 22 December 1941;
       Playfair, op cit, Vol III, p 95.

and delay in taking Bardia held up the capture of Halfaya till 17 January – a further delay which was one of the principal reasons why Eighth Army decided that it could not be ready to attack El Agheila before mid-February. But more important than these distractions was the serious under-estimation of the enemy's capacity that led to the assumption that he was too weak to be able to take the offensive before the middle of February.

In the weeks following Rommel's attack this miscalculation was attributed to incompetence on the part of the Middle East intelligence staffs. 'I cannot help thinking', wrote the CIGS to the C-in-C after the loss of Benghazi (29 January), 'that over-optimistic intelligence played a large part in accounting for your troubles'.[282] In February the C-in-C replaced his DDMI with Colonel de Guingand, a member of his planning staff, who protested that he had no experience of intelligence. The C-in-C replied: 'Excellent, that's why I have appointed you'.[283] It is to be noted, however, that with this appointment the senior MI officer in the Middle East, hitherto designated DDMI, was made DMI; and this change may indicate that commanders and operations staffs in the Middle East were recognising that they themselves were partly at fault. Certainly it was only from the early months of 1942 that they began to abandon the habit of consulting 'I' only when they felt they needed information about the enemy's situation, and to tackle the problem of integrating intelligence with plans and operations in the process of appreciation and decision-making.[284]

Whatever we may feel on this question it is clear that on one subject – the strength of the Axis ground forces in north Africa after Rommel's retreat – the optimistic assessment made by the intelligence bodies in the Middle East was challenged in Whitehall, but not by the Middle East commanders, before Rommel's attack. On 12 January in an appreciation sent to the Prime Minister the C-in-C estimated that 'not more than one-third of the original German-Italian forces got away . . . totalling 17,000 German and 18,000 Italian'.[285] This was based on GHQ's calculation of the enemy's losses after the study of half a dozen units whose losses were estimated from captured documents and low-grade Sigint, but whose condition was believed to be 'not abnormal'. On this basis GHQ set the losses at 24,500 battle casualties (25 per cent of an original strength of 98,000 men) and 63,000 total casualties (battle casualties plus POW). On 13 January the Chiefs of Staff informed the C-in-C that the JIC preferred a higher starting figure of

282. A Bryant, *The Turn of the Tide* (1957), p 280.
283. F de Guingand, *Operation Victory* (1964), p 105.
284. WO 208/3575, passim.
285. CAB 105/16, No 81; Churchill, op cit, Vol IV (1951), p 21.

108,000 men and the more modest estimate of 11,000 battle casualties and 49,000 total casualties, leaving Rommel with 59,000 men.[286] But on 14 January Cairo rejected these casualty figures as 'much too low' and went on to stress that, whereas its own figures were based on the detailed analysis of known facts, the JIC was working, as it had itself admitted, only on general assumptions.[287] It was during these exchanges that the CIGS wrote to the C-in-C, this time before Rommel's counter-attack, a letter in which it is said that he warned him against 'the highly coloured optimistic reports' of his intelligence staff and of its 'exaggerated estimates of casualties'.[288] The facts were that the enemy's ground forces, which had totalled 119,000 men (65,000 German and 54,000 Italian) at the beginning of *Crusader*, had sustained 8,400 battle casualties (2,300 German, 6,100 Italian) and total casualties including POW of 38,300 (14,600 German, 23,700 Italian), and thus numbered in January about 80,000 (50,000 German, 30,000 Italian).[289] Partly as a result of under-estimating the enemy's original strength, but mainly as a result of greatly exaggerating his casualties, Cairo under-estimated his total remaining strength in north Africa by more than 100 per cent.

On the subject of enemy casualties the intelligence authorities had received no help from high-grade Sigint. This was also true for the extent of the enemy's disorganisation. In his appreciation of 12 January the C-in-C reported that the Axis forces were 'much disorganised, short of senior officers, short of material and . . . certainly not as strong as their total strength, 35,000, might be thought to indicate'. 'I am convinced', he concluded, that 'the enemy is hard-pressed more than we dared to think'. This was certainly true of the Italians. But in support of it the C-in-C quoted only 'very full and interesting records of daily conversations between our prisoner-Generals Ravenstein and Schmitt',* who were speaking of 'great losses in the recent fighting, mismanagement and disorganisation, and above all [discontent] with Rommel's leadership'.[290] Apart from a captured document referring to bread shortage[291] no other evidence was received for the view that the Germans were seriously disorganised. Yet this view was universally accepted in the Middle East, by intelligence and operations staffs alike. Just before 21 January the DDMI is

---

* General Schmitt had been captured at Bardia. The conversations were recorded clandestinely in the special quarters for senior officers at the CSDIC in Cairo.

286. CAB 105/16, No 89.
287. ibid, No 93.   288.   Bryant, op cit, p 279.
289. Playfair, op cit, Vol III, p 97. Compare CAB 44/95, AL 1200/61, p 57 for slightly different figures.
290. CAB 105/16, No 81.
291. WO 169/3803 of 10 January 1942.

reported to have been confident that 'we have Rommel in the can'. The presumption that the enemy was in difficult straits extended to the interpretation put upon the two Axis troop movements that were noticed. On 10 January Army Y revealed that the incomplete Sabratha Division was relieving the Bologna Division at Agheila; Eighth Army judged that the change was possibly 'indicative of enemy weakness'.[292] The DMI in Whitehall put a similar interpretation on the news from the GAF Enigma that a paratroop battalion had been sent to the front from Tripoli:* on 6 January he signalled to the Middle East the comment that this move was 'presumably owing to lack of sufficient army units'.[294]

It was perhaps on this account that on one matter on which they were still getting information from Sigint – the supplies and reinforcements that Rommel was now receiving by sea – the Middle East authorities saw no significance in the information. They did not overlook the fact that supplies were arriving. The C-in-C's appreciation of 12 January was provoked by a signal in which the Prime Minister, then in Washington, had expressed anxiety at, among other things, an air reconnaissance report to the effect that nine ships of 10,000 tons had recently arrived in Tripoli. In his reply the C-in-C, relying on the C 38m, gave the correct composition of the convoy that had reached Tripoli on 5 January† – 'six ships recently arrived . . . averaging 7,2000 tons'.[295] In an earlier appreciation of 8 January he had already conceded that the convoy's arrival should 'ease' the enemy's supply situation.[296] By then C 38m had revealed that, as well as a large consignment of fuel for ground and air forces, the convoy was carrying material 'of great importance to the DAK', and the Middle East authorities had concluded that this must have included motor transport and ammunition.[297] On 15 January, however, the C-in-C was still reporting to London that the enemy's supply situation 'appears to be acute' and was judging that Rommel would stand where he was until forced to withdraw by the British offensive or by supply difficulties.[298] His advisers, who knew that the convoy that had reached Tripoli on 19 December had carried 300 MT, stocks of

---

* It was later learnt from the Enigma that it had been sent to test new equipment.[293]
† See above, p 330.

292. ibid, 10 January 1942.
293. CX/MSS/669/T1.
294. MKs 1547 of 2 January, 1661 of 6 January 1942; CX/MSS/600/T12.
295. CAB 105/8, No 285; CAB 105/16, Nos 79, 81; Churchill, op cit, Vol IV, pp 19–20.
296. CAB 105/16, No 67.
297. MK 1639 of 6 January 1942; ZTPI 4352, 4354, 4359; WO 169/3803 of 7 January 1942.
298. CAB 44/96, p 2.

88 mm ammunition, some fuel and other stores,[299] presumably believed that these supplies were doing no more than provide temporary relief to a well-nigh desperate Rommel.

This conclusion is supported by the fact that in his appreciation of 15 January the C-in-C commented that Rommel was unlikely to receive any new German formations for some time, though a fresh Italian division with some 140 tanks might be available in a month or so. His advisers were clearly discounting the possibility that the forces already at Agheila, reformed and supplied, would be sufficient for a counter-attack. Equally clearly, they were watching for evidence as to whether Rommel was being reinforced with new formations, and relieved at finding none; but they did not allow for the possibility that the convoy which arrived on 5 January might have brought in tank reinforcements.

It is true that whereas the convoy in fact carried a considerable number of tanks – 54 by one account, 80 (40 German and 40 Italian) according to another[300] – the Sigint information about its cargoes made no mention of tanks. To make matters worse, the other high-grade Sigint sources that might have given information about tanks had dried up. But it is still remarkable, especially after the shock of discovering at the end of December that tank reinforcements had reached north Africa in the previous convoy, that British estimates did not allow for further arrivals. On 15 January they put Axis medium tank strength at about 90 (42 German, 45–50 Italian).[301] On 17 January Axis strength was actually 173 (84 German and 89 Italian).[302] As British calculations were underestimating the number of Axis tanks destroyed during *Crusader*, putting it at 305 when the actual number was 340,[303] the error at mid-January was almost wholly due to the failure to allow that the important convoys which were known to be getting through to north Africa had brought tank reinforcements.

□

During the first three days of the advance which began on 21 January 1942 the Axis forces scattered the British forward units, inflicting sizeable losses and sustaining few themselves. These initial successes, to which the C-in-C Middle East later attributed Rommel's victory in the rest of the battle, they owed to the fact that they had caught the British unprepared. When British intelligence

---

299.   MKs 1000 of 18 December, 1111 of 20 December 1941; ZTPI 3600.
300.   Playfair, op cit, Vol III, p 139; CAB 44/94, p 104.
301.   CAB 44/96, pp 1–2; Churchill, op cit, Vol IV, p 22.
302.   CAB 44/94, p 104 (n); Playfair, op cit, Vol II, p 140.
303.   CAB 44/95, p 58.

had failed to give warning of the possibility of an enemy move, let alone of its timing and scale, not even an immediate improvement in intelligence, had Rommel's counter-offensive produced that, could have helped the British forces at this first stage.

As it happened, no such increase was vouchsafed. The RAF's reconnaissance, hindered now by the loss of forward airfields as well as by bad weather, produced little of value. Army Y identified some enemy units[304] but was unable to provide information about their movements and intentions despite the fact that, as usual, they relaxed their security precautions during their advance. The only Y unit capable of exploiting battle communications on a useful scale was attached to HQ XIII Corps and was hampered by its frequent withdrawals; the other such unit was at Eighth Army HQ, 150 miles in the rear. Sigint, still confined to what could be learned from the C 38m and the GAF Enigma, provided no information of operational value – except about the movement to Tripoli of the latest Axis convoy* – until 23 January. On that day the GAF Enigma showed that Rommel had advanced with his whole force in three columns, the DAK on the right, the Italian mobile divisions in the centre and on the coast Gruppe Marcks,[305] whose composition was unknown but which included elements of a newly-formed division, probably 90th Light, since evidence that Division zbV Afrika was being reformed and renamed 90th Light Division was now confirmed.[306]

When this evidence was received in the Middle East the British forward formations were already making the further withdrawal that would by the following morning take them 100 miles back. It accordingly did no more than finally dispose of Eighth Army HQ's first assessment of the enemy's intentions, which had been to the effect that Rommel was using only Italian divisions for a reconnaissance in force,[307] without disclosing what his intentions were. More than that, it was ambiguous about these intentions. Perhaps because he had attacked without consulting Berlin and Rome, one of the Enigma messages of 23 January had emphasised that he had made use of his temporary superiority to make an advance in order to forestall the coming British attack. After considering this information DDMI Middle East remained convinced that Rommel's move was only a reconnaissance in force – 'a typical operation of the 14 September type'† – though he also based this

---

* See above, p 330.   † See above, pp 294, 296.

304. M Carver, *Tobruk* (1964), p 152; WO 169/3803 of 22 January 1942.
305. MKs 2013, 2024 and 2030 of 23 January 1942; CX/MSS/633/T3, 636/T4, 638/T2, 645/T11.
306. WO 169/1107 of 28 December 1941; MK 2047 of 24 January 1942; CX/MSS/646/T13, 647/T10.
307. CAB 44/96, p 17.

view on the appreciation that Rommel had begun with only seven days' supplies at El Agheila.[308] The C-in-C also continued to be optimistic that it was no more than a spoiling attack[309] and Eighth Army commander still held that the enemy was near his limit.[310]

XIII Corps commander, in command of the forward units, was much less sanguine. On 24 January, having earlier suggested precautionary preparations for the evacuation of Benghazi, he pressed for the evacuation and for permission to withdraw to Mechili, and warned that the enemy's striking power had been seriously under-estimated. On 25 January, having been given discretion to do so if necessary, he ordered this withdrawal. His decision was overruled from Eighth Army HQ, which assured him that the enemy's advance was not a counter-offensive, and that intelligence appreciated that it had already over-reached itself, and instructed him to take 'the most offensive action' and 'the greatest risks' to stop its further progress.[311] At this juncture intelligence had added nothing to what Eighth Army had learned about the enemy from XIII Corps' experiences or from other sources up to 23 January. Eighth Army and GHQ ME, which had estimated that Rommel had started with 75–82 tanks, including 45–50 German, still believed that at most he now had 90, including 40–45 German.[312] In fact he had started with 173 (84 German and 89 Italian) and all the Italian and at least 61 of the German tanks were still intact at the end of 23 January.[313] By that date XIII Corps, which had begun with 141 tanks, had suffered considerable casualties, though the real state of its main formation, 1st Armoured Division, was not yet known at higher HQ.

From 26 January the intelligence situation, already poor enough from the British point of view, deteriorated rapidly. On the one hand Rommel, pausing at Msus, received valuable assistance from his intelligence staff. By reading some of the traffic in which the British were making their arrangements for the attack that they had planned to make south of Benghazi on 29 January, Rommel's intelligence staff learned that there were serious differences of opinion among the British commanders, that the British were contemplating the need to evacuate Benghazi and that they expected Rommel to advance north-eastwards from Msus to Mechili.[314] In the light of this intelligence he decided to forestall the British move by converging his three columns in a north-westerly swoop on Benghazi on 27 January, and meanwhile to confirm the

308. CAB 105/16, No 122.   309.   ibid, Nos 118, 127.
310. Playfair, op cit, Vol III, p 146.
311. CAB 44/96, pp 44–45; Playfair, op cit, Vol III, p 147.
312. WO 169/4005, XIII Corps Intelligence Summary of 23 January 1942;
      CAB 105/16, No 123; CAB 44/96, pp 28–29.
313. Playfair, op cit, Vol III, p 145 (n).   314.   ibid, p 147.

British in their belief that he was making for Mechili by having the DAK make a feint in that direction.[315] On the British side, on the other hand, the intelligence received, such as it was, only added to their difficulties.

During 27 January, in very bad weather, RAF reconnaissance sighted only one of the enemy's movements, the feint to Mechili,[316] and Sigint, in the first reference it had made to Rommel's latest plan, gave disastrously misleading information about it. The information was obtained from the decrypt of a commentary which the Italian Air Command in Libya had transmitted in the C 38m. Perhaps because the Air Command was confused by Rommel's cover-plan, perhaps because it was not privy to it, it announced that the Axis forces would continue their offensive thrust towards Mechili and attempt to reach Benghazi. Perhaps because Rommel was concerned to provide some reassurance that he would conform with Mussolini's demand that he give priority to preparing positions from which to defend Tripolitania, it added that 'the Axis forces will later withdraw to a line Sidi-el-Azeili–Antellat–Gialo which will be held . . . as a line for further attack'.[317]

Of these two items of information, the first, by the prominence it gave to the thrust to Mechili as compared with the attempt to reach Benghazi, appeared to justify the dispositions ordered by Eighth Army on 27 January – dispositions as a result of which 1st Armoured Division, sent away from Benghazi to meet the Mechili thrust, and 4th Indian Division, ordered to operate against other forces moving towards Benghazi, were irretrievably separated during 28 January and unable to prevent Rommel's capture of Benghazi on the following day. The second item appeared to confirm the accuracy of the appreciation in which on 27 January GS Int Eighth Army had concluded that Rommel would not make a large advance beyond his present line.[318]

A second commentary from the Italian Air Command was issued later on 27 January and relayed to the Middle East on 28 January. As well as giving now – but too late – an accurate account of Rommel's plan to swoop on Benghazi, it announced that he would then withdraw his motorised troops and air forces to the line Gialo–Antellat–the coast and keep contact with the British by reconnaissance forces only.[319] With this information to the effect that the enemy was unlikely to continue to attack in strength the C-in-C and Eighth Army commander made plans to deny more

---

315. ibid, p 148; CAB 44/96, p 55.
316. Playfair, op cit, Vol III, p 149; Carver, op cit, p 159.
317. MK 2118 of 1320/27 January 1942; ZTPI 5263.
318. WO 169/3803 of 27 January 1942.
319. MK 2136 of 1115/28 January 1942; MK 2142 of 28 January 1942; ZTPI 5311.

ground to Rommel. But they were frustrated by operational limitations and eventually decided, on the recommendation of Eighth Army's force commanders, to stand on the Gazala position.[320]

By 6 February the withdrawal to Gazala had been completed. By 9 February it was clear that Rommel had decided after much hesitation to occupy the ground up to Gazala in strength. Enigma decrypts during the night of 8–9 February revealed that he was planning to move XX Corps forward from south of Benghazi and the DAK forward from Msus. Further decrypts showed in the next few days that these movements were taking place and, on 18 February, that the enemy was mining and building strong points along a chosen line and intending to rest and reorganise his main forces.[321]

320. Playfair, op cit, Vol III, p 151; Carver, op cit, p 160.
321. MKs 2434 of 9 February, 2710 of 18 February 1942; CX/MSS/697/T2, 725/T4.

CHAPTER 22

The Mediterranean and North Africa from February to July 1942

AFTER THE return of Rommel's forces to Gazala in February 1942 Germany's main concern on the southern front was how best to use the sea and air supremacy that she had established in the central Mediterranean. She had not abandoned the hope of linking an advance on Egypt from Libya with a larger offensive against the Arab oil lands from the north. But the larger offensive hinged on the still uncertain outcome of the next campaign in Russia, and she had meanwhile to decide whether Rommel should continue his advance before she had consolidated the position in north Africa by capturing Malta.

At the end of 1941, on his appointment as Oberbefehlshaber Süd (OBS), Kesselring had revived the earlier proposal for an invasion of Malta but had received no support in Berlin. From January 1942 he accordingly concentrated on neutralising the island by air attack. In February, however, under pressure from OKM, Hitler authorised him to begin planning the capture of Malta in conjunction with the Italians, who were already training for the operation. During March and April there followed much discussion as to whether capture was essential – or whether neutralisation by bombing would suffice – and as to whether an invasion of Malta should precede or follow an attack by Rommel on Tobruk, with Kesselring and Rommel favouring an invasion and preferring that it should come first and with the Italians arguing that preparations for an invasion could not be completed before July. At the end of April a change of mind on Rommel's part brought the discussion to an end. Partly because of delay with the plans for taking Malta, and partly because his own supply position had so improved that he judged it best once again to anticipate a British offensive, he now urged that the attack on Tobruk should come first. Kesselring supported him, persuaded that the GAF's attacks had already sufficiently reduced Malta's power to threaten the north African supply routes. On 4 May, following a meeting between Hitler and Mussolini, a directive laid it down that Malta and Tobruk were both to be taken before Rommel advanced to the Nile, but set late May or early June as the date for Rommel's offensive and July for the capture of Malta.[1]

---

1. Playfair, *The Mediterranean and Middle East*, Vol III (1960), pp 175, 193–195; Gwyer and Butler, *Grand Strategy*, Vol III Part II (1964), pp 443–445.

Of this debate in the enemy camp, as of the enemy's intentions on the northern front in the Middle East, the British authorities received no information apart from rumours and a few hints in Axis diplomatic decrypts. With regard to the northern front the authorities in Whitehall remained reasonably confident on the basis of strategic considerations that there was no danger of an early German offensive. At the end of 1941 the JIC and the Joint Planners took the view that Germany would not attack Turkey until she had won a spring campaign in Russia and that, since that campaign could not begin before the end of April, the further threat would not develop before August. By the end of January 1942, after some hesitation by the CIGS about its first premise, the Chiefs of Staff had accepted this conclusion. So had representatives from the Middle East Defence Committee at meetings in London.[2] In the middle of March the JIC reviewed the situation and adhered to its earlier conclusion: the major German offensive in Russia would probably not start before 15 May and there would be no attack on the Middle East through Turkey or the Caucasus before Russia had been defeated.[3] In the second half of that month the intelligence bodies discounted a spate of reports to the effect that Germany intended to attack Egypt by air and sea via Greece, Syria or Cyprus as well as from Libya.[4] In Cairo assessments of the northern threat remained more cautious. By 20 February the Middle East Defence Committee, having severely reduced British forces on the northern front, was 'relying on this attack not taking place'.[5] As for the C-in-C Middle East, 'the weak northern front continued to harass and distract him'.[6] On 18 March he asked London to keep him supplied with all information about Germany's intentions as policy in Libya would have to be reconsidered in the event of a threat to Turkey.[7] On 20 March Sir Stafford Cripps, en route to India from the UK, reported from Cairo that 'the danger of which Auchinleck is apprehensive is that an attack should develop in Syria, from the north via Caucasus and Turkey, or upon Cyprus, while the operation was on in the Western Desert, in which event it would be necessary to withdraw a considerable proportion of the air forces from the desert . . . This would mean

2. CAB 84/39, JP (41) 1093 of 25 December; JIC (42) 19 of 17 January; JIC (42) 34 of 25 January; CAB 79/19, COS (42) 22nd Meeting of 20 January and 30th Meeting of 27 January; CAB 69/2, DO (41) 76th Meeting, 31 December; Churchill, *The Second World War*, Vol III (1950), pp 480, 564, 574.
3. CAB 121/412, SIC file D/Germany/ 1 Vol 1, JIC (42) 75 of 14 March, COS (42) 85th Meeting of 25 March.
4. WO 208/3573, MI 14 Appreciations for the CIGS, 23 March and 6 April 1942; CAB 84/43, JP (42) 296 of 23 March, para 14.
5. CAB 105/9, Hist (B) 9, No 23.
6. Gwyer and Butler, op cit, Vol III, Part II, p 448.
7. CAB 105/9, No 76.

abandoning the battle with extremely serious results'.[8] Until May, however, this anxiety did not figure much in Auchinleck's discussions with Whitehall, for they were dominated by arguments about his wish to delay his offensive on other grounds,* and it was meanwhile only too obvious that the enemy was giving high priority to maintaining control of the central Mediterranean and eliminating Malta as a base for the attack on his north African supplies.

From the beginning of 1942 the Chiefs of Staff allowed for the possibility that the enemy would try to eliminate Malta by invading it. On 12 January they directed that reinforcements against an invasion attempt should be sent to Malta in the January convoy from Alexandria. As well as being impressed by the strengthening of the GAF in Sicily and the beginning of its bombing of Malta, they were influenced by rumours from POW and diplomatic sources that the Axis was planning an invasion, and they were made uneasy by rumours of troop movements in southern Italy about which they had no reliable information.[9] The intelligence bodies in Whitehall did not disagree that the enemy was determined to neutralise Malta, or even that he was preparing an invasion. Until the end of March, however, by judicious use of the negative evidence of Sigint, aerial reconnaissance and other sources, they correctly resisted the conclusion that an invasion of Malta was imminent.

On 3 January the JIC appreciated that the enemy was unlikely to try to capture Malta until he was convinced that he was failing to neutralise the island by progressively intensified air attack. While there was good reason to believe that the build-up of the GAF in Sicily – where there were already 320 Italian aircraft – would reach 285 aircraft by mid-January and 550 by 1 February, there was no evidence yet of the accumulation of troops or assault craft in any of the likely assembly areas, and transport aircraft were not likely to be available while the fighting continued in Libya.[10] Should the enemy decide to invade, moreover, the JIC felt that it 'would surely get some weeks' warning'.[11] Rumours continued to come in during the next two months of troop movements in southern Italy and of the arrival of assault craft there.[12] More important, the GAF Enigma provided a firm indication of invasion preparations for the first time on 7 February, when it referred to the establishment at Reggio Calabria of a supply base for Fliegerkorps XI, the air

---

* See below, p 350 et seq.

8. CAB 69/4, DO (42) 31 of 26 March.
9. Playfair, op cit, Vol III, p 156.
10. JIC (42) 3 of 3 January.
11. CAB 105/8, Hist (B) 8 No 230 of 3 January 1942.
12. WO 208/3573 of 19 January and 1 February 1942.

landing command that had carried out the invasion of Crete.[13] But on 23 February the JIC adhered to its view that an invasion attempt was less likely than a continuation of the bombing.[14] Nor was it until the end of March that it changed its mind.

One reason for the change was the receipt of further information from the GAF Enigma. This had recently referred to the presence in Rome of a senior parachute general, who had taken part in the Crete operation, and had indicated that paratroop units were being moved from Russia.[15] In addition, from 'a good source', who was known to have contacts in the German High Command and who believed his information to be 'absolutely reliable', the SIS had obtained a report to the effect that Hitler had decided to capture Malta in April in order to safeguard the supplies for a subsequent offensive by Rommel against Suez. At a time when the GAF build-up in Sicily was at its height, and when unprecedentedly heavy GAF attacks on Valetta and the RAF's bases were severely eroding Malta's defences, the JIC understandably decided that this report must be taken seriously. On 31 March it warned that, with Malta severely weakened by air bombardment, it must be assumed that Germany had decided to capture it, and that the attempt would probably be made in April.[16]

The JIC still insisted, however, that there was no evidence that Fliegerkorps XI had yet arrived in Italy, that the GAF Enigma had not yet mentioned the destination of the paratroop units that were to be moved from Russia, and that no assemblages of transport aircraft, shipping and assault craft had yet been detected by the routine reconnaissance of Sicily now being flown from Malta.[17] These qualifications produced some mutterings from the Chiefs of Staff, who found it 'difficult to assess the likelihood of invasion'.[18] But before long the intelligence bodies were again treating with considerable scepticism the continuing rumours of an imminent invasion attempt.[19] That they were able to do so was primarily because their negative evidence – the fact that their main sources had not yet disclosed the moves and preparations that the operation would call for – was now supplemented by positive indications that the danger of invasion was receding.

Chief among these indications was the reduction of the GAF in Sicily. While the scale of the GAF's bombing effort against Malta continued to mount – the GAF Enigma indicated that 750 tons of

13.   CX/MSS/739/T10.
14.   JIC (42) 61 of 23 February.
15.   WO 208/3573 of 30 March 1942.
16.   JIC (42) 106 (o) of 31 March; WO 208/3573 of 30 March 1942.
17.   AIR 41/7, *Photographic Reconnaissance*, Vol II, p 105.
18.   CAB 79/20, COS (42) 104th Meeting of 2 April.
19.   WO 208/3573 of 6 and 20 April 1942.

bombs were dropped in February, 2,000 tons in March and 5,500 tons in April – Whitehall knew from Fliegerkorps II's regular strength and serviceability returns by the beginning of April that, at 425 aircraft, GAF strength in Sicily remained well below the ultimate figure of 650 which the Germans had originally intended to transfer there.[20] It knew, too, that the figure had been kept down by Germany's need to retain aircraft on the eastern front against Russia's winter offensive. As early as 23 March Air Intelligence was coming to the view that the GAF would have to go further, and reduce its strength in the Mediterranean, if it was to have enough forces in Russia for its spring offensive.[21] On 26 April the GAF Enigma disclosed, at last, that units of Fliegerkorps II were preparing to leave Sicily.[22] On 2 May the same source showed that two Gruppen were already withdrawing and that more were to follow.[23] On the same day the Chiefs of Staff used this evidence to reassure the Governor of Malta – where the authorities had recently been alarmed by the appearance in air photographs of what they judged to be new glider strips in Sicily[24] – that he could discount the danger of an invasion.[25]

Later in May it became clear that the wholesale withdrawal of Fliegerkorps II from Sicily was taking place, and the fact that some of the units were sent to reinforce Fliegerführer Afrika was one of the signs that Rommel was preparing to take the offensive. Other indications to the same effect, of which the earliest were received during April,* also suggested that, for the present at least, the threat of a descent on Malta was receding. As it happened, they included the only direct references to the Axis plan for the invasion of Malta that British intelligence obtained from Sigint traffic. On 2 May one decrypt disclosed that, an 'intended operation' having been postponed, Panzerarmee Afrika (the new name for Panzergruppe Afrika since the battle of Gazala) had requested that the San Marco battalion, which had been sent to north Africa in November 1941 to assist in the intended attack on Tobruk, should be retained for north African operations. In Whitehall it was impossible to guess at the nature of the 'intended operation'. Nor did the intelligence authorities realise that when they received a second decrypt, which revealed that the Italians wanted two ferry barges

---

* See below, p 360 et seq.

20. AIR 41/10, *The Rise and Fall of the GAF*, p 134.
21. WO 208/3573 of 23 March 1942.
22. MK 4686 of 26 April 1942; CX/MSS/926/T24.
23. WO 208/3573 of 4 May 1942.
24. AIR 41/26, *The RAF in the Middle East Campaigns*, Vol III, p 118; AIR 41/7, p 105; Playfair, op cit, Vol III, p 186; CAB 105/9, No 185 of 1 May 1942.
25. CAB 105/9, No 186 of 2 May 1942.

to return to Italy 'for exercises in connection with operation *Herkules*', they were handling the first and the last mention of the code-word for the invasion of Malta.[26]

□

Although Malta was thus spared an Axis landing attempt, it suffered immensely in the early months of 1942 from air bombardment and blockade and intelligence could do little to assist it during its ordeal.

For tactical intelligence during the air raids Malta relied mainly on the local RAF Y unit. From January 1942 GC and CS obtained from the Enigma some of the GAF's orders for operations over Malta, and the earliest of them showed that the RAF bases were to be the enemy's chief targets.[27] But such orders were by no means regularly intercepted, since much of the traffic between Italy and Sicily went by land-line, and it was rare for them to be decrypted in time for Malta to receive advance warning. The tactical intelligence derived by the Y unit from its interpretation of the R/T and W/T traffic of the German and Italian air forces was of greater value to Malta's fighter pilots; but neither the Y unit nor the island's radar could guarantee to give adequate warning of approaching raids.[28] So great, moreover, was the enemy's superiority in the air, so frequent his raids, that even advance notice did little to reduce the problems of the defence.

In the task of keeping Malta supplied, as in that of defending it in the air, there was little scope for using intelligence to reduce the brunt of the enemy's attack. In this case there was no lack of intelligence. The moment a convoy left for Malta from Gibraltar or Alexandria decrypts became available in profusion. From these Whitehall was able to provide the naval authorities with some valuable information about the dispositions and strengths of the enemy's air forces, about his reconnaissance routines and about the armament and tactics of his bomber and torpedo aircraft.* In

---

* It was at this time that the GAF Enigma provided the first intelligence that the Germans intended to form a torpedo bomber force using, among other weapons, the LT 350 or circling torpedo. LT 350 was first mentioned by the GAF in Greece in January 1942, when the British correctly appreciated that it was designed to be dropped by parachute in confined spaces and to do a slow circling run. At the end of February the decrypts disclosed that LT 350s were being sent to Sicily.[29] In April they disclosed that the GAF intended to use the weapon against Suez, but the plans appear to have come to nothing. It was used, ineffectively, against the June 1942 convoy from Alexandria to Malta, this being the first

26. MK 5209 of 11 May 1942; CX/MSS/968/T16.
27. MKs 1649 and 1656 of 6 January 1942; CX/MSS/600/T15 and 21; D Richards, *The Royal Air Force 1939–1945*, Vol II (1954), p 190.
28. AIR 41/26, Appendix XXIII, p 9; Clayton, *The Enemy is Listening* (1980) p 164, et seq.
29. MK 2838 of 23 February 1942; CX/MSS/739/T10.

addition, each convoy was preceded by intensive RAF photographic reconnaissance which provided further information about the latest dispositions of the enemy air forces.[30] But Whitehall and the commands could use the intelligence only to watch in great detail how a convoy was faring. For early warning of air attacks, which caused most of the losses, the escorts depended wholly on air patrols, radar and look-outs until May 1942. Thereafter, ships in the Mediterranean began to be fitted with ship-borne Y – naval 'Headache' and RAF 'computer' parties accompanied a Malta convoy for the first time in June 1942 – but the results were of marginal importance despite occasional successes. Against the ever-present threat of intervention by the Italian Fleet the Sigint was supplemented by PR; but as this was good only as far north as Naples, and as the C 38 m, when it did yield information about fleet movements, did so only after the enemy had sailed, it was not possible to rely on advance notice. Nor was there any room for surprise and flexibility in the sailing of the convoys. The enemy knew their destination. From reconnaissance and from agents he also invariably knew when a convoy was being assembled; and it can only have added to the frustration of the British authorities that, from reading the messages from the network of Axis agents established around the Straits of Gibraltar, and primarily those in which the Abwehr passed the intelligence back to Berlin via Madrid, they knew how much the enemy knew.* A great deal of diplomatic effort was expended in the attempt to curtail the activities of these agents, but as yet with little success.[31]

Not surprisingly in these circumstances, it became a progressively more difficult and costly undertaking to get the supplies through. The January 1942 convoy lost one of its four ships and one of its escorts was sunk by U-boat. In February the next convoy lost all its three ships to air attack. During the sailing of the March convoy the escort received advance notice from a submarine report and from the C 38m[32] that the Italian Fleet had left Taranto, and CS 15 fought a brilliant action against the battleship *Littorio* and two Italian cruisers, forcing them to retire with only slight damage to his own ships and none to the convoy.† But two of the convoy's four

---

time the Enigma showed that it had been employed operationally. The Mediterranean commands had been alerted to its existence and possible use.

* See Appendix 15.

† The C 38 m decrypts after this encounter, the second battle of Sirte, reported damage to one of the Italian cruisers but made no reference to the battleship, on which the British force had claimed hits. It later became clear that the *Littorio* had suffered no damage.[33]

30.   AIR 41/7, p 106.
31.   Woodward, *British Foreign Policy in the Second World War*, Vol IV (1976), p 8; CAB 79/21, COS (42) 155th Meeting, 19 May; CAB 80/62, COS (42) 140 (o) of 17 May. See also D McLachlan, *Room 39* (1968) pp 204–206.
32.   MK 3600 of 22 March 1942; ZTPI 7673.
33.   Naval Headlines 263 of 25 March 1942; Dir/C Archive 9047; Roskill, *The War at Sea*, Vol II (1957), pp 51–55.

merchant vessels were sunk by aircraft as they approached Malta and the other two were sunk by air attacks on Valetta harbour before discharging most of their cargo. Thereafter, although fighter aircraft were ferried to Malta by aircraft carrier from Gibraltar, the island depended on submarines for aviation fuel, and by early May the supply outlook was so grim that the need to sail another convoy in June determined the date chosen for the beginning of Eighth Army's offensive.*

Early in May C 38 m was immediately useful in helping to avert a further disaster at Alexandria. On 5 May it gave precise warning that there was to be another attack on that base by Italian human torpedoes, the chief target being the floating dock in which the *Queen Elizabeth* was being made seaworthy. The attack was made on 14–15 May and was duly frustrated.[34] By that time the scale of the GAF attack on Malta and its supplies was on the decline. This more than compensated for the fact, also disclosed by the C 38 m, that in preparation for a more aggressive policy against Malta's supply routes the Italian Fleet was basing more units at Messina and contemplating the use of Suda as a base.[35] Nor was it long before Malta was able to resume its own offensive against the Axis supplies to north Africa.

Between the middle of December 1941, when Force K was eliminated, and the end of May 1942, while the island was neutralised by the GAF's attacks, this offensive was virtually suspended, and it was obvious from the C 38 m traffic that most of the increased amount of shipping that the Axis was despatching to north Africa was getting through unscathed. On 23 February 1942 another large convoy, the fourth since mid-December 1941 to be escorted by the Italian Fleet, reached Tripoli intact. From January C 38 m showed that the Axis exploited Malta's shortage of reconnaissance aircraft, and the reduction of its naval and air attack forces, by sailing supply ships independently or in small groups at frequent intervals without escorts; by the end of February it was known that 11 ships had made the crossing in this way.[36] In these circumstances the fact that the Italians introduced a new indicator for the C 38 m signals at the beginning of March, and that GC and CS temporarily read only a small proportion of the traffic and that with considerable delay, made little difference. Nor did matters improve from the end of March when GC and CS regained its ability to read the C 38 m currently.

During April and May C 38 m gave details of 26 Axis shipping movements between Italy and north Africa. Only 9 of them were

* See below, pp 358, 363 et seq.

34.   Playfair, op cit, Vol III, p 192.
35.   MK 5334 of 15 May 1942; ZTPI 9684.
36.   NI/MSS/16 and 17.

sighted by British air reconnaissance.[37] At the same time the British anti-shipping operations had become no less costly than the sending of supplies to Malta. On 14 April five of Malta's few remaining strike aircraft were lost in a brave but unsuccessful attack on a south-bound convoy of which the C 38 m had given advance warning.[38] Attempts by the Mediterranean Fleet to supplement Malta's dwindling air and submarine attacks also ended in disaster. On 10 March the cruiser *Naiad* was sunk by U-boat when CS 15 was returning to Alexandria after following up unconfirmed air reports of damage done to an Italian cruiser.[39] On 10 May four destroyers sailed from Alexandria without air cover in a desperate bid to intercept a southbound convoy whose departure from Taranto had been reported in C 38 m signals; two days later three of them were sunk by aircraft of Fliegerkorps X. Very full intelligence of this attack was obtained from the GAF Enigma, but it was obtained too late to be useful. In an attempt to intercept the same convoy the submarine *Upholder* was sunk off Tripoli with all hands.[40]

The collapse of the British anti-shipping offensive is reflected in the following figures. In February and March 1942 the enemy lost only 9 per cent of the supplies he sailed to north Africa. In April and May only 13 Axis ships were sunk in the whole Mediterranean and the enemy's losses on the north Africa route fell to a negligible level. In April they were less than 1 per cent. In May they were 7 per cent, the improvement over the previous month being wholly due to the fact that aircraft from Malta sank a 7,000 ton ship off Tripoli on the last day of the month.[41] The success on the last day of May was achieved with the help of the C 38 m.[42] It marked the recovery of Malta's strike capacity, the beginning of a period in which that recovery was combined with anti-shipping intelligence to produce another sustained and decisive attack on Rommel's supplies.* For the present, however, the Axis had won the race for reinforcements and supplies in north Africa. During the four months to the end of May they succeeded in landing 236,500 tons of general military cargo and 106,500 tons of fuel.[43] During the first half of May it became increasingly obvious that Rommel intended

---

* See below, p 419 et seq.

37.   CAB 105/9, No 253 of 25 May 1942.
38.   Playfair, op cit, Vol III, p 190; MKs 4227 of 13 April, 4233 of 14 April 1942; ZTPI 8451 and 8458.
39.   Playfair, op cit, Vol III, p 163.
40.   ibid, p 190; MKs 5251 and 5256 of 12 May 1942; CX/MSS/972/T4,7,8 and 12.
41.   Playfair, op cit, Vol III, pp 163, 173–174, 189.
42.   MK 5949 of 28 May 1942; ZTPI 10268.
43.   Playfair, op cit, Vol III, pp 163, 189.

to anticipate the planned British offensive by resuming his advance.

☐

The discovery that Rommel was planning to take the offensive brought to an end a long debate between Whitehall and Cairo in which, as in the summer of 1941, Whitehall had pleaded that the C-in-C Middle East should launch an offensive at an early date and Cairo had counselled delay. As in the previous debate, the C-in-C's arguments were influenced by his anxiety about the northern front, which Whitehall thought excessive, while Whitehall appealed even more emphatically than in 1941 to the danger to Malta and the risk that the enemy would exploit his neutralisation of Malta to reinforce his position in north Africa. But what now dominated the debate was a further divergence: Cairo and Whitehall saw in different lights the undoubted fact that the enemy's supplies were getting through unscathed. For Whitehall the overriding consideration was that the enemy's reinforcements would make it progressively more difficult to dislodge him from his position in north Africa. In Cairo the chief problem was that the reinforcements were giving the enemy an immediate superiority in tanks.

In the period before Rommel's counter-offensive in January 1942 the authorities in the Middle East had overlooked the possibility that the enemy was getting tank reinforcements to north Africa.* So had the authorities in Whitehall, as is revealed by the fact that the Prime Minister's first response to the news of Rommel's success was to ask the C-in-C Middle East whether 'our fresh armour' had been unable to compete with 'the resuscitated German tanks'.[44] In Cairo, at least, this mistake was not repeated after Eighth Army had been forced back to Gazala. In consequence of this setback, moreover, another consideration, over and above the calculation of the number of enemy tanks, acquired great prominence. On 30 January, in reply to the Prime Minister, the C-in-C stressed for the first time that from now on he would need a superiority of two to one in tank numbers if he was to counter Germany's technical and tactical superiority.[45]† On 7 February the Cs-in-C Middle East jointly urged a similar argument on the Chiefs of Staff: the date on which they could resume the offensive in north Africa would depend on the rates at which they and the enemy could build up

---

* See above, p 335 et seq.

† See Appendix 14. From now onwards there was to be continuing evidence of the arrival in Africa of new models of German tanks with improved armour and armament.

44.   CAB 105/16, Hist (B) (Crusader) 2, No 136 of 24 January 1942; Churchill, op cit, Vol IV (1951), p 25.

45.   CAB 105/16, No 162.

armour, and because of British inferiority in tank performance they must have a three to two numerical superiority.[46] In the ensuing debate Whitehall did not question this requirement.

What Whitehall did question – often, and sometimes acrimoniously – was Cairo's estimates of the rate at which the enemy was receiving new tanks. The reasons are not far to seek. Quite apart from Whitehall's anxiety that the British advance should take place as soon as possible, the work of calculating the enemy's growing tank strength was open to disagreements and misunderstandings on two grounds. First there was no firm evidence about the number of tanks the enemy had been left with after the recent hard fighting: since they had retreated, the British could not count the enemy's casualties; in any case they did not know what his tank numbers had been when he began his advance. In the second place, until 11 March, during a period in which it was making it abundantly clear that Axis supply shipping was now reaching north Africa without difficulty, Sigint yielded little information about the arrival of tank reinforcements.

By 18 February Cairo had calculated that the enemy had a total tank strength of 227 (42 German and 185 Italian). Its argument was that ground and air observation had indicated 50–60 German and about 50 Italian tanks forward, and that to these it was necessary to add some 140 belonging to the Littorio Division.[47] The reconstitution of the Littorio Division had been the subject of rumours since December 1941; the C 38 m had in January 1942 revealed that an officer from the division had been in the latest convoy to Tripoli; Army Y had recently located its HQ and that of its tank regiment at Tripoli; nor was there any disagreement between MI and GS Int GHQ ME that 138 was the tank establishment of an Italian armoured division.[48]

On 26 February the Prime Minister ignored the Littorio Division and used the calculation that the enemy had 100–110 tanks in the forward area, against Eighth Army's 160, to urge on the C-in-C that the British had 'substantial superiority in the air, in armour and in other forces'.[49] This appeal crossed with a telegram of 27 February in which the C-in-C raised his estimate of total Axis tank strength in Libya from 227 (the figure given on 18 February) to about 475. This figure was made up of 260 in the forward area (160 German and 100 Italian), together with the 140 tanks of the Littorio Division – for which it was now admitted, however, that

---

46.   ibid No 194.

47.   ibid No 194 of 7 February, No 217 of 18 February 1942.

48.   WO 169/1107, XIII Corps Intelligence Summary of 25 December 1941; CAB 69/4, DO (42) 31, p. 6; Playfair, op cit Vol III, p 159; MK 2065 of 24 January 1942; ZTPI 5155.

49.   CAB 105/16, No 237; CAB 44/96, AL 1200/71, p 98.

there was an 'almost complete lack of confirmatory evidence' – and 71 German 'replacement tanks' which, as the Enigma had recently reported,[50] had arrived in a convoy at Tripoli on 23 February. The C-in-C added that, although it was not known whether other tanks had arrived with that convoy, the total Axis strength might reach 630 by 1 April. After admitting that this was a 'worst case' estimate, and that the enemy could not maintain as many as 630 tanks in the forward area, he concluded by announcing that he would be unable to reach the required numerical superiority until 1 June – and that even this assessment did not allow for the possibility of having to supply tanks for his northern front.[51]

In Whitehall MI found Cairo's estimate of 630 tanks by 1 April to be 'arbitrary and unexplained'. As for the estimate that the enemy already had 475 tanks in north Africa, it protested that this required that he should have shipped some 400 since the beginning of the year, and that this was 'barely even theoretically possible'. In particular, it cast doubt on the estimate that the Italians already had 240 tanks: if the number of these in the forward area had now jumped to 100, and if, as it pre-supposed, Cairo had reached this figure by assuming that 50 Italian tanks had been ferried over – as well as the German – and been sent to the front during January, this assumption made it less likely that the Littorio Division had received its tanks.[52] The Chiefs of Staff shared these views. On 27 February – the day on which they received the C-in-C's unwelcome news, and a week after the complete failure of the latest attempt to get a convoy through to Malta* – they had urged him to time his offensive so that it could regain the Cyrenaican airfields in time for the next Malta convoy, at the latest during April.[53] On 3 March, after a full discussion in the Defence Committee, they told him that his estimates were heavily biassed in favour of the enemy. Over and above allowing for the admitted technical superiority of the Germans, he was assuming that every Axis tank became effective as soon as it landed in Tripoli, whereas he reported that only 298 of his own 1,271 tanks were effective. They reminded him that, as was known from the GAF Enigma, the GAF in north Africa was being reduced by transfers to Sicily, and warned him that his superiority in the air might not last. And they urged that on this and other strategic grounds he should reconsider his decision. 'An attempt to drive the enemy out of Cyrenaica in the next few weeks is not only imperative for the safety of Malta, on which so much depends, but holds out the only hope of fighting a battle while the enemy is still

---

* See above, p 347.

50.   MK 2898 of 25 February 1942; CX/MSS/745/T20.
51.   CAB 105/16 No 240.
52.   CAB 44/96, pp 5–6.
53.   CAB 105/9, No 36.

comparatively weak and short of resources of all kinds.' Moreover, 'we have to think what may happen in the summer. We do not see what hope there will be at that time for the Levant-Caspian front, already denuded by the unavoidable calls of the Far East, if we have meanwhile allowed the enemy to build up in Africa a force which will pin down our remaining strength'.[54]

The Cs-in-C Middle East resisted this appeal. On 4 March they repeated that the necessary tank superiority could not be achieved before late June, or even early July, unless by some stroke of fortune the Axis ceased to be able to send reinforcements to Tripoli.[55] On 5 March they rebutted the charge that their latest tank estimates had been biassed in favour of the enemy: they had no choice but to allow for the fact that reinforcements were reaching Tripoli.[56] And on 13 March GC and CS provided evidence for the accuracy of part at least of those estimates by decrypting in the GAF Enigma an enemy tank return – the first to be obtained since the previous November* – which gave the number of Italian tanks as 87 and the number of German tanks of specified types as 159.[57]† If these were the numbers of serviceable tanks in the forward area – and in Cairo there was no doubt that this was so – they conformed closely to the estimates of such tanks (100 Italian and 160 German) which Cairo had made on 27 February.

The Prime Minister, using this tank return as an opportunity to return to the attack, put a different gloss on it, though whether or not he did so because he thought the return referred to all Axis tanks, not only tanks in the forward area, is not now clear. He pointed out to the C-in-C on 15 March that its total of 246 tanks was 'barely half the number you credited them with by 1st March' barely half, that is, of the 475 which had been Cairo's estimate of all Axis tanks in Libya – and compared it with the number of medium tanks – 430 – that the C-in-C had said he would have serviceable by 1 April. He went on in more general terms, urging that the enemy might be able to 'reinforce faster than you, so that, after all your waiting, you will find yourself in relatively the same, or even in a worse, position', and adding that a very heavy German counter-stroke upon the Russians must be expected soon.[58]

The C-in-C having recently declined a request from the Prime

---

* See above, p 297.   † See Appendix 14.

54. CAB 69/4, DO (42) 7th Meeting of 2 March; CAB 105/17, Hist (B). (Crusader) 3, No 7 of 3 March 1942.
55. CAB 105/17, No 10.
56. ibid, No 13.
57. MK 3324 of 13 March 1942; CX/MSS/793/T4.
58. CAB 69/4, DO (42) 31 of 26 March, p 6; CAB 105/17, No 31 of 15 March 1942; Churchill, op cit, Vol IV, p 263.

Minister that he should come to London for talks, the VCIGS, armed with questions from Whitehall, stopped off at Cairo to pursue the argument. During this visit the C-in-C agreed to accept parity with Rommel's Italian tanks, though still insisting that he must have a 50 per cent superiority in numbers over German tanks. In addition Cairo again conceded that its estimate that the Axis would have 630 tanks at 1 April and 650 by mid-May was the 'worst case' calculation, and that the 'best case' for 1 April was 320 serviceable and 70 in workshops; of these perhaps 350 would be serviceable by mid-May. These concessions enabled the C-in-C so far to fall in with London's wishes as to accept mid-May as the target date for his offensive. But he accepted it with the huge reservation that the enemy received no further reinforcements. If the Axis forces continued to receive reinforcements, and were able to bring all their formations up to establishment, they would have 650 tanks by 1 May; in this event a British offensive would not be possible before August.[59] On 2 April the Cs-in-C Middle East reaffirmed his view. They would seize any favourable opportunity to attack, before or after 15 May, but they could not bind themselves to this date. It would be feasible only if the enemy's tank strength turned out to be less than 650.[60]

The lower estimate of 320 Axis tanks plus 70 in workships at 1 April was in fact an estimate of the number of tanks already at the front. It was based on the assumption that the Enigma return of 246 tanks on 11 March referred to serviceable tanks in the forward area, on the calculation (for which captured documents had provided good evidence)[61] that the enemy would then have had about 25 per cent of his forward tanks (say 61) in the workshops, and on the fact that the Long Range Desert Group had on 14 March sighted a further 85 tanks, apparently German, on the Cyrenaica/Libya border moving east. 246 plus 61 plus 85 yielded a total of 392 tanks forward.[62] With this conclusion Whitehall did not greatly disagree. MI also accepted as reasonable Cairo's estimate of 10 April that by that date the total of Axis tanks had increased from 390 to 450, of which 380 might be serviceable.[63] It was otherwise with Cairo's estimate of the further build-up that would take place by 1 May. Both sides agreed that the Axis was unlikely to send more formations to north Africa, MI now having good evidence that the German Army was fully extended. Both agreed that the enemy nevertheless had enough tanks to bring the formations in north Africa up to full establishment. But whereas

---

59.   CAB 69/4, DO (42) 31, p 8; CAB 44/96, p 100.
60.   CAB 105/17, No 57.
61.   WO 169/3803, Eighth Army Intelligence Summary of 28 February 1942.
62.   CAB 69/4, DO (42) 31, p 6.
63.   CAB 44/96, p 104.

Cairo, now claiming to have conclusive evidence that the establishment of a German division was 180 tanks and strong evidence that that of an Italian division was 156, deduced that the enemy's target for two German and two Italian divisions was 672 tanks, or 650 in round figures, and feared that he could reach it by 1 May if his supply ships continued to arrive at the present rate, MI insisted that the establishment figures were 133 for a German and 138 for an Italian division.[64] These conjectures were equally faulty – for example, the establishment of a German division was not in fact constant[65] – but for lack of further evidence to stimulate it the argument was not pressed until the third week of April.

On 21 and 22 April the Enigma produced further evidence in the shape of two more tank returns. These were the earliest important consequence of the momentous fact that on 10 April GC and CS had again broken into Chaffinch, the Enigma key used for communications between Rommel's HQ and supply bases in north Africa and Europe, and north Africa and Berlin, and was now – though only with prodigious effort – reading just over half of the available traffic with delays amounting sometimes to a week or more.* The first return, for 21 April, referred merely to 161 serviceable tanks.[66] The second return, for 22 April, was much fuller: it specified the number of German tanks by type totalling 264, and also gave the figure for Italian tanks as 151.[67] Grand total 415.

Interpreted as the number of serviceable tanks in the forward area, the second return confirmed that Cairo's previous estimates of such tanks were of the right order. On 17 April Cairo had increased its calculation of their number to 396 serviceable and 70 unserviceable, total 466, after the Long Range Desert Group had sighted a further 44 Italian tanks moving up to the front.[68] On 25 April the C-in-C gave London his current estimate, as follows –

	Runners	Non-Runners	Total
German	265	45	310
Italian	132	24	156
	397	69	466[69]

---

* See below, p 374.

64. Playfair, op cit, Vol III, p 199; CAB 69/4, DO (42) 31, pp 4–6; CAB 84/43, JP (42) 296 of 23 March, para 9; WO 208/2573 of 2 March 1942.
65. Müller-Hillebrand, *Das Heer*, Vol II, (1954) p 107, Table 26.
66. MK 4508 of 22 April 1942; CX/MSS/912/T23.
67. MK 4815 of 30 April 1942; CX/MSS/935/T30 of 22 April 1942.
68. CAB 105/17, No 97 of 2 May 1942; CAB 44/96, p 104.
69. CAB 44/96, p 105; CAB 105/17 No 86.

In Whitehall, however, the first of the two returns, which had been a report from a GAF liaison officer with a single, unspecified unit or formation, had attracted the Prime Minister's attention. In the signal conveying the return to Cairo MI had incautiously added the comment that it seemed to refer to the number of German serviceable tanks in the forward area.[70] On 26 April, but presumably before he had studied the second return, the Prime Minister relied on this comment in a personal signal in which he challenged the C-in-C's tank estimates of the previous day. 'Your [estimate] of 25th instant attributes to the enemy in E. Cyrenaica German tanks 265 runners plus 45 in workshops, whereas the special information which has been sent you states that on 21st there were only 161 German tanks serviceable in the forward areas. I should be glad to know how this important correction strikes you'.[71] The C-in-C replied on 27 April. Whatever else it was – and Cairo had thought of several plausible alternatives – the figure 161 could not represent the number of serviceable German tanks in the forward area. As long ago as 11 March the Enigma had given this number as 159;* since then the Long Range Desert Group had seen 112 German, 46 Italian and 27 unidentified tanks moving into the forward area.[72] The Prime Minister conceded the point on 30 April: 'later most secret information . . . confirms your [estimate] of 25 April'.[73]

The fact that Whitehall and Cairo were coming to agree in their estimates of the Axis tank build-up did nothing to reduce the divergence between their views on strategy. On the contrary, on 3 May, in response to a recent sombre appreciation sent by the Chiefs of Staff of the Japanese threat to India, the C-in-C Middle East went so far as to suggest that it might be wise to stand on the defensive in the Middle East, abandoning the idea of an offensive in north Africa in the summer of 1942 and sending all possible land forces to India. In support, he now argued that no threat from the north would materialise before August, and probably later, and that withdrawals to India would in any case make little difference on the northern front should Germany overcome the Russian resistance on which he was depending for the defence of that front. He also urged that the enemy's resources were unlikely to permit Rommel to make a serious attack in the next three months.[74] As this judgment would otherwise conflict with a mass of intelligence and with appreciations that he himself had recently issued,† it must be supposed that by 'a serious attack' he meant an advance on

---

    * See above, p 353.   † See below, pp 362–363.

    70.   CAB 105/17, No 90 of 27 April 1942.
    71.   ibid, No 88.
    72.   ibid, No 90.
    73.   ibid, No 94.
    74.   CAB 105/9, No 189.

Egypt, as distinct from an attack on Tobruk. In all probability, however, he was in these remarks only embroidering on his central preoccupation, which was the fact that, in view of the tank situation, he was still unwilling to fix an early date for his offensive. On 24 April the Middle East Defence Committee had reaffirmed its warning to Whitehall that no specific date could be guaranteed.[75] And on 6 May – before receiving the Prime Minister's reply to his recent suggestion, a reply which asserted that he could give most help to all theatres by attacking Rommel on 15 May[76] – the C-in-C used Cairo's current estimates of relative tank strengths to justify a proposal that was less radical but still startling for its effects in Whitehall.

The proposal was that he should defer the offensive at least to 15 June. He supported it with the following argument. The enemy, whose tank formations were believed to be nearly up to establishment, would be able to produce on the battlefield on 1 June 360 German tanks and, even disallowing the Littorio Division, 156 Italian tanks. To off-set these numbers Eighth Army needed 700 medium tanks – 540 against the 360 German tanks in the proportion 3 to 2 and 156 to equal the Italians. In fact, however, Eighth Army would have only 460 tanks by 1 June and the number would rise to only 600 by 15 June. Because there would be an additional 250 medium tanks in reserve, this reduction of the superiority on 15 June could be accepted, 'though it necessarily reduces chance of success, and especially of quick success'. On the other hand, there would have to be a longer postponement to August if it turned out that the Littorio Division with its 156 tanks had to be allowed for; and if air forces had to be withdrawn from Libya to meet an emergency in Turkey or elsewhere on the northern front, the Libyan offensive either could not take place or would have to be called off.[77]

To the estimate of the enemy strength that it made on 6 May, Cairo, with the aid of another Enigma return of 6 May[78] and of detailed sighting reports from the Long Range Desert Group, continued to make slight upward amendments at intervals up to 22 May. The estimate of 22 May allowed the enemy 515 serviceable tanks (325 German, 190 Italian) disregarding any reserve. Rommel actually began his offensive on 26 May with 332 German and 228 Italian tanks, a total of 560, and he also had 77 German tanks 'in reserve but not immediately available'.[79] We cannot but be impressed with the Cairo figures, given the difficulty and the novelty

---

75.   ibid, No 162.
76.   Gwyer and Butler, op cit, Vol III part II, p 458.
77.   CAB 105/17, No 103.
78.   MK 5059 of 7 May 1942; CX/MSS/956/T13 of 6 May.
79.   Playfair, op cit, Vol III, p 220.

of the intelligence exercise which had produced them.* Nor did Whitehall dispute them when it responded to the C-in-C's message of 6 May. The Chiefs of Staff felt that the C-in-C should be ordered to make his attack at an early date because of Malta's plight and 'indications of an early German offensive' in north Africa, considerations to which he was paying 'insufficient attention'.[81] In a personal message of 8 May the Prime Minister stopped short of giving an order, but he insisted that risks must be run to help Malta and urged that, having regard 'to the fact that the enemy may be himself planning to attack you early in June', it would be right to take the offensive in May.[82]

The reply to the Prime Minister, sent by the Middle East Defence Committee on 9 May, was no less emphatic. Malta was not vital to the security of Egypt, and while the recovery of Cyrenaica could not guarantee the early revival of Malta's offensive capacity, a premature offensive against Rommel would entail risks in Egypt more serious than the loss of Malta. As for Rommel's intentions, there were some indications that he might attack early in June but they were not very definite. Moreover, 'if the enemy could be induced to attack us, with the forces now at his disposal, in our existing strong positions, while we retain our existing armoured forces in reserve behind them, it might very well be the best thing that could happen'.[83]

□

During this intense debate, as was perhaps inevitable, both sides from time to time cast critical eyes on the system under which the high-grade Sigint was being transmitted from GC and CS to the Middle East authorities. From February 1942 the DMI in Cairo sent a series of telegrams asking for more information and questioning some of the information he was receiving, and this with reference not only to the dispute about tank assessment but to other issues as well. During March and April it emerged that the chief complaint of the Middle East recipients was that they did not always know whether the comments added by GC and CS to its summaries of the decrypts were subjective or based on factual information which GC and CS had withheld from them. For his part the Prime Minister occasionally voiced a similar complaint,

---

* They are the more remarkable in that the historian of army intelligence admits that photographic reconnaissance of enemy armour was quite inadequate before Gazala because only 20″ lens cameras were available and low flying was practically impossible.[80]

80. Mockler-Ferryman, *Military Intelligence Organisation*, p 188.
81. Gwyer and Butler, op cit Vol III, Part II, p 459.
82. CAB 105/17 No 108.
83. CAB 105/9, No 205; CAB 44/96, AL 1200/71, p 39.

maintaining that a GC and CS summary had failed to convey to the Middle East the flavour or the full significance of a decrypt.

In May 1942 steps were taken which went far towards eliminating this kind of misunderstanding. The Senior Air Adviser at GC and CS spent a few weeks in the Middle East – the first GC and CS representative with experience of the Enigma to do so – inducting the intelligence authorities there into GC and CS's problems and methods. From the time of this visit, the Service intelligence branches, GC and CS and the main customers overseas regularly exchanged telegrams in which they freely discussed the doubts and differences they encountered when interpreting the Sigint material. And then the Prime Minister, having instructed 'C' on 30 May to see that the texts of two German situation reports were sent verbatim to General Auchinleck, directed that 'during the present battle [Gazala] . . . messages of strategic importance giving enemy intentions or situation are to be sent to General Auchinleck personally, verbatim . . . ', over and above the normal GC and CS service, thus lifting the ban under which GC and CS had hitherto been required for security reasons to paraphrase all decrypts before transmission.[84] The ban was never formally revived; instead, while normal service continued for reasons of speed and wireless economy to consist of summaries, GC and CS was able to adopt a more relaxed and efficient approach in all its reporting.

The reduction in these ways of what were mainly difficulties of communication by no means removed all possibility that the authorities in the United Kingdom and those in Cairo would reach different conclusions on the basis of the same Ultra clues. It may be noted, however, that they did so for the last time on any important issue during May 1942 – and that the divergence which then developed about Rommel's intentions was not a divergence between London and the intelligence authorities in the Middle East, but a divergence between London and the operational commanders in Cairo, who were reluctant to accept the views of their own intelligence advisers.

Until the middle of April the authorities in London, though aware of and impressed by the rate at which the Axis was building up its supplies to north Africa since achieving Malta's neutralisation, had never supposed that Rommel might become so strong that he could take the initiative. Nor had they had reason to do so. There had been rumours from Axis diplomatic decrypts and SIS reports to the general effect that Germany intended to attack Egypt from Libya, as well as from the Caucasus, Syria and Cyprus,[85] but some of these had said that the attack would not come before

---

84.   Dir/C Archive, 9619 and 9621 of 30 May and 1 June 1942.
85.   WO 208/3573 of 23 March and 4 April 1942.

Russia had been defeated, and the most impressive of them had stated that the capture of Malta would come first.* As early as 10 March the GAF Enigma had given the news that Fliegerführer Afrika was asking for photographs of Tobruk's fortifications, as he had done when Rommel was preparing for an offensive in November 1941, and was also reporting that Rommel's HQ wanted information about all fortifications, anti-aircraft positions and electricity and water installations between the Egyptian frontier and Suez.[86] But this had been an isolated decrypt, unaccompanied by other reliable indications of preparations for an enemy offensive. In a strategic appreciation in the middle of March the JIC concluded that Axis forces in Libya would not be strong enough to exploit their position there before mid-June, and that an earlier British offensive in the desert would be the best way of helping the Russians.[87] But during the second half of April the intelligence authorities in Whitehall were persuaded, as were those in Cairo, that Rommel was preparing to attack first and that he would move before mid-June.

MI's first warning to Whitehall that this was possible came on 20 April.[88] It drew attention to two items in Cairo's situation report of 17 April[89] – the first, the fact that the enemy had recently made local moves that facilitated concealment of concentrations for 'a possible future offensive'; the second, an estimate that the enemy might have in the forward area by May sufficient reserve supplies for 30 days' operations. On 22 April, basing itself on this same estimate, on Cairo's calculations of relative tank and air strengths and on information about enemy order of battle, the JIC ME,† in an appreciation cabled to Whitehall, issued a similar warning: the enemy might consider his superiority in armour sufficient for an attempt to seize Tobruk 'from May onwards'; an earlier offensive would be too risky for him owing to the strength of the Gazala defences; an attempt to move on into Egypt was improbable before September without additional formations; the availability of these would depend on the course of operations in Russia.[91] In the following week these warnings were confirmed by the Enigma.

The Enigma evidence, much of it produced by GC and CS's

---

* See above, p 344.

† This self-constituted body, which brought the heads of Service intelligence in Cairo together at informal drafting meetings, was now making its first appearance. It was not until 1944 that a formal JIC (ME), recognised by Whitehall and chaired by a member of the Foreign Office, was set up in Cairo.[90]

86. MK 3235 of 10 March 1942; CX/MSS/783/T8.
87. JIC (42) 75 (Final) of 14 March.
88. WO 208/3573 of 20 April 1942.
89. CAB 105/17, No 76.
90. Mockler-Ferryman, op cit, p 161.
91. CAB 105/9, No 156.

recovery of Chaffinch, began to accumulate on 19 April, a few days after Rommel had decided to fix his offensive for the end of May.[92] It was learned on 25 April that a parachute rifle brigade was to be brought up by the end of May 'for operations against the British field army and attack on Tobruk'.[93] Another Enigma message, decrypted on 30 April, contained the Panzer Army's reply to a warning from the German general who represented the OKW in Rome to the effect that operations on the Russian front would prevent the despatch of reinforcements to Africa after mid-June; the Panzer Army listed the supplies it needed as a matter of priority, and asked that they should arrive by the end of May.[94] On 24 April GC and CS had deciphered an appreciation from Kesselring referring to information he had received from a reliable source* to the effect that a British attempt to advance to Benghazi was not possible before the beginning of June and concluding that, 'since it is not possible before June, it will come too late'. This might have implied an earlier German attack either on Malta or in north Africa, but the latter interpretation was supported within a day or two by the Enigma evidence that the GAF was being withdrawn from Sicily.[95]† Other important clues were provided by the Enigma before the end of April. On 22 April it disclosed that the Panzer Army was to receive a further 80 tanks during May.[96] Messages of 28 April between the Panzer Army and Rome showed that the Panzer Army had shortened its priority list of 23 April and that it had been assured that an effort would be made to transport the whole of the shortened list by 10 May, and referred to the Panzer Army's 'known next intention'.[97] Some doubt remained as to whether the estimate that the enemy had sufficient supplies for 30 days' operations applied to fuel. On 2 May a further Chaffinch message removed this uncertainty; it stated that the 'consumption unit' – the basic measurement used by the Panzer Army's Quartermaster General in his fuel calculations – would be raised substantially by 1 June.[98] This immediately suggested that the Germans expected to receive further tanks and other vehicles by that date and were assuming that they would have sufficient fuel for them. The longer-term implications of the message took some

---

* This was the cypher of the American Military Attaché in Cairo, see above, p 331 and Appendix 1 (Part (i)), p 640.

† See above, pp 344–345.

92. Cabinet Office Historical Section, EDS/Appreciation/9, Part IIIA, p 33.
93. MK 4594 of 25 April 1942; CX/MSS/921/T14.
94. MK 4827 of 30 April 1942; CX/MSS/935/T9, 936/T11.
95. MK 4570 of 24 April 1942; CX/MSS/919/T4.
96. MK 4815 of 22 April 1942; CX/MSS/935/T30.
97. MK 5066 of 7 May 1942; CX/MSS/955/T2 and 3.
98. MK 5051 of 6 May 1942; CX/MSS/945/T12 of 2 May 1942.

days to work out, but eventually showed that there would be enough fuel for 38 days' operations.

After the receipt of this information the authorities in Whitehall no longer doubted that Rommel intended to attack by the end of May. On 4 May MI summarised the Enigma pointers to this conclusion in its weekly summary for the CIGS,[99] and he reported it to the War Cabinet on 8 May.[100] On 6 May GC and CS drew attention to still later evidence in an appreciation submitted to AI. 'A German offensive in Cyrenaica with the object of taking Tobruk . . . will probably be staged about 20 May. If this limited offensive meets with success an attempt will then be made to build up for a major attack on Egypt during the winter'. By disclosing enemy requests for maps and photographs the Enigma had now confirmed that Tobruk was the immediate objective,[101] and on 5 May it had produced a message from Kesselring ordering the preparation of paratroops, gliders and towing equipment in two stages, with 20 May and 20 June as the target dates.[102] On 9 May the JIC issued its appreciation of the same evidence. The enemy's attack on Tobruk was likely at any time after the third week of May; despite the indications that the enemy was interested in some further operation in June, an advance to the Delta would be ruled out during the summer by Rommel's fuel restrictions after the middle of June.[103]

It was with this appreciation before them that on 10 May the War Cabinet received from Cairo the signal of 9 May in which the Middle East Defence Committee, still resisting Whitehall's pressure for an early British offensive, expressed the view that the indications that Rommel would attack early in June were 'not very definite'.* As the JIC ME had drawn attention to these indications as early as 22 April, and as all the subsequent Enigma evidence had been sent to Cairo as soon as it was received, the Cabinet must have been puzzled by the Middle East Defence Committee's statement. There had, however, been earlier indications that the C-in-C was reluctant to reach the unwelcome conclusion that Rommel might attack first. In his situation report to London of 25 April he had allowed that the enemy might try an offensive against Tobruk in 'early May', but had added that, 'against this, May was likely to be a bad month for operations'.[104] In his report of 2 May

---

* See above, p 358.

99.   WO 208/3573 of 4 May 1942.
100.   CAB 65/30, WM (42) 59 CA of 8 May.
101.   eg CX/MSS/783/T8, 919/T10, 974/T20, 978/T10, 979/T11 and 986/T1.
102.   MK 5038 of 6 May 1942; CX/MSS/953/T5 and 8.
103.   JIC (42) 175 (0) of 9 May 1942.
104.   CAB 105/17, No 86.

he had recognised that increased enemy activity might point to preparations for an eastward thrust, but had concluded that it was primarily defensive.[105] On 3 May, in the signal in which he canvassed the possibility of remaining on the defensive during the summer of 1942, he had asserted that Rommel's resources were unlikely to permit him to make a serious attack during the next three months; and even if he was here referring to an advance on Egypt, and not to an attack on Tobruk, it is noticeable that he had made no reference to the possibility of an attack by Rommel on Tobruk when announcing on 6 May that his own offensive must be delayed till mid-June at the earliest.*

On 10 May the War Cabinet decided to bring the debate to a close. The Prime Minister replied to the message from the Middle East Defence Committee by stressing that Rommel was preparing to attack, and by instructing the C-in-C to attack during May if possible, and 'the sooner the better'; he added that the very latest date for engaging the enemy which he could approve was one which provided a distraction in time to help the passage of the June dark-period convoy to Malta.[106] There followed, in Mr Churchill's words, 'a considerable pause during which we did not know whether he would accept or resign'. By now, however, the timing of the British offensive had become an academic issue. It could not begin before Rommel delivered his attack if, as the intelligence evidence warned, that attack was to be expected in the last week in May; and on 13 May the JIC ME stressed in its own appreciation of the evidence that Rommel's timing was probably dictated by his wish to forestall the British. The Enigma references to his 'projected operation' must mean that he was not prepared to 'surrender the initiative and choice of time to us' by counter-attacking when the British moved, but was determined to strike first.[107] Two days later the C-in-C informed the CIGS that he accepted this conclusion – the evidence had convinced him that the enemy intended to attack about 20 May, possibly earlier, but more probably between that date and the end of the month – but went on to give the assurance that 'our plans to meet such an attack are made, all preparations are in hand.'[108] But there was still some resistance to the evidence in Cairo. On 17 May, the AOC-in-C Middle East telegraphed his 'personal reading of the situation' to the Chief of the Air Staff; it was to the effect that the evidence, which appeared 'to fit snugly', pointed to an Axis attack on Malta. He was at once informed that the CAS did not agree.

---

* See above, p 357.

105.   ibid, No 97.
106.   Playfair, op cit, Vol III, p 204; Churchill, op cit, Vol IV, p 276.
107.   CAB 121/620, SIC file F/Libya/3, JIC ME telegram TOO 1710 of 13 May 1942.   108.   CAB 44/96, p 140.

On 19 May the C-in-C, in another signal to London, recorded that there were 'strong signs that the enemy intends to attack us in the immediate future'. In the same signal – it was his reply to the Prime Minister's message of 10 May – he avoided reference to the request that he should attack in May by agreeing to choose a date that would provide distraction for the June convoy to Malta, and he asked the Prime Minister's consideration of the fact that, owing to the narrowness of his superiority over the enemy on land and in the air, the success of his offensive could not be guaranteed.[109]

By that time Eighth Army's planners had been overwhelmingly preoccupied for several days with meeting the enemy's attack and with preparing a counter-offensive. The preparations provoked another clash between Cairo and Whitehall, this time about the threat to the northern front. In April the authorities in Whitehall had reaffirmed their earlier conclusions on the subject: even if a German offensive in south Russia began by the middle of May, and even if Turkey acquiesced after a rapid German victory, no threat to Syria would develop before mid-July; a German move against Cyprus was also unlikely until Germany had defeated Russia.[110] During May Russian operations in the south delayed the German offensive, and on 22 May the Prime Minister informed the Russian government that the 'intelligence available' suggested that Germany had delayed the offensive from May to June.[111] Two days earlier he had invited the C-in-C Middle East to assume direct command of Eighth Army and had suggested that he should move the New Zealand Division from Syria to Libya.[112] On 22 May General Auchinleck declined both suggestions: in view of such things as a possible threat to Cyprus, he was already weakening the northern front as much as possible, and 'a situation may arise almost at any time when I shall have to decide whether I can continue to reinforce and sustain Eighth Army . . . or whether I must hold back and consider the building up of our northern front . . .'[113]

This problem apart, the appreciations of Cairo and London were now in alignment. On 19 May the JIC ME appreciated that with his present resources Rommel could not hope to do more than throw the British back to the Egyptian frontier.[114] Except that the JIC ME thought that the Germans would invade Malta if Rommel succeeded in taking Tobruk, whereas the intelligence bodies in

---

109. CAB 105/17 No 120.
110. CAB 66/23, WP (42) 158 (JIC (42) 121 of 6 April); JIC (42) 137 of 14
        April; JIC (42) 152 of 25 April.
111. CAB 66/24, WP (42) 219 of 10 June; Churchill, op cit, Vol IV, p 299.
112. CAB 105/17, No 125 of 20 May 1942.
113. ibid, No 129.
114. ibid, No 121.

London remained sceptical on this point, this appreciation coincided with Whitehall's view. Whitehall concurred on 20 May with the comment which the Cs-in-C Middle East attached to the appreciation when relaying it to London – a comment to the effect that, since it was 'most probable that the enemy does not know that we are so fully aware of his proposed action and is hopeful therefore of achieving a large measure of surprise', they should do nothing to show that they expected his attack.[115] In the light of further evidence received during the past few days, neither London nor Cairo now doubted that the attack was imminent.

The Enigma had disclosed that a battle HQ was being prepared for Kesselring at Derna on 17 May,[116] that on 18 May GAF fighters and bombers were about to move from Sicily to Crete and Cyrenaica, where they were to wait at Derna for orders to move forward in 'a few days', and that preparations were being made for a seaborne landing.[117] The details it gave about the seaborne landing showed that this involved only a few hundred men and that it had been hastily thrown together.[118] In addition, indications had begun to come in from the front; the enemy was increasing his reconnaissance and his bombing of British airfields and lines of communication, and his ground and air patrols had begun to put up active opposition to British reconnaissance. In its appreciation of 19 May the JIC ME repeated its view that 'the enemy is preparing an offensive to be launched soon after 20 May'.[119] On 22 May, in the signal to the CIGS in which he gave Cairo's latest estimate of the enemy's tank strength and listed the reinforcements he had brought to the front from Syria, Egypt and elsewhere in preparation for the enemy's attack, the C-in-C struck a more cautious note about its date: it would come 'early, possibly before the end of May, almost certainly before middle June'.[120] But on 22 May XIII Corps, in the northern sector of the Gazala line, expected the attack within 48 hours and on 25 May XXX Corps, which controlled the British armoured striking force, was brought to four hours' readiness.[121] And by the morning of 26 May the units of Eighth Army had been warned that the enemy might be expected to attack that night.[122]

The expectancy of the British forces reflected the fact that although the Enigma did not specify in advance the time of

---

115.   CAB 79/21, COS (42) 156th Meeting, 20 May.
116.   MK 5414 of 17 May 1942; CX/MSS/986/T23.
117.   MK 5487 of 18 May 1942; CX/MSS/991/T7.
118.   eg MKs 5065 of 7 May, 5432 of 17 May, 5603 of 21 May, 5638 of 22 May, 5808 of 25 May 1942; CX/MSS/957/T4, 988/T5, 996/T7 and 15, 1001/T7, 1012/T2.
119.   CAB 105/17, No 121.
120.   ibid, No 128.
121.   CAB 44/97, AI 1200/69, pp 39–40.   122.   ibid, p 51.

Rommel's attack – the night of 26–27 May – it left no room for doubt from 22 May that it would come within the next few days. On 22 May the GAF Enigma revealed that Kesselring had on 21 May summoned a conference at Derna for the following morning and had ordered that all GAF preparations were to be completed by 24 May.[123] On the same day a Chaffinch decrypt gave notice that General Crüwell, the DAK commander who had been on leave in Berlin, was to be back in north Africa on 24 or 25 May.[124] On 23 May another decrypt gave Rommel's instructions that the San Marco battalion, which was to undertake the seaborne landings, was to move to the front at once.[125] On 25 May GC and CS decrypted three messages that suggested an attack in a matter of hours. It was able to send only one of them to the Middle East in advance of the beginning of the offensive,[126] but this warning was supplemented by Army Y, which on 26 May, more than 24 hours before the ground forces made contact, intercepted the code-word *Venezia*, and correctly interpreted it as being the enemy's pre-arranged signal for the start of his attack.

□

Despite having good general warning of the imminence of Rommel's attack, the British lost the battle of Gazala. They might have avoided this setback and its far-reaching consequences – the surrender of Tobruk, the retreat to Alamein and the evacuation of the naval base at Alexandria – if they had delivered an earlier or more effective counter-attack. That this proved beyond them has been attributed generally to defects in organisation, planning and operational decisions.[127] This conclusion makes it difficult to decide how far intelligence affected the course of events, as is clear from the contradictory comments that have been made on the subject. One of them maintains that, although there were operational delays and mistakes, these have to be judged in the light of the fact that 'there are always "might-have-beens" after a battle is over and we know exactly what the enemy was up to'.[128] Another makes no such allowance, but insists that 'sources of information and the means of transmitting it were subject to considerable delay' and that 'decisions . . . were often taken on information which was misleading and out of date'.[129] Over and above the difficulty of

---

123.   MK 5641 of 22 May 1942; CX/MSS/1001/T15.
124.   MK 5654 of 22 May 1942; CX/MSS/1002/T14.
125.   MK 5732 of 23 May 1942; CX/MSS/1006/T1.
126.   MK 5812 of 25 May 1942; CX/MSS/1012/T17.
127.   CAB 105/17, No 209 of 11 June 1942; CAB 44/97, p 111; Churchill, op cit, Vol IV, p 324.
128.   de Guingand, *Operation Victory* (1947) p 117.
129.   Carver, *Tobruk* (1964) pp 251, 252.

deciding how much allowance to make for the uncertainties of battle and for the fact that there were indeed delays in obtaining intelligence,* there are other obstacles which probably mean that the subject is one that will always elude final judgment – the difficulty during battle of separating defects in intelligence about the enemy from defects in information about one's own forces; the problem of distinguishing between having intelligence about the enemy and being able to use it. From such detailed analysis as can be made, however, it is fair to say that, in so far as it applies to information that was available about the enemy, each of the above comments needs to be revised.

To begin with, intelligence failed to divine Rommel's operational plan in advance of his offensive, and was slow to grasp it after the offensive had begun. Despite this, the British forces recovered from the shock of his initial assault. An enormous improvement in intelligence then followed, but did not come in time. By the time the improvement took effect Rommel had succeeded in extricating his own forces from a precarious situation, and had recovered the initiative to an extent that was proof against even plentiful intelligence.

Rommel decided to make his main thrust, with all his mobile forces, round Bir Hacheim at the southern end of the British line. While the Ariete Division took Bir Hacheim, 15th and 21st Panzer Divisions would strike north behind the British forward defences, destroying the British armour, and 90th Light Division's motorised units would race to the high ground dominating the eastern approaches to Tobruk with the task of seizing British supply dumps and delaying the arrival of British reinforcements. All this during 27 May. On 28 May the two Panzer divisions would turn against the rear of Eighth Army's defensive positions at the northern end of the Gazala line while the Italian XXI Corps (infantry) joined 90th Light's non-mobile units in a frontal attack on the same positions from the west.[130] On the afternoon of 26 May, at the start of the main thrust, the Italian infantry supported by some German tanks were to advance in the north, and during the night of 26–27 May they were to keep up noise and movement in order to give the impression that the main thrust was to be a frontal attack north of the Trigh Capuzzo. To reinforce the deception plan the units taking part in the southern sweep were to deceive the British reconnaissance by leaving their tents behind, by facing east during halts and by observing complete wireless silence, and some of them were to thrust north-eastward during 26 May and turn south only after dark.[131]

---

* See above, p 22.

130. EDS/Appreciation/9, Part III A, pp 36, 40, 45.
131. Playfair, op cit, Vol III, p 219; WO 169/3936, Eighth Army Intelligence Summary No 220 of 30 May 1942.

That Rommel had the choice between a frontal attack and an outflanking movement to the south was obvious to the British commanders. So was the fact that unless his operational plans were disclosed in the Enigma traffic – the nature of which was such that this could not be expected – they would have to infer them from what they could learn from reconnaissance and front-line intelligence, supplemented with luck by fragmentary Sigint, about the movements and last-minute locations of his formations. In the event the Enigma yielded no comprehensive statement, and during May they failed to detect the radical changes which Rommel made in his order of battle in preparation for his outflanking attack.

If we discard the benefit of hindsight it is no easy matter to decide whether this failure was the penalty they paid for mistakes in assessing the evidence or is, rather, entirely attributable to the fact that the evidence they obtained was incomplete and ambiguous.* In the last resort, however, the failure was less crucial than the confusion which accompanied the evidence that came in when Rommel began to move. Although the final British dispositions were much influenced by Cairo's initial judgment that the enemy would probably make an attack aimed directly against Tobruk, they allowed for considerable uncertainty as to which course he would adopt. 22nd and 2nd Armoured Brigades of 1st Armoured Division were stationed against a frontal attack and it was emphasised that it was their primary task to deal with that. But XXX Corps' most powerful brigade, 5th Armoured Brigade of 7th Armoured Division, was deployed 15 miles further south primarily against the possibility of an outflanking movement. In the event of a frontal attack it was judged that the British defence lines and minefields would delay the German armour while 4th Armoured Brigade joined up with 1st Armoured Division. In the event of an outflanking attack it was judged that British ground and air reconnaissance would give sufficient warning to enable 4th Armoured Brigade to move south and be joined by one or both of 1st Armoured Division's two brigades. On the evening of 26 May, moreover, when XXX Corps obtained the first indications that the enemy was on the move, it accepted that, although it was still probable that the enemy's main weight was in the north, the Germans had a considerable battle group in the south; that on this account 'a thrust south of Bir Hacheim becomes more of a threat than a diversion'; and that 'we must be prepared, as we are, to meet an attack on both of the Corps' fronts'.[132] To this extent, while correct appreciation of Rommel's preliminary changes of disposi-

---

* See Appendix 16.

132. WO 169/4033, XXX Corps Operational Instruction No 46 of 26 May 1942; CAB 44/97, p 38.

tion would have given the British a decisive advantage, the failure to detect them was less responsible for Rommel's achievement of surprise than was the breakdown of the assumption that if he did move a large force round the flank there would be adequate notice from British ground and air patrols.

This assumption broke down when 7th Armoured Division's commander doubted whether the indications of the enemy's movements during the night of 26–27 May were sufficient to justify committing 4th Armoured Brigade to its southerly battle position and when 1st Armoured Division's commander proved reluctant to part with 22nd Armoured Brigade. Both of these pieces of hesitation have been related to the feeling of Eighth Army's commanders that the C-in-C, with his 'extensive and usually very accurate sources of intelligence', had good grounds for expecting a frontal attack.[133] It is true that the C-in-C was still expecting a strong attack in the north on 27 May and that on 28 May he was surprised that it had not come.[134] On the other hand, it was as much the responsibility of the Eighth Army commander as it was of GHQ to determine the direction of the enemy's attack; and it must be added that the early indications of the enemy's movements were far from conclusive.

The first of these indications came during the afternoon of 26 May with the enemy's feint in the north. The tanks involved in this attack were recognised as German, but it was observed that they were less numerous than had been expected and that no thrust developed.[135] Later that afternoon, however, the RAF's tactical reconnaissance sighted further to the south a considerable force of tanks moving north-east towards the centre of the British line, and this was unfortunately the part of the enemy's main force that was taking this route during daylight for deception purposes before turning south-east. XXX Corps thought it represented a reconnaissance in force and that the direction of the enemy's main thrust could not yet be determined.[136] At 2300, with reports of both these movements to hand, the Eighth Army commander concluded that the enemy's offensive had begun, but that it was still too early to deduce where the main attack would come.[137] During the night there followed several reports from British armoured car patrols of enemy columns moving south-east, but it was impossible to tell how big these columns were, or whether they were German or Italian, or whether they represented the only enemy line of

---

133.   Carver, op cit, pp 168–169, 175.
134.   CAB 105/17, No 136 of 27 May, No 142 of 28 May 1942.
135.   CAB 44/97, p 48; CAB 105/17 No 134 of 26 May; WO 169/3936, No 217 of 27 May 1942.
136.   WO 169/4033 of 26 May.
137.   CAB 44/97, p 75.

advance.[138] By 0230 on 27 May the reports had persuaded 7th Armoured Division's commander that the enemy was making a very strong thrust round the south. His 4th Armoured Brigade was warned to be ready from first light and 1st Armoured Division was ordered to be ready to send 22nd Armoured Brigade to join 7th Armoured Division. But because 7th Armoured Division's commander had become uncertain[139] no movements had been ordered by dawn, when a tactical reconnaissance aircraft sighted what was obviously Rommel's main force – a mass of vehicles including some 400 tanks – south of Bir Hacheim.

XXX Corps ordered 4th and 22nd Armoured Brigades to their southern battle positions when this report was received, but before they could move they were surprised by the enemy who had already overrun the modest force which had been sent south at the last moment to guard against a flanking attack. 4th Armoured Brigade suffered heavy damage in an attack by 15th Panzer Division. 22nd Armoured Brigade was attacked by both Panzer divisions and lost many tanks. By 1000 on 27 May 90th Light Division's motorised units, which had parted company with the DAK to make a dash to the north-east, had overrun the HQ of 7th Armoured Division and scattered 7th Motor Brigade.

Despite their initial successes, Rommel's forces encountered heavy resistance during 27 May and by the evening of that day, widely scattered, short of their objectives and with their supply lines threatened, they were themselves in a precarious position. On 28 May, however, Rommel successfully started to concentrate them in the Knightsbridge area. At that juncture he still hoped that they could resume the offensive when he had forced a supply route through the minefields, but on 29 May they used up most of their remaining fuel and ammunition in further heavy fighting and Rommel, with his supply routes still insecure, was forced to go over to the defensive in a more concentrated area behind a screen of anti-tank guns. On 30 May and 1 June costly British attacks on this position failed, and on 5 and 6 June what was intended to be the definitive attack on the position ended in a decisive defeat for Eighth Army – a defeat which the C-in-C called 'the turning point of the battle'[140] and later commentators have accepted as 'the blow from which Eighth Army was not to recover'.[141]

During this crucial phase of the battle intelligence, though it was improving, was doing so only slowly. Mainly from accurate air reconnaissance, the British knew by the evening of 27 May that

---

138.　ibid, pp 55, 75; Carver, op cit, pp 174–175.
139.　Carver, op cit, p 175.
140.　CAB 44/97, p 92.
141.　Carver, op cit, p 205.

they had checked Rommel's thrusts, that he had lost about 100 tanks and that he had not breached the minefields.[142] From Army Y, captured documents and POW they knew that the main thrust, checked in the Knightsbridge area, had been made by 21st Panzer Division, that 15th Panzer Division was in the same area, and that the sweep to El Adem had been made by strong elements of 90th Light Division.[143] Until the evening of 28 May, however, when this information was confirmed and amplified by the capture of the operational orders for Rommel's offensive,[144] they continued to think that the bulk of 90th Light and about 100 German tanks remained west of the Gazala position, ready to make a frontal attack.[145] And as late as 29 May, though no longer expecting a heavy frontal attack, they remained apprehensive about seaborne and airborne attacks against the Gazala line in the north. This anxiety was the result of earlier Enigma references to preparations for such attacks.[146] On the other hand, since the opening of the battle the Enigma had remained virtually silent about the enemy's plans and situation. Until 30 May all but two of the decrypts dealt with GAF operations and shipping movements. Of the exceptions the first, sent to the Middle East on 27 May, showed Kesselring ordering the GAF to prepare for a move to Acroma or El Adem[147] and the second, sent out on 28 May, showed that the Italian mobile corps had been ordered on 27 May to move north-east from Bir Hacheim.[148]

During 29 May it became clear from air and ground sightings that the enemy was digging in behind protective gun and infantry positions and trying to open up an additional gap through the minefields,[149] On the same day Army Y provided evidence of his supply difficulties, disclosing that 15th Panzer Division had started with water for only four days and that other formations were running short of petrol,[150] and a captured document showed that 15th Panzer Division had been urged to economise with ammunition.[151] On the basis of this evidence it was judged during 30 May that the enemy was weakening, and perhaps preparing to

142. CAB 44/97, p 76; WO 169/3936, No 218 of 28 May 1942; AIR 41/26, pp 147–149.
143. WO 169/3936, No 218 of 28 May 1942.
144. CAB 44/97, p 76; CAB 105/17, No 143 of 28 May 1942; WO 169/3936, No 219 of 29 May 1942.
145. CAB 105/17 Nos 132, 136, 142, and 143 of 28 May 1942; WO 169/3936, No 218 of 28 May 1942.
146. CAB 105/17, No 121 of 19 May 1942.
147. MK 5911 of 27 May 1942; CX/MSS/1019/T16.
148. MK 5923 of 28 May 1942; CX/MSS/1020/T30.
149. WO 169/3036, No 220 of 30 May 1942.
150. ibid, No 219 of 29 May and No 221 of 31 May 1942.
151. ibid, No 220 of 30 May 1942.

withdraw, and estimates of his remaining tank strength added to the feeling of confidence.[152] These estimates were based entirely on visual evidence, mainly RAF sightings, but they calculated with some accuracy that there were 150 German and 100 Italian tanks in the battle area. As against this force, Eighth Army had 240 medium tanks, plus 160 Infantry tanks, and expected 150 more medium tanks by 2 June.[153] In the course of 30 May, moreover, Eighth Army at last began to receive Army Enigma in quantity from GC and CS. The first decrypts – the product of the Chaffinch traffic of 27, 28 and 29 May – included the Panzer Army's evening reports for these three days. There was also an Italian summary of the land fighting up to 29 May. They gave no support to the view that Rommel was withdrawing, but they emphasised the serious-ness of his position.[154] The Eighth Army intelligence summary of the morning of 31 May appreciated that 'the only question . . . is how much of his force the enemy will be able to extricate'.[155] Rommel was no less optimistic, but it is to be noted that his own staff found his optimism 'scarcely comprehensible' at this stage.[156]

By the morning of 1 June Eighth Army had received from the Enigma firm evidence that Rommel was not intending to withdraw. During 31 May the decrypts disclosed that he had learned that the British planned a counter-attack for that night and that he planned to stand and meet it.[157] A further decrypt, sent out from GC and CS at 0604 on 1 June, announced his further intentions: the Panzer Army would let the British attack its strong position and would counter-attack after destroying the British tanks with its anti-tank screen.[158] Of the effectiveness of the screen, which was the basis for Rommel's confidence and which was to play a decisive part in the developments of the following week, Eighth Army had already received a foretaste. During the night of 30–31 May the German guns, particularly the 88 mm, had repulsed the first attack on the Cauldron – as Rommel's defensive position had come to be called – and administered heavy losses; and on the morning of 1 June Eighth Army's intelligence summary emphasised for the first time the importance of the screen.[159] The same intelligence summary also reflected the contents of the latest Enigma information: it

152. CAB 105/17, Nos 148, 149, 150, 152 of 30 May, No 153 of 31 May; CAB 44/97, p 80; Carver, op cit, p 163; WO 169/3936, No 221 of 31 May 1942.
153. CAB 105/17, Nos 150 and 152 of 30 May 1942; Carver, op cit, pp 187–188; CAB 44/97, p 78; Playfair, op cit, Vol III, p 220 (n).
154. MKs 6012, 6054 of 30 May, 6064 of 31 May 1942; CX/MSS/1026/T4, 1028/T7.
155. WO 169/3936, No 221 of 31 May 1942.
156. EDS/Appreciation/9, Part IIIA, pp 91, 98.
157. MKs 6077 and 6104 of 31 May 1942; CX/MSS/1029/T18, 1030/T22.
158. MK 6146 of 1 June 1942; CX/MSS/1032/T21.
159. WO 169/3936, no 222 of 1 June; CAB 105/17, No 159 of 1 June 1942.

appreciated now that the enemy intended to stand and if possible to resume his advance. By this time the Eighth Army commander and the C-in-C had concluded that Rommel's plan was to form a bridgehead, rather than to effect a withdrawal, and that they would have to liquidate the Cauldron position before launching a counter-offensive.[160]

The Eighth Army commander welcomed the opportunity of destroying Rommel's force which now seemed to be opening up.[161] However, after a second assault on the Cauldron had failed on the night of 1 June, again with heavy losses, he postponed a definitive attack until the night of 5 June. During the interval the Enigma made it plain that the enemy expected the attack.[162] It also established that the total number of tanks in the German formations was 129 on 1 June and 133 on the following day.[163] An inaccurate sighting report by tactical reconnaissance to the effect that there were 180 German and Italian tanks west of the minefield, and only 120 in the Cauldron, gave colour to the belief that 21st Panzer Division had been withdrawn and thus produced some uncertainty about the composition of the enemy forces.[164] But this uncertainty did not impede the preparation of the British attack, which was planned to begin with the destruction of the anti-tank screen by heavy artillery bombardment and infantry assault, and it contributed nothing to its failure, which sprang from the fact that the screen escaped the initial artillery bombardment.

How far the screen owed its survival to a British mistake in plotting the enemy's defence positions, and how far this was an operational mistake and not an intelligence matter, are questions that are not easily answered. The enemy positions were determined by infantry patrols and tactical reconnaissance – there was no Sigint information and there is no evidence that PR was employed – but they in fact lay further to the west than had been thought.[165]

□

With the resumption of the fighting, and most notably after the failure of the British attack of 5–6 June, British intelligence underwent a pronounced – not to say a dramatic – improvement.

160. CAB 44/97, pp 80–81; Playfair, op cit, Vol III, p 229.
161. CAB 44/97, pp 80–81, 85.
162. MKs 6171 and 6189 of 2 June, 6210 of 3 June, 6272 of 4 June 1942; CX/MSS/1037/T8, 1039/T34, 1045/T3.
163. MKs 6392 of 7 June, 6526 of 10 June 1942; CX/MSS/1055/T6, 1064/T19.
164. CAB 44/97, pp 84–85; WO 169/3936, Nos 223 of 2 June, 226 of 5 June 1942; CAB 105/17, No 170 of 3 June 1942.
165. CAB 44/97, p 85; Playfair, op cit, Vol III, p 233; WO 169/3936, No 223 of 2 June 1942.

Contact with the enemy naturally produced an increase in the yield from the non-Sigint sources – POW, captured documents, air and ground reconnaissance. More important, the capacity to exploit a wide variety of Sigint sources, a capacity which had been developing steadily if slowly during previous months, expanded enormously as soon as battle had been joined.

Until the end of May 1942 GC and CS was breaking the daily Chaffinch settings at least a week late – often with greater delay – and until Rommel began his attack the Chaffinch decrypts were providing only fragmentary information of operational value. From the beginning of June these settings were being broken with an average delay of 24 hours and were thus yielding more advance information about the enemy's intentions, the reduction in delay being directly due to the enemy's increased use of W/T for his cypher traffic. Even when the delay was more than 24 hours the greater density of the traffic still produced a fuller picture of the enemy's supply and operational situation. Nor was Chaffinch any longer the only Army Enigma key to be read. Since November 1941, when it had been read for a week with the help of captured material,* the key used by the Panzer Army for communications between army, corps and division (Phoenix) had resisted GC and CS's best efforts; the signals being mainly tactical and transmitted on low power, by no means all of them could be intercepted in the United Kingdom, and great administrative difficulties delayed the receipt at GC and CS of the signals intercepted in the Middle East. But these problems were so far overcome by 1 June 1942 that from that date GC and CS was able to decrypt much of the Phoenix traffic. The result was a great increase in intelligence despite the fact that, more so than the Chaffinch traffic, the Phoenix decrypts continued to be subject to interruptions and delays. Another Army Enigma key broken at this time, and named Thrush by GC and CS, carried very full information about the transport by air of supplies and troop reinforcements to north Africa.

As always during the course of operations, the GAF Enigma keys were hardly less valuable than the Army traffic as a source of information about the land battle. The GAF general purpose key – the Red – was being broken early each day. From the beginning of the fighting this was producing a great deal of ground intelligence in addition to regular information about the order of battle, serviceability, operations and intentions of the GAF; and after 21 June, when the Panzer Army was advancing beyond Tobruk, well ahead of the GAF's bases, it was to throw even more light on the ground fighting than it usually did. Of the separate Fliegerkorps keys that had been introduced at the beginning of

---

* See above, pp 295, 310.

1942* those of Fliegerkorps II – Locust – and Fliegerkorps X – Gadfly – were read less regularly than the Red until the end of 1942, but Primrose, the key of Luftgau Afrika, the formation responsible for the administration and supply of the GAF in Africa, was a prolific source of information about the enemy's logistic situation. Together with Chaffinch it was to become especially valuable from the end of June, when the enemy had reached Alamein and was beginning once again to encounter grave supply difficulties.

Even more valuable was the fact that just before the opening of the Gazala battle GC and CS had broken the key – named Scorpion – introduced for communications between on the one hand Fliegerführer Afrika's close support units and, on the other, the GAF's liaison officers[†] with the Panzer Army, the DAK and the Panzer divisions. Until it was withdrawn in February 1943 this key was regularly read with very little delay, GC and CS having discovered that on the first day of each month it could predict the settings which would be used in a scrambled order for the rest of the month. Partly for this reason and partly because little of the traffic could be intercepted in the United Kingdom, the decision was taken to have the traffic decrypted in the Middle East as well as at GC and CS, and its decryption at CBME in Heliopolis began on 12 July. In June and July 1942, during the British retreat to Alamein and the first round of fighting there, it yielded not only intelligence about GAF plans, but also a greater amount of current information about the ground fighting, including the location and intentions of the German divisions, than any other Enigma key.

The opening up of these new sources of high-grade Sigint from the end of May meant that the British now had access, if with different degrees of completeness, to every Enigma key used in the African fighting.[‡] This great achievement did not mean, however, that they knew everything about the enemy. Given the flow of decrypts reaching Cairo and the Western Desert, the British commanders should have been able to get an accurate grasp of the enemy's general position. As the fighting wore on, indeed, they more and more succeeded in doing so, their intelligence staffs becoming adept at using the Enigma to correct their first appreciations of recent operations and the enemy's latest moves, to track the whereabouts of his important formations and maintain a well-nigh perfect check on his order of battle, and to build up an excellent

---

* See above, 331.

† Fliegerverbindungsoffiziere (Flivos).

‡ The Enigma key introduced for use by surface ships in the Mediterranean and the Black Sea (named Porpoise by GC and CS) was an exception. GC and CS began to read this regularly in September 1942, having first broken it in August, see above, p 28 and Appendix 4.

knowledge of his supply and administrative situation. Even in these directions, however, the Enigma did not close all the gaps in their knowledge at once. For example, their supply information improved in July, when the Panzer Army began to include a short supply summary in its daily report; but the full ten-day returns of Rommel's Quartermaster now used a new pro-forma which was not sufficiently unravelled to provide information to the Middle East until the eve of the second battle of Alamein.

A more serious limitation, and an enduring one, was the fact that, while the sheer bulk of the Enigma intelligence made a vital contribution to the general grasp of the operational situation, not many of the decrypts directly illuminated the enemy's intentions and of these some necessarily reached the Western Desert too late to be of immediate use. This limitation was most pronounced in the case of the most tactical of the Enigma signals. Thus, most of the Scorpion traffic could only be intercepted locally and had to be sent back to Cairo and the United Kingdom for decryption. This difficulty applied less to the GAF general traffic, since this was almost invariably read with little delay and GC and CS was often able to give the Middle East some hours' warning of the GAF's intentions; but warnings based on this information were liable to be delayed in transmission from Air HQ Western Desert to No 211 Group, which controlled the RAF's forward fighter operations. With the other Enigma keys these difficulties were compounded by delay in breaking the daily settings. The Chaffinch delay was usually 24 hours; and with a whole day's traffic being broken a day late, there was further delay while GC and CS scanned and sorted the signals and prepared summaries of them for transmission to the Middle East. In these circumstances it was something of a luxury for the British commands to get advance notice of the movements and intentions of the enemy's ground forces.

When they did get such advance notice via the Enigma they owed it largely to the fact that the Panzer Army's daily report could be recognised externally at GC and CS and was given high priority there. The report was normally issued late in the evening, just before the Chaffinch setting changed. From the middle of June, when GC and CS began on most days to break the Chaffinch settings in the small hours of the following day, it was not uncommon for the decrypt of the report to reach Eighth Army HQ within 12 hours of its transmission by the Germans, and the report sometimes contained a summary of Rommel's intentions for the day following its transmission. Except when they were in this way exceptionally fortunate, however, the commands had to deduce the enemy's reactions and intentions from the accumulating evidence on his general situation. This came from the Enigma, POW and captured documents, but was amplified and brought up to date by ground and air reconnaissance and now, for the first time, also by the contribution received from Army and RAF Y.

In the lull in the fighting before the Gazala battle Army Y had begun to undergo considerable improvement in resources and organisation. The interception and exploitation of enemy low-grade and medium-grade codes and cyphers was expanded, DF facilities were increased, Traffic Analysis of the German signals system was organised at Eighth Army HQ; and steps were taken to ensure that the Y work done at Cairo, Eighth Army HQ and at corps level was better co-ordinated and its results exchanged. The improvement was far from complete at the beginning of the Gazala battle – it was to continue up to the second battle of Alamein in October, when the Army Y organisation in the Middle East comprised 2,400 all ranks as compared with 1,300 in May 1942. It was in any case off-set by the fact that the intelligence staffs of the Y units – those who were responsible for interpreting Y evidence – remained understrength and cut off from the operational intelligence staffs and from other sources of information.* But the Gazala battle showed up these defects, and within a fortnight Army Y was fully integrated into the operational intelligence process at Eighth Army HQ. Thereafter it produced such a flow of tactical intelligence about even the enemy's smaller units that, in the opinion of the officer who was to become the head of Eighth Army's operational intelligence, 'Ultra [i.e. the Enigma] and Ultra only put intelligence on the map' in the Western Desert, but in battle it was the Army Y service that was usually more valuable than the Ultra.[166]† This was also true of the Italian ground forces, for while the Italian Army's high-grade cypher had finally ceased to be readable at the end of 1941, the Army Y organisation continued to exploit several of its lower grade codes and cyphers and to obtain useful information from them.

Though it took place on a smaller scale, the expansion of RAF Y, an organisation which was employing 1,000 people by the end of 1942, also played its part in off-setting the delays which restricted the value of the Enigma as a source of operational intelligence – and in compensating for the fact that, although GC and CS was able to read much of it till the end of 1942, the north African traffic in the high-grade cypher of the Italian Air Force was now yielding information only about reinforcements and transfers, and that only in occasional messages. Unfortunately, for W/T purposes the GAF had from 1 April 1942 changed the code used for air to ground communications (Auka), which could be decyphered only at Cheadle and at the RAF Y base unit at Cairo with the help of

---

* See Appendix 16.
† But it was found that German tank R/T was too highly tactical to be of much value.

166.   WO 208/3575, Williams, The Use of Ultra by the Army, pp 3, 8.

information signalled to it from Cheadle. On this account the two RAF Y units which were at Sidi Barrani and Alexandria had to confine themselves to intercepting the GAF W/T traffic and sending it back to Cairo for decryption. Cairo was still able to provide advance warning of attacks on British convoys, raids on Alexandria and the Suez Canal and enemy aircraft movements generally, including the important transport flights across the Mediterranean. In relation to the fighting on land, however, delay in getting the results from Cairo to the forward areas robbed the W/T traffic of much of its operational value. On the other hand, the two mobile R/T units which the RAF had formed by June 1942 now came into their own as a source of tactical intelligence in the battle area.

Soon after their arrival in the desert they were re-sited, in April 1942, so as to be in touch by telephone with the operations room of No 211 Group. When the land fighting was resumed this arrangement, which had produced useful results in the shape of advance warnings of GAF attacks and emphasised the importance of exploiting the GAF's voice traffic, proved inadequate. Like their counterparts in the Army, the RAF Y authorities had not solved the problem of interpreting the Y material for the operational intelligence authorities and the operational intelligence authorities were not integrating its results with the intelligence coming in from other sources. After the battle of Gazala, however, though not until nearly a month had passed since Rommel had begun his offensive, the RAF, like the Army, integrated Y with operational intelligence by placing the R/T units under the direct operational control of No 211 Group and ensuring that the R/T information was dove-tailed into other intelligence about the battle situation as a whole.

Thereafter the R/T units made an important contribution to the growing body of information about the organisation and state of the GAF by reporting regularly on such things as its order of battle, the serviceability of its airfields, its casualties and replacements, and its fuel stocks.[167] More important, with assistance on the one hand from the RAF base unit in Cairo, whose Traffic Analysis determined which GAF units were using which frequencies, and on the other hand from the fact that the GAF made free use of R/T during active operations, the units were a major source of current operational intelligence. As with that of their counterparts during the Battle of Britain,* it is difficult to illustrate the impact of their work on particular operations. But it is clear that the operational authorities relied on them for warnings as to when enemy aircraft

---

* See Volume I, p 179 et seq.

167.   AIR 40/2323, Humphreys, The Use of Ultra in the Mediterranean and West African Theatres of War, p 2.

were airborne, for information as to their types and approximate positions, for locating the GAF's control stations and observer posts, and for finding gaps in the enemy's radar system. As during the Battle of Britain, again, they were able in these and other ways – notably by intercepting enemy pilots' reports of the height at which they were flying, by distinguishing between true and diversionary raids, by sometimes revealing the enemy's objectives and by reporting low-flying aircraft – to supply crucial data that could not be obtained by the RAF's own radar network.

If Y, in the RAF as in the Army, was thus from June 1942 becoming more experienced and better organised, its improvement as a source of tactical intelligence was the more rapid because it took place within the framework of the steadily increasing familiarity with the enemy – with his organisation and his normal behaviour, with the composition and the history of his main formations, with even the personal characteristics of his commanders – of which the major source was the high-grade German Sigint. This was especially the case in the RAF, where intelligence staffs had been receiving the product of the GAF Enigma for over two years and were now turning their experience of it to account when they handled other information and took their decisions. It was less true in the Army, which had benefited much less from the Enigma before the Gazala battle and which even now, on account of the greater delay in breaking the Enigma settings and the greater importance of field codes and cyphers in the ground fighting, relied more heavily than the RAF on the independent contribution of its Y units. Even in the Army, however, the great improvement in the Y service from June 1942 was due not only to its own expansion and not only to the great increase in the volume of enemy traffic that accompanied the heavy fighting, but also to the fact that the regular supply of Enigma was at last laying down a firm framework within which the Y product could be better assessed.*

Nor was this complementary advance, so crucial for the better use of both sources, confined to Y and high-grade Sigint. It applied also to the relationship between Sigint and the other sources of intelligence. On some subjects, if not on all, the exploitation of the other sources – POW, captured documents, ground patrols, visual and photographic air reconnaissance – increasingly profited from guidance derived from Sigint; and in consequence they made an increasingly valuable contribution to the sum total of information.

---

* Unfortunately the restrictions remained by which the Y authorities were not privy to the Enigma information and were thus less useful than they could have been. GC and CS nevertheless transmitted to the Middle East, for the use of the local Y units, both Army and Air, details of call-signs, frequencies and routines derived from the Enigma. This was of great help to field Sigint and contributed substantially to its success.[168]

168.   Clayton, op cit, p 215.

Photographic reconnaissance of the desert, for example, was steadily increased by a variety of measures and a variety of units. The Army's tactical reconnaissance squadrons were flown with fighter escorts, and received further protection from the extension of the early warning radars. No 2 PRU, which had been re-equipped with Spitfires in February, operated a Flight in the Western Desert for long-range strategic sorties; No 60 SAAF Survey Flight, re-equipping with Baltimores, was to survey and map territory behind enemy lines, and in addition there was visual reconnaissance from the so-called Strategic Reconnaissance Unit operating under the direct control of Air HQ in the desert.[169] At the end of May Air HQ and Eighth Army HQ set up a joint HQ to control PR operations; this step produced economy and efficiency, through better co-ordination in meeting the demands for PR coverage and in handling the conduct of sorties. But it did not ensure that the results of air reconnaissance were fully integrated with what was being learned from other intelligence, and with what was known of the battle situation as a whole. It was not until July that No 240 (later 285) Reconnaissance Wing RAF was formed to co-ordinate all reconnaissance effort, visual and photographic, in the Western Desert.*

□

These advances on the intelligence front ushered in a period in which, beginning during the battle of Gazala and ending only with the expulsion of the Axis forces a year later, the British forces in north Africa were supplied with more information about more aspects of the enemy's operations than any forces enjoyed during any important campaign of the Second World War – and, probably, of any earlier war. In time, the intelligence helped them to turn the tide in the north African campaign. General Auchinleck received the more important of the high-grade decrypts verbatim from 1 June, as we have seen;† it was on this account that he took an SCU party to his Command post when he left Cairo to take personal command of the Eighth Army on 25 June.‡ He believed that, but for the Sigint, 'Rommel would certainly have got through to Cairo'.[170] Nor does an analysis of the fighting in July leave much doubt that the Sigint did indeed make a significant contribution to his last and greatest victory, the first battle of Alamein.§ But it did

---

* See below, pp 402–403.
† See above, p 359.
‡ This became a regular practice in later battles in all the theatres of war.
§ See below, p 392 et seq.

169.   AIR 41/26, p 99; AIR 41/7, pp 60–61.
170.   AIR 40/2323, p 7.

not help Eighth Army to avoid the reverses, the most serious it ever sustained, that followed when Rommel had halted the British attack of 5–6 June.

The outpost of Bir Hacheim fell on 11 June. During Rommel's attack on it from 2 June the Enigma gave advance notice of some of the GAF's raids[171] and carried complaints from the GAF about the heavy losses it was sustaining and the lack of support from the Panzer Army.[172] Army Y revealed the intentions of the enemy ground forces for 4 June,[173] and from 7 June much information about the mounting scale of their attack. The Y information was valuable to the RAF during its many attacks on 4 June, both on the dive-bombers and against the land assault.* Except for helping the RAF, however, none of the intelligence could be put to operational use: Eighth Army was in no position to relieve the garrison.

The resistance of the Bir Hacheim garrison was a further setback for Rommel's plan. Having captured his operational orders, Eighth Army knew that he had hoped to seize Tobruk on D plus 4. By 8 June it knew from the Enigma that he had been giving priority to the Bir Hacheim assault from 6 June, when he assumed personal command of it.[174] On the other hand, on 9 June it learned from the Enigma that he was refusing to use tanks against Bir Hacheim lest this should prejudice his ability to advance to Tobruk with the least possible delay.[175] Another Enigma message of 12 June outlined his next move: as soon as he had disposed of the British armour in the Knightsbridge area, and of Bir Hacheim, he intended to roll up the Gazala position by cutting the coast road and to strike at Tobruk via Acroma and El Adem.[176] At the same time, the Enigma left no doubt about his urgent need for reinforcements and supplies. The Panzer Army's evening report of 7 June, received on 8 June, had revealed that its tank strength was down to 40 per cent, though it would recover to 60 per cent in a few days, and that personnel strength was down to 60 per cent.[177] On 6 June Rommel had asked for 6,000 men immediately. On 9 June he ordered every fit man to the front, and further decrypts spoke of 15th Panzer Division's

---

* It was on this occasion that the Free French garrison signalled 'Merci pour le RAF' and the RAF replied 'Merci pour le sport'.

171.   MKs 6235 of 3 June, 6252 of 4 June, 6284 of 5 June, 6357 of 6 June, 6411 of 8 June, 6440 and 6473 of 9 June 1942; CX/MSS/1042/T8, 1043/T15, 1047/T11, 1052/T22, 1058/T1, 1060/T12, 1061/T15.

172.   MKs 6277, 6297 and 6299 of 5 June, 6328 and 6329 of 6 June, 6375 of 7 June, 6403 of 8 June, 6549 and 6555 of 11 June 1942; CX/MSS/1047/T4, 1048/T2 and 6, 1050/T1 and 10, 1053/T15, 1057/T1, 1065/T18, 1066/T10.

173.   AIR 41/26, p 154.

174.   MK 6431 of 8 June 1942; CX/MSS/1059/T6.

175.   MK 6473 of 9 June 1942; CX/MSS/1061/T15.

176.   MK 6645 of 12 June 1942; CX/MSS/1071/T16.

177.   MKs 6423 of 8 June, 6494 of 9 June 1942; CX/MSS/1059/T1.

desperate need for replacements.[178] By 11 June, moreover, the Enigma had also put an end to speculation that a further German light division might have been sent to north Africa. The speculation had been started by hints from POW at the end of May; the Enigma established that what had arrived were four battalions of general replacements each a thousand strong.[179]

On 11 June, in the light of this evidence, GS Int GHQ ME produced an appreciation of the German intentions which was largely accurate and which envisaged an all-out attack on Tobruk.[180] Eighth Army commander's appreciation of the same day assumed that if Rommel continued his advance he would limit his attack against Tobruk to air and sea raids, stressed the difficulties he must be having after 15 days of continuous fighting, and still allowed that the enemy might decide to withdraw. Eighth Army's aim was 'not to let the enemy withdraw and reorganise'.[181] By the morning of 12 June it was clear that Rommel was not withdrawing and had no intention of doing so. During the previous day tactical reconnaissance and Army Y had warned that his forces in the Bir Hacheim area were moving north-east in the direction of El Adem, and had established the number of tanks taking part in the advance and the fact that Rommel was personally leading them. Reporting on this evidence on the morning of 12 June, Eighth Army's intelligence summary judged that Rommel was bent on pressing his original plan, but that the attempt to do so 'with depleted forces is an act of great boldness'. 'A second reverse would not be so easily retrieved by an improvisation of the kind at which the German commander is adept'.[182]

Eighth Army received the Enigma decrypt of Rommel's orders for the advance of 11 June on the morning of 12 June. Planning this advance in the light of his field Sigint unit's intercepts of Eighth Army's radio communications,* he instructed 90th Light Division to make for El Adem, and 15th Panzer Division for the airfield there, while 21st Panzer Division and the Ariete Division pinned down XXX Corps west of the Knightsbridge area. After taking the airfield and the RAF fuel dump the forces operating against El Adem were to swing round and complete the envelopment of the Gazala position.[183] The news was followed, not by a second reverse for Rommel, but by another decisive defeat for the British forces.

---

* See above, pp 298–299.

178. CX/MSS/1071/22, 1076/T14.
179. WO 169/3936, Nos 220, 221 and 232 of 30 and 31 May and 11 June 1942.
180. CAB 44/97, p 128.
181. ibid, pp 128–129.
182. WO 169/3936, No 233 of 12 June 1942.
183. MK 6612 of 0610/12 June 1942; CX/MSS/1069/T16.

Exploiting the confusion that accompanied a first brush between XXX Corps and 15th Panzer Division early on 12 June, Rommel ordered 21st Panzer Division to join the battle. The German attack destroyed 105 British tanks – about half those engaged – and 'the balance of tank strength passed finally and firmly to Rommel'.[184] British Army Y learned of 21st Panzer Division's intervention too late to give warning.[185] In contrast, Rommel's field Sigint alerted 15th Panzer Division of the approach of XXX Corps in time for it to take up a defensive position and to make the first attack.[186] But XXX Corps commander was well informed about the positions of the German formations before the engagement,[187] and it is safe to say that Rommel owed his victory less to the performance of his field intelligence service than to his superiority in direction in battle and in the quality and handling of his tanks.

Eighth Army's commander had conceded Rommel's superiority in these directions, as in artillery and anti-tank weapons, in his appreciation of 11 June, but had set against it his own superiority in the air and in tank numbers. With 250 medium tanks of his own, he was well informed of the enemy tank strength. By 11 June, although the Enigma had yielded no complete tank return since 2 June, Army Y was frequently intercepting the daily tank returns of 15th and 21st Panzer Divisions.[188] On 11 June, when the Panzer divisions had 123 medium tanks serviceable, Cairo calculated on this evidence that they had between 130 and 140.[189] But the important fact was that, in terms of the quality of his tanks, Rommel's position was now improving and Eighth Army may not have realised the full extent of the improvement. On 6 May an Enigma tank return had mentioned the inclusion in the total of 42 Pzkw III Special and Pzkw IV, and on 7 June the Middle East was told on the basis of another Enigma return that the ratio of Pzkw III Special, Pzkw IV and Pzkw IV Special to Pzkw IIIs was 1 to 4.[190] Not until 10 June, however, did Eighth Army's intelligence summary refer to this new development. It then announced that 'it is now established with reasonable certainty from captured documents that Mark 3 and Mark 4 Special tanks are present in Libya', and gave an outline of their characteristics drawn up by GS Int (Technical) GHQ ME.[191] Up till 11 June, moreover, neither Cairo's assessments of enemy tank numbers nor Eighth Army's references to the Army Y returns distinguished between types of

184. Playfair, op cit, Vol III, p 241 (n).
185. WO 169/3936, No 234 of 13 June 1942.
186. Playfair, op cit, Vol III, p 240.   187.   CAB 44/97, p 145.
188. Hunt, *A Don at War* (1966), p 103; WO 169/3936, No 230 of 9 June 1942.
189. Playfair, op cit, Vol III, p 239; Carver, op cit, p 211.
190. MK 6389 of 7 June 1942; CX/MSS/1055/T6.
191. WO 169/3936, No 231 of 10 June 1942.

tank, perhaps because the Army Y intercepts did not then specify them; and it was not until the morning of 12 June that the Eighth Army intelligence summary circulated a POW report on the organisation of 21st Panzer Division's Panzer regiment which mentioned the number of Specials it had received.[192] The next full Enigma return, showing that the ratio of Specials to older types of tanks had risen to 1 to 1, was not to be received until 31 July.[193]*

On the evening of 12 June, on learning that the battle had gone against him, Eighth Army's commander judged that he had either to stand and fight or withdraw his whole force to the frontier. With the agreement of the C-in-C and the Prime Minister, he decided to stand. It is impossible to say whether the decision was influenced by the fact that the remaining Enigma decrypts received on 12 June either illustrated the enemy's difficulties, by reporting shortages of ammunition, rations and water, or showed his anxiety about British reinforcements.[194] Twenty-four hours later, after Eighth Army had been reduced to 50 medium tanks in further heavy fighting, the decision was reversed and orders issued for the evacuation of the Gazala position. Except that it provided currently a plea from the GAF that Rommel should move against the main forward RAF airfield at Gambut – a plea that Rommel declined[195] – the Enigma evidence received during 13 June dealt with the armoured battle of the previous day; and, to judge from Eighth Army's intelligence summary, Army Y contributed no operational information. On 14 June intelligence improved. For the first time GC and CS was able to send out in the early hours an emergency message based on the Panzer Army's day report of the previous evening; it contained the news that Rommel would strike north that day in an attempt to seal off the Gazala front.[196] By noon Eighth Army had from the Enigma full details of Rommel's intentions for the day.[197] At nightfall Army Y reported that Rommel had observed the beginning of the British retreat from Gazala and had ordered his forces to cut the coastal road at once.[198] It is clear, however, that this information contributed little to the fact that most of the British force got away. The DAK was too tired to respond to Rommel's urging and the GAF was wholly occupied

---

* See Appendix 14.

192.   ibid, No 233 of 12 June 1942.
193.   MKA 799 of 31 July 1942; CX/MSS/1254/T10.
194.   MKs 6632, 6636, 6646, 6647, 6650 of 12 June 1942; CX/MSS/1070/T13, 1071/T8, 9, 15 and 17, 1072/T3.
195.   MKs 6677 and 6685 of 13 June 1942; CX/MSS/1072/T32, 1073/T1.
196.   MK 6747 of 0626/14 June 1942; CX/MSS/1075/T31.
197.   MK 6760 of 1141/14 June 1942; CX/MSS/1075/T31.
198.   WO 169/3936, No 236 of 15 June 1942.

until 15 June in attacks on the mid-June convoy from Alexandria to Malta.

From 15 June, when Rommel penetrated the El Adem defences, it was even more the case that intelligence could do nothing to restore a fast deteriorating situation. In the early hours of 16 June Eighth Army learned from a Scorpion decrypt that Rommel planned to extend his hold over the heights around Tobruk and take the huge Belhamed supply depot during the day.[199] But the British had begun to destroy stores at Belhamed on 14 June. In the early hours of 17 June Eighth Army again received, again from Scorpion, the DAK's instructions for the day – it was to take the Gambut airfield and cut the road east of Tobruk to complete the encirclement of the fortress – together with information on the current dispositions of the Panzer Army and on the GAF's intentions.[200] By then the RAF was out of touch with Eighth Army, and it was already evacuating Gambut. In addition to these advance warnings of the enemy's intentions, Eighth Army was now receiving a stream of Enigma decrypts and Y reports about the enemy's recent movements and operations. But on 17 June, in its final attempt to stop Rommel's onrush, its last effective armoured brigade suffered another defeat and lost 32 of its 90 tanks.

□

The continuing retreat of Eighth Army left Tobruk surrounded. On 14 June the Eighth Army commander, realising that he might be unable to prevent this, had requested permission to accept the investment of the fortress if necessary: his only other course was to prepare for its evacuation, which would be difficult. But the C-in-C had ordered him not to let Tobruk be invested. As far back as February he had decided that he would not accept another siege, which would lock up troops he might need on his northern flank. More important, he now believed that the enemy was nearing exhaustion[201] and that Rommel's capacities were not 'so great as to make it necessary to abandon Tobruk'.[202] On 16 June he argued that 'to invest Tobruk and mask our troops in the frontier positions the enemy would need more troops than our information . . . shows him to have'.[203] On 18 June the intelligence officers at Eighth Army HQ still shared this view.[204]

---

199.   MK 6860 of 0311/16 June 1942; CXMSS/1085/T3.
200.   MK 6924 of 0600/17 June 1942; CX/MSS/1089/T9.
201.   CAB 105/17, No 225 of 14 June; CAB 44/97, p 168.
202.   Playfair, op cit, Vol III p 247.
203.   CAB 105/17, No 239 of 16 June 1942.
204.   WO 169/3936, No 237 of 18 June 1942.

There was not much positive intelligence to support this conclusion. Such as it was, however, it may have reinforced the C-in-C's inclination to defer a decision. On 13 and 14 June several Enigma decrypts indicated serious shortages of ammunition in the DAK and of fuel in the GAF,[205] and one showed the Panzer Army summoning reserves from Naples.[206] On the evening of 17 June another decrypt revealed that the Panzer Army had urgently requested that 8,000 replacements should be flown to Africa, but had been told that shortage of transport aircraft would limit the number to 75 a day.[207] More unusually, two decrypts cast some light on the enemy's high-level strategic decisions. On 14 June one of these informed the Panzer Army that, as a result of a review of the situation by Mussolini, Kesselring and Cavallero on 9 June, Bastico, Rommel's titular superior, had received new orders to the effect that he should aim at the capture of Bir Hacheim and the Gazala position and at the destruction of the British armour; that the immediate encirclement of Tobruk should not necessarily be the next step, though it might be possible; that the situation would have to be reconsidered after the fall of Hacheim and Gazala; that the casualty and supply situation needed careful watching; and that exhausted troops must not be thrown into a new attack. The message added that Kesselring envisaged operations continuing for four or five days beyond 20 June, but that it was generally agreed that a temporary halt would then have to be called.[208] On 18 June the second message told the Panzer Army that Hitler had on 13 June approved the orders given to Bastico.[209] These messages were, it is now clear, a manifestation of the anxiety of the Axis leaders, and especially of Mussolini – an anxiety which on 1 May had led them, when deciding that Rommel should attack at the end of May with the object of taking Tobruk by 20 June, to lay it down that he should not move further east than the Egyptian frontier until the Axis had taken Malta.[210] They indicated that the Axis leaders were now dubious as to how far Rommel should press his attack on Tobruk. With hindsight, we may reasonably suppose that their transmission to Africa by W/T indicated that the Axis leaders were also dubious about Rommel's readiness to obey the orders recently sent to Bastico. But the British authorities had received no inkling of the strategic decision taken by the Axis at the beginning of May.

---

205. For example MKs 6719 and 6729 of 13 June, 6786 of 14 June 1942; CX/MSS/1074/T9, 1075/T3, 1076/T21.
206. MK 6720 of 13 June 1942; CX/MSS/1074/T11.
207. MK 6947 of 17 June 1942; CX/MSS/1091/T1.
208. MK 6774 of 14 June 1942; CX/MSS/1078/T11.
209. MK 6977 of 18 June 1942; CX/MSS/1093/T7.
210. Playfair, op cit, Vol III, p 219; EDS/Appreciation/9 Part IIIA, pp 146–147; EDS/Appreciation/10, p 199.

Furthermore, on 10 June an officer POW had stated that Rommel intended to by-pass Tobruk and make straight for the Egyptian frontier.[211]

From the morning of 16 June the C-in-C had been forced by events to change his ground. He then agreed that, though it was not to be invested, Tobruk might be isolated for short periods, and thus allowed Eighth Army's commander to keep a force there that would be adequate to hold it.[212] On 17 June he allowed the evacuation of El Adem. Tobruk was then surrounded, and with this setback British assumptions were to receive a still greater shock. During the earlier discussions no one, with the apparent exception of DMI Cairo,[213] had doubted that, if it was invested, Tobruk would be able, as before, to hold out. Enigma information that Rommel was preparing to attack Tobruk reached the Middle East in the afternoon of 18 June.[214] It gave no date for the assault, but was followed by an order of the day from Kesselring on 19 June which was relayed to the Middle East on the same day, and which announced that 'the fate of north Africa now depends on Tobruk; every man must know this tomorrow and act accordingly'.[215] On the afternoon of 19 June air reconnaissance reported that an east-bound enemy column, 15 miles long, had turned north and then west and was moving towards Tobruk on the coastal road from Bardia.[216] On this evidence, and because Rommel had adopted this approach in November 1941, as was known from the capture of his plan at that time, Cairo concluded that the attack would come from the east.[217] But Eighth Army commander and the forces in Tobruk remained uncertain on this point until the DAK, after making a lengthy forced march through the night, attacked at 0700 on 20 June, far sooner than anybody had expected.[218]

During 20 June Army Y and Enigma decrypts, army and air, provided a running commentary on the progress of the German land and air attack on the fortress, though the RAF Y unit gave no warning of the heavy air attack because its R/T set was unserviceable.[219] As in so many battles since 7 June, however, intelligence could do nothing to affect the outcome; and on the evening of 20 June, Eighth Army received from a message signed

---

211.   WO 169/3936, No 232 of 11 June 1942.
212.   Carver, op cit, p 232.
213.   de Guingand, op cit, p 122.
214.   MK 6999 of 18 June 1942; CX/MSS/1089/T9.
215.   MK 7056 of 19 June 1942; CX/MSS/1099/T13.
216.   CAB 105/17, No 260 of 20 June.
217.   ibid, No 262 of 20 June; de Guingand, op cit, p 123.
218.   Carver, op cit p 242; CAB 44/97, pp 206, 226, 229.
219.   AIR 41/26, p 188.

by Rommel and intercepted by Army Y the startling news that the garrison and capitulated.[220]

□

On 22 June, having taken Tobruk and captured large quantities of British supplies, Rommel asked for permission to pursue Eighth Army deep into Egypt. On 23 June Mussolini approved under pressure from Hitler and at the cost of postponing the invasion of Malta to September – though he stipulated that in the meantime Malta must again be suppressed by intensive air attack. At the previous Axis review of the north African fighting which had produced the instructions of 9 June* the capture of Malta had already been deferred from July to August. On the morning of 24 June, as soon as he had received approval, Rommel ordered the Panzer Army to continue its advance.[221]

On 20 June the Cs-in-C in Cairo had appreciated that, even if he took Tobruk and the frontier positions of Sollum and Halfaya, Rommel would not try to advance into Egypt unless he decisively routed the British forces in the field and received considerable reinforcements.[222] Later that day, however, in the belief that the enemy would have seized fuel and other stocks in Tobruk, and because the fall of the fortress had removed the enemy's need to keep any of his armour in the Tobruk area, Eighth Army's commander expected him to advance into Egypt and recommended that, rather than make a stand on the frontier, he himself should gain time and space for re-building Eighth Army by retiring the 120 miles to Mersa Matruh.[223] On 21 June the Middle East Defence Committee accepted this recommendation without being wholly convinced that Rommel would move into Egypt; it ordered that some force should be left at the frontier to delay Rommel 'should he try to advance eastwards'.[224] On 22 June the War Cabinet questioned this decision: it was a decision that gave insufficient emphasis to the difficulties which confronted the enemy in staging an attack on the frontier defences; on the other hand, Mersa Matruh might be quickly overrun if there was no more than a delaying action at the frontier.[225]

The British authorities received no information about the

* See above, p 386.

220.   WO 169/3936, No 239 of 21 June 1942; Hunt op cit, p 105; CAB 44/97, p 242.
221.   EDS/Appreciation/10, pp 98–103, 113.
222.   CAB 105/17, No 262 of 20 June 1942.
223.   CAB 44/98, AL 1200/70, p 243.
224.   CAB 105/17, No 269 of 21 June 1942.
225.   CAB 105/18, Hist (B) (Crusader) 4, No 5 of 22 June 1942.

exchanges that were taking place on a high level on the Axis side between 22 and 24 June. But they learned from the Enigma on the morning of 22 June that Kesselring and Rommel had agreed that their forces would be assembled for an attack on Maddalena, Halfaya and Sollum by 24 June and that Rommel intended his infantry to make a feint against Eighth Army's frontier positions while the DAK went south to outflank them. In the same message – it was a report to Göring – Kesselring added that 'as from 26 June I intend to transfer the Schwerpunkt [of the GAF effort] from Africa to Sicily, first because the transport crisis has become even more acute, and secondly because the GAF must have a certain space of time in which to regroup before entering on major operations'.[226] In the absence of other intelligence, the Middle East Defence Committee took this to be an indication that the enemy would pause after the attack on the frontier positions, and thus as a vindication of the plan to pull back the bulk of Eighth Army to Mersa Matruh and either prepare for a decisive battle there or regroup for an offensive.[227] Eighth Army's withdrawal was ordered to begin on the evening of 22 June.

During 23 June the Enigma gave in advance full details of Rommel's plan for outflanking the frontier positions[228] and revealed that, because there were no bombs or fuel in the forward area, such GAF support as could be provided would have to come from Crete.[229] At the same time, it contained the first indications that Rommel might not after all pause at the frontier. One message confirmed that he had captured considerable supplies at Tobruk.[230] Another stated that in the next few days the Panzer Army was to receive maps of Sollum, Sidi Barrani, Matruh, El Daba and Alexandria.[231] A third informed the GAF that Sidi Barrani, halfway to Matruh, was free for bombing on the nights of 23–24 June, and thus suggested that the Axis forces might be expecting to occupy it thereafter.[232] Early on 24 June Sigint revealed that the Germans were aware, from decrypts of his signals, that in the opinion of the US Military Attaché in Cairo* the British had been decisively beaten and that this was a suitable moment for Rommel to take the Delta.[233] Later in the day another decrypt revealed that

---

* See above, pp 331, 361 and Appendix 1 (Part (i)), p 640.

226. MK 7241 of 0846/22 June 1942; CX/MSS/1107/T28.
227. Playfair, op cit, Vol III, p 250; CAB 105/18, No 10 of 23 June 1942.
228. MKs 7288, 7289, 7322 of 23 June 1942; CX/MSS/1111/T9, 12 and 15, 1112/T11.
229. MK 7302 of 23 June 1942; CX/MSS/1111/T19.
230. MK 7306 of 23 June 1942; CX/MSS/1110/T23.
231. MK 7313 of 23 June 1942; CX/MSS/1111/T26.
232. MK 7348 of 23 June 1942; CX/MSS/1113/T15.
233. CX/MSS/1114/T10.

Hitler had ordered petrol to Tobruk 'with utmost despatch'[234] By
the end of that day air reconnaissance, Y and Eighth Army's own
sightings had established that the enemy's main body, comprising
the two Panzer divisions, 90th Light Division, the Ariete Division
and reconnaissance units, was 50 miles west of Mersa Matruh and
heading east at high speed.[235]

On 25 June the C-in-C ME personally assumed command of
Eighth Army and ordered a change of plan. Instead of a decisive
battle, only a delaying action was to be fought at Matruh: the
armour was not to be committed unless a favourable opportunity
arose; all infantry divisions were to be re-organised into battle
groups; surplus infantry was to be sent back to prepare positions in
the Alamein-Qattara gap as a rallying point; and a mobile battle
was to be fought between Matruh and the gap.[236] The new plan
was based on his assumption that his inferiority in tanks was such
that he would be unable to prevent Rommel from piercing his
centre or enveloping his southern flank. At this point, however, he
had received no reliable evidence about the enemy's tank strength
since 19 June, when Army Y had disclosed that 15th Panzer
Division had 60 serviceable. On 20 June Cairo had estimated that
the enemy might have as many as 519 serviceable by 30 June (of
which 330 German), though 339 (including 220 German) was more
probable, and that Eighth Army would, when reinforced, have 327
(plus 114 Infantry tanks) on the same date.[237] In fact the DAK's
strength was only 104 on 26 June (60 German, 44 Italian) as
compared with 155 in Eighth Army.[238] The over-estimate stemmed
partly from the conjecture that the Germans would be able to bring
forward 150, through recovery and repair, and partly from the fact
that, the Enigma having revealed that the Littorio Division was
being sent forward from Tripoli, it was assumed that it would
arrive with a full complement of 120 tanks; it in fact arrived with
only 36.[239]

During 25 and 26 June the enemy's approach to Matruh was
observed by air and ground reconnaissance,[240] and Y indicated
that, while 90th Light Division would thrust against the defences,
Rommel's main force would probably pass to the south.[241] During
the enemy's attack, however, which scattered the forward British
defences on the evening of 26 June and the next day cut off two

---

234.   MK 7400 of 24 June 1942; ZTPI 11522.
235.   WO 169/3936, Nos 241 and 242 of 24 and 26 June 1942.
236.   CAB 105/18, Nos 28 of 26 June, 34 of 27 June 1942.
237.   CAB 105/17, No 262 of 20 June 1942.
238.   Playfair, op cit, Vol III, p 286 (n).
239.   MK 7097 of 20 June 1942; CX/MSS/1101/T9; WO 169/3936, No 239 of 21
       June and No 241 of 24 June 1942; EDS/Appreciation/9, Part IIIB, p 282.
240.   AIR 41/26, p 198 et seq.
241.   WO 169/3936, No 242 of 26 June 1942.

divisions in Matruh and surrounded another division to the south, the British forces had to depend on what they could observe for themselves. Nor would advance intelligence have been of value to them if it had been available. The tactical situation was changing so fast and the signals communications of Eighth Army were badly disorganised.[242] The situation is exemplified by a signal issued by the C-in-C at 1145 on 28 June, on the strength of a C 38 m decrypt sent out from GC and CS at 0515. This warned that Rommel intended to cut off Matruh from the south and east; and the C-in-C insisted that the force there was on no account to let itself be trapped. The force had already been surrounded the previous evening and was now having to fight its way out.[243] In the process part of its Sigint unit and a large quantity of its records were captured.

On the morning of 29 June Rommel drove on by a forced march to the defence line at Alamein. At that stage the occupation and fortification of the line was far from complete and it by no means constituted a continuous defensive position. On the other hand, the Enigma left no doubt about Rommel's intentions. In one decrypt which reached Eighth Army early on 27 June the Panzer Army had asked Fliegerkorps X on Crete to supply plans of the Alamein fortifications 'as quickly as possible'.[244] Another announced on the next afternoon that the GAF had completed its reconnaissance of the Alamein-Qattara area.[245] By the evening of 28 June the C-in-C had learned from further decrypts that Rommel would attack the 'new position' as soon as possible.[246] At 1821 on 29 June he was sent Rommel's signal of that morning ordering the forced march.[247] To him, as to Rommel, it no doubt seemed clear that if the Panzer Army were able to make another strong attack without delay it would succeed in forcing its way through to the Delta. But the Panzer Army had met with stronger resistance than it had expected at Mersa Matruh, as the Enigma revealed during 28 June,[248] and it had also been weakened by increasing RAF attack since 24 June – all the more so since, as was known from Enigma, the GAF had been unable to assist it, and, as had been revealed by Y, the enemy's ground forces were suffering from a serious shortage of Flak.[249]

242. CAB 44/98, pp 295, 317.
243. MK 7651 of 28 June 1942; ZTPI 11718; CAB 44/98, p 297; Playfair, op cit, Vol III, p 294.
244.   MK 7560 of 27 June 1942; CX/MSS/1127/T17.
245. MK 7682 of 28 June 1942; CX/MSS/1131/T17 and 19.
246. MK 7717 of 28 June 1942; CX/MSS/1132/T21.
247. MK 7811 of 29 June 1942; CX/MSS/1135/T18 and 19.
248. MK 7677 of 28 June 1942; CX/MSS/1131/T13.
249. WO 169/3936, No 241 of 24 June, No 242 of 26 June 1942.

Until 27 June the RAF's all-out effort – an effort which was, for the first time, supplemented by USAAF heavy long-range bombers and could now be extended to Benghazi – had met with virtually no GAF resistance, and had profited from good intelligence from Army Y, the Enigma and reconnaissance about the enemy's supply columns, the positions of his HQs and the movements of his formations.[250] On 25 June the Enigma had testified to the RAF's effectiveness by showing that the enemy was taking urgent steps to bring up two fighter Gruppen to Sidi Barrani;[251] and on 27 June it had revealed that Kesselring had ordered the GAF to provide all-out support in the hard fighting for Mersa Matruh.[252] But the GAF effort there had turned out to be a pale reflection of those it had made against Bir Hacheim and Tobruk. The Enigma established that while this was partly because of the extent to which Rommel had raced ahead of Fliegerführer Afrika, it was mainly because the German squadrons were exhausted: from this time the Fliegerführer's routine returns showed that, although they were not sustaining heavy losses, their serviceability was consistently low.

□

As well as pointing to the enemy's mounting difficulties, Sigint now contributed intelligence of immediate operational value. It is not easy to judge precisely how decisive this was for the outcome of the first battle of Alamein, but of two things there is no doubt. On account of the complicated operational situation, the intelligence was more plentiful than usual. And on account of the fact that Rommel was being slowed down, it arrived in time for Eighth Army to turn it to good account.

During 29 and 30 June the GAF Enigma gave details of the GAF units that were being moved forward and of the airfields they were occupying, and Army Y provided numerous identifications and positions of the enemy's ground formations.[253] More important – for despite an all-out effort by the RAF to damage and delay him while Eighth Army got into its defensive positions, the enemy continued to advance more rapidly than was expected – Eighth Army received during the night of 29–30 June, from decrypts in the general GAF Enigma, the news that Rommel intended to attack at 1500 on 30 June, the earliest moment at which he could expect full GAF support, and that he would make a feint

---

250.   AIR 41/26, p 200.
251.   MKs 7414 and 7418 of 25 June 1942; CX/MSS/1118/T11 and 15.
252.   MK 7568 of 27 June 1942; CX/MSS/1127/T34.
253.   WO 169/3936, No 244 of 29 June 1942.

attack against the Alamein position in the forenoon, before launching the main assault.[254] In the light of this information orders were issued on the morning of 30 June that 'all defensive arrangements are to be completed at once on the supposition that the Alamein position might be attacked at any time from noon'.[255] About noon, however, in a message that left GC and CS at 1050, Eighth Army got from the GAF Enigma the Panzer Army's start line and the further information that the GAF doubted the ability of the Panzer Army to attack as planned, as the troops had failed to reach their positions.[256] From further decrypts it emerged that 90th Light Division was still 15 miles from Alamein, that 21st Panzer Division was immobilised for lack of fuel, and that a sandstorm had delayed the GAF's move to its advanced airfields.[257]

The re-arrangements thus forced on Rommel were disclosed in Enigma decrypts which reached Eighth Army HQ from the afternoon of 30 June. The attack was now to take place on 1 July, probably at 0100.[258] Further messages gave the pre-attack locations of several of the Axis formations, stated that the intended direction of attack for 15th Panzer Division was between Alamein and Bab el Qattara, and contained the news that the GAF would attack the key Alamein position between 0400 and 0600 on 1 July, when enemy ground formations would be 'east, south and west' of the area.[259] On this evidence the C-in-C stood the whole army to in the early hours of 1 July and made his dispositions in the expectation that the main attack would come between Bab el Qattara and Alamein, with the object of cutting off Alamein, and that there would be only minor thrusts south of Bab el Qattara and frontally against Alamein.[260] But the German forces got off to a slow start: by dawn the only development was the beginning of an infantry attack on the Alamein position. As for Rommel's plan of attack, the Enigma information was far from complete; but it had been sufficient to correct the evidence of Army Y and of sightings, which during 29 and 30 June had indicated that Rommel was sending his main force south-east for an outflanking attack in the southern sector, south of Bab el Qattara.[261] In the afternoon of 1 July it would emerge from the decrypt of his day report for 30 June that he had simulated an armoured thrust to the south, in the hope that the

254. MKs 7818 of 2209/29 June, 7828 of 0125/30 June, 7842 of 0510/30 June 1942; CX/MSS/1135/T30, 1136/T16 and 34.
255. CAB 44/98, p 323.
256. MK 7852 of 1050/30 June 1942; CX/MSS/1137/T5 and 28, 1136/T2.
257. MKs 7863, 7881 and 7890 of 30 June, 7971 of 1 July 1942; CX/MSS/1137/T17, 1139/T16 and 29, 1140/T27.
258. MK 7868 of 1439/30 June 1942; CX/MSS/1139/T1.
259. MKs 7893 and 7906 of 30 June 1942; CX/MSS/1139/T31, 1140/T6.
260. CAB 105/17, No 70 of 0880/1 July 1942.
261. WO 169/3936, No 245 of 30 June 1942.

British armour would move to meet it, and had planned that his main force, attacking further north, should turn south to engage the British from the rear while 90th Light Division and an Italian division cut off the Alamein position.[262]

In the event, at first light Rommel's main thrust was sighted where it was expected, between Alamein and Bab el Qattara, by air reconnaissance and attacked by the RAF.[263] It was held up by the infantry box at Deir el Shein for most of the day, while Y intercepts showed that the enemy plan was to turn south after Deir el Shein and take Qattara in the rear,[264] and was then prevented from advancing by British armoured resistance and night bombing of its supply columns. The thrust by 90th Light Division made even slower progress against the infantry box at Alamein – it was stopped by the end of the day – and was assumed to be only the feint attack mentioned by the Enigma until the Army Y organisation intercepted at 1300 a message from Rommel urging the division to get on with cutting the coast road east of Alamein.[265]

In the fighting of 1 July, in which the successful resistance of the infantry boxes played so large a part, intelligence was probably of no direct assistance. It is clear, however, that Y gave early information about most of the enemy's moves,[266] and, though often received with some hours' delay the Enigma evidence, must have been invaluable in keeping Eighth Army HQ abreast of the situation, particularly as its own information from the battlefield was decidedly sketchy. By the late afternoon the HQ had been given the morning positions of the enemy's formations, and had learned that 90th Light Division's advance had been halted, that the Littorio Division had lost its way, that 15th Panzer Division was being 'subjected to continuous bombing attacks' at 0930 and that the task of that division was to attack Bab el Qattara from the rear.[267] It was also able to discount a claim made in one of Rommel's signals that 90th Light Division had broken through – on the basis of which Berlin issued a communiqué saying that the occupation of Egypt was imminent.[268] More important still, Y now established the truth about Rommel's tank strength.

---

262.   MK 7947 of 1423/1 July 1942; CX/MSS/1141/T11; Liddell Hart, *History of the Second World War* (1970), p 281.

263.   WO 169/4006, XIII Corps Intelligence Summary of 3 July; WO 169/4054, XXX Corps Intelligence Summary of 1 July 1942.

264.   WO 169/4054, of 1 July 1942.

265.   ibid, 1 July 1942; WO 201/2154, Eighth Army Intelligence Summary No 246 of 1 July 1942.

266.   WO 169/4054, Intelligence Summary of 1 July 1942.

267.   MKs 7956, 7959, 7960, 7961 and 7963 of 1 July 1942; CX/MSS/1142/T5, 11, 13 and 14.

268.   MK 7985 of 2 July 1942; CX/MSS/1143/T10 and 12; WO 201/2154, No 247 of 2 July; WO 169/4054 of 2 July 1942.

Since making the huge over-estimate of 20 June,* Eighth Army had had only visual evidence on this subject. This evidence had credited Rommel with 100 to 150 German tanks and 40 to 50 Italian tanks on 27 June, with a total of 130 on 28 June, and with 120 German and 100 Italian on 30 June.[269] On 28 June the C-in-C had still assumed that the enemy had a 'marked superiority' in tank numbers.[270] During 1 July Y intercepts showed that 21st Panzer Division was down to 37 serviceable tanks and 15th Panzer Division down to 17.[271]† The information was borne out by the testimony of two British officers, captured and brought forward by the DAK, who made their escape during the assault on Deir el Shein.[272] In addition to this revelation – and the fact that the Y intercepts consistently reported on the DAK's low strength during July – another factor must have been important in determining the C-in-C's subsequent conduct of the battle. This was the fact that Y and Enigma decrypts during 1 July made numerous references to the RAF's considerable interference with the enemy's operations.

On 2 July Rommel at first tried to repeat the operations he had failed to carry out on the previous day. During the morning, however, 90th Light Division again failed to break through, and Rommel switched his main force to the attempt to reach the coast road. The movement was reported by Y and by air reconnaissance.[273] At this juncture the C-in-C decided to counter-attack, and by the time Y had shown that the DAK had started to move at 1800, 90th Light had been driven back by the British armour.[274] By the end of the day Y had picked up evidence that the enemy was beginning to experience fuel and ammunition shortage, had observed that 15th and 21st Panzer Divisions were being forced to work in close co-operation because of their losses, and had established that 15th Panzer Division was reduced to 18 serviceable tanks.[275] No tank return was obtained for 21st Panzer Division; in fact, the combined tank strength of the two divisions had shrunk to 26.[276]

Notwithstanding these losses, Rommel decided to renew on 3

---

* See above, p 390.
† No information was obtained about the Italian tanks, but these were by now a negligible factor and little attention was paid to them.

269. CAB 105/18, No 34 of 27 June, No 53 of 29 June 1942; WO 169/4006, 1st Armoured Division Operational Order No 22 of 1 July 1942.
270. CAB 105/18, No 45 of 28 June 1942.
271. WO 201/2154, Nos 246, 247 and 248 of 1, 2 and 3 July 1942.
272. WO 169/4054, of 1 July 1942.
273. AIR 41/26, p 23; WO 201/2154, No 247 of 2 July 1942; WO 169/4054 of 2 July 1942.
274. WO 201/2154, No 247 of 2 July; WO 169/4054 of 3 July 1942.
275. WO 201/2154, No 247 of 2 July; WO 169/4054 of 3 July 1942.
276. Playfair, op cit, Vol III, p 343.

July the attempt to break through the Alamein defences and cut the coast road. The Enigma disclosed his intention, together with the thrust lines to be adopted by the two spearhead formations, 90th Light and 21st Panzer Divisions, and the information was signalled to the C-in-C in the early hours.[277] Before the attack developed at 1700, the C-in-C having decided to wait for it before renewing his counter-attack, Y gave last minute information about it.[278] After fierce fighting the British retained the edge in armoured strength and the enemy withdrew under cover of smoke. Before the main attack Rommel, for the first time, had decided to use his Italian forces in an independent thrust and had sent them against British positions further south: this advance was revealed by a chance air sighting[279] and had ended in the rout of the Ariete Division, whose withdrawal from the battle was disclosed by Enigma decrypts just after midnight.[280] To compound Rommel's difficulties, the RAF scored big successes, especially against the GAF, during 3 July – though the RAF's own account of the battle complains that Eighth Army missed the opportunity to have it bomb the German ground formations which had been sighted in their assembly areas.[281] How far target selection was being influenced by Sigint and Y as well as by local information is not recorded. But it is known that the Scorpion Enigma signals of the GAF liaison officers with the Panzer Army were being decyphered in Heliopolis from 12 July,* and that the number of Enigma decrypts signalled out to the British HQs from GC and CS had by 3 July reached the figure of more than a hundred a day. Over and above those of outstanding operational importance, which have already been noted, most of these gave details about the enemy's ground positions, the locations of his HQs, his supply movements and the intentions and state of the GAF. In addition, several Enigma decrypts revealed that tension between Kesselring and Rommel was now high.[282]

The news that Rommel would not attack on 4 July, but would be looking to his supplies, was conveyed to Eighth Army HQ in the early hours of that day in a signal based on decrypted Panzer Army orders of the evening of 3 July.[283] Although the report did not say so, he had already decided that he would have to go over to the defensive for at least a fortnight.[284] During 4 July, on the other

---

* See above, p 375.

277.   MK 8067 of 0225/3 July 1942; CX/MSS/1147/T18.
278.   WO 201/2154, No 248 of 3 July 1942.   279.   AIR 41/26, p 34.
280.   MKs 8146 and 8167 of 4 July 1942; CX/MSS/1151/T3, 8 and 17.
281.   AIR 41/26 pp 28–30.
282.   For example, MK 8186 of 4 July 1942; CX/MSS/1153/T17.
283.   MK 8137 of 0015/4 July 1942; CX/MSS/1151/T6.
284.   Playfair, op cit, Vol III, p 344.

hand, the C-in-C kept up the pressure, and Eighth Army completely regained the initiative which had been passing to it gradually
since the German attack of 1 July. Indeed, it now encountered
some evidence of severe overstrain, and even of demoralisation,
among the German troops. Some authorities have concluded that it
missed the opportunity to deliver a general decisive attack because
it failed to realise how close the enemy was to defeat.[285] Others,
however, suggest that Rommel's field intelligence again enabled
him to check Eighth Army's initial moves. The evidence is
debatable.[286] The appreciation issued by Eighth Army's intelligence staff on the evening of 4 July was that, since the enemy was
trying to bring up fuel and ammunition behind his anti-tank
screen, his slight withdrawal might give way to 'a still more
determined thrust later'.[287]

On the Axis side expectations had meanwhile been running high.
During the last days of June it emerged from the decrypts that the
Italians were arranging to transfer naval units to Aegean bases[288]
and that the Axis powers were making plans for the exploitation of
Egypt.[289] On 1 July the decrypts showed that the Panzer Army had
urgently requested 10,000 copies of maps of the chief Egyptian
cities.[290] On 3 July C 38 m revealed that the Axis had learned that
Alexandria had been evacuated[291]* and were discussing arrangements for sailing the French squadron there to a French port.[293] On
the same day the decrypts showed that the Italians intended to
deploy between three and five cruisers to escort troop convoys from
the Aegean to Egypt, and that the first convoy had been due to
leave Taranto on 2 July.[294] But on the morning of 4 July the
authorities in Berlin and Rome received the Panzer Army's much
delayed day report for 3 July. This stated that 'British strength, low
Axis fighting strength and very strained supply position "compelled" temporary suspension of a large-scale attack'.

The decrypt of this signal reached the British authorities in the
Middle East on the afternoon of 5 July.[295]

---

* Preparations for the evacuation of the ships and HQ of the Mediterranean Fleet had
begun on 25 June. But negotiations with the French squadron were still continuing on 4 July
when a decrypt showed that Kesselring had been informed that the British authorities had
issued an ultimatum to Admiral Godefroy.[292]

285. AIR 41/26, p 43; Liddell Hart, op cit, p 284.
286. WO 169/4054 of 4 and 5 July; WO 169/4006 of 5 July 1942; CAB 105/18,
      Nos 92 and 93 of 5 July 1942; Hunt, op cit, p 112.
287. WO 201/2154, No 249 of 4 July 1942.
288. MKs 7467, 7472, 7475 of 25 June 1942; ZTPI 11573, 11581, 11583, 11675.
289. MK 7159 of 29 June 1942; CX/MSS/1133/T7, 1142/T15.
290. MK 7935 of 1 July 1942; CX/MSS/1141/T3.
291. ZTPI 12011, 12012, 12038.
292. CX/MSS/1150/T6.   293. ZTPI 12043.
294. Naval Headlines No 364 of 3 July 1942; ZTPI 11988.
295. MK 8247 of 1352/5 July 1942; CX/MSS1141/T3.

CHAPTER 23

The Mediterranean and North Africa from July 1942 to the Capture of Tripoli January 1943

ALTHOUGH ROMMEL had been forced to go over to the defensive by 4 July, he by no means gave up his attempt to break through to the Delta. Within two days he was probing the south of the British line and on 7 July, having met with little resistance, he launched a small-scale attack there. For the rest of the month, on the other hand, he was reacting to repeated British attacks. Despite their heavy cost in men and material, and despite the fact that they could rarely be properly prepared, the C-in-C Middle East kept these up in an attempt not merely to stop Rommel but to destroy his forces *in situ*.[1]

That this was his objective, and that he clung to it for so long, was due mainly to developments on his northern flank. The early success of the offensive launched by Germany in south Russia on 28 June persuaded the Cs-in-C Middle East by 9 July that they might have to meet a German advance into northern Iran in the first half of October and, though this was less likely, a German attack through Syria to Iraq as early as 10 September,[2]* But if this prospect alone made it imperative to try to destroy Rommel, and to do so 'as far east as possible' in order to avoid the need to lock up British forces in pursuing him westward,[3] another consideration pointed hardly less strongly in the same direction. The Cs-in-C knew that the enemy's forces were temporarily greatly reduced, and handicapped by enormous supply difficulties, but would be receiving sizeable reinforcements from the end of July.

The information about the enemy's supply position and reinforcement plans came almost entirely from the Enigma traffic between the Panzer Army and the Axis authorities in Rome and

---

* See above, pp 101–102 for Whitehall's assessments of the timing of this threat.

1. CAB 44/98, AL 1200/70, p 345; CAB 105/18, Hist (B) (Crusader) 4, Nos 138 of 15 July and 165 of 24 July 1942.
2. CAB 105/10, Hist (B) 10, No 23 of 9 July 1942.
3. CAB 105/18, No 138 of 15 July 1942; Playfair, *The Mediterranean and Middle East*, Vol III (1960), p 364.

Berlin, which now discussed these matters by W/T in greater detail than usual. It disclosed on 30 June that the Axis had resumed the air-lifting of troops,[4] and by the end of July it had reported the arrival of 23,000 men. More important – for these were known to be inexperienced troops who hardly replaced the heavy casualties of May and June – it revealed the response to Rommel's pleas for reinforcements. It announced on 7 July that while Rommel was to be reinforced by a new formation from Crete (382nd Regiment of 164th Infantry Division) OKH could otherwise spare only 'isolated' units over and above normal replacements, and that their assembly 'would take some time'.[5] By 12 July it had established that the regiment had arrived without transport and practically without weapons.[6] On 16 July, however, the Enigma gave the news that Hitler had ordered that 90th Light Division should be brought up to strength as a first priority, followed by 15th and 21st Panzer Divisions, that the Panzer Army was to be reinforced by troops from the Balkans beginning with the remainder of 164th Division, and that artillery was to be sent over.[7] On 17 July it reported that the rest of 164th Division would arrive before the end of the month, also without its heavy equipment.[8] At about that time further urgent pleas from Rommel produced the decision to send the Italian Folgore Division of paratroops – the Enigma showed it arriving in Libya within a week[9] – and a miscellaneous collection of German paratroop units called the Ramcke Brigade.

The Enigma report of the intention to send German paratroop units caused some anxiety about the possibility of an airborne attack on the airfield complex in the Delta, for it did not emerge till August that they were intended for use only in the ground fighting.[10] Sigint also failed until August to disclose that the Italian Pistoia Division had arrived in Libya by sea by the end of July. With these exceptions the Enigma – supplemented by, but more often camouflaged as, POW evidence – kept Eighth Army fully abreast of the enemy's manpower situation. It was the Enigma, too, supplemented on this subject by Army Y, which showed that

---

4. MK 7866 of 30 June 1942; CX/MSS/1137/T4.
5. MK 8500 of 7 July 1942; CX/MSS/1168/T10; WO 201/2154, Eighth Army Intelligence Summary No 255 of 10 July 1942.
6. MK 8603 of 12 July 1942; CX/MSS/1168/T34, 1174/T1; WO 201/2154, No 257 of 12 July 1942.
7. MKs 9066 of 16 July and 9222 of 17 July 1942; CX/MSS/1196/T26, 1203/T26.
8. MKs 9151 and 9222 of 17 July 1942; CX/MSS/1201/T7, 1203/T26.
9. WO 201/2154, No 269 of 24 July 1942.
10. MK 9393 of 19 July 1942; MKA 2274 of 20 August 1942; CX/MSS/1212/T17, 1308/T3; AIR 41/50, *The RAF in the Middle East Campaigns*, Vol IV, pp 150, 160; WO 208/3573, MI 14 Appreciation for CIGS, 17 August 1942; WO 201/2154, Eighth Army Intelligence Summary No 302 of 26 August 1942.

Rommel would be receiving tank reinforcements by the end of July. On 26 June it showed that Hitler had three days earlier ordered that 40 tanks (30 Pzkw III and 10 Pzkw IV) were to be sent to Africa with the greatest possible speed, together with 49 anti-tank guns and 30 heavy howitzers.[11] On 30 June it showed that the number of tanks 'scheduled for July' had been raised to 90 (60 Pzkw III and 30 Pzkw IV).[12] Thereafter the total rose to 110 and the Enigma tracked their progress through Italy and across to Mersa Matruh – where the Royal Navy and the RAF attacked their transports on 20 July and sank one before it could unload – and thence to the point of their delivery to the Panzer Army at the end of July.[13] Hardly less ominous was the news received from an Enigma decrypt on 23 July that 180 tank engines were arriving:[14] by that time it was known from Army Y that while the DAK had only 40 serviceable tanks, 21st Panzer Division alone had 44 tanks in its workshops,[15] and it could be presumed that 15th Panzer Division was in like state.

The C-in-C's anxiety to destroy Rommel's forces by all means, however desperate, was also fed by his knowledge that Rommel's wish to resume the offensive was being frustrated by the serious supply problems of the Panzer Army and the GAF. On 10 and 11 July the Enigma disclosed that the GAF in north Africa was suffering from a shortage of fuel.[16] By mid-July the shortage had reached such proportions that, as was also shown in the Enigma traffic, the air transport system in north Africa was being brought to a standstill and the GAF could be used only sparingly in operations until matters were improved by the arrival of a tanker in Tobruk on 25 July.[17] On 13 July the Enigma showed that the Panzer Army's need for fuel and ammunition was also becoming urgent.[18] This was partly the result of heavy fighting in the past few days, and partly because naval and RAF attacks on Axis shipping in the forward area had done considerable damage. The Enigma confirmed that one ship was sunk by the RAF in Tobruk on the night of 10–11 July.[19] During 11 and 12 July, alerted by Sigint references to their crucial importance, the RAF and the Navy sank off Mersa Matruh two large coastal vessels that had been brought

---

11.   MK 7490 of 26 June 1942; CX/MSS/1122/T8.
12.   MK 7851 of 30 June 1942; CX/MSS/1136/T40.
13.   MKA 937 of 4 August 1942; CX/MSS/1261/T4.
14.   ibid.
15.   WO 201/2154, Nos 263 of 18 July and 270 of 25 July 1942.
16.   MKs 8632 of 10 July and 8690 of 11 July 1942; CX/MSS/1175/T11 and 21, 1177/T28.
17.   eg MKs 9262 of 18 July, 9595 of 22 July 1942; CX/MSS/1206/T15, 1220/T11.
18.   MK 9042 of 13 July 1942; CX/MSS/1196/T19.
19.   AIR 41/50, p 141; MK 8742 of 12 July 1942; CX/MSS/1180/T30.

forward to ply between Matruh and Tobruk.[20] Enigma showed
that this action blocked Matruh even to supply submarines and
that the Panzer Army considered one ship in Tobruk worth several
in Benghazi.[21]

After 15 July, with naval bombardments and RAF attacks
continuing against Matruh and Tobruk and on shipping between
the two ports, and with the RAF harrying the Panzer Army's road
and rail communications, Rommel's supplies rapidly diminished.
As Eighth Army HQ learned from its report of that day, the Panzer
Army confessed on 18 July that the situation was critical, that the
discharge of ships then expected at Tobruk would relieve it only
temporarily, and that it would not be secure until naval self-
propelled lighters, less vulnerable to attack, had arrived in the
forward coastal area.[22] Nor was the crisis surmounted before the
middle of August. On the other hand, Rommel reported on 21 July
that his supplies, though too precarious to permit a large offensive,
were sufficient for his present operations[23] and – while the Enigma
traffic did not contain this report – it was only too clear from the C
38 m and the Enigma decrypts, which regularly gave the details of
sailings and the figures for unloadings, that shipping across the
Mediterranean was not being seriously interrupted and that,
despite damage and congestion there, large stocks were being built
up at Benghazi and Tobruk.

□

During the July fighting Eighth Army was as well supplied with
operational intelligence as with the essential facts about the state of
the enemy's forces and his plans for improving it. Once again the
Enigma was the chief source, but Army Y was scarcely less
important.

POW, captured documents and captured equipment were making a valuable contribution to technical intelligence,* but were of
less value at this stage for operational purposes. Air reconnaissance, both visual and photographic, was of less value than usual
for several reasons. The Western Desert Air HQ had become
separated from that of Eighth Army during the retreat. Nor was it
until the middle of the month that No 240 (later 285) Reconnaissance Wing RAF was set up to co-ordinate the work of No 2 PRU,
No 60 SAAF Survey Flight, the Army Air Photographic Unit and
the ME CIU's detachment with Eighth Army with the activities of

---

* See Appendix 14.

20. AIR 41/50, pp 141–142; MK 8554 of 9 July 1942; ZTPI 12475, 12476.
21. Dir/C Archive, 2–12 July 1942; CX/MSS/1171/T17 of 9 July 1942.
22. MK 9364 of 19 July 1942; CX/MSS/1211/T7.
23. Playfair, op cit, Vol III, pp 338–339.

the tactical reconnaissance squadrons, which remained under the operational control of the Army, and to cut the delay in distributing the results of reconnaissance to the subordinate formations. Even then the two HQs remained separate for another month and air reconnaissance continued to be handicapped by shortage of aircraft, by determined enemy opposition and by the persistence throughout the month of cloud and dust storms.[24]

With few exceptions, the Enigma decrypts from GC and CS continued to arrive too late to give advance notice of the enemy's movements. As fighting was continuous throughout July, however, they gave a full account of the changing battle situation, about half of the 100 messages a day dealing with it in some way, and the delay in getting this to Eighth Army HQ was off-set in two ways. The Scorpion traffic, invaluable for its frequent locations and identification of the enemy's divisions, was being decrypted at CBME from 12 July. Not less important, the steps taken in June to integrate Y with operational intelligence at Eighth Army and Corps levels* were now yielding dividends. The intelligence summaries of Eighth Army and of XIII and XXX Corps, with their pre-attack estimates of the enemy's strengths and dispositions, leave no doubt that during July Y, complemented by the Enigma and co-ordinated with other intelligence collected locally, gave the C-in-C all the evidence he needed for the planning of his attacks by following the moves the enemy made in response to them, by locating the enemy's formations and by showing up his weak points. It was at this time that Y first obtained in full measure the results which enabled it, during the rest of the African campaign, to contribute to 'the rounder pattern which Ultra could not achieve' and, by 'building up a day-to-day knowledge of the enemy which enabled us to handle Ultra with more confidence', brought the intelligence staff at Eighth Army HQ to the point at which it could feel that 'we had not done our day's work unless we had beaten the Ultra, unless we knew what was happening and could appreciate what would happen before it could arrive'.[25]

Without laborious analysis, it is impossible to tell at this distance in time how much of the Y data came from cryptanalysis, how much from plain language and how much from DF and Traffic Analysis. It is equally hard to establish precisely when and how either it or the Enigma influenced the C-in-C's tactical and operational decisions. But a brief account of his conduct of the fighting suffices to show that he followed the Sigint closely.

By 8 July, when the C-in-C decided to attack at Tel el Eisa at the

---

* See above, p 377.

24. AIR 41/25, *The RAF in the Middle East Campaigns*, Vol II, pp 136, 294; AIR 41/26, ibid, Vol III, pp 98, 219; AIR 41/50, p 103.

25. WO 208/3575, Williams, The Use of Ultra by the Army, pp 1, 8.

extreme north of the line on 10 July, he knew from both sources that Rommel had moved the bulk of his forces – 90th Light Division, 21st Panzer Division and the Littorio Division – to the southern sector,[26] and the news that Rommel intended to press his advantage there, received from the Enigma on 9 July,[27] did not divert him from his own attack. This was delivered against a position that was known from Y to be held by two Italian infantry divisions.[28] It virtually annihilated one of these divisions – and captured part of Rommel's field Sigint Unit[29]* – and forced Rommel to switch 21st Panzer Division back to the north to prevent a complete breakthrough.

The transfer of 21st Panzer Division was at once reported by Army Y and confirmed by the Enigma after some delay,[31] and both sources closely followed its activities during the operations up to 14 July in which it recaptured Tel el Eisa.[32] Nor is there any doubt that the C-in-C used this information and other order of battle intelligence when planning his next move, the attack on the Ruweisat ridge on the night of 14–15 July. The attack was decided on on 13 July, when Y established that 21st Panzer Division was in the extreme north, close to the Alamein position.[33] An hour or so after it was launched the C-in-C revealed his thinking in a signal to the CIGS: 'German troops now seem greatly stretched with 21st Panzer Division in the north, 15th Panzer Division in the centre and 90th Light Division in the south, thus opening apparently favourable chance of hitting hard in the centre against the Italians. My policy is to hit the Italians wherever possible in view of their low morale and because the Germans cannot hold extended fronts without them'.[34] The deployment of the Pavia and Brescia infantry

---

* This was 621st Signals Battalion, the source of much of Rommel's order of battle and operational intelligence. The consequent reduction in its effectiveness was a severe blow to Rommel who depended during the remainder of July on inadequate information from local sources. By the battle of Mareth in March 1943, however, it had been reformed and was again providing Rommel with important tactical intelligence. Throughout the African campaign German estimates of British order of battle based, on field Sigint and other sources, were regularly obtained from the Enigma and signalled to Cairo for use by the deception authorities.[30]

26. WO 201/2154, Nos 251 to 255 of 6–10 July 1942; eg MKs 8239 and 8260 of 5 July 1942; CX/MSS/1155/T17.
27. MKs 8623 and 8664 of 10 July 1942; CX/MSS/1175/T3 and 12, 1176/T1.
28. WO 201/2154, No 255 of 10 July 1942.
29. ibid, Nos 255 and 256 of 10 and 11 July 1942.
30. Hunt, *A Don at War* (1966), p 113; CAB 44/98, p 398.
31. WO 201/2154, No 256 of 11 July 1942; MK 8832 of 13 July 1942; CX/MSS/1185/T25.
32. WO 201/2154, Nos 257–260 of 12–15 July 1942; MK 8916 of 14 July 1942; CX/MSS/1189/T19.
33. CAB 44/98, p 367.
34. CAB 105/18, No 136 of 15 July 1942.

divisions on and around the Ruweisat ridge had been established by Y on 10 July.[35] It was during this fighting that under fire the Army Technical intelligence staff made the first examination of a Pzkw III Special and arranged with 1st Armoured Division a diversionary action which enabled it to recover the tank.*

Although it was launched without adequate preparation – and unavoidably so, for reasons that have already been discussed – this second British attack routed the two Italian divisions. By 18 July, in conjunction with a renewal of the attack in the Tel el Eisa sector, it had cost Rommel the equivalent of 3 Italian divisions and had forced him to bring all his German armour from the south to the rescue. Intelligence did not disclose that he had already decided on the evening of 14 July that he must abandon the attempt to break through to the Delta until the Panzer Army was fully replenished,[36] but it now showed that it was only with the greatest diffficulty that he again prevented a breakthrough by Eighth Army. While Y reported all his movements,[37] the Enigma threw much light on his problems. On 15, 16 and 17 July it disclosed that serious shortages of fuel and ammunition had developed at the front, that the supply columns were over-taxed and suffering heavy casualties from RAF attacks, and that the weakness of the Italian divisions had made it necessary to lay mines in front of their positions and to stiffen them with pockets of German troops.[38] As for Rommel's tank strength, no tank return was obtained from the Enigma until the end of the month, but the Enigma showed that the Italian armour had remained in the south and Y established that 21st Panzer Division was down to 10 serviceable tanks on 17 July,[39] and on 19 July it showed that 15th Panzer Division was down to 13.[40]

It was with this intelligence before him that the C-in-C decided on 18 July that 'the best way of inflicting a major defeat would be to strike strongly again in the centre', this time – deliberately – against the German armour, and that on 19 July he ordered a further attack on the Ruweisat ridge for the night of 21–22 July.[41] Despite his own heavy losses in the recent fighting, and whereas the tank reinforcements he was receiving consisted mostly of obsolete Valentines, he had at this time 61 Grants, which nearly matched Rommel's armour. It was thus with some confidence that he awaited the outcome. Nor was his optimism wholly misplaced.

---

* See Appendix 14.

35. WO 201/2154, No 255 of 10 July 1942.
36. EDS/Appreciation/9, Part IV, p 18.
37. WO 201/2154, Nos 260–262 of 15–17 July 1942.
38. MKs 9042 of 15 July, 9128 of 16 July, 9177 and 9195 of 17 July 1942; CX/MSS/1196/T19, 1199/T29, 1201/T21, 1203/T27.
39. WO 201/2154, No 263 of 18 July 1942.
40. ibid, No 264 of 19 July 1942.
41. Playfair, op cit, Vol III, pp 353–354.

During 22 and 23 July Rommel at last doubted his ability to hold out and was seriously considering a withdrawal as the only alternative to losing north Africa;[42] and although he did not report these anxieties by W/T, both Y and Enigma showed that the Panzer Army was sustaining heavy infantry losses and suffering from lack of reinforcements and that the GAF had again run into a fuel crisis.[43] But by the morning of 24 July it was clear that the British assault had been a costly failure, not least because 23rd Armoured Brigade had fallen foul of the enemy's mines and lost 100 out of its 150 Valentines, and that Rommel had lost very few of his tanks. The Enigma had warned on 15 July that minelaying on a very large scale was about to take place.[44]

Despite the fact that Eighth Army's losses had now reached an alarming level the C-in-C attacked again on 26 July, this time from the Tel el Eisa salient. In his order for the assault he stressed that a quick decision was essential since the enemy, although he had no general reserves, had suffered heavy casualties and was short of equipment, ammunition and transport, was now receiving reinforcements daily.[45] In addition to the evidence he was receiving to this effect,* he knew from the Enigma that Rommel was stiffening the Italian units with pockets of German troops.[46] Before the attack began Eighth Army learned from a decrypted signal from Flieger-führer Afrika that the Germans expected it; and it adopted a cover plan in an attempt to deceive them into thinking that the attack was to be delivered further south.[47] To no avail. Largely, again, as a result of the extensive mining that the Germans had carried out – the Enigma had carried further requests for mining by 25 July[48] but little or nothing was known about the whereabouts of their minefields[49] – the assault was a total failure. By 27 July, with Eighth Army itself close to exhaustion, the C-in-C knew that he had been denied the objective he had pursued for nearly a month. In his attempt to destroy the enemy where he stood he had been well served by intelligence, but had been frustrated by the sheer fighting ability of the Germans and by Rommel's brilliance in

---

* See above, pp 399–400.

42.   EDS/Appreciation/9, Part IV, pp 30–32.
43.   MKAs 7 of 23 July, 84 of 24 July and 173 of 25 July 1942;
      CX/MSS/1224/T1, 1226/T32, 1230/T6; WO 201/2154, Nos 267–269 of
      22–24 July 1942.
44.   MK 9011 of 15 July 1942; CX/MSS/1193/T19.
45.   CAB 44/98, p 398.
46.   CAB 105/18, No 155 of 21 July 1942.
47.   MKA 150 of 25 July 1942; CX/MSS/1229/T21 and 22; CAB 44/98, p 399.
48.   MKA 231 and 311 of 26 July, 448 of 28 July 1942; CX/MSS/1232/T3,
      1234/T28, 1239/T6.
49.   CAB 44/98, p 404.

discerning the crucial area in any battle and in switching his tired but dedicated troops.

□

On the same day – 27 July – the C-in-C issued an appreciation in which he recognised the risk that Rommel would resume the offensive before Eighth Army was ready to do so. Unless he decided to adopt a defensive posture, Rommel would be under compulsion to attack as soon as possible because he would know that the British position must improve, and he would want to do so before the end of August when he would again have a superiority in effective tanks. Eighth Army could not be ready to attack before mid-September at the earliest; it would thus in the meantime have to prepare for a defensive battle.[50] GS Int, Eighth Army had no reservations about Rommel's intentions. In the intelligence summary of 28 July it noted that the enemy was organising and rationalising his defences, but, aware that he was receiving reinforcements, concluded that 'the fundamental question becomes how soon can the forces behind these defences be made ready for attack'.[51]

During the first half of August this fundamental question remained unanswered, and such intelligence as was received about it only intensified the speculation. Early in the month GC and CS decrypted two reports from the operational staff of the Panzer Army which indicated that it contemplated an offensive, but which also stated that as yet an offensive was beyond its capabilities. The first complained that 'supply arrangements at present cover only day-to-day needs of troops' – that 'bringing up supplies for large-scale operations, let alone offensive, is not possible' – and went on to suggest remedies. The second complained that, whereas the Germans had so far borne the brunt of the fighting and would again do so in 'the coming operations', the Italians were receiving the bulk of the reinforcements.[52] A few days later another signal informed the Panzer Army that Warlimont, whose arrival in Africa had been reported by the Enigma on 25 July,[53] had now submitted a report and that Hitler had agreed to his 'suggestions'.[54] There followed other tantalising references in the Enigma traffic, including two requests that important guns and ammunition should be supplied by 15 August.[55]

50.   ibid, pp 415–418.
51.   WO 201/2154, No 273 of 28 July 1942.
52.   CX/MSS/1254/T5.
53.   MKA 191 of 25 July 1942; CX/MSS/1230/T20.
54.   MKAs 1067 of 6 August, 1381 of 9 August 1942; CX/MSS/1265/T17, 1271/T17.   55.   CX/MSS/1264/T7.

These requests suggested to GHQ, ME at Cairo that 15 August might be Rommel's date. In Whitehall MI was inclined to agree because another source 'who may be well informed' had given similar information.[56] In all probability this was a reference to a diplomatic decrypt from Rome of 5 August, which had mentioned that the Axis would attack on 15 August and – as MI knew to be correct – added that Rommel had been reinforced by two divisions. GS Int, Eighth Army remained sceptical of such other sources. On 9 August it reported that 'various bits and pieces are beginning to point to 15 August as a possible zero day ... Some of these, however, are from sources which in the past we have all too often found to be plants and, in general, neutral sources offer ample opportunity for this form of military horticulture'. But GS Int, Eighth Army did not rule out the possibility that Rommel might risk attacking on 15 August despite his continuing difficulties with supplies.[57] By 13 August, moreover, it had noticed that the GAF was strongly contesting the RAF's reconnaissance of the enemy's positions,[58] and that the enemy's supply position in the forward area was improving so fast that it would probably soon be as good as it had been before his Gazala offensive. On 16 August Eighth Army's intelligence summary stated that, 'while there is nothing to denote preparations for an attack on any one sector, air reconnaissance has shown in the last three days rather larger concentrations of MT than have been seen for some time past, particularly in the south'.[59]

At this point, on the evening of 17 August, GC and CS brought the speculation to an end by sending out to the Middle East what was perhaps the most important single item of information that the Enigma had yet contributed to the desert campaign. The decrypt of a Panzer Army appreciation of 15 August, it contained an outline of Rommel's intentions for the coming offensive. After mentioning that the supply position had eased, that reinforcements had arrived, that the Italians had been rested and reformed, and that a mobile defence in depth had been created and field works and minefields almost completed, the appreciation went on to say that a British attack was possible in late August, more likely after mid-September, in a strength of 3 armoured and 6 or 7 infantry divisions. The supplying and equipping of the German troops and the preparation of all the Axis forces for a further offensive would be largely completed when stores already loaded in Italy had arrived, and after this no further real improvement could be expected. Comparison of strengths showed that until the end of

56.   WO 208/3573 of 10 August 1942.
57.   WO 201/2154, No 285 of 9 August 1942.
58.   ibid, Nos 288 and 289 of 12 and 13 August 1942.
59.   ibid, No 292 of 16 August 1942.

August the Axis, with a 50 per cent superiority in medium artillery and 450 to 500 tanks against an estimated 400, would be strong enough to 'make a quick penetration of the front' in the south; but that in September 'the situation will change considerably to the advantage of the Eighth Army'. The Panzer Army would have to re-group before an attack, and this must be done on moonlight nights because of British air superiority; full moon was on 26 August, and the supply services of the Panzer Army and the German Air Force could just manage to be ready by then, provided convoys arrived on time. Only an attack about 26 August had any prospect of success, because any postponement must of necessity be 'a postponement for a whole month, at the end of which prospects would be remote'. On the other hand, Rommel stressed that his ability to move at that time depended on two things: the immediate despatch to Tobruk or Benghazi of supplies already loaded in Italy; and an assurance that thereafter the despatch by sea of ammunition and fuel to Cyrenaican harbours would be continuous. In the same way, he added, Kesselring considered 26 August a favourable date provided that GAF fuel arrived in the meantime.[60]

□

On 13 August, four days before this signal reached the Middle East, General Montgomery had assumed command of Eighth Army, and on 15 August General Alexander had succeeded General Auchinleck as C-in-C. No basic change was made to Eighth Army's plans following the change of commanders – nor was any required by the intelligence given in the signal of 17 August. In the appreciation he had made on 27 July, in which he had recommended that the command of Eighth Army 'should be put on a permanent footing', General Auchinleck had concluded that while the first priority was to prepare for a defensive battle in the El Alamein-Hamman area, Rommel might be tempted to seek a battle of manoeuvre by striking at the southern flank, the weakest part of the British line.[61] His successors retained his general plan for holding the main Alam el Halfa feature while countering an attempt by Rommel to penetrate in the south.[62]

General Montgomery's appointment did, however, produce a change in style. In a strenuous tour of visits the new Eighth Army commander told his men with remarkable assurance not only that Rommel was going to be defeated but also what he expected Rommel to do – and so much so that Whitehall, already disturbed

60.   MKAs 2094 and 2095 of 17 August 1942; CX/MSS/1300/T16.
61.   CAB 44/98, pp 415–418.
62.   Liddell Hart, *History of the Second World War* (1970), p 291.

by other indications of insecurity, was alarmed lest the enemy
should suspect the security of the Enigma.*

The new style of command, which did so much to raise the
morale of Eighth Army and to form the psychological background
conditioning its subsequent victories, thus owed something directly
to the possession of advance intelligence. Hardly less important,
however, was the fact that the new commander took over as his
intelligence staff a team that had been formed during July by the
transfer of DMI Cairo to be Chief of Staff, Eighth Army, and the
appointment of new men to the posts of GSO I(1)A and GSO
2(1)A.[63]† During the hard fighting between the end of June and the
end of July the new team had already assisted the C-in-C Middle
East to make the maximum use of intelligence. From the beginning
of August it was profiting from its experience during the recent
fighting by introducing further improvements into Eighth Army's
intelligence arrangements. Having noticed how quickly the Army
Y authorities disseminated information from enemy sources about
the whereabouts of British troops, Eighth Army HQ now set up
machinery to reduce the delay in obtaining and distributing
information from its own forward and reconnaissance units. 'We
had found', writes the new Eighth Army Chief of Staff, 'that
information took too long to reach us . . . We therefore established
a network of reporting centres which were echeloned down from the
most forward points of interest to Corps HQs. They gathered and
relayed information direct to Army HQ . . . A special section [at
Army HQ] sifted and passed on all the information received'.[64]
The results of the system, known as the J service, were of course not
only disseminated throughout the Army but also correlated at HQ
with information about the enemy from all sources. At the same
time – the change was announced on 1 August[65] – GS Int altered
the lay-out of the daily intelligence summary which it circulated to
Eighth Army's formations.

Hitherto the summaries had largely been an accumulation of
factual items, and interpretations and conclusions had frequently
been obscured by much complex detail. From now on the details
were relegated to a Part II, for the attention of intelligence officers
only, and the summaries began with a general, jargon-free,
appraisal which sought to ensure that the operational significance
of the latest evidence was not lost on commanders and their staffs.

---

* See below, pp 413–414.
† (1) A denotes Intelligence Operations, (1) B Intelligence Security.

63.   WO 208/3575, p 3: de Guingand, *Operation Victory* (1947), p 138: CAB
       105/18, No 183 of 30 July 1942.
64.   de Guingand, op cit, pp 145–146.
65.   WO 201/2154, No 277 of 1 August: Mockler-Ferryman, *Military Intelligence
       Organisation*, p 180.

Not less important, these general appreciations intended for unin-doctrinated as well as for indoctrinated readers, while taking all sources into account, made better use than before of Sigint. Indeed, 'Ultra was the background to these appreciations, it coloured the whole essay'.[66]

This step, taken from the need to ensure that Eighth Army's officers at HQ and in the subordinate formations were kept abreast of events, reflected the fact that the situation was being more and more fully illuminated by Sigint. From the beginning of August 1942 Sigint was at last providing on the state of the German ground forces in Africa a standard of reporting the equal of that which had been provided about the GAF since the early months of 1941. In particular, two new series of reports, which were to be made by the Panzer Army at regular intervals during the remainder of the north African campaign and which constituted the essential and virtually complete framework for the appreciation of all other Army intelligence, had been decrypted in the Enigma for the first time in the first week of August. One signal gave the complete return of the current strengths in officers, NCOs and men, and in guns, tanks, vehicles and other equipment, of the Panzer Army's divisions and Flak units as at 1 August, together with the establishment strengths.[67] Two other decrypts were a comprehensive tank return of 31 July for German and Italian formations and another tank return of 1 August which gave the current strength in fit tanks for each Panzer division and, for the first time, a firm figure for the establishment of each division.[68]

The complete divisional return of 1 August had shown that the total of German combat troops, about 34,000, was then less than three-quarters of the establishment of 52,000. Three weeks later the decrypt of the Panzer Army's day report for 20 August revealed that the strength of the Army still fell short of what it required for its offensive. Despite the arrival of the troops of 164th Infantry Division, reported by the Enigma in the middle of August,[69] and of most of the Ramcke paratroop brigade, reported on 17 August,[70] the day report complained that the German forces were 15,000 men below strength.[71] Even so, further decrypts during August made it clear that as a result of the arrival of these new formations – and of the Italian Folgore and Pistoia Divisions – the Axis forces were beginning to consume more maintenance stores than could be ferried over with the existing resources.

---

66. WO 208/3575, p 6–7.
67. MKA 1083 of 6 August 1942; CX/MSS/1266/T14.
68. MKA 799 of 31 July 1942; CX/MSS/1254/T10.
69. MK 2137 of 18 August 1942; WO 208/3573 of 10 August 1942.
70. WO 208/3573 of 17 August 1942.
71. MKAs 2604 and 2623 of 24 August 1942; CX/MSS/1320/T21.

The Enigma provided Eighth Army during August with an equally full but more disturbing account of Axis tank reinforcements. The return of 1 August had given the establishments of 15th and 21st Panzer Divisions as 203 and 216 and their strengths in serviceable tanks as 65 and 68. GC and CS then decrypted a signal of 1 August from OKH which announced that over and above the 110 tanks sent to Africa by 23 July, and the fit tanks that were now emerging from the workshops, 82 Pzkw III and 20 Pzkw IV tanks would be despatched in August.[72] During the month of August five further comprehensive tank returns for the Panzer Army were decrypted, and all of them specified type as well as numbers of tanks. They enabled Eighth Army HQ to watch the rise in the number of serviceable German tanks from 133 at the beginning of the month to 234 by 28 August, by which date the number of Pzkw III Specials amounted to 171 and Pzkw IV Specials to 26 as compared with 41 and 14 on 31 July, and also showed the number of Italian tanks rising from 96 to 281 (of which 234 were medium, the rest light) over the same period.[73]

The evidence about GAF strength in the Western Desert was no less complete. The strength was built up during August to the remarkably high figure of 298 aircraft – as compared with 210 before the battle of Gazala – by transfers, largely of fighter aircraft, from Sicily and Russia. The transfers were all recorded by the Enigma, which also reported the strengthening of Fliegerkorps X in Crete,[74] and the intelligence estimate of the number of German aircraft available in north Africa by the end of the month was 310. The Italian Air Force was also reinforced – in fact it was brought up to the number of 460 aircraft[75] – and although its build-up was less thoroughly covered by Sigint, it was clear enough that the enemy air forces were being prepared for an all-out effort.

It was thus with a continuous and comprehensive knowledge of the general state of the enemy's preparations that Eighth Army HQ received and interpreted the clues to his intentions that came in after the Enigma had warned on 17 August that he planned to attack on 26 August.

□

Until 24 August the evidence continued to suggest that the enemy would attack, as planned, on 26 August. On 17 August it was learned from the Enigma that, to avoid arousing British suspicions,

---

72.   MKA 937 of 4 August 1942; CX/MSS/1261/T4.
73.   MKAs 1012 of 5 August 1942, 1741 of 13 August 1942; CX/MSS/1263/T17, 1288/T21.
74.   CX/MSS/1313/T14; AIR 41/50, p 163.
75.   AIR 41/50, p 163.

the Panzer Army had prohibited reconnaissance near the Qattara depression.[76] Kesselring referred to an operation beginning on 26 August in a decrypt of 20 August.[77]* On 24 August the Enigma reported that Mussolini had approved 26 August as the date for the opening of the offensive.[79] By that time Y had detected that Rommel had withdrawn the Panzer divisions from the front line and relieved them with infantry,[80] and air reconnaissance and POW interrogation had provided further evidence that re-grouping was taking place.

On 21 August, interpreting this other evidence in the light of the Enigma, Eighth Army's intelligence summary concluded that 'the parallel to mid-May begins to be pointed' and that 'any advance to gain surprise must begin at night, and probably therefore when the moon is most helpful'.[81] On 22 August it announced that 'the exact time and place the enemy will break through is still open to conjecture', but added: 'We should not expect, on past practice, a concentration of enemy armour except . . . at the eleventh hour for the advance. The presence of 21st Panzer Division in the north or of 15th Panzer Division in the centre is therefore not significant. That an immobile division like 164th sits in the north while 90th Light Division, so often the crust-breaker, is waiting south, points an obvious moral. It would be surprising therefore, though the evidence is still too slight to be conclusive, if the enemy did not advance in the south at full moon'.[82]

At this juncture, on 24 August, GC and CS decrypted a message of 21 August in which Rommel had announced that he was unwell and asked to be relieved by Guderian while he took 'fairly long' leave.[83] Rumours of Rommel's illness appeared in the world Press in the first week of September, by which time there had already been indications in military decrypts that the Germans, alarmed by Axis shipping losses in the Mediterranean, had set up an inquiry into the security of their cyphers in that theatre. The leakage about Rommel's illness accordingly produced considerable alarm, the more so as Axis diplomatic decrypts indicated that the source was in London. On 9 September the Prime Minister asked Sir Edward

---

* On 25 August a further decrypt showed that Kesselring was to move to his battle HQ within the next few days. The Prime Minister, just back from Egypt, instructed that this decrypt should be sent textually to General Alexander, the new C-in-C ME.[78]

76. MKA 2096 of 17 August 1942; CX/MSS/1301/T24.
77. MKA 2274 of 20 August 1942; CX/MSS/1308/T13.
78. Dir/C Archive, 507 of 25 August 1942; MKA 2704 of 25 August 1942; CX/MSS/1323/T20.
79. MKA 2604 of 24 August 1942; CX/MSS/1320/T4.
80. WO 201/2154, No 288 of 12 August 1942.
81. ibid, No 297 of 21 August 1942.
82. ibid, No 298 of 22 August 1942.
83. MKA 2615 of 24 August 1942; CX/MSS/1320/T17.

Bridges to conduct an inquiry into the source of the leak. There followed on 11 September a decrypt which showed the Germans to be highly suspicious as a result of learning from POW that Eighth Army had known the outline and original date of the Alam el Halfa attack from Italian POW and that the news had been given to British troops in advance of the battle. The Prime Minister suspected that General Montgomery had been too free with the Enigma intelligence, using Italian POW statements as cover, and that this cover was far from adequate. In the event cover proved adequate but the Middle East authorities were warned to be more secure and special procedures were introduced for the handling of decrypts that were liable to lead to gossip.[84]* At Eighth Army HQ the news of Rommel's illness was carefully guarded and appreciations unaffected. The intelligence summary for 25 August suggested that 'certain administrative arrangements were not yet complete', but felt certain that these 'will be accelerated so as to allow [the enemy] to strike in the next two days'.[85] The next summary, issued on the evening of 26 August, introduced an Italian POW who had been expecting to take part in an attack on the night of 25–26 August, but warned that, although the attack had been put off, 'the imminent threat of an enemy advance has not diminished. Unless something untoward delays him, such as the continued sinking of his fuel-carrying ships, he is expected to advance before the month is out'.[86] The decrypt of Berlin's reply to Rommel's request to be relieved had reached Eighth Army HQ by emergency signal at midnight on 25–26 August: as there was no Panzer general available to replace him, the DAK's commander would take over and Kesselring would have the supreme command.[87]

Two days later the Prime Minister mentioned to the C-in-C Middle East that MI was now doubtful whether Rommel could start before 3 September unless he obtained fuel 'by methods not at present known to us'. The C-in-C replied that the offensive was 'equal money every day from now onwards. Odds against increas-

---

* These procedures required that no item considered by GC and CS as likely to lead to gossip be teleprinted to Whitehall or signalled to commands without highest authority. When permission was given such items went only to 'C' and the Directors of Intelligence personally in Whitehall or, abroad, only to individual commanders or to their senior intelligence officers in person. The system led to some complaints that high authority saw too much and junior intelligence officers too little.

84.   Dir/C Archive, 672, 674, 675 of 9 September 1942, PM minute of 11 September and PM telegram to Middle East, CXG 314 of 18 September 1942; CX/MSS/1391/T1.
85.   WO 201/2154, No 301 of 25 August 1942.
86.   ibid, No 302 of 26 August 1942.
87.   QT 40 of 2229/25 August 1942; CX/MSS/1326/T14.

ing till 2 September, when it can be considered unlikely'.[88] Eighth Army intelligence summaries maintained the same theme as the C-in-C. On 27 August the summary announced that full-scale attack was less likely to come that night than on 28 or 29 August.[89] The summary issued on the evening of 28 August reported that the enemy was still 'not quite ready'.[90] It gave in support of this conclusion the fact that Y units had heard 15th Panzer Division asking for as much fuel as possible, 'a demand not acceded to today'. The summary for 29 August quoted another Italian POW to the effect that the enemy 'apparently intended to attack this moon' and went on 'there is no evidence that he has yet abandoned the idea . . . The temporary delay may be due to a hitch in supplies as a result of our successful interference . . . and to the tardy arrival in the forward area of essential material especially fuel'.[91] The evidence for this estimate had come from the Enigma. The Enigma had not revealed, however, that Rommel had decided on 29 August that he must limit the scale of his offensive because of attacks on his shipping.*

In a message decrypted on 26 August the Enigma disclosed that the Panzer Army had ordered that motor transport sent as an emergency measure to pick up fuel and ammunition was to rejoin its units by 28 August.[92] On 26 and 27 August other decrypts reported that disruption to shipping had upset the Panzer Army's fuel supply programme and forced the Germans to give up fuel to the Italians.[93] A further decrypt indicating that an immediate offensive was not likely reached the Western Desert in the early hours of 28 August: it was a signal of the morning of 27 August in which the GAF had announced an extensive reshuffle of its senior commanders in the Mediterranean and north Africa, including the transfer of Fliegerführer Afrika to be AOC Fliegerkorps X.[94] Two other decrypts received on the morning of 28 August reported, on the other hand, that the Ramcke Brigade was to be sent forward that day, and that speed was imperative, and that emergency arrangements were now being made to airlift petrol from Crete.[95] And then, on the morning of 29 August, when the full moon period was drawing to an end, the Enigma confirmed that the enemy had

---

* See below, p 419 et seq.

88. Churchill, *The Second World War*, Vol IV (1951), p 489; WO 208/3573 of 31 August, 1942.

89. WO 201/2154, No 303 of 27 August.

90. ibid, No 304 of 28 August 1942.

91. ibid, No 305 of 29 August 1942.

92. QT 101 of 26 August 1942; CX/MSS/1330/T21.

93. QTs 66 of 26 August and 142 of 27 August 1942; CX/MSS/1327/T5, 1332/T16.

94. QT 194 of 2357/27 August 1942; CX/MSS/1331/T10.

95. QTs 226 and 227 of 28 August 1942; CX/MSS/1335/T6 and 23.

still not cancelled his offensive. In one decrypt – of a signal transmitted on 26 August – Rommel told Berlin that on medical advice he could retain command during the coming operation, though he would need lengthy treatment in Germany later.[96] In another – of a signal transmitted on 27 August – the Panzer Army informed Berlin and Rome that because of delays to a convoy 'the decision about carrying out the known intention will not be notified until 29 August'.[97]

In the event the offensive got under way during the night of 30–31 August, though Rommel did not decide to start that night until 1600 on 30 August.[98] Intelligence gave no last-minute alert. During 30 August, however, Y disclosed that 15th Panzer Division was moving south[99] and at last light – and in the area as well as at the time of day and within the period announced by the Enigma as long ago as 17 August – the RAF sighted the enemy's final concentrations.[100]

□

Deprived of the advantage of surprise, Rommel's thrust failed to make the quick penetration he had hoped for. During the night of 30–31 August it was subjected to heavy RAF bombing attacks while passing through the British minefields. In the afternoon of 31 August, Rommel having been forced to abandon his original intention of trying to outflank the position to the south, it turned north in an attempt to capture the Alam el Halfa ridge, consuming abnormally large amounts of fuel in this manouevre.* It was repulsed by gunfire from artillery and tanks which had been concentrated solely on the assumption that an enemy offensive could not succeed unless it captured the ridge. Rommel resumed the attack on the morning of 1 September, but at noon he decided temporarily to go over to the defensive where he stood.

The Enigma decrypt announcing this decision was the first important intelligence to be received about the conduct of the battle. It did not reach Eighth Army HQ until the early hours of 2

---

* A deception plan had been prepared by the intelligence and survey branches responsible for the production of 'going' maps. This was designed to lead Rommel up to the ridge by the route he eventually adopted. But the fact that his original plan would have sent the DAK over ground marked on this map as bad 'going' suggests that he was not influenced by the deception.[101]

96. QT 300 of 29 August 1942; CX/MSS/1339/T12.
97. QT 301 of 29 August 1942; CX/MSS/1339/T25.
98. EDS/Appreciation/9, Part IV, p 84.
99. WO 201/2154, No 306 of 30 August.
100. Playfair, op cit, Vol III, p 385.
101. Hunt, op cit, pp 124–125; de Guingand, op cit, p 148; Playfair, op cit, Vol III, p 384; Carver, *El Alamein* (1962), p 39; AIR 41/50, p 170.

September,[102] by which time GS Int, Eighth Army had already observed that the enemy did not seem to be intent on an all-out assault[103] and Eighth Army's commander had begun to prepare for a move to cut off a possible enemy retreat.[104] On the same morning Rommel ordered a withdrawal, to be spread over several days, to positions just west of the British minefield.[105] Army Y did not intercept this order – during 1, 2 and most of 3 September, indeed, it intercepted scarcely anything – nor did Rommel's announcement of his intention to OKW appear in the Enigma decrypts. On the morning of 3 September, however, air reconnaissance reported that three large columns were moving west, leaving behind large numbers of damaged tanks, and later that day Y revealed that 90th Light Division was leading the movement.[106] During 4 and 5 September Rommel defeated a belated and, as it turned out, costly attempt to interfere with his withdrawal, of which Y and reconnaissance were now supplying plentiful details.[107] In the afternoon of 6 September Eighth Army learned from the Enigma that the Panzer Army had already reached positions west of the minefields and was going over to the defensive there.[108]

On the same day the Enigma carried the Panzer Army's report on the battle of Alam el Halfa, though the report was not decrypted till 8 September.[109] It announced that only 36 German tanks and 11 Italian tanks had been total losses. This report was to be borne out by a comprehensive tank return of 20 September which gave the German figure as 193 (as against 234 on 28 August) and the Italian as 231 (as against 242).[110] Though the Panzer Army admitted to severe losses in guns and motor transport, and attributed them to air attacks, it had indeed abandoned its offensive less on account of battle losses than of supply difficulties, and it was to these that its report gave the greatest prominence.[111]

□

The supply difficulties which played so large a part in forcing Rommel to abandon the battle of Alam el Halfa had already delayed his offensive, forced him to reduce its objective and all but forced him to cancel it at the end of August. They owed something

102. QT 585 of 0306/2 September 1942; CX/MSS/1355/T10.
103. Playfair, op cit, Vol III, p 387.
104. ibid. 105. ibid, p 388.
106. WO 169/3937, Eighth Army Intelligence Summary No 310 of 3 September 1942.
107. ibid, Nos 311 and 312 of 4 and 5 September 1942.
108. QT 844 of 1206/6 September 1942; CX/MSS/1372/T7.
109. QT 941 of 8 September 1942; CX/MSS/1378/T19.
110. CX/MSS/1434/T10.
111. QT 941 of 8 September 1942; CX/MSS/1378/T19.

to the administrative problems created by the length of the Axis supply lines in north Africa and the restricted facilities of the forward ports. Above all, however, they were brought about by the revival, especially from the middle of August, for the first time since February 1942, of intensive British attacks on Axis shipping.

Attacks on coastal shipping and supply columns in the forward area had already been among the factors which forced Rommel to accept 'a temporary cessation of attack on a large scale' at the beginning of July.* From the end of July, when the ground fighting stopped, the RAF had devoted a major effort to destroying supplies on the roads and off the coast east of Benghazi and Tobruk, and to bombing Tobruk and Mersa Matruh. But by the middle of August Axis administrative improvements and increased GAF protection on the forward supply routes had so restored the situation that Rommel had decided that he could risk going over to the offensive so long as there was no interruption in the despatch of supplies from Italy to north Africa.† At that point British attempts to interrupt the trans-Mediterranean shipping had met with only occasional successes since February.

At the end of May the withdrawal of Fliegerkorps II from Sicily had at once been followed by the resumption of supply convoys to Malta and the reinforcement of Malta's strike and reconnaissance aircraft. During June two convoys had sailed, one from Gibraltar and one from Alexandria. But only two ships had succeeded in getting through, and Malta had continued to be short of aviation fuel. During July the GAF, in a successful effort to prevent the arrival of reinforcements, had resumed its assault on the island. At the same time the Axis had begun to sail ships to Tobruk, beyond the range of Malta's strike aircraft, and an attempt to extend the range of those aircraft by refuelling them in the desert behind the enemy's lines had proved unsuccessful. Although 12 Axis ships had been sunk in the last 10 days of June and during July, all had been sunk on the coastal run between Tobruk and the front. Nor did matters improve during the first half of August. The GAF assault on Malta was now faltering, British submarines had returned to Malta, and at the request of the Middle East Defence Committee further submarines were being sent to operate from Malta and Beirut; but only three ships were sunk in these two weeks – and all by submarine – largely because Malta was again short of fuel until it received five ships, the first to arrive since June, from the mid-August supply convoy from Gibraltar.‡ At that point, on the other hand, with the replenishment of Malta's supplies and

---

* See above, p 397.   † See above, p 409.
   ‡ There was a great volume of Enigma evidence about the high priority that the GAF gave to stopping this convoy, but very little of it was of immediate operational value to those defending it. The next convoy to reach Malta arrived in November; it was the first to sustain no casualties.

the reinforcement of the Mediterranean submarines, another sustained attack on Axis shipping became possible.

The attack began with the sinking of two large freighters – the *Lerici* by submarine on 15 August, the *Pilo* by the RAF on 17 August. Their loss came at a time when, as the Enigma revealed, the Panzer Army's consumption had been exceeding intake since the beginning of the month and stocks were sufficient to last only until 26 August;[112] it thus posed a serious threat to Rommel's plan to attack on that date, which he had announced as recently as 15 August.[113]*

On 19 August, two days after receiving the decrypt of Rommel's announcement, the Chiefs of Staff instructed the authorities in the Mediterranean to make a supreme effort, by every means, to interrupt the enemy's supply shipping during the next ten days.[114] On 21 August the RAF torpedoed the *Pozarica*, a tanker carrying fuel for the Italians, and directly as a result of this sinking, as the Panzer Army reported on 25 August, the Italian supply situation became 'likewise very strained'.[115] In another decrypt obtained on 26 August the Panzer Army complained that the sinking of the *Pozarica* had delayed the sailing of the *San Andrea*, another tanker whose cargo had been a 'key factor' in its fuel programme.[116] Although it did not emerge from the Enigma, it was these setbacks which led Rommel to decide on 24 August that he could not yet fix a date for his offensive.[117]

On 26 August the Enigma provided full details of an ambitious programme drawn up on 24 August and involving the arrival of 20 ships in north Africa between 25 August and 5 September.[118] The bombing of the Corinth canal by the RAF on 26 August disrupted this programme and led the Axis commanders in Africa to make the date of their offensive dependent on the arrival of a further fuel convoy.[119] This decision was reflected in the Panzer Army message of 27 August, the decrypt of which informed Eighth Army on the morning of 29 August that because of the non-arrival of fuel and ammunition it could not announce the date of its attack until 29 August.[†]

---

*See above, pp 408–409.   † See above, p. 416.

112. MKA 2282 of 20 August 1942; CX/MSS/1308/T22.
113. EDS/Appreciation/9, Part IV, pp 79–80.
114. CAB 79/22, COS (42) 240th Meeting, 18 August; CAB 79/57, COS (42) 94th (o) Meeting, 19 August: CAB 105/18, No 131 of 19 August 1942.
115. QT 142 of 27 August 1942; CX/MSS/1332/T16.
116. QT 66 of 26 August 1942; CX/MSS/1327/T5.
117. EDS/Appreciation/9, Part IV, p 83.
118. QT 66 of 26 August 1942; CX/MSS/1327/T5.
119. EDS/Appreciation/9, Part IV, p 84.

On 28 August the Enigma gave the details of the fuel cargoes of eight ships and announced a new emergency programme for getting them to Africa between 28 August and 2 September;[120] and on 29 August C 38 m announced that in addition the *San Andrea* had just sailed from Taranto.[121] More important, the Enigma had already provided information about the times and routes of some of the ships.[122] Two of the eight – the *Dielpi* with 2,200 tons for the GAF and the *Istria* with 200 tons for the Italians – and one other ship – the *Camperio* – had already been sunk on 27 August.

As a result of these sinkings Rommel decided on 29 August that he must limit his offensive to a local operation aimed at destroying British forces in the Alamein position.[123] This decision was not revealed by the Enigma. During 30 August, however, the decrypts produced two reports from the Panzer Army of 28 August – one announcing that of the 2,400 tons of fuel promised for that day only 100 tons had arrived, so that stocks were sufficient for only six days' fighting; the other announcing that 'particularly important' tank and anti-tank ammunition were also needed with 'utmost urgency'.[124] Late on 30 August the GAF Enigma confirmed that the Axis supply programme had suffered another blow, the torpedoing of the *San Andrea*.[125] Much later on, in October, the Army Enigma disclosed that the fuel and ammunition shortage had not been overcome when Rommel decided at 1600 on 30 August to proceed with his advance: his troops moved off with fuel for only $4\frac{1}{2}$ days' fighting when they had required enough for 15, and with sufficient ammunition for only four to six days.[126] We can only speculate as to whether Rommel's decision sprang from the expectation that he would still get supplies by capture or arrivals, rather than from the hope of achieving surprise and from the fear that he would be overwhelmed by Eighth Army's growing superiority if he did not attack.

At all events, the Enigma showed that Kesselring had by 29 August improvised an emergency air-lift of fuel from Italy to Crete, from Crete to Tobruk, and from Tobruk to the front, and on 30 August, when two of the remaining six ships of the emergency sailing programme had got through to Tobruk,* it was still possible to think that the other four would arrive. But as a result of RAF

---

* The Enigma disclosed that the 1,500 tons of aircraft fuel carried by one of these – the *Giorgio* – was found to be contaminated and unusable.[127]

120.   QT 232 of 28 August 1942; CX/MSS/1335/T29.
121.   QT 289 of 29 August 1942; ZTPI 16078.
122.   QT 100 of 27 August 1942; CX/MSS/1330/T13.
123.   EDS/Appreciation/9, Part IV, p 84.
124.   QT 396 of 30 August 1942; CX/MSS/1344/T26.
125.   QT 425 of 30 August 1942; CX/MSS/1346/T27.
126.   CX/MSS/1375/T26; AIR 41/50, p 165, quoting the DAK War Diary.
127.   QT 430 of 31 August 1942; CX/MSS/1346/T20.

attacks on 2 September one of them – the *Picci Fassio* – was sunk, another – the *Abruzzi* which had been promised for 30 August but was sailing late – was damaged and the sailing of a third, the *Bianchi*, was delayed. On 4 September, when the *Bianchi* was also sunk by air attack, the sixth ship got through with the first fuel the Army had received by sea since 30 August.[128] By then, however, at mid-day on 2 September, Rommel had ordered the withdrawal. On 3 September the Enigma disclosed that it was because of the sinking of the *San Andrea* and the non-arrival of the *Abruzzi* that he had already on the afternoon of 1 September gone over to the defensive.[129] His account to OKW of his decision to withdraw, which was not revealed in the Enigma, attributed the decision to the delay imposed by mines, to the incessant day and night attacks by the RAF and to the shortage of petrol: he had now heard of the loss of the *Picci Fassio* which meant that fuel supplies could not be assured before 7 September even if other ships got through.[130]

On 29 August, as the Enigma revealed on 30 August, Rome had advised the Panzer Army that although 'Malta's new lease of life' ruled out the transport of troops by sea, five more ships with running supplies would sail in the first few days of September.[131] By 5 September three of these had been sunk. The others were delayed and it was not until three ships from a heavily guarded convoy reached Tobruk on 8 September that the Panzer Army could be certain even of holding its new defensive positions. Until the same date the GAF's difficulties were no less acute. Partly because it had to divert much of its effort to shipping protection from the beginning of September, but mainly because of a shortage of fuel, of which the Enigma provided full details,[132] the GAF's daily sortie rate in the land battle had dropped steadily from 310 on 31 August to 130 on 6 September, the day on which the Panzer Army completed its withdrawal.

The successes against Axis shipping before and during the battle of Alam el Halfa contrasted sharply with the British inability to disrupt Rommel's supply lines before the battle of Gazala – an inability which the Cs-in-C Middle East had singled out as having contributed significantly to their defeat in that battle when they reported on it at the end of June.[133] Nor did the rest of September see any decline in the British attacks. Eleven ships were sunk in all in that month, containing some 20 per cent of the total cargo

---

128.   EDS/Appreciation/9, Part IV, p 84; Playfair, op cit, Vol III, p 382(n).
129.   QT 658 of 3 September 1942; CX/MSS/1359/T21.
130.   Playfair, op cit, Vol III, p 388.
131.   QT 417 of 30 August 1942; CX/MSS/1344/T30, 1346/T1.
132.   eg QTs 596 and 624 of 2 September 1942; CX/MSS/1351/T9, 1355/T5, 1358/T19.
133.   CAB 105/18, Nos 16 of 24 June and 25 of 25 June 1942.

despatched.* By the end of September Ciano was complaining that 'at this rate the African problem will automatically end since we shall have no more ships with which to supply Libya'.[136] In October the Axis sustained comparable losses.* Nor is there any reason to disagree with GC and CS's conclusion that it was these losses, and particularly the sinking of three tankers in the closing days of October, that finally undermined Rommel's ability to resist the British offensive in the second battle of Alamein.†

As in the period before their curtailment in February 1942, the British attacks were guided by intelligence derived mainly from the C 38 m traffic with help from the GAF Enigma. In June, when it once more became possible to act on its advance notice of shipping

* I *Cargoes disembarked in Libya, and the percentage lost on passage during June–December 1942*[134]

1942	Cargo type	Cargo disembarked (tons)	Percentage lost on the way
June	(a)* (b)	26,759 5,568	22
July	(a) (b)	67,590 23,901	6
August	(a) (b)	29,155 22,500	33
September	(a) (b)	46,165 31,061	20
October	(a) (b)	33,390 12,308	44
November	(a) (b)	42,005 21,731	26
December	(a) (b)	4,093 2,058	52

* (a) = General military cargoes
  (b) = Fuel

II   *Number and tonnage of Italian and German merchant ships over 500 tons sunk at sea or in port in the Mediterranean June–December 1942*[135]

June	6	20,016
July	7	15,588
August	12	65,006
September	11	33,446
October	17	54,804
November	17	54,584
December	33	94,526
Total	103	337,970

Note: It must be remembered when considering these statistics that they do not reflect the full importance of the critical cargoes sunk as a result of the policy of the attack on ships, as explained in the text.

† See below, p 439 et seq.

134. Playfair, op cit, Vol III, p 327, Vol IV (1966), p 210.
135. ibid, Vol III, p 327, Vol IV, p 210; Naval Historical Branch letter to Cabinet Office Historical Section, 10 March 1978.
136. Quoted in Richards, *The RAF 1939–45*, Vol II (1954), p 231.

movements, and again in September, this fact revived the suggestion that the C 38 m traffic should be deciphered in the theatre, at
Malta or Alexandria. On both occasions the suggestion was again
rejected, mainly on security grounds, but the system by which the
decrypts were transmitted to the commands from GC and CS
worked well enough. Of the 48 Axis ships sunk in the period from 2
June to 6 November, by which date the second battle of Alamein
had been won, only one (766 tons) was not reported to the Middle
East by GC and CS, while for all but two of the remaining 47 GC
and CS provided either the location in port or anchorage, or the
timing or routeing of the final voyage,* in good time for the
operational authorities to reconnoitre and attack.

In the case of most of these ships Sigint also supplied details of
the cargoes carried. That these details were more readily available
than before was due to the fact that from the early summer of 1942
the C 38 m and GAF Enigma decrypts were being supplemented
by those of the German Army Enigma traffic. It was the Army
Enigma Chaffinch decrypts that provided most of the intelligence
about cargoes.† At the same time Chaffinch built up for the British
authorities an ever-growing knowledge of the German Army's
supply situation. It was not until towards the end of October that
GC and CS was able to unravel with complete confidence the
elaborate pro-formas used by the Army's Quartermaster in his
ten-day reports, and thus to enable the authorities to bring a
statistical approach to their calculations. But by August they were
already able to mate the intelligence about individual cargoes with
their knowledge of the enemy's general supply position in such a
way as to economise their limited operational resources and obtain
the maximum damage from each sinking by directing attention to
the most valuable ships.

At first the target selection, and the work of combining the
Enigma with other information, was done by naval intelligence at
Alexandria and by the Army and RAF intelligence staffs in Cairo.
In September, however, the offices of C-in-C Mediterranean and of
No 201 Wing RAF – the command responsible for anti-shipping
operations from Egypt – were combined into a single HQ and the
selection of targets was made the responsibility of an inter-Service
group in Cairo which had been formed early in 1942 to study the
enemy's supply situation in detail. The group collated the Sigint
with information from all other sources, issued daily to all commands a summary of shipping movements, a statement of the

---

* See Appendix 17.

† Only about half of what was available of the Chaffinch was broken until September when
GC and CS was able to get much closer to its goal of 21 Chaffinch breaks a week. This
success brought about a stiffening of German cypher security which made the breaking of
Chaffinch much more difficult at the end of 1942.

enemy's supply position and a list of priority targets, and conducted a running correspondence with the commands on the SCU/SLU link about the planning of their attacks. In this way, to take a hypothetical example, Malta might allow a ship carrying rations to pass unscathed to Tripoli because ration stocks in Africa were known to be large, and might take on instead a tanker on the west coast of Greece, at the extreme limit of Malta's range, in order to allow Alexandria to give its undivided attention to ships leaving the Piraeus with ammunition cargoes that were badly needed in preparation for the fighting at Alamein.[137]

Bombing attacks on ships in port – mainly at Tobruk and Benghazi, but also at intermediate harbours like Navarino – were similarly guided by what Sigint had to say about the value to Rommel of their cargoes. By way of illustration, a heavy air attack against Benghazi was carried out on the night of 22–23 September after the C 38 m decrypts had revealed the arrival on 21 September of the *Apuania* with a large quantity of ammunition and rations and 10 tanks.[138] The ship blew up with the loss of almost all her cargo, as the Army Enigma decrypts soon revealed, and with great damage to the port installations and to other ships in harbour.[139]

The effectiveness with which the intelligence was exploited did not fail to arouse Axis suspicions. In October 1942 the Italians introduced new indicator settings for the C 38 m machine, and for a week or two the decryption of the traffic at GC and CS was subject to considerable delays. Fortunately, the October delays did not greatly reduce the flow of timely intelligence; during September the greater part of the GAF bomber force in the eastern Mediterranean was diverted to convoy escort in a desperate attempt to reduce shipping losses, and with this diversion the GAF Enigma became a prime source of intelligence about Axis shipping movements. Nor did the level of British sinkings undergo any decline in the period between the battle of Alamein and the end of the war in Africa. In December 1942 they accounted for no less than 52 per cent of the cargo the Axis sailed;* and at about that time, in a letter to an officer in OKH, a German staff officer attributed them to 'the excellent British network of agents' in Italian ports. 'Immediately after a ship is loaded our enemies get complete details sent to Cairo and Alexandria of the type, quantity and importance of the whole cargo. The convoy sets sail from Naples quietly and peacefully, escorted by three Italian torpedo-boats; then just before it gets to Tripoli the British come flying over and of course it is only the

---

* See above, p 422, fn*.

137.   ADM 223/89, Titterton, Report of Mediterranean Intelligence Centre, Section III.
138.   QT 1826 of 21 September 1942; ZTPI 17676.
139.   QT 1879 of 21 September 1942; CX/MSS/1429/T30 and 34, 1431/T6.

German steamer that gets hit, and it carries a cargo for which Rommel is eagerly waiting. Nothing happens to the Italian ships. The German security service should get to work on this problem . . .'

□

Between the battle of Alam el Halfa and the second battle of Alamein Sigint was not only valuable for its contribution to the success of the offensive against the enemy's supply-line to north Africa, an offensive that was intensified as part of the British preparations for the coming British assault.[140] What was scarcely less important, it also established the precise effect of the offensive on the enemy's logistic and manpower position. The British authorities would in any case have judged that the enemy could not hope to match the resources of Eighth Army, which had now been strongly reinforced and re-equipped. It was quite another thing that they should have known that down to 23–24 October, the date selected for their own attack, the enemy's supply position was progressively deteriorating, after a temporary recovery from the crisis experienced early in September, and that the Panzer Army was being deprived of freedom of operation.[141] And this knowledge they derived from GC and CS's decrypts of the Panzer Army's own running commentary on the situation.

On 6 September the Panzer Army reported that it had rations for 23 days, ammunition for only 14 days' fighting and sufficient fuel for only 8 days even at the current level of consumption: its long supply columns from Benghazi and Tobruk to the front required huge quantities of fuel, coastal traffic being inadequate and the railway taking only a small proportion of the total load. It warned that a serious supply crisis threatened and, since 'the continued uncertainty of the sea route must be assumed', requested the ferrying of general maintenance stores by air. Worried by the continuing reinforcement of Eighth Army, it also requested the despatch of 22nd Division from Crete, of German troops who had been kept waiting in Italy and of the long-overdue motor transport of 164th Division and the Ramcke Brigade, though these arrivals would only increase the supply problem.[142]

In response to this plea the Germans discontinued the air transport of fuel to north Africa, started during the Alam el Halfa emergency, and took the drastic step of temporarily stopping the air transport of troop replacements to make possible the flying-in of

140. AIR 41/50, p 223; Hunt, op cit, pp 128–129.
141. Howard, *Grand Strategy*, Vol IV (1972), p 64; eg QT 4077 of 22 October 1942; CX/MSS/1562/T23.
142. QT 941 of 8 September 1942; CX/MSS/1378/T19.

daily supplies. Some slight improvement was also brought about by the fact that the Italians managed to get ships across, though they were now driven by the RAF's heavy raids on Tobruk to ignore German protests and to send more of them to Benghazi, much further to the rear.[143] By 18 September, however, the Panzer Army was again complaining that the supply situation was becoming 'highly critical',[144] and on 24 September, reporting that over and above the serious fuel shortage the difficulty of taking stocks forward from Tripoli and Benghazi had made it necessary to cut the bread (and pasta) ration, it insisted that until the railway and coastal shipping replaced truck transport to the front it could not hope to build up fuel stocks from its existing receipts.[145]

In a rare Enigma reference to Germany's over-all fuel difficulties, OKH replied that supplementary fuel could not be sent to north Africa at once in view of the general fuel situation.[146] On 1 October, on the other hand, the Panzer Army was admitting that it had managed to build up its fuel stocks to 10.5 consumption units.[147] On the assumption which had been found to be reliable by the Middle East intelligence staffs – the assumption that Rommel's forces consumed two-thirds of a unit per day during full-scale operations – this was sufficient for 16 days at full scale.* On the same date, by reference to another tested assumption, the Enigma disclosed that the Panzer Army had ammunition for only six days' full-scale operations – 3.5 issues – and that its stocks of 50 mm anti-tank ammunition (1.5 issues), of 76.2 mm anti-tank ammunition (2.0 issues), of 50 mm tank gun ammunition (1.0 issue) and of 75 mm tank gun ammunition (1.3 issues) were below the general stock figure. Moreover, GC and CS had worked out that that figure (3.5 issues) represented stocks held throughout north Africa, not stocks held forward. In the same message of 1 October the Panzer Army reported that, because of difficulties in moving stocks forward, its food supplies were 'far from sufficient' and that particularly severe cuts were being applied to rations of vegetables, fruit, flour and drinks.[148] On 6 October the food situation had worsened, the Panzer Army reporting that the troops were 'suffering from undernourishment, a sharp decrease in efficiency and a high rate of sickness', and fuel stocks were down to 8.5 consump-

---

* But Rommel equated one unit with one day's full-scale consumption. See below, p 432.

143.   QTs 1822 of 21 September, 1989 of 23 September, 2091 of 24 September 1942; CX/MSS/1429/T32, 1437/T1, 1438/T3; AIR 41/50, p 229.
144.   AIR 41/50, p 229; QT 2091 of 24 September 1942; CX/MSS/1438/T3.
145.   QT 2256 of 27 September 1942; CX/MSS/1447/T11.
146.   QT 2242 of 26 September 1942; CX/MSS/1446/T9.
147.   QT 2644 of 2 October 1942; CX/MSS/1470/T2.
148.   CX/MSS/1470/T2.

tion units.[149] No fuel had reached north Africa in the first week of October, thanks mainly to successful RAF attacks near and in Navarino on two large ships, the *Unione* and the *Nino Bixio*, details of whose routes and cargoes had been provided by GC and CS.[150]

On 8 October, GC and CS decrypted a personal appeal from Stumme, Rommel's temporary replacement.* Fuel was very strained, ammunition quite insufficient, rations at 'an unsurpassably low level', motor transport and spares a cause of extreme anxiety. 'Contrast Eighth Army, considerably superior to us . . . and ready to attack.' If the Panzer Army was to maintain the north African theatre of war it must receive about 30,000 tons of supplies a month, including 12,000 of fuel, 9,000 of ammunition and 6,000 of rations. In addition, it needed as a matter of urgency 9,000 personnel replacements a month by air and the shipment of the supply and unit MT that had long been waiting in Italy.[151] A few days earlier the decrypt of a Panzer Army return had disclosed that it had received 11,200 tons of fuel, 2,500 tons of ammunition and 1,806 tons of rations during September.[152] A few days later another temporary improvement in the fuel situation, brought about by the arrival of the *Ankara* on 10 October, was coming to an end. On 20 October the Panzer Army signalled that by 25 October fuel stocks would be down to 3 consumption units ($4\frac{1}{2}$ days' battle supply), of which only 2 units (3 days) were east of Tobruk, and that it 'did not possess the operational freedom of movement which was absolutely essential in consideration of the fact that the British offensive can be expected to start any day'.[153] In contrast, transport by submarines and aircraft was doing something to relieve the shortage of ammunition, especially of anti-tank ammunition, and on 19 October the Panzer Army reported that total stocks in the battle area had risen to over 16 days' supply.[154] On the same day, however, it warned that since the RAF attacks had considerably reduced the efficiency of the railway, and coastal shipping remained inadequate, 'an impossible strain is still being thrown on transport in the forward area', and that storms in Cyrenaica were making matters worse by damaging water supplies and imposing long hauls to and from wells further to the rear.[155]

---

* See below, pp 440–441, fn *.

149. QT 3024 of 8 October 1942; CX/1492/T21.
150. MKAs 1914 of 15 August, 2028 of 17 August 1942; QT 66 of 26 August 1942; CX/MSS/1298/T29 and 33, 1327/T5; ZTPI 15177; AIR 41/50, p 231.
151. QTs 3059 of 8 October, 3117 of 9 October 1942; CX/MSS/1499/T1 and 12.
152. QT 2644 of 2 October 1942; CX/MSS/1470/T2.
153. QT 4077 of 20 October 1942; CX/MSS/1562/T23; Howard, op cit, Vol IV, p 64.
154. QT 3973 of 21 October 1942; CX/MSS/1556/T14.   155. ibid.

To complement the intelligence they received up to the date of the British attack, Eighth Army HQ and Cairo knew that, apart from Flakdivision 19, a GAF formation sent over on the eve of the attack in response to appeals for more protection against the RAF, the Panzer Army had not been reinforced since the Alam el Halfa battle. Speculation about the possible arrival of 22nd Division, which the Panzer Army had requested on 6 September, was ended on 12 September when the Enigma revealed that in view of 'the changed situation in the eastern Mediterranean', Hitler had decreed that the reinforcement of Crete must be accelerated and that 22nd Division was to be earmarked for that purpose.[156] It then emerged from the decrypts that the Panzer Army had been offered one of 22nd Division's infantry regiments (IR 47) but that transport and other delays were holding up its arrival.[157] As for replacement troops, the Enigma showed that these were arriving at the rate of 100 a day, and that this was insufficient to cover the sickness rate; thus 950 replacements arrived in the first fortnight of October and 1,500 men fell sick in the same period.[158] Just before the British attack GC and CS decrypted a second complete strength return from the Panzer Army. Dated 20 October, it showed that the forward German units and formations numbered 49,000 men, as compared with 34,000 on 1 August, and that the number of Italian troops in the Panzer Army was 54,000.[159] Eighth Army's fighting strength on the same day was 195,000 men.[160]

The Enigma, supplemented by Army Y intercepts of the regular returns made by 15th and 21st Panzer Divisions,[161] kept Eighth Army equally well informed of the enemy's tank strength. An Enigma decrypt revealed that 224 German and 270 Italian tanks were operational on 30 September.[162] Reporting this on 2 October, GS Int, Eighth Army assumed that the German number might increase by as much as 100.[163] But a further return of 14 October gave the German figure as 234, and on 22 October GS Int calculated that the number of German tanks was unlikely to have reached 270.[164] On the first day of the battle it learned from a further Enigma return dated 23 October that the DAK had 238

---

156.   WO 169/3937 No 317 of 10 September 1942 and its Appendix A.
157.   QTs 4487 of 27 October and 5250 of 4 November 1942;
        CX/MSS/1585/T31, 1628/T28.
158.   QT 3638 of 16 October 1942; CX/MSS/1531/T12.
159.   QT 4342 of 25 October, 4543 of 28 October 1942; CX/MSS/1576/T25,
        1590/T10.
160.   Playfair, op cit, Vol IV, p 300.
161.   WO 169/3937, No 322 of 15 September 1942.
162.   QT 2607 of 2 October 1942; CX/MSS/1467/T19.
163.   WO 201/2155, Eighth Army Intelligence Summary No 336 of 2 October
        1942.
164.   QT 3533 of 15 October 1942; CX/MSS/1526/T5.

tanks, of which 30 were Pzkw II unsuitable for battle, and the Italians 279 medium tanks.[165] Eighth Army then had 1,029 tanks fit and 200 available as immediate replacements, and a further 1,000 were being repaired or modified in workshops.[166] More important, the return for 23 October specified the number of each type of German tank. It showed that the total included 86 Pzkw III Special and 30 Pzkw IV Special, and confirmed a reassurance which Eighth Army had received a few days earlier to the effect that a new and heavier tank had not yet reached Africa. The Enigma had made its first obscure reference to the existence of the new tank, the Tiger (Pzkw VI), as long ago as 20 May 1942.[167] On 16 September it had associated the new tank with north Africa for the first time in a message in which OKH advised the Panzer Army of its dimensions.[168] In a further decrypt dated 16 October the Panzer Army had enquired about the whereabouts of the 40 Pzkw III and of the 40 Pzkw VI which it expected for 164th Division and for Panzer Abteilung 90, a new armoured unit destined for 90th Light Division whose possible despatch to or creation in north Africa had been hinted at in Enigma decrypts in August.[169] But the reply to this signal had stated that 10 Tiger tanks would be sent in November and 10 in December.[170] In the event, they were sent to Tunisia – and during the battle of Alamein only the Pzkw IV Special, 30 in number, was comparable in performance with the Grants and Shermans, of which Eighth Army had 500.[171]*

□

Valuable as it was for confirming that the supply situation and the balance of forces were tipping increasingly in Eighth Army's favour, this intelligence had less influence on the planning of the British offensive than did two other considerations. Eighth Army's first plan, dated 19 September, envisaged an assault on the enemy's powerfully prepared defensive position with an immensely superior force and a powerful encircling movement with the object of trapping and destroying him. But overwhelming superiority for

---

* The Shermans had by now received capped ammunition for their main armament. This greatly improved their performance against German armour.[172]

165.   QT 4234 of 24 October 1942; CX/MSS/1572/T14.
166.   Playfair, op cit, Vol IV, pp 9, 30.
167.   CX/MSS/1143/T5.
168.   QT 2004 of 23 September 1942; CX/MSS/1435/T3.
169.   WO 201/2155, No 330 of 2 October 1942.
170.   QTs 3413 of 14 October, 3639 of 16 October 1942; CX/MSS/1519/T13, 1531/T9.
171.   Liddell Hart, op cit, p 298.
172.   Playfair, op cit, Vol III, p 438.

Eighth Army was secured only by taking a calculated risk in relation to the possibility of a German attack against the northern flank of the Middle East and by deferring the offensive, while the date selected for the offensive, 24 October, incurred the further risk that it would give the enemy time to improve his defences.

During the month of September the development of an early German threat to Iran and Iraq could not be ruled out. On 2 September, when German forces were only 40 miles from Grozny in the Caucasus, the JIC assessed that they were nevertheless unlikely to reach Baku by the end of October or Tiflis before mid-November but that, if Russian resistance flagged, they could reach northern Iran by the end of December; after that date the winter weather would rule out any further operations before the spring.[173] The Chiefs of Staff were less sanguine;[174] and in Cairo on 14 September the intelligence authorities were allowing that Rommel might still be able to take the offensive before the beginning of November if forces had to be withdrawn from Eighth Army to meet a German advance from the Caucasus through Turkey.[175] On 9 September and again on 26 September General Wilson, the C-in-C of the new Persia and Iraq Command (PAIC), sought permission from London to make preparations against this threat – preparations which would have involved the transfer of considerable resources from north Africa.[176] But on 2 October the JIC repeated its earlier opinion: the Germans had made no further progress and 'a threat in force against Persia and Iraq before the spring of 1943 is most unlikely'.[177] On 6 October the Chiefs of Staff instructed General Wilson to recast his proposals in the light of the JIC's assessment.[178]

On the same day – 6 October – General Montgomery recast the plan for Eighth Army's attack. The original plan had envisaged that an assault by the infantry of XXX Corps on the enemy's defensive zone would establish a bridgehead during the first night, and that the newly formed X Corps, with the bulk of Eighth Army's armour, would pass through the bridgehead to challenge the enemy's armour while XIII Corps and 7th Armoured Division, with less powerful armour, attacked in the south and swept round the enemy's rear. In the revised plan emphasis was placed on fighting a battle of attrition; X Corps was not to seek an armoured encounter much beyond the bridgehead, but was to remain closer

173.   JIC (42) 332 of 2 September.
174.   CAB 79/23, COS (42) 255th Meeting, 4 September.
175.   Quoted in CAB 44/100, AL 1200/28/1, Section 5, pp 1 and 3.
176.   Howard, op cit, Vol IV, p 56.
177.   ibid, pp 55, 57; JIC (42) 383 of 2 October.
178.   Howard, op cit, Vol IV, p 57; CAB 79/23, COS (42) 279th Meeting, 6 October.

to Eighth Army's infantry while the infantry continued to 'crumble' the enemy's forward troops, and was to destroy the enemy's tanks when they attacked the infantry.[179] There was an operational reason for this change of emphasis: the standard of Eighth Army's training was turning out to be less good than had been hoped. But there can be little doubt that it was also prompted by the discovery that the date set for the offensive was giving the enemy, despite his many difficulties, time to prepare defences of unprecedented strength and depth.

The Prime Minister had singled out this risk on 23 September. In his comments on the plans for the initial assault he had not only reminded Cairo of the need for the earliest possible victory, to bring relief to Malta and to impress the French and Spanish authorities well in advance of the Allied landings in French north Africa, but had also made 'a point about the fortifications which the enemy will make in the interval. Instead of a crust through which a way can be cleared in a night, may you not find 25 miles of fortifications with blasted rock, gunpits and machine gun posts?'[180] But by that time the Enigma had provided only general references to the fact that the enemy was constructing fortifications and minefields,[181] whereas on 5 October, the day before the revision of the battle plans, GS Int Eighth Army, in major analysis of the enemy's defences, showed conclusively for the first time that they had been made especially formidable. In particular, it warned of the existence of what seemed to be a third line of fortifications behind the two that had already been detected.[182]

Despite this analysis and the consequent revision of the British plan, the enemy's defences and his powers of resistance were still to be far stronger than was allowed for. The miscalculation was in no way due to lack of intelligence about his dispositions. These began to change radically within a week of his retirement from Alam el Halfa; but by 20 September the Enigma had established the new order of battle.[183] Moreover, on the order of battle and on the minor changes that were subsequently made to it the Enigma evidence was so much duplicated by the other sources – Y, PR, captured documents and the occasional POW – that it was freely used in the intelligence summaries circulated to Eighth Army's formations.[184] A complete and virtually accurate order of battle of the German and Italian forces, drawn up by GS Int Eighth Army

---

179.   Playfair, op cit, Vol IV, pp 5, 6.
180.   Churchill, op cit, Vol IV, pp 528–529.
181.   Hunt, op cit, p 128.
182.   WO 201/2155, No 338 of 5 October 1942.
183.   QT 1777 of 20 September 1942; CX/MSS/1428/T4.
184.   eg WO 169/3937, Nos 323 and 331 of 16 September and 24 September 1942.

on 13 October, was issued to the intelligence officers of all
subordinate units and formations.[185] At the same time Eighth
Army's technical branch at GHQ in Cairo issued a booklet giving
photographs and descriptions of all the principal types of weapons
and equipment likely to be encountered.* But it is true that as
regards the location of the enemy units intelligence indicated only
the general areas occupied and that, despite the effort to supplement the information by air reconnaissance and ground patrols, the
exact locations of the enemy's units remained in some cases
unknown and were in others wrongly assessed.

A still more important problem was to discover how the enemy
intended to fight his defensive battle; but on this subject Eighth
Army could only make inferences from what was known about his
dispositions and his defensive layout. As early as 11 September
Rommel had issued an appreciation in which he concluded that he
would not only be unable to resume the offensive, but also had no
chance of fighting the kind of mobile defensive battle he
preferred.[186] He calculated that 30 consumption units of fuel at a
consumption rate of one unit a day were the minimum essential for
such a battle: 'without it the army was crippled and could not react
to the enemy's moves'.[187] Neither Rommel's appreciation nor the
calculation underlying it appeared in the Enigma decrypts. In the
same way, neither the Enigma nor any other source disclosed the
battle plan which, in the light of his fuel shortage and his
knowledge of Eighth Army's greatly superior force, he laid down
before going on sick leave in the middle of September.

Contrary to his predilection for concentrating his armour, this
plan spread the Panzer Army's armour in six battle groups spaced
equally behind the whole line, within striking distance of all parts
of the front, in the hope that by early and small-scale intervention
they would be able to pinch off any penetration of the defences by
Eighth Army and obviate the need to mount large-scale armoured
counter-attacks. He designed his static defences with the same
object, that of localising and restricting any British penetration, of
depriving the British armour of room for manoeuvre and of
checking the attack before it reached his anti-tank defences. Two
more or less continuous belts of mines, about 5 kilometres apart,
lay in front of his main defensive positions and were connected by
other minefields at intervals in such a way as to form boxes. The
front of each box, lightly held by battle outposts, guarded the
foremost minebelt; the rest of each box was sown with explosive

---

* See Appendix 14.

185. WO 201/2155, No 342 of 13 October 1942, Appendix A.
186. Playfair, op cit, Vol IV, p 26.
187. AIR 41/50, p 287 quoting *The Rommel Papers* (1953). See also Carver, op cit,
      p 101.

devices of every kind and covered by enfilading fire. The main anti-tank defensive zone, about 2 kilometres deep, lay behind the second minebelt. The depth of the whole, from the battle outposts to the larger anti-tank guns at the rear of the main defensive zone was between $2\frac{1}{2}$ and $4\frac{1}{2}$ miles. In the northern half of the front, where the main British thrust took place, some of the armour was dug in so that it could join in the defensive fire.[188] It was an essential part of the plan that the main defensive zone should be shifted to the rear and that the move should be concealed from the British. Initially the greater part of Rommel's troops were deployed behind the forward (eastern) minebelt; by 20 October the bulk of them had been withdrawn behind the western minebelt, leaving only the battle outposts manning the forward line.[189]

In the task of detecting and describing the enemy's field works, down to the point of locating his minefields, machine gun nests, wire defences and gun-pits with the precision required for the planning of the initial bombardment for which no prior ranging was possible, and for the subsequent infantry assault, intelligence was highly successful. As with the precise location of the enemy's units within his general order of battle, little of the information came from the Enigma, Army Y or captured documents; the chief sources were PR, other air reconnaissance and ground patrols, with occasional help from POW.[190] The RAF's contribution was particularly effective. PR produced a mosaic of the entire battle line and also many obliques of the front from a height of 5,000 feet. In spite of intense Flak it enjoyed greater freedom than ever before from GAF interference.[191] On the other hand, there is some evidence that GS Int Eighth Army did not wholly solve the problem of determining the extent to which each of the enemy's two main defence lines was manned on the eve of the battle, and thus of discovering the part they were intended to play in Rommel's plan.

GS Int realised by 16 September that a new continuous line, manned by battle outposts, was replacing the series of strong points on which the enemy's defences had previously relied.[192] On 17 September it concluded that the enemy was paying less attention to his defences in the south than in the north, and that in the north a

---

188. Playfair, op cit, Vol IV, pp 26–27, 29 fn; Carver, op cit, p 101.

189. WO 201/2155, No 351 of 30 October, Appendix A.

190. WO 201/648, Eighth Army Memo to Corps Commanders, 6 October 1942; WO 169/3937, Nos 315 of 8 September, 323 of 16 September, 328 of 21 September, Appendix A, 331 of 24 September, 332 of 25 September 1942; WO 201/2155, No 337 of 4 October, 340 of 8 October 1942; CAB 44/101, AL 1200/28/2A, pp 30, 167; Playfair, op cit, Vol IV, pp 19, 29; Montgomery, *The Memoirs of Field Marshal Montgomery* (1958), p 13.

191. AIR 41/50, p 238; AIR 41/7, *Photographic Reconnaissance*, Vol II, p 61; Mockler-Ferryman, op cit, p 188.

192. WO 169/3937, No 323 of 16 September 1942.

two-line defence system was emerging.[193] From an Enigma decrypt of 20 September it then learned that all the enemy's armour had been taken out of the line and put into reserve.[194] By 2 October, Y having disclosed that in the southern sector the armour behind the line was organised in three mixed battle groups located at equal distances apart, it was assuming, correctly, that the enemy had spaced his armour out in the same way along the entire length of his line.[195] In its next analysis on 5 October, GS Int established that there were '2 main defensive belts' connected by lines of defensive positions running east and west and forming 'hollow areas', thus identifying 'the boxes', and it correctly interpreted their purpose as being to hold up the forward attacking troops and to dissipate the remaining force of the attack within the defensive system itself. But it still expected that the enemy would concentrate his armour and deliver 'that smashing armoured counter-attack upon which German defensive principles are based'; and failing to realise that the enemy had deployed his northern armour close behind his main (westernmost) defence line, it placed it too far to the rear and suspected the emergence of yet a third defence line.[196] By 17 October it recognised that this line consisted of dug-in tanks, but was more inclined than before to think that it represented a third defence line.[197] Neither on 17 October, moreover, nor in its final pre-battle analysis of 22 October[198] did GS Int call attention to the general pull-back from the forward line to the main defence zone, leaving only the battle outposts to hold the western minebelt, which Stumme ordered to be completed by 20 October.[199] Y and PR did not detect this move and there was no reference to it in the Enigma.

Subsequent research has shown that the possibility that GS Int did 'not seem to have realised that the enemy had shifted his main line back behind the second minebelt' is supported by comparison between the map attached to the analysis of 22 October and the map captured from the Panzer Army during the fighting. 'Instead of a thin chain of dispositions along the front belt of mines and a thick chain behind the main belt, as shown on the Panzer Army map, the British map carries two thick chains'.[200] As against this, there is considerable evidence that Eighth Army knew that the

---

193. ibid, No 324 of 17 September 1942.
194. QT 1777 of 20 September 1942; CX/MSS/1428/T4.
195. WO 201/2155, No 336 of 2 October 1942; WO 201/650, XXX Corps Notes for Divisional Commanders' Conference 19 October 1942; Hunt, op cit, p 134.
196. WO 201/2155, No 338 of 5 October 1942; AL 3000/D/1–6, Notes on Chapter 56 of Playfair, op cit, Vol IV.
197. WO 201/2155, No 343 of 17 October 1942.
198. ibid, No 344 of 22 October 1942.
199. ibid, No 351 of 30 October 1942; Playfair, op cit, Vol IV, pp 26, 27.
200. WO 201/2155, No 351 of 30 October 1942; AL 3000/D/1–6.

enemy's western line was the main one. A memorandum from Montgomery to his corps commanders on 6 October referred to 'the second or main position'.[201] A document of XXX Corps dated 19 October stated that 'most of the enemy's field guns are beyond the main defences'.[202] XXX Corps' intelligence summary of 1000 on 24 October, describing the first night of the battle, would report that 'after a pause [after taking the forward defence line] the advance was continued against the enemy's main defences'.[203] But on 30 October, in its comments on the captured map, GS Int claimed only that 'the gaff was largely blown by RAF photographs and AAPIU before these instructions were issued'.[204] Perhaps the best conclusion in all the circumstances is that, while it had established that the main defence line was in the rear, intelligence did not reveal the extent to which the rear had been reinforced from the forward line – and that in mistaking the forward line of armoured troops for a third defence line, and assuming that the enemy's armour lay still further to the rear, it further under-estimated the strength of the main defence zone.[205]

□

Whatever the difficulties of British intelligence before the second battle of Alamein, and whatever its imperfections, they were as nothing compared with those experienced by the Panzer Army. Thanks to the work of the RAF, the enemy was denied any aerial observation of the British forces between 18 and 22 October, when Eighth Army took up its final positions, and during 23 October, immediately before Eighth Army's advance; as was confirmed in the Enigma decrypts of the Fliegerführer's daily reconnaissance reports, no GAF aircraft succeeded in over-flying the British area of concentration.

The success of the RAF in suppressing the GAF flowed from the British command of the air, but that was accentuated by the fact that during September and October, as during the battle of Alam el Halfa, the greater part of the German bomber force in the eastern Mediterranean was diverted to convoy escort in a desperate attempt to reduce the shipping losses, and by the fact that for the same purpose, and on Hitler's orders, the GAF was diverted for another intense attack on Malta, its third and its last, from 10

201. WO 201/649.
202. WO 201/650, Notes for Divisional Commanders' Conference 19 October 1942.
203. WO 169/4035, XXX Corps Intelligence Summary of 1000/24 October 1942.
204. WO 201/2155, No 351 of 30 October 1942.
205. AL 3000/D/1–6.

October. On 28 September the state of fatigue among the GAF crews was already so great that Kesselring redistributed and reduced the GAF effort throughout the Mediterranean and north African theatre. Despite this measure, which was at once disclosed in the Enigma,[206] convoy escorting continued in October, and the Enigma showed that, while most of it was done by Fliegerkorps X from Crete, the forces belonging to Fliegerführer Afrika were often forced to supplement the aircraft from Crete. This was especially the case after the beginning of October, by which time the Enigma had reported the move of bomber formations to Sicily from Crete, Russia and elsewhere 'for a short-term attack on Malta';[207] and even at the height of the battle of Alamein the greater part of the bomber force continued to be employed on convoy escort work.

The GAF's assault on Malta lasted from 10 to 19 October. It was largely ineffective. Malta's aircraft were sent out on anti-shipping operations on all but one of these nights; that night, notes the RAF narrative in an unconscious tribute to the value of the high-grade Sigint to these operations, was the one night when no Axis shipping passed within Malta's range.[208] The GAF Enigma also showed that the GAF was using fewer bombers and more escorting fighters as the assault proceeded. On 19 October, on the other hand, when it began its all-out offensive against aircraft on the GAF's north African airfields, the RAF knew that two-thirds of the bombers that the GAF normally kept in Crete were still deployed in Sicily. It was not until 25 October that, as the Enigma revealed, they began their transfer back to Crete and north African bases in response to Eighth Army's offensive, then two days old.[209]

The RAF's pre-battle offensive, the first of many that were to be undertaken in the remainder of the war with the object of 'softening up' the GAF by attacking its aircraft on its airfields, was further assisted by the knowledge, derived from PR from 9 October, that Fliegerführer Afrika's major bases at Daba and Fuka were flooded by rains, which grounded his aircraft.[210] But PR's chief contribution to the effectiveness of the RAF's strikes was its detailed photography of the lay-out of the enemy airfields.[211] The Enigma was no less valuable: as well as disclosing which GAF units were based at which airfields at any one time, the Fliegerführer's strength returns and reports on operations kept the RAF informed of the effect of its attacks. On 22 October the return reported that the Fliegerführer had 90 serviceable aircraft (40 dive-bombers, 40

206. QT 2454 of 29 September 1942; CX/MSS/1456/T6.
207. QT 1721 of 19 September 1942; CX/MSS/1426/T2.
208. AIR 41/50, p 242.
209. ibid, p 291; QT 4398 of 26 October 1942; CX/MSS/1580/T23.
210. AIR 41/50, p 236; Richards, op cit, Vol II, p 233.
211. AIR 41/50, pp 243–244.

fighters, 10 fighter-bombers),[212] whereas a month earlier the RAF had estimated that the GAF had 195 serviceable aircraft in north Africa out of an establishment of 300.[213] During the intervening month the Enigma had shown that the Fliegerführer had received no reinforcements to replace losses – that he had, indeed, had to transfer about 30 aircraft to Sicily[214] – and that the drop in serviceability was still more striking. On 22 October Enigma also revealed that the low state of serviceability had prompted a rebuke from Kesselring.[215]

The effect of the RAF's preliminary offensive was to be important during the fighting. On 24 October, the first full day of the battle, the GAF could fly only 107 sorties compared with the 1,000 flown by the RAF; nor did the GAF effort increase before 26 October. But it was no less important that, because no GAF aircraft succeeded in over-flying Eighth Army's concentration area up to and including 23 October, the enemy remained unaware of where and when the British attack would come.[216] At 1800 on 23 October GS Int informed Eighth Army Commander that the enemy showed no sign of expecting the attack that night.[217] The judgment was presumably based on the negative evidence provided by the RAF's visual observation, and possibly by Y, for there had been no positive intelligence on the subject since breakfast, when Eighth Army had received the decrypt of the Fliegerführer's report of the previous evening to the effect that all was quiet and that the British line was unchanged.[218] But its accuracy was confirmed shortly after midnight, when Eighth Army received the decrypt of the report of his intentions for 24 October which the Fliegerführer had issued on the previous evening.[219] Eighth Army obtained no advance intelligence to the effect that the enemy commanders, though by no means unanimous, leaned to the view that the main attack would come against the northern point of the southern sector.[220]* But on the afternoon of 24 October it learned from the Fliegerführer's report for 23 October and from the first Enigma

---

* This conclusion may have owed something to the elaborate British deception plan which was designed to suggest that the main thrust would be made in the south.[221]

212. QT 4147 of 23 October 1942; CX/MSS/1566/T26.
213. CAB 44/100, p 19.
214. eg QTs 2880 of 5 October, 2901 and 2903 of 6 October 1942; CX/MSS/1483/T1, 1485/T3 and 4.
215. QT 4106 of 22 October 1942; CX/MSS/1565/T21 and 24.
216. Playfair, op cit, Vol IV, p 32; AIR 41/50, pp 243, 262.
217. Playfair, op cit, Vol IV, p 31.
218. QT 4142 of 0820/23 October 1942; CX/MSS/1566/T19.
219. QT 4195 of 2344/23 October 1942; CX/MSS/1570/T21, 25 and 26.
220. AIR 41/50, p 270, quoting Panzer Army War Diary; Playfair, op cit, Vol IV, p 27; WO 201/2155, No 357 of 5 November 1942.
221. Playfair, op cit, Vol IV, pp 18, 19.

decrypts to mention the fighting that the Panzer Army had expected the main thrust to be in the south,[222] and GS Int Eighth Army's first report on the battle, issued at 1900 on 24 October, was able to say that 'apparently we gained complete surprise'.[223]

□

Despite Eighth Army's achievement of tactical surprise, the first phase of the battle did not go well. General Montgomery's plan had laid it down that, starting at 2200 on 23 October after an unprecedentedly heavy bombardment of the enemy's field and anti-tank artillery positions, XXX Corps and X Corps were to take the enemy's forward defence line, a mile behind the forward edge of his western minebelt, by 2355 on 23 October and establish a bridgehead to the west of the second minebelt before dawn on 24 October.[224] In the event, although the bombardment was 'extraordinarily accurate' and highly effective,[225] only about half of XXX Corps's infantry reached its objective by daylight on 24 October and X corps's armour had nowhere succeeded in breaking through. During the next two days the infantry largely completed the capture of its bridgehead, and the armour succeeded in establishing itself a short distance beyond the infantry; but by 26 October the armour had still not broken through to open country beyond the bridgehead. At that point, because the offensive was flagging, the Eighth Army commander changed his plan, maintaining attacks in some sectors but otherwise withdrawing some formations and going over to the defensive for a week while they prepared for a further large-scale assault.

How far this initial setback, with all its consequences for the length and costliness of the battle, was due to miscalculation of the strength of the enemy's main defence line, and to the possible over-concentration of the initial artillery bombardment on the forward defence line, it is impossible to judge, the more so as it is clear that it owed much to other considerations – the quality of the enemy's resistance and the difficulty of negotiating his formidable fixed defences, a difficulty which advance intelligence, however good, could do little to remove. During 24 and 25 October, however, while the enemy's policy of launching counter-attacks with smallish groups of tanks enabled the British aircraft, tanks and guns to inflict heavy casualties on him, intelligence performed

---

222. QTs 4242 and 4243 of 24 October 1942; CX/MSS/1572/T17 and 18.
223. WO 201/2155, No 345 of 24 October (mistyped 25 October in original).
224. Playfair, op cit, Vol IV, pp 34, 37, 49, 77; Carver, op cit, p 105; AIR 41/50, p 275.
225. Playfair, op cit, Vol IV, p 36; Carver, op cit, p 128; Liddell Hart, op cit, p 299; CAB 66/31, WP (42) 569 of 7 December.

valuable services first by keeping the counter-attacks under close observation by air and from Y and secondly by establishing that the enemy was not concentrating his armour. Eighth Army had reckoned on an immediate move forward of 90th Light Division from the position 15 miles west of Alamein, where it was guarding against a seaborne landing,* and on the concentration of all of the DAK by D + 1 through the diversion of 21st Panzer Division and the Ariete Division from the south to join 15th Panzer Division and the Littorio Division in the north.[227] But on 24 and 25 October the RAF's first-light tactical reconnaissance of the battle area, all the more effective in that the known weakness of the GAF in fighters allowed it to be carried out unescorted, established that none of the enemy's outlying armour had moved.[228] And throughout 25 October, and again on the morning of 26 October, General Montgomery's intelligence staff was able to assure him that it had still not moved.[229]

The enemy's policy was conditioned by several factors: continuing anxiety about the southern sector; the acute shortage of fuel, which prevented major movements; the death of Stumme, who was killed early on 24 October.[230] As we have seen, the fuel shortage had led Rommel himself to lay down the policy before going on sick leave in September. But after his return to north Africa on the evening of 25 October he abandoned it. In an attempt to restore the position in the north he ordered 15th Panzer Division and the Littorio Division to counter-attack early on 26 October against the dangerous salient that was being created at the northern end of XXX Corps' bridgehead. When the counter-attack was frustrated by artillery fire and RAF attacks, he decided to move 90th Light Division forward and, at 2100 on 26 October, ordered 21st Panzer Division to move north with one-third of the Ariete Division and a half of the artillery from the southern sector. He was aware that having moved 21st Panzer Division, he would be unable to move it back to the south for lack of petrol. His

---

* During September the British had carried out raids on Tobruk and Benghazi, the first seaborne and the other over land, with the object of interrupting Rommel's supplies. Though they failed, largely because of faulty intelligence from local sources, they strengthened the enemy's fear of British landings in his rear.[226]

226. CAB 105/19, Hist (B) (Crusader) 5, No 31 of 17 September 1942; CAB 44/100, pp 19, 30, 33–38; Hunt, op cit, pp 129, 132–134.
227. AIR 41/50, p 273; WO 201/650, Notes for Conference 19 October 1942; WO 201/648, de Guingand's Memo to Eighth Army Corps Commanders 7 October 1942.
228. AIR 41/50, p 278; WO 201/2155, No 345 of 24 October 1942 (mistyped 25 October in original).
229. CAB 44/102, p 463.
230. Carver, op cit, p 129; WO 201/2155, Nos 346 and 347 of 25 and 26 October 1942.

personal Kampfstaffel (Kasta O B), a battle group of assorted arms normally responsible for protecting Panzer Army HQ, was ordered north at the same time.[231]

Except that Y by the evening of 26 October had detected the northward move of a battle group later identified as 'the enemy commander's recce unit',[232] Eighth Army obtained no advance notice of these moves. During 27 October, moreover, while it learned from a signal timed 0626 from GC and CS that 90th Light was moving up and being relieved by the Trieste Division at Daba,[233] it remained uncertain for some time about the move of the southern armour. About noon GS Int was informed that DF had identified 21st Panzer Division at a point halfway between its southern position and the north;[234] and the intelligence summary it issued at 1900 claimed that Y had detected as early as 0800 that the division was on the move.[235] At 1230, however, it thought that the weight of evidence was against the suggestion that 21st Panzer Division was moving north.[236] It took this view because it had now captured a document which established that in mid-October the enemy's policy had been to wear down the expected attack without carrying out large-scale armoured counter-attcks,[237] and partly, perhaps, because the Enigma did not confirm the Y evidence until the evening[238] and did not divulge until 28 October precisely which units had left the south.[239] At 1315 on 27 October, however, Y again located 21st Panzer Division's HQ; it was on the northern front with 90th Light Division now somewhat to the north of it.[240]

Once the uncertainty had been cleared up, Eighth Army was alerted to the danger of an early enemy counter-attack.[241] This was all the more expected because the Enigma had disclosed on 25 October that Stumme was dead and Rommel on his way back to north Africa and, in the early hours of 26 October, that Rommel had resumed his command the previous evening.[242]* Neither the

---

* This information was sent out to a restricted distribution in accordance with the new anti-gossip procedure. The new procedure had already been adopted for reporting the Enigma intelligence about command changes in the Panzer Army during September,

231.   Playfair, op cit, Vol IV, pp 50–51; Carver, op cit, pp 144, 149; AIR 41/50, pp 289–290.
232.   WO 201/2155, Nos 347 of 26 October, 352 of 31 October 1942.
233.   QT 4478 of 0626/27 October 1942; CX/MSS/1585/T25.
234.   CAB 44/103, AL 1200/28/3A, p 39; de Guingand, op cit, p 204.
235.   WO 201/2155, No 348 of 1900/27 October 1942.
236.   CAB 44/103, p 39.
237.   WO 201/2155, No 347 of 26 October 1942; CAB 44/102, p 534.
238.   QT 4516 of 1815/27 October 1942; CX/MSS/1586/T15.
239.   QTs 4545 and 4550 of 28 October 1942; CX/MSS/1586/T15, 1590/T18.
240.   CAB 44/103, p 39.
241.   Carver, op cit, p 148.
242.   QTs 4259 of 1922/24 October, 4374 of 2311/25 October, 4394 of 26 October 1942; DEFE 3/573, CX/MSS/C 54, 57, 58 and 59; AIR 41/50, p 282.

Enigma nor Y gave any tactical warning of Rommel's first counter-attack, in the late afternoon of 27 October, but it was broken up by air attack and artillery fire with heavy losses. About mid-day on 28 October RAF bombing of the enemy's concentrations foiled Rommel's second attempt to counter-attack, his concentrations having been detected by tactical air reconnaissance.[247] This was Rommel's last attempt to take the initiative, and its defeat was the turning-point of the battle.[248]

During the lull in the fighting between the evening of 28 October and the renewal of the main British assault on 2 November the Enigma left no doubt about the parlous state to which the enemy had been reduced. By midnight on 28 October the British knew that Rommel had at 1300 requested Kesselring to send GAF reinforcements in view of the 'extremely critical situation'[249] and that, 'in view of the extremely tense fuel situation of the Panzer Army', Kesselring had ordered the GAF to transport fuel to Africa 'day and night down to the last crew and the last aircraft'.[250] On the morning of 29 October they learned that Rommel had ordered every available vehicle to bring fuel forward from Benghazi[251] and had issued an order of the day urging a supreme effort in a 'life and death struggle'.[252] In the evening of 29 October they received the Panzer Army's day report for 28 October: this described the situation as 'grave in the extreme', fuel stocks at the front being down to 1.3 consumption units, serviceable tanks being down to 81 German and 197 Italian, and there being signs that very strong British forces were preparing to break through in the north, by way of Sidi Abd el Rahman.[253]

Late on 29 October, disquieted by the news that some of Eighth Army's formations had been withdrawn from the front, the Prime

---

including the appointments of Stumme, Nehring and von Thoma.[243] It was also used for reporting Rommel's departure for Germany in September and for announcing on 23 October that the Enigma had revealed that he was in Austria on 17 October.[244] It had not prevented Eighth Army's intelligence summary from reporting on 19 October that Rommel was in Austria;[245] similarly the intelligence summary of 28 October reported that Stumme was dead and that Rommel had been seen on the battlefield.[246] For the introduction of the procedure see above, pp 414.

243. DEFE 3/573, CX/MSS/C 19.
244. QT 4152 of 23 October 1942; DEFE 3/573, CX/MSS/C 52.
245. WO 201/2155, No 343 of 19 October 1942.
246. ibid, No 349 of 28 October 1942.
247. CAB 105/19, No 103 of 9 November 1942; AIR 41/50, p 301; Playfair, op cit, Vol IV, p 57. Cf Churchill, op cit, Vol IV, pp 531–534.
248. CAB 105/19, No 103 of 9 November 1942; AIR 41/50, p 301.
249. QTs 4592 of 2108/28 October and 4603 of 2235/28 October 1942; CX/MSS/1594/T15; DEFE 3/573, CX/MSS/C 62.
250. QT 4599 of 2218/28 October 1942; CX/MSS/1594/T5.
251. QT 4642 of 0846/29 October 1942; CX/MSS/1595/T17.
252. QT 4644 of 0937/29 October 1942; DEFE 3/573, CX/MSS/C 63.
253. QT 4682 of 2056/29 October 1942; CX/MSS/1599/T23.

Minister referred to these items of intelligence in a signal to the C-in-C ME.[254] He used them as evidence that the enemy could not stand up to a prolonged large-scale attack and added that 'the brilliant success of the Air Force in sinking the vitally needed tankers . . . gives us solid grounds for confidence in your final success'. Sigint had contributed directly to the sinking of further tankers since the opening of the battle, and thus to the multiplication of the enemy's difficulties. As early as 23 October an Enigma decrypt of 21 October from the Panzer Army had revealed that although the next tanker, the *Proserpina*, was due on 25 October, its fuel could not reach the front before 29 October; the Army must receive fuel by air at once as its stocks at and east of Tobruk would otherwise be exhausted by that date by current consumption alone.[255] On 24 October in another decrypt the Panzer Army warned that battle requirements would exhaust its fuel stocks before 29 October and stressed the critical situation that would arise in the event of 'failure of seaborne supplies'.[256] A decrypt of 26 October confirmed that the Panzer Army's stocks were down to 3 consumption units on 24 October, a third of the total being at Benghazi, and that the GAF had begun the transport of fuel by air.[257] By then – in the early hours of 25 October – GC and CS had signalled to the Middle East the details of the *Proserpina*'s route, together with the fact that she carried 4,500 tons of fuel, and in the evening of 26 October it reported that she was ablaze and that in the same air attack an accompanying ship had been blown up.[258] The second ship, the *Tergestea*, had carried 1,000 tons of fuel and 1,000 tons of ammunition.[259]

Early on 28 October, together with reports of the dangerous fuel situation brought about in the Panzer Army by the loss of the *Proserpina* and the *Tergestea*,[260] the decrypts alerted the Middle East to the fact that the *Luisiano*, the next ship in the Axis supply programme, whose route, cargo and escort arrangements had been known for some days,[261] would leave Navarino at 1600 that day with 2,500 tons of army fuel.[262] At 2200 she was sunk by the RAF

---

254.   Playfair, op cit, Vol IV, p 60; Howard, op cit, Vol IV, p 67.
255.   QT 4119 of 23 October 1942; CX/MSS/1565/T36.
256.   QT 4258 of 24 October 1942; CX/MSS/1575/T9.
257.   QT 4383 of 0210/26 October 1942; CX/MSS/1579/T5.
258.   QTs 4211 of 24 October, 4421 of 1645/26 October, 4447 of 2246/26 October 1942; DEFE 3/582, ZTPGM 2441; ZTPI 19971; CX/MSS/1584/T19.
259.   Playfair, op cit, Vol IV, p 50, fn 1.
260.   QTs 4533 of 0108/28 October and 4599 of 2218/28 October 1942; CX/MSS/1585/T17, 1594/T5.
261.   QTs 4201 of 24 October, 4424 and 4578 of 26 October 1942; DEFE 3/582, ZTPGM 2597; CX/MSS/1571/T9, 1591/T19.
262.   QT 4537 of 0237/28 October 1942; ZTPI 20081.

in 'a superbly economical action',[263] and her loss – though not the fact that Rommel regarded it as 'shattering'[264] – was confirmed by the Enigma in the early hours of 29 October.[265]

It was known by then that another tanker, the *Morandi*, had succeeded in reaching Benghazi on 28 October with a small cargo of 300 tons.[266] But Benghazi was 1,000 miles from the front, and it was also known that the *Tripolino*, with a cargo 'of decisive importance for the situation at the front', and the *Ostia*, with a large quantity of ammunition, were preparing to sail from Benghazi to Tobruk.[267] On 1 November the RAF sank both ships, GC and CS having supplied in good time the details of their routes and sailings.[268] Their loss, which GC and CS at once reported to the Middle East,[269] was followed on the same day, again as a result of timely information from GC and CS, by the sinking of two Italian naval auxiliaries, brought in to augment the emergency supply of fuel and ammunition.[270] This completed the dependence of the Panzer Army on the air transport of fuel from Crete to airfields in the Tobruk area and on land transport from Tobruk to the front, and increased the effectiveness of the intensified attack which the RAF made on those transport routes in the final stage of the land battle.[271]

To the course of the land fighting between 28 October and the renewal of the main British assault on 2 November the high-grade Sigint made no such decisive contribution. A stream of decrypts reporting on operations by the Panzer Army enabled GS Int Eighth Army to keep its enemy order of battle intelligence up to date by confirming which units had made which attacks. Others revealed that while advanced elements of Infantry Regiment No 47, flown in from Crete on 27 October, were soon in action,[272] other valuable fighting units – Sonderverband 288, Recce Units 33 and 580 and the Trieste Division – were being kept back on the coast well west of Alamein because of the enemy's continuing fear that the British would attempt seaborne or airborne landings in the rear

---

263. AIR 41/50, p 303.
264. AIR 41/50, p 303, quoting *The Rommel Papers*.
265. QT 4588 of 29 October 1942; DEFE 3/582, ZTPGM 2728.
266. QT 4589 of 28 October 1942; CX/MSS/1594/T6, 7 and 8.
267. QT 4425 of 26 October 1942; DEFE 3/582, ZTPGM 2599; Playfair, op cit, Vol IV, p 53; AIR 41/50, p 314.
268. QTs 4790 of 30 October, 4861 and 4864 of 31 October 1942; DEFE 3/582, ZTPGM 2820; CX/MSS/1699/T4.
269. QT 4911 of 0531/1 November 1942; ZTPI 20341.
270. QTs 4915 and 4959 of 1 November, 5051 of 2 November, 5083 of 3 November 1942; CX/MSS/1610/T14, 1613/T23, 1618/T36; DEFE 3/582, ZTPGM 3024; AIR 41/50, pp 317–318, 323.
271. AIR 41/50, pp 307, 308, 309; Playfair, op cit, Vol IV, p 63.
272. eg QTs 4385 of 26 October, 4487 of 27 October 1942; CX/MSS/1579/T28 and 29, 1585/T31.

areas.[273] But the Enigma did not directly influence the timing and the direction of the coming British thrust; these had been settled before the decrypts threw any light on the preparations that Rommel was making against the time when the British would resume their assault.

On the morning of 29 October, on hearing of the loss of the *Luisiano*, Rommel seriously considered a general withdrawal but decided that, as this was ruled out by fuel shortage, he must make one more attempt to fight off the attack and prepare to pull back as many as possible of his tanks and weapons to Fuka, but only if retreat was forced on him.[274] At the same time he decided to make redispositions to counter the expected British thrust on the assumption that it would come in the north, along the coast road towards Sidi Abd el Rahman.[275] Of these decisions, and of the appreciations which underlay them, Eighth Army learned nothing before the evening of 29 October, when the Enigma reported that the Germans were expecting the break-through to come towards Sidi Abd el Rahman.* Nor was it until the early hours of 31 October that the Enigma divulged that Rommel was effecting the most important of his redispositions by withdrawing 21st Panzer Division, hitherto strengthening the front about 15 km south of Sidi Abd el Rahman, to operate as a mobile counter-attack force in the north; it was to be relieved in the line by the Trieste Division.[276] Confirmed by Y and circulated by GS Int to Eighth Army on the evening of 31 October,[277] and conveniently given cover by POW during 1 November,[278] this last intelligence was, even so, of immense value, as may be judged from the fact that when it was received the British were preparing to break through on the night of 1–2 November on that part of the front where the Italians were relieving 21st Panzer Division.[279] In other circumstances, indeed, the intelligence might have been crucial. As it was, however, it necessitated no change in British plans: General Montgomery, who had initially intended to make the break-through along the coast road, had changed its direction to the point further south at 1100

---

* See above, p 441.

273. QTs 4415 of 26 October, 4478 of 27 October, 4651 of 29 October 1942;
      CX/MSS/1581/T17, 1585/T25; DEFE 3/582, ZTPGM 2771; WO
      201/2155, Nos 347 of 26 October, 350 of 29 October 1942.
274. Playfair, op cit, Vol IV, p 59; Carver, op cit, p 156; EDS/Appreciation/9
      Part VI, pp 65, 66.
275. Playfair, op cit, Vol IV, p 59; EDS/Appreciation/9 Part VI, p 65.
276. QTs 4821 of 0534/31 October, 4853 of 1339/31 October, 4860 of 1608/31
      October 1942; CX/MSS/1605/T17, 1607/T8; CAB 44/104, AL
      1200/28/3B, p 525.
277. WO 201/2155, No 352 of 31 October 1942.
278. CAB 44/104, p 525.
279. ibid, p 525.

on 29 October, apparently because during the night of 28–29 October Y and POW had enabled GS Int to establish, on the basis of its knowledge of the composition of 90th Light Division, that the whole of the division had reached its new position and was now deployed across the direction of the projected British thrust towards Sidi Abd el Rahman.[280] Every effort was made during the next two days to convey the impression that the break-through would be attempted in the north, by keeping up the attacks of 9th Australian Division northwards towards the coast; and certainly it was hoped in Eighth Army that if the German formations could be separated from the Italian, which they had hitherto bolstered or 'corsetted', the break-through would be made against Italian troops.

In the event the British attack 'did not hit the Italians, as expected initially and claimed afterwards'.[281] 21st Panzer Division had left behind a battalion from one of its Panzer Grenadier Regiments (PGR) to stiffen the Trieste Division;[282] and Rommel had split the Trieste Division and 15th Panzer Division, interspersing their formations in a further attempt to maintain the 'corsetting' of his weaker forces. These facts had not been reported by the Enigma. Nor did the combined resources of field intelligence – tactical air reconnaissance, captured maps, POW and Y, the last of which was now functioning as well as it was ever to do in the course of the war – suffice to provide accurate and up-to-date information about the whereabouts of the various battlegroups into which the enemy had divided his main formations in such a way that their components were often separated from, and easily confused with, their parent formations. As always in battle conditions, it had also proved impossible to keep track of the enemy's tank strengths. On 1 November the DAK had a total of 102 effective tanks (7 with HQ, 51 in 15th Panzer Division, 44 in 21st Panzer Division), there were 15 to 25 with 90th Light Division near the coast, the Littorio and Trieste Divisions had 65 between them, and Rommel had sent back the Ariete detachment to the south on 28 October.[283] In Eighth Army, which had received no intelligence on the subject from the Enigma since the Panzer Army's tank return of 29 October,* and only scraps of information from Y, it was estimated on 1 November that the enemy had a total of 140 German and 130 Italian effective

---

* See above, p 441.

280.   de Guingand, op cit, p 206 and *From Brasshat to Bowler* (1979), p 12; Carver, op cit, p 158; Montgomery, *El Alamein to the River Sangro* (1949), p 22; WO 201/2155, Nos 349 of 28 October, 350 of 1900/29 October 1942; Playfair, op cit, Vol IV, p 59.

281.   Carver, op cit, pp 198–199.

282.   Playfair, op cit, Vol IV, p 64.

283.   ibid, p 64.

tanks on or near the main front – 15 with 15th Panzer Division, 125 with 21st Panzer Division, 60 with Littorio, 30 with Trieste and 40 with the Ariete Division.[284] But Eighth Army's over-estimate of the total number of enemy tanks did not alter the fact that the renewed British assault met German tanks in greater numbers than had been expected.

In other respects the attack was made according to plan and Eighth Army knew from the Enigma that every circumstance was favourable. The Enigma had shown an increase in the number of sorties flown by the GAF from 107 on 24 October to 242 on 31 October as a result of the reinforcements sent in response to Rommel's desperate appeal of 25 October.[285] But on 1 November it showed that, despite the reinforcements, the Fliegerführer's strength stood only at 36 dive-bombers, 50 fighters, 8 fighter-bombers and 10 reconnaissance aircraft.[286] As for the Panzer Army, on 30 October Eighth Army learned from GC and CS that, while the enemy's fuel position had not improved, his ammunition stocks had fallen to 0.7 of an issue by 29 October, and that the GAF had brought in transport aircraft from outside the Mediterranean in an attempt to maintain supplies.[287] On 31 October it learned that his troop strengths had 'fallen still further on account of considerable losses' and that on the previous day the Panzer Army had appreciated that the British were re-grouping for 'the actual grand attack in the northern sector'.[288] At breakfast on 1 November, more than 12 hours before the start of the attack, it received the decrypt of the Panzer Army's day report of the evening of 31 October. This contained the news that Rommel had ordered 'powerful elements' of 90th Light Division and 21st Panzer Division to renew on 1 November the full-scale attacks which they had been making in the north to relieve PGR 125, and thus advised the British that these forces would be tied down some distance from the area chosen for their own attack. And by also stating that there were 'no definite signs so far of an attack by further British forces on the remainder of the front', it further reassured them that in the course of preparing their attack they had maintained the element of surprise.[289]

□

Despite these advantages – and largely as a result of the fact that, owing to uncertainty about the enemy's order of battle and the

284.   CAB 44/105, AL 1200/28/3C, p 657.
285.   QT 4592 of 28 October 1942; CX/MSS/1594/T15.
286.   QT 4950 of 1 November 1942; CX/MSS/1613/T6.
287.   QTs 4732, 4735 and 4750 all of 30 October 1942; CX/MSS/1600/T23 and 32, 1601/T1.
288.   QTs 4853 and 4854 of 31 October 1942; CX/MSS/1607/T8.
289.   QT 4921 of 0849/1 November 1942; CX/MSS/1610/T22, 23 and 24.

fighting quality of the German tank crews, the offensive met greater resistance than had been expected – the situation looked gloomy on the morning after the beginning of the attack,[290] and the final break-through was achieved only at great cost. The infantry – the reinforced New Zealand Division under XXX Corps – had reached its objectives on time; despite difficulties created by scattered mines, which were virtually unplottable, the work of locating the enemy's minefields and defended positions had been well done, mainly by PR.[291] But the armour, the anti-tank guns and the artillery which the enemy had *in situ* obstructed the planned breakout of the armour, 9th Armoured Brigade and 1st Armoured Division, from the infantry bridgehead until the DAK counter-attacked. The outcome was the fiercest and most prolonged tank engagement of the whole battle, with heavy casualties on both sides.[292]

Weight of numbers decided the issue; by the evening of 2 November, Rommel's losses were so heavy, the DAK being down to 35 serviceable tanks, that he was forced to retire to the Fuka position. But Army Y did useful service first by contributing to the delaying of the DAK's counter-attack and then by giving good warning of it. The delay was brought about by the dislocation of the enemy's communications, partly by the British artillery barrage and partly by the use of airborne jamming against his wireless channels,[293] but it has been attributed particularly to a heavy RAF attack on the DAK's advanced battle HQ in the early hours of 2 November which destroyed its telephone communications and slightly wounded the DAK commander, and this followed from Y's success during 1 November in locating the HQs of the enemy's principal formations including the DAK.[294] The orders for the counter-attack in a signal to 21st Panzer Division were intercepted by Y at 0911 on 2 November, would have been known at GS Int, Eighth Army at practically the same time as they were received by 21st Panzer Division, and appropriate instructions had been passed to XXX Corps and the New Zealand Division before 1000.[295] Their interception was a good example of the tactical value of Y: although the orders had been transmitted as early as 0700 in the GAF's liaison officers' Enigma (Scorpion), which was being decyphered at Cairo, Cairo was unable to forward the decrypt to

---

290.   Liddell Hart, op cit, p 304.
291.   Playfair, op cit, Vol IV, pp 63, 66; AIR 41/50, p 318; WO 201/2155, No 350 of 29 October 1942.
292.   Carver, op cit, p 170.
293.   AIR 41/50, pp 319 fn, 321 fn 2, quoting *The Rommel Papers*.
294.   WO 201/2155, No 354 of 2 November, Part 2, para 1(a).
295.   Carver, op cit, p 167.

Eighth Army before the counter-attack took place, and it was not until the evening that GC and CS sent the substance of it to the Middle East.[296]

During the night of 2–3 November, however, Enigma decrypts reporting the enemy's assessments of the fighting reached Eighth Army in a steady stream. At noon on 2 November the Panzer Army had reported that the situation was tense in the extreme: all German mobile forces were committed, leaving the rest of the front denuded; the great British superiority in armour made the outcome uncertain; British tanks had broken through and were constantly being reinforced, and armoured cars were attacking HQs and lines of communication in the rear areas.[297] At 1730 the Fliegerführer had considered the situation as 'threatening in the extreme'; about the same time Kesselring had described it as one of 'most extreme crisis'.[298] More explicit and more striking was an emergency situation report to OKW in the early evening in which Rommel had announced that his army was exhausted. 'The army will therefore no longer be in a position to prevent a further attempt by strong enemy tank formations to break through, which may be expected tonight or tomorrow. An ordered withdrawal of the six Italian and two German non-motorised divisions or brigades is not possible in view of the lack of MT vehicles . . . But also the mobile troops are so intricately involved in the battle that only a part of them will be able to extricate themselves from the enemy. The stocks of ammunition still available are in the front area, while there are no stocks worth mentioning in the rearward area. The slight stocks of fuel do not allow of a movement to the rear over great distances. On the one available road the army will certainly be attacked night and day by the Royal Air Force. In this situation, in spite of the heroic resistance and the excellent spirit of the troops the possibility of the gradual annihilation of the army must be faced.'[299]

Rommel's report was sent from GC and CS at 0555 on 3 November; in accordance with the special procedure applied to decrypts which might evoke gossip and rumour, it was sent only to Cairo for the personal attention of the C-in-C ME. But at 0835 GC and CS repeated the gist of it in a signal to all its Middle East recipients in which it also sent the substance of a later decrypt of 2 November. This had announced that Rommel was preparing to retire fighting step by step from 3 November, withdrawing his infantry divisions during the night of 2–3 November, and that the

---

296.   QT 5032 of 1946/2 November 1942; CX/MSS/1618/T19.
297.   QTs 5073 of 0213 and 5077 of 0420/3 November 1942; CX/MSS/1619/T6.
298.   QT 5039 of 2047/2 November, 5063 of 0055/3 November 1942; CX/MSS/1618/T27 and 41.
299.   QT 5086 of 0555/3 November 1942; DEFE 3/573, CX/MSS/C 68.

Fliegerführer was to move units to rear airfields in conjunction with the withdrawal. It had added that fuel stocks at the front were down to 1.7 consumption units, that the complete removal of the ammunition depot at El Daba seemed impossible and that stocks in Matruh and to the west were very small.[300]

Early in the afternoon of 3 November Rommel received from Hitler an appeal or an order to the effect that he must hold out, 'not yielding a step and throwing in every weapon and every man available'; Rommel 'could show no other road to his troops than the road leading to death or victory'. GC and CS decrypted this signal early on 4 November, but did not transmit its contents to the Middle East until the afternoon and then only to the C-in-C.[301] When Rommel received it he had already been 'relieved and surprised' by reports from the DAK that Eighth Army had not yet renewed its offensive, as he had expected it to do, but seemed to be engaged in reorganising and replenishing.[302] And on receiving it he cancelled the orders he had issued for the withdrawal of his infantry and decided that after dark his armour should only move back a few miles in order to improve the chances of further resistance.

Eighth Army had indeed delayed the continuation of its attack. At a conference on the morning of 3 November it had been decided that a deep attack to the south-west by the infantry of 51st (Highland) Division and 5th Indian Brigade should start that evening as a prelude to the massive armoured break-out which would bring 'the final reckoning with the Panzer Army'.[303] During 3 November, on the other hand, the plans for cutting off the enemy's forces, by sending the New Zealand Division from the break-out point to Fuka while three armoured divisions of X Corps swung north to cut the coast road between Sidi Abd el Rahman and Daba, were drawn up in the belief that Rommel would be withdrawing, fighting step by step, from 3 November, as the Enigma had announced that morning. The Enigma vouchsafed no information about Rommel's decision during the afternoon to change his plan and to make a further stand; and the intelligence obtained from other sources was inconclusive. Air reconnaissance reports that the enemy was withdrawing in the north were coming in by mid-day, and during the afternoon the Italians in the south were observed to be retiring to the north-west, but an Italian POW taken in the north claimed that although the Italians were getting out, the Germans were staying, and Y indicated that the German HQs had not moved.[304] By off-setting the British delay during 3 November,

---

300.   QT 5098 of 0835/3 November 1942; CX/MSS/1619/T10 and 28.
301.   QT 5027 of 1411/4 November 1942; DEFE 3/573, CX/MSS/C 69.
302.   Carver, op cit, p 177.
303.   ibid, p 177; Playfair, op cit, Vol IV, p 74.
304.   AIR 41/50, p 325; WO 201/2155, No 355 of 3 November 1942.

Rommel's decision to make an intermediate stand should thus have enhanced Eighth Army's chances of cutting off the remains of the Panzer Army.

At first light on 4 November, when the British infantry thrust had broken through at the point of division between the German armour and the Italians, and the British armour was moving forward to exploit the gap, Eighth Army at last received from the Enigma news of Rommel's change of mind. At 0538 GC and CS sent out the decrypt of an announcement made by the Panzer Army at 1900 on 3 November that its motorised forces would not withdraw unless the British broke through with superior forces.[305] Thereafter, the fact that little traffic was observed on the coastal road confirmed that the enemy's withdrawal remained suspended during most of 4 November.[306] At 1000 the British armour came up against the re-formed screen with which Rommel was masking Sidi Abd el Rahman and Daba. By mid-day Rommel had asked Hitler's permission to withdraw;* at 1730, not waiting for an answer, he ordered all his forces to withdraw at once except the DAK, 90th Light Division and the remains of the Italian armour, which were ordered to retreat at dark.[307] Although his orders were not intercepted, Army Y soon detected preparations for withdrawal by 15th and 21st Panzer Divisions and other formations, and by 1845 it had established that 33rd Recce Unit was retreating to Fuka and that 15th Panzer Division was to pull back 70 km, probably to the same destination.[308]

The fact that, even so, Eighth Army failed to cut off all of what remained of the Panzer Army has been attributed generally to the slowness of the British armour, which, to the surprise of the enemy, halted for the night at darkness on 4 November when it was well beyond the bulk of Rommel's forces,[309] and more particularly to the diversion of the two most powerful and experienced British formations, 1st and 7th Armoured Divisions, to Daba, halfway to Fuka, on the morning of 5 November.[310] In accounting for the slowness of the pursuit it is perhaps unnecessary to look beyond operational delays, except that the New Zealand Division's slowness in starting for Fuka was partly caused by a Y intercept which told it that it

---

* Rommel's request and Hitler's approval of it, which was sent from Berlin later in the evening of 4 November, were not decrypted at GC and CS until early on 6 November.

305.   QT 5175 of 4 November 1942; CX/MSS/1624/T27.
306.   AIR 41/50, p 333.
307.   Playfair, op cit, Vol IV, p 85; DEFE 3/573, CX/MSS/C 72; Dir/C Archive 1295 of 6 November 1942.
308.   WO 201/2155, No 356 of 4 November 1942.
309.   QT 5229 of 4 November 1942; CX/MSS/1628/T16; Liddell Hart, op cit, p 305.
310.   Liddell Hart, op cit, p 305; Playfair, op cit, Vol IV, p 84; Carver, op cit, pp 186, 187, 202, 203.

would meet 15th Panzer Division there and caused its commander to concentrate his scattered units before advancing.[311] The diversion of 1st and 7th Armoured Divisions, which was too late to catch the retreating armour at Daba and which so greatly delayed Eighth Army's wider-sweeping pursuit that failed to catch it south of Matruh, is more difficult to explain. Apart from the Y intercepts of the evening of 4 November referring to a retreat to Fuka, there were RAF reports of dense road traffic between Daba and Fuka in the early hours of 5 November. But Sigint made no reference to the enemy's movements or intentions during the night of 4–5 November and it cannot be ruled out that in these circumstances GS Int, Eighth Army continued to attach undue weight to an Enigma decrypt which it had received in the early hours of 4 November. In this the Fliegerführer, discussing the Panzer Army's withdrawal, had referred on the evening of 3 November to its hope 'to gain some time at the next intermediate position, El Daba'.[312]

In the event, although the remains of the Italian XX Corps were caught between Daba and Fuka at noon on 5 November, losing about 40 tanks, mostly Italian, the rest of Rommel's forces reached Fuka by the morning of that day, and although he first thought of making a stand there, Rommel decided at 1400 to pull back 50 miles further west to Matruh.[313] At about the same time – 1340 on 5 November – 7th Armoured Division was sent to try to cut off the enemy between Fuka and Matruh, and 1st Armoured Division was ordered to make a wide sweep, starting at once and moving through the night so as to be able to attack at Matruh on 6 November. Twenty miles west of Fuka 7th Armoured Division stumbled on 21st Panzer Division, which was halted for lack of petrol, and destroyed 16 of its few remaining tanks, and numerous guns.[314] But 1st Armoured Division, slow to start and itself delayed by running out of petrol, was still 20 miles south of Matruh when, in the evening of 6 November, unable to attack because it had again exhausted its fuel, it saw what was left of the Panzer Army, about 1,000 vehicles, moving away from it in the distance.

Sigint was of no assistance to the land pursuit up to this point. During the night of 4–5 November GC and CS was decyphering the Enigma of 3 November. The decrypts informed Eighth Army that by the evening of 3 November the DAK had been reduced to 24 serviceable tanks and the Littorio Division to 17, that the Panzer Army's fuel stocks were then down to 1–2 consumption units,[315] and that on account of the MT fuel position the Panzer Army

311.   Carver, op cit, p 186.
312.   QT 5161 of 0221/4 November 1942; CX/MSS/1624/T7.
313.   AIR 41/50, p 373; Carver, op cit, p 189.
314.   Playfair, op cit, Vol IV, p 90.
315.   QT 5265 of 0333/5 November 1942; CX/MSS/1629/T10.

would be unable to continue mobile fighting beyond 'the area east of Matruh';[316] but they cast no further light on the enemy's plans or future movements until the afternoon of 6 November. Moreover, although Eighth Army then learned from the Enigma that Rommel was preparing to stand at Halfaya, where Italian formations were being brought up to protect the southern flank,[317] it is improbable that this intelligence in any way assisted the British pursuit force which, moving from Matruh on 7 November, dislodged the enemy from Halfaya and narrowly missed intercepting him at Capuzzo on 10 November.[318] Nor did Y add anything of value after notifying Eighth Army on the evening of 4 November of the enemy's preparations for withdrawal and his references to Fuka.

It remains to consider the possibility that, as the Enigma may have contributed to the wasteful diversion of two divisions to Daba on 5 November, so it may help to explain why on that most crucial day of the pursuit, when most of the Panzer Army was within range of the RAF's airfields, the RAF made so little use of its complete control of the air to bomb much more heavily than it did a disorganised enemy whose retreat was confined to a single escape road. Rommel had expected and feared an all-out RAF effort.* But to the astonishment and to the irritation of the pilots, sorties by the RAF's bombers and fighter-bombers, 350 during 3 November, were reduced to 120 during 5 November.[319] According to the RAF narrative of the campaign, the reduction was necessitated in part by the RAF's supply problems, which were dominated by the desperate need to seize airfields near Benghazi as soon as possible in order to cover the next Malta convoy, and in part by the expectation that the GAF was about to send strong reinforcements to north Africa – an expectation which produced the order that the RAF's primary mission from 5 November must be to provide fighter cover for the van of Eighth Army's pursuit and which thus inevitably reduced bomber activity.[320] The narrative adds that this expectation was based on 'previous experience' and respect for the exceptional flexibility of the GAF.[321] It may also have been influenced by the receipt in the Middle East on 4 November of the Enigma decrypt of Hitler's 'victory or death' appeal to Rommel: this had assured Rommel that 'important air reinforcements were being sent in these very days'.[322]

---

* See above, p 448.

316.   QT 5277 of 0625/5 November 1942; CX/MSS/1629/T7, 24 and 25.
317.   QT 5397 of 1206/6 November 1942; CX/MSS/1635/T7.
318.   Playfair, op cit, Vol IV, pp 94–95.
319.   ibid, p 88.
320.   AIR 41/50, pp 362, 367–368.
321.   ibid, pp 362, 366.
322.   QT 5207 of 1411/4 November 1942; DEFE 3/573, CX/MSS/C 69.

During 4 and 5 November, however, the Middle East authorities received other decrypts which were more explicit about the state and intentions of the GAF. GC and CS informed them early on 4 November that the GAF was preparing to transfer forces to the western Mediterranean for use against the large convoys it had detected at Gibraltar;[323] early on 5 November they learned that on account of the mounting threat at Gibraltar, not yet identified by the enemy as preparations for the Allied landings in north-west Africa, bombers previously transferred to Crete from Sicily had been ordered back to Sicily;[324] and during the course of 5 November the decrypts, while providing them with that day's strength return from the GAF in Africa, and showing them that only 5 fighters were serviceable,[325] continued to yield no evidence that reinforcements were on the way. It seems unlikely that they were influenced by Hitler's rhetorical promise and not impressed by these subsequent and far more substantial indications that the promise would not be fulfilled. If, as the narrative concedes, the RAF missed a unique opportunity during 5 November,[326] and if, as it claims, the opportunity was missed as a result of an expectation about the enemy, as well as on account of operational limitations, the expectation probably sprang not from paying undue attention to a part of the available intelligence, but from ways of thought that were too deeply ingrained to be influenced by intelligence – the cautiousness which arose from over-estimating the flexibility of the GAF and stood in marked contrast to the enterprise of the RAF when it moved forward.

□

After failing to cut off Rommel's forces at Capuzzo on 10 November 1942, Eighth Army might still have prevented them from withdrawing to Tunisia and exerting a powerful influence on the Tunisian campaign. Up to 19 November it might have cut the coastal road ahead of them, at a point south of Benghazi, if it had not delayed before ordering a strong enough force south-westward across the desert. If it had not delayed till 14 December before attacking at Agheila, and then till 15 January before assaulting Rommel's next defence line at Buerat, it might on each of these two further occasions have overcome the difficulty of cutting him off. This difficulty was substantial: Eighth Army's own supply problems mounted as it advanced; Rommel displayed his accustomed ability on the one hand in delaying his retreat and, on the other, in

---

323.   eg QT 5186 of 0747/4 November 1942; CX/MSS/1624/T55.
324.   QT 5270 of 0445/5 November 1942; CX/MSS/1629/T1.
325.   QT 5354 of 5 November 1942; CX/MSS/1629/T3.
326.   AIR 41/50, pp 362–363, 366–371.

extricating himself when attacked. Perhaps, indeed, it was insurmountable. But it owed nothing to the lack of intelligence. Throughout the pursuit General Montgomery was fully apprised by the Enigma, by air reconnaissance and by Army Y of the state of Rommel's forces and, more important, the Enigma gave him advance notice of Rommel's intentions.

On 11 November air reconnaissance showed that the enemy was evacuating Bardia and Tobruk.[327] At this point, given the probability that fuel shortage and his dependence on such fuel as lay at Benghazi would force him to hug the coast, Eighth Army briefly toyed with the idea of sending armoured cars by the shorter route across the desert to cut him off.[328] At the same time GOC X Corps went further and suggested that he should himself take this shorter route with a larger force.[329] Air Marshal Tedder, AOC-in-C Middle East, also urged such a move by substantial forces and offered to supply them with transport.[330] But General Montgomery had ruled on 10 November that his main bodies should not move west of Capuzzo lest they should outrun his ability to maintain them and court the risk of another of Rommel's counter-attacks. He hoped to overwhelm Rommel at Agheila, where he expected him to make his next stand.[331] Nor was he deflected from this plan when he learned from the Enigma during 10 November that 21st Panzer Division was down to 11 serviceable tanks, that 15th Panzer Division had no tanks left and that the Panzer Army had only one quarter of an ammunition issue and fuel for only 4–5 days.[332]

In the next few days the Enigma decrypts revealed considerable alarm in the Panzer Army – and on the part of Hitler – that the British would make a south-westerly drive across the desert to cut off its retreat south of Benghazi.[333] The decrypts also directly contributed to the sinking on 13 November of a tanker bound for Benghazi from which on 10 November the Panzer Army had been expecting early relief.[334] In the early hours of 16 November a special situation report from Rommel for Hitler showed that the fuel situation was 'catastrophic'[335] and that the Army was virtually

---

327. CAB 44/108, AL 1200/94B, p 458.
328. ibid.
329. Hunt, op cit, p 156.
330. AIR 41/50, pp 415–417, 420–421; de Guingand, *Operation Victory*, p 218.
331. Playfair, op cit, Vol IV, p 97.
332. QTs 5758, 5794 and 5822 all of 10 November 1942; CX/MSS/1654/T25, 1655/T11, 1658/T18 and 19.
333. QTs 5932 of 12 November, 6015 of 13 November, 6122 of 14 November, 6173 of 15 November 1942; CX/MSS/1664/T26, 1669/T14, 1674/T39, 1678/T31; AIR 41/50, p 420 fn, quoting *The Rommel Papers*.
334. QTs 5760 and 5772 of 10 November, 6001 of 13 November 1942; CX/MSS/1654/T34; DEFE 3/583, ZTPGM 3441, 3627.
335. QT 6253 of 0524/16 November 1942; CX/MSS/1684/T18 and 20.

immobilised, and partly for these reasons and partly because its alarm about the British advance was subsiding, the Panzer Army had decided that it would not pass through Benghazi till 19 November.[336] The following morning, two more tankers having been sunk by then with the assistance of Sigint, the decrypts reiterated that the Panzer Army was virtually immobilised in the Benghazi area.[337] On the morning of 18 November it was learnt that Rommel had decided to evacuate Benghazi that evening, abandoning its ammunition stocks, because British armoured cars had been sighted south of Benghazi.[338] X Corps had been ordered to send two columns of armoured cars across the desert on 15 November to harass the enemy south of Benghazi.[339] But this diversion apart, Eighth Army continued to follow up the enemy's retreat along the coast with light forces until, later on 18 November, General Montgomery ordered X Corps to strengthen its southern thrust and proceed at 'utmost speed' to cut off the enemy.[340] The order came too late: on 19 November the Panzer Army slipped past X Corps's armoured cars on its way to Agheila.[341]

How far GHQ Eighth Army delayed the order for a strong southerly thrust from anxiety about its own supply difficulties,[342] and how far it did so from confidence in its ability finally to overwhelm Rommel when it assaulted the Agheila position, is difficult to determine. It is clear, however, that its confidence was high. The Allied forces which had landed in Tunisia were now beginning to advance south-east; and on 14 and 15 November the Enigma revealed that the German authorities were switching to Tunis not only replacement battalions originally destined for the Panzer Army but also the transport aircraft which had hitherto supplied the Panzer Army with fuel.[343] Since Malta was being replenished – the long-awaited convoy arrived there intact on 20 November – and since Tripoli was about to become Rommel's only remaining port, it in any case seemed unlikely that the Panzer Army would receive much in the way of fresh manpower, tanks and fuel. On 13 November, and again on 16 November, GHQ Eighth Army emphasised these favourable developments in its intelligence

---

336. QT 6288 of 1536/16 November 1942; CX/MSS/1687/T21.
337. QT 6374 of 0913/17 November 1942; CX/MSS/1689/T21.
338. QTs 6412 of 0326/18 November, 6429 of 0629/18 November 1942; CX/MSS/1694/T19 and 56.
339. Playfair, op cit, Vol IV, p 97.
340. CAB 44/108, p 633; AIR 41/50, p 420; Hunt, op cit, p 156.
341. Hunt, op cit, p 156; CAB 44/108, p 656.
342. de Guingand, *Operation Victory*, pp 216–217.
343. QTs 6148 of 14 November, 6209 of 15 November 1942; CX/MSS/1675/T8, 1680/T23.

summaries.[344] And from 18 November its expectations seemed to be fully justified by further Enigma decrypts. On the evening of 18 November GHQ received Rommel's reply to a directive in which Mussolini had ordered him to defend Tripolitania on the Agheila line. Rommel stated categorically that he could defend the position, which was only slightly mined and void of natural flank defences, only if he was given artillery replacements (notably 122 heavy anti-tank guns) and 50 Pzkw IV tanks, if the GAF was strengthened, and if his fuel and ammunition situation could be fundamentally improved in the two to three weeks before Eighth Army was likely to attack.[345] On 19 November he had added in a further signal decrypted on 22 November that unless he also received more motor transport his non-motorised Italian formations would suffer 'the fate of their comrades at Alamein'.[346] On 24 November, Hitler having backed up Mussolini's decision that Agheila must be held 'in all circumstances', Rommel warned him that it was unlikely that he could hold it for any length of time and that 'the probability of the annihilation of the remaining elements of the army . . . must therefore be faced'. To the Prime Minister, who drew General Alexander's attention to the decrypts of Rommel's signals, another decrypt of 24 November also seemed to be 'of profound importance'; it stated that the Panzer Army's fuel would be exhausted in a few days.[347]*

Comforting though it was, this intelligence, coupled with the appreciation that Rommel was unlikely to receive the replacements and supplies he had requested, cannot but have alerted Eighth Army to the considerable risk that if he was subjected to a long-prepared direct assault, the enemy, while standing as long as possible, would again retreat and make good his escape as soon as superior force was brought against him. Nor did this risk decline in the next ten days. Sigint did not reveal that early in December, after a visit by Rommel to Berlin, Mussolini and Hitler had agreed

---

* During the remainder of the pursuit the Prime Minister's scarcely suppressed impatience was revealed in further signals to the C-in-C Middle East as follows:[348]

6 December 1942; 'Presume you have read the Boniface numbers QT/7789 and QT/7903 which certainly reveal a condition of weakness and counter-order among the enemy of a very remarkable character.'
27 December 1942; 'Boniface shows the enemy in great anxiety and disarray at Buerat . . .'
2 January 1943; 'Boniface 1897/T of 13 December shows enemy will certainly get away his now immobile troops . . .'

344.   WO 201/2155, Nos 362 of 13 November and 363 of 16 November 1942.
345.   QTs 6387 of 17 November, 6433 of 18 November 1942;
        CX/MSS/1690/T12, 1694/T59.
346.   QT 6714 of 22 November 1942; CX/MSS/1713/T17 and 18.
347.   QT 6839 of 24 November 1942; CX/MSS/1721/T25.
348.   Cabinet Office file 82/43/1 Part 2, T 1667/2 of 6 December, OZ 2338 of 27 December 1942, OZ 22 of 2 January 1943.

that preparations might be made for a retreat to Buerat, 250 miles west of Agheila and half-way to Tripoli;[349] but it did disclose that soon after his return to Africa on 3 December Rommel, though protesting at first, had concurred in a decision already taken by Bastico, C-in-C Libya, to withdraw the Italian infantry formations to Buerat.[350] By then, however, General Montgomery had made his plans. After 'wondering whether by bluff or manoeuvre on the open flank I could frighten the enemy out of his positions',[351] he issued on 29 November the orders for a frontal attack: it was to take place on the night of 16–17 December together with a wide outflanking movement by the New Zealand Division to a point 80 miles south of Agheila from which it might cut off the enemy in the rear. Starting on 11–12 December, the outflanking movement was to be accompanied by bombardment and infantry raids against the enemy's forward positions with a view to distracting his attention from the flank.[352]

The intention to pause until 16–17 December was dictated in part by the supply difficulties of Eighth Army's forward troops and in part by General Montgomery's insistence on building up an overwhelming superiority for his assault. During the pause, Eighth Army made a study of the terrain and of the enemy's order of battle, fixed defences and gun positions that was hardly less thorough than that which had preceded the battle of Alamein, and Army Y provided full and accurate details about his order of battle.[353] At the same time, however, the Enigma confirmed the appreciation that Rommel's requests for supplies and reinforcements for his much reduced forces would not be met. On the one hand the Axis authorities were now giving priority to supplying their forces in Tunisia; on the other hand, the Allies maintained their successful campaign against Axis shipping. Although the amount of shipping sent to Tripoli was further restricted by the presence of warships at Malta, three-quarters of it was sunk during November. By 5 December five shiploads of stores for the Panzer Army were waiting in Italy, but only two medium-sized ships were available. Furthermore, heavy RAF and USAAF raids on Tripoli sank further ships and disrupted port activity. By 6 December supplies for Tripolitania were having to be sent through Tunisian ports;[354] on 16 December Tripoli was closed to traffic and all supplies for the Panzer Army were diverted to Tunis and Bizerta.[355]

---

349. Playfair, op cit, Vol IV, p 219.
350. QT 7772 of 1904/4 December 1942; CX/MSS/1772/T10.
351. Montgomery, *El Alamein to the River Sangro*, p 29.
352. ibid.   353. See intelligence summaries in WO 201/2155.
354. QT 7898 of 6 December 1942; CX/MSS/1779/T3.
355. AIR 41/50, pp 430–431.

On 5 December the Enigma disclosed the complete strength and supply return for the Panzer Army and the GAF for 1 December.[356] The Panzer Army, now reduced to 54 tanks and to a little Italian armour (42 medium tanks), had no reserves of fuel and was desperately short of ammunition. The GAF had fuel and one day's operations and could not undertake adequate reconnaissance. On 8 December further decrypts informed Eighth Army that the GAF throughout Libya was 'immobilised' and that the Panzer Army had sufficient fuel to enable it to pull back from its forward positions to its main defence line, but not enough to permit it to counter-attack.[357] On the evening of that day Eighth Army finally received Rommel's announcement of his intentions: against the British assault, expected at any minute, he would hold out as long as possible, but would retire in the face of strong pressure.[358]

On 9 December GHQ Eighth Army, feeling that 'time was getting short', discussed the measures it would adopt if the enemy showed 'definite signs of withdrawal'.[359] But no such signs had been obtained by the early hours of 12 December when Eighth Army launched the raids on the Panzer Army's outposts that had been planned with the intention of distracting attention from the outflanking march of the New Zealand Division, which was now timed to begin on 13 December.[360] The Panzer Army, taking these raids to be the start of the British attack, at once started to withdraw.[361] At 1030 on 12 December, when British patrols had reported that the enemy was thinning out,[362] General Montgomery ordered the New Zealand Division to speed up, and brought forward Eighth Army's main assault by 48 hours, to the night of 14–15 December.[363] His change of plan again came too late. The New Zealand Division managed to catch the rear of 15th Panzer Division, but otherwise the Panzer Army, its movements charted in detail by Army Y,[364] escaped unscathed to the Buerat lines, to which it had completed its withdrawal by 28 December.[365] Rommel's subsequent comment on his escape is perhaps worth repeating: 'Experience should have told [the British commander] that there was a good chance that we should not accept battle [at Agheila]. He should not therefore have started bombarding our strong points and attacking our line until his outflanking force had

356.   QT 7829 of 5 December 1942; CX/MSS/1773/T7.
357.   QTs 8048 and 8055 of 8 December 1942; CX/MSS/1788/T19 and 32.
358.   QTs 8109 and 8115 of 8 December 1942; CX/MSS/1790/T7.
359.   CAB 44/109, AL 1200/94C, p 966.
360.   ibid, p 1000; AIR 41/50, p 438; Liddell Hart, op cit, p 308.
361.   AIR 41/50, p 438; Liddell Hart, op cit, p 308.
362.   CAB 44/109, p 981.
363.   ibid, pp 997, 1000; Playfair, op cit, Vol IV, p 224.
364.   WO 201/2155, Nos 384 to 393 of 13–25 December 1942.
365.   QT 9869 of 30 December 1942; CX/MSS/1885/T2.

completed its move and was in a position to advance on the coast road in timed co-ordination with the frontal attack'.[366]

General Montgomery reached the same conclusion at the time. His plans for the assault on the Buerat position called for simultaneous frontal and outflanking attacks without preliminary probing.[367] They have not on that account avoided severe criticism. He decided to 'plan for the Buerat battle on the basis of ten days' heavy fighting, using four divisions, and calculated that the necessary dumping would take some three weeks. I therefore intended to resume the offensive in mid-January'.[368] When reported to Whitehall this delay produced so much impatience that on 27 December the Prime Minister sent the following personal and most secret telegram to General Alexander: 'Boniface [the Enigma] shows the enemy in great anxiety and dissarray at Buerat, and under lively fear of being cut off there by an enveloping movement from the south which he expected might become effective as early as December 26. Reading Boniface after discounting the enemy's natural tendency to exaggerate his difficulties in order to procure better supplies, I cannot help hoping that you may find it possible to strike earlier than the date mentioned . . . Thus the great honour of taking Tripoli would probably fall to the Eighth Army'.[369] But his intervention had no more effect on Eighth Army's plans than did the fact that Enigma soon added to its reports on Rommel's situation a clear statement of his intentions.

On 31 December Eighth Army learned from the Enigma the outcome of a protracted debate between Rommel and his superiors. He was determined to get his army to Tunisia before his line of retreat and supply west of Tripoli was cut in his rear; the Axis High Command, anxious to deny the Allies the shipping route through the Mediterranean by reinforcing Tunisia, was determined that he should delay Eighth Army's advance at all costs.[370] The outcome was a compromise: repeating the tactics he had used at Agheila, Rommel was to withdraw his non-mobile troops to the Homs-Tarhuna line, between Buerat and Tripoli, to which his motorised divisions would retire after holding the Buerat line for as long as possible.[371] During the first week in January, while Army Y detected the fall-back from Buerat of his Italian formations,[372] the Enigma showed that the enemy was expecting two attacks about 13

366. AIR 41/50, p 438 fn, quoting *The Rommel Papers.*
367. Liddell Hart, op cit, p 397.
368. Montgomery, *El Alamein to the River Sangro*, p 32.
369. Cabinet Office file 82/43/1 Part 2, T 1761/2 of 27 December 1942.
370. VM 111 of 1 January 1943; CX/MSS/1897/T12.
371. VM 298 of 4 January 1943; CX/MSS/1909/T19 and 28.
372. AWLs 315 of 21 January, 323 of 27 January 1943; GAD 260 of 22 January 1943.

January – one by Eighth Army on Buerat, the second by US forces from Gafsa against Rommel's lines of communication on the coast – and was regarding a forestalling attack on Gafsa as 'of decisive importance in the Panzer Army's struggle for survival'.[373]* On 12 January the decrypts reported the outcome of a further discussion: Rommel had proposed the despatch of 21st Panzer Division and 580th Reconnaissance Unit to the Sfax/Gabes area and his superiors had approved the move on condition that 21st Panzer Division left its 34 tanks with 15th Panzer Division, and provided that Rommel still imposed as much delay as possible on Eighth Army in order to give time for preparation of defences at Mareth.[374]

Thereafter Army Y and the Enigma traced the westward move of 21st Panzer Division[375] and kept an accurate tally of the Panzer Army's tank strength. When Eighth Army attacked at Buerat on 15 January with between 7 and 8 divisions and 700 tanks it knew that it was faced by the equivalent of one and a half German divisions with 34 tanks and 6 Italian battalions with 57,[376] the tanks left behind by 21st Panzer Division being at the Homs-Tarhuna line for lack of fuel,[377] and that the enemy still lacked sufficient fuel and ammunition for heavy fighting.[378] It is scarcely surprising that Rommel withdrew immediately. But perhaps, to quote one official account of the desert campaign, 'it is surprising that after the enemy commander had declined action [at Agheila] it should be thought probable that he would choose to defend the much weaker position at Buerat . . . His forces . . . were only the battered remnants of the Panzer Army against which when intact at El Alamein, which was an infinitely stronger position, hardly more than twice that number of divisions had been employed'. The account concluded: 'Now that Rommel's supply difficulties and the weakness of his forces are so apparent from captured enemy documents, the Eighth Army commander's plans for the assault . . . seem . . . most ponderous . . .'[379] What it would have concluded had its author known that the Enigma was currently revealing not only Rommel's situation, but also his intentions, is best left to the imagination.

General Montgomery was not to be presented with another opportunity to cut off the enemy's retirement. After his withdrawal

---

* See below, pp 578–579.

373.   VM 633 of 7 January 1943; CX/MSS/1927/T12.
374.   VM 1068 of 12 January 1943; CX/MSS/1952/T16.
375.   eg GAD 260 of 22 January 1943.
376.   Howard, op cit, Vol IV, p 187.
377.   VMs 1209 of 14 January, 1281 and 1307 of 15 January 1943; CX/MSS/1959/T1, 1963/T31, 1964/T12.
378.   eg VMs 401 of 5 January, 542 of 6 January 1943; CX/MSS/1919/T15, 1922/T14.
379.   AIR 41/50, p 448.

from Buerat Rommel fought a number of rearguard actions with the object of delaying Eighth Army's advance, but Eighth Army had to content itself with repeatedly dislodging him, and its entry into Tripoli on 23 January 1943 was but a stage in a long and onerous pursuit that was not to end before the old Panzer Army was rounded up in Tunisia.

CHAPTER 24

Operation *Torch* and the
Campaign in Tunisia to
the end of 1942

DURING THE planning of the Anglo-American descent on French north Africa, as on the decision to undertake it, the influence of intelligence was subordinate to that of logistic, strategic and political considerations. It was so for obvious reasons. The chief requirement from intelligence in these stages was that it should predict enemy reactions to a major Allied initiative; this was an unaccustomed task and one in which reliability could not be guaranteed. The scale of the Allied undertaking was without previous parallel in the war, indeed in the history of warfare: never before had states collaborated in despatching such huge armadas over thousands of miles of ocean and landing so large an expedition in hostile or potentially hostile territory. It would have been surprising if both the decision to launch the operation and the detailed planning of it had not been the outcome of a process of compromise in which intelligence considerations took second place to discord on wider issues.

The President and the Prime Minister took a political decision when, in June 1942, after much inconclusive debate about the preferability and practicability of attempting a cross-Channel expedition, they agreed that early action must be taken against French north Africa with the object of drawing German forces away from the Russian front. The decision was taken in the teeth of opposition from the President's military advisers, whose sights remained set on an early cross-Channel invasion. During July the US Chiefs of Staff still prevailed on the British Chiefs of Staff to agree that the north African operation should take place 'at the earliest possible date before December 1942' only if by 15 September the situation on the Russian front indicated such a collapse or weakening of Russian resistance as to make Allied landings in Europe impracticable. Nor was their resistance finally overcome till 24 July, when the President and the Prime Minister insisted *tout court* that the operation should be launched 'at the earliest possible date'.*

---

* See above, pp 100–101 and for a detailed account of the strategic decision to mount operation *Torch* see Howard, *Grand Strategy*, Vol IV (1972), prologue.

This final decision to proceed as soon as possible was no doubt influenced by British intelligence assessments of the state of Germany's armed forces in Europe. According to an official US Army History, the preference of the US Chiefs of Staff for a cross-Channel invasion had been prolonged by a JIC assessment of 1 June to the effect that there might be a quick shift in the Russian campaign to the advantage of the Russians. By 16 July, in contrast, the JIC was calculating that, even if Germany did not eliminate Russia, she could and would withdraw to France and the Low Countries sufficient land forces to be able to count on resisting any Allied landing in Europe.[1] In the same paper, however, an appreciation entitled 'German Strategy in 1942–43', the JIC implied that there were powerful arguments in favour of early action against French north Africa; and strictly speaking these were strategic arguments, not intelligence assessments.

The paper of 16 July stated that 'if the United Nations concentrate their main effort during the winter in building up for invasion of Europe from the west next spring, Germany will . . . appreciate that this is the present intention of the United Nations, and her knowledge of the slowness with which the democracies change their plans and come to great decisions will induce in her the belief that she will not be effectively attacked, at least until it is too late, in the one theatre in which she is at present vulnerable, namely, the Middle East'. It stated that should she succeed in 1942 in defeating Russia and in exploiting Rommel's successes by advancing into Egypt and beyond, Germany might herself occupy French north Africa, thus greatly increasing the threat to Allied shipping. It urged, on the other hand, that if Russia were still fighting at the end of 1942 the Mediterranean would be Germany's Achilles heel if the Allies 'copied the German policy and occupied neutral territory.'

Whether or not this paper influenced the final decision to proceed, it did no more than recapitulate the views that had long been held by the British authorities, and the JIC's first comprehensive intelligence appreciation for the attack on north Africa followed the decision. Issued on 7 August, but incorporated into a Joint Planning Staff paper of 5 August, it dealt with three issues: the probable reaction of the forces of Vichy France; the threat to and through Spain; the form and extent of the other retaliation that might be expected from the Axis powers. Under each of these headings it provided in support of its conclusions a mass of detail which will be considered later on. Its general conclusions were as follows.[2] The French Army and Air Force would resist in com-

---

1. Matloff and Snell, *Strategic Planning for Coalition Warfare 1941–1942* (Washington DC 1953), pp 236–237; JIC (42) 200 of 1 June; CAB 121/412, SIC file A/Germany/1, JIC (42) 265 of 16 July.
2. CAB 121/497, SIC file E/North Africa/3G, JIC (42) 304 (0) of 7 August.

pliance with orders from Vichy to the point where they could plead *force majeure*; in the face of a resolute attack they would probably collapse speedily. The French Navy would resist only in the Mediterranean; the Dakar-based force would probably not be involved. If only because of her dependence on the Allies for essential imports, Spain would resist German pressure to move against Gibraltar unless it was backed with force. This would be possible only if Germany made withdrawals from Russia, since the German Army lacked a strategic reserve and was fully stretched, and such withdrawals would take time. Nor would there be any Axis air threat from southern Spain or the Balearics in the first month after the Allied landings. As for more immediate Axis responses, the Italian Army and Air Force were unlikely to be sent to Tunisia; Italian naval opposition to the assault convoys would not be pressed to the point of risking heavy forces outside the range of shore-based aircraft; Axis submarines in the area, which included between 16 and 20 German U-boats, could not be materially increased without some delay, though a subsequent build-up was to be expected; but what additional action Germany would take would depend on the speed with which the Allies advanced into Tunisia after the landings and, still more important, on the date of the landings.

The views of the JIC on this last point were that landings would place Germany in a strategic quandary. Unable at once to disengage any substantial forces from Russia, uncertain whether the Allies might not also land in Europe and faced with the need to maintain Rommel, she would try to avoid the extra commitment of occupying Vichy France, though pressing for maximum Vichy resistance in north Africa and supporting Vichy's air effort with Axis bombers operating from Sicily and Sardinia. It was unlikely that she would move reinforcements to the central Mediterranean before D-4, by which time it was assumed that she would have become sure of the destination of the assault convoys.* Even then, although it would be in her interest to do so, she might hesitate to try to forestall the Allies in Tunisia with the limited reinforcements available to her if the Allied advance from Algeria was developing fast. Should she make the attempt, it was unlikely that she would operate the GAF in Tunisia, with the possible exception of some fighter aircraft if she moved land forces in, and her capacity to move land forces in would be limited. She would have no trained air landing formations available other than those already in Libya; the demands on her transport aircraft for the supply of Rommel might make it impossible for her to move from France the 14,000 lightly-armed infantry that could theoretically be in Tunisia two

---

* But see below, p 478 et seq.

weeks from the order to move; and that force would have to be maintained by sea. As for seaborne troops, the first elements of one division could be in Tunisia two weeks after the Allied assault, but a complete division could not be operationally effective before four to seven weeks.

In contrast to what the JIC said about the threat from Spain and the reaction of the French forces, its assessment of the probable scale of Axis intervention turned out to be an under-estimate in every respect. Worse still, since it was accepted by the JPS[3] and remained unchanged throughout the planning period, it guided the expectations of the operational commanders with results that were to say the least unfortunate. According to a member of the JIS, in a note that is undated but that was written after the unfortunate consequences had materialised, the assessment differed from that which was offered by the JIS. The note says that the JIS weighed two considerations against each other, first the calculation that 'on the grounds of sound military strategy the arguments against further German forces being sent to North Africa . . . held most water'; secondly the belief that Hitler would intervene powerfully in Tunisia, even at the expense of other threatened theatres. It goes on to say that the JIS firmly concluded that 'to give an opinion based solely on what was considered sound military strategy was wrong': Hitler would do his utmost to resist the Allies and prevent them from opening up a new theatre in Tunisia. And it asserts that it was the JIC, meeting by itself, which reshaped the JIS draft into the paper which, as issued, conveyed the overall impression that, as sound military strategy would prevail even over Hitler's predilection for action, the Allied expedition would meet with serious opposition only from the French forces in the initial stages.[4] But if this were the whole story, it would still be necessary to explain why the JIC, far from merely watering down a JIS appreciation, as it often did, virtually reversed it.

Over and above the possibility that in its own draft the JIS had left the balance more even than the note allows between the belief that Hitler would act at once, and powerfully, and the considerations of prudent strategy, the explanation lies in the two provisos which figured in the JIC's paper of 7 August. The first of these provisos has been discussed already: the paper concluded that Germany, with the limited reinforcements that would be at her disposal, might hesitate to try to forestall the Allies in Tunisia if they advanced into Tunisia rapidly. The second had to do with the date on which the Allies carried out the landings. The paper only touched on this by warning that by the beginning of November

---

3. CAB 121/490, SIC file E/North Africa/3A, vol 1, JP (42) 721 of 5 August.
4. McLachlan, *Room 39* (1968), p 260.

Germany might find it easier to bring up substantial reinforcements because her fears of a cross-Channel invasion during 1942 would be at rest. But the JIC had on 3 August already issued an interim appreciation in which it gave two other reasons for believing that it was vital that the landings should take place at the earliest possible date. Not later than mid-October, whatever the result of the summer campaign in Russia, Germany would be withdrawing substantial land and air forces from the eastern front for rest and refitting. And, secondly, 'October may be a month of critical decisions by the Russian government' on which Anglo-American action, even if outside Europe, would exert an influence.[5] It seems safe to assume that when in the paper of 7 August the JIC stressed that German resistance would be limited, it was not merely assuming that the landings would be carried out early in October but was hoping that its assessment would show the need for not delaying the landings beyond that date.

This was certainly how the British planners understood the JIC's appreciation. On 2 August the JPS was working to an early-October date.[6] On 4 August the British Chiefs of Staff considered that, whereas up to the end of October Germany would have no forces available for coercing Spain and few for over-running Vichy France, by November these favourable conditions might have ceased to exist.[7] On 5 August the JPS send its appreciation, incorporating the gist of the JIC paper, to General Eisenhower, but they did so with some changes of emphasis. The JPS accepted the conclusion that the Axis would hesitate to commit ground and air forces to Tunisia 'provided our operations are rapid'. But it reduced the JIC's estimate of the ground forces that Germany would be able to send to Tunisia in the early stages if she did decide to intervene: it lowered from 14,000 to 8,000–10,000 the number of lightly-armed troops that could arrive by the end of the second week; it considered that they would be 'of low category and without motor transport'; and whereas the JIC had estimated that the leading units of an armoured or infantry division could arrive by sea about two weeks after the Allied landings, and that one division might be operationally effective in four to seven weeks, the JPS calculated that the first seaborne troops would disembark within 28 days of the decision to send them and that it would be six to seven weeks before one division could be operationally effective. On the other hand, the JPS, believing that the number of German divisions could rise from one to four within 14 weeks if the enemy were not forestalled, was emphatic in warning that 'the most

5.   CAB 121/497, JIC (42) 299 (o) of 3 August.
6.   CAB 121/490, JP (42) 720 of 2 August.
7.   CAB 121/490, COS (W) 237 of 4 August 1942; AIR 41/33, *The North African Campaign*, p 11.

effective Axis counter-move would be the move of Axis forces to north Africa by sea'. After noting that it would be difficult to deny the enemy the use of Tunisian ports in the early stages, and that Axis convoys would be making a short sea passage under cover of land-based air forces, the planners insisted that 'every effort must be made to delay the arrival of Axis forces by means of naval and air forces operating from Malta and from bases in north Africa as these become available'. More than that, they urged that it was so crucial to forestall the transfer of Axis forces to Tunisia that the key points there must be occupied within 26 days of D-4, when the Allied convoys would pass Gibraltar, and if possible within 14 days.[8]

On these grounds, and also on account of the poor state of land communications in French north Africa, the British authorities advocated that the Allied expedition should be carried as near as possible to Tunis and Bizerta, with landings as far east as Bône, and that a landing at Casablanca should receive lower priority, and perhaps be deferred to a later date, and they hoped the Mediterranean landings could be made on 7 October.[9] But General Eisenhower's draft outline plan of 9 August set the date of the operation at 5 November.[10]* The forces which, direct from the United States, were to carry out the Casablanca landing simultaneously with the landings in the Mediterranean could not be ready before that date, and the US authorities had urged that he should give priority to landings at Casablanca and Oran even at the expense of omitting an attempt to land at Algiers. They had done so from the fear that in the interval between landings in the Mediterranean, which would be possible early in October, and the landing at Casablanca, which could not be made until early in November, the GAF might trap the Allied forces in north Africa by mounting attacks from southern Spain against the Straits of Gibraltar.[11]

US official accounts make it clear that the US position paid little regard to intelligence assessments. The USAAF had indeed carried out an 'intelligence study'; but this was in fact only a contingency study which stressed the danger from overwhelming air attack that would arise during the assault phase if the Germans should obtain the use of Spanish and Spanish Moroccan bases.[12] And the determination of the US authorities to guard against this contingency derived from strategic considerations. Apart from the

---

* For the development of the *Torch* planning see Howard, op cit, Vol IV, p 119 et seq.

8.   CAB 121/490, JP (42) 721 of 5 August.
9.   Howard, *Grand Strategy*, Vol IV (1972), pp 118–120.
10. CAB 121/490; Outline Plan of 9 August 1942.
11. ibid, COS (42) 96th (o) meeting, 21 August.
12. Howe, *North-West Africa* (Washington DC 1957), p 16 fn 3, p 21 fn 5.

fact that the *Torch* operation was still opposed in some quarters, the US Chiefs of Staff were not wholly confident that Russia would be able to hold out or that the British would defeat Rommel; looking to the long-term interests of the United States, they were thus concerned that *Torch* should give them a powerful bridgehead in north-west Africa which bordered on the Atlantic and were convinced that the British plan, with its emphasis on the importance of pre-empting the Axis in Tunisia, ran too great a risk.[13] Against such arguments it was to no avail that the JIC, which had excluded the threat from Spain on 7 August,* adhered to its view in further appreciations on 14, 19 and 20 August.[14] Or that the British Chiefs of Staff, with Whitehall all but unanimous in judging the threat from Spain to be far less than the danger of allowing the Axis to get a foothold in Tunisia, insisted in response to the first draft plan that 'the whole concept of *Torch* may stand or fall on this question'.[15] Or, even, that General Eisenhower drew up a second plan, circulated on 22 August, in which, while reserving a high proportion of his available air forces against the air threat from Spanish bases, he eliminated the Casablanca landing and set 15 October as the date for the Mediterranean landings.[16] The American authorities would not budge from their insistence that there must be simultaneous landings at Casablanca and in the Mediterranean.

On 23 August, in their comments on the second draft plan, the British Joint Planners finally abandoned the hope of convincing their US counterparts that the US assessments were exaggerating the threat from Spain. At the same time, they noted the existence in the new plan of another serious defect: the schedules were so tight that in the event of any serious French resistance the timetable in the plan calling for the occupation of key points in Tunisia by between D+24 and D+28 would not be met.[17] In concluding on 7 August that the French forces would resist only to the point where they could plead *force majeure* provided they were subjected to resolute and powerful attack – and in calculating that 'the only serious resistance from ground forces was likely to be met during the assault or first phase', that is between D−4 and D+14† – the JIC had relied heavily on a wealth of reports about the morale and the political attitudes of the French forces, for the intelligence available about their composition, equipment and whereabouts left

* See above, 465.
† See above, pp 465–466.

13. Howard, op cit, Vol IV, pp 124, 125; Matloff and Snell, op cit, p 291.
14. JIC (42) 310 (o) of 14 August, 320 (o) of 20 August; CAB 121/497, JIC (42) 316 (o) of 19 August.
15. CAB 121/490, COS (42) 86th (o) meeting, 11 August, Annex.
16. ibid, COS (42) 239 (o) of 22 August.
17. ibid, JP (42) 763 of 23 August.

no doubt that if they offered all-out resistance it would take the Allies three months merely to secure the bases and the lines of communication for an advance into Tunis. In the weeks that followed the JIC appreciation the US diplomatic and intelligence organisations in north Africa, which produced most of the information under a long-standing agreement by which they looked after contacts with Vichy France while Great Britain handled relations with Spain, had propagated the view that French resistance would in any case be minimal, and had reported encouragingly on the project for fostering in advance a conspiracy which centred on bringing General Giraud to north Africa at the time of the landings.[18]* But Washington had been sceptical of the enthusiastic reports it was receiving from its representatives in Algiers, and Whitehall, being more sceptical of them in view of the American determination to reduce the reach and weight of the Mediterranean assaults in order to allow for the Casablanca landing and guard against the threat from Spanish bases, had been reduced to such despair that doubt was cast on whether the *Torch* project should go forward. The Joint Planners included in their commentary on General Eisenhower's second plan the bleak statement that 'the success of this plan depends on either the early collapse of French resistance or the ability of the Royal Navy and the RAF to prevent the passage of Axis forces, particularly seaborne forces, to Tunisia'.[20] On the same day – 23 August – General Eisenhower confessed to the Combined Chiefs of Staff that while the plan could succeed provided it met with neither French nor Spanish resistance, these were the most favourable conditions and that, if they did not materialise, the expedition would turn out to be insufficiently powerful.[21]

There followed two weeks of transatlantic argument in which the two governments hammered out a compromise. In the agreement which was reached on 5 September the US authorities accepted that landings at Casablanca and Oran by US troops should be accompanied by a landing at Algiers by British troops spearheaded by Americans. Thus far they yielded to the British anxiety about Axis intervention in Tunisia, to their own growing doubts about the prospects of winning over the Vichy French forces without subjecting them to powerful attack and, on the other hand, to the

---

* After his escape from prison in Germany General Giraud had got in touch with SIS in Switzerland and it was with the help of SIS that he reached Algiers the day after the Allied landings. The hue and cry following his escape was reflected in Abwehr decrypts[19] and in decrypts of signals from the German Security Police, see Appendix 5, p 672.

18.   Howard, op cit, Vol IV, pp 131, 132, 135, 146, 147-149, 159: Churchill, *The Second World War*, Vol IV (1951), pp 478, 480.

19.   Dir/C Archive 892 of 28 November 1942.

20.   CAB 121/490, JP (42) 763 of 23 August, para 8.

21.   ibid, COS (42) 242 (o) of 23 August.

suggestion, for which evidence was provided by the SIS and strongly urged by the Prime Minister, that Algiers was 'the most friendly and hopeful spot' from this point of view. But from the wish to establish the most powerful possible force at Casablanca they continued to veto landings nearer to Tunis; and they obtained last-minute support for their stand from the CIGS and the British Ambassador to Madrid. The CIGS conceded that it would be militarily unsound to attempt to by-pass Morocco; he argued, further, that a landing at Bône would be too exposed to Axis air attack.[22] The Ambassador, visiting London in connection with the *Torch* planning, emphasised to the JIC on 27 August the importance of a quick Allied success for the attitude of Spain; and on 29 August, in a note to the Chiefs of Staff, stressing that Spain would be under 'very great temptation' to cut the Allied lines of communication and share the spoils with Germany, he urged the formation of a striking force that would be ready to retaliate if Spain attacked directly or indirectly.[23] Presumably the CIGS and the Ambassador were not uninfluenced by the fact that the German summer offensive in Russia was now making rapid progress.

The shift in emphasis that had taken place since the initial decision to launch the operation was reflected in General Eisenhower's subsequent draft plans. On 14 August his directive from the Combined Chiefs of Staff had stated that the purpose of *Torch* was to obtain complete control of French Morocco, Algeria and Tunisia with a view to extending operations eastwards against the rear of the Axis forces in the Western Desert and with the ultimate objectives of completing the annihilation of these forces, of ensuring communications through the Mediterranean and of facilitating operations on the European continent. In his final draft plans the over-all objectives of *Torch* were to secure French Morocco and Algeria 'with a view to the earliest possible occupation of Tunisia' and to establish in French Morocco a striking force to control the Straits 'by moving, if necessary, into Spanish Morocco'.[24] And this shift of emphasis, in its turn, was reflected in the contingency planning and the operational decisions that were made in the final stage of preparations for the operation.

Contingency planning had begun when, on receiving the warning from the British Ambassador to Spain, the Chiefs of Staff ordered the Joint Planners to examine the consequences for *Torch* should all the political hypotheses on which it was based be falsified

---

22. Howard, op cit, Vol IV, p 125. See also, for NID's comments on the views of the CIGS and DMI, McLachlan, op cit, p 260.

23. CAB 80/64, COS (42) 248 (o) of 27 August; CAB 121/495, SIC file E/North Africa/3E, note by Sir S Hoare, 29 August 1942.

24. CAB 121/491, SIC file E/North Africa/3A, Vol 2, for plan of 20 September: CAB 44/113, AL 1200/10, for plan of 8 October.

by events.[25] The Joint Planners continued the enquiry into October and, assisted by the JIC, widened it so far as to take into account the risks that would then follow not only for *Torch* but for the whole strategic position of the Allies in the Mediterranean and west Africa;[26] but they still confined it to the dangers that would result and the steps that would have to be taken in the eventuality of a hostile Spain – an eventuality which on 5 October, in reply to a question by the Joint Planners about a possible declaration of war by Spain before the *Torch* convoys had passed the Straits, the JIC at last pronounced to be 'highly unreal'.[27]*

Meanwhile, the requirement of simultaneous landings at Casablanca, Oran and Algiers having compelled the acceptance of 8 November for the date of the landings, the Ambassador's warning had competed for influence on the operational decisions for *Torch* with the JIC's belief that there would be no immediate Axis threat from Spain,[28] and in the end the worst case hypothesis was adopted. In addition to allotting the bulk of the available troops to Casablanca and Oran, the final plan of 8 October provided for the transfer of a strategic bombing force from the United States for attacks on enemy air forces assembling at Spanish bases.[29] And whereas the British commanders of the Algiers landing (the Eastern Task Force) had urged the immediate seizure by airborne forces of the airfields at Bône, Tunis and Bizerta as the only way of forestalling the arrival of German air-transported troops, the plan rejected this project in favour of the seizure of the big airfield at Oran as a base from which to resist an Axis advance through Spain.[30]

The worst case hypothesis was also accepted with respect to the degree of opposition to the landings to be expected from the Vichy French forces, at least in the initial stages. The scale of air support for the landings took into account the importance of providing a display of overwhelming force at the outset;[31] and the estimated scale of Vichy air opposition was set far higher than in the original appreciations by the JIC and the Joint Planning Staff.[32] In the same way, the invasion convoys were assault-loaded with infantry

---

* For a fuller account of this contingency planning see Howard, op cit, Vol VI, p 112 et seq.

25. CAB 121/495, COS (42) 109th (o) meeting, 2 September.
26. ibid, JP (42) 793 of 7 September, expanded into JP (42) 817 of 20 September, JIC (42) 344 (o) of 10 September.
27. JIC (42) 390 (o) of 5 October.
28. Eisenhower, *Crusade in Europe* (1948), pp 102–104.
29. CAB 44/113; Air Plan, Annexes 1(a) and 1(d): Playfair, *The Mediterranean and Middle East*, Vol IV (1966), pp 126, 128.
30. Playfair, op cit, Vol IV, pp 129–130.
31. CAB 44/113, Air Plan Annexes I(a) and I(d).
32. ibid, Annex I(e).

units in the lead, in the expectation of heavy ground opposition; at
Algiers this meant delaying the disembarkation of the mobile forces
that would make the advance into Tunisia, but 'the disadvantages
that would arise if a rapid eastward advance proved possible had to
be accepted'.[33] Furthermore, the timetable set for the advance of
the Eastern Task Force into Tunisia allowed for two contingencies:
the first, assuming that French resistance would be full and
continued, provided for the occupation of Bône and Constantine by
D+20; the second, assuming French acquiescence or assistance,
envisaged that Bône would be held 'as a pivot' for pushing forward
armoured units to Tunis and Bizerta from about D+24,[34] and that
Tunisia would fall into Allied hands by D+46.[35]

Although the final plans thus cut to the narrowest of margins the
possibility of forestalling Axis intervention on the scale and at the
speed forecast for it by the JIC and the JPS at the beginning of
August,[36]* and although they for that reason laid great emphasis
on the vital need for urgency in pushing on to Tunisia, they by no
means assumed the worst in relation to Axis intervention. At the
beginning of August, in the light of the JIC and JPS appreciations,
the British Chiefs of Staff had insisted that 'the whole concept of
Torch may stand or fall on this question'.[†] Since that date the whole
concept of *Torch* had changed; deferred in date and shorn of
landings east of Algiers, the operation was different from that
which, in making those appreciations, the JIC and the JPS had
assumed or advocated. And yet on 6 October, in a paper that
brought up to date its original brief for the JPS of 7 August, the
JIC did not revise its original estimates of the scale on which the
Axis might intervene in Tunisia.[37] The paper reaffirmed the JIC's
original assessment of the resistance to be expected from the Vichy
forces; resistance would probably collapse quickly before a resolute
Allied attack. It reaffirmed, also, the original assessment of the
threat by or through Spain. Spain would remain on the side-lines
unless German pressure on her was backed by force or unless she
was confident of an early German victory in the war. These
conditions were unlikely to obtain; Russia's resistance at Stalingrad
and in the Caucasus was still tying down German forces on the
eastern front; Germany was also beginning to feel the effects of
increasing pressure by the Russians along the rest of the front; and
the strain of the war in the desert upon the Axis was becoming

---

* See above, pp 465–468.
† See above, p 469.

33. Playfair, op cit, Vol IV, p 126.
34. CAB 44/113, p 10.
35. Playfair, op cit, Vol IV, p 309.
36. Howe, op cit, pp 28–30.
37. CAB 121/497, JIC (42) 386 (0) of 6 October.

critical. For these same reasons, however, the JIC no longer felt the anxiety which in August had led it to qualify its estimates of Axis intervention with the proviso that Germany might be able to bring up far more substantial reinforcements if *Torch* were delayed beyond early October. On the contrary, the paper noted that there was still no sign of any substantial reinforcement of the GAF in the Mediterranean, let alone of preparation for a move into Spain or Tunisia, despite the fact that Germany was known to be apprehensive of Allied landings in the Mediterranean area. The JIC was never to change this view. However, on 30 October it did modify its August appreciation with regard to a German occupation of Vichy France, concluding at this last minute that, although there was no evidence of imminent occupation, this might follow in reaction to *Torch*.[38] It had probably been led to do so by Bertrand's reply to SIS enquiries at the beginning of October: he had then said that the Germans would react to a landing in north Africa by over-running unoccupied France – and thus put an end to his cryptan-alytic and espionage activities on behalf of the Allies.

In August the JIC had made a second proviso about its estimates of Axis reaction. But this had concerned not the esti-mated scale of Axis intervention in Tunisia but only the question whether the Axis would intervene at all – Germany might hesitate to do so if the Allied advance into Tunisia was rapid – and it was the JPS who, arguing that the most effective Axis counter-move would be the move of Axis forces to north Africa by sea, had stressed that 'every effort must be made to delay the arrival of Axis forces'. The JPS, again, had warned that the success of General Eisenhower's second outline plan 'depends on either the early collapse of French resistance or the ability of the Royal Navy and the RAF to prevent the passage of Axis forces, particularly seaborne forces, to Tunisia'.* In October the JIC made no further reference to the second of its earlier provisos and the earlier warnings of the Joint Planners were not renewed during the final planning of *Torch*.

The final plans allowed for considerable French opposition but made little provision against the intervention of German troops. No air forces were allocated for maritime strike and sea reconnaissance.[39] In the air plan strategic bombing was envisaged only against targets outside north Africa, particularly in southern Spain, so that bombers were not at first available against Tunis and Bizerta.[40] Hardly any steps were taken to include Malta's air strike forces in the general strategic plan, and during November they

---

* See above, p 470.

38.   JIC (42) 428 (o) of 30 October.
39.   Playfair, op cit, Vol IV, p 204.
40.   CAB 44/113, p 34.

continued to give priority to attacking the traffic to Tripoli.[41] Although the naval plan called for a surface ship effort from Malta against convoys,[42] none was mounted until the beginning of December.[43] Moreover, there was a further omission, the failure to make adequate Sigint arrangements, and while this may have arisen from inexperience and from the fact that the *Torch* plans were finalised without any attempt to make use of the experience of Cairo and the Western Desert HQs, it had the result that field intelligence was virtually non-existent and little operational use could be made of the high-grade Sigint that was made available.*

Since these omissions so clearly indicate a decline in the anxiety about the threat of Axis intervention, it is perhaps not surprising that when the Spanish threat had failed to materialise and it became evident that French resistance would not be prolonged, reluctance to prepare for the worst in relation to Axis intervention gave way to confidence that the Allies would have no difficulty in establishing themselves in Tunisia before the Germans could move in in any strength. In August the Prime Minister had allowed that 'all these data [the estimates of the scale of Axis intervention] may prove erroneous, in which case we shall have to settle down to some hard slogging'; in the same month he had cautioned the President that 'we cannot of course be sure of getting to Tunis before the Germans'.[44] But on 17 November, after the quick collapse of French resistance, he wrote to General Eisenhower that Cyrenaica would be conquered in November and added that 'we must also assume that in the same period or not long after the US and British forces will become masters of the whole of French north Africa including Tunisia. . . .'[45] The President, too, was 'inclined to think of French north Africa as conquered and occupied' when a formal agreement had been signed with the French in north Africa on 22 November.[46] Nor was the euphoria confined to the political leaders. The official Air Ministry account of the *Torch* fighting reveals how widely it was shared when it laments that 'the military promenade to Tunis which the Allies had anticipated became a soldiers' battle reminiscent of World War One'.[47]

□

If the Allied authorities had by October persuaded themselves that the expedition would surely meet with no great difficulties once it

---

* See Appendix 18.

41. Air Historical Branch, *The Middle East Campaigns*, Vol XI, p 507.
42. CAB 44/113, p 51.   43. ibid.
44. Churchill, op cit, Vol IV, pp 474, 475.
45. CAB 121/127, SIC file A/Policy/Middle East/2.
46. Howe, op cit, p 270.   47. AIR 41/33, pp 71, 202.

was disembarked, they were far from confident about its safety during the ocean passage, and during its progress from Gibraltar they had to accept that it would be unable to avoid severe attacks.

With regard to the passage across the Atlantic, formidable risks were indeed involved in taking hundreds of merchant vessels and warships from their normal duties and sending them across thousands of miles of ocean at a time when the number of U-boats in service had reached an unprecedented figure, when the U-boats had left the American seaboard and were again registering pronounced successes against Atlantic convoys – and when GC and CS and its US Navy counter-part remained unable to break into the U-boat Enigma. The risks were all the greater because it had to be assumed – and it soon became known – that the preparations which necessarily preceded the departure of that part of the expedition that was to sail from the United Kingdom could not be concealed from an enemy who was aware that something was afoot. During the first three weeks of October the GAF flew a daily reconnaissance of the south coast ports.[48] From the middle of the month it reconnoitred the assembly of the convoys in the Clyde, and the Enigma disclosed that its reconnaissance of Greenock on 22 October had detected an increase from 8 to 43 ships in the past week. At the end of September, moreover, intelligence showed that the Germans had instituted a daily GAF reconnaissance of Gibraltar and alerted their reporting agents in the area after receiving reports of British intentions in the western Mediterranean and rumours of a Malta convoy. The First Sea Lord had good reason to warn the Prime Minister that 'the U-boats might well prove extremely menacing' to 'the most valuable convoys ever to leave these shores'.[49]

This warning was based on the appreciations of the OIC. In ways that we have already described, the U-boat Tracking Room could still, despite the lack of the U-boat Enigma, make reliable estimates of the numbers of U-boats in service and at sea.* On 2 November, when the convoys were approaching Gibraltar, it put the number in service at 228[50] (it was, in fact, 212)[51] and the number in the north Atlantic and on passage at 94[52] (it was, in fact, 94).[53] During October its estimates of the numbers that were west of 25°W between Iceland and the Azores (42) and in the Mediterranean (17) were also entirely correct.[54] In the absence of the U-boat

---

* See above, pp 230–231.

48.   ibid, p 21.   49.   Roskill, *The War at Sea*, Vol II (1957), p 317.
50.   ADM 223/96, OIC SI No 415 of 2 November 1942.
51.   Roskill, op cit, Vol II, pp 218, 333.
52.   ADM 223/96, OIC SI No 415 of 2 November 1942.
53.   Roskill, op cit, Vol II, p 125.
54.   ADM 223/95, OIC SI No 394 of 12 October 1942.

Enigma, however, it had to rely on operational and DF reports, and on such evidence could only guess at the precise whereabouts and movements of the U-boats on patrol. And in the light of this fact, and of the above figures, it warned that 'it is remarkable that any convoy should pass through the area without being intercepted;'[55] and it calculated that if the enemy got wind of the departure and destination of the convoys 50 U-boats could be deployed against them by the end of October, and another 25 by 6 November.[56]

The Admiralty thus had no choice but to route the convoys as cautiously as possible, to provide them with escorts and air support on a lavish scale and to lay on intensive reconnaissance to give warning of U-boat attack as well as to keep watch on the French and Italian surface ship ports. The six slow advance convoys, of which the first left the United Kingdom on 2 October, were sent well east of the main Atlantic U-boat concentration but kept as far as possible from the Bay of Biscay. The assault convoys, mostly fast, left the Clyde, and Virginia and Maine, between 22 and 26 October; they followed the meridian of 26°W so as to be out of range of GAF reconnaissance and to pass through the Atlantic U-boat concentration where it was thought to be least dense.

In the event, the Mediterranean portion of the expedition, numbering some 340 ships, passed through the Straits of Gibraltar between the evening of 5 November and the morning of 7 November as yet unscathed.[57] This outcome was all the more remarkable in that during their passage to Gibraltar the enemy had sighted the convoys no less than five times. An FW 200 had sighted the carrier force on 31 October; during 2 and 3 November U-boats four times reported the assault convoy when it was steering for Gibraltar some 600 miles to the westward of the Straits.[58] The outcome must be attributed to some extent to good fortune, though it also testified to the effectiveness of the steps taken to improve the security of British naval cyphers and W/T communications.* OIC had correctly appreciated on 26 October that a group of U-boats had arrived in the Cape Verde–Azores area.[59] These boats would have contributed the chief threat, had they not made contact with a Freetown–UK convoy on 27 October off Madeira; their savage attack on this convoy had lasted till 31 October and had taken them far to the

---

* See below, pp 557–558 and Appendix 1 (Part (i)).

55. ibid.
56. Roskill, op cit, Vol II, p 317.
57. ibid, p 320.
58. ibid, p 319; Playfair, op cit, Vol IV, p 137.
59. ADM 223/96, OIC SI No 407 of 26 October 1942; JIC (42) (o) of 28 October.

north by the time the *Torch* expedition was sighted during the approach to Gibraltar.[60]

If intelligence thus made little direct contribution to the safe passage as far as Gibraltar, it was invaluable, together with the security of British signals communications, to those who formulated and carried out the Allied deception measures. That these measures were successful may be seen from the fact that German forces in north-west Europe remained on alert and none were moved to the western Mediterranean before the beginning of November.* They owed their success largely to the fact that the German intelligence machine was now, as the British had been in the first year of the war, incapable in the absence of reliable intelligence of discriminating between the many rumours and reports it was receiving about enemy intentions. As well as seeking to tie down Axis forces in Europe and discouraging Axis and Vichy defensive preparations in French north Africa, the deception plan aimed at concealing the destinations of the expedition both before and after it had passed Gibraltar. It played on the knowledge that the Germans were on the look-out for Allied landings in Norway and on the Channel coast as well as in the Aegean and in north Africa; and when the build-up at Gibraltar could no longer be concealed, and once the assault convoys had entered the Mediterranean, the plan explained these developments as being intended for the relief of Malta or for a descent on Sicily or southern Italy.[61] The existence of these enemy anxieties was firmly and currently established by the high-grade Sigint, which throughout the summer and autumn made frequent references to the threat to Norway and north-west Europe[62] and showed that the Axis was conspicuously worried by the threat to Tripoli, Benghazi and the Aegean.[63] It need not be doubted, moreover, that, had the deception measures been ineffective, a whole range of Sigint sources – Abwehr, C 38m and Axis diplomatic decrypts as well as the army, air and naval Enigmas – would have established that the enemy was not being deceived and, by showing what he was expecting, would possibly have enabled the Allies to make some adjustments to their plans.

It so turned out that, instead, the Sigint sources and PR enabled the intelligence authorities to dismiss reports from other sources that might otherwise have suggested that the cover plans had failed. On 15 September the Prime Minister assured the President

---

* For GAF moves from northern Norway, see below, p 480.

60.   AIR 41/33, p 40; Roskill, op cit, Vol II, pp 213, 320; Playfair, op cit, Vol IV, p 131; Beesly, *Very Special Intelligence* (1977) p 150.
61.   CAB 80/66, COS (42) 416 (o) of 26 November.
62.   eg CX/MSS/1327/T10.
63.   eg CX/MSS/1286/T16, 31 and 50, 1434/T14.

that 'the secret matter' gave no sign that the enemy was 'aware'.[64] At the end of September an RAF aircraft carrying a courier with details about the *Torch* build-up crashed off the Spanish coast; the Abwehr decrypts revealed that an attempt had been made to recover papers from the aircraft but without success. From 7 October, at the request of the Chiefs of Staff, the JIC made weekly reports on any new intelligence developments that might bear on *Torch*; in these reports it appreciated correctly, and with increasing confidence down to 3 November, that the enemy remained uncertain of the destination, the timing and the scale of the coming attack.[65] At the same time MI was using reliable intelligence to dismiss rumours as they arose, and its activities indicate the type of scare reports that the JIC was discounting in its summaries. On 19 October MI commented on reports which alleged that the Germans were despatching troops and preparing for air attacks to meet a descent on north Africa, that they had requested free passage through Tunisia and Algeria to Morocco for four divisions which had already moved to the Tunisian border and that they were making preparations to occupy French airfields on the Franco–Spanish frontier. MI pointed out that the first two reports were belied by the Enigma and that PR provided no confirmation for the third.[66] As for the origin of these rumours, they came from far and wide, but the substance of them had been reported to General Eisenhower by General Marshall on 16 October in telegrams which also recounted that Admiral Darlan had approached the US authorities in Algiers to warn them that Germany had got wind of forthcoming assaults on Dakar and/or Casablanca and to tell them that he feared Germany would retaliate with an invasion of French north Africa through Spain.[67]

Long before the convoy passed Gibraltar, on the other hand, the Allies were fully aware that, as they had expected, the enemy was on the alert against developments in the Mediterranean. They knew that he had received the news that a large convoy was approaching Gibraltar from the Atlantic on 11 October[68] – this was the first *Torch* supply convoy, which arrived at Gibraltar on 13 October, ten days before the British offensive at Alamein. On 21 and 28 October, after they had learned that the Italians had noted 'very heavy W/T communication of an operational nature between Malta, Gibraltar and the Admiralty' and that Kesselring thought a Gibraltar–Malta convoy 'possible', the GAF Enigma told them

---

64. CAB 121/491, PM telegram to President, T 1225/2 of 15 September 1942.
65. CAB 121/497, JIC (42) 405 (o) of 14 October; JIC (42) 415 (o) of 20 October, 424 (o) of 28 October, 432 (o) of 3 November.
66. WO 208/3573, MI 14 Appreciation for the CIGS, 19 October 1942.
67. CAB 121/497, folio 229A; Howard, op cit, Vol IV, p 153.
68. ZTPI 18989.

that, on orders from Hitler, nine U-boats in the western Mediterranean had been deployed on a line from Cartagena to Oran to intercept Allied convoys and that, on orders from Kesselring, the GAF had been put at short notice in anticipation of a movement from Gibraltar.[69] And by the end of October, as the days passed without the expected Malta convoy operation, it became obvious that the Axis was beginning to suspect that the concentration of shipping at Gibraltar was in preparation for Allied landings in the Mediterranean, and that the GAF in the western Mediterranean was being heavily reinforced. On 2 November RAF Y, confirmed by the GAF Enigma, disclosed that I/KG 60, a Gruppe of Ju 88s that had specialised in anti-shipping operations, was moving to the Mediterranean from Banak in north Norway. And on 4 November the Enigma added that I/KG 60 and another Ju 88 Gruppe, III/ KG 26, had been ordered to the western Mediterranean.[70] On 5 November the same source revealed that all GAF bombers that had been detached to the eastern Mediterranean from Sicily were to return there when Kesselring issued the code-word 'Gibraltar'[71] and that the GAF was moving yet a third Gruppe of Ju 88s, III/KG 30, from Europe to Sardinia and 25 Ju 87 dive bombers from Italy to Sicily.[72]

At the same time, intelligence showed that while the reports reaching the enemy now included some that were uncomfortably close to the truth, he remained uncertain of the destinations of the Allied convoys after they had passed into the Mediterranean* On 26 October a German agent's report from Turkey quoted a US diplomatic source as saying that an Allied attack on Libya from French north Africa was possible at some later date;[74] and by 3 November GC and CS had decrypted a report of 30 October from a German agent in Lisbon to the effect that the Allied naval concentration at Gibraltar incorporated 70,000 troops and foreshadowed an attack on Spanish Morocco and French north Africa,

---

* It was learned after the war that the Italians by the end of October had a shrewd idea that the Allied destination was French north Africa, but that their anxieties were overruled by the Germans.[73]

69.   ADM 223/105, Ultra signals 1020/28 October, 2217/5 November 1942; PK 10 of 5 November 1942. All GC and CS signals now bore a QT number, QT being the current digraph for SCU messages, but the signals addressed to Algiers and other *Torch* SCU units were given an additional PK number.
70.   QT 5186 of 4 November 1942; CX/MSS/1624/T55.
71.   CX/MSS/1625/T19.
72.   QT 5426 of 7 November 1942; CX/MSS/1638/T6. For an analysis of GAF moves to the central Mediterranean see ADM 223/96, OIC SI No 433 of 19 November 1942.
73.   Playfair, op cit, Vol IV, pp 135–136; Howard, op cit, Vol IV, pp 65–66; Howe, op cit, pp 73–74.
74.   CX/MSS/1639/T46.

timed to coincide with landings at Casablanca and Dakar.[75] On 5 November another decrypt disclosed that the Italian Consul at Punta Delgada had reported to the Italian Naval Attaché at Lisbon that an American convoy had passed the Azores bound for Africa. On 2 November, however, the GAF circulated in the Enigma a report from 'a trustworthy US source' that an invasion of Italy was planned for that month.[76] On 5 November the Enigma showed the GAF command suspecting either that the battle of Alamein, then reaching its climax, might point to the expedition's objective, or that the Allied objective might be the Aegean.[77] On 7 November it was learned that the German Military Attaché in Madrid had reported that the Spanish authorities thought that the intended expedition was to be an attack on Rommel's rear and that French north Africa or Italy were improbable targets; the Germans forwarded the report without comment to Rommel.[78] And at midday on 7 November, the Enigma having disclosed that GAF reconnaissance had established the strength and composition of the Allied force during 6 November,[79] GC and CS decrypted an appreciation of the same day by the German naval authorities.

As late as 4 November – this was revealed after the war – OKM had held that Malta supply convoys were the most likely explanation of the Allied build-up at Gibraltar; and it had discounted landings in the Mediterranean in the immediate future on the ground that the build-up included relatively few landing craft and passenger liners. In the appreciation of 7 November, however, it warned that the Allied force could be off Cape Bon at 1500 on 8 November if its intention was to break through the Sicilian channel, and that its strength and composition were such that 'apart from supplying Malta, the possibility has to be taken into account of a landing in the Tripoli–Benghazi area or in Sardinia or Sicily; and it added that the Allied movement derived further significance not only from the British land advance from Egypt but also from the fact that Allied air force and air-landing troop concentrations had been sighted in Palestine, Syria and Cyprus.[80] This decrypt was obtained from a recent addition to GC and CS's sources – the naval traffic in the Porpoise key of the Enigma.* From now until the end of the Tunisian campaign and beyond Porpoise was to be read continuously and currently, and, despite the fact

---

* See Appendix 4.

75. ADM 223/105, Ultra signal 0230/3 November 1942.
76. CX/MSS/1613/T33.
77. ADM 223/105, Ultra signal 2217/5 November 1942; PK 10 of 5 November 1942.
78. CX/MSS/1656 para 15.
79. QT 5460 of 7 November 1942; CX/MSS/1639/T14.
80. PK 47 of 1306/7 November 1942; DEFE 3/583, ZTPGM 3276.

that by no means all of it could be intercepted, it was to constitute an additional important fount of intelligence about trans-Mediterranean shipping.

It was presumably as a result of the enemy's uncertainty – an uncertainty that was sustained by deception measures which included sailing the fast Algiers convoy on a deceptive course and adopting W/T ruses based on the knowledge that the enemy had come to associate certain British W/T behaviour with preparations for a Malta convoy – that after their first contact with the convoy the U-boats in the western Mediterranean were ordered to withdraw to the eastward. Of this decision the Allies, lacking the U-boat Enigma, remained unaware at the time, as they did of the advantage they derived from the fact that the convoys had reached Algiers and Oran before the U-boats were ordered to reverse course at 0830 on 8 November.[81] Before being withdrawn the U-boats had been severely hampered by the heavy anti-submarine escort accompanying the convoys and by intensive Allied air patrols; they had made only two attacks and had succeeded in damaging only one ship. And this ship, torpedoed but not sunk just after entering the Mediterranean, was the sole Allied casualty. Force H, steaming to the north of the convoys to ward off intervention from the Italian and French fleets, drew off the bulk of the Axis air effort.[82]

There was little opposition during the landings and this makes it difficult to judge the quality of the intelligence about the defences and shore installations provided by the ISTD. But there is little doubt that its reports on defences, and on the landing beaches and the general terrain, were of high quality. As we have seen already, the ISTD and the IS (O) received the compliments of General Eisenhower after the *Torch* landings.* Another bouquet came from the naval commander of the expeditionary force, Admiral Cunningham, who said that 'ISTD's work gave a flying start to the North African operation'.[83] And a third came from the First Sea Lord when he was shown by the DNI the ISTD reports on Algeria and Tunisia.[84] Indeed, in all the accounts of the landing operations, including those of the accompanying naval and air bombardments and certain of the air landing operations, there is only one reference to a serious obstacle whose existence was not included in the intelligence reports. This was encountered by landing craft approaching a sector of the beach at Les Andalouses, near Oran, where a sand-bar unlocated by air photography or preliminary reconnaissance caused losses and delay.[85]

---

* See above, p 13.

81. Playfair, op cit, Vol IV, p 156.   82. AIR 41/33, p 47.
83. ADM 223/90, NID Memo on Handbooks, para 91.
84. ibid, NID 0831/17 November 1942.
85. Roskill, op cit, Vol II, p 326; Playfair, op cit, Vol IV, p 147.

This result can be accounted particularly satisfactory in that the ISTD, in its first major test, had had to prepare its reports at very short notice and to overcome an initial lack of topographical intelligence on ports and airfields.[86] In meeting the demands of the *Torch* planners it therefore had to widen its sources considerably. The Service departments supplied both the ISTD and the IS (O) with information on coast defences and airfields and some topographical information came from the SIS. There was also extensive PR of the African coast. From August 1942, when a considerable amount of intelligence about the beaches and the defences in the landing areas was assembled from photographs taken in previous routine PR sorties, the PR Flight at Malta, aircraft based in west Africa and No 1 PRU operating from the United Kingdom and from Gibraltar, flew many sorties to supply missing details and to ensure that the intelligence was kept up to date. These PR activities made a large contribution to a series of models of the landing beaches, of which the CIU produced no less than 46 for the British and American authorities from the middle of September.[87] But in addition the ISTD had the benefit of two new sources. Firstly, it used the results of the celebrated BBC appeal in 1941 for private photographs – often family beach scenes – of places of potentially military interest. Instead of the 10,000 hoped for, this produced no fewer than 80,000 replies, so laying the foundations of a photographic library whose filing staff was to increase from 20 to many hundreds before the war was over.[88] The second innovation was the Contact Register which, also started in 1941, was getting into its stride in 1942. This listed the names of a large number of people in commerce (especially in insurance and shipping), industry, professions such as mining and engineering, geographers, travellers and explorers who might be able to provide information about the terrain and installations of military interest in foreign countries.[89] General Eisenhower himself and Colonel Donovan also made useful contacts with town planning architects, interpreters of commercial aerial surveys and others who could not be recruited in the United Kingdom.[90] Finally the ISTD met its deadlines for the *Torch* planning by working in day and night shifts, the printing of the most secret parts of its reports being carried out by the Oxford University Press after the departure of the day staff.[91]

□

86. Matloff and Snell, op cit, p 113.
87. AIR 41/7, *Photographic Reconnaissance*, Vol II, pp 107–108, 113.
88. ADM 223/90, Memo on Handbooks, para 81.
89. ibid, para 82.
90. ibid, para 88 with accompanying undated minute by DNI.
91. ADM 223/90, NID 0831/17 November 1942.

The reactions of Vichy's forces to the landings conformed closely to the JIC's expectations. At Algiers fighting ceased on the evening of 8 November on orders from Darlan; Oran surrendered on 10 November, and Casablanca the next day, after bitter fighting; by 11 November, after first repudiating it, Pétain had by personal cypher given covert approval to the cease-fire which Darlan had negotiated with the Allied forces during 10 November; and on 13 November, the Vichy leaders in north Africa having come to an understanding among themselves as to the extent to which they would collaborate with the Allies, Darlan concluded a provisional settlement with General Eisenhower.[92]

Allied Force HQ (AFHQ) – the main body of which did not move from Gibraltar to Algiers until 25 November, following the signature of a more formal agreement with Darlan[93] – was well supplied with intelligence on these developments at a time when poor communications and local confusion restricted the information it was obtaining from its own subordinate HQs. It received from GC and CS a stream of decrypts of operational signals and situation reports from the French naval authorities at the landing ports, together with occasional messages to those authorities from Vichy, these being decrypts from the main French naval cypher which the British had acquired at the time of the defeat of France and which GC and CS had since read currently with only occasional interruptions. In addition, the group which had been attached to AFHQ from GC and CS to exploit the French Air Force codes and cyphers at Gibraltar supplied from that source, and from plain language transmissions, regular situation reports from Algiers to Vichy and valuable operational intelligence. Few decrypts appear to have been made of signals passing between Vichy and the authorities in French north Africa, but GC and CS provided AFHQ with extensive intelligence on the reactions of the French government from decrypts of the signals from the Sicherheitsdienst's authoritative agent at Vichy. On 9 November the Allied authorities learned from this source, and from the decrypt of a report from the Japanese Ambassador in Berlin, not only that the Toulon fleet had not sailed by 8 November, and was being deterred from sailing by its lack of aircraft carriers, but also that the Germans had approached the Vichy authorities with an offer of military support in north Africa and that Pétain had agreed to their intervention in Tunisia.[94] Between 13 and 16 November they obtained from the same source detailed reports of the vacillating course that was being followed by the Vichy government after

---

92. Howard, op cit, Vol IV, p 173; Playfair, op cit, Vol IV, pp 161, 163; Howe, op cit, p 265.
93. Howe, op cit, p 309.
94. Dir/C Archive 1351 of 11 November 1942.

its receipt of the news that Darlan had concluded an armistice and Germany had decided to occupy its European territory.

The German decision to occupy Vichy France and Corsica, an eventuality which the JIC had allowed for at a late stage in the planning of *Torch*, was disclosed in the Porpoise decrypts within hours of its implementation at midnight on 10–11 November.[95] At the same time, the fact that the JIC had been right in predicting that no threat would develop from or through Spain* was being suggested by the absence of Sigint indications of Axis preparations, and it was soon to be confirmed by Axis diplomatic decrypts, not to speak of Spanish assurances to the British government. On 13 November GC and CS decrypted a report from Madrid to the effect that Germany had assured the Spanish government that she would not demand right of passage for her armed forces; and on 19 November it informed AFHQ that Ciano had told the Japanese that, as Spain's attitude was negative, Germany and Italy were unlikely to move against her at present.[96] By then, moreover, GAF Enigma decrypts had established that the GAF was taking over major air bases on the French Mediterranean coast for defensive reasons.[97]

These developments had little immediate bearing on the course of the Allied operation. As for their longer-term consequences, intelligence failed to disclose that the German Army has used ten divisions for the occupation of France,[98] but Sigint made it plain that the occupation was making heavy demands on the over-stretched resources of the GAF and it provided useful information about Axis efforts to acquire French warships and to take over merchant shipping in French ports. On 15 November a decrypt in the Home Waters naval Enigma instructed the occupying forces to handle the French fleet at Toulon considerately;[99] it was followed on 30 November by one carrying Hitler's order of 27 November to the effect that 'owing to the uncertain attitude of the French' the fleet was to be seized.[100] By then, however, the Allies had received the rumour that the fleet had been ordered to scuttle and on 28 November the GAF Enigma reported that the ships were sinking and photographs obtained by No 1 PRU, which had kept a close watch on Toulon since 7 November, confirmed that many of the

---

* See above, p 474.

95.   PK 165 of 0840/11 November 1942; CX/MSS/1660/T1; DEFE 3/583, ZTPGM 3528.

96.   AWL PK 16 of 19 November 1942.

97.   ADM 223/96, OIC SI No 436 of 22 November 1942; PK 288 of 16 November 1942; CX/MSS/1679/T37.

98.   Howe, op cit, p 257.

99.   PK 282 of 15 November 1942; DEFE 3/205, ZTPG 86961.

100.   DEFE 3/208, ZTPG 89527.

ships were being scuttled.[101] The first decrypts about merchant shipping in French ports had meanwhile become available on 17 and 18 November; they had revealed that the Germans had taken over Danish, Norwegian and Greek ships in Marseilles and that OKM was making preparations to acquire further shipping space.[102] In the next few days the decrypted reports of the German agent in Vichy contained the news that Laval was prepared to release additional tonnage at once for the Tunis supply route.[103]

It may have been this intelligence that prompted the Admiralty decision of 21 November to extend the 'sink at sight' zone in the Mediterranean to the waters between the south of France and Italy.[104] But the Allied authorities scarcely needed intelligence to alert them to the enemy's interest in acquiring additional merchant ships – the more so as, within hours of his taking it, they had learned of his decision to commit air and ground forces to Tunisia. At about 1700 on 9 November the French colonel commanding El Aouina, the main airfield just outside Tunis, flew into Algiers with the news that 40 German bombers had arrived there.[105] This first intelligence of the German intention to intervene was confirmed the same evening by signals from GC and CS warning the Allied commanders that the GAF would move dive-bombers and fighters to Tunisia during 9 November[106] and that the Germans were establishing a sea transport office in Tunis.[107] On 10 November the Enigma and RAF Y from Cheadle reported the transfer of GAF units to the west and central Mediterranean and to Tunisia from every front including Russia, and the GAF Enigma revealed that Vichy had agreed to the establishment of a GAF HQ in Tunis.[108] On 11 November PR from Malta identified large numbers of transport aircraft and gliders at Trapani, the most westerly airfield in Sicily, and on 12 November, having seen nothing there on the morning of 9 November, it reported the presence in Tunis of 100 German and 20 Italian aircraft.[109] On 11 November a message from the German Naval Command, Italy, in the Porpoise Enigma informed a German S-boat flotilla which had been ordered to Tunis

101. AIR 41/7, pp 108–110; QT 7210 of 28 November 1942; CX/MSS/1743/T5.
102. PK 332 of 17 November 1942; DEFE 3/206, ZTPG 87123, 87250.
103. ADM 223/105, Ultra signal 1556/19 November 1942.
104. Playfair, op cit, Vol IV, p 202.
105. CAB 44/113, p 150.
106. PKs 117 and 121 of 9 November 1942; CX/MSS/1653/T11, 12, 28, 35 and 36.
107. PK 116 of 9 November 1942; DEFE 3/583, ZTPGM 3370.
108. PKs 134 and 149 of 10 November 1942; CX/MSS/1654/T32, 1658/T10.
109. Playfair, op cit, Vol IV, p 152; WO 204/978, AFHQ Daily Intelligence Summary No 4 of 11 November 1942.

from Sicily that as well as occupying France and Corsica, the Axis intended to form a bridgehead in Tunisia.[110]

In general terms we have already seen how the risk of Axis intervention in Tunis had been under-estimated, if not entirely discounted, while *Torch* was being planned.* In order to make plain how far the speed and scale of the intervention exceeded Allied expectations, we must now go back to the detailed intelligence assessments that were drawn up in advance and compare them with the actual Axis effort.

In August AI had advised the JIC that the strength of the GAF in Sicily and Sardinia, a total of 185 aircraft, could be reinforced by 60 long-range bombers from western Europe by D+14.[111] In a revised appreciation early in October it had predicted that by D-day this strength might be raised to as much as 385 aircraft by further transfers from western Europe 'in case of need';[112] and this estimate tallied well enough with the actual strength of the GAF – 395 aircraft – in the theatre on the eve of the landings.[113] Nor had AI been much less accurate in calculating the D-day strength of the IAF in Sicily and Sardinia. This was actually 574 aircraft; in August AI had estimated that it might be 525 by D+14, and at the beginning of November it had advised that it was already 530.[114] But AI had not foreseen the extent to which, as a result of the preparedness of the Axis to weaken all other fronts in its effort to hold Tunisia, even these figures would be exceeded after D-day. And still less had it believed that enemy air forces would operate from Tunisia. Its advice to the JIC in August had been that the GAF was unlikely to operate more than 515 aircraft against *Torch*, since reinforcements would be taken only from western Europe and facilities in Sicily and Sardinia were limited, and that, 'whether or not an attempt is made to move land forces into Tunisia, it is not considered likely that . . . the enemy would operate air forces in Tunisia (with the possible exception of some fighter aircraft if land forces are moved in) . . . In the event the number of GAF aircraft operating against the Allied forces exceeded the figure of 515 by 12 November; and by 12 December, after a stream of transfers from north Norway and Russia as well as from western Europe, no less than 850 German aircraft were operating against the Allied forces, out of a total of 1,220 in the Mediterranean theatre as a whole, and

---

* See above, p 465 et seq.

110. PK 157 of 11 November 1942; DEFE 3/583, ZTPGM 3502, 3528.
111. CAB 121/497, JIC (42) 304 (o) of 7 August, para 54 and Appendix C.
112. ibid, JIC (42) 386 (o) of 6 October.
113. Playfair, op cit, Vol IV, p 116; Air Historical Branch, *Air Ministry Intelligence*, p 173.
114. Playfair, op cit, Vol IV, p 116.

the GAF was operating strong ground attack forces (fighter-bombers and dive-bombers) from all-weather airfields in Tunisia itself.[115]

Together with the despatch of Italian Air Force units to Tunisia, another eventuality which had been ruled out by the JIC, the GAF's measures gave the Axis air superiority during the later stages of the race for Tunis, whereas the *Torch* air plan of October had provided for an Allied air superiority of two to one over the expected Axis scale of opposition. Nor was it solely because the GAF established numerical superiority that it played so large a part in halting the Allied advance. AI, armed with the plentiful evidence from Enigma of its low morale, fatigue and general ineffectiveness in the Libyan and eastern Mediterranean theatre, had reckoned in August that the GAF would be 'at a low ebb': 'it will be a force without depth and in need of a period for re-equipment; difficulty will be experienced in making forces available for sustained operations in a new theatre of war'. But the Germans overcame this difficulty and the fighting quality displayed by the GAF during the Tunisian campaign was of a high order.

The GAF also played a vital part in the early stages in ensuring the rapid move of German forces to Tunisia by providing protection for the Axis reinforcement convoys and by the operations of its transport aircraft.* AI's contribution to the JIC's August appreciation had not included any estimate of the extent to which the GAF might reinforce its fleet of transport aircraft in the Mediterranean, or of the speed at which it might do so. By as early as 10 November, however, by transfers from Russia as well as from bases and training schools in Germany, the GAF increased the number of transport aircraft in the Mediterranean to 673,[116] when it had earlier stood at 205, and it was not least as a result of this impressive, indeed astonishing, achievement that Allied estimates of the extent to which Germany would be able to transfer troops and equipment to Tunisia were falsified.

MI's original advice to the JIC had been that 14,000 lightly-armed troops might be moved in by air within 14 days of the decision to send them; the Joint Planning Staff had reduced this estimate to 8,000–10,000 men who would be of low category and without motor transport.† The number of German troops to arrive within 14 days was indeed 10,800. But they included small units of the kind that had proved their effectiveness in desert warfare – crack paratroopers and Panzer Grenadier regiments of high quality – as well as low quality troops originally intended as replacements

---

* See below, p 490 et seq.   † See above, pp 465–467.

115.   AIR 41/33, pp 192, 202.
116.   ibid, p 196; Playfair, op cit, Vol IV, p 171.

for Rommel. Moreover, they were accompanied by heavy equipment including motor transport. As for the JIC's predictions about the arrival of German troops by sea, it says much for the excellence of MI's order of battle intelligence that these had included an accurate estimate of the forces that might be used: one armoured division from Russia that was resting in France; one infantry division from France; miscellaneous units adding up to one more division; and possibly an SS division. MI had also been accurate when advising the JIC that the leading units of the first division could arrive by about two weeks after the Allied landings. The Joint Planning Staff had raised this estimate to 28 days from the German decision to send troops, and had taken the view that it would be six to seven weeks before one division could be operationally effective in Tunisia, whereas the JIC had assessed this delay as likely to be from four to seven weeks.* In the event, the JIC was to be nearer the mark on the first of these points, while on the second even the JIC's assessment was to be an under-estimate. The commander and HQ staff of 10th Panzer Division arrived by air on 24 November, 16 days after the Allied landings, and the first armoured elements of the division, coming by sea, had disembarked by 29 November and had gone into action at once.† For the JIC, however, if not for the JPS, these assessments had been something of a routine exercise: its August appreciation had stated that the Germans had had their fill of Italian inefficiency, and would not wish to be dependent on Italian-run sea communications, and that even with French collaboration they would still encounter 'delays, difficulties and misunderstandings'. To complete the account, the JIC had further concluded that the Axis would not send Italian troops to Tunisia, but in fact Italian troops arrived both overland from Tripoli and by sea.

Of the Axis decision to intervene in Tunisia by air and sea we have already seen that the Allies received early notice. Thereafter they received prompt, full and completely reliable intelligence of the rate of the Axis build-up and of the extent to which it was exceeding their expectations. Much of the intelligence was received from the GAF Enigma, for Kesselring commanded all three services in Tunisia and until mid-November even the ground forces there were under GAF command. The GAF cover was particularly full since GC and CS, having for the first time been given advance notice of a major Allied operation, had made special arrangements to ensure the rapid solution of the GAF Enigma key (Locust) used

---

* See above, pp 465–467.
† See below, p 492.

by Fliegerkorps II, the formation based in Sicily and Sardinia.* In addition the IAF high-grade book cypher, which GC and CS continued to read until the spring of 1943, was useful and Porpoise provided valuable shipping intelligence in the first few weeks, as did the C 38m once the Italians had organised themselves in the wake of the Germans. Mainly from these cyphers, which were being read without delay, but also from Malta-based PR and from SIS agents in Tunisia reporting via Malta, who supplied the SIS stations attached to AFHQ and First Army with a valuable series of reports from 11 November, it was known from 10 November that troops and equipment were arriving by air.[117] The Enigma revealed on that day that elements of Panzer Grenadier Regiment 104, belonging to 21st Panzer Division, had been ordered to Tunisia from Italy on 9 November,[118] while PR detected the unloading of light tanks from aircraft.[119] On 11 November the Enigma referred to the formation of a 'recce company T' composed of armoured cars and machine gun carriers.[120] On 12 November it disclosed that Para Regiment Hermann Göring, like Panzer Grenadier Regiment 104 a formation of high quality, was being sent to Tunisia.[121] And from 12 November the warning of 9 November to the effect that the Germans were setting up a sea transport office in Tunis was followed by the first Enigma references to the actual arrival of ships. The arrival of two ships carrying troops and a military cargo which included 17 tanks and motor transport was reported on 12 November,[122] the expected arrival of two further ships with troops on 14 November was disclosed on 13 November,[123] and on that day GC and CS sent out the first of a long series of Enigma decrypts giving the daily unloadings at Tunisian ports.[124] On 14 November the Enigma announced that four more ships, some with troops, were due by 17 November,[125] and the SIS organisation in Tunisia warned AFHQ that tanks had

---

* From operation *Torch* onwards arrangements to facilitate such priority treatment were put on a permanent basis and the system by which GC and CS's priorities were guided by the needs of future Allied operations worked almost without friction down to the end of the war.

117. PKs 128, 130 and 131 of 10 November 1942; CX/MSS/1654/T14, 16 and 21.
118. PK 170 of 11 November 1942; CX/MSS/1660/T3.
119. CAB 121/497, Malta telegram to Eisenhower at Gibraltar G-226 of 11 November 1942.
120. PK 170 of 11 November 1942; CX/MSS/1660/T3.
121. PKs 174 and 196 of 12 November 1942; CX/MSS/1664/T6, 1668/T23.
122. PKs 172, 176 and 179 of 12 November 1942; CX/MSS/1664/T8; DEFE 3/583, ZTPGM 3558, 3565; Howe, op cit, p 258.
123. PK 208 of 13 November 1942; DEFE 3/583, ZTPGM 3637, 3648, 3652.
124. PK 204 of 13 November 1942; DEFE 3/583, ZTPGM 3646, 3648.
125. PK 249 of 14 November 1942; DEFE 3/583, ZTPGM 3722.

been disembarked.[126] Further Enigma decrypts of 14 November indicated the intended scope of the army build-up. They disclosed that General Nehring, who had been Commander DAK until he was wounded at Alam el Halfa, had arrived as Senior Army Commander and that his Corps was to comprise, in addition to the scratch German division into which the ground forces already in Tunisia had been grouped, 'the Italian divisions' and 'later further divisions'.[127]

Evidence of the continued arrival of troops and equipment by air and sea, and of the transfer of further GAF units to Tunisia from the Mediterranean and beyond, continued to flow in from high-grade Sigint sources. On 15 November, when they disclosed that all air transport space had been diverted from Rommel to Tunisia since 9 November[128] and reported that 3,000 troops had already arrived,[129] they provided a long list of the units that were in process of being diverted from Rommel; they included Panzer Abteilung 190, a unit long promised for 90th Light Division.[130] On the same date they referred to the possible despatch of Panzer Abteilung 501, the Tiger tank unit also long promised to Rommel.[131] On 17 November they revealed that elements of the Italian Superga Division had been disembarked with 557 vehicles on 15 November.[132] On 16 and 17 November they announced the arrival of numerous cargoes of 88 mm guns, motor transport, fuel, ammunition and other bulk cargoes, including two ships carrying 26 tanks.[133] Other decrypts disclosed that a large-scale movement of fighters and fighter-bombers to Bizerta, including FW 190s,[134] had begun on 15 November; like the Me 109G, which had already been reported as arriving, the FW 190 outclassed anything the Allies had in north Africa at that time, but, despite this early warning, there was delay in releasing the latest types of Spitfires for the Mediterranean,[135] with the result that the GAF's superiority was 'unnecessarily prolonged'.[136] On 17 November it was learned that the whole of KG 76 – 90 bombers – was in the course of being transferred from the Caucasus.[137] By that time the shipping

---

126. WO 204/978, No 7 of 14 November 1942.
127. PK 231 of 14 November 1942; CX/MSS/1673/T44.
128. PK 280 of 15 November 1942; CX/MSS/1680/T23.
129. PK 279 of 15 November 1942; CX/MSS/1680/T17.
130. PK 274 of 15 November 1942; CX/MSS/1679/T32 and 33.
131. CX/MSS/1693/T32.
132. PK 336 of 17 November 1942.
133. eg PKs 293, 298, 303 and 305 of 16 November, 329, 336, 339 and 340 of 17 November 1942; CX/MSS/1693/T6; DEFE 3/583, ZTPGM 3792, 3827, 3829, 3830, 3841, 3887, 3943, 3944.
134. PK 271 of 15 November 1942; CX/MSS/1679/T20 and 26.
135. AIR 41/33, p 197.
136. Playfair, op cit, Vol IV, p 283 fn.
137. PK 321 of 17 November 1942; CX/MSS/1689/T3 and 18.

intelligence had provided sufficient detail – about dates of sailing, ports of departure and arrival, routes, cargoes and escorts – to establish the general pattern of the enemy's supply system. From 21 November it revealed that, in addition, troops were being ferried over in Italian destroyers and that stores were being brought in by unconventional ships – auxiliary sailing vessels, landing craft, ferries and a new type of small and versatile military transport vessel designated KT (Kriegstransportschiff).[138]

Meanwhile, on 19 November, the Enigma and SIS's agents had established that an Italian force had crossed into Tunisia from Tripoli with 21 tanks to secure the coastal road through Sfax and Gabes.[139] Nor was it long before more disturbing intelligence was received about the Axis army build-up. On 23 November the Enigma disclosed that the commander and HQ staff of 10th Panzer Division – a seasoned formation – had arrived in Tunis by air.[140] During 23 and 24 November it showed that three of the four Tiger tanks of Pz Abt 501 had arrived in Bizerta under conditions of great secrecy;[141] and on 26 November GC and CS decrypted a signal from Kesselring to Nehring relaying Hitler's order that the purpose of the Tigers was to turn the tide of battle and that Nehring was so to use them.[142] In addition, the first regular tank return for the force in Tunisia revealed that 30 German tanks were serviceable on 24 November.[143] A further decrypt of 28 November established that armoured elements of 10th Panzer Division had arrived by sea on 27 November; it was a signal from Kesselring of 27 November insisting that, to ensure that these troops were available for operations without delay, the deck cargo of all ships arriving in Tunis was to be unloaded at once, if necessary by night.[144]

□

After the event General Anderson, the commander of the Eastern Task Force, called (British) First Army after the assault, maintained that, in the absence of Allied landings east of Algiers, the race for Tunis was lost before it had begun,[145] and Admiral

138.   PK 439 of 21 November 1942; DEFE 3/584, ZTPGM 4124.
139.   CAB 121/497, JIC (42) 463 (0) of 27 November; WO 204/978 of 22 November 1942; PKs 406 and 429 of 19 November 1942; CAB 44/114, AL 1200/11, p 35; CX/MSS/1699/T23; DEFE 3/584, ZTPGM 4099.
140.   PK 493 of 23 November 1942; CX/MSS/1713/T1, 1718/T10; WO 208/3573 of 23 November 1942.
141.   PKs 486 of 23 November, 551 of 24 November 1942; CX/MSS/1717/T6; DEFE 3/584, ZTPGM 4294, 4296.
142.   QT 7033 of 26 November 1942; CX/MSS/1731/T3 and 26.
143.   QT 7018 of 26 November 1942; CX/MSS/1731/T32.
144.   QT 7148 of 28 November 1942; CX/MSS/1741/T13.
145.   CAB 121/502, SIC file E/North Africa/7, General Anderson's despatch, Operations by First Army in North Africa November 1942–May 1943, p 3.

Cunningham, the naval commander of the expeditionary force (NCXF), took the same view.[146] Other accounts have suggested that the Allies might have won the race, instead of losing it by the narrowest of margins, if their settlement with the Vichy leaders in north Africa had not been delayed by hesitations and disagreements on the part of the French.[147] These verdicts should not be detached from the suppressed condition on which they hinge. It was the Germans who won the race; and neither the distance from Algiers to Tunis nor the delay in reaching an accommodation with the French would have been of much moment if the Allies had prevented the German intervention in Tunisia – or if they had succeeded in limiting its scale and effect. As we have seen, the Germans intervened with a rapidity and a determination far in excess of what the Allies had allowed for. At the same time, we have also seen that the intelligence the Allies received about the character and scale of the Axis intervention was prompt and plentiful. Why, then, did they not do more to forestall the enemy when they learned that their prior assumptions about him were being belied?

All concerned, in Whitehall no less than in Algiers, were slow to grasp the significance of the intelligence that was available about Axis movements into Tunisia by sea and air. Beginning with the references to the establishment of a German sea transport office in Tunis on 9 November,* this intelligence began to flow in from 10 November. But apart from the fact that British submarines in the western Mediterranean, disposed north of Sicily since the beginning of the month against possible attacks by hostile surface fleets, were redisposed against the enemy's supply route to Tunisia on 11 November,[148] no action was taken for over a week to rectify the failure to provide in advance for the interdiction of traffic to Tunisian ports and airfields. The first expression of anxiety came from Admiral Cunningham on 19 November; he then asked AOC-in-C ME in Cairo whether the RAF could bomb the Bizerta supply line, as 'we have no aircraft'.[149] Thereafter proposals and decisions came thick and fast. On 20 November the Chiefs of Staff ordered Malta's bombers to suspend attacks on the Tripoli route and give top priority to stopping reinforcements to Tunisia, to bombing Tunisian airfields and to intercepting enemy transport aircraft; and on 22 November they decided to reinforce Malta with

---

* See above, p 486.

146. Playfair, op cit, Vol IV, p 152.
147. Howard, op cit, Vol IV, pp 179–180; AIR 41/33, p 69.
148. Playfair, op cit, Vol IV, p 207.
149. CAB 121/500, SIC file E/North Africa/5, telegram of 1747/19 November 1942.

torpedo bombers.[150] On 22 November the Admiralty proposed that a surface ship striking force should be based on Bône;[151] and on 24 November, after the Enigma had disclosed that the enemy was now sending Rommel's supplies via Tunisia,[152] it urged that this force should be supplemented by a similar one based on Malta.[153] The *Torch* plans had envisaged the creation of such force at Malta, but had made it dependent on air cover; until this intervention by the Admiralty the naval authorities in the Mediterranean had judged that air cover was inadequate.[154] On 23 November a conference at AFHQ decided to divert some of the heavy bombers of the Twelfth USAAF to assist the drive on Tunis by bombing the harbours in Bizerta and Tunis; and on 3 December General Eisenhower called for US heavy bombers from the UK to increase the attack on enemy ports and communications.[155]

Weeks passed before some of these measures had any effect. Torpedo bombers did not reach Malta till December; nor was it until the middle of that month that the submarines, severely handicapped by heavy GAF activity, scored their first success.[156] The others produced results with less delay. RAF attacks from Malta on enemy transport aircraft and on their terminal airfields, attacks which made use of high-grade and low-grade Sigint notifications of GAF movements, supplemented by PR,[157] were inflicting appreciable losses by the end of November. The first effective heavy bomber raid by the Allies on the harbours of Bizerta and Tunis took place on the night of 23 November, the Enigma disclosing that two ships had been sunk,[158] and thereafter the frequency and scale of such raids created considerable problems for the Axis. And successes from operations by British surface ships followed early in December.

Force K was reformed at Malta on 27 November from three cruisers and four destroyers taken from the escorts of the latest convoy to Malta. Force Q, three cruisers and two destroyers, was based at Bône from 30 November, as soon as adequate air protection could be provided. By 28 November they were receiving instructions from NCXF based on Enigma and C 38m decrypts in Ultra signals from the Admiralty. On that day, prodded by the Prime Minister, the Admiralty alerted NCXF, Malta and the flag

---

150.   Air Historical Branch, *The Middle East Campaigns*, Vol XI, p 523.

151.   CAB 105/32, Hist (G) 1 No 84 of 22 November 1942.

152.   QT 6743 of 22 November 1942; CX/MSS/1714/T9.

153.   CAB 105/32, No 96 of 24 November 1942.

154.   CAB 44/113, p 51; Air Historical Branch, *The Middle East Campaigns*, Vol XI, p 523.

155.   CAB 105/32, No 155 of 3 December 1942.

156.   Playfair, op cit, Vol IV, p 207.

157.   AWL 205 of 13 November 1942.

158.   PK 530 of 24 November 1942; CX/MSS/1721/T10.

officers afloat to the crucial importance of C 38m decrypts which showed that on 1 December one convoy of four ships was due at Tunis and a second, of six ships, was due at Tunis and Bizerta, and which gave the routes for both convoys. The alert was unnecessary; NCXF had made his dispositions before receiving it.[159] On 1 December, after the C 38m decrypts had disclosed that the arrival of the six-ship convoy had been put back by 24 hours,[160] Force Q sank all four ships of the Bizerta section, together with an escorting destroyer. On the night of 2–3 December, off Sfax, Force K sank three ships from the four-ship convoy, which had by then apparently been diverted to Tripoli, together with a further ship and a destroyer from a Tripoli-bound convoy of which the decrypts had provided full details during 28 November.[161] Another success, one that was at this stage as important as the winning of a land battle on the Tunisian front, followed on 4 December. Sigint then established that the SS *Menes* had blown up with a cargo including 17 Pzkw III and 17 Pzkw IV tanks in the area where HMS *Manxman* had mined the gap between two Axis minefields after earlier decrypts had disclosed the precise area of Axis minelaying, and thus of the whereabouts of the gap, between 21 and 26 November.[162] The significance of the loss of the *Menes* may be judged from the fact that the Enigma had shown that the total of serviceable German tanks in Tunisia on 30 November was 64.[163]

Although they continued to operate on most nights, Force K and Force Q had no further success till the night of 20–21 December, when Force K sank one ship off Djerba. As a result of their operations, the enemy had stopped sending his convoys across at night until he had completed the extension of his minefields, and while his convoys were crossing by day the GAF escorts acted as a deterrent to Allied intervention.[164] When he had extended his minefields he resumed night convoys; but his extensive minelaying, of which Sigint provided the exact whereabouts between 5 and 11 December,[165] severely restricted the activities of Force K and Force Q. Nor did British mines cause further casualties during December. But regrettable as it was, the decline in the effectiveness of the

159. ADM 223/105, Ultra signals 1940/28 November, 0151/29 November, 0005/2 December 1942; QT 7151 of 28 November 1942; ZTPI 22060.
160. QT 7241 of 29 November 1942; ZTPI 22120.
161. QTs 7146 and 7151 of 28 November 1942; ADM 223/105, Ultra signal 0112/2 December 1942; ZTPI 22053, 22060.
162. PK 442 of 21 November 1942; ADM 223/105, Ultra signals 2000/26 November, 0311/3 December 1942; DEFE 3/584, ZTPGM 4127; ZTPI 22424.
163. QT 7542 of 2 December 1942; CX/MSS/1758/T44.
164. Dir/C Archive 1717 of 12 December 1942, covering CNS to Prime Minister 9 December 1942.
165. ADM 223/105, Ultra signals 1310/5 December, 1436/9 December, 0150 and 0414/11 December 1942.

surface ships was less important than the fact that their short-lived successes at the beginning of December and the sinking of the *Menes* had come too late to affect the course of the land fighting. Had their operations begun but a few days earlier, and had they prevented or delayed the arrival of the armoured elements of 10th Panzer Division, the Allies would have broken through to Tunis. As the official British historian has observed: 'Had the Allies been able to get a tighter strangle-hold on the Axis communications immediately after the "Torch" landings, they might have won the ... Tunisian campaign by the end of 1942, and victory in Africa as a whole might have been close.'[166] As it was, not a single Axis ship on the run to Tunisia was sunk during November and, the more so as the Allied bombing of Tunis and Bizerta and of the Tunisian airfields had also begun too late to bring about an appreciable interruption in the flow of Axis supplies before the end of that month, the enemy was just able to save the situation on land by driving First Army out of its advanced positions near Tunis on 2 December.

□

It goes without saying that since the enemy had established powerful air forces in Tunisia, and was able to get supplies to the chief airfields and the major ports, the Allies laboured under a grave disadvantage in the land fighting. The Axis lines of land communications were short; the Allies had to advance a great distance, and bring up reinforcements and supplies, on inadequate roads and railways, and to do so in the face of determined air attack on a scale for which they were quite unprepared. It may well be that in these circumstances their advance could not have made better speed even if they had made better use of such intelligence as was available to them. At the outset, indeed, the unexpected news that GAF units had arrived in Tunisia acted as a check on the Allied commanders at Algiers even while it underlined for them that 'the greatest possible speed was essential in advancing east to forestall the German and Italian moves'.[167] On the evening of 9 November General Anderson considered a simultaneous attack on Bougie and Bône for the following night;[168] and landings by airborne troops at Bône, Bizerta and Tunis on 11, 12 and 13 November were also contemplated. But partly because of the intelligence about the GAF in Tunis and partly because of uncertainty about the attitude of the French – subsequent official accounts of the campaign differ as to the relative importance of

166.   Playfair, op cit, Vol IV, p 419.
167.   CAB 44/113, p 150.
168.   ibid.

these arguments[169] – these projects were abandoned. The earliest Allied move was thus the despatch by sea of a force from Algiers to Bougie, 300 miles west of Tunis, early on 11 November.

This expedition ran into difficulties. Probably on the basis of the first report to reach the SIS station at Algiers from its agents in Tunis – it was received on 11 November and warned that the French did not intend to resist the Axis[170] – it was advised soon after sailing that, contrary to earlier expectations, the French might not welcome it. Instead of making for Bougie harbour, it accordingly disembarked on the beaches. Although Algiers had been informed on 10 November from GC and CS that the GAF had ordered reconnaissance of coastal waters east of Algiers and attack on any Allied force that might make for Bougie and Philippeville,[171] it proved impossible to provide the air cover that had been planned for the expedition. During the disembarkation, a more protracted operation than had been envisaged, it was attacked by the GAF and lost valuable ships carrying stores and equipment for the overland advance.[172] A second Allied thrust – the seizure by paratroops of the airfield at Bône to coincide with a seaborne landing and the arrival there of an overland force – was no more fortunate.* The departure of the overland force from Algiers was delayed by uncertainty about the attitude of the French. When Bône was occupied on 12 November it was at once subjected to devastating GAF attacks.[175]

The first forces properly equipped for moving overland began to disembark at Algiers on 12 November from the first follow-up convoy: they included a contingent of 6th Armoured Division (Blade Force) which was to be the main striking force. On 15 November First Army began its advance on Tunis in three groups – one along the coastal highway from Bône, and, advancing along two different axes to the south of it, two groups of Blade Force. The

---

* It has been claimed that this parachute drop was made to forestall a similar German operation of which details had been learned from the Enigma on 10 November.[173] The Enigma made no such disclosure. During 10 and 11 November it reported only that German troops being sent to Tunisia included a parachute company and that the Germans thought the Allies were sending a seaborne force to Bône or Tunis.[174]

169. Playfair, op cit, Vol IV, p 154; Howe, op cit, p 277.
170. CAB 121/497, telegram from Malta to AFHQ G-246 of 11 November 1942.
171. PKs 128, 130 and 131 of 10 November 1942; CX/MSS/1654/T4, 14, 16 and 21.
172. Playfair, op cit, Vol IV, p 153; CAB 121/502, Anderson, op cit, p 4; CAB 44/113, p 156.
173. FW Winterbotham, *The Ultra Secret* (1974), p 105; R Lewin, *Ultra goes to War* (1978), p 271.
174. QT 5788 of 10 November 1942; PK 162 of 11 November 1942; CX/MSS/1655/T13, 1659/T22.
175. Playfair, op cit, Vol IV, p 153.

spearhead of the coastal force, which was without tanks, made very rapid progress towards and across the Tunisian frontier until it was held up by a German force, which it reported as containing tanks and lorried infantry, at Djebel Abiod, 40 miles west of Bizerta, on 17 November.[176] By that date Blade Force had reached Souk Ahras, 400 miles from Algiers and about 100 miles west of Tunis and Bizerta. In the meantime, a battalion of British paratroops had landed near the Tunisian frontier and had joined up with Blade Force; and American paratroops, landed near Tebessa, had penetrated to Gafsa, where they were to be stopped by Italian troops. On 18 November, however, General Anderson ordered the commander of 78th Division, who controlled the advance, not to commit his whole force until the greater part of it was concentrated in the forward area in preparation for renewing the drive on Tunis and Bizerta on 22 November.[177]

The decision by First Army's commander to pause and concentrate was taken while he was still at Algiers. When he took it he had received not only considerable intelligence about the continued arrival of German troops and aircraft,* but also several Enigma decrypts disclosing the enemy's operational intentions. On 14 November the first of these had reported that Nehring had on the previous day ordered his *ad hoc* force forward to a line from Bône to Tebessa, where it was to block road crossings.[178] On 15 November an order from Kesselring to Nehring had indicated that the German ground forces did not intend to remain on the defensive: it demanded that the occupation of territory not occupied by the British should be followed by mobile reconnaissance in preparation for attacks on Bône and other British-held areas.[179] On 16 November further decrypts had disclosed that a German battle group was advancing from Bizerta towards Djebel Abiod and that the GAF had reported that the Allied force in that area had no AFVs.[180] On the following day the Enigma reported signs of enemy alarm at the advance of this force; the German naval authorities were preparing to evacuate Tunis[181] and Nehring was warned that the Allies might drop paratroops there.[182] But it also announced that the Allied advance had been stopped by GAF attacks.[183] It was presumably the news that the advance had been checked, coming on top of the

---

  * See above, p 490 et seq.

176.   ibid, p 173.
177.   CAB 44/113, pp 32, 35.
178.   PK 244 of 0422/14 November 1942; CX/MSS/1674/T21.
179.   PK 278 of 15 November 1942; CX/MSS/1678/T29.
180.   PKs 292 and 311 of 16 November 1942; CX/MSS/1684/T30, 1688/T31.
181.   PK 319 of 17 November 1942; DEFE 3/583, ZTPGM 3880, 3881, 3884.
182.   PK 325 of 17 November 1942; DEFE 3/583, ZTPGM 3898.
183.   PK 375 of 18 November 1942; CX/MSS/1697/T8.

shock of learning that a German battle group with tanks and vehicles had reached the area, so many miles from its disembarkation ports, that produced General Anderson's decision to pause and concentrate.

On 21 November General Anderson, who had left Algiers for the forward area on 19 November, renewed his decision to remain on the defensive 'because of shortage of supplies, lack of air support and bad signals communications'.* He added that 'information about the enemy was scanty',[185] and it is clear that the Allies now suffered the consequences of inadequate intelligence preparations. The British and US Air Commands – Eastern Command (RAF) and Western Command (USAAF) – had each been provided with a new and independent PR unit; but the unit formed for Eastern Command, No 4 PRU, lost most of its six Spitfires and all its ground and interpretation equipment in the GAF raid on Algiers on 20 November, within a week of its arrival from Gibraltar.[186] As for Eastern Command's tactical reconnaissance squadrons, their activities were severely limited throughout November and December by the scale of GAF opposition; moreover, they had not benefited from a lesson learned in the Western Desert and were not equipped for photography.[187] Army Y was too disorganised to make up for the lack of PR and air reconnaissance, and it was not until February 1943 – following an advisory visit in late December 1942 by the head of the military cryptanalytic unit at Heliopolis – that it began to produce intelligence of operational value.† In these circumstances, General Anderson's information about the battle situation was limited to reports from his own troops and to the Enigma decrypts; but reporting in the forward area was also poorly organised until the arrival of V Corps in December, while the benefit General Anderson might have received from the Enigma was greatly reduced by the fact that after leaving Algiers he was constantly on the move and in poor signals communication with AFHQ.[188] To make matters worse, his senior operational intelligence officer – his GSO 1 (I)A – had been left behind in Gibraltar and did not arrive until the end of November.

---

* Enemy estimates of the Allied position at the time included on 18 November a decrypt which said the British intended no important operations for ten days, and on 19 November an appreciation, which was not decrypted until 25 November, that Allied forces were weak and that the Axis could therefore hold Bizerta and Tunis.[184]

† See Appendix 18.

184. PK 413 of 19 November 1942; AWL PK 24 of 25 November 1942; CX/MSS/1701/T10.
185. CAB 44/114, p 39.
186. Playfair, op cit, Vol IV, p 174 fn; AIR 41/7, pp 62, 108; Mockler-Ferryman, *Military Intelligence Organisation*, p 189.
187. AIR 41/33, p 80.
188. ibid.

General Anderson had been sent on an improvised SCU/SLU link in the forward area intelligence both about the uninterrupted flow of Axis reinforcements and supplies to Tunisia and about the land front, but apart from the fact that he would have received it with long delay, he may have had difficulty in assessing it in the absence of his GSO 1 (I)A and in view of the need to burn signals as soon as they had been read; indeed on account of his movements he may not have received all of it. If he had received it he would have learned from this source that Nehring was consolidating a front between Djebal Abiod and Medjez el Bab, a key junction and river crossing on the road to Tunis, and occupying Djedeida, a key point ten miles from Tunis, but was showing no signs of resuming the attack.[189] In addition, from his contacts with the French – if not from the GC and CS signals which carried the German reports – he would have known that the French Tunisian Division, which had been temporising with the Germans while it edged westward in the hope of making contact with the Allies, had declared for the Allies on 19 November but had then been attacked by the Germans and driven out of Medjez el Bab on 20 November. From the reports that were reaching him from the SIS network in Tunisia he also knew by 19 November that a force of 1,500 Italians had crossed into Tunisia from Tripoli with 21 tanks; and from the GC and CS signals he could have learned that other Italian troops were being sent from Tunis to join up with them and that, in order to strengthen the Italians, Kesselring had despatched a small German detachment to Sbeitla, a road junction south-west of Kairouan.[190] And on 21 November he should have received on the SCU/SLU link an appreciation from AFHQ which correctly assessed the objective of these last developments as being to guard the coastal road between Tunis and Tripoli against the US paratroops who were patrolling from Tebessa, so as to prevent the Tunis position from being turned and to allow Rommel to withdraw.[191] On the evening of 22 November, however, he reported to AFHQ that he must return to Algiers 'to appreciate fully the latest news which has reached me here only in the form of rumours'.

In this report he explained that a temporary halt had been forced on him by 'great administrative difficulties', which had been aggravated by 'a considerable intermingling with French troops and ... a confused situation arising from the rapidity of our advance and local duality of command', and by the fact that 'my forces available for the final rush on Tunis are woefully weak'. He

189.   CAB 44/114, p 39; PKs 364 and 367 of 18 November 1942; CX/MSS/1695/T24 and 25.
190.   CAB 44/114, p 35; CAB 121/497, JIC (42) 463 (o) of 27 November; PKs 403 and 404 of 19 November 1942; CX/MSS/1699/T9, 12, 18 and 19.
191.   GAD PK 5 of 21 November 1942.

then expanded his comment on the state of current intelligence. 'Before committing [the forces] to a risky adventure I must be sure of a good start and a clearer understanding of the odds against them than I have at present. . . . My principal anxiety is to assess rightly the importance to be given to the Axis thrust from the south-east and its implications on the key situation opposite Tunis'.[192] But the report as a whole makes it clear that, in so far as it was intelligence considerations which deterred him, he had been influenced less by the lack of current information than by the knowledge that, as was agreed at the conference he attended in Algiers on 23 November, 'the rapid build-up and the numbers of armoured vehicles and defensive weapons which were believed to be at the enemy's disposal greatly exceeded the estimates of the pre-invasion planners'.[193]

It was on this account that the conference of 23 November settled that First Army should be strengthened for its advance on Tunis by mobile US units – artillery, light and medium tanks, tank-destroyers – from Algiers and Oran, and that fighter and bomber squadrons of Twelfth Air Support Command, the ground-support elements of the Twelfth US Army Air Force, should be shifted east 'in small numbers' to reinforce the RAF.[194] But by no means all of these reinforcements had arrived when the advance was resumed on 25 November after a pause of six days, and those coming up from Oran arrived only in the last stage of the offensive.[195] It is easy to see that the Allies were now on the horns of a dilemma. On 20 November AFHQ's intelligence staff and MI in Whitehall had agreed in estimating that some 7,000 German and 3,000 Italian troops had already arrived, with 50 tanks, and that a further 8,000 Germans and 7,000 Italians would arrive shortly, with 80 more tanks, making a total of 25,000 men and 130 tanks.[196] During 23 and 24 November Enigma disclosed that the commander and staff of 10th Panzer Division and the first Tiger tanks had arrived.* The arguments for moving forward with the minimum of further delay, before the enemy's position had further improved, must therefore have been powerful. On the other hand, there were arguments for delaying the advance until First Army had received all the agreed reinforcements, and perhaps for increasing those reinforcements. But these were weakened by a continuing tendency to under-estimate the enemy's capacity for speed and improvisation. On

---

* See above, p 492.

192. CAB 44/114, p 41.   193. Howe, op cit, p 291.
194. ibid.   195. ibid, p 292.
196. AWL PK 18 of 20 November 1942; Dir/C Archive 1440, covering
      CX/MSS/1698/T32, and 1462, CIGS to Prime Minister, 21 November
      1942.

receiving the intelligence about the arrival of 10th Panzer Division's staff, for example, M I in Whitehall allowed that 10th Panzer Division itself might follow, but it thought it equally likely that the staff had been sent to command tanks already in or en route to Tunisia.[197] And whereas General Nehring had in fact accumulated 24,575 troops – 15,575 German and 9,000 Italian – by 25 November,[198] General Eisenhower's Chief of Staff was on 24 November assuming that the number of Axis troops in Tunisia had as yet risen only to 12,000.[199]

Whatever may be thought of these respective arguments, the Allied advance on Tunis was subjected to a series of checks; and the most crucial of them arose when Blade Force encountered the leading elements of 10th Panzer Division, with 34 tanks, at Djedeida on 28 November, before all the US armoured follow-up had arrived.[200] On 25 November First Army advanced 35 miles and a US armoured group, raiding 10 miles ahead of the main force, did serious damage at the enemy-occupied airfield at Djedeida before withdrawing. On 26 November a southern prong of the advance came close to the main thrust by reaching Tebourba, 10 miles west of Djedeida; but after first making rapid progress the main thrust was held up by an engagement with German tanks. On 27 November the southern prong was ordered to take Djedeida, but it was counter-attacked throughout the day by Pz Abt 190 with 15 tanks, including two of the four Pzkw VI Tiger tanks belonging to Pz Abt 501, while Nehring completed his withdrawal by pulling back from Tebourba to Djedeida. As a result of this check, the Allied assault on Djedeida by the southern prong, now strengthened by armour from the main thrust, was put off to 28 November, when it was hoped that it would also be reinforced by the balance of the US armour. On 28 November, however, the remaining US armour, part of the US 1st Armoured Division, was still coming up from Souk el Arba, 100 miles away, and the drive for Djedeida, begun before its arrival, was brought to a stop by constant GAF attack and resolute defence by the leading elements of 10th Panzer Division. It failed again when it was renewed on 29 November; in an Enigma decrypt of 30 November the Germans claimed to have destroyed 30 out of 50 Allied tanks.[201] On the evening of 29 November the commander of 78th Division was given permission to call off the attack for a few days pending the provision of increased air support.

---

197. WO 208/3573 of 23 November 1942.
198. Howe, op cit, p 294.
199. CAB 121/127, COS (42) 413 (o) of 24 November.
200. Howe, op cit, p 306.
201. QT 7295 of 30 November 1942; CX/MSS/1745/T11; Dir/C Archive 1596 of 30 November 1942.

The Allied forces, lacking tactical intelligence, had as yet also received very little of immediate operational value from the high-grade Sigint. The GAF Enigma had made it clear that the enemy expected the attack and was relying heavily on his air power;[202] during the advance it had given prior warning of some GAF operations,[203] but such was the superiority of the GAF over the battlefield, and their own lack of co-operation, that the Allied army and air commands were unable to make use of this intelligence.[204] About the intentions of the enemy's ground forces there had been hardly any Enigma decrypts since the resumption of the Allied advance. With Nehring's assumption of command the Germans had introduced a new Enigma key for the communications between the army in Tunis and Berlin, Rome, Kesselring and Rommel. GC and CS broke this key (which it named Bullfinch) towards the end of November but by then the Allied advance was virtually at an end.* Moreover, most of the operational Enigma traffic of the forces in Tunisia passed on MF networks in yet another key (Dodo); and as it was intercepted with difficulty in the UK and no provision had been made for intercepting it nearer the theatre[†], this traffic was not yet broken and was indeed read only on one or two days during the whole of the Tunisian campaign. At this juncture, moreover, the Germans were applying additional complications to the Army Enigma keys in use in Africa; these slowed down GC and CS and sometimes completely interrupted its daily solution of the settings. In these circumstances the number of decrypts about the enemy's ground situation had been few compared with what was customary in the desert. The most dramatic of the decrypts was the situation report of the evening of 25 November in which Nehring announced that he had been withdrawing all day, that he had already used up all available reserves and that it was 'therefore doubtful if Tunis can be held for long if the enemy continues his attack on 26 November with the same superiority'. It had been sent out from GC and CS at 0823 on 26 November.[205] But Kesselring's reply, which would have been still more useful, to the effect that Nehring was to withdraw only to an inner perimeter line round Tunis running through Djedeida, had not been decrypted and transmitted back to the Allied commands until

---

* See Appendix 4.
  † See Appendix 18, and above, p 21, fn † for the activities at CBME of the Fort Control Officer.

202. PKs 504 of 23 November, 533 of 24 November 1942; CX/MSS/1718/T25, 1721/T4 and 6.
203. eg QT 7155 of 28 November 1942; CX/MSS/1740/T32 and 33.
204. Howard, op cit, Vol IV, pp 116–117.
205. QT 7008 of 26 November 1942; CX/MSS/1731/T21.

28 November,[206] and it was not until 1134 on that day that GC and CS had been able to send out the news that the leading elements of 10th Panzer Division had reached Tunis.*

It was from decrypts of the GAF Enigma that on 30 November, when they were intending to resume their own assault as soon as possible, the Allied commanders learned of the German decision to go over to the offensive. Early that day they were informed that Göring had ordered Kesselring to see that the Tunis bridgehead was extended to the west and south-west as soon as possible, to prevent the Allies from building up superior forces.[207] And at 0452 on 1 December they were warned by GC and CS in a special priority signal that 10th Panzer Division had at 2000 the previous evening been ordered to attack at Tebourba at dawn.[208] As to whether or not First Army was able to profit from the warning, which gave it considerable details about the location of the attack, there is no record. Either way, the German attack, which began at 0800, was wholly successful: by 3 December First Army had been roughly handled and driven well clear of Tebourba. This withdrawal effectively ended the Allied command's attempt to take Tunis before the onset of the rains.

Reporting on the setback on 3 December, General Eisenhower insisted that the advance need not be abandoned 'provided we can prevent Axis ground reinforcement . . . , something we have not been able to do', and announced his intention of bringing out US heavy bombers from the UK to operate against enemy ports and communications.[209] Urgent efforts to step up the air attack from Algiers on the Tunisian supply route followed in the next few days, as did urgent appeals to Alexandria, Malta, Cairo and Whitehall for assistance.[210] In Whitehall on 5 December the Admiralty proposed, and the Chiefs of Staff accepted, that an additional cruiser should operate against the route, a course of action that the JIC had urged on 30 November.[211] Like the first, belated, recognition in November of the importance of cutting the supply route, these measures were to no avail. The Allied attack on the route underwent no marked improvement before the second half of December; nor was it until then that the Chief Air Intelligence Officer at AFHQ recognised that 'when it became apparent that

---

* See above, p 492.

206.   QT 7195 of 28 November 1942; CX/MSS/1741/T35.
207.   QT 7339 of 30 November 1942; CX/MSS/1747/T22.
208.   QT 7455 of 0452/1 December 1942; CX/MSS/1753/T22.
209.   CAB 105/32, No 155 of 3 December 1942.
210.   CAB 121/500, Cs-in-C ME telegram to COS, CC 148 of 4 December, Eisenhower telegram to COS NR 1311 of 6 December 1942, COS (42) 339th Meeting, 8 December.
211.   CAB 121/497, JIC (42) 465 (o) of 30 November.

the Allied ground forces would not succeed in over-running Tunisia till the following spring', [I] 'turned to the intensified local exploitation of intelligence (almost exclusively from Ultra) on Axis reinforcement and supply traffic to North African ports and along Tunisian roads and railways towards Libya. . . .'[212] By 12 December, on the other hand, two more German counter-attacks had overtaken General Eisenhower's hope of resuming the offensive on 9 December and had driven his forces back almost to Medjez el Bab. After a series of postponements, some of them imposed by the difficulty of bringing up supplies in increasingly bad weather, he then fixed on 24 December as the day for the advance. But on that day, after the failure of preliminary attacks on the German Army's new and strongly defended perimeter, he put off the attempt to take Tunis until the weather improved.

---

212. AIR 40/2323, Humphreys, The Use of Ultra in the Mediterranean and North-west African Theatres of War, p 10.

PART VII

The First Half of 1943

CHAPTER 25

The Air War in Western Europe in the First Half of 1943

THE GAF resumed its offensive against the United Kingdom on 17–18 January 1943 when, in retaliation for a raid on Berlin, it flew 100 bomber sorties over London and at once followed up this first major attack on the capital since May 1941 with a daylight raid by escorted fighter-bombers. The new campaign continued throughout the first half of 1943, small, infrequent and invariably ineffective night raids, distributed against a wide range of targets, being supplemented by weekly daylight attacks by fighter-bombers against London and coastal towns and, from the beginning of April, by fighter-bomber raids at night. From the outset it was clear that the night-bombing threat had been seriously blunted by a further shift in the balance of forces to the advantage of the British defences. As well as being ineffective, the long-range bombers, out-dated and manned by inexperienced crews, sustained heavy losses, as did the fighter-bombers in their night operations. The daylight operations by the fighter-bombers continued to be more effective – so much so that Fighter Command was forced to institute standing patrols against them from Kent to Devon – but they became infrequent from June, when the greater part of the units involved were again drawn away by the needs of the Mediterranean.

The Enigma gave good notice of the new offensive by disclosing from the end of 1942 that various GAF units that had been called away to other theatres in the previous autumn were returning to France and that bomber Gruppen were being re-formed there.[1] Order of battle intelligence provided reasonably accurate forecasts of the scale of the coming threat. The JIC calculated that the fighter-bomber daylight raids in 1943 were unlikely to involve more than 30–40 sorties over a period of three days;[2] this was roughly the size of the weekly raids carried out by the fighter-bombers from March 1943. The Air Intelligence Branch forecast that the GAF bomber force would be able to sustain between 15 and 20 sorties

---

1. ADM 223/101, OIC SI 420 of 7 November 1942, 467 of 20 December, 490 of 16 January 1943; ADM 223/102, OIC SI 514 of 13 February, 525 of 27 February, 541 of 13 March; Air Sunset 53 of 1 April 1943.
2. AIR 41/49, *The Air Defence of Great Britain*, Vol V, pp 171, 181, Appendix 21; JIC (43) 16 of 11 January.

every 24 hours until the summer months and 30 sorties thereafter.[3] In fact the long-range bombers carried out raids about every ten days during 1943 using about 50 aircraft in each attack. The Enigma also disclosed that from the beginning of March the German authorities, dissatisfied with the results of the offensive, began to make determined but in the end unavailing efforts to increase its effectiveness.

By that time the Enigma decrypts were referring with growing frequency to the GAF's shortages, especially in manpower.[4] In the middle of February they had disclosed that the GAF had ordered the transfer of all men aged 35 or below from staff posts to fighting units; commenting on this intelligence at the request of the Prime Minister, the CAS had noted that 'training is already being sacrificed and the removal of experienced HQ staffs of the Gruppen will increase inefficiency at a time when the strain on the GAF is very great'.[5] A week later another decrypt had revealed that Luftflotte 3, the formation in charge of the offensive against the United Kingdom, was being handicapped by shortage of personnel.[6] By 17 March, on the other hand, it had not only emerged that Göring had interviewed the commander of Luftflotte 3 about the failure of his aircraft to press home their night attacks on the United Kingdom between 1 and 10 March;[7] it was also clear that some effort was being made to lighten Luftflotte 3's difficulties. On 7 March the Enigma showed the GAF making enquiries for bomber crews with experience of operations over the United Kingdom.[8] By 16 March it had reported that three Gruppen of FW 190 fighters had moved to airfields in Belgium and Holland, specified as advanced landing grounds for fighter-bombers, and that supplies of incendiaries and of large HE bombs of a new type were to be sent to Belgium and France.[9] On 16 March, on the strength of this intelligence,[10] the Prime Minister gave orders that Britain's air defences were to be brought to the highest state of readiness against reprisal raids.[11] On the following day the Enigma revealed that a Colonel Peltz had been appointed to a special post of Angriffsführer England from 1 April to take charge of bombing attacks on the United Kingdom.[12] In April the Enigma added the

3.   AIR 41/49, p 189.
4.   For example, CX/MSS/2175/T42, 2225/T28, 2277/T11, 2300/T24 and 2388/T17.
5.   CX/MSS/2132/T7; Dir/C Archive, 2337 of 19 February 1943, covering CAS comment.
6.   CX/MSS/2175/T42; Dir/C Archive, 2396 of 26 February 1943.
7.   CX/MSS/2277/T28.   8.   CX/MSS/2231/T35 of 7 March.
9.   CX/MSS/2266/T16 and T20, 2272/T4.
10. CX/MSS/2266/T20 and 2268/T19; Dir/C Archive, 2566 and 2576 of 14 and 15 March 1943.
11. AIR 41/49, p 189.   12. CX/MSS/2436/T4.

further news that three officers were being recalled from Russia to carry out under Peltz's command experimental flights with a new aircraft;[13] this was later discovered to be the Me 410 fast bomber. In the event, however, these measures failed to put new vigour into the bombing offensive before June 1943 when, to meet more pressing requirements there, Peltz and a part of his command were transferred to the Mediterranean.

As in 1942 the effectiveness of the offensive was much reduced by the fact that the counter-measures authorities had acquired such familiarity with the equipment and procedure of the GAF's navigational beams that they were able to take immediate action against them whenever the GAF tried to use them for operations.

The new *Knickebein* frequencies were now intercepted for the first time during GAF operations, but it soon became clear that the *Knickebein* was being of little assistance to the night-bombers. In January 1943 the beams were set up on three occasions when the GAF was operating, but except on the night of the first raid, against London, when there was in any case no proof that the beams were actually used, the beam setting did not coincide with the main areas of the GAF's activity; in addition, presumably for 'spoof' purposes, the beams were set up when there were no raids.[14] In the following months there was no increase in the activation of the *Knickebein* beams during operations, but an increase in non-operational transmissions suggested that the GAF might be intending to organise 'spoof' beam settings on so large a scale as to enable it to use *Knickebein* in real attacks with little or no warning. This danger did not materialise, however.[15]

From the re-introduction of the *Y-Gerät* system the GAF similarly derived little benefit. During the spring of 1943 the PRU and the CIU detected increasing activity at known and suspected *Y-Gerät* sites; and by April it was recognised that the system was being extended in such a way as to require a complete reorganisation of the disposition and the method of operation of the jamming transmitters.[16] Meanwhile, *Y-Gerät* transmissions had appeared to be associated with GAF operations, though only with a single aircraft, during a raid on 7 February. On 7 March there was evidence that a single aircraft had again made use of *Y-Gerät*. Not until May, however, was it possible to confirm that the system was back in operational use; the crew of an aircraft shot down over London then revealed that *Y-Gerät* was being used with complicated procedures designed to evade the British jamming.[17] Subsequent POW interrogations showed that despite these procedures

13.　CX/MSS/2420/T24; Dir/C Archive, 2960 of 14 April 1943.
14.　AIR 41/46, No 80 Wing RAF Historical Report, p 43.
15.　ibid.　　　　16.　ibid, p 46.　　　　17.　ibid, pp 34, 46, 47.

the interference with *Y-Gerät* was being effective, and the interception of it showed that it was used only sporadically, and never to such effect that the transmission could be related to aircraft tracks during the German raids.[18]

Except to the counter-measures authorities, intelligence was of little assistance to the defence organisation. The daylight raids normally 'took the defences by surprise'.[19] In their night raids the bombers and the fighter-bombers were 'seldom engaged before dropping their bombs' and successful interceptions were 'rare'.[20] The Enigma rarely gave advance warning – exceptionally, it gave some hours' notice of Luftflotte 3's orders for an attack on Grimsby on 15 March[21] – and while Cheadle's watch on the enemy's low-grade W/T traffic, the prime source of intelligence about the GAF's bomber order of battle, produced some information, it was evidently either too delayed or too imprecise to be useful for operational purposes. After May 1941 the bombers rarely used R/T. The fighter-bombers, which began their night raids in April 1943, were controlled during their operations over south-east England by R/T, and Kingsdown's intercepts provided evidence that British radio counter-measures were deflecting the enemy from his targets, but it does not appear that they otherwise helped the defences. Perhaps because their intelligence was not sufficiently precise and timely they added little to the radar warnings and the same applies to a new source of early warning that opened up at this time – decrypts of signals sent in the Enigma to naval recipients to warn them of the times at which GAF bombers would cross the German coast on their missions to the United Kingdom.

It was these decrypts, however, which prompted the Air Section at GC and CS to suggest in April 1943 that it should institute a service to carry direct to the home commands of the RAF all grades of Sigint, from any of the German armed forces, that might have a bearing on enemy air activity over the United Kingdom and in north-west Europe. This proposal was watered down in discussion; as well as clashing with the Air Intelligence Branch's reluctance to be short-circuited, it coincided with a growing recognition that it was essential to improve the direct supply to the commands of current interpreted tactical intelligence about the GAF's defensive fighter activities, and that could be done only by centralising the interpretation at Kingsdown. But in July 1943 it led to the amalgamation of SALU and a sub-section of the Naval Section at GC and CS into the Air Operational Watch, which by the end of the year was reporting to Coastal and Fighter Commands all

---

18.   ibid, p 58.
19.   Collier, *The Defence of the United Kingdom* (1957). p 316.
20.   ibid, p 316.   21.   CX/MSS/2272/T5, Too 1330, of 15 March 1943.

intelligence about the GAF's offensive and reconnaissance activities in western Europe.

The Air Operational Watch, which remained in existence until the end of the war, was to become important with the approach of *Overlord*, and it was to provide valuable experience against the time when, as part of the preparations for *Overlord*, an SCU/SLU link was established from GC and CS to some of the operational authorities in the United Kingdom.*

□

While the GAF offensive was faltering there was a steady increase in Bomber Command's strategic offensive against Germany. This now benefited, moreover, from the introduction both of more effective technical aids to navigation and bombing and of countermeasures against the enemy's night-fighter defences. But from neither of these developments did Bomber Command derive decisive advantages in the first half of 1943.

A modified form of 'Gee', the first navigational aid, was brought into use by Bomber Command in February, and in April further improvements were made to it – one of them enabled the aircraft to change to a new frequency when they reached the target area and this remained undetected by the Germans until June 1943, the other altered the pulse coding. From the beginning of January 1943 the first scientific aid designed specifically as a bombing aid was introduced into Bomber Command. Known as 'Oboe', it was used by Pathfinder Mosquitoes and was not jammed by the enemy until November 1943 and then without serious effects. The next development, a device known as H2S, was an airborne radar to aid navigation and bomb aiming by producing a cathode ray tube (CRT) picture of the terrain beneath the aircraft. This too was available for limited operational use from the end of January 1943.†

With the arrival of the new equipment and the accompanying development of new bombing tactics the Air Staff hoped that area bombing would give way to selective night attacks on precise targets, whereas Bomber Command continued to believe that more effective area bombing of cities and towns remained the most profitable – indeed, the sole practicable – policy. In the early months of 1943 this was a growing difference of opinion that remained unresolved. Photographic reconnaissance, and to a smaller extent night photographs, were still the only reliable sources of visible evidence about bomb damage; up to the opening of the

---

* See Volume III.

† For details of 'Oboe' and H2S see Webster and Frankland, *The Strategic Bombing Offensive against Germany* (1961) Vol IV, Annex I.

Battle of the Ruhr in March the evidence they produced was insufficient to permit firm conclusions on either the value or the limitations of the new aids and tactics.[22] In the same period, however, Bomber Command's freedom of action was considerably restrained by other pressures.

On 11 January 1943 a campaign sustained by the Admiralty since the previous October in favour of the diversion of Bomber Command against the U-boat pens and other facilities at Lorient, St Nazaire, Brest and La Pallice received the approval of the War Cabinet.[23] On 21 January the decision to give special priority to the destruction of the Biscay U-boat bases was confirmed in the Casablanca directive of the Combined Chiefs of Staff. Moreover, while the Casablanca conference did not settle all differences between the British and American Chiefs of Staff, the Combined Chiefs of Staff nevertheless defined the strategic aim of the bombing effort against Germany in such a way as to show that they agreed in seeing it only as a prerequisite, though an essential one, to land operations against Germany. Over and above the special paragraph in which it approved an air offensive against the U-boat pens in the Biscay ports, the Casablanca directive stated with regard to bombing that its 'primary object will be the progressive destruction and dislocation of the German military, industrial and economic system, and the undermining of the morale of the German people to the point where their capacity for armed resistance is fatally weakened'. Within that definition it listed as the prime objectives, in an order of priority that should be varied only by reference to weather conditions and tactical feasibility, the U-boat construction yards, the aircraft industry, transport, oil plants, and other war industries.[24]

Intensive raids were carried out against the U-boat bases and construction yards between the beginning of February and the beginning of April 1943 with inconclusive results.* And from early in March 1943, this evidence reinforcing its continuing scepticism about the value of attacks on precision targets, Bomber Command availed itself of the control of operations and the discretion as to the feasibility and priority of targets that had been left to it by the Casablanca conference to move into the Battle of the Ruhr.

The Battle of the Ruhr, which absorbed most of its night-

---

* See Appendix 20.

22.   Webster and Frankland, *The Strategic Air Offensive against Germany* (1961) Vol II, pp 99–107.
23.   CAB 65/37, WM (43) 6 CA of 11 January.
24.   AIR 41/43, *The RAF in the Bombing Offensive against Germany*, Vol V, Appendix I; CAB 80/67, COS (43) 33 (0) of 28 January (CCS 65th meeting and CCS 166/1/D, both of 21 January); Webster and Frankland, op cit, Vol II, pp 10–11.

bombing effort during the next five months, opened on 5 March when, in a raid on Essen, 'Oboe' and other new aids were used for the first time to provide target marking to guide a large force (442 aircraft) to its target. The battle lasted till 25 July, by which time 15,504 aircraft sorties had dropped 42,349 tons of bombs with the loss of 718 aircraft.[25] Estimates of the damage done, based on the PR and night photographs, testified to a marked increase in the accuracy of the bombing and associated it mainly with the operational effectiveness of 'Oboe'.[26] But while these estimates themselves improved in accuracy with the expansion of PR and refinements in the methods of assessment, subsequent comparison with German records revealing a degree of error of between 10 and 20 per cent, they could measure only visible damage: the number of houses and factories destroyed and, by deduction, the number of people rendered homeless. In the absence of reliable intelligence on these subjects, such as reports direct from Germany or comprehensive references in Sigint sources, the effects of the recognisable damage on the enemy's economy and morale remained matters of speculation. All that could be said with certainty was that, though appreciable, the results of the severe damage done to the towns in the main centre of German heavy industry were not sufficient to prevent a general rise in the enemy's armament production at the time.[27]*

Though to a smaller extent than before 1943, the damage was still being exaggerated in Whitehall, but, on the other hand, determined efforts to avoid exaggeration were now being made. MEW and Research and Experiments Department 8 (RE/8) of the Ministry of Home Security, which were jointly responsible for the estimates, arrived at them by making rigorous calculations of the effects on production, from such things as destruction of dwellings, injury to factories, disruption of gas, electricity and water supplies, and other causes, that were based on the British experience of German bombing in 1940 and 1941, and they treated POW interrogations, SIS agents reporting at second-hand, the European Press, diplomatic evidence and the occasional Sigint item – the only available intelligence sources for the non-visible effects of the bombing – with much more caution than in earlier years.[28]

As well as becoming more cautious in their estimates of the damage done by the bombing offensive, the Whitehall authorities

---

* For details of the intelligence on the effects on the German economy, see above Chapter 18. For details of the intelligence that was coming in about morale at this time, see Volume III.

25. AIR 41/43, p 36.
26. Webster and Frankland, op cit, Vol II, p 134.
27. ibid, pp 256–259.
28. ibid, pp 244–246; AIR 41/43, pp 18–19.

were forced to recognise that the counter-measures that had now been adopted against the enemy's radar and night-fighter defences were not yet off-setting the increasing efficiency of the GAF's expanding defence organisation. The introduction of these counter-measures inaugurated, from the end of 1942, the running battle against extensions and improvements to the enemy's systems which continued down to the end of the war. It was a battle in which the intelligence sources – particularly the Enigma and the study of the night-fighter R/T traffic by GC and CS's Air Section – provided most of the evidence about the effects of the counter-measures and the GAF's operational and organisational response to them.[29] And in the first half of 1943 this evidence, backed up by Bomber Command's operational reports, indicated that the initial counter-measures had at most achieved some limited success during short periods of surprise.*

Still more decisive evidence to the same effect was provided by Bomber Command's casualties, which became heavier and heavier as the Battle of the Ruhr proceeded, and by the fact that, as well as imposing an increasing wastage rate on Bomber Command, the growing strength of the enemy's night-fighter force was driving its bombers to operate at higher altitudes and on darker nights. The enemy's actual strength in twin-engined fighters (mostly night-fighters) on the western front having risen from 180 to 349 between the beginning and the end of 1942,[30] it increased further to 478 by July 1943 and was to reach 682 by the following October.[31] This increase was made possible by the great expansion of aircraft production which had been inaugurated by Speer and Milch in 1942,† and it took place despite the high priority the expansion programme gave to the output of single-engined (day) fighters to redress 'the crippling lack of day fighter strength' that had developed by the end of 1942 as a result, among other things, of US Eighth Air Force's daylight offensive against western Europe.[32]‡ By July 1943 the monthly production of single-engined fighters had reached the figure of 1,000 aircraft and that of night-fighters the figure of 200 aircraft – both figures representing more than twice the output of the previous January – and the total first-line

---

* For details of the counter-measures see AIR 41/2, *The RAF in the Bombing Offensive against Germany*, Vol IV, pp 87–90; AIR 41/46, p 85 et seq; A Price, *Instruments of Darkness* (1977), p 128 et seq.

  † See above, p 145.

  ‡ See above, p 271.

29. AIR 20/1665, ASI Report No III of 29 March 1943.

30. AIR 41/10, *The Rise and Fall of the German Air Force*, pp 188, 220; Webster and Frankland, op cit, Vol I, p 490.

31. Webster and Frankland, op cit, Vol II, p 46 fn.

32. AIR 41/10, p 233.

strength of the GAF, raised to 5,396 aircraft as compared with 4,000 at the end of 1942, included 1,800 single-engined fighters (1,250 at the end of 1942) and 666 twin-engined fighters (495 at the end of 1942).[33]

Although Whitehall considerably under-estimated the rate of increase in the enemy's aircraft production programme during 1943,* its order of battle intelligence amply explained the experiences encountered by Bomber Command. It showed that by April 1943 Germany's offensive fighter strength was 44 per cent higher than in December 1941.[34] It showed, further, that the GAF had radically altered the distribution of its fighter forces. In August 1942, 38 per cent had been deployed on the western front as against 43 per cent in Russia; by April 1943 these percentages had become 45 and 27 respectively.[35] As for the twin-engined fighter force in the west which directly opposed the night operations of Bomber Command, Air Intelligence, which had estimated in November 1942 that it stood at 365 aircraft,[36] assessed its strength in July 1943 as 470 aircraft (actual figure 478).[37] And intelligence about the German Flak organisation, undertaken by an inter-Service and inter-Allied organisation called MI 15 which had developed out of MI 14(e) by July 1943,[38] revealed a comparable increase in the total deployment of guns and searchlights and a comparable concentration in the Reich at the expense of other theatres, from the beginning of 1943.[39]

It was in these circumstances, as the outcome of an intensified search for more effective techniques and tactics against the enemy's defences, that in July the decision was finally taken to resort to the use of 'Window'. This device – the dropping of metallic strips to produce false signals on enemy radar – and the controversies which delayed its introduction against the *Würzburg* from the spring of 1942 to the summer of 1943 have been fully discussed elsewhere.†
It is necessary here only to mention the part played by intelligence in resolving these controversies, which hinged on judging whether the RAF would profit or suffer.

Initially the main problem was to know whether the principle of

---

* See above, pp 142 et seq.
† See Price, op cit, pp 124–127, 140, 148; Jones, *Most Secret War* (1978), Chapter 33; Webster and Frankland, op cit, Vol II pp 142–145.

33.　ibid, pp 289, 301 (Table); Webster and Frankland, op cit, Vol II, pp 46 fn, 295 fn.
34.　AIR 41/43, p 69.
35.　ibid, p 71.
36.　Air Sunsets 17, 22 and 25 of 20, 25 and 28 November 1942.
37.　Webster and Frankland, op, cit, Vol II, p 46 fn.
38.　Mockler-Ferryman, *Military Intelligence Organisation*, p 274.
39.　Webster and Frankland, op cit, Vol II, p 295 fn.

'Window' was already understood in Germany; if not, its exploitation would provide the enemy with a counter-measure which he could use to the disadvantage of the RAF. As it happens, the Germans were conducting experiments during 1942 with a system similar to 'Window' and were faced with the same problem; such was their anxiety for the effects it would have if used against their defences that they suspended their trials and took other precautions to prevent the existence of the system from coming to the knowledge of the British. But Whitehall learned nothing of the German system (*Düppel*) or of the German precautions until October 1942, when a SIS agent reported that he had heard from a woman employed at a German GCI station that a British aircraft over the Rhineland had 'deceived a German control station by throwing out aluminium dust and then changing its altitude . . . The German night-fighters . . . are said even to have opened fire on the dust cloud'. Assessing the significance of this report, ADI(Sc) dismissed the idea that it had been 'planted', on the ground that the enemy would not make Whitehall a present of the 'Window' principle, and insisted that, whether the informant had been relaying facts derived from British POW* or giving a garbled account of German experiments, it proved that the principle was known to the Germans.[40] He has recently pointed out that 'the value of the report was independent of whether it was genuine or a 'plant' . . . In either case, it proved that someone in Germany knew of the Window principle and therefore the argument based on the premise that the Germans did not know of it was now substantially demolished'.[41] But this conclusion did not at the time meet with universal acceptance in the scientific community or from the operational authorities.[42] Debate about the relative advantages and disadvantages of using 'Window' continued to be fuelled throughout the winter of 1942–43 by uncertainty as to whether the enemy was aware of it as well as by the argument that the British defences were much more vulnerable to it than were those of Germany.

It was not further intelligence, moreover, but operational considerations which brought the debate to a close. By the beginning of April 1943 the casualties incurred by Bomber Command were mounting alarmingly in the Battle of the Ruhr and the Air Staff was correspondingly increasing its estimates of the losses that would have been avoided if 'Window' had been in use. On the other hand, the fear of German retaliation was dwindling under the argument that the GAF bomber force was a constantly declining threat. It

---

* The RAF had not in fact experimented with 'Window' over the Rhineland.

40.   AIR 20/1632, ASI Report No 16, German knowledge of 'Window', 24 October 1942.
41.   Jones, op cit, pp 293–294.
42.   Price, op cit, p 126.

was on these grounds that on 1 May the Chiefs of Staff approved the introduction of 'Window' for 1 July, subject to an investigation of the implications for other Allied projects, especially the invasion of Sicily (operation *Husky*) planned for 10 July. And it was mainly from concern for the success of the Sicily landings that the Prime Minister, advised by Lord Cherwell, delayed his approval of the recommendation of the Chiefs of Staff until 15 July.[43]*

By that date the intelligence sources had provided no indication since the previous October that the Germans were familiar with the 'Window' principle, or feared or intended its exploitation. Naval Enigma decrypts had indeed disclosed that, following experiments involving a U-boat, an ASV aircraft and the release of balloons since the middle of April 1943, the U-boat Command had authorised the use of some new device (code-name *Aphrodite*) from 15 June. But what *Aphrodite* was remained a mystery until the decryption and elucidation of a signal dated 9 July in which the Command, advising U-boats how to release the balloons, warned that their mooring wires and metal foil strips should not be allowed to get wet.[44] NID/DSD 9 then realised that *Aphrodite* was an application of the 'Window' principle which used the reflective property of metal strips in an attempt to protect U-boats against radar detection.†

In the Allied daylight offensive over western Europe Fighter Command and the light bombers of Bomber Command continued their sweeps over northern France and the Low Countries on a reduced scale from the beginning of 1943 and some of Bomber Command's major raids on the U-boat bases were day raids. But the chief development was the steady increase in US Eighth Air Force's precision bombing of industrial and military targets. From the beginning of 1943 US Eighth Air Force extended its operations

---

* For intelligence on the effects of the introduction of 'Window' on the bombing campaign see Volume III.

† A further report on 'Window' from ADI (Sc), who was in close touch with NID/DSD9, records that this discovery was arrived at only on 15 July: 'It is a noticeable coincidence that a few hours after the final decision was taken on 15.7.43 to use "Window", it became clear that the Germans had just anticipated us by using a similar device for their submarines to confuse our ASV aircraft'.[45] However, the US naval intelligence authorities had already come to this conclusion. On 23 June they had informed the US operational command, on the basis of the Enigma decrypts and of their interpretation of the code-name *Aphrodite*, that 'it is believed that "Aphrodite" refers to deception equipment of submarines in combating aircraft radar'. They then went on to describe the use in this device of metal strips and balloons.

43. CAB 80/69, COS (43) 227 (0) of 1 May; CAB 120/293, PM File, 406/1, Cherwell minute to PM 18 June and PM Personal Minute M 432/3 of 2 July 1943; AIR 41/43, p 87.

44. DEFE 3/268, ZTPG 124679 of 17 April 1943; DEFE 3/287, ZTPG 143424 and 143609 of 30 June; ZTPGU 14797 of 15 June 1943, and 15147 of 16 June.

45. AIR 20/1661, ASI Report No IV of 3 August 1943.

from the occupied territories to the fringes of Germany itself; its first attack on Germany was a raid on the U-boat facilities in Wilhelmshaven on 27 January 1943. From April 1943 it began to penetrate deeper into Germany – and thus to undertake an increasing proportion of its raids without fighter escort – and to place greater emphasis on the destruction of GAF fighters. In May the 'Trident' conference in Washington agreed that with the aim of softening up Germany in preparation for *Overlord*, the task of the daylight campaign should continue to be the reduction of the GAF's fighter forces by engaging fighters and attacking fighter production plants.

By July 1943 the determination with which US Eighth Air Force extended its raids ever deeper into Germany forced the GAF to make the defeat of the day-bomber its first concern.[46] From the same date, on the other hand, the fact that an increasing number of its raids were taking place without fighter escort raised US casualties to an alarming level, and in October, recognising temporary defeat, US Eighth Air Force was forced to suspend operations until it had acquired longer range fighters. Its offensive was not to be resumed until February 1944.

One reason why the offensive was maintained for so long in the face of mounting casualties lay in US Eighth Air Force's continuing lack of a reliable method of checking the claims of its bombers to have destroyed enemy fighters. Fighter Command had become more cautious in its assessment of its own claims by the end of 1942; in the first half of 1943, when it claimed to have destroyed 249 enemy fighters, the number actually destroyed was 235.[47] But US Eighth Air Force's estimates of the casualties it had inflicted on the GAF continued to be enormously exaggerated.[48] In the summer of 1943 its estimate of the number of enemy aircraft it had destroyed in the first 12 months of its operations exceeded the British estimate of German aircraft casualties on the western front from all causes in the same period.[49] As late as October 1943, in the second great raid on Schweinfurt which brought its offensive to a close, it claimed to have destroyed 186 fighters for the loss of 60 of its own bombers; but the GAF's casualties in the raid totalled only 38.[50] Until then, moreover, it had a second reason for continuing the offensive. It clung to the belief that, partly as a result of the enemy's heavy casualties and partly because of the heavy damage it was inflicting on German aircraft production, the GAF was not merely over-stretched, but was in its 'death-throes'.[51]

---

46.   AIR 41/10, p 289.   47.   AIR 41/49, p 268.
48.   AIR 41/10, p 288.
49.   Craven and Cate, *The Army Air Forces in World War II*, Vol II (Chicago, 1949), p 710.
50.   ibid, pp 704, 708, 711.   51.   ibid, pp 708, 711.

Evidence that the GAF was over-stretched had been received from the Enigma during 1942.* It was upheld at the end of 1942 when the Air Intelligence Branch detected a decline in the enemy's fighter strength in the west. Such a decline in fact occurred: the actual strength of the GAF's single-engined day-fighters in the west, which had risen from 292 at the beginning of 1942 to over 500 by the autumn, had dropped to 453 by the end of the year, when AI calculated that it stood at 485.[52] The decline was only temporary. As we have seen, by July 1943 the great increase in German aircraft production inaugurated by Milch and Speer early in 1942 had raised the GAF's total first-line strength to 5,396 from 4,000 at the end of 1942, of which some 1,800 were single-engined fighters as compared with 1,250 at the end of 1942.† At the same time, the effects of increased production being intensified by redeployments at the expense of the Russian and Mediterranean fronts, the number of single-engined fighters in the west increased steadily; it was 810 by July, 964 by October 1943.[53] This recovery, like the temporary decline, was soon detected by Air Intelligence. In March it recognised that the GAF as a whole was 'recuperating slowly'[54] and noted for the first time that the fighter force in the west was being reinforced at the expense of the Russian front.[55] On 1 April it observed that this reinforcement was being accelerated and that the fighter force in the west was now drawing formations from the Mediterranean as well as from Russia; and it also noted that the GAF was using twin-engined night-fighters to supplement its day-fighters in operations against the US Eighth Air Force's attacks.[56] By the end of April Air Intelligence realised that the GAF's build-up of single-engined fighters in the west was proceeding faster than it had expected; it calculated that total strength had reached 575 aircraft (the actual figure was then 507)[57] and expected it to rise ultimately to 700.[58] In May it correctly appreciated in advance of the Kursk offensive‡ that Allied operations in western Europe and the Mediterranean were reducing the effectiveness of the GAF in Russia and forcing it to use obsolete aircraft there and to rely on the air forces of the satellite powers.[59]

---

* See above, p 238.   † See above, p 517.   ‡ See below, p 625.

52. Webster and Frankland, op cit, Vol I, p 490; Craven and Cate, op cit, Vol II, p 234; Air Sunsets 17, 22 and 25 of 20, 25 and 28 November 1942.
53. Webster and Frankland, op cit, Vol I, p 490; Vol II, p 46 footnote.
54. Air Sunset 49, undated but evidently early March 1943.
55. Air Sunset 52 of 27 March 1943.
56. Air Sunset 53 of 1 April.
57. Webster and Frankland, op cit, Vol II p 295 footnote.
58. Air Sunset 56 of 25 April.
59. Air Sunset 49, undated early March, 57 and 64 of 3 and 25 May.

From that time, largely because of its under-estimate of the increase in the rate of German aircraft production during most of 1943 despite its generally reliable order of battle intelligence, Air Intelligence's calculations of the current and prospective strength of the enemy's day-fighter strength in the west, as of the GAF as a whole, began to fall behind actuality. As for single-engined fighters, it estimated on 9 May that the total strength had been 1,095 at the beginning of the year and that the GAF aimed at a first-line of between 1,400 and 1,450 by the end of the year.[60] In August it calculated that the figure had already reached 1,340.[61] But the figure had actually risen from 1,245 on 1 January 1943 to 1,504 by May, and was to reach 1,739 by February 1944.[62] Of this total strength, 810 fighters were deployed in the west by 1 July and 964 by 1 October, but the Air Ministry estimated the figure at 600 on 1 August and 780 on 21 September;[63] nor was it until November that it retrospectively raised the estimate for July from 600 to 740.[64] As against these under-estimates, however, the Enigma evidence of GAF re-deployments and the low-grade Sigint evidence on order of battle continued to show that the GAF was giving high priority to combating US Eighth Air Force's offensive. In June Air Intelligence learned that a large proportion of the day-fighters in the west were moving from France and Belgium to German bases, that intermediate landing grounds were being developed to give the fighters a greater effective range and that experiments were taking place with bombing the American bombers from the air.[65] In the same month it received indications that two Gruppen of single-engined fighters were being withdrawn from Leningrad to the west.[66] Between the end of July and the middle of August it learned that two further Gruppen were moving to north-west Germany from the Orel front, where the fighting was then at its height,[67] in response to the intensification of US Eighth Air Force's raids. In August it calculated that the force of 600 single-engined fighters in the west included 90 transferred from Russia and 60 from the Mediterranean.[68]

The authors of the history of US Eighth Air Force, drawing attention to the under-estimates of the day-fighter strength in the west and to the 'much larger error' in estimates of enemy aircraft

60.   Air Sunset 59 of 9 May.
61.   Air Sunset 282 of 9 August.
62.   AIR 41/10. p 301; Webster and Frankland, op cit, Vol II p 295 footnote.
63.   Air Sunset 282 of 9 August and 327 of 21 September.
64.   Webster and Frankland, op cit, Vol II, p 46 footnote.
65.   Air Sunset 67 of 7 June.
66.   Air Sunset 70 of 20 June.
67.   Air Sunset 279, 282 and 290 of 5, 9 and 17 August.
68.   Air Sunset 282 of 9 August.

production from which the under-estimates derived, have suggested that, had these mistakes been avoided, US Eighth Air Force would have realised sooner than it did that the casualties it was inflicting on the GAF's fighters and the damage it was doing to fighter aircraft factories were at best slowing down the increase in German output and front-line strength.[69] It seems unlikely, however, that the disparities that emerged between actual and estimated enemy front-line strengths were in themselves large enough to have had an influence on strategic decisions. Despite their short-fall, the estimates indicated a continual increase in the enemy's resources. They were accompanied by unmistakable evidence from the Enigma and other sources of order of battle intelligence that the GAF was giving highest priority to the defence of the Reich; and they were accompanied also by enormous and mounting losses in US bombers. It was in the light of these two considerations that the decision was taken to suspend US Eighth Air Force's deep-penetration raids on Germany in October. And when these considerations failed to prompt an earlier suspension, it may be doubted whether completely accurate estimates of current and future fighter strength would have done so.

Meanwhile, as well as forcing the GAF to give priority to its defences in the west and adding to the over-all wastage of its total fighter forces, US Eighth Air Force's offensive of 1943 had forced the Germans to undertake the dispersal of their aircraft factories. The dispersal put the industry in a better position to withstand the daylight offensive when that was resumed in February 1944. But it also delayed the enemy's planned fighter production by three months, and the US Strategic Bombing Survey later calculated that this delay contributed significantly to the outcome of the later air battles.[*]

---

* See Volume III.

69.   Craven and Cate, op cit, Vol II, pp 708–709.

CHAPTER 26

The War at Sea from November 1942 to the Summer of 1943

I N SEPTEMBER 1942, influenced by the demands of operation *Torch* as well as by the heavy losses that had to be expected on the Arctic passage, the Admiralty decided to suspend the Russian convoys until January 1943. By the end of October, however, with the withdrawal of the *Tirpitz* to Trondheim and of the *Scheer* to the Baltic, only the heavy cruiser *Hipper* and the light cruiser *Köln* of the enemy's main units remained in the north, and it was known by 11 November that, with the wholesale removal of the GAF's offensive forces in north Norway to the Mediterranean, the only aircraft suitable for anti-shipping operations in the north were a few He 115 torpedo-carrying float-planes.[1]* The Admiralty accordingly revised its plans. In order to reduce the number of supply ships building up in Russia, convoy QP 15 was sailed from Archangel on 17 November with 28 ships and the east-bound convoys were resumed with the sailing of convoy JW 51A on 15 December.† Before the resumption of the convoys a number of ships had attempted the passage to and from Russia independently. Another factor leading to the return to convoys was the relative failure of this experiment. By the middle of November 13 ships had sailed, of which five arrived: four had been sunk, one wrecked, three turned back.[2]

By 9 November the number of U-boats in the Arctic theatre had grown to 25,[3] a larger number than ever before. Throughout the winter intelligence made it clear that it remained at about that level. As before, indeed, the Enigma provided a reliable indication of how many of the U-boats were on patrol, together with a considerable amount of information about their positions and

---

* See above, p 227.
† The Arctic convoy designations now became JW/RA in place of PQ/QP, and those that sailed in 1943 were smaller than the earlier ones.

1. ADM 223/112, Ultra signals 0054 and 1130/25 October 1942; ADM 223/113, Ultra signal 1557/11 November 1942.
2. Roskill, *The War at Sea*, Vol II (1957), p 289; ADM 223/88, Colpoys, *Admiralty Use of Special Intelligence in Naval Operations*, pp 135–136.
3. ADM 223/96, OIC SI 423 of 9 November 1942.

movements. Use was made of this intelligence to the extent that the Admiralty timed the sailings of the convoys and adjusted the strength of their escorts in the light of the OIC's estimates of the seriousness of the U-boat threat, but the convoys derived little benefit from it once they had sailed. The foul weather and the narrowness of the northern seas in winter allowed little scope for evasive routeing; in any case, the Arctic U-boats were not disposed in patrol lines until a later stage in the war. As before, on the other hand, the U-boat threat to the convoys was less grave than that posed by the GAF and the enemy's surface ships. In November a strong force of U-boats attacked QP 15 but, hampered by severe storms, they sank only two ships.[4] In the second half of December 1942, while convoys JW 51A and JW 51B were at sea, the Enigma showed that the number of U-boats on patrol had dropped to at most three.[5] JW 52 got through without loss in January 1943; though U-boats sighted it and claimed two successes, they were fought off by the escort.[6] By March, when RA 53 lost three ships to U-boat attack,[7] the U-boats on the Arctic route had sunk about a dozen ships during the winter of 1942–1943.

In January 1943 the enemy attempted to revive the GAF threat which had disappeared in the previous November. The Enigma disclosed that two Gruppen of Ju 88 long-range bombers had returned to north Norway and would be used against convoy JW 52.[8] In the event they did no damage and on 26 January a decrypt showed Fliegerführer Lofoten complaining of the inadequacy of his striking force and asking for torpedo-carrying Ju 88s.[9] He received no further reinforcements.

Though temporarily reduced by the withdrawal of the *Tirpitz*, the threat from the surface ships was by no means removed. The British Naval Attaché Stockholm had reported before the end of September 1942 that the *Tirpitz* needed a refit. Although the Enigma had by then established that the German anxiety about Allied landings in Norway was again on the increase,[10] the OIC was unaware that the main reason why she was retained in Trondheim was Hitler's obsession with the defence of Norway.[11] Before the end of November, however, it was estimating that she

---

4. ADM 223/113, Ultra signal 1314/20 November 1942; Naval Headlines No 505 of 21 November 1942; Roskill, op cit, Vol II, p 289.
5. ADM 223/96, OIC SI 408 of 21 December 1942; Naval Headlines No 540 of 26 December 1942.
6. Roskill, op cit, Vol II, p 399.
7. ibid, p 400.
8. ADM 223/114, Ultra signals 0755/24 January, 1258/26 January 1943.
9. CX/MSS/2022/T22.
10. CX/MSS/1562/T17.
11. Roskill, op cit, Vol II, pp 289–290; D Woodward, *Tirpitz* (1974), p 80.

would be operational by mid-December and on 5 January 1943 the Enigma reported that she was beginning her post-refit trials.[12] On 31 October, meanwhile, after revealing that the GAF had sighted 45 ships in Iceland on 22 October, the Enigma showed that the *Hipper* had moved from Narvik to join the *Köln* at Altenfjord;[13] and during 6 and 7 November it disclosed that she had sailed to operate against independent ships, of which some had been attacked or sighted by U-boats.[14] She was back in Altenfjord by 9 November, having attacked some Russian ships but having found none of the independents; in a long Enigma report that was decrypted on 14 November she attributed her failure to lack of surprise and recommended that no publicity should be given to her sortie.[15]

Three days later the Enigma warned that the Germans were aware that QP 15 was about to sail.[16] And on 20 November it disclosed that Admiral Commanding Cruisers had been ordered to prepare to sail his entire force, including the *Köln*, at 0400 that day. The Admiralty promulgated this intelligence at 1354 on 20 November.[17] QP 15 had sailed with cruiser cover, and the Home Fleet had stationed four submarines off Altenfjord against a break-out by the *Hipper* and the *Köln*. Had they sailed, the Enigma notice might, in view of its timeliness, have proved to be of great value. By 1515 on 20 November, however, the Enigma had disclosed that the sortie had been cancelled on account of the weather.[18]

Of the next movements by German main units to Norway from the Baltic, movements which confirmed the enemy's determination to maintain the offensive against the Arctic supply shipping, the Enigma again gave timely warning. Late on 13 November it disclosed that the light cruiser *Nürnberg* was leaving the Baltic; by 0611 on 14 November it had added that she had passed Bergen a few hours earlier.[19] But an RAF strike on 15 November failed to find her at Stadtlandet between Bergen and Trondheim. She had been forced by bad weather to anchor between Bergen and Stadtlandet earlier that day, but this information, together with the fact that she had moved on to Trondheim after dark on 17

12. ADM 223/96, OIC SI 441 of 24 November 1942; ADM 223/114, Ultra signal 1742/5 January 1943.
13. ADM 223/112, Ultra signal 0228/31 October 1942; Naval Headlines No 477 of 24 October 1942.
14. ADM 223/112, Ultra signal 1223/6 November; ADM 223/113, Ultra signals 0230 and 1020/7 November 1942.
15. ADM 223/113, Ultra signal 2020/14 November 1942.
16. ibid, Ultra signal 1851/17 November 1942.
17. ibid, Ultra signal 1354/20 November 1942.
18. ibid, Ultra signal 1550/20 November 1942.
19. ibid, Ultra signals 1006 and 2345/13 November, 0611/14 November 1942.

November, was unfortunately not divulged by the Enigma decrypts until 18 and 19 November.[20] More fortunately, the Germans, while appreciating that the strike had been against the *Nürnberg*, assumed that the British had learned of her movement from agents.[21] By the time the *Nürnberg* had reached north Norway in the first week of December, after several postponements of her departure from Trondheim had been reported by the Enigma decrypts,[22] the OIC had deduced from Enigma references that the *Lützow* and the *Prinz Eugen* might leave the Baltic about 5 December and be followed soon after by the *Scharnhorst*. Reporting this on 24 November, the OIC noted that these ships had, like the *Nürnberg*, been taking part in exercise attacks on convoys, and that Enigma and PR evidence of the state of the enemy's repair programmes indicated that the *Tirpitz*, the *Hipper*, the *Prinz Eugen*, the *Lützow*, the *Scheer* and four 6″ cruisers, and possibly the *Scharnhorst*, were all likely to be operational by mid-December.[23] But no further intelligence was received until 11 December, when the Enigma decrypts of 9 and 10 December revealed that one large and three small warships had been due to pass Bergen northbound on the previous day.[24] It added late on 11 December that the formation was proceeding to Vestfjord and, on 13 December, that the large ship was the *Lützow* and that she had arrived in the Narvik area on 12 December.[25]

Although the Germans intended to send the *Lützow* to the Atlantic, they planned to do so only after attacking the next Arctic convoy; her movement along the Norwegian coast was accordingly not accompanied by evidence of enemy reconnaissance of the Denmark Strait and, as was only to be expected, the Enigma made no reference to her future plans. Even so, the C-in-C Home Fleet now re-established the Denmark Strait patrol and sent HMS *Anson* to Iceland.[26] At the same time, it was decided to proceed with the decision to resume the Russia-bound convoys without delay. Convoy JW 51A sailed on 15 December; it arrived at Kola on Christmas day without being sighted.[27] JW 51B, however, following on 22 December, was sighted by U-boat south of Bear Island about noon on 30 December and, as we now know, the *Hipper* and

---

20. Naval Headlines Nos 502 of 18 November, 503 of 19 November 1942.

21. ibid, No 502 of 18 November 1942.

22. ibid, Nos 512 of 28 November, 515 of 1 December 1942; ADM 223/113, Ultra signals 2220/25 November, 1315/28 November 1942; ADM 223/96, OIC SI 455 of 7 December 1942.

23. ADM 223/96, OIC SI 441 of 24 November 1942.

24. ADM 223/113, Ultra signal 0938/11 December 1942.

25. ibid, Ultra signals 2340/11 December, 1025/13 December 1942.

26. Roskill, op cit, Vol II, p 290.

27. ADM 223/96, OIC SI 468 of 21 December 1942; Roskill, op cit, Vol II, pp 291, 398.

the *Lützow*, whose move to Altenfjord on 19 December had been
disclosed by the Enigma,[28] at once sailed to intercept it.[29]

JW 51B was accompanied by six destroyers and five other
escorts under Captain Sherbrooke in HMS *Onslow* and covered by
the cruisers *Sheffield* and *Jamaica*, which had taken JW 51A through
to Kola. Admiral Burnett, commanding the cruisers, knew that the
Lützow had reached Altenfjord, that the German squadron there
could be expected to intervene, that two U-boats were at sea in the
area and that two others were in the vicinity of the ice-edge.[30]
During 28 and 29 December he had been informed by Ultra signal
of the details of the ice-edge, as reported by these U-boats, and of
the fact that on 28 December the Germans knew of his own
departure from Kola and were expecting shipping through the Bear
Island Channel.[31] On 30 December he received only one Ultra
signal; it told him there were strong indications that up to 0045 on
that day the German Admiral Commanding Cruisers was still in
Altenfjord.[32] As luck would have it, moreover, no Enigma was
decrypted during 31 December, so that at 0830 that day, when the
German force was close to the convoy, he did not know it had sailed
or, indeed, that the convoy had been reported by a U-boat on 30
December.

In the ensuing engagement, one in which the forces on both sides
were impeded by the poor visibility and atrocious weather of the
Arctic winter, the German force crippled the *Onslow* and the
Achates, which later sank, and also sank a minesweeper before the
British cruisers reached the scene at 1130, but it then suffered an
early hit on the *Hipper* and the loss of a destroyer before withdrawing at 1200, and the convoy's only casualty was damage to one
merchantman. The Enigma of 31 December, broken about midnight, confirmed that the German force had consisted of the *Hipper*,
the *Lützow* and six destroyers, and that one of the destroyers had
been sunk.[33] Early in January 1943 the Enigma disclosed that the
Lützow was undamaged, but nothing was learned about the *Hipper*
till 18 January when the Naval Attaché Stockholm reported that
she had been hit. An 'officer-only' Enigma signal, decrypted after a
delay of three weeks, confirmed on 24 January that her No 3 boiler
room had been flooded by a hit from one of the British cruisers.[34]

28.   ADM 223/113, Ultra signal 2140/19 December 1942.
29.   Naval Headlines, No 540 of 26 December 1942; Roskill, op cit, Vol II, p
      292.
30.   ADM 223/113, Ultra signals 1241 and 1915/23 December, 1216 and
      1846/25 December 1942.
31.   ibid, Ultra signal 1216/25 December 1942; ADM 223/114, Ultra signals
      1738/28 December, 1235/29 December 1942.
32.   ADM 223/114, Ultra signal 2015/30 December 1942.
33.   ibid, Ultra signals 0140, 0757 and 0912/1 January, 2242/3 January 1943.
34.   ADM 223/88, p 138; ADM 223/114, Ultra signal 1040/24 January 1943.

Following this engagement, which the Germans accepted as a British success,[35] the *Lützow*'s Atlantic cruise was cancelled,[36] and the *Hipper* was withdrawn with the *Köln* to the Baltic. Nothing was learned of the *Lützow*'s change of plan, but on 25 January the Enigma and the SIS ship-watchers warned that the *Hipper* and the *Köln* were leaving Altenfjord for Narvik and the Enigma indicated that no immediate movement beyond Narvik was intended,[37] The RAF had made special preparations for search and attack by the time the Enigma disclosed at about midnight on 4–5 February, after several days of uncertainty, that the ships were to leave Trondheim that night. But despite the preparations and the timely warning, the weather prevented an attack.[38] The *Hipper* and the *Köln* reached the Baltic on 6 February.[39]

Their withdrawal from Norway, in part an immediate consequence of the engagement of 31 December, also reflected the fact that Hitler's dissatisfaction with the performance of the surface ships had precipitated his replacement of Raeder by Dönitz and a decision to bring the main units back to Germany and suspend all work on, and new construction of, capital ships. While remaining adamant against further new construction,* Hitler was later persuaded by Dönitz's promise of success within three months to restore highest priority to surface ship action against the Russian

---

* One of the results was the final suspension of work on the aircraft carrier *Graf Zeppelin* in the spring of 1943. In March 1942, after the *Tirpitz*'s narrow escape off Vestfjord, Hitler ordered the immediate completion of the carrier. Neither this order nor the fact that it was not followed by any serious work on her came to the notice of the OIC, and from the summer of 1942 to the summer of 1943 the Admiralty's anxiety about her was kept alive by several references in the intelligence sources. In July 1942 a GAF Enigma decrypt reported that the GAF was shortly to inspect an aircraft carrier berth at Trondheim. On 16 January 1943 the Admiralty distributed to the Home Fleet and the US Chief of Naval Operations – and also to the Prime Minister at the Casablanca conference – the contents of another Enigma signal to the effect that dive-bomber pilots for the air units detailed for the *Graf Zeppelin* were to be ready by 1 March 1943. On 2 March the Naval Attaché Stockholm reported that, while her air personnel were to have been ready by the end of March, delays were now probable; and in May he added that her trials had begun in April. By then the GAF Enigma had disclosed that she had been transferred from Kiel, where PR had located her in March, to Swinemünde; and the OIC, still uneasy about her, requested a PR search for her. She was located by PR off Stettin on 23 June 1943. Thereafter the intelligence sources rarely referred to her and it became clear that work on her had been abandoned.[40]

35.   Roskill, op cit, Vol II, p 299.   36.   ibid, p 298.
37.   ADM 223/114, Ultra signals 0106 and 2125/25 January 1943; AIR 41/48, *The RAF in Maritime War*, Vol IV, p 347.
38.   ADM 223/114, Ultra signal 1350/31 January 1943; ADM 223/115, Ultra signal 0136/5 February 1943; AIR 41/48, pp 348, 351.
39.   ADM 223/115, Ultra signal 1348/7 February 1943.
40.   Roskill, op cit, Vol II, p 124 and fn; AIR 41/48, p 353; ADM 223/96, OIC SI 441 of 24 November 1942; ADM 223/97, OIC SI 592 of 15 May 1943; ADM 223/114, Ultra signals 1645 and 1745/16 January 1943; CX/MSS/1143/T34, 1968/T16, 2471/T1; last item covered by Dir/C Archive, 3066 of 23 April 1943.

convoys. Dönitz then decided to bring ineffective ships back to Germany, to keep the *Scheer* and the *Prinz Eugen* in the Baltic because of serious fuel shortage, but also to begin a more vigorous campaign with the remaining ships as soon as the *Scharnhorst* had joined the northern squadron.[41]

Except that a Japanese diplomatic decrypt revealed towards the end of January 1943 that Hitler had decided to give priority to U-boats at the expense of capital ships, Whitehall received no intelligence about these exchanges with Dönitz; and except that the Enigma was beginning to make occasional references to naval fuel shortage, no intelligence on Germany's final policy towards the future of her surface fleet was obtained until March. Early in March, however, a British POW in Germany reported by coded message that he had heard from a high German naval official that the big ships might have to give up men to meet the shortage of U-boat crews, and an Enigma decrypt of 10 March disclosed that crews of surface ships were being medically examined to see if they were fit for U-boat service. By the end of March the interrogation of U-boat POW had produced further evidence that a comb-out of surface-ship crews was taking place, beginning with the smaller ships.

Despite the evidence that fuel and manpower shortages were affecting the surface ships, the Home Fleet assumed that Dönitz's appointment would be followed by greater enterprise in the use of the German main units, either in attacks on the northern convoys or in the form of 'a desperate break-out' into the Atlantic.[42] On 8 January, moreover, after giving several indications that the *Scharnhorst* was engaging in fleet exercises in the eastern Baltic and might leave the Baltic before the ice formed, the Enigma announced that she and the *Prinz Eugen* had returned to Gdynia and that 'final decisions' were to be taken that day.[43] On 9 and 10 January the OIC followed up its earlier warnings that the departure of these ships might be imminent; on 9 January emergency signals to them suggested they were already moving[44] and on 10 January the Enigma referred to the existence of a special operation and to minesweeping in such a way as to indicate that they might be passing through the Great Belt.[45] Although the intelligence picture was complicated by the suspicion that an auxiliary cruiser, subsequently identified as the *Togo* (Raider K), might be leaving the

---

41.   AIR 41/48, pp 337–338; Roskill, op cit, Vol II, p 299.
42.   Roskill, op cit, Vol II, p 399.
43.   ADM 223/114, Ultra signals 1742/5 January, 1010/6 January, 0710/8 January 1943; AIR 41/48, pp 338–339.
44.   ADM 223/114, Ultra signal 1905/9 January 1943.
45.   ibid, Ultra signal 1543/10 January 1943.

Baltic at this time,[46]* submarines had been deployed off south Norway, Coastal Command was flying special patrols and the Home Fleet was ready to make a destroyer sweep there, and also to send a squadron on to Iceland to guard against a possible break-out into the Atlantic or an attack on the next Russia-bound convoy, when the *Scharnhorst*, the *Prinz Eugen* and destroyers were sighted off the Skaw steering north-west at 1300 on 11 January.[47] The German formation turned back on intercepting the RAF sighting report.[48] But this remained unknown until the forenoon of 13 January, when the Enigma disclosed that the *Scharnhorst* had returned to Gdynia, and an intensive and anxious search for the *Prinz Eugen* went on until the Enigma added on 15 January that she had returned with the *Scharnhorst*.[49]

A second unsuccessful attempt to move these ships to Norway followed later in January. The Enigma again gave good notice. As early as 20 January a signal from C-in-C Fleet on board the *Scharnhorst*, decrypted late, revealed that he would repeat the attempt when the weather was suitable.[50] Decrypts on the following day stated that the *Scharnhorst* and the *Prinz Eugen* would exercise until 23 January;[51] and on 23, 24 and 25 January further decrypts established that they were leaving the Baltic.[52] Coastal Command PR sorties and strikes were planned in advance, and all else was ready when the ships were sighted off the Skaw at 1415 on 25 January.[53] Again the enemy turned back on intercepting the sighting report; and again there was a period of suspense until – this time with less delay – the Enigma disclosed in the early hours of 26 January that the operation had been cancelled.[54] It added, on this occasion, that the ships had been making for Narvik.

By that time convoy JW 52 had reached Russia without loss, and the Enigma had by 24 January given the assurance that the remaining surface ships in the north – the *Lützow* and the *Nürnberg* – would not sail against it.[55] But on 19 February, four days after the sailing of the next convoy, JW 53, the Enigma disclosed that the GAF had reconnoitred Scapa Flow on 17

---

* See below, p 539.

46.   ADM 223/113, Ultra signal 1308/13 December 1942; ADM 223/114, Ultra signal 1800/7 January 1943.
47.   ADM 223/114, Ultra signal 1015/11 January 1943; Roskill, op cit, Vol II, p 398; AIR 41/48, p 339.   48.   AIR 41/48, p 340 (fn).
49.   ibid, pp 340–341; ADM 223/114, Ultra signals 1355/11 January, 1206 and 1829/12 January, 1054/13 January, 0732/15 January 1943.
50.   ADM 223/114, Ultra signal 1644/20 January 1943.
51.   ibid, Ultra signal 0857/21 January 1943.
52.   ibid, Ultra signals 1106 and 1544/23 January, 1412/24 January, 0834, 1033 and 1119/25 January 1943.   53.   AIR 41/48, pp 341–342.
54.   ibid, p 343; ADM 223/114, Ultra signal 0458/26 January 1943.
55.   Naval Headlines, No 569 of 24 January 1943.

February and planned intensive reconnaissance for the convoy; and on the following day it added that reconnaissance was taking place of the sea areas between Scotland, Norway and Jan Mayen.[56] On 10 and 27 February, and again on 3 March, the Enigma also carried unusual instructions to U-boats to report on British air and sea patrols and radar cover in these areas.[57] The enemy in fact made these arrangements in connection with his attempt to pass a blockade-runner through the Denmark Strait but the OIC, having no other intelligence about this unusual plan until the end of March,* necessarily associated them with a further attempt to send warships from the Baltic to Norway, and possibly into the Atlantic.[58] And the *Scharnhorst* did indeed pass through the Great Belt in the evening on 6 March. On this, her third attempt, she evaded the British surveillance, and it was not until 11 March that the Enigma established that she had reached Narvik.[59]

Although the GAF Enigma had disclosed on 5 March that, as often happened when a main unit was on passage, arrangements had been made to move fighters to Norway,[60] the naval Enigma for the few days preceding the *Scharnhorst's* move was not decrypted till 7 March. Its contents then proved to be inconclusive; they revealed that the *Scharnhorst* had been at sea in the Baltic on 4 March, but also that the Great Belt was to be closed during 6 and 7 March, and they made references by code-name to an operation off the Skaw on 5 March which might or might not be the movement of a main unit, but which in fact was an operation by minelayers.[61] In its uncertainty the OIC estimated on 7 March that the enemy force might break out into the Atlantic through the Iceland-Faroes gap on 7–8 March, unless it had done so on 6–7 March,[62] but also warned that the *Scharnhorst's* departure from the Baltic might have been delayed.[63] Air patrols of the northern exits of the Atlantic and of the Norwegian coast had found nothing by the evening of 9 March when PR established that the *Scharnhorst* had left Gdynia without the *Prinz Eugen*.[64] By that time, while the Admiralty decided not to give priority to fleet reconnaissance, so great was the need for aircraft protection for the Atlantic convoys, the Home

---

* See below, p 545.

56. ADM 223/115, Ultra signal 0900/20 February 1943.
57. ADM 223/97, OIC SI 530 of 5 March 1943.
58. ibid; ADM 223/115, Ultra signal 0900/20 February 1943.
59. ADM 223/116, Ultra signal 1030/11 March 1943; AIR 41/48, pp 343 (n) 345 (n2).
60. ADM 223/115, Ultra signal 1846/5 March 1943.
61. ibid, Ultra signals 0256, 0517 and 1651/7 March, 1815/10 March 1943.
62. AIR 41/48, p 343.
63. ADM 223/115, Ultra signal 1651/7 March 1943.
64. Roskill, op cit, Vol II, p 400; AIR 41/48, p 343.

Fleet had sent HMS *Anson* to Iceland and brought ships to short notice on 8 March, and Force H at Gibraltar was being kept at short notice against a possible Atlantic break-out.

At that point confusion was deepened by the late decrypt of another naval Enigma signal. It showed only that on 6 March the *Scharnhorst*, still in the Baltic, had been informed that air escort for her could not be arranged until 9 March.[65] In spite of the ambiguity of the decrypt the OIC on 9 March adhered, correctly, to the view that an important ship, which 'at first appeared to be the *Scharnhorst*', had passed through the Great Belt in the past few days; but to the earlier evidence suggesting that the ship intended to break out into the Atlantic it now added the further pointer that four enemy fleet destroyers had moved westward through the Straits of Dover on 6 March: they might have moved to act as a screen for a main unit returning from the Atlantic, or to escort blockade-runners, or to attack Allied convoys.[66]

On 10 March, when the Enigma established that the *Scharnhorst* was at sea off Norway on the previous day but had not yet excluded the possibility that she was making for the Atlantic[67] – it did not report her arrival in Narvik until 11 March[68] – it became clear from GAF Enigma decrypts about reconnaissance arrangements that another warship, possibly the *Lützow*, would soon be moving south.[69] The next day, when it learned from the naval Enigma that a number of signals, using a special cypher that was unreadable at GC and CS,* had been exchanged between the *Lützow*, the *Tirpitz* and German naval commands on 10 March, the OIC judged that the *Tirpitz* would be associated with the forthcoming movement;[70] by the beginning of February the Enigma had disclosed that the *Tirpitz* had completed her principal repairs and the Naval Attaché Stockholm had reported that she was preparing to leave Trondheim, and on 27 February an agent had reported that she was exercising in Trondheim. Later on 11 March the OIC received a report from the agent that she had passed the entrance to Trondheim fjord at 0830 that morning, course unknown, together with further decrypts concerning GAF escort on that day for a movement 'between Trondheim and Narvik or vice versa',[71] but perhaps

---

* This was the fleet cypher called Neptun by the Germans and Barracuda by GC and CS, see Appendix 4.

65.   ADM 223/115, Ultra signal 1740/9 March 1943.
66.   ibid, Ultra signal 1939/9 March 1943.
67.   ibid, Ultra signal 1435/10 March 1943.
68.   ADM 223/116, Ultra signal 1303/11 March 1943.
69.   ADM 223/115, Ultra signal 0130/10 March 1943.
70.   ADM 223/116, Ultra signal 1220/11 March 1943.
71.   ibid, Ultra signal 1810/11 March 1943; AIR 41/48, p 346; Roskill, op cit, Vol II, p 400.

because the Naval Attaché Stockholm had advised towards the end of February that there was no reason to think she would move to Narvik, it at first believed that she had gone south. Coastal Command carried out reconnaissance south of Trondheim and prepared for a strike in the Skagerrak.[72] On 12 March, however, the OIC suspected that she had moved to Narvik;[73] and on 14 March the Enigma did indeed disclose that she had joined the *Scharnhorst*, the *Lützow* and the *Nürnberg* in the Narvik area.[74]

Although the Admiralty could not rule out the possibility that the enemy had concentrated his ships in preparation for a break-out into the Atlantic – a possibility which prompted the US Navy to assemble a task force in Casco Bay (Maine) and agree to place it under the command of C-in-C Home Fleet if a break-out took place[75] – the OIC noted on 24 March that except that the *Ucker-mark* (ex-*Altmark*) had been reported in the Far East in November 1942, the Germans had no tankers at sea.[76] By then, moreover, it had received positive indications of an intention to use the ships against the convoys in the Arctic, where the hours of daylight were now rapidly lengthening. On 22 March it learned that the *Tirpitz*, the *Scharnhorst* and the *Lützow* had moved on from Narvik to Altenfjord,[77] and on 24 March the Enigma disclosed that the enemy believed that a convoy had sailed for Russia and was flying reconnaissance patrols to look for it.[78] In these circumstances the Arctic convoys were again suspended after the arrival of RA 53 in the second week of March. The C-in-C Home Fleet continued to be reluctant to use his battle fleet in the Barents Sea; by this time every escort vessel that could be spared from the Home Fleet was being transferred to the western approaches to form support groups for the Atlantic convoys;* and cruisers and destroyers from the Home Fleet were also being attached to the Plymouth Command to operate against blockade-runners and protect convoys against possible attack by the German fleet destroyers which had moved down to the Biscay ports.[79]†

Until the Arctic convoys were resumed in November 1943 the movements of the German main units, though remaining a major preoccupation, produced few alarms. At the end of April the *Nürnberg* was withdrawn to the Baltic, the reason being, as we now

---

* See below, p 565.   † See also above, p 534 and below, pp 542, 544.

72. AIR 41/48, pp 346–347.
73. ADM 223/88, p 112; ADM 223/116, Ultra signal 1155/12 March 1943.
74. ADM 223/116, Ultra signal 1440/14 March 1943.
75. Roskill, op cit, Vol II, p 400.
76. ADM 223/97, OIC SI 552 of 24 March 1943.
77. ADM 223/116, Ultra signal 0020/22 March 1943.
78. eg ADM 223/116, Ultra signal 1310/24 March 1943.
79. Roskill, op cit, Vol II, p 400.

know, her uneconomical fuel consumption.[80] Although there was
no indication of her departure from Narvik, where she had been
seen by PR on 27 March, the Enigma gave sufficient notice of her
departure from Trondheim to enable Coastal Command to sight
her twice, but an attempted strike against her came to nothing.[81]
On 7 May on the suspicion that the *Scheer* had left the Bight,
reconnaissance of the Norwegian coast was ordered; but it was
cancelled before it was carried out and PR then established that she
was still in the Baltic.[82] On 13 May the Enigma disclosed that the
entire squadron in Altenfjord – the *Tirpitz*, the *Scharnhorst*, the
Lützow, 5th and 6th Destroyer Flotillas and 5th Torpedo Boat
Flotilla – had been brought to three hours' notice on the strength of
a false report that a convoy had left Kola; two weeks later the
Enigma added that the squadron would only sail if it had firm
evidence based on air reconnaissance.[83] On 18 June the OIC had
no choice but to issue a warning that the enemy might be
attempting a break-out into the Atlantic when, following an
increase in GAF reconnaissance towards the Denmark Strait, DF
bearings on a signal in the cypher used by the German C-in-C Fleet
(Barracuda) placed it at sea north of North Cape. By 21 June,
however, no further evidence having emerged, it was concluded
that the enemy must have been on exercises.

□

Along the Norwegian coast operations against the movements of
the German main units were the chief call on the activities of the
British strike forces, mainly Coastal Command's No 18 Group, but
they also gave more attention to the enemy's coastal shipping from
the spring of 1943. As well as seeking to disrupt the important
coastal traffic, these activities and the carrier strikes of the Home
Fleet, which were to become more frequent, were intended to tie
down enemy forces, exploiting his known fear of an Allied landing.
At this time this fear was being given increasingly explicit emphasis
in the Enigma traffic in signals like that issued by Dönitz to the
German Navy's coast defence service on 23 March 1943:

'If our enemy attempts to set foot on our coasts, it will first of all be up to
you. Make no mistake – the hour of decision when each one of you will be
called upon to defend honour and homeland, may come very soon. I
expect that true to the glorious traditions of your units, you will display

---

80.   AIR 41/48, p 350 (fn 3).
81.   ibid, pp 351–352; ADM 223/117, Ultra signal 1541/30 April 1943.
82.   AIR 41/48 p 350.
83.   ADM 223/117, Ultra signals 2320/13 May, 1030/15 May, 1645/31 May
       1943.

the utmost vigour and resolution and squeeze the last ounce from yourselves and your weapons to give the enemy a bloody reception and deny him his break into Europe.'[84]

In April and May 1943, when No 18 Group was temporarily reinforced by a Strike Wing of torpedo aircraft, the RAF sank 19 of the total of 22 ships that it destroyed in Norwegian coastal waters during the first half of 1943.[85] For these operations, as for those carried out by Norwegian MTBs based on Lerwick, which now operated frequently in the Leads, and by occasional Home Fleet submarines, the background intelligence was obtained mainly from the non-Sigint sources. As well as keeping NID abreast of changes in the enemy's coastal defences, full details of which had been captured in the Vaagsö raid in 1941,* these sources were providing an increasing amount of information about shipping lanes and sailing patterns. They also disclosed a good deal about the counter-measures and precautions the Germans were taking not only against the attacks on shipping but also against the increasingly frequent raids made by SOE, which were evidently creating considerable strain. Regular reports reached Whitehall on these subjects, which were also referred to in the Enigma decrypts to an increasing extent.

The attacks on the Norwegian coast formed part of an intensified programme of direct air and sea attacks against the enemy's coastal shipping throughout Europe. As before, however, direct attack on this target was hampered by the lack of suitable strike aircraft until April 1943, when the Strike Wing of torpedo aircraft, formed in November 1942, began to operate effectively. Even after that date, moreover, direct attack continued to produce less good results than the aerial minelaying operations of Bomber Command. In the last five months of 1942 the minelaying programme, more successful than ever before, had accounted for 93 enemy ships as compared with 18 sunk by direct air attack.† In the first half of 1943 it produced still better results. The total number of German ships sunk by mine in the twelve months ending June 1943 was 275, most of them in the Baltic; in the same period 68 ships were sunk by direct air attack, and the RAF in 10,767 sorties lost 369 aircraft in direct attacks as compared with 283 minelayers in 6,055 sorties.[86] To a far greater extent than the direct attacks, the minelaying operations depended for their effectiveness on Sigint; they were guided almost entirely by the research carried out by the OIC and GC and CS on Sigint evidence about the enemy's swept ways, shipping channels and minesweeping capabilities.‡ Not less impor-

---

* See above, p 200.   † See above, p 198 Table.   ‡ See above, p 193 et seq.

84.   Naval Headlines, No 627 of 23 March 1943.
85.   Roskill, op cit, Vol II, pp 259, 390.   86.   ibid, p 395.

tant, it was from Sigint, and above all from the naval Enigma, that the Admiralty obtained the indisputable evidence of the scale of enemy losses which had fully persuaded the RAF of the effectiveness of minelaying by the end of 1942 and which now encouraged Bomber Command to maintain the programme in the face of considerable casualties and despite its other commitments.

The operational offensive against enemy coastal shipping was supplemented by successful diplomatic action to reduce the iron ore trade from Bilbao to the Biscay ports. The possibility of attacking the shipping on this route was very limited, but much was known about it from the British Naval Attaché Madrid, and it was as a result of his intervention with the Spanish authorities that the amount of ore shipped fell from 70,000 tons a month in the spring of 1943 to 22,000 tons in June 1943.[87] This reduction followed the decline of one million tons, according to MEW's calculations, in Germany's imports of Swedish iron ore during 1942, as compared with 1941, as a result of Swedish obstruction and of Germany's growing shortage of shipping. At the beginning of March 1943 MEW attributed the shortage to three main causes. Germany's increasingly heavy naval and military commitments were producing a shortage of skilled personnel, slowing down the rate of new construction and making it impossible for her to repair more than a fraction of her damaged shipping. Lack of fuel was immobilising a large number of her diesel vessels. Above all, however, the stringency was due to the heavy losses of ships and disruption of shipping brought about by Allied operations. In June the MEW reported that new construction remained 'negligible by comparison with current losses' and that the enemy's shipping resources were continuing to fall behind his military requirements and his first-priority economic needs.

Meanwhile, the German attack on shipping in British coastal waters had all but ceased. Minelaying and air attacks on shipping dwindled away from the beginning of 1943, the GAF concentrating its exiguous resources in north-west Europe on fighter-bomber attacks on British coastal towns.* It was otherwise with the offensive striking forces which Great Britain could make available in the Channel; their increase now played an important part in putting an end to German efforts to send auxiliary cruisers to sea by the Channel route. After the destruction of Raider B off Cherbourg in October 1942,† the Germans succeeded in the

---

* E-boat raids continued, and even increased; but while the Enigma and PR were still unable to give much assistance against them to the shipping defences, which continued to rely for warnings chiefly on shore-based radar and R/T intercepts, these sources made it clear that the number of E-boats was not being increased.[88]

† See above, pp 190–191.

87. ibid, p 391.   88. ibid, p 254.

following month in moving Raider A up-Channel. The Enigma gave warning that she was at sea off Le Havre, but bad weather saved her from being attacked.[89] In February 1943 they made another attempt to pass a raider down-Channel, but this time they were again frustrated. On 13 February in another illustration of Great Britain's growing control of the Channel – the result of the increase in her striking forces and the continuous reading of the Enigma, which had again, from as long ago as the previous December, provided the essential advance intelligence – *Togo* (Raider K) was so badly damaged by air attack off Boulogne that she had to be withdrawn to the Baltic.[90] She was the last raider to try to break out.

The difficulty the Germans encountered in getting the ships to sea was not the sole reason why they abandoned raiding by auxiliary cruisers. Now that the operational U-boat fleet was expanding fast and able to operate in distant waters, it was ceasing to be worthwhile to convert and man the ships. Furthermore, those raiders that had succeeded in getting to sea in the first half of 1942 were meeting with less success as a result of the improvement in Allied precautions and the growth of Allied activity on the oceans. For the same reasons, finally, they were leading a more hazardous existence. Of the three that were operating after the middle of 1943, the *Stier* (Raider J) was sunk in an engagement with an American liberty ship in September 1942 and the *Thor* (Raider E) was destroyed by fire in Yokohama in November.[91] The third – the *Michel* (Raider H) – survived until October 1943, when she was sunk by a US submarine off Yokohama.[92]

To the declining success of the raiders, as to their destruction, intelligence made next to no contribution. In view of the fact that the Enigma key used by the raiders was unbreakable, there continued to be little evidence about their movements beyond DF of their rare signals, the distress reports of their victims and reports, usually received with great delay, from survivors and German prisoners. Until April 1943, indeed, the OIC was not able to be sure that Raiders E and J had been eliminated; final evidence that this was so came from the diary of a prisoner, taken from an intercepted blockade-runner, and from a censored letter written to another prisoner.[93] An additional source of occasional information

---

89. ibid, p 257; ADM 223/113, Ultra signal 1745/8 November 1942.
90. Roskill, op cit, Vol II, p 387; ADM 223/113, Ultra signal 2301/8 December 1942; ADM 223/114, Ultra signals 1216/19 January, 1937/23 January, 1744/24 January, 1747/27 January, 1928/2 February 1943; ADM 223/115, Ultra signals 0937/8 February, 0118 and 1723/10 February 1943; ADM 223/97, OIC SI 534 of 8 March 1943.
91. Roskill, op cit, Vol II, pp 266, 267 and Appendix M.
92. ibid, pp 411–412.   93. ADM 223/97, OIC SI 570 of 12 April 1943.

was opened up when GC and CS broke the U-boat Enigma.* This became available only from December 1942, too late to help against the activities of Raiders E and J. In April 1943 it disclosed that a U-boat was to transfer mail for Raider H to a Japanese submarine in the southern Indian Ocean,[94] and in August it reported that torpedoes were being sent to the Far East for her.[95] But Sigint threw no further light on her until October, when the decrypt of a diplomatic telegram from Tokyo revealed that a German auxiliary had been sunk by submarine in Japanese waters.[96]

Against Axis blockade-runners, in contrast, the Admiralty now benefited from a considerable increase in intelligence from Sigint sources. From the autumn of 1942 Japanese diplomatic decrypts provided advance information about the blockade-running programme. From the beginning of 1943 advance notice of the movements of some of the ships, obtained from the U-boat Enigma, contributed directly to Allied success against them.

The Admiralty received advance warning from the Japanese diplomatic cypher that the Germans were planning an expanded programme of blockade-running between Europe and the Far East for the winter of 1942–1943. By 28 September 1942 this source had disclosed that ten tankers were preparing to leave Biscay for Japan to collect 150,000 tons of vegetable oil that was vital for the maintenance of Germany's food ration. On the basis of PR of the Biscay ports, and of reports from Japanese diplomatic decrypts, naval reporting officers and other observers about ship movements in the Far East, the Admiralty also had a good idea of which ships were available for the enemy's programme. It confirmed that, over and above those that might be needed for supplying U-boats and raiders, ten tankers were available in Biscay, and it calculated that eight ships might be expected to arrive from the Far East.[97] But until the beginning of 1943 it continued to know nothing about the routes used by the blockade-runners on the high seas, so that it could only guess at their approximate positions on the basis of their reported dates of sailing and their likely speed of advance, while the warnings it received from the Enigma, PR and the SIS of Biscay arrivals and departures continued to be imprecise or delayed.[98] The fact that operations against the blockade-runners met with

---

* See below, pp 551–552.

94. ibid, OIC SI 575 of 19 April 1943.
95. Morgan, *NID History 1939–1942*, pp 236–238.
96. ibid, p 238.
97. ADM 223/112, Ultra signals of 19 or 20 September 1942 (no TOO), 2047/28 September 1942; ADM 223/95, OIC SI 358 of 18 September 1942.
98. ADM 223/95, OIC SI 358 of 18 September 1942; ADM 223/96, OIC SI 401 of 19 October 1942.

greater success from the middle of November 1942 thus owed less to intelligence than to a combination of good luck and increasing Allied activity at sea.

Although the Enigma revealed the movement of escorts from the Biscay ports on 1 November, intensive search by Coastal Command and submarines failed to prevent the arrival of three inward-bound ships in the next few days.[99] And although the Enigma promptly disclosed the arrival of these ships,[100] it did not disclose until 7 November that two outward-bound ships had sailed on 5 November;[101] they were sighted by aircraft, but the Enigma showed they had not been prevented from continuing their passage.[102] But one of them was sunk by a US warship on 21 November – the first interception since 1941 – and just before and after that date other ships fell victim either to ill-luck or to increased Allied operational activity. In the middle of November two ships about to leave for the Far East were sighted and attacked in the Gironde by Coastal Command and prevented from sailing.[103] At the end of the month another outward-bound ship was sunk when she ran into one of the *Torch* convoys,[104] and on 12 December yet another scuttled on running into a north-bound convoy from Gibraltar.[105] No warning had been received of the departure of any of these ships, and the two that had got away from port had evaded the routine Biscay patrols. On 7 December the fact that something was known about the whereabouts and state of readiness of the ships in harbour was again put to good use when a party of Marine commandos, well briefed from PR and other sources, attached limpets to four ships in the Gironde, putting them out of action for several months.[106]

These losses disrupted the blockade-running programme from Biscay for nearly three months. On 24 November 1942, having learned from the Japanese diplomatic cypher that an agreement for the supply of Japanese vegetable oil to Germany had finally been completed, the Admiralty had warned the commands that further sailings by blockade-runners from Biscay were to be expected in the near future.[107] On 22 December, however, the decrypt of a signal from the Japanese Naval Attaché in Rome disclosed that the

---

99.   ADM 223/112, Ultra signal 0556/1 November 1942; ADM 223/96, OIC SI 425 of 9 November 1942.
100. ADM 223/112, Ultra signal 1615/3 November 1942.
101. ADM 223/113, Ultra signal 1147/7 November 1942.
102. ADM 223/96, OIC SI 425 of 9 November 1942.
103. ADM 223/112, Ultra signal 1201/17 October 1942; ADM 223/96, OIC SI 432 of 16 November 1942.
104. AIR 41/47, *The RAF in Maritime War*, Vol II, pp 457–461.
105. ibid, p 461.   106.   Roskill, op cit, Vol II, p 275.
107. ADM 223/113, Ultra signal 1735/24 November 1942.

Germans had postponed further sailings to Japan; and during January and February 1943, as we now know, no ships left Biscay.[108]

Towards the end of January 1943 the Japanese diplomatic decrypts yielded further information about the blockade-running programme. Sailings from the Far East would be suspended for an unknown period from early in February. Sailings from Biscay would be suspended after the end of March until October. But no effort was to be spared in despatching ships before the suspensions took effect.[109] Then, early in March, the decrypt of a signal from the Japanese Naval Attaché in Berlin reported that four ships were to leave Biscay at the end of the month under strengthened air and U-boat escort. It was followed by the arrival of four German fleet destroyers in Bordeaux about 8 March and by an increase in FW 200 reconnaissance of the approaches to Biscay from mid-March.[110]

By that time Coastal Command had instituted systematic air searches of Biscay and the cruiser *Newfoundland* had been ordered to Plymouth. But except that the Enigma disclosed by 18 March that the four destroyers had been brought to short notice,[111] no further intelligence had been received when an outward-bound blockade-runner was sighted by an air-sea rescue plane on 29 March. Identified as the *Himalaya* from PR photographs, she mistook for British warships the four German destroyers, which had sailed to escort an inward-bound ship, and returned to La Pallice.[112] Later on 29 March the Enigma indicated that three other blockade-runners had been preparing to leave Biscay on 28 March.[113] Not till 4 April, however, did PR of the Biscay ports establish that these ships had sailed;[114] all three cleared Biscay, only one of them being sighted.[115] On 9 April the RAF detected that the *Himalaya* had sailed again.[116] There had again been no advance notice of her movement, but on 11 April the Enigma disclosed that she had been ordered to return to port so as to draw attention away from an inward-bound ship.[117] She was attacked by the RAF on 10 April and never sailed again.[118] She was the last ship to attempt the outward passage in the 1942–1943 programme.

108.   Roskill, op cit, Vol II, p 484.
109.   ADM 223/114, Ultra signal 1805/23 January 1943.
110.   AIR 41/48, pp 302–303.
111.   ADM 223/116, Ultra signal 0924/18 March 1943.
112.   ibid, Ultra signals 0925, 1334 and 1845/31 March, 1254/1 April, 1210/4 April 1943.
113.   ibid, Ultra signal 2000/29 March 1943.   114.   AIR 41/48, p 307.
115.   ibid, p 307 and fn.   116.   ibid, p 310.
117.   ibid, p 313 and fn; ADM 223/116, Ultra signal 1125/11 April 1943.
118.   AIR 41/48, pp 311–313; ADM 223/97, OIC SI 570 of 12 April 1943.

Although intelligence remained unable to give advance notice of departures from Biscay, there had been a considerable improvement since the end of 1942 in intelligence about the whereabouts of the blockade-runners on the high seas. During November 1942 the Enigma had provided for the first time details of the limits, admittedly fairly wide, within which the blockade-runners shaped course between Biscay and 40°S; in November 1942 and again in February 1943 these were promulgated by the Admiralty to all relevant Ultra recipients.[119] Still more important was the fact that from the middle of December GC and CS's success in breaking the U-boat Enigma key (Shark), and thus in decrypting signals to the Atlantic U-boats for the first time since the previous February, had opened up a source of information about the movements of individual ships. The Shark decrypts disclosed the approximate positions of the ships in advance by prohibiting attacks by U-boats on single merchant ships beween certain dates in stated areas. From time to time, moreover, U-boats were ordered to rendezvous with blockade-runners, and on these occasions the decrypts gave the assumed name and a detailed description of the disguise adopted by the ship as well as exact positions.*

It was almost certainly on the basis of this type of intelligence that, although two of the three ships which got through Biscay early in April reached the Far East, the third (the *Portland*) was sunk by a Free French cruiser in the south Atlantic on 13 April:[120] at the end of March the Shark decrypts revealed that attacks by U-boats on single ships were prohibited within the passage limits in that area,[121] and on 8 April they gave a less imprecise indication of the position of one of these ships.[122] From the beginning of 1943, moreover, the Shark decrypts proved invaluable for operations against blockade-runners bound for Biscay from the Far East. One such ship (the *Ramses*) had been intercepted in the Indian Ocean without benefit of intelligence on 28 November.[123] On 31 December 1942, when no ship had reached Biscay since early November but the OIC believed that two or three others were on passage,[124] it was learned from the Shark decrypts that an inward-bound ship escorted by U-boats would cross 10°W at about 2000 on 1

---

* But the Enigma key (Sunfish) used by the blockade-runners themselves for their occasional transmissions, as well as by supply U-boats and supply ships in Far Eastern waters, was not to be broken till August 1943, see Volume III.

119.   ADM 223/113, Ultra signals 1230/13 November, 1531/15 November 1942; ADM 223/115, 1318/14 February 1943.
120.   Roskill, op cit, Vol II, p 409.
121.   ADM 223/116, Ultra signal 1334/31 March 1943.
122.   ibid, Ultra signal 1023/8 April 1943.
123.   ADM 223/96, OIC SI 447 of 30 November 1942.
124.   ibid, OIC SI 471 of 28 December 1942.

January.[125] An air search followed which sighted the ship (the *Rhakotis*) and homed HMS *Scylla* on to her. She scuttled.[126] On 14 February the Enigma again disclosed that U-boats had been forbidden to attack independents within the passage area between 10° and 35°N up to 23 February, and by 17 February it had added that the ship in question was the tanker *Hohenfriedberg*, which was known to have left Singapore on 19 December. By 25 February it had provided her approximate position, no less than seven U-boats having been ordered to rendezvous with her and bring her in 'at all costs'.[127] On 26 February, as a result, she was sighted by intensive air patrols and sunk by HMS *Sussex*.[128]

At the end of February, in the light of the improvement in the intelligence and of these successes in exploiting it by better co-operation between air and surface forces, it was decided to station a cruiser and Home Fleet destroyers at Plymouth.[129] But the next casualties to inward-bound blockade-runners owed nothing to intelligence. The now familiar restrictions on U-boats, this time for the period up to 26 March, were again decrypted on 1 March. But one of the ships thus provided for, the *Dogger Bank*, had made faster time than the Germans expected; she was thus already north of the restricted area when on 3 March – though this was not known till the end of the war – she was sunk by a German U-boat.[130] A week later the *Karin* (ex *Kota Nopan*) scuttled on being intercepted by US warships in 7°S, but no intelligence had been received about her departure for Europe: indeed nothing was learnt of her movements until, on 27 March, U-boats were told that they might meet her.[131]

By 11 March, without knowledge of these two enemy losses, the OIC calculated that only six blockade-runners were now likely to try to reach Biscay before the end of April, rather than the 13 it had expected: high-grade Sigint had recently reaffirmed that sailings from Japan were to be suspended from mid-February.[132] On 15 March the Japanese diplomatic traffic added the further informa-

125. ADM 223/113, Ultra signal 1435/31 December 1942.
126. AIR 41/47, pp 462, 464; ADM 223/96, OIC SI 469 of 21 December 1942; Roskill, op cit, Vol II, p 276.
127. ADM 223/96, OIC SI 469 of 21 December 1942; ADM 223/114, Ultra signal 1805/23 January 1943; ADM 223/115, Ultra signals 1720/9 February, 1318/14 February, 1148/17 February, 0101/21 February, 2131/23 February, 1726/24 February, 1855/25 February 1943.
128. AIR 41/47, pp 465–466; Roskill, op cit, Vol II, p 408; ADM 223/116, Ultra signal 2150/26 February 1943.
129. Roskill, op cit, Vol II, p 408.
130. ADM 223/97, OIC SI 570 of 12 April 1943; Roskill, op cit, Vol II, pp 409–410.
131. ZTPGU 9378.
132. ADM 223/97, OIC SI 537 of 11 March 1943.

tion that on 11 March four blockade-runners which had already left the Far East had been recalled at Germany's request, owing to the increasing dangers of the passage of the Atlantic; and the OIC, while guessing that such ships as had already reached the Atlantic would continue their journey, could no longer say how many might be expected.[133] Its uncertainty increased towards the end of March. It then learned from a delayed Shark decrypt that the U-boats had been instructed on 4 March to refrain from attacks in the restricted area and informed that 'several' Axis ships were to enter it in the near future. There was no means of knowing whether and to what extent this intelligence had been superseded by the more recent Japanese information.[134] On 29 and 30 March, however, the immediate situation was cleared up by Enigma decrypts which led directly to attacks on two inward-bound ships. On 29 March the Shark decrypts contained U-boat sightings of a ship off Greenland together with orders to U-boats to refrain from attacking her; HMS *Glasgow* sank the *Regensburg* north of Iceland the following day.[135] This was the first attempt to pass a blockade-runner through the Denmark Strait since 1939.[136] On 30 March Shark disclosed that the four German destroyers in Biscay had left port to rendezvous with an inward-bound blockade-runner and that a U-boat had met the ship in 41°N 38°W.[137] This ship, the *Pietro Orsoleo*, was sighted by air on 31 March, when the submarine *Shad* was ordered to take station at the entrance to the known swept channel across Biscay. On 1 April, as was subsequently revealed by the Enigma, the *Shad* scored hits on the ship and on one of the destroyers. But she failed to stop them reaching the Gironde, where PR confirmed their arrival.[138]

The *Pietro Orsoleo*, the first blockade-runner to reach Europe since the beginning of November 1942, was also the last ship to reach Europe in the 1942–1943 season. By the beginning of April the Enigma showed that the Germans, unaware that she had sunk on 10 March, had ordered the *Karin* to return via the Denmark Strait,[139] and the Home Fleet maintained patrols there for some weeks in case other ships attempted that route.[140] None did. From the beginning of April precautions were increased in the Biscay area also, in the belief that at least one more inward-bound ship

133.   ADM 223/116, Ultra signal 1608/15 March 1943.
134.   ADM 223/116, Ultra signal 1242/27 March 1943.
135.   ADM 223/116, Ultra signals 1544 and 2331/29 March 1943; Roskill, op cit, Vol II, p 410.
136.   ADM 223/97, OIC SI 558 of 5 April 1943.
137.   ADM 223/106, Ultra signal 0925/31 March 1943; ZTPGU 9407.
138.   AIR 41/48, pp 306, 307; ADM 223/116, Ultra signal 1644/1 April 1943.
139.   ADM 223/116, Ultra signals 1116/30 March, 1056 and 2220/6 April 1943.
140.   Roskill, op cit, Vol II, p 410.

was at large. On 9 April, when PR showed that the four destroyers and the *Himalaya* had sailed, it was conjectured that the destroyers would pick up an inward-bound ship on dropping the *Himalaya*, and priority was given to attacking the *Himalaya* in the absence of any firm evidence about another ship.[141] On 10 April, however, the day on which the *Himalaya* was bombed and ordered back to port, the inward-bound ship was sunk by HMS *Adventure*, who had been diverted in an attempt to intercept the *Himalaya*.[142] The ship, identified as the *Irene* (ex-*Silva Plana*), had not been among those reported to have left the Far East.[143] As the Japanese report of 15 March about the recall of four ships to the Far East proved to be correct, she was the last ship in the enemy's 1942–1943 sailing programme to attempt the inward passage.

At the end of April 1943 MEW noted that the 1942–1943 blockade-running programme had been conspicuously less effective than that of the previous year. It estimated that whereas up to June 1942, mostly since January of that year, Germany had received between 55,000 and 60,000 tons of cargo from the Far East, she had received only 28,500 tons of rubber since the autumn of 1942, less than one-third of what she had tried to import, and that Allied successes against the blockade-runners had cost her about 30,000 tons of rubber, 25,000 tons of oils and fats and smaller quantities of tin, tungsten and tea.[144] In July it noted with satisfaction that Germany had been frustrated in her attempt to relieve her supply deficiencies by blockade-running.[145] And, as we have seen, this Allied success is largely attributable to intelligence. More losses were incurred by the inward-bound ships than by those which left Europe for the Far East and, of the total losses, the bulk was sustained after the end of 1942; and the influence of intelligence is easily detectable in each of these directions. Between the autumn of 1942 and April 1943 17 blockade-runners left Biscay, of which ten made the passage, three turned back and four were sunk; but only five of the 17 sailings occurred after the end of 1942, only two of the five succeeded and intelligence played some part in stopping two of the sailings and sinking the third ship. In the same period 15 ships attempted the passage from the Far East. Of these seven were sunk and four recalled; but of the seven losses no less than six occurred after the beginning of 1943, after which date only one ship got through.[146] And four of the six sinkings were brought about directly or indirectly by the fact that it was above all against the inward-bound blockade-runners that, thanks mainly to the breaking of the

---

141.   AIR 41/48, pp 309 fn 3, 310, 311.
142.   ibid, p 314; ZTPGU 10526, 10803, 10804.
143.   ADM 223/97, OIC SI 558 of 5 April 1943.
144.   FO 837/17, MEW Weekly Intelligence Summary No 63 of 29 April 1943.
145.   ibid, No 72A of 3 July 1943.   146.   Roskill, op cit, Vol II, Appendix N.

Shark Enigma, the beginning of 1943 had seen a striking improvement in the supply of operational intelligence.

□

Useful as it was against the blockade-runners, the breaking of the Shark Enigma was of far greater importance for the contribution it made, at a crucial juncture, to the struggle with the U-boats in the Atlantic.

The operational consequences of GC and CS's inability to read the U-boat traffic after the beginning of February 1942 had been less than drastic for some months. During the first half of 1942 the U-boats had been concentrated close to the eastern seaboard of the Americas, and the density of shipping and the lack of defences there were such that it may be doubted whether better intelligence about their movements and dispositions would have helped to reduce their successes.* From June 1942 till the end of the year, moreover, large numbers of U-boats continued to operate against independent shipping, mostly in remote areas in which it would have been impossible to provide escorts or adopt evasive routeing even if good intelligence had been available; the U-boats were still sinking more independents than ships in convoy during these months. To these facts must be added the consideration that when the U-boats were not operating against convoys they worked more independently of orders from the U-boat Command, so that less operational intelligence would have been derived from the decryption of the signals to them.

From July 1942, however, the sinking of Allied ships in convoy again reached a serious level. In August, September, October and November 1942, respectively, 50, 29, 29 and 39 ships were lost in attacks on convoys, in addition to 51, 58, 54 and 70 independents.† From November 1942, moreover, the strain on Allied merchant shipping and escorts was enormously intensified by the demands of the Tunisian fighting. To begin with, the sailing of the *Torch* convoys necessitated the diversion of the shipping that plied between the United Kingdom and the Cape; and since this shipping was sent up and down the east coast of the Americas before and after crossing the north and south Atlantic, the diversion added to the volume of north Atlantic movements. Thereafter, instead of obtaining the use of the Mediterranean after a quick campaign, the Allies were forced by the success of the Axis holding operation in Tunisia not only to continue to use the Cape route, but also to sail extra convoys to north Africa and find escorts for them

---

* See above, p 230 et seq.   † See Appendix 8.

at the expense of the north Atlantic convoys.[147]* To make matters worse, the opportunities of the U-boats on the north Atlantic route were thus expanding at a time when, as the Admiralty estimated by the beginning of 1943, the number of operational U-boats had reached nearly 230 and the number in commission was about double that figure.[149]

In all these circumstances, Whitehall was deeply apprehensive by the end of 1942 that unless they could be reduced appreciably, sinkings by the U-boats would continue to outstrip the construction of new Allied tonnage, and that the available UK-controlled shipping and the new tonnage promised by the US would together be insufficient for the minimum imports – 27 million tons per annum – required to maintain rations and sustain industry in the United Kingdom.[150] It thus comes as no surprise to learn that the Admiralty looked with mounting impatience to GC and CS for a break-through in the struggle against the U-boat Enigma, and regarded this as being of crucial importance for its own struggle against the U-boats. On 22 November 1942, the OIC urged GC and CS to focus 'a little more attention' on the Shark problem: the U-boat campaign was 'the one campaign which Bletchley Park are not at present influencing to any marked extent – and it is the only one in which the war can be lost unless BP *do* help. I do not think that this is any exaggeration'. Nor is there any mistaking the relief with which, together with anxiety that every precaution should be taken to keep the fact secret, the First Sea Lord informed the US Chief of Naval Operations on 13 December that, at long last the four-wheel Enigma key (called Shark at GC and CS) used by the U-boats since the previous February had yielded to GC and CS's efforts.†

It by no means follows from the Admiralty's impatience that GC and CS's success in reading the U-boat Enigma from the end of 1942 actually played a decisive part in defeating the second great U-boat campaign against the convoys which was unleashed in December 1942 and called off in May 1943. The presumption, to quote a German historian of the U-boat war, that but for that success, and the use to which it was put, 'the turning point in the

---

* The planning for *Torch* had assumed the need for 66 sailings a month in November and December 1942 and January 1943, and 30 a month thereafter. In the event, 105 sailings a month were necessary to the end of January 1943, 92 in February, 75 in March and 38 in April.[148]

† See above, p 233.

147.   Howard, *Grand Strategy*, Vol IV (1972), p 291.

148.   ibid, p 291.

149.   ADM 223/97, OIC SI 504 of 1 February 1943; ADM 223/107, NID 01730/15 March 1943; Op-20-G History, Vol X, p 38.

150.   Howard, op cit, Vol IV, pp 292, 296.

Battle of the Atlantic would not have come as it did in May 1943 but months, may be many months, later'[151] is naturally powerful. There is, for one thing, the fact that, while total sinkings by U-boats were increasing again until the Shark key was broken in December 1942, they thereafter declined: November 1942 turned out to be the month in which the U-boats sank more merchant shipping than in any other month in the war.[152] Furthermore, although half a year was then to pass before the U-boats retreated from the convoy routes, and although they came close to gaining the upper hand before they retreated, the very fact that the struggle was so prolonged and so finely balanced suggests that the ability to read their communications must have been an asset of crucial importance to the Allies. Still more to the point, the Admiralty did not doubt at the time that this was so. In March 1943, in personal signals for the CNO in Washington about Ultra security precautions, the First Sea Lord stressed how anxious he was that 'we should not risk what is so invaluable to us', and in April, resisting the US proposals for using the Shark intelligence for attacks on the rendezvous points of the supply U-boats, he argued that 'if our Z [Enigma] information failed us at the present time it would, I am sure, result in our shipping losses going up by anything from 50 to 100%'. But the battle which was fought in the Atlantic between December 1942 and May 1943 was the most prolonged and complex battle in the history of naval warfare, and when its outcome clearly hinged on many factors it is not easy to establish the extent to which it was influenced by the Allied decryption of the signals of the U-boat Command.

There is no difficulty in understanding the value the Admiralty placed on the decrypts. The great bulk of them consisted of immediate operational intelligence about the departure and return of U-boats, the numbers and types of U-boats at sea, the movements and dispositions of their patrol groups and their operational orders. That the operational decrypts were so numerous and informative was a consequence of the U-boat Command's control of the north Atlantic offensive, a control which was even more rigorous now than in 1941. Not only did returning U-boats always signal their expected time of arrival; every outward-bound U-boat reported on clearing Biscay or, if leaving from Norway or the Baltic, after crossing 60°N. Except when a U-boat sailed for a special task or a distant area, it received its destination point and its operational orders by W/T after it had put to sea; these were matters which had to be settled in the light of the latest situation

151.   J Rohwer, Ultra and the Battle of the Atlantic: the German View, Presentation to the US Naval Academy, October 1977, pp 12, 13.
152.   Roskill, op cit, Vol II, p 485.

and of which all U-boats at sea had to be informed. No U-boat could deviate from its orders without requesting and receiving permission, and without requesting and receiving permission none could begin its return passage. In every signal it transmitted the U-boat was required to quote its present position; if it failed to do so, or if it did not transmit for several days, it was ordered to report its position. To each of its signals, again, the U-boat was expected to append a statement of the amount of fuel on hand.* As well as determining the order to a U-boat to return to base, this information enabled the U-boat Command to exercise detailed supervision of the refuelling of U-boats from supply U-boats at sea.† For this undertaking it signalled the refuelling rendezvous well ahead of time and issued precise instructions as to which U-boats were to be serviced by what amounts at what hours, and on completion the supply U-boat confirmed that the orders had been carried out and reported the state of its remaining supplies.

The control of the U-boat Command over the U-boats while they were searching for and attacking convoys was no less complete. It ordered the formation and re-formation of the patrol lines between specified geographical positions at regular intervals, addressing by name each U-boat commander who was to take a place in a line and giving him his exact position in it. It informed each line of U-boats what to expect in the way of approaching convoys and, in addition, supplied for the attention of all U-boats at sea a steady stream of situation reports and general orders. When a convoy was sighted the Command decided the time, the direction and the order of attack. The exercise of this degree of remote control meant that in return for its own situation reports – and over and above the homing signals they transmitted on medium frequencies for the benefit of other U-boats – it required U-boats in contact with the target to transmit on high frequencies detailed descriptions of the situation. Only when interception conditions made it difficult to receive high frequency signals was its control relaxed, and even then it normally nominated other U-boats as W/T relays in an effort to retain some supervision over the attack.

---

* The following is an example of a decrypt of the German text of a U-boat signal and its full translation:

Von SCHULZE:

Qu 8852 1 Dampfer, 1 Tanker wahrscheinlich. Am 15.10. Tanker Fackel. Stehe 8967 69 cbm 2 plus 1 Aale *SW* 3 bis 4 996 mb plus 21
An Bef Ubte.

From: Schulze (U 432)
To: Admiral Commanding U-boats
In square 8852 have sunk one steamship (for certain) and one tanker probably. Set one tanker on fire on October 15th. My present position is square 8967. Have 69 cubic metres of fuel oil left. Have two (air) and one (electric) torpedoes left. Wind south-west, force 3 to 4. Pressure 996 millibars. Temperature 21 degrees (above freezing point).

† For the introduction of supply U-boats see above, p. 229.

To carry the enormous burden of wireless traffic generated by this system the U-boat Command developed a signals network which, for complexity, flexibility and efficiency, was probably unequalled in the history of military communications. By the same token, however, it could not prevent the interception of the traffic or conceal its signals routines from the attention of Allied Traffic Analysis and, from the time when GC and CS broke the Shark key, it presented the Allies with an unprecedentedly rich flow of operational intelligence. Some of the uses to which the intelligence could be put will be obvious from the foregoing summary of its contents. The failure of U-boats to respond to requests to report their positions provided a nearly infallible guide to U-boat casualties. From their reports of the amount of fuel on hand their type could be identified when it was not already known. Above all, the Tracking Rooms* possessed a reliable basis for estimating the number and whereabouts of all U-boats at sea and for establishing the intentions of the U-boat Command. Nor was their knowledge limited to the mere texts of the decrypts. These were in such continuous supply that in the Tracking Rooms, as at GC and CS, there were men who acquired so great a familiarity with the temper, habits and character of the U-boat Command staff and of the individual U-boat commanders that they could anticipate what the enemy would and would not do – could judge which members of his HQ staff were on duty, and which of his U-boat commanders were least effective, and even detect misunderstandings between the staff and the commanders before the enemy had cleared them up – and route Allied convoys accordingly.

In one respect, however, and one that constituted a serious handicap for so long as the Allies were on the defensive and valued the Enigma chiefly for the contribution it made to their ability to route convoys clear of the U-boat positions, the knowledge of the Tracking Rooms was far from perfect on account of delays in breaking the settings. On 13 December 1942, when GC and CS reported that it had broken the Shark key by means which led it to believe that the traffic would soon be read with some regularity, its confidence had not been misplaced. By the beginning of 1943, after quickly breaking the settings for eight days of November 1942 and

---

* For the establishment of the Tracking Room in Washington see above, p 48. The Canadian authorities did not share in the combined Anglo-American programme for breaking the Shark settings but their intercept stations and DF organisation had made an indispensable contribution to the Allied north Atlantic Sigint network since the early days of the war. In May 1943 as well as receiving the intelligence summaries issued by Whitehall to the naval commands at home and overseas, the Tracking Room in Ottawa began to receive a full service of Enigma decrypts and from that time it carried on a completely free exchange of ideas and information by direct signal link with the Tracking Room in the OIC.[153]

153. Beesly, *Very Special Intelligence* (1977), p 169.

the early part of December, it was on some days reading the traffic in time for it to be of operational value. Thereafter, in partnership with the cryptanalytic branch of the US Navy Department, which made an ever-increasing contribution to the joint effort, it steadily completed its mastery over the Shark settings.* This mastery was to be total by August 1943, from which time till the end of the war all the traffic for each day was read as a matter of course with little or no delay. During the first half of 1943, however, while the traffic was read with delays that were sometimes less than 24 hours, and rarely exceeded 72 hours except on days when the settings proved to be unusually stubborn or intractable, such days unfortunately were not uncommon. By 17 February, for example, the settings had not been broken for ten days in January, and no traffic had been read since 10 February. And between 10 March and the end of June the settings for a further 22 days were either not broken at all or broken only after a long delay.[154]

To make matters worse, the need to decode the disguise that was added to all geographical positions referred to in the Shark decrypts created uncertainty and further delay from time to time. The 'address book' system introduced by the U-boat Command for this purpose in November 1941[†] was found to be still in use when the Shark key was recovered; it remained in use until the end of the war. Until the spring of 1944, however, it proved impossible to establish whether or not the periodic changes in the method of coding the book were carried out on a fixed principle. GC and CS then discovered that there was a fixed principle, and developed a partial solution to it, a few weeks before a copy of the book was finally captured from U 505. But throughout 1943 every change of code for positions given in the Enigma decrypts had to be solved by *ad hoc* research; and although the OIC and GC and CS, working in close co-operation on such evidence as DF findings, contact reports from Allied forces, and mistakes on the part of the enemy, commonly got the right solution without great delay, they were unable to avoid uncertainty or error in some cases, particularly in the early stage of a new code-period.[155]

Delay in reading and in elucidating the Shark signals reduced the contribution of the decrypts to effective evasive routeing for a number of reasons. A convoy could at best cover 240 miles in 24 hours, whereas the U-boats might cover between 320 and 370 miles in the same period. A delay of as much as three days in learning that U-boats had been ordered to move to new positions could thus

---

* See Appendix 19.   † See Appendix 9.

154.   Dir/C Archive, 2223 of 7 February, 2691 of 23 March, 2724 of 25 March, 2788 of 31 March 1943; Op-20-G History, Vol II, p 4 fn.
155.   Beesly, op cit, p 164.

mean that the intelligence was received too late to be of use in diverting convoys.[156] Moreover, it became increasingly likely that this would be so throughout the period from December 1942 to May 1943 because there was a steady increase from 212 to 240 in the total number of operational U-boats,[157] and because the proportion operating on the northern convoy routes rose still more sharply. At the end of 1942 25 were operating between Iceland and Newfoundland and 40 in the Biscay-Gibraltar-Azores area,[158] but on the northern routes alone the number on station rarely dropped much below 60 after the beginning of March 1943. At the same time, and most particularly from the beginning of March, the Allied convoy cycles had to be shortened to carry the increasing flow of American troops and war material to the United Kingdom. And if the combination of increasingly numerous U-boats and increasingly frequent convoys progressively accentuated the need of the Allies for up-to-date intelligence about U-boat movements and dispositions – and thus progressively reduced the length of delay beyond which the Shark decrypts ceased to be of operational value for evasive routeing – another development, one that was not so obvious at the time, told in the same direction. The German Navy's cryptanalytic service (the B-Dienst) was supplying the U-boat Command with accurate intelligence about convoy movements.

Throughout 1942 the B-Dienst had achieved considerable success against the British Naval Cypher No 3, known to the B-Dienst as the 'convoy cypher'.* On 15 December 1942 changes introduced to this and other British cyphers interrupted the German programme; nor is there any doubt that the improvement in the Allied position in the battle of the Atlantic during the next few weeks owed as much to this enemy setback on the cryptanalytic front as it did to GC and CS's success against the Shark key, with which it so fortuitously coincided. By February 1943, however, after switching most of its cryptanalytic effort on to it, the B-Dienst was again breaking the 'convoy cypher'. Thereafter, until 10 June 1943, when Naval Cypher No 3 ceased to be used, it was again able to read on most days the daily Admiralty U-boat disposition signal and could thus forecast the areas through which the convoys would probably be routed. In addition, it regularly read other convoy traffic, not excluding the orders diverting convoys which the Allied

---

* See Appendix 1 (Part (1)).

156.   ibid, pp 196–197.
157.   ADM 223/96, OIC SI 478 of 4 January 1943; ADM 223/97, OIC SI 559 of 5 April 1943; Roskill, op cit, Vol II, p 475.
158.   ADM 223/96, OIC SI 463 of 14 December, 468 of 21 December 1942; Beesly, op cit, p 155.

commands were basing on the decrypts of the Shark traffic; and it did so on occasions so quickly that it was providing movement information from 10 to 20 hours in advance. Nor did the U-boat Command fail to utilise the results of cryptanalysis, which for it as for Whitehall were more plentiful and far more valuable than the reports obtained from other sources. An authoritative German history of the U-boat war makes it clear that nearly all the U-boat dispositions ordered in this period by the U-boat Command were based either directly on the B-Dienst's decrypts or, when these were delayed or incomplete, on the knowledge of convoy periods and routes which the U-boat Command had built up from its study of earlier decrypts.[159]

Between February and June 1943 the battle of the Atlantic hinged to no small extent on the changing fortunes of a continuing trial of cryptographic and cryptanalytic resourcefulness between the B-Dienst and the Allies. It was a struggle in which the Allies prevailed in the end. In part they owed their victory to a long-standing anxiety on the part of the signals security authorities in the Admiralty about the cryptographic security of their cyphers, particularly the heavily used 'convoy cypher' – an anxiety which had induced them to plan, with the aid of GC and CS, from as early as April 1941, the introduction in the long term of more secure cyphers, and also to prepare a number of stop-gap measures to improve the security of the existing cyphers. They owed it also to the cryptanalytic success of GC and CS against the German cyphers; from the beginning of 1943 GC and CS's decrypts of 'officer-only' signals from the U-boat Command in the Shark key presented positive proof that the B-Dienst was reading the 'convoy cypher'.[160] It was as a result of these revelations that on 10 April 1943 the Admiralty took emergency action to advance the date for the introduction of the stop-gap measures it had prepared.* In the U-boat Command suspicions about the security of the Enigma were being revived at this time, but, unlike the Admiralty, it was ultimately persuaded, once again, that these suspicions were

---

* See Appendix 1 (Part (i)).

159.   Naval Historical Branch, BR 305 (2), The U-boat War in the Atlantic (German Naval History Series), Vol II, eg pp 89, 109. See also Beesly, op cit, p 161.

160.   DEFE 3/185, ZTPG 66769 of 23 July 1942; DEFE 3/199, ZTPG 80569 of 13 October 1942; DEFE 3/200, ZTPG 81422 of 20 October 1942; DEFE 3/585, ZTPGM 5772 of 18 December 1942; DEFE 3/586, ZTPGM 6287 of 28 December 1942; ZTPGU 7420 of 27 February, 8669 of 18 March, 10852 of 11 April, 13898 of 7 May, 14228 of 11 May 1943; ZTPG(T) of 0935/24 September 1942.

unfounded.* It must be emphasised, however, that it was not until June 1943, too late to influence the outcome of the great convoy battles, that the Admiralty was able to replace Naval Cypher No 3 and finally put an end to the benefit the U-boat Command had for so long derived from the B-Dienst's reading of the 'convoy cypher'.

In the light of these many considerations – the delays that accompanied the reading of the Enigma; the increasing frequency of convoys; the growing number of U-boats; the extent to which the U-boat Command was itself being helped by Sigint – it is easy to see why convoys continued to fall victim to U-boat attack in the months after the Shark key had been recovered. It is easy to see, indeed, that the value of the Enigma to evasive routeing must be judged not by its failure to eliminate disasters to convoys, but by the extent to which it reduced the frequency and the scale of the disasters. It may be added that since a large proportion of Allied shipping losses was sustained by a few convoys, and so much so that the severe mauling of a convoy was the equivalent of a lost battle on land, its value would still have been enormous even if its influence had been decisive only from time to time. But for all that we have stressed that there were delays in acquiring it, and despite the fact that they reduced its impact, we can see that its influence was more pervasive than this.

By no means all of the many convoys that escaped detection between 1 January and 31 May – nearly a half of those that sailed[†] – owed their escape directly to the Enigma. Some were successfully diverted when the decrypts were running late and the Allied Tracking Rooms were on that account 'blind', just as some were sighted when the decrypts were virtually current. Whether or not a gap in the breaking of the Shark settings coincided with a redisposition of the U-boat patrol lines was a matter of sheer chance, and not even advance intelligence about U-boat movements could guarantee that convoys would not be sighted by

---

* For it, as for the Allies, it was difficult, in a series of movements as complicated as those that made up the battle of the Atlantic, firmly to associate the enemy's orders and dispositions with the enemy's possession of Sigint unless he explicitly referred to decrypts in signals that were themselves decrypted. But the B-Dienst was not able to read the Allied Ultra traffic, which, like the Enigma 'officer-only' signals that were being decrypted at GC and CS, was used for disseminating the products of cryptanalysis. The U-boat Command, after again requesting an investigation into whether its disappointments might be due to the insecurity of the Enigma, accepted the assurance that the cypher could not have been compromised and concluded that the Allies were obtaining their intelligence about U-boat dispositions by other means – partly from French agents of the SIS, but mainly through the use of ASV and DF.[161] The Enigma showed that whereas at the end of December the Command was urging the U-boats to disregard Allied radar as being 'ineffective',[162] it was on 5 March, as a result of its suspicions, ordering them to ensure that their patrol lines were concealed from Allied airborne radar.[163]

† See Appendix 8.

161. BR 305 (2), p 88; Roskill, op cit, Vol II, p 364; Beesly, op cit, pp 162–163.
162. ZTPGU 1425.   163. BR 305 (2), p 89.

U-boats on passage. By no means every convoy that was sighted by
U-boat in these months suffered heavy losses; and nine out of the 38
that were contacted got through unscathed.* Like the convoys and
their escorts, the U-boats were hampered by operational conditions. The winter of 1942–43 was exceptionally violent, the ice
coming down almost as far as Newfoundland and hurricanes and
severe gales prevailing throughout the north Atlantic. Not less
important, they had to contend with the convoy escorts and with
the fact that the increase in their own numbers was being countered
by significant additions and improvements to the Allied defences.
But if the battle in the north Atlantic was more than a duel between
the cryptanalysts and intelligence staffs of the two sides – was an
unremitting struggle in terrible weather conditions to sink or save
ships – one conclusion still stands out when its course is reviewed
up to the end of March 1943. But for the contribution of the
Enigma to evasive routeing, the planned mass assaults of the
U-boats would have achieved in January and February 1943 the
enormous success that they secured only in March.

□

The decline in the number of Allied ships sunk in convoy in
December 1942 – 19 were lost compared with 39 in November
1942 – owed something to the fact that U-boats had been diverted
from the north Atlantic against operation *Torch*. It clearly owed
something to other factors also, for on the one hand the diversion
had taken place from the middle of November and, on the other
hand, the number of U-boats between Iceland and Newfoundland,
which had dropped from 17 to 10 between 2 November and 16
November, had climbed back to 21 by 14 December.[164] Equally
clearly, these other factors did not include the Enigma; the first
break into the Shark settings did not come till the middle of the
month, and the delay in breaking them was initially considerable.
Thus on 25 December no settings had been broken for the previous
six days. From the evening of 26 December, however, GC and CS
succeeded in reading the U-boat traffic for the period from noon on
25 December to noon on 1 January virtually currently. This short
period of near-currency began too late to avert the month's biggest
setback. Convoy ON 154, sighted on 26 December, lost no less than
14 ships.[165] But it provided the Tracking Rooms, for the first time
since January 1942, with the basis for forward assessments of the

---

* See Appendix 8.

164. ADM 223/96, OIC SI 415 of 2 November, 430 of 16 November, 463 of 14
December 1942.
165. BR 305 (2), p 69.

general situation and reasoned estimates of the future movements of the U-boats, and together with the fact that the settings were broken with considerable regularity, if with more or less delay, for the next five weeks, it was this which enabled the Enigma to make a decisive contribution to the further decline in U-boat successes that occurred during January 1943.*

During December the Shark decrypts had given warning that the U-boat Command was preparing to step up its offensive by revealing that it was introducing W/T arrangements for 'two convoy battle circuits'.[166] By 18 January 1943 the number of U-boats on the north Atlantic convoy routes had increased sharply to 40, from 25 in the early days of the month.[167] For the greater part of January, however, 'they swept and re-swept [the north Atlantic] . . . and found nothing'.[168] The number of Allied ships they sank in convoy dropped to 15; the number of independents to 14. So great, indeed, was the success of Allied evasive routeing that (though this was not to be discovered till after the war) the U-boat Command, suspecting that its failure was not to be explained by the appalling weather, and commenting on the fact that there had been a striking departure from the stereotyped routine practised by the British during the previous six months,[169] concluded in its log for 2 February that 'the fact of a continued partial compromise of our intentions must for a time be taken into account' and decided to adopt 'loose, mobile dispositions, widely spaced, which the enemy will not be able to evade as he would a contracted, fixed disposition'.†

The change in the north Atlantic situation was all the more marked in that the most serious attack on convoys during January took place in the south. Up to the middle of December 1942 the U-boat Command had had no success against the convoy routes to north Africa despite concentrating a large number of U-boats against them; although the Allies were not yet profiting from the decryption of the U-boat traffic, they were benefiting from the secure cryptographic and W/T arrangements they had made for

---

* The settings were read to 9 January with variable degrees of delay. From then till 19 January they were read reasonably currently. Thereafter the reading began to drop behind again. But by 10 February all but two days since 13 January had been broken.

† German suspicions were also aroused when Allied destroyers were sighted near a refuelling rendezvous between a supply U-boat and an Italian submarine in the south Atlantic on 12 January.[170] The Admiralty had issued the intelligence about the rendezvous by Ultra signal on 9 January.[171]

166. Op-20-G History, Vol II, p 5.
167. ADM 223/96, OIC SI 492 of 18 January 1943.
168. Op-20-G History, Vol II, p 16.
169. ibid, p 17; BR 305 (2), p 73.
170. BR 305 (2), p 88.
171. ADM 223/105, Ultra signal 1608/9 January 1943.

operation *Torch* and the follow-up convoys from the United Kingdom. But of the 15 ships sunk in convoy in January no less than seven were lost from TM 1, a convoy of tankers bound from Trinidad to Gibraltar for Tunisia – a setback due in part to the continued use of the 'convoy cypher'. On 26 December, expecting eastbound *Torch* convoy traffic on the basis of its own Sigint, the U-boat Command formed a new group to patrol along its expected route. But nothing had been found when, on 3 January, TM 1 was sighted by chance by a U-boat in transit in a position 900 miles south of the patrol area. Although the convoy shook off this U-boat with the loss of only one ship it ran into a patrol line formed by the group to the north of it. After various distractions this had been sent across hundreds of miles of ocean to an area where the U-boat Command estimated that it might meet the convoy. In the battle which followed TM 1 lost 6 more tankers out of the original 9. Shark decrypts were available by then, but were of no assistance. Early on 29 December they disclosed the orders for the original patrol, but the OIC was unable to determine its disguised positions with certainty. They revealed early on 3 January that the patrol had been abandoned on the previous day and the U-boats ordered to make for Brazil. But not until 9 January did they reveal that on 5 January, following the sighting of the convoy, the U-boats had been ordered to move back eastwards again and form a new patrol line ahead of TM 1.[172]

The enemy's success against TM 1 was a salutary reminder of the danger that still faced north Atlantic convoys despite the decryption of Shark and the contribution it had made in January to successful evasive routeing; it was pointed to at the time as 'indicative of what was still to be expected on the N Atlantic lanes'.[173] At the same time, it may have played some small part in inducing the U-boat Command to keep more U-boats on the New York-Gibraltar route than on the route to the United Kingdom during February and March – a decision which substantially reduced the threat in the north Atlantic during those months. We may be sure, however, that the U-boat Command maintained this policy reluctantly, under the insistence of the highest authorities in Germany that the highest priority should be given to delaying the Allied advance in Tunisia, for the U-boats operating against the more southerly route were severely disadvantaged. The convoys had more sea room than those further north. Perhaps on this account the hard-pressed B-Dienst gave priority in its work on the

---

172.   ibid, Ultra signals 1715, 1121 and 1755/27 December, 0225/31 December
         1942, 1431/3 January, 1205/9 January 1943; ADM 223/96, OIC SI 476 of
         3 January 1943; ADM 223/97, OIC SI 513 of 12 February 1943; ADM
         223/88, pp 228–235; BR 305 (2), p 79; Beesly, op cit, p 159.
173.   Op-20-G History, Vol II, p 18.

'convoy cypher' to signals relating to the north Atlantic, so that German Sigint about US-Gibraltar convoys, though gradually improving, continued to be fragmentary.[174] For both of these reasons the Allies found it possible on the southern route to carry out evasive routeing effectively even when they were reduced to relying on sightings and DF findings to supplement belated Enigma intelligence. From the middle of January, moreover, they frequently diverted convoys with the aid of current or nearly current Enigma decrypts; and this was not the least reason why the U-boats scored only two further successes against convoys between the US or the Caribbean and Gibraltar or the north African ports and why the more substantial of these did not occur until the middle of March.* The consequences of this poor performance by the U-boats for the fighting in Tunisia were significant enough. On the battle of the Atlantic its effects were still more profound. The division of the U-boat effort in the Atlantic meant that the number of U-boats on the north Atlantic route, where their opportunities were markedly greater, were markedly fewer than would otherwise have been the case.

During February, even so, the daily average of operational U-boats in the Atlantic as a whole reached 116 and the number in the north Atlantic rose from about 40, the number reached soon after the middle of January, to about 60.[175] Nor was this the sole reason why they were more successful than in the previous two months, sinking 34 ships from the convoys as compared with 19 in December and 15 in January. The German naval cryptanalysts had by now brought their success against Allied 'convoy cypher' traffic in this area to the high level at which it was to remain till June; they provided exact intelligence about a number of convoys in time for the U-boat Command to act on it.[176] The U-boat Command, seeking to close the gaps in its patrol plans which had become apparent in January, adopted a new strategy in the north Atlantic from the beginning of the month, one which concentrated on intercepting the eastbound convoys at an early stage by having advance, mobile and widely-spaced patrol lines make frequent sweeps south-westward from 30°W.[177] Yet the Allied losses were nearly all sustained by only two convoys because the Shark decrypts continued to make an effective contribution to evasive routeing. For most of the month the delays in breaking the Shark settings, although seldom less than 24 hours, were well within the

---

* See below, pp 561, for their attack on convoy UGS 6.

174. BR 305 (2), pp 66, 81.
175. ADM 223/97, OIC SI 504 of 1 February, 526 of 1 March 1943.
176. Rohwer, Presentation to the US Naval Academy, p 9; BR 305 (2), pp 58, 89.
177. Op-20-G History, Vol II, p 20, Vol X, p 47.

limit beyond which the decrypts ceased to be of operational use in evading planned U-boat patrol lines.

The decrypts came too late, even so, to help the Tracking Rooms to avoid sightings by stray U-boats or guard against sudden U-boat redispositions when these were ordered on the basis of German intelligence. It was on this account that the Tracking Rooms, operating with what amounted to a half-knowledge of the current situation, diverted convoy HX 224 away from the U-boats in the western Atlantic at the end of January only to have it contacted by U-boats further to the south-east.[178] And whereas HX 224 escaped with the loss of only two ships because the U-boats were not expecting it, on 4 February convoy SC 118 ran into a patrol line of 21 U-boats which, though it was hastily formed, had advance intelligence about its route. SC 118 was heavily protected; some of the U-boats had been brought up over considerable distances and they carried out a large part of the operation within the range of Allied air cover. Three of the U-boats were sunk and two seriously damaged.[179] But they had sunk 13 merchant ships by 9 February – fewer than the U-boat Command had hoped for from so many U-boats, as the Shark decrypts disclosed,[180] but sufficient to provide the OIC with another foretaste of what would happen if, evasive routeing having failed again, a convoy were 'to be picked up in circumstances more favourable to the enemy . . .'[181]

The attack on SC 118 was the first significant U-boat success since the end of December. The next was deferred till 20 February. Convoy ON 165 was sighted by a U-boat in transit on 17 February, but it lost only two ships and the enemy lost two U-boats. With help from Shark, which was read currently for a short period up to noon on 17 February, convoy HX 226 was at that time being diverted away from U-boat patrol lines which had been formed against it with the help of the B-Dienst. But during 18 February, while the U-boat Command was using later intelligence in an effort to intercept convoy ON 166, the Shark decrypts for the 24 hours to noon were not available. And although they became available with a delay of less than 24 hours, they came too late. ON 166, sighted in the forenoon of 20 February, was powerfully attacked up to 25 February, 14 of its ships being sunk for the loss of one U-boat.[182] The U-boat Command secured no further success on this scale until the second week of March. Convoy ON 167, the only other convoy to be attacked in this interval, was sighted by chance on 21

---

178.   ibid, Vol II, p 21; BR 305 (2), p 75.

179.   BR 305 (2), p 75; Roskill, op cit, Vol II, p 356.

180.   ADM 223/88, p 246; ZTPGU 5550.

181.   ADM 223/97, OIC SI 533 of 7 March 1943.

182.   Roskill, op cit, Vol II, p 357; BR 305 (2), pp 77–78.

February and lost only two ships to an improvised group of U-boats.

From the contrast between the results of these encounters with HX 224, ON 165 and ON 167 and, on the other hand, the heavy losses sustained by SC 118 and ON 166, we can see now what was concealed from the Allied authorities at the time. The effectiveness of the U-boat assaults was far higher when they were delivered from positions taken up on the basis of advance intelligence than when they had to be improvised in response to chance sightings of convoys that had not been expected or had been turned away.[183] It is accordingly important to note that the battle on the intelligence front turned significantly against the Allies from the beginning of March. The B-Dienst continued to supply good convoy intelligence to the U-boat Command. But the Shark settings were read with greater than average delay for all but three of the first ten days of the month, and between 10 and 19 March the decryption of the traffic suffered the longest interruption that GC and CS had experienced since the beginning of the year.*

The Shark setback probably goes far to explain why the U-boats intercepted a convoy on the southern convoy routes between the USA and Gibraltar where, except for a chance sighting which had led to the loss of three tankers at the end of February,[184] they had had no success since early January. The B-Dienst helped them to make contact with convoy UGS 6 on 12 March when the effort to divert it had failed for lack of tolerably recent Enigma intelligence about their orders and dispositions. Even so, some 20 U-boats succeeded in sinking only four of its 40 ships; in a running battle across the Atlantic which lasted till 19 March the US escorts, helped by ship-borne radar, repeatedly drove off shadowing U-boats and frustrated mass attacks.[185]

For the battle on the northern routes the consequences of the interruptions experienced in breaking the Shark settings are more difficult to assess. They certainly deprived the Allies of any reliable basis for the evasive routeing of the convoys during much of that month. On the other hand, there are good grounds for thinking that, just as the defence of UGS 6 foreshadowed the not too distant time when the convoy escorts would establish a decisive superiority over the U-boats, so the month of March marked another crucial turning point – that at which, as a result of the frequency of convoys, the number of U-boats at sea and the activities of the B-Dienst, the Allied authorities were ceasing to be able to affect the

---

* See Appendix 19, p 750.

183. Op-20-G History, Vol II, p 29.   184. BR 305 (2), p 83.
185. ibid, pp 97–98; J Rohwer, *The Critical Convoy Battles of March 1943* (1977), p 79 et seq.

battle in the north Atlantic by successfully diverting convoys even when the U-boat Enigma was currently available. After March, as we shall see, the U-boats would still be sighting convoys more frequently than before – as frequently as one every four days – despite the fact that the delay in decrypting the Shark traffic had by then been reduced to the levels that had previously obtained. But they would no longer be pressing home their attacks.

At the beginning of March, a month in which the OIC's estimate of the U-boats in the north Atlantic rose to the record number of 66[186] and the Allies convoyed twice as many ships as in February, the increase being largely due to the fact that with the stepping up of the flow of US troops and war material to the UK the north Atlantic convoy cycles had to be further shortened,[187] the U-boats, still intent on pressing the attack, were deployed in the north according to the strategy adopted during February. While two other groups patrolled in mid-Atlantic to complete the encirclement of any convoy that was detected, 30 swept every available route north of 50°N in the western forward area in the effort to secure the early interception of eastbound convoys.[188] Good luck and poor visibility deferred till 6 March the detection of convoy SC 121, whose course instructions had been decrypted by the B-Dienst,[189] but the convoy lost 13 ships between 7 and 11 March.[190] HX 228 fared less badly. Sighted on 10 March after good B-Dienst intelligence had frustrated the attempt to divert it in the light of Shark decrypts for 5–7 March, it lost four merchant ships and one of its escorts, and the escorts sank two U-boats.[191] ON 170 fared better still; shore-based and ship-borne DF helped it to evade the U-boats that were waiting off Newfoundland for the next HX convoy.[192] But the attempt to divert HX 229 on the same kind of information during 14 and 15 March was unsuccessful and its detection on 16 March was followed by the biggest convoy disaster of the war. The U-boat Command had already moved the western patrol line to intercept the convoy; it now ordered up the two reserve groups of U-boats from the mid-Atlantic, and as they streamed towards HX 229 they also encountered SC 122.[193] By 20 March 21 ships from the two convoys had been sunk for the loss of one U-boat. On 22 March, after digesting the Shark decrypts for the period from 15 to 19 March that had begun to reach it since 19

186.   ADM 223/97, OIC SI 544 of 15 March 1943.
187.   Op-20-G History, Vol X, p 48; Rohwer, *Critical Convoy Battles*, p 38.
188.   Op-20-G History, Vol II, pp 32–33, 37; Rohwer, *Critical Convoy Battles*, p 51.
189.   Rohwer, *Critical Convoy Battles*, p 51.
190.   Op-20-G History, Vol II, p 33; ZTPGU 8000; Roskill, op cit, Vol II, p 365.
191.   Op-20-G History, Vol II, pp 36–37.
192.   ibid, p 39; Rohwer, *Critical Convoy Battles*, pp 96–98.
193.   Op-20-G History, Vol II, pp 39–40; ADM 223/88, pp 247–257.

March, the OIC noted that the two convoys had been attacked 'by the largest pack of U-boats which has ever been collected into one area for the same operation'.[194]

In what remained of March there were no further serious encounters. In that month as a whole, however, the Allies had lost 42 ships from the Atlantic convoys,* compared with 26 in February,[195] while the number of U-boats sunk by convoy escorts or by aircraft operating in support of convoys had dropped back from 17 in February to only six. By this time, moreover, it was clear that the attempt to cripple the U-boat offensive by bombing the U-boat pens in the Biscay ports and the U-boat construction yards in Germany had had little, if any, effect. The emergency air offensive against these targets which was mounted at the end of January was abandoned at the beginning of April.†

Looking back on these experiences later in the year some members of the Admiralty staff thought that in March it had 'appeared possible that we should not be able to continue convoy as an effective system of defence' and judged that 'the Germans never came so near to disrupting communications between the New World and the Old . . .'.[196] At the time, the First Sea Lord attributed the crisis to the fact that conditions rendered evasive routeing impossible. On 8 March he and the CAS noted, with reference to an operational research project for increasing the size of convoys which had been developed by Professor Blackett during January and February, that 'conditions now are very different from those from which the majority of the data . . . was collected'.[197] On 22 March he noted that with the increase in the number of U-boats operating 'we can no longer rely on evading the U-boat packs and, hence, we shall have to fight the convoys through them',[198] On 30 March he told the Cabinet's Anti-U-boat Warfare Committee that the terrible shipping losses, though partly explained by the exceptionally bad weather, which had cut back air support, reduced the efficiency of the escorts and made for less room for manoeuvre in routeing convoys, were mainly due to the 'failure of evasion based on DF intelligence. The Atlantic is now becoming so saturated by U-boats that the practice of evasion is rapidly becoming impossible'.[199] This was a prophetic judgment. Evasive routeing bassed on Direction Finding, a euphemism for the Enigma decrypts, would not after the end of March regain the influence on the

---

* See Appendix 8.   † See Appendix 20.

194.   ADM 223/97, OIC SI 551 of 22 March 1943.
195.   Howard, op cit, Vol IV, p 310.   196.   Roskill, op cit, Vol II, p 367.
197.   CAB 86/3, AU (43) 68 of 8 March, para 16(e).
198.   ibid, AU (43) 90 of 22 March, para 1(c).
199.   ibid, AU (43) 103 of 30 March.

battle that it had exerted in the first two months of 1943. But no less prophetic were the First Sea Lord's further remarks. He found grounds for cautious optimism in the fact that the weather was improving, that support groups and escort carriers from Tunisia and the supply route to north Russia were being re-deployed to the Atlantic and that, still more important, more aircraft were becoming available. And it was indeed as a result of additions and improvements to the Allied defences that the U-boats, which had been kept at bay during January and February but had seemed set to win during March, would be defeated during the next two months.

□

The improvement of the Allied defences included some developments which increased the ability of the convoy escorts to undertake intelligence on their own account. In the early months of 1943 surface escorts were in short supply in the north Atlantic, so many ships having had to be diverted to other areas – to US waters, to the Arctic route and then to the Tunisian theatre. Since July 1942, however, so many escort vessels had been fitted with seaborne HF/DF that by the beginning of 1943 it was a standard item of equipment – and one which enabled them in good conditions to locate for themselves, and with greater accuracy than was possible from shore-based DF stations, the sighting reports and homing signals transmitted by U-boats. The U-boats were forced to make these transmissions by the fact that they operated in packs under the centralised control of the U-boat Command, and it appears that the U-boat Command either did not or could not take steps to prevent the escorts from intercepting and DFing them.[200] In some of the convoy battles of February the escorts made effective use of HF/DF and their experiences produced further refinements in the apparatus and the tactics that went with it.[201] Subsequent analysis of the convoy battles has shown that especially after March 1943, when more escorts were available, the escort commanders, with the aid of HF/DF and the information supplied to them about the enemy's W/T frequencies and procedures, were often able to estimate the direction and the rough range of U-boat transmissions and, either by forcing a shadowing U-boat to submerge or by detecting that U-boats had sighted a convoy ahead of them, to re-route their own convoys into safety.[202] Except in heavy seas,

200.   Roskill, op cit, Vol II, p 112.
201.   BR 305 (2), p 78 fn.
202.   Roskill, op cit, Vol II, p 112; Op-20-G History, Vol X, p 28; Rohwer, *Critical Convoy Battles*, p 37.

moreover, when it was less reliable than HF/DF, the escorts had the advantage of being able to locate U-boats with the shorter-range but more accurate 10 cm radar; most of them were fitted with this by the beginning of 1943, when more and more of Coastal Command's aircraft were also acquiring it, whereas the U-boats, which had been fitted with search receivers against the old 1.5 metre radar, had no protection against it.

The impact upon the convoy battles of HF/DF and centimetric radar, as also of the new weapons – improved depth charges and the first ahead-firing weapon (Hedgehog) – which had been coming into use since the beginning of the year,[203] increased as more escorts became available, and particularly when it became possible to form support groups and provide escort carriers (CVEs). Support groups had first been formed in the autumn of 1942, with the object of destroying U-boats once they had been located near convoys, but like the CVEs, which had also become available in the autumn, they had been absorbed by operation *Torch*, by the Arctic convoys and by the Tunisian campaign. At the end of March, however, CVEs started accompanying Atlantic convoys, and new support groups were formed round destroyers from the Home Fleet. By that time, also, very long-range (VLR) shore-based aircraft (Liberators) were beginning slowly to close the great gaps south of Greenland and north of the Azores which, beyond the range of air cover, had hitherto been the favoured operating areas for the U-boats; and as the number of such aircraft increased, so did closer collaboration between the aircraft and the surface escorts extend the efficiency of both.

With the arrival of these additions to the defence forces the Allied escorts and patrols, supplementing their growing ability to contain and throw off the attacking U-boats, began to make a decisive advance in the more positive direction of sinking them when they pressed their attacks. In November 1942, as the First Sea Lord then informed the Cabinet's newly-formed emergency Anti-U-boat Warfare Committee, U-boats were being destroyed at only one-third of the rate at which they were being constructed.[204] There was no change in the next two months: 13 U-boats were sunk in December, six of them on the convoy routes; 11 in January 1943, of which five were accounted for by the convoy escorts or aircraft operating in their support. In February matters improved. 17 U-boats were sunk on the convoy routes together with six others, as against 25 new U-boats taken into service.[205] And despite a relapse in March – 16 U-boats sunk, and only six of them in the convoy

---

203. Roskill, op cit, Vol II, p 207; eg ADM 223/97, OIC SI 595 of 17 May 1943.
204. CAB 86/2, AU (42) 1st Meeting, 4 November.
205. Roskill, op cit, Vol II, p 469; ADM 223/97, OIC SI 526 of 1 March 1943.

battles – the OIC was able to report on 24 May 'for the first time in any 3-month period . . . a net decrease in operational numbers', 56 having been sunk as against 51 which had started their first war cruise.[206]

It was thus from the beginning of April, so soon after it had taken place, that the reinforcement of the escorts with escort carriers, support groups and additional VLR aircraft began to exert its effect both on U-boat casualties and in terms of the U-boats' successes. At the same time, if the number of ships sunk in convoy dropped to 25 in April from the critical level reached in March, it did so because the U-boats were being driven on to the defensive by the escorts. Despite a temporary decline in the total number at sea, April saw no reduction in the number of U-boats in the north Atlantic; there was, instead, a reduction of the U-boat effort on the US-Gibraltar routes. The B-Dienst continued to serve the U-boats well.[207] As in March, on the other hand, evasive routeing continued to be ineffective despite the fact that the decrypting of the Enigma now suffered from less serious interruptions. Even though the decrypts made some successful diversions possible, the U-boats contacted many convoys – as many as in the time and with their numbers they could conceivably have attacked on any scale. Nor did these conditions change before the end of May, the month in which the U-boats still claimed 26 ships from convoys, but in which they were at last forced out of the north Atlantic.

To illustrate the winning of the initiative by the Allied defences we shall end with a survey of the main convoy battles of April and May. Before we undertake this it remains to enquire to what extent the escorts and the support forces benefited from the Enigma, as well as from their own tactical intelligence, in these months in which they drove the U-boats on to the defensive. From the beginning of 1943 the all but continuous reading of the Shark traffic had yielded a vast amount of information about the equipment and the characteristics of the U-boats, including the endurance, fuel consumption and speed of the various types. It was known that by the spring they were acquiring the ability to dive to greater depths and were being equipped with such new devices as an improved magnetic torpedo pistol and a pattern-running or circling torpedo (the FAT).* Delay in reading the Shark signals was no impediment when it came to studying such developments or to establishing which tactics the U-boats were employing at any time – submerged night attack, surface attack by day, frontal attack and so forth. The forcefulness with which additional reinforcements

---

* See Appendix 10.

206.   ADM 223/98, OIC SI 600 of 24 May 1943.
207.   BR 305 (2), pp 103, 105, 109–111.

were being deployed and new techniques developed for convoy defence – a spirit 'which created an atmosphere very different from the bitter, inconclusive arguments of the previous summer'[208] – owed something to the creation in November 1942 of the Anti-U-boat Warfare Committee, but it owed much, also, to the fact that the deliberations of that Committee were now being guided by this intelligence. As for the extent to which the intelligence assisted the Allied escorts and support forces in the Atlantic, this is a matter for surmise. It was not until the end of May 1943, that, making direct use of the operational intelligence obtained from the Enigma, and paying special attention to the destruction of the enemy's fleet of supply U-boats at their refuelling points, they went over to the offensive against the U-boats;* until then, apart from the fact that the Admiralty was unwilling to rouse the enemy's suspicions by exploiting the Enigma intelligence about U-boat refuelling operations,† they were tied down by the need to defend the convoys. But it is reasonable to suppose that during April and May 1943, when they got the upper hand in this defensive struggle, they were profiting not only from the fact that they had been reinforced and supplied with new weapons and devices, but also from the existence in the Admiralty and at the commands which supervised their operations of an ever-growing body of Enigma intelligence about all aspects of the U-boat effort.

□

The first intimations of what was to be the outcome of these developments had appeared in the Shark decrypts in February. Inexperienced U-boat commanders – a growing band – had then occasionally reported torpedo failures, made unsubstantiated claims‡ and betrayed signs of timidity, particularly fear of air attack,[210] and there had also been a noticeable increase in the occasions on which U-boats developed incapacitating defects during their outward passage of the Bay of Biscay.[211] But it was from the last days of March that, both in the course of convoy operations and from the decrypts of the comments made on the operations by the U-boat Command, the Allies obtained the first substantial evidence of a decline in U-boat morale.

Forty U-boats attacked convoy HX 230, which was sighted on 27

---

* See Volume III.   † See above, p 549.

‡ Exaggerated claims by the U-boat commanders in the early months of 1943 caused over-confidence in the U-boat Command and contributed to its unpreparedness for the sudden collapse of the U-boat offensive in May.[209]

208.   Howard, op cit, Vol IV, p 303.   209.   BR 305 (2), p 100.
210.   Beesly, op cit, pp 175–176.   211.   ibid, p 174.

March, but they were beaten off by the escorts, which included for the first time both an escort carrier and support groups, and succeeded in sinking only one straggler. Convoy SC 123 was sighted at the end of March but its escorts, again reinforced by a support group, passed it safely through the U-boat patrol line.[212] On 4 April convoy HX 231 was sighted. When ordering the U-boats to attack it the U-boat Command stressed for the first time the importance of attacking on the first night; on 4 February, during the attack on SC 118, it had assured them that this was not important as the 'heavy blow' would come later.[213] After the engagement against HX 231 it expressed itself dissatisfied that so many U-boats had sunk only six ships and reprimanded them for excessive use of wireless.[214] Four days later convoy ON 176 ran into a group of U-boats, but it lost only two ships.[215] On 11 April, when convoy HX 232 was sighted, the U-boat Command again voiced the suspicion that the U-boats were not pressing home their attacks: having ordered two groups to form up in readiness for this convoy it now called on them to display 'the healthy warrior and hunter instincts'. These signals were decrypted too late to save the convoy, but it lost only three ships, all on the first night of the attack.[216] On 15 April an outward-bound U-boat sighted convoy HX 233 despite the fact that it had been routed away from the U-boat patrol line; four other U-boats managed to attack it; but the convoy lost only one ship and the escort, reinforced by a support group, sank one of the U-boats.[217] The next attempt to divert a convoy was frustrated by B-Dienst intelligence, which enabled the U-boat Command to put a group in contact with HX 234 on 20 April. In the course of moving up to HX 234 the U-boats also contacted during 20 and 21 April convoys ONS 3 and ON 178. But in the attacks on all these convoys three U-boats were sunk for the loss of four merchant ships.[218]

In what remained of April there were no more U-boat successes in the attacks on convoys. Nor was this solely because SC 127 was successfully diverted during the operations against HX 234, ONS 3 and ON 178, and because ONS 4 and ON 179 evaded attack despite being sighted by U-boats outward-bound from Biscay.[219]

---

212. Roskill, op cit, Vol II, p 366; ADM 223/97, OIC SI 555 of 29 March 1943.
213. Dir/C Archive, 2244 of 9 February 1943; Naval Headlines, No 583 of 7 February 1943.
214. Op-20-G History, Vol II, pp 59–60; ZTPGU 10192.
215. BR 305 (2), pp 96, 97.
216. Op-20-G History, Vol II, p 62; ZTPGU 11044; BR 305 (2), p 97; Beesly, op cit, p 179.
217. Op-20-G History, Vol II, p 63; BR 305 (2), p 103.
218. Op-20-G History, Vol II, pp 64–65; BR 305 (2), p 103.
219. Op-20-G History, Vol II, pp 67–78.

Since the beginning of the month the decrypts of signals from the U-boats had contained increasingly frequent references to their fear of air attack and to the efficiency of the Allied surface escorts in following up aircraft sightings.[220] More recently they had also disclosed that the U-boat Command was seriously perturbed by these reports. From the middle of the month, while enjoining the operational patrol lines to maintain strict W/T silence, it had instructed some U-boats to make dummy signals to simulate the presence of U-boat groups.[221] By 19 April it was conceding that the U-boats could not effectively use pack tactics against convoys which had air support.[222] This confession constituted a considerable retreat from the new tactics it had adopted at the beginning of the month when, in order to bring them into a position to make quick surprise attacks, it had ordered the U-boats to sweep ahead on the surface. It had discovered, indeed, that the new tactics had made the U-boats all the more vulnerable to air attack.

It was on the basis of this intelligence that on 19 April the OIC Tracking Room drew attention to the 'incipient decline in U-boat morale', as manifested in their 'concern for vulnerability to air attack',[223] and that on 26 April, in a report which singled out the effectiveness of the escort aircraft carrier HMS *Biter* in the defence of ONS 4, it stressed that a lack of boldness had spread to most of the U-boat commanders.[224]

From the beginning of May the total number of U-boats at sea was approaching its peak; on 10 May the OIC estimated it at 128, 'the highest ever known', no less than 98 having sailed during April, most of them during the second half of the month.[225] Of this total, the number identified by the OIC on the north Atlantic routes still exceeded the 60 mark on 3 May,[226] and although their exact positions were not then known, the Shark settings having proved intractable since 26 April,[227] there was enough Enigma intelligence to show that the U-boat Command was more than ever intent on so disposing them as to eliminate all chance of missing the eastbound convoys. 'On the basis of the available information and an appreciation of the new pattern [of patrol lines] it was estimated on 1 May that by 3 May all routes would be blocked from 53°N, 48°W around to 46°N, 38°W'.[228] By 1 May, moreover, the U-boats

220.   ibid, pp 56–57.
221.   Op-20-G History, Vol II, p 63; ZTPGU 10856.
222.   ADM 223/97, OIC SI 576 of 19 April 1943.
223.   ibid, OIC SI 576 of 19 April 1943.
224.   ibid, OIC SI 580 of 26 April 1943.
225.   ibid, OIC SI 590 of 10 May 1943; Roskill, op cit, Vol II, p 372.
226.   ADM 223/97, OIC SI 583 of 3 May 1943.
227.   ibid, OIC SI 583 of 3 May 1943.
228.   Op-20-G History, Vol II, p 69.

had already sighted convoy ONS 5 at the northern tip of their patrol lines, and on 1 May itself, with help from the B-Dienst, they made contact with convoy SC 128.[229] But if reliance could no longer be placed on evasive routeing, it was also the case that the U-boats were no longer exploiting their sightings. ONS 5 lost one ship before they lost contact with it on 1 May; from 1 May to 4 May they searched in the vicinity of convoys ONS 5, HX 235, SC 128 and ON 180 without success;[230] and on 2 May the U-boat Command admonished them: 'With 31 boats something can and must be accomplished.'[231]

By the time the decrypt of this signal was in Allied hands the U-boats had done something to restore their flagging fortunes. Resuming contact with ONS 5 on 4 May, they sank 12 of its merchant ships in a long and complicated battle. But they achieved this success, their last on this scale, at the expense of seven U-boats sunk and five damaged. The extent of the loss and damage they sustained was disclosed by the Shark decrypts, which also produced further evidence that their fear both of Allied aircraft and of the surface escorts was on the increase.[232]

In the next encounter, the attack on convoys HX 237 and SC 129, the odds swung even further against the U-boats. The U-boat dispositions were known from the Shark traffic and the convoys were being routed accordingly. But it was also known that evasive routeing was being frustrated by the B-Dienst. This detected the diversions in such good time, and enabled the U-boat Command to concentrate so large a force of U-boats that on decrypting the Command's orders in 'officer-only' Shark signals, Allied intelligence concluded that 'no U-boat group operation ... was so evidently guided by continuing intelligence of the convoy movements'.[233] With 36 U-boats assembled against them the convoys should have been enveloped with ease, and had conditions been what they were in March they would have sustained appalling losses. But in a straight fight with the surface escorts, the escort carrier's aircraft and shore-based aircraft between 7 and 14 May the U-boats sank only two merchant ships in return for the destruction of two U-boats and severe damage to several others.

At the end of the battle the U-boats, temporarily dispersed in small groups to evade detection, were admonished by the U-boat Command: 'We can see no explanation for this failure'.[234] In the Tracking Room in the OIC it was clear that whatever might be the immediate reasons, the failure had 'provided further evidence that U-boat efficiency and morale were declining'.[235] Nor did it have to

---

229.   ibid, p 69; BR 305 (2), p 105.
230.   BR 305 (2), p 105.   231.   Op-20-G History, Vol II, p 69.
232.   ADM 223/88, p 258 et seq.   233.   Op-20-G History, Vol II, p 72.
234.   ADM 223/97, OIC SI 595 of 17 May 1943.   235.   ibid.

revise this conclusion in the light of the two convoy battles that took place in the next few days – the last such battles of the whole war. By 17 May it had learned from Shark decrypts that U-boat patrol lines were being re-formed and it was trying to route convoy SC 130 through a gap between the lines.[236] With 33 U-boats lying in wait, the convoy was nevertheless sighted on 18 May. But its escorts destroyed five U-boats and the convoy lost no ship. In the course of the encounter the U-boat Command was scathing about its 'inexperienced captains'; but it also ordered the U-boats to make dummy transmissions as a means of hiding their true movements, and in further signals on 18 and 19 May it admitted that 'the enemy had gained a few lengths on us in his efforts to deprive the U-boat of its most important attribute, its invisibility'.[237] A group of 22 U-boats had meanwhile been formed to catch convoy HX 239. The convoy was routed south of them on the basis of Shark intelligence[238] but, the B-Dienst having detected the diversion, it was nevertheless sighted on 22 May. The previous evening the U-boat Command had exhorted the U-boats in the following signal: 'If there is anyone who thinks that combating convoys is no longer possible, he is a weakling and no true U-boat captain. The battle of the Atlantic is getting harder but it is the determining element in the waging of the war . . .'.[239] In the ensuing battle, however, the U-boats suffered so heavily that on 23 May the U-boat Command decided to withdraw them to avoid further damage.[240] On the following day, when the number of U-boats sunk in the attacks on SC 130 and HX 239 had risen to eight and neither convoy had sustained any loss,[241] Admiral Dönitz issued a series of signals to the U-boats explaining the reasons for their withdrawal and giving them new disposition orders. He attributed their withdrawal 'primarily to the present superiority of the enemy's location devices and the surprise from the air which these have made possible'. 'All my efforts are directed towards the improvement of our own location, of counter-measures against the enemy's location and of our Flak armament'. 'Practical results will reach the front in the shortest possible time'. Until then 'the present situation . . . must be tided over by special precautionary measures both on passage and in waiting positions . . . Orders have been issued to this end, and I shall be drawing my own further conclusions in the choice of attacking areas'.[242] In its log for the same day the U-boat Command recorded that 'the situation in the

236. ibid.
237. Op-20-G History, Vol II, p 75; ZTPGU 13520.
238. Op-20-G History, Vol II, p 76.
239. ibid, pp 76–77; ZTPGU 14246.
240. Op-20-G History, Vol II, p 77.
241. ibid.   242. ZTPGU 14191.

North Atlantic forces a temporary withdrawal to areas in which there is less danger from aircraft'. All but a few of the U-boats – which were left behind and ordered to transmit dummy signals to delay the Allied discovery of the retreat[243] – were sent by the disposition order of 24 May to the area 600 miles south-west of the Azores in the first instance.

Confirmation of their victory was indeed briefly withheld from the Allies by the fact that the Shark signals of 24 May were not decrypted for a week, and the true significance of the signals was even then obscured for a few more days by delays in the OIC and at GC and CS in decoding the disguised references to the new dispositions.[244] As early as 2 May, on the other hand, GC and CS had decrypted a significant telegram from the Japanese Ambassador in Berlin. In January he had reported that Hitler had hopes of the new U-boat offensive on account of the improvement in U-boat capabilities. Now, however, the Ambassador reported that Hitler was complaining that because the war had started too soon 'we have been unable to dominate the seas'.

---

243.   ADM 223/98, OIC SI 603 of 31 May 1943, quoted in Beesly, op cit, p 183.
244.   Op-20-G History, Vol II, p 103; ADM 223/98, OIC SI 614 of 14 June 1943, quoted in Beesly, op cit, p 183.

CHAPTER 27

The End in Africa

DURING THE weeks following the suspension of the Allied advance in Tunisia the volume of enemy supplies and reinforcements reaching Tunisia continued to be a source of great anxiety. On 6 January General Eisenhower reported that unless it 'can be materially reduced the situation both here and in Eighth Army area will deteriorate without doubt'.[1] On 9 February he drew attention to the fact that the Axis was still getting 75 per cent of its requirements into Tunisia, and he warned that 'the termination of the Tunisian campaign depends on the extent to which we can disrupt enemy lines of sea communications'.[2] The warning was based on the knowledge that after registering an improvement during December 1942, when intelligence had shown that over a quarter of all Axis ships sailed for Tunisia were sunk, and with them nearly half of the known fuel and ammunition cargoes, Allied successes against the traffic had again declined.

It is true that in January 1943 the Allies again sank about a quarter of the ships which left Italy and Sicily for Tunisian ports. They included, at long last, the *Ankara*, mined on 18 January with a large cargo of motor transport and ammunition,[3] two other ships each carrying 10 tanks which were sunk on 17 and 22 January,[4] and several smaller landing craft and ferries. But the sinkings now accounted for only about one-seventh of the fuel shipped, and only about one-ninth of the ammunition. The low fuel figure was explained by the failure to intercept the *Thorsheimer*, a tanker which reached Bizerta with 10,000 tons of fuel on 28 January and which also escaped damage in two bombing attacks on the port.[5] Correspondingly, the sinking of the *Thorsheimer* on 21 February, with a further large cargo, raised the proportion of known fuel cargoes destroyed to 70 per cent during February. This sinking was directly

---

1. CAB 105/33, Hist (G) 2, No 39 of 6 January 1943.
2. ibid, No 140 of 7 February 1943.
3. VM 1609 of 18 January 1943; ZTPI 25616.
4. VMs 1736 of 19 January, 2000 of 24 January 1943; ZTPI 25983; DEFE 3/587, ZTPGM 7723.
5. VMs 2589 of 28 January, 2684 and 2688 of 29 January, 2806 of 30 January, 2981 of 1 February 1943; CX/MSS/2024/T18, 2028/T6; ZTPI 26333, 26488; DEFE 3/588, ZTPGM 8352, 8514.

attributable to advance notice from high-grade Sigint.[6] But the proportion of total ships sunk en route to Tunisia or on their arrival there dropped to less than 20 per cent in that month, mainly as a result of the fact that attacks on the ports were greatly reduced from the middle of the month when the Allied bombers were diverted to the land fighting. It was not until March, indeed, that the Allies succeeded in administering a serious check to the Axis flow of supplies.

There were several reasons for their failure to achieve this before the land fighting was resumed. The weather was bad, especially during January. The enemy's defence measures were effective. His strength in the air and his extensive mining restricted the British surface ship operations to attacks on the coastal traffic off the east coast of Tunisia, and severely hampered air and submarine operations in the Sicilian channel. For some of his supplies, moreover, he made increasing use of smaller – and safer – ferry craft; from the last week of January, for example, on Hitler's orders, as the Enigma showed, tanks were shipped only in these craft and only from Sicily.[7] Not less important was the fact that the confused state of the command structure of the Allied air forces did not permit an efficiently co-ordinated attack on the Axis supplies before the middle of February, when all Allied air forces in the Mediterranean were subordinated to a single commander directly responsible to General Eisenhower.[8] A special force for attacks on ship targets was formed from bombers of Twelfth USAAF at the beginning of January; but it did not begin operations until the middle of the month, and decisions as to whether to use bombers against the supply route or against ground targets were still being made with difficulty after that date.[9] Until March, again, when Cairo's specialist staff was transferred to Algiers,* the decisions were being taken without assistance from an intelligence group which specialised in the study of the supply situation and the selection of shipping targets. But it is clear that they were usually taken by the various air commanders – and sometimes by General Eisenhower himself – after extensive exchanges on the SCU/SLU channels in an effort to maximise their effect,[10] and that shortage of intelligence was not among the problems is shown by Whitehall's response to

---

* See Appendix 18.

6. Playfair, *The Mediterranean and Middle East*, Vol IV (1966), p 249; VMs 4492 of 1 February, 4580 of 20 February, 4715 of 22 February 1943; CX/MSS/2144/T3, 2148/T1; DEFE 3/589, ZTPGM 9978.
7. VM 2241 of 24 January 1943; CX/MSS/2012/T1.
8. AIR 41/33, *The North African Campaign*, pp 161–162.
9. ibid, pp 111, 126, 146–147, 160, 161–162; AIR 41/50, *The RAF in the Middle East Campaigns*, Vol IV, p 479.
10. GAD PKs 65 and 68 of 1 and 3 February 1943.

General Eisenhower's request for more air reconnaissance at the beginning of January. It disputed the need for larger reconnaissance forces 'in view of other sources of information'.[11]

Of these other sources of information, the high-grade cyphers – GAF Enigma and the Porpoise Enigma – and the C 38m were the most valuable, though they were supported by the SIS and PR. Taken together, these sources provided a virtually complete record of the shipping making for and arriving at Tunis and Bizerta from Italy and Sicily. As before, Sigint gave advance notice of the movements and routes of almost all the ships; in addition they now gave better information about cargoes. During November 1942 cargo intelligence had been scarce. By the end of January 1943 GC and CS was supplying full details of 60 per cent of all cargoes – a less perfect service than it had provided during the desert war, and one that somewhat declined again in February, but impressive nevertheless. From the beginning of January, the first month in which Rommel, also, was wholly supplied through Tunisia, an increasing amount of high-grade intelligence was obtained about the movement of supplies by road, rail and sea from Tunis and Bizerta to Sousse, Sfax and the smaller ports in central and southern Tunisia, and the decrypts confirmed that this local traffic was suffering from Allied air attacks. But these attacks could not be decisive so long as the enemy kept up the flow of supplies into Tunisia.

The fact that the Axis was succeeding in doing this, and the extent to which it was meeting his requirements, was known from Army Enigma decrypts as well as from the shipping intelligence. At the beginning of January they disclosed that the monthly target for German deliveries was 60,000 tons but that the actual rate of delivery of rations was barely meeting current needs; that fuel, also, was sufficient only for current use; and that ammunition shipments had built up stocks for only a fortnight's full-scale operations by three divisions.[12] On the other hand, they showed that at least 49,600 tons of stores were landed, German plus Italian, during February, as compared with 40,000 in the previous December.[13]* The source of the information about these deliveries was a series of daily unloading returns for Tunis and Bizerta. GC and CS began

---

* But it should be noted that there is a considerable discrepancy between these figures and those provided by the Italian authorities after the war. The latter say that the total delivered (military cargo and fuel) was 58,763 tons in December, 70,000 tons in January and 59,000 tons in February.[14] The discrepancy is probably due to the Italian inclusion of such items as guns and vehicles which were not incorporated in the German returns.

11. CAB 105/33, No 46 of 8 January 1943.
12. eg CX/MSS/1914/T55, 1927/T22.   13. CX/MSS/2195/T7.
14. Playfair, op cit, Vol IV, pp 210, 250.

to decrypt these in December; from the end of December it decrypted them virtually every day, thus providing a continuous commentary on the enemy's general supply position.

Thanks mainly to the Army Enigma – though on these subjects the decrypts were again supplemented by the SIS, POW interrogation and captured documents – there was similarly no shortage of intelligence about the enemy's order of battle and the arrival of enemy ground reinforcements in Tunisia. It was known that the forces in Tunisia had been reorganised as Panzer Army 5 (Pz AOK 5) under General von Arnim in mid-December, and that it then comprised an impromptu division under General von Broich, 10th Panzer Division, the Italian Superga Division and numerous smaller units.[15] During January the Enigma established that Panzer Army 5 was to receive a Corps HQ, 334th Division, the Hermann Göring Division – a GAF formation that had developed from a GAF regiment and was later to become a full Panzer division – and other units including 999th Afrika Brigade, which was also to acquire divisional status before its arrival.[16] Early that month the SIS reported the arrival of the first elements of 334th Division; and by the end of the month the Enigma showed that 21st Panzer Division had been subordinated to Panzer Army 5 after arriving in the Sfax area.* In the absence of references to other arrivals before March, when the Enigma was to report that the Hermann Göring Division and 999th Brigade had begun crossing to Africa,[17] it was thus known during February that Panzer Army 5 comprised four German and one Italian divisions.

For information on the growing military capability of these formations AFHQ depended on calculations of the number of troop reinforcements that were arriving by air and in Italian destroyers, and on deductions from Enigma reports on the state of the enemy's guns and ammunition. The movements of the troop-carrying destroyers, begun in December,[18] were fully covered by the C 38m and the high-grade decrypts. On the air transport programme, the GAF Enigma and GAF and IAF low-grade traffic provided considerable information, though it was not complete. From time to time Enigma decrypts of manpower and ration returns provided a check on the calculations.[19] AFHQ's manpower estimates in fact attained a high degree of accuracy. It estimated

---

* See above, p 460, and below, pp 579, 581–582.

15.   QTs 8234 of 10 December, 8327 of 11 December 1942;
        CX/MSS/1795/T38, 1798/T4, 1803/T13.
16.   VM 2122 of 23 January 1943; CX/MSS/2007/T18.
17.   VMs 5914 of 8 March, 6299 of 12 March 1943; CX/MSS/2230/T14,
        2253/T32.
18.   CX/MSS/1918/T18, 1919/T10.
19.   eg GAD PK 63 of 31 January 1943.

the number of German troops under von Arnim, including GAF personnel, as being 75,4000 at the end of January, whereas the actual total was 74,000.[20] On 13 February – the eve of the German offensive – high-grade decrypts checked and supplemented the calculation by disclosing that total strength in the Panzer Army 5 area was 110,000 men, including 20,000 GAF and naval personnel and 33,000 Italians.[21]

On the tank strength of the individual units AFHQ was less well informed; nor was any overall tank return for Panzer Army 5 decrypted between 17 December and 28 January. But AFHQ was able to calculate from the daily unloading reports for Tunis and Bizerta that the total number of serviceable tanks had increased to 140 by the end of December and to 200 by the end of January, when the decrypt of an overall return for 28 January showed that the figure stood at 194.[22] Tank returns always listed the number of Pzkw VI (Tiger) tanks separately; 11 of the 194 were Tigers.* On 24 January the Enigma disclosed that OKW was dissatisfied that, because of lack of crew training, the Tigers in Tunisia were not achieving the 'decisive effect' of which they were capable. From the same signal, in which OKW ordered intensified training, intelligence obtained the first reference to the Pzkw V (Panther) tank: the signal announced that on Hitler's orders Tigers and Panthers were to be shipped in larger numbers 'in coming months'.[23]

☐

Despite the anxiety they felt at their inability seriously to reduce the flow of the enemy's supplies and reinforcements, the Allied authorities in Tunisia did not suppose that this was permitting him to recruit his strength and build up his capacity to the point at which he would be able to take the offensive on any large scale, but only that it was adding to the difficulties they would encounter when they themselves resumed their attack. On 30 January 1943 General Eisenhower concurred in the text of an appreciation of 4 January sent to him from London by the JIC which concluded that the Axis forces, while they might carry out local attacks on a limited scale, would remain on the defensive.[24]† On 9 February he

---

* See Appendix 14, pp 715–716.
† See below, p 579.
20. CAB 105/33, No 114 of 3 February 1943; Howe, *North-West Africa* (1957), p 370.
21. VM 3924 of 13 February 1943; CX/MSS/2109/T25 and 27.
22. VM 3090 of 2 February 1943; CX/MSS/2051/T17.
23. VM 2221 of 24 January 1943; CX/MSS/2008/T30.
24. CAB 121/500, SIC file E/North Africa/5, JIC (43) 3 (0) of 4 January; CAB 121/502, SIC file E/North Africa/7, folio 2.

judged that any attacks the enemy might launch would have 'limited objectives'.[25] Between these dates, in the reports which he rendered at regular intervals to Washington and Whitehall, he made no reference to the possibility that a more powerful threat might develop. As for the appraisals of the enemy's capabilities on which his reports were based, the full records are not available in the United Kingdom, but the British official history has stated that in the few days before the Axis attack on 14 February the intelligence staffs at AFHQ and First Army believed that the enemy was 'over-stretched, that he would improve his defence positions, and at present husband his few mobile reserves'.[26]

In the light of what was known of the supply position and the rate of reinforcement, this was not an unreasonable conclusion. It may be noted, indeed, that some German authorities, knowing still more about those subjects, shared it. As late as 7 February von Arnim told Warlimont, then on a visit from OKW, that his army was unfit for large offensive operations on account of lack of ammunition, fuel and transport, and Warlimont on his return to Germany reported that the Axis position was 'a house of cards' as a result of the supply problem.[27] As for the size of that problem, von Arnim and Rommel were informed at the beginning of January that to meet their combined needs they would be sent 80,000 tons of supplies per month, of which it could be assumed that 60,000 tons would arrive; but they had assessed their needs at 150,000 tons, of which 70,000 tons would go to daily maintenance.[28] Like the views of von Arnim and Warlimont, these exchanges were not revealed to the Allies at the time, but their intelligence was not at fault when it depicted the Axis supply situation as being precarious.

Even so, the supply position had not invariably been an infallible guide to the enemy's intentions; and it was no doubt with this consideration in mind that in the first half of January the British Chiefs of Staff counselled against General Eisenhower's plan to despatch US II Corps from Tebessa to the coast at Gabes and Sfax on 22 January. The rationale of the plan was General Eisenhower's view that in the interval before he could resume the offensive – an interval he thought might last two months – he must limit the build-up of the Axis bridgehead by cutting the land route between Rommel and the main Tunisian ports, as well as by intensifying the attack on the Tunisian supply line. The Chiefs of Staff, less sanguine than the JIC, urged, instead, that he should concentrate on bringing forward the date at which he could take the offensive in the north; they thought it unwise to assume either that the enemy

25. CAB 105/33, No 130 of 9 February 1943.
26. Playfair, op cit, Vol IV, p 289.
27. ibid, p 274.   28. ibid, p 274.

would wait as long as two months before himself attacking from Tunis in force or that Rommel would be unable to act effectively against an American thrust to the coast.[29]

On 13 January the Enigma justified the second of their arguments. It disclosed that the Axis High Command had requested the strengthening of the Sfax area and that Rommel proposed to send 21st Panzer Division there,* and by 15 January Ultra recipients, of whom the most important were then assembled at the Casablanca conference, had learned that 21st Panzer Division was already on the move.[30] It is safe to assume that this intelligence did much to persuade the conference to cancel II Corps's projected advance.[31]

In support of the first argument of the British Chiefs of Staff – their anxiety that the enemy would go over to the attack in Tunisia if the Allies delayed their own offensive – there was as yet no positive intelligence. It was plain enough from the continuing despatch of supplies and reinforcements to Tunisia that the Axis was determined to impose the greatest possible delay on the Allies, and it was possible from knowledge of the Axis order of battle and of the capacity of the Tunisian ports to estimate the size of the forces it would devote to that aim. On 4 January the JIC had correctly assessed that by mid-February Rommel's army would be occupying the Mareth line and that the enemy's total ground forces in Tunisia would amount to 2 full-strength and 4 weak German divisions and 2 or 3 full-strength and 3 weak Italian divisions. With these forces, which were smaller than those available to the Allies and which would have less armour and be short of motor transport, petrol and administrative services, the JIC had calculated that the enemy would be unable to carry out a large offensive either towards Algeria or Egypt; he would confine himself to local offensives to improve and give depth to his bridgehead.[32] On 6 January, in deference to the more guarded judgment of the Chiefs of Staff, it had modified its conclusions to the extent of adding that the Axis would 'exploit any opportunity for vigorous action which offers, despite difficulties of weather and terrain, shortage of transport and maintenance problems'.[33] But no intelligence suggesting that the enemy might be intending more than local attacks had been obtained beyond the decrypt of a telegram from the Japanese Ambassador in Berlin. He had reported that Ribbentrop had told

---

* See above, pp 459–460.

29. Howard, *Grand Strategy*, Vol IV (1972), p 182; CAB 105/32, Hist (G) 1, Nos 296 and 308 of 29 and 31 December 1942; CAB 121/500, COS (W) 430 of 5 January 1943.
30. VM 1209 of 14 January 1943; CX/MSS/1959/T1.
31. CAB 121/152, SIC file A/Strategy/8, COS (43) 33 (o) of 28 January; Howe, op cit, p 353.
32. CAB 121/500, JIC (43) 3 (o) of 4 January.   33.   Howe, op cit, p 353.

him on 18 December that the Axis was considering taking the initiative in north Africa if the supply problem could be solved. MI had brought his message to the attention of the CIGS on 4 January.[34]

There is no difficulty in accounting for the lack, at this stage, of pointers to the enemy's coming offensive in southern Tunisia. At the end of November Rommel had put forward a plan by which his army would at once withdraw to Tunisia, there to join with Panzer Army 5 in striking at the Allies before their build-up could match the combined Axis strength. Rommel's proposal was not referred to in the Enigma decrypts and, although it was one of the factors which eventually persuaded Mussolini to permit a retreat from Tripolitania,[35] the Axis command during December and January was more concerned first that Rommel should impose the maximum delay on Eighth Army* and then, while he was struggling to reach the Mareth line and to consolidate there, that a serious thrust might develop from the Allied forces in the Gafsa/Tebessa area.[36] It was not until late in January that the enemy's thoughts turned to launching a strong spoiling attack on those forces. And even when this attack was launched in mid-February the Axis had still not got as far as thinking of extending it into an operation for turning the flank of the Allies' general position in Tunisia.†

From the third week of January it became apparent that the Axis command structures were being changed. The reorganisation of the GAF commands was simple enough and fully covered by the Enigma.[37]Fliegerführer Afrika amalgamated his forces with the southern elements of the GAF in Tunisia on 25 January. On 11 February he assumed command of Fliegerkorps Tunis, with HQ near Gabes, and at the same time Fliegerführer 2, in northern Tunisia, and Fliegerführer 3, in command of the forces in the south, were subordinated to him. The army changes were more complex and, the decrypts on the subject being unusually difficult to interpret, the Allied commanders in Tunisia did not receive a summary of them till 9 February.[38] As well as announcing that Bastico had laid down his command on 30 January, that Panzer Army 5 had been subordinated for operations to Comando Supremo in Rome with effect from 26 January, and that Kesselring would ensure that German influence was exercised on Comando

---

* See above, pp 459–460.   † See below, p 583 et seq.

34.   WO 208/3573, MI 14 Appreciation for the CIGS, 4 January 1943.
35.   Howe, op cit, pp 324, 364.
36.   VMs 111 of 1 January, 291 of 4 January 1943; CX/MSS/1897/T12, 1909/T1.
37.   VM 3798 of 12 February 1943; CX/MSS/2068/T15, 2069/T28, 2072/T6, 2090/T8.
38.   VM 3613 of 9 February 1943; CX/MSS/2090/T5 to 12.

Supremo's orders, the summary assumed that von Arnim had already taken unified command over Panzer Army 5 and Rommel's army. In one of the decrypts, which perhaps as a precaution against gossip was not mentioned to the Allied commanders, Hitler had indeed so ordered on 26 January and had given the reason: 'unified command of both armies is essential and must be assumed by one of the commanders; since Rommel is sick this can only be Generaloberst von Arnim'.[39] The summary also reported that the Italian General Messe was to relieve Rommel as GOC of the Axis ground forces on the Mareth line and that on 26 January his arrival had been expected 'within a few days'. In the event, though this was not learned at the time, Messe on his arrival on 2 February refused to take command because of the uncertain operational situation, Rommel decided not to relinquish his post until ordered to do so and Messe did not relieve him till 20 February;[40]* but numerous decrypts of signals originated by Rommel down to 20 February established that he remained in charge at least of his old army. Down to the resumption of large-scale fighting on 14 February, however, the Enigma failed to disclose that the order for the establishment of a unified command had not yet been implemented.

Even without the attendant confusion, it would have been difficult to deduce anything of value about the enemy's intentions from these command changes. Joint command over the Axis armies was urgently called for now that Rommel's supplies were going through Tunisia and 21st Panzer Division was moving there. Other decrypts had shown that after wrangling between Rommel and von Arnim about the control of the division, it had been subordinated to Panzer Army 5 on 28 January,[42]† Other Enigma references to the division were sufficiently explained by the revival of Axis fears about an Allied threat to the coast road as a result of the build-up of US II Corps at Tebessa. It was learned on 18 and 19 January that 21st Panzer Division would receive 34 tanks when it reached Sfax[43] and on 26 January that Kesselring had directed that 21st Panzer

---

* In October 1942 Rommel's Panzer Army Africa had been re-named German-Italian Panzer Army. On 20 February 1943 it became First Italian Army under General Messe. For some time before and after this date there was confusion among the German signallers as to what name they should use and they often described the Army as Panzer Army Rommel.[41] In this account First Italian Army is used from February onwards.

† Together with the Italian Centauro (armoured) Division, but the transfer of this division was not disclosed by the Enigma till later.

39.   DEFE 3/573, CX/MSS/C 96.
40.   Playfair, op cit, Vol IV, p 269.
41.   ibid, pp 50 fn. 269.
42.   VMs 2122 of 23 January, 2319 of 25 January, 2533 of 27 January, 2574 of 28 January 1943; CX/MSS/2007/T18, 2015/T12, 13 and 14, 2024/T6 and 28.
43.   VM 1667 of 19 January 1943; CX/MSS/1983/T24.

Division and Rommel's Panzer Army were to be rested and refitted with all possible despatch.[44] By 28 January the Enigma showed that the division had been immediately re-equipped on its arrival at Sfax on 26 January.[45]

To the extent that it did take place, the Axis reorganisation, and particularly the winding up of Bastico's command, seriously incommoded GC and CS by disrupting the pattern of the enemy's routine signals. Ever since the beginning of the fighting in north-west Africa the Enigma settings (Bullfinch) used by Panzer Army 5 at army level and above had sometimes been broken by GC and CS with long delays, while the settings used between Panzer Army 5 and its subordinate formations (Dodo) had gone largely unread owing to the lack of provision in the north African theatre, unlike the Middle East, for intercepting the traffic and sending the intercepts back to Bletchley.* From the beginning of December 1942 the Germans had resorted to security precautions which tightened up the encypherment of signals in all the Army Enigma keys used in north Africa, and this also added to GC and CS's difficulties. Although its work had suffered from more frequent delays and occasional gaps, GC and CS had despite these problems still managed during December 1942 and January 1943 to maintain a high level of success against the Bullfinch settings and against the settings (Chaffinch) used by Rommel's Panzer Army at army level and above. Following the lapse of Bastico's command at the beginning of February 1943, however, breaks into these settings became less and less frequent, with the result that the Enigma threw little light on the enemy's intentions at a time when these were generating more exchanges by W/T between the Axis commanders and their superiors in Europe.† This development was to some extent off-set by the fact that GC and CS read from January 1943 for three months and then, after a brief interruption, from April 1943 until the end of the Tunisian campaign the Fish setting (Herring) that was introduced in December 1942 for traffic between Rome and Panzer Army 5.

The difficulty that was experienced with the Enigma settings made it especially unfortunate that Allied Y and tactical reconnaissance had not yet overcome the problems created for them by

---

* See Appendix 18 and above, p 503.

† From April 1943, on the other hand, GC and CS broke another Enigma key (which it named Sparrow), that used by the German Army Sigint Service. By providing information about the German field Sigint staff, this sometimes gave clues as to coming German operations; it was also useful to Allied cypher security and, above all, by throwing light on enemy assessments of Allied order of battle it increased the value of the Enigma as a guide to those responsible for Allied deception measures.

44.   VM 2406 of 26 January 1943; CX/MSS/2018/T31.
45.   VMs 2533 and 2574 of 27 and 28 January 1943; CX/MSS/2024/T6 and 28.

insufficient advance preparations.* Moreover, they were impeded by complications and changes in the Allied command structure. In the middle of January, to help him to control military operations along the whole Allied front, General Eisenhower established a forward command post at Constantine but the intelligence staff at AFHQ continued to collate at a distance of hundreds of miles the intelligence reports of the three separate national commands – of the British First Army in the northern sector, the French in the centre and the Americans in the south. During the third week of January this system was shown to be operationally inadequate when Panzer Army 5 made a number of small-scale but important attacks on the French central sector; on 21 January General Eisenhower accordingly decided that the commander of the First Army must 'co-ordinate' the British and the US forces, and on 26 January, overcoming the objections of the French, he put General Anderson in command of all Allied forces on the Tunisian front. Changes even more abrupt were meanwhile being made in the Allied air commands.† Although they were unavoidable, such changes contrived to keep the field intelligence staffs less than efficient at the work of collecting and co-ordinating the results of air reconnaissance, POW interrogation, agents' reports and Y – work which was difficult enough in operational conditions at the best of times and which could not be done effectively in the absence of a stable organisation and clear channels of communication. Between the end of January and the bigger German attack that came in the middle of February, for example, the US, French and British formations continued to send their intelligence reports back to AFHQ because General Anderson's HQ lacked adequate communications and staff.

Over and above these considerable handicaps a further problem made it difficult to form an accurate appreciation of the enemy's intentions. The enemy's plans were being developed with frequent changes of mind and a large element of improvisation within an uncertain structure of command and against the background of confused local fighting that had gone on since mid-January in the mountainous area of the French-held sector of the Allied front. On 28 January, as part of a programme for strengthening the Axis front in the centre and south, von Arnim was instructed by Comando Supremo to undertake the destruction of the US forces in the Tebessa area as a sequel to a planned attack on Faid and then to seize the Gafsa basin. 21st Panzer Division overwhelmed the French garrison at Faid on 30 January, but von Arnim had doubts about the further stages of the plan. On 4 February Rommel, in a memorandum to Comando Supremo, repeated his earlier proposal

---

* See Appendix 18.   † See above, p 574.

that both Panzer armies under a unified command should make a concentrated attack against Gafsa before Eighth Army could attack Mareth. Rommel's plan was rejected as impracticable; instead, he was ordered on 8 February to attack Gafsa with such elements of the two Panzer armies as were not absolutely indispensable for other tasks, and he was told that his object must be primarily the destruction of enemy forces and only secondarily the taking of territory. On 9 February Kesselring, von Arnim and Rommel met to discuss the most recent instructions and to settle their differences; and as the latest reconnaissance reported that the US forces were leaving Gafsa, they agreed on a revised plan for two limited offensive-defensive operations that would be related but carried out under separate command. 10th and 21st Panzer Divisions would first join forces to destroy the US forces in the Sidi Bou Zid area west of Faid; this was operation *Frühlingswind*. 21st Panzer Division would then join a battle group from Panzer Army Rommel in an attack on Gafsa (operation *Morgenluft*) while 10th Panzer Division moved north to attack in the area west of Kairouan. It was settled that operation *Frühlingswind* should start between 12 and 14 February.[46] This is a brief summary of what the Allies learned after the event about the chief developments on the Axis side. At the time, as a result of the difficulties already discussed, the Enigma provided evidence about them that was so incomplete as to be wholly misleading.

An intimation of the enemy's general plan was obtained on 26 January from the decrypt of a signal from Kesselring of 24 January. This said that the Axis must regain the initiative as soon as possible by operating from the south of Panzer Army 5's front in the general direction of Tebessa and also, perhaps, from the Mareth zone. It added that Rommel's army would have to be rested and refitted as rapidly as possible to ensure the defence of the Mareth line against an attempt by Eighth Army to interfere.[47] On 30 January there followed two further decrypts. The first was from an unidentified authority, thought by GC and CS to be in Tunis. It stated that two divisions were not enough for an operation against Tebessa and that, although two divisions would be enough for an attack against Gafsa, they were not available; 10th Panzer Division could not be spared from the north and the rest of 21st Panzer Division (presumably that part of it which had not been used to take Faid) was not ready for operations. The second, from the GAF authorities, stated that in their opinion Rommel was having doubts

---

46.   Playfair, op cit, Vol IV, pp 287–289; Howe, op cit, pp 405–407.
47.   VM 2406 of 26 January 1943; CX/MSS/2018/T31.

about an attack on Gafsa.[48] These signals actually referred to Comando Supremo's instructions of 28 January and those instructions had not been decrypted by GC and CS – if indeed they had been transmitted in the Enigma – but there was no difficulty in interpreting the signals in the light of Kesselring's signal of 24 January. Moreover, all seemed to fall into place when on 1 February, from the decrypt of a signal from Fliegerführer Afrika of 31 January, GC and CS obtained full details of a forthcoming operation involving both 10th and 21st Panzer Divisions west and south-west of Kairouan to advance the main defence line in the Ousseltia–Fondouk area.

This operation, code-named *Kuckucksei*, was to be carried out by Korpsgruppe Fischer (Fischer was the commander of 10th Panzer Division) with powerful elements of 10th Panzer Division, including a 'Tiger Gruppe', and by 21st Panzer Division. From Medjez el Bab and Faid respectively, they were to move up to given assembly areas, 'probably' from dawn on 2 February. From there on 'A-day' Korpsgruppe Fischer would attack the Allied positions, and attempt to take them in the rear, while 21st Panzer Division and Fliegerführer Afrika shielded it against Allied intervention from the south-west.[49]

These details about operation *Kuckucksei* had also been issued on 30 January in Panzer Army 5's day report, which was decrypted on 3 February. On 8 February, moreover, the Enigma confirmed that, as was indeed the case, the enemy was still intending to carry out the operation by disclosing that GAF reinforcements were to be sent to Kairouan to operate in support of Panzer Army 5, probably on 10 February, in an offensive west and south-west of that place.[50] Two days earlier the Allies had learned from another decrypt that there was some disagreement among the Axis commands; in a signal to Kesselring on 6 February Fliegerführer Afrika had complained that neither Panzer army believed it could release the necessary forces for the Gafsa undertaking, and had requested that they should be given explicit orders to take Gafsa while the situation was 'still favourable'.[51] But between 8 February and 14 February, the day of the German attack, the Enigma gave no indication that *Kuckucksei* had been superseded by *Frühlingswind* and *Morgenluft* on 9 February; the signals giving the intentions to carry out these two operations were not decrypted and sent to the commands until late on 14 February.[52] Nor did the other intelli-

48. VMs 2824 and 2855 of 30 January 1943; CX/MSS/2036/T1, 2039/T7.
49. VM 2955 of 1 February 1943; CX/MSS/2043/T29.
50. VMs 3128 of 3 February, 3485 of 8 February 1943; CX/MSS/2055/T2, 2081/T36.
51. VM 3396 of 6 February 1943; CX/MSS/2075/T11.
52. VM 4001 of 14 February 1943; CX/MSS/2118/T13.

gence sources make up for the deficiencies of the Enigma, information from PR, tactical air reconnaissance, Army Y, POW and the Allied ground patrols being either non-existent or insufficient to correct the appreciation that on the northern front the enemy intended to carry out operation *Kuckucksei* through Fondouk, rather than the operation which Rommel and von Arnim were now planning against Sidi Bou Zid.*

On 13 February the Enigma disclosed that HQ 21st Panzer Division was to move forward that day[53] and indicated that the following day was to be A-day for an operation by Panzer Army 5.[54] This was the basis for 'the word . . . flashed from First Army HQ late on the 13th that an attack would be made by the enemy the next day'.[55] First Army's warning was a general one; the Enigma did not state where the attack would come. Nor were the Allies quick to discern the enemy's intentions when, beginning in the early hours of 14 February, 10th Panzer Division, with 111 Pzkw III and Pzkw IV tanks and a dozen Tigers, and 21st Panzer Division, with 91 Pzkw III and Pzkw IV tanks, moved against Sidi Bou Zid.[56] During the morning of 14 February US 1st Armoured Division[57] and II US Corps HQ[58] did not regard it as a major offensive and requested only 'modest reinforcements'.[59] As late as the evening of 14 February, when Combat Command A of US 1st Armoured Division had retired badly mauled, with the loss of 44 tanks, and other US formations had been surrounded,[60] it was thought that the enemy had employed only 21st Panzer Division with between 90 and 130 tanks.[61] Partly on this account and partly, no doubt, because of the lingering influence of the *Kuckucksei* decrypt, AFHQ and First Army HQ reasoned that 10th Panzer Division remained to the north, ready to attack in the Ousseltia–Fondouk area.[62]† Nor did the Enigma save them from the consequences of inadequate field intelligence during the following day; it did not mention 10th Panzer Division between 12 February‡ and 16 February, and even then it disclosed only that 10th Panzer

---

* For the details see Appendix 21.

† It is arguable that they could have deduced that 10th Panzer Division was involved from the latest Enigma tank return of 9 February, which had stated that 21st Panzer Division had only 63 serviceable tanks out of Panzer Army 5's total of 181 plus 15 Tigers.[63] But in the absence of regular checks on tank strengths from Army Y this is difficult to maintain.

‡ See Appendix 21.

53. VM 3889 of 0836/13 February 1943; CX/MSS/2111/T24.
54. VM 3883 of 0753/13 February 1943; CX/MSS/2111/T21.
55. Howe, op cit, p 405.						56. ibid, p 406.
57. ibid, p 413.				58. ibid, p 417.			59. ibid, p 417.
60. ibid, p 412.				61. ibid, p 417.			62. ibid, p 417.
63. VM 3573 of 9 February 1943; CX/MSS/2122/T21; DEFE 3/589, ZTPGM 9171.

Division was to receive fighter cover from Kairouan.[64] General Eisenhower was still under the impression that 10th Panzer Division had not been committed when, on the evening of 15 February, he agreed with General Anderson that US 1st Armoured Division's Combat Command B must be retained in the north.[65]

By that time the Allied counter-attack on Sidi Bou Zid had been repulsed with heavy US losses. In addition the Allied commanders had known from the Enigma since the morning of 14 February that Panzer Army Rommel considered that it could begin the Gafsa undertaking on the morning of 16 February only if the weather did not hold up the 'previous attack elsewhere' of 21st Panzer Division.[66] On the evening of 14 February, as a result of this decrypt, General Anderson had ordered the US forces at Gafsa to retire to Feriana, adding that they need not expect to be attacked for another 36 hours. On the evening of 15 February, in the light of a further decrypt and of the repulse of the counter-attack at Sidi Bou Zid, General Eisenhower and General Anderson agreed that the whole Allied front line should be pulled back while the threat of an enemy attempt to outflank it from the south was countered by a strong concentration of armour in the Sbeitla-Sbiba area.[67] The further decrypt, sent out from GC and CS on the evening of 14 February and consisting of a directive from Comando Supremo dated 11 February, had stated that, immediately following the attack by Panzer Army 5 on Sidi Bou Zid, First Italian Army* with a mobile Battle Group from Panzer Army 5 was to make a pincer thrust towards Gafsa and, dependent on the development of the tactical situation, to continue its attack on Tozeur after securing the Gafsa basin, while Panzer Army 5 itself concentrated, by a fairly strong thrust on its right wing, on extensively harassing the Allied concentration in the Sidi Bou Zid area.[68]

The Allies carried out a drastic withdrawal to a new line running through Sbiba, Kasserine and Feriana on the night of 16 February. By that time Rommel had ordered his southern Battle Group, which had taken Gafsa late on the previous night, to press on to Feriana, and von Arnim had started 10th and 21st Panzer Divisions for Sbeitla. At Sbeitla the main Axis advance was delayed by Combat Command B, First Army's sole remaining coherent armoured formation in the southern sector, which on 15 February

---

* See above, p 581, fn *.

64.   VM 4131 of 16 February 1943; CX/MSS/2127/T20.

65.   CAB 105/33, No 166 of 15 February 1943; CAB 44/115, AL 1200/8, p 178; Howe, op cit, p 423.

66.   VM 3962 of 0538/14 February 1943; CX/MSS/2117/T10 and 18.

67.   CAB 105/33, No 166 of 15 February 1943; CAB 44/115, p 178; Howe, op cit, p 423.

68.   VM 4001 of 14 February 1943; CX/MSS/2118/T17.

General Anderson had decided to bring south from Maktar, 50 miles to the north, where it had been masking Fondouk. On 17 February 21st Panzer Division drove Combat Command B out of Sbeitla, the southern Battle Group took Feriana and Rommel proposed to von Arnim that they should advance together with the two Panzer divisions to capture the huge American depots at Tebessa and then to move north to turn the Allied position in Tunisia. At midnight on 17–18 February von Arnim replied that no further considerable advance was possible because of supply difficulties and that 10th Panzer Division had already been ordered to Fondouk to carry out a modified version of *Kuckucksei* west of Kairouan. During the morning of 18 February, however, on learning that patrols of 21st Panzer Division and the southern Battle Group had met at Kasserine and that Axis air reconnaissance had shown that the Allies were not yet assembling for a strong counter-attack, Rommel appealed direct to Comando Supremo for authority to take 10th and 21st Panzer Divisions under his command and advance at once on Tebessa. His request was approved at midnight on 18–19 February, though with the major modification that he must in the first instance advance on Le Kef, an important communications centre for First Army. He began attacking through Kasserine on 19 February.[69]

Of these developments on the Axis side the Allied command received a good deal of Enigma about the movement up to Gafsa, and its decision to evacuate Feriana on 17 February was influenced by a decrypt of 16 February in which First Italian Army announced the intention of pushing on from Gafsa to Feriana.[70] From a further decrypt, sent out to it in the afternoon of 16 February, it could have deduced that the southern thrust might run out of fuel if it penetrated beyond Feriana; this gave it the news that fuel stocks available for 21st Panzer Division and the southern Battle Group on 15 February had been sufficient for 100–150 kms 'if the fighting is continued to the west'.[71] In the same decrypt the Quartermaster of First Italian Army had added that the carrying out of the 'special undertaking' was assured provided it was over in two days. But until 17 February, beyond what was being reported by their own troops, the Allies had next to no intelligence from the rest of the Axis front.* On 16 February GC and CS had decrypted Panzer

* The difference between intelligence about the southern Battle Group and the rest of the Axis front was due not only to the greater difficulty which GC and CS had with the Bullfinch (Panzer Army 5) than with the Chaffinch (First Italian Army) Enigma settings, but also because the Phoenix settings as used by First Italian Army for communications below army

69. Howe, op cit, pp 426–428, 440; Playfair, op cit, Vol IV, pp 293–295; Liddell Hart, *History of the Second World War* (1970), p 410.
70. VM 4133 of 16 February 1943; CX/MSS/2128/T1.
71. VM 4149 of 1450/16 February 1943; CX/MSS/2128/T9.

Army 5's day report for the previous day; it reported the destruction of 97 tanks at Sidi Bou Zid and the capture of numerous prisoners together with documents giving the entire US order of battle.[72] During 17 February the Enigma had disclosed that 10th and 21st Panzer Divisions were proceeding on 16 February to an unidentified position[73] and, though AFHQ still thought that its 'main strength' had remained near Kairouan, Army Y had at last located a portion of 10th Panzer Division near Sbeitla.[74] Nor was it until 17 and 18 February that, in the light of a series of decrypts of GAF Enigma signals from Fliegerführer Tunis, they were able to do more than guess at the nature of the special undertaking.

On the morning of 17 February the first of these signals told them that the Fliegerführer had informed Kesselring the previous day that an advance on Feriana and Tebessa, to put Allied air bases out of action, was possible.[75] On the evening of 17 February the next signal showed that the GAF had been ready since that morning for operations against Tebessa, Le Kef and on the northern front in support of a further advance.[76] In a third signal, sent out by GC and CS early on 18 February, the Fliegerführer reported to Kesselring on the evening of 17 February that a further advance was possible as air reconnaissance had disclosed that the Allies were withdrawing.[77] On the afternoon of 18 February he informed Kesselring that Rommel wished to advance with 21st Panzer Division to a position which GC and CS could not identify, but that Panzer Army 5 had refused to give up any troops; this decrypt reached the Allied commanders the same evening.[78]

The Fliegerführer's signals were interspersed with decrypts of signals from Rommel. Just before midnight on 17–18 February GC and CS decrypted a signal from him announcing that his intention for his Panzer Army on the following day was 'to hold the position reached'.[79] On the evening of 18 February the Allied commands received the decrypt of his day report for 17 February. It expanded on the previous signal by stating that his intentions for 18 February were to hold his bridgehead at Thelepte and to withdraw consider-

---

level were more easily decrypted than those for Dodo, the equivalent settings used by Panzer Army 5. See above, pp 503, 562, and also Appendix 18 for the failure to arrange for the interception of the frequencies carrying Dodo.

72. VM 4184 of 16 February 1943; CX/MSS/2130/T7.
73. VM 4216 of 0403/17 February 1943; CX/MSS/2132/T11.
74. CAB 44/115, p 192; WO 204/978, AFHQ Daily Intelligence Summary No 102 of 17 February 1943.
75. VM 4221 of 0459/17 February 1943; CX/MSS/2132/T14.
76. VM 4270 of 1751/17 February 1943; CX/MSS/2136/T5.
77. VM 4327 of 0627/18 February 1943; CX/MSS/2137/T2.
78. VM 4387 of 2009/18 February 1943; CX/MSS/2139/T11.
79. VM 4299 of 2333/17 February 1943; CX/MSS/2136/T43.

able elements to Mareth, and it announced that 'there seemed to be
no possibility either of continuation of the attack on Tebessa or
even of holding the area Thelepte–Feriana for any length of time'.
But it also announced that decisions about the southern Battle
Group depended on Panzer Army 5's situation in the Sbeitla area.
It added that 21st Panzer Division had 65 serviceable tanks.[80] But
Rommel's proposal to von Arnim of 17 February for a joint
advance, and his proposal to Comando Supremo of 18 February for
an advance by 10th and 21st Panzer Divisions under his own
command, were not decrypted until the afternoon of 19 February,[81]
and Comando Supremo's authorisation for the second of these
proposals was not decrypted till the evening of 20 February.[82]

While the Axis command hesitated between midnight on 17
February and midnight on 18 February, when Rommel received
permission to advance to Le Kef, the Allied command ordered
immediate measures for the defence of the pass at Kasserine and
the reinforcement of the southern sector. British armour – 6th
Armoured Division and 1st Guards Brigade – was despatched from
the northern sector to the Sbiba–Thala area and US 9th Division's
artillery was ordered to move up from Morocco. During this
period, in addition to what the Allies learned from the signals from
Fliegerführer Tunis and Rommel about their plans and their
uncertainties, they were informed by the GAF Enigma that 10th
Panzer Division was moving north-east through Fondouk on the
morning of 18 February but that a southern Gruppe of Panzer
Army 5 was advancing on Kasserine.[83] But while the threat from
Kasserine was clear enough, and while the Allies thus knew that it
would be a day or more before 10th Panzer Division could join up
with any advance, they had no firm intelligence about Rommel's
immediate intentions, and in particular about the direction in
which he would make his main thrust, until, some time after
midnight on 19–20 February, they received the decrypt of Fliegerführer Tunis's situation report for the evening of 19 February. This
disclosed that the GAF's orders for 20 February were to carry out
reconnaissance southwards from Le Kef and to be ready to support
21st and 10th Panzer Divisions.[84]

On the morning of 19 February Rommel had ordered the
southern Battle Group to advance through Kasserine and Thala to
Le Kef while 21st Panzer Division made for the same objective
through Sbiba, and had summoned 10th Panzer Division back

80. VM 4390 of 2115/18 February 1943; CX/MSS/2136/T16.
81. VMs 4473 of 1407/19 February, 4487 of 1743/19 February 1943;
     CX/MSS/2141/T15 and 20.
82. VM 4592 of 20 February 1943; CX/MSS/2148/T11.
83. VM 4373 of 1719/18 February 1943; CX/MSS/2139/T3.
84. VM 4513 of 2357/19 February 1943; CX/MSS/2145/T2.

from Fondouk to Sbeitla to await developments. 21st Panzer Division was halted by the greatly superior Allied strength at Sbiba. The southern Battle Group failed to achieve a surprise attack on Kasserine on the morning of 19 February, the American defenders of the pass having been alerted by the British Y party attached to US II Corps, but thereafter made progress through the pass. Rommel having decided to use 10th Panzer Division to reinforce its advance, an all-out attack at 1630 on 20 February succeeded in capturing the pass. On the morning of 21 February Rommel waited in preparation for an Allied counter-attack.[85] On the morning of 20 February, meanwhile, the planned take-over of command of the Allied forces by the newly-formed 18th Army Group under General Alexander had taken place, and he had decided to concentrate the Allied armour south of Thala, astride the road from Kasserine, to bring up Combat Command B from Tebessa to Thala, and to stiffen the defensive position with further armour, artillery and infantry from the northern sector.[86] With regard to these decisions it has been said that, had Rommel in fact turned west towards Tebessa, the Allies would have been caught badly off balance;[87] but it has also been claimed that 'there never was much doubt' that Rommel would thrust towards Thala rather than against Tebessa.[88] It may well be that this was clear enough from the course of the fighting since the previous morning; and there is no evidence to show whether the decisions were influenced by the receipt, hours before, of the decrypt giving the GAF's intentions for 20 February. But the omission of any reference to Tebessa in that decrypt makes it not improbable that the decrypt helped to persuade General Alexander's intelligence staff that Thala-Le Kef was 'the vital area'.[89]

About midnight on 20–21 February, from the decrypt of Comando Supremo's reply to Rommel's request of 18 February, the Allied command received confirmation that 10th and 21st Panzer Divisions were to make for Le Kef 'in the first instance'.[90] From the same decrypt they learned that the scope of the enemy's objectives greatly exceeded what intelligence had led them to expect. It announced that, since the 'low fighting value' shown by the Allied troops offered a unique opportunity to gain a decisive success by cutting off British V Corps or compelling the Allied forces in the south to withdraw, Panzer Army 5 was to prepare to attack on the front in northern Tunisia so as to tie down the Allies there while

85. Howe, op cit, pp 441, 452, 456, 470.
86. ibid, p 457; CAB 44/115, p 201.
87. Liddell Hart, op cit, p 406.
88. Hunt, *A Don at War* (1966), pp 161, 162.
89. CAB 44/115, pp 198–199.
90. VMs 4592 and 4602 of 20 February 1943; CX/MSS/2148/T11.

Rommel advanced, and that, since no major British attack at Mareth was expected for at least a week, only minimum mobile reserves need be kept there. It was followed by the decrypt of Rommel's orders for his further advance, which reached the commands from GC and CS about noon on 21 February.[91] 21st Panzer Division was to attack through Sbiba to Ksour. 10th Panzer Division, 'at only half battle strength since considerable elements were still operating elsewhere', was to attack along the road to Thala. The southern Battle Group was to advance towards El Hamma on the fork road to Tebessa. But when this intelligence was received, while 21st Panzer Division remained blocked on the Sbeitla–Sbiba road, 10th Panzer Division, elements of which had already been identified by Army Y among the forces that were attacking through the Kasserine pass, was fighting its way to Thala.

By the end of the day 10th Panzer Division had been repulsed, after heavy fighting, by the larger Allied force that had been assembled in the Thala area. At the same time, Combat Command B, recalled to Tebessa and strengthened by other US forces from the Ousseltia area,[92] had checked the subsidiary thrust which Rommel had sent towards Tebessa; and by 22 February the southern Battle Group was sustaining heavy losses. On the evening of 22 February Army Y, which was at last beginning to make a useful contribution, intercepted an order to withdraw addressed to one of its leading units. This was the first indication to be received of the general Axis withdrawal on which Rommel and Kesselring had decided during the afternoon. Other indications followed. At 0145 on 23 February, with quite remarkable speed, GC and CS issued the decrypt of Comando Supremo's order, timed 2130 on 22 February, for the attack to be halted and for the withdrawal of Rommel's forces to their starting positions.[93] During the remainder of 23 February Army Y and air reconnaissance[94] provided plentiful evidence that the withdrawal was in progress.[95]

□

Despite General Eisenhower's 'anxiety to take instant advantage of the fleeting opportunity for trouncing the enemy before he could recover from his embarrassing position' – an anxiety which led him

---

91.   VM 4634 of 1016/21 February 1943; CX/MSS/2151/T2.
92.   Howe, op cit, p 457.
93.   VM 4762 of 23 February 1943; CX/MSS/2160/T5.
94.   AIR 41/33, p 127.
95.   WO 169/8519, Eighth Army Intelligence Summary No 440 of 23 February 1943.

to assure the commander of US II Corps on the evening of 22 February that 'he was perfectly safe in taking any reasonable risk in launching local counter-attacks that could be properly supported by his artillery'[96] – II Corps was, to quote the US official history, 'extraordinarily hesitant' in making use of this intelligence.[97] It was not until late on 23 February that it gave orders for a general counter-attack to be mounted on 25 February. By that time the enemy had withdrawn through the Kasserine bottleneck and Rommel, as he had agreed with Kesselring on the afternoon of 22 February, was concentrating in southern Tunisia for an attack on Eighth Army which would catch it off balance while it was assembling its forces for an assault on the Mareth line.[98]

GC and CS excelled itself in giving good notice of Rommel's new intention. On 25 February it decrypted the day report for 22 February in which he gave his reasons for the sudden abandonment of the westward offensive: Allied reinforcements, bad weather, difficult terrain, low Axis fighting strength – and the fact that the situation at Mareth made it necessary to collect his mobile forces for a swift blow against Eighth Army before it had completed its preparations.[99] More important – for it had all along been obvious that the enemy had to take account of the danger at Mareth, and Comando Supremo's calculation that a British attack there was not expected for at least a week from 18 February had been decrypted on 20 February* – GC and CS now redeemed the shortcomings the Enigma had displayed before the enemy's February offensive by providing details of the preparations and plans for the assault on Eighth Army's positions at Medenine.

The Axis had by now established the unified command in north Africa that it had tried to introduce at the end of January.† General Messe took over command of Rommel's army – which was now named First Italian Army – on 20 February, but Rommel retained command of the forces under him in the fighting zone. On 23 February a directive from Comando Supremo laid it down that, to ensure unified control of future operations, Army Group Africa was to be formed under Rommel at once, and that Rommel would decide when the command of the Army Group was to be handed over to von Arnim. From the text of this directive, which was decrypted and sent out to the Allied operational authorities on 25 January, it could be presumed that, notwithstanding the references in January in the Enigma to Rommel's continuing illness,‡ the

---

* See above, p 592.   † See above, pp 580–581.   ‡ See above, p 581.

96.   Eisenhower, *Crusade in Europe* (1948), p 161.
97.   Howe, op cit, p 470.
98.   ibid, p 470.
99.   VM 4931 of 25 February 1943; CX/MSS/2172/T20.

hand-over would not take place before the attack in the Mareth area: it went on to say that, in addition to an offensive by von Arnim in the north, Army Group Africa would, on completion of the withdrawal from Kasserine, 'smash the attacking spearheads of Eighth Army in the first days of March', and that for this purpose 10th Panzer Division was to be prepared at Sfax and the remainder of the motorised formations at Gabes.[100]

The enemy's command changes, disclosed by the Enigma between 22 and 25 February,[101] did not put a stop to friction between von Arnim and Rommel. In the hope of taking Medjez el Bab and extending Panzer Army 5's front, but with the professed object of drawing off the Allies during Rommel's retreat from Kasserine, von Arnim launched an attack in the north on 26 February. It had some success but had incurred heavy losses, particularly in tanks, by the time it was called off on 4 March.* The Enigma gave notice of the opening of this attack,[102] and while it lasted the Enigma and Army Y† provided some tactical intelligence.[104] But the Enigma also revealed that Rommel was trying in vain to stop it. In a report of his plans issued on 27 February, and decrypted on 28 February, he referred to the intolerable dissipation of forces that was resulting from von Arnim's initiative.[105]

On 26 February Rommel had already asked First Italian Army to make a reconnaissance in preparation for an encircling attack on Medenine, 20 miles south of Mareth, by two to three Panzer divisions; this request was decrypted on 27 February.[106] As outlined in Rommel's report of 27 February, which was decrypted on 28 February, his plan was to attack at the latest on 4 March with 10th, 15th and 21st Panzer Divisions; 10th and 21st Panzer Divisions were to move south from Gabes well inland so as to 'deceive Allied air reconnaissance'. Apart from a fuel return for Army Group Africa which showed that on 1 March Rommel had fuel for at most three days[107] – enough to do great damage in a

---

* See below, p 598.

† The Enigma containing the notice to attack was decrypted at 0342 on 26 February. AFHQ's acknowledgement was received back at GC and CS at 0507. The DMI commented to the Prime Minister: 'A very good performance.'[103]

100.   VM 4967 of 1846/25 February 1943; CX/MSS/2173/T17.
101.   VMs 4697 of 22 February, 4967 of 25 February 1943; CX/MSS/2154/T8, 2173/T17.
102.   VM 5007 of 0342/26 February 1943; CX/MSS/2177/T14.
103.   Cabinet Office file 82/43/1, Part 2, DMI to the Prime Minister 26 February 1943.   104.   WO 208/3573 of 8 March 1943.
105.   VMs 5197 of 1416/28 February, 5207 of 1646/28 February 1943; CX/MSS/2190/T14.
106.   VM 5095 of 27 February 1943; CX/MSS/2183/T22.
107.   VM 5440 of 3 March 1943; CX/MSS/2204/T27; WO 208/3573 of 8 March 1943; WO 169/8519, No 445 of 3 March 1943.

surprise spoiling attack, but not for another offensive on the scale of
Kasserine – these two decrypts were the last to throw light on
Rommel's plans. But they were of decisive importance. As late as
26 February Eighth Army had no more than the equivalent of one
division up forward at Medenine, most of its armour was with X
Corps at Benghazi and General Montgomery, who was planning
an Alamein-type offensive against the Mareth line for 20 March,
estimated that 7 March was the earliest date at which XXX Corps
could be made ready to meet an enemy attack.[108] But after rushing
up guns and tanks during 'three days and nights of feverish
activity' beginning with the receipt of the decrypts on 27–28
February,[109] the strength of XXX Corps at Medenine had been
quadrupled by 4 March, and when Rommel eventually attacked
with 160 tanks and 200 runs he was opposed by 400 tanks, 350 field
guns and 470 anti-tank guns. By then, too, the RAF had brought
its forward strength up to double that which was known to be
available to the enemy.[110]

4 March passed without incident. Nor was it until the morning of
6 March that GC and CS sent out to Eighth Army the thrust-line
for the German attack and the news that it was to begin at 0600
that day. This decrypt was despatched at 0536 and would have
been received after the battle had begun.[111] Already, however, it
had been 'apparent at Medenine that the enemy would attack
before 7 March and, on the eve of the assault, that it would be
delivered on the morning of 6 March'.[112] Army Y had detected the
movement southward of Rommel's forces. Air sightings of 10th
Panzer Division and other armour had by 4 March suggested that
his main thrust would come from the west, from the southern end of
the enemy line.[113] Thereafter conflicting evidence was received
from various sources as to the direction from which Rommel would
attack. In the end the British artillery was 'so positioned that the
majority of our guns could bring down concentrations upon the
enemy from whatever sector he attacked'.[114] But by piecing all
these clues together Eighth Army was at least able to conclude by
the end of 5 March that the offensive would begin the following
morning.[115]

108. Playfair, op cit, Vol IV, pp 316, 320; Howe, op cit, p 514; Liddell Hart, op cit, p 416.
109. CAB 44/116, AL 1200/63, p 58; Montgomery, *El Alamein to the River Sangro* (1949), pp 54–55.
110. Playfair, op cit, Vol IV, p 324; Howe, op cit, p 516; Liddell Hart, op cit, p 411.   111.   VM 5722 of 0536/6 Mar 1943; CX/MSS/2220/T25.
112. Howe, op cit, p 514.   113.   AIR 41/50, p 493.
114. de Guingand, *Operation Victory* (1947), p 245.
115. VMs 5620 of 0612/5 March, 5665 of 1746/5 March, 5676 of 1954/5 March 1943; CX/MSS/2215/T20, 2218/T2, 8 and 9; Hunt, op cit, p 165.

Had Rommel defeated Eighth Army at Medenine the whole sequence of future Allied moves in the Mediterranean would have been set back but, in the event, attacking at 0600 on 6 March Rommel's forces sustained very heavy losses. By the end of the morning, as the Enigma soon disclosed,[116] he had decided to break off on account of the superior artillery and unexpected strength of the British defences. By the evening the three Panzer divisions had lost some 50 of their 140 tanks.[117] Surprise had been indispensable for the success of his plan, and Rommel had indeed attacked in the belief that Eighth Army was unready. Even though he had not detected its preparations, this belief is not easy to understand in view of the fact that Rommel's armour had been sighted by air reconnaissance, and had even been bombed during its approach.

General Montgomery used this argument in his own defence when – as after the battle of Alam el Halfa* – Whitehall rebuked him for taking insufficient precautions in making use of the Enigma. Decrypts of 9 March had revealed that, from POW statements and captured documents, the Germans had concluded that Eighth Army had been aware in advance not only of Rommel's intention to attack, but also of the strength, place and time of the attack.[118] The decrypts contained no evidence that the Germans assumed that the Enigma had been the source of this intelligence, as indeed it had not been as far as the time of his attack was concerned; and time was soon to show that they still did not suspect that their machine cyphers were vulnerable. But the revelation naturally caused alarm in Whitehall; as the CIGS pointed out, while the references to prisoners' statements and captured documents did 'not necessarily mean that matters of highest secrecy have been compromised', they did point to 'an alarming lack of security' which 'might well produce German cypher security counter-measures which would deny us all use of Ultra'.

In the wake of this and other recent alarms,† Whitehall was more than usually careful to withhold the news from the commands when it learned from the Enigma of Rommel's final departure from north Africa. Rommel handed over to von Arnim and left for Germany on 9 March. The Germans did not make the news public, nor was it until after the middle of March that it surfaced in the Enigma decrypts. On 18 March a decrypt mentioned that an officer had been given permission to undergo a cure at Semmering 'in company with Generalfeldmarschall Rommel';[119] the first signal

---

* See above, pp 413–414.　　　　† See Appendix 1 (Part (ii)).

116.　VM 5892 of 8 March 1943; CX/MSS/2230/T3.
117.　Playfair, op cit, Vol IV, pp 325, 326.
118.　VM 6021 of 9 March 1943; CX/MSS/2236/T33.
119.　DEFE 3/573, CX/MSS/C 110.

signed by von Arnim as C-in-C Army Group Africa was decrypted on 19 March; and early in April another decrypt referred to the despatch of Rommel's luggage.[120] These decrypts, which were given a severely limited circulation in Whitehall, were not forwarded even in restricted signals to the commands, where the intelligence staffs were left to themselves to conjecture at the end of March and the beginning of April from the evidence of a captured document and Army Y[121] – evidence that was even then undermined by the remarks of a POW[122] and not finally confirmed by further captured documents and circulated by the Allied commands until 21 April[123] – that Rommel might have been recalled before the battle of Mareth.

□

General Montgomery's plan for the battle of Mareth called for a frontal attack on the line by the infantry of XXX Corps, designed to make a gap through which the armour would head for Gabes and Sfax, and for a powerful outflanking move by the New Zealand Corps – the New Zealand Division augmented by 170 tanks – which would debouch into the main battle area through the gap between Djebels Melab and Tebaga. An extension of the enemy's defences across this gap – code-named *Plum* in Eighth Army – had been detected by the Western Desert Air Force during its PR coverage of the formidable defences of the line and the exceptionally difficult terrain around which they had been constructed.[124] Moreover – presumably at the suggestion of French officers who had prepared the Mareth defences before the war and who now assisted the planning of the assault[125] – the Long Range Desert Group had carried out ground reconnaissance of the rough country west of the Matmata hills, at the inland extremity of the Mareth line, and had established that this outflanking route to the *Plum* gap, though difficult, was not impossible.[126] Before the battle began PR detected, and patrols of 4th Indian Division confirmed, that viable tracks round the flank of the line ran through the Matmata hills themselves.[127]

During the last two weeks of the preparations it remained

120. ibid, CX/MSS/C 111 and 114; Dir/C Archive, 3066 of 23 April 1943.
121. Hunt, op cit, pp 167–168.　　122. WO 169/8519, No 473 of 4 Apr 1943.
123. WO 208/3581, 18th Army Group Intelligence Summary I/309 of 21 April 1943.
124. Playfair, op cit, Vol IV, pp 318, 331; WO 169/8519, No 449 of 7 March 1943.
125. Playfair, op cit, Vol IV, p 332; Howard, op cit, Vol IV, p 347; GAD PK 33 of 4 January 1943.
126. Playfair, op cit, Vol IV, p 316; Hunt, op cit, p 170; AIR 41/50, p 498.
127. Playfair, op cit, Vol IV, p 332.

uncertain how the enemy intended to respond to the coming attack, though the Enigma made it clear that he expected it.[128] Army Y and Enigma currently reported the frequent moves of 10th and 21st Panzer Divisions,[129] but threw no light on why the moves were being made. The Allied authorities estimated, correctly, that the enemy had lost 50 tanks at Medenine and a further 50 on First Army's front,* and knew that he was getting few replacements; their estimates were confirmed on the first day of the battle when Enigma disclosed that on 19 March 21st Panzer Division had 74 tanks, 10th Panzer Division had 57, 15th Panzer Division 38 and the Centauro Division 27:[130] a total of 196 tanks. The Allies were thus able to conclude that on the southern Tunisian front he could fight only a defensive battle.[131] But they could not rule out the possibility that he would go over to the attack before Eighth Army was ready, if only to spoil the advance against the rear of First Italian Army by US II Corps that was planned to begin from the Gafsa area on 17 March.[132]† At the same time, they were equally anxious lest, as at Agheila and Buerat, the enemy would abandon his line as soon as Eighth Army attacked in strength.[133] At the end of January the Enigma had disclosed that Rommel, when instructed to stand at Mareth, had pointed out the danger of being outflanked at Mareth, and had pressed to be allowed to fall back on the Akarit position.[134] Except that PR detected the beginning of a new defence line along the Wadi Akarit,[135] however, no further intelligence was obtained about the enemy's intentions until the eve of the assault; the Enigma made no reference to the fact that on his return to Germany Rommel had renewed his pressure for the immediate withdrawal of the 'marching' formations to Akarit and had again failed to get his way.[136]

Not until the evening of 19 March did the Enigma begin to resolve some of this uncertainty. The decrypt of Army Group Africa's day report of 19 March disclosed that 10th Panzer Division

---

* See above, p 594.

† All the more so since they were unaware that Rommel had left (see above, pp 596–597) and felt that it would be unlike him to wait on events.

128.   eg VM 6964 of 20 March 1943; CX/MSS/2294/T13.
129.   WO 169/8519, No 454 of 13 March 1943; WO 208/3581, No I/139 of 9 March 1943; VM 6845 of 19 March 1943; CX/MSS/2290/T10.
130.   VM 6911 of 19 March 1943; CX/MSS/2291/T21.
131.   WO 169/8519, Nos 449 and 450 of 7 and 8 March 1943; WO 208/3581, No I/137 of 8 March 1943; CAB 105/33, No 232 of 8 March 1943.
132.   WO 169/8519, No 453 of 14 March 1943; WO 204/967, AFHQ Weekly Intelligence Summary No 29 of 15 March 1943.
133.   WO 169/8519, No 454 of 14 March 1943.
134.   VM 2359 of 26 January 1943; CX/MSS/2016/T13.
135.   WO 169/8519, No 455 of 16 March 1943.
136.   Playfair, op cit, Vol IV, p 330.

was to remain near Kairouan as Army Group reserve till further notice, while 21st Panzer Division and HQ DAK were to move as mobile reserve to a position south-west of Gafsa.[137] This information assured the Allied commands that 10th Panzer Division would be unable to reach the Mareth line until a day or more after Eighth Army's assault, though they remained uncertain whether, as they now hoped, the enemy would commit his armour against US II Corps's advance, which had taken Gafsa on 17 March.[138] On the evening of 20 March, however, a few hours before beginning its frontal assault, Eighth Army learned from the decrypt of a report of the previous day from General Messe that the enemy intended to stand at Mareth. In this signal Messe, expecting Eighth Army to attack in three or four days' time, said that he expected a main frontal attack, a powerful outflanking attack by armoured and motorised troops and a simultaneous attack in superior force from the Gafsa area, but that 'faced with this situation I once more confirm my intention to defend the Mareth line to the uttermost'. He added that he was making provision for a withdrawal to the Akarit line 'should stubborn defence seem to be leading to complete annihilation'.[139]

At midnight on 20–21 March, after much evidence from Y and Enigma, and from observation of his own activities, that the enemy was concerned for his Mareth flank,[140] another Enigma decrypt disclosed that the GAF had sighted New Zealand Corps, on the afternoon of 19 March, well on its way to the *Plum* gap.[141] Arriving in sight of the gap at last light on 20 March, the Corps made contact with the Italian forces there on the following day, captured an important height during the night of 21–22 March, but its commander, General Freyberg, then decided not to push forward. Eighth Army had not by then learned that General Messe had on 19 March ordered 164th Division to move to the gap to reinforce the Italians; on the evening of 22 March it thought that the Division was still in the Mareth line and its presence in the gap, which it reached during 22 March, was not reported by Y and Enigma until 23 March.[142] On the other hand, during 21 March the Enigma had revealed that 21st Panzer Division had moved from Gabes to 'behind the Mareth front',[143] Y had established that

---

137. VM 6845 of 19 March 1943; CX/MSS/2290/T10.
138. WO 169/8519, Nos 457 and 459 of 18 and 20 March 1943; WO 208/3581, Nos I/155 and I/181 of 15 and 20 March 1943.
139. VM 6964 of 20 March 1943; CX/MSS/2294/T13.
140. eg CX/MSS/2288/T20; WO 169/8519, No 451 of 10 March 1943.
141. CX/MSS/2297/T6.
142. VM 7238 of 23 March 1943; CX/MSS/2307/T15 and 16; WO 169/8519, No 461 of 22 March 1943; WO 208/3581, No I/197 of 21 March 1943.
143. VM 7005 of 21 March 1943; CX/MSS/2298/T2.

a battery of 88 mms normally belonging to 21st Panzer Division had been sent to the gap,[144] and Eighth Army's intelligence staff had concluded that 21st Panzer Division would be following it.[145] It may be presumed that General Freyberg's decision to delay his assault on the *Plum* gap was taken in the light of this intelligence as well as of the fact that by the morning of 22 March Eighth Army's frontal assault had not yet made a break-through.

The frontal assault, preceded by an artillery barrage as at Alamein, had begun at 2315 on 20 March. The point of attack – the sector on the enemy's left that was manned by the Italian Young Fascist Division – had been selected in the light of accurate information from Y, POW, captured documents and the Enigma about the enemy's deployment in the line.[146] But the attempt to deflect the enemy's attention from the threatened sector had come to nothing, not least because the German field Sigint organisation, in what it considered to be its most important achievement, had obtained advance information of the Allied plans for Eighth Army. Diversionary raids during the night of 16–17 March had, as so often before, fallen foul of unsuspected minefields,[147] and shortly before the opening of the assault Eighth Army had learned from the Enigma that the Young Fascists were being stiffened by German troops.[148] By the morning of 22 March, slowed down by the arrival of further German reinforcements, the infantry had made a partial lodgement, but it was then beaten back by a counter-attack by 15th Panzer Division; good notice of this counter-attack was given by Y and air reconnaissance, but it proved impossible to break it up.[149] By nightfall on 22 March Eighth Army had accepted that the frontal attack had failed, and in the early hours of 23 March General Montgomery decided on a change of plan. Going over to the defensive on the Mareth line, he threw his main weight into the outflanking move, sending 1st Armoured Division round the Matmata hills, ordering 4th Indian Division to open up a shorter route around the enemy positions, and calling for an assault (*Supercharge II*) by the New Zealand Corps and 1st Armoured Division at the *Plum* gap. It was following this change of plan that General Montgomery urgently requested reinforcements from Egypt and Syria even 'at expense of *Husky*'.[150]* There was no new

---

* *Husky* was the cover-name for the Allied invasion of Sicily, see Volume III.

144. WO 169/8519, No 460 of 21 March 1943.   145. ibid.
146. Playfair, op cit, Vol IV, p 333; de Guingand, op cit, p 252; WO 169/8519, No 456 of 17 March 1943.
147. Playfair, op cit, Vol IV, p 335; de Guingand, op cit, p 252.
148. Playfair, op cit, Vol IV, p 335; VM 6995 of 0617/21 March 1943; CX/MSS/2297/T13; WO 169/8519, No 459 of 20 March 1943.
149. AIR 41/50, p 502; WO 169/8519, No 461 of 22 March 1943.
150. CAB 105/33, No 264 of 26 April 1943; Howard, op cit, Vol IV, p 351.

development in the intelligence available to him when he made this request.

Soon after making the change of plan Eighth Army learned from the Enigma that it could continue to discount intervention by 10th Panzer Division. It was informed early on 23 March that this division, which Army Y had located as still being at Kairouan on 21 March,[151] had been ordered to join with the Centauro Division in restoring the position on US II Corps's front,[152] where the Americans had been attacking since 20 March. 10th Panzer Division counter-attacked at El Guettar at 0630 on 23 March, but was repulsed after suffering heavy losses by US 1st Infantry Division, which had received precise warning of the enemy's intention from the British Y unit with US II Corps.[153]* For the next fortnight the Enigma and Army Y, which was now providing an excellent service, regularly revealed that 10th Panzer Division was being held in the El Guettar area and was for the most part in dire straits.[155] On the other hand, Eighth Army also knew that it could not expect relief from a further thrust made by US II Corps to the coast through Maknassy. II Corps's advance was held up by the fanatical resistance of a small German force that was identified by Enigma and Army Y as comprising Reconnaissance Unit 580 and the unit – Kasta OB – which had been Rommel's bodyguard.[156]† Y and POW later showed that this force was being strengthened by reinforcements from northern Tunisia.

On Eighth Army's own front the Enigma showed during 24 March that the enemy, realising that powerful forces were assembling for a major attack on the *Plum* gap, had sent 21st Panzer Division and 164th Division to that area, with orders to counter-attack only if they were attacked, and was doubting whether he could hold 'the new thinly-occupied main defence line',[157] During 25 March, as was disclosed by air reconnaissance and DF, 15th Panzer Division was also transferred from Mareth to the gap[158] and there were further important Enigma decrypts. 164th Division, in

---

* The Enigma also gave notice of the German attack[154] but it is not possible to say whether General Patton, who commanded US II Corps, was alerted on the Enigma evidence as well as by Army Y. He was not a recipient of Ultra at the time.

† See above, p 440.

151. WO 208/3581, No I/186 of 21 March 1943.
152. WO 169/8519, No 462 of 23 March 1943; VM 7181 of 0419/23 March 1943; CX/MSS/2306/T31.
153. Howe, op cit, p 562; K Strong, *Intelligence at the Top* (1968), p 90.
154. VM 7181 of 23 March 1943; CX/MSS/2306/T31, 2307/T17.
155. eg CX/MSS/2318/T22, 2319/T3, 6 and 11, 2324/T14, 2331/T3, 2361/T6.
156. eg VM 8230 of 2 April 1943; CX/MSS/2359/T1.
157. VM 7302 of 0342/24 March, 7357 of 1649/24 March 1943; CX/MSS/2312/T8, 2315/T1.
158. WO 208/3581, No I/198 of 25 March 1943.

command in the sector, reported that 21st Panzer Division might not be strong enough to recover the high ground that had been lost, appreciated that it might be impossible to repulse Eighth Army's expected mass tank attack and requested reinforcements and air support.[159] A GAF decrypt announced that FW 190 reinforcements were being sent from Italy.[160] And in the evening 164th Division was told that if it became too hard-pressed it might withdraw to El Hamma and to the north.[161] But not until 26 March, when the RAF in any case first noticed signs of a general withdrawal,[162] did Eighth Army learn that the enemy had decided to pull his infantry divisions back from the Mareth line to the Akarit position, thus converting the task of his forces in the *Plum* gap from all-out resistance into a temporary holding action to cover the withdrawal. An Enigma decrypt received on the afternoon of 26 March disclosed that von Arnim had made this decision on 24 March against opposition from Kesselring and Messe, his main reason being that he might need the forces in the gap to reinforce those that were holding up US II Corps at Maknassy.[163]

The withdrawal denied Eighth Army, once again, the opportunity to cut off the enemy's main body. Beginning on the night of 25–26 March, 24 hours earlier than originally intended, it was already in full swing when 4th Indian Division arrived behind the Mareth positions,[164] and the opening of *Supercharge II*, ordered for 25 March, had meanwhile been delayed by the local commanders. Their knowledge of the identity and condition of the forces opposing them was complete; it included the fact that 15th and 21st Panzer Divisions possessed only 73 serviceable tanks,[165] less than a quarter of their own. But they judged that in view of their shortage of field artillery the strength of the enemy's defensive positions made a frontal attack impossible, and that an outflanking move would take ten days.

It was in these circumstances that the AOC Western Desert Air Force proposed a massive preliminary air strike against the enemy's gun positions, defence posts and land-line communications.[166] This strike, involving practically all the tactical aircraft in the theatre in an operation hitherto without parallel, took place during daylight on 26 March. Its immense effectiveness,

---

159. VM 7395 of 2311/24 March 1943; CX/MSS/2315/T22.
160. VM 7406 of 25 March 1943; CX/MSS/2318/T9.
161. VM 7492 of 2228/25 March 1943; CX/MSS/2321/T31.
162. WO 169/8519, No 465 of 26 March 1943; WO 208/3581, No I/200 of 26 March 1943.
163. VM 7559 of 1345/26 March 1943; CX/MSS/2324/T14.
164. Playfair, op cit, Vol IV, pp 345, 348, 353 and fn.
165. VM 7537 of 26 March 1943; CX/MSS/2323/T21.
166. AIR 41/33, p 176; AIR 41/50, p 507; Playfair, op cit, Vol IV, p 348; de Guingand, op cit, p 256; Liddell Hart, op cit, p 419.

which was indispensable to the success of the armoured break-through, depended on the preparation for the pilots of details about a large number of precise targets. The information came from 'air photographs and other intelligence',[167] the other intelligence being RAF Y. The thoroughness of the intelligence preparations was all the more remarkable as they had to be undertaken unexpectedly at short notice.

The armoured advance started late in the afternoon on 26 March. By daybreak on the following morning it had passed through the defile to El Hamma. It was then held up by 15th and 21st Panzer Divisions and the enemy's anti-tank screen for two days during which the enemy's infantry completed the withdrawal to Akarit. 15th and 21st Panzer Divisions withdrew late on 28 March, their intention to do so having been disclosed by the Enigma early in the day.[168]* On 29 March Eighth Army occupied Gabes.

On 30 March General Montgomery decided against continuing the advance, electing to build up his strength for a later attack which was eventually launched on the night of 5–6 April.[170] At the time he made this decision his intelligence staff had received the decrypts of several Enigma reports of 28 March from Army Group Africa. One stated that the fighting on all fronts had consumed its reserves; a second that the supply situation was desperate and that 'a few hours might make all the difference'; a third that the holding of the front depended on the immediate arrival of supply ships.[171] In more detail, it knew from Y that 15th Panzer Division was down to either 3 or 9 tanks,[172] but it had no information about 21st Panzer Division's latest losses; and, influenced, perhaps, by another Enigma decrypt which had ordered Italian labourers to be sent from Akarit to develop a position at Enfidaville,[173] it believed that the enemy would hold the Akarit line only temporarily.[174] On the other hand, the main strength of US II Corps was still being held up at Maknassy, and a further Allied attempt to break

---

* On the morning of 28 March General Montgomery used his SCU/SLU channel to send news of his victory direct to the Prime Minister, copied only to the CIGS.[169] This procedure he was to use with increasing frequency as the war proceeded.

167. de Guingand, op cit, p 256.
168. VM 7733 of 0943/28 March 1943; CX/MSS/2335/T65.
169. Cabinet Office file 82/43/1, Part 2, unnumbered signal of 1130/28 March 1943.
170. Playfair, op cit, Vol IV, p 357.
171. VMs 7720 and 7841 of 28 and 29 March 1943; CX/MSS/2332/T4, 5, 7, 16 and 19, 2341/T12 and 13.
172. WO 208/3581, No I/215 of 29 March 1943.
173. CX/MSS/2351/T34.
174. WO 169/8519, No 469 of 30 March 1943; WO 208/3581, Nos I/200 of 26 March, I/222 of 30 March 1943.

through from the central mountain chain towards the coast
behind the Akarit line had been halted by the Germans at Fondouk
since 27 March.

By early April intelligence had provided further details about the
state and location of the enemy forces. The Enigma showed that
15th and 21st Panzer Divisions had withdrawn their tanks to a
point halfway between Gafsa and Gabes from which they might
intervene at either Akarit of Gafsa.[175] It also showed that they
together possessed only 23 tanks by 30 March,[176] a fact which led
Eighth Army intelligence to conclude that the two divisions were
'probably no longer effective'.[177] By 5 April, however, Y and air
reconnaissance had located 21st Panzer Division at El Guettar on
US II Corp's front, in company with 10th Panzer Division and
Panzer Abteilung 501, a fact which suggested that the enemy might
still make a strong attack there but was not expecting an immediate
attack at Akarit.[178] As for the forces at Akarit, POW taken at
Mareth had left no doubt that the Italians had little fight left,[179]
and the Enigma had confirmed that 164th Division had suffered
severe losses.[180] This meant that 90th Light Division was the only
unmauled formation in the line.[181] On 2 April an Enigma decrypt
gave the tank strengths of the German forces in the whole of
Tunisia for 30 March. 10th Panzer Division and Panzer Abteilung
501 had between them 78, including 8 Tigers; 15th Panzer Division
had 10; 21st Panzer Division had 13; and beyond that, in Panzer
Army 5, there were only 9 tanks, including 5 Tigers.[182] A total of
110 tanks.

By the time it opened its attack on the Akarit line on the night of
5–6 April, Eighth Army had built up a force of well over 500 tanks;
and its hopes of delivering a knock-out blow were high when, before
dawn on 6 April, its infantry succeeded in making a two-pronged
penetration of the enemy's positions. Later that morning, however,
90th Light Division counter-attacked and partially closed the
breach before the armour of X Corps had begun to move in, and in
the afternoon X Corps's advance was checked by a counter-attack
from 15th Panzer Division, the enemy's only available reserve. Y

---

175. VM 7970 of 30 March 1943; CX/MSS/2348/T13.
176. VMs 8005 and 8021 of 31 March, 8242 of 2 April 1943;
     CX/MSS/2350/T12, 2351/T4, 2359/T16.
177. WO 169/8519, No 470 of 31 March 1943; WO 208/3581, No I/223 of 31
     March 1943.
178. WO 208/3581, Nos I/244 and I/248 of 4 and 5 April 1943; WO 204/978, No
     149 of 6 April 1943.
179. WO 169/8519, No 465 of 26 March 1943.
180. ibid, No 472 of 3 April 1943; VM 7681 of 28 March 1943;
     CX/MSS/2332/T32.
181. WO 169/8519, No 467 of 28 March 1943.
182. VM 8242 of 2 April 1943; CX/MSS/2359/T16.

had given good notice of both of the enemy's counter-attacks.[183] General Montgomery then prepared to complete the armoured break-through on the morning of 7 April, preceding it with heavy air attack and artillery bombardment. But before the attack was resumed, air reconnaissance and Y were reporting the withdrawal of 'all elements' from Akarit, as also of 10th and 21st Panzer Divisions and all other enemy forces from the El Guettar–Maknassy area.[184] The Allies had renewed the attack from Fondouk towards Kairouan on 4 April in anticipation of this withdrawal, but no prior warning of the retreat had been obtained from any source. The Enigma decrypts about the retreat did not become available until 8 April.

On 10 April the Enigma decrypts reported that large parts of 21st Panzer Division, of 164th Division and of 90th Light Division were able to withdraw only on foot, without their heavy equipment, for lack of fuel, and that unless the fuel situation could be improved they might not be able to reach the Enfidaville line.[185] When British IX Corps with 6th Armoured Division reached Kairouan from Fondouk, however, in the afternoon of 10 April, 10th and 21st Panzer Divisions had already passed through on their way north. Still more remarkably, though leaving much equipment behind, the greater part of Messe's army succeeded in reaching Enfidaville from Akarit by 13 April.

□

The success of the Axis in once again extricating the bulk of its forces was a source of serious disappointment to the Allies. On 28 March, at the height of the battle of Mareth, the Chiefs of Staff had stressed in a signal to the commanders in Africa that it was essential to bring the Tunisian campaign to an end in April so that convoys could again be routed through the Mediterranean and full use be made of 'the limited shipping at our disposal'.[186] By that time, by increasingly heavy attacks on the enemy's bases in Sardinia and Sicily, which included Sigint-based intruder raids,*

---

* Only general accounts survive of the use made of intelligence in these operations by the combined operations room in AFHQ, but it is clear that RAF Y and the Enigma both made a valuable contribution.[187]

183. WO 208/3581, No I/249 of 6 April 1943; WO 169/8519, No 474 of 6 April 1943.
184. WO 169/8519, Nos 475 and 478 of 7 and 10 April 1943; WO 208/3581, No I/262 of 9 April 1943; AIR 41/50, p 515.
185. VM 8984 of 10 April 1943; CX/MSS/2402/T1.
186. CAB 105/33, No 267 of 28 March 1943.
187. Air Historical Branch, *Air Ministry Intelligence*, p 172; see also AIR 40/2323, Humphreys, The Use of Ultra in the Mediterranean and North-West African Theatres of War.

the Allied air forces had all but eliminated the GAF's threat to Allied supply convoys to such ports as Algiers and Bône. At the end of March the Enigma disclosed that practically all the aircraft of the three Gruppen of KG 26 – the torpedo-bomber unit which had led the assault against the Allied shipping – had been made unserviceable.[188] In April Allied losses dropped to five ships, all sunk by U-boat. From the middle of April, as Eighth Army moved north of Akarit, it became possible to supply it, also, from the western Mediterranean ports, and thus to begin reducing the amount of shipping sent round the Cape. But the U-boats had now resumed the offensive in the Atlantic, where the convoys were again sustaining serious losses,* and every delay in clearing the enemy from north Africa prolonged the strain on Allied shipping.

On 7 April, on the other hand, the day on which the enemy began his retreat, the Chiefs of Staff, in a report to the Combined Chiefs in Washington on the possibility that the Axis might be preparing a large-scale evacuation from Tunisia, had stated that the need to prevent this was already 'engaging the earnest attention of the North African Command in all its branches – naval, military and air'.[189]

In the view of the British Chiefs of Staff the enemy had not only not yet decided to evacuate his land forces; he would decide against doing so from the wish to retain a foothold in north Africa for as long as possible. This appreciation proved to be correct: on 16 April, after discussion with the Axis commanders, OKW ruled against a large-scale evacuation and decided that not even the withdrawal of specialist personnel was to be contemplated.[190] Although the Enigma decrypts made no reference to this discussion or to its outcome, they were forthcoming about the GAF. By 23 March it was known that the GAF in Sicily was suffering from exhaustion and low serviceability and that it had decided to abandon the bombing of ground targets in Tunisia because of its inability to guarantee fighter protection.[191] On 1 April it was learned that the enemy was withdrawing his dive-bombers from Tunisia.[192] But the Enigma left no doubt that the GAF was still making every effort to retain a fighter and fighter-bomber force in Tunisia. This may have influenced the Chiefs of Staff's appreciation. But there can be little doubt that the appreciation was based mainly on the fact that the Axis was not concentrating small craft

---

* See above, p 562 et seq.

188.   VM 8149 of 1 April 1943; CX/MSS/2354/T33.
189.   CAB 105/33, No 286 of 7 April 1943.
190.   Playfair, op cit, Vol IV, p 432.
191.   CX/MSS/2309/T5.
192.   AIR 41/33, p 175; WO 204/967, No 35 of 27 April 1943.

in Tunisia or north of the Narrows, and on the plentiful Sigint evidence that it was continuing to do its utmost to get supplies and reinforcements to Tunisia.

After the first week of April this evidence became all the more telling in that, in his effort to keep Tunisia supplied, the enemy now met with rapidly increasing difficulties. During March he had responded to the reorganisation and intensification of the Allied attack on the supply lines by making still greater use of ferries and landing craft – especially of the custom-built KT ships of about 800 tons – for his more valuable cargoes. Although Sigint provided full details of their sailings, such craft were harder to sink on passage than were the bigger ships, and the Allied bombing of ports interfered less with their loading and unloading. In this way, and by dint of more frequent sailings, the enemy succeeded in unloading 43,125 tons of cargo in Tunisian ports in March, compared with 49,600 in February.[193] Even so, Sigint showed that of the merchant ships reported to have sailed for Tunisia in that month the proportion sunk on passage or in port rose to 50 per cent, as compared with less than 20 per cent in February. It showed, further, that no cargo at all was unloaded in Tunis on 16 days of the month – including the period from 23 to 30 March, when no ships docked in any Tunisian port[194] – and that of the fuel despatched by sea only 30 per cent got across, the bulk of the remainder being in a tanker that was damaged and forced to turn back towards the end of the month. In these circumstances the enemy was being forced to rely for the transport of fuel, as of troops, ever more heavily on naval vessels and transport aircraft. Well before the end of March, when it disclosed that an additional Gruppe of 30 transport aircraft had arrived at Mediterranean bases,[195] the Enigma made it plain that his higher rate of fuel consumption and the increasing destruction of his shipping had made the enemy critically dependent on air supply,[196] and this intelligence contributed to the rapid and all but decisive worsening in his supply position that was brought about from the early days of April.

Post-war figures show that in April as a whole the Allies destroyed 41.5 per cent of the seaborne cargoes despatched to Tunisia – the same proportion as in March – but that, as a result of a decline in the amount of shipping sailed, the tonnage disembarked in Tunisia fell from 43,125 in March to 29,233 tons.[197] The decline in sailings became more pronounced as the month proceeded: Sigint established at the time that the average daily

193.   Playfair, op cit, Vol IV, p 417.   194.   Howard, op cit, Vol IV, p 350.
195.   VM 7644 of 27 March 1943; CX/MSS/2329/T35.
196.   AIR 41/50, p 522.
197.   Playfair, op cit, Vol IV, pp 416, 417, table.

unloading dropped from 1,300 tons at the beginning to 700 tons at the end. It was due partly to the growing shortage of merchant ships at the enemy's disposal – those he obtained from French ports being insufficient to off-set his continual losses[198] – and partly to the enormous risks that now attended the crossings. How great these were was illustrated early in the month. Sigint having disclosed details of a five-ship convoy that was due in Tunisia on 6 April, the day of the British assault at Akarit, one of the ships (a tanker carrying 2,000 tons of fuel) was sunk before the convoy had collected, a second ship was torpedoed soon after the convoy had sailed, two others were blown up off Bizerta, and the arrival in Bizerta of the single survivor was delayed till 17 April. In these circumstances it is hardly surprising that, while PR from Malta showed that the enemy forwarded increasing supplies to Sardinia and Sicily, fewer ships attempted to cross to Africa. On this account the total shipping sunk by the expanding Allied forces, which now included three-quarters of all British submarines as well as large contingents from the USAAF and the RAF, remained at the level achieved in March, and a greater number of the sinkings were of ships supplying Sardinia and Sicily. But it was still the case that, as Sigint showed, only four ships of over 3,000 tons succeeded in reaching Tunisia, and the enemy was thus depending more than ever on air transport for his fuel when the Allied air forces opened a sustained campaign against his large and heavily escorted air transport convoys and against his transport aircraft on airfields in Sicily and Tunisia.

The intelligence used during the planning and execution of this campaign (operation *Flax*) came partly from the GAF Enigma, which gave details of cargoes, variations of the convoy routes, flight cancellations and other enemy defensive measures. Even more important, however, was the interception by RAF Y of the tactical signals of the air transport systems of the GAF and the IAF, both of which played a large part in supplying north Africa in the last phase of the fighting there. From the study of this traffic the intelligence staffs derived their familiarity with the points of arrival and departure, the time taken to unload and turn round, the normal routes and the strength of the escorts.[199] The campaign began with an attack on a convoy of transport aircraft on 5 April. Until 17 April it was carried out by Allied aircraft operating from bases in northern Tunisia and Algeria, and by that date it had destroyed about a quarter of the total Axis transport fleet – over 100 aircraft.[200] On 17 April it was taken over by the fighters of the Western Desert Air Force; operating from newly occupied bases between Akarit and Enfidaville, these completed what, with pardonable exaggeration, has been described as 'the annihilation of the enemy's transport fleet'.[201] More prosaically, the GAF's transport fleet in the Mediterranean area, 263 aircraft at the beginning of the month, had lost 157 aircraft by 27 April, when operation *Flax* was concluded and when the Western Desert Air Force fighters were switched to the attack on seaborne supplies, and the Allies had also destroyed Italian transport aircraft and a large number of operational aircraft that the enemy had pressed into service for the ferrying of fuel and ammunition.[202] Whatever the enemy's total losses – one estimate is that they amounted to 432 aircraft[203] – this reduction of the German transport fleet, coming on top of that effected at Stalingrad, crippled it for the rest of the war. More immediately, the operation intensified the strangulation that was now rendering the enemy's supply position in Tunisia critical. At the beginning of April it was estimated that the GAF transport fleet was bringing in 250 tons of fuel daily, and the total daily delivery by air, by the GAF transports, by Italian transports and by bombers, was perhaps about 400 tons. On 10 April the Allies learned from the Enigma that Kesselring had warned that unless they received 400 tons of fuel daily the retreating German formations might not be able to reach the Enfidaville line.[204] On 25 April the Enigma disclosed that, on Göring's orders, transport flights to Tunisia were henceforth to take place only at night;[205] a change of policy which brought the Allied operation to an end, but which also greatly reduced the scale of Axis air deliveries.

□

It was thus in the knowledge that the enemy's supply position was deteriorating rapidly but that he nevertheless intended to prolong his resistance – in confirmation of the COS appreciation two days earlier the C 38m had disclosed on 9 April that he would make a stand at Enfidaville, and this had been reaffirmed in Enigma decrypts on 10 and 14 April[206] – that the Allied forces planned the final stage of their advance. This opened when Eighth Army assaulted the Enfidaville line on 19 April and First Army and US II Corps, four corps in all, began to move on Bizerta and Tunis from the south, south-west and west on 22 and 23 April.

Eighth Army failed to gain its two objectives, which were first to

201. ibid, p 523.   202. ibid, p 525.
203. D Richards, *The Royal Air Force 1939–42*, Vol II (1954), p 269.
204. VM 8984 of 10 April 1943; CX/MSS/2402/T1.
205. ML 305 of 25 April 1943; CX/MSS/2482/T12.
206. VMs 8971 of 10 April, 9302 of 14 April 1943; ZTPI 30095; CX/MSS/2401/T11, 2422/T18.

prevent the Panzer divisions with First Italian Army from joining forces with Panzer Army 5 on First Army's front and then to cut off First Italian Army's retreat by lunging across the neck of Cape Bon. Meeting with fanatical resistance, it was reduced to keeping up local attacks until 29 April. On the day of the assault, however, Y detected that part of 10th Panzer Division was moving to the Plain of Tunis from behind the Enfidaville line,[207] leaving only 15th Panzer Division there with about 15 tanks,[208] and AFHQ had by then put together various other indications that the enemy might be planning an attack against First Army's preparations.[209] On 17 April it had pointed out that a POW had alleged that the Hermann Göring Division would attack in the near future and that as that was the freshest of the German divisions, and was known to be up to strength except that on the evidence of the Enigma it lacked its armoured regiment, 'it might reasonably be employed in a spoiling attack' in its sector, south of Medjez el Bab.[210] On 19 April AFHQ suspected that 21st Panzer Division, as well as 10th Panzer Division, might be involved,[211] and 18th Army Group noted that the movement of enemy artillery might be connected with the attack.[212] The attack was delivered early on 21 April, in the area that had been predicted by AFHQ, by the Hermann Göring Division, the armoured component of 10th Panzer Division (7th Panzer Regiment) and Panzer Abteilung 501. Using a total of 80 tanks, including the few remaining Tigers, it temporarily threatened the artillery preparations for First Army's advance but was brought to a halt within hours after losing 25 tanks.[213]

On 22 April the main Allied advance on First Army's front was launched as planned. On the following day Y disclosed that the enemy was transferring 15th and 21st Panzer Divisions to this front;[214] and on 24 April the GAF Enigma revealed that Flieger-führer Tunis had called for reinforcement by 20 Me 109s.[215] But it was estimated from Enigma returns that the Germans had less than 100 serviceable tanks, that the Fliegerführer had 115 serviceable aircraft[216] and little chance of receiving reinforcement, on account of Axis fears of attack elsewhere in the Mediterranean, and that the

207. WO 204/978, No 162 of 19 April 1943.
208. ibid, No 163 of 20 April 1943; WO 169/8519, No 486 of 20 April 1943; ML 20 of 22 April 1943; CX/MSS/2465/T10.
209. Playfair, op cit, Vol IV, p 434.
210. WO 204/978, No 160 of 17 April 1943.
211. ibid, No 162 of 19 April 1943.
212. WO 208/3581, No I/307 of 20 April 1943.
213. ibid, No I/309 of 21 April 1943.
214. ibid, No I/327 of 24 April 1943; WO 169/8519, Nos 489 and 490 of 23 and 24 April 1943.
215. ML 175 of 24 April 1943, CX/MSS/2475/T1.   216. ibid.

enemy's combat strength was about 60,000 men. And since the Allies advanced with 1,400 tanks and over 300,000 men and the Mediterranean Air Command disposed of 3,241 aircraft, of which the bulk could be used in Tunisia if needed, this intelligence about the enemy's movements did not reduce the widespread expectations of a rapid conclusion to the Tunisian campaign. On 23 April the intelligence staff of 18th Army Group believed that 'with the limited resources at present available to the enemy he is unlikely to be able to offer prolonged resistance to our continuous and increasing pressure'.[217] On 25 April it repeated that 'the enemy is unlikely to be able to stand our pressure' – and not without reason, for Y had established that all the enemy formations were reduced in strength and hard pressed.[218] But it now added that the enemy would 'resist stubbornly till troops exhausted',[219] and by 26 April, having driven the enemy back several miles in some of the fiercest fighting of the whole war, the Allied thrusts had themselves ground to a halt.

On 29 April 18th Army Group and Eighth Army both acknowledged that they had been checked[220] and 18th Army Group recognised that on its fronts 'the enemy's counter-attacks are succeeding and are likely to continue'.[221] Y had by then established that the enemy had moved his last remaining tanks (two German reconnaissance units and some Italian AFVs) from the Enfidaville front;[222] The Enigma was soon to confirm the arrival of a new German armoured formation, Panzer Abteilung 504, and shown that it was already operating with the Hermann Göring Division;[223] and on 30 April the C 38m disclosed that Italian destroyers were still arriving in Tunisia with full complement of troops.[224] Together with the enemy's increased expenditure of fuel and ammunition, however, every additional reinforcement he received intensified his supply problem, and from the end of April, while the Allies paused until 7th Armoured Division and 4th Indian Division were brought round from Eighth Army to join First Army in a renewed drive on Tunis, this finally reached crisis proportions.

On 28 and 29 April the Allied commands learned that Army Group Africa expected 'a complete supply breakdown' if sea

---

217. WO 208/3581, No I/322 of 23 April 1943.
218. ibid, No I/327 of 24 April 1943.
219. ibid, No I/331 of 25 April 1943.
220. Playfair, op cit, Vol IV, pp 430, 441; WO 169/8519, Nos 494 and 495 of 28 and 29 April 1943.
221. WO 208/3581, No I/343 of 29 April 1943.
222. WO 204/978, No 173 of 30 April 1943.
223. ML 890 of 2 May 1943; CX/MSS/2514/T10.
224. MLs 612 of 29 April, 652 of 30 April 1943; ZTPI 31104, 31121.

supplies did not at once improve.[225] This information was obtained from the Porpoise decrypts from the German Naval Command in Tunisia, whose reports were at this time especially useful because the Army Enigmas had been read with less regularity since March. On 29 April Army Group Africa's decrypts furnished the details: such supplies of fuel and ammunition as were still arriving by sea were being immediately absorbed by the urgent needs of its formations, whose fuel holdings were now sufficient only for distances varying between 6 and 37 miles.[226] On the same day the GAF Enigma disclosed that the fuel situation was so catastrophic that the GAF could no longer find the 35 gallons a day that it needed to operate its radar.[227] By 4 May, according to a Porpoise decrypt, the Army Group could no longer guarantee to get rations, water and ammunition to the troops,[228] and the SIS and Army Y disclosed that the enemy had no reserves and that medical staff were being put into the line.[229] The last Axis merchant ship to reach Tunisia arrived on 3 May;[230] Sigint had given no notification of her sailing. But it was after receiving advance warning from Sigint that the destroyers of Force K sank the *Campo Basso* off Cape Bon on 4 May,[231] and that on 5 May the USAAF sank the *San Antonio*, 6,000 tons, on her way from Naples to Tunis, off Sicily.[232] These were the last two merchant ships to try to reach Tunisia, though smaller craft continued to ply and, as was disclosed in the GAF Enigma on 6 May, the German Naval Command was planning to use even U-boats to ferry fuel.[233]

It was in this way that the Allies brought about on 6 May a sudden collapse of Axis resistance. When they renewed the advance on that day von Arnim was unable to organise his defence for lack of fuel,[234] and on 7 May, when units of First and Eighth Armies burst into Tunis and US II Corps entered Bizerta, GC and CS was decrypting a signal from the Quartermaster of Army Group Africa which announced that supplies of ammunition were no longer to be sent as he lacked the petrol to move them.[235]

---

225. MLs 490 of 28 April, 594 of 29 April 1943; DEFE 3/595, ZTPGM 15639, 15787.
226. CX/MSS/2457/T17.
227. ML 558 of 29 April 1943; CX/MSS/2496/T5.
228. ML 1024 of 4 May 1943; DEFE 3/596, ZTPGM 16489.
229. WO 169/8519, No 499 of 4 May 1943; Dir/C Archive, 3138 of 30 April 1943.
230. Playfair, op cit, Vol IV, p 423.
231. MLs 977 and 1021 of 4 May 1943; CX/MSS/2519/T22; DEFE 3/596, ZTPGM 16523.
232. ML 1119 of 5 May 1943; DEFE 3/596, ZTPGM 16696.
233. CX/MSS/2525/T9.
234. Liddell Hart, op cit, p 429.
235. CX/MSS/2524/T2.

It was similarly the desperate supply position which prevented the considerable Axis forces which remained in the mountainous country south and south-east of Tunis from moving into Cape Bon to prolong their resistance or attempt evacuation. That this would be so was appreciated by the Allied intelligence staffs from 8 May.[236] There was nevertheless much anxiety about this prospect among the Allied commanders when the force they had despatched to seal off the land approaches to the Cape was held up for two days at the narrow defile of Hamman Lif by the two GAF Flak units which had fought with distinction as anti-tank screens throughout the Tunisian campaign. By then, moreover, several items of intelligence had been received which could be interpreted as indicating enemy preparations for evacuation or a last stand. During April PR had reported, and the Enigma had confirmed, that piers and other installations were being constructed on the Cape;[237] on 2 May the German Naval Command had reported in the Porpoise Enigma that it was moving its HQ to Cape Bon;[238] as early as 10 April the GAF Enigma revealed that an airfield for transport aircraft was being constructed on the Cape and that others were contemplated.[239] From 8 May, when the German radio announced that the African campaign was over and that Axis troops would be evacuated in small boats,[240] 10 destroyers, greatly aided by the full intelligence available, mainly from the C 38m, about the enemy's minefields, constantly patrolled the waters off Cape Bon: operation *Retribution*.[241] But air reconnaissance, which was covering the whole theatre very fully, detected no sign of preparations for a general evacuation,[242] and GC and CS provided further reassurance. On 8 May the decrypt of a telegram from the Japanese Ambassador in Rome disclosed that Mussolini had told him that evacuation was not possible,[243] and the Enigma revealed that the remains of the Hermann Göring Division were almost without motor transport and fuel and that 334th Division was withdrawing north-east of Tunis on foot for lack of fuel.[244] AFHQ accordingly announced on 11 May that 'to effect a major withdrawal into Cape Bon is not indicated by the enemy's intentions' and

236. WO 169/8519, Nos 503 and 505 of 8 and 10 May 1943; WO 204/967, No 37 of 11 May 1943; WO 204/978, No 183 of 10 May 1943; WO 208/3581, No I/372 of 9 May 1943.
237. VM 9924 of 20 April 1943; DEFE 3/594, ZTPGM 14659.
238. ML 841 of 2 May 1943; DEFE 3/596, ZTPGM 16169.
239. VM 9080 of 11 April 1943; CX/MSS/2408/T6.
240. WO 169/8519, No 503 of 8 May 1943.
241. Playfair, op cit, Vol IV, p 425.
242. WO 169/8519, No 501 of 6 May 1943; WO 204/978, No 182 of 9 May 1943.
243. Dir/C Archive, 3233 of 8 May 1943.
244. ML 1482 of 8 May 1943; CX/MSS/2544/T21 and 29.

that because of lack of fuel and ammunition the enemy's final surrender could not be long delayed.[245]

Von Arnim's report of his surrender, the last Army Enigma message from Africa, was decrypted on the following day.[246] Messe also surrendered on 12 May. Their troops, both Italian and German, had fought to the last.[247] The Enigma later showed that only 632 officers and men had been evacuated by air and sea.[248] A final count of prisoners showed that the number taken was somewhat under 250,000[249] and the intelligence authorities came in for criticism for under-estimating; they had calculated that the number would be 200,000.[250] Whatever may have been the reasons for the discrepancy, it was in the last resort thanks to the intelligence authorities that the problem of feeding the extra 50,000 was solved without great difficulty. As a result of the provision by GC and CS of regular Sigint notification of the sailings and the cargoes of the Axis supply ships, and of the efficiency of the Allied forces since February in using this intelligence to select priority targets for their anti-shipping attacks, Axis ration stocks had been rising and it was found that the enemy's food dumps held plentiful supplies.[251]

245. CAB 105/33, No 343 of 11 May 1943.
246. CX/MSS/2563/T18.
247. WO 169/8519, Nos 506 and 507 of 11 and 13 May 1943; WO 204/967, No 38 of 15 May 1943.
248. CX/MSS/2588/T4.
249. CAB 105/33, Nos 167, 369, 389 of 17, 19 and 27 May 1943.
250. Hunt, op cit, p 182; Strong, op cit, p 91.
251. Hunt, op cit, p 182.

CHAPTER 28

The Eastern Front in the First Half of 1943

WHITEHALL grew steadily more confident from the beginning of 1943 in its assessments of the prospects on the eastern front. In December 1942, when the *Torch* landings had been followed by the beginning of the Soviet counter-offensive, the JIC had suggested that Germany might seek peace with Russia when, on top of her difficulties in Russia, she was faced with the Allied clearance of north Africa – and had warned that Stalin might welcome a peace overture by the spring of 1943 if the Russian advance had not matched his hopes and the Allies had not followed up their Mediterranean initiative.[1]* In the middle of February 1943, after the German defeat at Stalingrad, the next JIC assessment concluded that Germany had at last to face the possibility that her recent defeat was irretrievable,[3] and on 9 March, when the Germans were counter-attacking in the Kharkov area in an effort to stabilise the front, the JIC felt that 'the prospect of a German defeat of Russia has receded to vanishing point'.[4] By 28 April it was confident that even if Germany gained territory in any further fighting, the point had passed at which she could hope to obtain a peace settlement with Russia; she was doomed to face a third winter of fighting on the Russian front.[5]

The growth of confidence was hardly a surprising development, such was the glare of publicity attending the disaster at Stalingrad and subsequent German setbacks, and it was not a process to which intelligence made much contribution. Although they were unfailingly shown to the Prime Minister, diplomatic decrypts to the effect that the German Army was criticising Hitler, or that Hitler was admitting that 'it would have been convenient . . . if the war

---

* According to decrypts of telegrams from the Japanese Ambassador in Berlin Hitler had tried to bring Japan into the war with Russia in August and Setember 1942 and again early in 1943, but had been rebuffed on each occasion. On 2 May 1943 the Ambassador reported that Hitler had recently told him that he had made peace proposals to Russia at the end of 1942, but that the Russians had summarily rejected them.[2]

1. CAB 121/412, SIC file D/Germany/1, Volume 1, JIC (42) 462 of 3 December, paras 22 (a), 29–30. 2. Dir/C Archive, 3171 of 2 May 1943.
3. CAB 80/39, COS (43) 55 (JIC (43) 64 of 15 February).
4. CAB 121/419, SIC file D/Germany/4, JIC (43) 99 of 9 March.
5. CAB 121/413, SIC file D/Germany/1, Vol II, JIC (43) 171 (o) of 28 April.

had started at least five years later . . .', or that Italy and the other satellites were losing heart, did not improve on reasonable inference.[6] An item of intelligence like the decrypt of an Enigma message containing a Führer directive of 27 February which stated that there had been cases of a serious lack of discipline during the recent retreats and ordered that future offenders were to be shot without court martial, added spice to what was public knowledge – and so much so that the circulation was restricted to 'C' and the Prime Minister[7] – but added little else. As we shall see, however, improvements were still being made to the intelligence from the Russian front, and these ensured that the British assessments, as well as becoming more confident, became more precise about Germany's strategic options and more accurate about her operational intentions.

By the beginning of March 1943, before they stemmed the Soviet offensive and succeeded in stabilising their line in the Kharkov area, the Germans recognised that they must adopt a defensive strategy on the eastern front for the rest of the year; the threat of an Allied cross-Channel invasion was regarded as being too serious to permit another all-out offensive and it was doubtful whether such an offensive could in any case succeed in view of Russia's ever-growing strength. At the same time, Hitler, vetoing withdrawal to a shorter line in Russia, was especially determined to hold on to the Crimea and early in March, the position in the Kharkov sector remaining perilous, OKH and Hitler agreed that after the thaw, and before the western Allies could mount an invasion, there should be a limited offensive against the Soviet salient in the Kursk area with the object of shortening the German line and reducing the threat of a Russian advance into the Ukraine.[8] Throughout the spring of 1943 the German view of the position was closely matched by Whitehall's assessments.

In the middle of February the JIC calculated that in the winter fighting to date Germany had lost 40 divisions from the total of 200 (including those of her satellites) with which she had begun.[9] After allowing for additional divisions transferred from France to Russia, her net loss on the eastern front was already some 25 divisions; but taking into account what part she would lose of her army in the Caucasus she would be left with at best a total of 160 divisions (the

6. Dir/C Archive, 2208 of 4 February, 2255 of 10 February, 2260 of 11 February, 2477 of 5 March, 2551 of 12 March, 3171 of 2 May 1943.
7. Dir/C Archive, 2424 of 2 March 1943; DEFE 3/573, CX/MSS/C 106 of 1 March 1943.
8. M Howard, Grand Strategy, Vol IV (1972), p 465; A Seaton, *The Russo-German War 1941–45* (1971), pp 353–354.
9. CAB 80/39, COS (43) 55 (JIC (43) 64 of 15 February).

actual number was 159)[10] which would be weaker and less well equipped than the 180 with which she had held her front in the winter of 1941–1942 and been able to take the offensive on only one sector in the summer of 1942. And they faced some 200 Russian divisions even assuming that Russia's losses had been as great as Germany's. Towards the end of February 1943 Stalin claimed that Germany had transferred 27 divisions to the eastern front from Germany and north-west Europe since the beginning of the year. MI's order of battle intelligence did not support this figure. By the third week of January MI 14 had increased its estimate of the total of German divisions on the eastern front to 186, as compared with 182 at the beginning of the year, in the light of reports of movements to Russia out of France.[11] By 22 February, when it calculated that Germany had lost 14 divisions at Stalingrad, it had raised her total number of divisions in Russia from the reduced figure of 172 to 176 and had lowered the number of divisions in France to 30, as compared with 39–40 at the beginning of 1943.[12] On 3 March, commenting on Stalin's claim, it allowed that only 18 of these 30 were capable of offensive operations, as compared with 26 out of 40 in the autumn of 1942, but argued that the number of divisions that had moved east totalled between 20 and 25, and added that 3 had returned from Russia to France and that 7 more had either arrived in France from Germany or were forming in Germany.[13] German documents were later to prove that 17 divisions moved from France to Russia between November 1942 and February 1943 and that 3 divisions had moved from Russia to France en route for Tunisia. [14]

As for the GAF in Russia, apart from transport aircraft* the Russian counter-offensive of the winter of 1942–1943 produced no transfers to the eastern front.[15] Before the counter-offensive began AI had detected from the GAF Enigma a large movement in the opposite direction. On 20 November 1942 it had estimated that some 410 aircraft (including 270 long-range bombers and 120 single-engined fighters) had left Russia for the Mediterranean since October, the bulk of them since the beginning of November; as a result the number of aircraft in Russia (550 bombers, 420 single-engined fighters and 80 twin-engined fighters) was then less than the number in the west and the Mediterranean (720 bombers, 730

---

* See above, pp 109–110.

10.   Howard, op cit, p 465.
11.   WO 208/3753 M114 Appreciations for the CIGS, 18 and 25 January.
12.   ibid, 22 February.
13.   CAB 121/460, SIC file D/Russia/1 (II), DMI to Ismay 3 March 1943.
14.   Howard, op cit, p 337.
15.   AIR 41/10, *The Rise and Fall of the German Air Force*, p 228.

SEF and 430 TEF).[16] By December, however, the number of aircraft on the Russian front was thought to total some 2,000,[17] and during January 1943 it was calculated that this figure had shrunk to 1,715.[18] In the middle of February the JIC estimated that the maximum strength of the GAF in Russia was 2,000 aircraft as compared with 3,000 in the summer of 1942. The Soviet Air Force, by comparison, was between 4,500 and 5,000 aircraft; though it was inferior to the GAF technically and in administrative efficiency, it was certainly adequate for support of the land forces.[19]

The JIC argued that although Germany could save a limited number of divisions by withdrawing to the shortest possible line – through Poland and along the rivers Niemen, Bug and Dniester – such a withdrawal would endanger her hold on the Balkans and so increase her defence requirements there as to absorb more divisions than she had released. It accordingly concluded that unless the current fighting between Kursk and the Sea of Azov went against her, she would try to hold on to her strongly prepared positions in the northern and central sectors, and in the south she would want to retain the Crimea in order to avoid Russian bombing of the Romanian oil.[20]

In March the Germans succeeded in stemming the Russian offensive and in stabilising the front in the Kharkov area, and before the end of the month Whitehall had received the first indications that they were preparing a counter-attack against the Kursk salient. But by 22 April the CIGS had ruled out the possibility of an all-out German offensive in Russia during the summer of 1943.[21] A week later the JIC, uncertain whether Germany or Russia would attack first in the Kursk area, was nevertheless quite sure that if Germany took the offensive, shortages of manpower and resources, particularly oil, aircraft and motor transport would prevent her from exploiting any success she might achieve.[22] It reached this conclusion after making a detailed comparison of the military and industrial strength of Germany and Russia. In making the comparison it was still handicapped by knowing much less about Russia than about Germany, particularly where military strengths and order of battle were concerned. But it now possessed evidence from 'most secret sources'[23] (no doubt a

---

16. Air Sunset 17 of 20 November 1942.
17. AIR 41/10, p 182.   18.   ibid, p 224.
19. CAB 80/39, COS (43) 55 (JIC (43) 64 of 15 February).
20. ibid.
21. CAB 121/412, CIGS notes, 22 April 1943.
22. ibid, JIC (43) 171 (o) of 20 April; CAB 121/413, JIC (43) 171 (o) (Revise) of 28 April.
23. CAB 121/512, SIC file E/Spain/1, JIC (43) 149 (o) of 30 April, Appendix A, para 11 (c).

reference to the increasing amount of information that was being obtained from decrypts of the Enigma traffic of the the GAF's Sigint organisation)* of the existence of considerable Soviet reserves, in striking contrast to the absence of German reserves in Russia and elsewhere, and it found the Soviet situation superior to Germany's in every respect except food supply.

The general accuracy of Whitehall's assessments, like their growing confidence, owed a good deal to the simple fact that Germany's options were now narrowing rapidly. At the same time, it also reflected further improvements in the supply of Sigint, which continued to be by far the most important source of intelligence about the Russian front.

Except in the Crimea and the Caucasus, where the Porpoise naval Enigma key was as valuable for its information on the ground fighting as for its naval intelligence, the GAF Enigma remained the most regular source of information about the enemy's ground forces, as well as about the GAF. Of the GAF Enigma keys, the general (Red) key continued to be the most productive, but additional specialised keys continued to appear and to be broken soon after their appearance: to name but a few, keys for GAF liaison officers in the Crimea (named Porcupine at GC and CS) and the Donets area (Hedgehog to GC and CS) by February 1943; a key for use both by Fliegerkorps and by liaison officers in the southern sector (Hedgehog II) from March; keys for Fliegerkorps I (Ermine) and Fliegerkorps VIII (Skunk), which were added to that of Fliegerkorps IV (Hornet) by the middle of the year; and, by then also, the key (Orchid) used by Luftgau XXV, the GAF administrative organisation in the Rostov area. From the beginning of 1943, moreover, GC and CS more than made up for the loss of the Army key (Vulture) at the end of 1942, and for its continuing inability to read other Army Enigma keys on the Russian front, by two other advances.

In the autumn of 1942 GC and CS had begun systematic research on the decrypts of Enigma traffic (known to it as Mustard) passed by the GAF's Sigint organisation in Russia. Up to this date the Mustard decrypts, though voluminous, had been very difficult to understand for several reasons including the fact that they were full of obscure geographical references. Even now, it was some time before they could be fully exploited. But from early in 1943 GC and CS was able to issue regular accounts of German appreciations of Soviet dispositions and intentions which were of great value both because they supplemented the still small stock of information obtained from Moscow about Russia's forces and for the light they threw on Germany's preoccupations. From the same date the work

* See above, p 69.

of intercepting and decrypting Germany's non-morse teleprinter transmissions* reached the point at which GC and CS, though still unable to read all of the intercepted traffic, produced decrypts of the highest operational significance. The earliest of the links to be identified had been intercepted in November 1942 and they were read with some regularity almost at once. These were those which connected OKH with Army Group E in the Balkans (Codfish to GC and CS) and with Seventeenth Army in the Crimea (Octopus). From the spring of 1943 GC and CS also read the link between OKH and Army Group South in Russia (Squid), the link between OKH and Memel (Trout) and the link used by the GAF mission in Romania (Tarpon). Though less voluminous than the Enigma, and more difficult to decrypt, this traffic made a valuable contribution to Whitehall's knowledge of the strategic situation on the Russian front; it revealed the planning, the appreciations and the supply difficulties of the German commands.

□

The Soviet offensive to free the Kharkov area† began on 1 February 1943. By the middle of February it had taken Kursk, Belgorod and Kharkov, and Hitler had had to fall in with Manstein's request that Army Group Don should withdraw to the defensive line of the Mius, west of Taganrog. By then, however, the Soviet armies were out-running their supplies and operating beyond the range of effective air support. On 19 February Army Group Don, now renamed Army Group South, counter-attacked from Krasnograd, south-west of Kharkov. It re-took Kharkov on 12 March, Belgorod on 18 March, and then came to a close with the Germans in the area bounded by the Mius and the Donets on much the same line as that which they had held in the winter of 1941 – nearly 500 miles back from Stalingrad.

Apart from disclosing on 15 February that an infantry regiment from Army Group A in the Caucasus was being transferred to Dniepropetrovsk by air,[24] Sigint gave Whitehall no advance warning of Army Group South's counter-offensive. In the course of the next three weeks, however, the GAF Enigma threw considerable light on the objectives of the German attack and on the effort that was put into it. By 1 March it had shown that the Germans hoped to destroy the Russian forces that were still south of the Donets and then advance on Kharkov;[25] somewhat later it reported that they

---

* See above, pp 28–30 and, for further details, Volume III.
† See above, p 111.

24.   WO 208/3573 of 15 February.
25.   ibid, 1 March.

intended to turn north after taking Kharkov, presumably to eliminate the Kursk salient.[26] It established that the attack was involving divisions recently arrived from France,[27]* and was being supported by a concentration of air striking power that represented, as Whitehall fully realised, a remarkable recovery by the GAF. 'All the indications' had suggested to AI that the retreat from the Don and the Caucasus had disorganised the GAF and seriously reduced its strength and serviceability; but the level of support it provided to Army Group South's counter-attack, the last operation in which Germany resorted to the principle of close army-air co-operation with which she had gained her victories in the west in 1940 and in Russia in 1941, showed that the GAF had succeeded in overcoming its worst problems, at least for the time being.[28] On the other hand, it was clear from the GAF Sigint that it had done so at the expense of other sectors of the eastern front, without recalling aircraft from the west and the Mediterranean;† AI calculated that the Kharkov operations were absorbing more than half of the total bomber and close support forces available in Russia.[29]‡

No doubt for this reason, in the belief that the point must soon be reached when the GAF would have to be rested for refitting and redistribution, Whitehall held that, although the Russian effort was also flagging, the German counter-offensive would be short-lived. In any case, it argued, the thaw and the mud would rule out any advance beyond the Donets.[31] And so it proved. By 25 March it was obvious from the German communiqués that, except in the Crimea and the northern Caucasus, the fighting was dying down and that another phase in the war on the eastern front was at an end.[32]

□

In the Caucasus by the end of February the Germans had halted the Russian advance to Novorossiisk and stabilised the front

---

* See above, p 617. † See above, pp 617–618.

‡ After the event it calculated that by the beginning of February some 950 of the total of 1,800 aircraft that were available on the eastern front, including the far north, had been concentrated on the Don sector – 53 per cent of the total compared with 36 per cent two months earlier.[30]

26. CAB 121/512, JIC (43) 149 (0) of 20 April, Appendix A, para 19.
27. CAB 80/39, COS (43) 63 (182nd Résumé), para 25.
28. AIR 41/10, pp 183–184, 225–227.
29. CAB 80/39, COS (43) 96 (186th Résumé), para 36.
30. AIR 41/10, p 225.
31. CAB 80/39, COS (43) 45 (180th Résumé), para 22, COS (43) 70 (183rd Résumé), para 29, COS (43) 84 (185th Résumé), para 26.
32. ibid, COS (43) 96 (186th Résumé), para 23.

sufficiently to enable them to complete the evacuation of Army Group A across the Kerch Straits by the end of March. At the end of March they were preparing a counter-attack on the Russian bridgehead at Novorossiisk.

During the second half of February the Porpoise Enigma had made it plain that Hitler attached the highest priority to the defence of the Crimea. In decrypts dated 18, 19 and 21 February he had impressed on Dönitz that 'the Kerch task', critical for the whole of the eastern front, was the most important the navy had faced since the Norwegian campaign, and the naval authorities had ordered that the Crimea was to be held.[33] By 28 February another signal had been decrypted which set out the German programme for sea transport in the Black Sea for the next two months.[34] On 8 March, moreover, the GAF Enigma disclosed that the Germans were planning the construction of bridges across the Dnieper and the Bug which would shorten the supply routes to the Crimea by some hundreds of miles.[35]

On 30 March, as soon as the Germans has shored up their position in the Kharkov area, the GAF Enigma reported that the bulk of the dive-bomber and bomber units in southern Russia, estimated by AI at about a half of the total of the 900 aircraft available in the area between Orel and the Sea of Azov, were to be concentrated in the Crimea.[36] The next day a Porpoise decrypt disclosed that the Germans intended to clear up the Russian bridge-head at Novorossiisk at the end of the first week of April with an attack involving three divisions and 'the mass' of Flieger-korps VIII;[37] on 3 April from the same source it emerged that an earlier decision to leave Novorossiisk in Russian hands had been reversed under pressure from the German naval authorities.[38] The British Military Mission in Moscow was instructed to advise the Soviet authorities of the German intention on 2 April: 'C' had referred the decrypts to the Prime Minister for a decision as to whether the Russians should be informed.[39]

Sigint gave no further warning of the German attack, which opened in the middle of April. By 4 May, however Porpoise and the GAF Enigma had established that, the GAF having failed to establish air superiority, the German ground forces were back at their starting points after suffering severe losses in men and tanks.[40]

33.   DEFE 3/590, ZTPGM 10007, 10472, 10813.
34.   ibid, ZTPGM 10218.   35.   CX/MSS/2196.
36.   CX/MSS/2346/T2; Air Sunset 53 of 1 April.
37.   DEFE 3/592, ZTPGM 12452.
38.   ibid, ZTPGM 12580; WO 208/3573 of 5 April.
39.   Dir/C Archive, Telegram to BMM, TOO 1300.
40.   DEFE 3/594, ZTPGM 14224, 15138, 15543; CX/MSS/2522/T17; Air Sunset 57 of 3 May; CAB 80/40, COS (43) 145 (191st Résumé), para 35.

Thereafter, until well into June 1943, Russian pressure forced the GAF to maintain a high level of activity in the Crimea and from such GAF Enigma decrypts as one at the end of May, which showed that three KGs – about 300 bombers – intended for the Kursk front were being transferred to the Kuban and Taganrog,[41] Whitehall realised that the GAF's effort was having adverse effects on the German build-up for an offensive in the Kursk area.[42] AI later calculated that in the spring and early summer of 1943 GAF sorties over the Kuban had averaged 400 a day – a larger effort than that which the GAF was making in Tunisia.[43]

At the end of June Sigint indicated that the German struggle to hold the Crimea had been in vain; the decrypts then reported that the Germans were expecting the Russian landings in the eastern Crimea that were before long to cut off the Kerch Straits and the Taman peninsula.[44] Still earlier the decrypts had shown that the GAF could not keep up its recent exceptional effort in the Crimea. On 17 June the GAF Enigma disclosed that some 30 Ju 87 dive-bombers were being transferred from the Crimea to Athens.[45] On 28 June it showed that 10 twin-engined fighters had been moved from the Crimea to Italy.[46] From as early as mid-May, moreover, the same source had made it clear that, as and when the situation in the Crimea allowed, the GAF was withdrawing close support forces to the Kharkov area.[47]

☐

In the Kharkov area the Germans had originally hoped to attack in the middle of April, but had repeatedly postponed their offensive. One reason for the postponements had been the diversion of the GAF to support the fighting in the Crimea. Another had been the difficulty of concealing the preparations from the Russians. Unimpressed by German deception measures which pointed to an attack in the Donets area, the Russians constructed a formidable defensive zone inside the Kursk bend; this activity induced Hitler to defer the offensive until his forces had received the new tanks (Pzkw V

---

41. CX/MSS/2654/T20.
42. CAB 80/40, COS (43) 148 (192nd Résumé), para 38, COS (43) 150 (193rd Résumé), para 40, COS (43) 172 (197th Résumé), para 39; Air Sunset, undated and unnumbered, between 13 and 17 May 1943.
43. AIR 41/10, p 232.
44. WO 208/3573 of 5 July; CX/MSS/2628/T23, 2831/T1.
45. CX/MSS/2747/T18; Air Sunset 70 of 20 June.
46. Air Sunset 71 of 28 June.
47. Air Sunset, undated between 13 and 17 May.

Panther and Pzkw VI Tiger)* and the new Ferdinand self-propelled gun.[48]

Whitehall had obtained the first intelligence about the German preparations in the third week in March, when the evidence – GAF Enigma decrypts about the movement of Panzer divisions on the central sector of the eastern front and a reorganisation of GAF commands which brought Fliegerkorps VIII back to the Kharkov front for close support operations – had suggested that the objective might be to cut off the Russian salient between Kharkov and Orel and that the offensive might be timed for about the end of April.[49] On 13 April, in a decrypt ordering GAF Command East to bring up advance detachments earmarked for the offensive, the GAF Enigma referred to the operation by its code-name (*Zitadelle*) for the first time.[50] Six days later the same source disclosed that Luftflotte 4 was sending forces allotted to *Zitadelle* to GAF Command East.[51] At that stage, as the CIGS reported to the Prime Minister on 16 April, it seemed clear that the operation involved an attack from the Smolensk-Orel area against the north side of the Kursk salient, but it was uncertain whether the attack was to be an army offensive or to be confined to the GAF.[52] But at the end of April GC and CS decrypted a comprehensive appreciation of Russia's strengths and weaknesses, produced in connection with *Zitadelle* and signed by von Weichs, C-in-C Army Group South, which confirmed that the German intention was to cut off the Soviet forces in the Kursk salient by attacking from the Orel and the Kharkov areas in a pincer movement and making an important subsidiary attack against Kursk from the east.[53]† This decrypt was derived from GC and CS's reading of the Squid link between Army Group South and Army Command, and it constituted the earliest example of the great addition to operational intelligence of the highest importance about the eastern front that the non-morse decrypts were to make for the rest of the war.

The substance of the decrypt was passed to Moscow on 30 April, together with estimates of the enemy's divisional strengths in the various sectors of the Kursk salient and the warning that the German attack was intended in the near future.[54] On 3 May,

---

* See above, p 577, for the earlier despatch of Tigers to Tunisia.
† See Appendix 24.

48.   Howard, op cit, pp 465–466; Seaton, op cit, pp 355–358.
49.   WO 208/3573 of 22 and 29 March.
50.   CX/MSS/2422/T28.   51.   CX/MSS/2451/T30.
52.   Dir/C Archive, 2960 of 14 April 1943, 2988 covering minute by CIGS of 16 April 1943.
53.   CX/MSS/2499/T14.
54.   Dir/C Archive, 3150 of 30 April 1943 covering DMI's MI 14/No 218 of 30 April.

however, by which time MI had received Sigint references to the presence of Second Panzer Army in the Orel area and of Fourth Panzer Army in the Kharkov area and had deduced that the subsidiary attack against Kursk from the east would be made by Second German Army,[55] AI did not think that the necessary fighter aircraft for *Zitadelle* could be transferred from the Crimea before the middle of the month.[56] By mid-May it had 'unimpeachable' evidence of a GAF build-up in the Kharkov sector, where it had located 800 out of the total of 1,830 aircraft on the eastern front, but it still judged that the close-support force in the sector, some 300 to 320 aircraft, remained too small for a major offensive, and it seemed that the operation would be further delayed. AI knew that the build-up of a close support force was being held up by the fighting in the Kuban, which was absorbing 120 out of the total of 190 single-engined fighters that were available south of Orel, and it noted that, because the GAF was being held back by the pressing needs of other fronts, there was no evidence that fighters or other aircraft were being sent in from Germany or elsewhere.[57] On 14 May the JIC team at the Washington conference produced an appreciation for the Prime Minister which quoted the presence in the sector south of Orel of 20 of the 22 Panzer divisions in Russia and the GAF build-up near Kursk as showing that Germany intended to bite off the Kursk salient, though it was sure that the offensive would be limited – not on the scale of those of 1941 and 1942 – and it, too, could not predict when fighting would begin.[58] Nor was it long before these appreciations were confirmed by Sigint. The next reference to *Zitadelle* occurred in a GAF decrypt of 22 May which dealt with the aircraft to be used by Luftflotte 4 in that operation but which also disclosed that aircraft were to be transferred to Luftflotte 6* for another operation named *Eule*;[59] on 28 May the GAF Enigma disclosed that the aircraft allotted to operation *Eule* were being transferred to the Kuban and Taganrog.†

On 31 May the CIGS, then at Algiers with the Prime Minister, thought 'a great battle' in Russia was imminent; he felt that Russia would attack if Germany did not do so.[60] But on 21 May the Head of the British Military Mission had reported that the Russians

---

* GAF Command East was re-named Luftflotte 6 at this time.
† See above, p 623.

55. WO 208/3573 of 3 May; Air Sunset 57 of 3 May.
56. WO 208/3573 of 3 May; Air Sunset 57 of 3 May.
57. Air Sunset, between 13 and 17 May.
58. CAB 121/153, SIC file A/Strategy/9, COS (43) 287 (o) of 7 June (COS (T) 16 of 14 May).
59. CX/MSS/2624/T12.
60. CAB 121/153, COS (43) 290 (o) of 5 June (Meeting on 31 May).

would await a German attack, being strongly placed for resistance in positional warfare.[61] In June the GAF Enigma, far from reporting the transfer of reinforcements to the Kursk sector, disclosed the movement of aircraft from Russia. Two Gruppen of single-engined fighters left the Leningrad front for north-west Germany,[62] the defence of which had already required the transfer of 40 fighters from Russia in March.[63] Two 'operational command stations' were moved from south Russia to Italy.[64] In a further response to the Allied preparations for amphibious operations in the Mediterranean and to the Allied deception measures which accompanied the plan for the attack on Sicily,* dive-bombers and twin-engined fighters were moved from the Crimea to Athens and Italy on the eve of the Kursk offensive.† On 20 June, in the light of this evidence, AI doubted whether Germany would undertake any major operation in Russia before she had gauged the scale and purpose of the next Allied thrust in the Mediterranean.[65] On 23 June the JIC, attributing the German delay in launching the offensive to the sudden Axis collapse in Tunisia, the continued Russian pressure against Taman and the intensification of the Anglo-American strategic bombing of Germany, agreed that Germany had been forced into a policy of 'active defence' in Russia at any rate until she could work out the extent of her growing commitments in the Mediterranean and the Balkans.[66] By then – indeed since the end of May – a number of diplomatic and SIS reports, some of them obviously reflecting German propaganda, had stated that Hitler had decided to defer the next, and the decisive, offensive in Russia until the spring of 1944.[67]

Except that AI derived some indication of the imminence of *Zitadelle* from the cessation of the GAF's preparatory bombing of industrial and communications centres in the Kursk sector which had begun during May,[68] intelligence gave no advance notice of the opening of the much delayed German offensive, of which the southern prong began on 4 July 1943, the northern thrust on the following day. In the south the Germans had nowhere penetrated more than ten miles by 6 July when Fliegerkorps VIII found itself unable both to support the German armour and to deal with the steadily increasing opposition of the Soviet Air Force. By 9

---

* See Volume III.			† See above, p 623.

61.	CAB 121/464, SIC file D/Russia/4, MIL 9136 of 21 May.
62.	Air Sunset 70 and 71 of 20 and 28 June.
63.	ibid, 52 and 53 of 27 March and 1 April.
64.	CX/MSS/2760/T1.
65.	Air Sunset 70 of 20 June.
66.	CAB 121/413, JIC (43) 259 of 23 June.
67.	WO 208/3573 of 31 May, 7, 14 and 21 June.
68.	CAB 80/40, COS (43) 192 (201st Résumé), para 34.

July – the day before the Allies landed in Sicily – the southern German advance was stopped some 90 miles short of the thrust from the north, which had failed to make progress after advancing six miles on the first day. On 12 July a Soviet counter-attack developed into one of the largest tank battles of the war. It was one in which the heavy German armour (Panther and Tiger) had little advantage over the Soviet T 34 and of which the outcome remained undecided when, on 13 July, Hitler called off the offensive and ordered the transfer of a number of divisions, including the SS Panzer Korps with Army Group South, to western Europe. By that time the Russians had opened an attack on the Orel salient, north of Kursk in the German rear, against which the GAF was unable to provide the Army with adequate support.

On the progress of the fighting Whitehall's intelligence was limited to GAF Enigma and what was supplied by the Russians to the British Military Mission. The GAF Enigma was not very illuminating. Not until 10 July did it make it clear that the Germans were carrying out operation *Zitadelle*.[69] Thereafter, while it enabled AI to work out that Luftflotten 4 and 6 were probably employing in the Orel-Belgorod area 1,000 aircraft, a half of the total GAF strength on the Russian front[70] – and a half, also, of the Russian estimate of that strength[71] – it disclosed little about the state of the battle until 22 July, when AI reported that the Soviet counter-attack against Orel had probably achieved a considerable victory by forcing the GAF to reduce its concentration against the Kursk salient.[72] Although they had withheld until 15 July the news that they were themselves counter-attacking at Orel[73] the Soviet authorities had begun to be forthcoming about the Kursk battle on 9 July, when the British Military Mission reported that the General Staff was 'reasonably confident'.[74] On 10 July the Mission reported that the General Staff had concluded that the fighting value and the equipment of the German divisions was much reduced, as compared with earlier offensives;[75] on 13 July that it was 'confident' that the German plan had failed.[76] Thereafter the Mission had frequent meetings with the General Staff and by 23 July it was able to send Whitehall an extended commentary on the Russian handling of the battle.[77] On the following day – when the Orel fighting was still at its height – Stalin publicly announced that the German plan for a summer offensive had been 'completely frustrated'.

---

69. CX/MSS/2882/T8; CAB 80/40, COS (43) 192 (201st Résumé).
70. Air Sunset 75 of 11 July.   71. CAB 121/464, MIL 9469 of 10 July.
72. CAB 80/40, COS (43) 205 (203rd Résumé), para 45.
73. CAB 121/464, MIL 9508 of 16 July.
74. ibid, MIL 9469 of 9 July.   75. ibid, MIL 9474 of 10 July.
76. ibid, MIL 9490 of 13 July.   77. ibid, MIL 9555 of 23 July.

APPENDICES

APPENDIX 1, PART (i)

British Cypher Security During the War

I *Organisation and responsibility in Whitehall*

When GC and CS was established in 1919 it was given two tasks, firstly to study the methods of cypher communication used by foreign powers and secondly to advise all government departments on the cryptographic security of the codes and cyphers to be used, and to assist in their provision.* As this History shows, GC and CS pursued its first task with outstanding success, but the weakness of many British cyphers at the outbreak of war in 1939 and for a long time afterwards, particularly of those used by the Royal Navy, calls for some examination of its performance of the second.

In 1926 an Inter-Departmental Committee was set up to consider the possibility of the use of cypher machines to replace the book systems then in use by the three Services, the Foreign Office and the Colonial and India Offices. After a prolonged study of the various machines available, including the German Enigma, two of which were purchased in 1928 at Admiralty initiative, the Committee recommended in January 1935 that the Air Ministry should arrange for the construction of '3 sets of cypher machines of an improved "Enigma" type through the agency of so-called "Type X" attachments'. This historic decision was the genesis of the secure Typex machine which was to be used so successfully by the three Services and other government departments for many years.

The War Office and Air Ministry adopted the Typex machine with enthusiasm, so that they were ready in September 1939 with a fully secure and efficient machine held down to Division in the Army and by all RAF Headquarters in the field. The Admiralty's earlier interest in cypher machines had, however, drained away so that at the outbreak of war communication between shore and ship remained wholly dependent on cypher and code books, recyphered by a number of subtractor tables, some of which were readily broken by the Germans. Similar systems were also used by the Army and Royal Air Force where the Typex machine was not available.

With the benefit of hindsight it is difficult to understand the Admiralty's reluctance to adopt the Typex machine for use in

---

* See Volume I, p 20.

ships. It was no doubt influenced by the fact that signals cyphered by machine are lengthier than those based on a cypher book. This was an important practical consideration in ship to shore communications and was perhaps given too much weight by GC and CS in its apparent acquiescence, from the security point of view, in the Navy's continued use of the subtractor system. GC and CS's confidence in the security of the subtractor system, which continued until the outbreak of war, was based on the assumptions that recyphering tables would be replaced at such intervals that sufficient material for cryptanalytic attack would never be provided, and that the rules for use would be faithfully complied with. It had apparently not been appreciated by the Admiralty or GC and CS that the volume of message traffic in war would make attainment of these conditions of use well nigh impossible, and this failure can in part be attributed to the divided control of the Navy's cypher organisation which then existed. DNI was responsible for security, relying on the advice of GC and CS, DSD for the communications organisation and the Paymaster Director General for the provision of cypher staff. As the war progressed, and it was seen that communications security was an essential element in the communications process, sole responsibility gradually passed to the Signal Division. It must also be said that in 1939 GC and CS lacked an organisation that was adequate to the task of co-ordinating its undoubted Sigint expertise with its responsibility for giving advice on the security of Britain's own communications.

Concentration on the defence of military convoys against surface attack, the concept of the battle fleet action – the scenario for the Fleet Exercises of 1938 and 1939 – and the doctrine of wireless silence may all have contributed to the Admiralty's failure to foresee the vast volume of message traffic which would be generated by the defence, the routeing and re-routeing of a large number of mercantile convoys in the face of continuous U-boat attack over a long period. It is of great interest that, if the Admiralty was unprepared for the great increase in naval message traffic, this mistake was shared by GC and CS from quite the opposite point of view; GC and CS feared that the outbreak of war might be followed, not by an increase in the use of wireless by enemy states, but by the imposition of wireless silence on their armed forces for all except tactical signalling, so making GC and CS's intelligence task even more difficult. It was, therefore, taken pleasantly by surprise to find such an enormous volume of operational information in the Enigma messages broken during the Norwegian campaign in 1940.*

Once war had begun it was the Admiralty, with the Royal Navy

---

* See Volume I, p 137.

suffering most from complete dependence on the subtractor system, which first became aware of its deficiencies. In the early months of the war there was an inclination to attribute the obvious German knowledge of the movements of HM ships to the capture of cypher documents which had to be assumed following the loss of submarines in shallow water in January 1940 and the loss of HMS *Hardy* in Narvik Fjord in April. With the problem of physical compromise in the forefront of their minds it is perhaps understandable that in these early days those concerned gave rather less attention to the actual cryptographic weakness of the long subtractor than it now appears that they should have done. But nevertheless action was taken not only to provide special tables for submarines and ships operating in 'dangerous waters', and so separate these from the main Fleet communications, but also to improve cryptographic security by procedural and other means.

This experience showed that communications security was not just a naval problem and that there was a lack of any proper organisation to co-ordinate the requirements and problems of the three Services with the cryptographic expertise of GC and CS. In December 1940, therefore, the Admiralty, in the persons of the Vice-Chief of the Naval Staff and the DNI, took the initiative in setting up an Inter-Service Cypher Security Committee, 'to keep under constant review the security of communications of the Services'. This Committee, with representatives from the Services and from GC and CS, which looked after the interests of the Foreign Office, began to operate under the chairmanship of the DNI on 17 February 1941. And in September 1941 it was again the DNI who proposed that the Committee should be reconstituted as a sub-committee of the JIC and its scope extended to cover the security of wireless behaviour and procedure as well as of cyphers; he pointed out that the study of British wireless security ought to be placed on an inter-Service basis in preparation for the time when the Services turned over to the offensive in large scale combined operations. The JIC accepted this proposal in October 1941, adding representatives from the Colonial, the Dominions and the India Offices to the membership of the new Inter-Service Cypher and W/T Security Committee. The new Committee delegated its work to two sub-committees, one for cypher security and the other for W/T security.*

It was not only in the field of communications security that

---

* No attempt is made here to give an account of the extensive work done by the British authorities to manipulate British wireless communications. Once adequate cypher security had been provided, this work was highly successful both in preventing the patterns of wireless traffic from betraying operational intentions and as an essential component in the art of strategic deception. Some reference to the contribution it made, notably in connection with the invasions of north Africa in November 1942 and of France in June 1944, will be found in the appropriate chapters of Volume II and Volume III.

awareness and organisation were lacking at the outbreak of war. General departmental security arrangements were primitive, there was no machinery for co-ordinating policy and methods and it was not until early in 1942 that the Security Panel, responsible to the Lord President with the Secretary of the Cabinet as chairman, was established to survey the whole field of security in all government departments.* The Security Panel initiated an investigation into arrangements for cypher security and by the end of 1942 membership of the Cypher Security Committee had been expanded to include the Ministries of War Transport, Food, Supply, Aircraft Production and Information and Censorship. This was only the first step in a fundamental re-organisation of the whole cypher security structure. The staff responsible for communications security at GC and CS was greatly strengthened and, to ensure co-ordination and direction at the highest level, the Cypher Policy Board, a Cabinet committee responsible to the Chiefs of Staff, was established in February 1944.

II *Results achieved by enemy cryptanalysis*

A full account of the work of the Axis cryptanalytic organisations is beyond the scope of this History. What follows is a brief summary of what was learned after the end of the war about the successes and failures of Germany's cryptanalysts against British high-grade cyphers, that is those cyphers which were intended to provide long-term security for the information passed in them. With the important exception of their success against merchant shipping communications, their performance against lower grade field cyphers and tactical codes is not dealt with; where it is relevant, however, an attempt has been made to take account of it in the operational chapters of the History.

A. THE ROYAL NAVY

By 1939 the Admiralty had rejected the use of the Typex machine in ships. At the outbreak of war the Royal Navy accordingly relied on the Naval Cypher, a 4-figure book used by officers, and the Administrative Code, a 5-figure book worked by ratings for less secret communications. The Navy thus had its own definitions of 'cypher' and 'code'; a 'cypher' was used by officers and a 'code' by ratings; both were recyphered/recoded – though the process was

---

* See above, p 7.

identical, the cypher was 'recyphered' and the code 'recoded' – by long subtractor tables. There was a variety of tables for use with each book.

1. *The Administrative Code and Naval Code*

Before the war the Administrative Code had been used both plain for non-confidential and recoded by long subtractor tables for confidential messages; and this practice had enabled the German naval B-Dienst to achieve its first success, the breaking of the Administrative Code and its tables. By the outbreak of war the Germans were reading traffic in this system extensively. They continued to do so, obtaining valuable operational intelligence, until 20 August 1940, when the Administrative Code was replaced by Naval Code No 1; this was a 4-figure book on the lines of the Naval Cypher, so that from this time all high-grade traffic was outwardly similar. Thereafter the Naval Code was subjected to the same improvements as were applied to the Naval Cypher; additional subtractor tables, more frequent change of tables, improvements in procedure, the use of one-time pads on an ever increasing scale and, later on, a more rapid change of the basic cypher and code books. In general, therefore, the B-Dienst's success in breaking the generally held tables used with Naval Code was similar to that achieved against the general tables used with Naval Cypher, although by the nature of the traffic the intelligence obtained was of less operational importance.

2. *The Naval Cypher*

The B-Dienst's experience in breaking the Administrative Code provided a most valuable start to its work on Naval Cypher. By April 1940 it was reading without great delay 30 to 50 per cent of the traffic intercepted, though it should be added that the evidence suggests that it had no success with traffic encyphered in the tables used by Commanders-in-Chief and Flag Officers. On 20 August 1940 Naval Cypher No 1 was replaced by No 2. It will have been noted that it was on this date too that Naval Code No 1 replaced the Administrative Code.

In the following months the Admiralty took further steps to improve the security of the long subtractor system, and· did so to some effect. The B-Dienst's success against Naval Cypher No 2 was comparatively limited until September 1941 when, for some unexplained reason, an indicator procedure which had caused the B-Dienst real difficulty was abandoned for one which was very much weaker. From then until 1 January 1942, when Naval Cypher No 4 replaced No 2, the B-Dienst again succeeded in reading a good deal of the traffic in generally held tables. By October 1942 the new No 4 book had been reconstructed to a fair extent, but against Naval Cypher No 4 the B-Dienst never achieved results comparable to its success against No 1 during the first year of the war and against No 2 during the last four months of 1941. Indeed, after the complete surprise achieved by the Anglo-US invasion of north Africa in November 1942 there was reason for the Admiralty to have some confidence that the long subtractor, thanks to all the action taken to improve it, was able to provide a reasonable degree of security for the Royal Navy's own communications.

Before the war no consideration had been given to the provision of secure communications between the Royal and United States Navies. When the need for this could be seen as a possibility late in 1940, the Admiralty, with the agreement of the US Navy Department, set aside one of its own reserve Naval Cypher Basic books, No 3, for this purpose and produced long subtractor tables for use with it. These were brought into use in June 1941 for use by the British, US and Canadian Navies in the Atlantic, for which purpose, for fear of unwieldiness, it was used to begin with without the improvements which had been applied to Naval Cyphers No 2 and No 4. This had serious consequences from October 1941, when the cypher began to carry an increasing amount of traffic. In January 1942, having realised that Naval Cypher No 3 had become the most important cypher for communications concerning arrangements for convoys and stragglers in the Atlantic, the B-Dienst concentrated most of its resources against it. By February 1942 it had reconstructed the book, and from then until 15 December 1942 it read a large proportion of the signals – sometimes as much as 80 per cent. From 15 December 1942 a change in the indicator procedure created a set-back for the B-Dienst, but it soon overcame this by increasing its staff. From February 1943 it was again reading a large proportion of the traffic, and was sometimes obtaining decrypts about convoy movements between 10 and 20 hours in advance. Throughout the period February 1942 to 10 June 1943 it frequently decrypted in this cypher the daily signal in which the Admiralty issued its estimate of U-boat dispositions.

The German success against Naval Cypher ended in June 1943, when the No 3 and No 4 books were replaced by Naval Cypher No 5, both for British and for British-Canadian-US use, and a novel and secure re-cyphering system was brought into use throughout the Royal and Royal Canadian Navies. It was not until 1 January 1944 that the US Navy could complete the distribution of this new re-cyphering system, so that for RN/USN purposes Naval Cypher No 5 had still to be used with the old system for some months. But on the strength of evidence derived from GC and CS's decrypts of

Enigma signals to the U-boats it was established that the Naval Cypher was no longer insecure after June 1943. From November 1943, moreover, the Naval Cypher was being progressively replaced for British-Canadian-US communications in the Atlantic by the Combined Cypher Machine (CCM) against which, as we shall see, the enemy made no progress.

It was the evidence of GC and CS's Enigma decrypts which established beyond doubt that the Naval Cypher was insecure. To this extent the Germans owed their prolonged success against the Naval Cyphers to the fact that their effective exploitation of Naval Cypher No 3 began at just the time, February 1942, when their introduction of the 4-wheel Enigma deprived GC and CS of decrypts of the U-boat traffic.* Since GC and CS kept a close watch on its own decrypts for evidence of enemy success against British and Allied cyphers, it was largely because it had read no U-boat signals since 1 February 1942 that it encountered no firm evidence of such success in the twelve months ending 1 July 1942. In the second half of 1942 a number of enemy naval signals were decrypted in cyphers other than the U-boat Enigma – they included occasional Italian and Japanese messages as well as decrypts in the German Home Waters and Mediterranean Enigma keys – which cast doubt on the security of Naval Cypher No 3 and No 4 and of the Naval Code; and at this time the Admiralty took steps to ensure that the basic cypher and code books could in future be changed more frequently. But it was not until GC and CS broke the 4-wheel U-boat Enigma at the end of 1942 that the Admiralty, the US Navy Department and GC and CS fully realised, from the decrypts and from the operational measures of the U-boat Command, the extent to which Naval Cypher No 3 had been broken.

In January 1943 the Admiralty warned all Flag Officers that due to the great load of traffic carried by the more generally held long subtractor tables it had to be assumed that some messages would be read with varying time lags and instructed them to adopt all possible precautions – a minimum of signalling, and the maximum use of one-time pads and of Typex, which by now was held by all naval commands ashore. Between then and June 1943, when it was able to bring into force Naval Cypher No 5 to replace Nos 3 and 4 and the new re-cyphering system, it had to fall back on further emergency measures, particularly the introduction of new cypher groups for giving positions and compass bearings in Naval Cypher No 3, as the Enigma evidence of insecurity accumulated.

Following the concern first felt in 1940 as to the adequacy of the long subtractor to carry the very large volume of message traffic which war experience had shown to be necessary, GC and CS had,

---

* See above, Chapter 26.

by April 1941, devised the new recyphering system which was not
to be introduced until June 1943. After consideration by the
Cypher Security Committee all three Services had decided to adopt
it after extensive trials which had ended in March 1942, before
Sigint began to provide solid grounds for anxiety. During the
remainder of 1942 difficulties in designing and manufacturing
devices for use with the new system and in printing the new tables
delayed the production of adequate stocks. Once produced these
had to be distributed world-wide and in those days of sea carriage
this would have taken anything up to six months, so that the new
system could not be ready for introduction before June 1943. The
fundamental explanation of the enemy's prolonged success is thus
to be found in the fact that it was not until the spring of 1941 that
GC and CS proposed the replacement of the existing re-cyphering
system and not until the spring of 1942 that the proposal was
adopted.

The first of these earlier and more significant delays arose from
GC and CS's misplaced confidence in the security of a re-
cyphering system which had been in use from well before the
outbreak of war. This confidence may seem all the more misplaced
in that GC and CS had itself achieved success against similar
systems before the outbreak of war, but after the summer of 1940 it
may well have seemed justified by the contrast between the
increasing difficulty which GC and CS experienced in breaking the
Italian high-grade book cyphers and the growing ease with which it
read the traffic encyphered on the German Enigma machine. The
second arose from a justified concern in all three Services that a
more complicated system might cause delays in message handling
and errors in transmission which might prove to be operationally
unacceptable. But even when due allowance has been made for
these mitigating factors, it remains the case that GC and CS and
the Service departments were slow to appreciate the weaknesses of
the long subtractor system; and the fundamental reason lies in the
fact that, having failed to establish close inter-departmental co-
ordination before the war, they continued to give insufficient
priority to the need for close co-ordination long after the war had
begun.

3. *Typex and CCM*

Although the Typex machine was not used at sea by the Royal
Navy during the war, the Combined Cypher Machine (CCM)
began to be used from November 1943 for British-Canadian-US
communications in the Atlantic; from then on use of the CCM
gradually increased and it was eventually held by all HM ships.
The machine was based on the US Electrical Cypher Machine and

the British Typex machine which had been made available to the Americans on their entry into the war. The US Navy was not able to provide the ECM for British and Canadian use, but by an agreement of June 1942 undertook to modify the ECM to work to the British Typex and to develop an adaptor for the latter, the modified ECM and Typex machines becoming different marks of the CCM. The speed with which this development work was done reflected great credit on the US Navy, but large numbers of the different marks of the CCM machine were required, and their production, undertaken both in the US and the UK, was necessarily a lengthy task. Like the Typex, the CCM proved to be totally secure; indeed the Germans made no serious attempt to solve either system.

4. *The Merchant Navy Code and Merchant Ships Code*

The cryptographic systems provided for communication with merchant ships were a prolific source of intelligence to the B-Dienst second only to Naval Cypher No 3 in their importance to the Battle of the Atlantic. The Merchant Navy Code replaced the International Code and Naval Appendix in January 1940. Like the earlier system it was used with a simple re-coding system so that by March the B-Dienst was having some success, and its work was greatly helped by the capture of copies of the Merchant Navy Code at Bergen in May 1940, after which it was able to read the bulk of the traffic with very little delay. Although this code was re-coded by a variety of tables (some for general use, some for independently routed ships, others for Commodores of convoys) all, other than the Commodores' table, which was little used, were readily broken by the B-Dienst. Nor were the tables issued to each inward and outward bound north Atlantic convoy from June 1941 an exception. In April 1942 the Merchant Navy Code was replaced by the Merchant Ships Code and there was a gradual change over to what was thought would be the more secure long subtractor as the recoding system. This change achieved little or nothing, the B-Dienst's entry into the new system being greatly aided by the capture of a copy of the new code book from a merchant ship in northern waters some four weeks before it came into force.

Apart from the fact that the reading of the Merchant Navy Code was of substantial assistance to the B-Dienst's all-important work on Naval Cypher No 3, the traffic contained operational intelligence about arrangements for convoys and stragglers. This was especially valuable after 10 June 1943, when the replacement of Naval Cypher No 3 by Naval Cypher No 5 ended the enemy's run of success against the Naval Cypher. However, the value of the Merchant Navy Code's decrypts was much reduced from December 1943, from which date positions mentioned in the signals, previously expressed in latitude and longitude, were disguised. From September 1944 an improvement to the recoding tables further increased the B-Dienst's difficulties: from then on it had 'neither route nor course'.

There was one other merchant ship system for communication with fast independently routed ships, each of which was provided with its own unique subtractor pad. This was introduced in August 1941 and achieved a reasonable degree of security. It appears that on the false assumption that the system was a truly 'one-time' one, which it was not, the B-Dienst did not work on the system until late in 1943, and it was not until May 1944 that it began to have some success. By that time positions in the signals were being disguised and the value of the decrypts was limited.

5. *The Naval Shore Code*

Against this system, introduced by the Admiralty in July 1941 for communication with Naval Attachés, Consular Officers and Reporting Officers, the B-Dienst had little success: much of the traffic passed by cable and the system made extensive use of one-time pads.

B. THE ARMY

The War Office adopted the Typex machine before the war and by September 1939 this system, which remained secure throughout the war, was in use between the War Office and commands, at home and overseas, and within the commands down to division level.

The War Office book cypher, re-cyphered by different long subtractor tables in different theatres, supplemented the Typex machine. The basic book was captured in Norway and at Dunkirk in 1940, but it appears that the Germans had no success against British cyphers, as opposed to field codes and radio telephony, during their western offensive in 1940.* In the Middle East they were solving the tables from at least August 1941 until January 1942, but from then on they were increasingly held up by improvements in procedure similar to those being introduced at the same time by the Admiralty and Air Ministry,† and in 1943, when the Army's long subtractor was replaced by the new system that was then adopted by all three Services, German success ended.

---

* But see Volume I, p 163 for their success against French cyphers up to the fall of France.
† But this set-back was off-set by the fact that at about this time they began to read the cypher used by the US Military Attaché in Cairo (see above, p 331).

C. THE ROYAL AIR FORCE

The Air Ministry adopted the Typex cypher machine before the outbreak of war, and by September 1939 this was in use at all RAF HQs. It proved to be completely secure. Although the Germans worked out its general principles after capturing the settings for a two-month period and a few machines (but without their wheels) during the retreat to Dunkirk in 1940, they never read its traffic; and they abandoned work on it at the end of 1941.

Although the Typex machine provided a completely secure system for the more important RAF ground-to-ground communications, the RAF was dependent on the RAF Cypher, a 4-figure basic book re-cyphered by a long subtractor, at lower levels of command where Typex was not available. This had all the weaknesses of the Navy's long subtractor systems and the GAF Sigint Service first broke this heavily used system early in 1940, when it read the traffic between the Air Ministry and Gibraltar, Malta, Habbaniya and Ismailia, and by the spring of 1941 it was also reading the traffic in north Africa. Although the GAF Sigint Service decrypted it with an average time-lag of between two and four weeks (messages being only occasionally broken within two or three days), this was sufficient to give valuable intelligence on the organisation, strength and deployment of the RAF in the Mediterranean. But improved procedures and more frequent changes of recyphering tables made their work gradually more difficult, and in November 1942 the traffic became unreadable. Work on the system continued, however, and in 1943, when the GAF learnt of the B Dienst's inability to break the Royal Navy's new re-cyphering system, it rightly concluded that it was faced with the same intractable problem. Interest in the system gradually died through lack of results, but at the end of the war the GAF had one man still doing his lonely best.

D. INTER-DEPARTMENTAL AND INTER-SERVICE CYPHERS

1. *Inter-departmental Cypher*

This system, a basic cypher book and long subtractor tables, was held in common by the Foreign Office, the Colonial, Dominions and India Offices and the Services. The Germans began work on it in the summer of 1940 after capturing the basic book at Bergen, and soon broke it. Until June 1943, when the Germans stopped work on it, it provided valuable political intelligence and information about merchant shipping, the Admiralty using it for communications with Naval Attachés, Consular Officers and Reporting Officers. For these last purposes, however, the Admiralty replaced it with the Naval Shore Code in July 1941 (see above, p 640).

2. *Inter-Service Cypher*

This basic cypher book, used with long subtractor tables, replaced the inter-departmental Cypher for inter-Service purposes in June 1942. The Germans appear to have had little or no success against it whether used with the long subtractor or the new system which, for use with this cypher, was introduced in June 1944.

E. FOREIGN OFFICE

1. *Main Cypher Books*

Despite an extensive attack in 1938 and 1939, the Germans failed to break the long subtractor system used to re-cypher the Foreign Office's basic cypher books. Against similar tables that were in force from November 1940 to January 1941 they had some limited success, but not enough to enable them to reconstruct the book before both the basic book and the tables were again changed. There is no evidence of later success, and according to German testimony after the war the main Foreign Office systems were never broken.*

2. *The Foreign Office R Code*

This book was used unrecoded for messages of a non-confidential nature. The Germans had already reconstructed the 1935 edition of the book when they captured a copy of it in Bergen in 1940. It took them about six months to reconstruct the new edition that came into force in 1941. It is unlikely that they obtained any valuable intelligence from this source.

---

* The discovery after the war in the archives of the German Ministry of Foreign Affairs of a 90-page volume of British diplomatic signals for the immediately pre-war period led to a Foreign Office enquiry in 1968. This established that a number of the signals had been despatched *en clair*. It also noted that there was reliable evidence that the Italians had obtained temporary possession of the cyphers of the Rome Embassy in 1935, and had photographed them, and that they had had fairly regular access to the cyphers at the Mission to the Holy See during the war, so that they might have read all telegrams to Rome up to the outbreak of war and telegrams to and from the Mission to the Holy See from the outbreak of war to the autumn of 1943. After the war the cryptanalysts of the German Foreign Ministry asserted that they obtained no information about British cyphers from the Italians.

APPENDIX 1, PART (ii)

Intelligence Bearing on the Security of Ultra

The British authorities responsible for Sigint and for communications security scrutinised all decrypts of enemy signals for indications as to whether the enemy was reading Allied codes and cyphers or was suspecting the compromise of his own.* From the time when intelligence from enemy decrypts began to be disseminated in any quantity they also scrutinised the signals traffic of the Allied operational commands, lest the enemy should derive from it by possible decryption or in other ways grounds for suspecting that his own codes and cyphers were not secure. Regulations designed to keep references to intelligence derived from decrypts out of Allied operational signals, unless those signals were using some totally reliable cypher, and out of documents that were liable to be captured were issued at regular intervals, and a watch was kept for cases of injudicious operational behaviour that might have betrayed that the commands were making use of Sigint. The regulations required that the possession of Ultra should never be jeopardised by a tactical operation that might arouse the enemy's suspicions. In the Navy, moreover, where the use of operational intelligence was most likely to arouse enemy suspicion, the Admiralty thought it best, soon after naval high-grade Sigint first became available, 'to exercise a more direct control over operations than was the usual practice' until it had gained some experience of the problems involved in making use of the intelligence for operational purposes.[1]

The Admiralty's decision was prompted by a series of alarms in the early stages. Fifteen supply or supporting ships at sea when the *Bismarck* sailed were sunk by the Navy between 7 May and 11 July 1941. The naval Enigma had disclosed the whereabouts of eight of

---

* Whenever the decrypts contained an item of intelligence about Allied forces Whitehall investigated with the commands whether the enemy's source might have been decryption of Allied signals. Investigation usually established that the source had been plain language or low-grade code signals, but see Appendix I, Part (i) for the extent to which Allied Sigint disclosed enemy success in reading Allied high-grade cyphers. During the period from mid-1941 to mid-1943 Sigint provided no positive evidence that the enemy suspected that his own high-grade cyphers were compromised, but see Appendix 19 for the evidence it provided about the improvement of his cyphers.

1. ADM 223/88, Colpoys, *Admiralty Use of Special Intelligence in Naval Operations*, p 12.

these; two of the eight were sunk despite the fact that the Admiralty, in an attempt to reduce the enemy's suspicions, had decided to allow them to escape.[2]* Not long after this episode the Admiralty was alarmed by two cases of carelessness. The C-in-C South Atlantic repeated to one of his destroyers the three U-boat positions which had been sent to him in an Ultra signal, and the officer commanding the submarines at Malta sent to one of his submarines virtually the exact text of a GC and CS decrypt giving full details of the arrangements made for sailing an Italian convoy to north Africa.[3]

Two further slips of the same kind were detected by the Admiralty in November 1941. The C-in-C Mediterranean transmitted to the Naval Attaché in Ankara – an unauthorised recipient of Ultra, and one based in a neutral country – the contents of a decrypt which had revealed that the enemy knew of an Allied plan to pass Russian tankers from the Black Sea into the Mediterranean.[4] And Flag Officer Commanding the North Atlantic at Gibraltar repeated to ships and authorities under his command three U-boat positions which had been sent to him by Ultra signal.[5] But no doubt as a result of the fact that the Admiralty had issued sharp rebukes on all the above occasions, and also sent out frequent reminders of the need for caution in the handling of Ultra, there were no further scares for nearly a year after November 1941; moreover, the next scares arose in north Africa in connection with the handling of Army Enigma.

The Prime Minister had meanwhile come to appreciate the importance of taking precautions when making operational use of high-grade Sigint. To begin with, he had been impatient about precautions, particularly with reference to the instructions which required GC and CS to paraphrase decrypts before passing them to the Middle East commands and to withhold non-essential intelligence. In April 1941, for example, he had criticised GC and CS for failing to mention that Hitler was taking a personal interest in Rommel's operations against Tobruk, and complained that its paraphrases were not reflecting the full flavour of the original decrypts. In July, having been briefed on the Admiralty's arrangements for sending Ultra about shipping movements to the operational authorities in the Mediterranean, he had sent the following minutes to the First Sea Lord: 'I hope Admiral Cunningham realises the quality of the information. If he cannot intercept on this

---

* See Volume I, pp 345–346.

2. ibid, pp 16, 18.
3. ibid, p 22.
4. ADM 186/801, BR 1736 (49) 2, pp 233–234; MK 121 of 23 November 1941; ZTPI 2416.
5. ADM 223/88, p 23.

we do not deserve success.' 'I wish I knew what he *did* when he received these messages.'[6] In August, again, in a minute connected with the formation of Force K at Malta,* he had pressed for more intensive exploitation of the Ultra intelligence.[7] At the beginning of September 1941, in contrast, he was expressing concern about decrypts of signals of the Italian Sigint service which had reported that Malta was sending orders to submarines about the interception of Italian convoys – and being reassured that the signals were based on Traffic Analysis, not on the decryption of Malta's orders[8] – and in November 1941 he expressed anxiety for the security of Ultra in a personal message to General Auchinleck. This asked the C-in-C not to allow any signals based on high-grade Sigint into the *Crusader* battle area 'except as statements on your own authority with no trace of origin and not too close a coincidence . . . There seems great danger of documents being captured in view of battle confusion. Excuse my anxiety.'[9]

Thereafter the Prime Minister was ready to relax the rules when the situation warranted. It was he who inaugurated the easing of the constraints on GC and CS's service to the Middle East commands by insisting in the summer of 1942 that General Auchinleck should be sent the verbatim texts of the more significant decrypts.[†] But he always lent his authority to the policy of insisting on the importance of security precautions, and sometimes his zeal in this matter exceeded that of his advisers. When the next alarms occurred in September 1942 – the first following the discovery that the enemy had learned that General Montgomery had had foreknowledge of Rommel's attack at Alam el Halfa, and the second occasioned by the leakage of intelligence about Rommel's illness – the Prime Minister played a leading part in rebuking General Montgomery, and it was he who ordered Sir Edward Bridges to set up an enquiry into Whitehall's responsibility for the leakage.[‡] And after the landings in French north Africa in November 1942 he more than once drew attention to the risks to the security of Ultra that might arise from the uncertain state of the fighting. On 21 November 'C' received this minute from him: 'Pray consider whether, at this period in the operation, it would not be wise to have a general campaign to reduce to one-third the

---

* See above, p 287.

† See above, pp 359, 380.

‡ See above, pp 413–414.

6. Dir/C Archive, 7202 of 29 July 1941, 7225 of 30 July 1941.

7. ibid, unreferenced minutes PM to CNS and reply, both of 24 August 1941, covering ZTPI 422 and 423.

8. ibid, 7472 of 2 September 1941; Naval Headlines 65 of 2 September 1941.

9. Cabinet Office file 82/43/1, Part 2, PM's personal telegram T/851 of 23 November 1941.

circulation of Boniface* here, in the Middle East and at the *Torch* Headquarters . . . There would be 2 classes of Boniface, starred and unstarred. The starred would only go to the new restricted circle. The unstarred would continue as at present, but would gradually die away, it being suggested that the hens are laying much less, or even not at all'.[10] On 6 December, when nothing had come of this proposal, he asked 'C' about the security of Ultra in the Tunisian battle zone, and was reassured that things were under control.[11] Early in 1943 he returned to the matter again and had to be reassured by a personal telegram from General Eisenhower stating that there was no danger that Ultra would fall into enemy hands.[12]

The last in this series of enquiries appears to have been occasioned by a report to the effect that General Anderson was taking copies of SCU/SLU signals forward of First Army's HQ. The resulting alarm was one of several which arose when the recipients of Ultra in Tunisia, many of them inexperienced in handling it, encountered heavier enemy resistance and more intense fighting than had been allowed for. It was this combination of circumstances which accounted for a serious breach of the regulations governing the use of naval Ultra, the first for more than a year. On 11 December 1942 the Naval Officer in Charge Bône delayed a convoy movement in a signal which was made in a cypher that Whitehall suspected of being insecure, and which gave as his reason the fact that he expected an E-boat attack. This expectation was based on a decrypt of which the gist had been sent to Algiers by GC and CS. To make matters worse, NOIC Bône was not an authorised Ultra recipient. To make matters worse still, it was now confirmed that the cypher used by the NOIC was being read by the enemy: the enemy cancelled the E-boat attack and it was an Enigma decrypt ordering the cancellation and reproducing the text of the NOIC's signal which brought the incident to Whitehall's notice.[13]† Another naval lapse followed a month later when the captain of the 10th Submarine Flotilla at Malta signalled to one of his submarines details of the movement of an enemy convoy that was subsequently cancelled. Reprimanding him, the First Sea Lord pointed out that his signal should have confined

---

* Boniface was the code-word for Ultra which the Prime Minister continued to use; it dated from the time when the earliest Enigma decrypts had been circulated in Whitehall as reports received from an agent of that name, see Volume I, p 138.

† So far as is known, the enemy, unlike the Admiralty, did not inquire into the source of the NOIC's intelligence.

10.   Dir/C Archive, unreferenced minute from the Prime Minister to 'C' of 21 November 1942.
11.   ibid, 1676 of 18 December 1942, answering PM's comment on CX/MSS/1783/T17 of 6 December.
12.   ibid, 2364 of 22 February 1943, enclosing SCU 172 of 17 February 1943.
13.   ADM 223/88, pp 27–30.

itself to giving patrol instructions, and added: 'This is a matter in which we cannot afford to have any, repeat any, slips.'[14]

In March 1943 the Enigma decrypts prompted further alarms by disclosing that the Germans were having qualms about their own security. A week before the battle of Medenine, while General Montgomery was preparing to meet the attack which the Enigma had predicted, the Prime Minister enjoined him 'to safeguard our precious secret so far as possible in your dispositions'.[15] In the event, Eighth Army's preparations left little room for safeguards, and after the battle the Enigma established that the Axis authorities suspected that General Montgomery had been forewarned of Rommel's attack.* Nor had Whitehall's anxiety about this news died down when further Enigma decrypts showed that the GAF had grounds for believing that, as was indeed the case, the Allies had had advance details about an important shipping movement. The high-grade Sigint had disclosed that four merchant vessels and a tanker, with cargoes which Kesselring had stated to be 'decisive for the future conduct of operations' would sail for Tunisia on 12 and 13 March in two convoys but in a single inter-locking operation; and the tanker and the two merchant ships were duly sunk by British air and naval forces. But before despatching these forces the British authorities had failed to provide full cover for the Sigint by making sure that air sightings were obtained, and as the enemy then delayed the convoy, the British forces were sighted by the GAF at the point where, but for the delay, they would have encountered their target.[16]

On 14 March, on the strength of an Enigma decrypt which indicated that the GAF had been made suspicious by this sighting, C-in-C Mediterranean was reprimanded by the First Sea Lord and the Prime Minister; the Prime Minister in his signal threatened to withhold Ultra unless it was 'used only on great occasions or when thoroughly camouflaged'. The C-in-C replied in the following terms:[17]

'. . . care was taken to arrange air reconnaissance in vicinity of both convoys.† Reconnaissance could not in fact reach northernmost convoy, but arrangements were made for dummy enemy reports to be made from vicinity. The convoy along north Sicilian coast was sighted by ASV

---

* See above, p 596.
† The Chief Air Intelligence Officer at AFHQ signalled on 13 March 1943: 'Convoys were both sighted by routine air sweeps varied from time to time in light of Ultra . . .'[18]

14. ibid, p 24.
15. Cabinet Office file 82/43/1 Part 2, Air Ministry telegram OZ 609 of 1 March 1943, from the Prime Minister to General Montgomery.
16. CX/MSS/2554/T1.
17. Dir/C Archive 2592 covering C-in-C Mediterranean telegram to CNS, 2030/15 March 1943 and CX/MSS/2265/T32.
18. ibid, CXG 209, TOO 1700/13 March 1943.

aircraft at frequent intervals and the information provided was more accurate than that of Special Intelligence.

2. As regards movement of warships, there have been warships in vicinity of Skerki Bank on average every other day for past fortnight. *Abdiel* has done 3 lays in this period accompanied part way by destroyers; 2 destroyers have gone through to Malta; and Force Q has operated. Enemy was aware of at least a proportion of these moves and reports of them.

3. While not minimising seriousness of arousing enemy misgivings, I consider his statement comes as much from a desire to cover his failure in protecting the convoy as from real base of suspicion. He did the same thing in excusing recent failure against 8 Army.*

4. The arrival of the convoy was of vital importance to the enemy and Tedder and I realise the equal importance of attacking it and concealing the source of the information. Short of failing to make proper effort against the convoy which I suggest would have been inadvisable, there appears to be no other action that could have been taken. I share your anxiety in this matter which is extremely difficult one to handle, but I can assure you it received the closest attention'.

The reply illustrates not only the rigour with which the operational authorities normally applied the prescribed precautions, but also the problems which sometimes confronted the users of Ultra in operational conditions. It is not without interest, either, for showing how complex those conditions might be; given the nature of Allied precautions, and bearing in mind that Allied lapses were relatively infrequent, this factor must have made it difficult for the enemy to elicit the truth even when his suspicions had been aroused. However that may be, neither after Medenine nor after the attack on the convoy did the enemy follow up his first suspicions. And the same was true when, this time in connection with the land fighting at El Guettar and Maknassy in the last week of March,† the Enigma decrypts again gave voice to suggestions that the Allies had had foreknowledge of Axis intentions. The decrypts made it clear that the suspicion was based on a 'sure source' – that is on interception of Allied wireless communications. They offered a variety of possible explanations for the Allied foreknowledge – the interrogation of POW and the cutting of landlines by the Allies, Allied air and ground reconnaissance, and Allied Sigint derived from the use of plain language or of careless signalling by Axis troops. But they contained nothing to suggest that the enemy connected it with the insecurity of the Enigma. Perhaps for this reason Whitehall took no action. Nor is there any evidence that on this occasion it was incautious use of Enigma intelligence that had aroused the enemy's suspicions; since the end of February the exploitation of the enemy's lower-grade codes by

---

* A reference to the security scare after the battle of Medernine.
† See above, p 601 et seq.

British field Y had greatly improved, Allied tactical air reconnaissance had become 'very efficient',[19] and it is reasonable to assume that these other sources were providing adequate cover for the Enigma. Y had indeed confirmed the Enigma warning of Axis intentions at El Guettar on 23 March 1943.*

For a period of 12 months after the end of March 1943 the records contain no evidence of further serious alarms in Whitehall. But in 1944, in a series of incidents which did indeed have severe consequences for Ultra, the Allies came nearer than ever before to alerting the Germans to the fact that they were reading the Enigma.†

---

* See above, p 601.
† See Volume III.

19. AIR 41/33, *The North African Campaign*, p 151.

APPENDIX 2

Developments in the Organisation of the Service Intelligence Branches, mid-1941 to mid-1943

I. *NID, Admiralty*

NID retained the system by which operational intelligence from whatever source was the preserve of the OIC and by which research and routine intelligence was carried out in (with few exceptions) country sections. The main changes to those sections were as follows:

NID 1 (the Northern Section, ie Germany and northern Europe): its great expansion was due partly to the great increase of intelligence, particularly PR, about the numbers and types of U-boats, but was chiefly brought about by the demands made upon it for the supply of intelligence for planning purposes. It developed close links with Combined Operations HQ, with the Combined Commanders Group which was studying the invasion of Europe from March 1942, and with GHQ Home Forces, which needed coastal intelligence both for its own long-term preparations for re-entry into Europe and for the small-scale raids that it was authorised to carry out independently of Combined Operations HQ. From the Home Fleet, also, it met a greatly increased demand for intelligence on targets and defences in Norway, and in August 1943 it appointed an officer to combined intelligence departments of the Norwegian Army and Navy.[1]

NID 3 (the Mediterranean Section): see NID 20, below.

NID 12: set up in July 1942, this incorporated NID 17P (see below) and NID 17M, the sub-section which had been responsible for handling on behalf of the Admiralty decrypts of the cyphers used by the German Secret Service and for contributing to the work of the bodies responsible for strategic deception. By October 1942 NID 12 was summarising some 400 items per day of German

---

1. Morgan, *NID History 1939–42*, pp 31, 54–55; ADM 223/107, Development and Organisation of the NID September 1939–April 1944, pp 14–16.

Enigma, diplomatic and Secret Service and various Italian de-crypts. These summaries were intended mainly to provide the First Sea Lord and the Board of Admiralty with a broad intelligence background for the taking of strategic decisions. They were also distributed to certain British and US operational commands in the United Kingdom.[2]

NID 16 (the Russian section): this was formed out of the Far Eastern Section (NID 4) in July 1941. It supervised the exchange of naval intelligence with Russia through the Soviet Military Mission in Britain and the British Military Mission in Russia.[3]*

NID 17P: this sub-section of NID 17 was formed in July 1941 to study and summarise for the Naval Staff the contents of the non-operational intelligence (and thus mainly non-naval intelli-gence, operational intelligence remaining the responsibility of the OIC) that was reaching the Admiralty from Sigint and the SIS.[†] By November 1941 it was issuing two or more summaries a day.

NID 20: this new country section was formed in December 1941 to be responsible for Vichy France, Spain and Portugal and their oversea possessions, which had originally been covered by NID 3 (the Mediterranean section). In the spring of 1942 it took over from NID 3 responsibility for east Africa and Rhodesia. In its early days its chief work was the provision of defence and topographical intelligence, including intelligence about the French Fleet, for the planning of operation *Torch* and of the landings in Madagascar (operation *Ironclad*).[4]

NID 23: this was the name given to the naval component of the joint NID/MI section that was established in the summer of 1943 to supply coastal defence intelligence for the whole of Europe (except the Channel, which had by then become the responsibility of COSSAC).[‡] Its establishment superseded the system by which since November 1942 the NID (through the Scandinavian sub-section of NID 1) and MI (through MI 14(h)) had been producing joint reports on coastal defences in Norway and, together with these Scandinavian sub-sections, it incorporated the coastal defence sub-section of NID 20.[5]

---

* See above, p 61.   † See Volume I, pp 286–287.   ‡ See above, p 192.

2. Morgan, op cit, pp 147–151; ADM 223/107, loc cit, p 40.
3. Morgan, op cit, p 105 et seq; ADM 223/7, loc cit, p 42 and Skeleton History of NID 16.
4. Morgan, op cit, pp 60–61, 87–90, 92, 100; ADM 223/107, Development and Organisation of the NID, p 45.
5. ADM 223/107, Development and Organisation of the NID, pp 46–47; JIC (42) 456 of 23 November.

II. *MI, War Office*

The main changes were the creation of new deputy directorships, as follows:

DDMI (PW) was established in December 1941 to take charge of MI 9 and the new MI 19.

DDMI (F) was the MI representative at SIS HQ appointed in March 1942.

DDMI (Y) was created in the spring of 1943 and made responsible to DMI and D Signals for the organisation of the Y service and controlling the work hitherto uneasily divided between MI 8 and Sigs 4. DD (Y) acted as War Office representative on the Y Committee, as the channel between DMI and GC and CS and as the formulator of general policy regarding the provision, administration and allocation of Army Y units. MI 8 implemented interception policy, disseminated information from Y and had operational control of fixed Y stations in the United Kingdom. Sigs 4 was responsible for all signals personnel and equipment, for the administration of fixed Y stations and for the requirements of Y communications. Another section of the Signals Directorate (Sigs 6) was responsible to DD (Y) on matters of technical security.[6]

Otherwise, while MI continued to be divided for the most part into country sections, some functional sections were established. The chief changes affecting the work of the sections were as follows:

MI 3 became responsible for all Europe (except Germany and German order of battle in occupied territories, the responsibility of MI 14) when it took over Russia, Scandinavia and eastern Europe from MI 2 in the summer of 1941.[7]

MI 15 (AA) was created in July 1943 to be responsibile for the collation and distribution of all intelligence on German anti-aircraft defences. This work had previously been carried out by a sub-section of MI 14 which had dealt directly with the Air Ministry and which from the summer of 1942 had had US officers attached to it. MI 15 (AA) continued the work as an inter-Service and inter-Allied organisation.[8]

MI 17 was established in April 1943 to act as the secretariat directly under DMI which presented to the CIGS the views of MI

---

6. Mockler-Ferryman, *Military Intelligence Organisation*, pp 18, 22.
7. ibid, p 20.   8. ibid, pp 18, 26.

on matters requiring Cabinet consideration. It incorporated MI (JIC) and MI (Co-ord), the two sections which had previously been responsible for co-ordinating the work of the Intelligence and the Operations Directorates. Like NID 17 in the Admiralty, it had a sub-section which distributed summaries of Sigint in the War Office.[9]

MI *19* was established in December 1941 to take over responsibility for enemy POW from MI 9, which continued to organise the escape and de-briefing of British POW.[10]

III. *AI, Air Ministry*

The reorganisation of AI on a functional basis, which was completed in August 1941,* remained unchanged until April 1944, when the subjects for which DDI 2 was responsible – aircraft industries, airfields and technical intelligence – were separated from operational intelligence and placed under a newly created Directorate of Intelligence (Research) which also took over DDI 4, responsible for RAF Y and low-grade Sigint. This made four directorates – security, operations, research and liaison – which remained in being till the end of the war and marked the final acceptance by the Services of the term 'Research' which had been regarded with misgiving at the beginning of the war. The few further changes that were made in the period down to mid-1943 were confined to the Directorate of Intelligence (Operations) and were of two kinds.[11]

First, the Director of Intelligence (Operations) became responsible to ACAS (I) for ADI (Sc) and ADI (Ph), and the POW section AI (K) was also placed under D of I (O) when it was raised to an assistant-directorate as ADI (K). By 1944, however, ADI (Sc) had again reverted to his former position of direct responsibility to ACAS (I).

In the second place, the deputy directorate which was responsible under D of I (O) for operational and organisational intelligence about all foreign air forces (DDI 3) made the following changes in and additions to its sections:

AI 3(b) remained responsible for covering the operational state of

---

* See Volume 1, p 284.

9. ibid, pp 18, 26–27.
10. ibid, pp 18, 52–53. See also M R D Foot and J M Langley, *MI 9* (1979).
11. Air Historical Branch, *Air Ministry Intelligence*, Vol II, Appendices C, D and E.

foreign air forces – order of battle, dispositions, strategy, operations, serviceability, wastage – but virtually confined itself to the GAF, the air forces of Germany's allies and satellites being easily dealt with by a single officer and a clerical assistant.[12]

AI 3(c) remained responsible for the assessment of bomb damage and enemy aircraft losses and for the preparation of operational target intelligence for the Allied air forces. From small beginnings in 1936 its Target Information Section (AI 3(c)1) built up a staff of 370 men and women by the end of the war. It had components in the Air Ministry and the CIU but its main production centre was at High Wycombe, close to the HQs of Bomber Command and US Eighth Air Force which made itself dependent on British facilities for target intelligence. AI 3(c)1 produced descriptive target lists used mainly by operational planners, and target maps, illustrations and information dossiers for the briefing of aircrew. Target lists were drawn up in consultation with the Service intelligence branches, MEW and the ISTD, and contained raw material supplied by the CIU as well as from a wide range of secret and overt sources. About 560,000 items per week were produced at the height of the combined strategic bombing offensive. Target material for tactical and clandestine air operations was also produced by the section.[13]

AI 3(e) was created in August 1941 to relieve AI 3(b) of certain non-operational subjects concerning the GAF where study was based primarily on the Enigma. These covered the ground organisation of the GAF, manpower, supply, maintenance, training and air transport.[14]

---

12. ibid, Vol I, p 104. See also The Work of AI 3(b) and The Use of Sigint in AI 3(b).
13. *Air Ministry Intelligence*, Vol I, pp 262–263, 280–283.
14. ibid, Vol I, pp 12, 164. See also Working Methods and Value of Ultra to AI 3(e).

APPENDIX 3

Letter from Cryptanalysts in Hut 6 and Hut 8, Bletchley Park to the Prime Minister, 21 October 1941

Secret and Confidential
Prime Minister only

Hut 6 and Hut 8,*
(Bletchley Park)

21st October 1941

Dear Prime Minister,

Some weeks ago you paid us the honour of a visit, and we believe that you regard our work as important. You will have seen that, thanks largely to the energy and foresight of Commander Travis,† we have been well supplied with the 'bombes' for the breaking of the German Enigma codes. We think, however, that you ought to know that this work is being held up, and in some cases is not being done at all, principally because we cannot get sufficient staff to deal with it. Our reason for writing to you direct is that for months we have done everything that we possibly can through the normal channels, and that we despair of any early improvement without your intervention. No doubt in the long run these particular requirements will be met, but meanwhile still more precious months will have been wasted, and as our needs are continually expanding we see little hope of ever being adequately staffed.

We realise that there is a tremendous demand for labour of all kinds and that its allocation is a matter of priorities. The trouble to our mind is that as we are a very small section with numerically trivial requirements it is very difficult to bring home to the authorities finally responsible either the importance of what is done here or the urgent necessity of dealing promptly with our requests. At the same time we find it hard to believe that it is really impossible to produce quickly the additional staff that we need, even if this meant interfering with the normal machinery of allocations.

We do not wish to burden you with a detailed list of our

---

* Hut 6 was responsible at Bletchley for the breaking of GAF and Army Enigma. Hut 8 was responsible for the breaking of naval Enigma.

† Responsible for all questions relating to cryptanalytic machinery.

difficulties, but the following are the bottlenecks which are causing us the most acute anxiety.

1. *Breaking of Naval Enigma (Hut 8)*

Owing to shortage of staff and the overworking of his present team the Hollerith section here under Mr Freeborn has had to stop working night shifts. The effect of this is that the finding of the naval keys is being delayed at least twelve hours every day. In order to enable him to start night shifts again Freeborn needs immediately about twenty more untrained Grade III women clerks. To put himself in a really adequate position to deal with any likely demands he will want a good many more.

A further serious danger now threatening us is that some of the skilled male staff, both with the British Tabulating Company at Letchworth and in Freeborn's section here, who have so far been exempt from military service, are now liable to be called up.

2. *Military and Air Force Enigma (Hut 6)*

We are intercepting quite a substantial proportion of wireless traffic in the Middle East which cannot be picked up by our intercepting stations here. This contains among other things a good deal of new 'Light Blue' intelligence. Owing to shortage of trained typists, however, and the fatigue of our present decoding staff, we cannot get all this traffic decoded. This has been the state of affairs since May. Yet all that we need to put matters right is about twenty trained typists.

3. *Bombe testing, Hut 6 and Hut 8*

In July we were promised that the testing of the 'stories' produced by the bombes would be taken over by the WRNS in the bombe hut and that sufficient WRNS would be provided for this purpose. It is now late in October and nothing has been done. We do not wish to stress this so strongly as the two preceding points, because it has not actually delayed us in delivering the goods. It has, however, meant that staff in Huts 6 and 8 who are needed for other jobs have had to do the testing themselves. We cannot help feeling that with a Service matter of this kind it should have been possible to detail a body of WRNS for this purpose, if sufficiently urgent instructions had been sent to the right quarters.

4. Apart altogether from staff matters, there are a number of other

directions in which it seems to us that we have met with unnecessary impediments. It would take too long to set these out in full, and we realise that some of the matters involved are controversial. The cumulative effect, however, has been to drive us to the conviction that the importance of the work is not being impressed with sufficient force upon those outside authorities with whom we have to deal.

We have written this letter entirely on our own initiative. We do not know who or what is responsible for our difficulties, and most emphatically we do not want to be taken as criticising Commander Travis who has all along done his utmost to help us in every possible way. But if we are to do our job as well as it could and should be done it is absolutely vital that our wants, small as they are, should be promptly attended to. We have felt that we should be failing in our duty if we did not draw your attention to the facts and to the effects which they are having and must continue to have on our work, unless immediate action is taken.

> We are, Sir, Your obedient servants,
> A M Turing
> W G Welchman
> C H O'D Alexander
> P S Milner-Barry

On receipt of this letter the Prime Minister minuted as follows to General Ismay on 22 October 1941:

'ACTION THIS DAY

Make sure they have all they want on extreme priority and report to me that this had been done'.

As a result of the Prime Minister's minute, staff requirements at Bletchley Park were given extreme priority and on 18 November 1941 'C' could report that every possible measure was being taken; though the arrangements were not then entirely completed, Bletchley's needs were being very rapidly met.

APPENDIX 4

Enigma Keys Attacked by GC and CS up to mid-1943

The individual keys allotted to Service and other users of the Enigma machine may be regarded as separate cyphers within a cypher. The tables set out below give details of the keys attacked by GC and CS, and the degree of success achieved, up till June 1943.

The tables show that the number of Enigma keys used by the German Air Force, Army and other organisations attacked up till mid-1943 greatly exceeded those used by the German Navy. Some 60 non-naval keys were broken before the end of 1942, by which time only 3 naval keys had yielded to attack. The reason for this was that it was not until late 1943 that the German Navy initiated a similar, but smaller scale, proliferation of its keys. By the end of the war some 200 non-naval keys had been identified and attacked. The number of naval keys scarcely exceeded 20. Details of the GC and CS attack on these will be given in Volume III.

On the other hand, every message that was intercepted in breakable naval keys was read by GC and CS. This was not always the case with those Enigma keys of the GAF, the German Army and other organisations attacked by GC and CS. Sometimes for technical reasons, and sometimes because the intelligence they yielded did not justify the expenditure of cryptanalytic resources, certain of these keys were not regularly broken. Certain other keys in this category were either not broken at all, or broken only rarely. But these were few in number and in general of less importance than the naval Enigma keys which defied attack. Examples are given in the tables.

As a means of ensuring the consistent identification of keys GC and CS adopted the following naming system:

Colours:	Initially the sole category, later used only for keys in very general use
Insects:	Fliegerkorps
Flowers:	Luftgaus
Birds:	Army
Fish:	Navy
Vegetables:	Weather and navigation
Others ad hoc	

Difficulties sometimes arose in applying the system. Keys sometimes split up or were resurrected and re-used later on. Once or twice, for internal reasons, GC and CS would give the same name to different keys. Each key had its own, often complex, history to which the brief references in the 'Remarks' column seldom do justice. The use of Roman numeral suffixes with certain keys calls for explanation. In the case of GAF keys a Roman I indicates the key in common use (Gebrauch key) and a Roman II the reserve (Ersatz) key. In the case of Army keys a Roman I indicated ordinary secret (Geheim) traffic, a Roman II indicated the staff (Stab) key (for top secret traffic) and a Roman III represented the Officer only (Offizier) key used only rarely for matters of the highest grade of secrecy. But both the Germans and GC and CS made exceptions to this practice.

Part 1   GAF Enigma Keys Attacked before the End of June 1942
Part 2   German Army Enigma Keys Attacked before the End of June 1942
Part 3   German Naval Enigma Keys Attacked before the End of June 1942
Part 4   GAF Enigma Keys Attacked between End June 1942 and End May 1943
Part 5   German Army Enigma Keys Attacked between End June 1942 and End May 1943
Part 6   German Naval Enigma Keys Attacked between End June 1942 and End May 1943
Part 7   Other German non-Naval Enigma Keys (SS, Railway etc) Attacked up to End May 1943

Part 1
GAF Enigma Keys Attacked before the End of June 1942

GC & CS Name for Key	Date Broken	Date First Identified by GC & CS and Duration	Remarks
Red	6.1.40	September 1939 (to end of war)	General purpose GAF key.
Blue	29.1.40	October 1939 (to end of war)	GAF practice key. Broken only rarely when occasion demanded.
Purple	26.5.40	May 1940 (to February 1941)	One day only broken. Unidentified.
Brown I	2.9.40	September 1939 (to end of war)	IV L N Versuchs-regiment.

GAF Enigma Keys Attacked before the End of June 1942 (contd)

GC & CS Name for Key	Date Broken	Date First Identified by GC & CS and Duration	Remarks
Violet	24.12.40	November 1940 (to January 1941)	General Luftgau key. Later replaced by separate Luftgau keys.
Light Blue	28.2.41	January 1941 (to end 1941)	Operational key for Africa. Lasted until introduction of separate Fliegerkorps keys 1.1.42.
Onion	8.5.41	March 1941 (to July 1941)	For navigational beam traffic: related to Brown.
Mustard	27.6.41	June 1941 (to end of war)	GAF Y Service key. From June 1944 there were two Mustards: Mustard I (W Front) Mustard II (Balkans).
Leek	31.7.41	June 1941 (to end of war)	A GAF weather key.
Brown II	17.12.41	December 1941 (to March 1943)	
Pink	1.1.42	February 1941 (to end of war)	Highest GAF command cypher. Intended for messages of highest secrecy, but only occasionally used as such, most highly secret traffic going by Red. Broken only occasionally by GC and CS.
Gadfly	1.1.42	1.1.42 (to end of war)	Initially Fliegerkorps X. Broken on day of its first appearance.
Hornet	1.1.42	1.1.42 (to December 1943)	Fliegerkorps IV. Broken on day of its first appearance.
Wasp	1.1.42	1.1.42 (to end of war)	Fliegerkorps IX. Broken on day of its first appearance.

GAF Enigma Keys Attacked before the End of June 1942 (contd)

GC & CS Name for Key	Date Broken	Date First Identified by GC & CS and Duration	Remarks
Cockroach	7.1.42	1.1.42 (to February 1945)	Fliegerkorps XII, later Jagdkorps I and Luftflotte Reich. A Western fighter key.
Locust	12.1.42	1.1.42 (to end of war)	Fliegerkorps II (Sicily).
Foxglove	12.1.42	November 1941 (to end of war)	Luftgau XVII (Ostfront): later LG VIII and LG Ost.
Primrose	17.1.42	1.1.42 (to September 1944)	Initially Luftgau West: later LG XXVIII (Med).
Beetle	4.3.42	1.1.42 (to end of war)	Initially Fliegerkorps VIII: later Luftwaffe Kommando Ost: then Luftflotte 6.
Snowdrop	7.4.42	April 1942 (to end of war)	Luftgau Westfrankreich later LG V.
Garlic	8.4.42	April 1942 (to end of war)	GAF weather key.
Scorpion	22.4.42	April 1942 (to February 1943)	Fliegerführer Afrika (ground-air co-operation)
Daffodil	9.5.42	May 1942 (to end of war)	Luftgau XI (Westfront)
Mosquito	8.6.42	1.1.42 (to end of war)	Fliegerkorps I: later Luftflotte 1 (Ostfront)
Skunk	16.6.42	May 1942 (to end of war)	Fliegerkorps VIII from May 1942 (Ostfront).

Part 2

German Army Enigma Keys Attacked before the End of June 1942

GC & CS Name for Key	Date Broken	Date First Identified by GC & CS and Duration	Remarks
Green (later Greenshank)	18.1.40	1939 (till end of war)	German Army Home Administration (Wehrkreis) key: Hut 6's toughest proposition. Only 13 breaks in whole war, latterly with some POW help. ('Such was the security of Enigma when properly used').
Yellow	10.4.40	April 1940 (till July 1940)	Army – GAF co-operation in Norway.
Gannet I	2.1.41	January 1941 (?)	German Army Command, Norway. Broken once only. Gannet II, broken 8.43, lasted till end of war.
Vulture I	27.6.41	April 1941 (till spring 1944)	Russian Front key.
Kestrel	9.7.41	June 1941 (to September 1942)	Broadcast key used for ground-air co-operation later split into 4 keys (see below). Ostfront.
Kestrel III	10.8.41		
Kestrel I	16.8.41		
Kestrel II	20.8.41		
Vulture II	21.10.41		
Chaffinch II	12.11.41	February 1941 (to May 1943)	First broken crypt-analytically in September and regularly from 12.11.41 to last week in November. Chaffinch keys captured in operation *Crusader* enabled whole month's traffic up to 23.11.41 to be read. Keys then changed and were not read again until April 1942. Chaffinch II

German Army Enigma Keys Attacked before the End of June 1942 (contd)

GC & CS Name for Key	Date Broken	Date First Identified by GC & CS and Duration	Remarks
			was key for communication between Panzerarmee Afrika and higher authority. Chaffinch I and III were general and administrative keys.
Chaffinch I	14.11.41		
Phoenix	23.11.41	November 1941 (to May 1943)	Operational key of Panzerarmee Afrika for use between Army, Corps and Division. Key captured during *Crusader* and all traffic for month up to 23.11.41 read. Then not broken again until summer of 1942 after which it was read with fair regularity.
Kestrel IV	27.11.41		
Kite	2.1.42	July 1941 (to April 1945)	Ostfront supply key.
Raven III	20.2.42	September 1941 (to April 1945)	Initially Twelfth Army; later Army Group E (Balkans)
Raven I	8.3.42		
Raven II	11.3.42		
Skylark	18.5.42	April 1942 (to May 1942)	Between France and Channel Isles.

Part 3
German Naval Enigma Keys Attacked before the End of June 1942

GC & CS Name for Key	Period of Use by German Navy	Date Broken by GC & CS	Remarks
Dolphin	September 1939 to end of war	With virtual currency from 1 August 1941	Called 'Heimisch' by Germans until 1.1.43 when it was renamed Hydra. Was general key for use by ships

German Naval Enigma Keys Attacked before the End of June 1942 (contd)

GC & CS Name for Key	Period of Use by German Navy	Date Broken by GC & CS	Remarks
			and authorities in home waters and Baltic, and by U-boats until 1.2.42. Traffic for February, June and July 1941 read from captured keys. Some other days before 1.8.41 also read. From that date all days read till 7.5.45 except 1–4 August 1941 and 18–19 September 1941. Atlantic U-boats changed to Shark (see below) on 1.2.42, but U-boats in Far North continued to use Dolphin until June 1944. 'Officer Only' (Offizier) of Dolphin, called Oyster by GC & CS, read regularly throughout the war, but often broke late.
Pike	September 1939 until an undetermined date late in the war	Not Broken	Used by raiders and other units in distant waters. Called 'Ausserheimisch' by Germans and, from 1.1.43, Aegir.
(None given)	September 1939 until end of war	Not Broken	Used by U-boats during exercises in Baltic. Called U-bootsübungsschüssel, later Thetis, by Germans.
Barracuda	May 1941 until end of war	Not Broken	Used for highest level communications during fleet operations. Called Neptun by Germans.

Part 4
GAF Enigma Keys Attacked between End June 1942 and End May 1943

GC & CS Name for Key	Date Broken	Date Identified in GC & CS and Duration	Remarks
Weasel	15.7.42	July 1942 (to April 1945)	Flakkorps I (Ostfront).
Narcissus	10.8.42	July 1942 (to November 1944)	Luftgau Norwegen.
Celery	2.9.42	Spring 1940 (to February 1945)	GAF weather key.
Crab	24.9.42	August 1942 (to October 1942)	A Luftflotte 1 key.
Porcupine	21.1.43	January 1943 (to March 1943)	Ground-air co-operation in south Russia.
Hedgehog	21.2.43	February 1943 (to July 1943)	Army-air co-operation key of Luftflotte 4.
Ermine	25.2.43	September 1942 (to end of war)	Fliegerkorps I (Ostfront).
Orchid	1.3.43	March 1943 (to November 1944)	Luftgau XXV (Ostfront).
Tulip	1.3.43	June 1941 (to February 1944)	Luftgau Holland.
Clover	1.3.43	March 1943 (to April 1945)	Luftgau I (Westfront).
Dragonfly	5.3.43	February 1943 (to May 1943)	Fliegerkorps Tunis.
Shamrock	9.3.43	March 1943	Almost certainly reserve for Blue till end March.
Lily	1.5.43	June 1941 (to April 1945)	Luftgau Belgien und Nordfrankreich.
Aster	12.5.43	May 1943 (to end of war)	Luftgau VII (Westfront).

Part 5

German Army Enigma Keys Attacked between End June 1942 and End May 1943

GC & CS Name for Key	Date Broken	Date first Identified in GC & CS and Duration	Remarks
Thrush	23.7.42	July 1942 (to November 1942)	Supply key Rome–Greece–Crete.
Bullfinch	20.11.42	November 1942 (to May 1943)	Special Panzerarmee 5 key Rome–Tunis
Mallard	28.11.42	August 1942 (to end of war)	A German Army Rome Administrative key
Goldfinch	2.12.42	December 1942	Related to Bullfinch: lasted one month only.
Dodo	8.2.43	November 1942	Initially Panzerarmee 5 Tunis: later resurrected when PzA 5 reformed in Europe when it lasted till April 1945. Not a very productive key in Tunisia.
Nuthatch	13.2.43	Mid-1942 (to February 1945)	Used on Berlin–Vienna–Belgrade link carrying Wehrkreis type traffic.
Sparrow	6.4.43	March 1943 (to May 1943)	Key of German Army Y organisation in Mediterranean.
Cormorant	8.5.43	April 1943 (to June 1943)	Special key used between Rome and Sardinia: broken only a few times.
Buzzard	16.5.43	April 1943 (to June 1943)	Special key used in south-east Europe.

Part 6
German Naval Enigma Keys Attacked between End June 1942 and End May 1943

Name of Key Given by GC & CS	Period of Use by German Navy	Date Broken by GC & CS	Remarks
Porpoise	April 1941 to 1 October 1943	August 1942 (broken currently from September 1942)	Called Süd by Germans. Used in Mediterranean by surface ships and shore authorities, and in Black Sea by surface ships, shore authorities and U-boats. Used by U-boats in Mediterranean 5.11.41 to 12.12.41: thereafter U-boats in Mediterranean used Shark until June 1943 when they acquired own key. 'Officer Only' (Offizier) of Porpoise, called Winkle by GC & CS, was read regularly but often broke late.
Shark	1 February 1942 to 24 May 1943	December 1942	Used by U-boats in Atlantic other than those in Far North. Called Triton by Germans. 'Officer Only' (Offizier) of Shark, called Limpet by GC & CS, read fairly regularly but often broke late.

Note: Several other Enigma keys, brought into use by the German Navy between June 1942 and May 1943, were identified and studied in this period by GC & CS but were not broken until afterwards.

Part 7
Other German Non-Naval Keys Attacked up to End May 1943

GC & CS Name for Key	Date Broken	Date Identified by GC & CS and Duration	Remarks
Orange I	10.12.40	1939 (till end of war)	General purpose SS key
Railway (known as Rocket from September 1943)	February 1941	June 1940	Reichsbahn key.
ISK	December 1941	December 1939 (to end of 1944)	Abwehr Enigma.
GGG	February 1942		Abwehr Enigma between Berlin and stations in Gibraltar area, passing via Madrid.
Orange II	February 1942	1.12.41	Used mainly between Berlin and SS divisions in the field.
Orange III	3.3.42		SS Kav. Div. (seldom used or broken).
Quince	14.8.42	August 1942 (to end of war)	Main SS general key.
Osprey	30.9.42	June 1942 (till April 1945)	Enigma key of Organisation Todt.
TGD	not broken	1939 (to end of war)	Gestapo Enigma key (named after its Berlin call-sign): its non-solution is 'to this day one of the classic mysteries of Hut 6'. The only other Enigma key used by the German police – that of the regular police – was introduced, and broken by Hut 6 as Roulette, in 1944. Otherwise the German police used hand cyphers.

APPENDIX 5

The German Police Cyphers

In the first two years of the war the non-Party uniformed police of the German Reich (Ordnungspolizei or ORPO) used a relatively simple hand cypher. This was read at GC and CS from before the beginning of the war; between February and June 1940 it was exploited jointly by British and French cryptanalysts at the French GQG on the Marne. In September 1941, by which time ORPO was active throughout occupied Europe, it adopted a more difficult hand cypher. Although in 1944 ORPO introduced an Enigma, called Roulette at GC and CS,* for its most secret communications the hand cypher remained in use and GC and CS read it with little delay from the end of 1941 till towards the end of the war.

This hand cypher was also used, though much more sparingly, by the other main arm of the German Police – the Security Police (SIPO), comprising the Criminal Investigation Branch (KRIPO) and the Secret State Police (GESTAPO) – and the related Security Service or Sicherheitsdienst (SD). For their most secret communications, however, these organisations used from an early stage in the war an Enigma key (called TGD after its Berlin call-sign)* which was never broken and was regarded by GC and CS as the key of the Gestapo.

The SS, the elite troops of the Nazi Party's private army, also made use of the Enigma machine. An SS Enigma key (called Orange I at GC and CS)* used for general administrative matters, including the organisation of concentration camps, was broken in December 1940, and read, with many ups and downs, until late in the war. Another key, Orange II,* which carried mainly administrative communications between Berlin and SS formations in operational areas, was broken from early in 1942 until it was replaced by another key – Quince* – later in the same year. This also was broken by GC and CS and read until late in the war. The SS also used other readable, but less important, Enigma keys and at least one valuable hand cypher.[†]

At GC and CS the Enigma traffic of the SS and the police was processed by the section responsible for the GAF and Army

---

* See Appendix 4.
† Intelligence about the operations of SS divisions was obtained from the Army Enigma keys used by the commands to which the divisions were subordinate.

Enigmas, which sent the decrypts to Whitehall in English translation. The police and SS hand cyphers were handled by the Military Section; this sent the decrypts in German to MI 14 but also produced a weekly summary in English of police operations behind the lines on the Russian front, of which 'C' sent a copy to the Prime Minister. The work done by the Military Section absorbed a considerable amount of time and labour, as may be judged from the fact that by the summer of 1944 some 500 people were engaged in intercepting, deciphering and processing the hand cyphers.

Among the reasons why GC and CS maintained so large an effort against the police hand cyphers, some were technical. The most important of them was the fact that decrypts of the hand cyphers often provided a means of entry into Enigma keys, but there were others. In the first place, the German Army and the GAF used for their medium-grade field communications, and also as a stand-by substitute for the Enigma, hand cyphers which were based on the same system as the main police hand cypher. Although these reserve cyphers were rarely used before 1944, this fact, which had been established by their occasional employment in emergencies on the Russian front, made it all the more important to keep abreast of the police traffic. In the second place, it was recognised from the end of 1942 that work on the police traffic was the best means of training additional staff for the exploitation of the medium-grade field communications of the German Army. Since the summer of 1940 little traffic of this kind had been intercepted from the European theatre, but Cairo had derived some benefit from its work on the medium-grade cypher of the German Army in north Africa and the Aegean, and Cairo's experience (reinforced by the failure to take advantage of it during the early stages of the campaign in French north Africa)* prompted preparations to exploit similar cyphers in the field when the Allied armies invaded the Continent.

Over and above these technical considerations, work on the police cyphers was not unimportant for the intelligence they yielded. With the outbreak of war the ORPO, always more military in character than western police forces, was formed into battalions or regiments and, equipped with artillery, tanks and aircraft, was used in close collaboration with the SS as an army of occupation in the subject territories and, in times of need, even as reinforcements for the Army. For most of the war the bulk of the wireless traffic of both organisations was accordingly concerned with German suppression of resistance and subversion, especially in Poland and the Baltic States, in the Balkans, in Russia and, after the fall of Mussolini, in Italy. From 1942, as earlier limited and

---

* See Appendix 18.

local anti-partisan operations grew into a bitter and specialised form of warfare, the increasing scale and effectiveness of the partisans evoking a correspondingly severe German response, the decrypts acquired increasing value for the light they threw on the training, the tactics and the detailed operations of the SS and the police and of the resistance forces. Although MI 14's appreciations do not refer specifically to information from the police cyphers this intelligence must have influenced its assessments of the situation in Russia.* In Russia, where SS and police formations fought along-side the Army for short periods during the winters of 1941–1942 and 1942–1943 and joined in the Army's retreat from the summer of 1944, the decrypts also supplemented the intelligence about the battle fronts that was being obtained from the armed forces Enigma.

In all the above areas the decrypts provided a good deal of information about the reprisals inflicted by the Germans in the course of their anti-partisan operations. They further disclosed the extent to which atrocities were being carried out in Russia as calculated acts of policy. On 13 September 1941, Daluege, Chief of the ORPO in Berlin, warned police commanders throughout Russia that there was a danger that matters of great secrecy, such as the exact number of executions, might be decyphered by the enemy; they should henceforth be sent by courier and not by wireless. But by then much of this nature had been transmitted by W/T and decrypted by GC and CS. Between 18 July and 30 August 1941 police decrypts on at least seven occasions gave details of mass shootings, in the central sector, of victims described variously as 'Jews', 'Jewish plunderers', 'Jewish bolshevists' or 'Russian soldiers' in numbers varying from less than a hundred to several thousand. On 7 August the SS Cavalry Brigade reported that it had carried out 7,819 'executions' to date in the Minsk area, and on the same day von dem Bach, commander of police in the central sector, reported that 30,000 executions had been carried out since the police arrived in Russia. In the southern sector between 23 and 31 August 1941 the shooting of Jews, in groups numbering from 61 to 4,200, was reported on 17 occasions. On one of these, on 12 September 1941 near Ovruch, Police Regiment South disposed of 1,255 Jews 'according to the usage of war'. Despite the ban on sending reports by W/T such incidents continued to be disclosed by the decrypts during the remainder of 1941 and throughout 1942 and 1943. The decrypts provided much detail about the associated German policy of colonising certain areas of occupied Russia, mainly the Ukraine, with settlers from Germany. They also referred to the activities of a special SS battalion which,

---

* See Chapters 17 and 28.

under Ribbentrop's guidance, was charged with plundering works of historical and artistic interest.

The decrypts showed that the police were helped in their work by various auxiliary bodies. They were joined, for example, by Flemish and Norwegian volunteer battalions. There was also a reference to the participation of Indians. Large numbers of Cossacks and Ukrainians were formed into auxiliary police battalions, known as Schützmannschaften, in 1942: they were active in all sectors and ultimately fought alongside the Germans at Warsaw. A certain amount of information was furnished by the decrypts about the relations between General Vlasov, commanding Ukrainian troops in German service, and Himmler and Hitler. Other Soviet minority races were similarly conscripted. In 1943 the Black Sea Police Command numbered 3,000 Germans and 18,000 auxiliaries of Soviet origin, including Tatars and Kalmucks. In some areas indigenous inhabitants of German origin (Volksdeutsche) were formed into auxiliary units. We have been unable to trace what circulation in Whitehall was given to these and other police decrypts by MI 14.

In contrast to the wealth of information it provided from eastern Europe, the police traffic revealed little about conditions in France, Belgium, Holland, Denmark, Norway and Greece until late in the war. This situation reflected the greater availability of land-lines and the fact that the police played a smaller part in occupation duties than they did in the east, the army taking the brunt, but it was also a consequence of the absence of widespread partisan warfare in these areas before 1944. From the middle of 1944, with the Allied invasion of western Europe, the situation changed – especially in France, where voluminous decrypts disclosed much intelligence about the activities of the Maquis and the measures taken by the Germans to counter them.*

For similar reasons, and also because GC and CS appears to have given higher priority to the traffic to and from the occupied countries until the end of 1943, the cyphers produced next to no intelligence from within the Reich before 1944. During that year the decrypts threw a great deal of light on the economic effects of Allied bombing and on Germany's worsening domestic situation, and in the final stages of the war they became one of the most important and interesting sources of operational intelligence.* Before 1944, however, the intelligence from Germany was limited to decrypts of signals from the Security Police about escaped POW – they began with the hue and cry following the escape of General Giraud from Königstein in April 1942 but did not beome regular until the middle of 1943 – and to information obtained on two other issues from short-lived hand cyphers.

---

* See Volume III.

Between 17 and 25 May 1943, following the breaching of the Möhne dam, a special but readable cypher was used in the Ruhr. It carried orders to police and other organisations in the affected areas; the decrypts showed that the emergency was quickly controlled.

From the spring of 1942 until February 1943, when it ceased to be sent by W/T, GC and CS decrypted in another cypher a daily return of prisoners at Dachau, Buchenwald, Auschwitz and seven other concentration camps – not all of them, but a good cross section.* The daily return consisted of a series of unheaded, unexplained columns of figures which GC and CS worked out to mean (a) number of inmates at the start of the previous day, (b) new arrivals, (c) departures by any means, and (d) number at the end of the previous day. It also specified the various categories of prisoner, such as politicals, Jews, Poles, other Europeans and Russians. GC and CS interpreted column (c) – 'departures by any means' – as being accounted for primarily by deaths. The returns from Auschwitz, the largest of the camps with 20,000 prisoners, mentioned illness as the main cause of death, but included references to shootings and hangings. There were no references in the decrypts to gassing. There were to be other references to concentration camps in the police traffic of later years, but they were infrequent.†

---

* Belsen did not exist at the time of the messages.
† See Volume III.

APPENDIX 6

Intelligence on the Threat of Chemical Warfare up to the beginning of 1942

At the outbreak of war it was known that Germany had the means of waging chemical warfare, and it was assumed that she was actively studying biological or 'bacterial' warfare and such other developments as flame weapons. But no reliable evidence was available about either her intentions or the technical aspect of her preparations.[1]

During the early months of the war reports on these subjects from a variety of sources were discussed by the War Cabinet or the Chiefs of Staff without, so far as can now be established, prior examination by the intelligence or the technical authorities – a fact which indicates the importance attached to the threat and also, perhaps, the continuing inability of those authorities to assess the value of the reports with any confidence. In September 1939 the COS considered a report from The Hague that Germany had developed a new toxic material, iron pentacarbonyl; they referred it to the Chemical Defence Research Department, which later advised that the material was unlikely to be effective.[2] In October the War Cabinet, on the basis of a report from the French that German Army gas masks were fitted for protection against arsenical smokes, authorised the modification of 400,000 Service gas masks.[3] In the same month its attention was drawn to repeated allusions in German broadcasts to the claim that the Polish Army had used gas supplied by the United Kingdom; as the claim was known to be false the Cabinet speculated on whether the allusions might imply that Germany was preparing to use gas on the western front in 'retaliation'.[4]

By the spring of 1940 MI 10 had accumulated sufficient technical detail about Germany's preparations to enable it to conclude that the gases she would most probably use were mustard and phosgene, and to say something about the performance of the various dissemination methods available to her – shells, cylinders,

---

1. CAB 4/27, CID 1383B of 20 January 1938, the last comprehensive pre-war report on the subject.
2. CAB 79/1, COS (39) 33rd Meeting, 30 September: CAB 80/4, COS (39) 82 of 17 October: CAB 80/5, COS (39) 116 of 9 November.
3. CAB 65/1, WM (39) 46 of 13 October.
4. ibid, WM (39) 48 of 15 October.

grenades, bombs, sprays – and about her own defensive measures. From the same date routine references in the Enigma to such things as nominations for anti-gas courses, reports of stocks of anti-gas equipment and the appointments of anti-gas officers established that she was well prepared for gas warfare. Not surprisingly, however, there continued to be no firm intelligence from any source bearing on Germany's policy regarding the first use of gas. In May 1940 the COS could only say that 'the fact that Germany has not yet used gas does not mean that she does not intend to initiate its use, but merely implies that up to the present she had not considered it expedient to do so'.[5] On 22 October 1940 the JIC took the same view.[6] A few days earlier, it had ended on an ambiguous, not to say evasive, note a comprehensive analysis of the increased number of warnings about Germany's intention to use gas that had been received from diplomatic, SIS and POW reports while Great Britain had faced the threat of invasion: 'On the evidence now available, it cannot be concluded that the use of gas is more imminent now than at any time since the beginning of the war'.[7]

Rumours that Germany planned to use gas in a renewed attempt to invade continued to arrive during the winter of 1940–1941, as did warnings that she was developing new gases, and Whitehall remained anxious about the threat. In January 1941 MI 14 reviewed the latest intelligence, such as it was; it felt that the discovery of new gases could not be ruled out and concluded that, as Germany appeared to be in a position to use gas in an invasion, 'the use of gas, therefore, is not unlikely'.[8] By that time the Prime Minister and the Chiefs of Staff had considered whether the threat might be reduced by a public statement of Great Britain's determination to retaliate if gas was used, and had concluded that there should be no statement until there was evidence that an attack was imminent.[9] On 3 March this conclusion was approved by the War Cabinet, which also reaffirmed existing policy: Great Britain would in no circumstances be the first to use gas but, since she could not rely on the enemy's undertakings not to use it, she must ensure that powerful and immediate retaliation was possible and take full defensive measures for the safety of her civilian population.[10]

During the remainder of 1941 the capture of German documents and military equipment in the Middle East and, more important,

---

5. CAB 80/10, COS (40) 319 of 4 May.
6. JIC (40) 62nd Meeting, 22 October.
7. JIC (40) 317 of 17 October: CAB 80/20, COS (40) 830 of 17 October.
8. WO 190/893, MI 14 Appreciation, of 17 January 1941, 'Possible Use of Gas by Germany'.
9. Churchill, *The Second World War*, Vol II (1949), pp 599, 633; Vol III (1950), p 942; CAB 79/8, COS (41) 1st Meeting, 1 January.
10. CAB 65/18, WM (41) 22 of 3 March.

on the Russian front[11] provided some reliable information about the weapons, the fillings and the procedures the enemy had developed for the use of gas. Summarising this in November, MI 10 concluded that it contained nothing that was very novel or very alarming. It showed that the Germans possessed gas shells and mortar bombs that were not readily recognisable; and it did not cover the use of gas from the air, a form of attack that might be heavily employed; but there was no evidence of new ground tactics and the indications were that no unexpected gases or ground weapons had been developed.[12]* The same captured material made it clear that the enemy was giving continuous and meticulous attention to his defence measures against gas. As to his intention to resort to gas, however, there continued to be no evidence beyond a trickle of rumours and these occasioned no unusual anxiety until the beginning of 1942, when they became more insistent with reference to the Russian front.

* In its next report in December 1941 MI 10 noted the first evidence that new weapons, the 'Nebelwerfer' and a projector later referred to as 'Wurfgerät', had been issued to Germany's chemical warfare troops. Thereafter, captured documents and field reports quickly established that the 'Nebelwerfer' fired rocket projectiles, and MI 10 suspected that its primary role might be the dispersion of gas as well as of smoke gas. This suspicion was abandoned at the beginning of 1943, but MI 10's study of the weapon laid the foundations for intelligence about the novel problem of rockets and their propellants which was to become so important when Germany developed the V-weapons.[13]

11. WO 208/3576, Porton File, CDR 5, p 868, Intelligence Summary No 90 of 25 January 1946, para 2(e).
12. WO 208/3577, MI 10 Summary of Technical Reports regarding Weapons, War Industry and War Transportation, No 58 of 8 November 1941.
13. ibid, Nos 61, 64, 68; WO 208/3578, No 86; WO 208/2287, Report No 98.

APPENDIX 7

German Meteorological Operations in the Arctic, 1940–1941

When the war put an end to the international exchange of synoptic meteorological reports, the Germans partly met their need for accurate weather forecasts by flying routine weather reconnaissance flights in all theatres and organising regular weather reporting by their own ships, particularly the U-boats, for which the Navy devised the short-signal (WW) weather reporting system. But because the weather in the Atlantic and the ocean-influenced areas of Europe is greatly influenced by the polar front, they had to try to augment these arrangements by special measures in the Arctic region. From September 1940 to June 1941, with consequences to which we have already referred,* the German Navy maintained weather trawlers on patrol as floating meteorological stations in the Greenland–Jan Mayen area. Thereafter, the Navy and the GAF set up automatic weather reporting installations at widely distributed points north of the Arctic Circle, a few of which worked successfully for long periods.[1] Although the Enigma disclosed the whereabouts of some of these automatic stations, it has not been possible to find out whether the Allies were able to intercept and exploit their transmissions. In addition, the Navy and the GAF sent several expeditions to operate weather stations at fixed points in Greenland, Jan Mayen, Spitzbergen and other Arctic territories.

The earliest expeditions were despatched in 1940. Because they were manned by Norwegian and Danish civilians they have been represented as being attempts by the Norwegian and Danish authorities to maintain their pre-war stations.[2] In fact they were organised by the Abwehr, and it was thanks largely to the fact that GC and CS had broken the Abwehr hand cypher by March 1940† that they were all frustrated.[3] A party of armed Danes was captured by the Free Norwegian gunboat *Fridhof Nansen* after being landed in east Greenland at the end of April 1940.[4] In September

---

* See Vol I, pp 337, 339.   † See Vol I, p 120 (n).

1. *The Polar Record* (Scott Polar Research Institute, Cambridge), Vol 6, No 42, July 1951, pp 202, 224–225.
2. ibid, p 225.
3. ibid, p 225; Morgan, *NID History 1939–1942*, pp 137–138.
4. *Polar Record*, Vol 6, No 42, p 225.

the *Fridhof Nansen* intercepted a sealer carrying a second party and forced a third ship to return to Norway. In October she stopped another attempt to put an armed party ashore in Greenland.[5] In November, sent to intercept a trawler which was taking a GAF meteorological party to Jan Mayen, she was herself wrecked, but the trawler was caught by the cruiser *Naiad* as she was putting her party ashore.[6] Its time of arrival had been disclosed by the Abwehr decrypts, as had the fact that Göring attached great importance to the success of the expedition.[7]

Despite these failures in 1940 – and despite the fact that a report of the *Naiad*'s coup found its way into the *Evening Standard* of 19 November – the Germans did not suspect that the Abwehr's cypher had been compromised. In August 1941 Abwehr decrypts again provided the advance intelligence which enabled the US Coastguard Service ship *Northland* to frustrate the next enemy expedition by intercepting the Norwegian ship *Buskö* on its arrival in Greenland from Alesund.[8]

The *Busko*'s party was the last to be organised by the Abwehr. It was also the last to be frustrated with the help of Sigint. In August 1942, after an interval in which the Germans confined their activities to Spitzbergen, they resumed their attempts to land meteorological parties in Greenland, but did so under naval command. Until the middle of 1944 these attempts were successful. Thereafter they were intercepted on their arrival in Greenland, but were so largely because of the improvement in US patrols. Before and after the middle of 1944 the Enigma provided a useful commentary on the activity of the enemy's meteorological parties and left no doubt about the importance the Germans attached to them, but it did not assist the Allies in their operations against the expeditions.*

---

* See Vol III.

5. ibid, p 225; Morgan, op cit, p 138.
6. *Polar Record*, Vol 6, No 42, p 226.
7. Morgan, op cit, p 138.
8. *Polar Record*, Vol 6, No 42, p 225.

APPENDIX 8

Allied Shipping Losses
1941 to May 1943

(i) *Losses of Allied Shipping and of U-boats 1 January 1942–31 May 1943**
(All Theatres)

Month	Allied ships sunk in convoy		Allied independently sailed ships sunk		Axis U-boats sunk by sea and air convoy escorts and support	Axis U-boats sunk by all other means	Remarks
	By U-boats only	By all enemies	By U-boats only	By all enemies			
1942							
Jan.	3	9	48	60	4	5	⎫ The
Feb.	9	16	67	78	2	0	⎮ U-boat
March	0	8	88	98	5	4	⎮ Campaign
April	4	11	69	104	1	3	⎬ on the
May	13	24	111	119	1	5	⎮ east
June	20	29	121	135	1	5	⎮ coast of
July	24	11	70	81	8	7	⎭ America
Aug.	50	60	51	56	9	8	
Sept.	29	39	58	62	6	7	
Oct.	29	33	54	56	9	8	
Nov.	39	46	70	75	9	8	
Dec.	19	25	33	38	6	7	
							⎫ The second
1943							⎮ U-boat
Jan.	15	18	14	19	5	6	⎮ campaign
Feb.	34	38	16	18	17	6	⎬ on the
March	72	77	23	25	6	10	⎮ Atlantic
April	25	29	22	24	9	8	⎮ convoy
May	26	31	19	19	28	19	⎭ routes
TOTALS	411	537	934	1067	126	116	

NOTE: During the same period 108 allied ships which were stragglers from convoy were sunk by U-boats and 114 by all enemies.

* Reproduced from Roskill, *The War at Sea*, Vol II, (1957) p 378.

(ii) *Losses from North Atlantic convoys January–31 May 1943**

Prefix letters	Description	No at sea	No contacted by U-boats	No contacted which had no losses
HX	Halifax/NY – UK	22	13	1
SC	Sydney (CB)/Halifax/ NY – UK (slow)	19	8	3
ON	UK – N America	20	6	2
ONS	UK – N America (slow)	21	10	3
UC	UK – NY (tanker convoys)	2	1	—
CU	Curaçao – UK (tanker convoys)	2	—	—
	TOTALS –	86	38	9

* Supplied by Naval Historical Branch.

(iii) *Losses from North Atlantic convoys March 1943***

British, Allied and neutral merchant ships

In convoy	Stragglers
7 (SC 121)	1 (HX 227)
4 (HX 228)	5 (SC 121)
13 (HX 229)	1 (SC 122)
8 (SC 122)	1 (ON 168)
Total 32	1 (ONS 169)
	1 (HX 230)
	Total 10
Escorts: 1 (HX 228)	
TOTAL (incl escort): 43	

** Supplied by Naval Historical Branch.

APPENDIX 9

Devices Adopted for Disguising U-boat Positions in Enigma Signals

On 16 June 1941 the U-boat Command took the first of several steps which showed that it was becoming disturbed that the U-boats were experiencing increased difficulty in intercepting convoys despite their increasing numbers.

The German measures consisted of tightening up the devices for coding positions which the Navy already used as a matter of course within its messages before they were encyphered. Previously the method of expressing positions at sea had been in terms of an irregularly constructed grid. The British had captured parts of the German naval grid – the part covering the North Sea and the Baltic and small portions of the north Atlantic area – in December 1939 and April 1940. In May 1941 they had acquired from U-110 that part of it which covered the whole of the north Atlantic and most of the Mediterranean; and by then, on the basis of the earlier captures and the Enigma traffic which had become available from the middle of March, the OIC and GC and CS had already gone a long way towards reconstructing the north Atlantic section of the grid. When the Enigma began to be read with up to a week's delay, during May, there was thus no difficulty in decoding many of the positions contained in the U-boat traffic. But on 16 June, when the Enigma was being read currently, the U-boat Command introduced a more complicated system of disguising its dispositions by relating positions at sea to fixed points of reference – Franz, Oscar, Herbert, etc – arbitrarily chosen and changed at short intervals. When decyphered a typical Enigma order to a U-boat now read: 'If boat is in fit condition for night attacks occupy as attacking area the northern halves of the 162-mile-squares [of the naval grid] whose central points lie 306 degrees 220 miles and 290 degrees 380 miles respectively from Point Franz. If boat is not in fit condition, report by short-signal "No".' Delay in solving this system somewhat reduced during June the operational value of what was derived from reading the Enigma currently. By July, however, the problem had largely been overcome.

It was not the last to be encountered. In August, partly as another internal security measure and partly as a means of boosting the morale of the U-boats, the U-boat Command began to address the U-boats by the names of their commanders instead of by the numbers of the U-boats. Since U-boat commanders shifted from time to time from one U-boat to another this made it harder for intelligence to keep an accurate check on the U-boat order of battle, but it did nothing to reduce the operational value of the Enigma intelligence. On 11 September, however, finding that the fixed reference-point system was too cumbersome, and the source of miscalculations by the U-boats, the Germans replaced it by one in which the digraphs of the naval grid squares were separately encyphered before the texts of their messages were encyphered on the Enigma machine. The OIC and GC and CS jointly solved this system, at least to the extent of eliminating most of the uncertainty, but there was some delay before they could do so.

On 24 November 1941 the U-boat Command testified to its continuing disquiet by introducing a still more troublesome way of disguising the positions. The new system was one by which the Christian name, surname and address of an imaginary person indicated the table that was in use at any one time for encoding the large square digraphs of the grid. By informing the U-boats that a new address was in force, the U-boat Command could bring a new table of digraph equivalents into use at once at frequent intervals; and since it did frequently change the addresses, the problem of decoding the positions given in Enigma signals was to resist systematisation and to require continuous ad hoc research until a copy of the address book was captured from U-505 in June 1944. Although the OIC and GC and CS had by then obtained a complete grasp of the Atlantic situation and of U-boat methods, it was not uncommon for them to fail to decode a position in the weeks between the end of November and the beginning of February 1942, when the Germans introduced the fourth wheel into the Enigma for Atlantic U-boat communications.

APPENDIX 10

Technical Intelligence on U-boats
1941 to March 1943

U-boat Types

By September 1941 the NID was able, mainly from POW interrogations, to construct a list of most of the various types of U-boat, using the correct German nomenclatures (I, IIA, IIB, VII, VIIB, VIIC, IXA, IXB and IXC), and to give for some 150 individual U-boats their type, tonnage, number of torpedo tubes and the yards where they had been built.[1] It knew by March 1941 that the Germans were developing supply U-boats, but did not know the type number and remained uncertain as to when the *Milchkühe* or supply U-boats (Type XIV) would become operational.

POW had disclosed in April 1941 the existence of UA, a 1,200-ton boat originally built for the Turkish Navy, and reported that she was capable of staying at sea for three or four months.[2] She went to the Atlantic as a supply boat with the first of the Type XIV boats in March 1942.[3] In June the OIC had no evidence that U-boats had been supplied at sea, and as late as August it thought it unlikely that any had yet been supplied.[4] In that month, however, survivors from U-379 reported that they had been refuelled and later in August POW from U-464, a Type XIV boat, gave her tonnage, 1,700 tons, and other details of the type.[5]

In June 1942 the naval Enigma revealed that three of another new type of four U-boats had carried out exercises under the Mining Experimental Command.[6] This was type XB of 1,700 tons, though these details were not yet established. In September 1942 PRU revealed the presence in St Nazaire of a new U-boat which the OIC suggested was a minelayer.[7]

---

1. ADM 186/806, Report No 27, September 1941.
2. ibid, Report No 20, April 1941, and No 23, July 1941.
3. Roskill, *The War at Sea*, Vol II (1957), p 102.
4. ADM 223/94, OIC SI No 216 of 1 June 1942; ADM 223/95, OIC SI No 321 of 24 August 1942.
5. ADM 186/807, Report No 47, September 1942 and No 50, November 1942.
6. ADM 223/94, OIC SI No 242 of 22 June 1942.
7. ADM 223/95, No 348 of 7 September 1942.

General Technical Characteristics

Although these were well understood for most types by 1941, uncertainty continued about underwater speeds and the depths to which U-boats dived. It was known that most types were designed to travel at between 7 and 8 knots submerged and it was expected that this would be increased in later boats, but no definite evidence of any increase was obtained during 1942. As for diving depths, POW reported in April 1941 that type VIIC, the one most commonly used in convoy attack, could dive to 30 m in less than a minute and that it did not normally dive deeper than 100 m; and in June 1941 they added that another type, IID, had a diving depth of 150 m and had once dived involuntarily to 210 m.[8] A depth of 200 m became a feature of later U-boats, but this did not emerge during 1942.

Mines

At the end of 1940 there had been reason to believe that U-boats were no longer laying mines. But all were equipped to do so and during 1942 there was Enigma evidence that type VIIC were carrying and laying mines.[9]

In February 1942 POW interrogation led the British authorities to suspect that the Germans had introduced a new non-contact mine.[10]

Torpedoes

In May 1941 POW provided the speeds and ranges of the two types of torpedo which, as had long been known, the U-boats carried. The electrically driven torpedo had a speed of 30 knots and a range of 5,000 m; the air-driven a speed of 30 to 44 knots and a range up to 6,000 m.[11]

In the same month a document taken from U-110 revealed that the Germans thought the British might be using an acoustically steered torpedo, and this reference caused the NID to keep a special watch for evidence that the Germans might introduce such a weapon. In June and December naval Enigma messages referred to FAT trials and FAT torpedoes, and in October a POW reported that the Germans were carrying out trials with an acoustic torpedo after suspecting that the British had introduced them. On 18 December 1942, after the evidence from these sources was put

---

8.   ADM 186/806, Report No 18, April 1941 and No 25, August 1941.
9.   ADM 223/95, OIC SI 330 of 30 August 1942.
10.   ADM 186/807, Report No 38, February 1942.
11.   ADM 186/806, Report No 21, May 1941.

together, the conclusion was reached that the Germans had probably got an acoustically steered torpedo to the operational stage. In March 1943 the Admiralty promulgated information to this effect. It was later to become clear that the FAT was in fact the zigzagging torpedo (*Federapparattorpedo*), but the misinterpretation had the advantage that counter-measures against the acoustically steered torpedo were prepared well in advance of its appearance.

Such-Gerät

It had long been known that the U-boats had this equipment, and that the Germans thought it inferior to the British Asdic. In October 1941 POW reported that experiments had been in progress as late as August 1941 to improve its maximum range to 500 m, and to give it a practical range of 300 m.[12]

Radar

No further information was obtained about radar in U-boats until 8 December 1942, when a naval Enigma signal referred to 80 cm horizontally polarised radar in connection with three U-boats which appeared to have been recently refitted.

In September 1942, however, it became known that the U-boats were using a radar search receiver to give them warning against the British $1\frac{1}{2}$ m Mark II ASV.[13] The Germans had introduced this receiver in August 1942 and it was fitted to all U-boats by the end of the year. By December 1942 a description of the equipment had been obtained from POW from U-352, which had been sunk in October.[14]

---

12. ibid, Report No 31, October 1941.
13. AIR 41/47, *The RAF in Maritime War*, Vol III, p 491.
14. ADM 186/809, Report No 103, December 1942.

APPENDIX 11

Admiralty Ultra Signals to the Home Fleet 30 June to 8 July 1942

(The times of origin of all Admiralty Signals
were in 'B' time = Double Summer Time)

30 June

0510: Information for 29th June now available, anticipate 30th June by about midday.

1050: Information for 30th will not now be available until about mid-day 1st July. 27th and 28th expected this afternoon.

1 July

1440: 30th up to noon 1st July now available.

2 July

2207: Information from 1200/1 to 1200/3 not yet available. Expected time uncertain, but probably by 0800/3.

3 July

0515: Information now available.

0810: 1. Shadowing aircraft were still in contact with PQ at 0200/3rd. Germans stated weather conditions made it doubtful whether it would be possible to continue shadowing.

2. At 2104/2nd British Battlefleet had not been located since 2100/1st. Unverified report had been received of a Skua 60 miles west of Trondheim at 1630/2nd, which led Germans to suggest that a carrier was possible off Trondheim.

3. At 0300/2nd, AOC Lofoten reported that close air escort for operation CONCERT would probably not be possible on account of weather.

4. GAF intentions for 3 July were –
    (a) renewed reconnaissance for convoy; and
    (b) operation KNIGHT'S MOVE.

Latter operation is special operation referred to in AM 1657B/28/6.

5. U-boats were in contact with PQ during 2 July.

Comment: Operations CONCERT and KNIGHT'S MOVE are probably concerned with enemy main units.

0950: At 0440/3rd July Admiral Commanding Cruisers reported 'LÜTZOW detached, remainder of formation at 0500 at Green 30.'

Comment: Position of Green 30 not known but probably in vicinity of Arstad or Andfjord.

1017: 1. Following signals were made in Offizier –
    At 2303/2   From Gruppe Nord to C-in-C Fleet Admiral Commanding Battleships.
    At 0326/3   From Admiral Commanding Cruisers to Admiral Commanding Northern Waters, C-in-C Fleet and Gruppe Nord.

Comment: This indicates TIRPITZ was at sea at 2303/2 possibly operation CONCERT.

2. At 1639B/2 U-boat group was told not repetition not to operate against westbound convoy.

1408: German aircraft maintained contact with a naval formation from 0210–0430/3rd, when position was 69 degs 27' North 0 degs 45' East course 085 degs.

1422: At 0748/3rd Germans estimated position of convoy at 0000/3rd as 74 degs 03' North 6 degs 10' East course 090 degs 8 knots.

U-boats told to search along this latitude. If no contact with enemy 'Bear Island patrol line' is intended.

1754: 1. At 0715/3rd GAF reported 2 cruisers in position 69 degs 12' North 16 degs 05' East, see AM 0950B/3.

2. At 1027/3rd LÜTZOW addressed a signal to Admiral Commanding Cruisers, so apparently was not in company with SCHEER.

3. At 0315/3rd Admiral Commanding Cruisers was informed certain memoranda would be dropped by aircraft 'at berth'.

4. At 1046/3rd Minesweeper on patrol in position about 67 degs 26' North, 14 degs 00' East reported 'formation has not yet passed'.

5. At 1115/3rd a large warship course east was reported by German Coast Station at Tennholmon believed near Bodo.

6. At 2258/2nd Air Officer Lofoten again reported close air escort for operation CONCERT would probably not be possible on account of weather. See AM 0810B/3rd para 3.

Comment: It appears certain SCHEER has moved northwards from Narvik, probably accompanied by destroyers. Movement of LÜTZOW is uncertain but she was independent of SCHEER. TIRPITZ and HIPPER may have left Trondheim area since 0001/3rd.

1819: All important information has now been studied. Information from 1200/3rd is not expected before 2359/4th.

4 July

0250: A sequence of signals since 1407B/3rd on the Kootwyk service transmitted once an hour appears to be cyphered on special settings from evidence of indicators. This may indicate the commencement of a special operation by main units, and contents of messages made to them may not become available.

1145: Coast station Hekkingen latitude 69 degs 36′ North, longitude 17 degs 51′ East reported at 0900/3rd repeat 0900/3rd 'one battleship, 5 destroyers, one supply ship passed from south-west to north-west'.

Comment: This was probably ADMIRAL SCHEER with tanker DITHMARSCHEN.

1918: C-in-C Fleet in TIRPITZ arrived Altenfjord 0900/4th July.

Destroyers and torpedo boats ordered to complete with fuel at once.

ADMIRAL SCHEER was already present at Altenfjord.

At 1622/3rd two U-boats were informed their main task was to shadow convoy.

1934: Noon 3rd to noon 5th now available.

2108: At 1327/4th you [ie CS I] were being shadowed by U-boat.

2110: 1. At 1130/4th U-boats were informed that no German surface forces were in their operational area then. Position of heavy enemy ships was not known but they were to be main target for U-boats when encountered. U-boats shadowing convoy were to keep in contact.

2. At 1458/4th U-boat B was ordered to continue shadowing convoy, and U-boat F to continue shadowing heavy forces which he had sighted at 1327/4th in 75 degs 51′ North, 23 degs 30′ East.

Comment: Heavy forces are presumably CS I.

5 July

0238: 1. It is not repeat not known if German heavy forces have sailed from Altenfjord, but they are unlikely to have done so before 1200B/4th.

2. It appears that Germans may be in some confusion whether a battleship is in company with CS 1.

3. Germans do not repeat not appear to be aware of position of C-in-C Home Fleet.

1517: At 1145/5th TIRPITZ stated that she would be ready in Rolvsöysund at 1430.

6 July

1015: 1200/5th to 1200/6th now available. 1200/6th to 1200/7th will not be available until pm/7th.

1317: 1. At 1340/5th U-boats were informed that attack on convoy was to take place on morning of 6 July.

2. At 2219/5th Gruppe Nord directed that operation KNIGHT'S MOVE was to be broken off.

3. At 0052/6th C-in-C Fleet was given details of sweeping operation and A/S patrols into Altenfjord.

4. At 0543/6th U-boats informed that operation in para 1 was cancelled. U-boats to search for convoy which was widely scattered as far as 70 degs North.

5. DITHMARSCHEN believed to be at Altenfjord, ordered to be at 1 hour's notice from 1200/6th.

Comment: This is assumed to mean that attack on the convoy by surface forces is abandoned and that TIRPITZ and ships in company are returning to Altenfjord.

LÜTZOW not located and it is not certain whether HIPPER or SCHEER was at sea with TIRPITZ.

8 July

0025: Now studying noon 6th to noon 8th.

APPENDIX 12

The Oil Target

At first sight intelligence would seem to have played a direct and decisive role in the discussions which led on 13 January 1941 to a directive to Bomber Command giving primacy to the oil targets. The Lloyd Committee's Fifth Report,[1] issued in December 1940, was undoubtedly so influential that it carried the day with the Chiefs of Staff Committee. Whether this influence sprang from intelligence or from the non-intelligence elements in the report is, however, a more open question.

The report was composed of four elements: a note by the Chairman, the main intelligence report, a summary of conclusions and three appendices. The main report said (in characteristic language): 'The present statistical position within the Axis is not by any means satisfactory enough to relieve them from serious concern for the future. Particularly, there must be an ever-present fear that, even on the existing relatively inactive scale of land operations, a more concentrated air attack on their synthetic plants, and a failure for any reason of their channels of supply from Roumania and Russia, might cause a critical deterioration in their position'. This was not a particularly strong conclusion but it pointed to the existence of a time factor. The Hankey Committee in fact drew the legitimate conclusion: 'The time factor is of the greatest importance. The Germans are now engaged in completing new synthetic plants and in reorganising transport of oil from Roumania with a view to greatly increasing their supplies. It is only by early action that we can obtain full value for our effort' (the last sentence a somewhat 'political' way of saying that action in the first six months was likely to produce a greater effect than action in the second six months). The main report also contained a sentence which was taken up and given great emphasis in the Chairman's introductory note. 'Apart from any stocks which still remain, Germany will be almost completely dependent for high grade octane spirit [ie aviation fuel] upon the output of her hydrogenation plants.' Upon this the Hankey Committee based the first of its own recommendations – that 'air attacks should be concentrated mainly on sources of synthetic production of oil in Germany'.

It was in relation to the synthetic oil plants that the report as a whole essayed the first approach to be made in any of the Lloyd

---

1. CAB 66/14, WP (41) 2 of 2 January (POG (L) (40) 18 of 16 December).

Committee series to the question of the effects of air bombardment. The main report stated that 'some allowance can be made for the effect of air bombardment in reducing supplies' and that 'the examination of the results of the air bombardment of the German synthetic plants on the basis of the period up to 4 October, during which time the plants were subjected to only 6.7 per cent (539 tons) of the total weight of aerial attack on all targets, indicates that the output of the plants attacked was reduced by 15 per cent'. The reader was then referred to Appendix III for details.

Appendix III was not in fact very informative except that it showed that British experience of German air raids had been used, and it was not until the issue of Appendix II to the next Lloyd Report[2] in May 1941 that the method used by the Oil Adviser to Bomber Command in reaching the figure of 15 per cent was fully explained. The assessment had in fact been built up by –

(a) analysing the hydrogenation process into groups of sub-processes;
(b) determining the importance of each sub-process to the operation of the whole plant;
(c) estimating the number of bombs required to cause complete stoppage of each sub-process;
(d) estimating the rate of repair to each sub-process after such damage;
(e) calculating the expectation of damage that would be caused on the average by bombing attacks of various weights;
(f) calculating the rate of recovery after attack.

(a), (b) and (d) had been discussed with experts of ICI's Billingham Hydro Plant, (c) was checked by an expert of the Home Office Explosives Department, (e) and (f) were calculated by Air Warfare Analysis, Harrow. After calculating the number of hits to be expected from dropping a given number of bombs with an assumed aiming error, the final outcome was a probable loss of production of 15 per cent.

Most of the factors listed above can only have been assessed by reference to known damage to British installations from enemy bombing, but they may not have been greatly in error. However, the final outcome also assumed that British air crew reports could be trusted when they claimed that the target had been attacked, and this was not always the case. Moreover, it assumed that the bomb-aiming error was 300 yards in good conditions at night – a figure that had been taken from pre-war trials of daylight bombing. Later it was realised that this error was far too small.*

---

* See above, p 260.

2. CAB 66/16, WP (41) 85 of 23 May (POG (41) 3).

Acknowledged by its author as an experimental and theoretical approach to the problem, and depending on data which owed virtually nothing to intelligence, the method thus yielded the highly optimistic estimate of bomb damage which perhaps more than anything else gave the report its influence. Yet this crucial appendix was prepared not by the Lloyd Committee itself but in Bomber Command, by the Oil Adviser who had been recruited to assess the damage caused.

The intelligence part of the Lloyd Committee report accepted these calculations for the purpose of making its own estimate of synthetic production in Germany up to the end of September 1941: 'On the assumption that further attacks are successful in sustaining a 15 per cent reduction . . . the total output will have been reduced from 3 to $2\frac{1}{2}$ million tons'. However, the calculation of the 15 per cent was given no place in the Lloyd Committee's summary of conclusions. Nor was it referred to either in the note by the Chairman (Mr Geoffrey Lloyd) or in the covering report of Lord Hankey's Committee.

On the other hand all parts of the Lloyd Committee's Fifth Report taken as a whole (ie the main intelligence report, Appendix III, and the note by the Chairman) urged the case for attacks upon the synthetic plants 'to produce the maximum effect on the Axis oil position'. In his personal note the Chairman added: 'I know the difficulties, but it is worth repeating that the only way to get a quick death clinch on the whole enemy oil position is both to destroy the synthetic plants and to interrupt Roumanian supplies'. 'My own view is that the Axis oil position is sufficiently important and sufficiently weak to justify a heavy effort against the strategic points.'* This view, which went well beyond the intelligence evidence, was endorsed by the Hankey Committee.

The fate of the short-lived oil offensive has already been referred to elsewhere.† Subsequent investigations by the Lloyd Committee and forceful recommendations by the Hankey Committee in relation to the German oil situation were powerless to re-instate it once it had been called off. Indeed the drift of the intelligence which followed the Lloyd Committee's December 1940 report tended if anything to add weight to the case against an immediate revival of the plan.

In the first place the Sixth Report of the Lloyd Committee issued in May 1941[3] threw some doubt upon the opinion expressed in its previous report that 'Germany would be almost completely dependent for high octane spirit upon the production of her hydrogenation plants'. Analysis by the Petroleum Board and by the Technical

* See Volume I, pp 243–244.
† See above, pp 258–259.
3.   ibid.

Panel of the Lloyd Committee had shown that the synthetic element in the samples of aviation spirit examined was less than expected. 'Thus', commented the Committee, 'the evidence from analysis, so far as it goes, does not fully bear out the deductions drawn in the last report'.

Secondly the calculation made in the Sixth report of the damage to be expected from air attack yielded much less encouraging results than that in the Fifth. Enlightened by the PR evidence on the effect of bombing at Gelsenkirchen and Scholven, the Oil Adviser to Bomber Command wrote in Appendix II to the Sixth Report: 'It is now realised that the synthetic oil plants are very difficult targets to see, except in exceptionally clear weather, and many of the sorties of last year were made in poor weather and without the help of the moon'. 'Perhaps, to make a conservative estimate, all the bombing reports hitherto should be gone through, discarding all sorties made without a moon and all sorties where results were not observed.'

Thirdly, the revised estimates of the German supplies forecast a smaller draft on stocks (1,240,000 as against 2,400,000 tons) and a higher 'margin'* after allowing for stocks immobilised in transit etc (1,560,000 tons as against 900,000 tons) than those of the Fifth Report, thus showing the German oil situation in a more favourable light. Moreover, the new estimates (made just before the German invasion of Russia) foreshadowed a general improvement in the German supply position after the spring of 1942.

Thus the intelligence case for the oil plan had weakened by May 1941. But it was operational difficulties rather than revision of intelligence that led the Joint Planning Staff in June to throw its weight against oil as the primary objective of strategic bombing.[4] Recalling that oil had hitherto been accepted as the ideal economic target, the JPS acknowledged that so long as the attack was restricted to night bombing the chances of real damage were small. Given the state of Bomber Command's resources and of the enemy's defences, and given also the requirement for extreme accuracy, effective attacks upon this target in the next twelve months would be rare. The JPS did not therefore recommend oil as the primary objective in the air offensive against the German economy.

The Hankey Committee continued throughout 1941 to press for an attack on German oil supplies, reinforcing its arguments by reference to the possibility of an 'oil war on two fronts' in its report of July 1941,[5] but to no avail. In its swan song in December 1941[6] it

---

* Tonnage available for immediate use, see Volume I, p 241.
4. CAB 84/31, JP (41) 444 of 14 June.
5. CAB 77/12, POG (41) 9 of 11 July.
6. ibid, POG (41) 23 of 15 December.

lamented that although the Defence Committee had invited the Air Ministry in June to arrange a heavy attack as soon as weather conditions permitted, the attack had not been made. At this stage of the German invasion of Russia the Lloyd Committee in the report covered by this, the last, Hankey Report[7] could not say that the oil shortage which it detected was having any military effect; it could find no sure indication that Germany regarded her reserves as inadequate for strategic needs.

As was almost invariably the case, the intelligence estimate of the German oil position charted comparatively slow movement upwards or downwards. Not until the last phase of the war was it possible to identify a situation so catastrophic that it could be exploited with decisive military effect. And by then the Allies were capable of delivering the blow.

---

7.   CAB 77/18, POG (L) (41) 11 of 1 December.

APPENDIX 13

Intelligence Before and During the Dieppe Raid

The purpose of the raid was to test the enemy's coast defences and discover what resistance would be met in seizing a port; it was also hoped to inflict wastage on the GAF, thereby giving some relief to Russia.[1] The outline plan, which was completed by 25 April 1942, provided for a frontal attack on the town of Dieppe, combined with two flank attacks, with the object of destroying the coast defences, the installations at the near-by airfield and such other targets as the radar stations, power stations, dock facilities and the invasion barges known to be in the harbour. It further provided that the assault would be preceded by heavy air bombardment and accompanied by airborne attacks. As planning proceeded the preliminary air bombardment was abandoned for operational and political reasons and, from weather considerations and on operational grounds, the accompanying airborne attacks were replaced by Commando landings.

The Chiefs of Staff approved the outline plan on 13 May, and on 1 June they confirmed that the operation (*Rutter*) should take place at the end of that month. But *Rutter* was subjected to postponements caused by the weather and unpromising training exercises, and on 7 July it was cancelled. The main reasons for the cancellation were continuing bad weather and a GAF attack on two assault ships which, loaded with troops, lay ready to sail for Dieppe at Yarmouth Roads.

When the Combined Report on the operation was written in October 1942 it was impossible to be certain whether the GAF attack had implied that the Germans had got wind of the plan from the frequent air reconnaissance sorties that they had carried out.[2] On the evidence of documents captured after October 1942 it appears that they had not done so. The documents showed that although they had for some months been expecting landings on the French coast at any time, and especially when tide and weather conditions would be most favourable, they had no particular grounds for expecting a major landing in the immediate future.[3] It

---

1. Gwyer and Butler, *Grand Strategy*, Vol III, Part II (1964), p 639.
2. CAB 98/22, The Dieppe Raid (Combined Report), p 8, para 36.
3. C P Stacey, *Six Years of War* (1957), pp 355–357 (Official History of the Canadian Army in the Second World War, Vol I); Gwyer and Butler, op cit, Vol III, Part II, p 639.

695

is true that the enemy's general anxiety about the western front was sufficient to persuade Hitler at the end of June to order the transfer to France of two SS divisions, and intelligence about these transfers reached Whitehall after *Rutter* had been cancelled.* It has been suggested that the cancellation was influenced by a report which indicated that 10th Panzer Division was in Amiens.[4] But Whitehall received that report, too, after *Rutter* had been cancelled.† Indeed, it was after the receipt of these intelligence reports that the decision was taken to revive operation *Rutter* in a revised form as operation *Jubilee*.

The Chiefs of Staff gave their approval to *Jubilee* on 12 August, only a week before it was carried out.[5] By that time, although the Allies had agreed to launch operation *Torch* and had abandoned plans for a cross-Channel invasion in 1942, the need to gain experience of conditions from a landing operation had not decreased, and in Russia the German summer offensive was making rapid progress. But there is no evidence that the case for reviving the operation was directly supported by arguments based on the strategic situation.‡ It has been suggested that the pressure for the revival came from Combined Operations HQ whose amour propre had suffered from the cancellation.[6] This is consistent with the fact that at the end of June, when the Chiefs of Staff were inclined to cancel *Rutter* from anxiety that its postponement would lead to security leaks, the Chief of Combined Operations had taken the view that cancellation was not necessary.[7]

Responsibility for the planning of the operation had from the outset been confined to Combined Operations HQ, to Home Forces Command, which delegated its authority to GOC-in-C South Eastern Command (General Montgomery) and to the three Task Force Commanders, and the intelligence staff of Combined Operations had taken exclusive charge of the collection, preparation and distribution of intelligence for the planners and the commanders. The JIC knew of the existence of the *Rutter* plan to the extent that it approved in June a proposal that an assault commando should be attached to the operation for the purpose of capturing enemy documents and cypher material.[8] On 20 July it

---

* See below, pp 700–701.
† See below, p 701.
‡ For the strategic debates which accompanied the decision to mount the raid see above, p 100 et seq.

4. Stacey, op cit, p 339.
5. CAB 79/22, COS (42) 234th Meeting, 12 August.
6. Stacey, op cit, p 340.
7. CAB 121/364, SIC file D/France/1, *Rutter* Folder, COS (42) 54th (o) Meeting of 21 June, 55th (o) and 58th (o) Meetings of 22 and 24 June.
8. ibid, JIC (42) 223 (o) of 13 June.

completed a large-scale review of the state of coastal defences in France and Belgium, concluding that the enemy was not yet expecting the Allies to attempt a major landing.[9] But it was not otherwise consulted; the first reference to *Jubilee* in its records occurred after the event, when the JIC was 'wondering whether', since such raids might affect German policy and dispositions, it ought not to be consulted before they were carried out.[10] The three Service intelligence branches each had a system for supplying intelligence to Combined Operations, but it decided not to ask for their assistance.[11] The exclusion of other staffs is presumably explained by the concern for secrecy; this certainly became a first consideration once *Rutter* had been cancelled. Knowledge that the operation had been revived as *Jubilee* was confined to the Prime Minister, the Chiefs of Staff and the staffs immediately involved, and in giving approval to the final plan on 12 August the Chiefs of Staff referred to it only as 'the future raiding operation'.[12] Nor was the Inter-Service Security Board informed of the operation beforehand; after it the Chiefs of Staff endorsed a JIC recommendation that the more secret the operation the more essential it was that the ISSB, as the organisation responsible for the preservation of secrecy, should be told and its charter was revised to require the Chiefs of Staff, the Joint Planning Staff and the CCO to inform it of impending operations.[13] The Sigint authorities, however, were given enough information about *Jubilee* to enable them to prepare special measures for the exploitation of low-grade Sigint during the operation.*

Combined Operations HQ applied directly to ISTD for topographical intelligence and to CIU for PR interpretation and the building and photographing of models, and it presumably relied on them to take account of what the SIS could add to their other sources of information. It made its own enquiries to the SIS about reports of enemy troop movements and no doubt also in connection with the special investigation it made into what was known about the extent to which the civilian population had been evacuated from the coastal area.[14] But from the Combined Report on the raid it is clear that it relied mainly on PR for such topographical

---

* See below, p 703.

9. JIC (42) 278 (o) of 20 July; CAB 79/22, COS (42) 213rd Meeting, 21 July.
10. JIC (42) 40th Meeting CA of 25 August.
11. eg JIC (42) 33rd Meeting, 17 July; CAB 106/3, History of the Combined Operations Organisation 1940–1945, p 41.
12. CAB 79/22, COS (42) 234th Meeting, 12 August.
13. CAB 121/364, (*Rutter* Folder), JIC (42) 468 (o) of 5 December; COS (42) 355th Meeting, 23 December. See also JIC (42) 44th Meeting of 8 September; 59th Meeting of 8 December.
14. CAB 98/22, p 3, para 19(i) and footnote.

intelligence about the area as went beyond general geographical information, and from subsequent criticisms of the intelligence preparations it is clear that it did not make adequate allowance for the limitations of PR as a source of information about terrain and defences. The Combined Report has this to say:

'Intelligence was provided by, and issued to the Planners by Combined Operations Headquarters Intelligence Section during all stages of the planning of operations "Rutter" and "Jubilee". By the 8th June, there had been prepared and issued to the Planners, in printed form (Confidential Book 04157 F), a full description of Dieppe, its port, military objectives, defences, RDF Stations, the enemy order of battle, scales of resistance, rate of reinforcement, and the German Air Force scale of attack. The Confidential Book also contained a full topographical and beach report, illustrated by photographs, as well as information on the approaches to, the tides and tidal streams off Dieppe. With the Confidential Book there was issued a series of General Staff Geographical Section standard and over-printed maps, town plans, defence traces, photographs and mosaics of the operational area. During the planning further intelligence was issued in the light of additional information procured from ground reports and air photographs. Amendments and additions were made to the defences and from time to time new defence traces were issued, together with the most recent air photographs and interpretations from the Central Interpretation Unit. These photographs were very comprehensive and provided a complete picture of the area. This was more clearly shown in detail by the building of special models of the whole area from Berneval to Quiberville on which were marked all batteries, beach defences, pill boxes, machine-gun posts, anti-tank blocks and the RDF Stations. This model was photographed from a very low angle from seaward, to represent the appearance of the coast at nautical twilight, and seven hundred and seventy copies of these silhouettes, on which were marked all chosen landing-places with their respective colours, were issued to Flotilla leaders and officers commanding all ships, at the request of the Naval Planners, as an aid to the recognition of the coastline. 140 Squadron, which, in conjunction with the Photographic Reconnaissance Unit, had flown reconnaissance flights throughout the whole planning period, made a very low sortie over the harbour entrance thirty-six hours before the raid. These photographs confirmed the suspected presence in the Eastern cliff of pill-boxes and also revealed a tank encased by a concrete wall at the end of the Western breakwater. They did not, however, disclose the type or calibre of the guns in the Eastern headland, nor did they show, what ultimately proved to be the fact, that there were similar pill-boxes built in the cliffs on the Western headland. Another method of defence was the mounting of anti-tank guns at certain road-blocks barring the way into the town. Though the air photographs revealed the presence of eight of these blocks on the Boulevard de Verdun, they could not show that behind some of these anti-tank guns were mounted, for the reason that when the photographs were taken, these guns were not in position. According to statements of prisoners of war, the guns were always removed just before daylight and put back into position just after dark, doubtless to prevent air reconnaissances from revealing them.

The Force Commanders were warned of the presence of a number of anti-tank guns whose position could not be definitely located by air photographs.

From statements of prisoners of war referring to the defences, these were shown to tally very much with the intelligence provided.

Combined Operations Headquarters Intelligence Section arranged its direct liaison service with the Force Commanders and right up to the time of the operation the latest intelligence was passed to them.'[15]

The subsequent criticisms include complaints that Combined Operations was slow in circulating the Confidential Book and inefficient in its efforts to up-date it.[16] These are to some extent off-set by evidence that care was taken to keep the forces engaged abreast of the results of the most recent PR,[17] and they are in any case of less moment than the claim that, from complacency in taking at its face value intelligence that was deficient and over-reliant on one source, PR, the planners and the intelligence staff at Combined HQ underrated the strength of the defences at Dieppe and the topographical difficulties that would be encountered by a landing there.

This claim has been made in the Canadian Official History[18] and in other accounts.[19] Not without some reliance on hindsight, they have based it mainly on the fact that the beaches proved to be quite unsuitable for a landing with tanks and on the fact that gun positions in the caves in the headlands, the prime source of the havoc inflicted on the frontal assaults, had gone undetected. The Combined Report did not contest the first of these charges; it appears to be the case that a photograph of a family group picnicking against a breakwater was the only basis from which to calculate the slope of the beach which tanks would have to climb.[20] But it should be noted that, although the General Staff of 2nd Canadian Division had made adverse comments on the suitability of the beaches when it was allocated to the operation, it had accepted the outline plan without pressing its criticism.[21] Against the second charge Combined Operations defended itself in the Combined Report, claiming that the gun positions could not have been detected in advance by PR, but only by agents, and that no

15. ibid, p 9, para 43.
16. Robertson, *The Shame and the Glory: Dieppe* (1962), pp 83, 89.
17. Stacey, op cit, p 345 and footnote.
18. ibid, p 398.
19. Robertson, op cit, pp 83, 89, 174–175; Lyman B Kirkpatrick, *Captains without Eyes* (1970), pp 170, 196, 197.
20. Montagu, *Beyond Top Secret U* (1977), pp 24–25.
21. Stacey, op cit, pp 331–332.

intelligence from agents about them was available.[22] While these points are not in dispute, and while it is true that at this stage SIS was severely handicapped by an intensive German security drive, it is reasonable to conclude that they do not invalidate the charge that in the planning of the raid too little care was given to the problem of the caves and, more generally, to the danger that the absence of firm evidence for defence positions did not preclude the possibility that Dieppe was more heavily defended than appeared to be the case. But that is not to say that these issues received no attention. The plentiful topographical intelligence made it plain that the beach at Dieppe itself was commanded by cliffs on either side, that rocky ledges on the smaller beaches restricted the state of the tide at which landing craft could approach, and that the town had a sea wall, with no breaches in it. The plans as finally revised for *Jubilee* were a compromise between GHQ Home Forces, which wanted a frontal attack in order to achieve the surprise that could not be expected from flank attacks, and Combined Operations HQ, which originally favoured flank attacks at points further away from the town than those eventually selected.[23] The question of the beaches and their defences, the earliest intelligence problem to arise during the planning of the Dieppe raid, and the one in relation to which the intelligence authorities incurred the most criticism, was touched on briefly in the conclusions of the Combined Report. They stressed that although beach reconnaissance for the operation had been 'very complete', such reconnaissance must in future be developed ahead of the development of a plan, to ensure that every detail, with photographs and silhouettes, was available at the Outline Plan stage, and that it and other sources should wherever possible be supplemented by naval reconnaissance.[24]

Mistakes and uncertainties about the German Army order of battle were of less moment than those concerning the beaches and their defences. The division holding the Dieppe area was wrongly identified as 110th Division, which was in Russia.[25] The HQ of the division, the target for some units from the flank attacks, was believed to be at Arques-la-Bataille, whereas it had moved to Envermeu, six miles to the east, on 27 April.[26] Neither of these errors had much influence on the course of the operation. The same is true of the uncertainty which prevailed as to whether 10th Panzer Division was at Amiens and of the knowledge that two SS divisions had arrived in France.

22.   CAB 98/22, p 22, para 190, and Annex 13, p 191, para 1225.
23.   ibid, pp 1–6, paras 1–24, pp 8–9, para 41; Stacey, op cit, pp 326, 331; Roskill, *The War at Sea*, Vol II (1957), p 241.
24.   CAB 98/22, p 46, para 366.
25.   ibid, Annex 2 Appendix A, p 90, paras 684, 685; Stacey, op cit, pp 357, 358; Robertson, op cit, p 176; Kirkpatrick, op cit, p 172.
26.   CAB 98/22, pp 8–9, para 41; Stacey, op cit, p 352 and footnote.

On 11 May Bertrand, who was still reporting regularly to the SIS, reported that 10th Panzer Division had arrived at Soissons from Russia; on 13 July, when MI had received indications that the division was to return to Russia, he replied to an enquiry from the SIS that it had moved the previous day to Amiens.[27] In August MI was doubtful whether it had remained in France after the end of July,[28] and the Detailed Army Plan for *Jubilee* stated that the departure of the division from France might be imminent. But the plan also allowed that if the division was at Amiens its armoured cars could be in Dieppe by between Z plus 3 and Z plus 5 hours and that its Tank Regiment could arrive there within Z plus 8 hours.[29] MI was wrong. In the event, von Rundstedt ordered 10th Panzer Division to move from Amiens to Dieppe half an hour before the British decision to evacuate such parts of the expedition as could avoid surrender. But its advance guard was still 10 miles away when the fighting finished.[30] As for the SS divisions, the Detailed Army Plan stated that one – Das Reich – had been located in Brittany and that the other, the Adolf Hitler Division, was believed to have reached Paris, perhaps as replacement for 10th Panzer Division.[31] This information also had come from Bertrand; it is now known that the Adolf Hitler, with only one brigade, was arriving there on 24 July.[32] But the Detailed Army Plan discounted intervention by either division. As early as 5 July the British had recognised that the Dieppe raid would have to be completed on one tide; the different tide conditions that followed from the deferment of the original date for the operation would otherwise have given the enemy the chance to reorganise on a scale that might prevent the withdrawal of the expedition's tanks.[33]

In these circumstances the points on which accurate assessments were most important were the rates at which the local enemy division and the GAF could bring up reinforcements. The Detailed Army Plan calculated that Dieppe town was held by an infantry battalion of 110th Division and ancillary troops, to a total of 1,700 men, that there would be no troop reinforcement for three hours, and that 850 men would be brought up by the fifth hour and 1,600 more by the eighth hour.[34] In the event, the Allied evacuation began at 1100, about six hours after all the flank and frontal attacks had gone in, and the Combined Report on the raid states that local

27. WO 208/3573 of 1 and 8 June 1942.
28. WO 208/3573 of 24 August.
29. CAB 98/22, Annex 2 Appendix A, pp 90–91, paras 684, 687, 688.
30. Stacey, op cit, p 390.
31. CAB 98/22, Annex 2 Appendix A, p 90, para 684.
32. Gwyer and Butler, op cit, Vol III, Part II, p 646; Stacey, op cit, pp 350–351, 355.
33. CAB 98/22, p 7, para 35.
34. ibid, Annex 2 Appendix A, pp 90–91, paras 684, 685, 687, 688.

German reinforcements reached Dieppe railway station just before the surrender on the beaches upon the completion of evacuation at 1220.[35] Estimates of the strength and rate of reinforcement of the GAF were also reasonably accurate. It was calculated that there were 260 first-line single-engined fighters between Texel and Brest (the actual number serviceable was 225) but that the initial fighter opposition was likely to be limited to 120 aircraft operating from Abbeville, Beaumont-le-Roger and Cherbourg, with a possible 75 further aircraft from St Omer and Courtrai, and that the number of fighter sorties would be only 50 in the first six hours and up to 250 in the next 24 hours.[36] In fact the fighters used at Dieppe were drawn chiefly from Abbeville, Beaumont and Courtrai; the number on patrol at any one time up to 0930, when the Military Force Commander took the decision to evacuate, was between 20 and 30; and the number of fighter sorties for the whole day was approximately 600.[37] As for long-range bombers, the total force available in the west was estimated at 220 (the actual strength being 175 plus 45 reconnaissance bombers) and it was calculated that the number of sorties would be 30 in the first six hours and 130 in the next 24 hours.[38] In the event, although the enemy committed all the bombers available in the theatre, it was 1000, after the decision to evacuate, before the first two arrived on the scene and AI estimated that the number of sorties during the rest of the day totalled 125.[39]

As may be judged from the slow response of the GAF, the raid achieved tactical as well as strategic surprise, and did so despite a chance encounter between the naval force for the eastern outer flank attack and the escort of a small enemy convoy.[40] But this encounter, which had a disastrous effect on the easternmost landing force by scattering its landing craft, might have been avoided but for failures in communications, and further such failures occurring throughout the short-lived operation impeded the commanders and greatly reduced the value of the current intelligence that was available. In the second of these directions the failures were compounded by suspicion on the part of the commanders that some of the intercepts of German R/T transmissions

35.   ibid, p 29, para 246; Stacey, op cit, p 373.
36.   AIR 41/49, *Air Defence of Great Britain*, Vol V, p 119 and footnote; CAB 98/22, p 30, para 260 and Annex 7 Appendix F, pp 163–164.
37.   AIR 41/49, p 124; CAB 98/22, p 30, para 268, p 31, para 273.
38.   AIR 41/49, p 119 and footnote; CAB 98/22, Annex I Intelligence Summary, p 87, para 658.
39.   AIR 41/49, pp 123–124; CAB 98/22, p 31, para 274, p 33, para 299, Annex 7 Appendix F, pp 163–164.
40.   CAB 98/22, p 15, para 106; Roskill, op cit, Vol II, p 246; Stacey, op cit, pp 358, 359, 369; Kirkpatrick, op cit, p 188.

consisted of bogus signals.[41] There was some justification for the suspicion; but subsequent analysis was to show that the enemy's attempts at deception on R/T were not effective and that he did not extend his deception measures to his plain language W/T transmissions, most of which were intercepted during the action.[42] It is clear that failure of organisation and of communications was the main reason for the breakdown of the plan that had been drawn up for supplying the expedition with operational Sigint about the GAF.

The raid against St Nazaire on 27/28 March 1942 had derived no benefit from the low-grade Sigint which Cheadle obtained during the operation: on security grounds the Sigint organisations had not been alerted in advance. On the initiative of the Sigint authorities it was agreed that this omission should be rectified in future operations, and for the Dieppe raid, despite the secrecy surrounding its preparation, the Sigint authorities were asked, for the first time, to make special arrangements for an Allied operation. The chief features of these arrangements were that interception of the most important W/T networks, notably those of the enemy's observer corps, his radar stations and his fighter control stations, was concentrated at Cheadle; that all intelligence derived by Cheadle from W/T was forwarded during the operation not, as was customary, to Fighter Command HQ, but direct to HQ No 11 Group RAF, the operational and intelligence centre for the expedition, which already received R/T intelligence direct from the HDU stations under normal arrangements; and that GC and CS's Air Section seconded two officers to Cheadle to ensure that only W/T intelligence of operational value was sent to HQ 11 Group and one officer to HQ 11 Group to interpret for the operational staff what was received from Cheadle and to work in close collaboration with the officer at HQ 11 Group who handled the R/T intercepts. At the outset it seemed that these measures would be adequate; there was little W/T traffic as no Observer Corps post reported the landings and the enemy's radar organisation broadcast no plots for several hours. But before long the War Room at HQ No 11 Group became so congested that it proved impossible either to fuse the W/T Sigint with the voluminous R/T coming from the GAF formations or to avoid serious delay in processing Kingsdown's R/T intercepts. Nor could Kingsdown, unable to relate its R/T intercepts to the operational situation, fill the gap. It failed, for example, to detect that the Dieppe area was being heavily reinforced by fighters from neighbouring sectors.

The failure of this experiment in providing up-to-the-minute tactical air intelligence from Sigint underlined the need for more

41. CAB 98/22, p 18, para 145, p 26, para 219, Annex 5, p 138, para 923, Annex 7, p 146, para 968; Stacey, op cit, p 367.
42. CAB 98/22, Annex 10, p 175, para 1085, p 176, para 1111.

efficient arrangements during future operations. In the discussions on this subject which followed the Dieppe raid it was recognised that there was no alternative to having all low-grade Sigint interpreted at one central point before it was presented to commands, and that, since GC and CS alone understood the material in all its intricacy and was able to interpret it in the light of high-grade Sigint, that central point must be the Air Section at GC and CS, or, for Mediterranean operations, a staff sent out from GC and CS to the Allied Command HQ. This conclusion, which was put into effect in time for the Normandy landings, but which before that time greatly improved the Sigint support given to the operations of Eighth US Army Air Force and, with less than complete success, was adopted for *Torch*,* was one of the chief lessons of the Dieppe operation.

Among the other lessons learned, one had a bearing on the provision of intelligence but arose out of the general breakdown of communications to and between the forces taking part in the raid; it was the need to set up in an HQ ship an inter-Service control and communications centre and to ensure that the field Sigint staff, responsible for local exploitation and for acting on intelligence received from the United Kingdom, were in close proximity to it.[43] HQ ships were provided in time for operation *Torch*, an operation which showed that much still remained to be learned in this direction but which provided further valuable experience.

It was in operation *Torch* that, also for the first time, an assault commando accompanied forward troops in an Allied offensive with the object of capturing enemy documents and cypher material. This measure, originally proposed by the NID in March 1942 during the planning of operation *Sledgehammer*, was incorporated into the planning of operation *Rutter* with the approval of the JIC on 12 June. But an inter-Service agreement on the composition and function of the commando was not submitted to the JIC until 11 August, too late for implementation during the Dieppe raid. For the Dieppe operation the NID briefed a special section of No 40 Royal Marine Commando on what material to look for, but this secret mission shared the failure of the whole operation.[44]

---

* See Appendix 18.

43. CAB 98/22, p 40, para 351.
44. CAB 121/364, (*Rutter* Folder), JIC (42) 223 (o) of 12 June, CCO correspondence with Colonel Hollis 15 and 16 June 1942; CAB 98/22, Annex 2 Appendix L, p 116, para 760; JIC (42) 32nd (o) Meeting of 14 July, 37th (o) Meeting of 11 August; JIC (42) 305 (o) of 5 August.

APPENDIX 14

Technical Intelligence on Tanks and Anti-Tank Weapons in North Africa

In February 1941 the Germans took with them to Africa four models of tank. Panzerkampfwagen (Pzkw) I and II no longer had much fighting value and only Pzkw III and IV, both medium tanks of the cruiser type, need be considered in this account.[1] In 1939 Pzkw III had been armed with 30 mm conventional armour and the 37 mm tank gun, but after the French campaign it had been re-equipped with the 50 mm short-barrelled tank gun and its armour had been strengthened at vulnerable points by the addition of 30 mm face-hardened plates.[2] Of the Pzkw IIIs that went to Africa, all had the larger gun and, though not all had the extra plates, the strengthened version began to arrive within a month or two; it is probable that they already formed a considerable proportion of the total by the time of operation *Battleaxe* (June 1941) and this was certainly the case during operation *Crusader* (November 1941).[3] Pzkw IV, which went to Africa in fewer numbers, was equipped with the 75 mm short-barrelled tank gun and its 30 mm armour was undergoing the same strengthening process, so that after the first arrivals those reaching Africa had the additional 30 mm face-hardened plates.[4]

Three types of German anti-tank gun need to be taken into account for the 1941 fighting.[5] At the time of *Battleaxe* two-thirds of German anti-tank guns were the 37 mm, developed five years before the war,[6] but a start had already been made with replacing these by the new, long-barrelled 50 mm anti-tank gun (called Panzerabwehrkanone (Pak) 38). During *Battleaxe* the Pak 38 made up one-third of the anti-tank arm and at *Crusader* this proportion had increased to over a half.* Although of higher penetration than

---

* During *Battleaxe* Rommel had fifty-four Pak 38 and twelve 88 mm out of a total of 155 anti-tank guns. By the time of *Crusader* he had thirty-five 88 mm and ninety-six 50 mm out of a total of 158.[7]

1. Playfair, *The Mediterranean and Middle East*, Vol II (1956), p 341; Vol III (1960), p 27.   2.   Playfair, op cit, Vol III, p 435.
3. Playfair, op cit, Vol II, pp 13, 341–344.
4. Playfair, op cit, Vol II, p 341; Vol III, pp 435–436.
5. Playfair, op cit, Vol II, p 341.
6. Playfair, op cit, Vol III, p 28 fn.
7. Playfair, op cit, Vol II, p 342; Vol III, p 28; B H Liddell Hart, *History of the Second World War*, (1970), p 177.

the corresponding short-barrelled 50 mm of Pzkw III, the Pak 38 could, with HE, penetrate the Matilda's armour only at short range.[8] But among the 88 mm dual purpose Flugabwehrkanone (Flak) guns which the Germans had also sent to Africa were a number which were intended for use as an anti-tank weapon and these were to be far more effective.[9]

A further point to be noted relates to the German ammunition. Although every German gun was issued with different kinds of ammunition, so that it could perform in different roles, for the anti-tank role the German tank and anti-tank guns used armour-piercing high-explosive shell which was capped for better penetration,[10] and later given ballistic capping. In addition, all tank and anti-tank guns (except the short 75 mm of the Pzkw IV) were eventually given a small issue of Panzergranate 40, a tungsten-cored shot of exceptional armour-piercing quality at medium ranges.[11]

With their face-hardened extra plates, incorporating a technique unused by the British, and their capped shell (not to mention Panzergranate 40), the Germans enjoyed a double advantage over the British forces in north Africa. In 1941 the British Army was equipped with two types of tank – the cruiser tank for rapid manoeuvre and a slow and heavily armed infantry (I) tank for supporting infantry in assaults on fortified positions – and its standard anti-tank and tank gun was the 2-pounder. Before the outbreak of war, when these weapons had been developed, gun-power had been considered to be a secondary consideration in the design of tanks and, in the belief that in a war with Germany the Army would be on the defensive in the early stages, priority had been given to the production of the I tank.[12] Following the loss of nearly all the Army's tanks and guns in France in the summer of 1940, there had been an emergency programme to produce more of the same weapons. The result was that the tank force in north Africa contained a disproportionately large number of I tanks (at this stage the Matilda), that it did not have the benefit of face-hardened armour and that the standard gun was a weapon that soon proved to be totally inadequate.* Moreover, like all

---

* As early as 1938 it had been recognised that the 2-pounder was insufficiently powerful and the design of a 6-pounder was well advanced in the summer of 1940. But the production of the 6-pounder was then delayed by the urgent need to produce large quantities of the 2-pounder, which remained the standard gun in north Africa until the second half of 1942.[13]

8. Playfair, op cit, Vol II, p 342.
9. ibid, p 341.
10. Playfair, op cit, Vol III, p 438.
11. Playfair, op cit, Vol II, p 342; Vol III, p 438.
12. Playfair, op cit, Vol II, p 174; L F Ellis, *Victory in the West*, Vol I (1962), p 545.
13. Playfair, op cit, Vol II, p 175; Vol III, p 214 fn.

Allied guns with two exceptions,* the 2-pounder used uncapped armour-piercing shot; it was unable to penetrate face-hardened armour. In contrast, the German 88 mm Flak gun could penetrate the Matilda at 2,000 yards[14] and, when firing Panzergranate 40, the German 50 mm Pak 38 could penetrate the Matilda's frontal armour at about 500 yards – a useful range in tank warfare.

The design of the British weapons had not been influenced by intelligence; they had been developed at a time when little or nothing was known about Germany's armoured fighting vehicles (AFVs) and when reports to the effect that she was producing a new and formidable type of anti-tank gun were being discounted.[†] Moreover, given the circumstances we have described, intelligence could not have made much contribution to the improvement or the replacement of the pre-war designs before 1941 even if it had greatly improved after the outbreak of war. In the event it did improve, but not so much that it was able to establish by the beginning of 1941 the extent to which the British weapons were inferior to the German.

By the opening of the French campaign MI's knowledge of the characteristics and performance of the four types of German tank was substantially complete. In particular, it knew that Pzkw III and IV had 30 mm armour and, respectively, the 37 mm and 75 mm gun; and it had correctly predicted that heavier tanks and larger guns would be developed.[15] During the French campaign it learned from the GAF Enigma that the 88 mm Flak gun was in use as an anti-tank gun.[16][‡] The Enigma did not throw any light on the efficiency of this gun,[§] but by the beginning of 1941 MI had received reports which led it to believe that it could penetrate

---

* One exception was the 37 mm gun of the US Stuart tank (and from May 1942 the secondary armament of the US Grant tank) which used light-weight capped shot. But the Stuart had only a short range and played only a minor role after operation *Crusader*. The other exception was the British 25-pounder field gun; this was not normally an anti-tank gun and it could not be counted on to be available for that role.

† See Volume I, p 77.

‡ The Flak units using the gun in the anti-tank role used the GAF Enigma. The decrypts provided a good deal of information about their organisation and order of battle and disclosed the efficiency of their co-operation with the Army; they also established that all Flak units were supplied with armour-piercing ammunition up to 88 mm.[17]

§ The Enigma rarely divulged information of this kind. Even when the Army Enigma was regularly broken, from the summer of 1942, the decrypts usually mentioned only the names and types of weapons and gave few details about their performance.

14. Playfair, op cit, Vol II, p 341 and table p 342.
15. WO 190/891, Appreciation No 22, undated but c February 1940; Playfair, op cit, Vol II, p 345.
16. WO 190/891, No 267 of 27 May 1940.
17. WO 190/891, No 267 of 27 May 1940; WO 106/1639, MI 10 Report No 14 of 13 June 1940; L F Ellis, *The War in France and Flanders*, (1953), p 87.

80–90 mm of armour at 400 yards;[18] although this was a serious under-estimate, the reports at least established that the Germans had an anti-tank weapon of greater penetration power than MI had previously allowed for.[19] But reports reaching Whitehall to the effect that the Germans were increasing the armour of their tanks after the French campaign, an inherently probable development, were judged by MI to be insufficiently detailed and reliable to merit dissemination.[20] The position at the time of the first contacts with the German forces in north Africa in March 1941 was that the British authorities did not know that Pzkw III and IV were being given additional face-hardened plates, or that the 37 mm gun of Pzkw III had been replaced by the short-barrelled 50 mm gun, or that the 37 mm anti-tank gun had been replaced by the long-barrelled 50 mm Pak 38. They may have assumed that the 88 mm Flak gun would be sent to Africa; in any case, the GAF Enigma disclosed that on 9 March 1941 Hitler had ordered the strengthening of the Afrikakorps anti-tank defences by Flak units. As we have seen, however, MI as yet under-estimated the performance of this gun.

Some of these facts were unearthed during April 1941, following Rommel's sweep through Cyrenaica and his two unsuccessful attacks on Tobruk. Captured documents showed that Pzkw III was armed with a 50 mm gun and that a 75 mm gun, which was no doubt associated with Pzkw IV, was in use; they identified the 50 mm anti-tank gun; and they confirmed the presence of the 88 mm Flak gun in one of Rommel's anti-tank units.[21] But captured documents, like Sigint, did not then yield reliable information about the performance of weapons, and since tank and gun crews could seldom say what had hit them, the same was true of battle reports. Thus it was only when the head of the Technical Intelligence section of GHQ, ME examined the guns and the AFVs abandoned by the Germans at Tobruk that such information began to emerge. The examination, of which the results were published in mid-May,[22] established that Pzkw III and IV had had their armour thickness doubled by the addition of extra plates, that Pzkw III's 50 mm gun could penetrate 60 mm armour at 400 yards and that Pzkw IV's short-barrelled 75 mm gun could penetrate up

---

18. WO 106/2258, WO Weekly Intelligence Summary No 79 of 20 February 1941; Cabinet Office Historical Section, AL 3000/B3 Part I, extract from WDF Intelligence Summary No 130 of 28 April 1941.
19. WO 106/2258, No 79 of 20 February 1941.
20. Playfair, op cit, Vol II, p 343.
21. AL 3000/B3 Part I, extracts from Cyrenaica Command Intelligence Summary No 12 of 13 April 1941 and WDF Intelligence Summary No 128 of 24 April 1941.
22. AL 3000/B3, Part I, extract from MI 10 Report No 41 of 8 May 1941; WO 106/2259, WO Intelligence Summary No 91 of 25 May 1941.

to 100 mm of armour at 600 yards.* By the end of 1941 it had not been established that the extra armour plates were face-hardened – to an extent which made the German tanks invulnerable to frontal penetration by the British 2-pounder – although armour specimens had been taken for despatch to the United Kingdom for examination. Capped shell and special armour-piercing shot (Panzergranate 40), which increased the performance of the German guns to well beyond these estimates, had been identified and given preliminary examination. The new long-barrelled 50 mm anti-tank gun, which had greater penetration power than Pzkw III's 50 mm gun, had been given preliminary examination, but there was no further information about the 88 mm Flak gun, the performance of which continued to be under-estimated.[24]

This being the state of intelligence in June 1941, there need be no doubt that under-estimation of the effectiveness of the enemy's weapons played a large part in the failure of the British forces in operation *Battleaxe*, the first occasion on which they sought to bring the German armour to battle on a large scale. On the eve of the offensive the C-in-C Middle East did indeed express anxiety about the vulnerability of the Matilda tank to the enemy's larger anti-tank guns.[25] But the inability of the Matildas to make headway against the 88 mm Flak gun still came as a surprise, and the heavy losses they sustained on the first assault went far to stultify the whole operation. The other German anti-tank guns, particularly the 50 mm Pak 38 with its 4½-pound shell and its Panzergranate 40, did much damage to the British Cruiser tanks. On the other hand, largely because the uncapped ammunition of the British 2-pounder was ineffective against the German face-hardened armour except at the closest range, German tank losses were only about one-eighth of the British losses.[26] It now emerged, moreover, that whereas the British had developed no organisation for this purpose, the Germans were able to off-set their inferiority in numbers of tanks by their efficiency in recovering and repairing battle-damaged tanks.[27]

Partly on this last account *Battleaxe* itself produced little new technical intelligence. But the set-back led the British authorities to adopt a more vigorous, if still improvised, programme for capturing and examining enemy equipment.[28] Up to operation *Crusader* the

* This was a serious over-estimate. Armed with the short 75 mm gun, as it was at this stage of the war, Pzkw IV was intended primarily for infantry support and not for anti-tank work. The short 75 mm gun could penetrate only about 45 mm of armour at 600 yards, although its high explosive shell could cause damage to British tanks up to 3,000 yards.[23]

23. Playfair, op cit, Vol II, p 341; Vol III, p 443.
24. WO 208/3580, MEF/9000(I)/MI 10 of 31 October 1943.
25. Playfair, op cit, Vol II, pp 163, 167.
26. ibid, pp 171, 173, 343.
27. ibid, p 174.
28. WO 208/3580, MEF/9000(I)/MI 10.

following equipment was captured and given a preliminary testing in the Middle East before being flown or shipped to the United Kingdom: a 50 mm Pak 38; a reasonably intact Pzkw IV with its 75 mm gun;* specimens of tank armour; a 28 mm s Pz 41 anti-tank gun,[†] and a range of armour-piercing ammunition, including Panzergranate 40. Also recovered was a captured document which disclosed that the 37 mm and 50 mm anti-tank guns were issued with special armour-piercing shot with which the 50 mm could penetrate the Matilda at 440 yards[‡] – and could thus deal with the lighter cruiser tank at much greater range. On this evidence the Pak 40 mm was superior to any other gun, not excluding the 88 mm Flak gun as it was then appraised, of which MI 10 had knowledge.

MI 10 recognised the significance of this last discovery: it noted that the armour-piercing shot was quite evidently something special and hoped that the examination of ammunition in the Middle East would produce more information about it.[32] But the significance does not appear to have been appreciated by some commanders in the Middle East, and the same applies to an additional piece of intelligence about the 88 mm Flak gun. Although nothing new was yet discovered about the performance of this gun, it was learned that it had been fitted with self-propelled mounting;[33] and yet it has been claimed that, having dismissed before the opening of operation *Crusader* reports that the gun was being used as an anti-tank gun, many commanders in the Middle East continued to believe that such a heavy gun could only be used in dug-in positions even after they had recognised its responsibility for many of their losses during *Crusader*.[34]

Whatever the truth about the progress of intelligence on the enemy's guns and ammunition, it is clear that preliminary examination in the Middle East of the armour and the Pzkw IV that had been captured, and tests carried out there against the latter

---

* For rescuing this at Suez when the SS *Georgic*, the ship that was transporting it, was bombed and set ablaze, Capt. D E Evans, head of GSI (Tech) and later of MI 10 (ME), was awarded the George Medal.[29]

† This gun had a novel tapered bore (on the Gerlich principle) which made it the German Army's most secret weapon,[30] but it did not play a significant part in the north African fighting.

‡ This was the Panzergranate 40. Compare the fact that when using HE shell the gun could not penetrate the Matilda's frontal armour at any range.[31]

29. ibid.
30. ibid: WO 106/2286, MI 10 Reports Nos 46 of 24 June and 49 of 21 July 1941; WO 106/2259, WO Intelligence Summaries Nos 98 of 2 July and 102 of 3 July 1941.
31. Playfair, op cit, Vol III, p 343.
32. WO 106/2286, No 50 of 1 August 1941.
33. ibid, No 52 of 29 August 1941.
34. Liddell Hart, op cit, p 181.

with the British 2-pounder, still failed to discover that the extra armour plates of the German tanks had been face-hardened. The report on the tests by GHQ ME's Technical Intelligence section stated that the 60 mm reinforced armour of the Pzkw IV was vulnerable up to a range of 500 yards and concluded that 'while the German armour plate has not been analysed, the results do indicate that it is not of a quality to prevent holes being made by existing British anti-tank weapons'.[35]

The state of technical intelligence at the beginning of operation *Crusader* in November 1941 may thus be summarised as follows. The British authorities had examined the Pzkw IV's 75 mm gun and knew that it was capable of doing great damage to their tanks even though the Pzkw IV was designed primarily for infantry support and not for the anti-tank role. They knew that the Pzkw III was equipped with a 50 mm gun which differed from the 50 mm Pak gun, both of which they had examined. They knew – at least they had received evidence to this effect – that the 50 mm Pak gun, like the 37 mm anti-tank gun, could use special shot, and that when using this the 50 mm Pak could penetrate the Matilda at 440 yards; but their evidence about the 88 mm Flak gun was that it had about the same capability, whereas it could penetrate the Matilda at 2,000 yards; and they did not know Rommel's strength in anti-tank guns or the proportions of his guns as between the 37 mm, the 50 mm and the 88 mm. They knew that some of the Pzkw IIIs and IVs had been fitted with extra plates but, although the Enigma had disclosed the number and types of tank available to Rommel, they did not know how many had been so fitted (it was in fact 'a considerable number' by this time[36]) and there was no evidence that they were face-hardened, making the front of both types of tank virtually proof against their own 2-pounder gun except at the closest range.

At the same time, considerable uncertainty still persisted about the respective roles of the tank and the anti-tank gun in German tactical doctrine. The Germans held that 'the primary use of tanks was to deal with troops and the task of destroying tanks was largely one for the anti-tank guns',[37] the smaller of which they pushed out into concealed positions ahead of their tanks; but the British forces, believing that the job of the tank was to counter tanks, attributed many of their tank casualties to tank fire when they were in fact caused by the anti-tank guns.[38]

It is beyond the scope of this study to attempt to assess how far and in what ways the planning and the course of *Crusader* would

---

35. WO 106/2259, No 96 of 15 June 1941; WO 106/2286, No 44 of 7 June 1941.
36. Playfair, op cit, Vol III, p 435.
37. ibid, Vol II, p 173.
38. ibid, pp 173–174; Liddell Hart, op cit, p 181.

have been altered by the existence of better intelligence about the enemy's weapons and tactics. Suffice it to say that the heavy tank losses suffered by the British in the first phase of the offensive – they were due chiefly to the 50 mm Pak 38, though the 88 mm Flak gun also caused heavy losses[39] – underlined the German superiority in these directions, and that in the end the vulnerability of the British tanks and the ineffectiveness of the British 2-pounder gun were outweighed only by the British ability to bring up far greater reserves than Rommel could. Nor did the balance of technical advantage change between *Crusader* and the battle of Gazala in May 1942. On the contrary, by February 1942, when Rommel's counter-offensive of January had forced the British advance back to Gazala and the superiority of his guns and tanks was causing acute concern throughout Eighth Army and in Whitehall, the enemy was introducing further improvements.

From the beginning of 1942 new models of Pzkw III and IV (Pzkw III J and Pzkw IV F 1), without extra plates but with their basic frontal armour increased to 50 mm and face-hardened, were reaching north Africa. Some of these arrived in time for Rommel's counter-offensive in January 1942 and by May 1942 they were available in considerable numbers.[40] By that time Rommel had also received a few Pzkw Special tanks; in these the 50 mm short-barrelled gun was replaced by a version of the long-barrelled 50 mm Pak 38 (Kampfwagenkanone (Kwk) 39) and the front was further strengthened by spaced armour; an extra 20 mm plate was separated by four inches from the 50 mm frontal armour, this again incorporated a principle not used by the British. Soon after the opening of his Gazala offensive Rommel received the first of the Pzkw IV Specials, which had the same spaced armour and carried a long-barrelled 75 mm gun in place of the short-barrelled 75 mm gun of Pzkw IV. More important – for the III and IV Specials were not available in significant numbers before July 1942* – were two other developments. By the end of May 1942 virtually all of Rommel's tanks had either the extra face-hardened plates or the new 50 mm face-hardened frontal armour. And by the same date the Germans had made great progress in turning existing anti-tank guns into self-propelled guns; the guns so modified included guns captured in Europe, especially one that was superior to the Pak 50 mm – the Russian 7.62 cm.†

---

* The ratio of new tanks to Rommel's Pzkw IIIs was 1 to 4 on 1 June 1942 but it rose to 1 to 1 by 31 July. See above, p 384, and below, p 715.

† Like the introduction of the Pzkw III and IV Specials, two other improvements in the enemy's artillery played no important part until after the middle of 1942. The first was the introduction of 'hollow-charge' ammunition, which gave infantry and field guns the capacity to attack armour; Eighth Army was warned of its existence on 10 May, and some

39.   Playfair, op cit, Vol III, p 28; Liddell Hart, op cit, p 180.
40.   Playfair, op cit, Vol III, p 436.

Although Rommel continued to enjoy technical superiority, his advantage was to some extent off-set from the beginning of 1942 by an improvement in British technical intelligence. In December 1941 GHQ, ME set up the AFV (Technical) Branch to study the technical factors affecting British AFV design and effectiveness. From March 1942 the Technical Intelligence section of GSI, greatly expanded and re-named GSI (Tech) GHQ, ME, developed novel methods of training staff in the collection and dissemination of information about enemy weapons, ammunition and equipment. German armour development was studied in depth so that by June 1942 the history of improvement, including reinforcement and face-hardening, was known in detail.[43] Meanwhile, in March, in tests against a Pzkw III, the AFV (Technical) Branch had appreciated the significance of its extra plates being face-hardened; and before the battle of Gazala it had established that the hardened plates were proof at all ranges against 2-pounder uncapped shot.[44]* By that time the capture of other tanks had established that Pzkw III and IV with 50 mm armour were arriving.[46] Also in March the British captured a specimen of the ex-Russian 7.62 cm gun which had been mounted on an improvised self-propelled chassis.[47] Another important discovery made before Gazala was established by captured documents; in mid-January 1942, when these confirmed that the 88 mm Flak gun could open effective fire at 2,000 yards, Eighth Army must have already been aware of that fact, but in mid-May they yielded precise figures of the penetration capacity of the gun at 2,000

---

performance details were quoted by GSI (Tech) from captured documents.[41] The second was the introduction of multiple barrelled mortars firing rocket-propelled projectiles. The best known of these was the Nebelwerfer, which did not begin to arrive in north Africa until late in 1942.[42] Like face-hardened armour and spaced armour, these developments incorporated novel principles with which the British forces in the field were unfamiliar.

* It also found that the plates were proof at over 500 yards against the uncapped shot of the British 6-pounder gun and the main armament of the Grant tank, both of which were used in the battle of Gazala for the first time, though whether or not this information was available before the battle is unclear.[45]

41. WO 169/3803, Eighth Army Intelligence Summary No 200 of 10 May 1942; Playfair, op cit, Vol III, p 438.
42. Playfair, op cit, Vol IV (1966), pp 500–501.
43. WO 208/3580, GHQ MEF GSI/6000/Tech of 29 June 1942.
44. Playfair, op cit, Vol III, pp 435–436; Cabinet Office Historical Section, AL 3000/B4, items 11A and 29, AFV Technical Report No 7 of 7 May 1942; WO 169/3803, No 240 of 24 June 1942.
45. Playfair, op cit, Vol III, pp 435–436.
46. AL 3000/B3 Part I, extract from XIII Corps Intelligence Summary No 54 of 1 December 1941; AL 3000/B4, Item 29, AFV Technical Report No 3 of 25 February 1942; WO 208/3578, MI 10 Technical Intelligence Summary No 73 of 21 May 1942; Playfair, op cit, Vol III, Appendix B.
47. WO 208/3577, MI 10 Technical Intelligence Summary No 70 of 23 April 1942; WO 169/3803, Nos 148 of 18 March and 188 of 27 April 1942.

metres and details of the ammunition with which the gun was supplied for its anti-tank and its anti-aircraft roles.[48]

As a result of these revelations the British knew the principal facts about their technical inferiority in weapons by the beginning of the battle of Gazala. By then, moreover, chiefly as a result of the regular reading of the Army Enigma from April 1942, Sigint was at last yielding valuable information about the numbers and types of Rommel's equipment. The decrypts disclosed that he had received 106 of the ex-Russian 7.62 cm guns before he opened his offensive, and they also established that he had received only a few Pzkw III and IV Specials when the battle began. Nor was it long before the discovery of the main facts about the specifications and performances of the Specials provided an early illustration of the way in which, from the summer of 1942, the Enigma and Army Y, though rarely disclosing technical details themselves, increasingly helped the technical intelligence authorities to obtain and interpret evidence from other sources.

The fact that III and IV Specials were reaching Africa had first been disclosed in an Enigma tank return in April 1942, at which time GSI (Tech) was already forecasting that the III Special would have the heavier (rather than reinforced) armour and mount a modified 50 mm Pak 38, while IV Special would be similarly armoured and mount the new long-barrelled 75 mm gun. A fortnight before the battle of Gazala a POW reported that the III Special had the long-barrelled 50 mm gun. Together with Enigma references to Pzkw III (long) and IV (long) which could be associated with the earlier references to Specials, and with captured document information, this enabled GSI (Tech) to provide Eighth Army in June 1942 with confirmation that the III Special had the long 50 mm anti-tank gun and the IV a new long 75 mm gun; the Enigma later provided explicit confirmation of this. In its June report Eighth Army also issued a POW statement that, as was correct, the new 75 mm gun could penetrate 45 mm of armour at 2,000 yards.[49] In the same report Eighth Army circulated accurate specifications of the spaced armour of the III Special which GSI (Tech) had obtained from interrogation reports; no Special was captured until a III Special was examined under fire in July and the gun and specimen spaced armour recovered from it.[50] At the

---

48.   AL 3000/B3, Part I, extracts from GSI GHQ ME Intelligence Summaries Nos 602 and 608 of 12 and 18 January 1942 and XIII Corps Intelligence Summary No 56 of 5 December 1941; WO 208/3578, Nos 72 of 12 May and 82 of 29 July 1942.

49.   CX/MSS/935/T3 and 9, 1083/T20 and 23, 1177/T1; WO 208/3577, No 69 of 14 April; WO 208/3578, No 77 of 20 June 1942; WO 169/3803, Nos 203 of 13 May and 234 of 14 June 1942; Playfair, op cit, Vol III, p 443.

50.   Playfair, op cit, Vol III, p 443: WO 208/3580, MEF/9000(I)/MI 10, para 21.

end of July an Enigma tank return revealed that the ratio of the new types of tank to Pzkw IIIs in Rommel's total armour had risen to 1 to 1; it had been given as 1 to 4 in a tank return of 1 June.*

The continuing improvement in intelligence made no difference to the fact that despite many attempts to improvise counter-measures, the British forces in Africa could do little to rectify the enemy's continuing superiority in quality of armour and armament before the end of the battle of Alam el Halfa in September 1942. In October, however, in time for the second battle of Alamein, the arrival in quantity of the Sherman tank at last gave Eighth Army equality in tank performance; and although it was not until January 1943 that, with their receipt of the British 17-pounder and of capped ammunition, the British forces acquired an anti-tank gun as effective as the German 88 mm, this disadvantage was off-set at Alamein in two ways. The first was the British numerical superiority in guns, as in tanks.† The second was the fact that before the battle technical intelligence had played an important part in British planning for the first time, MI 10 (ME) – as GSI (Tech) had now become – being able to issue well in advance correct details of the enemy's principal guns and tanks[51] and the Enigma establishing the essential facts about the numbers and types of tanks at his disposal. The Enigma failed to show that by the time of the battle all Rommel's Pzkw IIIs were Specials, with spaced armour,[52] but it had disclosed the growing proportion of Specials in the Panzer Army and the gradual disappearance of the old type Pzkw III and IV. Moreover, on the negative evidence of the Enigma tank returns Eighth Army knew that Tiger tanks had not reached north Africa in time for the battle.

In September 1942 the Enigma had provided the first confirmation of the existence of a new tank, Pzkw VI (Tiger), revealing that it was expected in north Africa but that existing unloading facilities there were inadequate to handle it. Together with Pzkw V (Panther), the Tiger tank had been under development since 1941 and rumours of the development of larger and more powerful German tanks had been abroad from an even earlier date.[53] But when the Enigma confirmed that the Tiger was operational nothing was known of its capabilities beyond the fact that the decrypt gave its

---

* See above, p 712.

† The British had five hundred and fifty-four 2-pounders and eight hundred and forty-nine 6-pounders against Rommel's two hundred and ninety Pak 38, sixty-eight 7.62 cm and eighty-six 88 mm anti-tank guns.

51. WO 208/3580, MEF/9000(I)/MI 10, para 26.
52. Playfair, op cit, Vol IV, p 500.
53. WO 208/3577, No 69 of 16 April 1942; WO 208/3580, MEF 6000/MI 10 of 12 August 1943, p 5, para 11; WO 190/891, No 276 of 5 June 1940; WO 106/2258, Nos 82 of 13 March and 86 of 10 April 1941.

dimensions.[54] As compared with Pzkw III and IV, weighing between 20 and 25 tons, it in fact weighed 54 tons, had 102 mm frontal armour and carried a tank version of the 88 mm Flak gun as its main gun, while the Panther, which did not come into operational use until 1943, weighed 45 tons, had 100 mm frontal armour and carried a 75 mm main gun.[55]

After the opening of the battle of Alamein the enemy made strenuous efforts to get the first Tiger tanks to the Panzer Army but met with difficulties, as the Enigma disclosed.[56] The Tigers were then diverted to Tunisia. This decision was disclosed by the Enigma decrypts a few days before the Allied forces first encountered Tigers there on 27 November 1942.[57] Thereafter, apart from the fact that battle experience, a photograph taken from a POW and Press photographs of the Tiger in Tunisia identified its main armament as being a tank version of the 88 mm Flak gun, no further intelligence about the tank was obtained until a Tiger was knocked out by a 6-pounder shot which penetrated its side armour at 900 yards on 31 January 1943.[58] As well as confirming existing information about its gun, its dimensions and its weight, examination of this tank established that the Tiger's frontal armour was 102 mm and that its side armour was 82 mm; it also indicated that while the Tiger was a formidable tank, its size, weight and complexity created difficulties and limitations in operational practice.[59] This conclusion was supported by an Enigma decrypt of 21 January in which Hitler attributed the limited success of the Tigers up to that date to the inexperience of their officers.[60]

In the event, the Germans were able to commit only a small number of Tigers to Tunisia; as the Enigma disclosed at the time, there were never more than 20.[61] As for their Pzkw IIIs and IVs, of which the great majority were by now Specials, the IV Specials with their long 75 mm gun had undergone no change, but in an increasing number of the more numerous III Specials the armour had been strengthened during 1942 and, from January 1943, the 75 mm short tank gun replaced the 50 mm long gun – the second of these developments being a response to the change in the nature of the fighting from primarily tank warfare to battles in which the overwhelming strength of the Allies in infantry and artillery could

---

54. CX/MSS/1435/T3 of 16 September, 1441/T11 of 21 September 1942.
55. Ellis, *Victory in the West*, Vol 1, pp 547–549.
56. CX/MSS/1643/T43 of 6 November 1942.
57. CX/MSS/1519/T13, 1531/T9.
58. Playfair, op cit, Vol IV, p 500; Mockler-Ferryman, *Military Intelligence Organisation*, p 168.
59. Playfair, op cit, Vol IV, p 500.
60. CX/MSS/2008/T30 of 21 January 1943.
61. CX/MSS/1758/T37 of 30 November, 1773/T26 of 2 December, 1782 of 5 December 1942; Playfair, op cit, Vol IV, p 500.

best be opposed by the 75 mm short-barrelled gun using HE with the new hollow-charge ammunition.[62] Technical intelligence had full knowledge of the Pzkw IV Special by the end of 1942[63] and it noted the changes made to Pzkw III as they occurred.[64] Thanks to Enigma, it also knew that the enemy realised that Pzkw III was becoming obsolete; a decrypt of March 1943 stressed that the Hermann Göring Division should bring Pzkw IV Specials to Tunisia as Pzkw III was no longer fit to fight there,[65] and this had been preceded since the previous November by other decrypts which made it clear that in the effort to meet appeals from Rommel for better tanks priority was being given to the Tiger and to the Pzkw IV Special.[66]

The German need for improved anti-tank guns was met by the despatch to Africa of a new 75 mm gun (the Pak 40, which was the counter-part of the gun carried by Pzkw IV Special), of an improved version of the ex-Russian 7.62 cm and, beginning in February 1943, of the latest model of the 88 mm Flak gun called Flak 41. With the performance of the first of these guns MI 10 had been familiar since October 1942, when tests carried out in the United Kingdom had shown that it could penetrate 87 mm of armour at 1,500 yards with its capped armour-piercing shell.[67] At the end of December 1942, in a comprehensive report on captured anti-tank guns which drew attention to the fact that the Germans were using a variety of anti-tank and dual purpose anti-aircraft anti-tank guns on self-propelled mountings, it noticed that they were experimenting with two forms of self-propelled armoured mounting for the long 75 mm gun and also referred to the existence of a self-propelled Flak 41.[68] Neither to the Flak 41 nor to the improved 7.62 cm gun are there any further references in the intelligence archives before the end of the Tunisian campaign. But at that stage, presumably as a result of further captures, MI 10 realised that the 88 mm Flak gun mounted in Tiger tanks in Tunisia, the most formidable tank armament yet developed, had been surpassed by the latest version of the 88 mm anti-tank gun, and appears to have suspected that this fact would influence the production of newer versions of the Tiger tank.[69]

This suspicion was to be confirmed in 1944, when MI 10's warning about the enemy's experiments with armoured self-propelled mounting for anti-tank guns was also vindicated. In

---

62. WO 208/2287, No 90 of 26 October 1942; Playfair, op cit, Vol IV, p 500.
63. WO 208/2287, No 95 of 25 December 1942.
64. ibid, No 90 of 26 October 1942.
65. CX/MSS/2253/T1 of 11 March 1943.
66. CX/MSS/1643/T43 of 16 November, 1836/T1 of 14 December 1942.
67. WO 208/2287, No 89 of 17 October 1942.
68. ibid, No 95 of 25 December 1942, Appendix B.
69. WO 208/3580, MEF/6000/MI 10.

Normandy the Allies did indeed encounter Tiger tanks mounting the tank version of the Flak 41, which proved to be more effective than any Allied weapon, and two forms of self-propelled armoured anti-tank gun – the Jagdtiger and the Jagdpanther – which turned out to be the most powerful armoured fighting vehicles yet developed, and it was principally by those means that the Germans had by then regained their lead in armour and armament.[70]*

---

* See Volume III.

70.   ibid; Ellis, *Victory in the West*, Vol I, pp 449–450.

APPENDIX 15

Axis Ship-Watching Activities
in the Gibraltar Area

The Axis naturally employed agents to supplement their chief sources of operational intelligence about Allied shipping, which were Sigint and aerial reconnaissance. The Allies knew from their decryption of the communications of the German secret services, primarily the Abwehr, that most of these agents constituted no danger; either they invented their material, which was a common practice in places like Lisbon and Madrid, or, like those installed in distant ports or Spanish merchant ships, they could not report in time to be useful.[1] But those who exploited Spain's position astride the Straits of Gibraltar were an exception. They could for most of the time observe shipping movements with the naked eye or collect information locally, and report without delay. Of the various forms of war-time assistance the Axis received from Spain,* its freedom to maintain a reporting organisation at the Western entrance to the Mediterranean was operationally the most important.

The Abwehr decrypts enabled Whitehall to observe the growth in the number of these agents and in their efficiency. By the autumn of 1941 they had stations at Algeciras (the most important), Tarifa, Cape Trafalgar, Malaga, Cape de Gata, Tangier, Ceuta, Tetuan, Cape Tres Forcas, Melilla and Alboran Island – though not in Gibraltar itself. Two of these stations were entirely Spanish, but the rest included German and Italian observers apparently in Spanish uniform. By the same time their initially incompetent service had developed into an efficient organisation. Algeciras alone was sending 20 messages a day; signals were usually reaching Berlin within an hour, so that the British Admiralty sometimes received the decrypt of the German report of an arrival in Gibraltar before it received the British notification signal; and except in low visibility

---

* These included the fuelling and repair of U-boats, the granting of W/T intercept and radio beacon facilities and the flying of occasional air reconnaissance on Germany's behalf.[2] Although Spain's assistance was cut back from the end of 1942, it continued on a smaller scale until it lost all operational value. The Germans also used Spanish and Portuguese fishing vessels for the reporting of shipping and weather information, as was also disclosed in Abwehr decrypts; in July 1942 two such vessels were arrested by the Royal Navy and on 1 November the radio operator of another was arrested on the high seas, his ship being then on a course which would have brought her directly into the route of a *Torch* Convoy.

1. Morgan, *NID History*, p 155.
2. ibid, p 156; McLachlan, *Room 39* (1968), p 193.

the reports were accurate to the extent that they usually named major ships correctly.[3] Against this system NID could do little beyond advising Gibraltar that particular arrivals and departures had been reported by the enemy, and the forces on the spot could do no more than sail when visibility was low and adopt evasive tactics based on advice from NID about the limitations of the enemy's reporting stations.*

From the autumn of 1941 the Abwehr decrypts showed that, in order to improve their observations at night and in low visibility, the Germans were installing an ambitious scientific detection system using infra-red or other short-wave apparatus supplemented by special night telescopes.[†] In an undertaking named operation *Bodden*, buildings were erected at nine sites north of the Straits and at five on the southern coast in the next six months, and it emerged that the system was to be brought into force on 15 April 1942.[4] But at least one of the northern stations was working by 28 February 1942, when it accurately reported the departure of Force H, and on 7 March the Admiralty warned the authorities in the area that ships were in future liable to be reported accurately in darkness.

In the second half of May, by which time PR of the new stations had been carried out and the SIS had begun to report,[5] the First Sea Lord proposed an attack on them by submarine. But the Chiefs of Staff, who also considered a landing by Combined Operations, rejected the idea of direct action for fear that it might provoke Spanish counter-action against Gibraltar.[6] Instead, the British Ambassador was instructed to protest to the Spanish government. He insisted on seeing General Franco in person.[7] The Abwehr decrypts thereafter revealed that, despite an attempt by Admiral Canaris to rally Franco, the Spanish government ordered the abandonment of the whole undertaking. An assurance to this effect was given to Sir Samuel Hoare by the Spanish Foreign Minister on 1 July 1942.[8]

---

* Examples were the evasive tactics adopted off Alboran by Force H in November 1941 before the attack on the *Ark Royal* (see above, p 327) and the deceptive course steered through the Straits by the fast convoy for operation *Torch* in November 1942 (see above, p 482).

† The principal method was one by which one or more bolometers used infra-red to detect the heat emissions of passing ships.

3. Morgan, op cit, p 155.
4. ibid, p 155.
5. Jones, *Most Secret War* (1978), p 255.
6. CAB 79/57, COS (42) 140th (o) Meeting, 17 May; Woodward, *British Foreign Policy in the Second World War* Vol IV (1976), p 8.
7. Dir/C Archive, FO/Madrid telegrams Nos 669 of 23 May, 677 and 765 of 25 May 1942, Foreign Secretary minute PM/42/134 of 10 June 1942; McLachlan, op cit, pp 205–206.
8. Woodward, op cit, Vol IV, p 8.

On 16 and 20 July, however, the Admiralty advised Ultra recipients that, although the Germans had for the present abandoned scientific observations, they were looking for new sites for the stations. The decrypts showed that they had already re-sited the bolometer near Algeciras and that since this could detect only movements in and out of Gibraltar, they were hoping to start another station near Ceuta. Within a month the Ceuta station was known to be operational. The stations had detected the passage of the Malta-bound convoy through the Straits in the second week of August despite bad weather and despite the fact that the convoy had been briefed as to how best to avoid them.[9] Following the enemy's attack on this convoy, the Chiefs of Staff on 25 August considered a plan concerted between the Governor of Gibraltar and SOE for putting the stations out of action and a proposal from the First Sea Lord that they should be jammed;[10] but although Whitehall was becoming anxious by then about the threat the stations would pose to operation *Torch*, action was again restricted to an approach to the Spanish government. A protest against the Algeciras and Ceuta stations was lodged in October.[11]

Despite this protest the stations continued to operate, though the files of the Abwehr decrypts do not record what they reported before and during the passage of the *Torch* convoys early in November 1942 or how much they contributed to the heavy German attacks on Allied shipping in the western Mediterranean during November and December 1942. But it was clear at the time that, even without the assistance of the stations, the Germans would detect the pre-*Torch* build-up at Gibraltar and the passage of the *Torch* assault convoys: at the end of September 1942, when they began to get rumours of Allied preparations, they instituted a daily air reconnaissance of Gibraltar* as well as alerting their ship-watchers.

The decrypts showed that the bolometers were dismantled at the end of 1942 and that the Spanish government had told Admiral Canaris on 29 December that all activity 'inimical to the Allies' must cease in order to give no pretext for the Allies to attack Spain. Even this did not dispose of the stations altogether. But, forced back on to visual observations and their trained German observers increasingly replaced by other nationals, they became less and less efficient. In the summer of 1943 the Germans briefly attempted to re-activate the scientific apparatus, but finally abandoned their efforts in July. The last recorded evidence of any activity by the stations was in January 1944.

* See above, p 476.

9. Morgan, op cit, p 156.
10. CAB 79/57, COS (42) 99th (o) Meeting, 25 August.
11. Morgan, op cit, p 156.

APPENDIX 16

Intelligence on Rommel's Dispositions before the Gazala Battle

No Enigma decrypt giving a comprehensive account of the Panzer Army's dispositions was obtained after 30 April 1942; that of 30 April – a Chaffinch decrypt – showed that the bulk of the enemy's armour was in the north, but mentioned that some elements of the DAK were 'at the moment' operating at the south of the line 'to secure the southern flank'.[1] While allowing that this activity in the south might be being undertaken with a view to an 'eastward thrust in future', Cairo judged at this point that it was 'primarily defensive'.[2] The interrogation of a major from Rommel's staff, captured while making a reconnaissance in the south on 29 April, did not alter this judgment. To a member of Eighth Army's staff, who had been disguised as a German officer, he spoke freely about Rommel's methods, but insisted that his reconnaissance had been a defensive measure against the possibility of a British move to outflank the Axis positions in the south; and this was not inconsistent with the documents taken from him.[3] During May it was obvious that German reconnaissance activity and defence construction in the south was continuing. 33rd Reconnaissance Unit was frequently located there by Eighth Army's Y units, which had read its code since the summer of 1941 and had been well aware of its close association with 15th Panzer Division. Some of the reconnaissance was observed by British ground patrols; on 22 and 23 May they reported that it was being carried out by German staff cars and, on 22 May, that an aircraft had picked up one of the German officers in the area.[4] Air reconnaissance provided further evidence. On 16 May Eighth Army drew attention to a tactical reconnaissance report of new camps, diggings and AA and vehicle concentrations in the Asida area and on 21 May, on receiving another tactical reconnaissance report of an unusually extensive concentration of tents and vehicles in the same area, it noted that this was evidence of a redistribution of enemy forces and an indication that

---

1. CX/MSS/939/T12.
2. CAB 105/17, Hist (B) (Crusader) 3, No 97 of 2 May 1942.
3. WO 169/3936, Eighth Army Intelligence Summaries of 3 May and 13 May 1942; WO 169/1005, XIII Corps Intelligence Summaries of 2, 16 and 25 May 1942.
4. WO 169/4033, XXX Corps Intelligence Summaries of 22 and 23 May 1942.

the enemy's interest in the southern desert was increasing.[5] But the extent to which redistribution was taking place remained unclear for lack of firm evidence from the rest of the enemy's lines.

During the second week of May Rommel made fundamental changes in his order of battle. He moved the motor regiments of 90th Light Division – its main fighting units – from the north to the Asida area, where they became the most southerly of his formations, and reversed the positions of the Italian XX (mobile) Corps and X (infantry) Corps so as to have XX Corps in the next most southerly position, next to 90th Light Division. At the same time he transferred HQ DAK and 15th and 21st Panzer Divisions from the north to a position about 20 miles further south, where they were opposite the centre of the British line.[6] Of these moves, which left the non-motorised units of 90th Light Division and the Italian XXI (infantry) Corps in the north, the British obtained only fragmentary information. The Enigma that disclosed on 7 May that the Ariete and Trieste Divisions of XX Corps were taking up the positions of X Corps,[7] hitherto the most southerly of the Axis formations, and that 155th Infantry Regiment – one of the motorised units of 90th Light Division – was being relieved by a regiment from the Trento Division. But it made no reference to the transfer of 90th Light Division's motor units to the south, and their transfer was not suspected when heavy movements in 90th Light Division's area were observed on 10 May: the movements were screened by shellfire and precautions to prevent British air reconnaissance, and Eighth Army concluded that the enemy was reinforcing or relieving his forces in the area.[8] As for the move by the DAK, the Enigma had located its HQ in its new area by 11 May and tactical reconnaissance aircraft made some sightings which suggested that a considerable force was moving into that area from the north between 7 and 9 May.[9] Thereafter, although the enemy opposition prevented all but partial attempts to get reconnaissance cover of the area, and although the Enigma made no reference to the whereabouts of 15th and 21st Panzer Divisions, it was assumed that one of the divisions had reached the new position.[10] From this position, however, which was roughly opposite the centre of the British line, the DAK was equally well placed for either a frontal or a flanking attack. In these circumstances the

---

5. WO 169/3936, of 16 and 21 May 1942.
6. EDS/Appreciation/9, Part III, A, p 53.
7. MK 5188 of 11 May 1942; CX/MSS/968/T12; WO 169/3936 of 21 May 1942; WO 169/4033 of 18 May quoting GHQ MEF's Weekly Review of the Military Situation of 11 May 1942.
8. WO 169/3936 of 11, 12 and 13 May 1942.
9. ibid; MK 5185 of 11 May 1942; CX/MSS/967/T19.
10. WO 169/3936 of 11 and 14 May 1942; WO 169/4033, Minutes of Staff Conference, 12 May 1942; WO 169/1005 of 10, 12 and 13 May 1942.

view that a frontal attack was more likely was supported by the feeling that the other Panzer division remained in the north. This view might have received further support from the numerous references in the Enigma to Rommel's preparations for airborne and seaborne landings as such operations could be more readily co-ordinated with an attack in the north. This feeling was perhaps strengthened when on 18 May a single Enigma decrypt located HQ DAK at Derna on 16 May.[11]* In return, the predisposition to expect a frontal attack perhaps strengthened the conviction that the whole of 90th Light Division remained where it had been located at the end of April.

In appreciations of 19, 20 and 22 May the C-in-C also leaned to this view on operational grounds: although it would be very costly, a frontal attack was the shortest way to Tobruk, whereas in the long detour round the Gazala line the enemy would expend an enormous amount of petrol and incur heavy wear and tear. The order of battle intelligence persuaded him that the frontal attack would be accompanied by a diversion against Bir Hacheim, but he judged that this would be made by Italian XX Corps since this formation had been located in the south and the two German Panzer divisions and elements of 90th Light Division appeared to be still in the northern sector.[12] At Eighth Army and XXX Corps HQs, on the other hand, it was thought at this stage just as likely, and perhaps even more probable, that Rommel would make his major thrust round the flank.[13]

This was the situation when, on 24 May, XIII Corps released what it called 'rather startling information'. It was obtained from an NCO attached to HQ 90th Light Division who was captured in the south on 23 May. He stated that his HQ Company and 90th Light Division's 155th Infantry Regiment were in the south; that 90th Light Division's two other motorised regiments had also moved from the coast to the south of the front; and that a very large number of German tanks – he estimated them at 300 and thought they belonged to 21st Panzer Division – were already concentrated there behind his company's position.[14]

In its comment on this interrogation XIII Corps noted that air reconnaissance in poor conditions during 23 May had indicated

---

* As HQ DAK was never at Derna at this time, this reference was presumably the outcome of a German error or a garbled intercept.

11.   MK 5490 of 18 May 1942; CX/MSS/992/T2.
12.   CAB 105/17, No 121 of 19 May and No 128 of 22 May 1942; Playfair, *The Mediterranean and Middle East*, Vol III (1960), p 218; Carver, *Tobruk* (1964), p 168.
13.   WO 169/3936, of 13 May, sent to XIII Corps and XXX Corps on 17 May 1942; WO 169/4033, Operational Order No 42 of 20 May 1942.
14.   WO 169/1005, 24 May 1942.

considerable north to south movement behind the enemy's line and that 'the possible move of 90th Light Division from its positions on the coast to the opposite flank of the line involves fundamental alterations in an appreciation of the most likely form of the enemy's attack'. But it added that 'beyond the information from this POW there are as yet very few indications that German Infantry [ie the three infantry regiments of 90th Light Division] have left the coast and, until confirmation of this move can be obtained, the possibility that the whole of 90th Light Division is in the south must be accepted with reserve'. As for his reference to 21st Panzer Division, this, too, 'should be treated with reserve'; it conflicted with the evidence that a substantial part of the German armour was still in the north. XIII Corps's conclusion was that 'the main German strength is still NORTH . . . but that Italian XX Corps has been strengthened by a German battle group from 90th Light Division . . .'[15] XXX Corps's view was much the same; it seemed definite that an 'HQ of 90th Light Division' was in the south, but the POW's statement that all the division's infantry regiments were in the south could not 'at present be accepted' and his statement that a large number of German tanks were there was unconvincing.[16]

Eighth Army HQ did not disagree. On 24 May, while admitting that the POW's statement that the division's 155th Infantry Regiment had moved south was supported by the fact that patrols had discovered Italians in 90th Light Division's original position during the night of 23–24 May, it announced that his evidence about 90th Light Division 'should be treated with reserve'.[17] It is a safe conjecture that this conclusion was strongly influenced by a recent reference to the division in the Enigma traffic; on 23 May a decrypt had located its signal's company in the original position, where it had left its non-motorised elements, and at least at GC and CS this 'appeared to indicate the continued presence of the division in that area'.[18] On 26 May, on learning from XIII Corps that the POW was 'still emphatic' that 300 tanks were supporting his division,[19] Eighth Army HQ suggested that since strategic recon- naissance had that morning sighted 30 in the area his figure should 'be divided by ten, although there may be more than those reported by Strat R', and noted that, while his statement that 90th Light Division was due to move south should not be forgotten, the greater frequency of tank sightings in the north still indicated that 'the German armour is in the northern sector'.[20]

15. ibid.   16. WO 169/4033 of 24 May 1942.
17. WO 169/3936 of 24 May 1942.
18. MK 5745 of 24 May 1942; CX/MSS/1008/T16.
19. WO 169/1005 of 26 May 1942.
20. WO 169/3936 of 26 May 1942.

Long after the event the GSO 3 I(a) of XIII Corps, who was present at the interrogation of the POW from 90th Light Division, recalled that the POW gave his information so 'very willingly', and made such 'strenuous efforts to recall as many details as he could', that 'some people thought it might be a plant'.[21] There is no reason to doubt that this suspicion goes far to explain why the information was received with so much caution. Equally clearly, caution was justified so long as the information was supported only by the few scraps of evidence from other sources that we have so far considered. But it has been claimed that Eighth Army HQ received further evidence before the beginning of the battle from the Army's Y organisation, that the evidence consisted of firm indications that Rommel's main thrust would be made in the south, and that Eighth Army gave little consideration to it.

There are several references to this claim in accounts by the intelligence authorities. They all depend on a statement by the Army Y organisation which is unfortunately vague as to when and in what form the evidence was submitted to Eighth Army's operational intelligence staff, and which does not give enough evidence to substantiate its claim that 'the grouping of the enemy and the implications thereof were quite clear from Sigint [ie Y]'. The evidence it provides in support of the claim consists of such items as the detection of W/T linkage between Italian X Corps and the tank regiment of 15th Panzer Division, a week or more before the attack, and the deduction, derived from reading a low-grade German field cypher, that 21st Panzer Division was moving well to the south. It is summarised in the following terms:

'It had been assumed that the German attack . . . would be delivered in the coastal sector from the west, and the Sigint indications of concentrations in the south were treated merely as showing apprehensiveness on the part of the enemy of an exposed flank. Sigint deduction further indicated that 21st Panzer Division was moving south.

These deductions were discredited, and when tactical reconnaissance reported vehicles, diggings, tracks and bivouacs in the old 21st Division area, it was assumed that Sigint must be wrong. In fact an elementary piece of deception had been achieved, and if reconnaissance had been made further south, the division would have been seen.

Enemy dispositions as seen by I(a) [Eighth Army's operational intelligence staff] and Sigint were widely divergent. Whereas the former believed that 21st Panzer Division and 90th Light Division and most of 15th Panzer Division were in the north preparing for a frontal attack . . ., Sigint sources had revealed that a large proportion of 15th Panzer Division and most at least of X Italian Corps, together with certainly some infantry elements of 90th Light Division, were in the south and that 21st Panzer Division had made a two-day journey almost certainly into the same sector, the object of the manoeuvre being fairly clearly the

---

21.   Hunt, *A Don at War* (1966), p 100.

outflanking of the minefield and of our own forward troops in the coastal sector.'

As stated, the claim that the Y evidence in itself left no reasonable doubt that Rommel intended to make his main attack in the south may be questioned. But it may be accepted that the evidence at least pointed in this direction, and that Eighth Army HQ was at fault in not marrying it with the information obtained from the POW on 23 May. From the account of the use of Sigint in the field by one of Eighth Army's operational intelligence officers it is clear, indeed, that GS Int Eighth Army recognised its mistake after Rommel had begun his attack. He not only concedes that the Y organisation was successful in locating 21st Panzer Division before the Gazala battle, when other intelligence sources had lost it,[22] but also confirms a statement in the Army Y organisation's report to the effect that from the early stages of the Gazala battle Eighth Army took steps to ensure that 'such blunders did not occur again'. The intelligence staffs of its Y groups – the men who were responsible for interpreting the Y evidence – were more closely integrated with its operational intelligence staffs. Except that the Y officers continued to be denied access to the Enigma, they were from that date made free of the information that the operational intelligence staff was receiving from other sources. The operational intelligence staff encouraged the Y staff to reciprocate.[23] It also took care to disseminate Y intelligence, as may be judged from Eighth Army's intelligence summaries. These now became full of information from low-grade Sigint. Up to 26 May, in contrast, they had carried no Y information relevant to Rommel's coming attack, with the result that while the Y intelligence officers at Eighth Army HQ had remained unaware of the evidence of the POW taken on 23 May – as they were unaware of the fact that Eighth Army was making desperate but unsuccessful efforts to locate the enemy's armour by air reconnaissance – XIII and XXX Corps and GHQ in Cairo had remained unaware of the Y information produced at Eighth Army HQ when considering the POW's evidence.

---

22. WO 208/3575, Williams, 'The Use of Sigint in the Army', p 7.
23. ibid, p 9.

APPENDIX 17

Contribution of Sigint to Axis Shipping Losses on North African Routes June to October 1942

Notes: (1) Shipping details below are taken from a captured document; every Axis ship there recorded as lost on north Africa traffic between June and October 1942 has been included. Signal details are a selection of the most valuable signals from GC&CS conveying Special Intelligence relating to shipping to Middle East Commands.

(2) ETA = Estimated time of arrival; ETD = Estimated time of departure; RV = Rendezvous.

(3) Dates are in the form 2/6 (= 2nd June) throughout.

	SHIPPING DETAILS				SIGNAL DETAILS		
Ship	G R T	Date Sunk	Where Sunk	Cause of Loss	Sigint References	Time of Origin	Summary of Text
ALLEGRI	6,836	2/6	Approaching Benghazi	Bombs	MK 5949 ZTPI 10268	2030/28/5	Due to leave for Tripoli 29/5.
GIULIANI	6,837	4/6	En route to Benghazi	Aircraft torpedo	MK 6114 ZTPI 10424 MK 6133 ZTPI 10445	1725/31/5 0124/1/6	Giuliani convoy postponed; route given. Escorting steamship Giuliani, torpedo-boats Pegaso and Partenope due Benghazi 4/6.
REICHENFELS	7,744	21/6	In area Pantelleria	Bombs	MK 7035 ZTPI 11222 MK 7087 ZTPI 11274	0715/19/6 0520/20/6	Due to arrive Tripoli 1930/21/6. Route given. Sailed from Naples 0030/20/6.
S. ANTONIA	1,480	23/6	Gulf of Sirte	Torpedo	MK 7164 MK 7234	0337/21/6 0519/22/6	In Circe convoy. ETA Benghazi 1030/24/6. Route given. Left Tripoli as arranged.

728

Ship	Tonnage	Date	Location	Cause	Reference	Date/Time	Remarks
REGULUS	1,085	24/6	Off Ghemines	Torpedo	MK 7164 ZTPI 11309, 11312	0337/21/6	In Circe convoy. To leave Tripoli 1700/21/6. ETA Benghazi 1030/24/6. Route given.
					MK 7234 ZTPI 11372	0519/22/6	Left Tripoli as arranged.
AVIONIA	1,122	26/6	Candia (Crete)	Fire	MK 7484 ZTPI 11594, 11596	0329/26/6	To leave Candia 0400/26/6. ETA Tobruk 1300/28. Route given.
					MK 7500 ZTPI 11610	1055/26/6	Departure postponed twenty-four hours due to loading difficulties.
					MK 7505 ZTPI 11615	1327/26/6	Morning 26th, on fire in Candia harbour.
SAVONA	2,120	28/6	Near Benghazi	Ran aground	MK 7714 CX/MSS/1132/T26	2047/28/6	To leave Benghazi 1700/28 for Tobruk.
					MK 7750 ZTPI 11787	0307/29/6	At 2100/28/6 ran aground near Sidi Sueiker.
BROOK	1,325	11/7	Mersa Matruh	Bombs	MK 8554 MK 9364 CX/MSS/1210/T34, 1211/T1 and 7	1025/9/7 18/7	Proceeding Mersa Matruh. Fuel shortage caused by loss of.
MAX BERENDT	766	11/7	Tobruk	Bombs			No evidence in Special Intelligence.
STURLA	1,397	12/7	Mersa Matruh	Torpedo	MK 8554 ZTPI 12475 MK 9364	1025/9/7 18/7	Proceeding to Mersa Matruh with Brook. Fuel shortage caused by loss of.
CITTA DI AGRIGENTO (Troopship)	2,480	20/7	Mersa Matruh	Aerial and naval attack	MK 9371 CX/MSS/1211/T21	1444/19/7	British air and naval bombardment of Mersa Matruh on 18th caused no damage to.
					MK 9594 CX/MSS/1220/T22	22/7	During bombardment on 20th, received four hits. Stern resting on bottom.

	SHIPPING DETAILS				SIGNAL DETAILS		
Ship	G R T	Date Sunk	Where Sunk	Cause of Loss	Sigint References	Time of Origin	Summary of Text
VETTOR PISANI	6,339	24/7	Off Cephalonia	Aircraft torpedo	MK 9637 ZTPI 13356	1701/22/7	Escorted by Antares, ETD Taranto 1000/23/7. Due Otranto 1800/28/7. 14 knots. Escort to be relieved at Sta. Maria di Leuca by Orsa and Calliope. ETA Navarino 1600/24/7.
					MKA 290 CX/MSS/1234/T4	26/7	Cargo: Army: 440 tons fuel, 548 mixed. Air Force: 488 tons fuel, 75 mixed. Navy: 50 tons fuel, 25 mixed.
DELOS	2,589	damaged 12/7 sunk 30/7	Tobruk	Bombs	MK 8650 MK 8970 MKA 630 ZTPI 12555, 12781, 140341 14036	1927/10/7 14/7 30/7	Arrived Tobruk at 1130/10/7. Immobilised by bomb. Hit by bomb, resting on bottom.
MONVISO	5,322	3/8	Off Benghazi	Submarine	MKA 553 ZTPI 13955	2045/29/7	Repairs to – at Navarino expected completed in about five days.
					MKA 865 MKA 900 CX/MSS/1258/T13 ZTPI 14239	1430/3/8 0131/4/8	Due Benghazi afternoon 2/8. Now known to have been due p.m. 3/8.
WACHTFELS	8,467	7/8	North-west of Milos	Submarine	MKA 914 ZTPI 14257 MKA 1079 CX/MSS/1254/T5, 1266/T16 MKA 1221 ZTPI 14581	0410/4/8 0539/6/8 1909/7/8	Leaving Suda for Tobruk 8/8 or 9/8. On 10.5 centimetre battery being loaded on. Convoy left Suda at 1710/6/8.

Ship	Tons	Date	Position	Cause of loss	Sigint references	Time of origin	Remarks
OGADEN	4,553	12/8	Off Ras el Tin (between Derna and Tobruk)	Submarine	MKA 1431	0158/10/8	Arrived Benghazi 9/8.
					MKA 1607	0233/12/8	To be off Derna at 0430/12/8. On passage to Tobruk. Speed 9 knots. Coastal route.
					CX/MSS/1278/T2, 1284/T7		Details of rendezvous of convoy and route to be taken. ETA Benghazi 0600/14/8.
LERICI	6,070	15/8	34°50′ North 21°30′ East	Submarine	MKA 1375 ZTPI 14732	0712/9/8	Convoy now to sail on 14th with route and time-table as in MKA 1375, but with forty-eight hours' delay. Due Benghazi 0600/16/8.
					MKA 1754 ZTPI 15050	1801/13/8	Details of German Air Force cargo.
					MKA 1686 CX/MSS/1286/T18	2230/12/8	
ROSALINO PILO	8,326	17/8	Off Pantelleria	Aircraft torpedo	MKA 1833 CX/MSS/1291/T13	1429/14/8	Ready to sail 12th. Cargo details included in tons: 431 diesel, 591 ammunition, 233 motor transport and tank spare parts, 917 rations, also guns and motor transport, including 3 tanks Mark III. Escorted by Maestrale and Gioberti to leave Trapani at 0400/17, ETA Tripoli 1030/18, 15 knots. Route given.
					MKA 2012 ZTPI 5262	1953/16/8	Position of convoy at 1200/27/8 given.
MANFREDO CAMPERIO	5,463	27/8	35 miles west of Cape Spada	Submarine	QT 100 CX/MSS/1330/T13	0003/27/8	Proceeding towards Benghazi. Speed 10 knots.
					QT 389 CX/MSS/1343/T13	1344/30/8	Cargo details.

SHIPPING DETAILS — SIGNAL DETAILS

Ship	G R T	Date Sunk	Where Sunk	Cause of Loss	Sigint References	Time of Origin	Summary of Text
ISTRIA	5,416	27/8	Off Ras el Tin	Bombs	QT 100 CX/MSS/1330/T13	0003/27/8	Position at 0300/27 given; proceeding towards Tobruk at 8 knots.
DIELPI	1,527	27/8	33°38' North 21°23' East	Bombs	QT 106 CX/MSS/1330/T13	0003/27/8	Position at 1200/27 given; proceeding towards Benghazi at 7 knots.
PAOLINA	4,894	27/8	Off Cape Bon	Mine	MKA 2634 ZTPI 15729	1123/24/8	Sagittario to escort Paolina from Sfax to Palermo by inshore route.
					MKA 2701 ZTPI 15805	0155/25/8	Sagittario to rendezvous Paolina at limits of French territorial waters off Sfax at 0400/26/8.
Tanker SAN ANDREA	5,077	30/8	39°49' North 18°15' East	Bombs, fire	QT 229 CX/MSS/1335/T29	0844/28/8	Loading at Taranto with army fuel, German and Italian. Loading to cease by p.m. 29/8. To leave at once for Tobruk arriving there 3/9.
					QT 425 CX/MSS/1346/T27	2139/30/8	Torpedoed and on fire. Cargo included 3,000 tons [believed cbm. meant] Otto fuel for Panzer Army Africa.
Tanker PICCI FASSIO	2,261	2/9	Off Derna	Bombs	QT 232 CX/MSS/1335/T29	0918/28/8	Cargo: 1,150 tons Italian army petrol 990 tons gas oil 800 tons paraffin.

(ISTRIA and DIELPI) Carrying in all 730 tons of fuel, 170 vehicles, and other supplies. QT 396

Picci Fassio contd

Ship	Tonnage	Date	Location	Cause	References	Time/date	Remarks
Picci Fassio contd					QT 581 CX/MSS/1354/T28	0105/2/9	Position of convoy and course at 0330/2/9 given. Due Tobruk 1600 hours.
DAVIDE BIANCHI	1,477	4/9	Off Tobruk	Aircraft torpedo	QT 695 CX/MSS/1362/T17	1956/3/9	Position of convoy at 0400/4/9 and course given, proceeding by coastal route to Tobruk. Cargo includes 960 tons German army fuel, 120 tons Italian army fuel.
PADENNA	1,589	4/9	Off Tobruk	Bombs	QT 747 DEFE 3/580, ZTPGM 154, 158, 160	1842/4/9	Ready to sail 2/9 with 340 cbm. Otto fuel and 60 cbm. diesel. Further cargo details.
					QT 417 CX/MSS/1244/T30, 1346/T1 QT 695 CX/MSS/1362/T17	2254/30/8 1956/3/9	Position of convoy at 0400/4/9 and course given; proceeding by coastal route to Tobruk.
ALBACHIARA	1,245	5/9	Ras el Tin	Submarine	QT 768 CX/MSS/1367/T16 QT 844 CX/MSS/1272/T7	0419/5/9 1206/6/9	By 1830/4/9 had left Benghazi for Tobruk. Sunk with 500 tons ammunition and rations.
CARBONIA	1,237	17/9	Ras Hammamet	Bombs	QT 1410 CX/MSS/1047/T8 and 11 QT 1514 ZTPI 17382	0448/15/9 1846/16/9	Left Naples 12/9. Cargo included 310 tons fuel. ETD Tunis 2200/16, passing Cape Bon 0600/17 then resume routeing laid down (to Tripoli).
LEONARDO PALOMBA	1,110	22/9	Off Kuriat island	Submarine	QT 1801 DEFE 3/186, ZTPG 75354 QT 1905 ZTPI 17748	1702/20/9 0544/22/9	To leave Palermo for Tripoli 2000/18/9. Driven aground in Gulf of Hammamet about 17/9; refloated 0900/21/9.

SHIPPING DETAILS   SIGNAL DETAILS

Ship	G R T	Date Sunk	Where Sunk	Cause of Loss	Sigint References	Time of Origin	Summary of Text
APUANIA	7,949	22/9	Benghazi	Bombs	QT 1533 ZTPI 17392, 17393, 17397 QT 1586 QT 1594 QT 1826 QT 1879 ZTPI 17463, 17464, 17475, 17676 CX/MSS/1429/T30 and 34	0214/17/9 2104/17/9 2312/17/9 0043/21/9 2257/21/9	Leaving Brindisi 1410/18/9. Escorts, route and speed given. Leaving Brindisi 1800/18/9. Route modified. Arrived Benghazi by 1500/20/9. Cargo details including 626 tons ammunition for Panzer Army Africa, 10 tanks, 465 tons bombs, ammunition for German Air Force. Note: most of cargo was destroyed in raid.
FRANCESCO BARBARO	6,343	27/9	Off Navarino	Submarine	QT 2480 CX/MSS/1459/T3	30/9	(1) No evidence in Special Intelligence prior to sailing. (2) Cargo included for Army: 489 tons ammunition 480 tons rations 96 tons mixed. For German Air Force: 553 tons ammunition 280 tons mixed. also 9 tanks Mark III, 9 self-propelled guns.
NINO BIXIO	7,137	1/10	Navarino roads	Aircraft torpedo	MKA 1914 ZTPI 15177	1822/15/8	ETD Benghazi 0500/16/8, ETA Brindisi 0100/18/8. Details of route and air escort.

Name	Gross tons total	Date	Position	Cause	References	Times	Remarks
					MKA 2028 CX/MSS/1298/ T29 and 33	0101/17/8	Position of convoy at 0300/17/8 given. Note: She was hit by a submarine torpedo off Cape Sapienza on 17/8 and towed into Navarino. Hit again in Navarino roads on 1/10, this time by an aircraft torpedo, she was abandoned. Refloated in August 1943, she was finally sunk as a blockship at Venice.
KRETA	2,359	8/10	Off Ras Hilal	Submarine	QT 2974 ZTPI 18383, DEFE 3/581, ZTPGM 1631	1058/7/10	Kreta and Calliope to leave Tobruk 0500/7/10 for Benghazi. Speed 5.5 knots. Positions given. ETA Benghazi 0730/9.
DANDOLO	4,964	8/10	Off Ras el Tin	Aircraft torpedo	QT 2899 CX/MSS/1484/ T16 and 18 QT 3006	0836/6/10 2150/7/10	Details of German Air Force cargo. Constant protection from first light until arrival Tobruk. Position of convoy 0400/8 given. Speed 8.5 knots.
ALGA	1,851	10/10	Ras Turguenes	Submarine			No evidence in Special Intelligence up to time of sinking.
LORETO	1,055	13/10	Cape Gallo	Submarine	QT 3044 ZTPI 18784 QT 3053 ZTPI 18784 QT 3129 ZTPI 18869 QT 3399 CX/MSS/1516/ T18 and 9	0746/8/10 1044/8/10 1508/9/10 1721/13/10	ETD Tripoli 0700/9/10, ETA Naples 0530/13/10. Route given. 7 knots. To carry about 350 prisoners (Indian). Tripoli confirms Loreto left at 0320/9. Cargo details.

SHIPPING DETAILS / SIGNAL DETAILS

Ship	G R T	Date Sunk	Where Sunk	Cause of Loss	Sigint References	Time of Origin	Summary of Text
AMSTERDAM	8,673	15/10	Misurata	Bombed and then torpedoed by submarine	QT 3425 CX/MSS/1520/T5	0221/14/10	Route of convoy given for 14/10.
					QT 3662	2244/16/10	Tripoli to arrange salvage of fuel oil on board.
					ZTPI 19325, 19332	0825/23/10	Salvaging operations going well. To be taken in tow early 24/10.
					QT 4141 ZTPI 19749, 19751	24/10	At 1400/23 hit by two torpedoes from submarine.
					QT 4203 ZTPI 19799		Vessel now resting on bottom.
BEPPE (Troopship)	4,859	18/10	Off Lampedusa	Submarine	QT 3675	0258/17/10	ETD Naples 1400/17/10. 8 knots; to RV another convoy at 1030/18/10. Combined convoy due Tripoli 1100/20/10. Route given.
					QT 3678 ZTPI 19346	0505/17/10	
TITANIA (Troopship)	5,397	20/10	Between Lampedusa and Tripoli	Aircraft torpedo then submarine torpedo	QT 3675 ZTPI 19346	0258/17/10	ETD Naples 1400/17/10. 8 knots. To RV convoy at 1030/18/10. Combined convoy due Tripoli 1100/20/10. Route given.
Tanker PROSERPINA	4,869	26/10	Off Tobruk	Set afire by bombs	QT 4211 DEFE 3/582, ZTPGM 2441	0442/24/10	Details of fuel cargo in tons: 888 B4 for German Air Force; 2,500 Otto for Panzer Army Africa; 1,165 Otto for Italians.
					QT 4300 DEFE 3/582, ZTPGM 2503	0352/25/10	Convoy due Tobruk 1500/26, or at 0800/26 if no stop at Ras Hilal. Route given. Speed 9 knots.

Proserpina contd

Ship	Tonnage	Date	Location	Cause	Reference	Time	Details
TERGESTEA	5,890	26/10	Near Tobruk	Aircraft torpedo	QT 4406 ZTPI 19956	0930/26/10	Convoy passed Derna at 0430/26 as arranged.
					QT 4300 QT 4406 DEFE 3/582, ZTPGM 2503, ZTPI 19956	0352/25/10 0930/26/10	Details as for Proserpina above.
Tanker LUISIANO	2,550	28/10	Off Navarino	Aircraft torpedo	QT 4201 CX/MSS/1571/T9	0124/24/10	To leave Italy for Africa with Porto Fino; to arrive on date Proserpina arrives Tobruk. Cargo to be 2,500 tons army fuel.
					QT 4424 DEFE 3/582, ZTPGM 2597	1754/26/10	Left Taranto 1700/26/10 with 1,460 tons Otto fuel.
					QT 4578 CX/MSS/1591/T19, ZTPI 20104	1616/26/10	ETD Navarino 1600/28. 7.5 knots. ETA Benghazi 1600/30. Route given.
					QT 4626 ZTPI 20152	0434/29/10	Sunk at 2200/28.
TRIPOLINO	1,464	1/11	Between Derna and Tobruk	Aircraft torpedo	QT 4790 DEFE 3/582, ZTPGM 2820	2048/30/10	Tripolino and Ostia to leave Benghazi for Tobruk 1400/30. Speed and route given.
					QT 4861 QT 4864 CX/MSS/1609/T4	1605/31 1717/31	Left Benghazi 1500/30. Tripolino cargo included: 440 tons rations 318 tons ammunition. Ostia cargo included: 57 tons rations 52 tons ammunition.
OSTIA	?	1/11	En route Tobruk	Aircraft torpedo	See above	See above	See above.

| | SHIPPING DETAILS | | | | | SIGNAL DETAILS | |
Ship	G R T	Date Sunk	Where Sunk	Cause of Loss	Sigint References	Time of Origin	Summary of Text
ZARA	1,976	2/11	Off Derna	Aircraft torpedo	QT 4959 QT 5059 CX/MSS/1613/T23, 1619/T1	2111/1/11 0014/3/11	Route given. Steps to be taken at Tobruk on 3rd to tow in Zara, which by 2030/2/11 had been torpedoed.
					QT 5083, DEFE 3/583, ZTPGM 3024	0516/3/11	By 2200/2/11, Zara had sunk about 27 miles from Tobruk.
BRIONI	1,987	2/11	Tobruk	Bombed and blew up	QT 4915 CX/MSS/1610/T14	0630/1/11	Brioni with 255 tons and arriving Africa 2/11.
					QT 5051 CX/MSS/1618/T36	2234/2/11	During air raid on Tobruk 1450/2/11, Brioni blown up.
					QT 3712 CX/MSS/1537/ T1 and 7	1554/17/10	Cargo envisaged: 3,000 tons Otto fuel 2,000 tons B4 aviation spirit.
PORTO FINO	6,424	6/11	Benghazi	Bombed and fired	QT 5392 CX/MSS/1634/ T23 and 26	1112/6/11	Harbour protection provided by German Air Force Staff Libya 4/11 for arrival Porto Fino.
					QT 5477 CX/MSS/1639/T41	0729/7/11	At Benghazi received direct hit 1400/6/11 and set on fire.
ETIOPIA	2,153	6/11	Tobruk	Fire	QT 5162 CX/MSS/1624/T9	0235/4/11	By 1700/3/11 had arrived Tobruk.
					QT 5387	1001/6/11	To be ready to leave 8/11.
					QT 5491 ZTPI 2065I; DEFE 3/583, ZTPGM 3258	1205/7/11	During air-raid on Tobruk 1430/6/11 Etiopia, in which remained 341 tons B4 aviation spirit, hit and set on fire.

Sigint Arrangements before and during the Tunisian Campaign

The selection and organisation of the intelligence staff for AFHQ took account of the fact that high-grade Sigint would be available and would be transmitted direct from GC and CS on an SCU/SLU link. Headed by a British Brigadier as Assistant Chief of Staff G-2, the staff included personnel from GC and CS to advise it on the handling, interpretation and operational use of the SCU/SLU material. An officer from GC and CS's Naval Section was attached for this purpose as SO (Y) to the Naval Commander Expeditionary Force (NCXF). Another officer from GC and CS was appointed Chief Air Intelligence Officer (CAIO) and given executive authority over the intelligence staffs at the two subordinate air commands, the British Eastern Air Command and the Twelfth US Army Air Force; and not only did he have assistants selected from AI and Fighter Command, but also an officer from GC and CS's Air Section to undertake the fusion of the high-grade Sigint with the low-grade air traffic that would be exploited in the theatre. GC and CS also provided two people from its Air Section to exploit Vichy Air Force tactical traffic at AFHQ. However, apart from the AC of S, G-2, himself, who had had some experience with it both in MI and at Home Forces HQ, AFHQ's intelligence staff did not include anyone skilled in the use of Army Sigint. The Army did not participate in the joint intelligence reporting centre which was set up at AFHQ by the Chief Air Intelligence Officer and the naval SO (Y) and which issued both immediate and long-term assessments of the air and maritime situations.

Until the Mediterranean part of the expedition had cleared Gibraltar the Admiralty sent the high-grade Sigint by Ultra signal to the naval commanders of the Western (Casablanca), Central (Oran) and Eastern (Algiers) Task Forces. Once the Mediterranean assault convoys passed 3° west the intention was that the naval commanders and Force H would receive the Sigint from NCXF, who would himself receive it from GC and CS on the direct SCU/SLU link to AFHQ. The service to AFHQ was inaugurated on 4 November, by which time NCXF, the operational commanders who were to serve ashore in Africa and part of the operational intelligence staff of AFHQ had arrived in Gibraltar. It was at once discovered that AFHQ had been provided with too little SCU/

SLU staff and equipment to enable it to handle the volume of intelligence that was transmitted to it, which included summaries of what was being learned about Rommel's retreat and the air situation throughout the Mediterranean, as well as intelligence directly affecting the convoys and, during the landings, much Sigint from local French sources. Nor was it until just before the landings were completed that the SCU/SLU organisation overcame the shortages and eliminated other difficulties, such as the fact that the GC and CS messages had to be carried by officer runner for a mile to AFHQ. Fortunately, however, the Admiralty continued during this interval to send out urgent intelligence by Ultra signal direct to the authorities afloat.

The arrangements made for transmitting high-grade intelligence to the Allied Army commands* after the landings similarly envisaged that it would be sufficient for GC and CS to send the material to AFHQ, which would select what it wished to forward to SCU/SLU units attached to the Eastern, the Central and the Western Task Forces. In the event, no SCU/SLU unit was sent with the Western Task Force to Casablanca and on 17 November, by which time it had transpired that it was not needed at Oran, the unit sent with the Central Task Force was transferred to Algiers. But delays were encountered in forwarding intelligence to the Eastern Task Force from Gibraltar, where it had to be paraphrased and re-encyphered before being transmitted to the SCU/SLU unit at Algiers. From 17 November, moreover, the 'unforeseen eventuality' that an additional SCU/SLU unit had to accompany First Army from Algiers created greater problems. Although the SCU/SLU party from Oran was attached to First Army, it received intelligence via Algiers; and Algiers, which had itself received it with delay caused by re-encypherment at Gibraltar, again re-encyphered it before transmitting it further forward. This double delay was eliminated from 25 November, when AFHQ and the SCU/SLU HQ moved from Gibraltar to Algiers, but other difficulties remained. SCU/SLU personnel and equipment in Algiers and with First Army was insufficient for the amount of traffic, which continued to be much heavier than had been expected. And after he had gone forward from Algiers, General Anderson, First Army commander, was moving about so much that it is impossible to say to what extent, if at all, he saw the intelligence which was forwarded to his SLU unit. These difficulties appear to have been largely overcome by early in December, by which time First Army was provided with two SCU/SLU units – one at its main HQ at Constantine and the other at General Anderson's command post at Ain Senour. By then, however, the

---

* See below, p 741.

critical period had passed, and the Axis powers had succeeded in reinforcing their bridgehead in Tunisia and consolidating their position there.

Once the initial difficulties with it had been overcome, the SCU/SLU service in north-west Africa worked well enough. Until February 1943 it preserved the principle that high-grade Sigint was transmitted by GC and CS only to AFHQ which re-transmitted selected items to First Army and other forward authorities. In February doubts harboured by Whitehall about the security of the high-grade material in the forward area were finally set aside[1] and arrangements were made for two newly formed commands – HQ Northwest African Air Forces and HQ 18th Army Group – to receive high-grade Sigint from GC and CS direct. Such a service continued, however, to be withheld from First Army. Except that he was for a time supplied from 18th Army Group, General Anderson continued to depend on signals from Algiers. It was not until April that he finally received high-grade Sigint direct from GC and CS.

The original inefficiency of the arrangements for transmitting high-grade intelligence, for reasons which may be subsumed under the fact that the Allies were unprepared for the nature and the scale of the enemy resistance they encountered, applied also to the organisation set up for the exploitation of tactical Sigint in the field, and this organisation took longer to get into its stride.

The planning of this part of the preparations for the campaign was undertaken by British Y authorities in co-operation with ETOUSA's signals section and the US Colonel who was to command the US field units in north Africa. They arranged that US officers should be trained at Army and Air Force Y units in the United Kingdom, and by MI 8, during the summer of 1942 and that these officers should in turn train the US Y units that were being formed for the operations. They further arranged that Cheadle should supply the solutions to the GAF low-grade codes direct to the US and the RAF Y units in the field,[2] and that a special section should be formed at GC and CS to help them to exploit the medium and low-grade codes and cyphers of the German Army by signalling cryptanalytic advice to them. To cover the period before and during the landings Cheadle's service to the Y units was extended to the HQ ship of the Eastern Task Force, *HMS Bulolo*, and to *HMS Duke of York*, the Force H flagship. The need for an HQ ship and the importance of collating GAF Sigint with radar information on the spot, during operations, had been among the lessons learned at Dieppe. *Bulolo* and *Duke of York* were

1. Dir/C Archive, 2364 of 22 February 1943, covering SCU 172 of 20 February 1943.
2. Air Historical Branch, *Air Ministry Intelligence*, p 63.

accordingly each provided with an RAF Y group which was trained to exploit GAF low-grade traffic with Cheadle's help; and *Bulolo* and three other ships were also given naval parties for the interception of enemy R/T on VHF, the value of which had been learned by experience during operations in support of Arctic and Malta convoys.[3] For the co-ordination and supervision of Y after the landings the CAIO at AFHQ, with his specialised staff, was made responsible on the air side. For the same work on the army side AFHQ was provided with a large section, Sigs I, G 2, AFHQ,* and it was intended that a similar section, I (s), should be attached to HQ First Army.

Despite the trouble taken to provide seaborne Y parties, neither W/T nor R/T produced noteworthy results during the actual landing operations. The *Bulolo* failed to receive Cheadle's signals, and it turned out that her W/T and R/T groups were too inexperienced, and perhaps too seasick, to be able to cope unaided. This mishap was of no great consequence: until 8 November, when the landings had been completed, the GAF concentrated its attacks on Force H and left the Algiers convoy alone. But it was otherwise with the problems which were encountered when, with the Allied advance to Tunisia, it was discovered that the Y units were inexperienced and poorly equipped and that the staff appointed to AFHQ and First Army HQ to direct their work was also inadequate.

The US Y units turned out to have had little training; such were their deficiencies that in January 1943 they had to be stiffened by British Y staff or temporarily integrated into the British units.[4] But the British units themselves were not much less inexperienced or any better organised during the first crucial month after the landings.

During that month, when the RAF in Algiers had no radar and warnings of enemy air attack from low-grade Sigint would have been especially valuable, the RAF units were in the first place slow to get into action. No 380 Wireless Unit arrived at Algiers on 12 November, but it did not become operational there until 20 November and did not begin to receive Cheadle's signals till 27 November. No official account of its activities has survived. But contemporary comments all point to the fact that its improvised staff was poorly trained, and the GC and CS officer who had been attached to AFHQ to undertake the fusion of low-grade Sigint with the SCU/SLU material reported that its effectiveness was 'extremely limited', partly because of poor interception conditions,

---

* Hereafter called I (s), AFHQ, the British term for it.

3. Roskill, *The War at Sea*, Vol II (1957), p 322.

4. WO 204/938, AFHQ A/COS G-2 Report of 17 March 1943, Intelligence Lessons from North Africa, p 10, para 23 (e).

and its communications 'lousily organised'. Until No 380 Wireless Unit was operational the naval R/T and the RAF W/T parties in the *Bulolo* did what they could with GAF traffic, and provided occasional warning of GAF attacks before the establishment of the radar early warning; but the service they provided was limited.* In addition, the RAF Y unit at Gibraltar is reported to have supplied AFHQ with 'extremely useful information on the GAF picture' and in an effort to improve the service at Algiers some of its staff was sent there when interception conditions at Gibraltar became poor.[6] Cheadle also did what it could to make up for the theatre's deficiencies by starting a special series of signals to Algiers in which, on the basis of such tactical air traffic as could be intercepted in the UK, it provided intelligence about the movements of individual enemy aircraft. Not surprisingly, however, this service was of little value for operational purposes.

Forward of Algiers no exploitation of low-grade air Sigint was undertaken before mid-December, when, again with disappointing results at first, an R/T unit was established on each of the two Allied forward airfields. Nor was it until January 1943, when the second RAF Y unit, No 381 Wireless Unit, was set up at Bône, that the GAF's tactical W/T transmissions were intercepted east of Algiers. Thereafter the service steadily improved, though there is no evidence that it made any substantial contribution to the fighting before March, when it began to have the help of Y experts from the Middle East. By mid-December, however, First Army had lost the race for Tunis and by January it had given up all hope of an early renewal of its advance; and while moving forward in the period up to the beginning of December the ground forces appear to have received no tactical Sigint warnings of the enemy air attacks which played so large a part in holding them up.

Ship-borne R/T was proving useful in giving advance information on enemy E-boats seeking to attack Allied convoys off the African coast from the beginning of 1943. By contrast, until February 1943, when experienced men arrived from Heliopolis and Eighth Army and it began to be the principle source of intelligence, Army Y has been described as being in 'disorder and confusion'. Over and above an all-American Army Y unit for the Casablanca force and a mixed US–British unit for Oran, neither of which had anything to do during the first phase of the campaign, British units were provided for First Army HQ and for the HQs of its two formations, V Corps and IX Corps. But since the planners had

---

* On the occasion of the first big GAF raid of 20 November on Algiers, however, the warning given by RAF Y in the *Bulolo* helped the defenders to reduce the severity of the raid.[5]

5. AIR 40/2323, Humphreys, The Use of Ultra in the Mediterranean and North-West African Theatres of War, p 10.
6. ibid, p 10.

decreed that these, the first such units to be involved in what might be an opposed landing, should be split in halves and loaded in different convoys for the passage, nearly a month had elapsed before any of them was fully operational. First Army's unit was not completely disembarked till 11 December and did not join First Army HQ, then at Constantine, till the end of the year. Part of V Corps's unit was landed on 12 November; but it 'could not assume its operational role until the arrival of its complementary part', and that did not take place till 8 December. Nor was it till late in December that the Sigint authorities in the theatre set up a local Y Board and embarked on attempts to improve matters in the forward areas by drawing on the unused resources at Casablanca and Oran, and in other ways.

It is scarcely necessary to look beyond these initial delays in order to account for the fact that before the Allied advance was halted and reversed, 'little intelligence was produced' by Army Y. Even after the middle of December, however, it remained ineffective until reinforcements were pulled in from the Middle East, and this was for reasons which further illustrate the incompetence or the misplaced optimism of the Sigint planners. No plan had been worked out in advance for co-operation between the US Y units and those with First Army. Among the staffs attached to First Army 'no one . . . had experience of Sigint in the field, and few of any Sigint at all'. The Y units themselves had been hastily assembled and poorly trained,* and they were sent out without all the available documentation and technical data that was relevant to their work. No less important, the I (s) section of AFHQ that was responsible for directing and co-ordinating their work was equally inexperienced, while the all-important I (s) section at First Army HQ was not effectively manned until January 1943. In the Middle East the Sigint authorities had found it essential to develop a Special Wireless Group which monitored the enemy's communications network throughout the theatre, so that CBME could identify the codes and cyphers in use and attack those which the field units could not exploit, and Eighth Army's I (s) section collated the intercepts of all the Army's Y units in order to ensure that the units were at all times following the most profitable interception programme. In the *Torch* theatre no Special Wireless Group had been provided for the first of these tasks and First Army's Y unit had to try to undertake it when it should have been concentrating on the tactical traffic that was of greatest use to First Army. The second of these tasks could not be undertaken before 1943.

To make matters worse, although it was well known that in the

---

* See above, p 742.

desert campaigns the Enigma communications between the German Army HQ and its subordinate formations were transmitted on medium frequencies which could be intercepted only with difficulty outside the forward area, the Sigint plan for Tunisia had committed what has been called the 'serious mistake' of making no provision for intercepting this traffic in the field or at Malta and Gibraltar, the only possible alternatives, and sending it back to GC and CS.* After a delay of seven weeks in which the traffic went unintercepted First Army's Y unit was instructed to take it at the expense of its proper tactical job, a job on which it 'never really started' before the end of the campaign.[7]

It thus comes as no surprise to learn that, even after First Army's Y units had become operational, their work continued to be ineffective until they were brought under the direction of experienced staff from Cairo and reinforced by a Y unit from Eighth Army in February 1943, upon the formation of 18th Army Group. At first they intercepted little traffic, and this was due to the inexperience of their operators as well as to the difficulties created by the mountainous terrain. Up to the beginning of January half of the traffic they intercepted was that of the German units facing Eighth Army, and they spent much time wrestling with codes which Eighth Army was already reading. Thereafter their interception programme was better organised and they began to issue regular Traffic Analysis summaries, but it was not until 20 February that they circulated their first operational decrypt. As a result of lack of equipment and training, and of proper co-ordination, their DF results were 'extremely poor'. Like the RAF Y groups, they had not been trained or equipped to intercept and exploit Italian traffic, another omission which turned out to be serious as the campaign developed and Italian forces played an increasingly active part in it. Furthermore, as was equally natural in these circumstances, the operational intelligence staffs, who had not been briefed in advance about what might be expected of field intelligence, gave them no guidance and placed no reliance on them until their performance improved.

The failure of Army Y was not entirely due to the lack of adequate planning. In the first two months of the fighting the German Army's signals network, itself under stress, behaved irregularly and was difficult to analyse; and from the end of November, when its layout became more conventional, the Germans took measures to improve the security of their tactical communications as they were also doing with their high-grade

---

* For the arrangements for the interception in the Middle East of networks exploitable at GC and CS see above, p 21, fn †.

7. Mockler-Ferryman, *Military Intelligence Organisation*, p 195.

communications.* First Army's Y organisation was severely handicapped by the difficulty of intercepting traffic and communicating
instructions and results over long distances in mountainous country, conditions very different from those in the desert. Even so, the
failure did stem to a large extent from inadequate preparation; and
while this was partly due to under-estimation of the possible scale
of the campaign, which no doubt infected the Sigint planners, and
partly to the fact that trained Sigint personnel was in any case in
short supply, it owed much also to the fact that GC and CS and MI
8 lacked the familiarity with the enemy's tactical traffic in operational conditions which – though even there only gradually and by
painful experience – had been acquired in Cairo and Eighth Army.
Not until August 1942, when they were instructed to begin to
prepare for *Torch*, did they examine the analyses of this traffic and
the reports on how to handle it, which had been submitted from the
Middle East but which had 'lain unregarded in the Military
Section at GC and CS', and call an officer back from the Middle
East to instruct Y units in the United Kingdom. They then
discovered that they themselves had insufficient knowledge or
material for training purposes, and the officer did not arrive till
October, too late to be of use before the landings. As we have seen,
these deficiencies were not made up until the *Torch* Y units were
strengthened with veterans from the desert campaigns in February
1943. Until then these units had to be content with Traffic Analysis
and cryptanalytic advice from GC and CS's Military Section, 2,000
miles away.

It may well be that, as well as arising from ignorance in the
United Kingdom, the omission to call on the resources of the
Middle East stemmed from the feeling that, either from the
knowledge that those resources were already over-strained or from
concern to preserve the security of the *Torch* project, it was
impracticable to do so. Whatever the true explanation, it was
an omission which was not rectified until February 1943 when the
full extent of the Y failure was recognised.

---

* See above, p 582.

APPENDIX 19

The Breaking of the U-boat Enigma (Shark)

The delay of nine months in breaking the U-boat four-wheel Enigma was regarded by GC and CS at the end of the war as having been 'the most serious cryptanalytic failure' in the record of its work on the German naval cyphers. It may be questioned whether 'failure' is the appropriate word, but what is beyond doubt is that every possible opportunity to reduce the delay was exploited to the limit of existing resources and that, given the nature of the opportunities and the state of the resources, the fact that the Shark problem was substantially solved by December 1942 represented an outstanding cryptanalytic achievement.

Before discussing the reasons for the delay, we should note that from as early as the spring of 1941 naval Enigma decrypts and captured material had referred to the possibility that a fourth wheel might be added to the naval Enigma machine, and minor modifications in the use of the three-wheel machine* had left little doubt that it would be used in the first instance to provide a separate key for the Atlantic U-boats. By the end of 1941, indeed, it was known that U-boats were being issued with a fourth wheel, and it had occasionally been used prematurely, by error, for signals transmitted on the U-boat frequencies. In December 1941, one such signal, together with the fact that the operator committed the further blunder of repeating it in the three-wheel setting, enabled GC and CS to recover the wiring of the fourth wheel.

Alarmed by these warnings, to which they drew attention as 'an ominous sign of worse things to come',[1] the naval Enigma experts at GC and CS also judged that sustained success in breaking four-wheel Enigma settings would be impossible without the development of a high-speed four-wheel Bombe. After the event they blamed themselves for the fact that, partly from wishful thinking, partly from fatalism and partly because they were preoccupied with the immediate task of thoroughly mastering the three-wheel Enigmas, they had not been more energetic in bringing the vital importance of this need to the attention of their superiors. It is clear, however, that their lack of drive, if such it was, was not

---

* See above, p 178.

1. Dir/C Archive 7731 and 7744 of 7 October 1941.

the sole reason why the work of designing and building a four-wheel Bombe did not begin as soon as the warnings were received. The management at GC and CS thought it would be unwise to divert to this formidable new task, the successful completion of which was problematical and would at best be prolonged, the scarce staff that was engaged in the construction of three-wheel Bombes – and did so on good grounds. Throughout 1941 GC and CS was faced with a steady proliferation of separate three-wheel Enigma keys for German Air Force and Army communications, and it knew that most of these could be broken currently provided the supply of additional three-wheel Bombes was maintained. Moreover, the attack on the Army keys was now intensifying and absorbing a prodigious amount of Bombe time.* As late as December 1941 Bletchley had taken delivery of only 16 three-wheel Bombes, of which only 12 were in action, but this number had risen to 30 by August 1942 and to 49 by the end of that year. Understandably the authorities did not consider approaching the United States for help: the United States was not yet in the war and, at least until she became a co-belligerent, several considerations made it a matter of high policy that Great Britain should retain her monopoly of work against the Enigma.

In these circumstances GC and CS secured a promise that an electronics expert from TRE would begin designing a four-wheel Bombe as soon as he could be released from other work; but he did not join GC and CS until the end of 1941. Nor was it until February 1942, when the blow had fallen and Shark had come into force, that the engineers who were engaged in producing three-wheel Bombes were brought in to supplement his work. There was a further delay until the summer of 1942 before the United States Navy's cryptanalysts were fully inducted into GC and CS's techniques for breaking the Enigma and were able to begin work on the Shark problem.[†] Thereafter, still longer delays ensued before the work was crowned with success. It was not until June 1943, after many disappointments and fresh starts, that Bletchley took delivery of the first workable British-built high-speed Bombe. The first of the Washington-based American high-speed Bombes became operational in August 1943.

At first sight these completion dates make the initial delays seem highly unfortunate. But since it is a reasonable assumption that the work would have taken just as long if it had started earlier, we may conclude that even if it had begun in June 1941, soon after the receipt of the earliest warning, the British programme would not have been completed until December 1942; and we may similarly conclude that if American assistance had been sought from January

---

* See above, 28.

† See above, p 57.

1942, soon after the United States entry into the war, instead of from July 1942, the United States programme would not have been completed before February 1943. In December 1942, however, GC and CS broke into the Shark key with its three-wheel Bombes. It should be added that its Enigma experts later took the view that in the interval between 1 February 1942 and the beginning of their regular success against Shark in December 1942, nothing less than the possession of between 10 and 20 four-wheel Bombes would have speeded up their attack. The existence of 'one or two fast Bombes would have made little difference'. Taking into account the rate at which four-wheel Bombes in fact became available, they further concluded that had the four-wheel Bombes begun to become available in the summer of 1942, instead of a year later, 'maximum gain' would have been 'intermittent reading of September-November 1942 traffic and reduction of time lag on some, but not all, days from November 1942. . .'

These judgments rested on two considerations. The first was the fact that in this interval no opportunity arose for capturing cypher material from a U-boat. The second was the fact that even if the wheel-wirings were known, it was necessary to be able to conjecture, and if possible to know precisely, the plain language text of an Enigma signal before Bombes could be set to work against each day's settings. It was in this way that, before making its major break into Shark, GC and CS broke the settings for three days, namely 23 and 24 February and 14 March 1942. The first of these days was broken on the basis of the conjecture that a decrypted 'Werft' signal* had been re-enciphered in a particular Shark signal. 14 March, to take another example, was broken because, Dönitz's message to the Fleet on being promoted Admiral having been decrypted in the Home Waters naval Enigma key, it proved possible to isolate the few Shark signals which included the one that carried that message. It took 6 three-wheel Bombes 17 days to break the setting for the day; a three-wheel Bombe had to work 26 times longer to test the text of a four-wheel signal than to test that of a three-wheel signal. Four-wheel Bombes, had they been available, would have been more expeditious. But the basic problem was that Dönitz was not promoted every day and that alternative god-sends were few and far between until the capture of cryptanalytic material made it possible for GC and CS to make effective use of the three-wheel Bombes against the Shark key from the middle of December 1942.

The U-boats regularly made weather reports, in the form of short signals using groups taken from a code-book which they enciphered on the Enigma machine. Until early in 1942 GC and CS

---

* See Volume I p 338.

had possessed this book, a copy of it having been among captures made early in 1941; up to that time, indeed, this fact, together with the discovery that the U-boat weather signals were re-broadcast by a German meteorological station in a weather code that was readable, though sometimes only after considerable delay, had frequently enabled GC and CS to reconstruct the unencyphered texts of the weather short-signals, and had thus been one of the means by which it had regularly broken the daily-changing three-wheel Home Waters naval Enigma settings.* But early in 1942 the U-boat Command had changed the book; and GC and CS's efforts to re-constitute the new book had not reached the point at which it could be used as a means of attacking the naval Enigma keys when a copy of it was taken from U-559, sunk north of Port Said on 30 October. It was this capture that enabled GC and CS, from 13 December 1942 to early March 1943, to break Shark settings with some degree of regularity. GC and CS at once discovered that the Germans had committed a further security blunder when bringing the fourth wheel into force. When used for encyphering plain language signals the fourth wheel changed its position from signal to signal. But because their short-signal books gave only three-letter settings, the U-boats set the fourth wheel at neutral when encyphering the weather signals, thus using the Enigma as a three-wheel machine. When it had short-signal texts of weather signals at its disposal GC and CS was thus able to break the three-wheel part of the daily Shark setting using three-wheel Bombes, and the remaining problem, that of finding the daily starting-position of the fourth wheel, gave it little difficulty.

On 10 March 1943 the U-boat Command brought into force a new code book for the short-signal weather reports, and it was at first feared that the consequences would be fatal. The First Sea Lord signalled the VCNS, then in Washington, 'U-Boat Special Intelligence has received a severe setback. After 10th March it is unlikely that we shall obtain more than 2 to 3 pairs of days per month and these will not be current. After 2 to 3 months the situation should improve considerably'. In the event, however, GC and CS recovered from the blow after a gap of only nine days. On 19 March, as 'C' then told the Prime Minister,[2] it broke the Shark settings for 16, 17 and 18 March; and from 20 March, with the interruptions and delays that we have already mentioned,† it resumed the regular reading of the Shark traffic.

Several factors contributed to this remarkable achievement. The number of three-wheel Bombes available at Bletchley, 49 by the end of 1942, was more than 60 by March 1943. Profiting from the

---

* See Volume I p 337.   † See above, p 552.

2.   Dir/C Archive, 2634 of 19 March 1943.

fact that the Shark traffic had been read since the previous December, GC and CS had worked out alternative stand-bys to replace the weather-signal texts that it now lost. It had been much assisted in doing so not only by the fact that the material from U-559 had included the current version of the short-signal book that was used by the U-boats for making sighting and battle reports and announcing their expected time of return – and by the fact that, unlike the weather book, this book remained in force – but also by the fact that at this time, when the convoy battles were at their height, the supply of such short signals was continuous. Of the 90 Shark days that were broken out of the total of 112 days from 10 March to the end of June 1943, the great majority were read with the aid of these short-signal reports, for which, as for the weather signals, the U-boats used the Enigma as if it was a three-wheel machine. Last but not least, the task of conjecturing or establishing the unencyphered texts of the reports, in order that they could be exploited by the Bombes, called for the most meticulous and urgent research to correlate the Shark evidence on U-boat activities and DF, RFP and TINA information on individual U-boat transmissions with operational reports by Allied ships and aircraft. This work derived much benefit from the intimate relationship that existed between the Tracking Room in the OIC and the Naval Section at GC and CS; but in the last resort its success depended on the Naval Section's complete familiarity with, on the one hand, U-boat behaviour and procedure and, on the other hand, the requirements of the cryptanalysts, with whom it had worked for so long in a single organisation.

During May 1943 the U-boats withdrew from the north Atlantic and, with the end of the convoy battles, their operational short signals ceased to be of service as a regular means of entry into the Shark settings. From 1 July, moreover, the U-boat Command introduced an additional complication into the four-wheel Enigma machine. Since 1 February 1942 the Shark key had utilised a single fourth wheel (Beta); from 1 July 1943 an alternative fourth wheel (Gamma) was brought into force. Despite these developments GC and CS continued to break the settings; indeed, from the summer of 1943 it did so with greater regularity than before. One reason for this was that the choice of fourth wheel as between Beta and Gamma was made by the Germans only monthly; once GC and CS had recovered the wiring of the new wheel, which it did cryptanalytically within a few days, it was only when making the first break of each month that it encountered the added difficulty of breaking the settings that was created by the extra wheel. Not less important, however, was the fact that when the supply of short-signal texts dwindled away GC and CS was able to profit from the growing German habit of re-encyphering in the Shark settings signals which had also been transmitted in the three-wheel Enigma or other more easily readable cyphers. These re-encypherments provided cribs into Shark that were longer and more reliable than such short-signal texts as still became available. For the reason which we have already given, they also took much longer to test on the three-wheel Bombes than did the short-signal texts. But from June 1943 the four-wheel Bombes began to operate, and from August, when the British high-speed Bombes were supplemented by the American ones, the breaking of the Shark settings became almost a daily routine.*

---

* The earliest British four-wheel Bombes proved to have a low serviceability, owing to the shortage of good quality raw materials. But the US Bombes made up for this and, also unhampered by shortage of skilled labour, the US programme produced them in greater numbers. By the end of 1943 the work of breaking the Shark settings had become wholly taken over by the US Navy which also, as already noted above (p 57) placed its spare Bombes at the disposal of GC and CS for work on other keys in a joint programme based on intimate relations and direct communications between the cryptanalysts.

APPENDIX 20

Bombing Operations against U-boat Pens and Construction Yards, February–April 1943

The War Cabinet decided on 11 January 1943, in response to pressure from the Admiralty since the previous October, that Bomber Command should give over-riding priority to attacks on the U-boat pens at Lorient, St Nazaire, Brest and La Pallice.[1] On 21 January, at the Casablanca conference, this decision was confirmed by the Combined Chiefs of Staff, who also listed U-boat construction yards among the high priority targets for the bombing campaign against Germany.[2]

That the enemy was starting to build pens or reinforced shelters for the U-boats at the Biscay ports was first reported by the SIS, but the reports were not credited until air photographs were taken in the summer of 1941.[3] Attacks on them at that time would perhaps have been effective, as was suggested by Coastal Command.[4] Some bombing attacks took place in 1942, without effect, and in November, when the U-boat threat was becoming acute, the problem was considered by the Anti-U-boat Warfare Committee. At that point there was some reluctance to sanction the bombing of the French population, and Bomber Command and the Air Staff were convinced that the shelters were impracticable targets and that attacks on them would have no appreciable effects on U-boat operations.[5] At the beginning of 1943 the Air Ministry remained sceptical and its scepticism was buttressed by SIS reports to the effect that the pens would be impregnable against air attack.[6] It was on this account that the Casablanca directive of the Combined Chiefs of Staff stated that while 'if these can be put out of action a great step forward will have been taken in the U-boat

---

1. AIR 41/43, *The RAF in the Bombing Offensive against Germany*, Vol V, pp 22–23; Webster and Frankland, *The Strategic Air Offensive against Germany* (1961), Vol II, p 97.
2. Webster and Frankland, op cit, Vol II, pp 10–11; Vol IV, Appendix 8 (xxviii).
3. Morgan, *NID History* 1939–42, p 243.
4. Roskill, *The War at Sea*, Vol I (1954), p 459.
5. Howard, *Grand Strategy*, Vol IV (1972), p 311.
6. McLachlan, *Room 39*, (1968), p 353.

war which the CCS have agreed to be a first charge on our resources . . . attacks on the pens should be continued so that an assessment of their effects can be made as soon as possible'.[7]

The immediate effects of the offensive vindicated the arguments of the air authorities. In the five weeks from the middle of January 1943 Bomber Command's night attacks on Lorient and St Nazaire consumed half of its total bombing effort; they destroyed almost everything except the pens. Smaller day-time raids by the USAAF on Lorient, St Nazaire, Brest, La Pallice and Rennes from the middle of February were no more effective. Nor were the intelligence sources slow to suggest that this was the case. By 25 January, after the earliest of the night raids, the Enigma, PR and the SIS had all reported that while the town and the facilities outside the shelters at Lorient had been severely damaged, the pens themselves had escaped harm.[8] On 17 February, following the first of the day-time raids on St Nazaire, the Shark Enigma disclosed that damage to the lock had delayed the escort for two U-boats but that U-boat operations had otherwise been unaffected.[9]

At that point the Air Ministry suggested that the offensive should be discontinued, but on 23 February, on the ground that evidence was still lacking about its effect in delaying the re-fitting and turn-round of U-boats, the Admiralty secured agreement for its continuation on a reduced scale for a further month.[10] In March, however, intelligence about the effects of the bombing on turn-round remained scarce. Regular reports by NID I on the subject, based on the non-Sigint sources, were inconclusive.[11] The Sigint evidence, such as it was, was conflicting. On 9 March a diplomatic decrypt from Vichy reported that, while it was failing to destroy U-boats in the pens, the bombing had completely destroyed Lorient and St Nazaire and that, since it was proving impossible to find workmen there even for high wages, the offensive could 'not fail to have an effect on the U-boat war'. In addition, by 11 March an Enigma decrypt had revealed that three hits on U-boat pens had reduced U-boat repairs by 25 per cent. On 8 March, on the other hand, a lengthy examination by the OIC of the Enigma evidence on U-boat turn-round times concluded that all that had been achieved so far was the loss of three U-boat cruises, or the saving of

---

7. Webster and Frankland, op cit, Vol IV, Appendix 8 (xxviii).
8. DEFE 3/246, ZTPG 102057; McLachlan, op cit, p 423.
9. ZTPGU 6110, 6115.
10. CAB 66/34, WP (43) 72 of 22 February; CAB 69/5, DO (43) 1st meeting, 23 February; CAB 86/2, AU (43) 7th meeting, 17 February; AIR 41/43, pp 24–25.
11. ADM 223/120, NID UC Reports, Nos 288, 306, 310 and 321 of 26 January, 8 and 17 March, 5 April 1943.

three to five Allied ships.[12] Perhaps for this reason, the idea had already been mooted of landing troops near the U-boat bases and enveloping them from the landward: though nothing came of this project, NID I compiled the intelligence that would be needed for this project and circulated it on 8 March.[13]

The OIC produced no further report until the middle of April; this concluded that the Biscay ports were congested with returning U-boats for whose refuelling at sea the few available supply U-boats had proved quite inadequate; that the reduction in the labour force brought about by the air raids must in these circumstances be slowing down turn-round times; and that 'the situation is likely to be aggravated provided raids are continued'.[14] But the offensive had already been abandoned earlier in April in deference to the Air Ministry's view that the bombing of Germany offered more profitable targets.

Concurrently with the attacks on the Biscay bases Bomber Command and the US Eighth Air Force had given first priority in the bombing of Germany to attacks on the U-boat construction yards, especially those at Wilhelmshaven, Kiel and Hamburg, on which NID I had accumulated a vast amount of detailed intelligence.[15] Some of the yards had already been attacked in the autumn of 1942 without appreciable results. PR, the main source of information as to the effects of the further attacks, established that the harbour areas and the shipyards had sustained severe damage. But as it was not possible from this evidence or from any other to show that they were delaying U-boat construction, these raids also ceased to be given priority from the beginning of April 1943. After the war the German records established that they had brought about no appreciable interruption in the monthly rate of U-boat commissioning;[16] they established, indeed, that no U boat was destroyed in a yard until April 1944 and that no bomb penetrated the roof of an assembly yard until just before the end of the war.[17] At the time NID I, basing itself on a wide variety of sources – POW, SIS, the enemy Press, radio and official publications, Allied naval attachés and PR – reached much the same conclusion. On 26 February it concluded on the basis of good PR of all the yards at regular intervals since 15 January that the former rate of U-boat construction was being maintained.[18] On 25 March it reported that US Eighth Air Force, in the first successful daylight precision raid

12. ADM 223/97, OIC SI 536 of 8 March 1943; Howard, op cit, Vol IV, p 314.
13. ADM 223/119, NID LC Report 606 of 8 March 1943.
14. ADM 223/97, OIC SI 572 of 15 April 1943.
15. ADM 223/107, NID 0831/43 of 4 February 1943.
16. AIR 41/43, pp 26–29; Webster and Frankland, op cit, Vol II, p 105.
17. Roskill, op cit, Vol II, (1957), pp 352–353.
18. ADM 223/118, NID LC report 592 of 26 February 1943.

on a yard, had possibly severely damaged several U-boats;[19] but a month later it recorded that the damage in that raid had been over-estimated and that the enemy had made rapid progress in repairing the yards that had been hit.[20]

---

19.   ADM 223/120, NID UC Report 313 of 25 March 1943.
20.   ibid, Report 325 of 24 April 1943.

APPENDIX 21

Intelligence on Enemy Intentions between 9 February and the German Attack on Sidi Bou Zid 14 February 1943

After 8 February, when they indicated that the Germans were intending to attack west and south-west of Kairouan in the near future but were undecided whether they could also move against Gafsa,* the Enigma decrypts continued to be virtually the only source of intelligence about the enemy's intentions. Between 1 and 13 February tactical air reconnaissance was severely restricted by bad weather and enemy air superiority.[1] For the same reasons, and also as a result of Allied disorganisation, no PR was available in this period or for some time afterwards.† For reasons discussed elsewhere, Army Y was scanty, and therefore unreliable, till the beginning of March.‡

As for the Enigma, a decrypt received on 9 February showed that the GAF was making arrangements to provide ground support for 21st Panzer Division.[3] This was followed on 11 February by Panzer Army 5's day report for 1 February, decrypted ten days late, which disclosed that the main body of 10th Panzer Division had then been at Sbikha, 25 miles north of Kairouan.[4] Early on 12 February GC

---

* See above, pp 584–585.

† In January 1943 the inadequacy of PR in Tunisia had prompted the decision to reorganise No 2 PRU, No 4 PRU and the Malta PR Flight as three PR squadrons and to equip them with the newest Spitfires (Type IX), but it was not until February that it was decided that the squadrons should receive the new aircraft as soon as possible and, for the first time, at the expense of requirements in the United Kingdom. As late as February the British and US photographic interpretation units were still struggling against the effects of enemy bombing and of communications problems, and during that month they were being amalgamated into a single North African Interpretation Unit (NAIU). It was not until March that all PR and interpretation units in Tunisia were placed under the central control of the North African PR Wing and that, apparently as an emergency measure prompted by the continuing deficiency of PR before and during the fighting at Kasserine, First Army was given its own PR Flight of P 38s, and only then did matters begin to improve.[2]

‡ See appendix 18.

1. CAB 44/115, AL 1200/8, p 167.
2. AIR 41/7, *Photographic Reconnaissance*, Vol II, pp 62–65; C Babington Smith, *Evidence in Camera* (1958), pp 160–161; Mockler-Ferryman, *Military Intelligence Organisation*, pp 177–178.
3. VMs 3498 of 8 February, 3572 of 9 February 1943; CX/MSS/2081/T36, 2086/T27.
4. VM 3706 of 11 February 1943; CX/MSS/2098/T19.

and CS decrypted a more recent signal from Panzer Army 5 which informed the GAF that A-day was to be 14 February.[5] The signal gave no details; GC and CS when despatching it to the theatre suggested only that it might be read in the light of the signal of 9 February about ground support arrangements, thus refraining from connecting it with the references to A-day in the *Kuckucksei* decrypt of 1 February 1943; but this connection would surely have been assumed by the intelligence authorities in the field. Later on 12 February two decrypts confirmed that 21st Panzer Division was to be associated with an operation planned by Panzer Army 5, as in *Kuckucksei*, and provided the first of two firm indications that there was also to be a serious German attack on Gafsa. One of them was Rommel's day report of 10 February which announced that 'according to development of situation with Panzer Army 5 (under-taking 21st Panzer Division) the forces intended for Gafsa under-taking will be despatched at the earliest on evening 11th'.[6] The other stated that fuel and ammunition for Battle Group DAK and Reconnaissance Unit 33 were available at Gabes and that RU 33 would leave on 11 February.[7]

The Allied command responded to this new development on 13 February; General Anderson ordered that Gafsa was not to be held in face of a strong enemy attack, but that the weak garrison there was to retire and counter-attack from Feriana.[8] But it made no change in its dispositions when it learned from further decrypts of 12 February that on 10 February 21st Panzer Division was still in the Faid area[9] and that by the evening of 10 February the mobile elements of 10th Panzer Division had reached a new assembly area in a coded position that GC and CS was unable to identify.[10] From Faid 21st Panzer Division was well placed for a move to the attack-area allotted to it in *Kuckucksei*, halfway between Faid and Kairouan, and – all the more so when DF evidence indicated that 10th Panzer Division had reached an area 'not far north of Kairouan' by 12 February – it was naturally assumed that the unidentified position lay on 10th Panzer Division's approach march for *Kuckucksei*. Equally naturally, the news in another decrypt of 12 February, to the effect that two Gruppen of fighter aircraft were due at Kairouan from the morning of 14 February, was taken as confirmation that the enemy intended to carry out *Kuckucksei*. So was the last decrypt issued before the German attack;

5. VM 3777 of 0436/12 February 1943; CX/MSS/2105/T8.
6. VM 3790 of 0758/12 February 1943; CX/MSS/2105/T29.
7. VM 3774 of 12 February 1943; CX/MSS/2105/T1.
8. Howe, *North-West Africa* (1957), p 403; Playfair, *The Mediterranean and Middle East*, Vol IV (1966), p 289.
9. VM 3832 of 12 February 1943; CX/MSS/2106/T21.
10. VM 3810 of 1546/12 February 1943; CX/MSS/2106/T21.

sent out at 0259 on 14 February, this said that Fliegerführer Tunis had been ordered 'to support 10th Panzer Division from Kairouan' on 14 February.[11] Kairouan was the airfield used by the GAF for *Frühlingswind*, there being no more suitable base; unfortunately for the intelligence staff at AFHQ, it was more suitable for *Kuckucksei* than for *Frühlingswind*.

On 13 February the Enigma disclosed that HQ 21st Panzer Division was to move forward that day[12] and confirmed that A-day referred to an operation by Panzer Army 5 that would probably take place on the following day.[13] This was the basis of 'the word . . . flashed from First Army's HQ late on the 13th that an attack would be made by the enemy the next day'.[14]

First Army's warning did not state where the attack would come; and by 13 February there was indeed an element of uncertainty on the part of the Allied authorities. In some quarters – the intelligence staff at US II Corps[15] and some air intelligence authorities[16] – it was felt that the main attack would be against Gafsa with a major diversionary operation west of Kairouan. This view may have been strengthened by the receipt during 13 February of another Enigma decrypt which showed that 'strong elements' of Rommel's army had been due to withdraw on 12 February from the Mareth line for a move against Gafsa.[17] On the evening of 13 February a further decrypt disclosed that Panzer Army 5 had requested a dawn attack by the GAF on Sbeitla in connection with its 'undertaking on the fourteenth'.[18] As Sbeitla, west of Faid, lay between US II Corps HQ's area and Sidi Bou Zid, 50 miles south-west of Kairouan, this item may have strengthened the view of the intelligence staff at AFHQ, as already expressed in its intelligence summary for the week ending 13 February, that an enemy 'thrust in the direction of Sidi Bou Zid might precede or coincide with an attack in the north on the Ousseltia valley, or in the south on Gafsa, in order to distract Allied reinforcements'. But if AFHQ thus left open the possibility that the main attack might be against Gafsa, it believed that, should the main attack be in the north, it would come west of Kairouan. It stated this in its summary of 13 February: the enemy would aim at 'the capture of Ousseltia and Pichon and the control of the passes west of the Ousseltia plain'. Nor is there much doubt that it believed a

11. VM 3953 of 0259/14 February 1943; CX/MSS/2117/T11.
12. VM 3889 of 0836/13 February 1943; CX/MSS/2111/T24.
13. VM 3884 of 0753/13 February 1943; CX/MSS/2111/T21.
14. Howe, op cit, p 405.
15. ibid, p 401.
16. Playfair, op cit, Vol IV, p 289.
17. VM 3868 of 13 February 1943; CX/MSS/2111/T9.
18. VM 3939 of 2101/13 February 1943; CX/MSS/2114/T9.

northern attack to be far more likely than an attack on Gafsa. In an appreciation which was dated 15 February, but which evidently reflected its expectations on the eve of the battle, First Army's principal formation, British V Corps, stated this conclusion firmly. It considered that, although it might be accompanied by a small-scale operation towards Gafsa, the main attack would be in the north; and although it differed from AFHQ about the objective of the northern attack, believing that, while it might be supported by 21st Panzer Division, possibly towards Pichon, it was 'likely to be directed south-westward and not westward from 10th Panzer Division's concentration area around Kairouan' (that is, towards Fondouk rather than towards Ousseltia), it did not question that it would be delivered roughly westward from Kairouan (that is, in the area specified in the Enigma decrypts about operation *Kuckucksei*).[19]

These appreciations were to be influential in persuading the operational authorities after the enemy attack had begun that there would be only a feint at Sidi Bou Zid, whereas the real blow was to come further north. After the event General Eisenhower was to be critical of the appreciation that the main attack was to come through Fondouk;[20] his naval aide was to state categorically that the intelligence authorities had misinterpreted the evidence;[21] the officer who became his new ACOS G2 at AFHQ from March 1943 was to imply that they had done so because they based their appreciations 'on one isolated piece of information in which they had come to believe implicitly and tended to disregard any contrary or alternative possibilities to the cherished theory'.[22] It will be evident from the foregoing analysis that there is no justification for these charges of misinterpretation in so far as they rest on the Enigma intelligence; this first disclosed that the enemy planned to attack in the north and subsequently gave no indication that the attack would come against Sidi Bou Zid through Faid. Moreover, while it is beyond question that ACOS G2 at AFHQ continued to be influenced by the outdated picture painted by the Enigma, AFHQ did allow for a 'thrust in the direction of Sidi Bou Zid . . . in order to distract Allied reinforcements,' and so much so that on 11 February it warned the garrison at Sidi Bou Zid to mount a 24-hour alert.[23]

These subsequent criticisms were supported by references to the

---

19. WO 204/966, AFHQ Weekly Intelligence Summary No 25 of 13 February 1943; CAB 44/115, p 252.
20. Eisenhower, *Crusade in Europe* (1948), pp 157, 158.
21. H C Butcher, *Three Years with Eisenhower*, (1946), pp 228, 229.
22. K Strong *Intelligence at the Top* (1968), p 81.
23. WO 204/966, AFHQ Weekly Intelligence No 25 of 13 February 1943; Howe, op cit, p 410.

existence of other evidence. General Eisenhower's post-war account stated that on 13 February he visited the commander of Combat Command B* (the equivalent of a British armoured brigade) opposite Fondouk, and found that in the light of reports from his reconnaissance patrols he was 'sure that there would be no attack at that point . . . he had reported these facts several times to his superior'.[25] General Eisenhower's naval aide similarly claimed that 'our own reconnaissance knew of the German build-up' opposite Faid.[26] The new ACOS G2 at AFHQ wrote that 'accurate reports of the strength and direction of the impending attack had been sent from the front, but it appears that they had been discounted both at First Army and at AFHQ as being an exaggeration on the part of green and untried troops'.[27] In the nature of things, it is not easy to assess the reliability of these references. If such reports were received and discounted, we should expect to find no mention of them in the surviving intelligence assessments. This is indeed the case. On 7 February AFHQ's daily intelligence summary had referred to 'French reports' of considerable enemy movement westward from Kairouan towards the mountain passes.[28] On 8 February Eighth Army's intelligence summary had quoted a reliable report to the effect that a force of 100 tanks was moving south from Tunis and 'reports from the front' about enemy preparations to capture Ousseltia and Pichon.[29] On 13 February AFHQ's daily intelligence summary reported that 12 tanks and some motor transport had been sighted that day east of Faid, but did not comment on the sightings,[30] and in its weekly intelligence summary for the period ending 13 February AFHQ referred to reports of fairly steady traffic on the Kairouan–Ousseltia road, including an unconfirmed report that civilians in that area were being evacuated, but reported no sightings that might have been construed as pointing to an attack from Faid or against Gafsa.[31] But three observations may be added to these necessarily inconclusive findings.

---

* The US 1st Armoured Division, which made up the bulk of US II Corps's strength, was divided into three Combat Commands which, partly on the evidence received about operation *Kuckucksei* on 1 February, were separated from each other over almost 90 miles of front when the Germans attacked.[24]

24. Howe, op cit, pp 388, 396, 406–407.
25. Eisenhower, op cit, p 154.
26. Butcher, op cit, p 229.
27. Strong, op cit, p 81.
28. WO 204/978, AFHQ Daily Intelligence Summary No 92 of 7 February 1943.
29. WO 169/8519, Eighth Army Intelligence Summary No 428 of 8 February 1943.
30. WO 204/978, No 98 of 13 February 1943.
31. WO 204/966, AFHQ Weekly Intelligence Summary No 25 of 13 February 1943, para 1.

The first is that a US official account, while mentioning that later on 13 February the garrison at Sidi Bou Zid noticed motor transport movement to the south-east and heard the faint sound of tank engines after dark, says nothing to suggest that the garrison had earlier detected a major enemy build-up in its area; it shows that, on the contrary, it was at first disposed to belittle the enemy attack when it came.[32]* In the second place, neither this official account nor any other gives due emphasis to the notable failure of Allied air reconnaissance to detect the southward movement to Faid of 10th Panzer Division with 110 tanks. It is known not only that bad weather and enemy air superiority had restricted air operations from 1 to 13 February, but also that it was air reconnaissance that sighted enemy motor transport on roads east and south-east of Faid on 13 February.[34] It is difficult to believe that if the Allied formations had suspected that the attack was to come through Faid, or were even uncertain whether it would come through Faid or Fondouk, they would not have been demanding more forceful air reconnaissance ahead of their positions. Finally, it seems clear that, in claiming that 'accurate reports of the strength and direction of the impending attack had been sent from the front', the ACOS G2 confused the situation before the battle with that which developed after the Germans had opened their attack. His comment echoes General Eisenhower's post-war account, but what that says is that while 'during the morning [of 14 February] frequent, and as it later turned out, very accurate reports were submitted by the American troops to General Anderson concerning the strength and direction of the German attack through Faid, these reports were discounted as the exaggeration of green, untried troops'.[35] After the battle General Eisenhower dismissed his chief intelligence officer. But his account leaves little doubt that he took this unusual, almost unprecedented, step† not from dissatisfaction with the pre-battle appreciations at AFHQ, but because after the beginning of the German attack 'the belief that the main attack was still to come through Fondouk persisted, both at Army HQ and, as I later learned, in the G-2 Division of AFHQ. The G-2 error was serious'.[36]

---

* This account draws attention to the fact that the military intelligence division of the War Department in Washington correctly appreciated that the enemy intended a major attack on the Sfax–Tebessa road through Faid, and suggests that it reached this conclusion before the battle. It may be noted, however, that the appreciation was sent to AFHQ somewhat later, in a signal dated 17 February.[33]

† See above, p 333 for the only precedent – General Auchinleck's replacement of his DDMI following Rommel's surprise attack at Agheila in January 1942.

32. Howe, op cit, p 411.
33. ibid, p 401.
34. CAB 44/115, p 167.
35. Eisenhower, op cit, p 158.
36. ibid, p 158.

A final comment may be made about General Eisenhower's claim that during the morning of 14 February very accurate reports were submitted by the American troops concerning the strength and the direction of the German attack. The claim is not supported by the US official account of the fighting to which we have referred. This shows that the garrison at Sidi Bou Zid was at first disposed to belittle the enemy attack and that the scale of the attack continued to be under-estimated at the battle front throughout 14 February.*

---

* See above, p 586.

APPENDIX 22

German appreciation for operation *Zitadelle*

On 25 April 1943 GC and CS decrypted a 'Comprehensive Appreciation for Zitadelle',* signed by Generalfeldmarschall von Weichs, C-in-C Army Group South, and addressed to the Supreme Command of the Army, Operations Section and Intelligence Section, Foreign Armies, East. It read as follows –

'In the main, the appreciation of the enemy remains the same as reported in Army Group South II No 0477/43 of 29 March† and in the supplementary appreciation of 15 April. The main concentration, which was already then apparent on the north flank of the Army Group in the general area Kursk-Sudzha-Welchansk-Ostrogoisk, can now be clearly recognised: a further intensification of this concentration is to be expected as a result of the continuous heavy transport movements on the lines Yelets-Kastornoye-Kursk, Povorino-Svoboda, and Gryazi-Svoboda, with a probable [increase] in the area Valuiki-Nevy Oskol-Kupyansk. At present, however, it is not apparent whether the object of this concentration is offensive or defensive. At present, in anticipation of a German offensive on both the Kursk and Mius-Donets fronts, the armoured and mobile formations are still evenly distributed in various groups behind the front as strategic reserves.

There are no signs as yet of a merging of these formations or a transfer to the forward area (except for II Guards Armoured Corps), but this could take place rapidly at any time.

According to information from a sure source,‡ the existence of the following groups of the strategic reserve can be presumed –

Two Cavalry corps – III and V Guards – in the area north of Novocherkassk. It can also be presumed that one mechanised corps – V Guards – is being brought up to strength here.

One mechanised corps – III Guards – in the area [north] of Rovenki.

One armoured corps, one cavalry corps and probably two mechanised corps – I Guards Armoured, IV Cavalry, probably [I] Guards Mechanised and V Mechanised – in the area north of Voroshilovgrad.

Two cavalry corps – [IV] Guards and VII Guards – in the area west of Starobyelsk.

One mechanised corps, one cavalry corps and two armoured corps – I

---

* CX/MSS/2499/T14.
† The 29 March appreciation never became available in Sigint.
‡ German Sigint.

Guards [Mechanised], I Guards Cavalry, II and XXIII Armoured – in the area Kupyansk-Svyatovo.

Three armoured corps, and one mechanised corps – II Armoured, V Guards Armoured, [XXIX] Armoured and V Guards Mechanised under the command of an army (perhaps 5 Armoured Army) – in the area of Ostrogoisk.

Two armoured and one cavalry corps – II Guards Armoured, III Guards Armoured and VI Guards Cavalry – under the command of an unidentified headquarters, in the area north of Novy Oskol.

In the event of Zitadelle, there are at present approximately ninety enemy formations west of the line Byelgorod-Kursk-Malo Arkhangelsk. The attack of the Army Group will encounter stubborn enemy resistance in a deeply echeloned and well-developed main defence zone (with numerous dug-in tanks, strong artillery and local reserves), the main effort of the defence being in the key sector Byelgorod-Tamarovka. In addition, strong counter-attacks by the strategic reserves from east and south-east are to be expected. It is impossible to forecast whether the enemy will attempt to withdraw from a threatened encirclement by retiring eastwards, as soon as the key sectors of the bulge in the front line at Kursk, Byelgorod and Malo Arkhangelsk have been broken through. If the enemy throws all strategic reserves on the Army Group front into the Kursk battle, the following may appear on the battlefield –

On day 1 and day 2 – two armoured divisions and one cavalry corps.

On day 3 – two mechanised and four armoured corps.

On day 4 – one armoured and one cavalry corps.

On day 5 – three mechanised corps.

On day 6 and/or day 7 – two cavalry corps.

Summarising, it can be stated that the balance of evidence still points to a defensive attitude on the part of the enemy, and this is in fact unmistakable in the frontal sectors of 6 Army* and 1 Pz Army. If the bringing up of further forces in the area before the north wing of the Army Group persists and if a transfer forward and merging of the mobile and armoured formations then takes place, offensive intentions become more probable. In that case, it is improbable that the enemy can even then forestall our execution of Zitadelle in the required conditions. On the other hand, we probably must assume complete enemy preparations for defence, including the counter-attacks of his strong motorised and armoured forces, which must be expected.'

---

* Sixth Army was reformed in the spring of 1943, after Stalingrad.

Index

France—cont.
divisions sent to, 696, 700–1; 10th Panzer Division reported in, 696, 700–1; Axis tanks and anti-tank weapons in battle of, 705, 707 & fn, 708; British tanks and anti-tank weapons in battle of, 706

Franco, General, 720

Freeborn, Mr, 656

Freetown, 171–2, 228, 476

French Air Force
Possible reaction of, to *Torch*, 464–6, 469–70, 472–5; Collapse of resistance by, to *Torch*, 475, 484; Cyphers of, read by GC and CS, 484, 739; Colonel of, flies to Algiers with news of GAF arrival at Tunis, 486

French Army
Possible reaction of, to *Torch*, 464–6, 469–70, 472–5; Collapse of resistance by, to *Torch*, 475, 484; Tunisian Division of, 500; Anderson in contact with, in Tunisia, 500–1; In centre of Allied front in Tunisia, 583; Sends information to AFHQ, 583, 761; Attacked by 5th Panzer Army, 583; Objects to co-ordination of Allied forces on Tunisian front, 583; Comes under command of Anderson, 583; Officers of, help to plan attack on Mareth Line, 597

French Morocco, 81 fn, 131, 471, 479, 590

French Navy
Possible reaction in, to *Torch*, 465–6, 469–70, 651; Possible attack by, on *Torch* convoys, 482; Cyphers of, read by GC and CS, 484; Toulon Fleet stays in port, 484–5; Axis efforts to take over, at Toulon, 485; Scuttling of Toulon Fleet by, 485–6; Sinks blockade-runner in south Atlantic, 513; Coverage of, by NID, 651

French north Africa, see also Operation *Torch*
SOE operations in, 14–15; SIS operations in, 19; Decrypting of German cyphers in, 31 fn, 582; Arrangements for POW interrogations in, 32; CIU arrangements for, 34–5; OSS operations in, 53; JIC suggests possible German attack on, 80, 464; PM favours allied occupation of, 84–5 & fn, 100; Possible Allied occupation of, by invitation (*Gymnast*), 85 fn, 89–91, 100; Loss of German oil stocks in, 137; PM presses for Middle East victory to influence authorities in before *Torch*, 431; Possible move of German forces to, 464–75, 478–9; Lack of land communications in, 468, 484, 496; Allied disagreements on landing points in, 468–9; US representatives in, predict minimal resistance to *Torch*, 470; Giraud escapes to, 470 & fn; Collapse of French resistance in, 475, 478, 482, 484; Formal agreement with the Allies signed in, 475,

484–5, 593; Hard fight for, 475; Success of *Torch* cover plan for, 478–9, 482; Agent reports possible Allied attack on Libya from, 480; Agent reports destination of *Torch* attack on, 480–1; Decrypts of messages from Vichy to authorities in, 484; GAF takes over bases in, 485; Delays to Allied settlement with French authorities in, 493; Allied attacks on Bougie and Bône fail, 496–7 & fn; Axis complications to cyphers in, 503, 582; RAF attacks on Axis communications in, 505; Lack of U-boat success against convoys to, 557, 559; Sigint on Axis intentions in, 579–80; Lack of provision in, for intercepting Axis Sigint, 582; Delays in, prolong strain on Allied shipping, 606; Possible Axis evacuation of, 606; Axis forces in, largely supplied by air, 608–9; Fears for security of Sigint in, 645; Decrypting of police cyphers in, 670; SCU/SLU arrangements in, 739–41; Allied Sigint organisation in, 739–46

Freya (German radar system), 245 & fn, 246–52, 254–6, 272

Freyberg, General Sir Bernard, 599–600

Fridhof Nansen, SS, 677–8

Frisch, Otto, 123

Frisian Islands, 247

Frühlingswind, Operation, 584–5, 759

Fuel, see also Oil, Coal, etc
German supplies of, 133–7, 265

FuGe 25, 254–5

FuGe 25A, 255, 257

Fuka, 436, 444, 447, 449–52

Fuller, Operation, 181–2, 185

Funk, Walther, 151

Gabes, 460, 492, 578, 580, 594, 597, 599, 603–4, 758

Gabr Saleh, 305

Gadfly (GAF Enigma key), 331, 375, 660

Gafsa, 460, 498, 580, 583–5, 587–8, 598–9, 604, 757–61

Galatea, HMS, 328

Gambut, 301, 308–9, 384–5

Gamma (Shark keys alternative fourth wheel), 751

Gannet I (Germany Army Enigma key), 662

Gannet II (German Army Enigma key), 662

Garlic (GAF Enigma key), 661

Gas see under Chemical Warfare

Gazala
Rommel's offensive from, 216 fn, 366–73, 386, 712; HQ Panzergruppe Afrika transferred to, 301, 313, 712; Anti-tank guns arrive at, 303, 712; Rommel retreats to, 311–13, 341; British advance towards, 313, 712; Battle of, 345, 358 & fn, 359, 366, 371, 375, 377–80, 386, 408, 412, 421,

Mediterranean Theatre—cont.
349, 721; Hitler lays down Axis priorities
in, 341; Enigma information sent to, on
torpedo bomber force, 346 & fn, 606;
Failure of British anti-shipping attacks in,
348–9, 418, 573–4; Sigint on Axis
transport flights over, 378; Movement of
Rommel's reinforcements across, not
seriously interrupted, 402, 418; German
enquiry into security of cyphers in,
413–14; Reshuffle of GAF senior
commanders in, 415; Changing situation
in Eastern area of, 428, 435; Kesselring
cuts GAF effort in, 436, 488; GAF
organises north African air lift, 446, 488;
GAF moves to Western area of, for
attacks on *Torch* convoys, 453, 480; OKW
anxious to deny Allies shipping route
through, 459; JIC views on strategy in,
464, 474; British plans for landings in,
468–74; *Torch* plans to clear north African
shore of, 471; Allies plan to re-open
communications through, 471, 547,
605–6; Political consequences of *Torch* in,
472, 474; Rumours of Allied action in
Western, reach GAF, 476; Allied *Torch*
convoys enter, 477–8, 482, 720 & fn, 721;
Enemy alerted in, by *Torch* convoys,
479–80; Hitler orders U-boats to Western,
480; Axis uncertainty on destination of
Torch convoys in, 480 & fn, 481; Heavy
GAF reinforcements for Western area of,
480, 486–8, 509, 511; GAF moves to bases
on French coast of, 485; Admiralty
extends 'sink at sight' zone in, 486; Move
of submarines in Western, 493; Colonel
Peltz moved to, 511; Axis mine-laying in,
574; Allied air effort in, co-ordinated
under Eisenhower, 574, 583;
Re-organisation of Axis commands in,
580–2; Influence of battle of Medenine on
Allied moves in, 596; COS stress need to
re-open route, through, 605–6; Less Allied
shipping sunk in, 606; Eighth Army
supplied through ports in Western, 606;
Strength of RN submarines in, 608;
Strength of Axis aircraft in, 609; Losses of
Axis transport aircraft in, 609; Axis fears
of Allied attack in, 610–11; Axis strength
in, in men and tanks, 610–11; Allied
strength in, in men and tanks, 611; Allied
air command in, strength in aircraft,
611; Future Allied moves in, 615,
626–7; Germany's growing commitments
in, 626; Air Ministry traffic to RAF
stations in, broken, 641; NID 3 coverage
of, 650–1; Allies capture German naval
grid for, 681; Arrangements in, for
interpreting Sigint, 704; Abwehr
reporting organisation at Western entrance
to, 719; Sigint arrangements in, 739–40

Medjez el Bab, 500, 505, 585, 594 & fn,
610
Memel, 620
Menes, Axis supply ship, 495–6
Merchant Navy code, 639–40
Merchant Ship's code, 639–40
Mersa Matruh, 388–92, 401–2, 418, 449,
451–2
Messe, General
  Takes over Rommel's Army at Mareth,
  581, 593; Commands First Italian Army,
  581 fn, 593; Intends to stand on Mareth
  Line, 599; Makes provision for
  withdrawal to Akarit, 599; Opposes von
  Arnim's withdrawal to Akarit, 602;
  Forces of, retreat to Enfidaville, 605;
  Surrender of, 614
Messina, 327 fn, 348
Meteorological Intelligence, 677–8, 749–50
MEW see under Ministry of Economic
Warfare
Mexico, Gulf of, 229
MF (Medium Frequency) Beacons, 194,
240–1, 259, 503
Michel (German Raider H), 190, 539–40
Middle East, see also separate countries
  SIS given close contact with C-in-C, 19;
  SIS (Algiers) links with, 19; Decrypting
  organisation in, 21, 279; High-grade
  cyphers intercepted in, 21 & fn, 374, 582;
  Liaison with GC and CS, 21 & fn, 22 &
  fn, 24, 284–7, 358–9, 644–5; Decrypts sent
  to, via SIS, 26; Naval decrypts sent to, 27
  fn, 644; Vichy cyphers in, 27 fn; German
  Army cyphers in, 28, 31 fn, 279, 299;
  POW interrogations in, 31–2; PR build
  up in, 38, 282–3; OSS operations in, 54;
  Possible threat to, via Caucasus, 67–8,
  80, 84–5, 91, 94, 98, 277–8, 341–2, 357,
  359, 364, 399, 430; PM presses for
  reinforcement of, 78; Riviera Conference
  discussions on, 81; Possible threat to, via
  Turkey and Iran, 83–5, 91, 103–4, 356–7,
  359, 364, 399, 430; Build up in, 85–6;
  Rommel's early offensive in, 89, 94, 111,
  278; JIC appreciation on Russian
  resistance sent to, 101; Exchange of
  telegrams with War Office on chemical
  warfare, 116; Discussions in, on
  forthcoming Allied offensive, 277; Threats
  to, discussed, 277–9, 342–3, 430; No
  reliable information on German
  intentions in, 278; Delay to Allied
  operations in, 278–9, 281–2, 287–8,
  300–1, 303, 343, 360, 364; Sigint
  authorities progress in, 279, 292; GAF
  codes broken in, 279–87; Axis supply
  problems in, 280–7, 292, 300–5, 309, 316
  & fn, 326, 399–400, 419, 422 & fn, 425–9;
  First C38m decrypts sent to, 283–7;
  Cs-in-C attribute anti-shipping successes

Royal Air Force—cont.

Recovers German aircraft with *Knickebein* device, 242–3; Balanced force of, in north Russia, 224; Information for, from many sources, 235–6; Encounters German air defences, 244–5; Early superiority of GAF aircraft over, 244; Delegation of, in USA, given photographs of radar apparatus, 249; German night fighter system used against, 252–7; Commands of, receive BMPs direct from GC and CS, 272–3, 512; Reinforces Malta, 282; Commitments of, in Middle East, 287–9, 290, 304, 309–10, 321–2, 325–6, 337, 339, 369–74, 377, 402, 416–28, 433, 435–7; Information for, in Middle East, 289; Establishes air supremacy in Middle East, 290, 304, 309, 435, 452; Strength of, in Middle East, 291; Reconnaissance by, of Rommel counter-attacks, 309–10, 331, 337, 339, 408, 413; Reconnaissance by, of Rommel withdrawal, 313–14, 318; AOC-in-C, Middle East, signalled by CAS on evacuation of Benghazi, 314; Bombs Italian Navy in Mediterranean, 321–2; Shadows Italian Navy in Mediterranean, 325–6; Loss of forward airfields hampers, 337, 352; Possible move of, from Western Desert to Northern Front, 342; Part played by, in protection of Malta convoys, 347, 452; Threat to air superiority of, in Middle East, 352, 357; Comparative strengths of GAF and , before Gazala, 360; Exchange of views between CAS and AOC-in-C, Middle East, on possible Rommel attack, 363; Reconnaissance by, during Rommel attack, 369–74, 377, 402, 416, 722, 725; Radar system of, in Middle East, 379; Intelligence staffs of, in Middle East, integrate Enigma and Y, 379 & fn; Reconnaissance by, in Western Desert, 380; Strategic Reconnaissance Unit of, in Western Desert, 380; Air HQ Middle East sets up joint PR HQ with Eighth Army, 380; Sigint aids, in Gazala battle, 381; GAF asks for special attack on Gambut airfield, 384; Evacuates Gambut, 385; Out of touch with Eighth Army, 385; Warns of imminent threat to Tobruk, 387; Attacks by, on Rommel's advancing forces, 391–2, 394–6, 405; Intelligence for, from Y and Enigma, 392, 396, 480; Attacks Axis transports at Mersa Matruh, 401–2, 405, 418; Attacks Axis communications in north Africa, 402, 405, 418, 443; Sights Rommel's concentration for (August) offensive, 416; Bombs Rommel's concentration for (August) attack, 416–17; Bombs Rommel withdrawal from Alam el Halfa, 417;

Renewed bombing attack by, on Axis shipping, 418–28, 442–3, 457; Inter-Service HQ for collating shipping information set up, 423–4; Flakdivision 19 sent to north Africa as defence against, 428; Success of PR by, before Alamein, 433, 435; Frustrates GAF reconnaissance, before Alamein, 435, 437; All-out attack on GAF airfields by, 436–7, 443; Estimates GAF strength before Alamein, 437; Keeps close observation during, and after, battle of Alamein, 439, 441, 449, 451, 454; Bombs Rommel's counter-attacking forces, 441, 447–8; Rommel fears attack by, 452; Failure of, to bomb Rommel's retreat, 452–3; Supply problems of, 452; Possibly misled by Enigma in failure to bomb Panzer Army, 452–3; Expects large GAF reinforcements in north Africa, 452–3; Ordered to attack Axis Tunisian convoys, 468, 470, 474, 504; Strength of air support for *Torch*, 472, 474; Plans for strategic bombing in support of *Torch*, 474–5; Aircraft of, carrying *Torch* courier, crashes off Spain, 479; Superiority of GAF over, in Mediterranean, 488, 491, 496, 499, 503; Requested to bomb Bizerta supply line, 493–4; Ordered to switch to Tunisian targets, 493–4, 504–5, 574; Loses PR planes and equipment in GAF raid on Algiers, 499; Reinforced by units of 12th USAAF, 501; Lack of high-grade Sigint for, in French north Africa, 503; Intensification of attack on Axis supply routes by, 505, 573–4; Air Operational Watch reports to, 512; Effect on, of use of 'Window', 517–18 & fn; Fails to attack *Nürnberg*, 527; Prepares for attack on German Northern Fleet, 530; Attacks German shipping in Norwegian waters, 537; Strike Wing of torpedo bombers operates in Norwegian waters, 537; Attacks Axis coastal shipping throughout Europe, 537; Comparative losses of, in direct attack and minelaying, 537; Success of minelaying operations by, revealed by Enigma, 537–8 Efforts of, in Mediterranean, co-ordinated under Eisenhower, 574, 583; Reconnaissance by, for AFHQ, 582–3, 595, 757, 762; Lack of information from, on Operation *Kuckucksei*, 586; Detects movement of Rommel's forces at Medenine, 595; Reconnaissance by, over Mareth Line, 600–2, 604–5; Reconnaissance by, after Mareth, 604–5; Reports withdrawal of Axis forces from Akarit, 605; Carries out heavy air attacks on Sicily and Sardinia, 605 & fn, 608 'Sigint-based intruder raids' by, 605 & fn; Lessens GAF threat to

Szilard, Professor, 126

T 34 see under Tanks, Allied
Tabun (Nerve gas), 119 fn
Taganrog, 75, 620, 623, 625
Taman Peninsula, 110–11, 623, 626
Tanks, Allied
  Inferiority of, to German models, 297–8,
    350, 352–4, 383–4; Ratio of, to Axis,
    needed in Middle East, 298, 350–2, 354,
    383–4; German knowledge of strength of,
    in Middle East, 298 fn; Heavy losses of, in
    Crusader, 306–8; Heavy losses of, in
    Rommel counter-attack, 338;
    Comparable strength of, in Middle East,
    350–8, 360, 365, 372, 382–4, 390; Losses
    of, in battle of Gazala, 383–4; Destruction
    of, ordered by Rome, 386; Losses of, in
    counter-attack at Alamein, 406; Strength
    of, before Alamein, 428, 715; Grants and
    Shermans arrive, for Eighth Army, 429 &
    fn; Losses of, in Djedeida attack, 502;
    Losses of American, in Axis Tunisian
    offensive, 586–7, 589; Strength of British,
    at Medenine, 595; Strength of British, in
    First Army advance, 610–11; Soviet T 34
    equal to German Panthers and Tigers,
    627; British/Canadian in Dieppe
    landings, 699; Types of Allied, in north
    Africa, 706–7 & fn, 709–10; US Grant,
    available for British, in Middle East, 707
    fn; US Stuart, available to British, in
    Middle East, 707 fn; Superiority of
    German over, in north Africa, 708–10; US
    Sherman, available to Eighth Army at
    Alamein, 715
Tanks, Axis
  Production of German, 145–6 & fn, 150;
    Anglo/US estimates of German
    production, 147 & fn, 150; Difficulty in
    identifying by PRU, 293; Assessments of
    Axis, in Middle East, 296–7, 351–8, 372,
    401; Tests made on captured, 297;
    Superiority of, over British models, 297–8,
    350, 352, 354, 383–4; British ratio to,
    needed in Middle East, 298, 350–2, 354,
    383; Losses of, over-estimated by Eighth
    Army, 306–7; Reinforcements of, in
    Middle East, 307, 315–16 & fn, 317–18,
    323–4, 330, 336, 350–1, 361, 401, 412,
    428–9, 712 & fn; Strength of, for
    Rommel's counter-attack, 308, 315–18,
    324, 336, 338, 360–1, 365, 372–3, 381–4,
    390, 394–5, 712 & fn; 'Specials' arrive for
    Rommel, 383–4, 401, 412, 429; 'Special'
    (Pzkw III) captured by British, 405;
    Strength of, after Alam el Halfa, 417,
    714–16, 724–5; Strength of, in second
    battle of Alamein, 428–9, 441, 445–6;
    First mention of Tiger (Pzkw VI), 429,
    715–16; Tigers sent to north Africa, 429,

491, 715–16; Losses of, in Alamein
    counter-attack, 447; Losses of, in Rommel
    withdrawal, 454–5, 458, 460; Rommel
    asks for 'Special' (Pzkw IV) to hold
    Agheila, 456, 717; Strength of, at Buerat,
    460; Disembarkation of, in Tunisian
    ports, 490–2, 501, 577; Tigers promised to
    Rommel sent to Tunisia, 491–2, 501, 716;
    Losses of, on Tunisian supply route, 495,
    573; Loss of Tigers on Tunisian route,
    495; Strength of, in Tunisia, 501–2, 577;
    Sent to Tunisia in special craft, 574;
    OKW dissatisfaction with Tigers (Pzkw
    VI), 577, 716; First Sigint reference to
    Panther (Pzkw V), 577, 715–16;
    Reinforcements of, for 21st Panzer
    Division, 581; Strength of 10th and 21st
    Panzer Divisions on eve of Axis attack,
    586 & fn, 590; Strength of, in Rommel
    attack at Medenine, 595–6, 598;
    Strength of, before Mareth, 598; Losses
    of, at Mareth, 603–4; Strength of, in
    spoiling attack against First Army,
    610–11; Panthers and Tigers sent to
    Russia for Kharkov offensive, 623–4, 627;
    Russian T 34 equals Panthers and Tigers,
    627; Technical intelligence on, in north
    Africa, 705–18; Tests carried out on
    captured, in UK and Middle East, 708,
    710–12; Superiority of armour of, 709–10,
    712–13 & fn; Hitler blames tank crews for
    disappointing Tiger results, 716; MI10
    expects new version of Tigers, 717–18;
    Jagdtiger and Jagdpanther encountered
    in Normandy, 718
Taranto, 320, 324, 397, 420, 732
Target Intelligence Section see under Air
    Ministry – AI: Target Intelligence
    Section
Tarhuna, 459–60
Tarifa, 719
Tarpon (Fish key), 620
Taub (Beam system), 243
Tebessa, 498, 500, 578, 580–1, 583–4,
    588–92, 762 fn
Tebourba, 502, 504
Technical Committee of Tube Alloys see
    under Tube Alloys, Technical Committee
Technical Intelligence Section see under Air
    Ministry – AI: Technical Intelligence
    Section
Technical Intelligence Section, GHQ,
    Middle East see under GSI(Tech)GHQ,
    ME
Tedder, Air Marshal Sir Arthur, 314, 454,
    493
Tel el Eisa, 403–6
Telecommunications Research
    Establishment (TRE), 247 fn, 250, 256,
    748
Terek, 107

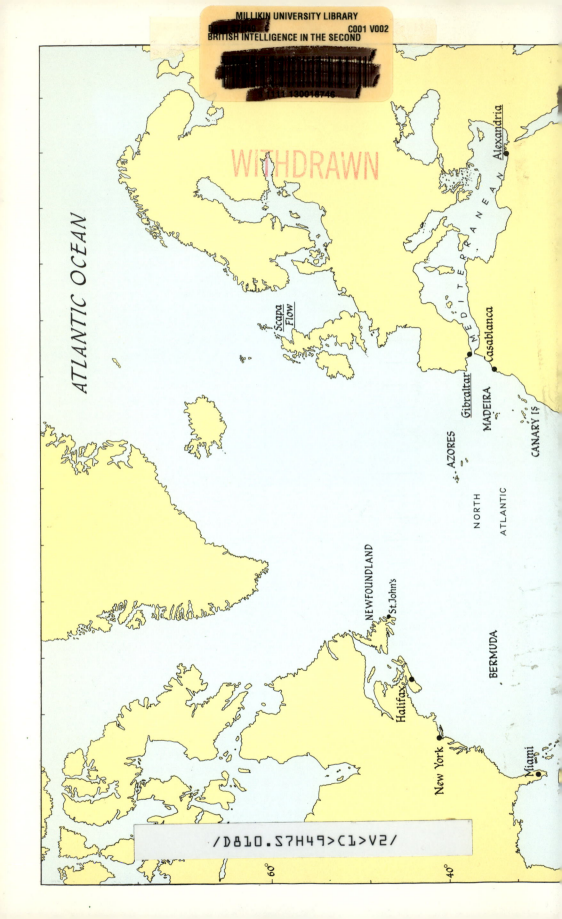

ATLANTIC OCEAN

Scapa Flow

Alexandria

MEDITERRANEAN

Casablanca

Gibraltar

MADEIRA

CANARY IS

AZORES

NORTH

ATLANTIC

NEWFOUNDLAND
St.John's

BERMUDA

Halifax

New York

Miami

60°

40°